ETHICS IN LAW

Lawyers' Responsibility and
Accountability in Australia

4th edition

ETHICS IN LAW

Lawyers' Responsibility and
Accountability in Australia

4th edition

YSAIAH ROSS
(FORMERLEY STAN ROSS)

BA , MA, JD
former Member Law Faculty,
University of New South Wales

Barrister (NSW), Lawyer (California)

LEXISNEXIS BUTTERWORTHS
AUSTRALIA
2005

LexisNexis

AUSTRALIA	LexisNexis Butterworths
	PeopleSoft House, 475–495 Victoria Avenue, CHATSWOOD NSW 2067
	On the internet at: www.lexisnexis.com.au
ARGENTINA	LexisNexis Juris Prudencia, BUENOS AIRES
AUSTRIA	LexisNexis ARD Orac GmbH & Co KG, VIENNA
BRAZIL	LexisNexis, SAO PAULO
CANADA	LexisNexis Butterworths, LexisNexis Quick Law, MARKHAM, Ontario
CHILE	LexisNexis Ltd, SANTIAGO
CZECH REPUBLIC	Nakladatelství Orac sro, PRAGUE
FRANCE	Juris-Classeur Groupe LexisNexis, PARIS
GERMANY	LexisNexis, FRANKFURT
HONG KONG	
GREATER CHINA	LexisNexis Butterworths, HONG KONG
HUNGARY	HVG-Orac Publishing Ltd, BUDAPEST
INDIA	LexisNexis, NEW DELHI
ITALY	Dott Giuffrè Editore SpA, MILAN
IRELAND	Butterworths (Ireland) Ltd, DUBLIN
JAPAN	LexisNexis, TOKYO
KOREA	LexisNexis, SEOUL
MALAYSIA	Malayan Law Journal Sdn Bhd, KUALA LUMPUR
NEW ZEALAND	LexisNexis Butterworths, WELLINGTON
POLAND	Wydawnictwo Prawnicze LexisNexis, WARSAW
SINGAPORE	LexisNexis Butterworths, SINGAPORE
SOUTH AFRICA	Butterworths Publishers (Pty) Ltd, DURBAN
SWITZERLAND	Staempfli Verlag AG, BERNE
TAIWAN	LexisNexis, TAIWAN
UNITED KINGDOM	LexisNexis Butterworths Tolley, LONDON, EDINBURGH
USA	LexisNexis Group, NEW YORK, New York
	LexisNexis, MIAMISBURG, Ohio

National Library of Australia Cataloguing-in-Publication entry

---

Ross, Ysaiah (formerly Ross, Stan)
    Ethics in law : lawyers' responsibility and accountability in Australia.
    4th ed.
    Includes index.
    ISBN 0 409 32144 3.
    1. Legal ethics — Australia. 2. Legal ethics. I. Title.
174.30994

© 2005 Reed International Books Australia Pty Limited trading as LexisNexis

1st edition 1995; 2nd edition 1997 (Reprinted 2000); 3rd edition 2001 (Reprinted 2003, 2004, 2005).

Inquiries should be addressed to the publishers.

Typeset in Goudy and Optima.

Printed in Australia by Ligare Pty Ltd.

Visit LexisNexis Butterworths at www.lexisnexis.com.au

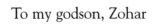

To my godson, Zohar

TABLE OF CONTENTS

PREFACE

Every chapter of this book has been modified for this fourth edition and there has also been a substantial increase in the amount of material presented because of rapid developments in the field of professional responsibility. Since the publication of the third edition in 2001, there has been important legislative change in most jurisdictions and a number of important High Court and other court and tribunal decisions. There has also been an important joint discussion paper in July 2005 on the Uniform Evidence Acts by the Australian Law Reform Commission, Victorian Law Reform Commission and New South Wales Law Reform Commission.

The drive towards the development of a national legal profession has continued, based on the Law Council's Legal Profession Model Laws Project published in April 2004. The success of the Project is seen by the enactment of statutes reflecting a uniform approach in most jurisdictions and the coming into force of the travelling practising certificate. The optimism that I held in the last two editions for a move towards common ethical rules based on the Law Council of Australia's Model Rules appears ready to materialise in the near future. There is a greater awareness within the legal profession of the importance of legal ethics and this is reflected by the professional and academic literature on the subject.

This edition has again expanded the Australian material, but still contains numerous overseas references. The main source is the United States, but the United Kingdom, Canada and New Zealand are also well represented. I have endeavoured to bring the text up-to-date as of September 2005.

I would like to acknowledge the following for their help: Noelene Lowes, my editor; Diana Piper, Elise Carney and Silke Kelly from LexisNexis Butterworths for all their help; the Mosman Art Gallery and Community Centre for use of its facilities. I would like to individually thank the following who have been of help: Professor Michael Asimow, Virginia Shirvington, Bruce Timbs and Commissioner Steve Mark.

There are numerous others I would like to acknowledge, who answered my questions and met my requests. These include officials and staff of state professional associations, LawCover, the Law Council of Australia and all the many other individuals, who are too many to mention by name.

I would also like to thank Marley and Trax for their continual love, devotion and affection.

Ysaiah Ross

Sydney

September 2005

TABLE OF CASES

References are to paragraph numbers

References are to paragraph numbers

References are to paragraph numbers

TABLE OF STATUTES

Australian Capital Territory

New South Wales

References are to paragraph numbers

Western Australia

United Kingdom

International

Canada

Indonesia

New Zealand

United States of America

PART ONE

Accountability and Responsibility
— The Framework

1

INTRODUCTION

HISTORY OF LEGAL ETHICS EDUCATION

University instruction for lawyers in Australia concerning their duties and responsibilities has been a recent development. Sydney University had a compulsory course on legal ethics in the 1940s, but from the 1950s on, law students in universities mainly received their training in professional responsibility from a few guest lectures, by judges or practising members of the profession. In more recent times only one law school, the University of New South Wales, had adopted a compulsory course on the subject that was introduced in 1974. Some other law schools until recently have only had optional courses on the legal profession or jurisprudence that deal with some aspects of professional responsibility. There have been brief segments also on legal ethics in the professional training courses, such as at the Leo Cussens Institute in Victoria and the College of Law in New South Wales. These courses are usually based on detailed provisions found in the state Legal Profession Act. Finally, the bar associations have also had an ethical component in their training courses based primarily on their bar rules.

1.1

Why did legal education historically rarely scrutinise lawyers and their responsibilities? I believe this occurred because the study of law in Australia was practice-oriented. Lawyers were trained in the new colonies by apprenticeship. This was the only avenue while living in the colonies for entry into the profession. Between 1857 and 1936 six law faculties were established in the capital city of each state,[1] but the apprenticeship approach still remained the main way to gain entry. Thus the law schools were influenced by and competed with the apprenticeship model during this period. The law schools were generally viewed as 'adjuncts to the legal profession, rather than truly academic institutions dedicated to liberal educational aims'.[2]

1.2

---

1. C Parker and A Goldsmith, '"Failed Sociologists" in the Market Place: Law Schools in Australia' (1998) 25 *J of Law Society* 33 at 34.
2. M Chesterman and D Weisbrot, 'Legal Scholarship in Australia' (1987) 50 *Mod LR* 709 at 711.

It was originally not necessary to do any training other than the university degree course in order to satisfy professional bodies on the substantive law training. Of course, this meant that the law course had required subjects such as evidence and procedure. The trade school mentality led to an emphasis on learning the law for the sole purpose of practising the law.[3] Furthermore, legal education in the universities was established not on the initiative of the universities but to meet the demands of the legal profession.[4] Within such a context there was little room for a course that critically examined the role of lawyers and their ethical responsibilities. This attitude prevailed until the early 1990s and is supported by the fact that the most important review of legal education, the 1987 Pearce Report, did not deal with the lack of ethical training of lawyers.[5]

1.3   Australian legal education has its origins in English methods but more recently North American teaching methods have become influential.[6] Australia is rapidly developing its own style of legal education that takes into consideration the economic and social context of the law.[7] Even with this change university education today still largely concentrates on studying the law reports and statutes to find out 'the law'. Within that context judges have the primary role and the lawyers are rarely mentioned. The lawyers' role in this system is that of the agent of the client and therefore their behaviour in handling the matter is of small importance.

1.4   There has been a more recent change in the attitudes of both the legal profession and the law schools concerning the importance of professional responsibility as a fundamental part of legal education.[8] This greater interest in legal ethics is shown by the following developments:

❑ The bar associations in all states and territories have adopted a uniform code of conduct based on the Barristers' Rules (NSW) 1995, which had important amendments adopted in 2000. The Barristers' Rules (NSW) have also become the basis for the advocacy rules in the Law Council of Australia's Model Rules of Professional Conduct and Practice.

❑ The Law Council's national Model Rules of Professional Conduct and Practice (the Model Rules) were adopted in 1996, revised February 1997 and March 2002. Almost all law societies have in the last few years revised their Professional Conduct and Practice Rules to bring them in line with these Model Rules. Ethical codes have also been adopted by Western Australia (last revision 2003) and in New Zealand.

❑ Furthermore, the Australian Law Reform Commission has recommended that: 'Legal professional associations and regulatory bodies should give

---

3.   M Chesterman and D Weisbrot (above).
4.   *Report of the Committee on the Future of Tertiary Education in Australia (Martin Report)* (1964) vol II, paras 11.9–11.10.
5.   D Pearce, E Campbell and D Harding, *Australian Law Schools: A Discipline Assessment for the Commonwealth Tertiary Education Committee*, AGPS, Canberra, 1987.
6.   C Bradley, 'Legal Education in Australia: An American Perspective' (1989) 14 *J of Legal Profession* 27.
7.   See Parker and Goldsmith (above). The authors also outline their proposal for an interdisciplinary law school at pp 43–50.
8.   See S Burns, 'Teaching Legal Ethics' (1993) 4 *Legal Education Rev* 141. This article quotes extensively from a major study on teaching professional responsibility in Canada. See W Cotter, *Professional Responsibility Instruction in Canada: A Coordinated Curriculum for Legal Education*, Joint National Committee on Legal Education of the Federation of Law Societies of Canada and the Council of Canadian Law Deans, 1992. See also C Parker, 'What Do They Learn When They Learn Legal Ethics' (2001) 12 *Legal Education Rev* 175.

priority to the development and implementation of national model professional practice rules.'[9] The Model Rules do state that it is 'anticipated that the model will be supplemented as necessary to meet the requirements of each Constituent Body'.

☐ There have been extensive amendments in 1996 to the Legal Practitioners Act 1981 (SA); in 1997 and 2004 to the Legal Practitioners Act 1974 (NT); and completely new Acts in Queensland (the Legal Profession Act 2004), Western Australia (Legal Practice Act 2003), New South Wales (Legal Profession Act 2004) and Victoria (Legal Profession Act 2004). Tasmania has a draft Legal Profession Bill 2005 which will soon be adopted.

☐ In legal education there has been a recent increase in the number of law schools holding compulsory and optional courses on legal ethics and professional responsibility. There was also a compulsory ethics course adopted in 1999 by the Legal Practitioners Admission Board (NSW).[10] Furthermore, in clinical legal education courses, students are confronted with ethical issues as a result of working in the programs and dealing with clients. Some of these programs, such as those at La Trobe, New South Wales and Newcastle Universities, have highlighted these issues in teaching legal ethics. The Law Council of Australia has also included ethics and professional responsibility as part of the compulsory practical training program in its *Blueprint for the Structure of the Legal Profession*, July 1994, and more recently in the development of the National Legal Profession Model Bill. A draft of the Model Bill was published in April 2004 and is available at its website, www.lawcouncil.asn.au. This project has been given the complete support of the Standing Committee of Attorneys-General.

It was therefore unfortunate that the Law Council in an extensive research paper, '2010: A Discussion Paper — Challenges for the Legal Profession', in Chapter 4 on the future of legal education, failed to discuss the importance and possible methods of teaching legal ethics.[11]

☐ The law schools at Notre Dame University (WA) and the University of Newcastle have adopted the pervasive approach to legal ethics, including ethics in all their courses.[12] The University of Newcastle has also established the first chair in legal ethics.

☐ The law school at Griffith University established a National Institute for Law, Ethics and Public Affairs, which has as one of its major objectives to research and conduct seminars on legal ethics.[13]

☐ The Centre for Legal Education, now located at the University of Technology Sydney, supported the conducting of workshops on the teaching of legal ethics. These workshops were conducted in 1999 under the auspices of Marlene Le Brun as part of a National Teaching Fellowship

---

9. Australian Law Reform Commission, Report No 89, *Managing Justice: A review of the federal civil justice system*, February 2000, para 3.71, recommendation 13.

10. The course results in a Diploma in Law and not a university degree. It is recognised as meeting admission requirements in New South Wales.

11. Published September 2001 and can be seen at www.lawcouncil.asn.au.

12. For the basis of the pervasive approach to teaching legal ethics see D Rhode, 'Ethics by the Pervasive Method' (1992) 42 *J of Legal Education* 31.

13. One of its first projects was a study of ethical issues encountered by Australian lawyers: see D Lamb, 'Ethical Dilemmas: What Australian Lawyers Say About Them' in S Parker and C Sampford (eds), *Legal Ethics and Legal Practice: Contemporary Issues*, Clarendon Press, Oxford, 1995, pp 237–55.

on teaching legal ethics. She also made a video and provided invaluable research information to aid teachers in the field.

❑ The Australian Universities Teaching Committee (AUTC) commissioned a report on legal education, which was published in 2003. The report, *Learning Outcomes and Curriculum Development in Law*, contains an extensive survey and analysis of the teaching of legal ethics.[14]

❑ The ALRC's discussion paper, *Review of the federal civil justice system*, released in 1999, found that there was still insufficient attention given to training in legal ethics and professional responsibility.[15] The ALRC did note: 'There is a growing support for clinical legal education programs, which provide opportunities to take a contextualised "ethics in practice" approach in the course of university study.' The ALRC also stated that many law schools had made 'considerable changes' in their curricula and course content to include ethical training.[16]

❑ The ALRC final report on the federal civil justice system, *Managing Justice* (released in February 2000), in its second recommendation, urges law schools to be involved in developing a 'high level of professional skills and a deep appreciation of ethical standards and professional responsibility'.[17]

❑ In 2000 the Law Admissions Consultative Committee (LACC) recommended that law students complete an ethics subject in their pre-admission practical legal training. The LACC felt that lawyers need to act ethically and develop a sense of professional responsibility and professional courtesy. In August 2003 the Standing Committee of Attorneys-General adopted the LACC recommendation.

1.5   Perhaps the most important reason for this shift is the increased interest in television programs, novels and films concerning legal ethical issues. Programs such as Geoffrey Robertson's *Hypotheticals*, the BBC's *Blind Justice*, the ABC's *Janus*, *Fallen Angels*, and recently in 2005 the telemovie *Hell Has Harbour Views*, the American series *LA Law*, *The Practice*, *Ally McBeal*, *Law and Order*, *Murder One*, *Picket Fences*,[18] *The Jury* and *Century City* and the English series *Rumpole of the Bailey*, and more recently *The Brief* and various other shorter series on lawyers by the ABC, have all sensitised large numbers of Australians to moral questions in a legal setting.[19] The

---

14.   R Johnstone and S Vignaendra, *Learning Outcomes and Curriculum Development in Law*, Chapter 5, AUTC, Canberra, 2003.

15.   Australian Law Reform Commission, DP 62, *Review of the federal civil justice system*, August 1999, Chapter 3.

16.   See n 15 (above), paras 3.28–3.29.

17.   Australian Law Reform Commission, see n 9 (above), para 2.89.

18.   For an interesting analysis of *Picket Fences* and *Murder One* see D McKie and S Walker, 'Learning Law from LA' (1997) 22 *Alternative Law J* 114. For a book on TV lawyers see P Joseph and R Jarvis, *Prime Time Law: Fictional Television as Legal Narrative*, Carolina Academic Press, Carolina, 1998.

19.   *LA Law* has been described as being 'about people and their responsibilities to each other; the responsibilities of lawyers to clients, partners, associates, and others; and the responsibilities of individuals to each other and of corporations (preferably large ones) to individuals … When done well, the "Law" part of the show is a series of moral questions that can be developed in a legal setting because, for better or worse, American society often presents moral questions that way': S Gillers, 'Taking *LA Law* More Seriously' (1989) 98 *Yale LJ* 1607, 1608. Perhaps the program was so successful on Australian television because we were presented with similar moral questions. Lamb's recent survey of law firms in Queensland found that the ethical problems were similar to those in the United States: Lamb, in Parker and Samford (eds) n 13 (above), p 237. It should be noted that one of the main script writers for *LA Law*, David Kelly (a lawyer), is the creator and writer for *Ally McBeal* and *The Practice*.

numerous American 'legal thrillers' by John Grisham (*Runaway Jury, The Chamber, The Firm, The Client, The Partner, The Street Lawyer, The Brethren,* for example) and others such as by Scott Turow (*Presumed Innocent, The Burden of Proof* etc), William Coughlin (*Shadow of a Doubt, Death Penalty, In the Presence of Enemies* and many more), Nancy Taylor Rosenberg (*Mitigating Circumstance, Interest of Justice* etc), Richard North Patterson (*Degree of Guilt, Final Judgment, Dark Lady* etc), the Australian authors Al Turello (*Wild Justice*), Richard Beasley (*Hell Has Harbour Views*) and Chris Nyst (*Cop This!*), also contain many examples of moral dilemmas for lawyers. Some of these novels have added to their huge audience by being made into films. Other important films in this area are the Australian films *The Castle, Brilliant Lies, The Man Who Sued God* and *Blood Oath,* and famous films such as *To Kill a Mockingbird, Presumed Innocent, The Verdict, In the Name of the Father, The Winslow Boy, Erin Brockovich, The Devil's Advocate, Legally Blonde, Chicago* and *Intolerable Cruelty.*[20]

1.6 If we compare developments in the United States to those in Australia during the last 31 years, we find that professional responsibility courses are compulsory in nearly all the American law schools. This is because the American Bar Association's (ABA's) accreditation standards for law schools have required, since 1974, instruction in 'the duties and responsibilities of the legal profession'.[21] The ABA requirements for such a course as part of a student's education[22] were a direct reaction to the Watergate scandal. Those involved in the break-in at the Democratic headquarters in the Watergate Building were almost all lawyers and were members of Nixon's staff.[23] These compulsory courses have led to a dramatic increase in research, which may be seen in the establishment of professional ethics journals and the publication of numerous articles, cases and materials, books and texts. Furthermore, the American Law Institute has undertaken the restating of the law governing lawyers as a major project.[24] Also in 1978 the ABA established a Center for Professional Responsibility to promote research and act as a conduit to bring together information and expertise from various committees dealing with professional responsibility issues. The Center has as one of its primary goals the fostering of communication between bar organisations and other agencies that supervise and regulate lawyers.[25]

1.7 In 1986 the ABA took a further step in professional responsibility education by requesting law schools to develop a pervasive approach to ethical and professional issues; that these issues should not only be explored in specific courses but should become a part of all other courses taught —

---

20. For a detailed description and analysis of 69 lawyer courtroom films see P Bergman and M Asimow, *Reel Justice: The Courtroom goes to the Movies,* Andrews and McMeel, Kansas City, 1996. A second edition will be published in 2006.

21. R Cramton, 'Teaching Legal Ethics: A Symposium — Introduction' (1991) 41 *J of Legal Education* 1.

22. See *Approval of Law Schools: American Bar Association Standards and Rules of Procedure,* Standard 302(a)(iv), 1983.

23. See R Wasserstrom, 'Lawyers as Professionals: Some Moral Issues' (1975) 5 *Human Rights* 1. A total of 29 lawyers were eventually gaoled or disbarred.

24. Cramton, see n 21 (above).

25. For information on the Center for Professional Responsibility's activities and publications, see its pamphlet *Center for Professional Responsibility: Resource Guide/ Publications and Services,* 1993.

both substantive and procedural. There has been a considerable amount of criticism of both the pervasive and specific course approach and strong student resistance. The training has been characterised as being either too narrowly focused on rules or not being realistic; that is, useless. In response to the criticism some law schools have adopted new creative approaches to teaching the subject. Almost all of these new programs have received some of almost $5 million in grants from the Keck Foundation, Law and Legal Administrative Grant Program given between 1991–95. For example, Columbia University School of Law conducts an intensive eight-day ethics course using practising lawyers discussing ethical problems that have occurred in their practice. The course includes videos showing clients and lawyers grappling with ethical issues. The students are required to take roles acting out the different ethical situations. Another experiment has been adopted at the College of William and Mary where students are divided up into law offices and confront each other in a litigation situation containing ethical problems.[26]

These experiments and several others are the exception to the norm. Most law schools in the United States do not take seriously the requirement of a compulsory professional responsibility course. The courses, even in some of the leading law schools, are not given the standing or the resources of the mainstream core courses and are considered unimportant by leading legal academics.[27] It is considered by many academics as the 'dog of the law school — hard to teach, disappointing to take, and often presented to vacant seats or vacant minds'.[28] By contrast, there are some legal academics who would argue that legal ethics is the most important subject given by a law school.[29]

1.8   Another development in response to Watergate was the establishment by the ABA in 1977 of the Kutak Commission on the Evaluation of Professional Responsibility to recommend changes to the ABA Model Code of Professional Responsibility. The new code, the ABA Model Rules of Professional Responsibility, was adopted in 1983 and important amendments enacted in 2002 and 2003. It adopts a far broader view of the lawyer's role and relationship to the legal system. The ABA Model Rules have changed the view of the lawyer as 'an officer of the court' to that of 'an officer of the legal system'. The Model Rules establish a framework where they help lawyers to determine and develop their own moral values. As of early 2004, 45 states and the District of Columbia have adopted some version of the Model Rules, while all of the remaining states except California have maintained the Model Code.[30] The ABA Model Rules are

---

26.   For detailed discussion on these programs and other innovative programs see Symposium, 'Teaching Legal Ethics' (1995) 58 *Law and Contemporary Problems*, Nos 3 and 4, pp 1–389.
27.   Symposium n 26 (above). The problems with professional responsibility courses are discussed in a number of the articles. See also D Luban and M Millemann, 'Good Judgment: Ethics Teaching in Dark Times' (1995) 9 *Georgetown J of Legal Ethics* 31.
28.   D Moss, 'Out of Balance: Why Can't Law Schools Teach Ethics?', *Student Law*, October 1991, p 19.
29.   See R Pearce, 'Teaching Ethics Seriously: Legal Ethics as the Most Important Subject in Law School' (1998) 29 *Loyola University Chicago LJ* 719.
30.   A few jurisdictions have combined the Rules with the Code. One major exception is California, which has adopted its own code of conduct.

cited as authority by the federal courts, including the Supreme Court, as the major authority on the conduct of lawyers. It should also be noted that almost every state has as a requirement for admission that a candidate pass an examination on lawyers' ethics. Furthermore, all law students have to pass the Multistate Professional Responsibility Examination, which is administered in 52 jurisdictions, in order to become a lawyer. The exam tests students' knowledge of the ABA Model Rules and the ABA Model Rules of Judicial Conduct.[31]

DEFINITION OF ETHICS

This book is intended as another contribution to the development of ethical training and ethical awareness in Australia. It assumes that someone can be ethical (a good person) and be a good lawyer.[32] What do we mean by 'ethical'? Ethics derives from two Greek words, *ethikos* which means 'practice and custom' and *ethos* which refers to 'character'. To conform to the customs and character of the community meant that you were acting ethically. Customs and codes of conduct throughout history have been closely connected. In the past, ethical codes had far more authoritative impact on our behaviour than they do today. This was because they came from sacred sources: for example, the Mosaic Code. Even the civil code of the Greeks, although created by humans, was considered sacred because it was sponsored by the gods of the *polis*. We look at our codes today with more critical eyes because we know they are the result of power struggles and represent special interests. We can always appeal to a higher moral law to modify or negate their provisions.[33] Knowing this allows lawyers to accept their professional rules and rulings as long as doing so does not deny them the right to place them within the higher moral law; that is, to give them a theological perspective.

1.9

How does a lawyer develop such a perspective? To begin with, lawyers have to define for themselves what they mean by ethics. Does it include taking into consideration the welfare of others or does it just concern one's own sense of self? If it is an individual's own view, does that then allow any criticism of another person's view of ethics? Koniac has succinctly separated law, ethics and morals. She says law depends for its effectiveness most heavily on force; ethics depends on education, membership and ostracism; morality uses membership and shame.[34] I believe that ethics is a system of conduct that sometimes is the same as the law, and supports its aims by giving publicity to rules of conduct, while at other times it goes beyond the law and sometimes conflicts with the law. Ethics includes concern for the

1.10

31. N McCarthy, 'Bar wants tougher ethics test, but not too tough', *California Bar J*, January 2005, p 1.
32. For a discussion by a philosopher of the moral implications of the term 'good' and what is needed to be a 'good lawyer', see S Wolf, 'Ethics, Legal Ethics, and the Ethics of Law' in D Luban (ed), *The Good Lawyer: Lawyers' Roles and Lawyers' Ethics*, Rowman and Allanheld, Totowa, NJ, 1984, pp 38–59.
33. E Shirk, *The Ethical Dimension: An Approach to the Philosophy of Values and Valuing*, Meredith Publishing Co, 1965, pp 62–5.
34. S Koniac, 'Law and Ethics in a World of Rights and Unsuitable Wrongs' (1996) 9 *Canadian J of Law and Juris* 11, 21.

welfare of others which combines with an inner reflection. The latter enables a lawyer to develop a sensitivity to what is appropriate behaviour in a given situation.

What I mean by inner reflection is not simply getting into one's head, or the use of reasoning. Although the human brain is a complex biocomputer, it needs to be programmed how to perform. Rational thought alone does not work to solve ethical problems because it operates only in one dimension. We need to allow that conscious entity which activates the brain — the human soul or spirit — to enable us to access a multi-dimensional energy source to give us insights.[35] This may not 'solve' the problem, but it will enable us to be sensitised to it and to show us possibly how to live with a paradox. An individual lawyer's ethical values will result from both a practical and a spiritual approach to the relevant legal rules and the development of sensitivity to his or her own morals, those of clients, those of the opposition and those of the community. Thus lawyers in finding their personal ethics must continually assess and reassess their assumptions, values and beliefs.

1.11   Evidently ethics is not easily defined. At its highest level ethical behaviour consists of universal principles (for example, the golden rule of do unto others as you would want others to do unto you), while in everyday practice it is modified by special circumstances frequently based on practical necessity. The heterogeneity of the legal profession is the reason that the profession issues formal ethical rulings and develops positivistic ethical codes. The latter provisions are usually broad and general in order to allow flexibility. This is because the profession recognises that in the area of ethics a practitioner may do something that can be technically unlawful but still ethically correct (from a universal perspective). By contrast it should be noted that a practitioner can also do something that is unlawful, for example the commission of simple negligence, yet not be in breach of the relevant ethical rules.

1.12   We are also dealing with difficult questions that sometimes cannot be resolved. These are questions that we confront in everyday life but which lawyers must deal with from within their professional roles. For example:

- ❑ Do you help a friend or relative who has lied to the police, or lied to the Australian Taxation Office, or lied to shareholders in a company in which he or she is a director?
- ❑ Do you conceal information that a product your company produces is defective and will kill people or that it will pollute the environment? Does it make a difference that by recalling the product the company may become insolvent and you and many others will become unemployed?
- ❑ Do you reveal to the relevant authorities that a friend, a student, a relative downloads child pornography from the internet? What if you know that a friend etc is using drugs? Does it make a difference that he or she has beaten up his or her spouse or partner after taking the drugs? That he or she has tried to commit suicide? That he or she steals to maintain the habit?

---

35.   This idea was developed from thoughts on alternative systems of medicine: see R Gerber, *Vibrational Medicine*, Bear & Co, Santa Fe, New Mexico, 1988, pp 32–3.

❑ What if you know that a neighbour, friend or relative beats his or her spouse, or abuses his or her children, or pollutes a local stream by dumping refuse into the water?

Lawyers are confronted with these issues within the professional context, mainly within the lawyer–client relationship. Lawyers are also important actors in public debate on these issues. Professional rules and codes can help in resolving some of these problems within the professional role. For the rest, and even for those where guidance is present, the lawyer will still have to reconcile his or her own personal ethical framework with that of the client and the community. Clients and the general public have the right to have high expectations of the legal profession. The state has granted lawyers a virtual monopoly over the delivery of legal services. A prominent Canadian Queens Counsel (QC) has said that the public has the right to expect the following professional and personal characteristics from lawyers:[36]

1.13

> 1. A thorough understanding of the law. 2. A recognition that the law is not immutable and that there is a need to have a continuing interest in changes in the law (indeed, the lawyer should continue to be a student of the law). 3. A demonstrated analytical ability. 4. Demonstrated written and oral communication skills. 5. Conscientiousness and a good understanding of human nature. 6. A strong interest in problem solving before there is a problem, in risk aversion and risk minimisation, and after there is a problem, in dispute resolution. 7. A good imagination for creative solutions. 8. Wisdom; good judgment; diligence; efficiency; competence; honesty; candour; discretion; care and prudence; and fearlessness. 9. That he or she is a person of utmost integrity.

These requirements form the basis of a lawyer's ethical framework. Perhaps carrying such a heavy burden of responsibilities is one of the reasons lawyers frequently like to use humour when talking about ethical problems. A good example reported in the press was a tale told by famous rugby player and lawyer, Nick Farr-Jones. He told the story of a lawyer doing conveyancing work for an elderly woman and due to her age and frailty the lawyer decided to reduce the charges. Instead of billing her at the scale fee of $1200 she sent an account for $1000. The client had misread the bill and sent the lawyer a cheque for $10,000, which left the lawyer with a terrible ethical dilemma. Should she share the windfall with her partners or keep it all for herself?[37]

1.14

Perhaps ethical issues will always provoke humorous ethical stories. There is no doubt though that the issues do provoke tension and conflict and are frequently difficult to resolve. The study of professional responsibility for law students is intellectually stimulating and at times emotionally confronting. Welcome to this exciting journey as we share the exploration of many of these difficult issues.

1.15

---

36. A Hunter QC, 'A view as to the profile of a lawyer in private practice' (1995) 23 *Alberta LR* 831.
37. *Sydney Morning Herald*, 28 March 1994, p 27. Reprinted in S Ross, *The Joke's on … Lawyers*, Federation Press, 1996, p 28.

2

THE ETHICAL FRAMEWORK

HOW ARE LAWYERS PERCEIVED?

2.1   One of the reasons for the increased interest in ethics is the public criticism of the behaviour of lawyers. Many leaders of the profession believe that by raising ethical standards, increasing penalties and by creating more efficient enforcement procedures there will be an improvement in the public perception of lawyers. Perhaps this may take place, but presently there is a sense of despair among leaders of the legal profession that no matter what they do or say the public does not understand who lawyers are and what they do. Various law societies have hired public relations officers and firms to improve their professional image but the poor image still persists. A survey in New South Wales revealed that successful institutional advertising is advertising that communicates information about lawyers' services rather than seeking to convert the public's negative feelings about the profession.[1] Research has also helped lawyers to understand better what kind of services are sought by their clients[2] and what their strengths and weaknesses are as perceived by clients.[3] The conclusion of the research is that the legal profession needs to take a positive position about the value of the services it offers, for example a logo in New South Wales states: 'Solicitors — helping you is their practice'.[4]

---

1.   D Stein, 'Learning More About Your Client-Base: Public Perceptions of Lawyers', November (1990) *Law Society J (NSW)* 46.

2.   See S Franks, 'What do corporate clients really think about legal services quality?' (1996) 34 *Law Society J (NSW)* 57 and 'How well do you understand your corporate clients?' (1996) 34 *Law Society J (NSW)* 57.

3.   J Brookman, 'Public perceptions of solicitors not uniformly bleak' (1996) 34 *Law Society J (NSW)* 78. The negative view of solicitors related to costs and client communication, while the positive views were for the solicitors' qualifications and that they had high skills and competence in the areas in which they were recognised to have expertise.

4.   J Cameron, 'Psychological Spring-Cleaning for the Law' (1991) 29 *Law Society J (NSW)* 64.

Ian Harrison SC, the then president of the Australian Bar Association and New South Wales Bar Association, stated: 'Barristers are not important people and have never thought they were. But in my experience as a barrister, people who need them think they are important.'[5] The heading for his article may be a good logo for barristers: 'A service clients are happy to pay for'.

Perhaps Norman Vincent Peale's 'power of positive thinking' approach will overcome the present situation where many lawyers feel isolated and think people hate them. Thus within this mind frame lawyers are quick to react when they are personally defamed. For example, a lawyer was recently awarded more than $80,000 in a defamation suit because a radio personality implied he was a 'heartless person'.[6] This problem of isolation is highlighted in an article revealing that more and more lawyers are dating each other, which says: 'Lawyers are attracted to each other because we repel everybody else.'[7] This article perhaps also supports Woody Allen's remark that: 'Some men are heterosexual, and some are bisexual, and some men don't think about sex at all — they become lawyers.'[8] In numerous recent films lawyers are portrayed as 'rats' and have personalities that make it impossible to live with them. They 'are presented in courtroom movies as money hungry, boozed-out, incompetent, unethical sleazebags'[9] and pathological liars.[10]

2.2

Media coverage

The vast majority of comments in the modern mass media cast lawyers in the mould of soulless people, or even worse, in conspiracy with the devil or even the devil incarnate. The latter ultimate portrayal of the fall of lawyers was the theme of the 1997 film *The Devil's Advocate*. In this film the head of an extremely successful law firm, that does not lose cases, is John Milton (an obvious reference to Milton's *Paradise Lost*). Al Pacino makes an excellent devil and brilliantly plays the part. When asked why he chose to play the role of a lawyer, he yells, 'because it is the ultimate backstage pass. It's the new priesthood'. He adds that lawyers with their immense egos are well suited for a central stage role in the twentieth century. A century ruled by avarice and amorality.

2.3

Depictions of lawyers working for the devil are more common and are found in many jokes. Here are two examples:[11]

2.4

---

5. I Harrison, 'A service clients are happy to pay for', *Australian Financial Review*, 18 July 2004, p 58.

6. *Australian Current Law News*, 10 June 1999.

7. M Kaufman, 'Lawyers in Love' (1993) 13 *California Lawyer* 46–7.

8. From his film *Love and Death* (1975).

9. M Asimow, 'When Lawyers Were Heroes' (1996) 30 *U of San Francisco LR* 1131, 1133. Asimow lists respectively for each category the following movies: (1) 'money-hungry' — Ed Concannon, the defence lawyer in *The Verdict* (1982); (2) 'boozed-out' — Frank Galvin, plaintiff's lawyer in *The Verdict*; (3) 'burned-out' — public defender Kathleen Riley in *Suspect* (1987) and several criminal defence lawyers in *And Justice For All* (1979); (4) 'incompetent' — defence lawyer Belinda Connie in *Philadelphia* (1992) and Frank Galvin in *The Verdict*; and (5) 'unethical sleazebags' — he states that there are many examples and cites nearly everyone in the courtroom in *Presumed Innocent* (1990) and also refers to *The Star Chamber* (1985) and *Class Action* (1990). See also M Asimow, 'Bad Lawyers in the Movies' (2000) 24 *Nova L Rev* 533 and 'Embodiment of Evil: Law Firms in the Movies' (2001) 48 *UCLA L Rev* 1339.

10. See *Liar! Liar!* (1997).

11. S Ross, *The Joke's on … Lawyers*, Federation Press, Sydney, 1996, pp 84 and 86.

God decided to sue the devil and to have impartial judges settle their differences once and for all. When Satan was served with the writ, he laughed and said, "And where do you think you're going to find a lawyer and where do you think the venue of the action will take place?"

~~~

A minister and a lawyer were chatting at a party:

"What do you do if you make a mistake on a case?" the minister asked.

"Try to fix it if it's big; ignore it if it's insignificant," replied the lawyer.

"What do you do?"

The minister replied: "Oh, more or less the same. Let me give you an example. The other day I meant to say 'the devil is the father of liars', but I said instead 'the devil is the father of lawyers', so I let it go."

2.5 Women trial lawyers are given special attention. They are stereotyped as being incompetent, promiscuous, too emotional (lacking objectivity), unethical, lacking judgment and even corrupt. According to Bergman and Asimow, 'It's almost as if filmmakers are scared stiff of powerful, successful women'.[12] This stereotyping of women is again present in *Erin Brockovich* (2000). Although the main role, the female paralegal, is portrayed in a glowing fashion, the main female lawyer is insensitive, condescending and lacks the ability to communicate with clients. Another negative portrayal is the uptight and insecure female lawyer in the recent film, *Laws of Attraction* (2004). There are exceptions to this female stereotype. For example, the woman barrister in *In the Name of the Father* (1993) and, more recently, the law student who goes to court in *Legally Blonde* (2001). She is intelligent, independent and skillful. One writer thinks lawyers 'seem to be a convenient device for highlighting the moral murkiness of life after the sexual revolution'.[13] What makes so many people develop such strong opinions about lawyers, which lead to so much media coverage of their activities and lives?

Historical background

2.6 Throughout history lawyers have been portrayed either as villains or heroes. Some of the former views are:

❑ Socrates' description in Ancient Greece in Plato's *The Dialogues*: '[T]he Lawyer is always in a hurry; there is [the clock] driving him on ... He is a servant, and is disputing about a fellow-servant before his master, who is seated, and has the cause in his hands ... The consequence has been, that he has become keen and shrewd; he has learned how to flatter his master in word and indulge him in deed; but his soul is small and unrighteous. His slavish condition has deprived him of growth and uprightness and independence ... He has been driven into crooked ways; from the first he has practised deception and retaliation, and has become stunted and warped ... and is now, as he thinks, a master of wisdom.'[14]

---

12. P Bergman and M Asimow, *Reel Justice: The Courtroom goes to the Movies*, Andrews and McMeel, Kansas City, 1996, pp 90–3.
13. P Hutchings, 'Why are Lawyers (almost) Always the Rats — and Why is it Always Michael Douglas?', Autumn (1990) *Bar News (NSW)* 11.
14. The quote comes from the *Theaetetus* (part of the *Dialogues*) and is quoted from T Overton, 'Lawyers, Light Bulbs, and Dead Snakes: The Lawyer Joke as Societal Text' (1995) 42 *UCLA LR* 1069, 1091.

❑ Edward Gibbon's description of lawyers in the Byzantine state in the third century: 'Some of them procured admittance into families for the purpose of fomenting differences, of encouraging suits, and of preparing a harvest of gain for themselves or their brethren. Others, recluse in their chambers, maintained the gravity of legal professors, by furnishing a rich client with subtleties to confound the plainest truth, and with arguments to colour the most unjustifiable pretensions ... Careless of fame and justice, they are described for the most part as ignorant and rapacious guides, who conducted their clients through a maze of expense and delay, and of disappointment; from whence, after a tedious series of years, they were at length dismissed, when their patience and fortune were almost exhausted.'[15]

❑ In the New Testament, St Luke states: 'Woe unto you also, ye lawyers! for ye lade men with burdens grievous to be borne ...'. This quote is widely used against lawyers, but it appears that Jesus was talking about the scribes–rabbis.[16]

❑ There is a famous quotation from Shakespeare's *Henry VI*: 'The first thing we do, let's kill all the lawyers.'[17] Although Shakespeare did make a number of derogatory comments about lawyers, this quote was intended as comic relief and not something to be considered seriously.[18]

❑ Finally, there are various accounts of utopian societies invariably without lawyers because they are 'a sort of people, whose profession it is to disguise matters'.[19]

Of course there are also numerous jokes which place lawyers in a poor light, for example: **2.7**

Question:

Why did the behavioural scientists substitute lawyers for rats in their laboratory experiments?

Answers:

Lawyers are more expendable. Lawyers do more harm to society than rats. The scientists are less likely to become attached or feel sympathy for them. Rats arouse more feelings of compassion and humanity. Lawyers multiply faster than rats. Animal rights groups will not object to lawyers being tortured. Rats have more dignity than lawyers. There are some things that rats just won't do.[20]

In California, the then president of the state bar suggested that a massacre of lawyers at a prominent San Francisco firm in 1993 was caused by the numerous jokes about lawyers. The president proposed amending California's hate crimes statute to provide for special prosecutions for offences against lawyers.[21] Of course, his request resulted in many more jokes about lawyers. In the United States criminal lawyers (especially public defendants) and family law practitioners are especially vulnerable to being

---

15. E Gibbon, *The Decline and Fall of the Roman Empire*, Vol 1, Collier Books, New York, 1962, Chapter 17, p 245.
16. The quote comes from Luke 11:46. See M Radin, 'The Ancient Grudge: A Study in the Public Relations of the Legal Profession' (1946) 32 *Virginia LR* 734, 745–6.
17. The quote comes from Pt II, Act IV, Scene 2.
18. See Overton (above), pp 1093–4.
19. T More, *Utopia*, cited in R Post, 'On the Popular Image of the Lawyer: Reflections in a Dark Glass' (1987) 75 *California L R* 379.
20. S Ross, *The Joke's on ... Lawyers*, see above, p 24.
21. (1993) 13 *California Lawyer* 53.

attacked. There have been a number of cases in recent years.[22] Lawyers are also in fear of disgruntled clients in Australia. For example, a solicitor in Sydney suffered 'horrific injuries' after being attacked by a former client 'wielding an axe'.[23] In January 2005 a type of airport perimeter security was adopted for the Law Courts Building, Queen Square, in Sydney.[24] Very tight security has been in force for the family law courts for a number of years.

Legislating to outlaw black-humour jokes about lawyers is not feasible. It will not stop the villain view of lawyers which sees them everywhere, multiplying at a rapid rate and inflicting pain wherever they go. It sees them as 'hired guns', 'mouthpieces', 'amoral', 'immoral', 'thieves' ... in other words, available to anyone as long as they have money. This view is reinforced by the legal profession encouraging the notion that lawyers are 'ruthless mercenaries' who seek to win at any price. This image brings in work because a lawyer can give you a psychological advantage by intimidating the opposition or by manipulating the law. In the United States the 'paid thug' image is summed up by a widely used bumper sticker: 'My Lawyer Can Beat Up Your Lawyer'.[25]

2.8 This mentality has spread to Australia. The then Queensland Attorney-General, Mr Wells, said we are developing a 'legal warrior caste'. He said: 'The Wall Street sue–litigate–liquidate–terminate mentality is just not forward thinking; these black-letter lawyers are the only professional group who are licensed to inflict pain — hip-pocket pain — on other people.' He saw this as a redistribution of wealth from 'down to up', and found that this approach is economically inefficient. He pointed out that the two most successful economies in the world, Japan and Germany,[26] have a ratio of engineers to lawyers of, respectively, 40:1 and 25:1. By contrast the ratio in Australia, the United States, New Zealand and the United Kingdom is 2:1.[27]

There is an element of truth to these figures but they are not accurate in relation to those actually doing the work of lawyers. The German figures do not include government lawyers, who make up a large percentage of their legal profession, and those for Japan are inaccurate. For example, in Japan in 1995 only approximately 700 out of 25,000 law graduates — 3 per cent — passed the national bar exam. The number who passed increased to 1000 in 1997, 1200 in 2003 and will be 3000 by 2010. This elite group predominantly become *bengoshi* (litigators — approximately 20,000 in 2003) who are usually cited as being the only lawyers, some *hanjiho* (associate judge) or *kenji* (prosecutor).[28] There exists a hotchpotch of other

---

22. D Curtis, 'Lawyering can be a dangerous job', *California Bar J*, March 2004, pp 1 and 18.
23. *Sydney Morning Herald*, 2 June 1998, p 2. There is also fear for the security of lawyers in other parts of Australia. See 'Solicitors at risk' (1996) 70 *Law Institute J (Vic)* 8.
24. *Bar Brief* (NSW), issue 117, October 2004.
25. A Kirsch, 'The Plague of Violence: Reflections after the Massacre in San Francisco' (1993) 13 *California Lawyer* 67.
26. The German legal profession is described by E Blankenburg and U Schultz, 'German Advocates: A Highly Regulated Profession' in R Abel and P Lewis, *Lawyers in Society, Vol Two: The Civil Law World*, University of California Press, Berkeley, 1988, pp 124–59.
27. M Robbins, 'Attorneys to put law in order', *Australian*, 27 October 1993, p 13.
28. C Wright, 'The Changing face of Japanese practice' (1996) 8 *Asia Law* 10, 13; H Nishiyama, 'Japan's Judiciary Reform', *Inside Outside Japan*, March 2001; and R Seeman, 'Japan Law: Legal Profession' (2003) www.japanlaw.info/lawletter/2003/2003_ Legal_Profession.html.

licensed lawyers, for example patent lawyer (*benrishi*), certified public tax accountant and lawyer (*zeirishi*), and licensed judicial and administrative scriveners who handle real estate and commercial registration matters and give legal advice (*shiho-shoshi*). Furthermore, there are numerous other legal tasks, such as in-house corporate work, done by law graduates who never bothered to pass the exam or who failed the exam. The vast majority of law graduates therefore cannot call themselves lawyers, but they still finish in a position to do legal work. It is estimated that Japan had around 125,000 suppliers of legal services in 1992,[29] and more than 200,000 by 2004.[30]

Under Justice System Reform Council proposals of 2001, 66 new law schools began in April 2004 resulting in about 6000 new graduates a year. It is the goal of the new reforms to have approximately 3000 pass the national bar exam by 2010.[31]

Even if the figures are not accurate as to the true ratio, there is no doubt that Japan and Germany both have a far higher ratio of engineers to lawyers than Australia.[32] Furthermore, there is some evidence that there is a significant relationship between economic growth and the number of engineering students as compared to the number of law students. A study undertaken between 1970–85 of the increase in per capita Gross Domestic Product (GDP) in 91 countries was first done by comparing the ratio of law students enrolled at university, and then doing the same comparison for engineering students. The study found there was a significant relationship between a higher proportion of engineering students and an increased GDP. By contrast, having a larger ratio of law students had a negative influence on increasing the GDP. Their conclusion was: 'Lawyers are indeed bad, and engineers good, for growth.'[33]

2.9

There are other studies which reach a similar conclusion but which have been highly criticised for failing to take into consideration other factors which are not included in conventional measures of economic development, such as GDP; for example, lawyers' contributions to the economic system that are not part of the market.[34] Posner gives as examples of such

2.10

---

29. See the survey of lawyers in 'The Legal Profession', *The Economist*, 18 July 1992, pp 13–15. It gives interesting comparative data on lawyers including the number of lawyers per 100,000 population in several countries. It states that there were 2 million lawyers worldwide. The latest figure of the International Bar Association in 1997 was that there are now 2.5 million lawyers. There is a detailed analysis of the Japanese legal profession as of the early 1980s in K Rokumoto, 'The Present State of Japanese Practicing Attorneys: On the Way to Full Professionalization' in Abel and Lewis (above), pp 160–224. For an older article on Japan see I Shapiro, 'Japan: Land of Law Graduates, If Not Lawyers', *New York Times*, 4 July 1983, p 18 extracted in S Gillers and N Dorsen, *Regulation of Lawyers: Problems of Law and Ethics*, 2nd ed, Little Brown & Co, Boston, 1989, pp 180–1.
30. Seeman and Nishiyama (above).
31. Ibid.
32. For example, see the figures published in *The Bulletin*, 23 July 1996, p 44.
33. See K Murphy, A Shleifer and R Vishny, 'The Allocation of Talent: Implications for Growth' (1991) 106 *Quarterly J of Economics* 503, 529 and J Nugent, 'Adversary Activities and Per Capita Growth' (1986) 14 *World Development* 1457.
34. For criticism of some of these studies see G Priest, 'Lawyers, Liability and Law Reform: Effects on American Economic Growth and Trade Competitiveness' (1993) 71 *Denver University LR* 115 and two articles by M Galanter: 'Predators and Parasites: Lawyer-Bashing and Civil Justice' (1994) 28 *Georgia LR* 633, 647–51 and 'News from Nowhere: The Debased Debate on Civil Justice' (1993) 71 *Denver University LR* 77.

contributions the regulation of pollution (cleaning up our air and water) and the deterrence of police brutality and corruption.[35] Posner makes another important point: a society led by lawyers increases access to legal remedies. This gives the public 'potentially valuable options to invoke those remedies should the need arise'. The need may never arise; and similar to having insurance without ever making a claim, there is value derived from knowing 'that should their legal rights ever be invaded they will be able to find a lawyer' to exercise their rights. Posner does modify this rosy picture, by pointing out that there is a greater threat of legal liability when it is easier to have access to lawyers to bring legal actions. He sees this as a 'negative option, or tax' and queries how the two option values balance out. He concludes that there is no clear answer whether lawyers contribute to or reduce economic output:[36]

> ... [T]here are many important questions about law that traditional lawyers, even when they are professors at the best law schools, do not and cannot answer, instead deferring to experts in other disciplines who may not know enough about law to answer them either.

2.11 The lawyer as the villain will always protect his or her own interests. Examples of this behaviour are found in media accounts, such as the barrister arguing for the court to grant the release of his client's funds (seized by the police) in order for the client to 'pay his counsel and feed his family'. This view also sees lawyers as a conservative force helping to maintain the inequalities in society, by the fact that lawyers have influenced law-makers (many of whom are lawyers) to grant them monopolistic practices, stifling desirable competition, maintaining the high cost of legal services and thereby restricting their services mainly to the rich.

The Australian Law Reform Commission has pointed out that there is abundant literature that criticises the role of the legal profession in 'obstructing meaningful reform of the civil justice system'.[37] The ALRC quotes from a major study of common and civil law countries that found: '[I]n all the countries represented in this volume the legal profession has tended to resist measures designed to simplify the litigation process, or to speed it up or to reduce its costs.'[38] Furthermore, even when there is change, lawyers will still profit from the reforms because they 'are needed to propose, resist, explain and litigate about new law'.[39]

2.12 Lawyers were not always regarded by society in such poor light. The first orators in ancient Athens during the fifth and fourth century BC were known as *synegorous*, who spoke on behalf of litigants, and also as *syndic* (friend).[40] These orators took over the case from the principal after the latter said a few words:

---

35. R Posner, *Overcoming Law*, Harvard University Press, Cambridge, Mass, 1995, p 89.

36. R Posner (above), pp 89–90.

37. Australian Law Reform Commission, Report No 89, *Managing Justice: A review of the federal justice system*, February 2000, para 1.177.

38. A Zuckerman, 'Justice in crisis: Comparative dimensions of civil procedure' in A Zuckerman (ed), *Civil Justice in crisis: Comparative perspectives of civil procedure*, Oxford University Press, 1999, p 52.

39. ALRC Report No 89, para 1.178 quoting J Leubsdorf, 'The myth of civil procedure reform' in A Zuckerman (above), p 61.

40. *The Joke's on ... Lawyers* (above), p 10 citing A Chroust, 'The Legal Profession in Ancient Athens' (1953–54) 29 *Notre Dame Lawyer* 339, 350–8.

These orators were chosen by the principal from among intimate friends, relatives, neighbours etc. The orator would not only present the facts and make the arguments but also express his personal belief in the honesty and integrity of the principal and in his cause. They were thus both advocates and character witnesses. An orator would not take on the case unless convinced in the client's cause. There was also a law that these advocates could not be paid, and it was considered to be disgraceful to both the litigant and the advocate if the latter was paid. These roles of *synegoros* and *syndic* were seen as a civic duty.

Modern lawyers like to see themselves as the chivalrous knight errant, the champion of just causes for people who are unable to defend themselves. The lawyer as hero is exemplified by Erskine's famous words justifying the defence of the unpopular Tom Paine, one of the leaders of both the American and French Revolutions. Erskine said:[41]   **2.13**

> From the moment that any advocate can be permitted to say that he will or will not stand between the Crown and the subject arraigned in the court where he daily sits to practise, from that moment the liberties of England are at an end.

Another famous quotation is Abraham Lincoln's view that 'as a peacemaker, the lawyer has a superior opportunity of being a good man'.[42] Of course, both Erskine and Lincoln were lawyers. From the earliest days of the legal profession, Cicero, a famous Roman philosopher and lawyer, saw lawyers as public servants whose house is 'without doubt the oracular seat of the whole community'. It was interesting for the author to find that almost all the quotations depicting the lawyer as a hero were written by lawyers or former lawyers. It is also rare to find the lawyer as a 'hero' in recent films,[43] but according to Asimow, in older Hollywood movies:[44]

> … lawyers were often described in glowing terms. Although there were a few scoundrels[45] or mouthpieces for the mob,[46] most film attorneys seem oblivious to the need to make a living. Untroubled by ethical conflicts, they fought hard but fair in court. We find them springing to the defense of the downtrodden, battling for civil liberties, or single-handedly preventing injustice. These stories reflect the popular culture of the time in which attorneys were widely respected.[47]

Perhaps the most famous lawyer film hero of this era is Atticus Finch, played by Gregory Peck, in *To Kill a Mockingbird* (1962). Atticus is a southern gentleman living in a small town at the time of deeply entrenched racial   **2.14**

---

41. Quoted by Lord Pearce in *Rondel v Worsley* [1969] 1 AC 191 at 274 (HL).
42. Quoted in I Kaufman, 'Utopia Without Lawyers?', *New York Times*, 14 August 1983, Section 4, p 19.
43. Exceptions are *In the Name of the Father* (1993), *A Time to Kill* (1997), *The Castle* (1998 — only the barrister), *The Winslow Boy* (1999) and *Legally Blonde* (2001).
44. Asimow (above), p 1132.
45. Asimow gives as an example the firm of Cedar, Cedar, Cedar & Budington in *Mr Deeds Goes to Town* (1936). Asimow, n 9 (above), fn 14 on p 1132.
46. Asimow (above), citing *Marked Woman* (1937).
47. Asimow (above): Asimow refers to the following: (1) 'springing to the defense of the downtrodden' — *Knock on Any Door* (1949); (2) 'battling for civil liberties' — *Inherit the Wind* (1960); (3) 'preventing injustice' — *Boomerang* (1947), *Compulsion* (1959) and *The Young Philadelphians* (1959).

prejudice, who decides to defend a black man accused of raping a white woman.[48]

Asimow sees great value in the old films because they portray 'our profession as we wish it really was and as it sometimes though rarely, really is'. He states that there have always been heroic lawyers and there are many practising today:[49]

> We find unsung heroes in law offices everywhere working competently for ordinary clients paying modest fees. We see numerous lawyers serving pro bono in public interest cases or volunteering in clinics. We find them doing underpaid jobs as public defenders, prosecutors, or legal service lawyers. They are toiling away for the government, protecting the environment, collecting taxes or enforcing worker safety laws. Pictures that focus on this kind of lawyer teach the public that there is a different model of professional conduct than the one they hear about in lawyer jokes. And such films teach lawyers that their profession entails something besides money-grubbing.

Asimow has incorporated several of these old films in his course on Law and Popular Culture. These films and others are discussed in great detail in a recent book he co-authored entitled *Law and Popular Culture*.[50]

2.15   Even if lawyers are usually no longer heroes in film and it is true that only the lawyers are making favourable comments about themselves, they do perform positive functions. Lawyers undertake many tasks that are deemed essential for the efficient functioning of modern society, such as enforcement of property rights, ordering relationships and advancing individual rights.[51] The role of lawyers in protecting civil liberties and human rights is widely known not only in Western society but in less well-developed countries where lawyers have led the opposition to oppression by dictators[52] or authoritarian regimes. For example, in 2000 there was a very highly publicised political trial in Malaysia of Anwar Ibrahim, the former Deputy Prime Minister. One of his lawyers and other lawyers have been cited for contempt and imprisoned for speaking out against the government's interference with the independence of the judiciary.[53]

---

48. The main character has basically been portrayed as a great hero. For example, Asimow says for lawyers: 'Atticus Finch is the patron saint. He is a mythic character. He is everything we lawyers wish we were and hope we will become' (Asimow (above), p 1138). For similar views see also T Shaffer, 'The Moral Theology of Atticus Finch' (1981) 42 *University of Pittsburg LR* 181. By contrast Osborn argues that Atticus did not act as a reasonable man who was an honourable lawyer would act in light of knowing his client would certainly be convicted no matter how strong the evidence was for acquittal. He should have 'gone to federal court seeking a writ of mandamus and asked that federal marshalls be called. He would have realized that this was a town where an appeal to reason was impossible. He would have fought for his client by all means possible … Atticus cannot see beyond his law books. Indeed, he seems scared to do so, as if it would unleash the real demons in the town. He plays along with the system. Atticus is a willing participant in a ritual that he knows to be absurd': J Osborne Jr, 'Atticus Finch — The End of Honor: A Discussion of *To Kill a Mockingbird*' (1996) 30 *University of San Francisco LR* 1139, 1141.
49. Asimow (above), pp 1133–4.
50. M Asimow and Shannon Mader, *Law and Popular Culture*, Peter Lang, New York, 2004.
51. I Ramsay, 'What Do Lawyers Do? Reflections on the Market for Lawyers' (1993) 21 *International J of the Sociology of Law* 355, 357–63.
52. See, for example, S Ross, 'The Rule of Law and Lawyers in Kenya' (1992) 30 *J of Modern African Studies* 421.
53. I Barber, 'President's Column' (1999) 62 *Stop Press* (newsletter of the NSW Bar Association) 1.

Ibrahim's lawyers were finally successful in the sodomy conviction appeal in 2004 and he was released from gaol. They then attempted to have his conviction for corruption reopened but this plea was rejected. There have also been a number of lawyers willing to represent Western prisoners who were captured while fighting for the Taliban in Afghanistan. These lawyers have questioned the legitimacy and composition of the military tribunals established to try these non-American Westerners. We will discuss this situation in more detail in Chapters 5 and 8. In this role lawyers, along with judges (former lawyers), act as a safety valve in controlling and modifying excesses of the executive and legislative branches of government.[54] Lawyers also act to defuse the anger of citizens abused by the injustices of the state, by channelling their complaints through the formal system of justice. The latter role maintains a peaceful society, but may be a barrier to more radical reform.[55] In Western society there are also many lawyers involved in legal aid and civil rights, but as one author has stated:

> Equal protection of the laws has certainly seen far more lawyers make more money in legal fees resisting claims of its violation than ever vindicated the rights of the oppressed. And the great mass of lawyers spend a predominant amount of their time making money from fee-generating clients, and do little else.[56]

There is also a widespread belief that lawyers are the main actors who profit from a lawsuit. Three American examples were successful class actions. The first, against the Ford Motor Company, was for possibly leaky 1983–86 Mustang convertibles. Each member of the class received a $400 non-transferable coupon, valid only for one year, towards the purchase of any new Ford. The lawyers for the class, by contrast, received approximately $1 million in fees and expenses. The second class action was brought against General Mills for their Cheerios and other cereals that had been contaminated with pesticides. Members of the class received a coupon good for a free box of any cereal when buying another box. The lawyers' proposed bill was $1.75 million.[57] The most recent settlement was against Bank of America where the lawyers received $2.1 million and $2.1 million went to a class of 1.9 million clients. As a result, after expenses, the clients received a 49 cent cheque.[58] Depending on your point of view 'the lawyers who file such cases are either tireless crusaders trying to keep big corporations honest or ambulance chasers exploiting the law to line their pockets'.[59]

2.16

In Australia a class action concerning potentially faulty pacemakers resulted in the firm Maurice Blackburn Cashman receiving $2.3 million. The members of a class of 482 clients received on the average less than $5000 each, with payments as low as $375. Dr Cashman defended the payout, blaming the company for the cost of litigation because they refused to settle

---

54. See generally M Glendon, *A Nation Under Lawyers: How the Crisis in the Legal Profession is Changing American Society*, Farrar, Straus & Giroux, New York, 1994.
55. R Wasserstrom, 'Lawyers and the Revolution' (1968) 30 *University of Pittsburgh LR* 125.
56. C Wolfram, *Modern Legal Ethics*, West Publishing, St Paul, Minn, 1986, p 3.
57. The cases and two others are from the *New York Times* in 1995 and described by B Hoffmaster, 'Hanging Out a Shingle: The Public and Private Services of Professionals' (1996) 9 *The Canadian J of Law and Jurisprudence* 127, 132–3.
58. D Smith, 'A Suit That makes More Cents for the Lawyers', *Los Angeles Times*, 11 April 2005, pp B1 and B6.
59. Ibid.

the matter. He said: 'At the end of the day, without the claim being brought, none of these people would have been compensated.'[60] Justice Ronald Sackville at first refused to sign off, but after the firm provided an independent cost assessment supporting its costs his Honour approved the settlement.[61]

2.17   The hero view of lawyers can also be seen in the role lawyers played in leading three of the major modern revolutions — the American, French and Russian. Some of the famous lawyers involved in revolutionary activity have been Robespierre, Lenin, Gandhi and Castro. It should be noted that when these lawyers became revolutionary leaders they ceased to be practising lawyers. Lawyers cannot be revolutionaries and at the same time uphold the legal system they seek to overthrow. If lawyers remain in the system they act as a moderating force that compromises revolutionary or radical goals.[62] Furthermore, lawyers who lead revolutionary movements may not always be idealistic. Lawyers are known for seeking power and the easiest and quickest way to achieving that goal is leading a successful revolution.

The basic philosophy of the legal profession contains an inherent conflict in its goals. The lawyer must serve the client to the best of his or her ability while also serving the high ideal of equal justice before the law. But how can the profession attain the goal of equal justice when it is structured to reflect and reinforce social inequality, that is, the best and most extensive service to those who are powerful and/or who can afford to pay? There is a great deal of truth in the question: how much justice can you afford?

Public perceptions

2.18   There is tangible evidence from various sources that the public holds lawyers in low esteem in relation to ethics and honesty.[63] What makes the public distrust lawyers?

---

60.   L Lamont, 'Victims get slim pickings as lawyers take $2m', *Sydney Morning Herald*, 10 November 2004, p 3.
61.   Private communication. For the settlement see *Courtney v Medtel Pty Ltd (No 6)* [2004] FCA 1598.
62.   Wasserstrom (above) (1968), pp 125ff.
63.   The Morgan Poll in December 2004 (Finding no 3809) showed Australian ratings for different occupations as to their ethics and honesty — rating them as either 'Very high' or 'High' — and found only a 33 per cent rating for lawyers. This was lower in order of highest rating than: nurses (90 per cent), pharmacists, doctors, school teachers, dentists, engineers, university lecturers, state supreme court judges, police, high court judges, accountants, ministers of religion, and bank managers. Coming in lower than lawyers were: public opinion pollsters, business executives, directors of public companies, federal MPs, stock brokers, state MPs, TV reporters, talk back radio announcers, union leaders, insurance brokers, advertising people, newspaper journalists, estate agents, and car salesmen (only 4 per cent). There are similar results in the Gallop Polls in the United States, which have found that the poor opinion the public has about lawyers has continued to get worse: see M Asimow, 'Bad Lawyers in the Movies' (2000) 524 *Nova Law Rev* 533, 538–40. Asimow also quotes two recent polls commissioned by the American Bar Association. The latter, ABA, *Perceptions of the US Justice System* (1999), according to Asimow, showed that the 'public seems to have moderate confidence in the justice system but almost none in the lawyers who make that system function'. In a November 2002 Harris Poll (#66) people were asked: 'Would you generally trust each of the following types of people to tell the truth, or not?' Lawyers came in next to last with 24 per cent would trust and 65 per cent would not, and 11 per cent not sure/refused. The lowest was stockbrokers at 23 per cent would trust and 66 per cent would not. The highest was teachers with 80 per cent would trust and 12 per cent would not, followed by doctors with 77 per cent would trust and 17 per cent would not.

❏ One good reason is the media coverage that concentrates on criminal law, especially criminal defence lawyers. Lawyers defending unpopular clients and causes have led to the notion that lawyers will do anything for anyone.

❏ Second, lawyers are portrayed as earning high incomes and manipulating complex law (made that way by lawyers) for the benefit of their rich clients.

❏ Third, lawyers are used as a dumping ground for clients to get rid of their own hostilities and guilt; for example, the lawyer acts out the client's emotional problems in areas such as family law. This results in lawyers having secret, highly personal, information that clients will not tell to anyone else. Clients often therefore fear and resent their lawyers for playing this role. Furthermore, within this role lawyers are required to be objective and will not empathise nor even, perhaps, sympathise with the client.

❏ Fourth, clients come to lawyers to solve their problems and thereby give lawyers control. This can lead to a feeling of being powerless. Lawyers compound this feeling by mystifying the law, using complex language that further alienates and confuses the clients.

❏ Fifth, lawyers lose many cases or make negotiated settlements that are not satisfactory to their clients, yet, whether the client wins or loses, the lawyer has to be paid.

❏ Sixth, there are bad and/or corrupt lawyers who may not only be unethical but also break the law. There are also lawyers who do incompetent work or who are neglectful by not doing the work (unnecessary delay). Clients who come across such lawyers often feel powerless and frustrated because the avenues for redress are usually through those who have access to the legal system — other lawyers. Psychologically, a client who is having trouble with his or her lawyer will not want to have to engage another lawyer to deal with the problem.

❏ Finally, even powerful clients hold lawyers in low esteem even if they help these clients achieve their objectives. Lawyers who do the bidding of these clients without regard to the clients' ethics, are treated as just another employee, and will not be deemed worthy of any respect.

A poll conducted in the United States by the *National Law Journal* found that the three main criticisms of lawyers were that they were too interested in money,[64] that they manipulated the legal system without any concern for right or wrong, and that they filed too many unnecessary lawsuits. In the same survey the most positive aspect of lawyers was that their first priority was to their clients and they knew how to cut through bureaucratic red tape. Lawyers are therefore praised for following the instructions of their clients while at the same time being criticised for using the law to satisfy these same clients by bringing too many lawsuits.[65] In Australia in June 2001 the Victorian Legal Ombudsman, Kate Hamond, did a phone survey of 300 people who had received legal services. The Ombudsman found that 71 per cent said they received good or very good service, while only 7 per cent said that the service was poor or very poor. The then Chief Executive Officer of the Law Institute, Ian Dunn, said: 'People love their own lawyers, **2.19**

---

64. A QC argued in court that his client's frozen assets should be partially thawed to enable the client to feed his family and 'pay his lawyers': *Sydney Morning Herald,* 2 April 1993, p 21.
65. Post (above), p 380.

but when asked about the legal profession as a whole, they have a very different view. It's one of those things.'[66]

Some believe that the poor public perception of lawyers has been based mainly on a criminal law mode. The mass media highlights the criminal system and the main actors in the system are lawyers. As long as lawyers are presented in the criminal context as their dominant public role they will continue to be distrusted. Lawyers have a very different perception of their role than that of the public. They believe as long as they uphold the proper procedures the system will provide the necessary safeguards for any accused. By contrast, the public believes that achieving justice means finding the truth and, for them, playing with procedural technicalities and safeguards is just lawyers' tricks.[67]

2.20   Asimow believes that the poor public image is based on many more factors than just the mass media criminal law image. Factors relating to the legal profession itself include rising incomes, increased numbers and increased litigation. He says highly publicised trials, for example the O J Simpson trial, showed too many 'perceived lapses and shortcomings of individual lawyers' that have been generalised as representing the whole profession. The changes in society with increased rates of divorce, crime and bankruptcy, caused many more people to be involved with lawyers in negative and unhappy circumstances. Furthermore, increased government regulation and expansion of the mass media has led to increased distrust of government and large institutions, such as the legal profession. The litigation process has been perceived as slow, expensive and too complex. Lawyer advertising has made law appear like any other business and there have been campaigns against lawyers by powerful groups in society. Finally, there has developed in the public perception negative stereotypes of lawyers; that lawyers are seen as 'dishonest, unethical, greedy, boorish, inconsiderate people who are impossible to deal with'.[68]

2.21   These distorted and at times contradictory public views give us an insight into why lawyers have such a poor public image — lawyers are identified in the public mind with the roles they perform for all of us. In reality lawyers reflect our own confusion with modern life. We have:[69]

> ... the desire for an embracing and common community and the urge towards individual independence and self-assertion; between the need for a stable, coherent, and sincerely presented self and the fragmented and disassociated roles we are forced to play in the theatre of modern life. In popular imagery the lawyer is held to strict account for the discrepancy between our own aspirations and our realities. This discrepancy is not the lawyer's alone, and once we understand this we may come also to see that in popular culture the lawyer is not so much our enemy, because his [or her] failings are so much our own.

Perhaps another reason for the unfavourable image is lack of communication. The legal profession 'has failed to educate the public about the complexity of the systems in which we live. We have a number of different goals ... and we can't realize all our ideals at the same time or to the same

---

66.   Law Institute of Victoria Media Releases, 23 July 2001.
67.   C Corcos, 'Presuming Innocence: Alan Pakula and Scott Turow Take on the Great American Legal Fiction' (1997) 22 *Oklahoma City University LR* 129.
68.   Asimow, 'Bad Lawyers in the Movies' (above), pp 543–49.
69.   Post (above), p 389.

extent'.[70] The fact that the legal profession is divided and not clear about its goals and objectives makes it an easy target to attack.

The mass media that has recently made lawyers so unpopular also may be making them more human and more acceptable to the public. One writer has stated the following about the very popular television program *LA Law*:[71]

2.22

> In the long run, the show's greatest impact may well be on the public's perception of the lawyer — characters as people with real emotions and sometimes difficult lives — people who do not always know the right path, people who do not always love their clients or their colleagues, people who sometimes lose ... Thus, if *LA Law* merely serves to sensitise the general public to the fact that lawyers are real people with real emotions, it will have served an important role for the profession.

LA Law is still having an influence on American law programs. In 2004 a new program, *Century City*, appeared and disappeared on American TV. It was modelled on *LA Law*, but set in 2030. *LA Law* was shown on Australian television for several years and has now been followed by more realistic programs, such as *The Practice*[72] and *Law and Order*. In Australia, we have also had a similar development with television programs such as *Janus* and *Fallen Angels* showing our lawyers to be very human. *The Practice* is excellent on presenting ethical situations. For example, in one episode a very upset client phones one of the lawyers. He has been drinking and has just run down a pedestrian. The bottle of whiskey is in the car. The lawyer suggests he get out the bottle and start drinking it openly in the street 'to calm his nerves'. Of course, he will flunk the breath test, but the police will not know if he was legally drunk before the accident. Was this ethical advice? Other members of the firm think it was not. Do they have an obligation to report the alleged unethical behaviour by this lawyer? See **7.84–7.87**.[73]

LEGAL EDUCATION AND LEGAL ETHICS

Even with the adoption of compulsory professional responsibility courses there will still be a need to change the educational philosophy in most of our law schools. An isolated course on professional responsibility may not by itself change the attitudes of the vast majority of law students. Students will have been moulded by community values and their individual upbringing. This does not mean that young adults cannot change their ethical values. Recent psychological research has shown that important changes can occur for young adults in dealing with ethical issues.[74] Rhode

2.23

---

70. Peter Shuck, quoted in H Samborn, 'Public Discontent: The Debate Goes Beyond Tort Law: It's About Lawyers: An ABA Journal Roundtable' (1995) 81 *ABAJ* 70, 75.
71. C Rosenberg, 'An *LA Lawyer* Replies' (1989) 98 *Yale L J* 1625, 1629. For a contrary view of *LA Law* which finds that it 'tends to sanitize the contradictions it deals with and wrap them up neatly', see the quote from Kathleen Rowe in D McKie and S Walker, 'Learning Law from LA' (1997) 22 *Alternative Law J* 114.
72. The creator of *The Practice* and *Ally McBeal*, David Kelly (a lawyer), was one of the main scriptwriters for *LA Law* and is married to Hollywood star Michelle Pfeiffer.
73. S Ross, 'Lawyers' ethics in TV serials' (January 1999) *Law Institute J* (Vic) 22.
74. D Rhode, *Professional Responsibility: Ethics by the Pervasive Method*, 2nd ed, Aspen Law and Business, New York, 1998, pp 6–7.

says that, by use of problem-solving and role-playing, students can improve their moral analysis skills and become more aware of the situational factors that affect their judgment.[75]

Perhaps a greater barrier to change is the present attitude of many legal academics and most law students that legal ethics is not an important subject. This approach to the subject does not help in developing strong ethical values. For many students it is not important because it is one of the least likely courses for making a living. Within the present positivist philosophy that permeates legal education in Australia and the United States,[76] subjects that are given attention by both staff and students are those that are considered practical and relevant to earning a living. Generally, law students have come to law school to learn to be good lawyers in order to make a good living and that is the main objective for learning the law. There is no conceptual framework that to be a good lawyer a student needs to learn and develop good ethics. This attitude leads to most students learning the law from cases and hypotheticals without placing human problems within a moral framework. This method encourages moral relativism. Most law teachers will not recognise that a moral problem exists in the cases they are discussing and even if they do they will not spend the time pointing out its ramifications. The reasons often given are that they do not have enough time to fulfil this role and cover the law in their course, that these problems can be examined in jurisprudence or legal ethics (if there is such a course offered) or these problems are not important. Rhode says:[77]

> For law schools to refuse, explicitly or implicitly, to address ethical issues that arise throughout the curriculum encourages future practitioners to do the same. One primary cause of unethical conduct, particularly in organizational settings, is the assumption that moral responsibility lies elsewhere. Legal education cannot afford to mirror this approach in classroom priorities. Although no law school course can fully mirror the pressures of practice, it can provide a setting to explore their causes. Particularly in areas where the interests of the profession and the public do not coincide, future lawyers can benefit from analyzing the gap before they have a vested interest in ignoring it.

2.24   Furthermore, the teaching at law school itself sets up a moral framework that upholds the notions of individualism, autonomy and competitiveness and adopts an adversarial, argumentative and rational approach to the material covered. Loyalty to the client is emphasised above moral and other concerns. There is a failure to teach our students that as lawyers we have responsibility to and for others. The control of the classroom dialogue and the dismissal of what we consider to be 'irrelevant' (not important to us) makes the students dependent and more passive and forever trying to 'psych out' the teacher: that is, telling the teachers what the students think we want to hear.[78] Finally, the language that we as teachers use to construct

---

75.   D Rhode, 'If Integrity Is the Answer, What is the Question?' (2003) 72 *Fordham LR* 333.

76.   The Australian attitude is shown by the courses needed for admission, which is very similar to what practitioners want law schools to teach. See (1996) 3(1) *ALTA Newsletter* 4. In the United States see T Shaffer, *Faith and the Profession*, Brigham Young University Press, Provo, Utah, 1986, p 3.

77.   Rhode, see n 74 (above), p 7.

78.   C Menkel-Meadow, 'Can a Law Teacher Avoid Teaching Legal Ethics?' (1991) 41 *Journal of Legal Education* 3, 7–8.

our stories and hypotheticals will also reveal what we think constitutes a good lawyer. By using sporting metaphors we portray the lawyer as competing, winning and so on. How often are the images used of the lawyer as a conciliator, friend and healer?[79]

Lawyers' professional responsibility

As was mentioned in Chapter 1 there appears to be a change taking place in Australian law schools in relation to teaching professional responsibility and legal ethics. In recent years a number of law schools have added an ethics component into their curriculum. This has been as a required or optional course. Some law schools have used their clinical legal programs to deal with ethical issues, for example University of New South Wales, University of Newcastle, University of South Australia. Others have incorporated ethics into the first year basic course, for example Sydney University. There has also been a suggestion that in courses such as corporations law there is a need for students to learn to be responsible corporate lawyers. This necessitates ethical reflection within a detailed and substantive course.[80] This does not mean that the positivist philosophy has been abandoned. In fact, it can easily become a component of a course on professional responsibility and ethics or any other course taking an ethics perspective.

2.25

Law versus morals

Positivist philosophy emphasises the separation of law from community and personal values and sees law as an objective organised system that applies authoritative force. This is the view expressed by famous philosophers of law, Austin, Kelsen and Hart.[81] Simon has said that adopting a positivist's definition of law leads lawyers, who want to apply what Simon calls a broader 'substantive' notion of law, to disobey the law in their everyday practice. Simon says positivism entails respect and obligation to the law and leaves no room for non-legal norms.[82] Although positivism has been intellectually repudiated, it still plays a role for lawyers in justifying their professional roles.[83] Furthermore, it is still very much alive within our judiciary.[84] Even legal educators who do not embrace positivism support its continuing influence by separating law from morals.

2.26

These teachers should not then wonder why their students become so unethical. The separation of law from morals leads to a very narrow view of law, which is corrupting to the human spirit. It is a view of law that is based on power and which may help to explain why so many law students find their law courses so inhumane. The effect on the students of their legal education highlights the inhumane nature of the course. A major study

2.27

---

79. Ibid, pp 8–9.
80. C Parker and P Redmond, 'Teaching good corporate lawyering' (1999) 3 *Flinders J of Law Reform* 97 and J von Doussa, 'Corporate law teaching and professional standards' (1999) 3 *Flinders J of Law Reform* 119.
81. For a concise description of positivist theory see W Simon, 'The Ideology of Advocacy: Procedural Justice and Professional Ethics' (1978) *Wisconsin L Rev* 30, 39–41.
82. W Simon, 'Should Lawyers Obey the Law?' (1996) 38 *William and Mary LR* 217.
83. Ibid.
84. See the views of the Chief Justice of the High Court of Australia (then Chief Justice of New South Wales), the Hon Murray Gleeson, 'The Law and Change' (1989) 27 *Law Society J (NSW)* 51.

done in the United States showed that many students develop personality distortions. They become increasingly anxious and develop feelings of being overwhelmed. This leads to stress and depression.[85] Furthermore, the unique stress of legal education is not overcome by counselling services since the general ethos of law schools does not encourage a student to seek such emotional support. Such actions would be viewed as 'manifestations of weakness and inadequacy'.[86]

2.28 Therefore, teaching law to students without a moral framework denies them the opportunity to develop healthy personalities. It gives them a perspective that leaves out consideration of the richness of all the various human problems that are associated with legal practice and which make legal practice interesting. Without a moral context legal education can only be contributing to the debilitation of the student's spirit by supporting the present dominant community attitudes of the overriding importance of power and money. Our present law teaching has not only failed to help the student develop good moral attitudes but instead has frequently imbued in students bad moral development.[87]

Buckingham says it is the responsibility of all law teachers to contribute to and promote the moral development of their students. This would include helping and advising students who seek them out concerning personal and ethical problems and focusing on ethical issues in the classroom:[88]

> If an institution is to encourage moral development, it should do so deliberately. It should create a vision, perhaps through the development of a mission statement, which outlines what the law school's objectives are with respect to the encouragement and development of moral growth amongst its students … Part of reinforcing the moral development of students would require adopting teaching methods that respect students. Intimidation, cynicism, bias and disrespect would be outside the objectives of any mission statement.

2.29 Perhaps it is unfair to fix the blame on the law schools. Our society is preoccupied with the importance of power and money. We have moved from a society that was 'inner-directed' to one that is 'other-directed'.[89] There is a widespread view that we can abnegate personal moral responsibility in deference to the mores of the society. Especially within the professional context that emphasises objectivity, lawyers will avoid any inner reflection because it is necessary to get on and do the job — performing a role as a competent and efficient worker. The large firms reveal this mentality by the importance placed on the need for each member of the firm to clock up enormous amounts of client-charged hours.

---

85. See Benjamin et al, 'The Role of Legal Education in Producing Psychological Distress Among Law Students and Lawyers' (1986) *American Bar Foundation Research J* 225.
86. M Carney, 'Narcissistic Concerns in the Educational Experience of Law Students' (1990) *J of Psychiatry & Law* 9, 25. The author quotes at p 31 the theories of Kohut on self-psychology which 'suggests that professional development optimally occurs in an environment that is both supportive and challenging — not eliminating anxiety and tension, but maintaining them at manageable levels'.
87. Shaffer (above) (1986), pp 3–4.
88. D Buckingham, 'Rules and Roles: Casting Off Legal Education's Moral Binders for an Approach that Encourages Moral Development' (1996) 9 *The Canadian J of Law & Jurisprudence* 111, 125–6.
89. D Riesman, *The Lonely Crowd*, Yale University Press, Newhaven, Conn, 1950, pp 13–25.

Christopher Lasch has said that this attitude has led to a culture of narcissism that is now endemic to Western society.

Lasch calls the modern person a psychological person — 'the narcissist':[90]

> ... he [or she] ... extols co-operation and teamwork while harbouring deeply antisocial impulses. He praises respect for rules and regulations in the secret belief that they do not apply to himself.

Lawyers seem to fit squarely into this definition. They believe that they are acting morally for their clients or themselves as long as they are following the rules (the law). Judith Shklar, a philosopher, calls this behaviour 'legalism'.[91] Shklar states:[92]

    2.30

> The dislike of vague generalities, the preference for case-by-case treatment of all social issues, the structuring of all possible human relations into the form of claims and counterclaims under established rules, and the belief that rules are 'there' — these combine to make up legalism as a social outlook ... [It] despises arbitration, negotiation, bargaining as mere politics, arbitrary and expedient ... Adjudication of private *lites inter partes* will remain the model for public rectitude, the best way to solve all social conflicts and 'the law' will remain 'there'.

Legalism

Forty-one years after Shklar expressed these views lawyers now embrace negotiation and will admit that politics is at times relevant and the 'thereness' of the law is no longer self-evident. Although some of the other aspects of Shklar's views are still present, such as the case-by-case treatment of social issues and the structuring of claims into the context of rules, Galanter states that the sources of rules and standards being applied are now so varied that:[93]

    2.31

> ... legal outcomes are contingent and changing: fixed rules are increasingly accompanied by shifting dialogic standards. Increasingly, outcomes are negotiated rather than decreed. Law is less autonomous, less self-contained, more absorbent, more open to methods and data from other disciplines.

Lawyers now recognise these changes for general practice but when they approach their own professional rules the traditional notion of 'legalism' still prevails. This technical application of 'the law' in interpreting ethical rules leads to a very narrow moral universe. It emphasises the use of logical or rational thought without giving proper concern for values.

The change referred to by Galanter has also been recognised more broadly by the social scientist community. The prevalent view for almost 50 years, reflected by Lasch's term 'narcissist' which emphasised that human behaviour is based on self-interest, started to change in the 1980s. In the 1990s and in the early 2000s many more social scientists 'argue for a more complex view of both individual behaviour and social organisation — a view that takes into account duty, love, and malevolence'. They say that many more individuals are committed to 'moral principles, concern for

    2.32

---

90. C Lasch, *The Culture of Narcissism*, Warner, New York, 1979, pp 22–3. See also generally Carney, n 86 (above).

91. J Shklar, *Legalism: An Essay on Law, Morals and Politics*, Harvard University Press, Cambridge, Mass, 1964.

92. J Shklar (above), pp 10 and 19.

93. M Galanter, 'Law Abounding: Legalisation Around the North Atlantic' (1992) 55 *Modern LR* 1, 24.

others, "we-feeling", and readiness to cooperate when cooperation does not serve self-interest narrowly conceived'.[94] Ridley would go even further, arguing that we have evolved an instinct for social harmony and virtue that has in modern times been blocked and negated by all-powerful organised religion and the state.[95] In order to recover 'social harmony and virtue ... it is vital that we reduce the power and scope of the state'. He argues for the devolution of this power to local institutions to help us draw out our instincts: 'We must encourage social and material exchange between equals for that is the raw material of trust, and trust is the foundation of virtue.'[96] This does not mean that self-interest is not important. As Mansbridge says:[97]

> Self-interest explains most of human interaction in some contexts, and it plays some role in almost every context. Institutions that allow self-interest as a primary motive, like the market and majority rule, are indispensable when vast groups of people who have no other contact with one another need to coordinate their activities or make collective decisions ... [But] when people think about what they want, they think about more than just their narrow self-interest. When they define their own interests and when they act to pursue those interests, they often give great weight both to their moral principles and to the interests of others ... [P]eople often take account of both other individuals' interests and the common good when they decide what constitutes a 'benefit' that they want to maximise.

2.33 Lawyers are similar to others in having benevolent and malevolent as well as self-interest motives. The teachers of law can reinforce this mixed motivation approach in their students by not using predominantly problem questions and hypotheticals purely based on self-interest examples. Of course, some self-interest examples are needed to maintain student interest, but we also need to emphasise altruistic, lofty and aspirational examples, especially in legal ethics and professional responsibility courses. 'If an important goal of legal education is to inspire a commitment to public service among future practitioners, then having faculty serve as role models makes obvious sense. As research on altruism makes clear, individuals learn more by example than exhortation.'[98]

THEORIES OF ETHICS

Four different approaches

2.34 How can we approach the question of whether one is acting correctly? There are moral sceptics who believe that when humans have to make a moral choice they do so without basing it on reason. Instead, forces beyond

---

94. J Mansbridge (ed), *Beyond Self-Interest*, University of Chicago Press, Chicago, Ill, 1990, preface p ix. This book is a collection of essays from various disciplines, almost all of them empirically based (two of them philosophical essays), representing the new thinking on human motivation.

95. M Ridley, *Origins of Virtue*, Viking, London and New York, 1996.

96. M Ridley (above), pp 264–5.

97. M Ridley (above), pp ix–x.

98. D Rhode and D Luban, *Legal Ethics*, 4th ed, Foundation Press, New York, 2004, p 1033. The authors refer to D Rhode, 'Pro Bono in Principle and in Practice' (2003) 53 *J of Legal Education* 413 and D Luban, 'Faculty Pro Bono and the Question of Identity' (1999) 49 *J of Legal Education* 58.

their control make the choice. Moral sceptics believe that people will not change their ways of acting by understanding moral issues.[99] In the legal context Hart calls them 'rule-sceptics' who believe that judges have unfettered power and that law is a game of 'scorer's discretion'.[100] These sceptics would also support the 'breakfast' theory of jurisprudence — what a judge ate for breakfast will determine the legal outcome of a case.

The breakfast theory of jurisprudence is the extreme view of an American school of thought — known as 'realism' or 'legal pragmatism'. One of its most important proponents was Cardozo. He said that the end use of law was for judges, by objective means, to use it for the 'welfare of society'. This means law is an instrument for change and used to mould society. Thus judges should use rules that function well and discard those that do not contribute to this goal.[101] Posner sums up 'pragmatic jurisprudence' as 'a rejection of the idea that law is something grounded in permanent principles and realized in logical manipulations of those principles, and a determination to use law as an instrument for social ends'.[102]   **2.35**

A third approach, known as ethical relativism, states that each of us has a correct conception of conduct that is equally valid. This approach can lead to extreme narcissism. An aspect of this approach is called 'ethical egoism'. It states that whatever action is in your own best interest is moral.[103] The problem with these views is that if everyone adopted them we would have a very dysfunctional society. Perhaps this is the reason why we have so much conflict in society — that these attitudes are now widespread. As we discussed above, Lasch has found that these attitudes have led to the 'culture of narcissism'.   **2.36**

A fourth approach is based on virtue or self-realisation. This tradition is a combination of Aristotelian thought and Judaeo–Christian philosophy. One develops virtues such as prudence, courage, temperance, fraternity and justice, according to Aristotle, by acting and judging according to 'right reason'. One develops right reason by our experience in everyday life. This will include our education and training and will help us create practical intelligence that leads to good habits — the unification of 'intellectual and moral insight'. By leading a life of right action a person contributes to 'human excellence'.[104] The main way of achieving 'virtue' is by 'observing and emulating the character and conduct of admirable people. Virtue develops and occurs in community, in relationship with others'.[105] Rhode says that feminist ethical theorists have adopted the virtue approach by arguing that ethical decision-making cannot be considered in the abstract. Instead it must be:[106]   **2.37**

---

99. Wolfram (above), p 71.
100. H L A Hart, *The Concept of Law*, Clarendon, Oxford, 1961, p 138.
101. B Cardozo, *The Nature of the Judicial Process*, Yale University Press, New Haven, 1921, pp 66, 88–103.
102. Posner (above), p 405.
103. Wolfram (above), pp 71–2.
104. Rhode (above), p 19.
105. R Cramton and S Koniak, 'Rule, Story, and Commitment in the Teaching of Legal Ethics' (1996) 38 *William and Mary LR* 145, 180.
106. Rhode (above), p 20. Rhode refers to C Card (ed), *Feminist Ethics*, Kansas University Press, Lawrence, Kan, 1991, and A Jaggar, 'Feminist Ethics' in L Becker and C Becker (eds), *Encyclopedia of Ethics*, Garland, New York, 1992, p 361. See also Carol Gilligan's famous book *In a Different Voice*, Harvard University Press, Cambridge, Mass, 1982.

> ... evaluated in context, with attention to the way individuals are embedded in roles, relationships, and communities. Morality, in this view, is not reducible to universal rules, nor are virtues reducible to those traits emphasized by traditional philosophy; rather, virtues such as care and concern for others, which are particularly associated with women and essential for community survival, deserve equal emphasis.

Analysing moral problems

Utilitarianism

2.38   Traditional moral philosophy has taken two basic approaches to analysing moral problems — teleological and deontological. The *Oxford Dictionary* defines teleology as the 'doctrine of final causes'. It is a view that 'developments are due to the purpose or design that is served by them'. This approach is best known under the heading of utilitarianism that examines a particular conduct to determine how it affects people's happiness and well-being. It is divided into two categories. The first is that of act utilitarianism, that requires one to choose the behaviour in a particular situation that leads to the greatest good for the greatest number. Within this category lawyers have developed 'decision utilitarianism' or 'show trial'. Shklar has stated that a show trial is judged from a 'non-legalistic political point of view ... in terms of its political value ...'.[107] She also says that the '[r]ules may be so vague (or judicial interpretation makes them so vague) that virtually any public action can be construed to appear to be criminal'.[108] 'Decision utilitarianism' is unique to the law and revolves around the court deciding the question of how the public welfare will be affected for the good rather than what is best for the individual parties involved in the case.[109]

2.39   The second category is called rule utilitarianism. It does not look at an individual case, but decides what course of action is appropriate for a group of similar situations. Utilitarianism has therefore as its final goal to prefer the course of action that generates more happiness or well-being for more people. Such a philosophy may be appropriate in an ethnically uniform society but in modern society with its multiculturalism it would lead to oppression of minority groups. Many lawyers use this approach to see if the 'law' or rule is working and whether or not people are better off. Both act and rule utilitarianism require a 'strict impartiality' that can oppose an individual's most profound moral concerns. Rhode says:[110]

> Few of us believe that we should subordinate all personal, professional, and family commitments in favor of the general welfare. Fewer still live in accordance with that principle.

Ethics

2.40   Deontology is defined as the science of duty or moral obligation: that is, ethics. Deontology is found in Kantian philosophy. It deals with first principles — God-given truths or truths arising out of natural law. First principles are defined in terms of either rights or duties, but in modern

---

107. Shklar (above), p 155.
108. Shklar (above), p 153.
109. For an example of 'decision utilitarianism', see R Bauer, 'Law and Ethics in Political Life: Considering the Cranston Case' (1993) 9 *J of Law & Politics* 461, 480–5.
110. Rhode (above), pp 21–2.

times the emphasis has been on rights. Once you have accepted a category as a maxim you then will it, at the same time, to become a universal law. To act morally would be to act according to these truths without usually taking into consideration the effects that are produced by such action. Kant called this a categorical imperative. For example, Kant has argued, under this concept, that if you accept that there is a duty of truthfulness, this would require you to tell the truth, that is, not lie. This is the objective approach. This would include telling the truth to a murderer of the location of an innocent person whom he intends to kill. For the vast majority of us such an action would be considered highly immoral and wrong by another universal or first principle — 'Thou shall not kill'. The latter I believe includes refraining from helping those who want to commit murder. Thus it would be far more appropriate to choose this first principle and break the first principle of truthfulness — and lie in such a situation.[111]

One could also reject truthfulness as a first principle. For example, Simon   **2.41**
has emphasised that there is a tendency to over-condemn lying. He argues that at times it is morally appropriate to lie and calls this 'virtuous lying'.[112] It could also be argued that if one lied, by giving the murderer a false location, the first principle of truthfulness could still be maintained from an emotional or feeling point of view, if not from a rational point of view. That is, the person giving the information is being truthful within himself or herself — spiritually — by telling the 'lie'. Finally, certain religions would allow you to lie in extreme circumstances. In Buddhism lying is prohibited when done for one's own self-interest. But lying is appropriate and necessary 'in order to protect someone on the point of being killed'.[113]

Nagel, a modern day deontologist, rejects Kant's use of universal maxims.   **2.42**
Instead he 'argues that one's agent–relative position will dictate whether an action is ethical based on the moral agent's specific relationship to the principal'. Nagel's approach is subjective and he places one important 'universal deontological constraint: a moral agent can never intentionally maltreat someone'.[114]

Within deontology actions can be morally correct according to people who are religious because the actions are 'God's will'. God's will — the first principle — can be determined either rationally or intuitively. When deontologists leave God out of the picture they focus on natural law; that human society has an intrinsic way of acting that is part of the nature of man and woman and that by conforming to this intrinsic order one is acting correctly. Kant had the notion of an ultimate principle — that each human being must always be treated as an end and not as a means to an end. This idea grants respect for each person as a rational creature.[115] Martin Buber would carry this further in his concept of the 'I and the thou', that is, that

---

111. Wolfram (above), p 74.
112. W Simon, 'Virtuous Lying: A Critique of Quasi-Categorical Moralism' (1999) 12 *Georgetown J of Legal Ethics* 433.
113. Patrul Rinpoche, *The Words of My Perfect Teacher*, Shambhala, Boston, 1998, p 126.
114. These views of Thomas Nagel come from L Greenwald, 'Moral Ethics' (1999) 12 *Georgetown J of Legal Ethics* 663, 664–5. Greenwald applies Nagel's principles to resolving conflict problems presented to an ethics committee of a large firm.
115. L Greenwald (above), p 75.

there is no separation between humans. Buber's approach recognises the spirituality in each of us.[116]

Posner states that people who believe in different schools of ethical thought may be able to 'agree upon a political principle such as wealth maximization, to govern a particular field of social interactions'. He chooses tort law as a field where wealth maximisation as its 'basic orientation' for the regulation of accidents could be accepted by 'an egalitarian, a Millian liberal, an economic libertarian, and an aficionado of Aristotelian corrective justice'.[117]

LAWYERS AND ETHICAL THEORIES

Prioritising interests

A moral lawyer

2.43   Several philosophers and legal philosophers have examined the behaviour of lawyers and have found little, if any, value in the way lawyers deal with ethical problems.[118] The main thrust of their approach has been to seek ways of limiting what lawyers do on behalf of their clients to the detriment of the interests of the community and other individuals. They argue that the professional rules and rulings cause lawyers to be client-oriented. This approach leads lawyers to do things for their clients that they would find immoral if they acted similarly for themselves or non-clients.[119] Wasserstrom has called this 'role-differentiated behaviour'. Thus the role of being a lawyer requires one to ignore moral considerations that otherwise would be crucial in relation to one's actions. Wasserstrom gives as an example of 'role differentiation' the role of being a parent. The parent is required by the mores of our society to prefer the interests of his or her child over those of children generally. His second example is the situation of scientists who have been involved or are involved in the development of atomic theory. The research has resulted in more lethal weapons that could destroy humanity. The dominant view among scientists was that they had the duty to expand the limits of human knowledge and it was not the scientist's role to investigate whether his or her discoveries were being put to 'improper, immoral, or even catastrophic uses'.[120] This approach to one's work can lead to the remarks made by the American comic Tom Lehrer while imitating an interview with a famous rocket scientist about his work: 'My job is to get the rockets up. Where they come down is not my department.' An amazing example of this approach was Rudoff Hess's

---

116. M Buber, *I and Thou*, Charles Scribner & Sons, New York, 1970 (trans) W Kaufmann.
117. Posner (above), p 404.
118. See T Schneyer, 'Moral Philosopher's Standard Misconception of Legal Ethics' (1984) *Wisconsin LR* 1529. He lists articles by Wasserstrom, Bayles, Goldman, Postema and Simon. For a collection of essays mainly by philosophers see D Luban (ed), *The Good Lawyer: Lawyers' Roles and Lawyers' Ethics*, Rowman and Allanheld, Totowa, NJ, 1984 and see also D Luban, *Lawyers and Justice: an Ethical Study*, Princeton University Press, Princeton, NJ, 1988.
119. Schneyer (above), pp 1531–2.
120. R Wasserstrom, 'Lawyers as Professionals: Some Moral Issues' (1975) 5 *Human Rights* 1, 3–4.

statement in 1946 to a United States army psychiatrist. He said: 'I didn't personally murder anybody. I was just the Director of Extermination in Auschwitz.'[121]

Wasserstrom says that role differentiation leads to lawyers being 'amoral'. That means that lawyers have no morals in dealing with their clients. Lawyers will disregard their own personal ethical views of the client's character and objectives. Furthermore, the lawyer is required to pursue with utmost skill, aggression and diligence the client's objectives, as long as they do not violate the law. The analogy has been made between lawyers and the traditional butlers who perform their tasks as professionals, never questioning what they are doing for their masters (clients). This attitude leads to a perverted form of professionalism which was highlighted in the 1993 film *The Remains of the Day*.[122] In this film the good butler always does what is required of him and never comments on the immoral actions of a master who becomes a supporter of Nazism.

2.44

Wasserstrom does approve the amoral approach in the area of criminal defence work because the 'amorality of lawyers helps to guarantee that every criminal defendant will have his or her day in court'. The community sanctioning lawyers to perform this role maintains the adversary system but it also means that defence lawyers help guilty clients to lie in court when they plead not guilty. The general community has difficulties understanding the representation of a guilty accused and we will discuss this in detail in Chapter 15.

2.45

Wasserstrom argues that this exception (allowing an amoral approach) should only be available for the criminal defence counsel. He finds that lawyers working in other areas should not use the amorality model because it is 'almost certainly excessive and at times inappropriate'. These lawyers need to be subjected to 'the demands of the moral point of view'.[123]

Wasserstrom points out four reasons why lawyers need to have a moral approach in non-criminal defence work:

1. The present institutional rules and practices are 'unjust, unwise or undesirable'.

2. An amoral approach will encourage 'competitive rather than cooperative; aggressive rather than accommodating; ruthless rather than compassionate; and pragmatic rather than principled' behaviour.

3. The work lawyers do is not like that of doctors. He says it is intrinsically good to cure a disease but it is not 'intrinsically good to try to win every lawsuit or help every client realise his or her objective'.

4. By being amoral in their professional lives lawyers pay a social price because this becomes for many of them the dominant role in their personal lives.[124]

---

121. *Weekend Australian*, 23–24 October 2004, p 25.
122. See R Atkinson, 'How the Butler Was Made To Do It: The Perverted Professionalism of *The Remains of the Day*' (1995) 105 *Yale LJ* 177; W Bradley Wendel, 'Lawyers and Butlers: The Remains of Amoral Ethics' (1995) 9 *Georgetown J of Legal Ethics* 161; and D Luban, 'Steven's Professionalism and Ours' (1996) 38 *William and Mary LR* 297. The film is based on Kazuo Ishiguro's novel *The Remains of the Day* (1989).
123. Wasserstrom (above) (1975), pp 4–6.
124. Wasserstrom (above), pp 5–6.

Wasserstrom re-examined his ideas more recently. He argued that role-differentiation behaviour results in better overall moral outcomes than leaving the decision to the moral universe of individual practitioners. Furthermore, the benefit to clients from the amoral approach is balanced by the influence lawyers can have on their ethical behaviour. Wasserstrom concludes that 'certain nagging dissatisfactions' still remain.[125]

2.46   Pepper has written an excellent article supporting the need for the amoral lawyer.[126] He argues that lawyers who adopt the professional requirements of being amoral are fulfilling a first-class citizenship model. The premise is that the law is a public good when it is made available to all. Lawyers who refuse to help a client because they believe such action to be immoral are substituting their beliefs for the individual autonomy and diversity of the client's views. The screening of clients places the lawyer in the role of a judge and results in rule by an oligarchy of lawyers. It denies a fundamental premise of first-class citizenship support for equality, that is, equal access to the law. It leads to no access or access subject to the moral judgment and veto of the lawyer. Such a situation also denies validity to the clients' moral views and destroys clients' autonomy.[127]

Pepper states that lawyers can enter into a moral dialogue with their clients. This allows the professional role to remain amoral as the lawyer still provides full access to the law for the client. The clients' decisions remain autonomous, but are affected by the lawyers' moral views. This places the lawyers in the role of moral educators. The clients can also bring to bear their moral universe which may modify the lawyers' advice which is based on amoral goals. Finally, Pepper says lawyers can, in extreme cases, take a conscientious objector position and that the amoral ethic can be ignored when the lawyer feels a higher moral obligation is involved than access to the legal system. He concludes by saying that a lawyer is a good person when he or she provides access to the law because by providing it the lawyer fulfils the moral values of supporting individual autonomy and equality for all.[128]

2.47   Kaufman criticises Pepper for limiting to exceptional circumstances the times when lawyers can escape the amoral role. He writes:[129]

> I wonder about a system of law that compels lawyers to be conscientious objectors, that is, which makes the law such that lawyers must break it in order to achieve what are conceded to be highly desirable moral ends. It is an insufficient answer to say that it enables us to put a satisfactory label — 'amorality' — on the role of the lawyer. And so, I think that the ethic of professional responsibility should and does recognise that it is entirely appropriate for the lawyer to refuse the amoral role in a significant number of situations — not just in the matter of choice of client, but also in the performance of the actual tasks the client wishes the lawyer to do.

125. R Wasserstrom in Luban (ed), *The Good Lawyer*, pp 25–34.
126. See S Pepper, 'The Lawyer's Amoral Ethical Role: A Defense, A Problem, and Some Possibilities' (1986) *American Bar Foundation Research J* 613.
127. Pepper (above), pp 615–19.
128. Pepper (above), pp 628–35.
129. A Kaufman, 'A Commentary on Pepper's "The Lawyer's Amoral Ethical Role"' (1986) *American Bar Foundation Research* 651, 653.

Other philosophical views

We have already pointed out that Simon's approach to the problem involves a broad substantive notion of law. Although Simon rejects positivism because it alienates lawyers from their commitment to legality and justice,[130] he does not find the answer in popular moral discourse. Instead, Simon believes that the tools of legal analysis are more structured and provide a clearer answer to providing lawyers with a moral framework. In his substantive approach there is no distinction between legal and non-legal norms. Simon thus wants to treat all norms as legal norms.[131] This approach enables lawyers to be committed both to upholding the law and fulfilling their notions of justice.[132] Wilkins states that he shares 'Simon's desire to create a morally attractive account of legal ethics that is grounded in the norms and practices of the lawyer's professional role'.[133] But Wilkins issues a warning that 'collapsing professional ethics into personal morality misses something important'. He points out that lawyers are different to other citizens in that they have been placed in a monopolistic position of trust by the state in relation to not only the interests of their clients but also for public purposes of the legal system. Therefore deliberations 'that may be appropriate in the realm of personal moral decision-making will not always produce the social goods that society legitimately expects from a regime of professional ethics'.[134]

2.48

Schneyer argues that many moral philosophers ignore the fact that the profession has promulgated rules and rulings to control what lawyers do for themselves and others to the detriment of their clients. He argues that these rules and rulings do not require the lawyer to act amorally — that there is enough flexibility in the rules for lawyers to apply their own ethical values. Furthermore, he says that it is not the professional bodies that cause lawyers to be client-oriented, but it flows from 'common financial, psychological and organisational pressures of law practice'.[135] In modern capitalist society one of the main objectives of any lawyer is to make a living but there can be exceptions. For example, many lawyers may reject a financially rewarding case if it will be generally bad for business, that is, making them unpopular and/or in opposition to the goals of important clients. They may refuse to act or, if they do act, play the role of mediator instead of zealous advocate. Lawyers will also often modify their client-oriented behaviour when the opposing lawyer or tax officer is someone with whom they frequently have contact. A trust relationship with the opposition may help many other present and future clients. Thus the relationship may become more

2.49

---

130. W Simon, 'Ethical Discretion in Lawyering' (1988) 101 *Harvard LR* 1083.
131. See D Luban, 'Legal Ideals and Moral Obligations: A Comment on Simon' (1996) 38 *William and Mary LR* 255, 261. Luban refers to Simon's article 'Should Lawyers Obey the Law?' (above), pp 226–7.
132. W Simon, 'Should Lawyers Obey the Law?' (1996) 38 *William and Mary LR* 217, 247.
133. D Wilkins, 'In Defense of Law *and* Morality: Why Lawyers Should Have a Prima Facie Duty to Obey the Law' (1996) 38 *William and Mary LR* 269, 272. Wilkins refers to his article 'Redefining the "Professional" in Professional Ethics: An Interdisciplinary Approach to Teaching Professionalism' (1995) 58 *Law & Contemporary Problems* 241.
134. D Wilkins, 'In Defense of ...' (above), p 274. He refers to his article 'Practical Wisdom for Practicing Lawyers: Separating Ideals from Ideology in Legal Ethics' (1994) 108 *Harvard LR* 458.
135. Schneyer (above), p 1543.

important than doing just what one client wants. Lawyers in these situations will feel that being fair is more important than winning.[136] Schneyer does not completely discount the insights of moral philosophy but finds that some of these insights are inappropriate because they lack an understanding of the 'real' issues lawyers face in their practice.

2.50   Perhaps the 'real' issues as described by Schneyer are that lawyers rarely think that they have any moral problem in dealing with clients. A survey of large law firms in Chicago found that 84 per cent of those who responded never found it necessary to refuse representation because it was contrary to their values. In fact, a vast majority of these respondents said they had not refused work because they were never presented with work they perceived as posing a moral issue or being in conflict with their values.[137] The conclusions that can be drawn from the survey are that lawyers do not closely look at moral problems or that the morality of their clients matches their own.

Lawyer as a friend

2.51   Even if we accept the Chicago survey it is still important to investigate a lawyer's moral world. It is obvious that the client-oriented model criticised by various philosophers is not the only consideration available if we are to investigate this world. There are far more moral complexities in the lawyer–client relationship than are revealed by the 'amoral' lawyer approach.[138] What is the nature of this relationship? The relationship has been described in various ways. Fried looks at it as one of 'friendship'. Fried believes that clients are entitled to receive from their lawyers the same special considerations, within the limits of the relationship, which we extend to friends or loved ones. The lawyer becomes the client's friend in a limited area, that is, in relation to the legal system.[139] Fried's approach has been criticised for the following reasons:

- ❑ He chooses to define friendship by reference to only one of its many attributes.
- ❑ He fails to recognise that a lawyer who conflicts with a client's view can get rid of the client.
- ❑ If a client lacks money the 'friendship' quickly ends. The relationship is looked at by other authors as being one of 'bureaucratic manipulation' — client of lawyer and vice versa.[140]

2.52   Fried's approach also conflicts directly with the dominant ethical requirements of the profession, which is the need to be 'objective'. A detached approach to the client's problem is the proper approach and rarely should they be friends.[141] If they do become friends the lawyer–friend must

---

136. Schneyer (above), pp 1545–7.
137. This survey is discussed in J Heinz, 'The Power of Lawyers' (1983) 17 *Georgia LR* 891, 902–3.
138. Schneyer (above), pp 1567–9.
139. C Fried, 'The Lawyer as Friend: The Moral Foundations of the Lawyer–Client Relation' (1976) 85 *Yale LJ* 1060, 1071–2.
140. Letters to Editor, Correspondence, 'The Lawyer as Friend' (1977) 86 *Yale LJ* 573.
141. Interviews of 13 of the 14 volunteer lawyers at the Fitzroy Legal Centre in Melbourne found that they thought that 'emotional attachment to a client's case' was either completely wrong or should be minimised: S Bothmann and R Gordon, *Practising Poverty Law*, Fitzroy Legal Centre, Melbourne, 1979, p 38.

take up the lawyer role when dealing with the legal problem and suppress the friend role model. There are three models that have been adopted to explain the relationship:

1. the lawyer-dominated model;
2. the client-dominated model; and
3. the cooperative model.[142]

Lawyer–client relationship

The legal profession by its rules and rulings follows the lawyer-dominated model. In that model the client comes to the lawyer for help and since the lawyer is the expert, the client should follow his or her advice. Implicit in this is that the lawyer is in control.[143] This model has been found to be valid not only in private practice but also in representing the disadvantaged at legal centres in Australia.[144] The profession's view ignores the fact that there are clients who are important and rich and who also are very sophisticated, for example in tax law, and will dictate to their lawyers (client-control model). These models will be discussed in more detail in Chapter 9. Furthermore, even if lawyers reject the lawyer-dominated model they need to be careful that they are not just manipulating their clients by being 'progressive', for example, when they defer to clients or client groups. Simon has pointed out that so-called 'progressive lawyering' has a dark side. He says that progressive lawyers who are effective 'cannot avoid making judgments in terms of their own values and influencing their clients to adopt those judgments'.[145] This can occur unconsciously when a lawyer fails to recognise that:[146]

2.53

> … the pace, pitch, tone, and volume, along with the level of detail that he provides with each option can unduly persuade or pressure a client into making a decision which a lawyer has predetermined that a client should make. Even in the ordering of options presented during discussion, the lawyer may manipulate a decision.

As Shaffer has pointed out, two of these models lack moral conscience. If the lawyer dominates and says the client needs to do something, the client is seen as having no right to exercise moral judgment; if the client dominates and wants the lawyer to do something then the lawyer has no

2.54

---

142. J Basten, 'Control and the Lawyer–Client Relationship' (1981) 6 *Journal of the Legal Profession* 17, 19; see also a different approach in A D'Amatu and E Eberle, 'Three Models of Legal Ethics' (1983) 27 *St Louis ULJ* 761.
143. See second part of Wasserstrom in Luban (ed), *The Good Lawyer* (above).
144. C Parker, 'The Logic of Professionalism: Stages of Domination in Legal Service Delivery to the Disadvantaged' (1994) 22 *International J of Sociology of Law* 145.
145. W Simon, 'Lawyer Advice and Client Autonomy: Mrs Jones' Case' (1991) 50 *Maryland L Rev* 213, 217.
146. P Zwier and A Hamric, 'The Ethics of Care and Reimagining the Lawyer/Client Relationship' (1996) 22 *J of Contemporary Law* 383, 412. The authors refer to R Bastress and J Harbaugh, *Interviewing, Counselling, and Negotiation: Skills for Effective Representation*, Little Brown, Boston, Mass, 1990, pp 296–7. Bastress and Harbaugh recommend that lawyers ask themselves the following questions to protect against transferring their irrational feelings onto their clients: '(1) How do I feel about the client? (2) Do I anticipate seeing the client? (3) Do I over identify with the client or feel sorry for the client? (4) Do I get extreme pleasure out of seeing the client? (5) Do I feel bored with the client? (6) Am I fearful of the client? (7) Do I want to protect, reject, or punish the client? (8) Am I impressed by the client?'

conscience — amoral model. Under both of these approaches the lawyer has a role in serving the legal system. If the system is basically fair — a source of goodness — then it can be argued that the lawyer's actions are morally justified. He or she is just doing a job that meets the needs of the community and has its sanction. Shaffer argues that this argument lacks merit because history has shown us that the legal system is based on power, not right or wrong, but on force and fear.[147] The correct approach according to Shaffer is the 'care' model (which I see as the cooperative model); that lawyers and clients talk to each other knowing that their conversations are almost always moral conversations:[148]

> Law-office choices and decisions often involve consideration of the social effect of what clients do and of the effect on the character of a particular institution, such as family or a business or the civil community.

2.55 The cooperative or care model overcomes the narrow focus of most professional moral discussions, that is, that the moral problems are only for lawyers — either doing what a client wants or refusing to act. When lawyer–client relationships are perceived as an exchange of moral views we overcome the perspective that we live in isolated moral worlds. Most lawyers operate in moral isolation by not seeing their clients as complete human beings. Clients are treated for their problem or problems and become objectified. These lawyers frequently assume that morals are not important and allow power to fill up the moral vacuum.[149] Lawyers who lead a moral life have open and frank discussions with their clients that include the moral issues of the problem. These lawyers approach their relationship with the client from a moral framework that results in making the lawyer and client interdependent and at risk:[150]

> It aspires to moral discourse as an exercise of love — that is, of what Aquinas called 'fraternal correction', what Barth called 'conditional advice', and what Martin Buber saw as the 'soul of relationships'.

2.56 In the Australian context the amoral, lawyer-dominated model is especially inapplicable in dealing with Aborigines. These clients will have a 'range of simultaneous issues that need to be addressed, such as discrimination, land rights, criminal justice, stolen generations, family law, high interest financial credit, housing and Social Security or Abstudy'.[151] The 'care' model is most appropriate, but few non-Aboriginal lawyers would know how to achieve the proper cooperation. At present there are not enough Aboriginal lawyers to meet the needs of their people, but even these lawyers will have trouble meeting the needs of their community. Dolman points out that Aborigines will come with high expectations to Aboriginal lawyers and these 'lawyers will burn out trying to meet these expectations. If the expectations are not met, it is possible the lawyer will experience a backlash within their own community'. Furthermore, Aboriginal lawyers are

---

147. T Shaffer, *On Being a Christian and a Lawyer: Law for the Innocent*, Brigham Young University Press, Provo, Utah, 1981, pp 7–9.
148. Shaffer (above), p 10.
149. Shaffer (above), pp 16–20.
150. Shaffer (above), p 22. See also Buber (above). Buber sees moral conduct not as something that is inherently profitable, but as a God-given set of commandments without which we could not exist.
151. K Dolman, 'Indigenous lawyers: success or sacrifice?' (1997) 4 *Indigenous Law Bulletin* 6.

frequently involved in their community and will be approached by clients in a social environment and these lawyers are expected to perform cultural duties such as attending funerals. Since these lawyers are scarce they are also placed on a 24-hour emergency alert. The demands made on the lawyers 'could be relentless'.[152]

The workplace environment

Many lawyers may wish to adopt the cooperative approach in their practice but feel that what Durkheim called 'market morality' dictates their actions; that they need to make a living and that clients are not interested in morals but only in achieving the best result for themselves. Is the definition of the lawyer as a 'good person' the one given by Pepper, that is, providing access to the law? What is important to lawyers in relation to their work besides making money? The legal profession extols hard work that stems from the Protestant ethic of good works and service to the community. In the modern large law firm, the enthusiastic worker who works many billable hours and is efficient in his or her work is considered by the firm as a good lawyer and a good person. By working hard and cooperating with others who are working hard, the young lawyer profits and so does the firm. There is a mutual contract — the firm cares for these workers and vice versa. 'Love becomes a metaphor for work' in these firms and because it is love it must be good for the lawyer, his or her family, clients and the community. But love as a metaphor for work is self-deceptive on the issue of what professionals do to their clients, to themselves, to their families and to the community.[153] A term has been given to this love of work — workaholism. An American lawyer–psychotherapist writes that this addiction to work is causing serious health problems because lawyers view their work as their personal identity. He states that unless lawyers see their work as an expression of the soul itself, they will continue to be dissatisfied.[154]

2.57

A survey taken in 1990 by the American Bar Association found that since the previous survey conducted in 1984:[155]

2.58

- ❏ [T]here have been increasing signs of lawyer dissatisfaction and burnout; ... and questions regarding the commercialism of the profession and its impact on professionalism have been raised.
- ❏ [I]ncreases in hours worked and the resulting decrease in personal time have become a major problem ... [and] the legal profession has in recent years become a less pleasant place to work ...
- ❏ Dissatisfaction has become a major problem throughout the profession.
- ❏ Other specific findings included findings that lawyers are working longer hours and three-fourths of firms with more than 30 lawyers have a billable hour requirement.

Lawyers seek a supportive and warm working atmosphere and the ABA survey found that this was an important part of job satisfaction.[156] This type

---

152. Dolman (above), p 6.
153. Shaffer, see n 76 (above) (1986), pp 150–4.
154. B Sells, 'Workaholism', *American Bar Association J*, Vol 79, December 1993, pp 70–2. See also his book *The Soul of the Law: Understanding Lawyers and the Law*, Element, Rockport, Mass, 1994.
155. American Bar Association Young Lawyers Division, *The State of the Legal Profession, Report #1: A Discussion of the Extent, Causes and Impact of Lawyer Career Dissatisfaction 1990 v 1984*, Chicago, Ill, 1990, pp 2, 7–12.
156. Ibid, p 10.

of atmosphere is difficult to create in the larger firms where greater emphasis is placed on billable hours. Computers have enabled management to monitor these work practices, which contributes to a situation where there always appears to be too much to do and never enough time to accomplish it.[157]

2.59   Lawyers in Australia are experiencing similar problems that are widely discussed in the media. In the *Australian Financial Review*'s Special Report on Corporate Legal Services it was stated that: 'One of the key issues yet to be addressed is the long hours worked by many lawyers.'[158] To meet some of the complaints many firms have adopted flexible forms of practice such as part-time work, job sharing, flexible working hours and working from home.[159] The most flexible example I found was Jennie Tzavaras, a partner in Phillips Fox, who works from her home in Colombo, Sri Lanka.[160] By contrast, in the same article the head of the Australian Women Lawyers, Jennifer Batrouney SC, stated that she knew of at least four instances where female partners in national law firms were forced out of the partnership for seeking flexible working arrangements.[161]

Perhaps becoming a partner is not important. New recruits in the large firms no longer have partnerships as their main goal and many will move on to other jobs. To meet the needs of the talented new recruits and try to retain their services, firms are seeking to develop a better working environment. Peter Hay, managing partner at Freehills, says the aim is to 'be a place where people love to come to work ... We try to make Freehills an attractive place to work ... [a] place where people are respected and treated well and given challenging work and helped in their development and learning ...'.[162]

Lawyers, by not facing up to the problems of the workplace, such as long work hours, are practising self-deception. This self-deception is more obvious from the health problems developed by lawyers who have followed the concept of the workaholic as the 'good lawyer'. Various articles written by health consultants and psychiatrists have begun to appear in lawyers' journals. The focus is on issues related to stress and change that are affecting many in their legal practice and in their home life.[163] The New South Wales Law Society recognised these problems by setting up LawCare in 1991. It is a 24-hour-a-day free counselling phone service for any member or their immediate family to discuss with a counsellor any personal or social

---

157. For a detailed discussion of how technology is creating a dissatisfying work atmosphere see W Braithwaite, 'How Is Technology Affecting the Practice and Profession of Law' (1991) 22 *Texas Tech Law Review* 1113 and (1992) 41 *Defense Law J* 285.
158. A Clelland, 'Family-friendly practice: team effort required', Corporate Legal Services, Special Report, *Australian Financial Review*, 14 November 2002, p 7.
159. Ibid. See also in this report, F Buffini, 'New practices to beat burnout', p 6.
160. K Towers, 'Working from home ... in Sri Lanka', *Australian Financial Review*, 20 August 2004, pp 1 and 53.
161. Ibid, p 53.
162. B Pheasant, 'Partnerships are no longer the only goal', Corporate Legal Services (above), p 4.
163. See, for example, D Tannenbaum, 'Stress and Change in the Legal Profession in the 1990s' (1990) 17 *Brief (Law Society of WA)* 7 and D Jansen, 'The Gulf Between the Professional and the Private: How Work Conflicts with Home Life', *The Proctor (QLS)* April 1993, p 15.

problem, for example those of stress management, marriage difficulties, drug and alcohol use, and so on.[164] This service is also available in South Australia, Western Australia, Victoria and Queensland. Lawcare columns now appear in several of the journals of the law societies.

More and more people are realising that they need to slow down and reflect on what they are doing. Carl Honore, in researching his book *In Praise of Slow*,[165] found that many people are reacting to the frenetic pace of modern life by seeking to slow down. He said people are establishing places where they can go slow, for example for doing exercise or for eating. In an interview concerning his book Honore said the whole notion of time has changed. 'There's the way Western culture views time — as linear and as a scarce resource and getting the most out of it. Time is valuable.' Honore says he is not 'anti-work' but he is 'anti that people should have no choice about working longer than is good for them or the organisation'. He concludes the interview by saying: 'When you are busy you can't confront the big things in life, ... so when you slow down it's asking you to go against the mainstream and ask the big questions about where you are going and who you are.'[166]   **2.60**

New technologies have also added to health problems by leading to less human contact. There is an obvious need to produce more human contact in the workplace. For example, I recall a colleague in the office next door sending me an email instead of knocking on my door to talk about the problem. Furthermore, technological developments have increased internal surveillance, placing more pressure on lawyers to produce and maintain profitability for their firm.[167] The need to know more continually and the increase in competition has led to a work situation where there is less and less meaning. This in turn has led to early 'burn-out' and/or unsatisfactory personal and family lives.[168] Finally, lawyers are being made aware that they cannot continue to rely solely on interpersonal communication skills. There is a need for lawyers to develop intrapersonally; that is, developing a self-awareness of their own behavioural patterns and preferences and the values and beliefs that they bring to their work, especially to the lawyer–client relationship. This is not an easy task but one that is worthwhile. It can enable lawyers not only to be of better service to their clients but also help them develop their sensitivities as human beings, which will lead to greater work satisfaction.[169]   **2.61**

It is not only from working hard that the lawyer gets his or her moral framework. The profession itself is a moral teacher and expects the   **2.62**

---

164. I Chung, 'Law Care Counselling' (1993) 31 *Law Society J (NSW)* 53. There are similar services in other jurisdictions. See also 'Stress: Symptoms and Strategies' in the LawCare column of the Law Society of South Australia *Bulletin*, February 1998, p 17.
165. HarperCollins, San Francisco, 2004.
166. C Fox, 'Busy, busy, busy', *Australian Financial Review, Boss*, October 2004, pp 20, 22 and 26.
167. A Clark, 'Information Technology in Legal Services' (1992) 19 *J of Law and Society* 13, 15.
168. See D Jansen, 'The Gulf Between the Professional and the Private' (April 1993) *The Proctor (QLS)* 15.
169. See the reasons why lawyers rationalise not making this change in B Blaustone, 'To Be Of Service: The Lawyer's Aware Use of Human Skills Associated With The Perceptive Self' (1990) 15 *The J of Legal Profession* 241.

practitioner to learn his or her morality by making friends with professional colleagues.[170] This is also for the good of the lawyer since the professional culture is regarded as connected with altruistic behaviour and generally for the public good. Many critics have called this professional rhetoric.[171] The fact that it may be rhetoric does not matter when so many lawyers have adopted the rhetoric as a justification for ignoring the broader moral framework in their lawyer–client relationships. Furthermore, there are now calls for lawyers to live up to the rhetoric and to bring altruism to their practice.[172]

Lawyer–client dynamics

2.63　Realistically, lawyers must face the fact that clients come to them for professional help. Frequently they do not see the lawyer as a complete human being. Since their main interest is to achieve their objective they only want one aspect of the lawyer, that is, his or her legal skills. In such situations it may be difficult and frustrating for a lawyer to attempt to apply the cooperative model. Even if it is difficult it is still necessary to apply this model because without it there would be no moral discourse.[173] Once there is a moral discourse, the fact that the lawyer and client do not agree, and may each have a morally defensible position, does not matter. Lawyers can still do their job knowing full well that their action is within a moral universe.[174] When both parties operate within a moral universe each one can affect the behaviour of the other and such a discourse will necessarily modify the amoral solutions and goals that were first voiced earlier in this chapter. Furthermore, if their moral universes are too far apart the lawyer can refuse to act. The duty to act will be discussed in more detail in Chapter 9.

2.64　When our discussions are within this moral universe we soon realise that the profession's ethos of neutrality, objectivity and non-friendship is just rhetoric. Many of our clients are friends, as seen by Fried, but within a limited context. We know that those clients who do operate within a moral framework are those whom we like and treat as friends. They therefore receive better service. Shaffer gives three reasons why friendship is justified in the lawyer–client relationship:

1. The love that exists in friendship benefits all other relationships.
2. Any friendship is a 'school for virtue'.
3. It is also the beginning for universal or 'civic' friendship.

2.65　Shaffer prefers the term 'earthy' friendship to 'civic' because the latter implies that the state can decide what is best — it makes the state a god. A good lawyer who is a good person will prefer community, family and religious values to those of the institutions, and will value friendship more than justice.[175] Our institutions, supported by an abstract concept of justice, have been tainted by Protestant enlightenment concepts. The professional rules and rulings stem from this culture and have led lawyers to

---

170. Shaffer, see n 76 (above) (1986), p 166.
171. See J Disney, J Basten, P Redmond and S Ross, *Lawyers*, 2nd ed, Law Book Co, Sydney, 1986, pp 73–91.
172. See C Menkel-Meadow, 'Is Altruism Possible in Lawyering' (1992) 8 *Georgia St ULR* 385.
173. Shaffer, see n 76 (above) (1986), p 31.
174. Schneyer (above), p 1564.
175. Shaffer, see n 76 (above) (1986), pp 31, 200–6, 223–4.

regard themselves as morally isolated individuals. This has resulted in lawyers being cut off from traditional community values and even at times from their own family values. By adopting a moral context for our work we become caring people — human lawyers.

For example, the profession says that we should be 'loyal' to our clients. This arises from the contractual lawyer–client relationship. It implies that we must follow the client's wishes, as long as they are lawful. Loyalty lacks ethical content and negates any possibility of friendship. A true friendship is based on fidelity. Being faithful has to do with mutual human relationship — a covenant as found in the Judeo–Christian tradition. If we apply fidelity to our lawyer–client relationships we achieve ethical clarity in doing our work. Loyalty would require us to help achieve unworthy or evil objectives. By applying fidelity, a lawyer can point out that he or she can still be faithful but cannot help the client to do evil. Instead, it can be an opportunity to present alternative actions.[176] **2.66**

Furthermore, lawyers uses the word fidelity as one of the main obligations of the relationship. We talk about the fiduciary duties and responsibilities of lawyers as an implied term of their contractual obligations. Lawyers can use this fidelity or fiduciary responsibility to then perform a role of moral educators and not one of amoral technicians. They can thus also be flexible in their relationship with their clients. They can show not only care for the client, but also for others involved with the client's legal problem and make the client aware of the broader ramifications of the situation. Of course, such an approach may not be feasible for many lawyers. These lawyers and law students hold deep-seated scepticism about the 'care' model, labelling it 'naive', 'too touchy/feely', and so on. The question these lawyers should examine is what beliefs they hold about human nature.[177]

One question many lawyers would ask is: 'If I want to adopt the care model how do I do it in practice?' The most important suggestion is become a good listener. Lawyers frequently stop a client's communication to give information on solving the problem. **2.67**

By doing this the lawyer stops being in a learning role and assumes one of control:[178]

> It subverts what the lawyer knows to what the client knows and feels … The more the client is listened to and understood, the more the client will likely listen and seek understanding in return.

Rusk lists the following as steps to good listening:[179]

> 1. Establish that your immediate goal is mutual understanding not problem solving. 2. Elicit the other person's thoughts, feelings, and desires about the

---

176. Shaffer, see n 147 (above) (1981), pp 87–90.
177. Zwier and Hamrie (above), pp 427–8 and fn 141.
178. Zwier and Hamrie (above), p 405.
179. T Rusk, *The Power of Ethical Persuasion*, Viking, New York, 1993, pp 70–1. Rusk elaborates on how to apply step three at p 89. He says: '1. Ask for a fair hearing in return. 2. Begin with an explanation of how the other person's thoughts and feelings affect you. Avoid blaming and self-defense as much as possible. 3. Carefully explain your thoughts, desires, and feelings as *your* truth, not *the* truth. 4. Ask for restatements of your position — and corrections of any factual inaccuracies — as necessary. 5. Review your respective positions.' Rusk's views are quoted extensively in Zwier and Hamrie (above), pp 404–5.

subject at hand. 3. Ask for the other person's help in understanding him or her. Try not to defend or disagree. 4. Repeat the other person's position in your own words to show you understand. 5. Ask the other person to correct your understanding and keep restating his or her position. 6. Refer back to your position only to keep things going. 7. Repeat steps 1–6 until the other person unreservedly agrees that you understand his or her position.

2.68   It is important to reiterate that the lawyer–client relationship has been adversely affected by professional rules and rulings that stem from Protestant enlightenment concepts. Abstract notions, such as 'justice', 'equality', 'fairness' and so on, have kept us from developing full human relationships with clients. It has led lawyers to regard themselves as morally isolated individuals because their work requires them to act in this manner. By adopting a moral approach to legal practice lawyers can become caring persons and make their work far more meaningful. This does not mean that this approach is feasible for all lawyers and law students.

2.69   We are still left with the nagging question as to which morals apply. What if the professional rules or rulings are opposed to the lawyer's ethics or to community or religious morals? What if the client's objectives are within the professional rules and community values but opposed to the lawyer's ethics or natural law? Should we look at the theological dimension of our actions? There are numerous other combinations of questions that could be posed. We know that each of us is subject to different moral claims at different times because we view the world from numerous perspectives. Frequently we will be faced with moral dilemmas and will have no clear idea of which to choose. This confusion stems from the significant gap that exists between our general moral principles and applying them in an everyday context. Aristotle said that we can overcome this gap by the use of practical judgment or what he called practical wisdom.[180] According to Postema, judgment entails taking 'a comprehensive view of the values and concerns at stake, based on one's experience and knowledge of the world'. He also points out that 'morality is not merely a matter of getting things right … but a matter of relating to people in a special and specifically human way'.[181] From a religious perspective we would say that when we relate to another human in a human way we are acknowledging that each person is a child of God.

Theological dimension

2.70   The theological dimension is usually missing from many lawyers' moral discussions. This stems from the non-religious philosophy that permeates our law schools. Positivism, Marxism, existentialism and other 'isms' all declare that God is dead or not relevant. They deny the basic essence of human feelings and human spirituality. By 'kicking out' God we have basically ousted moral discussions from our classrooms. There seems to be strong opinion that it is not polite to argue about religion or human spirituality, nor make moral assertions, because they sound 'airy-fairy' and

---

180. Aristotle, *Nicomachean Ethic, bk VI* (trans) H Rackham, 1962, cited in G Postema, 'Moral Responsibility in Professional Ethics' (1980) 55 *NYULR* 63, 68.
181. Postema (above), pp 68–70.

cannot be 'proven'.[182] Instead we deal with the eternal questions concerning the nature of our existence within the isolated discussion of various philosophical schools. We do this without placing these questions in a theological or human spiritual dimension. This usually leads to an unsatisfactory conclusion to any moral discussion that does take place.

For example, in classroom discussions on the amoral lawyer, for many years I referred to Sartre's views without bringing in the theological dimension. Sartre says that every individual is responsible for shaping her or his own existence. This responsibility is not met when we identify with our roles. 'I am a lawyer and that is why I pursue my client's greedy objectives.' By shifting responsibility to the institution a lawyer is able to act consistently within his or her assigned role. By adopting this kind of reasoning we evade our freedom and deny responsibility for who we are and what we do. We blame the legal profession and its rules for our actions. This can lead to the kind of remarks made by the comic Tom Lehrer about the famous rocket scientist quoted earlier in the chapter.

    2.71

Sartre says that in order to be free we must act according to our own conscience and to act otherwise is a form of 'bad faith'.[183] Students frequently posed the question that if their conscience felt comfortable in doing what society would consider morally reprehensible were they acting in 'good faith'? The answer was that few would feel comfortable in adopting that position but if they did, then they were acting in 'good faith'.

Sartre also said that human beings are responsible not only for themselves but for everyone else. This is because our impact on others may influence them. If we choose to act in 'good faith', we can never choose evil. Thus we always choose the good, and what is good for us has to be good for all.[184] Again we run into the problem of how self-choosing individuals can refrain from being egotistically oriented. Furthermore, we are confronted with Sartre's atheistic view that our existence is futile. He says that 'man [and woman] loses himself as man in order that God be born. But the idea of God is contradictory and we lose ourselves in vain. Man is a useless passion'.[185] Sartre's view is we are alive by recognising our Being but this still leads to 'nothingness'.[186]

    2.72

The answer to dealing with Sartre's philosophy appears to lie in the theological or spiritual context. There are philosophers who find in Sartre's existential philosophy a means for the rediscovery of God and for the rediscovery of love. Jacques Maritain says this rediscovery is found in the

    2.73

---

182. Shaffer, see n 147 (above) (1981), p 173. For the need to include moral theology in the study of legal ethics, see T Shaffer, 'Moral Theology in Legal Ethics' (1982) 12 *Capital University LR* 179.

183. See generally J P Sartre, *Existentialism* (B Frechtman trans), Philosophical Library, New York, 1947 and J P Sartre, *Existentialism and Humanism* (P Mairet trans), Methuen, London, 1948. It should be noted that Goffman states that there is no self outside of our roles. We all play roles by being part of society and part of a family: see E Goffman, *Encounters*, Bobbs-Merrill, Indianapolis, 1961, pp 105–12, cited in Rhode (above), p 133.

184. Sartre, see n 183 (above), generally.

185. J P Sartre, *Existential Psychoanalysis*, translation of several chapters of *L'Etre et le Neant*, New York, Philosophical Library, 1953, p 199.

186. This is the theme throughout Sartre's *Being and Nothingness*, New York, Citadel Press, 1966.

awakening of humans to the concept of Being. He states: 'I see the universal whole, whose part I am, is Being-with-nothingness, from the very fact that I am part of it; so that finally, since the universal whole does not exist by itself, there is another Whole, a separate one, another Being, transcendent and self-sufficient and unknown in itself and activating all beings, which is Being-without-nothingness, that is, self-subsisting Being, Being existing through itself.'[187]

There also appear to be certain ethical absolutes that extend across many cultures and which transcend positivistic human laws. These eternal truths have value in deciding our moral behaviour independent of our human preferences.[188] When we conduct our lives according to these truths we bring meaning to our existence.

2.74   Our society is based on Judeo–Christian traditions and within their general precepts we find many examples to help us find a spiritual framework in making our moral decisions, for example the Golden Rule of do unto others as you would have others do unto you. For many the answer is found by turning and praying to God. God, for most people, is found within traditional religion, which usually includes going to a religious house of worship. Sometimes we also know the 'answer'[189] when we turn to our 'inner self' (intuition) and listen calmly to find guidance from God. Some will find it by sitting on a beach watching the waves, entranced by a beautiful sunset, and some when they go fishing. When we enter deep within ourselves we find this stillness or silence. This method of seeking God has been the path of many 'mystics and spiritual visionaries ... who have been able to reconcile themselves with institutional authority'. This alternative approach has been 'the way of Gnosis, an acquaintance with, or knowledge of, the God within'.[190] Those who do not believe in God can apply this same approach and give whatever name they choose to the guidance they receive from within, for example 'the Force', the 'Buddha voice', 'intuition' and so on. We can place any name to the process of turning 'inward' and seeking calm guidance that comes from our spirit or soul, for example meditation or prayer. This approach is essential in our busy world. We sometimes do not have a chance to reflect on what we are thinking or doing. Invariably if we act impulsively we later regret our actions. The need for reflection and calm helps us to hear the deeper voice within. Only then do we know what rings true! As Jesus said to his

---

187. Jacques Maritain, *The Range of Reason*, New York, Scribner's, 1952, pp 88–91.

188. E Shirk, *The Ethical Dimension: An Approach to the Philosophy of Values and Valuing*, Meredith Publishing Co, 1965, p 60.

189. I believe that sometimes there is no answer — just a paradox. What usually happens is that we have to live with that paradox in a situation of conflict. As long as we remain open to an answer in such situations frequently one does come, or the problem dissolves without any action.

190. H Bloom, *Omens of the Millennium*, Fourth Estate, London, 1996, pp 1–2, 173–253. Bloom states on pp 13–14: 'If you seek *yourself* outside yourself, then you will encounter disaster, whether erotic or ideological ... Seeking God outside the self courts the disaster of dogma, institutional corruption, historical malfeasance, and cruelty ... You know the self primarily by knowing yourself; knowing another human being is immensely difficult, perhaps impossible ... Whether you can encounter God himself or herself depends upon yourself ...'.

disciples: '… you will know the truth and the truth shall set you free'.[191] Helprin has written a vivid and poetic definition of truth:[192]

> Truth is not anchored to the ground by driven piles. It can float and take to the air; it is light and lovely and delicate. It is feminine as well as masculine. It is often gentle, and, sometimes, it can even make a fool of itself — but when it does it calls down God (who protects weak creatures), and suddenly its foolishness becomes a blazing, piercing light.

Maritain says: 'Thus it is that when a man [or woman] has been really awakened to the sense of Being or Existence, and grasps intuitively the obscure, living depth of the Self and Subjectivity, he [or she] experiences, by virtue of the inner dynamism of this intuition, that love is not a passing pleasure or a more or less intense emotion, but the root tendency and very meaning of his [or her] being alive.'[193]   **2.75**

When I chose the spiritual perspective and brought it into the classroom I found that many students were able to resolve the problems that were presented by Sartre's views. The fact that the modern world has dulled our ability to be sensitive and aware does not absolve us from our moral responsibilities. Students do recognise the need to have a moral universe and, without such a framework, concern over the reason for their existence could make life quite difficult. We must have a moral context to both our private and public spheres if we are to live psychologically satisfying lives.

Obviously, the above approach can be an easy target for sceptic rationalism. Postema suggests that practitioners should incorporate their own sense of moral responsibility into their legal role and make their own assessment of what duties they should perform.[194] Schneyer made a witty response to this suggestion. He said that 'only when the legal profession abandons its ethical canon or orthodoxy in favour of a priesthood of all believers can lawyers be restored to a state of grace'.[195]   **2.76**

It is not the objective of this section to have lawyers aim to achieve the status of priesthood — few could or would choose such a path. Most lawyers are not engaged in criminal defence work and are therefore rarely required by the profession or the law to do things for their clients that conflict with both their personal values and those widely held in the community. The vast majority of lawyers have the flexibility within their practice to exercise moral judgment and to develop a moral framework. Even the small number of criminal defence lawyers have opportunities to exercise moral judgment, but they will find at times their choices more difficult and perhaps inconsistent with community values.

---

191. The Gospel of St John, 8:32, *The Living Bible*, Tyndale House Publishers, Wheaton, Illinois, 1971.
192. M Helprin, *Ellis Island and Other Stories*, in *Ellis Island*, Harvest Book, Harcourt Brace & Company, New York, 1981, p 192.
193. Maritain, *The Range of Reason*, see n 187 (above), p 92.
194. Postema (above), p 82.
195. Schneyer (above), p 1538.

CAN LAWYERS ACT MORALLY?

2.77   How can lawyers act morally? Rest and Narvaez give lawyers some guide-lines as to what is needed to act morally. They have established a four component model which consists of:

1. *Component I*: Moral sensitivity — 'It involves imaginatively constructing possible scenarios and knowing cause–consequence chains of events in the real world; it involves empathy and role-taking skills.'

2. *Component II*: Moral judgment — 'Once the person is aware of possible lines of action and how people would be affected by each line of action (Component I), then Component II judges which line of action is more morally justifiable.'

3. *Component III*: Moral motivation — 'Component III has to do with the importance given to moral values in competition with other values. Deficiencies in Component III occur when a person is not sufficiently motivated to put moral values higher than other values — when other values such as self-actualization or protecting one's organization replace concerns for doing what is right.'

4. *Component IV*: Moral character — 'This component involves ego strength, perseverance, backbone, toughness, strength of conviction, and courage. A person may be morally sensitive, may make good moral judgments, and may place high priority on moral values, but if the person wilts under pressure, is easily distracted or discouraged, is a wimp and weak-willed, then moral failure occurs because of deficiency in Component IV.'

The inability to meet any of the four components will result in a failure to act morally.[196]

2.78   There are many situations which will arise in practice that are not clearly covered by the professional rules. In fact, moral codes, including profess-ional codes, are normally kept more vague than legal codes. They usually have as their basis aspirational goals, which are couched in broad language. Thus the grounds for moral disapproval are frequently not clearly specified. This can result in lawyers applying their skills to their professional rules and interpreting them in a technical and narrow fashion to suit their needs. Most codes of professional conduct contain specific admonitions to their members to the effect that they are not inclusive — they do not deny the existence of other moral provisions not specifically mentioned. There exists within all professions unwritten conventions that help as a guide and control the behaviour of their members. Furthermore, most practitioners know that they supplement written and conventional rules of conduct with their own unwritten ones, which are frequently at a higher level of conduct than those specifically enumerated or those followed by convention. The professional rules 'are signposts at the crossroads not a fence along the entire length of the highway'.[197] Experienced lawyers develop these private moral codes that are a system of unwritten customs that are applied by using

---

196. J Rest and D Narvaez (eds), *Moral Development in the Professions: Psychology and Applied Ethics*, L Eulbaum Associates, Hillsdale, NJ, 1994, pp 23–4, as quoted in Buckingham (above), p 120. Buckingham applies the four components to legal education at pp 121–3.

197. F Oatway, 'Motivation and Responsibility in Tax Practice: The Need for Definition' (1964–65) 20 *Tax Law Review* 237, 239–40.

their intuition and instincts. Many legal practitioners follow what the Chinese call 'Li'. That is, a set of ethical precepts that are:[198]

> ... rules, partly defined and partly undefined of correct conduct and good manners, based more on moral principles than on conventions, and enforced not by legal sanction but by social reprobation.

It has become obvious from our discussion that to become both a good **2.79** person and a good lawyer we cannot just adopt a legalist position and strictly follow the ethical rules and conventions of the profession. First, these rules allow a large degree of interpretation by the individual practitioner. Second, there are many situations that they do not cover. Finally, even if the problem is clearly covered there may be a higher moral or theological principle that governs the situation and overrides the rule. This does not mean that we should throw out either the ethical rules of the profession or our own private rules. Rather, we should use these rules as a basis in helping us to recognise and become sensitised to the presence of ethical problems. Shirk has said:[199]

> One of the most difficult tasks of ethics is to help individuals recognise and be sensitive to the presence of an ethical problem. Sensitivity to others and to the nuances of human interaction is not inborn. It is not something easy to learn, and perhaps it is impossible to teach ... Ethical problems do not announce themselves as such. They must be noticed and felt to be problems ...
>
> Each and every serious answer in ethics or in religion is likely to represent an attempt to solve an urgent issue. As such it is worthy of respect regardless of how foolish or inappropriate it may be.
>
> To seek the better is to take a risk ... We might be wrong, we might have overlooked consequences of a serious nature; we might fail altogether. But to try is to have well-founded faith that nature can support our hopes and schemes.

All this discussion can be dismissed as being 'other worldly', that is, **2.80** unrealistic. One can easily argue that the term 'good', in being a good lawyer and a good person, is purely relative. By tasting the apple, Eve forever established in our Western tradition that we are doomed only to get partial answers to what is good and what is evil. The fall from grace established the dichotomy of good and evil — before this fall there was no separation. Judeo–Christian ethics have established for us that good is only revealed when we are pure in heart and then follow our intuitions. It cannot be found by reason.

Lawyers find this a hard pill to swallow. They will only accept an answer if it is based on reason. It is why lawyers argue that 'friendship, prudence and largeness of soul are not realistic in practice'.[200]

Shaffer says we should look at reality:

- ❑ the reality of who helps whom;
- ❑ the reality of who corrupts whom;
- ❑ the reality of who serves his own selfish needs and who doesn't.[201]

By looking at these realities we finally see the true nature of legal practice.

---

198. T Cheng, *China Moulded by Confucius: The Chinese Way in Western Light*, Stevens & Sons, London, 1947, p 37.
199. Shirk (above), p 127.
200. Shaffer, see n 76 (above) (1986), p 274.
201. Shaffer (above).

One author, who is a lawyer and psychologist, believes that you can maintain your soul in practising law. In fact, Benjamin Sells has called his book *The Soul of Law: Understanding Lawyers and the Law*. He points out that 'even more than feeling lonely, lawyers sense they have been exiled by being rejected by their fellow humans'. The sense of exile contributes much to the psychology of lawyers, from their 'quiet depression to their aggressive incivility, from their defensiveness to their addictions'.[202]

Sells finds the answer for lawyers in finding a soul in the practice of law is for increased acceptance and appreciation of the facts of communal existence. Furthermore, they need to make the facts in their work real and not abstract. By paying more attention and respect to facts lawyers can make a soul connection. Sells says that 'facts are the Law's only visceral connection to soul. Lawyers must resist the temptation to manipulate facts to obtain an advantage over their opponents'. The law is already good, maybe too good, at inventing defensible theories. It needs to become better at making imaginative connections with a given set of facts and then crafting suitable legal responses based on those facts. In other words, the law needs to 'make more art and fewer knock-offs'.[203] He ends by saying:[204]

> The way to the soul is through a radical appreciation of the imaginative dimensions of legal practice. The sources for this imaginal revolution are already there in daily practice: in messy cases that refuse categorization, in the mysterious search for motives, the cathedraled architecture of the courthouse, the dance of negotiation, and the lawyer's carefully reasoned fictions. But we have to pay close attention or we'll miss the soul's many quiet voices.

Achieving a sense of balance

Finding the lawyer's soul

2.81   What are lawyers doing to avoid the soulless nature of much of the law? How can they avoid burn-out, make an adequate living, feel fulfilled and feel that they have not sold their soul to the devil? I find that generally as a group, lawyers are sensitive to the issues of maintaining their integrity and seeking guidance in developing a more meaningful life. Many are exploring alternative therapies to maintain their health and also seeking out different types of courses that will enrich their lives. Some of the courses pursued include general courses on inner well-being and specific courses such as yoga, tai chi, meditation, reiki, pranic healing, massage, nutritional cooking and so on. These courses are not only beneficial in their private lives but flow naturally into making their work easier and less stressful. For example, courses on meditation teach not only relaxation skills, but also breathing techniques. The latter is an effective tool for developing better advocacy and negotiation skills.

2.82   Another important development in the salvation of their souls is the willingness of more and more lawyers to practise tithing. All major religions in the world emphasise the need to give to others freely our services or some of our wealth without the expectation of any financial or spiritual reward.

---

202. B Sells, *The Soul of Law: Understanding Lawyers and the Law*, Element, Rockport, 1994, p 176.
203. B Sells (above), p 184.
204. B Sells (above), pp 184–5.

There are lawyers who donate their time to various legal programs in order to obtain new clients or advance their careers within professional associations, but there are also a number of lawyers who willingly do pro bono and other services without seeking reward or recognition. The latter are fulfilling a deep soul connection that enriches their lives and enables them to be at peace with themselves in both their work and private lives. These lawyers have truly found and maintained their soul while practising the law. They can honestly feel and find meaning in the practice of law no matter what is said about lawyers by the mass media.

There is implied in the changing nature of practice a sense and need of group identification. Within the context of group identification there necessarily is a need for group responsibility.[205] The notion of group ethical responsibility for lawyers is a recent development. The responsibility of a firm for the actions of its members has not until recently been the concern of the disciplinary authorities. I believe that this approach of individual responsibility flows from the lawyer–client relationship; that lawyers find themselves in a one-to-one situation. The client has one lawyer responsible for his or her problem and that lawyer is the one who is accountable if anything goes wrong.

2.83

In class over a number of years I used an article in the *Harvard Business Review* to highlight the lack of group responsibility in Western society. The article helped my students to see the need for changes within the legal profession to develop group responsibility. The article is 'The Parable of the Sadhu' written by Bowen McCoy.[206] McCoy had been given a six-month sabbatical from his business job with Morgan Stanley and decided to use three months of leave to follow one of his dreams — mountain climbing in the Himalayas in Nepal. He went with an anthropologist friend, Stephen. They had camped at 14,500 feet before attempting to accomplish the highlight of the trip, a climb over an 18,000-foot mountain pass. Four New Zealanders camped with them and just below them were two Swiss couples and a Japanese hiking club. They had to leave very early in order to avoid the sun melting the steps that were cut in the ice. They departed at 3:30 am with the New Zealanders going first. The Swiss then followed and the Japanese were still in their camp. When they arrived at 15,500 feet one of the New Zealanders came down the mountain carrying a near naked body. He dumped the body of a sadhu (an Indian holy man) at their feet and angrily said he had done what he could do; that he had to get back to join his friends.

The sadhu was just barely alive and McCoy and his friend and the Swiss dressed him in warm clothes. The sadhu still could not walk. McCoy was worried about withstanding the problems of breathing in the altitude he needed to climb to and told Stephen and their guide that he wanted to go ahead. He made it to the top of the pass and when Stephen arrived some time later he ran to congratulate him as he was overjoyed by their

2.84

205. The following is extracted from my ethics column in the *Law Institute Journal*, December 1999, p 45.
206. *Harvard Business Review*, September–October 1983, reprinted in R Zitrin and C Langford, *Legal Ethics in the Practice of Law*, 1995, The Michie Company, Charlottesville, Virginia, pp 16–21.

accomplishment. Stephen said: 'How do you feel about contributing to the death of a fellow man?' McCoy asked him if the sadhu was dead. Stephen told him he did not know.

What had happened was that when the Japanese had arrived Stephen had asked them for the use of their horse to take the sadhu down a thousand feet to a hut. The Japanese had refused but offered the sadhu drink and food. Stephen then asked their guide to ask the Sherpas (porters) to carry him down to the hut but they could only take him down 500 feet. They needed to return because they would not have the energy to climb the pass if they went down any further. Stephen last saw the sadhu sitting on a rock in the sun throwing stones at a dog belonging to the Japanese.

Stephen was upset that although every group had given the sadhu some help they did so as long as it was not too inconvenient. There was not one group that would take total or ultimate responsibility for the sadhu. The groups were only interested in getting over the pass and/or their own individual well-being. McCoy started to question his own actions. Near the end of the article he asks: 'Is there a collective or institutional ethic beyond the ethics of the individual? At what level of effort or commitment can one discharge one's ethical responsibilities?' McCoy will probably be haunted by whether or not the sadhu survived for the rest of his life. It is obvious from his article that the story has affected him in his everyday business life.

When I used this story in class I asked my students the following question: 'What if the nearly dead person dropped at your feet was a famous Western actor or actress such as Brad Pitt or Nicole Kidman?'

We are living in a time of individualism, which deters group identification and group responsibility. Clive Hamilton, the executive director of the Australian Institute, states that the social groupings of last century 'are no longer relevant (or at least of greatly diminished relevance)'. He says we have become 'highly individualistic, in the sense of self-focused, a product of the combined impact of the liberation movements, neoliberal ideology and the market'. He states social groupings are still being constructed for utilitarian reasons — greater efficiency, lower costs etc — but these groups cannot be the basis for reconstruction of a new social world. The individual within these convenient groupings is still hostile to being social. Hamilton concludes: 'We must reconstruct the idea of solidarity not on the basis of economic benefit but on the basis of our common humanity.'[207]

2.85   Group ethical responsibility within the legal profession is a current issue. Already there are rules to allow firms to be disciplined. For example, in Victoria firms are held responsible under the disciplinary system. I will discuss this in more detail in Chapter 7. Generally the professional authorities in Australia have emphasised individual responsibility. By choosing to seek to discipline only one or two partners or an associate of a firm that has committed a serious ethical breach, the profession allows the firm to disassociate itself from these individuals, and to escape responsibility. By enforcing ethical rules that hold the whole group

---

207. C Hamilton, 'Diseases of affluence and other paradoxes in a time of plenty', *Australian Financial Review, Review*, 15 October 2004, pp 8–9. For a longer version of the essay go to www.tai.org.au.

responsible I believe we can develop better ethical practices within the organisations and that will improve the total image of the profession.

One may ask: 'Why me? Everyone else is acting amorally or immorally and all that will happen is that I lose my clients.'[208] The fact is that everyone else is not acting amorally or immorally. There are already a number of practitioners who practise within a moral framework and seek meaning in their work. There is also another reason for pursuing this path. The more practitioners that adopt the human and moral position, the easier it is for the rest of the profession to learn to act in this way. There is scientific evidence that says: 'If a certain critical number of people learn to do something well, then it will be far easier for the rest to learn.'[209]   **2.86**

Thus there are two alternatives to legal practice. One is the present lawyer–client model, the professional 'realistic' approach. The other is to place our work in a truly moral and meaningful context. The former leads to the present inhumane system that now prevails. The latter leads to an environment where one can be human: where one can reconcile being a good lawyer with being a moral person. If this dichotomy is a too contrasting approach there is a third path — to apply from time to time a moral and meaningful context to your legal work. This path can eventually lead you to reject for most of your work the 'realistic' approach and create a meaningful context in your working life.   **2.87**

---

208. For an interesting tale where the law firm does lose the client, see G Cooper, 'The Avoidance Dynamic: A Tale of Tax Planning, Tax Ethics, and Tax Reform' (1980) 80 *Columbia LR* 1553.

209. F Wolf, *Star Wave: Mind Consciousness and Quantum Physics*, Collier Books, New York, 1984, p 170.

3

PROFESSIONALISM

INTRODUCTION[1]

Lawyers as a profession

3.1   Lawyers are considered to be members of a group of occupations known as professions. Occupations that have been given special status have been in existence since the Roman Empire, but the term 'profession' and the distinctive features associated with it date back to the sixteenth century.[2] According to the *Oxford Dictionary* 'profession' comes from the Latin *professionem* which means making a public declaration, which came to mean taking a public vow or oath on entering a learned occupation. We frequently associate professional groups with notions of expertise, status and power. A good example was the action of the American Psychiatric Society in 1974, when by a majority vote at their convention they decided that homosexuality was no longer an illness. Ian Kennedy, in discussing this action, said:[3]

> ... so, since 1974 it [homosexuality] hasn't been an illness. How extraordinary, you may think, to decide what illness is, by taking a vote. What exactly is going on here?

3.2   Kennedy was showing by this example the great power that professional organisations have in defining our social reality. Were homosexuals really any different before or after the vote? The fact that certain occupational groups, such as lawyers, exercise enormous power over their areas of expertise is a cause for concern. We should ask immediately — how did these groups amass this power? What kind of controls does the public have in the exercise of the power?

---

1.   A number of the ideas in this section come from the chapter I wrote in J Disney, J Basten, P Redmond and S Ross, *Lawyers*, 2nd ed, Law Book Company, Sydney, 1986, pp 73–91.

2.   G Hazard Jr and D Rhode, *The Legal Profession: Responsibility and Regulation*, 3rd ed, Foundation Press, Westbury, NY, 1994, p 2.

3.   I Kennedy, The Reith Lectures, 'Unmasking Medicine', *The Listener*, 6 November 1980, p 600.

There is an assumption in our society that lawyers are professionals. Such   **3.3**
an assumption avoids the question of why lawyers may legitimately call
themselves professionals. When we think of the traditional professions,
lawyers and doctors immediately come to mind. In medieval times, being a
priest or a soldier would have been considered a profession, but few would
think of them as such today. During the fourteenth century, surgeons, who
have high status today, came after the barbers in the guild parades, which
reflected their relative status. Obviously, the latter were considered less
dangerous in the use of their scissors than the surgeons who probably killed
half of their patients with their knives. For centuries the clergy and military
were considered professions and suitable occupations for the children of the
upper class and later those of the rising middle class. Today we do not think
of the clergy nor the military as professionals. There is, therefore, historical
evidence of the rise and fall of the status of occupations. So how did the
present professionals obtain their status and extraordinary powers over the
area of their expertise?

Historical origin

The modern legal profession finds its historical origin within the church.   **3.4**
For hundreds of years the role of education was tied to ecclesiastical
functions. The main source and disseminators of knowledge were priests.
Lawyers, like priests, were among the few groups in medieval society who
had the ability to read and write. Since few had these skills lawyers became
an important reservoir for the accumulation of knowledge. The trans-
mission of this knowledge was limited. It took centuries, after the invention
of the printing press by Gutenberg in the fifteenth century, for printed
information to become readily available to the masses. The identification
with the clergy was clearly recognised by Voltaire, the famous eighteenth-
century French philosopher, poet and dramatist, who said: 'La loi, n'est pas
une profession, c'est un sacerdose' — the law is not a profession, it is a
priesthood.[4] The connection to religion is still present in France. On a visit
in April 2005 to La Rochelle, an old sea port, I noticed that the main court
house has etched into its old nineteenth-century facade the words 'Temple
de Justice'.

When the first Inns of Courts were created in England in the fifteenth   **3.5**
century they sought to be secular and to divorce themselves from the
church. In reality they were a halfway-house between the clerics and the
craft guilds, combining the skills and knowledge of both these groups.
During the seventeenth and eighteenth centuries the legal profession
became an important avenue for the children of the new middle classes to
achieve the status of 'gentlemen'. The industrial revolution of the nineteenth century destroyed the guilds as the skills of artisans were replaced by
machine-production, but the personal service offered by lawyers could not
be easily removed. It is only now that lawyers' skills are being threatened by
the post-industrial computer age. The modern legal profession is now
associated with the universities but this connection has not destroyed
aspects of the profession's historical link with the church. The legal

---

4.   Coming from Voltaire this is not a compliment for lawyers. Voltaire was notorious for his
      witty anti-clerical remarks.

profession still has a mystical aura that is evident in its ceremonial functions, its dress and its monopoly over esoteric legal knowledge. Anyone who has attended any of the opening of judicial calendar year ceremonies in Sydney, that take place in several of the main religions' houses of worship, would be impressed by the grandeur and solemnity of the occasion.

WHAT DETERMINES A PROFESSION?

Trait theory

3.6   During the 1950s and 1960s sociologists decided to examine what traits lawyers and doctors thought they had that made them different from other occupations. Millerson, in comparing the different traits found by 21 authors, found 23 elements, the most frequently cited of which were:

- ❑ skill based on theoretical knowledge;
- ❑ the provision of training and education;
- ❑ testing the competence of members;
- ❑ organisation;
- ❑ an ethical code of conduct; and
- ❑ altruistic service.[5]

It is obvious that sociologists could not agree on the definition of what constituted a profession. The term professional can still be used to evoke strong feelings and to promote status for an occupational group. It is also used as part of an implicit syllogism: 'academics are professionals — professionals do not go on strike — therefore academics should not go on strike to obtain higher wages'.[6] Or, 'barristers are professionals — professionals control their own fees — therefore barristers should be allowed to set their own fees'. Of course, traits or attributes are always in flux. For example, many academics in the twenty-first century no longer feel it is 'unprofessional' to take strike action. Finally, the trait theory helps us to understand how professionals see themselves, as traits are frequently gathered from claims made by the professionals as to what makes them unique.

3.7   The trait or 'inventory' approach was discredited because other occupations have many of the characteristics of the established professions; that is, technical skills, high incomes, consensus, distinctive traits and organisational support to achieve common objectives. In fact, these characteristics, as sociologists have pointed out, could be found to be common also to diverse groups such as 'professional' thieves[7] and jazz musicians.[8] Furthermore, occupations have sought to gain the status of the traditional professions by requiring certification and adopting codes of ethics. The

---

5.   G Millerson, *The Qualifying Associations: A Study in Professionalism*, Routledge and Kegan Paul, London, 1964, p 5. The most often cited article on the trait theory is E Greenwood, 'Attributes of a Profession' (1957) 2 *Social Work* 44.

6.   Another example of a professional trait is the abnegation of forming or joining unions. This attribute is no longer present in certain professional groups, for example academics — many of whom have been union members for a long time and also support the union when it asks its members to strike.

7.   See E Sutherland, *The Professional Thief*, University of Chicago Press, Chicago, 1937.

8.   H Becker, 'The Professional Jazz Musician and His Audience' (1951) 57 *American J of Sociology* 135.

enforcement of the standards set out for certification by these groups was sometimes almost non-existent.

A good example is the case of a cat (Oliver Greenhalgh) whose owner applied to have him certified as a fellow of the English Association of Estate Agents and Valuers. Oliver's application was approved even though his owner described him on the application as a 'rodent operative'. At the time this association obviously was more interested in collecting fees for issuing certificates than in maintaining any standard of knowledge of estate agencies and valuation.[9]

Another criticism was that the trait approach involved a high degree of circular reasoning and self-justification. The Anglo–American legal and medical professions were used as the model for other occupations to emulate in order to achieve the highest status of an occupation. Such an approach ignores other societies. Finally, the trait theory did not consider the historical context. It ignored the question: 'What are the circumstances in which people in an occupation attempt to turn it into a profession and themselves into professional people?'[10]   **3.8**

Power and resource theory

Sociologists in the 1970s and 1980s abandoned the trait approach to see how the professions achieved their economic power and control over the market for their services. Johnson developed the 'resources of power' theory. He stated: **3.9**

> The resources of power available to any single occupational group are rarely sufficient to impose on all consumers its own definitions of the content of production and its ends, except where these resources are articulated with other and wider bases of power.

He saw that professionalism is:[11]

> … a peculiar type of occupational control rather than an expression of the inherent nature of particular occupations. A profession is not, then, an occupation, but a means of controlling an occupation … [M]iddle class power provided the base from which the expanding 'professions' created their own autonomous organisations.

By exercising control over their clients and over their area of expertise, occupations achieve the status of profession. The resources of power approach thus gives support to the notion that there really is such a thing as a profession and, indirectly, sanctions control by the professionals over their clients and their area of expertise. It also sees the groups that achieved the status of a profession as being homogeneous and uniformly pursuing power as their major goal. This is true sometimes, but not always. Also, groups will sometimes make alliances with other groups to help them achieve their goals. The aim of the resources of power studies is to emphasise which resources and strategies give rise to control and power. There is little room for subjective experience and social action by members of the group. At times members will pursue nobler goals than just control and power. This

9.   *The Times*, 10 December 1967.
10.   E Hughes, 'Professions' (1963) *Daedalus*, No 4, p 92.
11.   T Johnson, *Professions and Power*, MacMillan, London, 1972, pp 45 and 52.

would be shown if the research looked at the actual activities of members of the group and not just at the goals of the leadership.[12]

3.10 According to Illich, Lasch and Gouldner, the resources of power theory was the basis for criticism of the professions for amassing extraordinary power and monopolising expertise, reducing the average person to dependence.[13] Illich called this the 'imperialism' of the professions.[14] Lasch argued that psychiatrists, social workers, penologists and educators saw themselves as the healers of a sick society and demanded and received broad medical authority to cure the problem.[15] Illich saw that the more the medical profession turned to the use of simple tools, that is, drug therapy, the longer the period of university education and practical training required before achieving the status of a doctor. Only then could one be granted the legitimate use of the simplest tools. Furthermore, the medical profession convinced the public that they needed doctors to cure them with their special knowledge of these tools and almost the entire population became dependent upon the doctor.[16]

3.11 Today, many people feel the 'helping' professions have more often been helping themselves to important positions with status and large financial rewards than helping to cure our illnesses. Of course, it can be argued that although professionals may have created the demand for their product, they have not created the social problems or illnesses that they attempt to control and cure.[17] The truth probably depends on who is dispensing the product and there are many that would point out numerous times when professionals have helped people.

In Australia there has been a strong reaction to the helping professions who are part of the new professional elite. They are seen to be out of touch with ordinary Australians. 'They have many names, including chardonnay socialists, the chattering class and … the moral middle class.'[18] The Howard Government has been very successful in exploiting this anti-elitism attitude to stay in government.[19]

There are many critics who believe that the professions are on the decline and that they are not in control but are controlled by others. This approach stems more from a class or structural perspective. A seminal work taking this approach is that of Larson.[20] Her objective was to see how professions

---

12. C Davies, *Professional Power and Sociological Analysis: Lessons from a Comparative Historical Study of Nursing in Britain and the United States* (1981) (unpublished PhD thesis, Dept of Sociology, University of Warwick), pp 231–3. See also T Halliday, *Beyond Monopoly: Lawyers, State Crises and Professional Empowerment*, University of Chicago Press, Chicago, 1987.

13. See C Lasch, *The Revolt of the Elites and the Betrayal of Democracy*, Norton & Co, New York, 1995 and C Lasch, *The Culture of Narcissism*, Warner, New York, 1979.

14. I Illich, *Tools for Conviviality*, Calder and Boyars, London, 1973 and I Illich et al, *Disabling Professions*, Marion Boyars, London, 1977.

15. C Lasch, *Haven in a Heartless World*, Basic Books, New York, 1977, p 15.

16. Illich (above) (1973), p 1.

17. A de Swaan, 'The Politics of Agoraphobia' (1981) 10 *Theory and Society* 359, 382ff.

18. M Sawer, 'The power of us and them', *Australian Financial Review*, Review, 22 October 2004, p 2.

19. Ibid. See also M Sawer and B Hindess (eds), *Us and Them: Anti-Elitism in Australia*, API Network, Sydney, 2004.

20. M Larson, *The Rise of Professionalism: A Sociological Analysis*, University of California Press, Berkeley, 1977.

organised themselves to attain power over the marketplace. She saw from her research that, historically, professionalism was a collective assertion of power by producers of special services to achieve upward social mobility, that is, special social status. They did this by control over a scarce resource — special knowledge and skills. This control was then translated into social and economic rewards.[21]

Historical background

Larson's work is important because she traced the history of lawyers, doctors and engineers not only in Anglo–American society but also in Europe. In the former, the professions such as law and medicine had a high status and power and reflected the dominant laissez-faire attitudes of those societies. In Europe, the long-standing state bureaucracies and strong centralised governments led to a different situation, with doctors and lawyers mainly working for the state. Those in private practice, unlike private practitioners in Anglo–American society, had a lower status than those working for the state. Furthermore, the medical profession in Russia was dominated by women, which also lowered its status.[22]

3.12

The history of the traditional professions shows a development from a predominantly economic function, focusing on organising and developing the ties between education in the universities and the marketplace, to a predominantly ideological function that justifies inequality of status and monopolistic practices. The professions today have adopted ideological functions to mystify and obscure real social structures. In order to achieve this position the professions had to develop a distinctive product. They did this by developing intangible goods; ones tied to the person and personality of the individual producer:[23]

3.13

> It follows, therefore, that the producers themselves have to be produced if their products or commodities are to be given a distinctive form. In other words, the professionals must be adequately trained and socialised so as to provide recognisably distinct services for exchange on the professional market.

The product then had to be standardised and made superior to competing products. This led to the need for monopolisation to eliminate competing products and thereby guarantee the market for its product. A monopoly was also needed to induce new recruits to accept the economic sacrifices of a long training period. The recruits knew that their investment was protected by market control that kept up the price of the product.[24]

Lawyers as bureaucrats

The traditional notion of a professional in our society has been that of the individual doctor and lawyer. We have a different situation today where the vast majority of the new members of these professions do not work alone and instead are employed by government departments, corporations or law firms as salaried employees. A good example of this trend was the requirement in New South Wales for newly qualified solicitors to work for three years as an employee before obtaining a full practising certificate. It

3.14

---

21. Larson (above), pp xvi–xvii.
22. Larson (above).
23. Larson (above), p 10.
24. Larson (above), p 10.

was changed, to bring it in line with other states, ensuring a uniform national standard, and the period was dropped to two years. Larson therefore argues that a better model of the modern *professional* should be based on the engineering profession. That profession is based on a techno-bureaucratic model with most of its members being employees. Although the professions push the image of individuality, the present situation is increasingly more that of salaried specialists in a large organisation. Promotion within these modern organisations does not lead to increasing power and control in decision-making. Professionals do have discretion in their actions at the level of everyday decision-making in relation to a project or individual client, but do not have real power nor freedom of choice in their work. Modern professionals function as agents of a power elite, who perpetuate the structures of domination and inequality which are essential to competitive capitalism. Professionals do this work for the elite without recognising that they are merely concealing their own collective powerlessness, subordination and complicity.[25]

3.15 Abel agrees with Larson that professionals are becoming bureaucratised and are more controlled than controlling of others. Abel has stated that the golden age of the legal profession has already passed and it is now in decline. He sees lawyers as losing areas of expertise to other groups. For example, legislation in New South Wales recently removed the legal profession's monopoly over conveyancing by issuing licences to lay conveyancers[26] and lay conveyancers operate in all jurisdictions except Queensland. In that state, it has been suggested that legislation be adopted to allow lay conveyancers,[27] but as of August 2005 no legislation has been adopted. The monopoly was removed in England and Wales in 1985.[28] Furthermore, the legal profession has been divided over the standards for admission and has lost control over admission to legal education to the universities. Thus the profession no longer controls the supply of lawyers and the present oversupply is devaluing its own status. The profession has tried to overcome this problem by increasing the public demand for its product, especially through legal aid and by opening new areas of work, for example administrative law and alternative dispute resolution, and by increased law-making to create many jobs, not only in the private practice, but also in government and the corporate sectors. Of course, reliance on government funding and employment leads to accountability to the government or control by the government. Furthermore, working in large corporations necessarily dictates loss of independent action as the corporation's policies will usually need to be followed.[29] These developments are in direct

---

25. Larson (above), pp 14–15 and 52.
26. See the Conveyancers Licensing Act 1995 (NSW). The 1995 Act replaced the 1992 Act and expanded the area of legal work that could be undertaken by licensed conveyancers. The new Act abolished the independently constituted Conveyancers Licensing Committee, and transferred the licensing function from the Law Society to the Property Services Council. See F Riley, 'The Conveyancers' Licensing Act 1995 (NSW)' (1996) 19 *UNSW LJ* 470.
27. Queensland Government Green Paper, *Legal Profession Reform*, June 1999, pp 26–28.
28. Administration of Justice Act 1985.
29. Loss of this independence and having two roles — professional and corporate — can negate legal professional privilege. See E Kyrou, 'Dual Roles: Implications for legal professional privilege' (April 2000) *Law Institute J (Vic)* 53.

opposition to the traditional values of an independent profession and, with the development of the large firms, large government and corporate legal departments, has led to a bureaucratisation of lawyers' work, which destroys the traditional notion of professionalism.[30]

Even with this new work there is limited scope for expansion. The legal product, unlike the medical one, is not so attractive to consumers and cannot be made universal. This is shown by a public that seems to be seeking less law rather than more law.[31] This was especially true during the economic recession of the early 1990s.[32] The large firms reacted by behaving in an 'ungentlemanly' manner in the smaller market, openly wooing each other's clients.[33] The pressures of competition for clients has become even greater in the beginning of the twenty-first century.

3.16

Furthermore, the large corporate clients are culling their panels of lawyers from whom they choose to give their legal work. This has placed a squeeze especially on middle-size firms.[34] This trend may be changing as some of the largest corporations, such as AMP, are giving more work to middle-size firms.[35] Finally, the profession, at least in New South Wales and Victoria, is no longer united over maintaining the status quo on restrictive practices. For example, the reaction of the Council of the Law Society in New South Wales to the New South Wales Government's initiative to reform the structure and regulation of the profession in 1992[36] was to criticise many of the restrictive practices of the bar.[37] The bar retaliated by attacking the Council of the Law Society for the views it had expressed for its members. The then President of the Bar, John Coombs QC, wrote to all solicitors, attaching a copy of the Law Society's submission to the Attorney-General, with a covering letter which was very critical of the position taken by the Council.[38] An extraordinary meeting of the Law Society was then called which repudiated the submission made by the Council. We will discuss these problems in more detail in the next chapter.

Growth of legal market and income

It should be noted that in the first few years of the twenty-first century there is anecdotal evidence that the market for legal services was growing faster than the rest of the economy in Australia. 'Law firm management consultant George Beaton said the fact that 13 leading corporate law firms expanded the ranks of their partnerships by an average 6.8 per cent was a positive forward indicator that was in line with strong growth across a

3.17

---

30. I Szelenyi and B Martin, 'The Legal Profession and the Rise and Fall of the New Class' in R Abel and P Lewis (eds), *Lawyers in Society, Vol 3: Comparative Theories*, University of California Press, Berkeley, 1989, pp 282–5.

31. R Abel, 'The Politics of the Market for Legal Services' in P Thomas (ed), *Law in the Balance: Legal Services in the 1980s*, Martin Robertson, London, 1982, pp 44–8.

32. K Maley, 'Top Lawyers Run Hard to Stay Still', *Sydney Morning Herald*, 8 May 1993, p 40.

33. Maley (above).

34. See *Business Review Weekly*, 10 March 2000, p 51.

35. S Moran, 'AMP looks beyond the top shelf', *Australian Financial Review*, 22 July 2005, p 51.

36. See the New South Wales Attorney-General's Department, *The Structure and Regulation of the Legal Profession*, Issues Paper, November 1992.

37. See K Gosman, 'Rumpole vs LA Law', *Sun-Herald*, 10 May 1992, p 33.

38. See also *Australian Law News*, September 1992, pp 7–8.

number of practice areas.'[39] In the United States the annual survey of the largest 100 firms in 2003 showed a 9.5 per cent increase in gross revenues and a 9.8 per cent increase in the average profit per equity partner to $930,700US. The American firms have been able to overcome the downturn in the general economy by the use of cost management.[40] In the first decade of the twenty-first century there also appears to be a development of a better job market for lawyers in the United States.[41]

In Australia the rate of growth of solicitors' income has fallen from the high increases in 2000 and 2001 of 15 per cent and 13 per cent respectively, but was still at a rate of 8 per cent for 2003.[42] It was estimated in late 2004 that the income of a partner in a top-tier law firm in Sydney was more than $820,000 while in Melbourne it was more than $700,000.[43]

Deprofessionalisation

3.18   Anleu agrees with Larson and Abel that 'more lawyers now perform specialized tasks and work in large bureaucratic settings'. She does not see the development as signalling:[44]

> ... the deprofessionalization or proletarianization of the legal profession. A major problem with ... [the deprofessionalisation argument] is the uncritical acceptance of the attribute model of the professions and the assumption that recent changes constitute deviations from an ideal-type profession. Alternatively, if professions are conceptualized as modes of organizing work, controlling a market, or making jurisdictional claims, then recent changes represent the assertion of control and consolidation of certain segments within the profession rather than an absolute reduction in professional autonomy.

Anleu also points out that the deprofessionalisation argument ignores the fact that salaried employees still have far more autonomy over their work than those lawyers in self-employment. The latter frequently do not have effective control of their position in the labour market. This means they lack the 'capacity to regulate and control work tasks and clients, even though the pace of work and the hours can be controlled to some extent'. These practitioners have always been vulnerable to market forces, which determine their 'ability to locate and retain clients, and clients frequently exercise some control over these lawyers'.[45] The argument that these clients exercise control seems somewhat dubious in light of the fact that these clients are often 'one-shot' clients, who rarely need lawyers' services.

---

39.   C Merritt and K Towers, 'Growth in law services outstrips economy', *Australian Financial Review*, 19 December 2003, p 45.
40.   K Scannell, *Wall Street J*, 29 June 2004. The article is based on the annual survey published in *The American Lawyer*, July 2004.
41.   'Better job market for attorneys', *California Bar J*, June 2004, p 1.
42.   K Towers, 'Slim pickings as firms tighten belts', *Australian Financial Review*, 8 August 2003, p 52. The figures are from the 2003 Mahlab survey.
43.   *Boss, Australian Financial Review*, November 2004, p 58.
44.   S Anleu, 'The Legal Profession in the United States and Australia: Deprofessionalization or Reorganization' (1992) 19 *Work and Occupations* 184, 199. Anleu also argues (p 200) that 'although professional employees are required to conform to organizational procedures and objectives and to coordinate their work with other employees, they maintain exclusive control over their own knowledge base, which preserves their autonomy and reduces managerial encroachments'.
45.   Anleu (above), p 199.

In contrast with Larson and Abel, Gouldner supports the views of Lasch   **3.19**
and Illich and others[46] that the professions do have power but only as
members of the 'New Class'. Gouldner sees professionals, including lawyers,
as leaders of the New Class who have taken power from the old class who
had control through economic power. The New Class rules our society by
controlling specialised knowledge or cultural capital. Gouldner says we are
now in the grip of the ideology of professionalism. Professionalism makes
tacit claim to:[47]

> … technical and moral superiority over the old class, implying that the latter
> lack technical credentials and are guided by motives of commercial venality.
> Professionalism silently installs the New Class as the paradigm of virtuous
> and legitimate authority, performing with technical skill and with dedicated
> concern for the society-at-large … In asserting its own claims to authority,
> professionalism in effect devalues the authority of the old class.

During the 1960s and 1970s, perhaps in response to loss of control and   **3.20**
deprofessionalisation of the legal profession, lawyers entered the New Class
in large numbers, for example in government employment. These
government lawyers were instrumental in the implementation of social
change through governmental programs and formed a group of lawyers
critical of traditional professional values. During the late 1970s and into the
1980s many lawyers abandoned the New Class, and there was a trend
towards reprofessionalisation of the legal profession. Szelenyi and Martin
state that:[48]

> Gouldner was wrong; he believed that the rise of the New Class was virtually
> inevitable, even imminent. Instead, the 'New Class' project failed, the
> radical middle class is gone, and the highly educated, including lawyers, have
> re-entered the Collective Mobility project of professionalism, which had
> served them so well in the past.

The 1990s and early 2000s have shown another change with a number of
professionals, including lawyers, seeking to maintain the collective mobility
of their profession and flexibility in work practices, while at the same time
finding meaning to their life within personal development courses, such as
those of the New Age movement. The question for this century is whether
notions of professionalism such as status and power can be maintained
while members of the professions are searching for the meaning of life. This
question is explored in detail in Chapter 16.

CODES OF PROFESSIONAL CONDUCT

Types of codes

Codes of professional conduct are one of the most important characteristics   **3.21**
of a profession. In recent times new codes for the legal profession have been

46.   See the views of McKinlay that the medical profession has amassed tremendous power:
      J McKinlay, 'The Business of Good Doctoring or Doctoring as Good Business: Reflections
      on Views of the Medical Game' (1977) 7 *International J of Health Services* 459.
47.   A Gouldner, *The Future of Intellectuals and the Rise of the New Class*, Seabury Press, New
      York, 1979, p 19.
48.   Szelenyi and Martin (above), pp 263, 276–82.

adopted in a number of Australian jurisdictions, in the United States and New Zealand: see Chapter 1.

These codes have already been amended in most Australian jurisdictions. Almost all of them are in the process of adopting a uniform code based on the Law Council of Australia's 1997 Revised Model Rules of Professional Conduct and Practice (as amended in 2002) that is to act as a uniform national code.[49] The Royal Commission on Legal Services in England recommended in 1979 the adoption of a written code.[50] Although the law societies in England and Scotland have begun work on adopting a code, as of August 2005 no comprehensive code was in force. The solicitors in England and Wales adopted a Publicity Code in 1990 which was replaced by a new code in 2001. The United Kingdom lawyers do come under the Code of Conduct for Lawyers in the European Community which was adopted in 1988, amended in 1998 and 2002. Finally, there have been calls to have an international ethical code to control the activities of Western lawyers operating in the developing world[51] which are not covered under the International Code of Ethics of the International Bar Association.[52]

3.22 A recent development has been ethical provisions for specialised areas such as a family law code,[53] a residential conveyancing code of practice,[54] a tax ethics code,[55] a code for government solicitors,[56] a code for expert witnesses[57] and a code for immigration lawyers.[58] There is even a code for employed solicitors in New South Wales to understand better the relationship between themselves and senior solicitors.[59] A new set of these employment guidelines was adopted by the New South Wales Law Society in 2003. The need for specialised separate codes of professional conduct is based on the argument that lawyers' duties vary greatly depending upon the area of practice.[60]

---

49. Information from the Law Council of Australia, December 2004.
50. *Final Report* (1979), paras 22.57–22.60.
51. J Daehler, 'Professional Versus Moral Responsibility in the Developing World' (1995) 9 *Georgetown J of Legal Ethics* 229.
52. For an interesting account of ethical requirements when practising in China, see C Langford and N Nicoll, 'Ethics Abroad: A Shanghai Surprise', *California Bar J*, November 2002, p 10.
53. See *Family Law Advisory Code of Practice*, Law Society of NSW, 1993.
54. See 'Residential Conveyancing Code of Practice' (1991) 29 *Law Society J (NSW)* 35. This Code was repealed by Council on 19 October 2000.
55. See S Ross, *Ethics for Tax Practitioners*, Australian Tax Research Foundation, 1993 and *Code of Conduct*, Australian Taxation Office, 1992.
56. 'Guidance on Ethical Issues for Government Solicitors (NSW)', 2003. See V Shirvington, 'Ethics: Guidance on ethical issues for government solicitors' (2003) 41 *Law Society J (NSW)* 34.
57. See the draft Uniform Civil Procedure Rules 2005 (NSW).
58. See Migration Agents Regulations 1992 (No 292) reg 5. These regulations were held not to violate the Constitution by being applied to lawyers who must meet their requirements to practise immigration law. See *Cunliffe v Commonwealth* (1994) 182 CLR 272. Meeting the requirements is not difficult for lawyers. It can be done by simply filling out an application showing they have an Australian law degree or that they are admitted to practice.
59. See 'Towards Better Understanding of the Contract of Employment' (1992) 30 *Law Society J (NSW)* 48.
60. See S Sporkin, 'The Need for Separate Codes of Professional Conduct for the Various Specialties' (1993) 7 *Georgetown J of Legal Ethics* 149.

For example, corporate practice or tax practice present totally different sets of problems to those of the criminal defence lawyer. Furthermore, an American judge has pointed out that 'the general ethical standards of the existing rules often do not make sense when applied to corporate and securities practitioners'.[61] In these areas there is often difficulty in deciding who is the client, what type of representation should be pursued before government regulatory bodies, what lawyers should do during corporate takeovers and what obligations are owed by lawyers to third parties, for example public shareholders.[62]

Code of ethics analysed

Lichtenberg has summed up what she calls the 'puzzling' idea of an ethical code. She says:[63]   **3.23**

> What is it, exactly, and how can it bind us? Or can it? Its status, normative if not ontological seems mysterious. Either its pronouncements are obvious (read 'platitudinous'), in which case it invites ridicule, or they are not obvious (read 'controversial') in which case it arouses suspicion. A third possibility is that its pronouncements are vague. In that case they are useless unless interpreted. When interpreted, they are either obvious, thus platitudinous; or not obvious, thus controversial.

Why the great need for an ethical code? Who benefits when an occupation adopts an ethical code? It has been argued that codes can be used to control lawyers from shady practices and also give the lawyers a weapon against clients who want them to do something that the lawyers consider too extreme. The mere existence of a code can raise the standard of ethical behaviour simply by clarifying what is deemed to be ethical conduct and expressing an occupation's commitment to a moral standard.[64] This idea is the basis of voluntary codes of conduct.[65] It can lead to morally acceptable or required behaviour by making people conscious of their actions and by threatening them with sanctions.[66] A code can also have aspirational aspects by providing a statement of ideals that can act as a framework for a more ethical-oriented profession.

Ethical codes can be criticised for their inability at times to resolve ethical   **3.24**
conflicts and for their limited ability to change human conduct. Codes can also be used to the detriment of the community and be used mainly for the interests of the profession. A code can enhance status, control the market for legal services and be used to defend the profession against attack. For example, if lawyers are accused of some kind of unsavoury behaviour the profession can say it will amend the code and that will cure the problem.[67]

---

61. Sporkin (above).
62. Sporkin (above), pp 150–2.
63. J Lichtenberg, 'What are Codes of Ethics for', in M Coady and S Bloch (eds), *Codes of Ethics and the Professions*, Melbourne University Press, 1996, p 15.
64. Studies of the 500 largest American corporations show a highly statistically significant link of better economic performance by those corporations who make a formal public ethical commitment to their stakeholders. L Preston, Letters to the Editor, *The Economist*, 13 May 2000, p 5.
65. See *Voluntary Codes*, Office of Consumer Affairs, Ottawa, March 1998.
66. Lichtenberg (above), p 27.
67. See A Daniels, 'How Free Should Professionals Be' in E Freidson (ed), *The Professions and Their Prospects*, Sage Publications, Beverly Hills, 1973, pp 31, 45–9.

Codes can only be effective if they are clearly stated and enforced against members. They must be able to 'permit the coercion of ethical delivery of professional services and ... offer a prospect of deterrence of professional misconduct'.[68]

3.25   There has been a lively debate in the United States as to whether or not the adoption of a new code of ethical rules makes any difference to the behaviour of lawyers and benefits their clients.[69] Abel has vigorously opposed the use of an ethical code to set standards for lawyers mainly because a code is used for the profession's own interest.[70] Since Abel stated his views a case study applying the United States ABA Model Rules came to the conclusion that the Rules over-emphasised zealous advocacy and thus 'license lawyers to engage in ethically questionable conduct by allowing them, for example, to disregard the moral rights of people other than their client'.[71] There is a need for a critical reappraisal of the present day lawyers' ethical codes[72] and for a continuing review to make sure that the codes meet the needs of the consumers of legal services.

3.26   An analysis done in Australia by Maley of the provisions of the ethical codes of three professions — architecture, engineering and medicine — and the statutory regulations and ethical rulings of the Law Society of New South Wales, found that the elements fell into two categories. Those that occurred most frequently had an intrinsic function. They were 'concerned with maintaining the solidarity of the professional group as such'.

The other category, extrinsic, was far less frequent and concerned:[73]

> ... maintaining 'proper' relations between the profession as a whole and those other groups and activities which, though important to it, are nevertheless 'external' to the professional group. These include the client, the community, and the art and science of the profession.

3.27   Maley also found that the 'essential extrinsic function of professional codes is their role as an act of public reassurance'.[74] Maley's study would appear to support the view that ethical codes are more beneficial to the profession than to their clients and the public. The study is now more than 30 years old and a new study would be valuable.

The nineteenth-century constitution (an aspirational code) of the American Medical Association supports Maley's views by stating the purposes of the professional association to be:[75]

---

68. I Freckelton, 'Enforcement of Ethics' in M Coady and S Bloch (eds) (above), p 130; and Lichtenberg (above), p 27.
69. See 'Ethical Codes and the Legal Profession: A Symposium' (1981) 59 *Texas Law Rev* 147ff which includes both points of view. See also N Moore, 'The Usefulness of Ethical Codes', *1989 Annual Survey of American Law*.
70. R Abel, 'Why Does the ABA Promulgate Ethical Rules?' (1981) 59 *Texas Law Rev* 639, also from the symposium in the previous footnote.
71. S Higgins, 'Ethical Rules of Lawyering: An Analysis of Role-based Reasoning from Zealous Advocacy to Purposivism' (1999) 12 *Georgetown J of Legal Ethics* 639.
72. See L J Potter, 'The Ethical Challenges Facing Lawyers in the 21st Century' (2001) 4 *Legal Ethics* 23, 29.
73. B Maley, 'Professionalism and Professional Ethics' in D Edgar (ed), *Social Change in Australia: Readings in Sociology*, Cheshire, Melbourne, 1974, p 393.
74. Maley (above).
75. Undated pamphlet of the AMA.

For cultivating and advancing ... for elevating ... for promoting, for enlightening and directing ... for exciting ... and for facilitating, and fostering friendly intercourse between those engaged in it.

There is nothing wrong with adopting aspirational codes. According to MacKenzie, they help 'to remind the profession and inform the public of the public service dimension of the practice of law'.[76] Codes that seek to regulate the profession cause more problems because they 'cannot help but at least dilute the public service orientation'.[77] Detailed codes to control ethical behaviour are doomed to fail. They will foment endless litigation because it is impossible to achieve any kind of certainty in the principles and rules to be applied. There is a need for flexibility which is destroyed when ethical codes become too specific. MacKenzie adds two further criticisms: (1) '[A]n exhaustive code of black-letter rules is unlikely to attract the support of a professional consensus' which 'is important in any system of self-government, partly because voluntary compliance is preferable to disciplinary sanctions'. (2) By specifying: 'minimum prohibitions for disciplinary purposes entails regulating to the lowest common denominator. If the standards that are established are calibrated too high, neither widespread compliance nor rigorous enforcement is likely ... Rules that embody minimal standards ... de-emphasize ethical aspirations and are certain to discourage lawyers from reaching beyond those minimums'.[78]

Advertising rules

An example of the general and flexible approach has been the changes made to advertising rules in Australia. There used to be many detailed rules forbidding most types of lawyer advertising.[79] Generally, today in most jurisdictions, the only restriction is that the advertising must not be of a kind that could reasonably be regarded as 'false, misleading or deceptive' and in contravention of the Trade Practices Act 1974 (Cth) or similar legislation concerning fair trading. The result has been an increase in advertising, but unlike in the United States, this advertising has generally not brought the profession into disrepute. An example of an advertisement that is considered within the new rules was the sending of a circular to real estate agents in a specific area by a Melbourne solicitor offering to pay a referral fee to any real estate agent who referred a vendor or purchaser for whom they did a conveyance.[80]

3.28

This Victorian attitude may not be as acceptable in New South Wales, Queensland or for national lawyers organisations. The Council of the Law Society in New South Wales in November 1996 was still requesting the Attorney-General to make a regulation prohibiting advertising which might be regarded as 'offensive, vulgar, obscene, sensational or unprofessional ... and might be reasonably regarded as bringing the legal profession into

3.29

---

76. G MacKenzie, 'The Valentine's Card in the Operating Room: Codes of Ethics and Failing Ideals of the Legal Profession' (1995) 33 *Alberta LR* 859, 869–70.

77. MacKenzie (above).

78. MacKenzie (above), pp 870–1.

79. S Ross, 'Lawyers and the Public — How to get them Together' (1979) 53 *ALJ* 184 and Disney et al, see n 1 (above), pp 355–82.

80. See Ethics Committee rulings (July 1999) *Law Institute J* (Vic) 41.

disrepute'.[81] The Attorney-General rejected this request, but in 2002 to meet the criticism of an explosion in personal injury claims the New South Wales Government enacted the Civil Liabilities Act which limited the scope of actions and restricted the heads and quantum of damages that could be recovered. Similar legislation has been adopted throughout Australia. In 2003 the New South Wales Government also issued a ban on personal injury and work injury advertising by personal injury lawyers. The regulations restrict advertising in this area to any 'product or service' offered by a legal practitioner. In 2005 the ban was extended to the employees of lawyers and to others advertising lawyers' services in this area.[82] This ban is an exception to the general lenient advertising rule of 'false, misleading or deceptive'.[83]

The Queensland Law Society, Bar Association and the Australian Plaintiff Lawyers Association (APLA) in September 1999 issued a press release that blasted 'ambulance chasing'. The Law Society requested power to discipline solicitors involved in touting schemes, and also wanted its powers to restrict 'vulgar, misleading, or false' advertising restored.

The APLA President Ian Brown complained about touting schemes based on a 'conveyancing-belt mentality'. 'Lawyers have arrangements with a whole array of people such as tow truck operators, intermediaries in the form of trauma advisory services and such like, public hospitals, doctors, physiotherapists etc.'[84]

The ban on advertising by personal injury lawyers has affected many solicitors and barristers who have sought other avenues of practice, especially family and migration law. The APLA changed its name to the Australian Lawyers Alliance and expanded membership to other areas of practice including migration, criminal, family and consumer law.[85] The New South Wales Bar Association also established a Practice Enhancement Scheme in 2004 that was designed to help members to broaden their area of practice. The Scheme was primarily intended to assist barristers who do predominantly personal injury work. To combat the loss of work the Law Council of Australia created a 'Tort Reform Hot Spot' on its website, www.lawcouncil.asn.au, to educate the public and convince governments to reconsider their recent changes to tort law. Finally, there was also legal action by APLA to have the advertising ban declared invalid. The High Court upheld the ban on personal injury advertising in New South Wales.[86] It appears that other states will adopt similar legislation.[87]

81. See F Riley, *New South Wales Solicitors Manual*, Law Society of New South Wales, Sydney, 1988, looseleaf, para 5060. In the latest edition, LexisNexis Butterworths, Sydney, 2002, the Law Society's request is no longer present.
82. Clauses 24–29, Legal Profession Regulation 2005 and cl 73D, Workers Compensation (General) Amendment (Work Injury Advertising) Regulation 2005. The Legal Profession Act 2004 s 85 allows for regulations that can place restrictions on the general lenient advertising rule in s 84, and s 85 refers to the restrictions enacted in 2003 and amended in 2005.
83. Section 84, Legal Profession Act 2004.
84. 'Lawyer's Groups Call for Ban on Touting', *Australian Current Law News*, 30 September 1999.
85. M Priest, 'Plaintiff work shrinks as reforms begin to bite', *Australian Financial Review*, 12 November 2004, p 57.
86. *APLA Ltd v Legal Services Commissioner (NSW)* [2005] HCA 44.
87. C Merritt, 'States face flak after ban on ads upheld', *Australian*, 2 September 2005, p 25.

Perhaps we are asking too much of ethical codes. We have to recognise that such codes, which are usually general principles, are only a beginning in determining ethical behaviour. The gaps are filled by: specific professional association rulings, disciplinary proceedings, statutes and case law. We also recognise that lawyers have an ethical framework outside the codes from conventions developed by the profession over many years. These professional community values are learned in everyday practice. Finally, lawyers have family, community, religious and personal moral predispositions. Hazard says:[88]

3.30

> ... each lawyer's ethical responsibilities are unique. From the choice-making viewpoint of the lawyer therefore, the realm of professional ethics is not a rule-determined domain. Rather, it is a domain where the lawyer has pervasive marginal discretion guided by a few fundamental legal rules and constrained by circumstances of practice.

THE FUTURE OF THE LEGAL PROFESSION

Number of lawyers

Whether or not today's students of law are entering a 'profession' or a commercial occupation that competes with other occupations in the open marketplace is of importance to those who make the arduous commitment needed to become qualified lawyers. The profession is growing rapidly. According to the figures of the Law Council of Australia (May 2000) the total number of legal practitioners was 36,348. In the latest figures as of June 2004 the total was 47,541.[89] This indicates that the profession has been losing control over the supply of lawyers. There are also indications that the profession in the near future will no longer be male dominated. One of the main reasons for the increase in the number of students has been the dramatic increase in the number of women law students and in the number of law schools. There are, as of March 2005, 30 law schools compared to 12 in the early 1980s. This may be compared to the situation since the 1980s in Canada where there have been no new law schools, and the United States where there have been only two new law schools.[90]

3.31

Status and public service

The oversupply of lawyers and the increase in female lawyers (who are more willing to work part-time) can only lead to lower salaries and fewer job opportunities and thus a lowering of the general status of the profession. A good example of this development is the fact that starting salaries in 2003, according to the Graduate Careers Council of Australia, of 40 leading occupations revealed that dentistry was the highest at $55,000 a year, while law was in 15th place at $39,480. The average starting salary of the 40 occupational groups was $37,000.[91] As we have stated, Abel sees this

3.32

---

88. G Hazard Jr, 'Ethical Opportunities in the Practice of Law' (1990) 27 *San Diego LR* 127, 128.
89. Figures provided by Bruce Timbs, Law Council of Australia in May 2000 and November 2004.
90. Information provided by Christopher Roper from the Centre for Legal Education, May 2000.
91. Graduate Careers Council of Australia, *Grad Files*, December 2003, www.gradlink.com.au.

loss of control over supply as an indication of a profession in decline. At the same time, the profession is making it more difficult to become fully qualified by establishing a two-year period of practical training in order to become fully qualified;[92] also, many students never intend to practise law. Many more students are seeking legal qualifications even with the increased entrance requirements to study law in university, which are the second highest behind those of medicine.

3.33 Lawyers still see themselves as having a very high status occupation, which they seek to maintain by frequently advocating their need for independence and by maintaining high fees. Their desire to perpetuate this high status is evident from various rulings of the profession to maintain the image of the profession; for example, solicitors may only engage in another business that is of a respectable character and which would be unlikely to bring the profession into disrepute.[93] These factors would tend to support the argument that the legal profession may still be in its 'golden era' and will not decline in the near future.

The debate over the importance of lawyers maintaining the attributes of professionalism is well covered in the United States. In 1986 the ABA's Commission on Professionalism issued a report dealing with the concern of the ABA Board of Governors that there had been a decline in professional standards. The report pointed out that only 6 per cent of corporations rated 'all or most' lawyers as being worthy of being called 'professionals'. It found that only 7 per cent thought lawyers' professionalism was on the increase, while 68 per cent thought that professionalism had decreased. Even 55 per cent of state and federal judges surveyed in a separate poll stated that 'lawyer professionalism was declining'. The report calls for lawyers to adopt higher standards of conduct than those required by disciplinary rules. The Commission viewed as the dominant feature of professionalism a devotion to public service. An important recommendation was that lawyers should resist adoption of the accumulation of wealth as their primary goal.[94] The ABA also established a standing committee on professionalism. In 1988 the ABA adopted the following proposals:[95]

❑ lawyers should perform at least 50 hours of pro bono or other community service per year;

❑ a statement of 10 aspirational goals on the use of lawyer advertising (for example, avoidance of inappropriately dramatic music, unseemly slogans, hawkish spokespersons and premium offers);

❑ two model codes dealing with professional courtesy.

3.34 In reviewing the Commission's report Moore points out that the claims made by the legal profession to a tradition of public service are a recent development which began in the nineteenth century.[96] Moore agrees with

92. This is the period established under the National Legal Model Code.
93. See (1990) 28 *Law Society J* (NSW) 23.
94. ABA Commission on Professionalism, *In the Spirit of Public Service: A Blueprint for the Rekindling of Lawyer Professionalism*, 1986, pp 10, 50 and 243.
95. N Moore, 'Professionalism: Rekindled, Reconsidered or Reformulated?' (1990) 19 *Capital University Law Rev* 1121, 1123. This article was part of a symposium on legal ethics published in that issue.
96. N Moore, 'Professionalism Reconsidered' (1987) *American Bar Foundation Research J* 773, 781.

Larson and other scholars that the 'professionalisation' process is little more than a self-interest drive to obtain sanction from the community of a monopoly for its services free from government interference.[97] In light of the historical evidence it is curious that lawyers and law students still consider that it is important that law be viewed as a profession and that public service is seen as an important element. In fact, there have been a number of recent calls for a return to 'old values' which would redeem the legal profession.

The nostalgia is most evident in Linowitz's memory of the profession he was admitted to in the late 1930s. He says when he entered practice he joined a family and the clients were also part of this family. He even recalls clients objecting to receiving legal bills that were too low![98]   **3.35**

Kronman also believes this redemption of the profession would be made possible by a return to old values, the 'lawyer–statesman'.[99] Kronman appears to associate what he believes to be the increasingly mercenary and indeed rapacious character of the practice of law with the opening up of jobs in large law firms to Jews, women, and persons from a working-class background.

According to Posner, the desire to return to a homogenous profession:[100]

> … in order to reduce price competition is a symptom of the guild mentality, and Kronman does not show that such a mentality is likely to serve clients or the society better than a competitive ethos would do.

Kronman has also been criticised for being anti-democratic and anti-egalitarian and seeking a 'meritocratic elitism, sometimes called "Corporatism"'[101] and for his choice of role model statesmen.[102] It seems that Kronman's redemption will not work.

One of the early critics of the notion of professionalism, Simon, has now called for the use of professionalism to propagate the 'ideals of law'.[103] If lawyers want to maintain their special place in society and retain the finer aspects of professionals they need to pursue the social good. They must refuse to pursue unworthy claims of clients that are in conflict with the social values embedded in the substantive and procedural law. For example, they need to educate their clients to conform to regulatory and legal requirements and not seek technical ways to circumvent them. This approach requires lawyers to be sensitive to wider social issues, while at the   **3.36**

---

97. N Moore (above), generally.
98. M Linowitz with M Mayer, *The Betrayed Profession: Lawyering at the End of the Twentieth Century*, Charles Scribner's Sons, New York, 1994, pp 52–62.
99. A Kronman, *The Lost Lawyer: Failing Ideals of the Legal Profession*, Belknap Press of Harvard University Press, Cambridge, 1993.
100. R Posner, *Overcoming Law*, Harvard University Press, Cambridge, 1995, p 93 referring to Kronman (above), pp 291–300. In contrast to Kronman's pessimistic approach see M Glendon, *A Nation Under Lawyers — How the Crisis in the Legal Profession is Transforming American Society*, Farrar, Straus & Giroux, New York, 1994. Glendon finds many positive developments in a society run by lawyers. She finds numerous examples of the law and lawyers triumphing over corruption and power.
101. J Bickenbach, 'The Redemption of the Moral Mandate of the Profession of Law' (1996) 9 *The Canadian J of Law & Society* 51.
102. R Cramton and S Koniak, 'Rule, Story, and Commitment in the Teaching of Legal Ethics' (1996) 38 *William and Mary LR* 145.
103. W Simon, 'Ethical Discretion in Lawyering' (1988) 101 *Harvard Law Rev* 1083, 1084.

same time continuing a viable legal practice. It calls for lawyers to live up to the rhetoric of the ideals of professionalism.[104] Bickenbach also criticises the new redemption approach:[105]

> Why waste our time redeeming the profession when we could be investigating more seriously the possibility that important social ideals can be better achieved in some different, nonprofessionalized manner?

3.37   Bickenbach could have added that the notion of being a 'professional' is itself anti-democratic and elitist. It separates that occupational group from the community, seeking to make its members superior in status and power. Hamilton has said that the 'metaphoric networks of gentility, religion, and the military' that help make up the image of lawyers' professionalism 'are all hierarchical'. He states:[106]

> The words we used and still use to describe the conduct required of lawyers contribute to the hierarchy, within the profession on the basis of class, gender and ethnicity. They may also contribute to the 'low esteem' in which the profession as a whole is held.

If lawyers truly want to be a moving force in achieving social justice they have to be perceived as being egalitarian.

Loss of power

3.38   The maintenance of an anti-democratic and elitist image may be an important reason the professions are under attack. Another important reason for the attacks is that the community has become more aware that 'professions' are just a description of a way in which an occupation has organised its work to control a market. Perhaps lawyers would be better off not being associated with the concept.[107] As Moore states:[108]

> ... I think that we will all be better off if [we] ... by-pass the idea of 'profession' and appeal directly to a spirit of public service among a group of citizens who happen to have special knowledge and skill in relation to the law and are thus in a position to make unique contributions to the community in which they live.

The history of Western society has charted the rise and fall of different professions. As we have stated, surgeons in the fourteenth century were members of a guild that merged with that of barbers and participated in processions with shoe-makers, glaziers and masons. The military and clergy were respected professions during the Middle Ages, while lawyers (as we know them today) were not. The threat of corruption by over-expansion and the development of competitive occupations is always present. Therefore, lawyers in the past guarded with vigilance their special knowledge and tried to prevent the dissemination of this knowledge to the mass media.

---

104. See Simon (above) and also R Gordon and W Simon, 'The Redemption of Professionalism?' in R Nelson, D Trubek and R Solomon (eds), *Lawyers' Ideals/Lawyers' Practices: Transformations in the American Legal Profession*, Cornell University Press, Ithaca, 1992, p 201; S Linowitz with M Mayer, *The Betrayed Profession*, Charles Scribner's Sons, New York, 1994; and Bickenbach (above), p 59.
105. Bickenbach (above), p 60.
106. J Hamilton, 'Metaphors of Lawyers' Professionalism' (1995) 33 *Alberta LR* 833, 856.
107. Moore (above) (1990), p 1131.
108. Moore (above), p 1133.

In recent years the profession has been unsuccessful in stopping the   **3.39**
revelation of its special knowledge in areas such as conveyancing and family
law. Conveyancing is now highly competitive within the legal profession, to
a certain degree because of the spread of non-lawyer licensed conveyancers
and do-it-yourself kits. Furthermore, conveyancing is now going online.
Victoria established a Land Exchange program in 2002 and the software was
set up in 2004. The program provides online 'processing of financial and legal
settlements and the lodgement of simple discharge, transfer and mortgages
into the Land Registry'. Electronic conversion of land titles has also been
established in New South Wales.[109] These developments will make easy and
cheap access to do-it-yourself conveyancing for the general public.

Family law has also been simplified; in straightforward divorces people can
now complete and file the forms on their own. The profession has also at
times been willing to help to educate the public and to simplify the law.
Furthermore, government legal services are at the forefront in their use of
online services to cut costs. Queensland Legal Aid in 1997 installed on a
trial basis kiosks that resemble cashcard machines. By following instructions
and pressing the right buttons people can seek help to do simple tasks such
as asking for legal advice, completing divorce forms and even filing some
court claims. The company that makes the machines states that it is:[110]

> … already possible to design a program to simulate legal reasoning which
> could judge a complicated civil case or even hear a murder trial, given all
> relevant law and precedents were available to the computer.

In the United States a number of jurisdictions have recognised by statute
the work of legal assistants who prepare documents. These assistants
can complete, file and serve forms. In California they are restricted from
giving any advice, while Arizona allows them to provide general legal
information.[111]

Even with these developments lawyers, and other professionals, still can
exercise considerable power. In 2004 the lawyers, accountants and other
professionals successfully opposed bankruptcy reforms by the Howard
Government. The reforms were aimed at removing artificial structures that
protect assets from creditors. Chris Merritt stated: 'The professions knew
that … their "traditional" method of hiding assets would be abolished. And
that was unacceptable.'[112]

The author also feels that the replacement of judges is still a long way in the   **3.40**
future, if it is ever to occur, because computers will never be able to
replicate exactly the human judgment and feelings that judges need when
dispensing justice. Anleu makes the following important observation:[113]

> The profession has become more complex, stratified, and rationalized. This is
> not synonymous with deprofessionalization or the absolute loss of autonomy
> and self-regulatory authority but points to the complexity of occupational
> groups continually seeking control over work in various work settings.

---

109. M Dunlevy, 'Get off the conveyance belt', *Weekend Australian*, 11–12 October 2003,
     p 43.
110. J Fife-Yeomans, 'Computer justice goes on trial', *Weekend Australian*, 5–6 April 1997, p 1.
111. D Rhode and D Luban, *Legal Ethics*, 4th ed, Foundation Press, New York, 2004, pp 778–9.
112. C Merritt, 'Abuse of the legal system', *Australian Financial Review*, 23 July 2004, p 8.
113. Anleu (above), pp 200–1.

Reform of the legal profession will inevitably be slow because those appointed to make these changes are usually leading members of the profession. If law is on the decline as a profession it will be a slow loss of power, authority and privilege.

PART TWO

Structure and Regulation

4

STRUCTURE

HISTORICAL OUTLINE

Importance of structure

The present structure of the legal profession has its foundation in the early development of Australia's history. The importance of understanding these developments is that present professional structures have a profound influence on the ethical behaviour of lawyers. These structures also determine how the profession exercises power and control over its members. The subject cannot be taught in isolation and any discussion of reform of that structure will necessarily include a discussion of the impact such changes will have on the behaviour of lawyers.[1]

4.1

The structure of the legal profession that developed in England had a great influence on Australia. The structural characteristics of the English profession included:

❏ a divided profession;
❏ boundaries between the different groups fixed by defined incompatibilities, preventing the undertaking of specific tasks;
❏ the exercise of strong control over its members by enforcing ethical standards.

Some examples of these features were: the inability to be a solicitor and barrister at the same time; the prohibition of barristers on engaging in commercial activities; the control of ethical behaviour by senior members exercised through the Inns of Court; and the use of general standards, not rules, frequently unexpressed.[2]

It would appear that the features of this structure would be those adopted in the colonies. Although several aspects of practice in England did affect the structure in some colonies, most of the early colonial legal professions developed unified structures. This was a natural structure because there were so few lawyers and thus lawyers had to be able to engage in the whole

4.2

---

1. H Glenn, 'Professional Structures and Professional Ethics' (1990) 35 *McGill LJ* 424, 425–6.
2. H Glenn (above), pp 426–9.

range of legal practice. The formation of the structure of the profession in Australia began in New South Wales. It was affected by the rejection in 1814 of the right to appear of the only qualified lawyers, ex-convicts, by the first judge, Jeffrey Bent. The Colonial Office responded to his request to have only free men appear before the court by sending out two solicitors. They did not arrive until 1816 and thus the Supreme Court remained closed for two years. The ex-convicts were not barristers and were mainly from Ireland.[3]

4.3 The history of the present Supreme Court began with the third Charter issued in 1823; it was established in 1824. The Charter empowered the court to admit lawyers 'to act as well in the character of Barristers ... as of Proctors, Attorneys and Solicitors'.[4] The Supreme Court in reality admitted barristers and solicitors separately, but allowed them once admitted to act in both capacities. The barristers, who numbered four out of the first nine free lawyers admitted to practice,[5] were insulted by this procedure and requested a change. At first they were refused and W C Wentworth, their leader, felt that he had been 'degraded'. Eventually the barristers prevailed and a ruling made by the Supreme Court in 1829 divided the profession. Approval by the Crown took until 1834 because of strong opposition by the solicitors. The barristers then formed their own restrictive practices. Although challenges to this division by bills before parliament occurred on several occasions during the nineteenth century, they were unsuccessful. Finally, solicitors were somewhat appeased with the granting of full rights of audience in all courts in 1892 and by the fact that transfer between the two branches was made easier.[6]

Recent reform of structure

4.4 This century there have been several attempts to achieve fusion in New South Wales. A bill introduced by the Labor Government in 1931 was vigorously opposed by the judges of the Supreme Court, the bar and the Law Institute (later the Law Society). As a result it quietly disappeared from the government's agenda. Recommendations in 1982 by the New South Wales Law Reform Commission to abolish the rigid division and replace it with a more flexible structure did not become law because of strong opposition from the Law Society and the bar.[7]

In 1993 the New South Wales Law Reform Commission again recommended the abolition of the rigid division[8] and the Liberal/National Government accepted most of the recommendations. Opposition to this reform came mainly from the bar. This opposition was successful in maintaining the division of the profession,[9] but could not stop some of the

---

3. See A Castles, *An Introduction to Australian History*, Law Book Co, Sydney, 1971, pp 106–8 and 110.
4. Third Charter of Justice, 1823, s 10.
5. S Ross, 'Legal Profession in Tasmania' (1975) 5 *University of Tasmania LR* 1.
6. Legal Practitioners Act 1892 s 2 and *The Structure of the Profession*, New South Wales Law Reform Commission, Discussion Paper (1981), pp 47–9.
7. J Disney, J Basten, P Redmond and S Ross, *Lawyers*, 2nd ed (1986), pp 29–30.
8. *Scrutiny of the Legal Profession: Complaints Against Lawyers*, New South Wales Law Reform Commission Report, 1993.
9. Legal Profession Act 1987 (NSW) s 38D.

reforms. There is a discussion below of the main features of the Legal Profession Reform Act of 1993 which amended the Legal Profession Act 1987, dealing with the structure of the profession. As of June 2004, according to the Law Council of Australia, there were 1764 barristers, 143 corporate and government barristers and 332 non-practising barristers in New South Wales. There were also 13,140 solicitors, 4598 corporate and government solicitors and 1634 non-practising solicitors. Of the barristers 327 were women (14.6 per cent) and of the solicitors 7845 (40.5 per cent). The total number of solicitors was 19,732 and barristers 2239.[10] The figures show a dramatic increase in numbers as reported in May 2000 when the total number of solicitors was 13,998 and barristers 1655.[11]

History in Victoria and Queensland

As both Victoria and Queensland were under New South Wales' jurisdiction, on becoming separate colonies in 1851 and 1859 respectively, they inherited the professional structure of New South Wales. In both states numerous battles took place over fusion and in Victoria fusion was achieved in 1891. The resistance to the legislation was very strong from the bar and the judges, and barristers formed an association to preserve the separate bar. Members took a pledge to practise solely in the style of a barrister, which included refusing to appear with non-members and refusing to accept briefs from amalgams (lawyers practising as both solicitors and barristers). The association was disbanded under strong criticism, but its boycott was effective. In 1900 a new bar organisation was formed which became the Victorian Bar Association in 1963.[12] The 1891 Act, up until the major reforms under the new Legal Practice Act 1996, resulted in a profession fused *de jure* but divided *de facto*. Under s 69 of the Legal Practice Act 1996 the bar still maintains its separation and its sole practice rules, although since 1994,[13] and under s 66 of the Act, barristers can appear with other advocates.

4.5

The 1891 reforms did achieve for solicitors and amalgams the right of audience in all courts in Victoria. This right has been rarely exercised because the judges required all lawyers to wear wigs and robes when appearing before the Supreme Court and because there existed a degree of hostility from the judges to these practitioners.[14] Under s 70 of the Legal Practice Act 1996, the wearing of wigs and gowns in non-jury proceedings is now optional.

4.6

In 1993 there were a number of suggestions made by the Victorian Law Reform Commission for reforming some of the restrictive practices that result from the structure of the profession. We will discuss these below. As of May 2000 there were 1343 barristers and 8208 solicitors in Victoria. By June 2004 there were 1774 barristers and 11,514 solicitors. The barrister figures included 1569 practising, 172 non-practising and 33 corporate and government. The breakdown for solicitors was 8753 practising, 1698

---

10. Bruce Timbs of the Law Council of Australia provided the statistics, November 2004.
11. Ibid, May 2000.
12. Disney et al (above), pp 31–2.
13. *Australian Financial Review*, 1 September 1994, p 20.
14. AFR (above), p 32. It is somewhat ironic that in New South Wales a solicitor is prohibited from wearing a wig and gown but there is a growing movement to allow solicitors to wear a wig and gown.

non-practising and 703 corporate and government. Female lawyers in Victoria were 3831 of the solicitors (34.3 per cent) and 293 of the barristers (16.5 per cent).

4.7   In Queensland similar opposition by the judiciary and the bar prevented fusion until it was adopted by the Legal Practitioners Act of 1881. The retention of the division was accomplished by making sure that the legislation did not interfere with the requirements of separate admission to practice, different education and a separate roll.[15] After the adoption of the 1881 Act only a few tried to practise as barristers while still being solicitors but they soon ceased this approach because of judicial hostility.[16] The *de jure* right to cross-practise was finally abrogated by legislation in 1938. Unlike Victoria and New South Wales, solicitors did not gain the right of audience in all the courts in Queensland until the Supreme Court Act was amended in 1973.[17] The division of the profession in Queensland is more rigid than in the other states and there is no strong movement to change this structure. A minor change took place from May 1993 when direct professional access to barristers from certain other professions was permitted in 'non-contentious' matters where that professional was acting on behalf of a client. The change in Queensland was adopted before the New South Wales and Victoria Bars decided to drop their opposition to direct access.[18] As of May 2000 there were 537 barristers and 4586 solicitors in Queensland. The figures for June 2004 were 796 barristers and 5733 solicitors. The barristers included 758 practising, no non-practising numbers were given, and 38 corporate and government. Among the solicitors 4985 were practising, 156 were non-practising and 592 were corporate and government lawyers. Female representation at the bar was 75 (9.4 per cent) and there were 2012 solicitors (35.1 per cent).

History in other jurisdictions

4.8   Unlike the main eastern states, Tasmania, South Australia and the territories did not develop divided professions. The reason for this in Tasmania may have been the absence of a group of barristers at the initial formation: only one of the first 45 lawyers was a barrister.[19] Other reasons were the sparse population, agricultural economies, isolation from the other colonies and a small number of practitioners. Today Tasmania still has a small profession. As of May 2000, although there were only 20 barristers out of a total profession of 490 practitioners, there is an Independent Bar Association of Tasmania. Furthermore, the President of the Australian Bar Association in 2000 was from Tasmania. The Law Council figures in June 2004 included the barristers in the solicitors' numbers. The figures were

---

15. J Bennett and J Forbes, 'Tradition and Experiment: Some Australian Legal Attitudes of the Nineteenth Century' (1971) 7 *University of Queensland Law J* 172, 187.
16. H Gibbs, 'Some Aspects of the History of the Queensland Bar' (1979) 53 *ALJ* 63, 64.
17. Section 38A.
18. For the reasons for rejecting direct access to the bar see *Victorian Bar News*, Winter 1993, No 85, pp 44–6. The Victorian Bar later adopted a broader rule on direct access than the Queensland Bar: *Weekend Australian*, 12–13 March 1994, p 7. The New South Wales section changes are found in the Legal Profession Act (1987). Section 38I (1) states: 'Barristers may accept any clients, subject to the barristers rules and the conditions of any relevant practising certificate.'
19. Ross (above), p 1.

490 practitioners of which 465 were practising, 13 were non-practising and 12 were corporate and government lawyers. The total of female practitioners was 130 (26.5 per cent). The Tasmanian Bar on its website states as of March 2005 there are 20 barristers.

4.9 South Australia was established as a colony in 1837 with its professional rules and practice received directly from England. The original South Australian Ordinance of 1845 called for admission under the title practitioner but it empowered the judges of the Supreme Court to separate the profession if they so chose. The judges never exercised this power and it was removed by s 6 of the Legal Practitioners Act 1981. With a small population, agricultural economy and few lawyers, fusion was the natural choice for South Australia. Furthermore, by adopting Torrens Title land law reforms and thereby losing their monopoly over conveyancing, there was less business for those few lawyers. Although efforts were made by the bench during this century to divide the profession, on both occasions the proposals were defeated in plebiscites conducted by the Law Society among its members.[20] There was, as of May 2000, a voluntary bar consisting of 162 barristers in a total profession of 1676 lawyers. It appears that without the conveyancing monopoly there is no drive to have a full division. The figures in June 2004 included the barristers with the solicitors' figures. The total number of practitioners was 2180 of which 1740 were practising, 440 were non-practising and no figure was given for corporate and government lawyers. There were 875 female practitioners (40.1 per cent).

4.10 The Northern Territory was transferred to the Commonwealth from South Australia in 1910 and, with a similar situation to South Australia, fusion was the basis of its professional structure. In recent years, a small bar has developed which, as of March 1997, consisted of only 29 barristers out of a total profession of 355 lawyers. The total in June 2004 was 400 solicitors and 31 barristers. There were 399 practising solicitors, one non-practising, and no figure for corporate and government lawyers. There were 190 female solicitors (47.5 per cent) and five female barristers (16.1 per cent).

Western Australia was founded in 1829 and being an isolated, agricultural colony with a small population and few lawyers, fusion was the obvious structure for the profession. Unlike Tasmania, most of the early lawyers were barristers. They did not oppose having one branch of the profession but they wanted it to be solely barristers. Since conveyancing was handled by land agents the need for solicitors was not as great as in the eastern states. In 1861, the Chief Justice issued an ordinance which called all practitioners barristers but this was disallowed by the Legislative Council. A fused profession subsequently developed.[21] Perhaps these historical roots are the reason that the body which controls admission and discipline for the profession was known up until 1993 as the Barristers' Board. The first voluntary bar was formed in 1962 but it accepted the fused structure and the fact that its members were subject to the powers of the Barristers' Board. One of the founding members, F T P Burt, later became Chief Justice and in this capacity he and other members of the judiciary encouraged the

---

20.   J Forbes, *The Divided Legal Profession in Australia*, Law Book Co, Sydney, 1979, pp 179–84.
21.   J Forbes (above), pp 185–6.

development of specialist advocates.[22] Its membership is still a small proportion of the profession and as of May 2000 consisted of 145 barristers out of 2755 lawyers. In June 2004 there were 2157 solicitors and 167 barristers. There were 1711 practising solicitors, 352 non-practising and 94 corporate and government solicitors. The figures for the bar were 164 practising, three non-practising and none as corporate and government lawyers. There were 678 female solicitors (31.4 per cent) and 22 barristers (13.2 per cent). It is obvious from these figures that the total number of lawyers has dropped dramatically from May 2000 and the proportion of barristers in the profession has increased substantially.

4.11 The Australian Capital Territory provides for a fused profession by common admission of lawyers as 'barristers and solicitors' under the Legal Practitioners Act 1970. Like the other fused states, in recent years a separate bar has been formed that as of May 2000 consisted of 48 barristers out of 745 lawyers. The figures for June 2004 were 1000 solicitors and 48 barristers. Among the solicitors 898 were practising, 102 were non-practising and no number was given for corporate and government lawyers. The barristers were all practising. There were 383 female solicitors (38.3 per cent) and six barristers (12.5 per cent).

4.12 As we have stated, the profession is growing rapidly. The figures of the Law Council of Australia as of June 2004 were 42,496 solicitors and 5055 barristers, which makes 47,551. The number of female solicitors was 15,944 (37.5 per cent) and barristers 728 (14.4 per cent). As of May 2000 there were 32,409 solicitors and 3939 barristers. This made the total number of legal practitioners 36,348 as compared to 32,576 in March 1997.

PRESENT RESTRICTIONS AND CHANGE

History of restrictions

4.13 Many of the most important restrictive practices developed in England during the eighteenth and nineteenth centuries were then adopted by the divided professions in the eastern Australian states. Solicitors and attorneys were granted a monopoly with respect to initiating litigation on behalf of clients by the Act of 1729. The Society of Gentlemen Practisers, the predecessor to the present Law Society, wanted to go further by having clients who wanted advice able to approach a barrister only through a solicitor. The Society's wishes were not completely effected.[23] In 1850 a court did hold that for more than a century it was uniform usage that barristers had to take their instructions from attorneys only,[24] but this was not the general practice. It was not until 1888 that the General Council of the bar confirmed the usage as applying for contentious matters.[25] This practice has only changed during the 1990s.[26]

---

22.   See G Sawer, 'Division of a Fused Legal Profession: The Australasian Experience' (1966) 16 *University of Toronto Law J* 245, 247 and D Malcolm, 'The Independent Bar: Origins and Functions of the Western Australian Bar Association' (1984) 11 *Brief (Law Society of Western Australia Journal)* 8.
23.   B Abel-Smith and R Stevens, *Lawyers and the Courts*, Heinemann, London, 1967, p 20.
24.   *Doe d' Bennett v Hale* (1850) 15 QB 171; 117 ER 423.
25.   Disney et al (above), pp 23–6.
26.   For a recent case where a barrister was disciplined for conducting a conveyance without an instructing solicitor see *Council of the NSW Bar Association v Frank Raleigh Witt* (1996) Legal Profession Disciplinary Reports No 3, p 27.

The solicitors' monopoly over conveyancing was granted to their 4.14
predecessor organisation, the Society of Gentlemen Practisers, by legislation
in 1804. In return the Society had to accept an increase in the duty on
practising certificates and articles in order to help finance the Pitt
Government's war against Napoleon.[27] This monopoly became very
valuable during the nineteenth century because of the industrial
revolution's development of land use, the easy access to rural land by the
development of the railroads and canals, and the enclosure movement and
expansion of trade. Two of the major restrictive practices at the bar were
the two-counsel rule — that a Queen's Counsel cannot appear without a
junior; and the two-thirds rule — that a junior receives two-thirds of the fee
of the QC. Both developed during the nineteenth century and by the end of
the century were accepted as long established custom.[28] The two-thirds rule
was abolished in England in 1971 and subsequently in all jurisdictions in
Australia. The two-counsel rule was abolished at various times throughout
Australia during the 1980s and 1990s.

Even without a two-counsel rule Queen's Counsel or Senior Counsel will 4.15
usually have cooperation from their solicitor to have a second counsel if the
case calls for one. The rules have also been modified to allow Queen's
Counsel (or the new Senior Counsel) to appear with a solicitor advocate.

There has been a long debate over the advantages and disadvantages of the 4.16
divided or rigid structure. The main advantages of having a separate bar
appear to be as follows: it leads to the development of a group of specialist
advocates who are free from conflicting interests, maintaining independence
and objectivity, and providing ready access to non-specialist solicitors,
especially those from sole practitioners and small firms. The disadvantages
are: frequent unnecessary use of two lawyers (barrister and solicitor) leading
to duplication, omission and confusion of function, and the lack of freedom
and incentive for lawyers, both solicitors and barristers, to develop new
methods of legal services so as to provide a better public service. The
disadvantages appear to outweigh the advantages according to the view
taken by the New South Wales Law Reform Commission,[29] the Victorian
Law Reform Commission[30] and the Trade Practices Commission.[31]

The historic outline has shown that reform of restrictive practices of the 4.17
legal profession has been a difficult task to accomplish in the states with
divided professions. The profession has a history of defeating efforts to
impose outside regulation and accountability. There was a major effort to
regulate the profession in New South Wales by recommendations resulting
from the New South Wales Law Reform Commission's long inquiry of
1976–84. At first it looked as though a major change would take place

---

27. Abel-Smith and Stevens (above), p 22.
28. See *Barristers' Services: A Report on the Supply to Her Majesty's Counsel Alone of Their
    Services* HMSO, London, 1976, pp 9–11 and Abel-Smith and Stevens (above), pp 223–4.
    Note that the two-thirds rule had different applications in Australia. For example, in New
    South Wales a junior could charge up to two-thirds, while in Victoria a junior had to
    charge two-thirds.
29. *First Report on the Legal Profession*, New South Wales Law Reform Commission, 1982,
    pp 59–73.
30. See **4.20**.
31. *Study of the Professions, Legal*, Final Report, Trade Practices Commission, March 1994.

when the Attorney-General submitted proposals to Cabinet based on the Law Reform Commission's recommendations. The Law Society announced its acceptance of the Attorney-General's proposals concerning common admission, removal of all distinctions between barristers and solicitors and the abolition and relaxation of some of the restrictive practices.[32] The then Attorney-General, Mr Paul Landa, died soon afterwards and the recommendations were shelved until the Opposition took office. The new government did enact the Legal Profession Act 1987, which did not bring in any drastic changes. In fact, as Weisbrot has stated, the Act resulted in an increase 'in the powers of the Councils of the Law Society and Bar Association and maintained most of the restrictive trade practices which had been identified and questioned'.[33] The profession in New South Wales has been able to maintain a degree of unity until recently despite the degree of fragmentation that actually exists over the type of work and degree of status involved. This unity was possible because of an adherence to the concept of the rule of law, for example 'independence of the profession'; a large degree of 'social homogeneity'; and a share in interest in wanting to maintain a monopoly over 'certain financially lucrative areas of work',[34] such as conveyancing for solicitors and advocacy for barristers.

4.18   In the 1980s, 1990s and early 2000s this unified front was showing signs of cracking under the pressure of renewed demands by the government and the public for reform. A new Legal Profession Act was adopted in New South Wales in 2005 and also in Victoria in 2005. Major reform of restrictive practices in the United Kingdom took place in 1990 with the enactment of the Courts and Legal Services Act. It adopted most of the recommendations in a White Paper issued by the Lord Chancellor in 1989. The major recommendations adopted were the abolition of the solicitors' monopoly over conveyancing and probate work; the abolition of the barristers' monopoly over higher court advocacy; the establishment of a Legal Services Ombudsman to monitor how complaints against lawyers were dealt with by professional complaint bodies; and an advisory committee on legal education and conduct under the auspices of the Lord Chancellor.[35]

4.19   In Australia during the 1980s, 1990s and in the early 2000s there have been numerous inquiries into various aspects of professional structure and regulation. All states have had inquiries (the latest one, under way in Queensland, started in 1999 and led to the Legal Profession Act 2004)[36] and at the federal level the Senate Standing Committee on Legal and Constitutional Affairs has inquired into the costs of justice, which dealt with aspects of restrictive practices; the Federal Trade Practices Commission (TPC) examined ways of eliminating the anti-competitive structures of the 'legal services industry'; and an inquiry in 1994 also calling for more competition was the Access to Justice Advisory Committee's Inquiry into

---

32. 'President's Message' (1984) 22 *Law Society J (NSW)* 265.
33. D Weisbrot, 'Competition, Cooperation and Legal Change' (1993) 4 *Legal Education Review* 1, 4. He refers to his book, *Australian Lawyers*, Longman Cheshire, Melbourne, 1990, pp 262–3 and 270.
34. Weisbrot (above) (1990), pp 4–5.
35. Lord Chancellor's Department, *Legal Services: A Framework for the Future*, Cmnd 740, 1989.
36. Queensland Government Green Paper, *Legal Profession Reform*, June 1999.

Access to Justice.[37] Finally, it should be noted that in 1997 and 1998 the Australian Law Reform Commission published several issue papers on the federal civil justice system. In August 1999 it published Discussion Paper No 62, *Review of the federal civil justice system*. The final report, Report No 89, *Managing Justice: A review of the federal civil justice system*, was released in February 2000. This inquiry has had important ramifications for the future form of legal practice in Australia and we will refer a number of times to its papers, especially to the discussion paper and final report, throughout this book.

Legal income and costs

Legal services are a significant part of our economy's infrastructure cost. In the financial year 1992–93 over $3000 million was spent on the legal services of barristers and solicitors in private practice, most of which sum comprised fees for professional services.[38] The amount that was estimated to have been spent according to the Australian Bureau of Statistics for legal services of private practitioners for 1995–96 was $5255.8 million, for 1998–99, $7035 million and for 2001–02, $10,600 million.[39] This is a dramatic increase in each of the new figures.

4.20

It is obvious with such large costs that the community has an interest in regulation which 'reduces or eliminates market distortions, or otherwise produces public benefits'. Thus the Law Reform Commission of Victoria in a discussion paper issued in July 1991[40] examined the rules of practice and professional conduct in light of the principle of whether they involved a net public benefit or were unnecessary restrictive practices. The Commission in looking at each rule determined whether there was a substantial public benefit in retaining the rule; the probable effect the rule had on costs; and whether similar benefits could be obtained with a less restrictive rule.[41] In its final report the Commission cited widespread community concern in relation to the costs of legal services and the need to find new approaches and solutions. The Commission said that the problem was 'rooted in some of the legal system's most cherished characteristics'.[42] The Commission in its discussion paper found that the restrictive practices of the bar were

---

37. The report is called *The Access to Justice Report* (1994). The committee was chaired by R Sackville QC, now Justice Sackville.
38. This figure is taken from the Trade Practices Commission's 1993 report *Study of the Professions*. This is an increase of 200 million from the 1987–88 figures: see *Legal Services Industry in Australia*, Australian Bureau of Statistics, 1987–88, 1990, pp 1–2.
39. Australian Bureau of Statistics, 1995–96 Services ABS Catalogue No 8678.0 1997, p 11, as quoted in ALRC, Discussion Paper No 62, August 1999, para 4.39. The ARLR has a detailed discussion and analysis of the legal costs for the federal civil law system at paras 4.38–4.91. The 1998–99 ABS figures were quoted in the *Sunday Telegraph*, 27 August 2000, p 36, and the 2001–02 figures are in ABS, 2001–2002 *Legal Practices*, ABS Catalogue No 8667. The ABS 2001–02 figures were released on 25 June 2003 and there is a detailed breakdown of the legal costs for private, public and legal aid lawyers. The ABS has a survey every three years and the next one should be released around June 2006.
40. *Restriction on Legal Practice*, Discussion Paper No 23, July 1991.
41. Law Reform Commission of Victoria, *Access to the Law: Restrictions on Legal Practice*, Report No 47, May 1992, pp 4–5.
42. LRC (Vic) (above), p 1, quoting from M Rosenberg, 'Devising Procedures that are Civil to Promote Justice that is Civilised' (1971) 69 *Michigan Law Review* 797, 816.

anti-competitive and did not produce any substantial public benefit which justified their retention.[43] The Commission was criticised for not having professional economic support for these findings, so for its final report it commissioned an independent economic analysis conducted by the Tasman Institute. The Institute's findings completely supported the Commission's assessment.[44]

Restrictive practices and reform — Victoria

4.21   The discussion paper made the following comments on restrictive practices at the bar:

❑ The restriction that a barrister must act only on instructions of a solicitor should be removed so that barristers may receive instructions from other professional groups, such as accountants, tax agents, insurers and professionals who provide planning advice, and perhaps receive instructions directly from lay clients in some contentious matters. (This latter restriction was removed in 1994 and under s 66 of the Legal Practice Act 1996 and Pt 3.2.3 of the new Legal Profession Act 2004.)

❑ It did *not* suggest that the restriction that barristers cannot perform solicitor's work be removed (this rule is retained).

❑ It said that the restriction of being a sole practitioner should be abolished and barristers be permitted to form business associations with other members of the bar, to practise as employees of other barristers and to incorporate their practice. (This recommendation was specifically rejected under s 69 of the 1996 Act and Pt 3.2.6 of the 2004 Act.)

❑ It did *not* suggest that barristers form business associations with other professionals, including solicitors.

4.22   It suggested that the following rules should also be abolished:

❑ that barristers can only appear with co-counsel who are members of the bar (abolished in August 1994 and under s 65 of the 1996 Act and Pt 3.2.2 of the 2004 Act);

❑ that barristers can only rent chambers from a corporation controlled by the Bar Council (abolished by s 68 of the 1996 Act and Pt 3.2.5 of the 2004 Act);

❑ that barristers can only conduct their administrative services by use of one of the 11 clerks approved by the Bar Council (abolished by s 67 of the 1996 Act and Pt 3.2.4 of the 2004 Act);

❑ the two-counsel rule (it was abolished by the bar in February 1992);

❑ that a barrister was not to attend the office of a solicitor except in a few exceptional circumstances, even if they are working together.[45]

In relation to both barristers and solicitors it was suggested that all restrictions on advertising fees and services should be removed. The Commission felt that existing restrictions on 'misleading and deceptive' forms of advertising provided sufficient protection to the public. (This suggestion has been adopted under practice rules.)[46] It also proposed that

---

43. LRC (Vic) (above), p 13. One member of the Commission, R Richter QC, agreed that the rules are anti-competitive but that some of them involve a net public benefit. See his dissent on p 73.
44. LRC (Vic) (above), pp 13–15.
45. LRC (Vic) (above), pp 6–7.
46. LRC (Vic) (above), pp 7–8.

contingent fees be allowed for both professions subject to rules made by their respective professional bodies. (This proposal was rejected under s 99 of the 1996 Act and Pt 3.4.29 of the 2004 Act, but ss 97 and 98 of the 1996 Act and Pts 3.4.27 and 3.4.28 of the 2004 Act do allow conditional costs agreements where payment is made only on a successful outcome — except in criminal and family law matters. These agreements involve a premium (or uplift) of up to 25 per cent above the normal legal costs in litigious matters.)[47]

Solicitors have the restriction that only solicitors can be directors or shareholders of their companies, and that the practice of law must be the sole purpose of the company's business. These restrictions serve as impediments to multi-disciplinary practices and are obstacles to national and international practice. The Commission proposed that these restrictions be removed but that the Law Institute should have the power to regulate the nature of the business associations formed by solicitors with others.[48] The 1996 Act under Pts 10 and 12 rejected this recommendation by prohibiting multi-disciplinary practices, but under s 293 legal practitioners had the right to have limited liability corporations. Under Pt 2.7.1–2.7.35 of the 2004 Act Victorian solicitors are allowed to incorporate and under Pt 2.7.37–2.7.51 to have multi-disciplinary partnerships (MDPs). MDPs have also been adopted in New South Wales,[49] in Western Australia,[50] in the Northern Territory[51] and Queensland.[52] Furthermore, controversial legislation that allows solicitors to incorporate was adopted in late 2000 in New South Wales[53] and later in Queensland,[54] the Northern Territory,[55] Western Australia[56] and, as stated above, in Victoria: see **10.28** for a discussion of incorporation. In October 2000 the Law Council of Australia adopted the New South Wales MDP system as the model for Australia.[57] Earlier in 2000 the American Bar Association rejected any form of MDP.[58] One interesting

4.23

---

47. LRC (Vic) (above), pp 8–9.
48. LRC (Vic) (above), p 8.
49. Legal Profession Act 1987 (NSW) ss 48F–48G, 48J and now under ss 165–180 of the new Legal Profession Act 2004 (NSW).
50. Legal Practice Act 2003 (WA) ss 74–85.
51. Legal Practitioners Act 1996 (NT) ss 35AZN–35AZZE.
52. Legal Profession Act 2004 (Qld) ss 123–142.
53. Legal Profession Amendment (Incorporated Legal Practices) Act 2000 (NSW) and now under ss 134–164 of the Legal Profession Act 2004 (NSW). There was strong opposition to the draft bill of the 2000 Act in the Upper House and it was opposed by the Bar Association. See M Saville, 'Lawyers pushed into the furnace', *Sydney Morning Herald*, 20 March 2000, p 37; C Merritt, 'NSW incorporation bill in danger', *Australian Financial Review*, 17 March 2000, p 30; J Shaw, 'Of legal practices under the Corporations Law: The Attorney-General expands on his proposals' (1999) *Law Society J (NSW)* 67. The bill was enacted in late 2000.
54. Legal Profession Act 2004 (Qld) ss 85–121.
55. Legal Practitioners Act 1996 (NT) ss 35AD–35AZM.
56. Legal Practice Act 2003 (WA) ss 47–73.
57. *Media Release*, 5 October 2000, Law Council of Australia. See National Professional Taskforce Multi-disciplinary Practices Working Group, *Multi-disciplinary Practices: Legal Professional Privilege and Conflict of Interest*, Issue Paper, Law Council of Australia, Canberra, ACT, 2000.
58. For the arguments against the adoption of MDPs and incorporation because they are mainly for business interests and not concerned with high ethical standards, see S Mark, 'Harmonization or Homogenization? The Globalization of Law and Legal Ethics — An Australian Viewpoint' (2001) 34 *Vanderbilt J of Transnational Law* 1173, 1188–1196.

development from the changes was the listing on the Australian Stock Exchange of the banking and finance division of a Sydney law firm — Noyce Legal.[59]

4.24　In its final report the Commission decided not to recommend to parliament that particular rules be abolished or modified. It decided that the legal profession could not be trusted to make objective judgments about whether restrictions on the market for its services served the public's interest. It stated that the Trade Practices Commission (now the Australian Competition and Consumer Commission (ACCC)) should be the sole body charged with the responsibility for administering competitive policy throughout Australia. The suggestions of the Victorian Law Reform Commission were adopted in New South Wales in late 1993 when the Opposition Labor Party with support of independents amended the Legal Profession Reform Bill to have the restrictive practices of the legal profession subject to the Commonwealth Trade Practices Act 1974.

4.25　Although most of the recommendations of the Law Reform Commission of Victoria have now come into existence, it did not survive the Labor Government's loss of office. Shortly after publishing its final report the Commission was abolished as one of the first cost-saving measures of the new Coalition Government. The Law Reform Commission only came back into existence under a new Labor Government in 2000.[60]

Conveyancy practice

4.26　The Legal Practice Act 1996 in Victoria did not change the practice of conveyancing in that state. Under Pt 13, conveyancers who are not licensed can still perform this work, but must now inform their prospective clients in writing and with large public notices of the nature of their insurance coverage and whether or not they will retain a practitioner to perform the legal work in the transaction. In the vast majority of transactions lawyers need to be involved to do the 'legal work'. The Legal Profession Act 2004 Pt 7.1 added further requirements and some control by the new Board, but conveyancing remains largely unregulated. There is no formal requirement or experience. 'In Victoria, anyone can walk off the street and set up a conveyancing business ... It's dangerous.'[61] The non-regulated conveyancers usually use a legal practitioner to finalise the transaction. After the collapse in late 2004 of a conveyancing practice, Grove Conveyancing, with losses of up to $9 million,[62] the Victorian Government established an inquiry concerning the general regulation of the conveyancing industry. The inquiry has a broad reference and will look at the system now established in New South Wales.[63]

The New South Wales licensing system was established in 1992, despite strenuous opposition by solicitors to maintain their monopoly over

---

59.　M Pelly, 'Law firm list itself', *Sydney Morning Herald*, 17 May 2004, p 22.

60.　Victorian Law Reform Commission Act 2000.

61.　K Towers, 'Victorian conveyancing laws "dangerous"', *Australian Financial Review*, 29 October 2004, p 56.

62.　For a discussion of the collapse of Grove Conveyancing, see C Merritt, 'Grove crisis sparks war of words', *Australian Financial Review*, 29 October 2004, p 56.

63.　C Merritt, 'Victoria launches conveyancing inquiry', *Australian Financial Review*, 12 November 2004, p 57.

conveyancing.[64] Solicitors have found that licensed lay conveyancers are very competitive, forcing many solicitors to discount their price.[65] Further changes in 1995 extended the rights of licensed conveyancers to commercial, retail and rural property transfers, as well as transfers of goodwill and stock in trade. These changes were again vigorously opposed by the Law Society, but were supported by the press.[66] There were further changes in the Conveyancers Licensing Act 2003. L J Hooker, the large real estate agency, proposed to establish its own conveyancing law firm, Summerlegal, in New South Wales in 2004. L J Hooker said that a one-stop service appealed to its clients. A similar law firm established in Western Australia has been extremely successful with 90 per cent of its customers using its services. In New South Wales, Steve Mark, the Legal Services Commissioner, opposed its establishment because it would place undue pressure on lawyers and not be in the interests of consumers. Mark said: 'If there is a dispute over a contract, the solicitor acting on behalf of either party [vendor or purchaser] is going to be in conflict with the agent.'[67] As a result of government pressure, when Summerlegal was established it distanced itself from L J Hooker.[68]

In Queensland in 1999 the government proposed removing the solicitors' monopoly over conveyancing and setting up a licensed conveyancers' scheme. The scheme proposed emphasised the need for adequate academic and practical training for conveyancers. It also proposed a Legal Practice Authority to be responsible for granting licences and for investigating any complaints. This scheme was strongly opposed by the Queensland Law Society on the basis of the high quality of service and reasonable price provided by its members.[69] The Queensland monopoly is being threatened from outside the state. Paul Sande, a New South Wales licence conveyancer, under the name Realty Conveyancing Services, gets around the monopoly by having his office just 70 metres from the border. He has 10 employees and does a booming business in Queensland. Also a group of Australian Capital

4.27

---

64. Conveyancers Licensing Act 1992 (NSW). The power still remained with the solicitors as they controlled the Conveyancers' Licensing Committee. There was considerable criticism that there were artificial barriers to entry: see the *Sydney Morning Herald*, 6 September 1993, pp 14, 15; 17 November 1993, p 9; 5 November 1994, p 2. The Conveyancers Licensing Committee and the power of the Law Society to issue licences was removed in 1995: see Conveyancers Licensing Act 1995 (NSW). The issuing of licences is by the Department of Fair Trading. The power to regulate licensed conveyancers is by co-regulation with this department and the Office of the Legal Services Commission. The Northern Territory also adopted a highly regulated licensed conveyancers regime under the Land and Business Agents Amendment Act 1991. Queensland remained the only jurisdiction without non-lawyer conveyancers as of August 2005.

65. See the survey conducted by the Law Foundation of New South Wales as to the changes to their conveyancing practice: *Tomorrow's Legal Services Bulletin*, August 1994.

66. The new Act, the Conveyancers Licensing Act 1995 (NSW) repealed the 1992 Act. For the politics concerning the adoption of the Act see *Sydney Morning Herald*, 28 September 1995, p 9 and Editorial, *Sydney Morning Herald*, 20 September 1995, p 14 and F Riley, 'The Conveyancers' Licensing Act 1995 (NSW)' (1996) 19 *UNSW LJ* 470, 471–2.

67. J Eyers, 'Fears over "inside" conveyancing', *Australian Financial Review*, 16 April 2004, p 56.

68. Communication from Commissioner Steve Mark.

69. Green Paper (above), pp 26–28.

Territory solicitors, in a division of the firm of Nicholas Dibbshas, have established a cheap online conveyancing service: www.ozpropertylaw.com.[70] As of August 2005 no new licensing scheme has been adopted in Queensland.

Restrictive practices and reform — New South Wales

4.28   In 1993 the Law Society supported the New South Wales Law Reform Commission's latest suggestions for reforming the restrictive practices of the bar. Throughout 1993 the Law Society Council and the Bar Association Council fought a public battle over reform of the structure of the legal profession.[71] The main changes which were finally adopted in relation to structure in the Legal Profession Reform Act 1993 (which amended the Legal Profession Act 1987), some against the wishes of both the solicitors and the barristers, include the following:

❑ direct access to barristers by any client;[72]

❑ common admission into the legal profession as a lawyer and then election as to whether one wishes to practise as a barrister or a solicitor but not both (this was changed in April 1997 by amendments to the Legal Profession Act allowing admission as a 'solicitor and barrister', but the separate bar is retained under this Act and the Legal Profession Act 2004);[73]

❑ abrogation of the appointment of Queen's Counsel by the Crown;[74]

❑ the right for a barrister to choose a solicitor advocate as a junior;[75]

❑ the right of a barrister or solicitor to be in partnership with a non-lawyer (but note the provision allows barristers' rules to stop this and they do prevent it);[76]

❑ the right to contingent fee contracts but not on a percentage basis.[77] The uplift fees in personal injury damages matters under s 338 of the new 2004 Act have limits for claims up to $100,000. The practitioner can receive only up to 20 per cent or $10,000, whichever is greater, of the amount recovered;

❑ a newly constituted Advisory Council, with five of the 11 members being lay people, not only to review the structure and functions of the legal

---

70.   *Hearsay*, C Merritt (ed), *Australian Financial Review*, 19 September 2003, p 53.

71.   For an interesting summary of some of this dispute and the role of the New South Wales Government see *Justinian*, August 1993, pp 7–16.

72.   Section 381 and now under s 83 of the Legal Profession Act 2004 (NSW); the Bar Association has still placed many restrictions on the work a barrister can do for a client that comes directly to the barrister: see rr 74–87, Barristers' Rules (NSW) 1995. These rules were challenged by two barristers before the Legal Profession Advisory Council, as either imposing a restrictive or anti-competitive practice, or as contrary to the public interest. The complaint was later dismissed by the Advisory Council: see NSW Bar Association, *Newsletter*, April 1995, p 1 and July 1995, p 3.

73.   Sections 25–26, 38A and 38D of the Legal Profession Amendment (National Practising Certificates) Act 1996 and now under ss 31, 34 and 41 of the Legal Profession Act 2004 (NSW).

74.   Section 38O and now s 90 of the Legal Profession Act 2004 (NSW). Those with the office do not lose the right to the title. The Bar Association has replaced the QC title with its own SC (Senior Counsel): *Sydney Morning Herald*, 14 October 1993, p 4.

75.   Section 38M and now s 88 of the Legal Profession Act 2004 (NSW).

76.   Section 48G and now ss 165–166 of the Legal Profession Act 2004 (NSW).

77.   The term used is 'conditional costs agreements' in ss 186–187 and now ss 323–325 of the Legal Profession Act 2004 (NSW).

profession but also to advise on professional standards, advertising and general regulation of the legal profession;[78]

❑ an independent Legal Services Commissioner to deal with complaints against any lawyers[79] but still leaving limited power with the existing system of the Law Society and Bar Association.[80] The Commission does have the power to receive almost all initial complaints and has a review role;[81]

❑ the right of a barrister or solicitor to advertise in any way he or she thinks fit as long as it is not 'false, misleading or deceptive' or contravenes the Trade Practices Act 1974, the Fair Trading Act 1987 or any similar legislation or contravenes any requirements of regulations.[82]

Competition policy

Amendments to the Legal Profession Reform Act 1993 which made the legal profession subject to the Commonwealth's Trade Practices Act 1974 were forced on the government by the Labor Opposition and independents: these represented a major defeat for the legal profession of New South Wales.[83] The provisions did not come into effect until Commonwealth law permitted the relevant bodies to exercise jurisdiction[84] and no legislation was ever enacted. The provision was repealed on 1 April 1997 by the Legal Profession Amendment (National Practising Certificates) Act 1996 because of the adoption of the Competition Policy Reform Act (NSW) 1995. The latter Act enacted the agreement reached between the Commonwealth and the other jurisdictions for the implementation of a national competition policy. This policy was in line with the Law Council of Australia's *Blueprint for the Structure of the Legal Profession* (1994) which stated that 'national competition policy principles apply to the legal profession'.[85] Other jurisdictions have also adopted legislation in line with the National Competition Policy Agreement, endorsed by all governments, to have Pt IV of the Trade Practices Act apply to all individuals and businesses, including legal practitioners.[86] All jurisdictions are now subject to a Competition Code which is found in the Competition Policy Reform Act 1995 (Cth). The Code is administered by the ACCC.

4.29

The major reforms in the 1990s of the restrictive practices of the legal profession that result from rigid structures came about because of the high degree of consumer awareness; community demands for increased accountability and responsibility for lawyers; and the realisation by legal

4.30

---

78. Sections 57H, 58–59 and now under ss 682–685 of the Legal Profession Act 2004 (NSW).
79. Sections 129–134, 147A and under ss 686–693 of the Legal Profession Act 2004 (NSW).
80. Section 148 and under ss 694–700 of the Legal Profession Act 2004 (NSW).
81. Sections 149–151 and under s 505 of the Legal Profession Act 2004 (NSW).
82. Section 38J and under s 84 of the Legal Profession Act 2004 (NSW).
83. Sections 38FC–38FD. Although the Trade Practices Act has applied since its enactment to the ACT and the Northern Territory it was not in force in other jurisdictions.
84. Section 38FA.
85. *Blueprint for the Structure of the Legal Profession: A National Market for Legal Services*, Law Council of Australia, July 1994, p 2.
86. For a summary of the effect of the application of the restrictive trade provisions, see S Corones, 'Solicitors subject to Trade Practices Act' (July 1996) *Proctor (Journal of Queensland LS)* 10–11.

professional associations that competition was generally a healthy development for the legal profession. There also exists today far greater client mobility and the days of client loyalty to a lawyer or group of lawyers no longer exist. More and more clients, including governmental clients, now ask for tenders on providing legal services or shop around for good service at the best price. Furthermore:[87]

> ... the emphasis on 'micro-economic' reform has reached the professions, with the attendant concerns about the elimination of restrictive trade practices and the promotion of increased competition within and between markets for goods and services — including professional services.

4.31 One aspect of the competition credo is the opening up of the Commonwealth Government's legal work to private tender. The Attorney-General's Department has had to compete for non-litigation commercial work from 1 July 1994. It maintained its monopoly over litigation work. Its Legal Practice unit is partly commercial and for the 1995–96 financial year it made an operating profit of $7.25 million.[88] The Commonwealth legal services market was estimated at March 1997 to be valued at about $198 million per annum but this may be an inflated figure.[89] The Legal Practice unit received $13 million funded by the budget and $80 million from billable hours. This gave it 47 per cent of the market share. Private counsel and private firms each received $20 million (10.1 per cent) of the market, while in-house government lawyers' cost was $60 million or 32.8 per cent.[90] The latest figures for 2003–04 have shown that government legal spending has dramatically increased. The research firm Interdata found that government's legal spending was $243 million of which $182.3 million was outsourced.[91] These figures do not include a number of government departments. The Australian National Audit Office states that 40 government agencies spent $446 million on legal services for 2003–04. Of this amount $216.2 million was outsourced to private lawyers. This is a huge increase from 1999–2000 when the total was $307.8 million.[92]

Australian Government solicitors

4.32 The government has also adopted the A-G's *Report's* general recommendation that in order to compete efficiently the Attorney-General's Department needs to be restructured. The restructuring took place in 1998. The A-G's *Report* pointed out that the department would have as its main functions the giving of policy advice, coordinating the provision and purchase of legal services, dealing with constitutional and international law problems and legislative drafting. There are civil, criminal and information and security law divisions and offices of legislative drafting, international law, legal services coordination and legal services purchases.

---

87. *Access to the Law: Restrictions on Legal Practice* (above), p 5.
88. *Report of the Review of the Attorney-General's Legal Practice*, March 1997, Chapter 6.5.
89. The Australian Bureau of Statistics estimate for 1995–96 was much lower at $75 million. See Australian Bureau of Statistics 1995–96 *Legal and accounting services* ABS Catalogue No 8678.0 1997 quoted in ALRC Report No 89, *Managing Justice: A review of the federal justice system*, February 2000, para 175.
90. ALRC Report (above), Chapter 4.27.
91. C Merritt, 'Bulging brief: fee bonanza for favoured law firms', *Australian Financial Review*, 6 August 2004, p 1.
92. C Merritt, 'Canberra's legal bill soars $138m', *Australian*, 21 June 2005, p 5.

All this work is funded by the government from its budget. The Legal Practice section became a statutory authority called the Australian Government Solicitor (AGS) under the Attorney-General's direction. So far as practicable, it charges fees and is totally competitive with the private sector. The AGS has a business and commercial section and offices of litigation and general counsel. It maintains regional offices in all capital cities and in Townsville. The AGS continues to provide legal services to government departments.[93] The monopoly over government litigation was also given to the AGS.

It was estimated that 49 per cent of the legal services of these government departments was provided by the Legal Practice section, while 39 per cent was provided by their own in-house lawyers and 12 per cent by the private sector.[94] Therefore the AGS inherited a core governmental clientele and according to the *A-G's Report* had a good chance of retaining this work:[95] **4.33**

> Client departments and agencies expressed satisfaction with services provided by the Legal Practice, and indicated that they had received improved service ... from the Legal Practice since the untying of some elements of work. The Legal Practice was perceived as having greater expertise and specialised knowledge of government law than private practices, with a competitive advantage over private firms because of its unique understanding and empathy with government perspectives, practices and processes, and accumulated knowledge and experience of departmental and agency needs. Major departments and agencies saw fewer conflicts of interest and confidentiality risks in using the Legal Practice ...

This prediction that the AGS would retain government legal services has proven to be more than accurate. According to a survey by Interdata in 2002–03 the AGS received over $77.7 million of the $144.8 million of the outsourced government work, which was 53.6 per cent of the total. In 2003–04 the legal fees of the AGS increased to $99 million, which constituted 54.3 per cent of the $182.3 million outsourced work.[96]

As of 1 September 1999 the AGS became a financially independent statutory authority within the Attorney-General's portfolio, with the Minister for Finance and Administration and the Attorney-General being joint shareholders. According to the then Attorney-General, Daryl Williams, mechanisms were put into place to remove any competitive advantage the AGS may have by its public ownership. He had its monopoly over government litigation removed as of 1 September 1999 and had the Office of Legal Services Coordination provide advice and directions so as to allow private firms to contribute to the delivery of most Commonwealth legal services. He said: 'Some areas of Commonwealth legal work (mainly Constitutional, Cabinet, national security and public international law) remain tied to government lawyers, to allow consistent interpretations and applications of these areas of law to be maintained.'[97] The corporate **4.34**

---

93. *Report of the Review of the Attorney-General's Practice* (above), Chapters 9 and 10.
94. van Leeuwen (above), fn 78.
95. *Report of the Review of the Attorney-General's Practice* (above), Chapter 7.30.
96. C Merritt, 'Bulging brief: fee bonanza for favoured law firms' (above), pp 1 and 57.
97. D Williams, 'Greater Competition for Commonwealth Legal Work' (November 1999) *Brief (Law Society of Western Australia)* 23 and see also L Dempsey and M Costello, 'A Slice of the Legal Pie — Outsourcing of Government Legal Work' (November 1999) *Brief (Law Society of Western Australia)* 6. The changes to the AGS were part of the Judiciary Amendment Act 1999.

statement of the AGS says it is a government-owned national law firm that serves the public interest. There is a possibility of a conflict in the policies of the AGS because the CEO is appointed directly by the minister, while the board is independent. Simon Konecny of the AGS said: 'If there should be disagreement between the CEO and the board, the entity could become dysfunctional.'[98] No such problems had taken place by August 2005. As of December 2004 it had over 360 lawyers.[99]

An important development has been the use of the outsourcing of government legal work to combat discrimination against female lawyers. The Victorian Government requires that firms who receive government work provide a fair share to female barristers. If a firm fails to adhere to these guidelines the Victorian Government will cease retaining that firm.[100]

4.35 Although the AGS and the private profession will compete for government business they must do so under model litigant rules. These rules were adopted by the Attorney-General's Legal Practice (which became the AGS) in 1995. In 1999 amendments to the Judiciary Act 1903 made it obligatory that all Federal Government litigation be conducted according to these rules. The rules set down ethical standards of fair play and are approved by the Australian Law Reform Commission (ALRC) in DP 62, *Review of the federal justice system.*[101] They are:

□ promptly dealing with claims and not causing unnecessary delay;
□ not taking advantage of a claimant who lacks the resources to litigate a legitimate claim;
□ not relying on technical defences unless the Commonwealth's interests would be prejudiced by the failure to comply with a particular requirement;
□ apologising where the Commonwealth is aware that it or its lawyers have acted wrongfully or improperly.

4.36 The ALRC said: 'If all parties acted as model litigants, the civil justice system would be more effective and efficient.'[102] In its final report, the ARLC pointed out that model litigant rules had been revised in 1999 and now apply to 'claims and litigation' and 'litigation (including before courts, tribunals, inquiries, and in arbitration and other alternative dispute resolution processes) involving Commonwealth agencies'.[103] The ALRC made as recommendation 23 in its final report that these rules 'should include commentary and examples explaining the required standards of conduct of lawyers (and others) representing government, and giving examples concerning "unnecessary delay", "technical defences", and avoiding "taking advantage" of a claimant who lacks resources'.[104]

---

98. C Jay, 'AGS debates public sector governance', *Australian Financial Review*, 22 October 2004, p 56.
99. See its website: http://www.ags.gov.au/
100. C Merritt, 'More briefs for female lawyers', *Australian Financial Review*, 29 August 2003, p 3 and K Towers, 'Warning to firms on briefing policy', *Australian Financial Review*, 21 November 2003, p 57.
101. Paragraphs 8.47–8.50.
102. Paragraph 8.51.
103. ALRC Report No 89, *Managing Justice: A review of the federal civil justice system*, February 2000, para 3.142.
104. ALRC Report (above), para 3.147.

Market forces have also led to intense competition to retain and attract clients in a way far removed from the model rules of fairness. Parker interviewed 41 practitioners to determine how they perceived the reforms to the regulatory system of the legal profession.[105] She found that lawyers claimed that market forces had made them more competitive even before the regulatory reforms were enacted. One lawyer said:[106]

4.37

> Partners were charging a particular bank $300, $315, $350 an hour, and last year that bank told them $200 an hour, take it or leave it. They don't always get away with it. It depends on supply and demand.

Another lawyer gave an even more troubling account:[107]

> At the top end it is absolutely cut-throat. They have been tendering for business and a while ago I heard that firms were tendering below cost … Practitioners are working too hard. They're literally killing themselves. Last week one of our leading superannuation lawyers died. She was only 37.

Competition policy influence on restrictions

The legal profession has accepted the need for competition, but with exceptions. For example, the Council of the Law Institute of Victoria in 1993 adopted a policy which 'commits Victorian solicitors to broad competition principles subject only to a "net public benefit" test which would ensure that competition policy principles do not override public or consumer interests'.[108] The President of the Law Institute said that the competitive policy must be subject to the fiduciary and other ethical duties of solicitors.[109] Parker found in her study that the profession was willing to accept competition reforms as long as it controlled the regulatory system.[110]

4.38

The Trade Practices Commission (now the ACCC) recognised this trend when it called for a major overhaul of the legal profession. It found that a divided legal profession reduces competition between solicitors and barristers causing economic inefficiency, and should be abolished. The Commission also recommended the following:

4.39

- ❏ that the law become more affordable by deregulation of fees;
- ❏ lawyers should be able to choose the most efficient business and management arrangements including forming businesses with other professions and having the ability to incorporate;
- ❏ the office of Queen's Counsel should be abolished as well as lawyers' monopoly over areas such as conveyancing, simple civil claims, family law and wills.

Such changes would also enable lawyers to provide better services and would lead to better access to the law.[111] Many of these changes have now

4.40

---

105. C Parker, 'Converting the lawyers: the dynamics of competition and accountability reform' (1997) 33 *ANZJS* 39.
106. ALRC Report (above), p 48.
107. ALRC Report (above), p 48.
108. Letter to the editor by D Denby, President of the Law Institute of Victoria, *Australian Financial Review*, 21 January 1994, p 26.
109. *AFR* (above).
110. Parker (above), pp 43–53.
111. Trade Practices Commission, *Study of the Professions, Legal*, Final Report, March 1994, pp 6–12, 78–80. Another Commonwealth report, *Access to Justice: An Action Plan*, 1994, pp 65–221, came to similar conclusions. It found that the present regulation of the legal profession denied consumers access to the legal system.

taken place, helping to develop more flexible structures. In the past the profession developed numerous ethical rules to maintain control over its members and thereby control over the product offered to the public. The development of national mega law firms,[112] the increased mobility of lawyers and intense competition has broken this control.

4.41 As we will discuss in Chapter 6 there is a drive by the Law Council of Australia and state and territory associations to adopt uniform admission and practice rules, which now exist in most jurisdictions. The need for uniform policy has resulted from the development of the national mega law firms. There now exists a travelling practising certificate. A lawyer admitted in one jurisdiction can carry on legal practice in any other jurisdiction, without the need to be formally admitted. This development has also probably influenced the Commonwealth and state governments to adopt competition legislation. 'These changes have given Australian lawyers the ability to develop the delivery of legal services to meet the demands of a national and international market and to compete in developing global-isation of legal services.'[113] These developments have also influenced the bar. One of the goals of the Australian Bar Association is to achieve recip-rocal rights of practice for its members throughout the Asia–Pacific. The easier admission of foreign lawyers by Australian jurisdictions, which we will discuss in Chapter 6, has paved the way for reciprocal rights throughout the Asian region.

4.42 The Commission's report can be criticised for failing to accept that some restrictions on organisation and structure can be beneficial to the consumers of legal services, by ensuring the provision of more efficient services. The High Court of New Zealand in *Fisher & Paykel Ltd v Commerce Commission*[114] dealt with an exclusive dealing arrangement (franchise dealers must sell only the products of the manufacturers or distributors in return for some marketing and efficiency gains). The court held that this kind of organisational and contractual way of improving efficiency could lead to an increased competitiveness of these firms and thus meet the objectives of competition law. Farmer QC used this case to support his argument that the dismantling of the structural features of the bar would decrease efficiency and thereby competition. He said that the bar's reputation for independence (avoiding conflict of interests) and advocacy expertise (efficiency in advocacy) benefited consumers by offering them a better product than one that would be available without the separate bar.[115]

4.43 Farmer ends his article with a warning that has been made by those supporting division of the profession in many of its past successful battles:[116]

> To anyone who truly understands and knows the importance of quality of the provision of legal services, including especially the quality of legal representation in court, the Report of the Trade Practices Commission is hard to take seriously. It borders on the nutty. But regrettably, the members of

---

112. See S Ross, 'Prospects for structural and economic integration of the Australian legal profession' (1997) 4 *International J of the Legal Profession* 267.
113. Ross (above), p 285.
114. [1990] 2 NZLR 731.
115. J Farmer, 'The Application of Competition Principles to the Organisation of the Legal Profession' (1994) 17 *University of New South Wales LJ* 285, 294–6.
116. J Farmer (above), p 297.

the Commission, although not understanding the nature of legal services, are not nutty. The Commission has great standing. Its report will be taken very seriously. There is great danger that its populist appeal will lead to legislative reforms that will be against the public interest. That will not matter to the many who dislike lawyers. It may not matter to politicians and to bureaucrats who do not welcome the greater use of judicial review proceedings by lawyers acting for citizens complaining of the abuse of governmental power. But it will matter to the quality of the legal system and ultimately to the maintenance of the Rule of Law.

5

REGULATION

INTRODUCTION

Self-regulation

<u>**5.1**</u>   The Law Society of New South Wales has eloquently stated the position for self-regulation:[1]

> The legal profession is one of those professions, designated '*consultant professions*', that are distinguished by a tradition of honourable service and are of particular value and importance to the community. Professional self-regulation is logical and efficient. The legal profession in New South Wales has demonstrated throughout its history that it is capable of setting, and enforcing compliance with, high standards of professional practice. The courts have constantly relied upon the professional practitioner of good repute and competency as the best arbiter of proper professional conduct. An informed understanding of a professional discipline is required to assess the standards of practice which should be observed by practitioners who profess competence in that discipline ... The independence of the legal profession from the influence or control of the executive arm of government is essential not only to its effective self-regulation but also to the very maintenance of the rule of law. One of the reasons for the perceived unpopularity of lawyers is their need from time to time to defend persons' rights under the law and to uphold the law. If the executive should wish to take action to circumvent the law, or diminish individual rights, the lawyers who may stand between the executive government and the achievement of its objectives should not be subject to the control of a government instrumentality.

<u>**5.2**</u>   This quotation contains the main reasons for maintaining the control and regulation of lawyers by lawyers:

- ❏ the service ideal — that lawyers have traditionally been altruistic and served the community;
- ❏ lawyers have historically set a high standard and this standard has been maintained by disciplining members;

---

1.   *Submission: Scrutiny of the Legal Profession: Complaints Against Lawyers*, Law Society of New South Wales, 31 July 1992, paras 2.1 and 2.3.

❑ non-lawyers cannot understand the applicable proper standards of the profession; and

❑ the ideology of the rule of law — that government control and regulation would interfere with lawyers doing their work properly and protecting their clients' rights against arbitrary governmental action.

These ideas have also been enshrined in the Law Council of Australia's *Blueprint for the Structure of the Legal Profession* issued in July 1994. The Law Council realised that self-regulation also carries with it certain responsibilities. The *Blueprint* states:[2]

> The self-regulation of the legal profession is subject to an external and transparent process of accountability to ensure that the rules of the professional bodies are not inconsistent with national competition policy principles; the protection of consumers of legal services through comprehensive education and training of the legal profession and the development of a uniform standard of client care; proper information is available for consumers of legal services as to quality and cost of legal services.

As we have seen in Chapter 3, professions, including the legal profession, have ethical codes to distinguish them from other occupational groups. We saw that codes are used as another means of maintaining self-regulation. We also discussed in that chapter how lawyers historically mobilised to receive the community sanction that gives them control over their own affairs. This control extends to the standards required for admission and those applicable to disciplining the profession's members. The rationale for maintaining control over these two functions is discussed in the next two chapters. In this chapter we will explore the institutions that regulate lawyers, how the power to regulate is distributed and the reasons for granting those powers.

5.3

REGULATORY INSTITUTIONS — NATIONAL ASSOCIATIONS

Historical background — Law Council

National bodies in Australia have limited power and influence. This stems from the historical context of states' rights, where the local state professional associations retain most of the power over their members. Individuals were unable to join the Law Council of Australia until 1984, and the right to individual membership was removed in 1994 on resolution of Council. Membership of the sections of the Law Council (see below) is now dependent on membership through constituent bodies or through prescribed categories of persons approved by Council.[3] The emphasis on local identity has also been accentuated by other features. These include:[4]

5.4

> ... the high degree of differentiation within the legal profession with institutional or structural differences ... as well as differences based on speciality, status, income ... the highly individualised nature of some styles of legal practice, particularly at the Bar and with sole practitioner solicitors; the split between the jurisdictions with divided private professions and those with fused professions; the fact that legal knowledge (of statute law and

---

2. *Blueprint for the Structure of the Legal Profession*, July 1994, p 2.
3. Fax from Margery Nicoll, Director, Legal & Policy, Law Council of Australia, 30 May 1997.
4. D Weisbrot, *Australian Lawyers*, Longman Cheshire, Melbourne, 1990, pp 188–9.

practice rules) is far more localised than is true of other professions, such as accounting or medicine; and the imbalance in the size of the various professions, which has engendered supply–control and reciprocity controversies.

5.5 This historical framework, emphasising local identity, has come under attack during the 1980s, 1990s, and early 2000s. It has been undermined by the development of national law firms, the granting by the High Court of reciprocal practice rights in other states and territories,[5] and the need for a national response to federal initiatives to control the profession federally; for example, the Trade Practices Commission (now the ACCC) and Access to Justice Advisory Committee suggestions, the development of international legal practice and the adoption of a National Legal Profession Model Bill as the basis of a national legal profession. These developments are discussed throughout the book.

5.6 The Law Council of Australia was formed as a federation of all law societies and the bar associations of New South Wales, Queensland, Victoria and the Australian Capital Territory in 1933. It has several functions as shown in cl 3 of its present Constitution: (1) a trade union function to promote the welfare of lawyers at a national level and coordination of various submissions by its constituent organisations; (2) a public function to promote the administration of justice and general improvement of the law; (3) a consumer function to develop and promote access to justice, insurance and assurance schemes and continuing education programs and conferences. It has only become influential in this role since the 1970s. In reaction to the Whitlam Government program of legal and social change (especially the establishment of the Australian Legal Aid Office), the constituent member organisations in 1975 established a permanent office in Melbourne that was moved to Canberra in 1983. It now has the power to represent the profession in the determination of fees within the federal jurisdiction, at important national forums (for example, the National Tax Summit in 1985); organises conferences, including the biennial Australian Legal Convention; and coordinates submissions concerning national legislation, for example opposition to the Australia Card[6] and commenting on important legal issues such as mandatory sentencing, capital punishment, legal rights of migrants, unfair trial for Australians being prosecuted as terrorists by the United States, anti-terror legislation and legal aid funding.

In 2004 the Law Council was concerned that Australian David Hicks, an alleged terrorist, would not receive a proper trial by an American military commission. It thus sent an observer, Lex Leary QC, to attend the initial hearing. On 14 September 2004, the Law Council released Mr Leary's report, which found that under the present rules the commission was not independent; that 'the rules of evidence are all but absent'; and that there was 'no viable appellate process which can impartially correct errors and remedy a miscarriage of justice'. Mr Leary's report showed that it was impossible for Hicks to receive a fair trial.[7] Mr Leary made a second report

---

5. *Street v Queensland Bar Association* (1989) 168 CLR 461.
6. D Weisbrot (above), pp 189–90.
7. See Law Council's Media Releases, 15 September 2004, www.lawcouncil.asn.au.

in July 2005 that again says Hicks will not receive a fair trial. He pointed out that there are no rules of evidence and that the military commission was unworkable.[8]

The Law Council has established various standing committees, which meet regularly, and also ad hoc committees to deal with specific objectives. Furthermore, it has five sections of substantive law practice which have substantial membership: business, family, federal litigation, legal practice, and international. Some of these sections publish newsletters to their members and some sponsor journals such as the *Melbourne Journal of International Law* and the *Australian Law Practice Management Journal*.[9] These areas of practice are along the lines of the influential sections of the American Bar Association. Until the late 1980s, the sections rarely met and consisted mainly of volunteers who were busy practitioners. In more recent times, the sections have been very active, conducting numerous continuing legal education programs; each has its own administrator who is part of the Law Council Secretariat. There is also more original research taking place, but it still does not compare to, for example, the American Bar Foundation.[10]

5.7

Modern role of Law Council

This may be changing as the Law Council has employed more permanent staff and the sections have become more active. The Law Council has been the moving force in the decision adopted by the Standing Committee of Attorneys-General to implement a national interstate practising certificate regime, as well as the adoption of the National Legal Profession Model Bill. The Bill has 11 principal areas of regulation. These include:

5.8

1. Reservation of legal work and legal titles;
2. Admission to practice;
3. Practising certificate requirements;
4. Trust accounts;
5. Fidelity fund cover;
6. Costs and costs disclosure;
7. Complaints and discipline;
8. External intervention;
9. Lawyers' business structures (namely incorporated legal practice and multi-disciplinary practices);
10. Legal profession rules; and
11. Foreign lawyers practising foreign law in Australia.[11]

The Law Council has also established an Australian Advocacy Institute. One setback was the Law Council's decision (motivated by cost cutting) to stop publication of its journal, *Australian Lawyer*. The journal went to all lawyers in Australia and was a valuable source of information for lawyers in both branches of the profession. It was replaced by a monthly four-page

---

8. Ibid, 21 July 2005, www.lawcouncil.asn.au.
9. See www.lawcouncil.asn.au.
10. See S Ross, *Politics of Law Reform*, Penguin, Ringwood, 1982, p 58.
11. See the Law Council website for more information on the National Legal Profession Model Bill, www.lawcouncil.asn.au.

newsletter also entitled *Australian Lawyer*, which ceased publication in December 2002. The Law Council now publishes information about its activities in local state journals and by maintaining an informative website at www.lawcouncil.asn.au. This is obviously not a completely satisfactory solution for a national organisation and can be contrasted with the American Bar Association's publication of a number of national journals.

5.9   The Law Council has had little control over the vested interests of its members. The right of constituent members to veto any Law Council action that affected their 'vital interests' has consistently kept the issue of division/fusion off the agenda. The Law Institute of Victoria threatened to withdraw in 1981 unless this clause was deleted from the Association's Constitution. A compromise was reached by the substitution of a new clause that precludes the Council from interfering with the domestic concerns of the constituent associations.[12]

The Law Institute of Victoria was responsible for pushing the Council into allowing the admission of individual members. It emphasised that the Council would only become a vibrant and influential body by having individual members and reflecting their views and opinions. The Institute pointed out the success of similar organisations overseas, which resulted from allowing individual membership; for example, the American Bar Association and the Canadian Bar Association.[13] In 1993 the Law Institute again threatened to become the first body to withdraw from the Law Council. The threat came about because of the Council's refusal to support the Institute's drive to have contingent fees implemented nationally, and also because of the cost of membership. The Institute did not withdraw.[14] The Queensland Law Society made another threat of withdrawal in 1996 and it was 'suspended' four months later. In the past the other threats to withdraw have been made by the Victorian and New South Wales Bar Associations.[15] In 2004 there was a movement by members of the Queensland Bar Association to sever their links. These members did not think they received value from their association for the annual capitation fee paid to the Law Council.[16] As of August 2005 there is no indication that the Queensland Bar intends to sever its ties.

Australian Bar Association

5.10   The other main national lawyers' body is the Australian Bar Association, formed in 1962 to represent those lawyers practising solely as barristers. At that time there were only separate bars in New South Wales, Victoria and Queensland. The Association has been successful in defending the divided structures in those states and has been influential in its support of the

12.   J Disney, J Basten, P Redmond and S Ross, *Lawyers*, 2nd ed, 1986, p 45.
13.   'Institute Wants Admission to be Australian Wide' (1983) 57 *Law Institute J* (Vic) 524–5.
14.   Communication from the office of the Law Council of Australia. There have been three other threats of withdrawal from the Council, all of them eventually removed (New South Wales and Victorian Bar Associations and in 1996 the Queensland Law Society).
15.   *Justinian*, May 1996, p 10.
16.   K Towers, 'Law Council "value" under fire in Qld', *Australian Financial Review*, 1 October 2004, p 49.

development of separate bars throughout Australia. Tasmania was the last jurisdiction to have an independent bar, joining in 1996. The Australian Bar Association's objectives, according to its Constitution, are to 'advance the interests of barristers', to 'maintain and strengthen the position of the Bar', to 'form a bond of union among members' so as to ascertain and express their views, exchange information and develop common standards or rules. The objectives also include maintaining and improving standards of instruction and training, making 'representations on behalf of barristers to Federal and other Government departments or bodies' and to 'maintain the rule of law'.[17] As Disney et al state:[18]

> With the more active role assumed by the Law Council of Australia in recent years and the extension of direct representation to Bar Associations upon the Council's central committee, the Australian Bar Association has become less prominent. It does, however, continue to make representations to the Commonwealth Attorney-General on matters of interest to barristers and in other matters of common concern such as the negotiation of professional indemnity insurance cover for members.

The Australian Bar Association also issues press releases, for example a statement was issued defending the High Court when it came under attack by prominent politicians for some of its decisions in early 1997,[19] and in 1998 and 1999 it took a strong stand against the New South Wales Government's use of part-time acting judges[20] and in 2000 opposed mandatory sentencing.[21]

5.11

It was also involved in the drafting, and adoption in 1993, of a uniform national bar code (Code of Conduct) which unified the ethical rules for barristers throughout Australia except for Tasmania.[22] This code has since been replaced by a new code based on the New South Wales Barristers' Rules 1995,[23] known as the Advocacy Rules. These rules have been approved by the Australian Bar Association and later by the Law Council as part of its Model Rules of Professional Conduct and Practice. Its membership has grown dramatically in recent decades. In 1983 it claimed to represent 2600

17. Australian Bar Association, Constitution, cll 3(a)–(c), (h), (k), (l).
18. Disney et al (above), p 46. See also (1983) 57 *ALJ* 438.
19. See also defence of the independence of the courts in Attorney-General and Minister for Justice Daryl Williams and Justice Dennis Mahoney, 'Who Will Defend the Courts?', *Australian Bar Gazette*, No 3, July 1997. This issue also has the statement on judicial independence by the eight state and territory Chief Justices: pp 3–7.
20. See 'From the President' (1999) 6 *Australian Bar Gazette* 1–2.
21. See 'From the President' (2000) 7 *Australian Bar Gazette* 1–2.
22. After its adoption the New South Wales Association decided to reject the new code and adopted its own rules. The bar associations in other states and the Law Council (for their advocacy rules) adopted the New South Wales rules of 1995. In 1995 the Code was drastically modified to bring it more into line with the New South Wales rules and at the same time the New South Wales rules were modified. The New South Wales rules were further amended in 1997.
23. The 1995 rules were not gazetted until June 1997 by which time they had additional amendments. As a result the Law Council of Australia and other bar associations who followed the 1995 changes are not identical with those eventually adopted in New South Wales in June 1997. In January 2000 a number of important amendments were adopted by the NSW Bar Association and the Law Council of Australia adopted these changes in 2002.

barristers,[24] and by April 1997 that number was 3675.[25] The individual bars pay membership by taking $20 from each of their members' dues and therefore its budget is not large. The increase in membership is a natural development as more practitioners go to the bar. By August 2005 it still did not have a permanent office; the office moves to the city of its incumbent president. For example, the President in 2004 was Ian Harrison SC from New South Wales and the office was in Sydney. In 2005 it was Ian Viner QC from Western Australia and the office was in Perth. It appears that the organisation does not want the office to stay in one city because it is believed that the bar in that state would then dominate its policies.[26]

Other national bodies

5.12 The Law Council of Australia and the Australian Bar Association are far less important as national bodies than similar bodies of other professions in Australia, such as the Australian Medical Association, the Australian Society of Accountants, the Institute of Chartered Accountants and the Australian Institute of Engineers. Also, in comparison to other national legal professional bodies in common law countries such as New Zealand, England and Wales, Scotland, Canada and the United States, the national legal bodies in Australia have little power. It can be argued that countries such as New Zealand and England do not have federal structures and so national bodies can function more efficiently, but Canada and the United States have federal structures and their national bodies:[27]

> ... play central roles in law school accreditation and standards, promulgation of codes of professional conduct and, in the United States, federal judicial selection. The North American professions are fused, and it may be that division in addition to federalism is too potent a recipe for sectionalism to be overcome, notwithstanding such unifying elements as common economic interests and adherence to the ideology of the rule of law.

5.13 The situation in Australia is similar to the localism that characterises the legal profession under civil law countries in Europe and Latin America. The tradition in those countries was the attachment of professional associations to the local courts that led to the formation of a large number of associations. In the twentieth century these groups integrated into national associations but these national bodies remain weak with the local organisations maintaining the most power over their members.[28]

A number of other national associations representing lawyers have been formed. Some of these are associated with the main professional bodies such as young lawyers' groups. Others have been formed for political reasons,

---

24. *Sydney Morning Herald*, 6 October 1983, p 15.
25. Private telephone communication from the Australian Bar Association, late March 1997. These figures include the 1996 membership numbers from the Northern Territory (14) and the ACT (47) because they had not paid by April 1997. The figure includes payment for 1997 for the 12 members from the new Independent Bar of Tasmania. Please note that the Law Council of Australia said there were 3785 barristers in Australia as of March 1997. For a more up-to-date figure of membership look at the figures for barristers in each state in Chapter 4.
26. For more information on the Australian Bar Association go to www.austbar.asn.au.
27. Weisbrot (above), p 192.
28. Weisbrot (above).

such as the now defunct Australian Legal Workers' Group,[29] the Lawyers' Reform Society and the Australian Society of Labor Lawyers that has strong ties to the Labor Party. There are also specialist interest groups such as the Family Law Association, the Women Lawyers' Association, the Australian Institute of Judicial Administration, the Australian Taxation Institute, the Environmental Law Association, the Commercial Law Association, the Australian Plaintiff Lawyers Association (changed in 2004 to the Australian Lawyers Alliance with expanded membership to include migration, criminal, family and consumer lawyers), Australian Lawyers for Animals and the Communication Law Association.

There are groups that look after the interests of the consumers of legal services (for example, the Law Consumers Association), and groups who represent other interests affected by the law, such as the Prisoners' Action Group, Amnesty International, the Council for Civil Liberties, the International Commission of Jurists, the Australian Lawyers for Human Rights, and so on. Furthermore, there are now various research centres to support some of these groups in areas such as communications law, tax law, human rights, privacy and commercial law. One interesting development is the Australian Council of Professions which represents the major professional organisations — architects, engineers, surveyors, pharmacists, lawyers, doctors, accountants, dentists, veterinarians and actuaries. The Council's main function is to safeguard the common interests of these professions in areas of liability insurance and to maintain their anti-competitive practices.[30]   **5.14**

REGULATORY INSTITUTIONS — STATE BODIES

Composition of state bodies

In each state and territory except Western Australia and Victoria there exist professional associations which are self-regulating. Western Australia had an independent statutory body called the Barristers' Board for 100 years; it was replaced in 1993 by the Legal Practice Board.[31] The composition of the Board is similar to that of the old Board and is composed entirely of lawyers: the Attorney-General, the Solicitor-General, all Queen's Counsel and nine practitioners. The number of legal practitioners was increased to 12 in 2003.[32] The Board is independent of the Law Society and is a body corporate.[33] The main change was the establishment of two separate bodies — a Complaints Committee and a Disciplinary Tribunal, both with lay representation — to deal with discipline.[34] The Law Society in Western Australia still has the same limited role it had under the   **5.15**

---

29. For a history of its formation see Ross (above), pp 43–53.
30. Weisbrot (above), p 192.
31. Legal Practitioners Amendment (Disciplinary and Miscellaneous Provisions) Act 1992 (WA).
32. Legal Practice Act 2003 (WA) s 7.
33. Ibid, s 6.
34. Legal Practitioners Amendment (Disciplinary and Miscellaneous Provisions) Act 1992 (WA) and Disney et al (above), p 38. For the present composition of the Disciplinary Tribunal see Legal Practice Act 2003 (WA) s 169.

Barristers' Board, such as bringing complaints against practitioners to the attention of these bodies and representation on the Legal Aid Commission.

5.16 The Legal Practice Act 1996 in Victoria established the most radical restructuring of the regulatory process for any legal profession in Australia. An independent Legal Practice Board with seven members was established under Pt 15 of the Act. The 1996 Act has now been replaced by the Legal Profession Act 2004 but the Board has been retained. The Chairman of the Board under the 1996 Act was a retired or serving judge; three members of the Board were lay persons as recommended to be appointed by the Attorney-General; at least one of the lay persons had to be experienced in risk management or prudential supervision; and the remaining three members were legal practitioners of not less than seven years' standing, elected as follows: one from the roll of advocates, one from the roll of non-advocates and one from the combined roll. Under Pts 6.2.8 and 6.2.9 of the 2004 Act the new Legal Services Board still has three lay persons and three elected lawyers — now two who are non-advocates and one a barrister. The lay appointments still include one with experience in risk management or prudential supervision and now another must be someone who can represent 'the interests of consumers of legal services'. Under Pt 6.2.6 the chairperson no longer has to be a judge or retired judge but anyone whom the Attorney-General wants to appoint. In all likelihood that person will be a judge or former judge. This is obvious by a special provision, Pt 6.2.7, which clarifies the ramifications for a judge if he or she is appointed. The most important change is that the new Legal Services Commissioner is the chief executive officer of the Board. Under Pt 6.3.4 he or she has to 'administer the affairs of the Board in accordance with the policies and directions of the Board'. This can cause possible conflicts of interest between the Board and the Commissioner.[35] Under Pt 6.2.19 the Board is at the apex of the new Victorian regulatory structure and can issue its own rules and delegate power to the Commissioner or his or her employees and anyone who is a member of a class prescribed by regulation. In all likelihood such a class will be the former recognised professional associations, the Victorian Bar Inc and the Victorian Lawyers RPA Ltd. Under s 299 of the 1996 Act the recognised professional association generally had to have as members or practising at least 200 legal practitioners. As a result the only recognised professional associations were the Bar Association, named the Victorian Bar Inc, and the Law Institute which was reconstituted as the Victorian Lawyers Recognised Professional Association Ltd and calls itself Victorian Lawyers RPA Ltd.

Characteristics of the professional bodies

5.17 The New South Wales Law Society was the only law society to be formed originally as a private corporation, but later receive statutory recognition. In the other jurisdictions the law societies (Victorian Lawyers in Victoria) have been incorporated by statute. The law societies' power stems from their articles of association granted to them by statute. They have the power to control admission, discipline, set ethical standards, audit trust

---

35. See A Evans and C Parker, 'Too close for comfort', *Australian Financial Review*, 10 December 2004, p 47.

accounts, set standards to continue practice (continuing legal education) and control other related matters. They also represent their members in relation to governments, the judiciary, admission boards, other occupational groups and fee-determining bodies. The regulatory powers are exercisable under their constitutions (or by statute) by their councils, elected by the members. In some jurisdictions the Attorneys-General or their representatives are members, but no law society has provided for non-lawyer representation.[36] This is very different from developments overseas and from other professional bodies where parliament has required non-professional representation and in some cases outside control.

Although membership of a law society is voluntary, all qualified practising lawyers are members. In most jurisdictions they are automatically granted membership without any additional cost when taking out a practising certificate. In New South Wales legal practitioners as of 1 July 2004 had to indicate whether they wanted to be members of the Law Society even though they are entitled to membership with their practising certificate.[37] Over 92 per cent retained or took out membership for 2004–05.[38] In the fused states many lawyers who practise as barristers are also members of the Law Society and even if they do not join they are subject to the power of the law societies. Furthermore, the Western Australian Bar Rules require members to maintain their membership in the Law Society.

5.18

The bar associations, except in New South Wales, are voluntary associations which do not exercise statutory powers. They have two sources of power — their articles of association, and the fact that their rules of conduct receive judicial recognition — which have also granted the associations standing to bring disciplinary action against any member or non-member barrister.[39] In New South Wales the right to bring actions and be heard is now vested in the Bar Council by statute.[40] The High Court has held that this section did not affect the inherent powers of the Supreme Court to give leave to appear to other parties. The High Court allowed the Bar Association to appear but did say that it should only be granted this right in exceptional circumstances.[41]

The bar associations have also established ethical committees. If one of these committees asks a non-member of the association to answer a complaint, he or she will respond to the request and submit to their jurisdiction rather than face the expense of a disciplinary proceeding initiated by an association in the Supreme Court. Bar associations exercise regulatory powers through a central committee or a council elected annually by their

5.19

---

36. Disney et al (above), p 39.
37. The Legal Profession Act 1987 (NSW) s 57M: a barrister or solicitor is 'entitled' to be a member of the professional organisations without paying any additional amount to the cost of the practising certificate.
38. Law Society Media Release, 1 July 2004.
39. See *Clyne v New South Wales Bar Association* (1960) 104 CLR 186. In New South Wales non-members as well as members are bound by the rules of the associations under s 57D of the Legal Profession Act 1987.
40. Legal Profession Act 1987 (NSW) s 16 and now under s 696 of the Legal Profession Act 2004 (NSW). Section 16 also vested this power in the Council of the Law Society and continues to do so under s 699 of the Legal Profession Act 2004 (NSW).
41. *Wentworth v New South Wales Bar Association* (1992) 106 ALR 624 at 627–31.

members. In some jurisdictions the Attorneys-General are ex-officio members and there is no provision for lay membership. The president of each association usually acts as spokesperson for the whole bar.[42]

5.20   The Legal Profession Act 1987 granted the New South Wales Bar Association the power to license and discipline all barristers and this power is retained under the Legal Profession Act 2004.[43] The legislation has enabled the New South Wales Bar to restrict practice to those who practise privately in the traditional manner. The requirement that all barristers do one year's pupillage has led to discrimination against academic, government and in-house corporate lawyers who are now not eligible for a full practising certificate. The Association refused to have a 'grandfather' clause by applying this requirement to part-time barristers already admitted to the bar.[44] The other traditional bar associations, in Queensland and Victoria, also oppose membership by barristers not willing to practise in the 'traditional, private, independent fashion', and the 'Queensland Bar Association has actively discouraged such membership'.[45]

THE ARGUMENTS FOR AND AGAINST SELF-REGULATION

Why are lawyers different?

5.21   According to sociologists, the defining characteristics which distinguish professions from other occupations include the notion of freedom from external control and the right to self-regulation,[46] but as we saw in **3.6–3.7**, the trait theory lacks validity. Even if the criticism of the trait theory is valid, the legal profession has adopted the view that self-regulation is an important feature for its members. In the introduction to this chapter we gave the principal justifications given by the profession for self-regulation. They are:

❑ the service ideal — that lawyers have traditionally been altruistic and served the community;

❑ historically, lawyers have set a high standard and this standard has been maintained by disciplining members of the profession;

❑ non-lawyers cannot understand applicable proper standards of the profession; and

❑ the ideology of the rule of law — that government control and regulation would interfere with lawyers doing their work properly and protecting their clients' rights against arbitrary governmental action.

5.22   A fifth reason frequently given is that the existence of an ethical code protects the public interest. We have discussed in **3.21–3.30** why this reason is unsound and the discipline rationale will be discussed in Chapter 7.

---

42.   Disney et al (above), p 44.
43.   Sections 27, 37–38A, 57D, 152 and 155 and under ss 41, 537, 702 and 704 of the Legal Profession Act 2004 (NSW).
44.   See D Weisbrot, 'Competition, Cooperation and Legal Change' (1993) 4 *Legal Education Review* 1, 19.
45.   Weisbrot (above) (1990), p 193.
46.   See A Carr-Saunders and P Wilson, *The Professions*, Clarendon Press, Oxford, 1933; E Greenwood, 'Attributes of a Profession' (1957) 2 *Social Work* 45.

Under the present system the legal profession councils act not only as regulatory bodies but also as governing bodies. As regulatory bodies the councils' main function is to protect the public interest, while as governing bodies they have to look after their own members, that is, fulfil trade union functions. Only in Victoria and Western Australia has separation of the regulatory body from the governing body occurred because the government recognised that a conflict of interest exists when the Law Society wants to perform both these functions.[47]

There is an erroneous view held by some practitioners that to take away the self-regulatory function of lawyers would be discriminating against that profession. A former president of the New South Wales Bar stated:[48]

    5.23

> ... all major activities should be fundamentally self-governing. Trade unions are run by the members ... not by consumers. Doctors manage their own affairs, as do chemists and accountants. Why should barristers have to endure a regime that no respectable trade union would tolerate for one moment?

In their private capacities professional associations are free from outside regulation but in their public functions there is outside regulation. In contrast, trade unions are subject to numerous laws and regulations in their private and public activities.

In the public sphere we have followed the English model of regulation whereby the legal profession is in a unique position. Abel-Smith and Stevens in their seminal work on lawyers stated, concerning English solicitors:[49]

    5.24

> The extent of self-government which Parliament granted to solicitors was exceptional. While the legislature had insisted on introducing non-professional members on the bodies responsible for the education and discipline of doctors, nurses, midwives, dentists, pharmacists and architects, no non-lawyer could interfere with the affairs of solicitors.

In Australia a similar situation developed with no other profession having its regulatory body composed entirely of persons elected directly or indirectly by its member practitioners. This was the situation in all jurisdictions until the changes under the Legal Practice Act 1996 and the Legal Profession Act 2004 in Victoria. The New South Wales Law Reform Commission has stated:[50]

> In ... other professions one or more professional associations exist, but they have no statutory powers of regulation. In no case is the Board part of, or directly associated with, a professional association, but in most cases some of its members are nominated by, or come *ex officio* from, an association or are elected directly by registered practitioners. Frequently, they are academic members, either *ex officio* or by University nomination. In every case some right of nomination is given to the government, or senior government officers are *ex officio* members. In some cases all members of the Board must belong to the profession concerned, in other cases there is a member of a related profession or the legal profession, and in some cases a Minister has an unfettered right of nomination.

47. T Joyner, 'Complaints and Discipline — The Legal Practice Board' (1993) 20(3) *Brief* (*Law Society of WA*) 19.
48. R Meagher, 'A Step Towards Anarchy' (1979) 15(2) *Australian Law News* 11.
49. B Abel-Smith and R Stevens, *Lawyers and the Courts*, Heinemann, London, 1967, p 192.
50. NSW Law Reform Commission (Discussion Paper), *General Regulation*, Sydney, 1979, p 72.

5.25   None of the boards has legislative powers, the power to make regulations being vested in the governor. In some cases, however, regulations can be made only on the recommendation of the board. The scope of the regulation-making power is much narrower than that conferred on the Council of the Law Society.[51] Although the New South Wales Law Reform Commission was describing the situation in that state, the situation is similar in other jurisdictions in Australia.[52] It is ironic that the legal profession, which prohibits outside influence except in Victoria, in its own regulation is highly involved in regulating other professions. 'Lawyers interfere in the practice of scientists, of economists, of physicians, and indeed of ordinary trade unionists.'[53]

5.26   The fear of government interference and the loss of independence, therefore, appears to be unique to the legal profession. It can be argued that lawyers are in a special position in protecting the community from oppressive institutions by being able to argue their clients' cases vigorously against government, other powerful institutions and against public opinion. As an ideal this goal is unachievable, but many lawyers have acted courageously for their clients on numerous occasions. The ideal must be balanced against the need for the public to obtain satisfactory legal services from the profession, which has an exclusive right over these services. It is the government's obligation to achieve this goal. If the profession has complete power over the latter goal by self-regulation there is no accountability. Therefore, in striking a balance between these two ideals there is a need for outside involvement in the regulation of the profession.

Community representation

5.27   Without outside representation community interests will not be heard, as the only perspective will be that of those working in the profession. For example, the profession has been under attack for not controlling its members who have provided services that are unduly slow, and as a whole for providing services that are too expensive.[54] There is no indication that the preservation of the independence of the legal profession will be in jeopardy if there is community representation on its governing board, especially if that representation is in the minority. It can be argued that such involvement can help the profession to become sensitised to community needs and by responding to these needs reduce the likelihood of government interference that would gravely weaken its independence. Furthermore, public confidence in the profession is more likely to increase if the public knows that non-lawyers have a significant voice in the regulation process and that the profession does not choose these members.[55]

Lay representation on the general regulatory body of a profession is not new. The General Medical Council in England has had lay members since

51.   NSWLRC (above).

52.   Disney et al (above), p 205.

53.   Editorial, *Australian Financial Review*, 7 April 1982, p 3.

54.   See the Trade Practices Commission, *Study of the Professions, Legal: Final Report*, 1994, Chapters 5 and 8 and the New South Wales Law Reform Commission Report 70, *Scrutiny of the Legal Profession: Complaints Against Lawyers*, 1993, pp 33–64.

55.   New South Wales Law Reform Commission, *First Report on the Legal Profession*, 1982, paras 3.7–3.30.

the nineteenth century.[56] In Canada, in a number of the provinces including Ontario and Quebec, there are substantial numbers of outside members on the governing bodies of legal professions. In Quebec, the Office of the Professions oversees all professions, including the legal profession. It has appointed four non-lawyers out of a total of 24 to the governing council.[57] Since 1977 the Californian legal profession has had six public members of a total of 23 (originally 21) on its Board of Governors and other states have followed this practice.[58] The election of 15 lawyer members is staggered with only five seats being contested at any one time. One other member is elected by the California Young Lawyers Association and the final lawyer member is the President elected by other board members.[59]

Government representation

Another fear expressed by the profession is having governmental representation on its regulatory bodies. The New South Wales Law Reform Commission agreed that it would be undesirable for government nominees to constitute a large proportion of the regulatory body's membership because it would interfere with the independence of the profession. It also argued that there is a strong case for some government role on the basis that the government is accountable to the whole community at regular intervals and is responsible for the whole range of different public policies for the community. Furthermore, the government may be more in touch with changing public needs and attitudes than the profession. Government representatives will have special knowledge, usually unknown to members of the profession, of how the profession will be affected by governmental policies in other areas.[60]

5.28

Service ideal — pro bono

The service ideal is the last rationale used by the profession for maintaining self-regulation. Service to the community contains the notion of altruism — disinterested service to the community. One of its foundations is the religious notion; that working as a lawyer is a 'calling' by God to do the particular work. The idea stems from the profession's historical connection with the church. By contrast, McKinlay has stated:[61]

5.29

> Since a disproportionate number of those dominant occupations are from families with members already in, or associated with them, it would appear that whoever is doing the calling, is doing it in a highly biased and self-protective fashion!

The notion of disinterested service must also be examined in light of the realities of everyday practice. The profession has to face business realities, especially of the 1990s and early 2000s, where:[62]

5.30

56. *First Report on the Legal Profession* (above).
57. Professional Code, Statutes of Quebec, 1973, C43. See Disney et al (above), pp 205–6.
58. Business and Professions Code, s 6013.5. The Board was increased to 23 members as of January 1994. Texas also has six lay people on its Board of Directors: Rules Governing the State Bar of Texas, art 4, s 3.
59. See www.calbar.org.
60. *First Report on the Legal Profession* (above), para 3.28–30.
61. J McKinlay, 'On the Professional Regulation of Change' in P Halmos (ed), *Professionalism and Social Change*, University of Keele, Keele, 1973, pp 66–8.
62. Weisbrot (above) (1990), p 196.

... private practitioners are unwilling to provide legal services irrespective of financial reward (nor are they obliged to do so by the profession's ethics),[63] and solicitors must operate their firms on sound business principles, often offering general business and investment advice as well as more traditional legal services.

There is, however, a trend for professional bodies to require their members to do pro bono work — free legal work for the public.[64] The Law Council of Australia has adopted this definition:

Pro bono work is defined to include situations where:

1. A lawyer, without a fee or without expectation of a fee or at a reduced fee, advises and/or represents a client in cases where
   (i) a client has no other access to the courts and the legal system; and/or
   (ii) the client's case raises a wider issue of public interest.
2. or, the lawyer is involved in free community legal education and/or law reform;
3. or, the lawyer is involved in the giving of free legal advice and/or representation to charitable and community organisations.[65]

Young, idealistic and enthusiastic new members of the profession have demanded since the late 1970s that the large firms provide them an avenue for doing pro bono work. For example, arrangements were made by some of the firms periodically to place some of their young lawyers in neighbourhood legal aid centres for several months or one or two days a week as part of their work.[66] The New South Wales Law Society established a pro bono referral scheme in July 1992[67] and the New South Wales Bar Association established its pro bono register in 1995.[68] There are also Public Interest Law Clearing Houses in New South Wales, Victoria and Queensland that receive hundreds of requests a year which they farm to lawyers on their rosters. The centres have on their rosters many prominent law firms and, in Victoria, every barrister.[69] Another important initiative was the establishment by the Public Interest Law Clearing Houses of the Homeless Persons Legal Services in Victoria in 2001, Queensland in 2002 and New South Wales in 2004.[70]

---

63. See, for example, the New South Wales and Queensland Barristers' Rules, rr 85(c) and 91(c).
64. Pro bono comes from the Latin phrase *pro bono publico* which means 'for the common good'.
65. Resolution adopted 5 September 1992 and amended 18 October 1995.
66. These arrangements originally took place at the Redfern Legal Centre and Kingsford Legal Centre in Sydney, but now occur in other cities. For a discussion of such a secondment in Melbourne, see S Moran, 'Pro Bono converts commercial to community', *Australian Financial Review*, 29 July 2005, p 59. In the United States similar developments took place: see M Galanter and T Palay, 'Large law firms and professional responsibility' in R Cranston (ed), *Legal Ethics and Professional Responsibility*, Clarendon Press, Oxford, 1995, pp 198–200.
67. Communication from the Law Society of New South Wales; see also Law Society of New South Wales, *Pro Bono 'For the Public Good': A Review of the Law Society of NSW's Pro Bono Initiatives*, September 1995.
68. See *Newsletter*, NSW Bar Association, July 1995, p 11.
69. J Fife-Yeomans, 'Lawyers do it for love, not money', *Weekend Australian*, 16–17 August 1997, p 11.
70. See National Pro Bono Centre's newsletters at www.nationalprobono.org.au. For New South Wales see M Pelly, 'Lawyers hit the streets for homeless', *Sydney Morning Herald*, 21 May 2004, p 5 and M Pelly, 'Legal service for homeless a victory', *Sydney Morning Herald*, 27 September 2004, p 4.

Victoria has also given awards for pro bono work and has coordinated its pro bono efforts under the Voluntas Pro Bono Secretariat.[71] Other states also give awards for pro bono work. In May of 2003 the Law Institute updated its Legal Assistance Scheme which then had 400 volunteer solicitors. The Scheme is now managed by the Public Interest Law Clearing House and the Victorian Bar.[72] There is also a movement by the Australian courts, especially the Family Court, to develop pro bono schemes. In conjunction with the profession, The First National Pro Bono Conference was held in Canberra in August 2000. There was a second Conference held in October 2003 with delegates not only from all over Australia, but also from overseas. As a result of the first Conference the National Pro Bono Resource Centre was established in 2002 at the University of New South Wales. It was funded by the Federal Government with a four-year grant. The Centre helps match the available pro bono resources with the needs of the community. In May 2004 it established a pro bono network which is a web-based internet link-up and support information exchange between pro bono professionals. The Centre provides a download for the Australian Pro Bono Manual, which helps firms to establish pro bono programs. The Manual is also available from the Victoria Law Foundation.[73] The funding for the Centre was renewed and increased for a further four years by the Federal Government in the May 2005 budget. The decision by the government was welcomed by the Law Council as recognition for the important work being done by the Centre.[74]

There is a need for even more widespread involvement within the profession. For example, less than 5 per cent of the profession are formally involved in pro bono work although many more do informal pro bono. This is supported by a 1997 practising certificate renewal survey of solicitors in New South Wales, which found that 42 per cent of respondents (3643 out of 8675) said that they were doing pro bono work at the time of the survey. One-third of these said they did up to 10 hours pro bono work in the month of March; 14 per cent said they did more than 11 hours in that month.[75] It was estimated under this survey that there was 63,000 hours of volunteer work with a value of about $74 million.[76] A later survey from the Australian Bureau of Statistics found that Australian lawyers average only 23 hours of pro bono work per year. The ABS figures in 2003 show that solicitors working outside the capital cities conduct approximately on the average more than twice the amount of pro bono work than those working in the cities.[77]

5.31

---

71. See the discussion of the Access to Justice subcommittee in the *Law Institute Journal*, May 2000, p 29.
72. 'Legal Assistance Scheme Launched', Media Release, Law Institute of Victoria, 14 May 2003.
73. Newsletters at www.nationalprobono.org.au.
74. Media Release, Law Council of Australia, 11 May 2005, www.lawcouncil.asn.au.
75. See Keys Young, *Practising certificate survey 1997–98 Final Report*, September 1997.
76. Keys Young (above), p 33 and New South Wales Law Society Media Release, 29 September 1997.
77. The ABS study ABS, 2001–2002 *Legal Practices*, ABS Catalogue No 8667 (2003), is discussed in D Hillard and J Corker, 'Pro bono: Australia needs to raise the bar on standards', *Australian Financial Review*, 17 June 2005, p 54.

5.32   A Victorian survey done in February 1999 showed that 91 per cent of those that responded did not keep a record of the amount of pro bono work they did. Those that did keep a record, on the average, did 28 hours per month, and the average for those who estimated a figure was 15 hours per month. Only 25 per cent of those who responded said they had a pro bono policy.[78] These figures are substantially higher than the figures given in 2003 by the ABS.

The legal profession can help the public to obtain better legal services not only by providing human resources, but also by making monetary contributions to legal aid organisations. Lawyers can also do non-legal work for organisations representing the poor, elderly and disabled members of the community. It should be noted that a survey of the profession in the late 1970s showed that substantial numbers do not see that 'lawyers are primarily motivated by a desire to serve the community'.[79] Only 20 per cent of recent law graduates surveyed in 1986 stated that they chose law as a career as 'a way of being useful in the community'.[80] This was the view of lawyers and students in the 1970s and 1980s but a more recent article by Goldsmith argues that many students maintain idealistic views of helping society throughout their law school education.[81] Several authors have stated that in the United States many law students are interested in seeking social justice.[82]

5.33   If more recent graduates are interested in doing pro bono work there may not be a need for the profession to push for mandatory pro bono as a way to maintain credibility in its arguments for retaining self-regulation. The New South Wales Law Society has recommended that its members do a minimum of 10 hours of pro bono work each year or the equivalent of 1 per cent of their billable work. They also recommended that law schools adopt pro bono requirements as part of the legal training.[83] The Australian Law Reform Commission commented favourably on the New South Wales Law Society's recommendations. The ALRC in their discussion paper proposed 'that all lawyers be required to undertake a prescribed measure of pro bono services each year'.[84] In their final report the Commission agreed with the criticism of mandatory pro bono:[85]

---

78.   'Building a pro bono culture' *Law Institute J (Vic)* June 1999, p 49. The survey was contributed by the Voluntas Pro Bono Secretariat.
79.   Only 46 per cent agreed with this statement. See R Tomasic and C Bullard, *Lawyers and Their Work*, Law Foundation of New South Wales, North Sydney, 1979, p 275.
80.   D Pearce, E Campbell and D Harding, *Australian Law Schools: A Discipline Assessment for the Commonwealth Tertiary Education Commission*, AGPS, Canberra, 1987, vol 4, Appendix 5, pp 55–8.
81.   A Goldsmith, 'Warning: Law school can endanger your health!' (1995) 21 *Monash University LR* 272.
82.   See R Granfield, *Making Elite Lawyers: Visions of Law at Harvard and Beyond*, Routledge, New York, 1992 and R Stover, *Making It and Breaking It: The Fate of Public Interest Commitment During Law School*, University of Illinois Press, Urbana, Ill, 1989.
83.   Law Society of NSW, *Access to Justice — Final Report*, December 1998, pp 15–16.
84.   Discussion Paper 62, *Review of the federal civil justice system*, para 6.46.
85.   Report No 89, *Managing Justice: A review of the federal civil justice system*, February 2000, para 5.20, recommendation 37.

It has no wish to sour the professional good will which supports the justice system. Nevertheless, in a world which sees lawyers in less charitable lights and where the financial and professional imperatives of practice are increasingly demanding, it is appropriate to emphasise the service ideals which characterise the legal professional ideal. The Commission sees considerable merit in the American example, which emphasises the ethical ideal of pro bono service.

Voluntary versus mandatory pro bono

The Commission then recommended that the legal professional associations adopt similar provisions to the American Model Rules of Professional Conduct, r 6.1. The Commission also recommended that law students be encouraged 'to undertake pro bono work as part of their academic or practical legal training requirements'.[86]   **5.34**

Although some local bar associations in the United States have imposed pro bono requirements as part of their membership,[87] a mandatory requirement has generally been strongly opposed, especially in large states like California.[88] In 1993 r 6.1 of the United States Model Rules was amended. It states: 'A lawyer should aspire to render at least (50) hours of *pro bono publico* legal services per year ...'. A substantial majority of these services are to be rendered without a fee to '(1) persons of limited means or (2) charitable, religious, civic, community, governmental and educational organizations in matters' concerning persons of limited means. Rule 6.1(b) also says that lawyers should provide any additional services for no fee or a reduced fee to individuals and organisations seeking to secure or protect civil rights and liberties and public rights. Subsection (3) of r 6.1(b) further adds that lawyers should have 'participation in activities for improving the law, the legal system or the legal profession'. An earlier draft of this rule had a 40-hour per year mandatory requirement.

By 2005 mandatory pro bono in the United States still only existed at the local bar level, for example Orange County Bar Association in California, and is strongly opposed by the state bars. In May 2003 the Nevada Supreme Court amended its rule 191 and now requires all lawyers to make annual pro bono reports. The rule asks lawyers to contribute 20 hours of free services and 60 hours of reduced fees. These requirements are only aspirational. The states of Florida and Maryland have also adopted mandatory pro bono annual reports.[89] It appears that commercial firms with more than 100 lawyers are more willing to do pro bono work.[90] Rhode accepts the fact that a number of lawyers make substantial pro bono contributions which is an expression of the highest ideals of the profession. She also states: 'Most

---

86.   Report No 89 (above), para 5.19, recommendation 38.
87.   Galanter and Palay (above), p 197.
88.   In Nevada mandatory pro bono was adopted and then removed because of strong opposition: see K Nitta, 'An Ethical Evaluation of Mandatory Pro Bono' (1996) 29 *Loyola of LA LR* 910. Nitta makes a strong argument for the adoption of mandatory pro bono. See also A Boon and R Abbey, 'Moral Agendas? Pro Bono Publico in Large Law Firms in the United Kingdom' (1997) 60 *Modern LR* 630.
89.   See ABA Standing Committee on Pro Bono and Public Service, www.abanet.org.
90.   See Hillard and Corker (above). The authors refer to a study, *Researching Law*, by the American Bar Foundation.

lawyers make no contributions, and the average for the bar as a whole is less than half an hour a week ... Moreover, much of what passes for "pro bono" is not aid to the indigent or public interest causes, but either favors for friends, family, or clients, or cases where fees turn out to be uncollectible.'[91]

5.35   The argument for mandatory pro bono is based on the idea that by granting lawyers a lucrative monopoly over legal services, the community and the state deserve something in return. As Luban states: '[T]he monopoly and indeed the product it monopolizes is an artefact of the community. The community has shaped the lawyer's retail product with her [and him] in mind; it has made the law to make the lawyer indispensable. The community, as a consequence, has the right to condition its handiwork on the recipients of the monopoly fulfilling the monopoly's legitimate purpose.' Luban sees this purpose as the slogan: 'Equal Justice Under Law'. By this I believe he means access to the system by proper legal representation. He argues without this 'equal justice' the legal system has no legitimacy.[92]

Two Australian legal academics, Bagaric and Dimopoulos, reject Luban's argument. They state that: 'The monopoly was never *granted* to the legal profession, rather, it exists because the law is complex and private citizens are often unable to assert their legal entitlements without professional assistance. Hence lawyers do not have a reciprocal obligation to grant something (namely pro bono services) in return. Quite simply, lawyers are the only people in the community with the requisite skills and knowledge to represent people in relation to legal matters. Doctors, plumbers and taxi drivers also have a monopoly over their respective areas of expertise and yet are not required to work free of charge. Why should lawyers be different?'[93]

They then point out that lawyers benefit from doing pro bono work in receiving a better image and more work. Thus by electing to do such work lawyers should not see it as an ethical responsibility but rather as something they voluntarily commit to do for a benefit for themselves and others. They then argue that the lawyers should not bear the burden of providing free services because government is responsible for the complex laws. In order for people to obtain the legal services they need, government has to step in and provide payment to lawyers. They believe to do this government should place a levy on taxpayers, like it does for medicare, to establish legicare.[94]

Rhode has a different suggestion for getting lawyers to provide more pro bono — give them continuing legal education credit for their work. She also believes that there should be mandatory pro bono. She would allow those who do not want to participate to meet the requirements by buying

---

91.   An extract from D Rhode, *Access to Justice*, 2004, in D Rhode and D Luban, *Legal Ethics*, 4th ed, Foundation Press, New York, 2004, p 884.

92.   D Luban, *Lawyers and Justice: An Ethical Study*, 1988, Princeton University Press, pp 286–7. Two other authors have developed the 'public assets theory'; that lawyers sell certain services to their clients only because these services have been provided by the state with the sanction of the community. This justifies the state requiring lawyers to pay back by way of pro bono work the increase in their income and market demand provided by the state and the community. See S Lubet and C Stewart, 'A Public Assets Theory of Lawyers' Pro Bono Obligations' (1997) 145 *U Pa L Rev* 1245.

93.   M Bagaric and P Dimopoulos, 'Legal Ethics is (Just) Normal Ethics: Towards a Coherent System of Legal Ethics' (2003) 3 *QUT* 21.

94.   Ibid.

out their obligation. They can do this by making an equivalent financial contribution to a legal aid program.[95]

In Australia recently there appears to be stronger support for providing pro bono work. It is estimated that most of the big law firms have budgets of up to $2 million for free legal services.[96] There are other kinds of pro bono work provided by lawyers. These include reducing fees, giving free services by being involved with community legal centres, working on various committees of their professional bodies and doing legal aid work which is paid at a substantially reduced fee. There also appears to be strong opposition to mandatory pro bono. I agree with Luban philosophically that lawyers need to seek to provide 'Equal Justice Under Law' but I do not believe that mandatory pro bono will achieve this goal. Such a requirement would not be in the public interest. Lawyers who are made to give free services will seek ways of meeting the requirements by doing the least possible work, will refrain from voluntarily doing other pro bono work and invariably will not perform as well as they can. Furthermore, mandatory pro bono can also be viewed by the public as another ploy by the profession to protect its privileged status and support its argument that it is serving the community.

    Finally, there may be a more mundane approach to stimulating lawyers to do pro bono work. It may provide them with financial rewards. The Victorian Labor Government's Attorney-General, Rob Hulls, stated in February 2000 that, in deciding who is to be given its $40 million in legal fees, the Victorian Government would assess firms by various criteria. He said: 'In assessing which firms are used, we also want their commitment to pro bono work taken into account. If the government has to choose between a number of equally qualified law firms, then each firm's commitment to pro bono work [will be] taken into account.'[97] Law firms appointed to the Victorian Government Legal Panel must make a commitment to do pro bono work as a condition of their appointment.[98] As for the legicare solution proposed by Bagaric and Dimopoulos, do you believe Australians would be willing to accept a tax levy to increase lawyers' incomes? I believe a levy to protect one's health is far easier to accept than one to protect one's rights.

5.36

CONCLUSION

Recommendations for reform

The New South Wales Law Reform Commission in its First Report on the Legal Profession in 1982 came to the conclusion that the Law Society and Bar Association should remain as the general regulatory bodies for their members. This recommendation was subject to the following conditions:[99]

5.37

---

95.   D Rhode, *Access to Justice*, 2004, extracted in D Rhode and D Luban (above), p 888. For the arguments for and against mandatory pro bono see the same extract on pp 885–94.

96.   Fife-Yeomans (above).

97.   N Reece, 'Pro bono work may give Victorian firms an edge', *Australian Financial Review*, 25 February 2000, p 32.

98.   Media Release, Law Institute of Victoria, 14 May 2003, see n 72 (above).

99.   Para 4.13.

(i)   There should be substantial and effective community participation in the system of general regulation, including community representation on the Law Society Council and the Bar Council ...

(ii) The Governor should have certain powers to make statutory regulations in relation to the profession and any regulation made by a general regulatory body should be subject to the approval of the Governor ...

(iii) The question of whether the Law Society Council and the Bar Council should continue as the general regulatory bodies should be subject to a periodic review initiated by the Attorney-General.

5.38   The final recommendations were a stepping-back from the earlier more drastic ones contained in the Commission's discussion paper. In that paper the Commission recommended the transfer of the regulatory authority to a body independent of the professional bodies, called the Legal Profession Council. A summary of its reasons follows:

a) the risk of lay members being so daunted or dominated by professionals in the councils of their own associations as to be ineffective or mainly cosmetic;

b) the symbolic value of the creation of an independent body, expressing the need for regulation to be directed towards the promotion of the public and not the professional interest;

c) the desirability of avoiding any suggestion of state interference in lawyers' trade union activities; and

d) problems arising from the private contractual nature of the associations' constitutions.[100]

Presently neither group of recommendations has been adopted in New South Wales but some are now in effect in Victoria. Lay representation is not present on any council regulating the legal profession in Australia except in Victoria, but is present on committees established by the regulatory bodies. New South Wales, as we mentioned in **4.28**, does have a Legal Profession Advisory Council (LPAC) with five lay people out of the 11 members. One of its powers is to review the structure and functions of the professional bodies by making recommendations to the Attorney-General. It can also review the profession's rules to see whether they impose restrictions or are anti-competitive and the Attorney-General has the power to declare any professional rule inoperative following this recommendation.[101]

5.39   The LPAC has very limited power and is dependent on the Attorney-General to carry out its recommendations. Parker has stated:[102]

> A more democratic regulatory structure for the profession might give [the] LPAC its own power to veto rules and might also give it a role in advising and overseeing the OLSC [the Office of Legal Service Commission is to be discussed in Chapter 7] in the way it decides to handle and address recurrent problems in the profession. Consumer and community groups need a forum where their voice will count in deciding how the profession operates on a day by day basis.

5.40   Perhaps it will take a number of years for Australian lawyers to enter what Halliday has called the phase of 'post-monopolism'. Once market control has been realised and institutionalised by various relationships with the

---

100. General Regulation (above), pp 149–52 as summarised in Disney et al (above), p 218.

101. Sections 57H and 57I of the Legal Profession Act 1987 (NSW).

102. C Parker, 'Justifying the New South Wales Legal Profession 1976–1997' (1997) 2 *Newcastle LR* 1, 26.

state, the powerful professions show less interest in self-regulatory activities. On the basis of a survey of state and major metropolitan bar associations undertaken in 1982 in the United States, Halliday found that some bar associations had few or no self-regulatory responsibilities and those that did concern themselves with such functions gave them a relatively low priority. Halliday also concludes that in a majority of American bar associations, where the monopoly position is secure, efforts to defend the monopoly are not given priority. These associations have only allocated a minimum amount of resources such as staffing, leadership time, budget, and committee activity to defending their position. Halliday concludes that the emphasis on self-regulation is only of importance during the developmental phase of professionalisation.[103] It appears that these bar associations are so firmly entrenched that the loss of important regulatory functions, such as control over discipline of their members to an outside body, does not entail their decline. Powell has stated:[104]

> One hundred years of bar association control had established the main contours of the process so that in surrendering control, these associations could be confident that the basic structure and focus would remain relatively unchanged. Bar Association control was no longer necessary to establish the legitimacy of the association nor to institutionalise the process. Immediate control over discipline by the collective embodiment of the profession may be viewed as historically contingent rather than as a necessary and defining feature of professionalism.

Trade Practices Commission report

It can be argued that losing control over discipline may not interfere with the essential regulatory functions of the profession. What if the profession lost control over other functions, including a number of areas of practice in which it has a monopoly, for example, advocacy? The report of the Trade Practices Commission, *Study of the Professions, Legal: Final Report* (March 1994) recommending removal of some of the monopolistic areas of practice did not receive support from the profession. The report stated:[105]

5.41

> There should be no necessary presumption that any area of legal work should be reserved to lawyers without scrutiny. Rather, all areas of legal work should be examined by an appropriate body to determine the areas, if any, where there are sound public interest reasons for continuing to reserve that work to qualified lawyers and those areas where it would be in the public interest to allow competition to non-lawyers.

The legal profession's response to the recommendations was tepid.[106] The President of the New South Wales Law Society warned:[107]

> Whenever there has been an opening up of so-called easy legal work, it has produced a far more regulated regime, not less, and no discernible improved access to justice.

---

103. T Halliday, *Beyond Monopoly: Lawyers, State Crisis and Professional Empowerment* (1987) and 'Professions and the Monopoly Motif' (unpublished paper, 1982) as cited in M Powell, 'Professional Divestiture: The Cession of Responsibility for Lawyer Discipline' (1986) *American Bar Foundation Research J* 31, 54.
104. Powell (above), p 54.
105. p 8.
106. *Australian*, 9 March 1994, p 14.
107. *Sydney Morning Herald*, 7 March 1994, p 3.

5.42   The Trade Practices Commission's report also came under strong attack from the Attorney-General of New South Wales and others for leading to 'over-regulation'.[108] The report can also be criticised for having a faulty economic premise. Removing market controls can lead to a form of increased competition that does not actually increase the quality of services and reduce costs. For example, firms may compete, like our banks, by using a great deal of advertising. The cost of legal services may have to increase, if the market does not expand sufficiently to meet this additional cost.

Even if the various criticisms of the Trade Practices Commission's report are correct there appear to be valid reasons for some changes. Some obvious areas are where database technology and other innovations make it easy for non-lawyers to do conveyancing, draft a will or negotiate simple taxation and civil matters.[109] In such situations there may be far less valid reason for maintaining the existing system.

5.43   Some members of the profession will oppose almost any changes, arguing 'Why change something which is working perfectly well?' As one barrister said:[110]

> You are talking about an institution which has been in existence in its current form for hundreds of years. It must have been doing something right.

Other members are more willing to bring in changes, which they recognise benefit not only consumers but also the profession. History has shown us that if effective change is to take place reformers will need the profession's cooperation. Parker has said that:[111]

> ... an element of self-regulation in the process of reform is an ingredient of co-operative change. Thus reformers should de-emphasise calls to abolish self-regulation and instead capitalise on the discontent with self-regulation which already exists within the profession. That discontent is a resource that can be harnessed through dialogue aimed at self-reform.

5.44   According to Powell, for Chicago lawyers the maintenance of self-regulation was perceived not to be as important as maintaining a good image and reputation for the profession and the legal system. The reforming of the lawyers' inadequate discipline system was deemed to be expensive and thus giving control over discipline to the courts was easily granted and perceived as the best method of reform. Thus the profession willingly accepted reform without any threat of imposed change by the government.[112]

Parker, in her case study of reform of the profession in Australia, has identified two broad dynamics — 'one of persuasion and dialogue resulting in conversion and acceptance of reform, and one of imposition and disrespect engendering resistance'.[113] She states that:[114]

---

108. *Sydney Morning Herald*, 12 March 1994, p 11.
109. Editorial, *Australian*, 9 March 1994, p 9.
110. See M Gunn, 'Lawyers put in the dock', *Weekend Australian*, 12–13 March 1994, p 7.
111. C Parker, 'Converting the Lawyers: The Dynamics of Competition and Accountability Reform' (1997) 33 ANZJS 39, 52–3. Parker has expanded these views in her book. See C Parker, *Just Lawyers: Regulation and Access to Justice*, Oxford University Press, 1999, pp 121–39.
112. Powell (above), pp 40–1.
113. Parker, *Just Lawyers* (above), p 124.
114. Parker (above), p 137.

... engaging the legal profession in dialogue proved effective in converting lawyers ... Some lawyers were responsive to such dialogue simply to maintain legitimacy in the eyes of the community. Others opened their minds to the ideas of reformers and were persuaded by their merits. Yet voluntary change was most common where persuasive dialogue was accompanied by a perception of the inexorability of the reform process ... When reformers seemed to assume that the profession had not and would not reform itself, or where reformers seemed to refuse to listen to lawyers' perspectives on their own profession, lawyers experienced reform proposals as illegitimate insult. The apparent inexorability of reform became a goad to defiance and reactance.

Parker concludes that 'the profession is complex, and in order to comprehend its ambiguity, lawyers must have the privilege and responsibility of deliberation with and accountability to government regulators and community groups'.[115]

---

115. Parker (above), p 139.

6

ADMISSION

INTRODUCTION

6.1 One of the main regulatory functions performed by the profession is deciding who can become a member. It is an important process for preserving its cultural identity and independence. The main rationale for maintaining control over admission, according to the profession, is to control the quality of services offered to the public — to protect the public against incompetent or fraudulent practitioners. Those opposed to these controls offer different reasons why the profession maintains control:

- ❑ the profession is seeking to prevent competition, thereby maintaining the high cost of legal services; and
- ❑ it wants to use this power to keep out undesirables and thereby control 'deviant' behaviour.

CATEGORIES OF OCCUPATIONS

6.2 There is a hierarchy of requirements for admission into an occupation or activity. The lowest stage is registration, followed by certification and finally by licensing. Under registration individuals are required to list their names in order to conduct an activity. Anyone listing his or her name can engage in the activity. There is usually a fee involved for maintaining the list. Examples of registration are taking out a fishing, dog or hunting licence and voting. In fact in many places you can get a dog licence without showing any proof that you own a dog.

The next stage is certification, where a governmental agency or an educational or occupational group certifies that an individual has certain skills. This does not prevent others who do not have such a certificate from performing the work. Professions such as architecture, psychology and accountancy in many jurisdictions are certified but others can also do the same work. The main protection is that others performing this work cannot use the title: they cannot call themselves architects, psychologists or accountants.

The highest stage is licensing. Those wanting to work in such occupations need to obtain a licence from a recognised authority that has been granted the power to issue the licence. To obtain the licence the person needs to demonstrate competency in the area. This may be by meeting certain educational requirements and/or passing a test. Anyone practising this occupation without taking out a licence will be subject to a fine or gaol sentence. The occupations that require licensing include medicine and law.[1] In Australia every jurisdiction has provisions to penalise any non-lawyer who does certain prescribed work reserved *only* for lawyers.[2] The penalty can be severe and result in a gaol sentence.[3]

6.3 Milton Friedman has stated that the drive to move from registration to certification and finally to licensure is a tool in the hands of the occupational group. It uses it to obtain a monopoly at the expense of the public. The people who are most concerned with obtaining the status of licensing will be those from the particular occupation. Once they attain licensure the leaders will ensure that people who might undermine their position of power will not obtain a licence. These people are denied admission and the group identity and monopoly position is maintained. Friedman prefers certification because if those who control certification in an occupation:[4]

> ... impose unnecessarily stringent requirements and reduce the number of practitioners too much, the price differential between certified and non-certified will become sufficiently large to induce the public to use non-certified practitioners.

6.4 The licensing of lawyers can therefore stifle innovation by removing competition. By formalising the requirements to be a lawyer, the profession denies the availability of other levels of legal services. The public can only buy one type of product and its choice is limited. The 1990s started to see a change in this situation due to the rise of consumer rights groups, the subjection of lawyers to restrictive trade practices laws, the increased willingness of the legal professional association to accept competition and the loss by the legal profession of its areas of legal monopoly, especially over conveyancing.

LEGAL PROFESSION ADMISSION

6.5 To gain full entry to the legal profession one must meet certain educational requirements at recognised educational institutions, be of 'good fame and character' and 'fit and proper', and obtain certain practical experience. The practical training includes either a period of time at a recognised institute after receiving a law degree, for example the Australian National University Legal Workshop (Australian Capital Territory), the College of Law (New

1. M Friedman, *Capitalism and Freedom*, University of Chicago Press, Chicago, 1962, pp 144–9.
2. See, for example, Legal Profession Act 2004 (Vic), Pt 2.2 and the Legal Profession Act 2004 (NSW), Pt 2.2.
3. In *Legal Practice Board v Ridah* [2004] WASC 263, the non-lawyer pretended to be a solicitor and made a number of court appearances. He was sentenced to 20 months in gaol.
4. Friedman (above), pp 148–9.

South Wales) or Leo Cussins Institute (Victoria);[5] or as an articled clerk in Queensland,[6] the Northern Territory, Tasmania and Western Australia.[7] There is a possibility for waiver of the practical training course if the applicant can show a history of sufficient practical experience.[8] If a graduate does one of the practical training courses he or she may still have to practise under the supervision of a fully qualified practitioner for one to two years (depending on the jurisdiction) to be entitled to a full practising certificate. As the Australian Law Reform Commission stated, the practical legal training requirements 'vary considerably in Australia from jurisdiction to jurisdiction, and range from two years of articles to sliding combinations of articles, work experience, and institutional training'.[9] Over the last 21 years other requirements such as nationality,[10] swearing an oath of allegiance to the Queen,[11] and residence in the jurisdiction[12] have all been removed or greatly diminished.[13] The refusal of a staunch republican to take an oath of allegiance to the Queen resulted in the Victorian Supreme Court refusing his application.[14] The Victorian Attorney-General in April 2000 stated he would have the law changed and remove this requirement.[15]

NATIONWIDE ADMISSION

6.6   One of the current issues concerning admission is the development of a common admission standard throughout Australia. This has resulted in a truly national legal profession. The Standing Committee of Attorneys-General worked with the state professional bodies in each jurisdiction to develop:[16]

    (a) The removal of any impediments to reciprocal admission to practise ... that were not based on non-discriminating character, educational and practical training requirements.

---

5.   For a discussion of the practical training system see D Weisbrot, *Australian Lawyers* (1990), pp 148–51 and ALRC, Report No 89, *Managing Justice: A review of the federal civil justice system*, February 2000, paras 2.09–2.12 and 2.102–2.114.
6.   Queensland also had admission based on 10 years of public service in certain qualifying departments. Both the articles of clerkship and the public service methods of qualifying are to be phased out. See Queensland Government Green Paper, *Legal Profession Reform*, June 1999, p 3.
7.   Green Paper, *Legal Profession Reform*, para 2.12.
8.   See the ACT case of *In the matter of An Application to be Admitted as a Legal Practitioner* [1999] ACTSC 4.
9.   *Managing Justice* (above), para 2.103.
10.   The requirement of being a 'British subject' was removed in *Re Howard* [1976] 1 NSWLR 641 and *Re Ho* (1975) 24 FLR 305, and by statute in some other states.
11.   This requirement was first diminished by courts allowing admission without the formal taking of an oath: see *Re Howard* [1976] 1 NSWLR 641 at 646. It has now been removed as a requirement for acquiring Australian citizenship.
12.   *Street v Queensland Bar Association* (1989) 168 CLR 461.
13.   For more details of past requirements, see J Disney, J Basten, P Redmond and S Ross, *Lawyers*, 2nd ed, 1986, pp 290–8.
14.   *Moller v the Board of Examiners* [1999] VSC 55. Beach J refused to exercise his discretion, as permitted by statute, to waive the oath. See also Y Ross, 'Can a republican be admitted to practice?' *Law Institute J (Vic)* October 1999, p 38.
15.   N Reece, 'Hulls ends forced allegiance to the Queen', *Australian Financial Review*, 14 April 2000, p 29.
16.   (1992) 18 *Commonwealth Law Bulletin* 617.

(b) The harmonisation of relevant educational and practical training requirements.

(c) The adoption of a scheme allowing for reciprocal admissions to be made without the need to personally attend in court.

The Attorneys-General's proposal was in line with the High Court decision in *Street v Queensland Bar Association*[17] that adopted the view that the practice of law in Australia is of national concern. McHugh J stated in that case:[18]

> It is a matter of national importance that, if they wish, interstate residents should have the services of legal practitioners from their own state when conducting litigation in the courts of another state. It is a matter of national importance that, if they wish, state residents should be able to utilise the services of interstate practitioners in conducting litigation in the courts of their state. The practice of law also plays an increasingly important part in the national economy and contributes to maintaining the single economic region which is a prime object of federation.

The Mutual Recognition Act 1992 (Cth) set the basis for uniform admission and was adopted by all jurisdictions by 1995. By 2005 a travelling certificate existed nationwide.

The Law Council of Australia has reconciled the different standards of admission and established a common standard, which was published in July 1994 as part of the *Blueprint for the Structure of the Legal Profession: A National Market for Legal Services*. The admission standards include a common requirement for university training including a list of required core subjects.[19] There were differences between jurisdictions over a common minimum standard of practical legal training. To overcome the problem, uniformity is imposed at the point when lawyers receive their unrestricted practising certificates.[20] The Law Council adopted a system of two types of practising certificates; one certificate for practice as a 'barrister and solicitor', and the other as a 'barrister'.

6.7

After completion of academic qualifications, in order to be eligible for admission in any Australian jurisdiction, each person must complete two years of practical training or have become entitled to practise without restriction as a barrister. The latter requirement is met by completing a reading course which includes 'procedure and ethics and those practical skills which are of particular relevance to a lawyer practising as a barrister' and a period of being in practice 'under the supervision of an experienced barrister'. The definition of restricted practice is practice performed as an employed lawyer which involves the application of legal knowledge and skills to the delivery of legal services and within a lawyer–client relationship. Professional training is defined as experience in a prescribed field of practice, acquisition of prescribed legal practice skills and understanding of prescribed areas of professional responsibility.[21] The

---

17.   (1989) 168 CLR 461.
18.   (1989) 168 CLR 461 at 589.
19.   The courses are: administrative law; company law; constitutional law; contracts; criminal law; equity and trusts; evidence; procedure; property and torts.
20.   C Merritt, 'The Quest for a Standard Lawyer', *Australian Financial Review*, 8 July 1993, p 3.
21.   *Blueprint for the Structure of the Legal Profession: A National Market for Legal Services*, July 1994, pp 7–12.

Uniform Admission Rules allow all jurisdictions to grant reciprocal practising rights to practitioners from other jurisdictions by a mere administrative enrolment procedure.[22] As a result, practitioners now have been issued the equivalent to a national practising certificate under the new uniform legislation (see below).

6.8 By early 2005 almost all the jurisdictions had adopted the Model Provisions of the Law Council of Australia (Model Act) as a basis for their own Acts.[23] The purposes of the Model Act as stated in Pt 1, para 103 are:

(a) to provide for the regulation of legal practice in this jurisdiction in the interests of the administration of justice and for the protection of consumers of the services of the legal profession and the public generally;

(b) to facilitate the regulation of legal practice on a national basis across State and Territory borders.

For example, Pt 2.6 of the Legal Profession Act 2004 (Vic) sets out the inter-jurisdiction provisions regarding admission and practising certificates. Part 3.5.2 requires all law practices to have professional indemnity insurance. Parts 4.4.32–4.4.38 give the regulatory authority in Victoria, and those in other jurisdictions, the power to deal with disputes and complaints, and the ability to discipline lawyers. It enables exchange of information and referrals between regulatory authorities to deal with disciplinary matters. Similar legislation has been adopted in the Australian Capital Territory, South Australia, New South Wales, Queensland, the Northern Territory and Western Australia. Tasmania is in the process of adopting the Model Act.

RECOGNITION OF FOREIGN LAWYERS

6.9 Lawyers' services need to be available to clients not only nationally, but also internationally. Many of our larger firms and overseas firms working in Australia need to serve their clients on an international basis.[24] The Commonwealth Attorney-General established in 1986 a Working Group on the Globalisation of Legal Services. The Law Council of Australia has in its *Blueprint on the Structure of the Legal Profession* (1994) encouraged globalisation of legal practice because it increases trade and investment activity.[25] In 1996 the Law Council of Australia adopted a Model Practice of Foreign Law Bill. In March 1997 the Standing Committee of Attorneys-General gave their commitment to ensure access to Australian jurisdictions by foreign lawyers. This Bill has now become part of the Model Act and adopted as part of the uniform legislation.

6.10 For example, provisions for legal practice by foreign lawyers is found in Pt 2.8 of the Legal Profession Act 2004 (Vic). Under Pt 2.8.6 foreign

22. See s 11 of the Legal Practitioners Act 1970 (ACT) which also extends the right to reciprocal practice to New Zealand lawyers. The latter have also been given the right in other jurisdictions in Australia.
23. The latest version was April 2004.
24. See M Langford, 'The Internationalisation of Legal Practice — Implications for Australia' (1992) 22 *Hong Kong LJ* 162 and S Ross, 'Prospects for structural and economic integration of the Australian legal profession' (1997) 4 *International J of the Legal Profession* 267, 282–4.
25. See p 24.

lawyers who are registered can do the following legal services: conduct work or transact business concerning the foreign law of the country in which they are registered; concerning those problems of foreign law that relate to arbitration, conciliation, mediation and consensual dispute resolution of a kind prescribed by the regulations; and in proceedings before bodies other than courts, where the rules of evidence are not required and where knowledge of the foreign law of their country is essential. To overcome these restrictions to a certain degree, under Pt 2.8.12 foreign registered lawyers can hire Australian legal practitioners.

There appear to be no problems in permitting foreign registered lawyers to practise the law of their home country in Australia. Under the Model Act there appears to be no longer a need for there to be reciprocity for Australian lawyers. Reciprocity had already occurred in many places before the recent enactment of the Model Act. There was originally concern that Australian lawyers would not be able to compete with foreign lawyers who could offer integrated services by virtue of being granted local admission.[26] These fears have not been justified as the new legislation restricts foreign lawyers to practising foreign law and has safeguards such as requiring professional indemnity insurance and subjecting them to local disciplinary procedures.[27] **6.11**

Admission to practice in many European and Commonwealth countries is also possible by a qualifying transfer examination established by the Law Society of England and Wales. In the United States the examination is offered by the Qualified Lawyers Transfer Test International (QLTTI) and information on its examinations can be found at www.QLTT.com. The QLTTI in its advertising states that by passing this open book exam an American attorney has the doors open to practice in 48 countries. It lists as the benefits the following: 'end dependence on outsourcing; better serve your clients with global interests; increase your billing rates; attract new clients with cross-border work'. The European Community allows lawyers from one member state to provide temporary legal services in another state. A lawyer from one state who practises the law of the European Union and that of another state for more than three years can be admitted to practice in the other state.[28]

The Commonwealth Government also established an International Legal Service Advisory Committee to help boost Australia's ability to export legal services. One of its objectives is to provide a hospitable environment for foreign lawyers seeking to practise foreign law in Australia. Its original chairman, Sir Laurence Street, former Chief Justice of New South Wales, sought to establish uniform guidelines with other Commonwealth countries to enable lawyers to practise throughout the Commonwealth.[29] The Law Council of Australia has signed formal Memoranda of Understanding with a number of Asian professional bodies in order to further liberalise access to Asian markets. The understandings are with associations in China, **6.12**

---

26. Working Group on Globalisation (above), pp 58–9.
27. Legal Profession Act 2004 (Vic) Pts 2.8.8 and 2.8.14.
28. R Goebal, 'The Liberalization of Interstate Legal Practice in the European Union: Lessons for the United States' (2000) 34 *International Law* 307.
29. See *Australian Law News*, September 1991.

Singapore, the Philippines, Vietnam, Indonesia, Taiwan, Korea, Thailand, Japan and Malaysia.[30]

John Tucker, Director of the International Legal Services Advisory Council (ILSAC) in the Commonwealth Attorney-General's Department, provided the author in 2000 with the following figures on trade in professional legal services. In 1987–88 Australia exported $74 million and imported $23 million making a surplus of $51 million. By 1995–96 exports were $173 million and imports $75 million; a surplus of $98 million. In 1996–97 the surplus fell as exports were $156 million and imports $88 million but in 1997–98 it rose dramatically, with exports $207 million and imports $83 million; a surplus of $124 million. The latest published figures of the ILSAC show the following: for 1999–2000 exports were $194 million and imports $58 million, a surplus of $136 million; and for 2000–01 exports were $245 million and imports $81 million, a surplus of $161 million.[31] These figures show that we have little to fear from competition by foreign lawyers.

In this chapter we will be concerned with the question of who should have the power over admission to the profession and what characteristics and standards should be required for admission.

ADMISSION CRITERIA

Educational requirements

6.13   The issue facing admission authorities is to determine which courses are to be taken as a condition of admission and which types of values and skills the applicant should develop in order to be admitted. The authorities have to avoid prescribing virtually the entire content of the legal course to maintain standards, which has the effect of stifling a liberal legal education. Queensland has had a history of very restrictive course requirements for admission, while New South Wales has been far more flexible. The latter permits students to choose more elective subjects during their legal education. New South Wales is also the only state that has continued to maintain the Admission Board system of education, which allows entry to the profession by taking a part-time course outside the university system. It caters for those who cannot gain entry into the highly competitive university system or who are unable to afford to enrol in full-time study.[32] With the development of uniform admission standards the compulsory courses will become identical throughout Australia.

Ethical education

6.14   The controlling authorities also have other criteria beyond academic prerequisites to consider. For example, they need to determine whether the applicants have acquired professional values. We will discuss below the

---

30. Law Council of Australia, *Overseas Liaison, Promoting and Facilitating International Legal Practice*, www.lawcouncil.asn.au.

31. ILSAC Report, 'Australian Legal Services Export Development Strategy 2003–2006' (2002).

32. For an account and criticism of the Admission Board system see D Weisbrot (above), pp 141–3.

problems of determining moral character. It should be pointed out that there is at present no requirement that all students pass a course or examination in professional responsibility. Although aspects of professional responsibility are taught in the practical training courses, there is no minimum national standard. In 2000 the Law Admissions Consultative Committee (LACC) recommended that law students complete an ethics subject in their pre-admission practical legal training. The LACC felt that lawyers needed to act ethically and demonstrate that they had developed a sense of professional responsibility and professional courtesy. In August 2003 the Standing Committee of Attorneys-General adopted the LACC recommendation of compulsory ethical training.[33] Whether such a requirement would raise moral values in the profession is debatable, but students can become sensitised to the issues involved. In the United States, where most states require students to pass an examination or questions on an examination in relation to professional responsibility, there is no indication that these examinations have led to a development of professional virtues.[34]

Skills and values

What fundamental skills and values need to be developed before an applicant should be admitted and how should they be determined? In Australia, receiving a law degree and completing the practical training course is deemed to meet these requirements. Do we also need the American format of an extensive examination on the different areas of the law (the bar exam)? Americans have been very critical of the examination system: it is seen as evaluating only some forms of competence needed to practise law; it is arguably incomplete and also discriminates against applicants who do not have similar skills to those being tested but who do have skills that are needed to be a competent lawyer. The examinations have also been criticised for discriminating against minority groups and women because they are drafted mainly by white males.[35] Do we need to include in these examinations the testing of lawyering skills?

6.15

In Alaska applicants are tested on their ability to write a memorandum on the basis of a given set of facts and materials. In California applicants are presented with a complete legal file containing letters, police reports, memos, and so on, and they must complete various assignments within three hours, including the drafting of pleadings and memoranda, the outlining of a deposition, and writing a closing argument.[36] These performance tests have been criticised for placing additional burdens on the applicants and applying them is expensive and time-consuming.[37] The arguments over testing for competence will continue, 'with everyone

---

33. Communication from Justice Priestley.
34. *Legal Education and Professional Development–Educational Continuum: Report of the Task Force on Law Schools and the Profession: Narrowing the Gap*, ABA, 1992, p 283 (the ABA Task Force Report). For an excellent summary of the report, see E Clark, 'Legal Education and Professional Development–Education Continuum: Report of the Task Force on Law Schools and the Profession: Narrowing the Gap' (1993) 4 *Legal Education R* 201.
35. See D White, 'The Definition of Legal Competence: Will the Circle Be Unbroken?' (1978) 18 *Santa Clara LR* 641, 644–9.
36. ABA *Task Force Report*, see n 34 (above), pp 280–1.
37. ABA *Task Force Report*, see n 34 (above), p 282.

agreeing that we need more of it, but no one knowing precisely how it can be tested or assessed'.[38]

6.16 Even if we were to adopt this approach, these assignments would only test a part of what an American Task Force (MacCrate Report) on legal education found to be the fundamental skills and values needed to be a lawyer. The fundamental skills were: problem-solving; legal analysis and reasoning; legal research; factual investigation; communication; counselling; negotiation; litigation and alternative dispute resolution procedures; organisation and management of legal work; and recognising and resolving ethical dilemmas.

The MacCrate Report said that the fundamental values of members of the profession should be: provision of competent representation; striving to promote justice, fairness and morality; striving to improve the profession; and professional self-development.[39] The MacCrate Report's approach to admission was that it is only one stage in the development of a lawyer. It adopted a holistic view of legal education that emphasises the need to develop the fundamental skills and fundamental values at all stages: pre-law school education, law school and legal practice.[40] The Report was criticised because, by seeking uniformity, it would undermine 'diversity and impair law schools' responsiveness to their own particular needs and strengths'. It also did not deal with the issue of cost. One Dean estimated that the adoption of a three unit skills and values course per semester could raise the law faculty's budget by 35 to 50 per cent.[41]

6.17 Most of the recommendations in the Task Force Report have been included in the Law Council of Australia's *Blueprint for the Structure of the Legal Profession*.[42] The focus in Australia still has been on the recommendations of the Priestley Report.[43] This report recommended 11 core substantive courses, including professional conduct. The Australian Law Reform Commission pointed out the difference between the 'Priestly 11' approach and that of the MacCrate Report. The latter 'would orient legal education around *what lawyers need to be able to do*, while the Australian position is still anchored around outmoded notions of *what lawyers need to know*'.[44] The ARLC makes suggestions for remedying this situation in its Recommendation 2. It states: 'In addition to the study of core areas of substantive law, university legal education in Australia should involve the development of high level professional skills and a deep appreciation of ethical standards and professional responsibility.'[45]

The ALRC Report only referred to 'Priestley 11', which lists the academic requirements for admission. Justice Priestley, the Head of the LACC, stated

38. G Hazard and D Rhode, *The Legal Profession: Responsibility and Regulation*, Foundation Press, Mineola, 2nd ed, 1988, p 467.
39. ABA *Task Force Report*, see n 34 (above), pp 138–41.
40. ABA *Task Force Report*, see n 34 (above), p 225.
41. D Rhode and D Luban, *Legal Ethics*, 4th ed, Foundation Press, New York, 2004, p 1010.
42. *Blueprint for the Structure of the Legal Profession*, Law Council of Australia, Canberra, 1994.
43. Justice Priestley was the head of the Consultative Committee of State and Territorial Admitting Authorities.
44. ALRC, Report No 89, *Managing Justice: A Review of the federal civil justice system*, February 2000, para 2.21. See also ALRC *Discussion Paper* 62, August 1999, para 3.23.
45. ALRC, Report No 89, ibid. See also DP 62, paras 3.26–3.48.8.

that 'Priestley 12' describes the Practical Training Requirements, which identify 12 skills or areas of practice. Thus, he said, a true comparison with the United States would have combined 'Priestley 11' and 'Priestley 12'.[46] The 'Priestley 12' standards were later refined by the Australasian Professional Legal Education Council (APLEC) and then were replaced by the *Statements of Competency Standards for Entry Level Lawyers* (*Competency Standards*). The *Competency Standards* were jointly developed by the LACC and APLEC and adopted by both bodies in November 2000. They reinforce and help clarify the recommendations of other bodies as to the requisite skills needed for uniform national admission. They were submitted in April 2001 to the Council of Chief Justices. The Justices resolved to encourage individual admitting authorities to give favourable consideration to the proposals.[47]

It should be noted, as I said elsewhere, that the recommendations by the ALRC, the APLEC, the LACC and the ABA Task Force Report 'give little attention to human and service aspects of lawyering. Concern and care for the well-being of clients and development of the emotional intelligence of law students do not appear to be considered very important'.[48]

TRANSNATIONAL LAWYERING

There is also an urgent need for legal education to consider the dramatic increase in transnational lawyering. We discussed above the increased exportation and importation of legal services. The ALRC in 2000 recognised the need for more emphasis in the curriculum on subjects like public international law and conflicts of law (private international law).[49] The Law Council of Australia in 2001 saw the need for the legal profession to further develop markets overseas.[50] By 2005 very few law schools have incorporated a transnational approach in their curriculum. In their 2003 report on Australian legal education, Johnstone and Vignaendra stated:

6.18

> Australian law schools ... have not developed coherent strategies to address the demands that globalisation will impose on lawyers in the twenty-first century. While some law schools have taken some firm steps towards 'internationalising' their LLB and postgraduate curricula, developing exchange programs, bringing in teachers from overseas jurisdictions, and focusing on a national rather than state-based curriculum, there is little sense of a systematic and co-ordinated strategy to prepare students for the challenges posed by globalisation. One major constraint is the space demanded in the LLB curriculum by the Priestley requirements ... The other constraint, however, appears to be that most law schools simply do not see the issue as a major priority.[51]

46. Letter to author from Justice Priestley.
47. Ibid. See also Y Ross, 'Debate over training more than academic', *Australian Financial Review*, 24 August 2001, p 54.
48. Y Ross and P MacFarlane, *Lawyers' Responsibility and Accountability: Cases, Problems and Commentary*, 2nd ed, LexisNexis Butterworths, Sydney, 2002, para 5.5.
49. ALRC Report No 89 (above), paras 2.82–2.84.
50. Law Council of Australia, *2010: A Discussion Paper — Challenges for the Profession*, September 2001, Chapter 3: The World in 2010, www.lawcouncil.asn.au.
51. R Johnstone and S Vignaendra, *Learning Outcomes and Curriculum Development in Law*, AUTC, Canberra, 2003, p 206. See Chapter 7 for a discussion of the globalisation issues.

CONTINUING LEGAL EDUCATION

6.19   It is also necessary for authorities to play a role at an earlier stage to help future lawyers develop these values and skills. It means a continuing policy of admission — continuing supervision not only of legal knowledge (continuing legal education) but also subjecting members to periodic check-ups to see that they are maintaining their skills and developing their professional values. The Law Council in its *Blueprint* recommends 10 hours per year of mandatory continuing legal education (MCLE).[52] Such a MCLE requirement has been in effect in New South Wales for several years.[53] In the United States there are a number of states with mandatory CLE including California. In many states it is unpopular and this was shown by a Californian poll where 66.7 per cent opposed MCLE.[54]

The ALRC in its discussion paper in August 1999 recommended mandatory continuing legal education.[55] In its final report, the ALRC discussed the problems with CLE[56] and then made the following recommendation: 'Recommendation 7: As a condition of maintaining a current practising certificate, all legal practitioners should be obliged to complete a program of professional development over a given three-year period. Legal professional associations should ensure that practitioners are afforded full opportunities to undertake, as part of this regime, instruction in legal ethics, professional responsibility, practice management, and conflict and dispute resolution techniques.'[57]

REFORM PROPOSALS

6.20   An interesting structure for providing continuing supervision has been adopted in England and Wales.[58] The Lord Chancellor's Advisory Committee on Legal Education and Conduct supervises legal education and admission requirements. The Committee was established under the Courts and Legal Services Act 1990 but has a purely advisory role.[59] It has 15 members, two practising barristers, two practising solicitors, two academic lawyers, a judge and eight members who are not practising lawyers. The government White Paper said that this composition was:[60]

> ... to ensure that the Committee primarily represents the views and interests of the user of legal services, but contains wide representation from those who have practical experience of providing them.

---

52.   *Blueprint*, see n 42 (above), p 13.
53.   Rule 42 of the Professional Conduct and Practice Rules. The requirements were extended in 2005 to include a mandatory component related to management of the practice of law. See Legal Profession Regulation 2005 cl 176.
54.   *California Bar Journal*, July 1999, p 1.
55.   DP 62 (above), para 3.58.
56.   Report No 89 (above), paras 2.131–2.146.
57.   Ibid, para 2.146.
58.   The original Green Paper, *The Work and Organisation of the Legal Profession*, 1989, Cmnd 570, paras 3.12–3.16, did give the Committee strong powers but these were rejected in the later White Paper.
59.   See Sch 2 of the Act.
60.   *Legal Services: A Framework for the Future*, 1989, Cmnd 740, paras 7.9–7.10.

The Committee has a continuing work program to examine activities in each of the main areas of legal education — academic training, vocational training, practical training and continuing education. It can therefore act as a unifying force for setting admission criteria and be a clearing house for ideas on reforming legal education.[61] The Legal Services Ombudsman, a lay person, is also authorised to work in association with the Committee.[62] This Committee was abolished in late 1999 and replaced by the Legal Services Consultative Panel which has similar responsibilities in relation to legal education and training.[63]

There has been a proposal by the ALRC for the establishment of a body to be called the Australian Council on Legal Education (ACOLE) 'to provide a degree of oversight and coordination to ensure that standards are developed and maintained, and a measure of quality assurance provided'. The ACOLE 'would be charged with developing model standards for legal education and training for lawyers and other key participants in the justice system'.[64] **6.21**

The Consultative Committee of State and Territorial Law Admitting Authorities (Consultative Committee) proposed the establishment of a National Appraisal Council (Council) for the legal profession. The Council would:[65]

> ... ensure national standards are developed and applied for —
> ❏ appraising the academic and practical training required of both Australian and overseas applicants for admission to practise law;
> ❏ determining any additional studies or practical training required by overseas applicants for admission to practise law in Australia;
> ❏ appraising the suitability of subjects offered by tertiary courses in law, in order to satisfy the national academic and practical training requirements developed by the Council.

The composition recommended for the Council was only two academics out of the 17 members. The Standing Committee of Attorneys-General rejected the proposal and the ALRC did not favour it. The ALRC said that it believed that: 'the public interest may be better served by the estab-lishment of a body which sets (appropriately high) national minimum standards for legal education. Once developed, such standards should be accorded great weight in determining whether a degree from a particular institution will be accepted for admission purposes. The formal auditing and accrediting process should remain at the State and Territory level.'[66] **6.22**

The ALRC did make a proposal for an Australian Academy of Law. It would be an institution 'which can draw together the various strands of the legal community to facilitate effective intellectual interchange of discussion and research of issues of concern, and nurture coalitions of interest. Such an institution should have a special focus on issues of professionalism (including ethics) and professional identity, and on education and training'.[67]

---

61. *Legal Services* (above), paras 9.1–9.7.
62. *Legal Services* (above), para 10.26.
63. Access to Justice Act 1999 (UK) s 35.
64. DP 62 (above), paras 3.66, 3.73.
65. See ALRC, *Managing Justice* (above), para 2.35.
66. ALRC (above), para 2.74.
67. ALRC (above), para 2.118. For recommendation 6 see para 2.128.

CONTROLLING AUTHORITIES

Composition of admission bodies

6.23   Although the judiciary under its inherent powers generally controls admission,[68] the actual standards have been developed by the local law societies and bar associations. These standards have varied from jurisdiction to jurisdiction. Within the judiciary's supervisory power over admission is the setting of educational requirements for admission. This power stems from the Third Charter of Justice in 1823 for New South Wales and is different from the position in England where the judiciary has left the questions of educational training to the Inns of Court and the Law Society.[69] The situation in the United States is similar to that in Australia. In most states, the state's Supreme Court sets the standards for admission under its inherent powers. Although the state's Supreme Courts make the rules, they adopt rules generated by committees of lawyers established under the authority of state bar associations.[70]

The judiciary's control over admission in Australia is being eroded in some jurisdictions. In 1979 the Bowen Report in New South Wales recommended removing the power from the Supreme Court judges and placing it in a broadly representative Council of Legal Education.[71] Finally, in 1994, the New South Wales Solicitors' and Barristers' Admission Boards, dominated by judges, were replaced by a Legal Practitioners' Admission Board. The latter still has four judges (the Chief Justice and three appointed by him or her), but also includes two solicitors and two barristers, the Attorney-General or his or her representative and two academics.[72]

6.24   Victoria's Council of Legal Education still has almost a majority from the judiciary (10), but also has academic (four), government (three) and practitioner representatives (four).[73] The Australian Capital Territory Admission Board has no judicial members but all five barristers and solicitors are appointed by the Chief Justice.[74] In Tasmania academics have one representative and appoint a legal practitioner on the Board of Legal Education.[75] In South Australia the Legal Practitioners Education and Admission Council was established in 1999. It is responsible for making rules prescribing the academic and practical training requirements for admission. The Council also has the power to decide what is needed for the issue and renewal of practising certificates and the requirements for post-admission education training or experience. It has two academic

---

68.   In New South Wales this inherent power to admit was originally revoked under the Legal Profession Act 1987 s 17(b) and is still revoked under s 34(2) of the new Legal Profession Act 2004. Under s 27 of that Act a referral to the Supreme Court can be made by the Admission Board.

69.   G Samuels, 'Control of Admission to Practice — Its Effect on Legal Education' in R Balmford (ed), *Legal Education in Australia*, National Conference on Legal Education in Australia, Conference Papers, Vol A, 1978, p 679.

70.   See R Huber, 'Entry to the Bar: Who is in Charge?' (1977) 14 *Houston LR* 25.

71.   *Report of the Committee of Inquiry into Legal Education in New South Wales (Bowen Report)*, 1979, pp 233–9.

72.   Legal Profession Act 2004 (NSW) s 680.

73.   Legal Profession Act 2004 (Vic) Pt 6.5.1.

74.   Legal Practitioners Act 1970 (ACT) s 7(1).

75.   Legal Profession Act 1993 (Tas) s 19.

representatives and four judges out of its 12 members. The Act was later amended to add a law student to its membership. The South Australian Board of Examiners, which controls the admission process, has 15 members. It is dominated by 12 practitioner members but does have two persons nominated by the Attorney-General.[76] Queensland has a new Legal Practitioners Admission Board with two barristers, two solicitors, a member appointed by the minister, and the Brisbane registrar.[77]

In Western Australia the Barristers' Board had power over admission for 100 years. The Board was independent from the judiciary and Western Australia is still the only jurisdiction where power over admission has been removed from the active judiciary. The Barristers' Board was replaced in 1992 by the Legal Practice Board, but there was no change to the membership.[78] The Board was composed of the Attorney-General, the Solicitor-General, all Queen's Counsel, nine practitioners and all retired Supreme Court judges.[79] Although the new Act adopted most of the recommendations made in 1983 by the Clarkson Commission Inquiry into the Future of the Legal Profession, it rejected having academic and lay representatives on the Board. Therefore control over admission still rests with practitioners and retired judges.[80] In 2003 the new Legal Practice Act removed the retired judges, made sure the QCs had their principal place of business in Western Australia and increased the number of practitioners to 12.[81] In the Northern Territory the Legal Practitioners Admission Board has seven practitioners appointed by the Chief Justice, of which at least two have to be practising on their own account.[82]

6.25

The need for broad representation on admission boards has become quite evident over the years from judicial interference over the composition and recognition of courses needed for admission.[83] For example, in 1983 the Barristers Admission Board in New South Wales, attended only by a few judges and without prior notice, decided that the course taught at the University of New South Wales, 'Law, Lawyers and Society', no longer satisfied the Board's standard for the study of legal ethics. Perhaps this was 'retribution for the mildly critical thrust of the subject and the involvement of some of its teachers in law reform activities'.[84] After vigorous protest from the Faculty of Law the decision was within a short time quietly rescinded.[85]

6.26

A judge has made perhaps the best argument for taking away the power over the control of admission to the judiciary. Samuels J stated:[86]

6.27

---

76. See generally the Legal Practitioners Act 1981 ss 14B and 14I.
77. Legal Profession Act 2004 (Qld) s 490.
78. Legal Practitioners Amendment (Disciplinary and Miscellaneous Provisions) Act 1992. See also *Brief*, Law Society (WA), Vol 20, April 1993, pp 16–21 and May 1993, pp 19–21.
79. *Brief* (above), April 1993, p 17.
80. *Report of the Committee of Inquiry into the Future Organisation of the Legal Profession in Western Australia (the Clarkson Report)*, 1983, p 171.
81. Legal Practitioners Act 2003 (WA) s 7.
82. Legal Practitioners Act (NT) s 8.
83. D Weisbrot (above), p 145.
84. D Weisbrot (above).
85. D Weisbrot (above).
86. G Samuels (above), pp 678–82.

Judges as a general class have no particular interest in, or knowledge of, the technical processes of legal education. They are not in direct touch with requirements of current practice. There is no valid reason to suppose that they are better able than practitioners of comparable talent and experience to determine what lawyers need to know to provide a conveniently adequate legal service to the community. The majority will have a tendency to frame educational policy in light of experience which the passage of the years will render increasingly irrelevant ... Since [an admission board] has a teaching and examining function it should include academics ... [A]nother reason for including academics [is they] increasingly assume the character of social conscience to the profession and the judiciary. It is a role for which they are well cast, since they are neither influenced by professional self-interest nor trammelled by professional responsibility ... [Their] work keeps them aware of the wider ranging currents of legal thought and experience, and they are constantly exposed to the irreverent reactions of students first encountering the more opaque areas of the law.

6.28 The present situation in Australia shows that there is no uniform representation in the bodies controlling admission. Generally, membership on the admission authorities includes judges, practitioners and academics. The consumers of legal services are not represented but it has been argued that the Attorney-General's membership protects consumers' interests. Also, the Attorney-General can choose to appoint lay representatives. Many would say that this is inadequate protection. The situation in the admission area is similar to that in the regulation of the profession; that is, that there is very little[87] or no lay representation on the various admission authorities in Australia. The arguments given in favour of such representation have been set out in **5.26–5.27**. Finally, one of the largest groups not represented is the law students. There was a provision for a law student representative in the Legal Practitioners Bill introduced in South Australia in 1976, but there was strong opposition from the Law Society and the bill was withdrawn.[88] This was recently remedied with the inclusion of one law student in the admission process. It is obvious that law students have a particular perspective, which is different from all the other interested groups. There is no reason why they should not have a voice in the process in all jurisdictions.

'GOOD FAME AND CHARACTER' AND 'FIT AND PROPER'

Preliminary investigation

6.29 The denial of admission is of obvious importance to an applicant. It means the loss of years of investment in educational costs and the loss of potential income. Furthermore, it is a denial of both the prestige associated with being a lawyer and the greater possibility of advancement in other areas related to the law, for example politics, government service and business. It can also have the negative effect of labelling the rejected person as being an

---

87. There is proposed lay representation on the Queensland new Legal Practice Committee and provision for lay representation by way of an Attorney-General's appointment in South Australia.

88. A Perry, 'Reforming the Profession: SA Legal Practitioners Bill 1976' (1976) 2 *Legal Services Bulletin* 46.

undesirable. The stakes are so high that it is necessary to make preliminary decisions regarding those law students who have been involved in past and present actions that may affect the suitability of their becoming lawyers; that is, those who may be lacking 'good fame and character' and are not 'fit and proper'.

Until 1993 two states, Queensland for barristers only and New South Wales for both branches,[89] required students to enrol as students-at-law before or shortly after beginning their law courses, or for a prescribed period before applying to be admitted.[90] The system was considered to be unnecessary and unsatisfactory and in 1979 the Bowen Report recommended that it be abolished in New South Wales.[91] It was abolished in New South Wales in 1993 for university students. Students-at-law still exist for those enrolled in a course of study required by the Law Extension Committee of the University of Sydney. **6.30**

The old system in New South Wales had been strongly criticised for applying inconsistent standards in screening applicants as to their good fame and character. The vast majority of applications were only examined to see if they had used the prescribed language formula requested by the Board. It was only if someone made a complaint about a student-at-law that the Board made a closer examination of what was contained in the application. A full disclosure of all activities on the student-at-law's application also did not bind the admission authorities that the applicant was now of the good fame and character needed for admission as a lawyer. This unsatisfactory situation was remedied in 1987 by the Legal Profession Act (NSW) and re-enacted in the 2004 Act. The Act allows an applicant to have consideration of the character requirements before admission by the Admission Board. A declaration can be obtained which binds the Admission Board that the applicant meets the requirements as to 'good fame and character' for activities up to that date unless the applicant does not make a full disclosure.[92] The Admission Board can also decide not to hear the application and have it heard by the Supreme Court.[93] In 2004 Queensland also adopted legislation on early consideration of character requirements.[94] **6.31**

The New South Wales[95] and Queensland[96] Supreme Courts have exercised their inherent power to decide whether to revoke the registration of a student-at-law. The court decisions in this area have not established any clear standards. Furthermore, the standards that have been applied appear to be harsher for students-at-law than for those already admitted to practice. The reason appears to be that students-at-law, unlike practising lawyers, have difficulty in showing positive activity to negate their wrongful actions. **6.32**

---

89. Rules relating to the Admission of Barristers of the Supreme Court of Queensland, r 34; Barristers Admission Rules (NSW), r 14; and Solicitors Admission Rules (NSW), r 4.
90. See the Rules (above).
91. *Bowen Report* (above), paras 5.8.3–5.8.4.
92. Sections 13–15 of the Legal Profession Act 1987 (NSW) and now ss 26 and 29 of the Legal Profession Act 2004 (NSW).
93. Section 13A of the Legal Profession Act 1987 (NSW) and now s 27 of the Legal Profession Act 2004 (NSW).
94. Sections 35–37 of the Legal Profession Act 2004 (Qld).
95. *Prothonotary v Ord* [1976] 1 NSWLR 421.
96. *Re Costello* (1889) 3 QLJ p 129.

Practising lawyers have had more time to accumulate support from other lawyers that they have a good reputation and they can argue that the offence is out of character with their previous conduct:[97]

> In this respect students suffer the disadvantage of having no professional experience and reputation to use in rebutting negative inferences drawn from a particular incident.

6.33 Furthermore, a number of cases show that only fines have been imposed in cases where solicitors have signed documents falsely, knowing full well that they will be acted upon.[98] When the Legal Profession Disciplinary Tribunal struck a solicitor off the roll for doing this, the Court of Appeal in New South Wales overruled the decision, imposing only a fine because the tribunal had deviated from the standard penalty in such cases.[99]

6.34 The tribunal has also been too lenient. In the widely reported case of Carol Foreman, one of the tribunal's findings against her was that she had falsified her timesheet and concealed the existence of the original from the Family Court. She was only fined for her professional misconduct, because of previous good conduct and the 'impressive support from her peers'.[100] The Law Society appealed and the Court of Appeal by a 2:1 decision struck her off.[101] Kirby J, in the minority, also felt the penalty of a fine was insufficient but he said she should only be suspended for four years. He also commented on the appalling amount Foreman had charged her client (almost $500,000) and said that the Law Society should investigate this issue. He added:[102]

> Little wonder that the legal profession and the methods of charging are coming under close parliamentary, media and public scrutiny. Something appears to be seriously wrong in the organisation of the provision of legal services in this community when charges of this order can be contemplated, still less made. Of course those charges were rendered not by Ms Foreman alone but by her firm. That firm has not been heard, in the nature of these proceedings, to defend its charges before the court.

6.35 As the *Foreman* case shows, courts may no longer be as lenient as they have been with practitioners who have a 'good reputation'. In the past, even a single non-professional action by a student was sufficient to deny that student a licence to practise law, while similar action or actions by members of the profession were not grounds for revocation of their licence. I believe that the incongruity between admission and disciplinary standards cannot be rationally supported and it appears that the courts have moved in this direction.

It should be noted that Professor Daniel believes that Foreman was a scapegoat for problems that were widespread within the profession. Daniel, in her book *Scapegoats for a Profession*,[103] describes how Foreman became

---

97. J Basten and P Redmond, 'Character Review of Intending Lawyers' (1979) 3 *Univ of New South Wales LJ* 117, 141. This is an excellent article on the student-at-law system.

98. See Kirby J in *Fraser v The Council of the Law Society of New South Wales*, Legal Profession Disciplinary Reports, No 5, 1992, p 16, supplement to *Law Society J* (NSW), September 1992.

99. *Fraser's case* (above).

100. *In the matter of Carol Anne Foreman*, The Legal Profession Disciplinary Tribunal, supplement to *Law Society J* (NSW), No 1, March 1994, pp 16–17.

101. *Law Society of New South Wales v Foreman* (1994) 34 NSWLR 408.

102. *Foreman's case* (above) at 421–2.

103. A Daniel, *Scapegoats for a Profession: Uncovering procedural injustice*, Harwood Academic Publishers, 1998, pp 77–90.

a tainted figure as a result of media coverage to the effect that she was a family lawyer who grossly overcharged. The tainting is obvious from Kirby J's comments set out above. But also note that Kirby J feels that Foreman's firm should have been made accountable. This did not happen and it further supports the notion that Foreman was the scapegoat. Daniel concludes that the scapegoating engaged in by the legal profession has not been successful. The legal profession is still criticised for the high cost of legal services and for blocking community access to legal services.[104] The appeal and the harsh sentence were intended to give the public a feeling that the profession was doing its job of properly disciplining its members.

The abolishment of the registration requirement for university law students in New South Wales removes the problem of the application of inconsistent standards. However, it does not remove the inherent power of the Supreme Court to have control over students enrolled in law. How the court would exercise this power is open to speculation. Furthermore, a preliminary request for a declaration by a student as to his or her character is still part of the Legal Profession Act and would be heard at the Admission Board and any appeal by the Supreme Court.[105]

6.36

In general, admission bodies in Australia have had a history of not making a comprehensive investigation of the past conduct and character of applicants. There is no provision for interviewing applicants. Applicants are usually only investigated because of disclosures made by the applicants or, rarely, when complaints are lodged against them to admission authorities. Some jurisdictions require applicants to declare that they have not acted in a way that is likely adversely to affect their 'good fame and character'. If they have so acted they must disclose the conduct in detail.[106] There is no indication on the applications of what activities can affect a person's good fame and character, and it is left to the applicant's discretion to decide what to include. In some jurisdictions the applicant needs to supply character references. There have only been a few hearings of 'wholly exceptional cases' in relation to admission in Australia.[107] Two of the most famous cases have been in New South Wales — the cases of *Wendy Bacon* and *Katherine Wentworth*, which are discussed in **6.47–6.50**.

General criteria

The following problem question raises a number of issues as to what criteria should be applied for admission:

6.37

> Jane's university years were characterised by a passing interest in studies and a passionate occupation with a variety of political causes. Her involvement was not purely theoretical. On one occasion she interceded to assist a fellow male gay rights demonstrator who was being assaulted by a bevy of policemen in the back of a paddy-wagon. This action resulted in her arrest for assault and for resisting arrest. This last incident, in which Jane caused substantial physical injury to two police officers, occurred in her final year of law school. The trial will not take place until she has completed the College of Law training.

104. A Daniel (above), pp 92–96.
105. Legal Profession Act 1987 (NSW) s 14 and now in the Legal Profession Act 2004 (NSW) ss 26 and 28.
106. Disney et al (above), p 274.
107. For a discussion of some of the cases see Disney (above), p 274.

Despite her arrest, Jane's political activities continued unabated. In the last six months she has been arrested on two further occasions for offensive behaviour arising out of public political demonstrations. The first conviction was for using unseemly words while under the influence of alcohol in a public place (calling a policewoman a 'pig') and the second was for trespassing after chaining herself to a tree to stop logging of a rain forest. She pleaded not guilty to both charges and was convicted and fined on each occasion. While appearing before a magistrate on one of these charges she told her: 'I feel disgusted by the political prejudice revealed in your comments today'. She was charged with contempt of court and fined for the comment. She refused to pay the fine and served two days in gaol.

The problem indicates some of the issues we face in determining what values we seek for members of the profession. Should they uphold the law on all occasions? Do they need to have a social conscience? Can they be aggressive? Can they be an alcoholic? Can they be politically active? Can they have a prior criminal record?

GOOD MORAL CHARACTER — CASE LAW

6.38   What is a 'fit and proper' person — one who is of 'good fame and character'? Good moral character as a requirement for being admitted to the legal profession dates back to the Roman Theodesian Code and has its common law roots from the thirteenth-century Inns of Court in England.[108] Certification as to having a good moral character is a prerequisite of practice not only in every jurisdiction in Australia, but in most other nations and in other licensed professions.[109] An applicant who is inactive, like a vegetable, just pursuing his or her studies, watching television and rarely leaving the house, such a person will meet the test. The test is therefore a negative one. An applicant will be presumed to be of 'good fame and character' and 'fit and proper' unless there is evidence of past misconduct. Justice Black of the United States Supreme Court in *Konigsberg v State Bar of California* has defined 'good moral character' in terms of 'an absence of proven conduct or acts which have been historically considered as manifestations of "moral turpitude"'.[110]

6.39   In the *Konigsberg* case Black J also said that the term 'good moral character' is 'unusually ambiguous'. He added:

> It can be defined in an almost unlimited number of ways for any definition will necessarily reflect the attitudes, experiences and prejudices of the definer. Such a vague qualification ... can be a dangerous instrument for arbitrary and discriminatory denial of the right to practise law ... [T]he question is whether on the whole record a reasonable man [or woman] could fairly find that there were substantial doubts about [the applicant's] ... honesty, fairness and respect for the rights of others, and for the laws of the state and nation ...

Frankfurter J has said that to be of 'moral character' an applicant must have 'those qualities of truth-speaking, of a high sense of honour, of granite

---

108. D Rhode, 'Moral Character as a Professional Credential' (1985) 94 *Yale LJ* 491, 494. See also the judgment of Frankfurter J of the United States Supreme Court in *Schware v Board of Bar Examiners* 353 US 232 at 247 (1957).
109. Rhode (above), p 491.
110. 353 US 252 at 262 (1957).

discretion, of the strictest observance of fiduciary responsibility ...'.[111] These are noble sentiments but to apply such a test to a student who has done little in life is totally unrealistic.[112]

It is also possible to be of 'good fame and character' but not be 'fit and proper'. The Victorian Supreme Court made such a decision in *Victorian Lawyers RPA Ltd v X*.[113] The applicant had pleaded guilty to six accounts of making a false report. She had made false accusations of sexual assault. She did not appear to have any appreciation of the impact of her offences on innocent people. She also had failed to inform the Board of Examiners of the relevant circumstances surrounding the charges she had made and thus seriously misled the Board. The applicant was otherwise found to be a person of good character and reputation. Harper J refused her admission because she was not a 'fit and proper person'. He said: 'One who is not capable of dealing appropriately with awkward facts of this kind in one's own life (that is, that she has or may have caused great harm to others) cannot be entrusted appropriately to advise clients who are similarly placed.'[114]

The test for admission causes serious problems for Aboriginal law students. These students usually have been and are politically active and some have a criminal record. Some of these students will have been involved in 'street marches, sit-ins, or blockading development on land with indigenous spiritual significance'. A study done by Dolman in 1997 of 50 Aboriginal law students (one-third of the total Aboriginal law student population) found that 68 per cent were 'concerned or very concerned' about meeting the 'good fame and character' test. Dolman wonders how many of these students will be discouraged by the test from seeking admission. He says: 'Indigenous law graduates may find the "good fame and character" test harder to pass, or at least have a perception that they will not pass such a test.'[115] I believe we need a different test to apply to Aborigines involved in political activities who are seeking admission.

6.40

A recent Australian Capital Territory Supreme Court case, the *Hinds* case,[116] allowed an applicant of Aboriginal descent to be admitted, even though he had a record of previous offences. When he was 17 Hinds was convicted of drunk driving; when he was 20, of making a false complaint to the police; and when he was 29, a further conviction of drunk driving. The court felt that these offences did not cast any light on the question of his present character because of his age at that time and the fact he was now 45. The court was more concerned with his convictions of breaching five domestic violence orders between 1993 and 1996. Hinds, having complete candour and cooperating with the court, negated these more recent convictions. Furthermore, the court was impressed by Hinds' community activities and found that he was considered a 'considerate and compassionate man'. Probably a very important point was that Hinds' references attested to the fact that there was 'absence of any propensity to

---

111. *Schware v Board of Bar Examiners* 353 US 232 at 247.
112. C Wolfram, *Modern Legal Ethics*, West Publishing, St Paul, 1986, p 860.
113. [2001] VSC 429.
114. Ibid, para 36.
115. K Dolman, 'Indigenous Lawyers: success or sacrifice?' (1997) 4 *Indigenous Law Bulletin* 5–6.
116. *Re The Legal Practitioners Act 1970; Re Application by Hinds* [2003] ACTSC 11.

aggressiveness' in his character. The court said he 'proved to be a quietly spoken man who gave evidence in a careful and apparently thoughtful manner. He was clearly ashamed of his previous behaviour and seemed to find it difficult to understand how he could have behaved so badly ...'.[117] I agree with the court's decision but hope that in the future courts would not base their criteria for admission on factors such as 'quietly spoken' and 'absence of any propensity to aggressiveness'. It is well known that within the legal profession there are few legal practitioners who would meet these criteria.[118]

6.41   The courts in Australia have rarely articulated what is meant by good moral character. In a case dealing with a medical practitioner seeking admission in New South Wales, Justice Homes stated in reference to good character:[119]

> Reputation is obviously relevant to the solution of the problem but cannot be the exclusive test. 'Good' is used also in the sense of 'moral strength' ... An inability to withstand the importunings of the evilly disposed would disqualify, as would the propensity to exploit the gullible. These and other defects in moral fibre may not be part of a man's reputation, but evidence of these traits must be weighed in estimating character. Even these characteristics cannot be looked at in isolation. The judgement as to character must be arrived at by giving due weight to all features. Finally, the judgement must be made of the person at the time when the court is asked to consider the application.

6.42   In the same case Walsh J pointed out that because good character is a negative test it was not necessary for the applicant to establish he was of high moral standing:[120]

> The question before the court is not whether it is satisfied affirmatively that the applicant is of bad character. The ultimate question for the court is whether it is satisfied that he is of good character.

It is obvious from these general statements that the principles of what constitutes 'good fame and character' are ambiguous and unclear and we must develop standards from individual cases. The cases can be divided into three main categories:

- dishonesty — includes theft, fraud, forgery and so on, and lack of candour;
- political activity — concerns activities with non-conformist political groups; and
- personal moral standards — includes use of drugs or alcohol, sexual activity, criminal offences and so on.

Specific criteria

Dishonesty

6.43   The most famous case of dishonesty leading to denial of admission to practice is the *Davis* case.[121] Davis had been convicted in 1934 on a charge of breaking, entering and stealing and failed to disclose the conviction on his application for admission in 1946. After being admitted the omission was discovered and he was struck off the rolls. He made four efforts to be

---

117. Ibid, paras 10–11.
118. See Y Ross, 'Quietly does it to gain admission', *Australian Financial Review*, 17 October 2003, p 53.
119. *Ex parte Tziniolis; Re the Medical Practitioners Act* (1966) 84 WN (Pt 2) (NSW) 275 at 300.
120. *Ex parte Tziniolis* (above) at 277.
121. *Re Davis* (1947) 75 CLR 409.

readmitted but was only successful in 1978.[122] Dixon J in turning down his appeal to the High Court in 1947 stated:[123]

> The Bar is no ordinary profession or occupation. The duties and privileges of advocacy are such that ... counsel must command the personal confidence, not only of lay and professional clients, but of other members of the Bar and of judges. It would almost seem to go without saying that conviction of a crime of dishonesty of so grave a kind as housebreaking and stealing is incompatible with ... admission to the Bar of the reputation and the more enduring moral qualities denoted by the expression, 'good fame and character' ...

Davis had argued that his crime was an 'aberration in the course of a life of highly commendable and very unusual effort and achievement'. Davis had come from a working-class family and had left school at 14. After working for several years he returned to school. He was eventually able, with the aid of a grant of financial assistance, to go to law school. He had an invalid sister and a brother who suffered disablement in a serious accident. At the age of 19, he suffered a nervous breakdown and was admitted to a mental hospital for eight months. A little over four months after his release he committed the crime. Davis testified that his recollection of that period of his life was hazy. He was 21-years-old and returned to law school three years later and finally received a degree in 1945. Dixon J recognised the difficulties faced by Davis and found them in his favour. He stated that to overcome the crime of housebreaking as a barrier to being admitted to the bar would be difficult, but a prerequisite would be to realise the need for complete candour to the court:[124]

6.44

> The fulfilment of that obligation of candour with its attendant risks proved too painful for the appellant ... In those circumstances, the conclusion that he is not a fit and proper person to be made a member of the Bar is confirmed.

Dixon J's judgment does not guarantee admission on complete disclosure of past crimes, but it did state that lack of candour would be a bar to admission.

In the following year the High Court admitted to practice an applicant, Lenehan, who had committed a number of dishonest acts. These acts were related to monetary matters and took place 20 years before his application, when he was working as an articled clerk in a law office.[125] He had tried for admission nine years earlier but had been refused and was refused again by the Supreme Court of New South Wales. The High Court in a joint judgment said that he was surrounded in his initial practice by evil examples and that this occurred at an early age formed some mitigation and extenuation. His later employment record was respectable and he completed a satisfactory war service including a promotion. During his war service he was responsible for handling, paying out and administering considerable funds. The court stated:[126]

6.45

> There must be a strong disinclination to admit to the profession of a solicitor any person who has been shown ever to have been guilty of improper conduct ... But the false steps of youth and early manhood are not always final proof of

---

122. Disney et al (above), pp 284 and 336.
123. *Re Davis* (1947) 75 CLR 409 at 420.
124. *Re Davis* (above) at 426.
125. *Ex parte Lenehan* (1948) 77 CLR 403.
126. *Ex parte Lenehan* (above) at 420.

defective character and unfitness. The presumption ... they may appear to raise may surely be overcome by a subsequent blameless career.

The present case discloses ... early manhood under bad influences without proper guidance and ... a fully adult life of seemingly correct and exemplary conduct and every outward manifestation of good character. A fine war record is something which ought to count in such a question.

6.46   In contrast to the High Court's judgment, Jordan CJ of the Supreme Court, who had the benefit of witnessing Lenehan's behaviour as a witness said:[127]

[W]henever the applicant was hard pressed, he showed himself unscrupulous in misappropriating money belonging to his aunt, to his employers and to his employers' clients as and when he got the opportunity, and was equally unscrupulous in giving false explanations in endeavours to exculpate himself.

Comparing *Davis* and *Lenehan*, the only satisfactory reconciliation of the decisions is that Lenehan fully disclosed his past misdeeds, while Davis lacked candour. Also, Lenehan had a fine war record while Davis did not serve in the military. It should be noted that full disclosure may not be enough if there is a consistent history of dishonesty.[128]

6.47   In 1981 a widely known political activist and journalist, Wendy Bacon, was denied admission. The New South Wales Court of Appeal gave as its principal ground her lack of honesty concerning her role in standing bail for a prisoner. The court found that the funds had been obtained from the prisoner, SS, or from sources associated with him. Bacon denied knowledge of SS's interest in the funds and alleged that the moneys had been obtained as a loan from a close mutual friend, VA. Bacon refused to call VA to testify. Moffitt J found that Bacon had not told the court the truth about important and critical aspects of the bail matter. He said he did not believe her story as to the source of the bail money and she had conspired with others to represent that the money was her own, knowing that this was improper. He found that Bacon was truthful in her dealings with many people, but lacked honesty in dealing with those in authority, if they stood in the way of a desired end considered a worthy cause. Moffitt J stated:[129]

The end now is to be admitted to the Bar. The purpose is to enable her in some way to pursue worthy causes having the status of a barrister or maybe practising as one. The bail matter presented for her a difficulty ... to be overcome if the end were to be achieved. Once again means did not matter. She was prepared to be untruthful and to mislead the court in pursuit of the desired end, namely to be a barrister so as to better pursue some of the causes which she espoused. That a person can be trusted to tell the truth and regardless of the ends not to participate in a breach of the law is fundamental to being a barrister ... The bail matter and her evidence in respect of it establish she is not fit to be a barrister ...

6.48   The *Wentworth* case[130] was widely discussed within the profession and extensively reported in the media. Kate Wentworth was notorious for bringing numerous legal actions. She stated in an interview that opposition to her admission was because she had sued a number of judges, barristers and solicitors and 'partly because I am a woman and the very male dominated legal profession doesn't like a woman ... questioning their superiority'.[131]

127. (1948) 77 CLR 403 at 421.
128. *Frugtniet v Board of Examiners* [2005] VSC 332.
129. *Re B* [1981] 2 NSWLR 372 at 394.
130. *Wentworth v The New South Wales Bar Association* (1992) ALRJ 663.
131. *Sydney Morning Herald*, 27 June 1992, p 9.

In opposing her application before the Supreme Court, the Bar Association claimed that besides being a frequent litigant she had lied under oath and had taken on a campaign to harass any members of the profession who opposed her. The Association said that Ms Wentworth demonstrated the 'inability or deliberate refusal to accept the authority of the court' that was 'not to her liking'. She had also engaged in a 'persistent course of conduct calculated or designed to bring into disrepute the court or members of the court who rule or find against [her]'.[132] Counsel for Ms Wentworth argued that there was no evidence that either judges or members of the profession would be unable to deal with her as counsel. Her 'notorious' reputation was not substantiated by evidence but only through untested innuendo. He said that there was no evidence of any convictions or any fraud or dishonesty. Her counsel argued that:

> What [the association] asks you to do is to embark on a court-conducted psychological profile and psychiatric examination of Ms Wentworth without evidence and come to a conclusion that she is not fit to practise.

He emphasised that she had a 'strong personality' and was:[133]

> ... fearless when fighting for her own interests, but she has obviously alienated some people in the legal profession and the judiciary. Her personal qualities as demonstrated should make her a courageous and, hopefully, a good barrister ...

6.49 In finding Ms Wentworth unsuitable for admission as a barrister, Campbell J of the New South Wales Supreme Court said that she habitually made 'grave allegations' against people without proper foundation in a 'long chain of litigation', which was not consistent with good character. He found that she lied in certain documents, in a television interview and in informing a judge about an adjournment. Campbell J also said that Ms Wentworth was unable to accept responsibility for any decisions that went against her and instead blamed 'wrongful conduct on the part of others, be they witnesses, lawyers or the presiding judges'. Because she refused to confess to her past errors and recant, Wentworth was denied admission.[134]

6.50 Replying to Campbell J's decision Wentworth said she found the judge's conclusions 'pretty astonishing'. She said she was being opposed because she told the truth and 'the real problem for them is the truth hurts and I tell truths they don't wish to hear'. She also said:[135]

> Anything that is closer to McCarthyism and the Star Chamber than what I have just been subjected to would be hard to imagine. Perhaps we could have another witches' trial ... Perhaps we've just had it.

Wentworth's appeals to the Court of Appeal[136] and the High Court failed. It was stated that the Bar Association had legal costs of an estimated $600,000 in fighting her application for admission.[137] In September 1994

---

132. *Sydney Morning Herald*, 15 October 1992, p 8.
133. *Sydney Morning Herald*, 13 October 1992, p 7.
134. *Sydney Morning Herald*, 15 October 1992, p 8.
135. *Sydney Morning Herald*, 24 December 1992, p 2. There are certain similarities to the *Wentworth* case in the denial of admission to an applicant in Arizona: see *Matter of Ronwin* 136 Ariz 566, 667 P 2d 1281, certiori denied (1983) 464 US 977.
136. *Wentworth v NSW Bar Association* (CA(NSW), No 40044 of 1993, 14 February, 1994, unreported).
137. See *The Australian*, 27 April 1994, p 5.

Ms Wentworth became the first applicant for admission before the new Legal Practitioners' Admission Board. She was denied admission.[138]

6.51   There have also been several unreported student-at-law cases where the students lied and lacked candour in dealing with the admission authorities, resulting in their being struck off the student-at-law rolls.[139] In one of these cases, *Larkin*, the accused had forged a document but failed to admit what he had done was a forgery. In striking him off the rolls the court seems to suggest that it was not the initial forgery that resulted in this action but his denial of the fact in the two proceedings brought against him. The court said:[140]

> Had he admitted the impropriety of doing what he did, we could have found much in the circumstances to palliate his conduct ... The defendant ... is unable to appreciate the nature of his behaviour — in which we include his purported explanation before this court — and is unfit to remain as a student-in-law.

Comparison of the cases

6.52   These cases appear to be consistent with *Davis*, *Bacon* and *Wentworth*, in that lack of candour and/or refusal to appreciate one's actions are decisive elements in denial of admission. Furthermore, there is no guarantee by the courts if the applicant admits everything that he or she will be admitted to practice. The cases do appear to be in conflict with another unreported decision, the *Rose* case.[141] Rose had been an employee solicitor who had falsified certificates of incorporation on two occasions because of work pressure and failed to lodge the proper certificates of incorporation with the Corporate Affairs Commission.

It was only a matter of time until his actions would be discovered, because of the statutory obligation of a company to file an annual return within 19 months of incorporation. When the Commission received a return from a 'company' not on its register it commenced an investigation. This did not occur until two years after the falsification of the second certificate. In the meantime, seven months after the second falsification, Rose had his name removed from the Roll of Solicitors and he was admitted to the bar. In seeking admission to the bar he swore an affidavit that he had not done anything to affect adversely his 'good fame and character' and was not aware of any facts that might affect his fitness to practise as a barrister. He also swore that he did not 'expect or apprehend' that any actions would be taken against him due to his practice as a solicitor.[142]

6.53   McClemens CJ found that Rose had 'perpetrated two acts of inexcusable misconduct'. The Bar Association counsel did not cross-examine Rose and

---

138. Private communication by a member of the Board.
139. See *The Prothonotary v Jai Ram* (CA(NSW), 11 May 1989, unreported) and *Prothonotary v Larkin* (CA(NSW), 24 October 1977, unreported). The *Jai Ram* case dealt with a law student refusing to admit that he had cheated in an examination. The court was divided over the length of removal from rolls — one judge saying up to 10 years, and two of the judges agreeing on three years. The *Larkin* case is discussed in detail in Basten and Redmond (above), pp 119–24.
140. Basten and Redmond (above), p 123.
141. *New South Wales Bar Association v Rose* (SC(NSW) 27 November 1974, unreported). Discussed in Basten and Redmond (above), pp 132–4.
142. The facts are taken from Basten and Redmond (above), pp 132–3.

the judge accepted Rose's explanation that he did not consciously advert to the two falsifications when swearing the affidavit for admission to the bar. It was pointed out to the court that the clients had suffered no financial loss nor had Rose made a gain. Rose was severely reprimanded and suspended from practice for three months, which included the whole of the summer vacation.[143] *Rose* can only be reconciled with judgments like *Davis* on the basis that Rose did not lack candour; that he did not intentionally leave out the information concerning his misdeeds. It would appear that the criminal *mens rea* element is a necessary component in finding lack of candour. Furthermore, Rose did accept and admit he had acted wrongly.

Another three cases support the need for a *mens rea* element. In the *Moore* case[144] a barrister was struck off the rolls for not disclosing that he had bribed a police prosecutor when applying for admission to the bar. The bribe had taken place in 1983 when he was a solicitor. Moore alleged that when he applied for admission in 1989 trauma had caused him to repress from his consciousness this conduct; that is, there was no *mens rea*. Moore used the evidence of a psychologist to support this allegation. The court rejected the evidence because it contradicted his evidence that the threat to his reputation of revelation of the bribe continually played on his mind. The court said his action was far more likely explained by his knowledge that disclosure of the bribe would lead to rejection of his application for admission and other criminal consequences might follow.

6.54

In *Barristers' Board v Khan*,[145] a solicitor who had been admitted to the rolls was struck off for not revealing a problem he had with the Law Society. When he had applied to be admitted as a barrister he failed to mention that a former client had made a claim against him for withholding funds and that the Law Society had suspended his practising certificate and appointed a receiver to deal with the matter. He also had unsuccessfully sought to have the suspension removed.

In *Re the Application of Del Castillo to be Admitted as a Legal Practitioner*,[146] the applicant acting on legal advice did not admit in his application that he had been acquitted of murder. The Full Federal Court found that there had been no deception but an omission based on poor legal advice. The court upheld the Australian Capital Territory Supreme Court's denial of admission until the applicant brought the admission to the attention of the authorities in New South Wales. He had been admitted in New South Wales, the admission board having knowledge of the omission, and the Full Federal Court felt that the matter had to be looked at in detail by the New South Wales admission board.[147] A Victorian court also said that being acquitted of a crime does not prevent a finding of not being a fit and proper person.[148]

---

143. Basten and Redmond (above), pp 133–4.
144. *NSW Bar Association v Moore*, CA(NSW), Legal Profession Disciplinary Reports, Supplement to *Law Society J (NSW)*, No 1, March 1994, pp 20–2, 29.
145. [2001] QCA 92.
146. (unreported, Fed C of A, Full Ct, No 126/98, 12 May 1999, BC9902973); [1999] FCA 626.
147. For an analysis of this case see Y Ross, 'Admission standards — the need for candour', *Law Institute J (Vic)*, November 1999, p 36.
148. *Frugtniet v Board of Examiners* [2005] VSC 332.

6.55   In the two most recent cases both applicants appear to have lacked candour, but still were admitted. In the *Law Society of Tasmania v Richardson*,[149] Crawford J held that the Law Society failed to meet the onus of proof in its case against Scott Richardson. A university committee had found Richardson guilty of academic misconduct. The committee also told him that he would be expected to disclose to the Supreme Court on his admission application that he had been reprimanded.

Richardson felt he had not done anything wrong and thought of appealing the committee's decision. He decided it was unnecessary because of the advice of his father, Gregory Richardson, a senior counsel, who said that the decision of the committee was 'bull shit'. He had also sought the advice of his legal ethics teacher and the Dean of the Law Faculty. He thought their advice was that there was no need to disclose and thus did not disclose. His father moved (with his mother's approval) his application for admission and said his son was a 'fit and proper person', but did not mention the reprimand. The Law Society sought to have Scott removed from the rolls for lack of candour.

After the action was filed, Scott Richardson had the academic committee's decision overruled because of a lack of natural justice. Crawford J discussed in detail the academic misconduct issue. It appeared likely that Scott did not do anything wrong. Furthermore, although the Dean and his ethics teacher denied telling Scott he need not disclosure, Crawford J came to the conclusion that they may have told him that it was Richardson's decision. The judge felt that a 22-year-old would act on this advice and what he did was only 'an error of judgment'. As a result he dismissed the charges. Crawford J said that Tasmania was different to some other jurisdictions that have court rules telling applicants what they have to admit. He said he might have made a different decision if there were specific rules prescribing matters to be disclosed. For example, South Australia in its rules requires disclosure of academic dishonesty such as plagiarism.

In applying the cases Crawford J argued that when the courts have said there is need to disclose they could not have meant that you had to disclosure every mistake in your life. I would argue that it was obvious that Richardson had the intention not to disclose a *serious* matter. Furthermore, there is no excuse that the applicant was given wrong advice (see *Del Castillo* above). I believe that the main focus for Crawford J should have been whether there was an intention by Richardson not to disclose. Instead, his focus was on the details of the misconduct, the advice given by others and not on candour.

In the second case, *Skerritt v The Legal Practice Board of Western Australia*,[150] the Court of Appeal sent back to the Board to review its decision to refuse Skerritt admission. At the rehearing he was admitted.[151] Skerritt, in his application for registration of his articles, admitted to a conviction for stalking. There was also a complaint made by a Ms Saggers, who said that Skerritt had been stalking her and had lodged an

149. [2003] TASSC 9.
150. [2004] WASCA 28.
151. Private communication from Claire Thompson, a former President of the Law Society of WA.

unwarranted complaint against her with her employer, the Australian Taxation Office. It was argued that Skerritt showed no remorse in relation to all these matters. The Board found that Skerritt firmly believed his innocence despite 'compelling' evidence to the contrary. The Board felt that sufficient time had elapsed since the various incidents and found him to be of 'good fame and character'. At his later application to be admitted to practice the issue under the Act concerned whether he was 'a fit and proper person'. The Board found him 'fit and proper' based on its earlier decision but a month later rescinded this finding on the basis of new evidence. The main new concerns were why he had ceased to be a member of the Australian army, why he had commenced the various dubious legal actions and complaints and whether he was involved with information published on the internet concerning his previous hearing. The Board finally decided that he was not a 'fit and proper person'. It based its decision on his failure to be truthful about his conduct in the army and the nature of his mental health (a suicide attempt) at that time, his ingestion of anti-depressant medication over a period of time, and his misconduct regarding the two women. The Board said it had changed its views from the previous hearing because of additional information.

The Court of Appeal said that there was no rational basis to conclude an isolated suicide attempt made 12 years before the application, combined with taking anti-depression drugs, renders a person unfit to practise. The court said depression *per se* 'does not seem to us necessarily to detract from a person's capacity to perform any of the duties required of a practitioner ... Many persons in the community — including no doubt many members of the legal profession — suffer from depression, and yet are able to fulfil their duties in an honest and competent way'. Severe depression causing a practitioner to act inappropriately can render the practitioner unfit,[152] but the depression here was not linked to Skerritt's behaviour towards the two women.

The court also found that the Board could have found a lack of candour in relation to information concerning Skerritt's conduct in the army. It said that the 'weight to be attached to that ... is a matter for the Board'. In sending the matter back it pointed out that the Board should, in relation to his suicide attempt, also 'take into account the sensitivity and distressing nature of the incident involved', that Skerritt eventually authorised disclosure and that the circumstances were not capable of a finding of unfitness. The court said that the Board's finding that he lacked insight into his wrongdoing and lacked remorse towards the two women for his actions was an appropriate finding. This finding was relevant to his fitness to practise. At the rehearing the Board decided not to find lack of candour resulting in Skerritt being unfit for practice.

6.56 The need for remorse, cooperation with the authorities and rehabilitation is a highly subjective requirement that is present in both the admission and disciplinary context. An attitude of rudeness, arrogance, argumentativeness, or unwillingness to accept that you have done wrong and the unwillingness to change your ways, can lead to being denied admission. It is therefore

---

152. The court cites for support *Barristers' Board v Young* [2001] QCA 556.

inadvisable for an applicant to argue that what they did was correct or was an expression of a high ideal or to protest innocence. Rhode states that:[153]

> Michigan's repentant bomber was admitted to the Bar despite several years in a maximum security facility, while North Carolina's unconfessed 'peeping Tom' was thought too great a public threat to be certified.

Rhode also points out that past conduct is no indication of future conduct:[154]

> Even trained psychiatrists, psychologists, and mental health workers have been notably unsuccessful in projecting future dishonesty or other misconduct on the basis of similar prior acts ... [N]ot only do examiners and judges generally lack clinical expertise, they are ... frequently drawing inferences ... based on one or two prior acts, committed on the basis of similar prior acts ...

Need for honesty

6.57   One other element that runs through most of the cases is that judges will deny admission to applicants who lie. Judges state that they rely on lawyers being truthful. Tribunals place a high importance on honesty within the legal profession.[155] Can it be said that lawyers are always truthful and, if they are not, is the requirement of being truthful in order to be admitted to the profession consistent with the standard applied to those already in practice? We have already pointed out there has been a double standard but this may be changing in light of the *Foreman* case: see **6.34–6.35**. The *Wentworth* case was widely discussed in the media as an example of a different standard being applied for those in practice than for those seeking to be admitted.[156] One letter to the newspapers questioned whether lawyers are always truthful:[157]

> Ms Wentworth would not arouse such fear and loathing among the barristers if she were merely threatening the public interest. Her crime is probably to suggest that lawyers may lie to advance invalid cases. They are very sensitive about such implications and they would not be so anxious if abuse of process were as rare as the dearth of disciplinary action related to it suggests ... [A] taboo has developed which prevents the institutions of the law from dealing with this problem [misleading the court] or even admitting that it exists and that there is unacknowledged and possibly unconscious fear among the lawyers that an investigation in this area might hurt some deemed to be honest ... People who conduct their own cases are likely to interpret as deliberate lying by an opposing lawyer, behaviour that another lawyer would consider normal, and would tolerate even if it did arouse suspicions. Thus they target the opposing lawyers and threaten to open the abuse-of-process can of worms. All the lawyers, including judges, close ranks against such people, deem them vexatious litigants and do all they can to prevent them pursuing their cases. The requirement that lawyers be of good character has turned into the deemed truth that all lawyers are of good character. This results in them lending spurious credibility to invalid cases and is unfair to the litigants on the other side. The requirement should be abolished and a lawyer should be deemed no more likely to be truthful than the client he represents.

153. Rhode (above), p 545.
154. Rhode (above), pp 559–60.
155. *Borg v Barnes* (1987) 10 NSWLR 734 at 737.
156. See J Slee, *Sydney Morning Herald*, 1 January 1993, p 8 and 15 January 1993, p 10.
157. Letters to the editor, C Moulton, 'Are Lawyers Always Truthful', *Sydney Morning Herald*, 6 November 1992, p 10.

Judges have stated in judgments that lawyers do tell untruths. A good **6.58** example is some of the comments made by Rolfe J in ordering nine former and present partners of the law firm Baker & McKenzie to repay $3.5 million. He referred to some of the evidence given by the lawyers with terms such as 'fabrication', 'untruthfulness' and 'gross inconsistency'. Such comments by judges are rare but perhaps the famous quote by Mark Twain is fairly accurate. He said: 'What chance has the innocent, uncultivated liar against the educated expert? What chance have I against a lawyer?'[158] In the United States at least there is a widespread belief that lawyers lie frequently. This notion was the basis of a recent Jim Carey film, *Liar, Liar*, where a lawyer is not allowed to lie for one full day. This results in destroying the lawyer's legal practice.

The need for lawyers to lie in the interest of their clients can be detrimental **6.59** to their self-esteem and health. Bok has pointed out that:[159]

> Liars usually weigh only the immediate harm to others from the lie against the benefits they want to achieve. The flaw in such an outlook is that it ignores or underestimates two additional kinds of harm — the harm that lying does to the liars themselves and the harm done to the general level of trust and social cooperation. ... The very fact that he *knows* he has lied, first of all, affects him. He may regard the lie as an inroad on his integrity; he certainly looks at those he has lied to with new caution. And if they find out that he has lied, he knows that his credibility and the respect for his word have been damaged.

We have already stated that the application by the profession of inconsistent standards for applicants as compared to members of the profession is untenable and perhaps the *Foreman* case (see **6.34–6.35**) shows that courts are now ready to apply more consistent standards. We will see in discussing the duties of candour and fairness in Chapters 14 and 15 that lawyers are rarely disciplined for misleading the courts. We will also discuss in more detail in Chapter 12 the fact that lawyers often lie to their clients.[160]

Political activity

Australian admission boards have rarely inquired into applicants' political **6.60** activities. In contrast, in the United States and Canada there have been a number of cases where admission authorities have denied entry to the profession to those who hold political beliefs that advocate the violent overthrow of the government or calls for disobedience to the law.

There are two main decisions dealing with this problem in Australia. In *Re Julius*,[161] decided in 1941 by the Supreme Court of Queensland, the court dealt with the allegation that the applicant was a member of the Communist Party. Being a member made him a disloyal subject of the King and his actions were prejudicial to the war effort. There was no evidence that he was a member of the Party and the applicant denied he was a member. He did admit selling the Party's newspaper and it was found that he possessed communist literature but that was held not to materially affect

---

158. M Twain, *The Mark Twain Reader*, Winward, Leicester, 1981, pp 823–4.
159. S Bok, *Lying: Moral Choice in Public and Private Life*, Pantheon Books, New York, 1978, pp 24–5.
160. See L Lerman, 'Lying to Clients' (1990) 138 *Pennsylvania LR* 659.
161. [1943] St R Qd 247.

his good fame and he was admitted as a barrister. Mansfield J said (at St R Qd 247 at 260):

> There is to my mind a difference between the advocacy and support of certain of the principles of Communism and the carrying out of those parts of communistic doctrines which call for the overthrow of the existing constitution by revolution and force. It does not necessarily follow that because a person agrees with one or more planks in a platform … that he must be taken to be wholly in accordance with the views of the body whose platform that is …

> The free and unrestricted expression of socialistic views is countenance to Queensland law, provided that the person … does not violate the laws relating to defamation, to sedition and to the suppression of subversive activities …

6.61   The second case dealt with Wendy Bacon. As discussed above, she was denied admission because the Court of Appeal held that she had lied concerning the source of bail money she had supplied. Two of the three judges of the Court of Appeal discussed her political activities. Moffitt J stated that:[162]

> [I]n itself being a radical in a political sense or being what might be regarded by some as an extremist in views on sex, religion or philosophy provides no bar to admission as a barrister, unless of course, the attitude of the [person] … renders him not a fit and proper person because his character, reputation or likely conduct fall short of the standards expected of a practising barrister. It is an open question subject only to the requirements of being a fit and proper person … Some matters in the past may be so incompatible with being a barrister, not only then, but also later when the application for admission is made, that the court will not be persuaded that the applicant is a person fit and proper … Character does not change readily and an applicant for admission or readmission may have some difficulty in persuading a court that his past character or past outlook manifested by conduct or the profession of ideas were incompatible with being a barrister, have changed.

> Some matters in the past may more easily be set aside, in particular the conduct of young persons, being conduct not seen in human experience as determinative or necessarily so of ordinary character or future attitudes or conduct. What a student may do as a student particularly of a student activist type in the exuberance of development and exploitation of new freedoms opened to his developing mind, might call for some scrutiny of a claim to present fitness, but could and mostly will provide little sound guides to his fitness to be a barrister … Many of the great have been radical in their youth and seen by others to be such. The Bar and other democratic institutions would be less, if such people had been or are excluded on some narrow minded, authoritarian or punitive basis.

6.62   Moffitt J found that Bacon had shown a continuation of her past political conduct and attitudes beyond her youth and this raised a real question of her fitness to be a barrister. Her continuing political activities were quite incompatible with being a barrister.[163]

Reynolds J in the other judgment pointed out that Bacon had been convicted of 10 offences and had 13 other charges in relation to her political activities over a period of eight years from 1970–77. She was 24-years-old when first charged and had had no charges laid against her for

---

162. *Re B* [1981] 2 NSWLR 372 at 380.
163. *Re B* (above) at 380.

the four years before the court proceedings. Reynolds said her record showed her to have been a professional protester and that she had shown herself not to be a fit and proper person to be admitted to the bar. He said:[164]

> It is not a question of any difference of view as to her political ideology or indeed a dislike of the vigour with which she has pursued the many causes she has espoused. It is rather a question of whether a person who aspires to serve the law can be said to be fit to do so when it is demonstrated that in the zealous pursuit of political goals she will break the law if she regards it as impeding the success of her cause. That she has done many times in the past, though it may be said that in those cases dishonesty was not involved.

The *Bacon* case raises serious questions over the standards being applied by the judges. The notion that radicalism is only correct in one's youth and that it is inconsistent with being a barrister would support the public perception that lawyers must be conservative — at least to be admitted. Furthermore, Bacon had not broken the law for four years before her case, but the court appears to accept the idea that she had not changed. Moffitt J states that 'character does not change readily' but gives no authority for such a broad statement. Rhode has collected various studies that indicate there is no basis to predict future behaviour from prior conduct.[165]   **6.63**

Australia is similar to the United States in upholding the right of a member of the Communist Party to be admitted to practice.[166] The United States Supreme Court has upheld the right of a state bar to ask questions concerning an applicant's political beliefs and whether he or she was a member of the Communist Party.[167] This decision can be contrasted with a much more recent decision of the Arkansas Supreme Court. It held that an applicant's right to freedom of speech is violated if they have to answer a state bar question as to whether they are a member or supporter of an organisation that believes in or teaches the overthrow of the government by force or by any illegal methods. Answering this question, according to that court, violates the First Amendment protection of the right to being politically active.[168] Only in British Columbia was a 'Marxist Communist' denied the right to practise but this occurred in 1950 at the height of the Cold War.[169]   **6.64**

The *Bacon* case can be contrasted to an applicant who had amassed 17 convictions related to activities to end the war in Vietnam. He was admitted on his first application, without objection, in New South Wales. Another applicant was admitted in Victoria despite a conviction for failing to register for national service during the Vietnam War.[170] In the *Hallinan*   **6.65**

---

164. *Re B* (above) at 387.
165. Rhode (above), pp 555–62.
166. The United States Supreme Court upheld this right in *Schware v Board of Bar Examiners* 353 US 232 and *Kongisberg v State Bar of California* 366 US 36 (1961). There are no reported cases in Australia but well-known Communists have been admitted to practice. In South Australia one has even been appointed as Queen's Counsel and then later on to the bench. On being appointed to the bench he resigned from the Party, but this is customary for any judge who is a member of a political party.
167. *Kongisberg v State Bar of California* 366 US 36 (1961) and *Re Anastaplo* 366 US 82 (1961).
168. *Carfagno v Harris* 470 Fed Supp 219 (D Ark 1979).
169. *Martin v Law Society of British Columbia* (1950) 3 DLR 173.
170. Disney et al (above), p 289.

case, a political activist with numerous convictions for non-violent civil disobedience actions was admitted by the Californian Supreme Court. Peters J held:[171]

> If we were to deny to every person who has engaged in a 'sit-in' or other form of non-violent civil disobedience and who has been convicted therefor, the right to enter a licensed profession, we would deprive the community of the services of many highly qualified persons of the highest moral courage.

In Illinois a racist, Matt Hale, was denied admission to the bar by the Bar's Committee on Character and Fitness because he used an Israeli flag as a doormat and, as leader of the East Peoria World Church of the Creator, hated blacks and Jews. In rejecting his application the bar panel said that the applicant, under the United States Constitution, was: 'free ... to incite as much racial hatred as he desires and to attempt to carry out his life's mission of depriving those he dislikes of their legal rights. But in our view he cannot do this as an officer of the court.'[172]

Jewish Law Professor Alan Dershowitz, in offering to represent Hale on his appeal, said: 'Character committees should not become thought police. It's not the content of thoughts I'm defending; it's the freedom of everybody to express their views and to become lawyers. Although I find his views utterly reprehensible and despicable, I don't believe anybody should be denied admission to the bar on the basis of their views.'[173] Hale eventually dismissed Dershowitz as his lawyer.

The Illinois Supreme Court denied Hale's petition requesting a full review and oral hearing of the conclusions of the Bar's Committee arguing that Hale's case was not a First Amendment problem. In his dissenting judgment Justice Heiple said the case was about Hale's First Amendment right to free speech. Furthermore, Heiple J stated that the Committee based its ruling on what Hale would do and not on any specific conduct that he had done that violated the disciplinary rules. Heiple J questioned whether, if Hale was already a lawyer, his statements would lead to his disbarment; that there appeared to be a double standard — one for admission and another for practising lawyers.[174] The United States Supreme Court also refused to review the decision.

Personal morals

6.66 Various critics have stated that the personal morals of an applicant are irrelevant to considerations for admission. The argument is that the application of such criteria would lead to subjective judgments based on the morals of the elite members of the profession controlling the admission process. Furthermore, society's morals are constantly in flux and older members of the profession, especially judges, would be out of touch with these changes.

---

171. *Hallinan v Committee of Bar Examiners of State Bar* 421 P 2d 76 (Ca 1966).
172. *The State Journal Register*, 30 January 1999; Associated Press, 9 February 1999; and CNN, 13 November 1999.
173. Ibid. See also the *Sydney Morning Herald*, 20 April 1999, p 10.
174. *Re Matthew F Hale*, 723 NE 2d 206 (1999 Ill) Supreme Court of Illinois.

The profession disagrees with these comments and has examined the behaviour of applicants in relation to two main areas:

❑ criminal conduct and abuse of legal process; and

❑ non-criminal conduct.

CRIMINAL CONDUCT

In relation to the former we have already discussed the *Wentworth* case (see 6.48–6.50) where being a vexatious litigant was considered to be one of the elements in her denial of admission. We have also seen that a consistent record of convictions can be a barrier, for example in the *Bacon* case, but not a barrier for those involved in convictions for protesting against the Vietnam War.

6.67

Courts appear to be willing to admit those with a prior conviction or convictions. The applicants have to admit to the action and accept responsibility for what they have done. In addition, the conviction(s) is less serious if it was an isolated incident, or happened during one's youth, or a number of years ago. How many years have to pass after committing a serious crime or how many years are needed after being struck off for rehabilitation is arbitrary. Four years without a conviction was not enough time for Wendy Bacon, nor was three years enough for Evatt in applying for readmission.[175] Evatt was finally readmitted on his third application after 13 years[176] and it took Davis 31 years to be readmitted (when he was 64-years-old).[177] Peter Clyne, a barrister who was struck off the rolls, was never readmitted. On an application for readmission the court said that Clyne:[178]

> … still exhibits a degree of casuistry, lack of humility and an intellectual arrogance which are incompatible with a sincere understanding of, and a genuine belief in, the code of honour of the Bar … [I]t is clear that he has not undergone that degree of moral regeneration which is essential before he can be re-admitted.

Clyne did finally admit in 1981, 19 years after this decision, that the judgments were correctly based and asked for forgiveness, but he had during that time continually attacked the judgments. He died a few years after finally showing remorse, never having been readmitted.

A student, David Kang, who fired two blank shots at Prince Charles in 1994 and attempted to attack him, eventually was admitted to practice. The headlines around the world called him a 'royal assassin'. By 2005 he was a practising barrister. It appears that after the incident Kang had complete remorse and lived an unblemished life.[179]

---

175. *Evatt v New South Wales Bar Association* (CA(NSW), 15 December 1981, unreported) extracted in Disney et al (above), pp 334–6. In the United States a law student's dishonesty in handling money stopped his admission because it only occurred one year before his application: *Re Mustafa* 631 A 2d 45 (DC App 1993).

176. *Evatt's* case.

177. Davis' applications for readmission had been opposed by the Bar Association and its view carried considerable weight: see *Ex parte Davis* (1963) 63 SR (NSW) 54 at 67.

178. *Clyne v New South Wales Bar Association* [1962] NSWR 709.

179. M Benns, 'He shot at a prince, now he's a barrister', *Sun-Herald*, 6 February 2005, pp 1 and 4.

6.68   An important element is the nature of the crime. Minor traffic violations or parking tickets would not be a bar to admission. Breaking or entering, theft, embezzlement, can be barriers, although a crime lacking *mens rea*, for example involuntary manslaughter, may be treated differently.[180] It has been stated that in Australia admission boards look carefully at cases involving indecent behaviour, driving under the influence of alcohol, smoking Indian hemp, but have a 'liberal attitude to offences, which do not directly relate to the practice of law, nor involve recent dishonesty'.[181]

In South Africa a Rastafarian applicant, who had two convictions for cannabis possession and avowed his intention to continue to use pot, was denied admission by the law society. He argued on appeal that he smokes the 'holy weed' as part of his religious practice, but this did not enable him to be admitted.[182] In the United States ex-prisoners who have committed serious crimes such as armed robbery,[183] manslaughter and sale of narcotics[184] have been admitted to practice. There was a law student in Arizona who served a lengthy sentence for murder and whose admission as a student resulted in some heated debate. He graduated near the top of his class and was later admitted to practice.[185] The California Supreme Court has stated that convicted murderers could be admitted if they had conducted themselves in an 'exemplary fashion over a meaningful period of time',[186] but there are cases of refusal of admission to convicted murderers.[187] An applicant who had three convictions for drunk driving was refused admission.[188] In only eight jurisdictions in the United States is conviction for a felony an automatic disqualification for admission.[189] In all other jurisdictions the courts will look at the nature of the crime and how many years ago it took place. The California Supreme Court overruled in August 2000 the Bar Court's admission of an applicant who was convicted of manslaughter on the basis that, even though he was on drugs, he was vicious in killing his sister. He had also continued to violate the law by committing other offences, including forgery, numerous driving offences, theft and possession of heroin. The court said his record displayed a lack of respect for the law. As stated above, the court did say in this case that convicted murderers could be admitted.[190]

---

180. *Ziems v Prothonotary of the Supreme Court of NSW* (1957) 97 CLR 279. In that case the High Court overruled the decision of a lower court striking off the roll a barrister who had committed a felony — involuntary manslaughter — because he did not commit a crime that had a *mens rea* element. Although it is a case dealing with discipline the notion of the requirement of a *mens rea* as an important element can be used for admission cases. The *Ziem* case can be compared to a United States case in New Mexico in which a lawyer who committed involuntary manslaughter was indefinitely suspended from practice because the crime was 'contrary to honesty, justice or good morals': *Re Morris* 74 NM 679 at 397 P 2d 475 (NM 1964).
181. Disney et al (above), p 289.
182. Reuters News Service (Johannesburg), 21 February 2000.
183. *Re Application of GLS* 291 Md 182, 439 A 2d 1107 (Md 1982).
184. *In Re Manville* 538 A 2d 1128 (DC 1988).
185. See Rhode and Luban (above), p 926.
186. *In Re Eben Gossage* 23 Cal4th 1080 (2000).
187. *Re Moore* (1983) 308 NC 771, 303 SE 2d 810 and *Re Roger MM* 466 NY S 2d 873, 96 AD 2d 1133 (NY 1983). See also L Gunn, 'Past Crimes and Admission to the Bar' (1980) 5 J Legal Profession 179.
188. *Frasher v West Virginia Board of Law Examiners* 408 SE 2d 675 (W Va 1991).
189. *ABA Comprehensive Guide to Bar Admission Requirements*, 1996–97, pp 10–11.
190. *In Re Eben Gossage* 23 Cal4th 1080 (2000).

NON-CRIMINAL CONDUCT

Australian admission boards and courts have rarely dealt with non-criminal conduct. It appears to be a factor in the *Wentworth* case (vexatious litigant, and so on) but most of these problems have arisen in the context of disciplining members of the profession. In Australia there appears to be a belief that inquiries into an applicant's mental health are an invasion of privacy. If a person has had a history of poor mental health it would appear that expert evidence would be requested to support his or her ability to practise. Psychiatric evidence was used to explain the mental health of Davis in an effort to mitigate his behaviour in his third readmission application[191] but not in any of the previous actions. In Victoria a solicitor seeking admission, after being suspended in New Zealand due to alcoholism, used psychiatric evidence to show that he had overcome his drinking problems. He was admitted but granted only a limited practising certificate.[192] In the *Skerritt* case (above) the Court of Appeal said that 'there is no rational basis for a conclusion that a suicide attempt some 12 years prior to the application, either alone or in combination with the taking anti-depression medication, renders a person unfit to practice'.[193]

6.69

In the United States there have been a number of cases dealing with psychological, financial problems (bankruptcy) and sexual relations. The standards concerning mental health are inconsistent, with some jurisdictions making no inquiries, while others require a certificate of a history of treatment from a psychiatrist regarding the applicant's ability to practise law.[194] In Nevada mental illness is not considered to be grounds for denial, while some states have excluded applicants who show 'religious fanaticism', and personality disorders involving 'hypersensitivity, unwarranted suspicion, and excessive self-importance', or a 'propensity to unreasonably react' to perceived opposition.[195]

6.70

The background of an applicant in relation to finances is obviously important because of the entrustment of clients' funds. In the *Lenehan* case it played an important role in denying him admission and in helping him gain admission. A defect in character has been found in the United States because of reckless business dealings and failure to honour financial commitments, such as not paying student loans despite having the ability to do so.[196] A person cannot, according to federal law in the United States, be denied admission solely for declaring bankruptcy.[197]

The problem of character in relation to sexual preference stems from the fact that certain sexual practices have violated the law throughout our history. Thus, being a homosexual was illegal throughout Australia and only ceased to be illegal in Tasmania in 1997. Can sexual behaviour that violates the law, for example sodomy or adultery, be relevant to the fitness to

6.71

---

191. See *Re Davis* [1962] NSWR 1110 at 1112ff.
192. Files of the Law Institute of Victoria in 1975.
193. [2004] WASCA 28 at para 43.
194. Rhode (above), p 540. See also *Matter of Ronwin* 136 Ariz 566, 667 P 2d 1281 at 1281–8.
195. Rhode (above).
196. *Florida Board of Bar Examiners v GWL* 364 So 2d 454 (Fla 1978); *Application of Gahan* 279 NW 2d 826 (Min 1979) and see generally Annotation, 64 ALR 2d 301.
197. Bankruptcy Act, 11 USC s 525.

practise law? There are no cases in Australia dealing with this problem but there are a number in the United States. In Florida a practising lawyer was disbarred because of his arrest for performing a homosexual act in public. He later applied for admission to practice in New York where the Court of Appeals held that homosexual conduct was a relevant factor in considering fitness for admission but it did not prevent his admission.[198] A Florida court in a later decision held that private, non-commercial homosexual acts between consenting adults, that violated the law, were irrelevant in deciding fitness to practise. Therefore there was no right to investigate or inquire into these activities.[199] In Virginia a state character committee's refusal to certify for admission an applicant who cohabited with another in violation of a state fornication law was reversed by the Virginia Supreme Court. The court held that although the living arrangements might be 'unorthodox and unacceptable to some segments of society, this conduct bears no rational connection to her fitness to practise law'.[200]

CONCLUSION

6.72   Throughout this section we have been highly critical of the criteria for determining fitness to practise law, that is, 'good fame and character'. Rhode has argued that the character review process legitimates a fundamentally illegitimate system. By retaining this system we support the profession's claims to regulatory powers, monopolistic practices and social status. She says we should either totally abandon the whole character process or limit disqualification to a few clearly specified offences and the money saved used in regulation of professional misconduct.[201] She concludes by stating:[202]

> As currently implemented, the moral fitness requirements both subvert and trivialise the professional ideals it purports to sustain. In seeking to express our aspirations, such rituals succeed only in exposing our pretences. While hypocrisy is often the bow vice pays to virtue, better forms of tribute may be available.

---

198. *Re Kimball* 33 NY 2d 584 (1973). The case is discussed in S Convissar, 'The Concept of Attorney-Fitness in New York: New Perspectives' (1975) 24 *Buffalo LR* 553. Kimball was later allowed to be readmitted but only if he passed the state bar examination and the costs were assessed against Kimball. See *Florida Bar In re Kimball* 425 So 2d 531 (Fla 1982).
199. *Florida Board of Bar Examiners Re NRS* 403 So 2d 1315 (Fla 1981). See also B Blackford, 'Good Moral Character and Homosexuality' (1980) 5 *J Legal Profession* 139.
200. *Cord v Gibb* 219 Va 1019, 254 SE 2d 71 (Va 1979).
201. Rhode (above), pp 584–92.
202. Rhode (above), p 592.

7

DISCIPLINE

INTRODUCTION

Historical background

Although the Charter of Justice of 1823 did not expressly confer on the Supreme Court the power to discipline lawyers, it has always been assumed that the court had this power as incidental to its powers over admission.[1] During the nineteenth century the State Supreme Courts developed, through the exercise of this jurisdiction, a body of principles that has established common law standards applied not only by the State Supreme Courts but also by all other disciplinary bodies. The High Court has also accepted that the decisions have a state basis. In the *Clyne* case the court said it would not interfere with the decisions of the State Supreme Courts except on 'the most compelling grounds'. To do so would impair the 'relationship of trust and confidence' between the state courts and the profession.[2]

By the latter part of the nineteenth century and in the early part of the twentieth century, the Supreme Courts gradually recognised that disciplinary matters concerning solicitors were to be heard first by the law societies and that cases of substantial concern or needing severe penalties came to the courts at the instigation of the law societies. The courts also directed the law societies to investigate complaints against solicitors, which came directly to them.[3] During the twentieth century statutory powers were conferred on the professional associations throughout Australia to investigate charges of misconduct against members. We will discuss below

7.1

---

1. See Rich J in *Kennedy v The Council of the Incorporated Law Institute of New South Wales* (1939) 13 ALJ 563 and see also *Re Davis* (1947) 75 CLR 409. The inherent power of the Supreme Court to admit practitioners has been revoked in New South Wales under s 17(c) Legal Profession Act 1987.
2. *Clyne v New South Wales Bar Association* (1960) 104 CLR 186 at 198.
3. J Bennett, *A History of Solicitors in New South Wales*, Legal Books, Sydney, 1984, pp 345–6. Although this describes the situation in New South Wales, a similar development took place in other jurisdictions.

the powers and jurisdiction of the professional associations and the disciplinary tribunals and boards.

Supreme Court inherent power

7.2   The State Supreme Courts still retain their inherent power over disciplinary affairs. This right is preserved by statute in all jurisdictions except Western Australia.[4] The Supreme Courts, along with their concurrent jurisdiction, at times act as appellate courts from decisions of disciplinary tribunals. We have pointed out in Chapter 6 that the courts also exercise their inherent disciplinary powers over those training to be lawyers.

7.3   The exercising of the power to suspend or disbar lawyers is supposed to be 'wholly protective' and not a punishment to the lawyer.[5] Who is being protected? The court said in the *Clyne* case that it was protecting the public and making sure that the abuse of the privilege of being a lawyer by lawyers, as in *Clyne*, would not lead to the profession losing its privileges. The latter element involves maintaining the integrity and standards of the profession, acting as a deterrent to other lawyers and ensuring that the profession does not lose the public's confidence. It can be argued that loss of the licence to practise from the perspective of the person being disciplined has a punitive aspect; that is, the loss of the licence usually leads to diminished status and income. A further punitive aspect is that lawyers can be severely fined by disciplinary tribunals, ordered to pay the professional association's costs and have to pay for their own legal costs in the disciplinary proceedings. If an appeal is taken, this can add on enormous legal costs if the practitioner is unsuccessful.[6] Furthermore, solicitors who make mistakes can be punished by the court ordering them to pay the costs of their own client and/or the costs of the opposite party:[7]

> The matter complained of need not be criminal. It need not involve speculation or dishonesty. A mere mistake or error of judgment is not generally sufficient, but a gross neglect or inaccuracy in a matter that it is a solicitor's duty to ascertain with accuracy may suffice.

7.4   Barristers are not mentioned but the court would have the power to penalise them for gross neglect and it appears the immunity doctrine would not bar a disciplinary proceeding.[8] As we will see in Chapter 10, barristers and solicitors have immunity from litigation for their negligence for matters 'intimately related to litigation'.[9]

---

4.   For example, see s 590 Legal Profession Act (NSW) 2004. Although statutory provisions reiterate this inherent power the power is not absolute and can be modified by specific statutory provisions. See the High Court's views in *Walsh v Law Society of New South Wales* [1999] HCA 33.

5.   *Clyne v New South Wales Bar Association* (1960) 104 CLR 186 at 202. In *Re Ruffalo* (1968) 390 US 544, 88 S Ct 1222 the United States Supreme Court has come to the opposite conclusion, stating that disciplinary proceedings were 'quasi-criminal' and constitute a 'punishment or penalty imposed on the lawyer'.

6.   See, for example, the disciplinary action against Antony John McDermott Macken, where the costs of the Law Institute before the tribunal and then on appeal were $150,000 and costs of the transcript provided by the Board were over $19,000: (1997) 71(2) *Law Institute J* 58.

7.   Lord Wright in *Myers v Elman* [1940] AC 282 at 317.

8.   See 'Unsatisfactory professional conduct in respect of a barrister. Report of the determination' (1998) 3 *Legal Profession Disciplinary Reports*.

9.   The test adopted in England and Australia is from the New Zealand case *Rees v Sinclair* [1974] 1 NZLR 180 at 187.

STANDARDS IN PROFESSIONAL CAPACITY

Introduction

The following is an example of a discipline problem:

7.5

> Peter is a well-respected solicitor, with a reputation for his skills and efficiency. He has been in practice as a solo practitioner for 12 years in a small country town. In the past three years he has run into severe family problems. His wife and he have been fighting and one time he even physically hit her. He also has problems with his son who stole a car and has been sent to a youth training centre. As a result he has not performed well in his legal work. He has taken time off to drink frequently with friends at the local pub. He is also seeing a psychologist about his personal problems. A few months after the 'trouble' in the family began there were two complaints against Peter to the discipline authorities for a delay in processing divorce matters. Peter replied promptly by completing the matters. Last year there were two more delay matters, this time in relation to conveyancing. Again Peter completed the work within a few weeks of being contacted.
>
> Far more serious has been the case of Grace, a 74-year-old widow, who went to Peter over injuries she suffered as a passenger in a car accident. He failed to file her complaint before the statute of limitations had passed. Grace has gone to another solicitor and is suing him for negligence. She has also gone to the disciplinary authority who, after investigating, has referred the matter to the disciplinary tribunal. Peter is charged with professional misconduct. Grace has made an application to the tribunal claiming $12,000 damages for her loss.
>
> The tribunal has to decide whether Peter's conduct constitutes professional misconduct and, if so, what is an appropriate penalty and how can Grace be compensated? The whole town knows about Peter's problems including this matter. Discuss the issues involved, including what Mary, Peter's counsel, should advise Peter.

As can be seen from the problem, the severity of the penalty for this behaviour would depend on whether one took the client's or the lawyer's perspective. The problem asks: what conduct the profession considers needs to be punished, how this should be done and what constitutes mitigation. Generally, cases receiving disciplinary treatment are misappropriation and commingling of clients' funds,[10] conviction for a serious crime,[11] lacking candour and honesty in dealing with the professional association, the court or tribunal[12] and sometimes cases of repeated minor violations.[13] Although

7.6

---

10. This can lead to being struck off even if no money is lost: see *Law Society of New South Wales v Moulton* [1981] 2 NSWLR 736. This decision was a departure from an earlier attitude that if no money was lost and the lawyer did not make a gain then there would be a lesser punishment: see *New South Wales Bar Association v Rose* (SC (NSW), 27 November 1974, unreported) discussed in Chapter 6. By contrast, in a more recent case the Court of Appeals (NSW) appeared to return to the earlier attitude that if clients are not upset and no money is lost, there should be a lesser penalty: *O'Reilly v Law Society of New South Wales* (1991) 2 Legal Profession Disciplinary Reports (NSW) 13, per Clarke JA at 26.
11. Although *Ziems v Prothonotary of the Supreme Court of New South Wales* (1957) 97 CLR 279 modifies this proposition for crimes lacking a *mens rea* element.
12. See *Re Veron; Ex parte Law Society of New South Wales* (1966) 84 WN (NSW) Part 1, 136.
13. Although *Clyne v New South Wales Bar Association* (1960) 104 CLR 186 does not mention this aspect of his behaviour, he had had various warnings by judges for his behaviour in court. Furthermore, a number of minor violations can be considered professional misconduct. See *In the matter of Ian Gordon Dunn* (1994) 3 Legal Profession Disciplinary Reports 5, where repeated offences were brought into consideration as a reason for giving a greater penalty.

there are many cases of delay and incompetence in dealing with clients' affairs, these violations usually receive less severe sanctions.[14] A new area considered to be in the less serious category is that of having sexual relations with a client.

7.7   No matter what breach may have occurred it is an extremely important matter for the practitioner. An accused practitioner needs to treat the accusation seriously and may have to seek proper legal representation. As two American lawyers who specialise in this area have stated, it is not the 'time to engage in any ethical or legal brinkmanship'.[15] As we will see, the main objective should be for the practitioner to cooperate and not to engage in confrontational tactics.

Professional misconduct and unprofessional conduct

7.8   It has been stated by the New South Wales Court of Appeal in a case dealing with readmission that the same ethical and professional standards apply for both branches of the profession.[16] The question that needs to be addressed is — what standards should be applied to professional conduct? Under common law the courts established certain categories to deal with breaches of professional standards. Although most jurisdictions have developed definitions for breaches of the standards, the common law definitions have either been basically adopted or have not been abrogated and still have relevance. The definitions fall into three categories: serious breaches; breaches falling short of the highest category; and breaches of etiquette (conventions) or written rules between members of the profession. The words used normally for the most serious are 'professional misconduct'. The definition of 'professional misconduct' stems from an English judgment dealing with a medical practitioner and later applied to lawyers. The English court stated that the 'Law Society are very good judges of what is professional misconduct by a solicitor'.[17] It said that the General Medical Council could:[18]

> ...[find guilty of] infamous conduct in a professional respect [a practitioner if] in the pursuit of his profession, [he or she] has done something with regard to it which would reasonably be regarded as disgraceful or dishonourable by his professional brethren of good repute and competency.

7.9   The High Court has elaborated on the definition in striking off the rolls a solicitor who had endeavoured to improperly influence a witness. Rich J said in the *Kennedy* case that:[19]

14. For a severe sanction see *In the matter of David Colin Hundt* (1992) 1 Legal Profession Disciplinary Reports (NSW) 1. The Disciplinary Tribunal found instances of gross neglect and some of slackness or casualness in acting for clients. The lawyer was suspended for two years and ordered to pay the Law Society's costs.
15. M Coffield and C Kendall, 'Tactics in a Disciplinary Proceeding' (1997) 24(1) *Litigation* 41.
16. *Re Davis* (CA(NSW), 27 October 1978, unreported).
17. Darling J, *Re a Solicitor; Ex parte The Law Society* [1912] 1 KB 302. Darling's judgment was adopted in Australia in *Re Veron: Ex parte Law Society of New South Wales* (1966) 84 WN (NSW) Part 1, at 136, 142. In *Veron* the court said at 147 that it would pay great regard to the view of the Council of the Law Society as to what constituted professional misconduct.
18. Lopes LJ, *Allinson v General Council of Medical Education and Registration* [1884] 1 QB 750.
19. *Kennedy v Council of the Incorporated Law Institute of New South Wales* (1939) 13 ALJ 563.

… a charge of misconduct as relating to a solicitor need not fall within any legal definition of a wrong doing. It need not amount to an offence under the law. It was enough that it amounted to grave impropriety affecting his professional character and was indicative of a failure either to understand or to practise the precepts of honesty or fair dealing in relation to the courts, his clients or the public.

Rich said that the solicitor's actions had to be judged 'as a whole' and it showed that he could not be trusted to discharge his duties as a solicitor and in relation to the court. McTiernan J in concurring said that professional misconduct might be involved because his 'anxiety to win the action for his client was more powerful than his attachment to the standards which a solicitor should observe', but this was no excuse for his conduct.[20]

The standard of 'professional misconduct' has been adopted in most jurisdictions but the Supreme Court of South Australia decided to use the expression 'unprofessional conduct' because it was broader than the English term 'professional misconduct'. The court stated that its definition broadened the term 'disgraceful or dishonourable' by not limiting it to the ordinary sense of the term. It includes conduct:[21]

7.10

… which may reasonably be held to violate or to fall short of, to a *substantial degree*, the standard of professional conduct observed or approved of by members of the profession of good repute and competency. [emphasis added]

'Unprofessional conduct' is adopted by legislation in South Australia as meaning:[22]

… an illegal act of any kind committed in the course of practice … and any offence of a dishonest or infamous nature committed … in respect of which punishment by imprisonment is prescribed or authorised by law; or any conduct in the course of, or in connection with, practice by the legal practitioner that involves substantial or recurrent failure to meet the standard of conduct observed by competent legal practitioners of good repute.

The Complaints Committee in South Australia supplements this definition with the common law one. In Western Australia statutory power is granted to the Complaints Committee to investigate the conduct of legal practitioners. The committee can determine whether the conduct may constitute 'unsatisfactory conduct'.[23] Western Australia differs from South Australia because unprofessional conduct is now part of this larger category, 'unsatisfactory conduct'. The latter has been defined as including: '(a) unprofessional conduct on the part of a legal practitioner, whether occurring before or after admission as a legal practitioner; (b) illegal conduct on the part of a legal practitioner, whether occurring before or after admission …; (c) neglect, or undue delay in the course of legal practice; (d) a contravention of this Act, the regulations or the rules; and (e) conduct occurring in connection with legal practice that falls short of the standard of competence and diligence that a member of the public is entitled to expect of a reasonably competent legal practitioner.'[24] There is no specific definition of 'unprofessional conduct' but Western Australia has also

7.11

---

20. *Kennedy's* case (above) at 563–4.
21. *Re R, a practitioner of the Supreme Court* [1927] SASR 58 at 60.
22. Section 5 of the Legal Practitioners Act 1981 (SA).
23. Section 164 of the Legal Practice Act 2003 (WA).
24. Section 3 of the Legal Practice Act 2003 (WA).

adopted the definition of 'unprofessional conduct' as expressed by the Supreme Court in South Australia.[25]

Confusion over disciplinary terms

7.12 There has been some confusion over the two basic terms. The Supreme Courts have sometimes used the terms as if they were the same. For example, in Queensland the legislation called for a hearing of charges of 'professional misconduct' or 'unprofessional conduct'.[26] Until 1997 there was no definition of the terms and thus the common law applied. There has also been some confusion caused by the Queensland Full Court of the Supreme Court adopting the South Australian Supreme Court definition of 'professional misconduct'.[27] The court was criticised for not recognising that the legislation included two separate definitions with different meanings.[28] Furthermore, Queensland courts have narrowly defined 'professional misconduct' as being limited to misconduct in the course of professional work.[29] An attempt to remedy this problem by legislation was by defining 'unprofessional conduct or practice' in s 3B of the Queensland Law Society Legislation Amendment Act (No 2) 1996. The definition was not exclusive.

In 2004 this definition was removed by section 245 of the Legal Profession Act 2004 (Qld). It adopts as the main term 'professional misconduct'. The definition is similar to that in New South Wales (see below). It is not exclusive, so the common law is still relevant and the old confusion of what falls under 'unprofessional conduct or practice' and 'professional misconduct' is still left open. Hopefully, the Queensland courts will now stick to using only 'professional misconduct'.

7.13 The confusion over defining the two terms has also been exacerbated in New South Wales, where 'unprofessional conduct' came to mean something amounting to a breach of professional standards but not amounting to professional misconduct. The High Court, in rejecting the Supreme Court of New South Wales' confirmation of the reprimand given to a solicitor by the New South Wales Statutory Committee, pointed out that the Supreme Court had the right to establish such a standard for unprofessional behaviour, falling short of professional misconduct, but only within its inherent jurisdiction and by giving proper notice to the lawyer.[30]

7.14 When the inherent jurisdiction of the court is involved it may be irrelevant what term is used. The ultimate determination for the court is whether the lawyer is fit to practise. Kitto J of the High Court said 'fit to practise' is not capable of a precise statement. He stated:[31]

> The answer must depend upon one's conception of the minimum standards demanded by a due recognition of the peculiar position and functions of a barrister [or solicitor].

---

25. *Brief* (WA) June 1984, p 9.
26. See Queensland Law Society Act 1952, s 6(2), (3), (3B), s 6AF(1)(a)(i) and s 6F(a).
27. See *Adamson v Queensland Law Society Incorporated* (1990) 1 Qd R 498 at 507.
28. D Searles, 'Professional Misconduct — Unprofessional Conduct Is There a Difference?' (1992) 23 *Queensland Law Society J* 239.
29. *Re Wheeler* [1991] 2 Qd R 690 at 697; *Queensland Law Society Incorporated v Smith* [2001] 1 Qd R 649 at para 10.
30. *Datt v Law Society of New South Wales* (1981) 148 CLR 319 at 330–1 per Mason J.
31. *Ziems v Prothonotary of the Supreme Court of New South Wales* (1957) 97 CLR 279 at 297–8.

The Supreme Court has complete independence in making the judgment as to whether professional misconduct or unprofessional conduct has been established and it has at times reversed the findings of a tribunal. The court can find that professional misconduct has been proven and still this will not lead to a finding of unfitness to practise.[32] In a New South Wales Court of Appeal decision the solicitor was found to have demonstrated a lack of candour to the Statutory Committee constituting a 'grave impropriety', but this was not enough to find him unfit to practise. The court pointed out that the Statutory Committee can also fine or suspend for professional misconduct and the court decided that the appropriate penalty was to fine the applicant.[33] There is also power in the Supreme Court just to reprimand or make a different disciplinary order for conduct that is a serious breach of standards but falls short of professional misconduct.[34]

New categories of breaches of conduct

Even if fitness to practise is the ultimate determination, tribunals need to be given guidance. It became obvious that a more precise definition was required for serious breaches of professional standards including those falling short of professional misconduct or unprofessional conduct. The New South Wales Law Reform Commission suggested that two categories be adopted:

7.15

- ❏ 'breaches which show a temporary or permanent unfitness to practise' entitled 'conduct showing unfitness to practise'; and
- ❏ 'all other breaches' called 'unsatisfactory conduct'.[35]

The latter was adopted into legislation in 1987 as a completely new category called 'unsatisfactory professional conduct'. It includes (as changed in 2004):[36]   S 496

> … conduct of an Australian legal practitioner occurring in connection with the practice of law that falls short of the standard of competence and diligence that a member of the public is entitled to expect of a reasonably competent Australian legal practitioner.

---

32. *Datt v Law Society of New South Wales* (1981) 148 CLR 319.
33. *O'Reilly v Law Society of New South Wales* (1991) 2 Legal Profession Disciplinary Reports (NSW) 13, per Clarke JA at 26. Clarke pointed out no client or borrower expressed any dissatisfaction with a conflict of interest over the use of their funds, nor did any client lose money. The clients had knowledge of the solicitor's involvement with the company, that he had invested their money and they were very satisfied with their dealings with him. Clarke distinguished earlier cases where solicitors were struck off the rolls for having a conflict of interest between the solicitor and his borrower client: see *Law Society of New South Wales v Moulton* [1981] 2 NSWLR 736.
34. *Prothonotary v Jackson* [1976] 2 NSWLR 457.
35. *Second Report on the Legal Profession*, New South Wales Law Reform Commission, 1982, p 53.
36. Section 496 of the Legal Profession Act 2004 (NSW). See also F Riley, 'Unsatisfactory Professional Conduct to be published in Tribunal reports', *Law Society J (NSW)* June 1998, p 64. The Australian Capital Territory has adopted similar definitions to New South Wales: see s 37 of the Legal Practitioners Act 1970 (ACT). South Australia amended the Legal Practitioners Act 1981 in 1998 by adding 'unsatisfactory conduct' to s 5. Unsatisfactory conduct is: 'Conduct in the course of, or in connection with, practice by the legal practitioner that is less serious than unprofessional conduct but involves a failure to meet the standard of conduct observed by competent legal practitioners of good repute.'

7.16   The 1987 Act also extended the common law definition of 'professional misconduct'. It was redrafted for clarity in 2004. It now states:[37] ~~s494~~

(1) For the purposes of this Act:

professional misconduct includes:

(a) unsatisfactory professional conduct of an Australian legal practitioner, where the conduct involves a substantial or consistent failure to reach or maintain a reasonable standard of competence and diligence; and

(b) conduct of an Australian legal practitioner, whether occurring in connection with the practice of law or occurring otherwise than in connection with the practice of law, that would, if established, justify a finding that a practitioner is not a fit and proper person to engage in legal practice.

(2) For finding that an Australian legal practitioner is not a fit and proper person to engage in legal practice as mentioned in subsection (1), regard may be had to the matters that would be considered under section 25 or 42 if the practitioner were an applicant for admission to the legal profession under this Act or for the grant or renewal of a local practising certificate and any other relevant matters.

7.17   The changes in New South Wales include, under s 498, specific examples of conduct capable of being 'unsatisfactory professional conduct' or 'professional misconduct' that do not limit the general definitions:

(1)

(a) conduct consisting of a contravention of this Act, the regulations or the legal profession rules;

(b) charging of excessive legal costs in connection with the practice of law;

(c) conduct in respect of which there is a finding of guilt for—

(i) a serious offence; or

(ii) a tax offence; or

(iii) an offence involving dishonesty;

(d) conduct of an Australian legal practitioner as or in becoming an insolvent under administration;

(e) conduct of an Australian legal practitioner in becoming disqualified from managing or being involved in the management of any corporation under the *Corporations Act 2001* of the Commonwealth;

(f) conduct consisting of a failure to comply with the requirements of a notice under the Act or the regulations (other than an information notice).

(2) Conduct of a person consisting of a contravention referred to in subsection (1)(a) is capable of being unsatisfactory professional conduct or professional misconduct whether or not the person is convicted of an offence in relation to the contravention.

7.18   There are almost identical provisions, Pts 4.4.2–4.4.4, in the Victorian Legal Profession Act 2004. The changes in Victoria, unlike those in New South Wales, also include specific provisions on what constitutes only 'unsatisfactory professional conduct' or only 'professional misconduct'. Part 4.4.5 states that 'unsatisfactory professional conduct' is:

(1) … failure by an Australian legal practitioner to comply with a condition of his or her practising certificate …

(2) Sub-section (1) does not apply if the failure amounts to professional misconduct.

---

37.   Section 497 of the Legal Profession Act 2004 (NSW).

Part 4.4.6 states that 'professional misconduct' is:

(a) wilful or reckless failure to comply with a condition to which an Australian practising certificate held by the practitioner is subject;

(b) wilful or reckless failure to comply with an undertaking given to a court, tribunal, the Commissioner or the Board.

The category of 'unsatisfactory professional conduct' created a new perspective on standards. They are no longer from the profession's point of view alone but include what the consumer of legal services can expect. The new category can also be used to discipline practitioners who have committed a less serious violation of the rules. Furthermore, repeated violation of this category now constitutes 'professional misconduct'. The definitions show that consumer-type complaints such as delay and negligence can no longer be ignored.   **7.19**

Consumer disputes

This consumer orientation was reinforced in New South Wales by amendments to the Act in 1993 with a new s 124. It adopted the New South Wales Law Reform Commission's recommendations on the need for a 'Complainants' Charter of Rights'.[38] It was redrafted and amended in the Legal Profession Act 2004. It now states in s 494:   **7.20**

(2) The objects of this Chapter relating to lay persons and the clients of legal practices are as follows:

(a) to give every person the right to complain about the conduct of lawyers,

(b) to ensure that information is readily available to lay persons about the means of redress that are available under the scheme,

(c) to give clients of law practices access to sufficient advice and assistance in order to make and pursue complaints in accordance with this Part and to understand their rights and responsibilities under this Chapter,

(d) to promote transparency and openness for lay persons at all levels of the operation of the scheme, subject to the need to preserve confidentiality in appropriate circumstances,

(e) to provide an opportunity for mediation of consumer disputes relating to legal services,

(f) to provide complainants with a reasonable opportunity to comment on statements of the lawyer against whom the complaint is made before the complaint is disposed of,

(g) to ensure that complainants receive adequate notice of the commencement and status of disciplinary proceedings at relevant stages of the process (including notice of the dismissal of complaints and the reasons for dismissal),

(h) to give complainants the right to seek an independent review of decisions of Councils to dismiss complaints or reprimand Australian legal practitioners.

The Act recognised that the majority of complaints consist of grievances about matters such as poor communications, delay, negligence, rudeness, discourtesy and so on, that do not amount to unsatisfactory professional conduct. A new category entitled 'consumer disputes' was created to allow   **7.21**

---

38.   See *Scrutiny of the Legal Profession: Complaints Against Lawyers*, New South Wales Law Reform Commission, Report 70, 1993, pp 135–6.

clients to seek redress and to have a remedy. These complaints can now be dealt with and can be referred to mediation.[39] The main criticism of the original provisions was that participation in mediation of a consumer dispute was voluntary. This was changed under s 517 of the Legal Profession Act 2004 (NSW) that gives the Commissioner the power to require compulsory mediation. There may not be a great need for forcing the parties to mediation as the Legal Services Commission, over a number of years, has solved many of its complaints by informal mediation. This includes disputes solved by staff by telephone mediation, without the lodging of a complaint; for example, a dispute regarding documents the client urgently needed from the solicitor.[40]

Negligence as misconduct

7.22   Although the Supreme Court in New South Wales recognised, in 1925, that sub-standard work, which consists of gross neglect and delay in conducting the affairs of a client, can be professional misconduct,[41] the Law Society rarely penalised its members for this behaviour. In 1974 the New South Wales Court of Appeal said 'there is no reason in principle why conduct which can be classified as negligence cannot amount to professional misconduct'.[42] This view is held throughout Australia and a more recent Western Australian Tribunal decision found an ethical breach and fined the practitioner for 'undue delay'.[43] The New South Wales Court of Appeal also stated, in a 1981 case, that clients had the right to expect a minimum standard of competence from a solicitor deemed to be a fit and proper person to practise. This minimum level means a solicitor needs to maintain a basic knowledge of the law, and keep in touch with developments in his or her field of practice. There is no excuse for ignorance by the solicitor of the changing requirements of practice or ethics, but rather such ignorance would be an aggravating factor.[44] In 1989 the court did state that mere professional incompetence or deficiency in professional practice in themselves do not amount to professional misconduct.[45]

7.23   In light of the new category of 'unsatisfactory professional conduct'[46] and the new consumer orientation, it would appear that mere neglect of a client's affairs can lead to disciplinary action. The *Ian Gordon Dunn* 1994 Disciplinary Tribunal decision came to this conclusion in finding unsatisfactory professional conduct for neglect and inattention to a client's affairs.[47] Such a rule has existed under statute for many years in Western Australia where 'any neglect or undue delay' in the conduct of legal work has been grounds for disciplinary action.[48] The Disciplinary Tribunal in

---

39.   Sections 143–144 Legal Profession Act 1987 (NSW), which can now be found in ss 514–524 of the Legal Profession Act 2004 (NSW).
40.   See, generally, Office of the Legal Services Commissioner Annual Reports.
41.   *Re W C Mosley* (1925) 25 SR (NSW) 174 at 175.
42.   *Re Mayes* [1974] 1 NSWLR 19 at 24 per Reynolds and Hutley JJ.
43.   The decision is outlined in *Brief (Law Society of WA)* February 1998, pp 14–15.
44.   *Law Society of New South Wales v Moulton* [1981] 2 NSWLR 736.
45.   *Pillai v Messiter (No 2)* (1989) 16 NSWLR 197.
46.   See s 496 of the Legal Profession Act 2004 (NSW).
47.   *In the matter of Ian Gordon Dunn* (above).
48.   Section 25(b) of the Legal Practitioners Act 1893 (WA). This provision is now found in s 3 of the Legal Practice Act 2003 (WA).

New South Wales also found in a more recent case that unreasonable delay in dealing with a client's workers' compensation claim constituted unsatisfactory professional conduct.[49]

In another New South Wales case a barrister was found guilty of unsatisfactory professional conduct for his neglect and delay in providing his instructing solicitor advice in respect of an appeal. The barrister presented a number of mitigating factors and only received a reprimand.[50]

Conventional rules

'Unsatisfactory professional conduct' or 'professional misconduct' also include violations of regulations and the rules that regulate members of the profession, such as advertising rules, retainer rules, etiquette rules and so on.[51] Some 'practice rules' are not written. This conduct would fall under what the High Court has called 'conventional rules'. The court said a breach of these rules can be considered serious, but would not warrant disbarment — at least unless it were shown 'to be part of a deliberate and persistent system of conduct'.[52] The conventions of etiquette, such as when to wear a wig, what is appropriate dress, what colour bag a junior can use (blue), and so on, are rarely breached because of peer pressure. It would be highly unlikely that someone would be able to breach them consistently and remain in the profession because of peer pressure and other penalties such as contempt of court.

7.24

Sexual relations

One area of lawyer misconduct that may be seen as constituting 'unsatisfactory professional conduct' or even 'professional misconduct' is having a sexual relationship with or sexually harassing a client. There is a 1972 case where a solicitor had a sexual relationship with a client after the decree absolute in a divorce case but before the decision had been made on custody and maintenance. Shortly after, when he was applying for admission as a barrister, the Queensland Supreme Court in considering his application found his actions constituted unprofessional conduct. The court said that 'her conduct with him might well affect the client adversely in the pending proceedings'. The court still held that the misconduct did not disqualify him from admission to the bar. In the appeal to the High Court it was held that while his conduct was reprehensible it fell short of unprofessional misconduct showing an unfitness to practise.[53] In New Zealand the commentary (3) to r 1.01 states the following: 'The relationship of confidence and trust may be breached where a practitioner and client enter into a sexual relationship.' A stricter attitude towards sexual relations with clients has been taken by medical disciplinary tribunals.[54] Perhaps it can be argued that doctors need a stricter standard as it would be extremely unusual for a lawyer's clients to take off their clothes!

7.25

49. *Re King* (1998) 1 Legal Profession Disciplinary Reports (NSW) 11.
50. *In the matter of David Ferdynand Libling* (1998) 2 Legal Profession Disciplinary Reports 27.
51. See Pt 4.4.4 of the Legal Practice Act 2004 (Vic) and s 498 of the Legal Profession Act 2004 (NSW).
52. *Clyne v New South Wales Bar Association* (1960) 104 CLR 186 at 199.
53. *Bar Association of Queensland v Lamb* [1972] ALR 285.
54. J Disney, J Basten, P Redmond and S Ross, *Lawyers*, 2nd ed (1986), p 332 cites *Battachayra v General Medical Council* [1967] AC 259 (Privy Council) to support this point. See also *Medical Board of Queensland v Martin* (2000) 2 Qld R 129.

7.26   Although there is little authority finding that having a sexual relationship or sexually harassing a client is misconduct, such action may be seen as falling under the broader category of conflict of interest and can lead to breach of fiduciary duty. An example of the latter was an American case where the lawyer obtained confidential information on the client's emotional and psychological state, then used that information to convince her to have sexual relations.[55]

7.27   There is thus a sound argument that lawyers' professional independent judgment will be affected because of their personal interest. Furthermore, their client will probably be placed under additional emotional stress, and they are breaching their fiduciary duty and are abusing their position of trust.[56] This is what occurred in a recent South Australian case where the practitioner, Ms Morel, was struck off for entering into several personal relationships with prisoners she represented. The Full Supreme Court pointed out that her client 'did not receive the independent legal advice that he needed. The confidentiality of his disclosures to his solicitor was compromised'. The court concluded that: 'The technical competence of Ms Morel ... is not the subject of complaint. What makes her unfit to practise is an apparent and continuing failure to discern the barrier between professional and personal relationships, to the detriment of her clients and her integrity as a legal practitioner.'[57] Many in the profession would still think that there is nothing wrong with having a sexual relationship with a client. The former president of the New South Wales Law Society, John Marsden, when questioned about such relationships, in his defamation action against Channel 7, said: 'A lot of my sexual partners have been clients of mine — one way or another.' He then said: 'There's nothing unethical about that' (having a sexual relationship with someone he was at the same time representing).[58]

7.28   In 1996 the Council of the Law Society of New South Wales narrowly rejected by an 11:9 vote (secret ballot) moves to adopt a specific professional conduct rule under which legal practitioners could be disciplined. It stated that practitioners in the course of their practice must not discriminate against any person and must not sexually harass a colleague, staff member, client or other person. Instead, the Council adopted a non-binding resolution which condemned:

> ... all forms of harassment and discrimination against any person on the basis of race, sex, marital status, political belief, sexual orientation or perceived sexual orientation, religion or ethical belief, mental or physical disability or the person's association with, or relation to, a person identified on the basis of any of the above.

The resolution did point out that behaviour detailed above could constitute 'professional misconduct' or 'unsatisfactory professional conduct'. The resolution did not satisfy many women lawyers and the Women Lawyers' Association resolved to press the society to adopt a specific

---

55.   This happened in *Tante v Herring* 264 Ga 694, 453 S.E.2d 686 (1994). The lawyer was suspended for 18 months.
56.   See L Akenson, 'Solicitor/Client Sexual Relations — An Abuse of Power' (1995) 69 *Law Institute J* (Vic) 450.
57.   *Legal Practitioners Board v Morel* [2004] SASC 168 at paras 45 and 50.
58.   *Sydney Morning Herald*, 17 June 2000, p 3.

professional conduct rule.[59] The move to adopt a specific conduct rule resulted from a report by Keys Young, *Gender Bias and the Law*,[60] which showed widespread sexual harassment and discrimination against women. The New South Wales Bar Council had in June 1995 adopted a similar resolution, later adopted by the Law Society.

Pressure continued from various women legal groups to have binding rules. In late 1999 a general regulation was adopted prohibiting legal practitioners from engaging in any conduct 'that constitutes unlawful discrimination (including unlawful sexual harassment) under the Anti-Discrimination Act 1977 against any person'.[61] The provision was extended in 2005 to interstate practitioners for actions in New South Wales and to local practitioners for actions in other jurisdictions.[62] In Victoria the Bar Association adopted sexual harassment regulations in 1999. By contrast, in Queensland a committee of the Law Society found 'substantial and ongoing sexual harassment' in the profession. The committee recommended that the Solicitors' Practice Rules be amended to have sexual harassment constitute professional misconduct. The finding of 'sexual harassment' and the recommended rule change were both rejected by the Queensland Law Society.[63] In March 2004 the Law Council of Australia issued a 'Model Equal Opportunity Briefing Policy for Female Barristers and Advocates' to overcome the bias against female advocates.

7.29

None of the above resolutions or proposed rules and regulations in New South Wales specifically deals with having a sexual relationship with a client. This is an area that is rapidly developing in the United States. In 1992 the ABA adopted Formal Opinion 92-364 which states:

7.30

> A sexual relationship between lawyer and client may involve unfair exploitation of the lawyer's fiduciary position, and/or significantly impair a lawyer's ability to represent the client competently, and therefore may violate both the ABA Model Rules of Professional Conduct and the Model Code of Professional Responsibility.

In 2002, r 1.8 of the ABA Model Rules of Professional Conduct was amended. Rule 1.8(j) states that: 'A lawyer shall not have sexual relations with a client unless a consensual sexual relationship existed between them when the client–lawyer relationship commenced.' Although a prior relationship is exempt, Comment [18] warns the lawyer that he or she 'should consider whether the lawyer's ability to represent the client will be materially limited by the relationship. See Rule 1.7(a)(2) [conflict of interest]'. Comment [19] prohibits a lawyer working for an organisation from 'having a sexual relationship with a constituent of the organization who supervises, directs or regularly consults with that lawyer concerning the organization's legal matters'.

---

59. *Justinian*, May 1996, p 4.
60. Department for Women, New South Wales Government, 1995.
61. Now found in cl 141 of the Legal Profession Regulations 2002.
62. Legal Profession Regulation 2005 cl 176.
63. *Courier-Mail*, Brisbane, 4 September 1998.

Some critics of the new ABA r 1.8(j) feel that the conflict of interest rule and the confidentiality rule can deal with any dangers,[64] but a number of states have adopted r 1.8(j) as part of their ethical code. In some states the State Supreme Court has issued rules prohibiting sexual relations similar to the ABA rule and a number of states, even before the adoption of r 1.8(j), had specific rules regulating lawyer–client sexual relations. A number of states had adopted complete bans on such relationships except if they existed before the commencement of the professional relationship.[65] Two of these states, Wisconsin and Minnesota, have the best rule because of the clear definition of sexual relations. It is defined as being 'sexual intercourse or any other intentional touching of the intimate parts of a person or causing the person to touch intimate parts of the lawyer'. The rule in both states also includes situations where the client initiates the relationship and covers organisational clients.

7.31   In 1989 California became the first state to have a law that permitted its Bar Association to regulate these sexual relations.[66] The bar later enacted Professional Conduct Rule 3-120. This rule prohibits sexual relations between a lawyer and a client. The definition is broad and similar to the one in Wisconsin and Minnesota. The Californian rule is different since it does not ask for a total ban. Rule 3-120 (B)(3) states: 'A member shall not; … continue representation of a client with whom the member has sexual relations if such sexual relations cause the member to perform legal services incompetently …'.

There is a similar provision under ABA Model Rule 1.7(b), which deals with conflicts of interest. It allows the lawyer to act if he or she can continue to act in a 'professional manner'. Under this rule it is lawyers who make the decision to continue to act according to their 'reasonable beliefs' that the representation is not 'adversely affected'. The Californian rule is more effective since it applies a general objective standard and not a subjective 'reasonable beliefs' one. The problem with the Californian rule is that it does not clearly enunciate what actions would result in a breach. Lack of competency can be broadly defined as leading to a complete ban as it can be argued such a relationship will always interfere with a lawyer's abilities to perform skilfully. It can also be interpreted narrowly and not find a breach because the lawyer acted competently but in reality not in the best interests of the client. Thus the vagueness of the rule has made it too difficult to apply and enforce.[67]

7.32   The legislation in California and elsewhere may affect scriptwriters. Many Hollywood films show lawyer characters acting for their lovers or becoming

---

64.   See L Mischler, 'Reconciling Rapture, Representation, and Responsibility: An Argument Against per se Bans on Attorney–Client Sex' (1997) 10 *Georgetown J of Legal Ethics* 209.

65.   These states are Iowa, Minnesota, Oregon, North Carolina, West Virginia, Utah and Wisconsin. This information comes from M Eckhause, 'A chastity belt for lawyers: proposed MRPC 1.8(k) and the regulation of attorney–client sexual relationships' (1997) 75 *University of Detroit Mercy LR* 115; A Award, 'Attorney–Client Sexual Relations' (1998) 22 *The Journal of the Legal Profession* 131; and from S Ross, 'Sex, lawyers and ethics', October (1998) *Law Institute J (Vic)* 38.

66.   California Business and Professions Code s 6106.9.

67.   Eckhause (above), p 138.

lovers while representing someone. For example, in *Jagged Edge* (1985) Glenn Close plays a lawyer having an affair with her client while defending a man charged with murdering his wife. During the trial her representation is hampered because of her knowledge of her client's affairs with other women.[68]

Women lawyers are invariably portrayed by filmmakers as 'looking for love in all the wrong places'.[69] The use of sex by women lawyers is a major theme in a number of films. It is one of the ways for them to get a better job. The implication is that they are manipulative, power hungry and possibly incompetent, that is, they couldn't get the job except for their sexuality. The female lawyer (Greta Scacchi) in *Presumed Innocent* is a character who had her whole career based on using sex to get to the top. The lawyer in *The Verdict* (Charlotte Rampling) left her position in a prominent Boston law firm to get married. Now that the marriage has ended she wants her job back. The firm is involved in defending a large negligence action and needs information on the strategy and witnesses of the plaintiff's lawyer (Paul Newman). The senior partner, (James Mason), is willing to oblige and offers her the job back and financial payment but only if she is willing to start a romantic sexual relationship with the plaintiff's lawyer to elicit the needed information.[70]

Jagged Edge and other similar films highlight some of the arguments for a ban on sleeping with clients. These relationships almost invariably result in breaches of the rules governing confidentiality and conflict of interest. The arguments for the ban, which are present in these films and go beyond the films, are: **7.33**

❑ the client is sometimes in a vulnerable position both emotionally and economically and easily coerced or unduly influenced into a sexual relationship;

❑ lawyers need to remain detached and objective in representing a client;

❑ sexual relations with a client can lead to incompetent legal services;

❑ there is an imbalance in the relationship because lawyers are in a position of authority.[71]

If the activities of Arnold Becker, the philandering divorce lawyer in *LA Law*, are any indication, sexual relations between lawyers and clients in divorce cases often occur in the United States.[72]

It appears that in the United States sexual relationships with a client can lead to suspension from practice but not disbarment. In a case in Georgia a lawyer was suspended for three years despite the fact that the sexual   **7.34**

---

68. For another film where a female lawyer becomes too emotionally involved, but not sexually involved, with her client, see Rebecca DeMornay in *Guilty as Sin* (1993).

69. P Bergman and M Asimow, *Reel Justice: The Courtroom goes to the Movies*, Andrews and McMeel, Kansas City, 1996, pp 90–3. A second edition of this book will be published in 2006. For another account of the role of women lawyers in film and a discussion of the favourable view of female lawyers in television, see M Asimow and S Mader, *Law and Popular Culture*, Peter Lang, New York, 2004, pp 185–90.

70. Bergman and Asimow (above), pp 217 and 304.

71. For a detailed analysis of the problem see J O'Connell, 'Keeping Sex Out of the Attorney–Client Relationship: A Proposed Rule' (1992) 92 *Columbia Law R* 887 and M Livingston, 'When Libido Subverts Credo: Regulation of Attorney–Client Sexual Relations' (1993) 62 *Fordham LR* 5. Also see the arguments and cases that are attached to ABA *Formal Opinion* 92-364.

72. See Akenson (above), p 451.

relationship began before there was a lawyer–client relationship. Perhaps this was because it was a divorce case where the client's case could be adversely affected in matters of custody, alimony and so on.[73] A number of jurisdictions exempt people who are married or if they had an ongoing relationship before entering into a lawyer–client relationship. In a case in Colorado, a lawyer defending a husband and wife initiated a sexual relationship with the wife. He also had other misconduct and was disbarred on the grounds of conflict of interest.[74] In a more recent Arizona case the lawyer in a domestic relations matter made inquiries concerning his client's sexual conduct, asked to see her breasts prior to a planned breast augmentation surgery and embraced her a number of times. He admitted to his actions. He was found to have violated the conflict of interest rule and was censured and made to pay costs.[75] A Virginian lawyer was suspended for two years for having sexual relations with a young client whom he set up in an apartment and employed as a legal assistant, while representing her in divorce proceedings.[76] In a more serious matter a public defender, Theresa Olson, was found by the prison guards having sexual relations with a client accused of a triple murder. She was removed from the case causing further delays in a trial that had already been delayed for six years. She had been representing him for two years and denied the charges saying she was only hugging him. She was suspended from practice for two years. Two of the judges dissented because of the lack of evidence of actual sexual intercourse.[77] Finally, there have been suggestions that lawyers who become involved with clients should face possible criminal sanctions.[78]

7.35 We may be entering an era where many lawyers will seek to have a secretary present or their door ajar when they are interviewing clients. This may cause some concern and be a blockage for clients who need to speak about sensitive issues. The Law Council of Australia may need to adopt a specific rule in the Model Rules concerning sexual relationships with clients. In my view, clients come to lawyers when they have a problem that they need professional help to deal with or solve. They are thus in a vulnerable position and should not have to be confronted with any kind of sexual pressure. They need to feel secure and be able to completely trust the lawyer. The problems of vulnerability are even more serious in the area of family law. There is an urgent need for an adoption of a complete ban on such relationships in this area. This could be done by the profession or by an order from the Family Law Court.

---

73. *Re Lewis* 415 SE 2d 173 at 174–6 (Georgia 1992).
74. *People v Gibbons* 685 P2d 168 (Colo 1984).
75. *In re Moore* 2002 Ariz. Lexis 36 (Ariz. March 5, 2002) cited in www.ethicsandlawyering. Com/Issues/0402.htm.
76. *In the Matter of Everett Michael Myers*, VSB Docket No 98-010-1787 (18 February 2000), cited and discussed in B Williams, 'Sex, Lies and Bar Complaints', *Virginia Lawyer Register*, November 2001, p 1. This article cites a number of other cases in Virginia.
77. See G Johnson, 'Lawyer Banned for Sex Incident', *Seattle Post-Intelligencer*, 9 September 2002 and G Johnson, 'State Supreme Court suspends Theresa Olson for two years', *Seattle Post-Intelligencer*, 7 April 2005. See also report from staff and news services 'Lawyer accused of sex with client suspended for two years', *Seattle Post-Intelligencer*, 8 April 2005, www.seattlepi.com.
78. L Langford Jr, 'Criminalising Attorney–Client Relations: Toward Substantive Enforcement' (1995) 73 *Texas LR* 1223.

Other ethical violations

The new category of unsatisfactory professional conduct has also given the   **7.36**
Administrative Decisions Tribunal in New South Wales flexibility to create
new ethical violations. For example, a barrister, who had not been cited for
contempt of court by a judge for being rude and arrogant, and for making
'reckless allegations' in court, was still found to have committed
unsatisfactory professional conduct. The tribunal said each case would have
to be looked at on its own to see if the behaviour constituted unsatisfactory
professional conduct.[79] This approach to defining the new category allows
the tribunal to exercise considerable discretion and may be unfair because it
does not give any clear guidelines to members of the profession. The
tribunal did state in this case that, generally, contempt of court could
amount to unsatisfactory professional conduct. It would seem inconsistent if
a practitioner is found in contempt and then not disciplined, while a
practitioner who has not been held in contempt is disciplined.

In a more recent Australian Capital Territory case a practitioner had
executed a certificate that he had explained documents to his clients. It was
found by the Professional Conduct Board he had falsely certified receiving a
memorandum and allowed the clients to sign the certificate. The Board
found him guilty of unsatisfactory professional conduct for bringing the
profession into disrepute. The Australian Capital Territory Supreme Court
on appeal upheld the Board's finding stating that there was no need to make
a finding of fraudulent intent.[80]

CONDUCT OUTSIDE PROFESSIONAL PRACTICE

Introduction

In the past, disciplining Australian lawyers for what they do in their private   **7.37**
lives was unusual. The professional associations in all jurisdictions, under
their power to issue annual practising certificates, can refuse, cancel or
suspend a practising certificate for a criminal conviction involving moral
turpitude, and in almost all jurisdictions for bankruptcy. There was
uncertainty in the past as to the power of disciplinary tribunals to hear
complaints for personal misconduct[81] but in recent times legislation has
given them this power.[82] The courts have the discretion to stay or not
invoke the disciplinary jurisdiction, until criminal proceedings are resolved.
It is unclear when the discretion should be exercised but Wootten J has
given certain guidelines in relation to civil matters (disciplinary matters).[83]
His Honour said that there is a prima facie right for a plaintiff to have his or

---

79. *New South Wales Bar Association v di Suvero* [2000] NSWADT 5 May 2000. The costs
    were awarded against di Suvero. The parties negotiated a compromise settlement of the
    costs while the case was on appeal. During the appeal process di Suvero retired from the
    profession.
80. *PG v Law Society of the ACT* [2004] ACTSC 99.
81. Disney et al (above), pp 327–8.
82. See, for example, ss 497 and 498 of the Legal Profession Act 2004 (NSW) and Pts 4.4.3
    and 4.4.4 of the Legal Profession Act 2004 (Vic).
83. See the guidelines adopted by Wootten J in *McMahon v Gould* (1982) 7 ACLR 202.
    Riley refers to this case and others: see Riley n 36 (above), para 3360.

her action tried and thus the burden is on the defendant to show 'that it is just and convenient that the plaintiff's ordinary rights should be interfered with'. There is no absolute right of the Crown or an accused to have a civil action 'stayed because of a pending or possible criminal proceeding'. Courts will have to strike a balance between the parties. Factors that are relevant will include examining whether or not there is a 'real and not merely notional danger' of injustice in the criminal case. This can occur if, for example, the person will be prejudiced in the criminal hearing by information revealed in the disciplinary one. The judge has to be sensitive to an accused's 'right of silence' in the criminal case, which may not be present or appropriate in the disciplinary matter. In the United States the judiciary has not hesitated in serious situations to initiate disbarment proceedings before and even in the middle of a lawyer's criminal trial.[84]

7.38   While disciplinary or criminal proceedings are underway the professional association has the power to suspend or refuse to reissue a practitioner's practising certificate. If the association denies a practitioner his or her certificate, an order can be sought to have the certificate granted while the matter is brought to a conclusion. A court hearing such a matter will look at all the circumstances, including how long a delay is involved before the disciplinary proceeding is to be heard, and on occasion will grant the practitioner a certificate.[85] There are now new provisions in Victoria[86] and New South Wales[87] that allow an application to the tribunal for an order cancelling or imposing conditions on a practising certificate when criminal proceedings are pending against a practitioner.

Types of personal misconduct

7.39   What kind of personal misconduct will lead to disciplinary action? In the United States political activities considered to be subversive have at times led to disbarment,[88] but Australia has been far more tolerant of its lawyers. Cases throughout the common law world indicate a tolerance for being fined, or paying for prostitutes, but allow disciplinary action for being involved in running a brothel. In an old English case, owning a house used as a brothel was enough to be struck off the rolls.[89] More recently, in 1992, a New South Wales solicitor was only reprimanded for being guilty of running a brothel, for making a misleading application, and using false names in opening and running a bank account. Cripps JA said that if all that had been established was that he ran a brothel he would have dismissed the summons.[90] A barrister was struck off in 1950 for consorting with known

---

84.   *Medrano* 956 F 2d 101 at 102 (5th Cir 1992). The lower court had disbarred the lawyer but the decision was reversed because the court had applied the 'clear and convincing' standard instead of the 'preponderance of evidence' one.
85.   See *In the matter of Cummings No 2; Re Legal Practitioners Act 1981* [1999] SASC 79.
86.   Part 2.4.16 of the Legal Profession Act (Vic) 2004.
87.   Section 51 of the Legal Profession Act (NSW) 2004.
88.   *Re Smith* 233 P 288 (1925) (disbarment for sympathetically addressing the International Workers of the World); *Re Margolis* 112 A 478 (1921) (disbarment for advocating anarchism and for avoiding the draft).
89.   *Re Weare* [1893] 2 QB 439.
90.   The other two judges agreed with the judgment of Cripps JA in *Prothonotary of the Supreme Court of NSW v Chapman* (14 December 1992, unreported). See also J Slee, 'Ins and Outs of Legal Practice', *Sydney Morning Herald*, 15 January 1993, p 10.

criminals,[91] although never charged or convicted of the allegation. The Victorian Supreme Court has held that the bankruptcy of a solicitor is not by itself a sufficient ground for striking off,[92] but it can be used as an excuse for suspending, cancelling or not issuing a practising certificate and for removal of a practitioner as a trustee of estates.[93] In recent years, there has been throughout Australia more thorough reporting requirements for lawyers who have become bankrupt.[94] Professional bodies have become more willing to suspend, cancel or not issue a practising certificate in these cases. If the bankruptcy was in order to avoid paying income tax, disciplinary actions have been instituted. In fact, a number of barristers in New South Wales have been struck off for income tax violations.[95]

The majority of a Western Australian disciplinary tribunal in 1996 found a practitioner guilty of unprofessional conduct for being involved in an organisation, and deriving financial benefit from its activities, which ran 'various parties known as rave parties'. A 'significant number (or, to use the practitioner's words, up to 40 per cent) of people attending such parties used illegal drugs in connection with their attendance'. The majority concluded that:[96]

> For a legal practitioner to organise for financial gain an activity which is, to a substantial degree, associated with drug use is not conduct in which a legal practitioner ought to partake.

Violent activities

In *The Law Society of South Australia v Le Poidevin*,[97] the Law Society sought to have a practitioner struck off for being guilty of offences of threatening to endanger life and for committing a common assault. The court said that there was 'no doubt that the practitioner's conduct amounted to a serious departure from a standard of behaviour acceptable for a member of an honourable profession'. It decided not to strike him off and only to suspend him from practice for two years because he had 'not been guilty of dishonesty'. The court said that the 'conduct complained of has been largely due to his inability to control his temper in circumstances which he found stressful. These proceedings are a clear reminder that the practitioner must guard his tongue and watch his conduct'. The court can be criticised for emphasising that primarily 'dishonesty' should be the grounds for disbarment.

7.40

---

91. *Re Foster* (1950) 50 SR (NSW) 149.
92. *Re a Solicitor* [1933] VLR 103 at 106.
93. *Howes v Law Society of Tasmania*, 18 September 1998 FCA 106/97, BC9804770.
94. For example, see cls 134–135 Legal Profession Regulation 2002 (NSW). The Legal Profession Amendment (Disciplinary Provisions) Act 2001 (NSW) made it mandatory for all practitioners to disclose to the professional associations any acts of bankruptcy and convictions for indictable offences or tax offences.
95. See *NSW Bar Association v Hamman* [1999] NSWCA 404 (understatement of income, sentenced to 14 months periodic detention); *NSW Bar Association v Somosi* [2001] NSWCA 285 (failed to file a return for 17 years); *NSW Bar Association v Cummins* [2001] NSWCA 284 (failed to file a return for 38 years); and *NSW Bar Association v Young* [2003] NSWCA 228 (failed to file a return for 16 years).
96. The matter is reported by the Registrar of the Tribunal in (1996) 23 *Brief* (Law Society of WA) 45.
97. [1998] SASC 7014.

By comparison with this case a solicitor, whose violence was more extreme, was struck off in *Law Society of New South Wales v McKean*.[98] The solicitor had been convicted of two counts of maliciously inflicting bodily harm with intent. He had stabbed his estranged de facto wife and one of her children, a five-year-old girl. The judge had found no provocation. The solicitor had spent three years in gaol and had long-term and ongoing psychiatric treatment. The tribunal pointed out in its determination that it was significant that the solicitor did not tender any evidence from his psychiatrist.

Personal dishonesty

7.41 An example of dishonesty outside of practice occurred in a more recent New South Wales case. A barrister was struck off the rolls for falsely swearing an affidavit with intent to mislead the Family Law Court in a matter in which he was a party. The court emphasised that the tribunal was clearly entitled to conclude that the barrister knowingly and falsely swore the affidavit.[99] A similar charge was brought against former President Bill Clinton for giving misleading evidence while under oath about Monica Lewinsky during the Paula Jones sexual harassment case.[100] The matter was referred to the Arkansas Supreme Court Committee on Professional Conduct with a recommendation that Clinton be disbarred. Before it was heard Clinton reached an agreement with the Arkansas Bar where he admitted that he had 'knowingly made false statements' that were 'prejudicial to the administration of justice'. Clinton also agreed to accept a $25,000 fine and a five-year suspension from practice.[101]

7.42 What if the Australian Tax Office makes a mathematical mistake in issuing a legal practitioner an assessment order — what should the practitioner do? The Deputy Commissioner issued a writ out of the Australian Capital Territory Supreme Court against a Canberra lawyer, Chamberlain. As a result of a clerical error the decimal point was moved one place and the amount became $25,557.92 instead of $255,579.20, which was the assessment made against the taxpayer. The writ was served and Chamberlain agreed to pay the mistaken amount. He then wrote to the Commissioner removing any objections to the assessment because of the negotiated settlement. The Commissioner later found the mistake and issued a writ for the unpaid balance which was unsuccessful in a number of actions because of Chamberlain's defence of res judicata.

  The Australian Capital Territory Law Society then brought charges in the Australian Capital Territory Supreme Court for professional misconduct. The Law Society alleged that Chamberlain had induced 'another to act on a mistake' to his 'own advantage'. The court by a 2:1 judgment found professional misconduct and Chamberlain was suspended from practice for six months and had to pay the Law Society's costs.[102] On appeal the Full

98. [1999] NSWADT 55.
99. *Coe v New South Wales Bar Association* [2000] NSWCA 13.
100. 'Panel Seeks December hearing over Clinton Disbarment', *Associated Press Release*, 5 September 2000.
101. D Rhode and D Luban, *Legal Ethics*, 4th ed, Foundation Press, New York, 2004, pp 258–9 and 261.
102. *Re Law Society of the ACT and Chamberlain* (1993) 116 ACTR 31.

Federal Court upheld the finding of professional misconduct because of his failure to communicate the mistake to the ATO (a fellow practitioner). It lowered the penalty because his conduct was at the 'lower end of the scale of professional misconduct' and was an isolated incident and out of character. Instead of being suspended he was given a reprimand.[103]

Commission of a felony

It was assumed at one time that conviction for a felony would automatically lead to striking off. This problem was looked at in the case of a barrister found guilty of involuntary manslaughter. In the *Ziems* case[104] a barrister had killed a motorcyclist while driving under the influence of alcohol. He was imprisoned for two years. The Supreme Court in striking him off declined to investigate the details of the action taken. They held it was incongruous for a barrister to be a person serving a sentence for a serious crime. The High Court by a 3:2 decision (Kitto, Fullagar and Taylor JJ) reversed the lower court decision by suspending him from practice during the term of imprisonment. The court decided by 3:2 (Dixon J joining two members of the majority) that it was appropriate to look at the circumstances of the offence and to examine in detail the trial of the barrister. Kitto J said at 297:

7.43

> ... it will be generally agreed that there are many kinds of conduct deserving disapproval, and many kinds of convictions of breaches of law, which do not spell unfitness for the bar, and to draw the dividing line is by no means always an easy task.

His Honour argued that there was no need to look at details of the trial but that the offence was an isolated one and:

> ... does not warrant any conclusion as to the man's general behaviour or inherent qualities ... It is not a conviction of a premeditated crime. It does not indicate a tendency to vice or violence, or any lack of probity. It has neither connection with nor significance for any professional function.

Fullagar J in his judgment stated:

> Personal misconduct, as distinct from professional misconduct, may no doubt be grounds for [disbarment] ... But the whole approach of a court to a case of personal misconduct must surely be very different from its approach to a case of professional misconduct. Generally speaking, the latter must have a much more direct bearing on the question of a man's fitness in practice than the former.

Fullagar J found that the barrister had been placed at a material disadvantage in the manslaughter trial because of the Crown's refusal to call a key police officer and a misdirection to the jury. By looking at these facts he said it was impossible to justify a finding that Ziems was an unfit and improper person.[105]

7.44

More recently the Western Australian Supreme Court stated that the Legal Practitioners Act 1893, s 31AA does not prohibit an inquiry as to the propriety of a practitioner's conviction. The tribunal still held that the conviction was correct. Although there had been some unsatisfactory aspects of the trial for theft of and fraudulent sale of a motor vehicle, they

---

103. *Chamberlain v ACT Law Society* (1993) 118 ALR 54.
104. *Ziems v Prothonotary of the Supreme Court of New South Wales* (1957) 97 CLR 279.
105. *Ziems* (above) at 288.

were insufficient to bring the jury's verdict into doubt. The Supreme Court refused to disturb this finding of the tribunal.[106]

7.45 The High Court judgment in the *Ziems* case is consistent with the criteria applied in the admission cases. The court shows that the past behaviour, reputation and especially the intent of the practitioner in the misdeed under investigation, would all be looked at before an order was made. Therefore, for example, in *Ziems* the *mens rea* element was not present, as he had committed an involuntary act. This was important to the court in reaching its decision. In contrast, in *Prothonotary of the Supreme Court of NSW v Pangello*,[107] a solicitor who was convicted of bribing a public officer was struck off the rolls because there was no doubt in the mind of the court that he had intended this action.

Income tax cases

7.46 In a very different tax case from the *Chamberlain* case, a barrister who pleaded guilty to five charges of falsely understating his income in income tax returns was struck off. Unlike *Chamberlain* this practitioner had shown 'significant and prolonged dishonesty for personal gain'. Although the barrister had demonstrated genuine contrition the court felt he should be struck off but did state 'that the door to readmission is never closed'.[108] A number of other barristers have also been struck off for failure to file their tax returns and/or concealing their income[109] and some had their practising certificates suspended because of taxation violations. In the *Murphy* case[110] the barrister had his practising certificate reinstated even though he had failed to lodge returns for several years and had gone into bankruptcy. The Court of Appeal found that Murphy was 'wrong to have taken advice to delay filing his taxation returns and should have addressed his situation earlier and filed for bankruptcy when his position was obviously hopeless, he should also have made more taxation payments ...'. The court accepted Murphy's acknowledgment that he had been wrong and that he should have addressed his financial situation at an earlier time. Furthermore, Murphy, unlike some of the barristers in other cases, did not attempt to conceal or understate his income or to avoid his tax obligations. By looking at all the circumstances the court found that there was not a sufficient deficiency in character or competence as a legal practitioner to remove his practising certificate. He was held to be a fit and proper person.[111]

The Bar Association appeared to be lenient to some of the barristers who had been suspended and they were reinstated within a year of their suspension. The then President of the New South Wales Bar Association, Brett Walker SC, when asked about the rapid reinstatement said: 'I take the view, that there is joy in the repentance of sinners.' The *Sydney Morning Herald* editorial commenting on his statement said: 'This facetiousness may go down well with other barristers, but it will hardly impress the public.' It

106. *Mullally v Legal Practitioners Complaints Committee* [1997] 250 WA 1.
107. (1993) 75 A Crim R 77.
108. *New South Wales Bar Association v Hamman* [1999] NSWCA 404.
109. See *NSW Bar Association v Somosi* [2001] NSWCA 285; *NSW Bar Association v Young* [2003] NSWCA 228; and *NSW Bar Association v Cummins* [2001] NSWCA 284.
110. *NSW Bar Association v Murphy* [2002] NSWCA 138.
111. Ibid, paras 157–8 and 171–2.

was unclear whether the barristers had cleared up their tax debts but they were reinstated because they had demonstrated, according to Mr Walker, 'insights into previous shortcomings' and a 'willingness and a capacity to do things differently in the future'. The editorial stated that the actions of the Bar Association brought the system of professional self-regulation into disrepute and perhaps it needed to be reconsidered.[112]

Other convictions

Lawyers have been disbarred for drug convictions[113] and for sexual child offences.[114] The latter offence was the basis for the most important recent case in this area. The New South Wales Court of Appeal[115] heard the case because of procedural problems in bringing it before the disciplinary tribunal. In exercising its inherent jurisdiction the Court of Appeal decided that the solicitor should be struck off for his conviction on four counts of aggravated indecent assault on two minors and for his lack of candour in not reporting a second conviction to the Law Society that occurred while he was under investigation by the Society. The solicitor was not named in order to keep unknown the identity of the two young girls who had been witnesses in the criminal action: s 11 of the Children (Criminal Proceedings) Act 1987.

7.47

The candour issue was important in this case. After the Law Society had lodged a complaint there were further charges against him by one of the girls. He was found guilty of the charges even though he denied the allegations and there was strong evidence from his wife and the other daughter that the alleged actions could not have occurred. On appeal these convictions were quashed. He failed to inform the Law Society of the new charges and convictions. His reasons were that he felt he was innocent and would win on appeal. There was evidence that he had the intention of keeping this information from the Law Society. It would appear that he was afraid that if he told the Society of this event his chances of being struck off would have dramatically increased.

The Court of Appeal felt that indecent assaults on minors was the kind of conduct that renders a solicitor unfit for practice and constitutes professional misconduct. Furthermore, the court felt that the solicitor lacked candour by not reporting the later convictions; that he had made a 'conscious decision not to disclose the convictions'. The court pointed out that the practitioner 'denied that he breached the duty of candour. That denial in itself indicates a failure to comprehend the duty of candour required of a solicitor when dealing with an investigation' of complaints made against him.[116]

7.48

In mitigation of his indecent actions the solicitor confessed promptly and fully to the allegations and helped the police in every way. Furthermore, at

112. Editorial, *Sydney Morning Herald*, 23 September 2003, p 12.
113. *Barristers' Board v Darveniza* (2000) 112 A Crim R 438.
114. *Barristers' Board v Pratt* [2002] QCA 532; *In re Boudreau* 815 So2d 76 (La 2002). In the latter case the lawyer had been sent to gaol for 21 years for bringing back from overseas explicit child pornography magazines.
115. *The Council of the Law Society of NSW v A Solicitor* [2002] NSWCA 62. The facts of the case set out in the text are taken from this judgment.
116. Ibid, at para 109.

that time he was under severe strain. He had lost his job as a solicitor and his father had just died. He also immediately went for psychiatric counselling. The psychiatrist testified that there was 'a great likelihood that such behaviour would never occur again'. The solicitor had excellent references from members of the profession and the incidents with his stepdaughters appear to have been an isolated case of deviant behaviour. The solicitor is now the stepfather of the two girls and father figure to them. He and his wife work in unskilled jobs with low incomes. He has lost his job as a solicitor and had to resign his position as a captain in the military reserve. The solicitor had to sell his only main asset, a unit, and used the equity to pay for the legal fees in defending the November 2000 allegations. In being struck off he had little chance to dramatically increase the income of the family. This is a case where inappropriate activity by a lawyer within the family context has resulted in not only punishment for himself but for the whole family.[117]

7.49   The High Court granted special leave in *A Solicitor v The Council of the Law Society of NSW*.[118] The judgment of the five judges upheld the finding of the Court of Appeals that the lack of candour and the indecent assaults combined constituted professional misconduct. The solicitor was not a fit and proper person to be a legal practitioner. The High Court rejected the separate finding that the appellant's indecent assaults constituted professional misconduct at common law. The court said that they 'did not occur in the course of the practice of his profession, and [they] had no connexion with such practice'. The court added that 'the nature of the trust, and the circumstances of the breach, were so remote from anything to do with professional practice that the characterisation of the appellant's personal misconduct as professional misconduct was erroneous'.[119] The High Court referred to the principle in *Ziems* that it was necessary to examine 'the whole position'.[120] The court thus decided that the facts did not warrant the solicitor being struck off but rather only being suspended. Since the solicitor had not had a practising certificate for five years the court considered that this period was a more than adequate penalty and held that the order removing his name from the roll be set aside.[121]

The High Court's decision was severely criticised. Ackland said: '[A]ccording to the reasoning of the High Court, it is far, far worse not to be candid with the Law Society, or even not to pay tax, than it is to be overly intimate with children.'[122] In writing about the Court of Appeal's decision, I said: 'On reading this decision I became very sad. I have advocated severe punishments for members of the profession who in their private lives violate common ethical standards ... The commission of any serious crime should lead to a sanction. I do not condone the solicitor's behaviour but sometimes there is a need for compassion and mercy ... The image of the profession

117. See Y Ross, 'Lack of candour cost solicitor livelihood', *Australian Financial Review*, 28 June 2002, p 59.
118. [2004] HCA 1.
119. [2004] HCA 1 at paras 32–34.
120. Ibid, at para 18.
121. Ibid, at paras 40–41.
122. R Ackland, 'The High Court and an indecent order of values', *Sydney Morning Herald*, 6 February 2004, p 11.

needs to be protected, but I believe that this was a case that warranted some mercy and a suspension from practise for several years would have been a sufficient sanction.'[123]

MITIGATING FACTORS

Certain mitigating factors will justify a reduction in severity of the sanction imposed. These include whether or not there is a record of prior disciplinary breaches, community and professional reputation, cooperation with the disciplinary authorities, willingness to accept that misconduct had been committed and the demeanour of the practitioner during the proceedings. Some practitioners argue substance abuse or mental illness to mitigate their actions but disciplinary authorities and the courts are hesitant in allowing such arguments unless it can be shown that this mitigating factor is sufficiently connected to the misconduct. The authorities cite that they must protect the public and the standing and reputation of the profession.[124] Lawyers face the problem that, by arguing they are not responsible for their actions because of substance abuse or mental illness (acting involuntarily), they reveal that they lack the ability to practise. Thus, this kind of mitig-ation argument may be used against the lawyer.

7.50

Mental illness

In the United States the ABA has recognised that chemical dependency and mental illness may be in the list of mitigating or aggravating factors in deciding what is the appropriate sanction to be imposed[125] and most courts have accepted chemical dependency as a mitigating factor.[126] Newman J said in *In re Kersey*[127] that 'when alcoholism has been a causal factor leading to professional misconduct, rehabilitation from that condition will be considered a significant factor in imposing discipline'. The judge concluded that 'the minimal deterence value of suspension upon other alcoholic attorneys is substantially outweighed by the likely salutary effect upon Kersey's continued rehabilitation that continuation of his professional career will have'. In light of the fact that revealing these habits can aggravate the situation, lawyers will often be hesitant about using such evidence. One lawyer, specialising in legal discipline cases, says he will only use such evidence if it is 'clear and convincing evidence that someone was operating in a fugue state'.[128]

7.51

In Australia there are a number of cases[129] that support this argument that such evidence must be carefully used to obtain mitigation. Hope J said,

7.52

---

123. Y Ross, 'Lack of candour cost solicitor livelihood' (above), p 59.
124. *Clyne v New South Wales Bar Association* (1960) 104 CLR 186 at 202.
125. ABA Standards, Sanctions Standards, 9.22, 9.32.
126. See B Workie, 'Chemical Dependency and the Legal Profession: Should Addiction to Drugs and Alcohol Ward Off Heavy Discipline?' (1996) 9 *Georgetown J of Legal Ethics* 1357, 1364.
127. 520 A2d 321 (CA, Dist of Columbia, 1987).
128. S Goldberg, 'Drawing the Line: When Is an Ex-coke Addict Fit to Practise Law' (1990) 76 *American Bar Association J* 49, 50.
129. See below.

when denying an appeal from the disciplinary tribunal of a striking off order:[130]

> ... although undoubtedly stress and health must have played a part in the solicitor's failings, those failings stretch over such a long period and are so repeated that I am unable to have any confidence that the public would be adequately protected ... Lawyers, and particularly those who appear regularly in courts, are continually subject to stress.

Goldberg had brought in psychiatric evidence to argue that his deficiencies in practice were in the past and that there would not be a recurrence of his previous failings. Hope J said that the psychiatrist's views were ambivalent in that the failings and deficiencies could be either due to temporary stress and ill health or maybe some more basic cause. His Honour took the view that the evidence suggested that the lapses stemmed 'from an essential unreliability and lack of responsibility'.[131]

7.53 In *Re The Legal Practitioners Act 1981; The Law Society of South Australia v Murphy*[132] a practitioner admitted unprofessional conduct which involved: failure to follow trust fund procedures; failure to communicate and to follow instructions; failure to reply to requests from the Complaints Committee and overcharging. The practitioner said that his conduct could be partly explained by 'depressive illness'. He requested that his offer to undertake not to practise law be accepted in substitution for being disbarred. Doyle CJ refused his request and said that 'the depression to which some of the conduct is attributable itself indicates that the practitioner is not presently fit to practise, and that there is no reason to think that the condition will be of short duration'.

Three more recent South Australian cases also refused to accept medical testimony of mental illness as an excuse. In *Legal Practitioners Board v Phillips* the court said:[133] 'Such a disorder may explain but does not excuse the practitioner's inappropriate attitude toward the client. The evidence provided did nothing to explain other aspects of the practitioner's misconduct, namely his dishonesty and lack of candour and frankness with the tribunal and the court. It does not explain his manipulation of the court process to obtain a personal advantage. It does little to explain why he retained a charge over the client's property when he was not entitled to do so.' In *Legal Practitioners Board v Hannaford* the court said:[134] 'Many practitioners are subjected to stress in their working lives. This is part of professional life. Practitioners must understand that personal stresses cannot ameliorate the seriousness with which professional obligations are viewed and need for strict compliance at all times. A practitioner's professional standards must not be compromised or eroded.' In *Legal Practitioners Conduct Board v Morel* (discussed above), Ms Morel tendered evidence that she had consulted a psychologist with LawCare, but the court found that her 'attempts at treatment appear to have led to little improvement'.[135]

---

130. *Goldberg v The Law Society of New South Wales* (CA (NSW)), (1991) 1 Legal Profession Disciplinary Reports 15, 28.
131. *Goldberg's* case (above).
132. [1999] SASC 83.
133. (2002) 83 SASR 467 at 475.
134. (2002) 83 SASR 277 at 281.
135. [2004] SASC 168 at para 63.

By contrast, the *Harrison* case[136] concerned a barrister who had failed to comply with 14 notices issued in relation to outstanding tax returns over the period 1982–94, and in 1995 he was convicted on 30 counts and sentenced to 200 hours community service. The New South Wales Legal Services Tribunal failed to find professional misconduct. Harrison admitted his behaviour was 'dreadful' and 'irrational'. He used evidence from a psychologist, which showed that he was suffering from depression, which had caused him to be irresponsible in relation to his financial affairs and his health. The tribunal found that Harrison had a psychological block about filing his tax returns. It was emphasised that his actions were not deliberate and the psychological problems had not affected his professional duties. The tribunal concluded that his inertia in relation to filing tax returns was therefore 'not relevant ... to a determination of those "enduring moral qualities" which constitute his intrinsic character'. I believe that the tribunal's view that Harrison's tax return block did not affect his professional duties is irrelevant to a finding of a breach of s 127 of the Legal Profession Act 1987 (now s 497(1)(b) of the Legal Profession Act 2004) for conduct outside of his professional practice. It can be used as an argument for diminishing the severity of the penalty but should not be the basis for finding no breach.[137] This has now been made clear under s 498 of the Legal Profession Act (NSW) 2004 where it is stated a conviction for a tax offence is capable of being unsatisfactory professional conduct or professional misconduct.

A recent case, *Law Society of Tasmania v Schouten*,[138] has some similarity to the *Harrison* case. The practitioner had a history of failing to file his tax return (1985–95) and failing to comply with orders to do so by the courts. He submitted doctor's evidence that he was 'suffering from a clinical depression which rendered him incapable of performing the tasks necessary to furnish the returns'. Cox CJ found that this taxation case was a result of inertia because of pressures and thus was different than the recent cases in New South Wales where the practitioners were motivated by a desire to cheat the revenue. Cox CJ stated: '[H]e has now, with medical assistance and counselling, improved his capacity to overcome [the inertia] ... I do not regard him at the present time as permanently unfit to practise ...'. The court did find that his conduct constituted professional misconduct at common law and approved of the Law Society limiting his right to practise only as an employed practitioner.[139]

---

136. *Bar Association of New South Wales v Harrison* (Legal Services Tribunal, June 1997, unreported).
137. There is another case were there was a criminal violation, prohibited importation of firearm parts and avoidance of customs duty, and the court held that the matter did not have any connection with the practitioner's legal practice and therefore did not reflect on his fitness to practise: *Re Kerin*, Supreme Court of South Australia, Full Court, November 1997, BC9706183. It should be noted that s 5 of the Legal Practitioners Act 1981 (SA) is much narrower than the provision in New South Wales. Under this section, to have a finding of 'unprofessional conduct' outside of practice there needs to be 'an offence of a dishonest or infamous nature ... which punishment by imprisonment is prescribed or authorised by law'.
138. [2003] TASSC 143.
139. Ibid, paras 22–24.

7.55   In *Himmelboch*, a Victorian barrister presented psychiatric evidence that he had a condition known as 'adult attention deficit disorder' which was exacerbated by an 'anxiety and depressive disorder'. O'Bryan J in rejecting the use of the striking off power took into account the mitigating circumstances of the barrister's psychological problems. He said that it was 'a grave step to find a person is not a fit and proper person to practise'. He upheld the tribunal's order of cancellation of his practising certificate and prevented him from applying for one year.[140]

7.56   The approach of O'Bryan J and the tribunal to cancel a practising certificate where there is a mental problem is also found in legislation. For example, Pt 2.4.20 of the Legal Profession Act 2004 (Vic) gives the Board the power to amend, cancel or suspend a local practising certificate if 'the holder is no longer a fit and proper person' and under Pt 2.2.4 not to issue a certificate if the Board finds the applicant is not a 'fit and proper person'. There needs to be satisfactory evidence that the practitioner is unfit to practise because of infirmity, injury or mental or physical illness and that it is in the public interest or interest of the barrister's or solicitor's clients that action be taken. Unfit to practise is found only if the practitioner's problem results in him or her being unable to carry out the inherent requirements of practice.

7.57   The cases show that psychiatric and medical evidence can be used to make a mitigation plea. It was also used by Davis to explain his behaviour when he was young, in his third readmission application[141] and by Moore, to explain his lack of disclosure of a bribe on applying for admission to the bar.[142] Both of these cases are discussed in Chapter 6. In several of the cases the use of such evidence was unsuccessful. In cases where it was successful it was because the practitioner's legal work was not affected, the practitioner had received successful treatment and in situations like *Himmelboch* because the judge felt that it was a 'grave step' to make a finding of 'not a fit and proper person to practise'. The decisions help to support the notion that Australian courts are hesitant but will at times accept psychiatric or psychological evidence as a mitigating factor. In the United States mental illness has been argued successfully as a mitigating factor in some cases[143] but not in others.[144] The American courts:[145]

---

140. *The Victorian Bar Incorporated v Himmelboch* [1999] VSC 222. See also Y Ross, 'Striking off the roll in Victoria', March (2000) *Law Institute J (Vic)* 39. The Court of Appeal in Queensland refused an appeal in the case of *Henry William Smith* by the Law Society to have a practitioner struck off who was suffering from a major depressive illness, the cause of his misconduct. The court upheld an order of the Statutory Committee suspending the practitioner until he could establish he was a fit and proper person to hold a practising certificate: *Bi-Annual Report of Disciplinary Action* (1998) 3 Supplement to *Proctor* 4.
141. See *Re Davis* [1962] NSWR 1110 at 1112ff.
142. *NSW Bar Association v Moore* (1994) 1 Legal Profession Disciplinary Reports, Supplement to *Law Society J (NSW)* 29.
143. For a discussion of various factors and cases involved in the area of mitigation, see J Wang, 'Improving Attorney Discipline' (1993) 6 *Georgetown J of Legal Ethics*, 1039, 1056–62. See, for an example of a successful case, *Re Wolf* 476 NW 2d 878 Wis 1991.
144. See, for example, *Re Bowers* 400 SE 2d 134 (S Carolina 1991).
145. Wang (above), p 1060; quoting the case of *Committee on Professional Ethics and Conduct v Robinson* 458 NW 2d 393 at 394 (Iowa 1990).

... seem willing to mitigate when there is clear medical evidence for the mental or emotional disability causing the misconduct, but seem less willing when the lawyer offers general stress, or depression as mitigating factors.

The American view seems similar to that in Australia; that a sufficient nexus is needed between the misconduct and the mental illness.

Chemical dependency

Psychiatric evidence can also be used in cases of chemical dependency; that is, dependency on drugs and alcohol. In Victoria a solicitor seeking admission, after being suspended in New Zealand due to alcoholism, used psychiatric evidence to show that he had overcome his drinking problems. He was admitted but granted only a limited practising certificate.[146] In the *Ziems* case (see **7.43–7.45**) the involuntary nature of the crime due to alcoholism helped Ziems to mitigate his punishment. The High Court emphasised that his misconduct occurred in his personal life and there was no evidence that it had affected his professional work.[147]   **7.58**

In Canada a lawyer who was addicted to cocaine and made defalcations from his trust account was only suspended for two years when he voluntarily revealed his habit. He was also required for five years after his reinstatement to remain under supervision, undergo random drug testing and have no authority to sign on the trust account.[148] The lawyer was impressed by the cooperation he received from the Law Society of Upper Canada (Ontario) and felt that he could advise other lawyers with substance habits that they could go with their problems to the Law Society.[149]   **7.59**

A similar matter occurred in South Australia. David Quick QC, a prominent practitioner, was charged with unprofessional conduct for the use of cocaine.[150] The Legal Profession Conduct Board ('the Board') alleged that Quick's actions constituted unprofessional conduct because: **7.60**

1. He committed an offence of an 'infamous nature' by taking injections of cocaine on at least nine occasions and heroin once on the mistaken belief it was cocaine;
2. The taking of the illegal drug affected Quick's 'ability to carry out his professional duties';
3. The practitioner breached an 'undertaking voluntarily given by him to the Board to make no further use of cocaine or any other illicit drugs'.

The evidence revealed that because of taking cocaine he missed a mediation in May 2001. On 26 June 2001, he took what he believed was cocaine but was in reality heroin and almost died. He was in intensive care

---

146. He was required to work as an employee solicitor. His case was found in the files of the Law Institute of Victoria during our research in 1975. See N Currall, 'The Cirrhosis of the Legal Profession — Alcoholism as an Ethical Violation or Disease' (1999) 12 *Georgetown J of Legal Ethics* 739.
147. *Ziems v Prothonotary of the Supreme Court of New South Wales* (1957) 97 CLR 279.
148. L Aisenberg, 'Staying Clean' (1990) 14(2) *Canadian Lawyer* 14.
149. Aisenberg (above), p 17.
150. I wrote a number of articles on this matter. See Y Ross, 'Lawyers, drugs and money: addressing substance abuse', *Australian Financial Review*, 6 December 2002; 'Coke disciplinary case lacks only a Quick decision', *Australian Financial Review*, 7 March 2003; 'QC's cocaine use a "victimless" offence', *Australian Financial Review*, 21 March 2003; and 'Cocaine a personal matter for commander', *Australian Financial Review*, 11 April 2003.

for a day and half and remained in a hospital for two more weeks. As a result he failed to appear in the Court of Criminal Appeal on 27 June. He missed two other professional commitments during the five years of using cocaine.

In early July 2001, Quick informed the Board of his cocaine habit and gave the Board an undertaking to refrain from taking cocaine or any other illicit drugs. He breached that undertaking 10 times from September 2001 until early May 2002.

Quick voluntarily ceased practice on 27 February 2002 but continued to do legal work for the Australian Defence Force. Quick was a commander in the Navy Reserve. From mid-July to August, while he was working in Canberra, it would appear for the Defence Force, on several occasions he took amphetamines. The Navy did not pursue any disciplinary action against him. In fact, it appears he was allowed to continue to do legal work for the Defence Force even after confessing to the use of cocaine. Quick did not resign his commission until 3 December 2002.

7.61 Two doctors and a psychologist, experts on substance abuse, testified and submitted reports. Their conclusions were generally that he was 'making great progress towards resolving his problem'. Dr Buttfield, a physician, said that Quick has 'never been addicted to the drugs cocaine or amphetamine, but there was an emotional dependence upon the process of taking cocaine'. He and Dr Gauvin, a psychiatrist, alleged that the emotional dependence that remained was stress that largely resulted from the failure of the tribunal to complete the proceedings. Dr Gauvin also said the delay in finalising the tribunal's decision had caused Quick to develop an 'Adjustment Disorder with Anxiety and Depression to a degree which has necessitated hospitalisation'.

Dr Gauvin said that Quick's cocaine use was the 'result of illness (depression) and not associated with intentionally using illicit drugs'. He said Quick had a problem with cocaine dependence, but not addiction. He said 'that if all control measures are in place, there is a 10 per cent chance' of Quick taking cocaine.

7.62 During the various hearings of the tribunal Quick accepted a six-month overseas academic position starting on 4 January 2003. Quick also made an apology to the profession and the Board; he undertook not to return to practice until 1 July 2003 and to submit himself to treatment by Dr Gauvin and Mr Minniti, and random urine testing by Dr Buttfield.

Quick admitted all the allegations but argued that the offence of taking cocaine was not 'an offence of an infamous nature'. The Legal Practitioners Tribunal, in its unpublished report of 17 March 2003, accepted Quick's submission. It looked at a number of cases which define 'infamous' and these cases say that it means 'shameful' or 'disgraceful'. For example, in *Le Poidevin*, behaviour of an infamous nature was found when the practitioner threatened to shoot someone and committed a common assault.

The tribunal said that in 'circumstances of this case, there is nothing particular in the facts that make the offence infamous'. The tribunal added that it was clear that Quick had committed offences under s 31(1)(b) of the Controlled Substances Act 1994, but that it was unaware of any previous decision that held that breach of that section amounted to commission of an offence of an infamous nature. '[The] relevant offence is victimless. It does not impact, per se, on any other person.' It concluded that in its opinion the actions of Quick did not constitute an offence of an infamous nature.

The tribunal also found that Quick is held in high regard by the profession and the judiciary. The tribunal referred to references from a number of judges, which established that Quick is 'hard working, honest, reliable, talented, personable, trustworthy, dedicated, passionate, conscientious, warm, friendly, courteous and honourable and that he enjoys a wide reputation for those qualities both in the legal profession and socially.' The tribunal accepted that the cocaine usage was 'out of character'.

The tribunal emphasised the practitioner's willingness to be rehabilitated and his cooperation with authorities; that he reported himself, acknowledged the facts of the charges against him, apologised to the profession and the Board. It concluded that his 'recovery process is well underway'. In determining an appropriate penalty the tribunal said that it had to consider that Quick was 'a person of considerable substance' whom it believed 'would be a significant loss to the profession and public if he was not permitted to practice again'. The tribunal did say that the public needs to be protected, but this could be met by regular urine testing. It suspended Quick's practising certificate for only three months and required regular certificates sufficient to indicate any illicit drug usage.

Under the Act it appears that Quick needed to be suspended from practice **7.63** for at least 12 months. The Board argued for such a penalty and that Quick's offences had affected the reputation and standing of the legal profession in the public eye. The tribunal said it agreed but found that in effect Quick had not practised for 12 months, had not used illicit drugs since May 2002 and medical evidence showed that he was rehabilitating. Quick was able to commence practice when he returned from overseas.

The doctors and the tribunal appear to accept the notion that Quick's cocaine habit was an illness and not done intentionally. It is as if they accept he had no *mens rea* to commit a crime. Perhaps this is also the reason Quick has not been charged by the authorities for committing a crime under the Controlled Substances Act. It should be noted that certain drugs, such as cocaine, act as a stimulus, and can help advocates to be more fearless and forceful in presenting their case. Like the use of performance enhancement drugs in sports, drugs can give an advocate an unfair advantage. Perhaps we may need to institute random drug testing to stop lawyers from using abusive substances and also to help them come forward and seek help for their problem.

In another recent case dealing with drugs, *Prothonotary of the Supreme Court* **7.64** *of NSW v P*,[151] a solicitor was convicted and sentenced to six months for importing cocaine. The New South Wales Court of Appeal stated 10 principles to look at to determine whether to strike off. One of the most important was that a practitioner should only be struck off when the probability is present that the practitioner is permanently unfit to practise. The fact that the practitioner has a conviction for a serious offence does not necessarily lead to a striking off. The court stated that the important

---

151. [2003] NSWCA 320.

question was to determine the present fitness to practise and not that of the fitness when the crime was committed. The court took into consideration that she was remorseful and had been rehabilitated and been drug-free for almost four years and was no longer a risk to her clients or the public. The court found no basis for removing her from the rolls.

Chris Merritt, writing two years after the decision, said: 'If "P" returns to practice, shouldn't her potential clients be given the opportunity to make an informed decision about whether they want their legal affairs handled by a reformed drug smuggler?'[152]

American substance abuse cases

7.65   In the United States the courts have been inconsistent in the application of penalties for substance abuse. The penalties range from disbarment for the use of marijuana[153] to only a 30-day suspension for driving under the influence of alcohol and causing the police to chase at dangerous high speed.[154] The marijuana case showed that a higher standard would be placed on a lawyer acting for the state in order to 'preserve the public trust'.[155] California has a regulatory proceeding under its Business and Professions Code s 6007(b)(3) which allows removal from practice of lawyers who are shown to be suffering from a mental illness or defect or cannot practise law competently because of drug or alcohol abuse. The ABA Model Rules for Lawyers Disciplinary Enforcement (1989) r 23 provides for placing lawyers on an indefinite period of 'disability inactive status' in case of their mental or physical incapacity.

7.66   The approach in North America has frequently been to mitigate the penalty because of substance abuse. It appears that too much weight has been placed on protecting lawyers' rights to earn a living at the expense of protecting the public. Of course, lawyers should be given the opportunity for rehabilitation but not when the public has been or can continue to be seriously harmed.[156] The Australian authorities have leaned more heavily towards protecting the public, except perhaps in the *Quick* case, than the authorities in North America.

LawCare

7.67   We mentioned in Chapter 2 that a number of articles written by health consultants and psychiatrists have begun to appear in lawyers' journals. They deal with stress and change which are affecting many in their legal practice and in their home life.[157] The New South Wales Law Society

---

152. C Merritt, 'Prejudice', *Australian*, 9 September 2005, p 26.
153. *Re Johnson* 488 NW 2d 682 (South Dakota 1992). In this case disbarment was based on the lawyer using marijuana 100 times and cocaine once but the lawyer was only convicted of one misdemeanour. The main factor against the accused was that he was a deputy state attorney and 'his position required of him a higher standard of conduct to preserve the public trust in our system of justice' (at 685).
154. *Re Eddingfield* 572 NE 2d 1293 (Indiana 1991).
155. *Re Johnson* 488 NW 2d 682 at 685 (SD 1992).
156. For an article arguing for stricter control over lawyers' chemical abuse, see Workie (above).
157. See, for example, D Tannenbaum, 'Stress and Change in the Legal Profession in the 1990s' (1990) 17 *Brief (Law Society of WA)* 7 and D Jansen, 'The Gulf Between the Professional and the Private: How Work Conflicts with Home Life', April (1993) *The Proctor (Law Society of Qld)* 15.

recognised these problems by setting up LawCare, a 24-hour free counselling phone service for any member or their immediate family to discuss
with a counsellor any personal or social problem, for example stress
management, marriage, drug and alcohol abuse, and so on.[158] In Canada
the Canadian Bar Association has started a program to coordinate the
different provincial law societies' and other law groups' programs which
offer lawyers access to personal counselling.[159] It has been estimated in the
United States that one-third of all lawyers suffer depression or substance
abuse. It has also been reported that lawyers have 'about three times the
rate of depression and almost twice the rate of substance abuse as other
Americans'.[160] In light of these figures it is not surprising that the ABA has
a Commission on Impaired Attorneys that works as a clearing house of
information on lawyer impairment issues and programs. It holds an annual
conference and maintains and sells a directory of lawyer assistance programs
and an up-to-date survey of such programs.[161] The Law Council of Australia should consider establishing a similar program in Australia.

Lawyers and community work

An unusual argument in mitigation was presented in the case of barrister   **7.68**
Paul Coe. Mr Coe was the first Aboriginal lawyer struck off the rolls in
Australia. The Legal Services Tribunal (NSW) found that he filed a
'substantially false' affidavit concerning his financial worth to the Family
Court. The tribunal noted that it had 'not received from Mr Coe any
acknowledgment that he recognises and regrets his wrongdoing, nor any
assurance from him that his conduct has not been and will not be repeated'.
It was argued that Coe should be treated with leniency because of the fact
that he had 'played a major role in advancing the interests of members of
the Aboriginal community, and that he is held in the highest regard by
members of that community'. The tribunal recognised his contribution but
decided that it was not 'appropriate to relegate broader issues in favour of
the interests of a segment of the community'.[162] Coe appealed but the
Court of Appeal upheld the disbarment order.[163]

In another case a barrister who had done extensive community work within   **7.69**
the Lebanese community was also disbarred for being involved in a sham
and fraudulent investment agreements. The barrister produced evidence
that he was a person of 'good fame and character, a loyal friend, a person
who gave active community service and someone who would suffer
considerable hardship' if he was disbarred. The tribunal weighed this
evidence against the need to protect the public and decided to issue a
striking off order.[164]

---

158. I Chung, 'Law Care Counselling' (1993) 31 *Law Society J (NSW)* 53.
159. (1990) 14(2) *Canadian Lawyer* 17.
160. D Rhode and D Luban (above), p 973.
161. (1990) 76 *American Bar Association J* 51. For a recent discussion of general drug addiction
     (including tranquillisers and sedatives) and the need to seek treatment to save your
     practice and your life, see D Sanchez, 'Abusing Illicit Drugs', August (1997) *California
     Bar J* 12.
162. *Sydney Morning Herald*, 4 July 1997, p 3.
163. *Coe v New South Wales Bar Association* [2000] NSWCA 13.
164. *In the matter of Richard Mitry*, Decision of the Legal Services Division of the
     Administrative Decisions Tribunal, 30 August 1999, unreported.

STRUCTURE AND OPERATION OF DISCIPLINARY SYSTEMS

Introduction — characteristics of the systems

7.70   There are major differences between the states and territories as to the composition, jurisdiction and powers of the disciplinary systems. The systems do have some common features. All the professional associations have great powers over the disciplinary system except in Western Australia where the disciplinary system is completely independent.[165] The systems are mainly reactive, although a Legal Service Commissioner (LSC) or a professional association can initiate an investigation. For example, under Pt 4.4.8 of the Legal Profession Act (Vic) this can occur if the Comm-issioner has reason to believe that a practitioner's conduct constitutes unsatisfactory professional conduct or professional misconduct. A complaint is usually filed, predominantly by clients, with the relevant professional association, complaints' committee or legal services commission. A number of complaints filed by lawyers against other lawyers are also received but they are a distinct minority of all the complaints filed.[166] Although complaints can be initiated by the LSC or professional associations, they are usually acting on information provided by a judge, a magistrate or a member of the profession who has not filed the information in the form of a complaint. All the authorities involved in the disciplinary process have refused to employ independent investigators to monitor and report on lawyer conduct. One exception in Australia is that professional associations have been empowered to employ auditors or investigators to conduct random audits of trust accounts to detect non-compliance.

7.71   The predominantly reactive discipline system in Australia may be contrasted with that of California. The California Bar Association had an enormous budget (over $40 million between 1992 and 1997) devoted to disciplinary matters that helped it maintain a large investigative staff in order to monitor members' behaviour and, more importantly, develop programs aimed at preventing incompetent or unethical behaviour.[167] This system came to a standstill by April 1998 when the then Republican Governor Peter Wilson vetoed the bill that authorised the collection of membership dues. As a result the vast majority of the staff was dismissed and discipline matters were not dealt with. When the crisis was finally resolved with the intervention of the State Supreme Court and the eventual election of a new Democrat governor, the authorised fees had been drastically reduced. As a result the money spent in 1999 on discipline was only 65 per cent of the 1997 allocation — approximately $26 million. Even with this large reduction the discipline system has started again its

---

165. The Law Society has only the ability to reprimand and has no powers to investigate the activities of its members: *Scrutiny of the Legal Profession: Complaints Against Lawyers* (above) (1992), para 3.74.

166. *Scrutiny of the Legal Profession* (above) (1992), pp 15–16 and 22–3. The discussion paper contains a detailed breakdown of the complaints filed against solicitors and barristers from 1988–91. The paper also has a description of the discipline systems in all of the Australian states and in England and California as of 1992. See also Office of Legal Services Commission (NSW) *Annual Report 1998–99*, p 55.

167. *Scrutiny of the Legal Profession* (above) (1992), para 3.146. The system in California is outlined in paras 3.147–3.151.

investigative role, although not as extensively as before the crisis.[168] As of 1 March 2005, California has more than 200,000 lawyers, which even with the reduced fees enables it to raise considerable funds. New York has the most lawyers in the United States — over 214,000.[169]

Another common feature is that most Australian systems now have lay people involved in some aspect of the disciplinary process. These include the use of lay observers to investigate, on the request of complainants, the handling of their complaint by the investigative authority.[170] In no jurisdiction are lay persons in a majority when sitting on a disciplinary tribunal. A recent development in which lay people play a more dominant role is the establishment of advisory councils, similar to the Lord Chancellor's Advisory Committee in England, discussed in Chapter 6. These committees can make recommendations and reports to the Attorney-General on any matter relating to the legal profession and this would include the ethical and professional standards to be applied and whether the profession's rules are anti-competitive.[171] Other advisory bodies with a similar role in some Australian jurisdictions are the Legal Ombudsman and the Office of Legal Services Commissioner (OLSC).[172] **7.72**

Several jurisdictions now have conciliation facilities that have been very effective in solving most complaints referred to them.[173] In England conciliation has been so successful that 90 per cent of all complaints received in 1991 were referred for conciliation.[174] Each jurisdiction has a disciplinary tribunal to hear formal complaints. These tribunals usually have the following sanctions which they can use: cost of litigation, fine, limitation on the scope of the practising certificate, certain undertakings such as requiring the lawyer to take corrective legal education, suspension from practice and striking off the rolls. In some jurisdictions an order can be up to a specific limit for the lawyer to compensate his or her client. **7.73**

Operation of the systems

Any person can make a complaint. The complaint has to be in writing, on a form provided by the disciplinary authorities or in the form of a statutory declaration. The complaint is filed with the professional association in some jurisdictions and in New South Wales, Victoria and Queensland it must be **7.74**

---

168. See Y Ross, 'The shutdown of regulatory functions', May (1999) *Law Institute J (Vic)* 33.
169. As of 1 March 2004 total membership was 200,269 — active members 148,885. See (April 2005) *California Bar Journal* 3. It should be noted that a number of the active members do not reside in California. The New York Bar, which has the greatest number of non-resident members, had 207,413 registered lawyers at the end of 2003 and another 7000 registered in 2004. See (February 2005) *California Bar Journal* 1.
170. There are lay observers or Ombudsmen in South Australia and Tasmania, while in Queensland, Victoria and New South Wales the Legal Services Commissioner fulfils this function.
171. See, for example, the Legal Profession Act 2004 (NSW) ss 683–684.
172. For example, the Legal Profession Act 1993 (Tas) ss 82–85, Legal Profession Act 2004 (Vic) Pt 6.3, Legal Profession Act (NSW) Pt 7.3 and Legal Profession Act (Qld) ss 412–427.
173. *Scrutiny of the Legal Profession* (above) (1992), paras 3.14 and 3.98. This refers to the Victorian system, but by 2005 provisions for mediation and conciliation are now available in all jurisdictions.
174. *Scrutiny of the Legal Profession* (above) (1992), paras 3.117–3.118. The complaints suitable for conciliation concern delay, poor communication, misunderstandings and carelessness.

filed with the OLSC. In the latter jurisdictions if it is filed with a professional association it must be referred to the OLSC.[175] The OLSC may decide to investigate the complaint or refer it a professional association. In South Australia and Western Australia independent complaints' committees have been established.[176] If the complainant cannot identify the legal practitioner, he or she can still complain by identifying the legal practice concerned.[177] The complaint is investigated by the staff of the investigatory authority that decides whether to proceed with more formal action. The lawyer under investigation is informed in writing and asked to comment on the allegations. Any practitioner (not only those who are the subject of the complaint) must provide information, produce documents and assist the investigation. A practitioner does have the right to decline to provide documents that are subject to confidentiality or legal professional privilege.[178] A practitioner can choose to breach his or her duty of confidentiality by producing these documents but only if the professional body or OLSC is satisfied that this action is necessary in order for the practitioner to rebut an allegation of the complaint. Requests for information need to be provided promptly and any excessive delay may be deemed a breach of the Legal Profession Act.[179] Furthermore, practitioners will also be in breach, which can constitute professional misconduct, if they wilfully mislead or obstruct the investigating bodies.[180] If a trust account matter is involved, an investigator will usually be appointed to deal with the complaint.[181] If the complaint is deemed to be valid it is then referred to the complaints' committee or the OLSC. The OLSC will usually refer trust account matters to the professional association's complaints committee. The committee's recommendation goes either to the council of the association, the Board or the OLSC, which will usually accept the recommendation. The appropriate authority can sanction the lawyer or refer the matter to a disciplinary tribunal or, far more rarely, to the Supreme Court.[182] The investigation and disposal of complaints are subject to review and supervision by a Legal Ombudsman in Tasmania and by the OLSC in New South Wales, Victoria and Queensland.[183]

---

175. Section 505 of the Legal Profession Act 2004 (NSW), Pt 4.25 of the Legal Profession Act 2004 (Vic) and s 256 of the Legal Profession Act 2004 (Qld).

176. Legal Practitioners Act 1981 (SA) ss 68–77 and Legal Practice Act 2003 (WA) ss 162–164. The South Australian Legal Practitioners Conduct Board has three lay persons out of seven members while the Western Australian one has two out of nine. The South Australian Board is discussed by its Director Chris Cocks: see September (1999) *Bulletin (Law Society of South Australia)* 30.

177. Legal Profession Act 2004 (NSW) s 504(3)(b).

178. *Gridger v The Council of the Law Society of New South Wales* [1999] NSWSC 904. See also, for example, the Legal Profession Act (Vic) Pt 4.4.11.

179. See B Murdoch, 'Failure to reply to Society: is it discourtesy?' *Law Society J (NSW)* September 1999, p 25.

180. See also *Law Society v Murphy* [1999] SASC 83 where Doyle CJ said that there 'can be no doubt about the obligation of a practitioner to assist [the Board] with its enquiries'.

181. For example, see Pt 3.1 of the Legal Profession Act (NSW) 2004.

182. Some of this description comes from D Weisbrot, (1990) *Australian Lawyers* 201–2.

183. See Legal Profession Act 1993 (Tas) s 85, Legal Profession Act (Vic) Pts 4.4.9–4.4.10, Legal Profession Act (Qld) s 273 and Legal Profession Act 2004 (NSW) ss 543–547.

Whistleblowing

One problem facing the profession is that the vast majority of the complaints come from aggrieved clients. Does the profession need to develop an ethos that is conducive for more lawyers to make complaints? What are the obligations of lawyers in reporting other lawyers for their wrongdoings? Should these lawyers be disciplined for failing to make such a report? In Australia there is a strong stigma attached to reporting on another even though under law failure to report a 'serious offence' is a crime.[184] The terms used include: narking, stooling, squealing, dobbing, blabbing, snitching, tattle-tailing, finking, peaching, and others. The people giving the information are known as: informants, rats, stool pigeons, pimps, snitches, dogs, super-grasses and so on.[185] The stigma is so strong that whistleblowing has led to severe social and economic penalties; that is, loss of job, isolation from one's peers and even psychiatric committal.[186] For example, in a study of 233 American whistleblowers 90 per cent lost their jobs or were demoted; 27 per cent were sued; 26 per cent had psychiatric or medical referrals; 25 per cent became alcoholic; 17 per cent lost their homes; 15 per cent became divorced; 10 per cent attempted suicide and 8 per cent became bankrupt.[187] Sometimes whistleblowers can even lose their lives.[188] A very good example is the reaction to the whistleblower in the recent film *The Insider* (1999). In this film justice triumphs and the tobacco industry eventually admits its deceit.

7.75

This extremely negative view of whistleblowing is disheartening, considering that whistleblowers are usually 'motivated by a desire to react against a harm or a potential harm to the organisation or the community; they are driven by a moral motive and will take a public stand'.[189] To overcome these reactions and to protect such high moral behaviour, legislation has been adopted. The first such legislation was in the United States, the Civil Service Reform Act 1978. The Act prohibited reprisals against federal employees who disclosed certain information. The protection was deemed inadequate and it was strengthened and improved by the

7.76

---

184. See s 316(1) of the Crimes Act 1900 (NSW). Serious offence under this Act is defined in s 311(1) as any offence punishable by imprisonment or penal servitude for five years or more. This section has been the subject of a report: see *Review of section 316 of the Crimes Act 1900 (NSW)*, New South Wales Law Reform Commission, Report 93, December 1999.

185. I can thank a number of my students for providing this list during class discussions and in their papers.

186. See B Sweeney, December (1983) *Legal Services Bulletin* 284. For a detailed account of a number of cases of whistleblowers and an analysis of the psychodynamics of whistle-blowing in our society, see Q Dempster, *Whistleblowers*, Penguin Books, Ringwood, 1997. For some interesting Australian cases see D Grace and S Cohen, *Business Ethics: Australian Problems and Cases*, 2nd ed, Oxford University Press, Melbourne, 1998, pp 148–61.

187. These figures are cited in J McMillan, 'Legal protection of whistleblowers' in S Prosser, R Wear and J Nethercote (eds), *Corruption and Reform*, Queensland University Press, St Lucia, 1990, p 205.

188. See J Garnaut, 'Whistleblower's death was murder, court told', *Sydney Morning Herald*, 19 October 2004, p 5.

189. I Blonder, 'Blowing the Whistle' in M Coady and S Bloch (eds), *Codes of Ethics and the Professions*, Melbourne University Press, Melbourne, 1996, p 166 at 169. This article is an excellent discussion of the topic and examines Australian legislation.

Whistleblower Protection Act 1989. In Australia legislation to protect whistleblowers was first enacted in Queensland in relation to the Fitzgerald Inquiry.[190] It protected people giving evidence to the Criminal Justice Commission. Legislation in Queensland (Whistleblowers Protection Act 1994), New South Wales (Protection Disclosures Act 1994), Australian Capital Territory (Public Interest Disclosure Act 1994), Tasmania (Public Interest Disclosure Act 2002), New Zealand (Whistleblowers Protection Act 1994) and Victoria (Whistleblowers Protection Act 2001) was adopted to protect public service whistleblowers.[191] South Australia enacted wider legislation which allows for protection for those making disclosures not only from within the public service.[192]

7.77 Victoria also has limited protection which is given to lawyers working in the public service by the Office of the Public Service Commissioner under the Code of Conduct for the Victorian Public Sector (1995). Section 22 urges the reporting of any 'unethical behaviour or wrongdoing' which 'may include behaviour that you believe violates any law, rule or regulation, or represents gross mismanagement, or is a danger to public health or safety'. Section 24 states that persons making such a report will be 'protected against discrimination ... providing your claim is reasonable and you have reported the matter to an appropriate person'. There are similar provisions for public servants in other Australian states and the Commonwealth.

7.78 The main focus of the legislative activity and the public service codes has been to protect whistleblowers making disclosure of corruption, waste and illegal conduct in the public sector, although some of them aim to encourage the disclosure of conduct adverse to the public interest; for example, the Australian Capital Territory and New Zealand legislation. The focus on protecting whistleblowers may be necessary in light of a survey by the Independent Commission Against Corruption (NSW) which found that nearly 75 per cent of the 1331 public servants surveyed feared they would suffer if they reported corrupt conduct.[193] Only the legislation in South Australia provides protection for disclosure of 'corrupt or illegal conduct generally'.[194] Only the legislation in New Zealand provides for an independent whistleblowing authority, although all the statutes allow disclosure to other authorities outside the relevant department. In 2004 the Australian National Integrity Study found a number of incidents of government corruption in the Federal Government had not been reported. It called for an independent national corruption watchdog and stronger protection for whistleblowers.[195] The need for an independent authority was also evident from a Queensland Whistleblower Study that reported that:

---

190. Whistleblowers (Interim Protection) and Miscellaneous Amendments Act 1989 (Qld).
191. For a discussion of the ramifications of whistleblowing, see the interesting articles by R Fox, 'Protecting the Whistleblower' (1993) 15 *Adelaide LR* 137 and W De Maria, 'Whistleblowing' (1995) 20 *Alternative Law J* 270. For a recent article see D Lewis, 'Whistleblowing Statutes in Australia: Is it Time for a New Agenda' (2003) 8 *Deakin LR* 16.
192. Whistleblowers Protection Act 1993 (SA).
193. L Morris, 'Fear paralyses PS Whistleblowers', *Sydney Morning Herald*, 28 April 1994, p 3.
194. Whistleblowers Protection Act 1993 (SA) s 3.
195. R Heffernan, 'Nation needs ethics watchdog, says study', *Courier Mail*, 14 October 2004, p 12.

Eighty-three per cent of their immediate superiors were ineffective in dealing with their disclosures and the effectiveness rating only marginally increased as whistleblowers went up the chain of command in their public sector unit.

More serious was the finding that by 'far the most common response to the question, "What happened when you took the matter to your supervisor?" was "A superior obstructed the complaint"'.[196] Finally, enacting whistleblowing laws may have little effect. A survey done on the effectiveness of the New South Wales legislation found that it was widely ignored by government departments and local councils, who also failed to inform their employees about their rights under the law.[197]   **7.79**

These surveys and an analysis of the whistleblowers legislation shows that whistleblowing lawyers will normally not be sufficiently protected from reprisal. Furthermore, there is little other legislative support for lawyer whistleblowers. Most jurisdictions have no formal rules governing whistleblowing but there are some lawyers who do make complaints. An analysis of complaints made in 1991 in New South Wales found that 16 per cent of those made against solicitors and 28 per cent of those made against barristers were made by other lawyers.[198]

Whistleblowing for lawyers

There is no general rule in any jurisdiction requiring lawyers to report other lawyers for their misdeeds except for trust account violations. It can be argued that there is a general rule under common law that lawyers as officers of the court have an ethical duty to uphold the rule of law. By taking the oath of admission to become practitioners they accept the ethical duty to uphold the rule of law. This would include reporting another lawyer who they know is breaking the law.[199] Under s 730A of the Legal Profession Act 2004 (NSW) the OLSC and the Councils of the Law Society and Bar Association must report any suspected offences they find during their investigations to the relevant law enforcement or prosecution authority. They also need to make available to that authority the relevant information and documents in their possession.   **7.80**

Most jurisdictions have statutory rules or rules of court known as 'pimp' rules that require the reporting of another lawyer for trust fund violations.[200] In Queensland and New South Wales, if solicitors have reasonable grounds for suspecting[201] another solicitor of mismanaging his or her trust account they have to report it to the President of the Law Society.[202] The breakdown of the complaints made by lawyers against

---

196. De Maria (above), p 273. De Maria refers to several of these studies in this article that he and C Jan have conducted and published. See footnotes 3 and 14.
197. N Vass, 'ICAC says law fails to protect whistleblowers', *Sydney Morning Herald*, 25 September 1996, p 7.
198. *Scrutiny of the Legal Profession* (above) (1992), pp 16 and 23.
199. This argument is presented by V Shirvington, ethics officer of the New South Wales Law Society. in 'Be careful of the "blind eye" syndrome' (1996) 34 *Law Society J (NSW)* 26.
200. Disney et al (above), p 338. For example, see cl 132 of the Legal Profession Regulation 2002 which requires a practitioner to report another practitioner if he or she has reasonable grounds for suspecting that practitioner of being dishonest or having irregular dealings with trust money or controlled money: for discussion of this provision see V Shirvington, 'There but for the grace of ...?' (March 1998) *Law Society J (NSW)* 25.
201. The Queensland provision's 'reasonable suspicion of misconduct'.
202. Legal Profession Regulation 2002 (NSW) cl 132 and Rules of the Queensland Law Society r 92.

solicitors does not indicate how many were made under the mandatory trust account provisions. The Law Society of New South Wales says most of the mandatory reports come from other partners in the same firm. The main reason for their actions is probably because they could also be liable to disciplinary action if they neglect the matter.[203]

7.81 From my inquiries in New South Wales no solicitor has been disciplined for failure to report a trust fund violation, although there have been numerous solicitors prosecuted for defalcations. It may become necessary for the professional associations to enforce or adopt rules requiring reporting of trust fund violations in light of recent huge payouts from fidelity funds. In New Zealand in 1992 a firm had a defalcation of $60 million which bankrupted the fidelity fund, while in New South Wales in 1997 violations by an Albury firm required the fidelity fund to make a payout of more than $40 million. These large payouts have to be met by raising a levy on all solicitors, which was estimated to be $10,000 over five years in New Zealand and $2000 a year in New South Wales.[204]

7.82 It is obvious that the Australian legal profession has too many large defalcations and too many cases of professional incompetence. These serious violations have harmed many clients. They have also resulted in higher professional indemnity insurance premiums and levies on all practitioners to cover the losses, and affected the funding of legal aid. Perhaps these violations would have remained undiscovered by a whistleblower, but supporting whistleblowing may eventually lead to future disclosures. The Professional Standards Council of New South Wales supports the need for more whistleblowing and says there is a need for legislation to extend protection from public servants to members of the private professions.[205] Perhaps there is also a need to provide a financial reward as an incentive for more people to report violations.[206] In the United States under the False Claims Act, whistleblowers can sue corporations and public counties for frauds against the Federal Government. They can receive up to 30 per cent of the judgment, as well as compensation for their costs.[207]

7.83 In England and the United States, the responsibilities of lawyers are much wider on reporting ethical violations. In England solicitors are under a duty to report to the Law Society another solicitor whom they believe 'falls short of the proper standard of conduct for the profession'.[208] The author has

---

203. See *Re Mayes* [1974] 1 NSWLR 19.
204. B Logan, *Sydney Morning Herald*, 1 March 1997, p 5; 7 March 1997, p 15 and 12 March 1997, p 5.
205. The paper is entitled 'Whistleblowing in the Professions' and is available at www.lawlink .nsw.au/psc. See *The Australian Financial Review*, 28 April 2000, p 28.
206. A Hepworth, 'Whistleblowing reward debate', *Australian Financial Review*, 16 July 2004, p 16 and 'Pitch to encourage whistleblowers, *Australian*, 18 November 2003.
207. The right to sue public local bodies was upheld by the United States Supreme Court in *Cook County v United States ex rel, Chandler* on 10 March 2003. See, for a discussion of the case and statute, J Hilden, 'A Unanimous Supreme Court Decision Means Whistle-blowers can go after Counties, Not just Companies', 18 March 2003, www.findlaw.com/ hidden/20030318.html.
208. Professional Conduct of Solicitors, Principle 14.04. The principle also says that, when reporting, the solicitor should 'where necessary' first obtain his or her client's consent.

been informed that such a report is rare.[209] In general, solicitors in England, like those in New South Wales, do not like to report other solicitors. Abel states that between 1973–78 only 14 per cent of all complaints against solicitors were filed by other solicitors.[210]

In the United States the ABA Model Code, DR 1-103(A) requires lawyers to report any violation by another lawyer,[211] while the Model Rules r 8.3[212] requires lawyers to report another lawyer's misconduct. Under r 8.3 there is no duty to disclose client information that is confidential under Model Rule 1.6(a). This requirement to maintain material deemed confidential is a major barrier to reporting lawyers in the United States.[213] This barrier was removed for reporting corporate misdeeds by in-house lawyers under the Sarbanes-Oxley Act in 2002. We will discuss this Act in detail in Chapter 11. There have been only very few disciplinary actions for failure to report another lawyer's misconduct and these have been mainly concerning trust funds.[214] Thus, having broader mandatory requirements than those in Australia has not made much difference. In the United States, like Australia, reporting a fellow lawyer is also hindered by fears of being labelled a 'rat-fink' and by fears of retaliation.[215]

7.84

As a result of these attitudes a major controversy developed when the Illinois Supreme Court in the *Himmel* case suspended from practice for one year a lawyer who knew of another lawyer's misappropriation of funds of a client. The court found that the information had been received in a situation where the privilege had been waived and the lawyer was ethically bound to report it.[216] The *Himmel* case sent a clear message to Illinois lawyers — report professional misconduct. In the first year after the case the number of lawyers reported by fellow lawyers increased by more than 500 per cent. Illinois lawyers report misconduct at a higher rate than any other state.[217]

7.85

---

209. In 1994 my students, David Katz and Eric Mappem, for their research assignment, telephoned the English Law Society and were informed by one of its officers that she had not encountered a single case of discipline for failure to report in the seven years she had worked at the Disciplinary Tribunal.
210. R Abel, *The Legal Profession in England and Wales*, N Blackwell, Oxford, 1988, p 251.
211. Rule 1-103 provides: 'Disclosure of Information to Authorities: A lawyer possessing unprivileged knowledge of a violation of [misconduct] shall report such knowledge to a tribunal …'.
212. Rule 8.3 provides: 'Reporting Professional Misconduct: (a) A lawyer having knowledge that another lawyer has committed a violation of the Rules of Professional Conduct that raises a substantial question as to that lawyer's honesty, trustworthiness, or fitness as a lawyer in other respects, shall inform the appropriate authority … (c) This rule does not require disclosure of information otherwise [privileged] …'.
213. D Richmond, 'The Duty to Report Professional Misconduct: A Practical Analysis of Lawyer Self-regulation' (1999) 12 *Georgetown J of Legal Ethics* 175, 184–213.
214. J Wang (above), pp 1039, 1045. See also J Mitchem, 'The Lawyer's Duty to Report Ethical Violations' (1990) 18 *Colorado Lawyer* 1915.
215. D Webster, 'Still In Good Standing: The Crisis in Attorney Discipline' (1987) 73 *American Bar Association J* 61, footnote 46.
216. *Re Himmel*, 533 NE 2d 790 (Ill 1989).
217. D Van Duch, 'Best Snitches: Illinois Lawyers' (1998) 27 *National LJ* A1 and A25.

7.86   There has been only one other decision for a failure to report another lawyer: *Re Condit*. Condit admitted violating Model Rule 8.3(a) and entered into a consent discipline order of public censure.[218] Since the *Himmel* decision a number of states have issued reports on the scope of the duty to report in their jurisdiction. In contrast, the San Diego Bar issued an opinion that lawyers have absolutely no duty to report the misconduct of another lawyer. This opinion was based on the fact that the California Rules of Professional Conduct does not include any reporting provision.[219]

7.87   Lawyers face a serious ethical problem in reporting the professional misconduct of a colleague. In *Wieder v Skala*[220] a young associate was fired because he insisted that the firm report one of his colleagues. The firm reported the colleague, but waited to fire the lawyer 'because he was in charge of handling the most important litigation in the firm'. He was fired a few days after filing motion papers in that important case. The reporting of professional misconduct of other lawyers is required under the New York State Bar's disciplinary rule DR 1-103A.[221] The court found that the firm had breached an implied term of the associate's employment contract. It said lawyer employment contracts have an implied understanding that neither the employer nor the employee will do anything to prevent each other from conducting the practice in accordance with the ethical standards of the profession. The court found that the rule in question was critical to the maintenance of the unique function of self-regulation. The court also said:

> ... by insisting that plaintiff disregard DR 1-103(A) defendants were not only making it impossible for plaintiff to fulfil his professional obligations but placing him in the position of having to choose between continued employment and his own potential suspension and disbarment ... Insisting that ... plaintiff must act unethically amounted to nothing less than a frustration of the only legitimate purpose of the employment relationship.

Operation of the system — procedures

7.88   We have discussed the need for fairness to the consumer of legal services, but there is also a need for the rules of natural justice such as procedural fairness for the practitioners being investigated. This includes the need to provide the practitioner with a copy of the complaint against him or her and an opportunity to respond to it. In the *Murray* case the failure of the Legal Services Commissioner to meet this requirement resulted in a denial of procedural fairness.[222] The need for procedural fairness has been recognised by legislation in New South Wales[223] and there is also a provision that grants practitioners immunity from civil liability for communications

---

218. Unreported Arizona decision, 14 March 1995. The case is cited and discussed in Richmond (above), p 183.
219. Private communication.
220. 609 NE 2d 105 (1992).
221. DR 1-103(A) provides: 'A lawyer possessing knowledge, not protected as a confidence or secret, of a violation of DR 1-103 that raises a substantial question as to another lawyer's honesty, trustworthiness or fitness in other respects as a lawyer, shall report such knowledge to a tribunal or other authority empowered to investigate or act upon such violation.'
222. *Murray v Legal Services Commissioner* [1999] NSWCA 70. This requirement is present in s 508 of the Legal Profession Act (NSW) 2004.
223. Legal Profession Act 2004 (NSW) s 591.

made by them in connection with a disciplinary investigation.[224] The disciplinary proceedings may be open to the public depending on whether it is in the public interest or the interests of justice. In New South Wales, hearings are to be conducted in public, but the tribunal can close the hearing under s 75 of the Administrative Decisions Tribunal Act. The tribunal may decide to close the hearing to protect legal privilege. There is also power for the tribunal to issue orders at any stage to protect the disclosure of information where it is subject to legal privilege or any duty of confidentiality.[225] There was a tradition in some jurisdictions of not reporting the name of the practitioner especially for less serious violations. This has now changed with the establishment of a national register of disciplinary actions.[226] Some jurisdictions have already established a register.[227] The strict rules of evidence are usually followed for serious breaches (professional misconduct), but the rules are relaxed for less serious ones.[228]

The problem with this approach is that a tribunal will sometimes not know whether it is dealing with a serious breach (professional misconduct) and therefore will adopt strict rules of evidence. Flexible rules of evidence are needed because the hearing is not like a normal common law trial. Disciplinary proceedings are considered to be protective of the public and the image of the profession and not punitive in nature.[229] As a result, the procedures are different from the normal adversary trial and have an inquisitorial aspect. This does not mean that they are not adversarial. They are *sui generis* because they combine the adversarial with an inquiry rather than a hearing based on information.[230] Similar to the admission cases there is an obligation for candour and cooperation that is foreign to the adversary system in relation to the disciplinary authorities investigating and adjudicating a case. The courts have repeatedly emphasised the need for lawyers to appreciate the appropriate professional standards and understand how they have departed from them in the present situation. As we mentioned (see **6.67**), Peter Clyne was never readmitted to the profession. Although at one point, 21 years after his disbarment, he accepted that the judgments against him were correct, he continued to attack these decisions in public and private until the end of his life. Thus, Clyne never truly showed proper contrition, nor understanding that he had done wrong. **7.89**

During the actual process of being disciplined, behaviour such as Clyne's can exacerbate the misconduct and lead to a more severe penalty. In the *Livesey* case Moffitt J said:[231] **7.90**

> … what is minor may become serious if the barrister or solicitor is unfrank about the matter or gives a false explanation concerning it … Regrettably, it

224. Legal Profession Act 2004 (NSW) s 601.
225. Legal Profession Act 2004 (NSW) s 560.
226. See Law Council of Australia, Model laws project (April 2004), Division 11.
227. For example, see Legal Profession Act 2004 (NSW) s 577, Legal Profession Act 2004 (Qld) s 296 and Legal Profession Act (Vic) Pt 4.4.26. In New South Wales detailed provisions are found in Legal Profession Regulation cl 173.
228. See, for example, Legal Profession Act 2004 (NSW) s 558. For the situation in Victoria, see A Albert, 'Statutory Professional Disciplinary Proceedings' (1994) 68 *Law Institute J* 168.
229. *Clyne v New South Wales Bar Association* (1960) 104 CLR 186 at 202.
230. *Law Society of NSW v Jackson* [1981] 1 NSWLR 730 at 734.
231. *New South Wales Bar Association v Liversey* [1982] 2 NSWLR 237 at 239.

has been common experience in cases before this court that professional unfitness would not have been established by the initial misdemeanour, but is revealed by the wrongful conduct that follows in an endeavour to rectify or conceal the initial wrong or error.

In the *Veron* case[232] the solicitor refused to give oral evidence in the witness box or file an affidavit in relation to the accusations. He treated the proceedings as if they were adversarial by meeting the charges with mere argument and at times when questioned refused to answer, arguing the privilege against self-incrimination. The court found that he used 'battle tactics' which was in stark contrast to his obligation, as an officer of the court, to cooperate with the court. The *Veron* principle of the need to cooperate was modified in the *Malfanti* case.[233] In that case it was held that a solicitor is not obliged to assist the tribunal by giving evidence in order for the Law Society to establish its case. If the evidence adduced against a solicitor is incapable of establishing any of the categories of misconduct, the solicitor has a right to argue that there is 'no case' and the matter should be dismissed.

7.91 These cases highlight the special character of disciplinary proceedings. In the *Kalaf* case the practitioner did not disclose that he had been 'severely reprimanded' by the Bar Council when dealing with the Solicitors' Admission Board. He had stated that the Bar Council held his 'conduct fell short of the standard required to be a barrister'. Kirby J in the majority in the Court of Appeal, in suspending him for one year, held that his disclosure lacked frankness, but was not dishonest. He found it fell short of the standard of disclosure that can be expected of a barrister in dealing with the court but was not a grave default. His Honour applied the *Kotowicz* case that said the duty of candour did not extend so far as to require the practitioner to volunteer all relevant evidence, especially if he considered some evidence placed him at risk.[234] Kirby J modified this statement by saying it did not negate the obligation of 'total honesty' on the part of the practitioner, but he did emphasise the need for the courts and the profession to practise 'forgiveness' as stated in the Bible.[235]

7.92 The disciplinary proceedings also depart from the adversary model in other respects. The doctrine of estoppel has been held to have no application where a disciplinary tribunal has dismissed charges and charges are later brought before a court exercising its inherent jurisdiction.[236] There is also provision in New South Wales for the OLSC, when it is reasonable to accept complaints out of the time limit of the three year Statute of

---

232. *Re Veron; Ex parte Law Society of New South Wales* (1966) 84 WN (NSW) Part 1 136 at 141. This case has been cited on numerous occasions for the need to cooperate and not to mislead the tribunal, court or law society: see Moffit J in *Johns v Law Society of NSW* [1982] 2 NSWLR 1 and *In the matter of Chris Christopher* (1991) 5 Legal Profession Disciplinary Reports (NSW) 18.

233. *Malfanti v Legal Profession Disciplinary Tribunal* (1993) 4 Legal Profession Disciplinary Reports (NSW) 17.

234. *Kotowicz v Law Society of New South Wales (No 2)* (unreported, CA(NSW), Kirby P, Samuels and Mahoney JJA, No 392/86, 7 August 1987, BC8701232).

235. *NSW Bar Association v Kalaf* (unreported, CA(NSW), Kirby P, Samuels and Mahoney JJA, No 588/86, 11 October 1988, BC8801429).

236. *Weaver v Law Society of New South Wales* (1979) 142 CLR 201.

Limitation,[237] to do so, and this provision was extended to the councils of the professional associations in July 2000 and incorporated in the new Act in 2004.[238] Furthermore, a plea of double jeopardy cannot be used in a disciplinary proceeding on the same facts for which the lawyer has been acquitted in a criminal matter.[239] The procedural rules will also vary for each jurisdiction. If an appeal is made to the Supreme Court from a tribunal, the court will treat the hearing as being de novo. It has been said that it will give 'great weight to and be slow to differ' from a tribunal's opinion.[240] The High Court has described a hearing de novo as one where 'the matter is heard afresh and a decision is given on the evidence presented at that hearing'.[241]

Amendments to the Act in New South Wales have changed the nature of the appeal.[242] It is no longer de novo but is treated as any appeal. This means the issues and facts as defined and found by the Administrative Decisions Tribunal cannot be changed by the appeal court.[243]

Hearing de novo

If the appeal is a hearing de novo, the court will still have the same approach of giving 'great weight to and be slow to differ' from the opinion of the tribunal, even though tribunals now include lay members.[244] This does not stop the court from forming its own assessment of the evidence and its own view of the principles to be applied. For example, the court is not bound by the tribunal's view of what is required for the protection of the public or by what its own view is of 'prevailing or appropriate standards of conduct of solicitors'.[245] A Victorian judge, Gillard J, recently said: '[The] Court decides the matter afresh, unfettered by anything that the Board has said. Because of the Board's wide experience, I note its conclusion. But having said that, in the end the appeal must be decided by this court on the evidence before it.'[246] The onus of proof does lie on the professional association or authority taking the proceeding but may easily shift to the lawyer because the proceedings are not adversarial. The court

7.93

237. Section 137 of the Legal Profession Act 1987 (NSW). This section was amended in July 2000 to overcome the decision in *Barrwick v Law Society of New South Wales* [1999] HCA 2.
238. Section 506 of the Legal Profession Act 2004 (NSW).
239. The disciplinary proceedings deal with fitness to practise and not the criminality of the action of the practitioner: see *Re Imrie and Institute of Chartered Accountants of Ontario* (1972) 28 DLR 3rd 53 at 55–6.
240. *Re Hodgekiss* (1962) 62 SR (NSW) 340 at 343.
241. *Coal and Allied Operation Pty Ltd v Australian Industrial Relations Commission* (2000) 203 CLR 194 at 203.
242. The *Re Hodgekiss* decision that the hearing was de novo on appeal was adopted under s 171F(4) of the Legal Profession Act 1987 (NSW). This provision was repealed effective from 8 March 1996 by the Courts Legalisation Further Amendment Act (NSW) 1995 and appeals now come under the Supreme Court Act 1970 s 75A. The nature of the appeal to the Supreme Court is found under s 729A of the Legal Profession Act 2004 (NSW).
243. *Walsh v Law Society of New South Wales* [1999] HCA 33.
244. Kirby P and Mahoney JA, *Law Society v Foreman* (1994) 34 NSWLR 408 at 412–13, 446.
245. *Foreman's* case, per Mahoney JA and Giles A-JA at 440, 471.
246. *Frugtniet v Board of Examiners* [2005] VSC 332 at para 8. It should be noted this is an admission case, but it is just as relevant for disciplinary cases.

can 'reformulate or add charges that the lawyer has to answer and the lawyer's response to them become part of the criteria for disciplinary action'.[247] Although these are mainly New South Wales cases, they can now provide guidance to other jurisdictions that have de novo hearings on appeal.

Standard of proof

7.94   Australian courts have accepted that the standard of proof applied in disciplinary matters is civil — that is, to the reasonable satisfaction of the court[248] or on the balance of probabilities — but:[249]

> ... the degree of satisfaction for which the civil standard of proof calls may vary according to the gravity of the facts to be proved [but need never] attain the degree of certainty which is indispensable to the support of a conviction upon a criminal charge.

An interesting problem arose in applying this standard of proof in a case involving a solicitor admitted in both Western Australia and England.[250] There was an allegation that the solicitor had sworn an affidavit in support of her application for divorce that contained material falsehoods. She denied the allegation in a disciplinary action brought against her. She was not present at the hearing, having permanently left Australia, but was represented by counsel. The Barristers' Board stated it had imposed on itself a high standard but not a criminal one and struck her off the rolls. A complaint was then brought in England and the Solicitors' Disciplinary Tribunal struck her off the rolls stating that it was 'far from convinced that any miscarriage of justice had occurred in Western Australia'. On an appeal to the Queen's Bench it was held that the tribunal had to determine whether an allegation of perjury had been proven. The alleged misconduct was tantamount to a criminal offence and the tribunal should require that it be proved beyond a reasonable doubt. The court said it was unclear what standard of proof had been applied by the tribunal or whether it had recognised that it was required to draw its own conclusion on the allegation. Therefore, the decision was quashed and the complaint remitted to the tribunal for redetermination and with the need to apply the criminal standard.[251] Forbes has said the English court's decision is inconsistent with the view in Australia and contrary to an earlier English case.[252]

7.95   In another decision on standard of proof the High Court in the *Smith* case[253] reversed the decision of the Court of Appeal (NSW), striking off the rolls a barrister who 'lied'. The High Court said the fact that a court does not *accept* the testimony of a lawyer does not lead to the conclusion that the lawyer has 'deliberately lied'. Lying in these circumstances would amount to perjury; however, there had not been a proper hearing because

247. Disney et al (above), p 321.
248. *Dewer v Dewer* (1968) 12 FLR 319.
249. *Reifek v McElvoy* (1965) 112 CLR 517 at 521–2.
250. *Re a Solicitor* [1992] 2 WLR 552.
251. *Re a Solicitor* (above) at 562.
252. J R S Forbes, *Disciplinary Tribunals*, 2nd ed, Federation Press, Sydney, 1996, pp 151–2. The English case that comes to a different conclusion is *R v Hampshire County Council; Ex parte Ellerton* [1985] 1 WLR 749.
253. *Smith v New South Wales Bar Association (No 2)* (1992) 66 ALJR 605.

Smith was not given an opportunity to answer the new charge that he had 'deliberately lied' to the Court of Appeal. Also, the Court of Appeal had failed to apply the appropriate standard of proof in coming to its determination. To prove the allegation (perjury), it would need to be shown that the barrister, Smith, deliberately misstated what took place. The High Court sent the matter back to the Court of Appeal for a new hearing on the issue of Smith 'deliberately' lying to that court. Such action by Smith, if proven, would constitute professional misconduct because he lacked candour. The High Court did not indicate the appropriate standard of proof to be applied, but the standard probably would have been higher than the balance of probabilities. Smith negotiated a settlement with the bar, never had a new hearing and returned to practice.

American rules

In the United States the strict rules of evidence are not usually applied in disciplinary hearings. In the individual states different standards of proof have been adopted. The different standards of proof are:

   ❑ clear and convincing evidence;

   ❑ preponderance of the evidence; and

   ❑ evidence beyond a reasonable doubt.

7.96

By far the most common standard used by the courts, following the ABA recommendations, is a 'clear and convincing' standard of proof. The courts have decided that property rights are involved and therefore the constitutional requirement in a criminal case of evidence beyond a reasonable doubt is not applicable.[254]

CRITIQUE AND PROPOSALS FOR REFORM

Reform of the system

The New South Wales Law Reform Commission said that a properly designed complaints system has multiple aims that include: redressing the complaints of dissatisfied consumers, ensuring that practitioners are diligent and competent, and establishing and maintaining a high standard of ethics and practice throughout the profession. In New South Wales the old complaints system was geared mainly to ensuring diligence and competence but did not even satisfy that objective in relation to 'lower level unsatisfactory professional conduct'.[255] In all jurisdictions the legal profession has failed to overcome the problem that lawyers and clients have a different perspective as to what is important in providing legal services. This has caused an 'underlying problem of misunderstanding and lack of communication'.[256]

7.97

Major reforms have taken place in recent years in dealing with complaints, 'notably participation by lay persons in the complaints process, and the increase in the range of sanctions available against legal practitioners'.[257]

7.98

---

254. C Wolfram, *Modern Legal Ethics*, West Publishers, St Paul, 1986, pp 108–10.
255. *Scrutiny of the Legal Profession* (above) (1993), para 4.2.
256. *Scrutiny of the Legal Profession* (above) (1992), para 3.97.
257. *Scrutiny of the Legal Profession* (above) (1992), para 3.98.

The states of Victoria, New South Wales, South Australia, Western Australia, Tasmania and Queensland have made other major reforms in seeking to overcome consumer dissatisfaction. There have been dramatic changes in the structure of the discipline system under the new legal profession Acts adopted in Western Australia in 2003 and in Queensland, New South Wales and Victoria in 2004.

However, even where reform has taken place, it has varied between states and there has been criticism of the changes. New South Wales is the only jurisdiction that legislated a Complainants' Charter of Rights (now incorporated as provisions in the Legal Profession Act 2004). Western Australia is the only jurisdiction that has taken the disciplinary process almost completely away from the professional associations. Finally, only Victoria has given lay people a prominent role in the regulation process. Victoria and New South Wales have also developed the best mediation system that includes compulsory conciliation. The Legal Ombudsman in Tasmania does not have such an active role in the disciplinary process as the offices of Legal Services Commissioner (OLSC) have in Victoria, Queensland and New South Wales. The Tasmanian Ombudsman has more of a monitoring role and is not involved at the initial stages — like the role of the OLSC in New South Wales, Queensland and Victoria.[258] Amendments to the Legal Practitioners Act 1981 in South Australia and the Legal Practitioners (Miscellaneous) Amendment Act 1996 dissolved the old Legal Practitioners Complaints Committee and established a Legal Practitioners Conduct Board. Under Pt 6 of the Act the new board is independent of the profession. In Queensland two separate bodies independent of the profession were established under the Legal Profession Act in 2004 — the Legal Practice Tribunal and the Legal Practice Committee.[259]

Office of Legal Services Commissioner

7.99 Many of the suggestions for reform by the New South Wales Law Reform Commission were adopted in the Legal Profession Reform Act 1993 which amended the Legal Profession Act 1987, including the 'centrepiece' of its reforms — an independent office. The Commission had pointed out that it had 'powerful concerns' about the independence and accountability of a complaints system left primarily in the hands of the profession.[260] It recommended the establishment of an Office of Legal Services Ombudsman (the Act uses Commissioner not Ombudsman) (LSC) with broad powers to receive, investigate and oversee the handling of complaints. The Commissioner would handle the initial intake of all complaints against legal practitioners, including non-lawyers offering legal services, for example licensed conveyancers.[261] The Act did adopt this idea of a separate office with powers to receive, investigate and review the processing of complaints but left out power over licensed conveyancers. Licensed conveyancers are

258. Section 85 of the Legal Profession Act 1993 (Tas). The role of the Commissioner in receiving all initial complaints in Victoria and New South Wales is discussed earlier in the chapter. In Queensland it is found under s 256 of the Legal Profession Act 2004.

259. Sections 429–448 (Tribunal) and ss 449–472 (Committee).

260. *Scrutiny of the Legal Profession* (above) (1993), paras 3.7–3.23.

261. *Scrutiny of the Legal Profession* (above) (1993), recommendation 7, pp 256–7.

disciplined under a separate system.[262] The new 2004 Act has continued the same structure and increased some of the powers — for example compulsory mediation and a register of disciplined lawyers. The OLSC has great power, including the right to dismiss complaints which it determines are 'misconceived or lacking in substance'. The OLSC is at the apex of the complaints handling system with all complaints except those initiated by either the bar or Law Society Councils coming immediately under its jurisdiction. The OLSC also has the power to monitor continuously the progress of all complaints through their different stages.[263] The New South Wales system has been in operation for more than 10 years with the same Commissioner, Steve Mark. It has been the pioneer in establishing an effective and cost-efficient system. It has been so successful that both Queensland and Victoria have adopted similar systems and it has been approved by commentators in the United States and the United Kingdom.

Reports of the New South Wales Commissioner

The fact that the OLSC has the initial contact with the consumers can only make them feel confident that in filing a complaint they are approaching a body that is clearly independent and impartial. There is no longer the psychological barrier of filing a complaint against lawyers with their own professional association (other lawyers). This may be one of the main reasons for an increase of 32 per cent in complaints against lawyers during its first year of operation in New South Wales.[264] Another reason could be a greater awareness by the public because of publicity by the OLSC, or it may mean that the publicity 'stirred up' the public to make complaints. For 1995–96, the second year of operation, written complaints went down slightly, telephone complaints increased by 31 per cent and there was an increase in successful resolution of complaints by mediation.[265] For 1996–97 written complaints increased by 23 per cent, for 1997–98 there was a small decrease in complaints,[266] for 1998–99 an increase of 6 per cent,[267] for 1999–2000 there was hardly any increase (only 32 more files),[268] for 2000–01 it decreased by about 9 per cent (the year of the Olympics),[269] for 2001–02 an increase of 11 per cent,[270] for 2002–03 it decreased by 5.5 per cent,[271] and for the most recent year, 2004–05, it fell by about 4 per cent.[272]

7.100

262. Licensed conveyancers are disciplined by the Director-General under s 133 of the Conveyancers Licensing Act 2003 (NSW). Under s 3 of that Act the Director-General is the Commissioner for Fair Trading in the Department of Commence or, if there is no such position, the Director-General of the Department.
263. See Legal Profession Act 1987 (NSW) Div 32 — Complaints about legal practitioners; and Div 5 — Investigation of complaints.
264. OLSC *Annual Report* 1994–1995 (1996), p 4. See also www.lawlink.nsw.gov.au/ OLSC. This link also has other information besides the annual reports.
265. OLSC *Annual Report* 1995–1996 (1997), p 5.
266. OLSC *Annual Report* 1997–1998 (1999), p 5.
267. OLSC *Annual Report* 1998–1999 (2000), p 5.
268. OLSC *Annual Report* 1999–2000 (2001), p 5.
269. OLSC *Annual Report* 2000–2001 (2002), p 4.
270. OLSC *Annual Report* 2001–2002 (2003), p 4.
271. OLSC *Annual Report* 2002–2003 (2004), p 4.
272. OLSC *Annual Report* 2003–2004 (2005), p 4.

The Commissioner in the latest report observed that the level of complaints had hardly changed in the last few years. Mr Mark felt that this was a significant development because the number of legal practitioners has substantially increased. Furthermore, the statistics from other jurisdictions in Australia, from New Zealand, the United Kingdom and several Canadian jurisdictions, indicate that fewer complaints are brought against lawyers in New South Wales than elsewhere. He concluded: 'This is evidence that our educational and problem solving approach appears to be working.'[273]

During the first two years of operation the OLSC still referred most of the complaints filed to the Law Society and Bar Association,[274] but in the last few years it then stabilised where it referred only around 30 per cent to the Law Society and around 40 per cent to the Bar Association,[275] and by 2004 it was only 22 per cent to both bodies.[276]

7.101 In the first two years of operation the fact that so many complaints were referred to the professional associations and the lack of sensitivity to consumer complaints by the associations possibly erected psychological barriers to initiating a complaint. In the last few years a large majority of the complaints are now handled by the OLSC and this change can only be beneficial for the OLSC in maintaining an independent image. It appears that the OLSC has realised it has to be careful in conducting a co-regulation system and that it does not become merely a 'symbol' of independence from professional influence, rather than truly independent.

Criticism of the system

7.102 The New South Wales Government did reject some important recommendations of the Law Reform Commission. The Act establishes a category called consumer complaints that are to be dealt with by mediation, but the Act calls for voluntary use of the system with agreement by both parties. This was remedied in the Legal Profession Act 2004 (NSW) where compulsory mediation was adopted under s 517, while in Victoria there is a back-up system if one party fails to appear or the mediation is unsuccessful.[277] By contrast, the Queensland Legal Profession Act 2004 adopted the old New South Wales system where there is no obligation to accept mediation.[278] Under the Queensland system there is no provision made for an alternative back-up system if one or both parties refuse to mediate or mediate in bad faith. There is provision in Victoria for compensation to be made by the practitioner to the complainant.[279] In New South Wales a compensation order can also be given even if the practitioner receives only a reprimand or caution under s 540 or s 545 of the

---

273. Ibid, p 2.
274. Approximately 61 per cent were referred in 1995–96 — 60 per cent to the Council of the Law Society and 76 per cent to the Council of the Bar Association: see OLSC *Annual Report* 1995–96 (1997), p 5. Approximately 62 per cent were referred in 1994–95 — 61 per cent to the Council of the Law Society and 82 per cent to the Council of the Bar Association: see OLSC *Annual Report* 1994–95 (1996), p 46.
275. OLSC *Annual Report* 1997–1998 (1999), p 5 and OLSC *Annual Report* 1998–1999 (2000), p 5.
276. OLSC *Annual Report* 2002–2003 (2004), p 4.
277. Legal Profession Act 2004 (Vic) Pts 4.3.12–4.3.14.
278. Sections 262–264.
279. Legal Profession Act 2004 (Vic) Pts 4.2.14 and 4.3.17.

Legal Profession Act 2004, but only if such compensation had been requested by the complainant.[280]

A second major criticism is that the Act does not legislate for:[281] **7.103**

- ❏ the introduction of an English-style 'client care' program;
- ❏ requiring the professional associations to provide a continuing legal education program for practitioners on legal ethics and professional responsibility;
- ❏ ensuring that the professional bodies provide adequate counselling and assistance programs.

The 'client care rule' was adopted by the Council of the English Law Society in 1990. The rule requires solicitors to keep clients informed and obliges law firms to establish procedures within the firm for handling complaints.[282] In New South Wales the Council of the Law Society of New South Wales adopted a similar rule to that in England, entitled a Client Care Guideline to Best Practice, effective 1 January 1996, but it is not binding. The guide has been modified and the latest version is June 2004.[283] In 1998 the New South Wales Law Society launched a Best Practice program that has as one of its aims to improve client satisfaction. The program is taught at the College of Law and includes as part of the training client management and quality assurance. Completion of this course enables practitioners to use the Law Society's 'Towards Best Practice' logo on letterheads and promotional material.[284] There are similar 'best practice' programs throughout Australia. In 2000 a national body for best practice was established and took the name Quality in Law (QL). The programs that are offered have been developed in association with the Australian Quality Council.[285]

The Act does state that one of its objectives of the complaints and **7.104** discipline system is 'to promote and enforce the professional standards, competence and honesty of the legal profession'.[286] The OLSC also has as one of its functions providing assistance to professional associations in promoting community education about the regulation and discipline of the profession and to help them to enhance professional ethics and standards.[287] The problem is that there are no requirements for specific programs. The Commission has during its first 11 years developed videos for consumers and for practitioners, to help them to obtain the best service by showing possible communication problems from each other's perspective. Furthermore, the OLSC produces an informative quarterly newsletter, *Without Prejudice*, and has published 16 different fact sheets and three brochures that explain how it handles and resolves complaints. 'The fact

---

280. Sections 570–571 of the Legal Profession Act 2004 (NSW).
281. For these recommendations and others, see *Scrutiny of the Legal Profession* (above) (1993), paras 5.1–5.31.
282. *Scrutiny of the Legal Profession* (above) (1992), para 3.130. Breach of this rule is not automatically a matter for discipline but it could constitute 'inadequate professional services' and a continuous breach could be professional misconduct.
283. See www.lawsociety.org.uk.
284. Office of the Legal Services Commission, *Without Prejudice*, April/May 1998, No 11, p 1.
285. *Without Prejudice*, OLSC (NSW), August 2001, p 2.
286. Section 494(1)(b) of the Legal Profession Act 2004 (NSW).
287. Section 688(1)(o)(p) of the Legal Profession Act 2004(NSW).

sheets provide information on legal issues for both practitioners and complainants.'[288]

7.105 Until October 1998 there were no judicial members of the tribunal. The Law Reform Commission had argued that judicial involvement would increase the public perception that the tribunal was independent and would help give recognition to the importance of the rights and issues at stake in a disciplinary hearing.[289]

This has now been remedied with the appointment of judicial members to the Administrative Decisions Tribunal. The composition of the tribunal comprises a judicial member; a barrister or solicitor — depending on whether the hearing is for a solicitor or for a barrister; and one lay member.[290]

7.106 There was also criticism of the changes in Victoria under the Legal Practice Act 1996. The government had hoped that new legal profession organisations would be created as competition to the Law Institute and the Bar Association. This is why it legislated for the creation of recognised professional associations (RPAs). The only organisations that became a RPA were the former Law Institute (Victorian Lawyers RPA Ltd) and Bar Association (Victorian Bar Inc) and it appears unlikely any other organisation will be created. The Act also created three bodies to regulate the profession: the RPAs, the Legal Ombudsman and the Legal Practice Board. As the former president of the Victorian Lawyers RPA Ltd, Michael Gawler, stated, these three bodies 'combined appear to be costing Victorian lawyers and the community many millions of dollars more than the total cost of regulation before the introduction of the [1996] Act'. He also complained that the Act is 'unnecessarily complex and difficult'.[291] There was a feeling among Victorian lawyers that the Ombudsman's office was too zealous in pursuing members of the profession. As a result the system was abandoned and one similar to that in New South Wales was adopted in 2004 with two main bodies — the Legal Services Board and the Legal Services Commissioner.[292]

7.107 The changes in New South Wales, and also those in Victoria and Queensland, appear to herald a new age of professional responsibility to the consumer. Future issues will continue to concern the need to provide a system of discipline that ensures the public's trust and confidence in the legal profession. Other jurisdictions in Australia need to reform or further reform their present systems. They can look to New South Wales, Victoria, Queensland or elsewhere in achieving this goal. For example, in California the profession has established a full-time 'bar court' to hear disciplinary

---

288. See www.lawlink.nsw.gov.au/OLSC. This link also has other information including the annual reports.
289. *Scrutiny of the Legal Profession* (above) (1993), para 4.176.
290. Administrative Decisions Tribunal Act 1997 (NSW) Sch 2, Pt 3, Div 3, cl 4.
291. M Gawler, 'The future regulation of Victorian lawyers', May (2000) *Law Institute J* (Vic) 3.
292. Parts 6.2 and 6.3 of the Legal Profession Act 2004 (Vic). For an excellent discussion of the problems of the Legal Practice Act 1996 and suggested alternative regulatory bodies, see P Sallmann and R Wright, *Legal Practice Act Review*, March 2001. The study was commissioned by the Victorian Government. Extracts from the report can be found in Y Ross and P MacFarlane, *Lawyers' Responsibility and Accountability — Cases, Problems and Commentary*, 2nd ed, LexisNexis Butterworths, Sydney, 2004, pp 91–101.

matters. The court is completely independent of the profession and is comprised of a presiding judge, six hearing judges and two review judges (one is a lay person). If the state bar decides not to file formal charges with the bar court the complainant can appeal to a Complainants Grievance Panel that has substantial lay representation. There exists also an independent discipline monitor who reports annually to the California State Legislature on how the system is operating.[293]

Lawyer ethics schools

An original alternative solution to disciplining lawyers in the United States, that we may follow, was the establishment of lawyer ethics schools. The ABA Commission on Disciplinary Enforcement recommended that all jurisdictions adopt educational programs for minor misconduct. Most states have substance abuse programs and several states have ethics schools. These ethics schools teach lawyers how to avoid future misconduct. They are similar to state-run traffic schools for motorists. A lawyer can choose to go to an ethics school as an alternative to receiving a sanction. The schools are only used for lawyers accused of minor misconduct, such as failure to return telephone calls.[294] The California Bar's school course consists of eight hours of instruction on professional responsibility. It includes questions and answers, a hypothetical, and information about substance abuse, stress management and a final examination. The sessions are interactive, concentrating on risk management strategies and various disciplinary cases. According to a 1995 survey only 6.6 per cent of the 1450 lawyers who successfully completed the course have had a subsequent ethics inquiry by the bar.[295] A more recent study in Arizona found that those who met the requirements of the ethics program had a lower likelihood of recidivism than those who did not.[296] The California Bar also conducts a client trust accounting school.[297] It would appear that lawyers face a future system of discipline that will be responsive to consumer demands and emphasise prevention and rehabilitation for professional misconduct.

7.108

---

293. *Scrutiny of the Legal Profession* (above) (1992), paras 3.147–3.151.
294. Resnick, 'Lawyer Ethics School Created: Florida is Third State', 29 June 1992, *National LJ* 3.
295. D Snyder, 'Bar's ethics school aids the errants', May (1996) *California Bar J* 31, 34.
296. D Ellis, 'A Decade of Diversion: Empirical Evidence that Alternative Discipline is Working for Arizona Lawyers' (2002) 52 *Emory LJ* 1221.
297. July (1997) *California Bar J* 27.

PART THREE

The Lawyer–Client Relationship

8

DUTIES OF
REPRESENTATION

INTRODUCTION

Within the lawyer–client relationship there are certain obligations for both the lawyer and the client. In this Part we will deal with the major general duties lawyers owe to their clients. These include the duties to act, to inform, to obey instructions, to be competent, to preserve clients' confidences and to be loyal. Of course, there are limitations on the scope of these duties, including certain restrictions on the behaviour of the client. Furthermore, as we will see in Part 4, where we will discuss the ethical duties of lawyers resulting from the adversary system, frequently these obligations will override the lawyers' ethical duties as discussed in Part 3. For example, if a client commits perjury in court the lawyer's duty of candour will override or modify his or her duty of confidentiality. **8.1**

In Parts 3 and 4 we are concerned with the applicable principles. Some of the principles are mandatory and are legally binding by either statute or common law. Some are not legally binding because they have only been adopted by professional associations and/or disciplinary tribunals, unless a statutory provision makes these principles binding in law. Those that do not have statutory backing can also be called mandatory because it is highly likely they will be followed by the courts. Others urge a certain kind of behaviour which will be likely to be adopted by disciplinary tribunals and/or courts and are therefore quasi-mandatory. There are some that are advisory and unlikely ever to have legal effect, but have considerable influence on how lawyers behave. Finally, there are some that are advisory, stating that lawyers may behave in a certain way. These principles are flexible and are therefore permissive.[1] Certain principles apply only to a particular category of lawyers (for example, barristers only). **8.2**

---

1. J Disney, J Basten, P Redmond and S Ross, *Lawyers*, 2nd ed, Law Book Co, Sydney, 1986, p 597. The categories and content have been modified according to the author's view.

8.3 Throughout both Parts it will be necessary to establish the existence of a client–lawyer relationship. In the United States s 14 of the Restatement of the Law Governing Lawyers 3rd states:

> A relationship of client and lawyer arises when:
>
> (1) A person manifests to a lawyer the person's intent that the lawyer provide legal services for the person; and
>
> (2) (a) The lawyer manifests to the person consent to do so, or
>
>   (b) fails to manifest lack of consent to do so, when the lawyer knows or reasonably should know that the person reasonably relies on the lawyer to provide the services ...

It should be noted that at times lawyers will be held responsible to non-clients who have reasonably relied on the lawyer.

Sources of guidance

8.4 Until recently lawyers have had little professional guidance to help them resolve ethical problems. In the early 1980s only South Australia and Western Australia and the bar associations in Victoria, Queensland and New South Wales had adopted formal codes of ethics. Now there are conduct rules for legal practitioners and barristers in all jurisdictions. The Law Council of Australia's Model Rules of Professional Conduct and Practice are also being used as a basis for the adoption of rules in most jurisdictions: see **1.4**. The rules are also becoming more effective in controlling the behaviour of practitioners. The solicitor and barrister rules in New South Wales now have some legal effect for disciplinary proceedings under the Legal Profession Act 2004 s 711[2] and a similar effect under Pt 3.2.17 of the new Legal Profession Act 2004 in Victoria. Furthermore, professional bodies are issuing many more rulings and official statements.[3]

8.5 Other sources of guidance include:

- ❑ legislation that is general, for example fraud under the Crimes Acts, or more specific provisions, such as the trust account provisions in the various Legal Practitioners' Acts;
- ❑ the general common law principles, for example the law relating to breach of contract, or specific principles such as lawyer–client privilege;
- ❑ judicial and disciplinary tribunal statements dealing with ethical issues which are not legally binding but which give guidance;
- ❑ the legal writings of judges, academics and lawyers;[4]
- ❑ conventions and customs, especially those followed by barristers.

8.6 Law students and lawyers have a difficult time applying the principles that are relevant to the behaviour of their profession. The vast majority are trained with the notion that a legal norm is either violated or complied with and there is then an appropriate sanction. In reality all areas of the law have grey areas and have a number of different sources to access in finding

---

2. Section 711 states that the professional conduct rules are binding on Australian legal practitioners and locally registered foreign lawyers. It states: 'Failure to comply with legal profession rules is capable of being unsatisfactory professional conduct or professional misconduct.' There is a similar effect in Victoria: Pt 3.2.17 of the Legal Profession Act 2004.

3. These rulings and statements appear in professional journals and/or are sent to the practitioners.

4. Disney et al (above), pp 597–8.

relevant principles. The main difference is that in other areas of law the drafting of principles and their enunciation by tribunals and courts is usually clearer and easier to access than those used to control lawyers' behaviour.

The numerous sources for the body of principles that governs lawyers' behaviour lack coherence. The principles:[5]

> ... are often stated in unduly vague or misleading terms, are in conflict with other principles or are of uncertain authority. In addition ... there is considerable uncertainty as to what sanction, if any, will be imposed for breach of a particular principle.

There is a greater challenge in learning and applying these principles. Students must avoid the 'black letter' approach and seek the 'spirit' of the rules. They should heed this advice from the Bible: 'The Letter killeth but the Spirit giveth Light' (II Corinthians 3:6).

8.7

In this chapter we will look first at the obligations of entering into a relationship, that is, the duty to serve. We will then examine the problems of representing unpopular or repugnant clients. We will conclude by looking at the duties relating to termination of the relationship and the clients' right of dismissal.

REPRESENTATION

Barristers — 'cab-rank' rule

Lawyers are the key-holders to the legal system because they have a monopoly over legal services. Without their help many people would be unable to exercise their legal rights. It is therefore essential that clients have access to lawyers' services. In Chapter 2 we quoted the famous statement of Erskine, to justify his unpopular defence of the revolutionary Tom Paine. He said:[6]

8.8

> From the moment that any advocate can be permitted to say that he will or will not stand between the Crown and the subject arraigned in the court where he daily sits to practise, from that moment the liberties of England are at an end.

Erskine was a prominent barrister. He took his stance with the knowledge that in accepting Paine as a client he had the support of the 'cab-rank' rule, that is, barristers, like cab drivers, must act on a first come, first serve basis. Rule 85 of the Barristers' Rules New South Wales and Rule 89 in Queensland state:

> A barrister must accept a brief from a solicitor to appear before a court in a field in which the barrister practises or professes to practise if:
>
> (a) the brief is within the barrister's capacity, skill and experience;
>
> (b) the barrister would be available to work as a barrister when the brief would require the barrister to appear or to prepare, and the barrister is not already committed to other professional or personal engagements which may, as a real possibility, prevent the barrister from being able to advance a client's interests to the best of the barrister's skill and diligence;

5.   Disney et al (above), p 598.
6.   Quoted by Lord Pearce in *Rondel v Worsley* [1969] 1 AC 191 at 274 (HL).

(c) the fee offered on the brief is acceptable to the barrister; and

(d) the barrister is not obliged or permitted to refuse the brief under Rules 87, 90 or 91. [In Queensland it is under Rules 91–93, 95–97.]

8.9   There is a similar rule in England from which the New South Wales and Queensland rule originate.[7] The mandatory requirement is only for briefs coming from a solicitor. There is no obligation to represent a client directly.

In Victoria Rule 86 is broader, requiring the acceptance of all briefs coming from a solicitor. This means it covers not only court work but also chamber work — to give advice or to draw pleadings.

Although the 'cab-rank' rule is mandatory it is also supported by anti-discrimination legislation such as the Commonwealth Racial Discrimination Act 1975. That Act makes it unlawful to refuse to act for a person 'by reason of the race, colour or national or ethnic origin'.[8] Anti-discrimination legislation in some states also prohibits discrimination in providing services because of sex, age or marital status.[9] In Queensland the bar has adopted Rule 130 which states:

> A barrister must not in conduct of the barrister's practice discriminate against a client, solicitor, or another barrister on the basis of the person's religion, age, race, impairment, political belief or activity, trade union activity, sex, marital status, pregnancy, parental status, lawful sexual activity or association with, or relation to, a person identified on the basis of any of the above.

Arguments for and against the 'cab-rank' rule

8.10   The 'cab-rank' rule analogy, requiring barristers to serve the next person in the queue, is not a particularly fitting one: cab drivers are licensed to ensure that adequate service is provided at a fair price, while lawyers are licensed for the very different purpose of ensuring competence. This means providing service at an appropriate standard. Furthermore, lawyers need to establish a relationship with their clients based on trust, which is not a consideration for cabbies. These arguments ignore the fact that the client is the main beneficiary of the relationship and has the freedom to choose the lawyer. If lawyers can pick and choose their clients there is a danger that some will go unrepresented or have access only to poorer lawyers, because these people have a bad reputation or are poor.[10]

Bagaric and Dimopoulos point out that the trust issue is one-sided and the lawyer is disadvantaged. While the lawyer is required by his or her fiduciary duties to create a relationship based on trust, the lawyer does not have enough time to determine the 'trustworthiness or general character of the client'.[11]

A number of commentators have pointed out that the 'cab-rank' rule is ineffective because it has so many exceptions. For example, Rule 85 (see above) has numerous exceptions besides that of needing to act only in areas in which the barrister practises or professes to practise. There are also

---

7.   Code of Conduct, para 209.

8.   Section 13. See also Equal Opportunities Act 1997 (Vic) s 26.

9.   See, for example, Anti-discrimination Act 1977 (NSW).

10.   J Basten, 'Control and the Lawyer–Client Relationship' (1981) 6 *Journal of the Legal Profession* 7, 34.

11.   M Bagaric and P Dimopoulos, 'Legal Ethics is (Just) Normal Ethics: Towards a Coherent System of Legal Ethics' (2003) 3 *QUTLJ* 21.

mandatory exceptions[12] and discretionary ones.[13] Many of the mandatory exceptions concern situations of conflict of interests or maintaining confidences.[14] Instances of refusals to act that are discretionary include: where the brief is one not offered by a solicitor; where the length of time needed to deal with the matter would prejudice the barrister's practice;[15] where the solicitor is on the 'blacklist' for not having another barrister paid reasonably promptly or in accordance with the costs agreement;[16] where there are reasonable grounds to believe that the fee may not be paid; and several other situations dealing with confidences and conflict of interests.[17]

Barristers' clerks have the authority to accept briefs for barristers. It is **8.11** obvious from all the exceptions that these clerks have tremendous discretion in protecting barristers from unwanted briefs.[18] Lord Steyn of the House of Lords said that the clerk had the ability to reject briefs and also raise the fee, within limits. He felt that the 'cab-rank' rule was not likely to oblige barristers to take unwanted work.[19] By contrast, in *D'Orta-Ekenaike v Victoria Legal Aid*[20] Callinan J stated that the Australian clerk system is different. He said that: 'It would be wrong for a barrister, or a barrister's clerk in Australia, and it is not the practice ... to raise a barrister's fee as a device to avoid an unwanted brief.' Furthermore, he stated that in only two of the states with a functionally divided profession do barristers employ clerks and their role 'is increasingly administrative, and removed from the fixation of fees'.

The New South Wales Law Reform Commission has stated:[21]

> In our view, the main practical effect of the [cab-rank] rule ... is not that it forces reluctant barristers into accepting unpopular cases, but rather that it reduces criticism of barristers who do take such cases.

Furthermore, although in all jurisdictions there is now direct access to barristers, access in the vast majority of cases (the exception is criminal cases) is through a solicitor who can also protect barristers from being briefed in unwanted matters. Without a solicitor the 'cab-rank' rule, in the vast majority of cases, does not come into effect as solicitors do not have any mandatory duty to accept work.[22] For example, there was a reported case where a plaintiff was successful in suing a psychiatric hospital for false imprisonment, assault and battery, and negligent treatment by a psychiatrist. The plaintiff said the hardest part of the case was going from solicitor to solicitor with no one wanting to take the case.[23]

---

12. Rules 87, 89–90.
13. Rules 91, 92.
14. Rules 87(a)–(j) and 89.
15. Rule 91(a) and (b).
16. Rule 92.
17. Rule 91(c)–(g).
18. See editorial, 'Taking sides', *New Law J*, 9 February 1990, p 157. For further comments on the editorial see the *New Law J*, 2 March 1990, pp 284–6.
19. *Hall & Co v Simons* [2000] 3 All ER 673.
20. [2005] HCA 12 at para 377.
21. First Report on the Legal Profession (1982), New South Wales Law Reform Commission, para 6.78.
22. See, for example, *Queensland Solicitors Handbook*, para 5.01(1), which states there is no duty to accept work.
23. G Turnbull, 'Former Psychiatric Patient Claims "Significant" Court Win', *Sydney Morning Herald*, 17 July 1980, p 18.

8.12 The 'cab-rank' rule is also open to abuse if a wealthy client ties up all the available legal talent in a certain area by being the first one to brief all the main barristers. This happened in Queensland where the plaintiff, by briefing 14 QCs, tried to corner the market in legal talent. Mackenzie J upheld the right of the plaintiff to take this course of action and to disqualify a QC who had given an opinion to the plaintiff from acting for the defendant.[24] According to Young J of the New South Wales Supreme Court there is also:[25]

> ... anecdotal evidence that in some fields where a limited number of experienced practitioners, such as being at the liquor bar, some clients will deliberately brief barristers giving them confidential information about their business activities, to make sure that the barrister can never appear against them.

Solicitors and overseas lawyers

8.13 As stated, there is no 'cab-rank' rule for solicitors in Australia but they are subject to anti-discrimination legislation. The Law Society of New South Wales has stated that there is a moral obligation to accept work 'in cases of dire emergency or unavailability of alternative practitioners'. The Law Society also said 'that in practice this subjective moral obligation [to accept work] felt by most solicitors is subject only to the same exceptions applying to ... barristers ...'.[26] More recently, in 1994, in its second draft of its aspirational code, the New South Wales Law Society said there is no obligation to accept work, although in the final draft this provision was omitted.[27] Furthermore, the 1996 and 1997 Law Council of Australia's Model Rules, proposed for state law societies, has no 'cab-rank' rule.

8.14 This attitude may be changing. The Council of the New South Wales Law Society in October 1997 in *Caveat News Bulletin* 187 sought its members' views as to adoption of a 'cab-rank' rule. The then president, Patrick Fair, argued that a rule was needed in light of the fact that in the 1997–98 Practising Certificate Renewal Survey, just under 10 per cent of solicitors spent more than one-quarter of their time doing adversary work. Some members have raised the issue of wearing wigs and gowns now that they are permitted to practise as 'solicitors and barristers'. While investigating this matter the Chief Justice raised the issue of whether solicitors who practise as advocates might be bound by a 'cab-rank' rule. Mr Fair also argued that the extensive participation by solicitors in pro bono schemes indicated 'a recognition of a duty to represent clients who would otherwise be unable to obtain representation'.

8.15 The arguments against a solicitor's 'cab-rank' rule are: there is a much greater supply of solicitors than barristers, and thus a client in all likelihood will find someone willing to act; and solicitors can act as a sieve by filtering out 'unmeritorious or irksome' matters. Thus, a 'cab-rank' rule would impose a far greater responsibility on solicitors than the rule imposed on barristers.

---

24. *Australian Commercial Research and Development Ltd v Hampson* [1991] 1 Qd R 508.
25. *Ng v Goldberg* (SC(NSW), August 1993, unreported, p 16).
26. 'Duty to Accept Work', Law Society of New South Wales submission to the New South Wales Law Reform Commission, 1979, pp 3–4.
27. Draft Code of Conduct (NSW) 1994, r 2.2. For the final draft where this provision was omitted, see *Law Society J (NSW)*, December, 1994, p 74.

The main argument for the rule is that solicitors are the main access for clients to be represented by a barrister. Recent changes allowing direct access to barristers will only relieve this problem on rare occasions, as the vast majority of the bar's work will still come from solicitors. A 'cab-rank' rule only for advocate solicitors would tremendously increase direct access to lawyers by the public. As of June 2005 no rule has been adopted.

There has been considerable debate in the United States as to whether to **8.16** adopt the 'cab-rank' rule. Such a rule was included in the draft Model Rules in an early version but was omitted from subsequent drafts.[28] The general rule in the United States and elsewhere in the world is that there is no duty for lawyers to accept work, except where their professional association or a court assigns them to the client. The International Code of Ethics of the International Bar Association states: 'Lawyers shall at any time be free to refuse to handle a case, unless it is assigned by a competent body.'[29] The International Bar Association's view is supported by Linowitz. He states:

> If you have the client simply because you were next on the cab rank, you can be truly convinced of the justice of his cause (and thus the injustice of his antagonist's cause) only by autohypnosis, which is not the mark of professionalism. And the best lawyers, the ones we should wish to regard as our models, have in the end accepted clients very largely through judgments as to whether or not they were willing to be associated with this person's cause.

Linowitz does say that the British barristers do not really religiously follow **8.17** the 'cab-rank' rule because the better barristers will not deal with solicitors they do not trust. I believe there is a similar attitude among leading Australian barristers.[30]

In the United States many states administer an ABA recommended oath upon admission. It includes a pledge: 'That I will never reject, from any consideration personal to myself, the cause of the defenceless oppressed ...'. This oath does not seem to have legal status. Model Rule 6.2 states the only mandatory requirement: 'A lawyer shall not seek to avoid appointment by a tribunal to represent a person except for good cause such as (a) representing the client is likely to result in violation of the rules of Professional Conduct or other law; (b) representing the client is likely to result in an unreasonable financial burden on the lawyer; or (c) the client or cause is so repugnant to the lawyer as to be likely to impair the client lawyer relationship or the lawyer's ability to represent the client.' Nothing is said about appointments by bar associations. Furthermore, Model Rule 1.2(b) states: '[R]epresentation of a client, including representation by appointment does not constitute an endorsement of the client's political, economic, social or moral views or activities.'

Unpopular and repugnant clients

Professional rules

The rules concerning duties of representation come under most strain in **8.18** dealing with unpopular or repugnant clients. The 'cab-rank' rule helps

28. Draft Model Rules, r 1.15, January 1980, cited in Disney et al (above), p 602.
29. See Rule 10, International Code of Ethics (International Bar Association).
30. S Linowitz with M Mayer, *The Betrayed Profession: Lawyering at the end of the Twentieth Century*, Charles Scribner's Sons, New York, 1994, pp 25–6.

barristers in Australia to take unpopular cases. Without the rule some 'could be deterred if such appearances were generally construed by professional colleagues and the public as expressions of sympathy for the client's cause'.[31] Bagaric and Dimopoulos see the main advantage of the rule as protecting barristers from choosing 'between their hip pocket and social condemnation ... [Thus] the principle may be an economic expedient as opposed to a moral prescription'. They conclude that: 'There appears to be no moral basis for maintaining the cab rank rule. The only benefit from it is that it assists lawyers to take on socially unpopular matters. If the rule is to remain, it should no longer be considered as an aspect of legal "ethics".'[32]

Until 1994 the New South Wales Bar Rules had as one of the exceptions rule 2(o). This provision allowed refusal to act when a barrister held 'a conscientious belief which on reasonable grounds he [or she] considers would preclude him [or her] from fairly presenting his [or her] client's case'. The removal of the rule provoked a lively debate for and against its revocation. As one barrister pointed out:[33]

> ... when a barrister conscientiously objected he or she would indicate to the client the nature of the problem of conscience and the client would normally not hire that barrister.

Bagaric and Dimopoulos would have argued against the revocation of rule 2(o). They state that the more persuasive argument against the 'cab-rank' rule is that it violates the barrister's personal right to liberty which includes the right of freedom of association. There are some barristers who will not want to represent certain clients and should be given this choice because there are still many barristers who are willing to represent anyone.[34]

8.19 Under the New South Wales and Queensland Barristers' Rules (r 6), barristers 'must accept briefs to appear regardless of their personal prejudices'. The Victorian Bar does not have an equivalent of r 6 but does have r 11 which is identical to r 16 in New South Wales and Queensland. It states that once a barrister takes on a case he or she:

> ... must seek to advance and protect the client's interests to the best of the barrister's skill and diligence, uninfluenced by the barrister's point of view of the client or the client's activities, and notwithstanding any threatened unpopularity or criticism of the barrister or any other person, and always in accordance with the law including these Rules.

In Germany there is a rule allowing lawyers to refuse to take a case 'against the lawyer's personal conviction as to its legal justification and against those rules of law and morals that he [or she] ought to take into account'. The rule does not apply in criminal defence matters.[35]

---

31. First Report on the Legal Profession (above), para 6.78.
32. M Bagaric and P Dimopoulos (above).
33. See M Sharp and D Killick, 'Conscience in the balance', *Sydney Morning Herald*, 8 March 1993, p 11.
34. M Bagaric and P Dimopoulos (above).
35. D Rueschemeyer, *Lawyers and Their Society*, Harvard University Press, Cambridge, Mass, 1973, p 125.

American professional rules

In the United States there has been a general proposition that there is an obligation to accept unpopular clients.[36] The comment [5] to Model Rule 1.2 states that:

> Legal representation should not be denied to people who are unable to afford legal services, or whose cause is controversial or the subject of popular disapproval. By the same token, representing a client does not constitute approval of the client's view or activities.

8.20

Unpopular clients are also discussed in the comment to Model Rule 6.2. It adopts a flexible approach to the matter. It states: 'A lawyer ordinarily is not obliged to accept a client whose character or cause the lawyer regards as repugnant.' By contrast, the same comment notes that a lawyer has pro bono responsibilities under r 6.1 that are met by 'accepting a fair share of unpopular matters or indigent or unpopular clients'.

In the older ABA Model Code, EC2-27 states that no matter what his or her personal feelings are, 'a lawyer should not decline representation because a client or a cause is unpopular or community reaction is adverse'. Model Code EC2-26 modifies this requirement by stating that a 'lawyer is under no obligation to act as advisor or advocate for every person who may wish to become his client', but modifies this by stating that 'a lawyer should not lightly decline' the representation. There are states that have mandatory representation. For example, all Californian lawyers take an attorney's oath when admitted. The oath is set out in the California Business and Professional Code. Under s 6068(h), it is a duty for every lawyer to 'never reject, for any consideration personal to himself or herself, the cause of the defenseless or oppressed'.

8.21

Moral issues — American perspective

There are a number of complicated moral issues involved in this area. The present drive to increase pro bono work is the recognition by the legal profession in Australia and the United States that the profession has a moral obligation to provide legal services to those who are in need. The moral duty stems from the monopoly lawyers have over providing services in relation to a complex system. Without these services many people would be denied their legal rights. If lawyers are allowed to choose their clients there will be situations where some clients may not receive any representation. But should every interest be heard? For example, do Nazis, racists, rapists, serial killers or child pornographers have the right to have lawyers represent them? A second issue is: if all interests should have representation, how can lawyers be protected from becoming identified with their clients even though their codes explicitly state they should not be so identified? A third issue is: how closely should lawyers identify with their clients' causes, for example zealous or fearless partisanship versus maintaining objectivity?

8.22

The duty to represent an unpopular or repugnant client has two aspects. The first stems from identification that results in loss of business and does not disturb the lawyer's moral universe. From a moral perspective this client

8.23

---

36. M Freedman, *Lawyers' Ethics in an Adversary System*, Bobbs-Merrill, Indianapolis, 1975, p 10.

should be represented in all situations where the lawyer is competent and available. The second situation can possibly also lead to the loss of business but includes the fact that the lawyer finds the views of the prospective client morally repugnant.

Wolfram's view is that a repugnant client should be represented only if:

❑ the client's claim is legally just;

❑ the client's claim is a morally important and compelling one; and,

❑ the client's need for this particular lawyer's services is truly pressing.[37]

8.24   The first thing to decide is who is repugnant. This is an individual decision based on objection to the client's goals, but not necessarily to the client *per se*. Wolfram rejects the argument that clients who are ethically worthless people should not be represented — ethical 'shunning'. Ethical shunning does not take into regard a person's human dignity and seems only appropriate in extreme cases of unrepentant moral agents. Thus, a prospective client who needs to protect a legal right to an 'essential human need' should be represented. For example, a Nazi deserves representation in a custody or murder case but should be denied representation for immoral purposes, for example seeking a permit to distribute hate literature.[38] Others would argue that even in the latter situation a Nazi should be represented because the lawyers are vindicating a broader principle, for example freedom of speech and freedom of the press.[39]

8.25   Wolfram does accept the fact that some lawyers would claim that their repulsion to Nazism (or to rape) was so strong they could not competently represent such a client in any matter. In the United States some significant identification occurs between lawyers and their clients. It is probably not as strong as the position taken by the famous radical lawyer William Kunstler. His view was that he represented only clients he loved.[40] Lawyers know that they are often identified with their client so most would refuse to represent a Nazi. A famous civil liberty lawyer, Charles Garry, while saying that Nazis should be represented, said they would not have his representation. He added:[41]

> In an ordinary criminal case with no political or racial overtones, I don't have to like my client or dislike him ... You've got to have empathy for him, though; you have to understand him, so that you can start relating to and explaining him.

8.26   A third criminal defence lawyer, Abbe Smith, describes her feelings if she had to represent an accused who intentionally killed a stranger, a woman, because he saw her making love to another woman. She concludes that she would use as a provocation defence the fact that he was homophobic; this might get the charges dropped from murder to manslaughter. She says the choice would be easier if she was the only available public defender:[42]

37.   C Wolfram, 'A Lawyer's Duty to Represent Clients, Repugnant and Otherwise' in D Luban, *The Good Lawyer: Lawyers' Roles and Lawyers' Ethics*, Rowman and Allanheld, Totowa, NJ, 1984, p 223.

38.   C Wolfram (above), pp 225–31.

39.   D Luban, *Lawyers and Justice: an Ethical Study*, Princeton University Press, Princeton, NJ, 1988, pp 160–2.

40.   D Luban (above), p 224.

41.   Basten (above), p 33.

42.   A Smith, 'On Representing a Victim of Crime' in G Bellow and M Minnow, *Law Stories*, University of Michigan, Ann Arbor, 1996, pp 163–4.

The role of a public defender is to defend poor people accused of crimes, not to judge them. In view of the public hostility most criminal defendants face, and their lack of choice in counsel if they are poor, public defenders ought to be steadfast. If our clients can't choose their lawyers, why should we be able to choose our clients? The accused criminal defendant should not have to face the charges alone, whatever the nature of the charge. Soon enough, if convicted, the defendant will have to serve the sentence alone. My answer is not simply intellectual … There is a defender in my soul … I have represented many clients alleged to have committed acts of hate and violence. I have represented some clients accused of bias crimes. I have represented some clients who seem to be almost heartless. I have never felt unable to provide zealous, even empathic advocacy …

The truth is, no matter what crimes my clients are accused of committing, once I become their lawyer I feel a connection to them. No matter who they are, there is almost always something to like about them, or at least something redemptive.

Wolfram points out that the American style of representation of intense client loyalty — zealous advocacy — means that a lawyer not committed to a repugnant client will present a flawed case. He concludes, however, that a flawed representation is still better than no representation at all, as long as the client chooses in full awareness of the lawyer's repulsion.[43]

Unpopular clients in Australia and the United States

In contrast to the American position, the English and Australian 'cab-rank' rule supports the 'accepted symbol of professional detachment'. Under its protection 'the Bar can perform its basic task of representation or counsel on a strictly professional and independent footing'.[44] The bar in Australia has on numerous occasions defended its members from attack for accepting briefs for unpopular clients. For example, the bar defended Dr Evatt in 1950 for taking a brief to contest the validity of the Communist Party Dissolution Act. Evatt, a King's Counsel, a former High Court judge and Labor Party Attorney-General, was strongly criticised for taking the case.[45] The committee of the bar defended his action by issuing a detailed statement in support of a barrister's right to accept a brief. It was stated at the time that the Bar Chairman had a subsequent sharp decline in his practice that was due to the committee's statement.[46]

8.27

A similar problem occurred for the American Civil Liberty Union (ACLU) when they were the only ones willing to represent a group of neo-Nazis. The Nazis (as they called themselves) were opposing Skokie Village's (Illinois) attempt to obtain an injunction to stop them from staging an anti-Jewish march. The ACLU pointed out that its lawyers did not agree with what the Nazis wanted to say, nor did these lawyers even necessarily believe that the Nazis had a right to say it.[47] These lawyers were representing abhorrent clients with repellent objectives in order to vindicate the broad important principle of the right to peaceful demonstration. The ACLU

8.28

---

43. Wolfram (above), p 224.
44. E Rostow, 'The Lawyer and His Client' (1962) 48 *American Bar Association J* 25, 29.
45. A Dean, *A Multitude of Counsellors*, Longman Cheshire, Melbourne, 1968, pp 161, 191 and 206, extracted in Disney et al (above), pp 604–5.
46. Disney et al (above), p 605.
47. D Goldberger, 'Would You Defend an Unpopular Cause?' (1978) 5 *Barrister* 46.

suffered considerable harm, especially loss of financial support from many Jewish contributors. Neither did the ACLU receive active support from the local or Chicago bar associations.[48]

Wolfram states:

> Setting aside any strategic decisions about defending civil liberties, would a duty to represent have existed if one could have foreseen the quite considerable harm that the ACLU suffered as a result of its decision to provide representation?

He also says sensible moral values have to include:[49]

> A desire not to ruin one's private practice or one's organisation; not to impair seriously the extent to which one can make credible arguments on behalf of other clients, not to bring public scorn upon one's family and friends — these and similar concerns are legitimately compelling.

8.29 The bar associations in the United States have been notorious throughout their history for not making sure lawyers are available for unpopular clients.[50] They have also failed actively to come to the defence of lawyers representing unpopular clients.[51] The ACLU and individual lawyers have borne the burden of making sure unpopular clients are represented. A recent example is the appointment by the ACLU of a black lawyer, Anthony Griffin, to represent the Texas Grand Dragon of the Ku Klux Klan. The ACLU had appointed him without knowing he was black to represent the Klan leader for seeking to deny the Texas Human Rights Commission access to the Klan membership list. Griffin cited in support of his representation a similar case where the NAACP was granted the right of privacy when the state of Alabama sought to obtain its membership list.[52] Griffin summed up his views for acting by stating: 'What is happening to him today can happen to us next. None of us can close our eyes to these issues. This has nothing to do with colour, but is free speech.'

Griffin has been criticised strongly by black groups for his action and the Texas National Association for the Advancement of Colored People (NAACP) demanded his resignation.[53] The story had a happy ending with Griffin winning the case and receiving the first annual William Brennan Award[54] for upholding freedom of expression. Griffin has stated: 'In our role as lawyers, we're not God. If lawyers backed off because someone is unpopular or hated, then our whole system of justice would just fall apart.'[55]

8.30 In the United States there was also the debate over the representation of Credit Suisse by the prestigious New York law firm of Cravath, Swaine & Moore. Twelve young associates in this firm protested that its representation added the firm's 'imprimatur' and gave 'legitimacy' to this client. Credit

---

48. D Goldberger (above).
49. Wolfram (above), p 231.
50. See, for example, Chapter 8, 'Cold War Conformity' in J Auerbach, *Unequal Justice*, Oxford University Press, New York, 1976.
51. D Goldberger, 'The "Right to Counsel" in Political Cases: The Bar's Failure' (1979) 43 *Law & Contemporary Problems* 321.
52. *NAACP v Alabama* 357 US 449 (1958).
53. S Krun, 'A black and white case of civil rights', *Australian*, 30 September 1993, p 9.
54. William Brennan was a famous liberal United States Supreme Court judge.
55. Quoted in R Zitrin and C Langford, *Legal Ethics in the Practice of Law*, the Michie Company, Charlottesville, Virginia, 1995, p 51.

Suisse was having a dispute with the families of victims of the Holocaust over deposits that had been kept hidden from those families. The argument by the Cravath 12 was that the adversary system required the firm to do its best for its client and this could only result in an injustice to the families of the victims. Their view was supported by a prominent Washington lawyer, Ronald Goldfarb, who argued that Credit Suisse deserved representation but not necessarily by lawyers who find their client's morals abhorrent. However, Alan Dershowitz, a famous Harvard law professor, defended Cravath's actions because of the need to have every client provided with adequate representation. Dershowitz argued that allowing lawyers to be the judges as to who deserves representation would establish a dangerous precedent. He said: 'Good lawyers should represent bad clients, just as good doctors should treat bad patients.'[56]

It has been argued that if a 'cab-rank' rule existed in the United States, action such as the ACLU's in *Skokie*, Anthony Griffin's representation in the *Klan* case and Cravath's in *Credit Suisse* might be more readily accepted. The reason given is that lawyers would be able to claim immunity from being identified with clients not only in the case of unpopular clients.[57] Against this argument is the fact that even in Australia, which has the 'cab-rank' rule, lay people will still often identify lawyers with their clients.[58] The problem was addressed by a former President of the Law Council of Australia, Alex Chernov. He stated:[59]

    8.31

> The labelling of the lawyer who has advised or acted in relation to a transaction which is rightly or otherwise condemned by so called public opinion as immoral, by inference denies to the client the right to seek legal advice in respect of that transaction. What is perhaps more important, it also puts pressure on lawyers to engage in moral judgment when asked to give legal advice or act for the client in respect of a transaction which is or may become unpopular. Moreover, it has a tendency to inhibit lawyers from providing independent legal advice or otherwise acting at all in relation to transactions which are perceived as being unpopular.

Leaders of the profession like Chernov are rightly concerned by the problem of the public identifying lawyers with their clients' morals. The author has received anecdotal examples on a number of occasions of this taking place and the lawyer being penalised. One example was that of a young junior barrister who was briefed in a number of industrial award cases from a Liberal/Country Party Government and when the Labor Party later took over government he was no longer briefed. He complained bitterly, saying he was only following the 'cab-rank' rule and that he was a Labor supporter, having grown up in the then working-class Balmain. Another example was that of a prominent QC who was not appointed to the bench by a Liberal/Country Government because he had become too involved in civil liberties causes, especially for Aborigines. He then took on more

---

56. See R Goldfarb, 'Guilt by Association: Lawyers Should be Judged by the Clients They Keep' and A Dershowitz, 'Defending the Offensive: Judging Who Deserves Representing Is Dangerous', *Washington Post*, 6 April 1997, C3.
57. Basten (above), p 36.
58. I Temby, 'Professional Conduct — Control or Conscience?', *Australian Law News*, April 1982, p 12.
59. A Chernov, 'The Lawyer and Morality' (1991) 18(1) *Brief (Law Society of WA)* 8.

conservative clients, including some large corporations and the Australian Medical Association, and a few months later received his appointment. Of course, his actions caused his old civil liberty clients to become suspicious of him and he lost some of their trust for a while.[60]

Hicks case and military tribunals

8.32   It appears that today the legal profession's national body, the Law Council, is willing to support unpopular clients such as alleged terrorists. As previously pointed out (see **5.6**), the Law Council has been in the forefront of seeking a proper trial and adequate representation for alleged terrorist David Hicks. The Law Council has also strongly opposed new federal anti-terrorist laws that remove the provision of basic civil liberties. It also issued a media release calling for a proper court, not a military tribunal, to try David Hicks,[61] when the Court of Appeals of the District of Columbia held that the military tribunals were constitutional.[62]

There are enormous problems in providing effective representation for terrorists. As Hicks's lawyer, Stephen Kenny, vividly pointed out: how can you take instructions from a client who is incommunicado? In the beginning he was receiving his instructions from Hicks's father.[63] There appear to be very few solicitors in Australia, like Kenny, willing to represent those accused of being associated with terror groups.[64]

In the United States the National Association of Criminal Defence Lawyers (NACDL), which has more than 11,000 members, first expressed its concern over the restrictive conditions imposed on lawyers defending the alleged terrorists incarcerated at Guantanamo Bay in Cuba. When these conditions continued the Association's President, Lawrence Goldman, wrote in its monthly publication *Champion* the following statement: 'In view of the extraordinary restrictions on counsel, however, with considerable regret, we cannot advise any of our members to act as civilian counsel at Guantanamo. The rules regulating counsel's behavior are just too restrictive to give us any confidence that counsel will be able to act zealously and professionally.'[65] In August 2003 the NACDL Ethics Advisory Committee issued Opinion 03-04 which states that:

> ... it is unethical for a criminal defense lawyer to represent a person accused before these military commissions because the conditions imposed upon defense counsel ... make it impossible for counsel to provide adequate or ethical representation. Defense counsel cannot contract away his or her client's rights, including the right to zealous advocacy ... which is what the government seeks ...

60.   Private communication.
61.   Law Council Media Release, 17 July 2005, at www.lawcouncil.asn.au.
62.   N Lewis, 'Ruling Lets US Restart Trials at Guantanamo', *New York Times*, 16 July 2005, p 1.
63.   J Macken, 'Dealing with the unknown client', *Australian Financial Review*, 14 November 2004, p 59.
64.   See F Walker and E Duff, 'I might represent Osama some day', *Sun-Herald*, 4 April 2004, p 58. The article gives profiles of two Sydney lawyers, Stephen Hopper and Adam Houda, who it alleges represent 'almost all those accused of being associated with terror groups in Sydney'.
65.   L Goldman, 'Guantanamo: Little hope for zealous advocacy', *Champion Magazine*, July 2003, p 4.

NACDL will not condemn criminal defense lawyers who undertake to represent persons accused before military commissions because some may feel an obligation to do so. If defense counsel undertakes representation and can abide by these rules, counsel must seek to raise, with knowledge of the serious and unconscionable risks involved ... including possible indictment ... every conceivable good faith argument concerning the jurisdiction of the military commission, the legality of denial of application of the Uniform Code of Military Justice (UCMJ), international treaties, and due process of law, including resort to the civilian courts of the United States to determine whether the proceedings are constitutional.

... The problem with these military commissions is that full zealous representation likely will not and cannot be achieved ... Criminal defense lawyers are severely disadvantaged in their duties to represent their clients. The loss of rights can only help insure unjust and unreliable convictions.[66]

There are presently a number of legal actions in the federal courts in the United States against the legitimacy of the military tribunals. In the case of *In re Guantanamo Detainee Cases*, Judge Green in the United States District Court in Washington, DC, declared that the tribunals were unconstitutional and that the prisoners had rights under the Constitution. By contrast, another judge, Judge Leon, in the same court in an earlier decision, decided that the detainees could have their cases examined by the United States courts.[67] Judge Green's decision was overturned by the Court of Appeals of the District of Columbia.[68] The issue may have to be settled eventually by the United States Supreme Court.

AIDS victims

It would appear that representing unpopular clients will be a continuing problem for the legal profession. One of the most recent issues is the problem AIDS victims have in obtaining legal representation for the various legal issues related to the disease. Many lawyers fear loss of business if they are seen to be identified with AIDS victims.[69] As a result, special legal centres dealing directly with AIDS litigants have been established.[70] Representing AIDS victims was highlighted in the film *Philadelphia*. The main character, a lawyer who is gay, is fired for having AIDS. He goes to a number of lawyers before finally finding one who will represent him in an action against his former firm for unlawful dismissal.

8.33

Moral activists

Luban sees the solution for the problem of lawyers representing repugnant clients to be lawyers adopting an attitude of responsibility and accountability for the ends sought by their clients. Luban calls his vision 'moral activism'. He says when lawyers disagree with the morality of a client's objectives they should not simply decline or withdraw representation, but instead they should try to influence the client for the better.

8.34

---

66. NACDL Ethics Advisory Committee, Opinion 03-04 (August 2003) approved by Board of Directors, 2 August 2003, www.nacdl.org.
67. C Banhan and agencies, 'Hicks has rights, rules US judge' *Sydney Morning Herald*, 2 February 2005, p 7. The heading for the article is misleading in that Hicks's case was not before the District Court.
68. Lewis (above), p 1.
69. See E Gold, 'Sometimes you cry ...' (1988) 12(8) *Canadian Lawyer* 16.
70. An example is the establishment of the HIV/AIDS Legal Centre in Sydney.

Only after lawyers have actively engaged their client regarding the morality of their projects should lawyers dissociate themselves if the projects are still immoral.

In this vision, lawyers will take on repugnant cases and be responsible and accountable for their client's ends until they decide that the immoral ends cannot be changed. Luban sees this as an alternative vision of legal practice. He says there are two situations that are exceptions where he wants to maintain the lawyer's non-accountability. The first is when lawyers represent abhorrent clients with repellent objectives in order to vindicate broad important principles. The second is when a lawyer has to represent 'the damned', for example a rapist, murderer, and so on.[71]

Defendants facing serious criminal charges

American cases

8.35   The High Court in 1979 in the *McInnis* case, with Barwick CJ representing the majority of 4:1, held that the 'accused does not have a right to be provided with counsel at public expense'. Nor does he or she have an 'absolute right to legal aid'.[72] We will discuss this decision in more detail later on: see **8.52–8.53**. The *McInnis* decision has been contrasted with the position in the United States. In 1963 the United States Supreme Court held that in serious criminal cases the accused is denied due process if he or she is not able to obtain legal representation.[73] This doctrine of the right to representation was extended in *Argersinger* to any case where, absent a knowing and intelligent waiver, an accused can be imprisoned, whether classified as petty, misdemeanour or felony.[74] In some proceedings where there is a possiblity of imprisonment, for example probation revocation hearings, the Supreme Court has delegated the decision on whether counsel needs to be appointed to the lower courts on a case-by-case basis.[75]

8.36   Even with the constitutional guarantees in the United States there is a problem finding enough competent criminal defence lawyers. This has become a serious problem in death penalty cases. California is notorious for having long delays in death penalty cases because of the shortage of competent criminal lawyers to conduct appeals.[76] There is an automatic right to appeal to the California Supreme Court and each accused facing the death penalty is given two assigned public defenders. Chief Justice George told me at lunch in April 2005 that the court spent a substantial amount of its time dealing with these appeals, but is still falling further behind. The situation has become so serious in having competent criminal counsel that the Californian legislature created and funded the Habeas Corpus Resource Centre in 1998. This helped alleviate to a certain degree the representation for direct appeals because there were many lawyers

---

71.   D Luban (above) (1988), pp 160–2.
72.   *McInnis v R* (1979) 143 CLR 575.
73.   *Gideon v Wainwright* 372 US 335 (1963).
74.   *Argersinger v Hamlin* 407 US 25 (1972). See also *Alabama v Shelton* 535 US 654 (2002).
75.   *Gagnon v Scarpelli* 411 US 778 (1973).
76.   'Politics at the Gallows' (1992) 12 *California Lawyer* 19–20 and K Beitiks, 'State Bar Appeals to Attorneys to Take on Indigent Defendants in Capital Cases', June (1997) *California Bar Journal* 1.

willing to do this work. The reason was that lawyers had more certainty as to what needed to be done. Many lawyers did not seek to do the habeas proceedings because they involved sniffing out information not found on the record, for example withholding of material evidence, inadequate representation, proving a client was mentally retarded etc. As a result, by late 2004 there were still 146 Californian inmates on death row who were not represented by counsel in habeas corpus proceedings.[77]

There were additional problems concerning representation as a much more conservative Supreme Court retreated from the *Argersinger* case. In *Scott v Illinois* the court stated that representation is not required in misdemeanour cases in which imprisonment could have been imposed, but was not imposed.[78] An American text has summed up the court decisions in demarcating the critical stages of a criminal case. It states that 'a defendant has a right to appointed counsel at a preliminary hearing at which probable cause is determined, at post-arrest lineup, at trial and sentencing and through a first appeal; but the right does not extend to discretionary appeals, habeas corpus proceedings, or other post-conviction remedies'.[79]

Right to representation in Australia

Ironically, a much more liberal High Court has in turn modified *McInnis*. In the *Dietrich* case[80] the High Court in a 5:2 judgment adopted the Canadian position. Sections 7, 10(b) and 11(d) of Canada's Charter of Rights and Freedoms guarantee counsel at public expense. The courts in Canada have interpreted these provisions as not an absolute right but only as one aspect of affording the accused a fair trial.[81] The High Court summarised the Canadian position:[82]

    8.37

> Where an accused has been denied legal aid, the trial judge may direct the appointment of counsel if satisfied that the accused is impecunious and the nature of the case is such that the accused cannot receive a fair trial without representation.

The High Court says that even without a Charter of Rights the approach of Australian courts resembles that of Canada.[83] The court stated that:[84]

> Australian law does not recognise that an indigent accused on trial for a serious criminal offence has a right to the provision of counsel at public expense. Instead, Australian law acknowledges that an accused has a right to a fair trial and that, depending on all the circumstances of the particular case, lack of representation may mean that an accused is unable to receive, or did not receive, a fair trial. Such a finding is, however, inextricably linked to the facts of the case and the background of the accused.

---

77. 'Habeas center needs help for death row inmates', *California Law J*, December 2004, pp 1 and 20.
78. *Scott v Illinois* 440 US 367 (1979). See Herman and Thompson, '*Scott v Illinois* and the Right to Counsel: A Decision in Search of a Doctrine' (1979–80) 17 *American Crim LR* 71.
79. G Hazzard Jr, S Koniak and R Cramton, *The Law and Ethics of Lawyering*, 2nd ed, The Foundation Press, Westbury, New York, 1994, pp 193–4.
80. (1992) 109 ALR 385.
81. See *Deutsch v Law Society of Upper Canada Legal Aid Fund* (1985) 48 CR (3d) 166 and *R v Rowbotham* (1988) 41 CCC (3d) at 65–6.
82. (1992) 109 ALR 385 at 395.
83. (1992) 109 ALR 385.
84. (1992) 109 ALR 385 at 396.

The court held in *Dietrich* that:[85]

> ... the desirability of an accused charged with a serious offence being represented is so great that we consider that the trial should proceed without representation ... in exceptional cases only. In all other cases of serious crimes, the remedy of an adjournment should be granted in order that representation can be obtained.

8.38   In *Dietrich* the accused was denied counsel for a serious offence and thus a miscarriage of justice did occur because Dietrich had been convicted without a fair trial. The High Court ordered a new trial.[86]

In light of the *Dietrich* case it is unlikely that a lawyer will be placed in a position of choosing to withdraw in a serious criminal case because legal aid has been refused. The High Court directed trial judges in such situations and other situations of no representation in serious criminal cases to request Legal Aid Commissions to reconsider their decision. The court also said that having a fair trial by providing counsel was not likely to impose a substantial financial burden on governments. It may only require a re-ordering of priorities on how legal aid funds are allocated.[87]

8.39   The problem of the level of skill and the adequacy of compensation for unrepresented indigent defendants came up in *Attorney-General for NSW v Milat*.[88] The Court of Appeal reversed the decision of Hunt J who had adjourned the case until the Legal Aid Commission had met the demands for higher fees by Milat's lawyers. The court said that the *Dietrich* doctrine did not permit a judge to interfere with the administration of legal aid funds. The doctrine said that legal representation had to be available, but did not dictate the level of compensation. The court pointed out that adequate representation was available when the practitioner regularly practises in the area of criminal law. The court found Milat's representation to be proper and that the settlement of the fees was to be decided by the Legal Aid Commission in its negotiations with the accused's lawyers.

8.40   In the *Milat* case the amount offered by the Legal Aid Commission, although below the amount sought by Milat's representatives, was still considered by the Court of Appeal as adequate compensation. But what if the amount offered is so low for the amount of work that needs to be done, as to jeopardise the continuation of representation? This occurred in *R v Malcolm John Souther*.[89] In this case neither the Legal Services Commission nor the South Australian Government were willing to provide the defendant's legal representative with a suitable fee. Olsson J followed the *Dietrich* case. His Honour said:[90]

---

85.   (1992) 109 ALR 385.
86.   (1992) 109 ALR 385 at 397–400; the High Court has held in *New South Wales v Canellis* (1994) 181 CLR 309 that *Dietrich* does not apply to tribunals, particularly where the tribunal has no power to grant a stay. In *R v Frawley* (1993) 69 A Crim R 208 *Dietrich's* application was restricted if the client refused to cooperate with his counsel. A number of other unreported cases have required the accused to take reasonable steps to obtain legal assistance before the *Dietrich* principle would be applied.
87.   *Dietrich* (1992) 109 ALR 385.
88.   [1995] 37 NSWLR 370.
89.   *R v Malcolm John Souther* (SC(SA), 22 May 1997, unreported).
90.   *Souther's* case (above).

The current intransigence of the Government and the Legal Services ... is quite unacceptable. It has the practical effect of continuing to deny the accused a fair trial by reason of lack of representation ... I therefore propose ... a stay until such time as that 'stand-off' situation has been resolved in a fair, satisfactory manner.

It appears a permanent stay under the *Dietrich* case will only be granted when an accused can 'demonstrate that his trial would be unfair because of his inability to find legal fees so that he could be adequately represented at the trial'. When the evidence shows that an applicant requires time for his 'circumstances to stablise and to prepare for his trial' the court will only issue a temporary stay.[91]

Souther, Milat and other cases[92] conclude that an accused is not guaranteed his or her first choice for legal representation, nor 'Rolls Royce' representation, but should have a person with the appropriate experience for their particular case who needs to be paid an adequate fee.

8.41

Another problem is: how far will the courts extend the doctrine? The Full Family Law Court decided in *Heard v De Laine*[93] that *Dietrich* did not guarantee separate representation under the Family Law Act. The High Court itself refused to extend the doctrine to tribunal proceedings in *New South Wales v Canellis*.[94] The court said that it applied only to grant a fair trial in serious criminal cases. In a recent Federal Court decision, *Rivera v United States*,[95] the three judges in corrigendum found that the *Dietrich* principle was not applicable in an extradition matter.

A South Australian court in *Fuller v Field and State of South Australia*[96] refused to extend the *Dietrich* doctrine to committal proceedings. It said that, even if the matter was a serious crime, being unrepresented at a committal was not as serious as at the stage of prosecution. The court did say it had the right to stay committal proceedings if it could be shown that the proceedings constituted an abuse of process. Such a finding prior to the conclusion of a trial would be rare.[97] In another South Australian case, *DPP v Fuller*,[98] it was held that the need for financial assistance to 'roof and call expert witnesses' could not be 'categorised as a legal representation problem'. *Dietrich* does not deal with such a problem.

In *Clarke v Commonwealth Director of Public Prosecutions*,[99] the Australian Capital Territory Supreme Court refused to extend the doctrine to a complex committal proceeding. Clarke, an American businessman with no previous criminal record, faced charges that arose out of the liquidation of Burns Philp Trustee Co (Canberra) Ltd. Clarke had been extradited from the United States. Higgins J pointed out that, if Clarke had faced these charges in the United States, he would have been guaranteed

8.42

91. *R v Joyce* [2003] NSWCCA 280.
92. See *Cummings v R* (Dist Ct(WA), 28 November 1994, unreported) and *R v Karounas* (1995) 77 A Crim R 479.
93. (1996) FLC 92-675.
94. (1994) 124 ALR 513.
95. [2004] FCAFC 154.
96. (1994) 62 SASR 112.
97. Miles J, quoted in *Clarke* (above), see fn 2 in that case.
98. [1997] SASC 6005.
99. [1999] ACTSC 42.

representation at all stages. He stated: 'It may well be that, had the extraditing authorities been aware that the applicant would be forced in this country, on complex committal proceedings (not less than seventy lever arch folders of documents and seventy witnesses — one witness statement being 322 pages) to proceed without a lawyer, extradition might have been denied.'[100]

Higgins J said that the case involved 'difficult legal issues involving evidence which may be unlawfully or improperly obtained or subject to client/lawyer privilege ... and very risky for a non-lawyer to attempt to deal with. The applicant might well find he has inadvertently waived privilege or made an admission against [his] interest merely by cross-examination, quite apart from so-called "without prejudice" conferences with the DPP's representatives'.[101] The judge did feel that if a trial was pending or the proceedings were at trial, there was a strong case for applying the *Dietrich* doctrine.[102] It appears that complicated serious criminal offences will result in a granting of legal aid. If a grant is refused judges may have to adopt the approach in the *Souther* case and issue a permanent stay of the proceedings. If they refuse to do so the *Dietrich* doctrine will be violated and an appeals court will in all likelihood grant some kind of remedy to the accused.[103] By contrast, Slicer J of the Tasmanian Supreme Court proceeded with a serious criminal offence where the accused was unrepresented because the case was not likely to be complex.[104] There are also some rare serious criminal offence cases where the issues are simple, the duration of the trial appears to be short and the ability of the accused to conduct the case could lead a judge to decide that a fair trial could be conducted without representation.[105]

The Victorian Court of Appeal found that there may also be no need for the accused to prove that there is a triable issue. The court found a miscarriage of justice because of an unfair trial in a serious drug case. The accused maintained his innocence at all times but was not given representation. The court held that without assistance 'he was clearly incapable of meeting the Crown case' and lacked the ability to test the Crown's evidence or give anything but a 'rudimentary' address to the jury. The court also stated in *obiter* that in all murder cases there was a need for representation.[106]

Legal aid problems

8.43   The realities of legal aid, with its limited funds, places tremendous pressure on judges not to use the *Dietrich* doctrine to negate the legal aid guidelines. A good example is the Victorian case of *Ronald Andrews v Victoria Legal Aid*.[107] Hampel J had to deal with an application for the grant of legal aid in an impending criminal trial, after its refusal by the Victoria Legal Aid (VLA). The VLA conceded that without representation the accused would not

---

100. *Clarke* (above), p 43.
101. *Clarke* (above).
102. Higgins J cited *Dietrich* and *R v Gakhar* [1999] ACTSC 31.
103. See *R v BK* [2000] NSWCCA 4.
104. For example, see *R v Pirmona* [1998] 250 Tas 2 (BC9801708).
105. See *Frugtniet v Victoria* (1997) 148 ALR 320 at 327 and *R v Fuller & Cummings* (1997) 69 SASR 251.
106. *R v Phung* [1999] VSCA 195.
107. [1999] VSC 281.

receive a fair trial or there was a substantial risk that this would occur. The refusal was based on the requirements dealing with whether the applicant was unable to afford the full cost of employing a private practitioner.

Hampel J said that it was 'an unusual case' and he felt that there was no relevant authority to help him make a decision. The facts are that Andrews, the accused, was 67-years-old with a sick wife who was 63, a daughter with a terminal condition whom he looked after and an unmarried granddaughter with two children whom he cared for part time. His assets consisted of a joint interest in a property with his wife worth $130,000 and a superannuation fund then worth $67,000 (after having spent $20,000 on the committal hearing). He was drawing $150 per week from this fund and he had a pension for himself and his wife of approximately $300 per week.

The judge recognised that the accused had accumulated over a long time a 'very small financial nest egg'. The issue was whether he had to use these limited funds to employ a practitioner to defend him. Andrews decided he wished to be represented, but would not use up his limited funds. Hampel J stated that if the only fund had been the superannuation money, he would have taken the view that it would be harsh and unjust to deprive him of that fund and would have granted him legal aid. But Andrews refused to sell his house or to take a charge over the property. The judge approved of this decision by the accused, but said that under the circumstances he was unable to find that the accused was indigent under the Act. He did comment that he was 'unhappy ... about the situation that a person in Andrews' position finds himself in our system at the moment'.

Hampel J did state that if at any stage before the trial the accused was willing to give a charge over the property for funds sufficient to enable representation by the VLA, the judge would make such an order. Until that happened the judge said that he regretted he could not act, 'as unhappy as the situation is, because the reality in this world is that even if acquitted, Andrews would get no compensation or repayment of the costs incurred'. He concluded: 'I think that provides a real problem in our society and in relation to our legal system. It is not a problem of the making of Legal Aid but it is nevertheless a real social problem and I am afraid the difficulties caused to the court by an unrepresented accused in this sort of case will be immense but we will just have to bear them.'

The problems with the legal aid system are numerous but they are also intertwined with inefficiencies within the general legal system. The Chief Justice of the High Court, Murray Gleeson, warned governments that 'unrepresented litigants are posing a threat to justice and the efficiency of the courts ... The cost of delays, disruptions and inefficiencies ... was borne largely by government ... Providing legal aid is expensive. So is not providing legal representation'. Chief Justice Gleeson said the lack of representation led to delay that further exacerbated the overburdened court lists. He pointed out that even in High Court proceedings, before single judges, 28 per cent of the litigants were unrepresented.[108] Furthermore, a recent report by the Family Court shows that most litigants are self-represented. This has caused burdens for the court and for its judicial

8.44

---

108. A Burrell, 'Not providing legal aid too costly: Justice Gleeson', *Australian Financial Review*, 11 October 1999, at p 3.

officers, leading to inefficient processing of cases.[109] The Australian Law Reform Commission has found similar problems in the Family Court.[110]

8.45   The comments by the Chief Justice and others were supported by the Law Council of Australia, which ran a partially successful lobbying campaign in November 1999 to obtain a $126 million increase in legal aid funding over the ensuing four years. The Federal Government in January 2000 granted an additional $72 million in funding to be allocated over the next four years, including $9 million for expensive Commonwealth criminal cases.[111] There now exists a National Legal Aid (NLA) organisation which comprises the eight independent Legal Aid Commissions from the states and territories. The NLA is the body that coordinates efforts to efficiently use legal aid funds and other resources. It has adopted a Strategic Action Plan for 2004–05 to achieve this goal. According to the NLA, for the year 2003–04 the eight Commissions received $128.5 million from the Commonwealth Government, $147.8 million from state and territory governments and $18.3 million from interest, contributions and fees. The Commissions provided legal services to over 750,000 Australians for 2002–03.[112]

Even with the continual increase in government funds there is a continuous crisis in legal aid funding. For example, in July 2004 the Attorney-General caused concern in rural areas affecting 820,000 people when he elected not to continue the funding of nine community legal centres. The money was reallocated to be used in capital city call centres.[113]

8.46   Within its terms the *Dietrich* doctrine does not apply to appeals and thus there is no guarantee of counsel to help in such appeals. It is only with legal aid or with pro bono assistance that applicants will have representation. Justice Kirby in the *Cameron* case[114] stated:

> The limitations on the resources of Legal Aid, in Western Australia, as elsewhere, make it inevitable that cases occur where legal representation before this Court is not provided. This Court cannot forfeit its judicial responsibilities to the decisions of legal aid bodies constrained by resource allocations of the Executive Government.

> Where an applicant is not legally represented, a heavy burden is cast on the Justices of this Court to scrutinise often voluminous and ill-expressed materials against the risk that an error of law or miscarriage of justice has occurred. As is perfectly proper, the Crown is commonly represented on the return of such applications by one and sometimes two counsel and by solicitors, as happened here. … Appellate courts, including this Court, are sometimes forced to rely on their own resources or voluntary assistance occasionally provided by legal professional bodies. Yet if *Dietrich* rests, as I think it does, on a broader, and possibly a constitutional, foundation … whether generally or at least in cases within federal jurisdiction, improved arrangement for the presentation of applications by indigent prisoners in

109. See, generally, Family Court of Australia, Research Report No 20, *Litigants in person in the Family Court of Australia*, 1999.
110. See Australian Law Reform Commission, Report No 89, *Managing Justice: A review of the federal civil justice system*, February 2000, Chapter 5.
111. *Australian Lawyer*, Newsletter of Law Council of Australia, February 2000, pp 1–2, 4.
112. See www.nla.aust.org.
113. 'National Legal Funds Cut', *Advertiser*, 7 July 2004, p 28.
114. *Cameron v The Queen* [2002] HCA 6.

custody may be required. If necessary, it would be open to the courts, by their orders, to ensure such arrangements in defence of the utility of their exercise of the judicial power in a just way to all persons invoking that power. Ultimately, in proper cases, such orders might be enforced by requiring the release of a prisoner on bail pending the provision of proper representation before the appellate court.[115] The courts of the Australian Judicature, including this Court, are not helpless in the face of a lack of provision of legal facilities to indigent prisoners who seek to enliven a right of appeal or of an application for leave or special leave that is now standard to prisoners who are not indigent or who can secure public legal assistance. ... The appellant's success in this appeal does not demonstrate that improved arrangements are unnecessary. On the contrary, it demonstrates the opposite. In my opinion, this Court should not be content with the present unequal arrangements for prisoner applications.

Justice Kirby's *obiter* comments emphasise the need for more legal funding to provide representation at the committal and appeal stages. The failure to extend the *Dietrich* doctrine and the inability to provide sufficient legal aid will at times lead to glaring injustices.

DUTY TO CONTINUE TO ACT

General rules

Luban's 'moral activism' vision, discussed above (see **8.34**), presents us with another problem. If after trying to change the client's immoral ends the lawyer fails, can he or she just quit? When can a lawyer stop acting for a client?

8.47

Western Australia has detailed rules on the termination of a retainer. Rule 17.3 states:

Subject to Rules 12.3 and 17.4, a practitioner may withdraw from representing a client:

(a) at any time for any reason if withdrawal will cause no significant harm to the client's interests and the client is fully informed of the consequences of withdrawal and voluntarily assents to it;

(b) if the practitioner reasonably believes that continued engagement in the case or matter would be likely to have a seriously adverse effect upon his health;

(c) if the client commits a significant violation of a written agreement regarding fees or expenses;

(d) if the client made material misrepresentations about the facts of the case or matter to the practitioner;

(e) if the practitioner has an interest in any case or matter in which he is concerned for the client which is adverse to that of the client;

(f) where such action is necessary to avoid commission by him of a breach of these Rules;

(g) where a grant of legal aid to the client is withdrawn or an existing grant is not extended by the Legal Aid Commission provided that:

(i) the practitioner gives reasonable notice to the client of the practitioner's intention to withdraw, and

---

115. Kirby J refers to *United Mexican States v Cabal* (2001) 75 ALJR 1663 at 1679 [77]; 183 ALR 645 at 668.

(ii) the client is unable to make any other satisfactory arrangements for the payment of the practitioner's fees; and

(h) where any other good cause exists,

provided that in all such cases the practitioner shall take reasonable care to avoid foreseeable harm to his client, including giving due notice to the client, allowing reasonable time for substitution of a new practitioner, cooperating with the new practitioner and subject to the satisfaction of any lien the practitioner may have promptly turning over all papers and property and paying to the client any moneys to which the client is entitled.

8.48 Rule 12.3 is an exception to the general rule. It states that if a client behaves in an offensive or improper manner lawyers shall continue to act unless there is justification to assume instructions have been withdrawn. It also says if the lawyer's professional standing is being or is likely to be impugned they can withdraw but only if it does not jeopardise the client's interests. The other exception, r 17.4, states that only in the 'most exceptional circumstances' shall a brief for a serious criminal charge be returned and then only if another lawyer has enough time to master the case.

8.49 The general rule in Australia is that lawyers contract to finish the entire business of their retainer. In New South Wales, the Law Society's model cost agreement helps solicitors to avoid the 'entire contract' rule. Many legal practitioners throughout Australia can also attempt to contract out by the use of r 6.1.1 of the Model Professional Conduct and Practice Rules. This rule states that practitioners do not have to complete their contracts where they and the client have 'otherwise agreed'. Another exception to the rule is under Model Rules r 6.1.3, that termination can take place 'for good cause, and on reasonable notice to the client'. There are special rules for court proceedings and for criminal trials that make it more difficult to present a 'good cause and reasonable notice'.[116] The Model Rules r 6.3 appears very liberal towards practitioners in allowing withdrawal on giving reasonable notice when a legal aid grant is withdrawn in criminal cases, but there still exists under r 6.2 the need for seven days' notice to withdraw if there are unsatisfactory arrangements for payment of the practitioner's cost.

8.50 New South Wales also has r 6B of its Professional Conduct and Practice Rules which is similar to r 6 of the Model Rules, but places a limit on the reasonable notice time period of 'not later than thirty (30) days' prior to the trial. South Australia had a rule, until it adopted the Model Rules, that stated that lawyers can withdraw if the client's instructions prevent lawyers from properly performing their duties.[117] This has been interpreted in a number of cases to include the situation where a client refuses to follow the lawyer's advice.[118] The latter may also fall under the Western Australian rule of 'any other good cause' or the general rule 'for good cause'. This situation is a problem of 'control' and such refusal by the client may not be good cause without the client's consent. Lawyers can also base their argument for withdrawing their representation on the fact that they cannot act in 'good conscience' on behalf of a client who, for example, refuses to reveal to the Australian Taxation Office a mathematical or other error that

---

116. For example, Supreme Court Rules, Pt 66, r 7 (NSW). There are similar Supreme Court rules in other jurisdictions.
117. Professional Conduct Rules (1993) r 9.10.
118. See *R v Frawley* (1993) 69 A Crim R 208 and *R v Promizio* [2004] NSWCCA 75.

has been discovered by the lawyer. I believe that in the vast majority of cases lawyers will have little difficulty withdrawing in the circumstance of the client not revealing a discovered tax error, as clients do not want to retain lawyers who will not fulfil their wishes.

The ABA Model Rules r 1.16 is similar to the Western Australian rule. It does include an interesting clause that allows withdrawal if 'a client insists upon pursuing an objective that the lawyer considers repugnant or imprudent'. The comment to r 1.16 states that a lawyer appointed to represent a client ordinarily needs the appointing authority's approval to withdraw.

The above rules show that although there are ethical rules inhibiting lawyers from withdrawing, there are many exceptions to these rules. There is enough scope for lawyers to threaten withdrawal if clients will not follow their advice. Lawyers' power over their clients is thus not placed in jeopardy by the ethical rules prohibiting withdrawal. The rules still place the lawyer in a position of control. **8.51**

A question that still remains open is: when does the lawyer–client relationship end? Some would say when the transaction or case is completed; for example, the conveyance or the will, the end of a trial, and so on. In some situations it is not clear when the obligations conclude. Duties towards clients, such as confidentiality and avoiding conflicts of interest, continue even when there is clearly no relationship. Other times lawyers will maintain a continuous relationship with certain clients even when they have little or no legal work from them. It is thus important for lawyers to clarify with their clients when the representation will end. This would include how settlement funds and trust account funds will be handled. It will also include how payment of the final bill and any other possible costs will be dealt with and how the client's confidential information will be preserved. There is also a need to clarify the responsibilities of the client in relation to payment of fees and production of documents.[119] An important area that needs to be looked at is the obligations towards criminal defendants, especially juveniles. Are there responsibilities towards such clients even after the judicial hearing? Are there ways lawyers can help these clients even when they are in gaol or to prevent them from committing future crimes? Under our present system very few criminal defence lawyers will feel any obligations after the client is either gaoled or set free.[120]

Consequences of breach

A breach of the above rules can lead to disciplinary action, but such action would be rare. A lawyer may also be sued for negligence but this would also be rare. A third possibility is that the lawyer will lose any moneys owed for work performed before the breach. Finally, in a trial situation, withdrawal shortly before or during a trial may result in the client being granted a new trial because he or she had to proceed without legal representation.[121] **8.52**

---

119. D Bell, 'Crossing the Bridge Before We Get There: Addressing Termination and Withdrawal Issues with Clients', www.calbar.ca.
120. For an interesting account of a lawyer working with juvenile offenders who continued his connection with his clients, see C Ogletree, 'Public Defender, Public Friend: Searching for the "Best Interests" of Juvenile Offenders' in Bellow and Minow (above), p 131.
121. Disney et al (above), p 610.

There are numerous examples where such a request for a new trial has been turned down. The most notorious was the *McInnis* case, referred to above (see **8.35**), where the High Court upheld the conviction on charges of rape, unlawful assault and deprivation of liberty. The trial judge had turned down his request for an adjournment because of the public inconvenience — jurors summoned and witnesses present. McInnis had argued that his lawyer had withdrawn on the day of the trial because he had been denied legal aid the previous evening. This left him without representation during the trial for a serious crime. As we stated, the High Court held that the 'accused does not have a right to be provided with counsel at public expense'. Nor does he have an 'absolute right to legal aid'.[122]

8.53   Murphy J in a strong dissent upheld the right to counsel. He pointed out that a practical solution for the trial judge would have been for that judge to have asked McInnis's counsel to continue to represent him to avoid both the public inconvenience and the injustice to McInnis. Murphy J stated:[123]

> Any lawyer, conscious of his responsibility as a member of a profession which has exclusive rights to represent others in court and has high ethical standards of public service, would not have refused. If he did refuse, then the judge should have adjourned the case and refused to allow it to continue until Mr McInnis had been provided with adequate representation.

There was a public outcry over the decision and McInnis's lawyer was criticised for deserting his client. The lawyer, Mr Singleton, withdrew because he was not being paid for the trial. Singleton supposedly stated:

> Re-enter [the case]? No. Why! I am amazed at the thought-process. I haven't got instructions from anyone. I take instructions on the basis that I'm going to be paid. I was not briefed.

The Barristers Board of Western Australia held that he had violated r 17.4 and fined him $1250 and $750 costs.[124] There have been other instances where lawyers have withdrawn in similar circumstances and not been disciplined.[125] In a South Australian case the Supreme Court refused leave to withdraw in a personal injury case when the legal aid grant was terminated. The court said that no good cause had been established, nor had reasonable notice been given.[126]

Barristers' rules

8.54   Barristers are notorious for returning briefs or transferring them to other barristers because they have double-booked. The practice exists because sometimes court-listing procedures cause the double-booking, or other times it occurs because barristers want to protect themselves in case one of the briefs is adjourned or settled.[127] This practice has been criticised:[128]

---

122. *McInnis v R* (1979) 143 CLR 575.
123. *McInnis* (above) at 585.
124. 'Lawyer Withdrawals — Client Unrepresented' (1981) 7 *Commonwealth Law Bulletin* 1032.
125. See Disney et al (above), p 611, citing *McIntyre v R* (Fed Ct, No NT G37 of 1981, unreported).
126. *Chisholm v State Transport Authority* (1986) 41 SASR 317.
127. R Megarry, *Lawyer and Litigant in England*, Stevens, London, 1962, p 77.
128. Disney et al (above), p 615.

[B]arristers have been known to accept a brief with the intention ... of returning it if a brief that is more interesting, remunerative or prestigious turns up later. On numerous occasions counsel have hung on to clashing briefs for far too long, and clients have been left in the hands of inexperienced and ill-prepared substitutes. Alternatively, they may adjourn or settle a case in a way which is contrary to the interests of their client but save the personal embarrassment (and loss of remuneration) of having to return a brief at the last moment.

The actions of barristers have been strongly criticised by solicitors and there has been a call for abuse of double-booking to constitute professional misconduct.[129] In the rare cases where disciplinary action has been taken, the sanctions imposed were very light, for example a fine for $300.[130] A good example was the case *In the matter of Glen Gould*.[131] Gould, a barrister, had been part heard in Local Court proceedings in relation to an apprehended violence order (AVO). He accepted a brief in the Family Court that conflicted with his obligation to be present for the resumption of the AVO hearing. Gould returned the brief for AVO on the Friday morning preceding the Monday hearing of both matters. The tribunal found he had committed professional misconduct by violating r 95 of the Barristers' Rules. He was publicly reprimanded and ordered to pay the Bar Association's costs.

8.55

The New South Wales Barristers' Rules (there are similar rules in Queensland and Victoria) meet some of the solicitors' complaints. Rule 95 applied in the *Gould* case states:

> A barrister must not return a brief to appear in order to accept another brief unless the instructing solicitor or the client ... in the first brief has permitted the barrister to do so ...

Rule 97 states:

> A barrister who wishes to return a brief ... must do so in enough time to give another legal practitioner a proper opportunity to take over the case.

The Rules also state in r 96 that, unless the solicitor consents, a barrister cannot return a fixed date brief in order to attend a social engagement. Where there appears to be a clash of briefs the barrister has to apply a number of rules to decide which to retain including whether a case has already been partly heard, which brief was accepted first and which one is more difficult for another barrister to master. Rule 98 states: 'A barrister must promptly inform the instructing solicitor or the client ... as soon as the barrister has reasonable grounds to believe that there is a real possibility that the barrister will be unable to appear or to do the work required by the brief in the time stipulated by the brief or within a reasonable time if no time has been stipulated.' There are several other rules, rr 99–102, on returning briefs.

8.56

Two other important rules are rr 93 and 94. Rule 93 states that, in defending in serious criminal cases, a brief shall not be returned except if:

> ... the circumstances are exceptional and compelling; and there is enough time for another legal practitioner to take over the case properly before

---

129. 'Duty to Accept Work', Law Society of New South Wales (Submission to the New South Wales Law Reform Commission), 1979, p 9.
130. See 'Ethics Committee Report', *Victorian Bar News*, Spring 1982, p 8.
131. (1998) 2 Legal Services Tribunal Disciplinary Reports (NSW) 2.

hearing; or the client has consented after the barrister had clearly informed the client of the circumstances ...

Rule 94 gives precedence to briefs defending serious criminal trials over those in civil trials if the barrister has been double-briefed.

8.57   The case of *R v White*[132] dealt with a proposed withdrawal of a barrister because the barrister said he had been dismissed by the client and it had become impossible to communicate with the client. The barrister had received advice from the Bar Council that he should withdraw. Barr AJ noted that the court had a general discretion as to whether or not to grant leave to withdraw. He said that the discretion may not be present when as a matter of professional ethics the barrister has been advised to withdraw. Barr AJ said even if that discretion is not abrogated by the professional ruling 'it ought not to be exercised against a grant of leave' in these circumstances.

It should be noted that the rules mainly concern the relationship between barristers and solicitors. The next section deals with the client's right to withdraw from the relationship.

Clients' rights of dismissal

8.58   Both Western Australia and South Australia (until adopting the Model Rules) had clear rules on clients' rights to dismiss. Rule 17.1 (WA) stated:

> A practitioner shall recognise that a client is entitled to change his legal adviser at any time without giving a reason and shall, subject to the satisfaction of any lien the practitioner may have, take all reasonable steps to facilitate such a change should his [or her] client so request.

The old rule 9.12 (SA) stated: 'A practitioner should not place any fetter upon or otherwise attempt to discourage a client from changing legal advisers at any time.' Rule 9.13 stated:[133]

> Subject only to such lien as may lawfully be imposed by a practitioner ... a practitioner shall offer all such assistance and give all such advice or information as may be necessary to enable any other practitioner instructed to take over a matter, to take such matter in hand promptly and expeditiously and with the least duplication in costs.

In the United States the Comment to Model Rule 1.1b has similar provisions.[134]

8.59   The right of the client to dismiss is based on the concept that the relationship is one of confidence and if clients lose confidence in their lawyer there is no reason for continuing the relationship. The client still must pay for any work already done and failure to do so can result in the solicitor enforcing a lien over the client's papers.[135] If the dismissal of the lawyer is for a good cause clients may be relieved of this obligation and may even have a suit for negligence.[136]

---

132. (1995) 77 A Crim R 531.
133. The Law Society of the Northern Territory Professional Conduct Rules, rr 9.8 and 9.9 are identical.
134. Rule 8.3 (NSW) allows solicitors the right to exercise a lien for unpaid costs when they have completed the retainer or the client has dismissed them or they have terminated the retainer for just cause and on reasonable notice.
135. There is a discussion by the Court of Appeal (NSW) on ownership of documents and what documents should be released to a client where a client terminates the relationship in *Wentworth v De Montfort* (1988) 15 NSWLR 348.
136. Disney et al (above), p 617.

It should be observed that it is not usually in the client's interest to dismiss a lawyer. Lawyers have detailed and intimate knowledge of clients' affairs and this may be psychologically disturbing. There are also expenses and delays involved in instructing new lawyers and familiarising them with the case. Finally, if a client wants to sue the lawyer for breach of contract or negligence, this can lead to even far greater complications than the original matter. Clients will therefore hesitate before dismissing their lawyer.

Right to choose counsel

Clients have the right to choose their counsel. For example, even if a solicitor agrees to allow another barrister to take over a brief because the original barrister has double-booked, the client can refuse to accept that barrister. In the English case of *R v Woodward*[137] the accused in a criminal trial was refused the right to defend himself. He had chosen to do this because he had not had the opportunity to see the counsel assigned to him. The trial judge forced him to accept the lawyer. In upholding his appeal the Court of Criminal Appeal stated that 'no person charged with a criminal offence can have counsel forced upon him against his will'.[138] The High Court of Australia has affirmed the general principle that a party to proceedings, civil or criminal, has the right to present his or her own case.[139]

8.60

American cases

The United States Supreme Court has also supported the English point of view in the *Faretta* case.[140] In that case the court held by a 5:3 decision that a defendant even in a serious criminal case cannot be forced to be represented by counsel. Stewart J said:[141]

8.61

> It is undeniable that in most criminal prosecutions defendants could better defend with counsel's guidance than by their own unskilled efforts ... The right to defend is personal. The defendant, and not his lawyer or the state, will bear the personal consequences of a conviction ... And although he may conduct his own defence ultimately to his own detriment, his choice must be honoured out of 'that respect for the individual which is the lifeblood of the law'.

The minority in *Faretta* found that broader philosophical issues were at stake at times preventing defendants from waiving their right to legal representation. Burger CJ, with Blackburn and Rehnquist JJ, joining the dissent said:[142]

> That goal [of achieving justice] is ill-served, and the integrity of and public confidence in the system is undermined, when an easy conviction is obtained due to the defendant's ill-advised decision to waive counsel. The damage thus inflicted is not mitigated by the lame explanation that the defendant simply availed himself of the 'freedom' to go to jail under his own banner ... The system of criminal justice could not be available as an instrument of self-destruction ... [E]very person accused of crime shall receive the fullest possible defense; in the vast majority of cases this command can be honoured only by means of the expressly guaranteed right to counsel, and the trial

137. *Woodward* [1944] KB 118.
138. *Woodward* (above) at 119.
139. *Collins (Hass) v R* (1976) 8 ALR 150.
140. *Faretta* 95 S Ct 2525 (1975).
141. *Faretta* (above) at 2540–1.
142. *Faretta* (above) at 2543.

judge is in the best position to determine whether the accused is capable of conducting his defense.

8.62   Sometimes others will interfere with the accused's wishes because of their own interests or broader public interests. This was highlighted in the Gary Gilmore affair which is dramatically portrayed in Norman Mailer's *Executioner's Song* (1979).[143] Gilmore was the first person to be executed in the United States in almost 20 years. There were various groups and people who had an interest in stopping the execution against Gilmore's wishes. Gilmore did not want to spend his life in a prison he found intolerable. He chose to die and ordered his lawyers not to file an appeal. He had shown competence to make this decision. The ACLU lawyers involved in the case had been dismissed by Gilmore because they opposed the death penalty. The ACLU opposed its former client's wishes because it felt that if Gilmore was executed the floodgates would open. They proved to be right. They tried to stop the execution as an *amicus curiae* (friend of the court) but this was denied. The Supreme Court initially did grant an *amicus curiae* petition for a stay by Gilmore's mother but lifted the order. The Supreme Court eventually affirmed his right as a competent person who knowingly and intelligently refused to appeal his death sentence. It can be questioned whether a person who chooses death can be deemed to be competent. Furthermore, how much authority does a client have in stopping his or her lawyer from using legal tactics to avoid the death penalty? In an Ohio decision the court denied a motion for a review of the competency of a death row prisoner's decision to cease all appeals.[144]

Australian cases

8.63   In Australia the issue of *amicus curiae*, stepping in to represent someone, was highlighted in several cases involving the Family Court and the High Court. In *Re a Teenager*,[145] parents sought to have a hysterectomy performed on their 15-year-old daughter, who had a mental age of two-and-a-half years. The Redfern Legal Centre Disability Unit's solicitor obtained a Supreme Court order restraining the operation at any time in the future. With the order a next of friend was appointed, the secretary of a disabled person society, to act for the child against the parents. This person had no personal knowledge of the child or her family. Cook J in the Family Court rejected the next of friend's application and allowed the parents to arrange the operation. He pointed out how well the child had been cared for and loved by the family. He was concerned how:

> ... a complete stranger to the child and the family could prosecute an action which ... involved most intimate and sensitive awareness and appraisal of that particular child's interests. It does not seem appropriate to the court that representatives of interest groups, no matter how well-intentioned or motivated can bring to all essential judgments, arising both before and during such litigation as the present, the cool and pragmatic approach required.

---

143. For a review of the book, see B Babcock, *Book Review*, (1980) 32 *Stanford LR* 865.
144. *State v Berry* 706 NE 2d 1273 (Ohio 1999). For a discussion of the cases and reasons for defendants choosing to be executed, see R Garnett, 'Sectarian Reflections on Lawyers' Ethics and Death Row Volunteers' (2002) 77 *Notre Dame LR* 796.
145. (1989) FLC ¶92–006.

Cook J concluded that it was important to avoid 'unnecessary and ill-advised interference in the family life that is the essence of our society'.

A case with very similar facts, *Re Jane*,[146] took place shortly afterwards in Melbourne. Nicholson CJ in the Family Court refused an injunction requested by the Victorian Acting Public Advocate to stop a hysterectomy operation. He commented that the Public Advocate:

8.64

> ... acted both responsibly and properly in making an application to the court
> ... I consider that it is vital that before procedures of this type are sanctioned
> by the court, it should have the benefit of an independent presentation from
> some disinterested third party on behalf of the child.

The High Court supported Nicholson CJ in *Secretary, Department of Health & Community Services (NT) v JWB and SMB*.[147] The High Court decided that in cases of children with intellectual disabilities the guardian of such a child cannot act independently to have the child sterilised. The court held that in all these cases court approval is mandatory:[148]

> Children with intellectual disabilities are particularly vulnerable, both
> because of their minority and their disability, and ... there is less likelihood
> of (intentional or unintentional) abuse of the rights of children if an
> application to a court is mandatory, than if the decision in all cases can be
> made by a guardian alone.

Brennan J clearly stated the fears of the court:[149]

> [T]he power to authorise sterilisation is so awesome, its exercise is so open to
> abuse, and the consequences of its exercise are generally so irreversible that
> legal controls are needed.

The Full Family Law Court has upheld and applied these High Court principles and formulated various guidelines to help practitioners.[150]

8.65

These ideas need to be applied also to children with intellectual disabilities facing criminal charges. These children are far more vulnerable than other juveniles and need effective representation and other help when questioned by the police. There have been recommendations for reforms in this area by both the New South Wales Law Reform Commission[151] and the Australian Law Reform Commission.[152]

Sometimes court approval will also be needed in other areas concerning the welfare of children. The New South Wales Supreme Court has gone even further in protecting the rights of children even before they are born. In *Re Baby A*[153] Young J ordered the mother of an unborn child not to breastfeed the child and that the child be given special medical treatment, because the mother had tested HIV positive. Young J used the court's inherent *parens patriae* jurisdiction to make this order which was also used in another

8.66

---

146. (1989) FLC ¶92–007.
147. *Secretary, Department of Health & Community Services (NT) v JWB and SMB* (1992) 66 ALJR 300.
148. *JWB and SMB* (above) at 312.
149. *JWB and SMB* (above) at 320.
150. *Re P and Legal Aid Commission (NSW)* (1995) 19 Fam LR 1.
151. See, generally, NSWLRC Report No 80, *People with an Intellectual Disability and the Criminal Justice System*, 1996.
152. Australian Law Reform Commission (with the Human Rights and Equal Opportunity Commission), Report No 84, *Seen and heard: priority for children in the legal process*, paras 18.122–18.124.
153. [1999] NSWSC 787, 26 July 1999.

Supreme Court case. In *DoCS v Y*,[154] Austin J held that the *parens patriae* jurisdiction had not been affected by the Family Law Act 1975 (Cth). Thus, various state legislation concerning the welfare of children was still in effect. In this case, a young teenage girl had been medically diagnosed as having anorexia nervosa. The parents and the child rejected the recommended treatment and believed that she was wrongly diagnosed. There was evidence that if the child was not force-fed she might die or that she could be permanently damaged. Austin J ordered that the child become a ward of the state and treatment be carried out.[155]

154. [1999] NSWSC 644, 30 June 1999.
155. See also J Eades, 'Parens patriae jurisdiction of the Supreme Court is alive and kicking', *Law Society J (NSW)*, February 2000, p 52.

9

COMMUNICATION AND CONTROL[1]

INTRODUCTION — CONTROL MODELS

In this chapter we will look first at the different control models that will help us define the nature of the lawyer–client relationship. We will then explore the duties lawyers have in supplying information and advice. Finally, we will deal with the rules concerning obedience to the client's instructions.

9.1

There are three models of control:[2]

- the lawyer-control model;
- the client-control model; and
- the cooperative model.

In the lawyer-control model the lawyer is in control because of his or her expertise. It assumes that because of lawyers' training they know the best approach to clients' legal problems; and that lawyers, by being detached and objective, will be able to handle the problem more clearly than clients who are emotionally involved with the situation. The attitude is that clients are in a weak position and have to place their trust in and be dependent upon lawyers.[3] This model predominates in lawyer–client relationships and is preferred by the profession. One Melbourne practitioner alleges that lawyers give advice with the expectation that it will be followed. If it is not, the lawyer expects the client to find another lawyer. If the client remains, the lawyer may 'treat the client with contempt by not answering telephone calls and by briefing barristers at the last possible minute'.[4] This model is

9.2

---

1. The framework in this chapter is adopted from J Disney, J Basten, P Redmond and S Ross, *Lawyers*, 2nd ed, 1986, Chapter 18.
2. The basic ideas come from J Basten, 'Control and the Lawyer–Client Relationship' (1981) 6 *J of the Legal Profession* 7, 16–24.
3. See, for example, para 5.02 of the *Queensland Solicitors Handbook*, QLS, Brisbane, 1995.
4. Letter from Martin Vink, 12 February 2005. Mr Vink also stated that if the client accepts the advice then this becomes the client's instructions. Thus the notion 'I am instructed by my client that ...' really is inaccurate.

probably even more prevalent when the client is poor and uneducated. Lawyers frequently believe that these clients seek dependency and are inferior. Even if they treat such clients differently, especially in certain neighbourhood legal aid centres, they may use:[5]

> ... the client dependency as a strategically necessary construction required to gain sympathy from adjudicators and to minimize client participation in case management, thus speeding the favorable disposition of a mass caseload. Whether his [or her] motivation flows from formal belief or instrumental knowledge, a poverty lawyer plans and manages the advocacy process — interviewing, counselling, negotiation, discovery, trial and motion practice — in a manner that restricts his [or her] client's opportunity to speak.

This model is not only preferred by the legal profession, but also by other professions. Psychiatrists, for example, have stated they must have unrestrained power over their patients:[6]

> From the very outset [the psychiatrist] influences the patient by virtue of his [or her], one may be permitted to say, holy presence, by the sheer strength of his being, his glance, and his will.

Tszasz adds that:[7]

> ... no special treatment should be attempted unless the physician can control the external surroundings, relationships, and influences on the patient ... [T]he physician must not apply any specific treatment unless he [or she] is master of the patient, and this he can only become if he is spiritually superior to him. Unless this superiority is established, all treatment will be in vain.

9.3   An even more powerful statement was made by Dr Alan Cregg in *Autopsy on the AMA*: 'A physician is so surrounded by frightened patients, adoring families, and obsequious nurses that he will not brook criticism by God or man.'[8] In the client-control model clients make the important decisions based on the technical information given to them by the lawyer. The lawyer has to carry out the client's decisions as long as he or she is not required to do something that is unethical or illegal. This model is usually present when the client is powerful because of position or wealth. This model does not deny that the lawyer has special skills and knowledge, or that the lawyer is better able than the client to conduct the client's legal affairs. It stops the lawyer from being overbearing and paternalistic to the client,[9] and allows the client to make the important decisions on the goals the client seeks to achieve.

This may mean placing the legal problem in a far broader framework, for example perhaps political, rather than the narrow confines of the legal context. In dealing with civil disobedience clients, one lawyer states:[10]

> ... the clients bear the consequences of their decisions and are in the best position to understand the full non-legal as well as legal significance of their choices. Accordingly, lawyers counsel clients best by helping them to explore all of the possible consequences of their actions so that the clients can make decisions that best suit their needs.

---

5.   A Alfieri, 'Welfare Stories' in G Bellow and M Minow, *Law Stories*, University of Michigan Press, Ann Arbor, 1996, p 38.
6.   T Szasz, *The Myth of Psychotherapy*, Syracuse University Press, Syracuse, NY, 1988, p 74.
7.   Szasz (above), p 77.
8.   A pamphlet that was not dated.
9.   Basten (above), p 20.
10.   N Polikoff, 'Am I my client? The role confusion of a lawyer activist' (1996) 31 *Harvard Civil Rights-Civil Liberties Review* 443, 458.

The author calls this form of lawyering 'client-centered counselling'. Other scholars argue that 'progressive lawyering' should involve lawyers helping to empower rather than seeking to control their clients.[11]

9.4

The cooperative model (also known as the 'care' model) is one where the lawyer and client learn as much as they can about each other's attitudes and goals, and seek to come to a common solution to the problem. There is open discussion and the parties are on an equal footing: 'Action will only be taken which is morally acceptable to both lawyer and client.'[12] In this relationship there is what Shaffer calls a moral dialogue — not only an exchange of information but also of moral views.[13] We have discussed the advantage of the cooperative model in overcoming the moral isolation faced by most lawyers in Chapter 2. We can add two other advantages:[14]

> ... it preserves the autonomy, responsibility and dignity of both parties ... and while the model sacrifices the alleged advantages of the lawyer's emotional detachment ... it substitutes the possibility of more informed, comprehensible and relevant advice based on a fuller understanding of the client's position.

The cooperative model can vary according to the clientele. For example, Aboriginal lawyers working for Aboriginal clients, as we mention in Chapter 2, have far more extensive obligations than other lawyers. They are more likely to 'be involved in matters involving family or friends, particularly because of the altruistic objective and the cultural duty associated with the "extended family" concept'.[15] Dolman says that the nature of Aboriginal culture causes the Aboriginal lawyer to 'desire to act "altruistically", that is, to make a contribution to the community'.[16] Acting 'altruistically', that is, becoming part of the community, expands the scope of the traditional cooperative or care model. In contrast, non-indigenous lawyers may have difficulty using the cooperative model because they do not understand the cultural requirements. In the United States it has been pointed out that the ABA Model Rules:[17]

9.5

> ... are inadequate to resolve the problems created by cultural differences between non-Indian attorneys and their tribal clients, the increased propensity for paternalism in tribal representation, and conflicts of interest in tribal representation.

On the other hand, the cooperative model can lack moral content when both clients and lawyers cooperate to structure arrangements or activities

9.6

---

11. L White, 'To Learn and Teach: Lessons from Driefontein on Lawyering and Power' (1988) *Wisconsin LR* 699. For criticism of the progressive approach see A Southworth, 'Taking the Lawyer Out of Progressive Lawyering' (1993) 46 *Stanford LR* 213.
12. Basten (above), p 23.
13. Shaffer calls his a 'care' model: T Shaffer, *On Being a Christian and a Lawyer: Law for the Innocent*, Brigham Young University Press, Provo, 1981, pp 7–10.
14. Basten (above), pp 23–4.
15. K Dolman, 'Indigenous lawyers: success or sacrifice?' (1997) 4 *Indigenous Law Bulletin* 6. Dolman says in footnote 18 that in the extended family 'aunties and uncles are regarded as mothers and fathers, and great uncles and great aunties are regarded as grandmothers and grandfathers'. This makes the Aboriginal immediate family much larger than often found in white Australian families.
16. Dolman (above).
17. T Zlock, 'The Native American Tribe as a Client: An Ethical Analysis' (1996) 10 *Georgetown J of Legal Ethics* 159, 161.

that are illegal or close to being illegal or silently agree to turn a blind eye to illegal activities. For example, during the 1980s many lawyers were involved with the 'Bold Riders', helping them rip off Australian society. Sykes states that:

> In most cases greed was the explanation for the readiness of the professions to lower their standards. Banks, directors, lawyers and accountants were all earning fat fees from the bold riders.

These entrepreneurs were able to boast of having the services of leading professionals including the foremost Australian law firms.[18] Tomasic and Bottomley support this view from their interviews with lawyers and accountants. They found that professional advisers played an important role in shaping 'the patterns of corporate conduct'. These professionals acted at times in a positive manner by making suggestions within the law, but at others they ignored or failed 'to detect or advise against fraudulent action'. Their actions were then 'interpreted by the corporate client as an implied sanctioning of conduct'.[19]

9.7   A fourth model can be suggested to exist when an employer or government agency would say to a person: 'We will provide you with a lawyer, but only if that lawyer does what we say is appropriate.' In that situation we would have what Basten says is 'a system that is foreign to certain basic values of our criminal justice system'. What usually happens is that the third party, for example a legal aid authority, lays down general guidelines, for example to control costs, and the lawyer (who is technically still in control) must restrict his or her legal work to meet these demands. There may also be a requirement that the client needs to cooperate with the appointed lawyer, and failure to do so would result in the lawyer withdrawing. A similar situation can happen when the client is a member of a political group and the group decides how a case should be run. This would constitute influencing the client within the client-control model. The main conflict of power is still within the lawyer–client relationship.[20] In Chapter 12 we will discuss third party influence and the conflicts that arise.

Who is in charge?

9.8   The question 'Who is in charge?' may not give us an accurate insight into what really takes place in lawyer–client relations. How the authority is generated and maintained by the parties in the relationship is also very important. In any lawyer–client relationship all three models may be present at some time in the relationship. Usually lawyers and clients will at different times manipulate each other in order to be in control. There will also be times when no one knows who is in control and in reality no one is in control. At these times both parties will be working towards solutions, but not in any way that could be termed cooperative. They may be acting towards different goals without properly communicating this information to each other. Generally, it can be said that the lawyer-control model is more

---

18.   T Sykes, *Bold Riders: Behind Australia's Corporate Collapses*, 2nd ed, Allen & Unwin, Sydney, 1996, pp 575–8.
19.   R Tomasic and S Bottomley, *Directing the Top 500: Corporate Governance and Accountability in Australian Companies*, Allen & Unwin, Sydney, 1993, p 88.
20.   Basten (above), pp 16–17. The fourth model was the author's idea but was deemed by Basten not 'necessarily' to constitute an additional model.

dominant in family, criminal and tort work, while the client-control model is more dominant in the corporate law context.

A study done in the United States by Sarat and Felstiner[21] of lawyer–client interaction in 40 divorce cases found that 'lawyer–client interaction in divorce occurs against a background of mutual suspicion, if not antagonism, between lawyers and clients'. The clients are frustrated by the lack of emotional responsiveness by their lawyers and 'worry that lawyers will be inattentive or disloyal'. Lawyers regard their divorce clients as emotional, irrational, demanding and unrealistic. The 'client is ... if not an enemy, an uncertain and unreliable partner and ally'. Emotional unresponsiveness to the clients and cynicism of the lawyers about the legal system work to enhance lawyer-control over divorce clients, yet both aspects contribute to client dissatisfaction with lawyers and the legal system. The authors conclude that this behaviour is not limited to divorce practice and it is important that law students gain greater understanding of the emotional aspects of their future interaction with clients.[22] Another more recent study of 69 lawyers working in civil rights and poverty law in Chicago found the whole spectrum from lawyers' extreme paternalism to strong deference to clients.[23]

9.9

INFORMATION AND ADVICE

Introduction

The major source of complaints against lawyers by clients is their failure to communicate, to follow instructions and to be courteous.[24] A study of the 1992 Supreme Court Special Sittings in New South Wales found that: 'With regard to information ... plaintiffs had a need for information about various aspects of their case, but ... this need was left wanting.' The study also found that: 'The main concern expressed was that they [plaintiffs] were excluded from the negotiations which ultimately resolved their case.'[25] In the last decade communication complaints has fallen to second place behind allegations of negligence. The Office of Legal Services Commission (NSW) for the year 2002–03 stated that: '[C]onsistent with previous years the majority of complaints included allegations of negligence (20.5 per cent), communication (15.8 per cent) and overcharging (10 per cent) ... The statistics gathered understate the part poor communication plays in

9.10

---

21. The survey was first published by A Sarat and W Felstiner in 'Law and Social Relations: Vocabularies of Motive in Lawyer/Client Interaction' (1988) 22 *Law and Society R* 737. The findings are also presented in 'Lawyers and Clients: Putting Professional Service on the Agenda of Legal Education' (1991) 41 *J Legal Education* 43 and in their book *Divorce Lawyers and Their Clients: Power and Meaning in the Legal Process*, Oxford University Press, New York, 1995. I will refer to the 'Lawyers and Clients: Putting Professional Service on the Agenda of Legal Education' article.
22. See n 21 (above), pp 47–53.
23. A Spitjwprtj, 'Lawyer–Client Decisionmaking in Civil Rights and Poverty Practice: An Empirical Study of Lawyers' Norms' (1996) 9 *Georgetown J Legal Ethics* 1101.
24. *Scrutiny of the Legal Profession* (1993) Report 70, New South Wales Law Reform Commission, paras 3.118–3.119.
25. *Plaintiffs and the Process of Litigation*, Report of the Civil Justice Research Centre, December 1994.

client dissatisfaction since it is often identified only after preliminary inquiries into a complaint have been made.' The Commission also received almost 10,000 calls to their inquiry line.[26]

A further indication of the problem of poor communication is the number of notifications to LawCover (Law Society of New South Wales professional insurer). According to Bruce MacDermott, General Manager, Risk Management Services for LawCover: '[In] the past 16 insurance years poor communication with clients has been the cause of 49 per cent of all notifications … "Poor communication" refers to those notifications where it is alleged the solicitor failed to advise the client adequately or provided incomplete explanation, did not follow the client's instructions, acted without obtaining instructions, and/or failed to define the extent of the retainer.'[27]

This is a problem not only found in Australia but also in other common law jurisdictions. For example, the California State Bar complaint hotline received more than 100,000 calls in 1993 and by 1995 the total was more than 128,000. Approximately 60 per cent of these calls concerned complaints by clients about lawyers who failed to return phone calls, failed to inform clients about the status of their case or failed to bring the client into the decision-making process.[28] Recent figures on calls in California are distorted because of the crisis in funding that took place in 1998. When the State Governor refused to sign a bill allowing the State Bar to collect dues, the bar had to lay off most of its staff. In April 1998 the bar closed down the Ethics Hotline and it was not reopened until early in 1999.[29] It recovered on reopening, reaching a peak of more than 156,000 calls in 2003, but had a dramatic decline to only about 96,000 in 2004.[30]

9.11   Failure to inform a client about important aspects of their legal matter can also lead to legal action. For example, in the *Micos* case[31] a client successfully sued a solicitor for negligence. The solicitor in acting for a purchase of land discovered a title defect and failed to notify the client. In a criminal matter, *R v Szabo*,[32] a client discovered after the trial that his counsel had been in a de facto relationship with the Crown prosecutor. The Court of Appeal found a miscarriage of justice and ordered a new trial. The fact that their relationship was in an interrupted phase did not affect the court's decision.

In the past, because this kind of conduct, lack of communication, did not constitute a disciplinary violation, the profession did little to correct the behaviour. Today, due to recommendations by law reform commissions and by the Trade Practices Commission (now the ACCC), the profession is starting to treat these 'minor' violations more seriously. If a practitioner has a history of such violations and they become chronic, he or she can be

---

26. Office of Legal Services Commissioner, *Annual Report*, 2002–2003, pp 4 and 6. For detailed figures see pp 24–31.
27. B MacDermott, F – 'Risk Management', F150–3, in C Laurie (ed), *Management of Australian Law Practice*, 2004. For detailed breakdown see Appendix 2, F50–15.
28. *California Lawyer*, December 1993, p 91 and *California Bar Journal*, March 1996, p 16.
29. For a description of the crisis see Y Ross, 'The shutdown of regulatory functions', *Law Institute J (Vic)*, May 1999, p 33.
30. See *California Lawyer*, April 2005, p 6.
31. *Micos v Diamond* (1970) 92 WN (NSW) 524 (C of A).
32. [2000] QCA 194.

severely disciplined. The legal profession has recognised that it is in a service business and must provide quality service to its clients. It has encouraged its members to pursue efficient business practices and to learn more about client relationship skills. In the past these rules have generally applied to solicitors and not barristers. Barristers did not have any contractual relationship with clients. This situation may now be changed with rules allowing direct access to barristers.

General principles

We have already discussed in Chapter 7 the 'client care' rules in New South Wales and the mandatory rule in England.[33] These rules incorporate a duty to keep clients periodically informed. The Law Council's Model Rules under its advocacy and litigation provisions state:

9.12

> **Rule 12.2** A practitioner must seek to assist the client to understand the issues in the case and the client's possible rights and obligations, if the practitioner is instructed to give advice on any such matter, sufficiently to permit the client to give proper instructions, particularly in connection with any compromise of the case.

> **Rule 12.3** A practitioner must where appropriate inform the client about the reasonably available alternatives to fully contested adjudication of the case unless the practitioner believes on reasonable grounds that the client already has such an understanding of those alternatives as to permit the client to make decisions about the client's best interests in relation to the litigation.

Western Australia also has general principles on keeping clients informed. Rule 10.1 states: 'A practitioner shall fully inform his [or her] client of his rights and possible courses of conduct regarding issues of substantial importance and shall keep his client apprised of all significant developments and generally informed in the matter entrusted to him by the client unless the client has instructed the practitioner to do otherwise.'[34] Western Australia also requires under r 5.2 that:

9.13

> A practitioner shall always be completely frank and open with his [or her] client and with all others so far as his [or her] client's interest may permit and shall at all times give his [or her] client a candid opinion on any professional matter in which he [or she] represents that client.

The ABA Model Rules r 1.4 states:

9.14

(a) A lawyer shall:

> (1) promptly inform the client of any decision or circumstance with respect to which the client's informed consent, as defined in Rule 1.0(e),[35] is required by these Rules;

> (2) reasonably consult with the client about the means by which the client's objectives are to be accomplished;

> (3) keep the client reasonably informed about the status of the matter;

> (4) promptly comply with reasonable requests for information; and

---

33. See V Shirvington, 'Client Care = happier clients, some salutary lessons from England' (1996) 34 *Law Society J (NSW)* 26.
34. See also r 10.3 (WA) which requires detailed continuing communications to the client concerning costs.
35. 'Informed consent' denotes the agreement by a person to a proposed course of conduct after the lawyer has communicated adequate information and explanation about the material risks of and reasonably available alternatives to the proposed course of conduct.

(5) consult with the client about any relevant limitation on the lawyer's conduct when the lawyer knows that the client expects assistance not permitted by the Rules of Professional Conduct or other law.

(b) A lawyer shall explain a matter to the extent reasonably necessary to permit the client to make informed decisions regarding the representation.

The Comment [5] to r 1.4 states: 'The client should have sufficient information to participate intelligently in decisions concerning the objectives of the representation and the means by which they are to be pursued, to the extent the client is willing and able to do so ...'.

These general principles, in the above rules, lay the foundation for lawyers' responsibility in initiating contact with clients and for maintaining a schedule for communicating with them throughout the processing of their legal problem. By having a planned series of periodic reports lawyers can convey to their clients a clear message that the lawyer is dealing with their problem. Such open communication leads to a better relationship based on trust and confidence and will greatly reduce the number of complaints made against lawyers. Furthermore, by providing enough information clients are able to help in solving the issue. For example, clients can help in investigation, in providing evidence, in taking notes at a hearing and by attending other similar hearings. These efforts will make clients feel they are part of their own case. It enables the lawyer and client to make more efficient use of the cooperative model.

Study of participatory model

9.15 A seminal study by Rosenthal shows that the cooperative model (he calls it the 'participatory model') can lead to better results for clients. The study was on the experiences of clients involved in personal injury claims. He compared the outcomes according to whether or not the client actively participated in the conduct of the case. Rosenthal then used an expert panel to determine if the outcome was good or bad. This was decided according to whether the damages recovered were higher or lower than the experts would have expected to be awarded in the case. The results showed that 75 per cent of the active clients, but only 41 per cent of the passive clients, obtained what were classified as good awards. Rosenthal concluded that his research showed that active participation can promote more effective problem-solving. His research indicated that:[36]

> ... clients can supplement the specialised knowledge of professions, fill gaps, catch mistakes, and provide criteria relevant for decision. Conversely, the collaborative task of having to explain and discuss the problem with the client can help the professional avoid mistakes and focus on the relevant aspects of the problem.

9.16 Rosenthal pointed out that client participation did place burdens on the lawyers and/or the clients and there were certain barriers to its implementation. The first was that confronting complex and uncertain problems with heavy risks is threatening to all of us. Therefore, many clients may find the threat too heavy a price to pay in emotional stress in return for the benefits. A second problem in implementing the model was that lawyers retain a disproportionate amount of resources that allows them to

---

36. D Rosenthal, *Lawyer and Client: Who's in Charge?*, Russell Sage Foundation, New York, 1974, p 23.

manipulate the client and thereby deny the client's effective collaboration. The lawyer has more extensive knowledge and experience and deals with the client in his or her own social setting, that is, their office, which clearly places the lawyer in a position of authority and power. A third limitation is the overwhelming acceptance by the public of the traditional lawyer-control model. The clients may feel that it is proper to place their trust in lawyers without questioning whether the lawyers deserve that trust. Furthermore, clients treat lawyers as technical experts and feel that the problems are too complicated for them to make a productive contribution. A fourth limitation in using the model is the inability of clients to deal with technical language and multifaceted decisions that are present in legal problems. A fifth barrier is that lawyers are ignorant about 'the proper scope and form disclosure leading to informed consent should take'.[37]

There is a need to develop 'effective techniques and standards of relevance for disclosure which neither waste the time of participants, unduly confuse the client, nor unduly threaten him [or her]'.[38] A sixth limitation on using the participatory model is that it is expensive. Lawyers will have to spend more time with clients. This may be advantageous in that it will lead to more efficient processing of the legal problem than the passive model where lawyers do not have enough information to provide an effective service. A seventh limitation is that it is time-consuming to use the participatory model. This is valid but it is a matter for people to establish their priorities of what is important. The final limitation of the model is that it will reduce the lawyers' domination in the relationship, which will result in a loss of ability to restrain clients from taking immoral or illegal actions. Rosenthal concludes that the costs of pursuing the participatory model do not outweigh the advantages gained by client participation.[39]

9.17

Offers of settlement

Professional rules

Comment [2] to ABA Model Rule 1.4 states that when a lawyer negotiates on behalf of a client, the client needs to be informed of all relevant facts. This includes communications from another party and the lawyer must take other reasonable steps that permit the client to make a decision regarding a serious offer from another party:

9.18

> A lawyer who receives from opposing counsel an offer of settlement in a civil controversy or a proffered plea bargain in a criminal case should promptly inform the client of its substance unless the client has previously indicated that the proposal will be acceptable or unacceptable or has authorized the lawyer to accept or to reject the offer ...

The California Rules of Professional Conduct have specific provisions on communication of settlement offers. Rule 3-510 states:

> (A) A member shall promptly communicate to the member's client:
>
> 1. All terms and conditions of any offer made to the client in a criminal matter; and
>
> 2. All amounts, terms, and conditions of any written offer of settlement made to the clients in all other matters.

---

37. Rosenthal (above), p 57.
38. Rosenthal (above), p 143.
39. Rosenthal (above), pp 154ff.

9.19 It should be noted that in California only *written* offers need to be communicated in non-criminal matters. In Australia r 10A.4 of the Rules of Professional Conduct and Practice in the Northern Territory states: 'A practitioner must inform and advise the client of any offers to compromise the client's case and always endeavour to achieve an appropriate resolution of the case at the earliest opportunity.' The Law Council's Model Rule 12.2 (above) requires the practitioner to provide the client with sufficient information and advice to enable the client to give proper instructions concerning any offers of settlement. In determining the rules relevant for offers of settlement in Australia it is still necessary to look at the common law. Barristers under common law had implied authority to consent to a verdict for the opposition in the absence of the client and without the client's express authorisation.[40] This principle has been followed in more recent cases where lawyers usually have implied authority to settle a suit without reference to the client as long as the compromise does not involve a matter 'collateral to the action'. Lawyers also have ostensible authority between themselves and the opposing party to settle cases on behalf of clients without showing actual proof of authority. If lawyers know that their clients have insufficient assets to meet an offer the lawyers have made, there would not be an implied authority to make that offer. This still would not negate the lawyers' ostensible authority and the clients are still bound by their lawyers' actions, but only if the lawyer making the settlement is 'on the record' with the court and it is not a collateral matter.[41] The rule appears to be that in order to invalidate an arrangement entered into by counsel it must be shown not only that counsel's authority was limited, but also that the limitation was known to the other side at the time.[42] In a more recent case the solicitor had the authority to bind the client and entered into a settlement. The client attempted to modify the settlement but the Queensland Court of Appeal rejected the appeal.[43]

Case law on offers of settlement

9.20 There are exceptions to this general principle where settlements made by lawyers have been set aside. Good examples of these exceptions are where no authority was present because the lawyer failed to discuss and communicate the terms of the offer of settlement with the client,[44] or the lawyer failed to follow the client's instructions.[45] In the latter English case the court held that a counsel has 'no authority, express or otherwise' to bind the client, when he or she does not follow explicit instructions of the instructing solicitor of the client's wishes not to enter into a consent order. The court set aside the order because these were 'special facts in a rather special case'. The court quoted *Halsbury's Laws of England*[46] as stating:

---

40. *Mathews v Munster* (1887) 20 QB 141 (Div Ct).
41. *Waugh v H B Clifford & Sons Ltd* [1982] 1 All ER 1095 at 1104–6. For a more recent case dealing with ostensible authority see *Von Schulz v Morriello* [1998] 15 Qld 2.
42. *Strauss v Francis* (1866) LR 1 QB 379 at 381 (Div Ct).
43. *von Schulz v Marriello* [1998] 15 Qld 2.
44. *Australian Direct Mail Advertising & Addressing Co Pty Ltd v Sukkar* (SC(NSW), Eq Div, No S1635 of 1981, unreported) cited in Disney et al (above), p 631.
45. *Marsden v Marsden* [1972] 2 All ER 1162 at 1164.
46. 3rd ed, vol 51, para 74.

… when, in the particular circumstance of the case, grave injustice would be done by allowing the compromise to stand, the compromise may be set aside, even although the limitation of counsel's authority was unknown to the other side.

A New Zealand case has held that a solicitor's retainer does not carry with it actual authority to settle an action he or she was retained to commence:[47]

9.21

… save only where there are expressed instructions to the contrary … [A]s between himself and his client the solicitor requires the authority of the latter.

In that case the solicitor was held liable for professional negligence for compromising an action contrary to the instructions of the client.

Under ABA Model Rule 1.2: 'A lawyer may take such action on behalf of the client as is impliedly authorized to carry out the representation.' Comment [3] to that Rule states: 'At the outset of representation, the client may authorize the lawyer to take specific action on the client's behalf without further consultation. Absent a material change in circumstances and subject to Rule 1.4, a lawyer may rely on such an advance authorization. The client may, however, revoke such authority at any time.' There is no comment concerning the situations where the lawyer goes beyond his or her actual authority.

Wolfram has stated the general rule in the United States:[48]

The rule that prevails in the great majority of jurisdictions is that the mere fact that a lawyer possesses the authority to represent a client gives the lawyer no implied authority. Thus a local court rule requiring a lawyer to appear at a settlement conference with authority to settle requires a lawyer to appear with express authorisation from the client to settle or with the client personally present. Settlement authority must be expressly or implicitly conferred by the client, or the client must ratify the settlement. Parties who contract with a lawyer in absence of one of those basis for validating the settlement in effect generally assume the risk that the client will exercise his or her power to repudiate.

Wolfram's view of the state courts has not been accepted by the federal courts. The Second Circuit Court held that if the lawyers have apparent authority their clients will be bound by the settlement agreed to by the lawyers.[49]

Lawyers have been criticised for failure to communicate offers of settlement to their clients.[50] Such failure can be considered negligent and/or a breach of contract, and can lead to a civil action[51] if it is not barred by the immunity doctrine.[52] Failure to notify clients of such information can also

9.22

47. *Thompson v Howley* [1977] 1 NZLR 16.
48. C Wolfram, *Modern Legal Ethics*, West Publishers, St Paul, 1986, pp 169–70.
49. *US v International Brotherhood of Teamsters*, 986 F2d 15 (2nd Cir 1993).
50. *Australian Direct Mail Advertising & Addressing Co Pty Ltd* case (above). It has been stated that approximately 5 per cent of all complaints to the Law Institute of Victoria concern whether or not there was authority for a solicitor to settle a case: G Lewis, 'Professional Practice' (1983) 57 *Law Institute J* 207.
51. *Waugh* and *Thompson* cases (above). In the United States a court held that failure to communicate a settlement offer constitutes malpractice and that there was no need for expert testimony to establish the lawyer's negligence: *State v James*, 48 Wash App 353, 739 P 2d 1161 (1987).
52. See *Biggar v Mcleod* [1978] 2 NZLR 9. In that case the immunity doctrine was held to apply to advice given by a practitioner about a settlement during the course of a trial. This case may be modified by the general doctrine adopted in *Donellan v Watson* (1990) 21 NSWLR 335. Both these cases are discussed in Chapter 10.

be grounds for a complaint to the professional association. In a recent Queensland case the failure to communicate and the settlement of the claims against the instructions of the client were part of the reasons for a finding of professional misconduct. The solicitor was struck off the roll.[53] It is obviously good practice for legal practitioners to obtain written instructions concerning offers of settlement. There is a need throughout Australia, whenever it is feasible, for an ethical rule requiring the communication of all offers of settlement and professional advice concerning the offer.

What if a practitioner advises a client to accept a settlement that turns out to be too low? Justice Handley held in *Studer v Boettcher*[54] that the practitioner who did this at an end of a formal mediation was not liable if he had acted 'with proper care and skill during the mediation, and that his advice to settle on the best terms then available was good advice'.

9.23 Barristers who settle a case immediately before trial will usually receive their full fee for the first day of the trial unless they failed to negotiate a cancellation fee. Cancellation fees are usually bargained for with solicitors before accepting a brief. Of course, if a long trial is involved barristers may not be supportive of an offer, especially if they have not double-briefed, because of fear of losing a large fee.

9.24 Another reason lawyers may be reluctant to support an offer or fail to communicate it is because they want to gain experience from conducting the trial and/or receive public recognition. In the United States, far more often than in Australia, lawyers have proceeded with 'test cases' to the detriment of their clients. In such instances the lawyers are seeking, by use of the courts, an appellate decision that changes the law, thereby benefiting many people and sometimes the lawyer's own reputation. Sometimes the defendants in such suits may make a very reasonable offer that would satisfy the client, but would defeat the purpose of the test case (often a class action), that is, achieving social justice by reforming the law. In such situations lawyers may endeavour either to persuade the client to continue the case by being biased towards the offer or fail to communicate the offer of settlement.[55] American lawyers also face difficult ethical issues in settling class actions. There may be irreconcilable differences between members of the class as to the aims of the action. There may also be a conflict between the lawyers and the class, for example a financial offer to settle that gives little to the class but provides the lawyers with large fees. Luban says that lawyers acting in these situations should act in a responsible manner. They need to act as a 'representative of the client class as a whole' as far as it is feasible to do so.[56] Luban's view seems idealistic by granting too much autonomy to lawyers. There is a need for specific ethical rules and sanctions to control how lawyers act in test cases and class actions.

53. *In the Matter of Andrew Charles Lauchland*, Annual Report of Disciplinary Action, No 5, Supplement to *Proctor*, December 1999, pp 5–6. The solicitor made several other serious breaches including the filing of false affidavits in the name of the client.
54. [2000] NSWCA 263.
55. See, for example, M Bloom et al, *Lawyers, Clients and Ethics*, Council on Legal Education for Professional Responsibility Inc, Chicago, 1974, p 72.
56. D Luban, *Lawyers and Justice: an Ethical Study*, Princeton University Press, Princeton, 1988, p 356.

Legal aid availability

Lawyers have financial incentives not to reveal to clients that they are eligible for legal aid. In some jurisdictions such advice will lead to the loss of the client to the legal aid service, while in others it means that the lawyer will retain the client but receive a lower fee. The latter takes place because the legal aid programs usually pay much lower than the scaled fees for the services rendered. Furthermore, these fees are not usually paid promptly and many lawyers charge above the scale fees that are minimum fees.

9.25

The profession has enacted rules and rulings to deal with communication in this area. In New South Wales there is no obligation for solicitors to inform clients of the availability of legal aid. The Council of the Law Society 'has made no formal pronouncement on the issue and declined to include in the Solicitors' Rules a specific rule on the subject'.[57] In New South Wales there is a requirement in criminal cases when accepting instructions to act, subject to obtaining a grant of legal aid, to assist the accused to apply for the grant.[58] By contrast, South Australian rr 34.1 and 34.2 oblige practitioners to inform clients of their eligibility and help them to make an application. Western Australian r 11.1 is similar but also states that the 'practitioner shall not be obliged to act for that client on a legally aided basis'. New Zealand and English Law Societies also have rules similar to those of South Australia.[59] Victoria adopted in 2000 r 12(2)(b) that required clients to be advised of any rights they 'may have to apply for legal aid unless there is no real possibility that the client is eligible'.[60] This rule was removed by the Professional Conduct and Practice Rules 2003, which were later slightly modified by the Professional Conduct and Practice (Amendment) Rules 2003. The latter came into operation on 1 March 2005. The new rules are based upon the Law Council's Model Rules.

The Queensland Law Society ruling states that 'there is an obligation on a practitioner to inquire as to the client's eligibility for legal assistance'.[61] This ruling was the subject of a lawsuit in the *Tydhof* case.[62] The plaintiff sought to have papers released by his former lawyers who refused to release them until he paid his bill. He argued that the firm had no valid lien because he had discharged them for just cause, for not informing him of his eligibility for legal aid. The court held that the firm had a valid lien. There was no indication in the client's original instructions that he had financial need. Instead, there was evidence that he had resources to pursue his claim. The judge said that merely being retained does not impose a duty on the solicitor to advise a client of the existence of legal assistance. And in this case, even if there was a breach of duty, it could not be used as a just cause for depriving the law firm of its lien. Failure to inform of the availability of legal aid was incidental or collateral negligence. The client's remedy is to claim in a separate action damages flowing from that breach of duty. Since this case

9.26

57. See F Riley, *New South Wales Solicitors Manual*, Law Society of New South Wales, Sydney, 2004 looseleaf, para 5425 (LexisNexis Butterworths, Sydney).
58. Rule 6A, Professional Conduct and Practice Rules (NSW).
59. Riley (above), para 5425.
60. Professional Conduct and Practice Rules 2000, r 12(2)(b).
61. (1977) 7 *Queensland Law Society J* 184.
62. *Re Elfis and Somers; Ex parte Tydhof* (SC(Qld), McPherson J, No 270/82, unreported) extracted in Disney et al (above), p 633.

the Queensland Law Society has adopted the Solicitors Handbook. Under para 14.01 practitioners who accept instructions from impecunious clients who have 'good prospects of success may either: (1) Conduct the action without legal assistance; or (2) Obtain legal assistance and accept the Legal Aid scale of fees'. In the first alternative the client has to be informed that he or she will be 'obliged to pay solicitor and own client costs. A client who does not agree should be referred to another practitioner'.

9.27 The rules and rulings and the *Tydhof* case indicate that failure to inform clients of their eligibility for legal aid may constitute negligence and/or breach of contract. This is not a satisfactory solution for impecunious clients. They will need to go to another lawyer and seek legal aid to pursue their civil claim for damages or pursue the matter by making a complaint against the practitioner with the professional association. In either situation there are various barriers for these clients in seeking redress. There is obviously a need for all jurisdictions to require lawyers to inform clients of the availability of and their eligibility for legal aid.

Other information and advice

9.28 Lawyers are required to inform their clients if they intend not to apply the full rigour of the law in dealing with the opposing party but they frequently fail to meet this requirement. As Disney et al state:[63]

> ... this duty is honoured more in the breach than the observance, especially in relation to granting opponents extensions of time beyond the deadlines for filing pleadings. There is a general tradition of 'courtesy' among the profession that these deadlines will not be enforced unless ample advance notice of a strict attitude has been given.

There is a Western Australian ethical rule relevant to the above matters. Rule 18.2 states:

> If a practitioner observes that another practitioner is making or is likely to make a mistake or oversight which may involve the other practitioner's client in unnecessary expense or delay, he [or she] shall not do or say anything to induce or foster that mistake or oversight and shall, except where so doing might prejudice his own client, draw the attention of the other practitioner to that mistake or oversight.

9.29 Clients are often not informed about statute of limitations defences, especially if their lawyer has a continuing and good relationship with the other lawyer. Such a defence will be treated as a mere technical loophole that should not be applied, nor is it in the lawyer's interest that the client be informed. Lawyers also may be held to be involved in a fraud with their clients. This can happen, for example, if they tell clients about a tax refund that is too high because the Australian Taxation Office made a mistake and the clients refuse to correct the mistake.

The last issue is whether lawyers have a duty to inform and advise clients about non-legal matters. Rosenthal in the study discussed above (see **9.15ff**) says the following:[64]

> A lawyer who defines his [or her] counselling role narrowly to exclude involving himself with the medical, emotional, employment, family, and

---

63. Disney et al (above), p 636.
64. Rosenthal (above), p 42.

financial problems the client may face as a result of the accident, may leave to the client a wide range of crucial choices. The client who assumes that the lawyer's role in the problem solving is a broad one, may anticipate attorney guidance in such 'nonlegal' areas as the kind and extent of medical attention; failing to get such guidance, he may assume, often erroneously, that his response to his medical needs, will have little eventual impact on the outcome of his claim.

Rosenthal points out that failure to give such non-legal advice may lose for the client both monetary compensation and emotional restoration.[65]

9.30

The ABA has recognised that lawyers' advice should be broad in scope. Model Rule 2.1 states:

… In rendering advice, a lawyer may refer not only to law but to other considerations such as moral, economic, social and political factors, that may be relevant to the client's situation.

The Comment to the Rule states:

[2] Advice couched in narrowly legal terms may be of little value to a client, especially where practical considerations, such as cost or effects on other people, are predominant. Purely technical legal advice, therefore, can sometimes be inadequate. It is proper for a lawyer to refer to relevant moral and ethical considerations … [because they] impinge upon most legal questions and may decisively influence how the law will be applied.

[3] A client may expressly or impliedly ask the lawyer for purely technical advice. When such a request is made by a client experienced in legal matters, the lawyer may accept it at face value. When such a request is made by a client inexperienced in legal matters, however, the lawyer's responsibility as advisor may include indicating that more may be involved than strictly legal considerations.

[4] Matters that go beyond strictly legal questions may also be in the domain of another profession. Family matters can involve problems within the professional competence of psychiatry, clinical psychology or social work; business matters can involve problems within the competence of the accounting profession or of financial specialists. Where consultation with a professional in another field is itself something a competent lawyer would recommend, the lawyer should make such a recommendation. At the same time, a lawyer's advice at its best often consists of recommending a course of action in the face of conflicting recommendations of experts.

There is no similar provision to r 2.1 and its Comment in Australia but it should be noted that r 2.1 is permissive. If it was mandatory it would conflict with the present perception of the lawyer's role in the adversary system. We will discuss this in detail in Part Four. Rule 2.1 does recognise that lawyers at times may not have the knowledge to give non-legal advice. There are lawyers who are very skilled in tax and financial advice but other lawyers attempting to do this work have caused financial hardship for their clients. Their lack of financial skill has at times led them to make trust account defalcations. Lawyers are also becoming adept in having a wide range of information as to where clients can obtain additional advice that will help their case.

9.31

One area in which lawyers have been given a role in providing non-legal advice is family law. Many lawyers have been criticised for being insensitive and adversarial in dealing with matters in this area. The Family Law Act

9.32

---

65. Rosenthal (above).

1975 (Cth) requires lawyers to inform the client of the legal and possible social effects of the proposed proceedings (including the consequences for the children of the marriage) and, under 1995 reforms, to point out to clients that the primary methods of resolving family law disputes are counselling, conciliation, reconciliation, mediation and arbitration and not litigation.[66]

DUTY TO OBEY

9.33   In this section we will first outline the general principles and then examine particular aspects of duties of obedience. In the latter part we will discuss the general conduct of a case, guilty pleas, family law situations and clients with disabilities. There are also problems faced by in-house lawyers who work for corporations and governments. Their problems in relation to obedience to instructions will be discussed in Chapter 12.

General principles

9.34   Lawyers are agents of their clients and are under contractual obligation to them. Therefore they are required to do what their clients instruct them to do within the terms of the contract. Failure to follow instructions can lead to disciplinary or civil action. Of course, the lawyers' obligation is subject to the general law and their obligations as officers of the court. Thus, lawyers do not have to take instructions that require unethical or illegal behaviour. Lawyers will also have to on occasions go behind clients' instructions. Clients may be lying when giving instructions and lawyers have the duty to tell the client that instructions do not make sense or are inconsistent with known facts.[67] ABA Model Rule 1.2 states:

>   (a) ... [A] lawyer shall abide by a client's decisions concerning the objectives of representation ... and shall consult with the client as to the means by which they are to be pursued ... A lawyer shall abide by a client's decision whether to settle a matter ...
>
>   ...
>
>   (d) A lawyer shall not counsel a client to engage, or assist a client, in conduct that the lawyer knows is criminal or fraudulent, but a lawyer may discuss the legal consequences of any proposed course of conduct with a client and may counsel or assist a client to make a good faith effort to determine the validity, scope, meaning or application of the law ...

9.35   Comments [1] and [2] to r 1.2 state:

>   [1] ... [T]he client has ultimate authority to determine the purposes to be served by legal representation, within the limits imposed by law and the lawyer's professional obligations. The decisions specified in paragraph (a), such as whether to settle a civil matter, must also be made by the client. ... With respect to the means by which the client's objectives are to be pursued, the lawyer shall consult with the client ... and may take such action as is impliedly authorized to carry out the representation.
>
>   [2] On occasion, however, a lawyer and a client may disagree about the means to be used to accomplish the client's objectives. Clients normally defer to the special knowledge and skill of their lawyer with respect to the means

---

66.   Family Law Reform Act 1995 (Cth) Pt III.
67.   V Shirvington, 'Going behind clients' instructions' (1998) *Law Society J* (NSW) 32.

to be used to accomplish their objectives, particularly with respect to technical, legal and tactical matters. Conversely, lawyers usually defer to the client regarding such questions as the expense to be incurred and concern for third persons who might be adversely affected. Because of the varied nature of the matters about which a lawyer and client might disagree and because the actions in question, may implicate the interests of a tribunal or other persons, this Rule does not prescribe how such disagreements are to be resolved ...

The American rule shows how vague and difficult it is to set boundaries on following clients' instructions. When applying Rule 1.2 it will be difficult to determine what constitutes technical and legal tactical issues. It is generally accepted that lawyers have the right to decide how to question a witness and what witnesses should be called.[68] In these situations, whenever it is feasible, lawyers should inform the client of what they intend to do. We have already discussed the fact that lawyers have implied authority and at times apparent or ostensible authority to act on behalf of their clients. This authority is based on the law of agency but can be expressly restricted by clients. We have also discussed in the previous chapter lawyers' right to withdraw if clients refuse to follow advice concerning preparation or conduct of the proceedings. In Chapter 15 we will discuss this right of withdrawal in relation to clients' perjury and confessions of guilt.   **9.36**

In order to avoid disputes over authority and over clients' instructions it is advisable for lawyers to obtain written instructions concerning the scope of the representation especially in relation to offers of settlement. There is evidence that the failure to have written instructions has led to many disputes.[69] Failure to have written instructions on the scope of the retainer, according to Lord Denning, will be held against the solicitor. The client's word will be preferred because the client is ignorant:[70]   **9.37**

> If the solicitor does not take the precaution of getting a written retainer he has only himself to thank for being at variance with his client over it and must take the consequences.

The Court of Appeal in New South Wales completely disagrees with Lord Denning's views.[71]

Particular aspects — general conduct of a case

Many lawyers in the United States assert that lawyers should control all of the important aspects of representation. These assertions are made in relation to the following situations: contingent fee cases, class actions, certain divorce actions, criminal cases and poverty law representation. The arguments for lawyers' control are based on the following: **9.38**

❏ Lawyers have superior learning, training and skill in legal matters. These traits could not be duplicated in a reasonable period of time by a client because of the client's emotional state and the mystifying complexity of law and legal institutions.

---

68. See 'Report from the Ethics Committee', *Victorian Bar News*, Winter, 1979, p 9.
69. See New South Wales Law Reform Commission, *Legal Profession Inquiry: Background Paper — III* (1980), pp 55–9.
70. *Griffiths v Evans* [1953] 2 All ER 1367 at 1369.
71. *May v Burcul* (CA(NSW), No 103/82, 18 October 1982, unreported) cited in Disney et al (above), p 639.

❑ In some situations 'a lawyer is an officer of the court and in that role may not permit clients to direct the lawyer to perform in a way that the court would not approve'.[72]

There are many Australian lawyers who would agree with the American views, especially in relation to conduct of a case in court. The Victorian Bar's Ethics Committee has stated:[73]

> There is no doubt that it is for counsel, and counsel alone, to determine how his client's case is to be presented to the court, so that it is within his complete discretion what witnesses he will call and what questions he will put in cross-examination. It is important that counsel should take steps to ensure that, as far as possible, the lay client understands the relevant procedure, nonetheless that final decision in this area rests with counsel ...

9.39   The Western Australian Professional Conduct r 13.1 states that counsel has the authority, subject to the rules, to 'conduct each case in such manner as he considers will be most advantageous to his client'. Rules 14.5 and 14.10 give freedom of choice for clients to decide as to what plea they will make to a criminal charge and whether or not they want to give evidence.

A prominent Canadian judge, Martin J, when he was a QC went further than the Victorian Bar or the Western Australian Professional Conduct Rule in relation to defending a criminal charge. He stated that counsel has 'total control and responsibility over the defence'. The decision on whether to plead guilty or not guilty rests with the client. Once that decision is made:[74]

> ... it is for the defence counsel to decide how the case is to be conducted in accordance with his best judgment as to what is in the best interest of the client.

9.40   The ABA Standards for Criminal Justice, 4-5.2 *Control and Direction of the Case* do not agree with Martin's views:

(a) Certain decisions relating to the conduct of the case are ultimately for defense counsel. The decisions which are to be made by the accused after full consultation with counsel include: (i) what pleas to enter; (ii) whether to accept a plea agreement; (iii) whether to waive jury trial; (iv) whether to testify in his or her own behalf; and (v) whether to appeal.

(b) Strategic and tactical decisions should be made by defense counsel after consultation with the client where feasible and appropriate. Such decisions include what witnesses to call, whether and how to conduct cross-examination, what jurors to accept or strike; what trial motions should be made, and what evidence should be introduced.

(c) If a disagreement on significant matters of tactics or strategy arises between the defense counsel and the client, defense counsel should make a record of the circumstances, counsel's advice and reasons, and the conclusion reached. The record should be made in a manner which protects the confidentiality of the lawyer–client relationship.

Allocation of authority

9.41   The case law has looked at allocation of authority rules to see whether they lead to a miscarriage of justice in criminal cases. In the New Zealand case of *R v McLoughlin and Isaacs*[75] a barrister refused to follow his client's

---

72.   Wolfram (above), p 155.
73.   'Report from the Ethics Committee' (above), p 9.
74.   *Problems in Ethics and Advocacy*, Law Society of Upper Canada, 1969, p 282.
75.   [1985] 1 NZLR 106 (C of A).

instructions to conduct a defence against a charge of rape based on an alibi. Instead, counsel conducted the case on a consent defence. The court held that the accused did not have the proper opportunity to place his defence to the jury and therefore did not receive the full client's instructions in reference to challenges made to jurors[76] and the making of admissions.[77] The old Australian Bar Association (1993), Code of Conduct Rule 7.2(f) supported the case. It stated that a barrister is under a duty to advise the accused of his or her rights. This includes advice such as the right to challenge jurors, the right to give evidence, the right to call evidence, to name but three, but it is for the client to make the decision as to the exercise of these rights.[78]

The Barristers' Rules are more general. Rule 17 (NSW and Qld; r 12 Vic; r 12.2 Model Rules) states: **9.42**

> A barrister must seek to assist the client to understand the issues in the case and the client's possible rights and obligations ... sufficiently to permit the client to have proper instructions, particularly in connection with any compromise of the case.

Rule 18 (NSW and Qld; r 16 Vic) states:

> A barrister must not act as the mere mouthpiece of the client or of the instructing solicitor and must exercise the forensic judgments called for during the case independently, after appropriate consideration of the client's and the instructing solicitor's desires where practicable.

The New South Wales Barristers' Rules were amended in March 2000 and include a new r 17B (r 19 Qld; r 12.4 Model Rules). It states:

> A barrister must (unless circumstances warrant otherwise in the barrister's considered opinion) advise a client who is charged with a criminal offence about any law, procedure or practice which in substance holds out the prospect of some advantage (including diminution of penalty), if the client pleads guilty or authorises other steps towards reducing the issues, time, cost or distress involved in the proceedings.

The Explanatory Notes (NSW) state that the policy behind this new Rule 'is to ensure that clients in this position must not be deprived of choices which should be theirs, and which may turn out to be very important for their lives, by a simple lack of information'. The Notes believe that in most cases it will be necessary for counsel to advise according to this Rule.

In *R v Birks*,[79] the accused was indicted for maliciously inflicting bodily harm with the intent to have sexual intercourse and having sexual intercourse without consent. The defendant's inexperienced counsel failed to ask the complainant during his cross-examination about the fact that no anal intercourse had taken place and that her physical injuries were not intentionally caused by the defendant's conduct. The failure of counsel to ask these two questions became the basis of a vigorous attack on the validity of the defendant's testimony. This was because the defendant gave a different version of the events than the complainant. Counsel still had an **9.43**

---

76. *R v Johns* (1979) 25 ALR 573 (HC).
77. *R v Balchin* (1974) 9 SASR 64 at 67.
78. This code, adopted in 1993, was no longer being followed in most jurisdictions by 1995. It was completely redrafted, based mainly on the New South Wales Barristers' Rules and adopted in July 1996.
79. (1990) 19 NSWLR 677.

opportunity to bring in evidence to show that he had been instructed by his client that no anal intercourse had taken place and that the physical injuries were unintentional. Counsel only brought this evidence to the attention of the court after the jury had retired to consider their verdict.

On appeal, Gleeson CJ (NSW) followed a decision of the Court of Appeal in England, *R v Ensor*.[80] In that case a leading counsel, defending his client on two charges of rape, refused to follow his client's instructions to make an application to sever the indictment, which would normally have been accepted. Lord Lane said that not following this instruction, even if erroneous, could not possibly be described as incompetent. Mistakes or unwise decisions made by counsel during a trial by itself are not sufficient grounds for an appeal. Lord Parker went on to say (in *R v Ensor* at 502):

> ... if the court had any lurking doubt that the appellant might have suffered some injustice as a result of flagrantly incompetent advocacy by his advocate, then it would quash the convictions ...

Gleeson CJ summarised the relevant principles to be followed:

1. A Court of Criminal Appeal has a power and a duty to intervene in the case of a miscarriage of justice, but what amounts to a miscarriage of justice is something that has to be considered in the light of the way in which the system of criminal justice operates.

2. As a general rule an accused person is bound by the way the trial is conducted by counsel, regardless of whether that was in accordance with the wishes of the client, and it is not a ground for setting aside a conviction that decisions made by counsel were made without, or contrary to, instructions, or involve errors of judgment or even of negligence.

3. However, there may arise cases where something occurred in the running of a trial, perhaps as the result of 'flagrant incompetence' of counsel, or perhaps from some other cause, which will be recognised as involving, or causing, a miscarriage of justice. It is impossible, and undesirable, to attempt to define such cases with precision. When they arise they will attract appellate intervention.

Gleeson CJ found that the inexperience of counsel resulted in a number of mistakes which gave rise to a miscarriage of justice. He therefore upheld the appeal. The High Court has held that incompetence of counsel in a criminal case is not separate ground for an appeal. The appellant has to show that there was a miscarriage of justice because of the incompetence.[81]

American cases

9.44   Cases in the United States have had an inconsistent approach to the problem of who controls what aspect of a criminal defence. In *Nelson v California*[82] the Ninth Circuit Court rejected an appeal based on the fact that the defendant's lawyer, for tactical reasons, declined the defendant's request to object to the introduction of seized evidence. The court said that only counsel is competent to make that decision and must be the manager of the case. If the defendants made such decisions they would be likely to do more harm than good, which would impair the constitutional guarantee to right to counsel. The United States Supreme Court in *Jones v Barnes*[83]

80.   [1989] 1 WLR 497.
81.   *TKWJ v R* (2002) 212 CLR 126 at 132–133 per Gaudron J, 157 per Hayne J.
82.   (1965) 346 F 2d 73 (9th Cir).
83.   (1983) 463 US 745.

adopted a similar approach. The Second Circuit had granted habeus relief to the accused because his lawyer, ignoring the client's request, had omitted several issues on appeal that he felt would not succeed. The Supreme Court overruled this decision. Chief Justice Burger stated: '[B]y promulgating a *per se* rule that the client, not the professional advocate, must be allowed to decide what issues are to be pressed, the Court of Appeals seriously undermines the ability of counsel to present the client's case in accord with counsel's professional evaluation ... Absent exceptional circumstances, he [the accused] is bound by the tactics used by his counsel at trial and on appeal.' The dissenters in *Jones* rejected the paternalistic approach of the majority and emphasised the need to maintain 'the dignity and autonomy of a person on trial'. The Alabama Supreme Court in the *Taylor* case[84] refused an appeal because counsel was incompetent for acceding to the defendant's insistence on a plea of alibi. Counsel had urged that self-defence was the defendant's only chance to win. The defendant argued that counsel had violated the ethical rule on not conducting the trial according to his professional view. The court said that the issue of what defence is to be asserted is for the defendant to decide.

In *People v Hunt*[85] an Illinois court refused to set aside a conviction because the trial court had acceded to the defendant's request. The defendant had requested, against his counsel's advice, that the defendant's brother be called as a witness. The brother's evidence pointed to a different alibi than one that had just been given by the defendant's other witness.   **9.45**

The appellate court stated:

> ABA Standards for Criminal Justice 4-5.2 should not be used to absolve the overzealous defendant who intrudes into this area of professional discretion by insisting on a contrary course of action after counsel has explained the possible disadvantages of the insisted tactic.

The court concluded that such behaviour estopped the defendant from claiming on appeal that adhering to his request constituted prejudicial error.

These American cases show that the lawyer does not always know what is best,[86] but if the client prejudices his or her own case the courts will not allow that behaviour to be grounds for an appeal. This view is supported by recent Australian cases applying the *Dietrich* doctrine. If clients interfere to such an extent that their lawyers cannot properly represent them they will not be able to argue they did not have adequate representation.[87] These cases are based on the issue of whether the defendant has received his or her day in court. This means that defendants have had the right to a fair and full trial and the opportunity to have the aid of competent counsel. Under the *Dietrich* doctrine failure to provide competent counsel will result in a miscarriage of justice.

Relationship with the system

The control lawyers have over clients, especially in criminal trials, is evident in an examination of relationships in the courtroom. Defence   **9.46**

---

84. *Taylor v State* (1973) 287 So 2d 901.
85. (1981) 426 NE 2d 1268. For a similar case see *People v Gadson* 24 Cal Rptr 2d 219.
86. See M Freedman, 'A Lawyer Doesn't Always Know Best' (1978) 7 *Human Rights* 28.
87. See, for example, *R v Frawley* (1993) 69 A Crim R 208 and more recently *R v Promizio* [2004] NSW 75.

counsels are often friendly to prosecutors and at times it may appear to the accused that all the actors — defence counsel, prosecutor and judge — are in a conspiracy against the accused. This may be more evident in the American setting because of the strong push for plea bargaining. In the United States, according to Blumberg, the client becomes a secondary figure in the court system:[88]

> The accused's lawyer has far greater professional, economic, intellectual and other ties to the various elements of the court system than he does to his own clients ... The defense attorneys ... ultimately are concerned with strategies which tend to lead to a plea. It is the rational, impersonal elements involving economies of time, labor, expense and a superior commitment of the defense counsel to these rationalistic values of maximum court organization that prevail, in his relationship with a client.

9.47   In the Australian context, Mack and Anleu[89] interviewed 64 defence lawyers, prosecutors and judges but generally did not find support for Blumberg's view of a 'group culture' acting against the interests of defendants. They did make a possible exception for Magistrates' Courts 'where volume of cases is much higher, resources are much less, and the role of police prosecutors, who lack legal professional training is greater'. They also found that some of the interviewees, especially those expressing views on the subject, thought that legal aid defence lawyers had less time and resources for extended discussions over a settled plea than private defence lawyers. The latter tended to prolong discussions and did not 'encourage early pleas because of financial considerations ... [P]rivate practitioners are more thorough, especially where they do not have the resource constraints of legal aid commissions'.[90] They warned that it was important that defence counsel have proper training and give sufficient time and investigation to defendants' cases 'so that the unprofessional legal culture described in other jurisdictions does not develop in Australia'.[91]

Mack and Anleu also found some similarities with Blumberg in the alienation from the system experienced by defendants. They state that the:

> ... accused may be fearful, anxious, confused, and intimidated by unfamiliar and formal court processes. For the accused, everything seems to happen very fast, whether in court or in conference with a legal representative. The accused may be affected by drink or drugs, lack of education, or may have a background which does not give familiarity with the practices and assumptions of the Anglo-Australian system of justice. The accused may not be able to speak or understand English adequately ...

Even with an interpreter there can still be great misunderstandings. Finally, these problems can be further 'aggravated by other characteristics, such as an intellectual disability'.[92]

---

88.   A Blumberg, 'The Practice of Law as a Confidence Game' (1967) 1 *Law and Society Review* 15, 19–25.
89.   They conducted 55 interviews (some interviews had more than one lawyer present), that included 52 men and 12 women. The study focused on District Court (or County Court) and Supreme Court practices: K Mack and S Anleu, *Pleading Guilty: Issues and Practices*, Australian Institute of Judicial Administration, Carlton South, Vic, 1995, pp 1 and 17.
90.   Mack and Anleu (above), p 30.
91.   Mack and Anleu (above), pp 114–15.
92.   Mack and Anleu (above), pp 107–8.

Blumberg's American perspective is supported by a study of criminal cases in Birmingham, England. In interviews the defendants said:[93]

> … that they found it difficult to decide which side their barrister was on, so closely involved did he appear to be with the prosecution. Many more felt they were not genuine parties to what took place in the court or to the decisions that were taken before it.

Ashworth states that in the English context at the negotiating stage of a criminal trial a defendant's dependence on their 'legal representatives is considerable, and this brings issues of professional ethics to the fore'.[94]

It can be argued that defence counsels have a vested interest in being on friendly terms with prosecutors and judges. The accused is almost invariably a 'one-shot client' while defence counsel has to maintain a continuing relationship with the other actors in the courtroom. Not all defence counsels have adopted this approach and it appears that in Australia they are proud of their independence. Furthermore, having a divided profession means that barristers find themselves switching sides more readily than their American compatriots. In the United States not every defence lawyer is involved in 'processing' clients. The radical or left-wing criminal defence lawyers are notorious for refusing to cooperate in 'processing' their clients. William Kunstler was widely quoted as stating that a lawyer is not a good defence counsel unless he or she has been cited for contempt of court. It would not be possible for an Australian barrister to adopt this attitude and remain on the rolls.   **9.48**

Problems of defence counsel

Recent American developments, especially in the representation of alleged terrorists, have made it more difficult for zealous defence lawyers. In fact, one of these lawyers, Lynne Stewart, has faced two trials alleging she conspired 'to provide material support and resources to a foreign terrorist orgainization'. The court found in the first trial that 18 USC s 2339B was too vague and broad to find Stewart had provided material support.[95] The government re-indicted Stewart on material support charges under the narrower 18 USC s 2339A. They had to prove under this provision that Stewart provided the material support or resources 'knowing or intending that they are used in preparation for, or in carrying out' terrorist designs. Stewart was found guilty under this provision of being a go-between by conveying her client's messages to his disciples in Egypt that urged them to use violence. Stewart's client is Sheik Omar Abdul Rahman, who is serving a life sentence for terrorist activities. The Sheik, a loyal supporter of Osama bin Laden, was in gaol for conspiring to blow up the United Nations, two Hudson River tunnels and the FBI building in New York. 'Stewart's case became a litmus test for how far a defense attorney could go in aggressively representing a terrorist client' and her conviction was condemned by civil liberties lawyers. Professor David Cole said: 'This will have a chilling effect on lawyers who might represent an unpopular client.' By contrast, Professor Steven Lubet, director of Northwestern University's program on advocacy   **9.49**

---

93. J Baldwin and M McConville, *Negotiated Justice*, Robertson, London,1977, p 85.
94. A Ashworth, *The Criminal Process: An Evaluative Study*, Clarendon Press, Oxford, 1994, p 264.
95. *United States v Sattar* 272 F Supp 2d 348 (SD NY 2003).

and professionalism, stated: 'There is nothing about "vigorous defense" that requires a lawyer to facilitate her client's political goals ... This case has nothing to do with zealous defense.' The case is on appeal.[96]

Furthermore, other lawyers working against the government have also been pursued. Several high-profile lawyers representing clients charged with drug offences were indicted. The prosecutors who obtained the indictment were also the prosecutors who opposed the accused lawyers representing their clients in the drug cases.[97] The indictment of criminal conspiracy alleged that these lawyers crossed the line of representation and instead were helping their clients break the law. The lawyers were convicted after several trials but all the convictions were thrown out except those for conspiring to launder money.[98] It has become riskier in the United States to defend not only political and drug violations but also all kinds of criminal defendants. For example, a lawyer was found guilty of conspiring with his client and obstructing justice, in relation to an investigation by the FBI, the grand jury and the federal district court. The investigation concerned the gambling operation and racketeering enterprise of his client. The accused argued he was zealously defending his client. The Court of Appeals upheld his conviction. The court said that he was motivated by 'corrupt endeavor to protect the illegal gambling operation and to safeguard his own financial interest ... [and] that separates his conduct from that which is legal'.[99] One concern for lawyers has been that clients have allegedly lied to prosecutors about their lawyers to get a better plea bargain deal. Thus, lawyers need to be careful in their discussions and also be able to rebut these accusations.[100]

Particular aspects — guilty pleas

9.50   The role of defence counsel just discussed seems at times to point to a strong push to 'processing' defendants, that is, pushing them to plead guilty by the use of plea or charge bargaining. As we saw in **9.42** the advocacy rules (r 17B NSW, r 19 Qld and r 12.4 Model Rules) require advocates to inform their clients about what advantages could result, including diminution of penalty, if the client pleads guilty. In the American context it has been said that without the strong institutional support for plea bargaining the whole criminal justice system would grind to a halt. The tradition of plea bargaining has been recognised by the ABA *Standards Relating to Plea Bargaining*. The attitude is that, because of the better results

96. M Powell and M Garcia, 'Sheik's US Lawyer Convicted of Aiding Terrorist Activity', *Washington Post*, 11 February 2005, p A01. For a more detailed discussion of why Stewart had acted to convey the information and that she had crossed the line, see A Smith, 'The Bounds of Zeal in Criminal Defense: Some Thought on Lynne Stewart' (2002) 44 *S Texas LR* 31. Smith states that he finds 'it hard to believe that Stewart acted as she did to promote or carry out terrorism in the name of the suffering people of Egypt ... There is no indication she had especially strong views about politics in the Middle East'.

97. D Lyoins, 'Feds Snare Lawyers in Cali Cartel net: The Defense Bar Sees, in Raids, Taps and novel Theories, an Unprecedented Attack', *National Law J*, 19 June 1995, A1. .

98. M Hlakdy, 'Two Lawyers' Convictions Junked: Federal Judge Reverses Jury on Some Florida Drug Counts, Though Others Stand', *National Law J*, 21 June 1999, A3.

99. *United States v Cueto*, 151 F3rd 620 (Ct of App, 7th Circuit, 1998).

100. R Chepesiuk, 'Guilty by Association?' (1997) 26(4) *Student Lawyer* 34.

that come from plea bargaining, defence counsel should 'as a matter of basic competence' try to plea bargain.[101]

This attitude can be contrasted to views found by Mack and Anleu in Australia.[102] They found that on the most part what occurs is:

> ... an informal, semi-adversarial/semi-cooperative process which attempts, in a situation of uncertainty, to identify the facts which can be proved beyond a reasonable doubt and the charge which most appropriately reflects the facts, to the satisfaction of both prosecution and defence.

Plea bargain is not an appropriate term in the Australian context. As Jacobs says: 'It carries notions of a done deal, and it also carries some baggage from its US origins, where the negotiations can include matters of penalty. This does not and cannot happen in Australia ... [What happens is the] prosecutors tell courts that they will not proceed on the more serious charges; the courts must deal, and only deal, with the charge that remains. The person charged pleads guilty to that lesser offence.'[103] Justice Samuels has suggested that a more appropriate term would be 'charge agreement'.[104]

It should be noted that Mack and Anleu did not interview defendants involved in the Australian criminal justice system. In all common law jurisdictions only the accused has the right to decide whether to plead guilty or not guilty. In Australia this was specifically stated in r 7.2 of the old Australian Bar Association's Code of Conduct (1993). The United States Supreme Court has supported this notion by holding that a guilty plea entered without the client's consent will be set aside.[105] The Supreme Court has not decided what remedy will exist for a defendant whose lawyer rejects a plea bargain without the client's consent. If the defendant is then found guilty of a more serious charge, is that ground for appeal? Is ordering a new trial the solution? The courts in the United States have gone both ways — ordering new trials or saying the accused had already had a fair trial.[106]

9.51

The innocent accused

Many defence lawyers in the United States feel that the accused has the right to make a plea only in a technical sense; that the lawyers' advice should prevail and if the client refuses to adhere to that advice they should find another lawyer.[107] But what should lawyers do for clients who maintain they are innocent and who in fact are innocent? Lawyers know the hazards of trials and if the evidence is strongly against an innocent client what should they advise? What if the innocent client decides to plead guilty against the lawyer's advice? Former Chief Justice Burger of the United States Supreme Court stated that:[108]

9.52

---

101. Wolfram (above), p 591.
102. Mack and Anleu (above), p 6.
103. M Jacob, 'Plea for rational thought', *Adelaide Review*, July 2004.
104. G Samuels, 'Review of the New South Wales Director of Public Prosecutions' Policy and Guidelines for Charge Bargaining and Tendering of Agreed Facts', Report, May 2002, para 14.1.
105. *Boykin v Alabama* (1969) 395 US 238.
106. For a discussion of these cases see G Hazard Jr, S Koniak and R Cramton, *The Law and Ethics of Lawyering*, 2nd ed, The Foundation Press, Westbury, New York, 1994, pp 529–30.
107. Alschuler, 'The Defense Attorney's Role in Plea Bargaining' (1975) 84 *Yale LJ* 1179, 1306–7.
108. W Burger, 'Standards of Conduct for Prosecution and Defense Personnel' (1966) 5 *American Criminal LQ* 11, 15.

A judge may not properly accept a guilty plea from an accused who denies the very acts that constitute the crime. However, he may do so if the matter is in such dispute or doubt that a jury might find him guilty in spite of his denials. When an accused tells the court he committed the act charged to induce acceptance of the guilty plea, the lawyer to whom contrary statements have been made owes a duty to the court to disclose such contrary statements so that the court can explore and resolve the conflict ...

9.53   Burger's views were opposed by Bowman. He stated that counsel should advise the accused that he or she can enter a guilty plea. This plea may be accepted if counsel points out to the court that there is sufficient evidence against the accused to justify a guilty verdict by a jury. Counsel should also advise the accused that the guilty plea may not be accepted without acknowledgment of guilt. The lawyer can then suggest that the accused can tell the court he or she is guilty even though this is false.[109] This approach appears to have tacit support under the recently adopted Australian advocacy rules: see **9.42**.

Bowman's views would cause considerable trouble for defendants, such as Aborigines, who usually because of cultural reasons do not like to answer personal questions, especially from police.[110] Furthermore, they are more likely to want to get out of gaol quickly and not go through the whole trouble of a trial and trying to raise bail. The easy solution will be to plead guilty to 'get it over with'.[111]

9.54   There does not appear to be any guidance under Australian professional conduct rules as to what a defence counsel should do when an accused maintains his or her innocence, but wants to plead guilty. The choices appear to be either for counsel to withdraw, or to continue to act, but with clearly stated and signed instructions from the client.[112] The Commonwealth Prosecution guidelines state that the prosecutor should not accept a guilty plea when the accused continues to maintain his or her innocence.[113]

[Handwritten margin note: Clear ex of ethical dilemma — u know C is innocent but wants to plead guilty.]

Trial judges in Australia faced with an accused wanting to plead guilty have been given some guidance by the High Court in *Maxwell v R*. Dawson and McHugh JJ stated:[114]

An accused is entitled to plead guilty to an offence with which he is charged and, if he does so, the plea will constitute an admission of all essential elements of the offence. Of course, if the trial judge forms the view that the evidence does not support the charge or that for any other reason the charge is not supportable, he should advise the accused to withdraw his plea and plead not guilty. But he cannot compel an accused to do so and, if the accused refuses, the plea must be considered final, subject only to the discretion of the judge to grant leave to change the plea to one of not guilty at any time before the matter is disposed of by sentence or otherwise.

---

109. A Bowman, 'Standards of Conduct for Prosecution and Defense Personnel — an Attorney's Viewpoint' (1966) 5 *American Criminal LQ* 28, 31.
110. My Aboriginal students have told me that it is impolite to ask direct questions about personal matters in many Aboriginal societies. This is not understood by the predominantly white policemen when pursuing their inquiries.
111. This view was expressed by some interviewees in Mack and Anleu (above), pp 13, 109.
112. Mack and Anleu (above), p 117.
113. *Prosecution Policy of the Commonwealth Department of Public Prosecutor*, 2005, para 5.16.
114. *Maxwell v R* (1996) 135 ALR 1 at 7.

> The plea of guilty must, however, be unequivocal and not made in circum-
> stances suggesting that it is not a true admission of guilt. Those circumstances
> include ignorance, fear, duress, mistake or even the desire to gain a technical
> advantage ... If it appears ... that a plea of guilty is not genuine, ... [the trial
> judge] must (and it is not a matter of discretion) obtain an unequivocal plea of
> guilty or direct that a plea of not guilty be entered.

Many Australian criminal lawyers, especially prosecutors, believe that:

> ... innocent people do not plead guilty; people who are arrested and charged
> are guilty of something. From this perspective, any discussions about charges
> and a guilty plea are a matter of fitting the correct charge to the actual offence.

Whether or not this is true there is no doubt that at times 'impecunious
and powerless defendants will plead guilty because their lawyer advises them
to do so',[115] especially if the lawyer says they will possibly receive a lesser
penalty. A good example of this occurring was the Victorian case of *R v
D'Orta-Ekenaike*.[116] The accused at all times believed he was innocent of
the rape charge but because of the pressure of his solicitor and counsel, he
pleaded guilty at the committal hearing. He had been told that 'he did not
have a defense', that if he pleaded guilty he would get a 'suspended
sentence' and if he did not 'he would receive a custodial penalty'. There was
also no requirement that he enter a plea at the committal hearing. On the
advice of new counsel he withdrew the guilty plea at trial. He testified that
he was 'virtually forced' to enter the guilty plea. The committal plea was led
as evidence and he was found guilty. On appeal the Court of Appeal
quashed the verdict because the lower court had failed to properly instruct
the jury on the use that might be made of the defendant's original guilty
plea. On retrial the evidence of his guilty plea was not admitted and he was
acquitted. The defendant later sued Victorian Legal Aid and the barrister
who had represented him at the committal hearing. He alleged that they
had negligently exercised 'undue pressure and influence' upon him. The
action ended up as a test case before the High Court concerning the
immunity of the barrister from being sued: see **10.83**.

Sometimes an accused who makes a voluntary deal later changes his or her
mind. This occurred in the famous American Unabomber case. The accused
had caused a number of deaths to get attention to his radical political views.
He accepted a deal that if the prosecution would not seek the death penalty
he would plead guilty. He decided to seek to vacate his conviction. He
alleged the guilty plea was involuntary because his counsel insisted on
presenting evidence of his mental condition which was contrary to his
wishes. His appeal was rejected on the basis that his original written and
oral statements at the time of his guilty plea showed that the plea was
entered into voluntarily.[117]

The American problems relating to plea bargaining have begun to appear in   **9.55**
England and Australia. The Australian Bar Association's old Code of
Conduct (1993) r 7.2 states:

> (c) It is the duty of a barrister representing a person charged with a criminal
>   offence to advise that person generally about any plea to the charge. It
>   should be made clear that whether the client pleads 'not guilty' or 'guilty',

---

115. Mack and Anleu (above), p 19.
116. [1998] 2 VR 140.
117. *United States v Kaezynski* 239 F3d 1108 (9th Circuit, 2001).

the client has the responsibility for and complete freedom of choice in any plea entered. For the purposes of giving proper advice, the barrister is entitled to refer to all aspects of the case and where appropriate may advise a client in strong terms that the client is unlikely to escape conviction, and that a plea of guilty is generally regarded by the court as a mitigating factor, at least to the extent that the client is thereby viewed by the court as co-operating in the criminal justice process.

...

(g) Where a client denies committing the offence charged, but nonetheless insists on pleading guilty to it for other reasons, the barrister may continue to represent that client, but only after advising what the consequences will be, and that submissions in mitigation will have to be on the basis that the client is guilty. Whenever possible in such a case, a barrister should receive written instructions.

Guilty plea — lesser sentence

9.56 There is no mention of plea bargaining except for the indication that the court may be more lenient when a guilty accused cooperates by pleading guilty. There is widespread judicial authority supporting this claim,[118] even though it is difficult for judges to gauge the degree of remorse. Furthermore, judges in some jurisdictions have statutory powers to take into account guilty pleas in deciding on reducing a sentence.[119] In New South Wales judges who do not reduce a sentence must give reasons for their refusal,[120] while in Queensland judges are required to state they have made a reduction in sentence because of the guilty plea.[121] In Western Australia the statute states explicitly that a guilty plea is a mitigating factor, which implies that a judge must discount a sentence.[122] The discounts in Western Australian are between 20 and 35 per cent when the guilty plea is 'fast tracked'. The earlier in the proceedings the plea is made the greater the mitigation. The High Court allowed an appeal in a Western Australian case where only a 10 per cent discount had been given.[123] In August 2000 Spigelman CJ issued guideline judgments in two cases that an accused should be given a 10–25 per cent discount on sentence for an early plea of guilty.[124] It was pointed out in these two cases the great variations in discounting that exist in Australia.[125]

In April 2005 the New South Wales Government announced a scheme of early discounts of 25 per cent if an accused pleaded guilty at the preliminary hearing before a magistrate. If the accused pleads guilty later in the District or Supreme Court, the discount would only be 12.5 per cent. The purpose of the changes was to reduce the expenses of the Director of Public Prosecutions by limiting the practice of last minute pleas of guilty and no

---

118. *R v Shannon* (1979) 21 SASR 442; *R v Holder* [1983] 3 NSWLR 245; *R v Morton* [1986] VR 863; *R v Harman* (1988) 35 A Crim R 447; and *R v Dowie* (1989) 42 A Crim R 234.
119. See, for example, Sentencing Act 1991 (Vic) s 5; Crimes Act 1900 (NSW) s 439; and Sentencing Act 1995 (WA) s 8(2). See also J Willis, 'Sentence Discounting for Guilty Pleas' (1985) 18 *ANZ J of Crim* 131.
120. Section 439(2) of the Crimes Act 1900 (NSW).
121. Section 13 of the Penalties and Sentences Act 1992 (Qld).
122. Section 8(2) of the Sentencing Act 1995 (WA).
123. *Cameron v The Queen* [2002] HCA 6. The decision was 4:1 with McHugh J dissenting.
124. *R v Thompson and Houghton* (2000) 115 A Crim R 104.
125. Ibid, at 137.

bills.[126] The problem with the changes is that an accused may decide at the late stage that a 12.5 per cent discount is so low, that he or she may decide to go to trial.

There are obvious practical considerations for discounting sentences, such as saving the community money and time, the latter helping relieve delays and backlogs in the court system, and sparing the emotional stress for victims and witnesses. There is not universal approval for the practice. It is not accepted in some jurisdictions and some judges and lawyers have raised serious questions of principle. The New South Wales Law Reform Commission lists as disadvantages that:[127]   **9.57**

> ... it penalises those who plead not guilty; it promotes pleas of guilty in cases where the prosecution should justly be put to proof, thus creating the risk that innocent persons will be pressured to plead guilty; it smacks of judicial participation in charge bargaining; it undermines the principle that a plea must be made voluntarily; it is wrong to allow a benefit for merely facing the inevitable or doing what the offender ought to do anyway; it is wrong to take into account matters which do not relate to the offence or the offender or the traditional theories of punishment, but relate solely to the administration of the criminal justice system; increasing guilty pleas will militate against public scrutiny of the police and law enforcers; and ultimately, it will create the risk that innocent people will plead guilty.

The requirement of a discounted sentence also leads to expectations and at times the granting of 'undue leniency'. This result is inconsistent with proper principles of sentencing.[128] Mack and Anleu find that the criticism of discounting is sufficient for them to recommend that there 'should be no formal sentence discount for a plea of guilty'.[129]   **9.58**

Discussions with the prosecution and/or the judge concerning the consequences of a guilty plea take place without the presence of the accused. In such circumstances lawyers:[130]

> ... may consciously or unconsciously mislead the client about the nature of these discussions, or in the course of them may act in a manner of which the client would have disapproved if he or she had known.

The Commonwealth and Queensland prosecution policies also explicitly oppose participation by their prosecutors in discussions with judges.[131] The disapproval under prosecution policies has led to considerably fewer discussions with judges by lawyers over guilty pleas than took place in the past, but those between defence lawyers and prosecutors are still   **9.59**

---

126. See the editorial concerning the changes, 'Dealing the hard reality of justice', *Sydney Morning Herald*, 7 April 2005, p 10.
127. *Sentencing*, New South Wales Law Reform Commission, Discussion Paper 33, April 1996, para 5.71.
128. Mack and Anleu (above), pp 165–70.
129. Mack and Anleu (above), p 172. The New South Wales Law Reform Commission in *Sentencing* (above), para 5.80, said that its 'tentative' view is that the argument, that weight should be given to guilty pleas for relieving the victim of the stress of giving evidence in irresistible cases as well as doubtful ones, is persuasive.
130. Disney et al (above), p 647.
131. *Prosecution Policy of the Commonwealth Department of Public Prosecutor*, 2005, para 5.13; Director of Public Prosecutions Queensland, Statement of Prosecution Policy and Guidelines, p 16. This policy is now the widely accepted view by those involved in criminal cases. See Mack and Anleu (above), p 5.

common.[132] These discussions take place in all jurisdictions and lead to a guilty plea in the majority of criminal cases without the need to go to trial. Mack and Anleu found in their interviews that these discussions are regarded as 'usual and appropriate'. The latter is known as charge bargaining which is recognised by the Commonwealth prosecution policy[133] and adopted by law. An example of the latter is that by statute the prosecutor in New South Wales has authority to accept a plea of guilty to a lesser charge.[134]

9.60   The issues of plea bargaining were discussed in the leading English case *R v Turner*.[135] The accused appealed because he said he did not have an opportunity to exercise a free choice in retracting his plea of not guilty and pleading guilty. There were long discussions with counsel who advised that a plea of guilty might lead to a non-custodial sentence. He also said that if he contested the matter his past convictions might be exposed and he ran the risk of a prison sentence. The counsel went on to discuss the matter with the trial judge and returned stating to the accused's solicitor that if he pleaded guilty he would receive a fine or some other non-imprisonment sentence. Although these were counsel's own views the solicitor and the accused received the impression, because counsel had just returned from the judge, that these were also the views of the judge. Lord Parker CJ found that although the accused was always warned that the choice was his own as to what to plead, in reality he did not have a free choice in the matter after it had been intimated that the information came from the judge. Therefore his appeal was upheld. Lord Parker made some observations on plea bargaining. They are:

1.   Counsel must be completely free to do what is his duty, namely to give the accused the best advice he can and if need be advice in strong terms. This will often include advice that a plea of guilty, showing an element of remorse, is a mitigating factor which may well enable the court to give a lesser sentence than would otherwise be the case. Counsel of course will emphasise that the accused must not plead guilty unless he has committed the acts constituting the offence charged.

2.   The accused, having considered counsel's advice, must have a complete freedom of choice whether to plead guilty or not guilty.

9.61   The *Turner* case has not been followed in Australia in allowing judges to receive information relevant to the sentence of the accused. But its basic principle — allowing free choice in deciding to plead guilty — is applied.[136]

---

132.   Disney et al (above), p 647. See also *R v Kolalich* (1990) 47 A Crim LR 71 at 79, which shows the willingness of courts to accept charge negotiations. A more recent High Court decision held that even after a charge negotiation is agreed to, the prosecution is entitled, before sentence, to withdraw its acceptance of a plea of guilty, but for the interests of justice only with leave of the court. This is because an accused may have prejudiced himself or herself in reliance on the prosecution's acceptance of his or her plea, for example by making admissions. If the accused has been prejudiced the judge should refuse withdrawal: per Dawson and McHugh JJ, *Maxwell v R* (1996) 135 ALR 1 at 10–11.

133.   *Prosecution Policy of the Commonwealth* (above), paras 5.12–5.15.

134.   See, for example, s 394A of the Crimes Act 1900 (NSW).

135.   [1970] 2 QB 321 (C of A).

136.   For a review of the cases and discussion of the principle see *R v Boyd* BC200004511; [2000] NSWCCA 110.

Former Chief Justice Barwick of the High Court has censured plea bargaining as being wholly undesirable because it leads to justice behind closed doors.[137] In *R v Marshall* the Victorian Supreme Court stated that sentence indication was objectionable:[138]

> ... because it does not take place in public, it excludes the person most vitally concerned, it is embarrassing to the Crown, and it puts the judge in a false position which can only serve to weaken public confidence.

The court said that it also went against the idea 'that judgment in the court is delivered only after the court has heard ... the evidence of both parties'. Furthermore, it was stated that by indicating a sentence a judge would be inhibited in passing a more severe sentence. If the judge did so the accused would feel he or she was not dealt with justly.[139] The *Marshall* case[140] emphasised the public image of the judges and did not consider other issues such as improving the efficiency of the system. There appears to be widespread support in Australia for the position that judges should not participate in the substance of plea discussions.[141]

Pilot scheme — sentence indication

In February 1993 a pilot scheme on sentence indication was started at Parramatta District Court,[142] and expanded to Downing Street, Sydney District Court in June 1993 and to all New South Wales District Criminal Courts in February 1994. A judge was able, on or before arraignment, to indicate at a sentence indication hearing what sentence the judge might give the accused, if he or she was to plead guilty to the offence charged or to another, lesser offence arising from the facts.[143] The application had to be made by an accused before or at arraignment. After the sentence was indicated the accused had to decide to plead guilty or not guilty. If the plea was guilty the judge who indicated the sentence stood over the matter for the usual sentence hearing following a plea of guilty. The judge was bound by the sentence indicated, if the facts and other relevant material presented at the indication hearing were not altered at sentence hearing. If they had altered the judge was able to decide to impose a lesser or greater sentence. The accused at that point was allowed to change his or her plea to not guilty and go to trial before another judge.[144]

9.62

The government decided in June 1995 to drop the scheme by not renewing the legislation as a result of a report by the New South Wales Bureau of

9.63

---

137. *R v Bruce* (HCA, Barwick CJ, 21 May 1976, unreported).
138. *R v Marshall* [1981] VR 725 at 732. See also the Federal Court decision taking a similar view in *Tait v Bartley* (1979) 24 ALR 473.
139. *Marshall's* case (above) at 734.
140. See also P Sallman and J Willis, 'The Judges' Role in Plea Bargaining' (1981) *Legal Services Bulletin* 132.
141. Mack and Anleu (above), pp 137–9.
142. The scheme was established under the Criminal Procedure (Sentence Indication) Amendment Act 1992 to the Criminal Procedure Act 1986.
143. Section 53(1) of the Criminal Procedure Act 1986.
144. Practice Note No 22, District Court — Sentence Indication at Parramatta in 1993. A recent study, the *Crown Court Study*, found that 11 per cent of 269 defendants surveyed had pleaded guilty even though they had not committed the offence: see Research Study No 19, RCCJ, HMSO, 1993, p 139 cited in M Aronson and J Hunter, *Litigation — Evidence and Procedure*, 6th ed, Butterworths, Sydney, 1998, para 12.153. See also paras 12.153–12.161 on aspects of plea bargaining.

Crime Statistics and Research. The bureau found that the scheme had failed to produce earlier and more frequent pleas of guilty. It had also failed to reduce the delay between committal and case finalisation where accused persons change their plea to guilty.[145] The scheme was expensive to run and by failing to meet its objectives it became an economic liability. These views can be contrasted with those expressed in the Mack and Anleu study. They found that most of those interviewed in New South Wales were 'very positive towards the scheme'.[146]

Mack and Anleu's study found that:[147]

> Plea discussion and agreements in Australia do not really involve a bargaining, bidding, haggling, horse-trading process ... [The] discussions do not appear to rely on unjustified relinquishment of some certain claim or advantage, nor a promise to give some undeserved advantage. The term bargaining is misleading. It implies that parties actually barter over the price to be paid for a desirable good — a guilty plea for a low sentence ... [G]uilty pleas are 'consensual outcomes of professional discussion' the emphasis being on 'settling the facts'.

As already stated they found in Australia an 'informal, semi-adversarial/semi-cooperative process' of plea discussion and that the accused sometimes is somewhat invisible in the discussion process that resolves the charges. Thus, impecunious and powerless defendants plead guilty after their lawyers have agreed to a deal which they are then advised to accept.[148]

9.64   Mack and Anleu did not interview any of the accused and thus there is no specific data concerning the influence of lawyers on the decision to plead not guilty. As discussed above, the study carried out in Birmingham, England, came to the conclusion that many defendants do not voluntarily plead guilty. Of those who decided to plead guilty, 60 per cent did so because they were guilty or because they had knowledge or believed that their barrister had plea bargained with the prosecution. The other 40 per cent pleaded guilty because of pressure from their barrister without any specific deal being made with the prosecution.[149] It may be that similar pressure is being placed on defendants by lawyers in Australia. There was a publicised case of a battered de facto wife, an Aborigine, who killed her de facto husband, whose conviction was quashed when it was shown that her solicitor from the Aboriginal Legal Centre had pleaded her guilty against her wishes.[150]

9.65   Mack and Anleu suggest that current practices in Australia can be improved by:[151]

❑ ensuring prompt, thorough professional evaluation of the merits of a criminal charge by prosecution and defence;

145. D Weatherburn, E Matka and B Lind, *Sentence Indication Scheme Evaluation*, New South Wales Bureau of Crime Statistics and Research, 1995.
146. Mack and Anleu (above), p 74.
147. Mack and Anleu (above), p 6.
148. Mack and Anleu (above), pp 6, 19 and 107–8.
149. Baldwin and McConville (above), pp 25–8.
150. T Hewett, 'Case of Aboriginal's guilty plea that wasn't', *Sydney Morning Herald*, 21 January 1989, p 15.
151. Mack and Anleu (above), pp 14–15.

❑ providing information the accused needs to make an informed decision — including likely sentence — as early as possible;

❑ requiring a written statement in court from prosecution and defence evaluating the case and describing any agreement;

❑ providing an opportunity for the accused to be heard;

❑ ensuring the victim's concerns are properly considered; and

❑ continuing to emphasise judicial independence in sentencing, with an opportunity for advance indication of sentence by the judge, and a significant de-emphasis on sentence discounts.

Particular aspects — family law and clients with disabilities

Lawyers are known for their adversarial skills. In the context of family law this can present serious problems for their clients. There are two types of lawyer in family law — settlers and fighters.[152] Settlers discuss the various options with their clients and advise not only what is the best that they can win, but also seek to reach an amiable agreement with the other side. Lawyers who are fighters seek to win on every point. They may manipulate their client into taking a much stronger stance against a former spouse than is necessary or is in the interest of the family.[153] Although fighters may be successful in the amount of child support, custody, and so on, the final result may be little cooperation between the ex-spouses. If the maintenance payments are too onerous it can also lead to eventual non-payment of support. Furthermore, an adversarial hearing adds to an already volatile emotional situation that can alienate clients from lawyers because of bad feelings they carry away from the experience.

9.66

A study of 40 divorce cases in the United States, which were taped and observed by the authors, found that the image of the lawyer as a fighter, stirring up contention and adversarial behaviour, was incorrect. Most of the lawyers the authors observed 'worked hard to sell settlement to their clients and to avoid contested hearings and trials'. The lawyers made it a professional practice to be emotionally unresponsive, preferring to focus on the financial aspects of the case. The conclusion was that this approach combined with the lawyers' cynicism about the law and legal system contributed to client dissatisfaction with their lawyers and the legal system.[154]

9.67

Therefore, lawyers acting in the Family Court have to be careful how they define doing 'the best' for their clients. Lawyers need to learn how to deal better with clients as complete people, learning about their personal needs rather than concentrating only on the financial aspects of their cases. They also have to stop themselves from coming to any quick conclusions as to the merits of their client's case.

Representation for children

There are special difficulties in acting for clients who are not fully able to give instructions; such clients include children, the mentally ill and

9.68

---

152. Of course, some lawyers move between the two model types.
153. The terms 'fighter' and 'settler' come from P Tennison, *Family Court — The Legal Jungle*, Patrick Tennison Enterprises, Ashburton, Vic, 1983, p 31.
154. Sarat and Felstiner (above), pp 46–53.

handicapped. We will first examine separate representation for children. The Family Law Act 1975[155] provides in s 60B that:

(1) The object of this Part VII is to ensure that children receive adequate and proper parenting to help them achieve their full potential, and to ensure that parents fulfil their duties, and meet their responsibilities, concerning the care, welfare and development of their children.

(2) The principles underlying these objects are that, except where it is against the best interests of the child:

(a) children have the right to know and be cared for by both parents ...; and

(b) children have a right of contact, on a regular basis, with both parents and with other people significant to their care, welfare and development; and

(c) parents share duties and responsibilities concerning the care, welfare and development of their children; and

(d) parents should agree about the future parenting of their children.

9.69   The terminology in the Act has been replaced with new terms in the 1995 amendments. Guardianship is now 'parental responsibility', custody is replaced with 'residence', access is replaced with 'contact', welfare of the child is 'best interests of the child', child agreement is replaced with 'parenting plan', order for guardianship, custody, access, or maintenance is now called 'parenting order', and so on. Under s 65E 'best interests' of the child is the paramount consideration in making a parenting order. Sections 68F–68K list the factors for determining the 'best interests'. They include, among others: any wishes expressed by the child, but the child's maturity and level of understanding are considered in giving weight to the wishes; the nature of the child's relationship with each parent and others; the effect on the child of changing the child's circumstances; family violence; the need to protect the child from physical or psychological harm; the child's maturity, sex and ethnic background; financial resources of each parent; each parent's attitude to the child and their responsibility to parenthood, and so on.

It should be noted that the 1995 amendments now restrict the paramount principle, the best interests of the child, to the making of a parenting order. In other areas, such as the kind of legal representation for the child, the paramount principle does not operate.[156]

9.70   The best interest approach has been criticised as still not giving the child enough consideration. There has been a shift from 'best interests' to 'expressed interests' in both Australia and the United States.[157] The new emphasis is to enable the child to express his or her views freely and to be able to express these views at any hearing. This is the approach of the

---

155. The Act was significantly amended in 1995 by the Family Law Reform Act 1995 (Cth): see R Bailey-Harris, 'The Family Law Reform Act (Cth): A New Approach to the Parent/Child Relationship' (1996) 18 *Adelaide LR* 83.

156. R Chisholm, ' "The Paramount Consideration": Children's Interests in Family Law' (2002) 16 *Australian J of Family Law* 87, 109–110.

157. A Taylor, 'Children in the legal system', September (1998) *Law Society J (NSW)* 62 at 63. Taylor refers as her American sources E Buss, 'You're my what? The problem of children's misperceptions of their lawyers' roles' (1996) 64 *Fordham LR* 1699 and the ABA, *Standards of practice for lawyers who represent children in abuse and neglect cases*, 1993.

Australian Law Reform Commission in its report *Seen and Heard* which is discussed in detail below.

The new terms that came into effect in 1995 have been under interpretation by a number of family law cases which are more appropriate in a family law text. Bailey-Harris summarised the main problem areas:[158]

1. *The exercise of parental responsibility*: what will this mean in practice to the parent with whom the child does not live, especially in respect of decisions concerning the day-to-day management of a child? How frequently will a specific issue order be used to modify decision-making about both long-term and day-to-day management of a child?

2. *Residence*: will shared residence orders become common, with a reduced scope for orders relating to direct contact?

3. *Contact*: will the new legislative provisions lead to even further emphasis on the desirability of a child maintaining contact with both parents? And will this be extended to (quasi-) presumption in favour of contact with other relatives, notably grandparents?

4. *Parenting plans*: will these be popular, or will parents who agree prefer to seek consent orders?

I would add the problem of freedom to move to another jurisdiction. How will this be affected by the need for joint parental responsibility?

Section 68L authorises the court to appoint a separate representative to protect the welfare of the child but is silent as to the obligations and duties of the lawyer appointed. The Full Family Law Court, as stated above (see 8.41), has also held in *Heard v De Laine*[159] that the *Dietrich* doctrine did not apply under the Family Law Act 1995 to guarantee separate representation for children. Furthermore, the Commonwealth Guidelines for granting legal aid for family law states that in 'no circumstances should this Guideline be interpreted to indicate that there is an obligation on the Commission to make a grant of legal assistance because a court has ordered that a child's representative be appointed. Due to lack of funds there has been a dramatic increase in lack of representation, not only as separate representatives for children, but also for other litigants in family law matters'.[160]

9.71

In the early 1980s the Chief Judge of the Family Court issued guidelines for separate representation of children.[161] These guidelines were withdrawn and never replaced. The Full Family Law Court in 1995 gave some guidance in *Re P and Legal Aid Commission (NSW)*.[162] It approved a submission from Judith Ryan of the Legal Aid Commission of New South Wales. She suggested that the separate representative ought to:

9.72

1. Act in an independent and unfettered way in the best interests of the child.

2. Act impartially, but if thought appropriate, make submissions suggesting the adoption by the court of a particular course of action if he or she considers that the adoption of such a course is in the best interests of the child.

---

158. R Bailey-Harris, see n 155 (above), p 101.
159. (1996) FLC ¶92-675.
160. Australian Law Reform Commission, Report No 89, *Managing Justice: A review of the federal civil justice system*, February 2000, paras 5.94–5.131.
161. *Australian Family Law*, Butterworths, looseleaf service, para 4070.4.
162. (1995) 19 Fam LR 1.

3. Inform the court by proper means of the children's wishes in relation to any matter in the proceedings. In this regard the separate representative is not bound to make submissions on the instructions of a child or otherwise but is bound to bring the child's expressed wishes to the attention of the court.

4. Arrange for the collation of expert evidence and otherwise ensure that all evidence relevant to the welfare of the child is before the court.

5. Test by cross examination where appropriate the evidence of the parties and their witnesses.

6. Ensure that the views and attitudes brought to bear on the issues before the court are drawn from the evidence and not from a personal view or opinion of the case.

7. Minimise the trauma to the child associated with the proceedings.

8. Facilitate an agreed resolution to the proceedings.

The court added two other suggestions: first, the separate representative should be appointed at an early stage of proceedings — usually at the first directions hearing; second, the separate representative should usually have the role to call expert evidence.

In March 2004, the Family Law Section of the Law Council of Australia and the Family Law Council of the Australian Government issued Best Practice Guidelines for lawyers doing family law. Part 6 of the Guidelines details how to deal with children. Some of the matters in the guidelines come from the Act, the rules of court, or Practice Directions. Some provisions require lawyers to point out to their clients the paramount position of the best interests of the children. The guidelines emphasise a cooperative approach and advise lawyers not to assist vindictive conduct by their clients. Part 1.6 emphasises the need for lawyers to warn clients not to encourage the children to 'take sides or become involved in their parents' disputes'. Part 1.7 requires lawyers to make their clients aware that negotiations in relation to the children are separate from negotiations concerning other issues. In the United States there are similar guidelines entitled 'Bounds of Advocacy Goals for Family Lawyers' that are issued by the American Academy of Matrimonial Lawyers.

9.73 Other cases have also helped to clarify the role of the separate representative. The separate representative is asked personally to investigate matters, but the Full Court has disapproved the practice of the separate representative becoming like an additional welfare worker.[163] The *Demetrious* case[164] describes the ideal role of these lawyers as being like a friend of the court. They should present additional evidence or arguments that aid the court in coming to a decision. In the *Bennett* case[165] the court said that the role of the separate representative is analogous to that of counsel assisting a Royal Commission. In gathering evidence lawyers should not only interview the child and explain their role, but also the parents and anyone else of significance, for example teachers.[166] It should be noted that unlike other clients the child has no power to dismiss the separate representative. The power lies with the court, and the child or any other interested party can ask

---

163. *Lyons and Boseley* (1978) FLC ¶90-423 and *E and E (No 2)* (1979) ¶FLC 90-645.
164. (1976) FLC ¶90-102.
165. (1991) FLC ¶92-191.
166. *Pagliarella v Pagliarella* (1993) FLC ¶92-400.

the court to exercise its power of dismissal.[167] The Family Court has also developed specific guidelines for the appointment of separate representatives that appear to be discriminatory. For example, in Re K[168] one criterion for appointing a separate representative was in situations:

> ... where there are real issues of cultural or religious differences affecting the child ... or where the sexual preferences of either or both of the parents are likely to impinge upon the child's welfare.

Recent developments

The new Family Court Chief Justice, Diana Bryant, wants judges to be taught the skills needed to properly interview children in difficult custody disputes. Chief Justice Bryant stated that presently it is extremely rare for judges to interview a child because the judges feel they do not have the proper experience and leave the interviewing to experts. The Chief Justice said that the new Children's Cases Program established in Parramatta and Sydney was a good place for judges to test their skills of interviewing.[169] The Children's Cases Program was a pilot scheme of 100 cases where children are the focus of the proceedings. It was established in 2004 under a less adversarial process. The only affidavits that were sworn were by the parents and expert reports were received in writing. Its aim was to provide a quick and effective means of resolving issues concerning children within three months of filing. The judge was given a larger role including the right to make proposals for settlement and control conduct and length of any cross-examination.[170]

9.74

Another major initiative in 2004 was the Commonwealth Government's proposed establishment of 65 nationwide Family Relationship Centres. These centres would take over some of the dispute resolution activities of the Family Courts. Chief Justice Bryant said: 'What we might do if these centres are properly funded in the community ... is that we will modify some of the mediation services in the Family Court so that we don't duplicate confidential counselling and we can put our resources into bringing children into the process.'[171]

An ALRC report, Seen and heard: priority for children in the legal process, has made some recommendations for child representation.[172] The following are some suggestions from Recommendations 70–72:

- 'In all cases where ... the child is able and willing to express views or provide instructions, the representative should allow the child to direct the litigation as an adult client would.' These traits should prevail over the representative's assessment of the 'good judgment' or maturity of the child.
- 'Every child should be seen except in those rare instances where it is physically impossible for the representative to see the child.' The child should be seen often enough so as to establish a relationship. The first

167. Pagliarella's case (above).
168. (1994) FLC ¶92-461 (Full Court).
169. L Scott, 'Children get their say on divorce', Australian, 28 September 2004, p 3.
170. M Pelly, 'Children to get voice in family cases', Sydney Morning Herald, 28–29 February 2004, p 5.
171. L Scott (above), p. 3.
172. Australian Law Reform Commission (with the Human Rights and Equal Opportunity Commission), Report No 84, Seen and heard: priority for children in the legal process, December 1997.

- meeting should be as soon as possible, usually well before the first hearing and sufficient time should be allocated to the representation in order to obtain clear directions.
- ❏ The child should be seen preferably face to face and in a place that is comfortable for the child. Even a non-verbal child should be seen.
- ❏ 'The lawyer should use language appropriate to the age and maturity of the child.'
- ❏ 'The representative should employ appropriate listening techniques and provide non-judgmental support.' The discussions on the case should include 'concrete examples' and provide the client with a 'road map' of the interview and the legal process.
- ❏ 'Under no circumstances should the representative proceed if he or she is uncertain of the basis of representing the child.'

The Report also included standards for acting in the best interests of the child. These standards basically require the advocate to thoroughly invest‑ igate and present the child's case. One interesting standard using the American term 'zealously' is 'to advocate zealously for the legal rights of the child including safety, visitation and sibling contact'.

Children in criminal cases

9.75 The problem of separate representation for children has developed in a similar manner in the United States.[173] One area of special attention has been the representation of juvenile delinquents. The original approach was for the lawyer to participate in the benevolent juvenile justice system in a non-adversarial manner by facilitating the court in finding the most suitable disposition for the child. This was known as the welfare model and emphasised the rehabilitation needs of the juvenile. This approach was rejected by the Supreme Court in *Re Gault*,[174] which held that due process rights under the adversarial system in criminal cases should be extended to juveniles. This approach, the justice model, focused on procedural fairness (due process) and accountability. It is the approach that has been endorsed by the ABA in its 1979 *Juvenile Justice* Standards. A third model, the restorative model, discussed below, is being explored both in the United States and Australia. The situation in Australia has been that children's rights in criminal matters have not been afforded the kind of protection provided in the United States.[175] The Australian Law Reform Commission has argued that the American situation is different from that in Australia. The considerations in the United States involve the constitutional right to counsel and due process. Furthermore, there has been a strong reaction in that country to the welfare orientation of juvenile courts.[176] There has been the recognition in Australia that children do need legal representation when charged with a criminal offence and most children do have access to

---

173. Wolfram (above), pp 159–62.
174. (1967) 87 S Ct 1428.
175. Juvenile criminal proceedings have been superimposed on the general criminal law, although special procedures have been enacted for children relating to the nature of the hearing, evidence and sentencing: see, for example, the Children (Criminal Proceedings) Act 1987 (NSW). For an example of some of the problems, see S Scarlett, 'Children's Statements to the Police: Admissible Evidence or not' (1992) 30 *Law Society J (NSW)* 38.
176. *Child Welfare: Children in Trouble*, Australian Law Reform Commission, DP 9, 1979, p 22.

legal representation in these cases in Australia.[177] Since this Australian report, juveniles' rights have been eroded in some states of the United States, especially California.[178]

In New South Wales representation has been provided under the duty solicitor's scheme in the Children's Court, which has been highly criticised for not properly representing the clients.[179] The criticism has led to improvement in the assistance provided. In metropolitan areas solicitors need to apply to be placed on a special children's duty roster. They also have to agree to certain performance standards and to attend specialist accreditation or specialist legal education. There are now procedures for removing those solicitors who fail to perform. In New South Wales the following centres provide youth legal services: the National Children's and Youth Law Centre, the Burnside Adolescent Legal Service and the Shopfront Legal Centre and, since 1987, the Legal Aid Commission's Children's Legal Service based at Cobham Children's Court in western Sydney. The main defect in New South Wales is the lack of services in rural areas. This is an especially serious problem for Aboriginal young people who make up approximately 25–30 per cent of those in detention. These were the findings of Report No 10, *Inquiry into Children's Advocacy*, carried out for the New South Wales Legislative Council's Standing Committee on Social Issues in 1996.[180] The report recommends that services of the Legal Aid Commission at Cobham be extended to all Children's Courts and that other services be extended throughout the state.[181]

9.76

In 1981 the Queensland Law Youth Advocacy Centre was established in Brisbane. The centre provides legal representation and advice, but also has an 'holistic' approach to children's legal problems. It sees that the legal problems do not exist in isolation and thus has social workers and solicitors working together to assist the youths. The Centre has as its policy that the child gives the instructions to the solicitors, but they make sure that the solicitors have enabled the children to understand the implications and consequences of their decision. The Centre believes that this approach instils in the children trust and confidence in its actions.[182] In Victoria there is a system of pre-hearing conferences in the Children's Court, which allows for legal representation for the child to help negotiate a settlement of the problem. Magistrates in Victoria are also required to adjourn criminal cases where children are not represented and not to proceed until they have had reasonable time to arrange representation.[183]

9.77

---

177. See *Speaking for ourselves: Children and the legal process*, Issues Paper 18, Australian Law Reform Commission, 1996, para 8.68.
178. Californian voters adopted proposition 21 in March 2000 which amended its Constitution to empower prosecutors to decide whether juveniles are tried as adults (juveniles tried in adult courts can receive sentences of up to life in prison): Associated Press Release, 6 September 2000.
179. C Simpson, 'NSW Children's Court Duty Solicitor Scheme' (1975) *Legal Service Bulletin* 300 and M Appleby, L Miller and R Moss, 'Legal Aid for Children' (1979) *Legal Service Bulletin* 95.
180. *Inquiry into Children's Advocacy*, carried out for the New South Wales Legislative Council's Standing Committee on Social Issues, Report No 10, 1996, pp 83–8, 90.
181. *Inquiry into Children's Advocacy* (above), p 89.
182. *Inquiry into Children's Advocacy* (above), pp 47–8.
183. See s 20 of the Children and Young Persons Act 1989. See also P Swain, 'Pre-hearing conferences: A step towards ADR for the Children's Court' (1995) 69 *Law Institute J (Vic)* 112–13.

9.78   The ALRC Report, *Seen and heard: priority for children in the legal process*, made a number of recommendations to deal with injustices in the juvenile criminal system. Recommendation 226 states that 'a child suspected of committing an offence should have a statutory right to access legal advice prior to police interview and that police must inform young people of this right at the time of apprehension'. Duty solicitor schemes should be appropriately resourced to enable practitioners to meet with their child clients before the first court appearance. Recommendation 228 says that 'Children should be legally represented at bail application proceedings'.

The report also states a third model for juvenile criminal cases, the restorative model, is now being followed. 'It does not overlook rehabilitation and punishment but places them in the context of individuals taking responsibility for their actions.' The report says that this model allows juvenile offenders to be diverted from the formal court system. It balances their rights against their responsibilities to the community.[184] The report recommends that standards for juvenile justice need to 'stress the importance of rehabilitating young offenders while acknowledging the importance of restitution to the victim and the community'.[185]

9.79   The role of legal representatives under the restorative model will still be to protect the rights of their clients but also to act to help them accept responsibility for what they did.

Even with improvements to the system there has been a campaign to achieve national minimum juvenile justice standards by having the Commonwealth Government implement Australia's full obligations under the Convention on the Rights of the Child.[186] As of August 2005 the Commonwealth has failed to implement the Convention. Furthermore, the High Court has stated that the Commonwealth immigration laws on detention prevail over any international obligations under the Convention.[187] Thus, the provisions of the Convention relating to fair trial for juveniles has no influence on trials in Australia.

The main objective of child representation, especially in criminal cases, is to have the child's views properly expressed. It is necessary for lawyers to be sensitive to the children's needs. Young people have to be viewed as 'persons of value' and lawyers 'should ensure that these clients are served with diligence and excellence'.[188]

Incapacitated clients

9.80   We have discussed already the problem of sterilisation for mentally incapacitated teenagers in the previous chapter: see **8.62–8.64**. What can a lawyer do when dealing with instructions from incapacitated clients? In such situations whom is the lawyer representing? The lawyer has to

---

184. Report No 84, *Seen and heard: priority for children in the legal process* (above), para 18.34.
185. Report No 84 (above), recommendation 198, p 477.
186. The relevant provisions under the Convention to provide a fair trial are arts 3(i), 9(ii), 12(ii), 37, 40(ii)(b). The campaign is under the auspices of the Anglican Social Responsibility Commission (WA).
187. *WACB v Minister for Immigration, Multicultural and Indigenous Affairs* [2004] HCA 50. The decision was unanimous.
188. B Lucas, 'Advocacy in Children's Courts' [1980] 4 *Crim LJ* 63, 77. This is an excellent article on the type of advocacy that is needed.

determine how capable the client is of making a decision. At common law the difference between capacity and incapacity is generally the ability of the client to understand the nature and effects of the legal matter.[189] There are problems in this situation in deciding who is the client because instructions may come from a third party on behalf of the incapacitated person. In any situation of dealing with such a client the lawyer must make an independent assessment of the capacity of the client and not just rely on information provided by the third party.[190] Failure to determine properly the capacity of the client and only following the wishes of the third party, for example a parent, can lead to a serious conflict of interest.[191] In a similar manner to the separate representative acting for a young child, lawyers acting for the incapacitated have an overriding duty to act in the client's best interests and must treat these clients the same as other clients. They have to take into account the client's views and preferences to the extent that they are communicated.[192] Sometimes this can become very difficult, for example with clients who have Alzheimer's disease. In such a case in New South Wales Young J found that an elderly lady did not have the mental capacity to instruct her solicitor and Young J warned solicitors from bringing actions where they have very vague instructions. The solicitor in this case was ordered to pay the defendant's costs.[193] Clients who are so mentally incapacitated that they cannot make a decision in relation to a legal matter will have, appointed by the court, a close relative to act as *amicus curiae*. The lawyer will then have to take instructions from this person on behalf of the client.[194]

In order to help solicitors to avoid the capacity problems raised by Young J and others, the New South Wales Law Society's Client Capacity Sub-Committee issued detailed client capacity guidelines in 2003.[195] The guidelines provide a detailed discussion under each section and the author only gives a few examples. The guidelines state: 'Adults are presumed to be competent to give instructions.' Solicitors have to ask themselves if 'there any reasons to doubt a client's competence'. The guidelines then give a number of 'common indicators of conditions that impair capacity'. They are acute depression; brain injury and organic brain damage; dementia; intellectual disability; manic-depression; and schizophrenia. Next the guidelines state: 'Consider whether you can obtain proper instructions after further explanation or education of your client. Are you satisfied you can get proper instructions?' For example, when a client has a mental illness,

189. P Fennell, 'Incapacitated Clients' (1993) 90 (15) Gazette, *Journal of the Law Society (UK)* 27.
190. P Fennell (above), p 28.
191. See the discussion of a recent case where the lawyer admitted that a conflict did exist between a 19-year-old quadriplegic and his father: *Cockburn v Gio Finance Ltd* (unreported, CA(NSW), Priestley JA, No 40580/84, 2 February 1996, BC9600068).
192. Fennell (above), p 28.
193. *Ranclaud v Cabban* (1988) NSW ConvR ¶55-385. In this case the woman had given six different powers of attorney during a 10-month period.
194. D Edwards, 'Acting for Brain-Injured Clients', November (1993) *Proctor (Law Society of Qld)* 12.
195. 'Client Capacity Guidelines: Civil and Family Law Matters' 41 *Law Society J (NSW)*, September 2003, p 50. It should be noted the author has only outlined the main questions facing a solicitor and the guidelines have an enormous amount of useful information and suggestions to help a solicitor to properly carry out his or her duties.

the solicitor needs to determine whether the 'illness temporarily impairs the client's capacity, or is a chronic illness permanently impairing capacity'. The next question posed is whether the solicitor can act without full formal instructions when a relative or friend can assist in clarifying the instructions in the client's best interest. It is also important, if the capacity of the client is in doubt, to get the client's consent to have a formal assessment by the relevant qualified professionals. If the client refuses such an assessment there are a number of legal options to compel the client to submit to an assessment. Finally, the solicitor may have to consider whether to terminate the retainer and refer the client to other agencies for help.

9.81 In representing mentally ill persons before the Mental Health Review Tribunals lawyers are supposed to make 'best interest' judgments. Lawyers in this situation, even with the advice of caring professionals, will frequently be fulfilling a highly paternalistic and inappropriate role:[196]

> The representative does not have the expertise and experience in clinical and social matters to make best interest judgments. Moreover, even if he [or she] were [sic] capable, any decision of this kind would pre-judge the disposal of the case ... that is a decision which the tribunal has itself to make.

Such a client cannot be wholly incapable because, as a patient already in an institution, that person has to have sufficient capacity to apply to the tribunal to have a hearing. Therefore it would be an exceptional case where such clients were totally unable to provide instructions to the lawyer:

> If the patient is capable of expressing a view as to the outcome he [or she] desires and can provide minimal assistance to the representative, this should suffice for the purpose of carrying out instructions.[197]

9.82 The representation of the intellectually disabled in a criminal case needs special rules. For example, there is no guarantee for these people to have a lawyer present during interrogation. The New South Wales Law Reform Commission recently recommended that there should be no interrogation of intellectually disabled suspects unless there is a lawyer present.[198] There are also serious problems when these accused come to testify as their competency is usually disputed.[199] This does not mean they are prohibited from testifying. They can still competently testify on some issues but not on others, and can make unsworn statements.[200] A recent example of these problems was a South Australian robbery case where a mentally ill man believed he was God; that he was from another planet and the Roman Empire; that his guitar spoke to him; and that he had a number one hit single on the United States music charts. Magistrate Rosanne McInnes would not let the police prosecute the man who, she said, was 'mentally incapable of instructing a solicitor'. The charges included theft of $13.65 of groceries. Commenting on the police policy of prosecuting the mentally ill

196. L Gostin and E Rassaby, *Representing the Mentally Ill and Handicapped*, Quartermaine House Ltd (for National Association of Mental Health and the Legal Action Group), Sunbury, 1980, p 4.
197. L Gostin and E Rassaby (above).
198. *People With an Intellectual Disability and the Criminal Justice System: Policing Issues* (1993) DP 27, New South Wales Law Reform Commission, p 105. See also the final report, *People with an Intellectual Disabiltiy and the Criminal Justice System* (1996) Report 80.
199. *People with an Intellectual Disability and the Criminal Justice System* (1994) DP 35, New South Wales Law Reform Commission, p 160.
200. Evidence Act 1995 (Cth) ss 12–13.

the magistrate said that this did not 'mean courts are then required to engage in long and expensive criminal justice processes resulting in people with mental illnesses being re-badged as criminals and institutionalised in jails instead of hospitals'.[201]

There are even more complicated problems with the questioning and the testimony of children who are disabled. They may need specially trained interpreters or appropriate technology.[202] Thus, police working in this area should be required to have specific training to be able to identify and communicate with various kinds of disabilities.[203] There are already special rules incorporated into the Commonwealth Crimes Act[204] that enable Indigenous people to have a support person, relative or friend or another suitable person, present during police interviews.

9.83 It is obvious from this discussion that lawyers acting for clients with disabilities must be extremely sensitive to the needs and wishes of their clients. This may take time and, above all, patience. These lawyers have to also be inventive in creating an atmosphere or situation to enable some form of communication to take place. These disabilities can also include problems of hearing, seeing and lack of understanding, cultural misunderstandings, especially for Indigenous people, or misunderstanding of a foreign language.[205] The need for accurate interpreters for foreign languages and for Indigenous people, especially from remote areas, is essential for lawyers to meet the needs of their clients.

We want to avoid situations where a defendant was involuntarily committed to a psychiatric institution for observation because, when asked by the magistrate how he felt, he used an expression which literally translated meant: 'I am God of Gods.' In fact he was using a colloquialism in his own language which if properly interpreted to English should have been 'I feel on top of the world'.[206]

Finally, in a recent Queensland Court of Appeal case, poor communication between an Aboriginal woman and her solicitor was grounds for finding that a miscarriage of justice had occurred in the lower court. At the trial for murdering her de facto spouse, no evidence was called and the accused did not testify. The Court of Appeal found that there were issues of provocation and self-defence that had not been presented. The court held that the exceptional difficulties in communication were caused by differences in cultural and psychological characteristics of the accused and her legal representatives.[207] The problems of communication with Aboriginal clients have led to the publication of a book to help lawyers.[208]

201. R DiGirolamo, 'Law row over man who thinks he's god', *Australian*, 30 July 2004, p 6.
202. Australian Law Reform Commission (with the Human Rights and Equal Opportunity Commission), Report No 84, *Seen and heard: priority for children in the legal process*, 1997, paras 18.122–18.124.
203. ALRC (above), recommendation 217, p 509.
204. Sections 23H, 23J and 23K.
205. ALRC (above), paras 18.114–18.121 and recommendations 215 and 216.
206. L Roberts-Smith, 'Communication Breakdown', Winter (1993) 73 *Victorian Bar News* 36.
207. *R v Kina* (unreported, CA(Qld), Davies and McPherson JJA, No 221/93, 29 November 1993, BC9303861).
208. D Eades (ed), *Aboriginal English and the Law — Communicating with Aboriginal English Speaking Clients: A Handbook for Legal Practitioners*, University of New South Wales Press, Sydney, 1992.

10

COMPETENCE AND CARE

INTRODUCTION

10.1   Lawyers have often been held responsible for the enormous increase in malpractice suits against other professionals. It is therefore not surprising that there has been a similar increase in malpractice suits against lawyers. In the United States there are certain firms that specialise in suing other lawyers. The trend was seen in England in the 1960s; *Cordery's*, the guide for solicitors, warned solicitors that:[1]

> ... the pursuit of actions for negligence, once rare occurrences, has now become the pastime of the disgruntled client whose affairs have gone wrong whether through ill luck, his [or her] own fault or otherwise, and no professional man or indeed technician is safe from them.

There is no indication in this quote that the solicitor may have been responsible for the client suing, but *Cordery's* was warning its readers to read the guide carefully! An example of the validity of this warning is the number of LawCover claims in New South Wales: under this scheme between 1980 and 1989 the number of professional indemnity claims against solicitors increased by 335 per cent.[2] This trend slowed down during the 1990s and between 30 June 1995 and 30 June 1996 the number of claim notifications varied between 807, the lowest in 1998, to 872, the highest in 1996.[3] Even with the large growth in the profession the increased number of claims until 1998 far exceeded in percentage terms the growth in the number of solicitors.[4] This trend has now changed between 1999 and 2003.

---

1.   *Cordery's Law Relating to Solicitors*, 6th ed, Butterworths, London, 1968, p 148.
2.   M Mills, 'Professional Negligence: the Expanding Liability of Lawyers' (1992) *Australian Bar Rev* 1, 6.
3.   *LawCover 1999 Annual Report*, LawCover, Sydney, 2000, p 7.
4.   There were approximately 5000 solicitors in New South Wales in 1976 (J Disney, J Basten, P Redmond and S Ross, *Lawyers*, 1977, p 79) and that number had increased to 5470 by early 1985 (Disney et al, 2nd ed, 1986, p 47), 10,464 by April 1993, 11,914 March 1997, 13,998 May 2000, and 17,738 by June 2004 (Law Council of Australia figures).

According to MacDermott, in 1999 the rate of notification to LawCover per solicitor in private practice was approximately one notification per 13 solicitors. In the last four years rate has fallen to one per 15 solicitors. As a result of these figures LawCover did an investigation in 2003 to find out the possible reasons for the fall in rate notifications. The factors appeared to be 'improved legal education, including legal practice training and practice management training, and improved risk management practices and culture in law firms contributed to the falling rate of notifications'.[5] We will also look at professional indemnity insurance in the last part of this chapter.

Since early 2002 legislation similar to the New South Wales Civil Liability Act 2002 has been adopted throughout Australia. These Acts aim to modify the common law principles of negligence. As Balkin and Davis state:

> [There] may be a splintering of certain aspects of the law of negligence into eight separate strands, each being similar to the others but each differing to varying extents from those others. It is to be regretted that the homogeneity which the common law system imposes upon so much of the law of torts in Australia may well be lost ... We can only hope that, in interpreting the legislation, the various state and territory courts strive for as much uniformity of outcome as possible.[6]

We will refer to the New South Wales Act as the basis for our discussion. The Act contains a new Pt 1A, Negligence. Under s 5 'harm' is defined as 'harm of any kind, including ... personal injury or death, damage to property, economic loss'. Negligence is defined as 'failure to exercise reasonable care and skill'. Section 5A states Pt 1A applies 'to any claim for damages for harm resulting from negligence, regardless of whether the claim is brought in tort, in contract, under statute or otherwise'. Section 5B, 'General Principles', states:

(1) A person is not negligent in failing to take precautions against a risk of harm unless:
   (a) the risk was foreseeable (that is, it is a risk of which the person knew or ought to have known), and
   (b) the risk was not insignificant, and
   (c) in the circumstances, a reasonable person in the person's position would have taken those precautions.
(2) In determining whether a reasonable person would have taken precautions against a risk of harm, the court is to consider the following (amongst other relevant things):
   (a) the probability that the harm would occur if care were not taken,
   (b) the likely seriousness of the harm,
   (c) the burden of taking precautions to avoid the risk of harm,
   (d) the social utility of the activity that creates the risk of harm.

Section 5D states the principles for determining causation and s 5E says that 'the plaintiff always bears the onus of proving, on the balance of probabilities, any fact relevant to the issue of causation'.

5.   B MacDermott, F – 'Risk Management', F50-8, in C Laurie (ed), *Management of Australian Law Practice*, LexisNexis Butterworths, 2004. See also Appendix 4, F50-17–20.
6.   R Balkin and J Davis, *Law of Torts*, 3rd ed, LexisNexis Butterworths, 2004, preface, p xvii.

These new statutory provisions will have to be compared and incorporated into the principles that developed in common law in order to determine lawyers' professional negligence.

This chapter is divided into the following sections: ethical duties, contractual liability, tort liability, immunity of advocates and compulsory insurance.[7]

ETHICAL DUTIES

10.2　Today the profession's attitude to competence is that it is an important ethical issue. This was not always the profession's view: historically, disciplinary action for lack of competence was extremely rare. *The New South Wales Solicitor's Manual* in 1975 summed up this view:[8]

> It seems superfluous to point out the fact, but it is nevertheless necessary owing to prevailing misconceptions, that the Law Society is not concerned with matters of mere negligence on the part of solicitors. Gross negligence, accompanied by something more, may amount to professional misconduct; but incompetence is something over which the Society has no control, not being the body by which admission was granted; and mere negligence is not a matter within its power to exercise disciplinary sanctions however much the Society may be concerned about the effect on public relations. Therefore the client must rely upon his [or her] Common Law rights.

A similar attitude existed in other common law jurisdictions. For example, competence was not explicitly made a professional obligation in the United States until 1969 when it was included in the ABA Model Code.[9] A 1943 California disciplinary case demonstrated the typical attitude, with the court saying that:[10]

> [A lawyer] must perform his [or her] duties to the best of his individual ability, not the standard of ability required of lawyers generally in the community. Mere ignorance of the law in conducting the affairs of his client in good faith is not a cause for discipline.

Even as late as 1980 the Florida Supreme Court stated that the fact that a lawyer's 'conduct might well be the basis of a negligence action ... is insufficient to warrant a disciplinary action'. The client had been bitten by a dog and the lawyer had failed to discover the dog's propensity to bite.[11]

10.3　Today the importance of competence as a professional obligation in both Australia and the United States is shown by the development of the ethical duty of competence and care as a disciplinary offence, as discussed in Chapter 7: see **7.15–7.24**. The professional conduct rules reinforce this attitude by including competence as the first rule. The Law Council of Australia Model Rules r 1.1 states:

> A practitioner must act ... with competence and diligence in the service of a client, and should accept instructions, and a retainer to act for a client only

---

7.　The format follows that in Chapter 20 of Disney et al (above), 1986.
8.　R Atkins, *The New South Wales Solicitor's Manual*, 3rd ed, Law Society of New South Wales, Sydney, 1975, p 45.
9.　DR 6-101(A).
10.　*Friday v State Bar* 144 P 2d 564 (Cal 1943).
11.　*Florida Bar v Neale* 384 So 2d (Florida 1980).

when the practitioner can reasonably expect to serve the client in that manner and attend to the work required with reasonable promptness.

The Western Australian rules covering competence (rr 5.4–5.6) are more complex. They include the general scope of the Law Council's rule and also state that practitioners shall not do unnecessary work increasing the costs, nor take instructions which are beyond their competence.

In the United States r 1.1 of the ABA Model Rules states:

> A lawyer shall provide competent representation to a client. Competent representation requires the legal knowledge, skill, thoroughness and preparation reasonably necessary for the representation.

The Comment [5] to the rule points out that the:

> ... required attention and preparation are determined in part by what is at stake; major litigation and complex transactions ordinarily require more elaborate treatment than matters of lesser consequence.

Model Rule 1.3 is also relevant. It states: 'A lawyer shall act with reasonable diligence and promptness in representing a client.'[12]

Competence and care is a very important area in the development of lawyer responsibility and accountability. Surveys conducted in New South Wales in the late 1970s and again in 1992 show that the two most frequent complaints about solicitors were negligence and delay. In the 1980 Background Paper III, the New South Wales Law Reform Commission found that the most common complaint was delay (29 per cent) and the second most frequent, negligence (13 per cent).[13] The figures provided to the New South Wales Law Reform Commission for 1988–91 by the Professional Conduct Department of the New South Wales Law Society showed a similar result. Complaints about delay constituted 20 per cent of the total while those for negligence were very close at 17 per cent.[14] The most recent figures by the Office of Legal Services Commissioner for 2002–03 have complaints against solicitors for alleged negligence at 20.5 per cent.[15] In the United States the ABA states that between 1990–95 malpractice claims constituted the greatest percentage of claims against lawyers.[16] It is obvious by the number of complaints of incompetence and delay that lawyers have to take their obligations in this area seriously.

10.4

CONTRACTUAL LIABILITY

Introduction

When a client offers to employ a lawyer, the lawyer 'expressly or by implication undertakes to fulfil certain obligations'.[17] There is a reliance

10.5

---

12. It is debatable whether the ethical rules on competence can be used to establish legal malpractice. See a note 'The Evidentiary Use of the Ethics Codes in Legal Malpractice: Erasing a Double Standard' (1996) 109 *Harvard LR* 1102.
13. p 12.
14. See *Scrutiny of the Legal Profession*, DP 26, New South Wales Law Reform Commission, 1992, para 2.30.
15. OLSC, *Annual Report 2002–2003*, p 6.
16. ABA Standing Committee on Professional Liability, *Legal Malpractice Claims in the 1990s*, 1997.
17. *Cordery's Law Relating to Solicitors* (above), p 49.

factor involved and the lawyer can still be liable in contract for promissory estoppel, even where he or she gives unpaid advice.[18] Without reliance, and where there is no fee and no other consideration, there may not be any contractual liability. Barristers in the divided professions did not have contractual capacity under common law. In Victoria this rule was abolished by the Legal Profession Practice Act 1981 and it has been clear that barristers in that state have a contractual relationship with clients.[19] For example, it has been held that a client can sue to recover a fee paid to a barrister to attend a hearing if the barrister fails to attend.[20] In England and Wales the Courts and Legal Services Act 1990 now permits barristers to enter into contractual relationships with their clients. Similar changes were adopted in New South Wales that came into effect in 1994 under s 381 of the Legal Profession Act (NSW) 1987. Those provisions were restated under the Legal Profession Act 2004. Section 83, Client access, states:

> (3) Contracts — A barrister or solicitor may enter into a contract for the provision of services with a client or with another legal practitioner. The barrister or solicitor may accordingly sue and be sued in relation to the contract.
>
> (4) Barristers' contracts — A barrister may enter into a contract with a client even though the barrister has accepted a brief from a solicitor in the matter.

The actual liability of barristers under a contract is unclear due to the lack of litigation. The Victorian Law Reform Commission has stated:[21]

> It is clear that the contract does not, under present law, contain the usual term in service contracts imposing an obligation to use the due care and skill or — which amounts to the same thing — the term is not enforceable on grounds of public policy; *Giannarelli v Wraith* (1988) 165 CLR 543. It is also clear that the extent to which a client can control the authority of an advocate to determine how the hearing should be conducted is limited by public policy. The content of the contract is also determined to some extent, no doubt, by the customary practices of the Bar.

Barristers can also be held responsible on equitable grounds for breach of confidence where no contract exists.[22]

Standard of care

10.6   It should be noted that some of the cases on the standard of care are also relevant in determining the scope of representation. At common law lawyers are under a contractual duty to the client to exercise a reasonable and competent degree of skill.[23] As we will see, this common law duty was later extended to tort law. Lawyers are not liable for errors in judgment in relation to matters of law or discretion. Every case has to depend on its own

---

18. Restatement (Second) of Contracts, s 90 quoted in fn 4 of the judgment in *Togstad v Vesely* (Minn 1980) 291 NW 2d 686.
19. See Pt 3.2.3 of the Legal Profession Act 2004 (Vic). The cases also support this view: see *Levy v Union Bank of Australia Ltd* (1896) 21 VLR 683 and *Re Melbourne Parking Station Ltd* [1929] VLR 683.
20. *Levy v Union Bank of Australia Ltd* (1896) 21 VLR 683.
21. *Access to the Law: Accountability of the Legal Profession*, Discussion Paper 24, Law Reform Commission of Victoria, July 1991, p 16, fn 39.
22. Disney et al (above), 1986, p 659.
23. *Lanphier v Phipos* (1838) 8 C & P 475 at 479 (KB).

specific circumstances.[24] Lord Diplock has reinforced these views and set out the general standard of care. He said:[25]

> No matter what profession it may be, the common law does not impose on those who practise it any liability for damage resulting from errors of judgment, unless the error was such as no reasonably well-informed and competent member of that profession could have made.

Specialisation and standard of care

The common law definition leaves certain questions unanswered. Practice today involves more and more specialisation. Should there be a different standard for a specialist? These lawyers have met higher standards in their area of expertise than other members of the profession,[26] as implied by the test being 'the standard of the ordinary skilled man exercising and professing to have that special skill'.[27] Certain specialisation programs only require someone to announce that they are specialising in that area. Should these practitioners who have had no additional training be held to a higher standard? What if a practitioner has a reputation for being, for example, an expert in tax law, or professes to be such an expert: is there a higher standard of care?

10.7

The latter question was asked in an English case that involved a solicitor of high standing and great experience in acting for publishers and writers. Although the court found that the solicitor did not fall below either a higher or normal standard of care, in dictum the court left the question open as to whether a client was entitled to a higher standard when employing such a person. Megarry J pointed out that the standard of care in tort is uniform. He said that this does not necessarily limit an action for breach of an implied duty of care in contract. There may be a higher standard because of the reliance the client has placed on the special skills of the lawyer.[28] Now that barristers who are experts in a particular field can enter into contracts it would appear that they are subject to a higher standard of care and liable for breach of contract for negligent advice.

Cole J applied the views of Megarry J in *Kleinworth Benson Australia Ltd*. The case concerned alleged negligence by solicitors concerning a loan security. The plaintiffs, merchant bankers, argued that there was a higher standard of care for solicitors who assert that they are experts in the field of legal work 'for the purpose of effecting commercial lending transactions'. Cole J said that 'in the absence of actual assent to a higher level of responsibility than that ordinarily imposed by the common law' there is no such duty. He added that it 'is a question of construction of the retainer' in each situation and 'not implication of a term'. Cole J refused to imply a

---

24. *Hart v Frame* (1838) 6 Clark & Fin 193 at 210 (HL).
25. *Saif Ali v Sydney Mitchell* [1978] 1 WLR 849 at 861.
26. Such a program has existed in New South Wales since 1993. See Law Society of New South Wales, *Specialist Accreditation Scheme*, Professional Development, June 1992. The program includes specialisation in the following areas: business, commercial litigation, immigration, personal injury and wills and estates. Other jurisdictions have also adopted specialist programs.
27. McNair J formulated this test followed by many courts in *Bolam v Friern Hospital Management Committee* [1957] 1 WLR 582 at 586. This test has been modified by the High Court in Australia: see *Rogers v Whitaker* (1992) 175 CLR 479.
28. *Duchess of Argyll v Beuselinck* [1972] 2 Lloyd's Rep 173 at 183 (HC).

term of higher knowledge in the case and found for the defendants. He said the basis on which these services were offered, and for which merchant banks and other commercial organisations employ these solicitors, is:

> ... the implicit understanding of both that in areas of complex commercial transaction, such firms have an expertise beyond that which one might expect from other solicitors.

His Honour said that whether or not a higher duty of care in tort existed for solicitors professing to specialisation or greater expertise was unnecessary for him to decide, as the claim was one in contract. In dictum he expressed an inclination to the view that there might be a higher duty in tort. This is because a claim to expertise 'is a material circumstance critical to the creating and existence of the relationship between the parties'.[29] Cole J based this view on a test stated by Windeyer J of the High Court in the Voli case.[30]

10.8 Mandie J of the Victorian Supreme Court came to a different conclusion to Cole J in *Toronto Dominion Australia Ltd v Mallesons Stephen Jaques*.[31] His Honour found a large commercial firm, Mallesons, liable for breaching their retainer by applying as the standard of care a 'reasonably competent solicitor practising in the commercial or banking and finance field'. Mandie J only awarded nominal damages because the breach did not cause any loss or damage to the plaintiff.

This higher standard has also been used in several recent cases. In *Yates Property Corp Pty Ltd v Boland* the Full Federal Court found that the solicitors had not carried out 'their retainer as would a reasonably competent solicitor expert in the law relating to resumption of land'.[32] In this case the solicitor was recently admitted and knew little about resumption of land law but the court found that the firm professed to have expertise in that area. Thus, a division of expertise in the large firms will result in having a higher standard for all practitioners working in that division.[33] Although the High Court overruled the Full Court's finding that the solicitor was negligent, it did not state whether or not there should be a higher standard or discuss the scope of representation.[34]

There were two other cases after the Full Court's decision in *Yates* but before the High Court's decision in that case. In *Montague Mining Pty Ltd v Gore*[35] the standard applied was for a solicitor with 'specialised expertise in resources law'. In *NRMA Ltd v Morgan* the solicitors and barrister 'professed to be and [were] expert[s] in corporations law'. The standard applied by Giles J was 'that appropriate to a member of the relevant profession having such specialist expertise'.[36] The advice given by the lawyers to the NRMA did not take into account the case of *Gambotto v WCP Ltd*,[37] which was

29. *Kleinwort Benson Australia Ltd v Armitage* (unreported, SC(NSW), Cole J, No 28114/88, 26 April 1989, BC8902252).
30. *Voli v Inglewood Council* (1963) 110 CLR 74 at 84.
31. (unreported, SC(Vic), Mandie J, No 2044/94, 26 July 1995, BC9506546).
32. (1998) 157 ALR 30 at 44.
33. B Zipser, 'Growth of professional negligence claims against legal practitioners' (October 1999) *Law Society J (NSW)* 68, 69.
34. *Boland v Yates Property Corp Pty Ltd* (2000) 74 ALJR 209.
35. (unreported, Fed C of A, Wilcox J, No 563/97, 23 October 1998, BC9805642).
36. [1999] NSWSC 407 at 409.
37. (1995) 182 CLR 432.

then on appeal to the High Court. The High Court's later decision in *Gambotto* made the advice given to the NRMA incorrect. In applying the higher standard Giles J decided the barrister and solicitors had been negligent.

The barrister, Mr Heydon QC, and the solicitors, appealed and the Court of Appeal found that they had not been negligent.[38] The case was heard by three judges from outside New South Wales as Heydon QC had been appointed to the Court of Appeal after the lower court decision. Justice Heydon was later appointed to the High Court. The Court of Appeal accepted that a higher standard of care did apply for practitioners professing to have a special skill but that standard was that of those of 'the ordinary skilled person exercising and professing to have that special skill'.[39] Even with a higher standard the court still found that the practitioners' advice was not negligent (see below). The NRMA's application for leave to appeal to the High Court was refused.

What if the legal practitioner has a reputation for being skilled in a certain area of law, but does not profess to having the special skill? It has been held that the practitioner will be held to the ordinary standard and not to a higher one.[40]

In the United States lawyers who hold themselves out as specialising in a particular field and as possessing greater than ordinary knowledge and skill in that field will be held to the standard of performance of other lawyers holding themselves out as specialists in that area.[41] A specialist who gives a reason for turning down a case (say, for example, a torts lawyer who turns down a case with the advice that there is no tort liability when in fact there is), should know that his or her advice will be relied on and that he or she will be held responsible to a higher standard than a lawyer who does not purport to be a specialist. If the lawyer turns down the case without giving a reason there will not be any responsibility.[42]

10.9

Lawyers acting in a trademark search where the firm did not hold itself out to be expert in trademark work were also held not to be liable.[43] The question here is whether lawyers should take on work that is beyond their capacity. It has been held in New South Wales[44] that it is no excuse for a lawyer to argue that he or she was inexperienced in litigation. The court held in this case that the solicitor should have told his client of his inexperience or briefed counsel. In a similar American case concerning the setting up of a trust as a tax shelter, the lawyer who was inexperienced in this field was held to be negligent. The court held that in certain circumstances lawyers who are general practitioners are under a duty to refer clients to, or recommend, a specialist. If lawyers fail to refer and undertake to perform the work themselves, without the aid of a specialist, there is a:[45]

---

38. *Heydon v NRMA* [2000] NSWCA 374.
39. Ibid, Malcolm AJA, para 146.
40. *Wooldridge v Sumner* [1962] 2 All ER 978 at 989.
41. *Walker v Bangs* 601 P 2d 1279 (Wash 1979).
42. *Procanik v Cillo* 543 A 2d 985 (NJ 1988).
43. *Mayo v Engel* 733 F 2d 807 (11th Cir 1984).
44. *Vulic v Bilinsky* (1983) 2 NSWLR 472.
45. *Horne v Peckham* 158 Cal Rptr 714 at 720 (1979).

... further duty to have knowledge and skill ordinarily possessed, and exercise the care and skill ordinarily used by specialists in good standing in the same or similar locality.

The Comment [3] to the ABA Model Rules r 1.1 does excuse lawyers acting in an emergency situation. There is no duty to brief a specialist in the area if such a referral would be impractical.[46] It appears that the standard to be applied in emergency situations is that the lawyer should exercise the skill and knowledge ordinarily possessed by lawyers under similar circumstances.

Location of practice

10.10   Another question is whether the standard of care that is applied should be determined by the appropriate practice of lawyers in a particular 'locality' as seen by lawyers practising in that jurisdiction. An English court has rejected the use of other practising lawyers as expert witnesses to the appropriate practice. The English High Court held that:[47]

> ... if there is some practice in a particular profession, some accepted standard of conduct which is laid down by a professional institute or sanctioned by common usage, evidence of that can and ought to be received ... The test is what a reasonably competent practitioner would do having regard to the standards normally adopted in the profession.

Cole J in *Kleinwort Benson Australia Ltd* (see **10.7** above) did not go this far. His Honour said:[48]

> Evidence of the practice of solicitors is not, in my view, determinative of the conduct necessary to discharge a solicitor's obligations under a duty of care, whether tortious or contractual.

The New South Wales Court of Appeal in a 1994 decision concerning the duty of care in advising on the purchase of a business said that evidence was admissible as to 'the common practise of solicitors of good repute who were given a retainer to act on the sale of a business'.[49] In the United States, expert evidence by lawyers practising in the field as to the standard of care does take place.[50]

10.11   This does not, however, resolve a situation where the practice as accepted by experts in the field or by the professional organisation is below community standards. A Canadian case held that general practice and custom in the City of Ottawa in 1969 was not to make a search of local planning records to ensure the usage desired by the client was allowed. A solicitor who failed to make such a check was held not to be negligent.[51] In discussing this case Keeler pointed out that the court was mistaken in that it did not assess common practice in the profession against the standard of reasonable care expected by the community.[52]

---

46. See also B Glesner, 'The Ethics of Emergency Lawyering' (1991) 5 *Georgetown J of Legal Ethics* 317.
47. *Midland Bank Trust Co Ltd v Hett, Stubbs and Kemp* [1979] Ch 384 at 402.
48. *Kleinwort Benson Australia Ltd v Armitage*, see n 29 (above).
49. *Macindoe v Parbery* (unreported, CA(NSW), Full Ct, No 40640/89, 17 August 1994, BC9402891).
50. See *Progressive Sales v Williams, Willeford, Boger, Grady & Davis* 356 SE 2d 372 (NC 1987) and *Togstad v Vesely, Otto, Miller & Keefe* 291 NW 2d 686 (Minn 1980).
51. *Hanck v Dixon* 10 OR (2d) 605 (1975).
52. J Keeler, 'Paying for Mistakes — Professional Negligence and Economic Loss' (1979) 53 *ALJ* 412, 416.

The view expressed by Keeler was adopted by the Privy Council in dealing with the Hong Kong style of completion in a land transaction.[53] It was normal and customary conveyancing practice for the purchase money to be handed to the vendor's solicitor in reliance upon undertakings by that solicitor. The solicitor in this case failed to honour the undertakings and left the colony with the money of the plaintiff. The bank sued their solicitors for breach of contract. Their Lordships found that the Hong Kong style of completion had a foreseeable risk that was readily avoidable. It therefore held that the common practice of the profession fell below a standard of reasonable care.

Courts decide standard of care

There have been similar decisions in relation to medical practitioners. In the English case of *Sidaway v Board of Governors of the Bethlem Royal Hospital*[54] Sir John Donaldson stated that the:[55]

> ... definition of duty of care is not to be handed over to the medical or any other profession. The definition of duty of care is a matter for the law and the courts. They cannot stand idly by if the profession, by an excess of paternalism, denies their patients a real choice. In a word, the law will not permit the medical profession to play God ...

10.12

Lord Scarman in a House of Lords decision[56] pointed out that the courts should not choose one expert group over another as to whether there is negligence. It is the role of the court to examine the exercise of skill that was involved. The High Court has adopted Lord Scarman's view following his dissenting opinion in the *Sidaway* case. In a joint statement in *Rogers v Whitaker*,[57] the court held that while evidence of accepted medical practice was a useful guide, it was for the courts to determine the appropriate standard of care demanded by the law. The court did emphasise that this case concerned what information needed to be provided to a patient in the assessment of the actual surgical performance. In such situations the view of professional opinion would be influential if not decisive.

In *Hodgins v Cantrell*[58] a barrister gave advice on the quantum of damages in a motor vehicle accident that the plaintiff could expect if the case was litigated. Based on this advice the plaintiff settled. The barrister was later sued for giving too low a figure. Testimony from four expert barristers was used to determine that the defendant barrister's estimate was very low and thus unreasonable and negligent. Branson J of the Federal Court in *Yates Property Corp Pty Ltd v Boland*[59] applied the principles from *Rogers*. In her decision on the appropriate standard of care she relied principally on the evidence of experts in the field (valuers and legal practitioners) in determining whether a breach of standard of care had taken place. She also considered her own opinion in the course of giving judgment.

10.13

53. *Edward Wong Finance Co Ltd v Johnson Stokes & Master* [1984] 1 AC 296 at 304 (PC).
54. [1984] 1 QB 493 (CA).
55. See n 54 (above) at 512. His Lordship was applying the views expressed in a Canadian case, *Reibl v Hughes* (1980) 114 DLR 3rd 1 at 12.
56. *Maynard v W Midlands Regional Health Authority* [1984] 1 WLR 634 at 639 (HL).
57. (1992) 175 CLR 479.
58. (1997) MVR 481 SC(NSW).
59. (1997) 145 ALR 169 at 197–8.

The Full Federal Court in the appeal in *Yates* also accepted the use of expert witnesses in helping to determine the standard of care in specialised areas. The court emphasised the change in nature of practice with the development of large firms and specialist small 'boutique' firms with one or two narrow areas of expertise. The court rejected the use of the views of experts in determining the more general standard of care. It said that 'such evidence [is] of little assistance ... We think that a court is well placed to determine the liability of a legal practitioner without the aid of such evidence where questions of particular practices do not arise. Moreover, a court runs a real risk of falling into error when it places principal reliance on the expert testimony of witnesses instead of forming its own view of ... the duties owed by barristers and solicitors and the appropriate standards in accordance with which those duties must be performed.'[60] On the appeal the High Court failed to comment on these views in its decision.[61] It is unfortunate that the court did not give its views on the application of a different standard of care for specialists and how expert testimony is to be used.

10.14 The previous cases highlight the problem of determining the appropriate geographical area to be applied. Should the standard be that of, for example, the practice in Brisbane or in Queensland or in all of Australia? Until recently it could be argued that the standard of that state would be the appropriate one as the practice of law was state-oriented. In light of the recent High Court case, *Street v Queensland Bar Association*,[62] where it was held that the practice of law in Australia is nationally oriented, we may need to develop a national standard of care. Furthermore, we are developing national practising certificates as discussed in Chapter 6. Perhaps even a national standard may not be considered an appropriate standard of care. The New South Wales Court of Appeal has held[63] that the prevailing practice of Sydney doctors was not enough to establish a standard of care; it was appropriate to have evidence of an overseas expert on what should have been done. A case in the United States has held that the standard to be applied was that of lawyers practising in the state of Georgia. The court did say that there was little difference between applying a local or national standard.[64] It has been argued that the locality requirement includes the need for lawyers to know local considerations essential to their client's representation. At other times a national standard may be appropriate in some areas of specialisation.[65]

There may be some help with these issues under the recent negligence legislation adopted throughout Australia. The Civil Liability Act (NSW) 2002 relieves a practitioner from liability under s 50(1) if he or she provided a service that 'was widely accepted in Australia by peer professional opinion as competent professional practice'. This standard can be overruled by a court under s 50(2) if the 'court considers the opinion is irrational'. What if there are differing opinions? Under s 50(3) such differing opinions, 'one or

60. (1998) 157 ALR 30 at 50 and 56.
61. (2000) 74 ALJR 209.
62. (1989) 168 CLR 461.
63. *Albrighton v Royal Prince Alfred Hospital* (1980) 2 NSWLR 542 at 562.
64. *Kellos v Sawilowsky* 322 SE 2d 897 (Georgia 1985).
65. R Mallen and V Levit, *Legal Malpractice*, West Publishing, St Paul, 1981, p 254.

more (or all)', that have wide acceptance can be relied upon by the court. The Act obviously must be applied within the context of the various aspects of the above discussion.

Scope of representation

We have discussed in the last chapter the fact that a lawyer has an obligation to carry out a client's instructions. Sometimes these instructions are far from complete in meeting all the legal requirements of the client. Clients are not experts in law and may not realise that other work needs to be done in relation to their problem other than what they have instructed their lawyers to do. Furthermore, sometimes the instructions are unclear as the client only comes in to deal with one aspect. Do lawyers have an obligation to go beyond instructions to perform additional work or at least find out if additional work needs to be done? If they do have such an obligation there will necessarily be a higher standard of care. The English Court of Appeals had to deal with such a problem in the *Griffiths* case.[66] The client came to the solicitor in relation to a work-related injury. The solicitor advised him only concerning his claim for workmen's [workers'] compensation and not in relation to his common law tort rights. The suit for negligence failed. Somervell LJ found no negligence on the basis that the variety of matters which solicitors have to deal with increases annually and they have to know too many areas of law. He said that it was a borderline case but solicitors could not be held to know all areas of the law. Romer LJ based his decision on the fact that the client only asked for advice in one area of the law and the solicitor was therefore only following instructions.

10.15

In a strong dissent, Denning LJ said if a workman goes to a solicitor and states he has had an accident, the first question the solicitor should ask is:[67]

> What is the man's legal position? Every solicitor ought to know that there is all the difference in the world between a case where the employer is to blame and a case where he is not. If the employer is not to blame, the man [or woman] gets only workmen's compensation. If the employer is to blame, either for negligence or breach of statutory duty, the man receives the much higher award given by the common law. I cannot think that it is right for the solicitor to escape by saying: 'You only consulted me about workmen's compensation, not about common law damages'. That attributes to the workman a legal knowledge of the difference between them. Many workmen do not know the difference, and it would be most unfair to attribute it to them.

In a later English case, *Midland Bank Trust Co Ltd v Hett, Stubbs and Kemp*,[68] a solicitor failed to check whether an option agreement had been registered. It had been drawn up six years before by another partner in the firm. The agreement between the father and his son giving the son an option to purchase a farm owned by the father had been executed. There had been a failure to register the option. The son had consulted the firm about the desirability of exercising the option. The solicitor looked at the agreement but failed to check whether it had been registered. In breach of

10.16

---

66. *Griffiths v Evans* [1953] 1 WLR 1424.
67. *Griffiths v Evans* (above) at 1427.
68. [1979] Ch 384 (HC).

the agreement the father subsequently sold the land and the son could not exercise his rights. The court held that the instructions did not relate to the registration of the option but to the agreement. The firm had not heard of any family discord. The failure to check the registration of the option was held not to be negligent, but the original failure to register the option was negligent. The firm was held liable because there existed a tort liability that arose only on the sale to a third party and which was independent of any contractual liability.[69]

10.17   Australian and English courts today would no longer follow the majority view in the *Griffiths* case, nor the limited scope of duty in *Midland Bank Trust*. In *Vulic v Bilinsky*[70] a New South Wales solicitor did not pursue the plaintiff's common law rights in a work-related injury. The original instructions did not include issuing a writ for damages against the employer. The action had become statute-barred. The solicitor had argued that he was not specifically instructed to bring that action and that he was inexperienced in litigation. Myles J said the client was only an injured worker who had some inkling that he might be entitled to money from his employer:

> His instructions to the defendants as it seems to me were to advise on and if necessary take such steps as were reasonable to obtain such recompense ... If the plaintiff had a clear cause of action they had firstly a duty to advise but also authority to proceed on his behalf ... If the plaintiff's cause of action was doubtful they had a duty to tell him so and let him know of the likely consequences of alternative courses of procedure and to allow him the opportunity of giving further instructions.

Miles J pointed out that even if he was a non-specialist in litigation, a competent non-specialist solicitor would know that the Workers' Compensation Act imposes a three-year limitation period for common law actions from the date upon which the worker first received payment of workers' compensation. Furthermore, the solicitor did not inform the plaintiff that he was inexperienced in litigation. The plaintiff was entitled to expect the proper standard of care of a reasonably competent solicitor who did not hold himself out to be a specialist in the field of personal injury litigation. If he was so inexperienced in litigation he should inform the client of his lack of experience. This would give the client the alternative to instruct another solicitor. If a solicitor accepts the instructions he or she should protect the client and himself or herself by seeking advice from counsel. Miles J held the solicitor to be negligent.[71]

10.18   The High Court in *Cook v Cook*[72] held that in particular circumstances a subjective standard may be applied. In that case circumstances existed where there was special knowledge of the skills of the negligent party which led to a decrease in the level of duty of care. In light of the *Cook* case, would the client in *Vulic* have had a lower standard of care applied to his situation if he had known that the solicitor was inexperienced in litigation and still retained him?

---

69. See n 68 (above) at 402–3.
70. [1983] 2 NSWLR 472.
71. See n 70 (above) at 474, 482–4.
72. (1986) 162 CLR 376.

In *Midland Bank Trust Co Ltd*[73] it was held that the scope of a solicitor's duties to the client 'depends upon the terms and limits of [the] retainer and any duty of care to be implied must be related to what he [or she] is contracted to do'. Thus, in *Park v Allied Mortgage Corporation Ltd*[74] Hill J in the Federal Court stated that a solicitor was obliged to advise the client:

> ... as to the purchase price of the property to be given as security; the total amount to be advanced on first and second mortgage to enable the purchase to be completed; and the fact that the moneys to be advanced exceeded 100% of the purchase price of the property. It is not a defence to a solicitor to say that he was entitled to keep these matters to himself and to rely only upon the valuation obtained ... [I]t could never be an absolute defence to a solicitor that he relied upon a valuation obtained when other circumstances known to the solicitor cast doubt upon that valuation.

Hill J found that the investment advice was understood to be part of the retainer and the solicitor thus had a duty of care, which he had breached.[75]

Outside the scope of retainer

Can a lawyer be held responsible outside the scope of the retainer? In **10.19** *Waimond v Byrne*[76] the New South Wales Court of Appeal rejected the view expressed in *Midland Bank Trust Co Ltd* and found that the lawyer had a duty that went beyond the scope of the retainer and included a duty in tort. This duty meant the lawyer had to instruct the client clearly on the ramifications of the proposed mortgage although it was not part of the original instructions. This was a borderline case and the court was evenly divided (2:2). In other cases the scope of the retainer has been important in finding no liability. In *Orszulak v Hoy*[77] the Queensland Full Supreme Court held that a retainer to perform only conveyancing did not include a duty to advise the client on investment aspects. The New South Wales Court of Appeal agreed with this view, holding that a solicitor acting in a conveyancing matter does not have an implied obligation to furnish financial or investment advice.[78] In another case, *Thors v Weekes*,[79] the Federal Court found that solicitors were not negligent when they were retained to perform what the court called 'mechanical' aspects of conveyancing. They owed no duty to conduct a search of old title land for Crown reservation, or to warn that no search had been undertaken.

In *Macindoe v Parbery*,[80] the New South Wales Court of Appeal did not find a solicitor negligent for not investigating the purchase of a licence when advising on the purchase of a surfboard hire business. A local council revoked the annual licence. The court did express 'a little unease' in

---

73. [1979] Ch 384 at 402–3.
74. [1995] ACL Rep 250 FC 4.
75. For an example of a retainer held not to include investment advice and thus no liability, see *Trust Co of Australia v Perpetual Trustees WA* (unreported, SC(NSW), McLelland CJ, No 5723/92, 9 July 1997, BC 9702915).
76. (1989) 18 NSWLR 642.
77. (1989) Aust Torts Reps ¶80–293 (Qld).
78. *Citicorp Aust Ltd v O'Brien* (1996) 40 NSWLR 398. For a discussion of this case see R Cichero, 'Solicitors' duties of care: *Citicorp v O'Brien* — Is there an obligation to give unsolicited financial advice?' (1997) 35 *Law Society J (NSW)* 27.
79. (1989) 92 ALR 131.
80. (unreported, CA(NSW), Full Ct, No 40640/89, 17 August 1994, BC9402891).

upholding the court's finding that the solicitor was not negligent. The New South Wales Court of Appeal in that case and in an earlier judgment[81] said that solicitors have to go beyond the specifically agreed professional tasks.

10.20 The High Court in a 4:1 decision[82] upheld the findings and decision of the trial judge[83] and the South Australian Full Supreme Court in *Austrust Ltd v Astley*.[84] In that case a solicitor was found to have breached his general retainer. The solicitor was an experienced practitioner with expertise in commercial and corporate law, who also had acted for the plaintiff for a number of years and knew its operations. The solicitor had failed to warn his client (a trustee) of the risk of personal liability for trust debts of a trading trust. The judge said the solicitor should have advised the plaintiff company of the desirability of excluding personal liability. The court did not find contributory negligence even though the plaintiff had its own employed solicitor involved in the matter and was 'an experienced and skilled trustee'.

The solicitor accepted his liability for breaching the retainer but appealed to the High Court on the contributory negligence issue. The High Court held that contributory negligence could be found even though the duty of the defendant was to protect the interests of the plaintiff. But in this case the issue of negligence turned on the scope of the solicitor's retainer and therefore involved a breach of contract. Since the apportionment statute in South Australia used the word 'fault', contributory negligence did not apply in cases of breach of contract. If the original action was in tort contributory negligence could have been sought. The High Court has been criticised for its excessive formalism in its decision.[85] The decision in *Astley* was negated in New South Wales where apportionment is allowed under breach of contract where there is contributory negligence.[86]

10.21 We have discussed *NRMA Ltd v Morgan*[87] and *Heydon v NRMA*[88] above, concerning the standard of care. In that case the advice was given by a solicitor and barrister, who were experts on corporations law, on the restructuring of a large motoring service organisation. The practitioners failed to advise that an appeal to the High Court, which had been granted, could render their proposed method of restructuring unlawful. Giles J in the New South Wales Supreme Court held the practitioners owed a higher standard of care and found them negligent for failing to advise the client concerning this risk. Giles J found that had the client received the proper advice it would have abandoned or ceased work on the proposed restructuring. The barrister was held liable even though he had not been specifically requested by the solicitor to advise upon the effect of the appeal of the *Gambotto* case to the High Court on the advice he had given.[89] The

81. Cousins v Cousins (unreported, CA(NSW), Full Ct, No 40366/90, 18 December 1990, BC9001586).
82. (1999) 161 ALR 455.
83. (1993) 60 SASR 354.
84. (1996) 67 SASR 207.
85. J Davis, 'Contributory Negligence and Breach of Contract: *Astley v Austrust Ltd*' (1999) 7 *Torts LJ* 117.
86. Law Reform (Miscellaneous Provisions) Act 2001 (NSW).
87. [1999] NSWSC 407.
88. [2000] NSWCA 374.
89. [1999] NSWSC 407.

Court of Appeal in *Heydon v NRMA* decided that the advice was not negligent. It was not in the scope of representation for the practitioners to have warned the NRMA that there was a risk involved in the advice given on the reconstruction because of a case on appeal to the High Court. The three judges had different reasons for their finding. Malcolm AJA found that the decision in *Gambotto* was outside the issues that would reasonably have been contemplated by a competent lawyer at that time.[90] McPherson AJA held that it was not reasonably foreseeable,[91] and Ormiston AJA said it could not be reasonably anticipated.[92] The judges felt that in *Gambotto* the narrow and unusual reasoning adopted by the majority in the High Court was the reason for their decision.

Many members of the New South Wales Bar were upset by the *NRMA Ltd v Morgan* decision. The fact that Giles J's decision was overruled on appeal does not negate the value of the interesting comments and suggestions made while the case was on appeal. Two members of the bar wrote that: 'The reaction of many barristers has been that, if Senior Counsel as eminent as that sued in *NRMA* could be found negligent, then the task for lesser mortals is close to impossible. The relationship of professional trust and respect between solicitors and the Bar takes a heavy blow when one must now assume that the solicitor sitting across the table today may tomorrow be suing one in court; and that the client for whom one does one's very best today may tomorrow be seeking to access one's insurance policy, in some cases one's assets and destroy one's reputation in the process.'[93]

Barristers should take due warning of the new dangers of practice. They include:

10.22

- ❑ the need to have detailed notes when providing advice or engaging in general discussion of matters in conference;
- ❑ the need to clearly and expressly state the qualifications or limitations upon the advisory task;
- ❑ on any matter involving complexity and/or large sums of money there are advantages and probably a need to retain two or more counsel;
- ❑ counsel need to examine closely the limits on their professional indemnity insurance so they are adequately covered;
- ❑ an hourly rate may not be appropriate and a premium should be charged because of the risks involved for matters that are complex and/or costly.[94]

Practitioners may still be concerned because both courts in the *NRMA* case held practitioners to a higher standard. Furthermore, the reasoning of the Court of Appeal in *Heydon v NRMA* at times is inconsistent with previous High Court cases.[95] It would appear therefore that the decision may not have a great influence in negating the need for practitioners to consider giving advice beyond the specific demands of their clients if it is reasonable

10.23

---

90. [2000] NSWCA 374 at para 309.
91. Ibid, at para 403.
92. Ibid, at para 612.
93. J Gleeson and G Kennett, 'Recent Decisions Concerning Liability of Counsel' (February 2000) *Australian Bar Gazette* 10 at 12.
94. See n 93 (above), pp 11–12.
95. For a detailed analysis of the court's reasoning see F Riley, *New South Wales Solicitors Manual*, LexisNexis Butterworths, Sydney, 2004, looseleaf, para 41,040.

to do so. Two other cases, from New South Wales and England, also require practitioners to be knowledgeable about tax law.

In *Bayer v Balkin* Cohen J found a duty on the solicitor who was a trustee to have a continuing supervision of the trust. He added that this included advising of the best way to avoid expenses to the trust of future high taxation. Cohen J in dictum added: 'It now seems to be accepted, with the imposition of high rates of tax ... that there is a duty on ... accountants and solicitors to advise their clients how they can avoid, as far as possible, making what the government regards as a proper contribution.'[96] In *Hurlingham Estates v Wilde & Partners* solicitors advised concerning the purchase of shares in a company. The solicitor involved, Mr Rowe, was the conveyancing and commercial partner but had next to no knowledge of tax law and failed to advise of adverse tax consequences from the transaction. Lightman J said: 'There were no specific terms of the solicitors' retainer limiting what would be the ordinary duty of a solicitor instructed on such transaction. There was no specific reference to tax [in the original instructions], but that does not mean that Mr Rowe did not assume responsibilities to advise as to tax ... In these circumstances I have no doubt that he owed a duty to advise how the transaction should be structured, and to advise that the structure in fact adopted exposed Hurlingham [the client] to the tax charge, which (by common consent) by alteration to form rather than the substance of the transaction could have been avoided.'[97] In the future, practitioners with little tax knowledge would be wise to tell the client and send the client elsewhere or seek help on the matter.[98]

10.24   If the advice is adequate but not followed by the client, the lawyer is not responsible for the client's actions. It is not the role of lawyers to force their advice on their clients. How far lawyers need to go in giving advice is unclear and will depend on the facts in each situation. It has been held that the experience and knowledge of the client in some cases can affect the scope of the retainer.[99] It would appear from these recent cases that lawyers in both Australia and England could be held negligent if they fail to know the basic remedies available to their clients. This will be required whether or not they have been instructed to pursue those remedies. Australian lawyers would be wise to inform their clients of the ramifications of their actions and obtain clearly written instructions as to their role.

American cases

10.25   In the United States lawyers are required to do a minimum amount of research in an area in which they have limited or no expertise if they advise the client that there is no cause of action. In the *Togstad* case[100] the lawyer in a medical malpractice case failed to check hospital records and consult with an expert before rendering an opinion. He also failed to inform the

---

96.   (1995) 95 ATC 4609.
97.   [1997] 1 Lloyd's Rep 525, 530.
98.   For comments on both cases and on Justice Cohen's views see R O'Connor, 'The Duty of Solicitors To Give Tax Advice — An Update' (February 1998) *Brief* (*WA Law Society J*) 25.
99.   See *Rybak v Senneh Pty Ltd* (CA(NSW), 40549/93, 18 October 1996, unreported).
100. *Togstad v Vesely, Otto, Miller & Keefe* 291 NW 2d 686 (Minn 1980).

client that there was a two-year statute of limitation. The court found him to be negligent. In a Californian case, *Smith v Lewis*,[101] it was held that a higher standard is required than just minimum research. The court said:

> If the law on a particular subject is doubtful or debatable, an attorney will not be held responsible for failing to anticipate the manner in which the uncertainty will be resolved ... But even with respect to an unsettled area of law, we believe an attorney assumes an obligation to his [or her] client to undertake reasonable research in an effort to ascertain relevant legal principles and to make an informed decision as to a course of conduct based upon an intelligent assessment of the problem.

Another important Californian case, *Nichols v Keller*,[102] involved a lawyer who drafted an agreement for his client to limit the scope of representation. The agreement stated that the lawyer was to deal only with the workers' compensation claim. There was no mention of a potential tort claim for the injured client in the agreement. The lawyer did not inform the client of the limitations on the scope of his representation, nor on the possible adverse implications, nor did he advise the client to seek another lawyer in reference to the tort claim. When the client discovered that his tort claim was statute-barred he sued the lawyer successfully for negligence. The Court of Appeal stated: 'Not only should an attorney furnish advice when requested, but he or she should also volunteer opinions when necessary to further the client's objectives. The attorney need not advise and caution of every possible alternative, but only of those that may result in adverse consequences if not considered.'[103] The court also said that: 'A trained attorney is more qualified to recognize and analyze legal need than a lay client, and, at least in part, this is the reason a party seeks out and retains an attorney to represent and advise him or her in legal matters.'[104]

Exclusions and limitations

Many contracts carry limitations from liability that have been agreed to by the parties. Can lawyers enter into such contracts with their clients? It would appear in these situations that there are unequal bargaining positions because the lawyer usually has far more knowledge as to the implications of such a contract and this will lead to a conflict of interest. Thus, the general rule is that lawyers cannot limit their liability by lowering the standard of care. For example, under the Conflict of Interest: Current Clients: Specific Rules, ABA Model Rule 1.8(h) states: 'A lawyer shall not make an agreement prospectively limiting the lawyer's liability to a client for malpractice unless permitted by law and the client is independently represented in making the agreement.' Lawyers do limit liability by rarely orally stating when giving opinions that the client 'cannot possibly lose', and so on. Instead of firm opinions about the law, lawyers modify their assertions with terms such as 'likely' or 'probably'. In written contracts lawyers do at times insert express disclaimers, but rarely, if ever, seek to limit their monetary liability. Furthermore, as was stated in the *Nichols* case, a lawyer can still be held to be negligent if the client is not given adequate

10.26

---

101. 530 P 2d 589 at 595 (Ca 1975).
102. (1993) 15 Cal App4th 1672.
103. Ibid, at 1683–4.
104. Ibid, at 1686.

information concerning the disclaimers that limit the scope of representation. Two more recent Californian cases have also rejected limiting the scope of representation. In *In the Matter of Valinoti*[105] it was held that counsel cannot have a 'limited' appearance in immigration proceedings. In *Janik v Rudy, Exelrod & Zieff*[106] it was held that a lawyer contractually limiting the scope of representation still is responsible for asserting claims arising out of the same facts that a client would reasonably expect in order to achieve the objectives of the representation.

Limits to liability

10.27   Unlimited personal liability for lawyers has, until recently, always been assumed. This assumption was maintained under recent changes allowing lawyers to practise as corporations, for example s 28 of the Legal Practitioners Act 1981 (SA) which states:

> Any civil liability incurred by a company that is a legal practitioner is enforceable jointly and severally against the company and persons who were directors of the company at the time the liability was incurred.

However, as we discussed in Chapter 4 (see **4.23**), legislation in a number of jurisdictions (Victoria, New South Wales, Queensland, Northern Territory) now allows solicitors to incorporate. Incorporation by lawyers opens up explosive ethical and liability issues: see **10.28**.

There is also a cap on professional liability under the Professional Standards Act 1994 (NSW).[107] Section 3(a) allows schemes to be created 'to limit the civil liability of professionals and others'. Under s 21, if such a scheme has been approved and is in operation, insurance companies in the policies can limit liability for professional negligence for members of this occupational association. Legal practitioners under s 5(1)(b)–(d) of this Act cannot limit their liability for any negligence or fault when acting in a personal injury claim. They cannot limit it also for a breach of trust, when there is fraud or dishonesty, or when there is death of or personal injury to a person. Occupational associations have to design a mandatory professional indemnity insurance scheme for their members which specifies the amounts of liability for different classes and/or different kinds of work. The association's scheme must contain a detailed list of risk management strategies and the means for them to be implemented by its members.[108] The Professional Standards Council has an educational and monitoring, development and educational role in maintaining the standards and creation of the occupational associations' schemes.[109] The Law Society of New South Wales scheme, based on LawCover insurance arrangements, was approved by the Standards Council in 1996[110] and that of the New South

---

105. (2002) 4 Cal State Bar Ct Rptr 498 at 521.
106. (2004) 119 Cal App4th 930.
107. Similar provision exists in the Professional Standards Act 1997 in Western Australia: see M Costello and S Unwin, 'The Natural Legal Services Market — Part 1, Brief' (1999) 26(1) *Law Society of WA Journal* 5. See also the Professional Standards Act 2003 (Vic) and Professional Standards Act 2003 (SA).
108. Professional Standards Act 1994 (NSW) ss 4, 7–11, 24 and 36(1).
109. See n 108 (above), s 43(1).
110. For a discussion of the proposal see (1995) 33 *Law Society J (NSW)* 77.

Wales Bar Association was approved in late 2004.[111] The Commonwealth Government has also adopted a scheme to limit professional liability under Commonwealth legislation such as the Trade Practices Act 1974, the Australian Securities and Investments Commission Act 2001 and the Corporations Act 2001.[112] The Federal Government will have to approve the schemes presented to it by the various state law societies and bar associations in order for their practitioners to obtain capped liability under Commonwealth law.

As we discussed in Chapter 4 (see **4.23**), several jurisdictions have adopted legislation allowing solicitors to incorporate and to have multi-disciplinary partnerships (MDPs). The Legal Profession Amendment (Incorporated Legal Practices) Act 2000 (NSW) allows lawyers to incorporate under the Corporations Law with limited liability and the right to public listing. These provisions are now found under ss 134–164 of the Legal Profession Act 2004 (NSW). Under ss 132 and 140 at least one director has to be a solicitor holding an unrestricted practising certificate; the solicitor or solicitors' directors are responsible for managing the legal services provided; and all the solicitors are individually responsible under the Legal Profession Act 2004 (NSW) for their actions, and are subject to the ethical rules of the Law Society of New South Wales. Thus, lawyers will not be able to hide behind the corporate veil and will still be subject to negligence actions and therefore need to carry professional indemnity insurance.[113] There are serious ethical problems presented by the new forms of practice. The questions that are posed are: (1) Will clients still receive high quality legal services? (2) Does incorporation and/or becoming a MDP increase the potential for breaches of confidentiality? (3) Will the new structures provide a greater risk of conflict of interest and a greater need for Chinese Walls?: see **12.83–12.94**. These problems will become clearer after several more years of practice under the new structures.[114]

10.28

In the United States, Model Rule 1.8(h) prohibits lawyers from making an agreement with a client to limit liability for malpractice unless it is permitted by law and the client has independent legal advice in making the agreement. The California Rule 3-400 is more absolute, prohibiting contracts that limit liability for professional malpractice. The enormous increase in the number of malpractice suits against professionals, many resulting in very large awards, has led professionals to lobby governments to bring in statutory limits to liability. We will discuss the problems of indemnity insurance in the last section of this chapter.

10.29

---

111. See *Bar Brief*, issues 118 and 119, November and December 2004.
112. Treasury Legislation Amendment (Professional Standards) Act 2004 (Cth).
113. See M Saville, 'Lawyers pushed into the furnace', *Sydney Morning Herald*, 20 March 2000, p 37.
114. For an excellent discussion of these problems see S Mark, 'Harmonization or Homogenization? The Globalization of Law and Legal Ethics — An Australian View' (2001) 34 *Vanderbilt J of Transnational Law* 1173, 1193–6. See also R Cocks, 'Ethical Ramifications of Corporatised Legal Practice' (2001) 8 *Deakin LR* 6.

TORT LIABILITY

Establishment of the duty

10.30   In 1939 the English Court of Appeal in *Groom v Croker*[115] established the principle that a solicitor's liability to a client for failure to perform was contractual. The court said that the solicitor–client relationship did not give rise to any tort liability. This rule was rejected in *Hedley Byrne*[116] in 1964. In a case dealing with the negligent misstatement of a bank Lord Morris of Borth-y-Gest summed up the view of the House of Lords:[117]

> ... that it should now be regarded as settled that if someone possessed of a special skill undertakes, quite irrespective of contract, to apply that skill for the assistance of another person who relies upon such skill, a duty of care will arise.

It was not clear that this decision applied to solicitors until the *Midland Bank* case in 1979: see **10.16**. In that case Oliver J found that the liability for the solicitor could be either in contract or tort.[118] This view that solicitors may have concurrent liability in tort and contract has been accepted in Australia.[119] If the action against a solicitor is statute-barred in contract Australian courts have accepted that there is still liability in tort.[120]

Contract or tort liability — does it matter?

10.31   The fact that concurrent liability now exists for lawyers in contract and tort can make a great difference in the choice of remedy to pursue.[121] We have already seen that sometimes a suit against the lawyer in contract is statute-barred and that the remedy has to be in tort. This can occur because the statute of limitations is usually longer for torts than for contracts. It is also important to determine when the injury is considered to have occurred. The rule according to the High Court is that:[122]

> ... damages for tort or for breach of contract are assessed as at the date of breach ... The rule will yield if, in the particular circumstances, some other date is necessary to provide adequate compensation.

The High Court has also held in a more recent decision, *Wardley Australia Ltd v Western Australia*,[123] that in relation to the negligent preparation of a document for a client the correct date for the statute to run is when the client actually suffered a loss and the damage is actually fulfilled. It will only start to run when the document is prepared if the chose of action acquired

---

115. [1939] 1 KB 194.
116. *Hedley Byrne & Co Ltd v Heller & Partners Ltd* [1964] AC 465.
117. See n 116 (above) at 502.
118. *Midland Bank Trust Co Ltd v Hett, Stubbs and Kemp* [1979] Ch 384 at 402–3, 411, 417 (HC).
119. See *Macpherson and Kelly v Kevin J Prunty & Associates* [1983] VR 573 and *Brickhill v Cook* [1984] 3 NSWLR 396.
120. *Aluminium Products Queensland Pty Ltd v Hill* [1981] 1 Qd R 33 and *Vulic v Bilinsky* [1983] 2 NSWLR 472.
121. The ideas in this section mainly come from two sources: D Ferguson, 'Professional Liability' (1973) 47 *ALJ* 592, 595, and J Sutton Jr and J Dzienkowski, *Cases and Material on Professional Responsibility of Lawyers*, West Publishing, St Paul, 1989, pp 144–5.
122. *Johnson v Perez, Creed v Perez* (1988) 63 ALJ 51 per Wilson, Toohey and Gaudron JJ.
123. (1992) 175 CLR 514.

by the client when the document was executed is regarded as a form of property which later loses value because of the negligence.[124]

There are a number of state court decisions which have stuck to the rule that the statute runs from the time the damages first occur and not from the time the client becomes aware of them.[125] For example, the New South Wales Court of Appeal in *Segal Litton & Chilton v Fleming* held that in a case of pure economic loss the statute started to run only when the plaintiff suffered an actual loss. Thus, it ran from when the property was sold in 1994 and not from 1989 when the solicitor negligently failed to remove certain rights of way from the title of land as instructed by the client.[126]

There is legislation in a number of jurisdictions stating the limitation period runs from the date which the plaintiff either knows, or ought with reasonable diligence to have found out, that damages have occurred and the defendant is at fault.[127] It would appear that this approach is more reasonable. Clients are usually inexperienced and will fail to recognise negligence when it occurs. It is for this reason that a cause of action for professional malpractice should not accrue until the client knows, or should know, all material facts that are essential to show that cause of action.[128]

It is very important that the time an action begins to run is when the client knows or should have known of the negligence, because it can take place many years before damage occurs. For example, as in the *Segal Litton & Chilton* case, the defect of title negligently not discovered or revealed by a solicitor can lead to damages many years later, when the client tries to sell the property and the defect is uncovered. In the area of malpractice many states in the United States have enacted specific statutes of limitations for malpractice actions. Another important difference between contract and tort liability is that a contract may have certain terms such as choice of the forum controlling the actions. If there is no such term an action in contract can be at the place of formation or the place of breach, or the place of the defendant's residence. In tort law such flexibility does not exist. Furthermore, a contract may contain clauses that may affect any suit on that contract (express disclaimer of liability), but will generally not influence a suit based in tort.[129]

10.32

There are also important differences between the two in relation to damages. A plaintiff can obtain a remedy in contract by proving only nominal damages and obtain costs. Plaintiffs suing in tort who fail to prove damages, except for defamation, will invariably have to pay their own costs as well as a large percentage of those of the defendant. In a malpractice suit

10.33

124. Ibid, at 531–2.
125. See, for example, the Full Court of the Supreme Court of Queensland in *Gillespie v Elliott* [1987] 2 Qd 509 and more recently *Martindale v Burrows* [1997] 1 Qld R 243.
126. [2002] NSWCA 262. See also *Walmsley v Cosentino* [2001] NSWCA 403 where the court said a client's action against a solicitor was not barred. The solicitor failed to advise his client of the client's right to sue him for failing to file the client's action within the statute of limitation for personal injuries in a motor vehicle accident.
127. For example, Limitation Act 1969 (NSW) s 50D.
128. A different view is that allowing a flexible approach to the statute of limitations is manifestly unfair to lawyers: see G Cross, 'Solicitors' Negligence and the Statute of Limitations — Can We Overcome the Injustices?' (October 1992) *Queensland Law Society J* 399.
129. See Barwick CJ, *MLC v Evatt* (1968) 122 CLR 556 at 570.

these legal costs are very high. The measure of damages may vary greatly between favourable decisions in tort as opposed to contract. For example, damages can be exemplary in tort and only nominal in contract. In tort law damages can be reduced because of comparative negligence, and no such defence exists under contract law. Finally, in tort law there may be statutory rights to obtain contribution from a joint tortfeasor but no such right exists under contract law.[130]

It should be noted that until recently barristers did not have any contractual capacity. Even with recent changes suits against barristers instructing solicitors, clients or others, will usually have to be taken in tort.

Non-client liability — wills

10.34   Historically, privity of contract requirements prohibited a cause of action against a lawyer by a third party.[131] *Donoghue v Stevenson*[132] destroyed the privity doctrine and the *Hedley Byrne*[133] decision ensured that liability applied to professionals. In recent years liability to third parties or non-clients has become one of the most important developments in extending the area of professional negligence. In the English case *Ross v Caunters*,[134] a firm of solicitors sent a will to the testator for execution. They instructed him that it should not be witnessed by the beneficiary, but failed to warn him that the beneficiary's spouse also could not witness the will. As a result of the solicitor's actions the will was invalid and the testator died with the beneficiary losing the bequest. The beneficiary claimed damages against them for the loss of benefits. The firm admitted negligence but argued that they owed a duty of care to the testator, their client, but did not owe such a duty to the beneficiary. The court found that a sufficient relationship of proximity existed so that it was in reasonable contemplation that carelessness on the part of the solicitors might be likely to cause damage to the beneficiary. The court did not find any consideration that ought to negate or limit the duty owed. Although the primary duty owed is to the client, extending that duty to the beneficiary 'far from diluting the solicitor's duty to his client, marches with it, and if anything, strengthens it'.[135] The doctrine in the *Ross* case was later approved by a 3:2 majority by the House of Lords in the *White* case.[136]

10.35   The *Ross* and *White* cases can be narrowly confined to negligence related to wills. They can also stand for the proposition that lawyers will be held liable to third parties if the intent of the client to benefit the third party was the primary or direct purpose of the legal transaction. The doctrine has obvious application in relation to wills. The New Zealand Court of Appeal,[137] the Supreme Court of British Columbia in Canada[138] and courts in the United

---

130. See, for example, *Macpherson and Kelly v Kevin J Prunty & Associates* [1983] VR 573.
131. *Winterbottom v Wright* (1842) 152 Eng Rep 402.
132. [1932] AC 562.
133. [1964] AC 465.
134. [1980] Ch 297 (HC). The principle in the *Ross* case has been approved of and followed by the House of Lords in *White v Jones* [1995] 2 AC 207; 1 All ER 691.
135. [1980] Ch 297 at 309 and 321.
136. *White v Jones* [1995] 1 All ER 691; [1995] 2 AC 207.
137. *Gartside v Sheffield Young & Ellis* [1983] NZLR 37.
138. *Smolinski v Mitchell* [1995] 10 WWR 68. See also *Earl v Wilhelm* (2000) 183 DLR (4th) 45.

States[139] have all extended solicitors' liability in relation to wills. The Supreme Court of Victoria adopted a different approach in the *Searle* case.[140] In that case the solicitor signed the will as one of the witnesses. The will was invalid because the solicitor and the other witness failed to sign the will in the presence of the testator. The beneficiaries' suit against the solicitor according to Lush J failed for the following reasons:

❑ The defendant owed no duty to the beneficiaries because the testator owed no duty to them to make the gift or to perfect the execution of his intention to make the gift. Therefore a question arises whether the solicitor acting on behalf of the testator should be subject to a duty of which the testator was free.

❑ The content of the solicitor's duties fell completely within the control of the testator. The latter could change instructions destroying any duty to the beneficiaries.

❑ There are serious problems of conflicting duties if solicitors owe a duty of care to any person other than their client in the discharge of their client's instructions.

❑ At the time of the gift the beneficiaries had no right or interest capable of protection at law or in equity or capable of enforcement by any remedy.

❑ There was no representation made to the beneficiaries. Furthermore, unlike bankers or auditors, solicitors are only concerned with their clients and it is irrelevant to them who the clients choose as beneficiaries.[141]

High Court cases

The High Court of Australia first considered solicitors' duties to third parties in *Hawkins v Clayton*.[142] The testatrix died in January 1975 and her solicitors made no attempt to locate the plaintiff until March 1981. The plaintiff, who was both the executor and beneficiary, was listed in the telephone directory during that period. During those six years the main asset of the estate, a house, had considerably deteriorated. A majority of 3:2 found that the solicitors had breached the duty of care they owed to the executor. Two of the majority, Deane and Gaudron JJ, applied the proximity test, with Deane J's judgment having the most detailed analysis. The third judge, Brennan J, did not use a proximity test. The minority judges, Mason CJ and Wilson J, also applied the proximity test but found that there was not a sufficient relationship of proximity. The majority holding was that solicitors assume a responsibility, and the client places a reliance on them, to make reasonable efforts to locate the executor named in the will on learning of the testator's death. Breach of this duty gives the executor the right to bring suit against the solicitors for any loss to the estate.

Deane J found that there was no settled practice on notifying executors at the death of a testator. His Honour therefore did not imply such a term under the lawyer–client contract. He said that the duty of care in tort transcends that contained in express or implied terms of contract and found that the primary relationship was between the firm and the testatrix, and not the plaintiff. The damages that resulted were pure economic loss.

10.36

---

139. For a discussion of these cases see *White v Jones* [1995] 2 AC 207 at 255.
140. *Searle v Perry* [1982] VR 193.
141. See n 140 (above) at 198–9.
142. (1988) 164 CLR 53; 62 ALR 240.

Deane J found that within the professional relationship there is an assumption of responsibility and reliance. These combined with the foreseeability of a real risk of economic loss, giving the relationship with the testatrix the necessary proximity with respect to the foreseeable economic loss. His Honour then said that this risk in relation to the executor was also foreseeable and therefore the proximity test was met. He found that at times there were special categories of cases where lawyers had to take positive steps to prevent economic loss. Deane J found such a category within a professional relationship because it involves 'the related elements of an assumption of responsibility and reliance'. Although he said that the present case was a borderline one, he found that the firm was under a duty, and had breached that duty, to take such positive steps.[143]

10.37 Gaudron J accepted the proximity test but unlike Deane J her Honour did not find that reliance was applicable. Instead, she stated her test of finding proximity as being:

> ... constituted by the reasonable expectation of a person ... that the other person will provide relevant information or give reliable information, if that expectation is known or ought reasonably to be known by the person against whom the duty is asserted.[144]

Her test does not answer the question whether or not the person has this duty. It also 'draws no distinction between the position of a solicitor and the position of any other person who is apprised of the facts'.[145]

Brennan J issued a curious judgment. He rejected the proximity test for determining the existence of a duty of care in cases dealing with pure economic loss. His Honour said that the *Hawkins* case was a new category of case. In determining the existence of a duty in those situations the court needs to determine 'whether there is some factor in addition to reasonable foreseeability of loss'. This factor Brennan J found present because 'a duty of disclosure arises from custody of the will and the purpose for which custody was accepted'.[146] Brennan J did not explain what it is about the nature of the will or the custody of the will, which could support a duty to disclose.[147] Furthermore, Brennan J's view that duty to disclose arises from the purpose of custody does not seem to lead to a duty:[148]

> For it is one thing to say that a purpose of holding a will in safe keeping is to ensure that the beneficiary benefits and it is another thing to say that the person who offers to hold it thereby accepts responsibility for achieving that purpose.

10.38 Mason CJ and Wilson J in their dissent reasoned similarly to Deane J except they did not find that the proximity test was met. They looked first at the nature of the contract and found that there were no express nor implied terms imposing the duty on the firm to take positive steps. Such a duty to take positive steps could only arise within the contract and not under tort law. They found that there was no necessary relationship of proximity, and the firm owed no duty of care to the executor.[149]

143. (1988) 62 ALR 240 at 255–7.
144. See n 143 (above) at 265.
145. F Field and R Gormly, '*Hawkins v Clayton* (1988) 164 CLR 53: Doubts Concerning the Ratio Decidendi' (1990) 12 *Sydney LR* 638, 649.
146. *Hawkins v Clayton* (1988) 62 ALR 240 at 244–6.
147. Field and Gormly (above), p 647.
148. Field (above).
149. *Hawkings v Clayton* (1988) 62 ALR 240 at 241–2.

The High Court in *Hill v Van Erp*,[150] by a 5:1 majority extended the liability to a solicitor who negligently executed a will, thereby denying a beneficiary the benefits under the will. The solicitor, Mrs Hill, in executing the will had the beneficiary's husband, Mr Van Erp, witness the will. This made the will invalid under s 15(1) of the Succession Act 1981 (Qld). The majority found that the solicitor was liable to the beneficiary in tort. The High Court referred extensively to the House of Lords decision in the *White* case. Brennan CJ stated that generally a solicitor's duty is owed solely to the client, but in the situation of testamentary instructions, the interests of both the client and the intended beneficiary are coincident. His Honour found that economic loss could be found in tort law even when there was no existing right or interest by the party seeking damages. It was sufficient to find damages if the plaintiff would have received a benefit but for the negligence of the defendant. Brennan CJ did not apply a proximity test, but did say that it was reasonably foreseeable that the beneficiary would be damaged by the solicitor's negligence. He held that the breach of the retainer for failing to carry out the client's wishes was also a breach to the intended beneficiary.[151]

10.39

Dawson J (with Toohey J agreeing generally with the reasons) applied the proximity test and found that solicitors who are employed to draw up a will have a relationship of proximity with the intended beneficiaries of those wills. A duty therefore exists to the beneficiaries by the solicitors to carry out the instructions with reasonable skill and care.[152] Dawson J in dicta tried to limit the scope of solicitors' liability. He said that the general rule is that solicitors do not owe a duty to anyone but the client. His Honour pointed out that the present case was different from such cases because it:[153]

10.40

> ... does not involve any conflict of duties on the part of the solicitor such as might occur in other situations, because the interests of the client are in all relevant respects the same as the interests of the intended beneficiary.

Gaudron J also applied a proximity test but in the context of the position of control. She said that the relationship between the solicitor and the beneficiary 'was not that characterised either by the assumption of responsibility or reliance. Rather, what is significant is that Mrs Hill was in a position of control over the testamentary wishes of her client and, thus, in a position to control' whether the beneficiary would receive the intended benefits of the testatrix. Gaudron J emphasised:[154]

> ... [the] importance of control as a factor in proximity and also as a factor governing the context of the duty of care. In the present case she finds that the loss of the legal right by the beneficiary was reasonably foreseeable by the solicitor. This combined with a duty of care resulting from the solicitor's position of control, makes the solicitor liable.

Unlike Gaudron J, Gummow J found that control is a factor, but not the dominating factor, in finding the solicitor liable. He said:

> Not only the foreseeability of harm to Mrs Van Erp ... but a complex of other factors combine to summon into existence a duty of care owed by Mrs Hill to

---

150. (1997) 142 ALR 687.
151. *Hill v Van Erp* (above) at 691–4.
152. *Hill v Van Erp* (above) at 699–703, 706–7.
153. *Hill v Van Erp* (above) at 707.
154. *Hill v Van Erp* (above) at 716–17.

Mrs Van Erp ... These matters include the extent to which the engagement of Mrs Hill by the testatrix plainly was designed to enhance the economic position of Mrs Van Erp as a particular individual, the control exercised (as a practical matter) over the realisation by the testatrix of her testamentary intentions towards Mrs Van Erp, and the closeness of the connection between the request by Mrs Hill to Mr Van Erp that he attest the will and the direct legal effect thereof, being the consequent failure of the gifts to Mrs Van Erp by the will.

His Honour then pointed out that:

There is also the public interest in the promotion of professional competence and the avoidance of disappointment of the wishes and expectations of testators and beneficiaries by negligent actions of solicitors.

Gummow J gave an extensive discussion of the proximity test. He said that his result in finding the solicitor liable 'may be expressed as consistent with a finding of sufficient proximity', but pointed out he did not apply the proximity doctrine as it is of 'limited use in the determination of individual disputes'.[155]

10.41   McHugh J in his dissent relied extensively on the reasons for not finding liability expressed in the *Searle* case. His Honour pointed out the difficulties in applying the proximity doctrine, and worried that the majority's decision would result in an increase in insurance premiums for legal practitioners, which would then result in increased costs of professional services.[156] He added that it:

... must also lead to a considerable, perhaps massive, expansion of the law of economic loss. Consider, for example, the case of the accountant who is paid a fee by a client to investigate the prospects of a business knowing that the client intends to purchase the business as a gift for a relative. Does the accountant owe the relative a duty of care? Is the accountant liable for the profits that the relative would have earned if, but for the accountant's negligence in assessing its viability, the business had been purchased? Does the insurance broker who is instructed to take out a life assurance policy for a client owe a duty of care to the proposed beneficiary? Is the broker liable to the beneficiary if, as the result of the broker's undue delay, the 'assured' dies before the policy is taken out? Moreover, it is difficult to see why the duty should be confined to gifts as opposed to benefits. In that event, professional persons, acting in purely commercial situations, may often owe duties to third parties who stand to benefit from the retainer of a professional person by a client.[157]

McHugh J then stated that the present case was no different to:[158]

... numerous other areas of social and business activity where a person is under no duty to prevent economic loss to another. Indeed, in many cases where the courts have held that there was no duty to prevent economic loss to the plaintiff, the plaintiff has actually relied on the defendant to perform a task. Individual investors, for example, rely on auditors and the Australian Securities Commission to monitor the activities of companies, and both have statutory duties in respect of their work. Yet in the absence of a representation and reliance or something similar, neither auditors nor the Commission owe a duty of care to prevent economic loss to investors.

---

155. *Hill v Van Erp* (above) at 744–5, 747–9.
156. *Hill v Van Erp* (above) at 725–6, 728.
157. *Hill v Van Erp* (above) at 728–9.
158. *Hill v Van Erp* (above) at 729–30.

The High Court's decision in *Hill* extends the liability for legal practitioners to non-client beneficiaries in negligent drafting and/or execution of a will. The *Hill* doctrine also includes liability to beneficiaries when a solicitor failed to carry out the deceased's instructions by direction when it became apparent that the testator could not sign his name and before he lapsed into unconsciousness.[159] It does not extend to a solicitor who failed to prepare a will when the testator at the time of her death had not finally determined to choose the appellant as the beneficiary. Although the Queensland Court of Appeal unanimously found no liability, two of the judges found that the solicitors had a duty to the 'hopeful' beneficiary.[160] This proposition that there is a duty to 'hopeful' beneficiaries appears to be incorrect.[161] It should also be noted that the *Hill* decision does not indicate how far the court is willing to extend this liability to other non-client areas of practice.

Non-client liability — other areas

As we have stated, the wills cases can be deemed to be an isolated extension of liability to non-clients. They can also stand for the proposition that lawyers will be held liable to third parties if the intent of the client to benefit the third party was the primary or direct purpose of the legal transaction. In *Hardware Services v Primac Association Ltd*,[162] the Queensland Supreme Court had to deal with duties to non-clients in a commercial case. The plaintiff had a three-year unregistered lease that contained an option to renew for three more years. Primac Association had given a covenant to the plaintiff to obtain from any purchaser of the property a covenant protecting the option. Primac had instructed its solicitors to register the lease and this covenant. The plaintiff had also orally and by writing requested Primac's solicitors to do this. The solicitors did not give any direct response to the request by the plaintiff. The plaintiff made no inquiry, nor employed anyone to check on the matter. The solicitors failed to register the lease and when the property was sold, the new owners evicted the plaintiff. The plaintiff sued Primac and its solicitors. 												**10.42**

Thomas J found that by disregarding the instructions the solicitors had breached their duty to the client but not to the plaintiff. He applied the reasoning of Lush J in the *Searle* case that there were serious conflict difficulties involving the owing of duties to non-clients. This, his Honour argued, was only a starting point as there are times:[163] 												**10.43**

> ... where a solicitor has contact with a non-client in which he [or she] creates reasonable expectations in that party, and where it is reasonable for that party to rely upon a duty of care being exercised towards him ... [I]t may well be that it is much more difficult for a third party to expect a solicitor to

159. *Summerville v Walsh* (unreported, NSW(C of A), 26 February 1998, CA40321/97, BC9800342).
160. *Queensland Art Gallery Board of Trustees v Henderson Trout II* [2000] QCA 93. For an excellent analysis of this case and the law relating to will-making duties see R Mortensen, 'Solicitors' Will-Making Duties' (2002) 26 *MULR* 4. A similar case to *Henderson Trout* in California came to the same conclusion: see *Radovich v Locke-Paddon* 35 Cal App 4th 946, 41 Cal Rptr 573 (1995).
161. Mortensen, ibid.
162. *Hardware Services v Primac Association Ltd* [1988] 1 Qd R 393.
163. *Hardware Services* (above) at 397–8.

take positive actions to advance or protect his interests than it would be to expect the solicitor to abstain from actions which might cause him harm ... [T]here is no reason why a solicitor will not be liable in tort to a non-client if he conducts himself in such a way as to raise reasonable expectations and reliance in that person that the solicitor will observe reasonable care towards him in the doing of an act or the omission to do an act.

10.44 Thomas J found that in the present case there was no response by the solicitors and thus the plaintiffs could not have had any reasonable expectations that the solicitors would act.[164] He based his views on a New Zealand Court of Appeal decision, *Allied Finance and Investments Ltd v Haddow*,[165] in which the solicitors were found liable to a third party where reliance by the plaintiff on the solicitor acting was contemplated. In that case the solicitor was not silent but had given a certificate to a money-lender that the client's yacht was free of any charges. A certificate is more than a mere statement but something less than an undertaking, but the solicitor's action had given the third party the wrong impression. Therefore a reasonable expectation that the yacht was unencumbered had been created for the third party.[166]

10.45 In a similar English case, *Gran Gelato Ltd v Richcliff (Group) Ltd*,[167] a High Court decision came to the opposite conclusion that there was no duty owed. In this case the defendant's solicitor had negligently answered the question as to whether there were any covenants or rights in the lease that could affect the plaintiff's interest. He had said that there were none to the lessor's knowledge. The answer was wrong and the plaintiff relied on this communication. The court found that the plaintiff already had a remedy. This was a valid reason for not extending the liability to the solicitors because of the fear of unforeseen consequences of an extension. The case appears to suggest that solicitors can be liable for negligent misstatements to third parties only when they expressly warrant either that the statement is true or that they have taken reasonable care. It also implies that solicitors only act as an agent for whatever their client tells them, and will not be responsible for the content of the information. This narrow decision seems to be in conflict with the rule established in *Hedley v Byrne*.[168]

10.46 The responsibility of solicitors to non-clients has been discussed in other cases. In *Thors v Weeke*[169] it was alleged by the applicants that the respondents' solicitors had an obligation to disclose to them that no title search had been taken or to have undertaken such a search themselves. Gummow J found that the applicants at the material times were represented by their own solicitors and that there did not exist an assumption of responsibility and reliance giving rise to a duty of care. In an English case, *Al-Kandari v JR Brown & Co*,[170] solicitors for the respondent (husband) in a custody matter

---

164. [1988] 1 Qd R 393 at 398.
165. [1983] NZLR 22 at 24–5.
166. See also *Eksteen v White* [2000] ANZ Conv R 128 where a reasonable expectation in a third party had been created by the lawyer.
167. [1992] 1 All ER 865.
168. The decision has been criticised for contradicting the *Hedley Byrne* rule. See M Whincup, 'Taking a solicitor's word' (12 June 1992) *New Law J* 820.
169. (1989) 92 ALR 131.
170. [1988] QB 665.

lodged its client's passport with the Kuwait Embassy to have the children's names removed. This action was against an undertaking of the husband that his passport would be retained by the respondent. The husband secured the passport from the Embassy and abducted the children to Kuwait. The appellant wife won in the Court of Appeal which held that the husband's solicitors owed her a duty of care. By agreeing to hold the passport the solicitors accepted responsibilities to their client, the appellant and the children. The court did point out that generally no duty of care is owed to an opposing party in an adversarial situation. The Tasmanian Supreme Court stated in the *Hagen* case that the possibility of liability to the opposing side does exist, but did not find any duty of care in that case.[171]

The New South Wales Supreme Court has held a firm of solicitors liable towards a non-client in a commercial situation. In *Hilton v Noss*[172] a cheque placed with a solicitor by a non-client for the purchase of a property with a client of the solicitor was deposited with the solicitor. The solicitor knew or should have known the purpose of the cheque and still negligently released it for his client's use and not for the purchase. Giles J held the solicitor liable for the misuse of the cheque because of his knowledge of the situation and because of various types of proximity between the non-client and the solicitor.

10.47

Two more recent cases in this area had different results concerning the liability of solicitors. In *Sainwill Pty Ltd v Williams*, the Western Australian Supreme Court held a solicitor who was acting for the purchaser of a business liable to the vendor. The solicitor had undertaken for the vendor to register the mortgage given as security. The vendor relied on the solicitor. As a result of his failure to carry out this task the vendor suffered damages.[173] In *Oakley Thompson and Co v Canik* the husband had failed to obtain secured consideration on transferring land. When the third party defaulted on the mortgage repayments the land was sold by the mortgagee. The husband blamed the third party's solicitor for transferring the land wrongly. The trial judge found the solicitor liable by applying the *Hill* case. The Full Family Court of Australia on appeal overruled, stating that the trial judge was wrong in extending the principles of a case dealing with beneficiaries to this situation.[174]

10.48

Non-client liability — United States

In the United States two approaches to liability to third party clients have been followed. The first is similar to that in Australia and England and is known as the third party beneficiary theory. The second approach is found in California and is called the balancing test. The balancing test recognises that an injured third party may deserve compensation even though there is no privity to the negligent lawyer. The California Supreme Court set out the test in a case not dealing with a lawyer, *Biakanja v Irving*.[175] The court held that:

10.49

---

171. *Hagen v McElwaine* (unreported, SC(Tas), Full Court, No 498/93, 16 September 1994, BC9400446).
172. (SC(NSW), Giles J, No 50261/94, 16 May 1995, unreported).
173. (unreported, SC(WA), Full Court, No 7363/97, 17 December 1997, BC9707363).
174. (1998) 145 FLR 438.
175. 320 P 2d 16 (Cal 1958).

The determination whether in a specific case the defendant will be held liable to a third person not in privity is a matter of policy and involves the balancing of various factors, among which are the extent to which the transaction was intended to affect the plaintiff, the foreseeability of harm to him [or her], the degree of certainty that the plaintiff suffered injury, the closeness of the connection between the defendant's conduct and the injury suffered, the moral blame attached to the defendant's conduct, and the policy of preventing future harm.

10.50   The balancing test has been used by California[176] and other jurisdictions in holding lawyers liable. For example, the Wisconsin Supreme Court applied the test in finding a lawyer liable to a beneficiary who suffered because of the lawyer negligently drawing up a will.[177] A later case in Wisconsin has limited the balancing test to cases involving negligent drafting of a will.[178] It has also been used in the state of Washington to find that no liability exists in the will area in relation to the legal representative of an estate. The Washington Supreme Court was not satisfied with a general balancing test and applied the following elements:[179]

(a) the extent to which the transaction was intended to benefit the plaintiff;

(b) the foreseeability of harm to the plaintiff;

(c) the degree of certainty that the plaintiff suffered injury;

(d) the closeness of the connection between the defendant's conduct and the injury;

(e) the policy of preventing future harm; and

(f) the extent to which the profession would be unduly burdened by a finding of liability.

In 2004 California extended its balancing test to include also 'the likelihood that imposition of liability might interfere with the attorney's ethical duties to the client and whether the imposition of liability would impose an undue burden on the profession'.[180] There are a number of other jurisdictions which have also accepted the balancing test.[181]

Section 73 of the Restatement (Third) Law Governing Lawyers 2000 deals with the 'duty to certain non-clients'. It states:

For the purposes of liability ... a lawyer owes a duty to use care ...

(2) To a non-client when and to the extent that

(a) the lawyer or (with the lawyer's acquiescence) the lawyer's client invites the non-client to rely on the lawyer's opinion or provision of other legal services, and the non-client so relies; and

(b) the non-client is not, under applicable law, too remote from the lawyer to be entitled to protection.

Under point (3) the lawyer owes a duty when:

(a) the lawyer knows that a client intends as one of the primary objectives of the representation that the lawyer's services benefit the non-client;

---

176. *Lucas v Hamm* 364 P 2d 685 (Cal 1961).
177. *Auric v Continental Casualty Company* 331 NW 2d 325 (Wis 1983).
178. *Green Springs Farms v Kersten* 401 NW 2d 816 (Wis 1987).
179. *Trask v Butler* 123 Wash 2d 835, 872 P 2d 1080 (Wash 1994).
180. *Boranian v Clark* (2004) 123 Cal App 4th 1002; 20 Cal Rptr 3d 405.
181. For example, see *Wisdom v Neal* 568 F Supp 4 (D NM 1982); *Licata v Specto* 225 A 2d 28 (Conn 1966); *Albright v Burns* 503 A 386 (NJ 1986); and *Traveler's Ins Co v Brees* 675 P 2d 1327 (Ariz 1983).

(b) such a duty would not significantly impair the lawyer's performance of obligations to the client, and the absence of such a duty would make enforcement of those obligations unlikely.

Under point (4) the lawyer's duty arises when:

(a) the lawyer's client is a trustee, guardian, executor, or fiduciary acting primarily to perform similar functions for the non-client;

(b) circumstances known to the lawyer make it clear that appropriate action by the lawyer is necessary with respect to a matter within the scope of the representation to prevent or rectify the breach of a fiduciary owed by the client to the non client, where

(i) the breach is a crime or fraud or

(ii) the lawyer has assisted or is assisting the breach;

(c) the non-client is not reasonably able to protect its rights; and

(d) such a duty would not significantly impair the performance of the lawyer's obligations to the client ...

The Comments to the section issue a warning as to its limited applicability. **10.51** They state: 'Making lawyers liable to non-clients, moreover, could tend to discourage lawyers from vigorous representation. Hence, a duty of care to non-clients arises only in the limited circumstances described in the Section and must be applied in light of those conflicting concerns ... Similarly, a lawyer representing a client in an arm's length business transaction does not owe a duty of care to opposing non-clients, except in the exceptional circumstances described in this Section.' The Comments also state that liability will only arise in transactional settings and not in litigation and point out that the cause of action of a non-client is in substance identical to a claim of negligent misrepresentation.

Under the third party beneficiary test:[182]

> ... [to] establish a duty owed by the defendant attorney to the non-client, the non-client must challenge and prove that the intent of the client to benefit the non-client third party was the primary or direct purpose of the transaction or relationship.

The test has mainly been used to find liability in the negligent drafting and execution of wills and has sometimes been limited to that area.[183] The test has also been applied in other kinds of cases.

In Illinois, the court applied the third party beneficiary theory in relation to a divorce case. The defendant lawyer had represented the plaintiffs' mother and the divorce settlement required the father to maintain all four children as the prime beneficiaries in his life insurance policy. The father named his new wife as beneficiary and the children sued their mother's lawyer for failing to ensure that the husband's employer and/or the insurance company was aware of the settlement provision. The court found that the primary purpose of the lawyer–client relationship was to obtain a divorce decree and not to guarantee the children's continued welfare.[184] In a later Illinois case, the court found the lawyer negligent when the lawyer representing the buyer sent an opinion letter to the seller stating that he had no reason to suspect buyers' representations and warranties were untrue

---

182. *Pelham v Griesheimer* 440 NE 2d 96 at 99 (Ill 1982).
183. See E Lorton, 'Attorney Malpractice: Negligence and Liability to Third-Parties' (1993) 6 *Georgetown J of Legal Ethics* 1097, 1103–6.
184. *Pelham v Griesheimer* 440 NE 2d 96 at 97–101.

or misleading. The duty was limited only to the opinion letter and did not extend to investigation and disclosure of matters beyond the scope of the letter.[185]

10.52 In a New York case the theory was applied in a commercial situation. A lawyer representing a group of limited partnerships issued an opinion letter that was sent directly to a creditor for the purpose of obtaining a loan. The lawyer's opinion indicated that the creditor and its assignee under a note purchase agreement could rely on his opinion. The information he provided turned out to be erroneous and the assignee successfully sued the lawyer for negligence. The court said that the specific purpose of the document was to benefit the third party and therefore there was a legitimate action.[186]

Although both tests are firmly entrenched as exceptions to the privity rule, according to one author the recent decisions are not expanding the exceptions already made. A number of cases have shown that the courts are restricting the scope of liability to third parties.[187] For example, a California Supreme Court decision held that while an accountant could be potentially liable for negligent misstatements in an audit, the accountant had no general duty of care to a non-client. The accountant would only be liable if the 'third party relied on the misrepresentation in a transaction that the accountant intended to influence'.[188] But if it is foreseeable that reliance will occur and the third party relies on misleading information of the lawyer, a duty will exist. This liability will occur when the lawyer prepares a misleading instrument such as a private offering statement for his or her client's corporate debenture.[189] Liability will also occur when a lawyer drafts a misleading report to help his or her client sell a property.[190]

Sometimes a court will not impose a duty on lawyers to exercise reasonable care towards a non-client if such a duty 'would potentially conflict with the duty the attorney owes to his or her client'. This view is based on the fact that: 'It would be inimical to the adversary system for an adverse party to be allowed to rely on an opposing party's attorney.'[191] This situation occurred in a Massachusetts divorce and child custody proceeding. The lawyer had represented the husband. The wife suspected the husband had sexually abused the children and in the lower court obtained an order denying the husband visitation rights. On appeal the husband had been granted supervised visitation rights and the supervisor appointed had been recommended by the husband's lawyer. In the course of the first visitation the husband forced the supervisor out of the car and fled the country with the children. The wife sued the lawyer, claiming the supervisor was incompetent and the lawyer knew or should have known about the husband's intent to abduct the children. Thus, he had breached his duty to the wife and the children. The Massachusetts Supreme Court rejected the

185. *Geaslen v Berkson, Gorov & Levin Ltd* 220 Ill App 3d 600, 581 NE 2d 138 (1st D 1991) at 607–8.
186. *Vereins-Und Westbank, AG v Carter* 691 F Supp 704 at 706–12 (NY 1988).
187. Lorton (above), pp 1106–10.
188. *Bily v Arthur Young & Co* 834 P 2d 745 at 770 (Cal 1992).
189. *Molecular Technology Corp v Valentine* 925 F 2d 910 (1991, 6th Circuit Court of Appeals).
190. *Petrillo v Bachenberg* 139 NJ 472, 655 A 2d 1354 (1995).
191. *LaMare v Basbanes* 418 Mass 274, 276 (1994).

wife's argument on the basis of the potential conflict with the duty the lawyer owed to the husband and the potential duty owed to the children.[192]

The courts have also relied on s 552 of the Restatement (Second) of Torts which states: 'One who, in the course of his business, profession or employment, or in any other transaction in which he has a pecuniary interest, supplies false information for the guidance of others in their business transactions, is subject to liability for pecuniary loss caused to them by their justifiable reliance upon the information if he fails to exercise reasonable care or competence in obtaining or communicating the information.' Section 552 was applied by the Texas Supreme Court and also by the 5th Circuit. In both cases the courts held the lawyers had a duty not to make negligent misrepresentations to a third party involved in the transaction.[193]

In the most recent Californian case in 2004, the California Supreme court said lawyers could be held liable to a non-client for malicious prosecution. In *Zamous v Stroud*[194] the California Supreme Court said that if lawyers continued to prosecute a lawsuit after they discovered that there was a lack of probable cause, the defendant had a right to sue those lawyers.

ADVOCATE'S IMMUNITY

Introduction

In 1860, barristers in England were granted unrestricted immunity from litigation for negligence. In *Swinfen v Lord Chemsford*[195] the court held:

10.53

> An advocate is not responsible for ignorance of law or any mistake of fact, or being less eloquent or less astute than he was expected to be; and ... if he [or she] is acting with perfect good faith with a single view to the interests of his client, he is not responsible for any mistake or indiscretion or error of judgment of any sort.

The immunity doctrine was not tested for over 100 years until the House of Lords upheld its validity in 1967 in *Rondel v Worsley*.[196] The scope of the immunity, including its application to solicitors, has been the major source of litigation since the *Rondel* case. The present status in Australia is that the immunity exists for all advocates, for work that is:[197]

> ... so intimately connected with the conduct of the cause in court that it can fairly be said to be a preliminary decision affecting the way that the cause is to be conducted when it comes to a hearing. The protection should not be given any wider application than is absolutely necessary in the interests of the administration of justice ...

The situation in Australia seemed likely to change in light of the decision of the House of Lords in *Hall & Co v Simons*.[198] This case totally removed

---

192. Ibid, at 277.
193. *McCamish, Martin, Brown & Loeffler v F E Appling Interests* 991 SW 2d 787 (Tex 1999) affirming 953 SW2d 405 (Tex App, Texarkana 1997) and *First National Bank of Durant v Trans Terra Corporation* 142 F 3d 802 (5th Cir 1998) adopting the Texarkana Court of Appeals view.
194. (2004) 32 Cal 4th 958, 960 and 973.
195. (1860) 5 H & N 890.
196. *Rondel v Worsley* [1969] 1 AC 191.
197. McCarthy J in the Court of Appeal in *Rees v Sinclair* [1974] 1 NZLR 180 at 187.
198. *Hall & Co v Simons* [2000] 3 All ER 673.

the immunity for lawyers in England and Wales. Instead of following *Hall*, the High Court in *D'Orta-Ekenaike v Victoria Legal Aid*[199] by a majority of 6:1 retained the immunity doctrine. We will discuss the *Hall* and *D'Orta-Ekenaike* cases below in detail.

10.54 The discussion of the immunity doctrine is set out as follows:

- ❏ the important cases that established the doctrine;
- ❏ the scope of the doctrine;
- ❏ the situation in Canada, the United States, Europe and other countries;
- ❏ arguments for and against the immunity;
- ❏ removal of the doctrine in England; and
- ❏ retention of the doctrine in Australia.

One vital question that should be present throughout is why lawyers, as compared to other occupations and professions, are the only group granted an immunity from litigation for negligence.

Establishing the immunity

10.55 The alleged negligence complained of in the *Rondel* case was that the barrister, in defending the plaintiff on a criminal charge of grievous bodily harm, failed to ask questions or call evidence to counteract the prosecution's evidence that the plaintiff had used a knife. The House of Lords on the basis of public policy upheld the barrister's immunity not only to work done in the conduct of the trial, but also to work where litigation was pending. The latter included the drafting of letters, drawing of pleadings and the interlocutory stages up to trial. The public policy reasons were:

- ❏ If barristers could be sued they would be so concerned for their clients' rights that they would not observe their duty to the court.
- ❏ That the 'cab-rank' rule meant that barristers in their field of practice had no choice but to represent anyone who could pay their fee.
- ❏ The fear of negligence suits would make barristers over-cautious and prolix in presenting cases, causing inefficient processing of court proceedings.
- ❏ That barristers should be treated as other actors in the judicial process, such as judges, jurors and witnesses, who are immune from civil litigation.
- ❏ Allowing negligence actions would result in relitigation of cases (sometimes with a different standard of proof), leading to lateral attacks on judgments. This would result in bringing the judicial process into disrepute.[200] The majority in *Rondel* in dictum said that solicitors acting as advocates had the same immunity as barristers.[201] This latter view was affirmed in the next House of Lords decision, *Saif Ali v Sydney Mitchell & Co.*[202]

These reasons will be revisited in the last part of this section when we look at the *Hall* and *D'Orta-Ekenaike* cases.

10.56 In *Saif Ali* the plaintiff had been a passenger in a vehicle involved in a collision. There was no doubt that he was entitled to compensation from one of the drivers involved in the accident. Due to the negligence of his solicitors and barrister an action was brought against the wrong party.

199. [2005] HCA 12.
200. The summary of the public policy reasons are stated by Wilson J in *Giannarelli and Shulkes v Wraith* (1988) 81 ALR 417 at 433.
201. *Rondel v Worsley* [1969] 1 AC 191 at 232, 243–4, 265–7 and 284–5.
202. [1980] AC 198 at 215, 224, 227.

Before this could be remedied the statute of limitations had run out and his avenue of redress was to sue his solicitors. The solicitors joined the barrister as a third party. The House of Lords by a 3:2 decision adopted and applied the 'intimately connected' to litigation test from the *Rees* case. It held that the barrister's action of giving the wrong advice leading to the expiration of the limitation period fell 'well outside the immunity area'. In upholding the immunity doctrine Lord Diplock specifically refused to list what type of work would satisfy the *Rees* test. He said that only two of the public policy reasons given in *Rondel* were valid. These were that barristers should be granted the same general immunity from civil liability as other persons participating in the proceedings; and in order to maintain the integrity of public justice, cases should not be allowed to be relitigated by collateral means.[203]

The decision in *Saif Ali* was based on the notion that if the client could never have his or her claim litigated there could be no connection of the matter to litigation. In reality this view is one based on hindsight. Until the statute of limitations passed there was no doubt that the matter fell within the scope of the immunity. All the work done was in order to litigate or to settle the matter based on the threat of litigation.

10.57 The *Rees v Sinclair* case took place in a fused jurisdiction, New Zealand. Another case in a fused profession took place in South Australia. The *Feldman* case[204] was decided before the *Saif Ali* case and Bray CJ's broad immunity doctrine has not been followed by the later High Court decision in *Giannarelli* discussed below. Bray CJ did point out that a solicitor–barrister was still liable for actions while acting as a solicitor:

> If as counsel he [or she] advised himself as solicitor at some stage in the pre-trial history that there was enough evidence on the topic then, even if he acted negligently, he would be immune from suit. If, however, as solicitor he failed to obtain material which it was within his power to obtain to put before himself as counsel for advice on evidence, or if he failed to obtain such material after being advised by himself as counsel that was necessary to do, then it may well be that he would be liable in negligence.

Australian position

10.58 The High Court upheld the immunity doctrine, adopting the test in *Rees v Sinclair* and negating a statutory provision in the *Giannarelli* case. In that case plaintiffs sued their solicitors and barristers who had acted for them on charges of perjury. They argued that the defendants had negligently failed to advise them. They had also failed to make a plea on their behalf that evidence given by them before a Royal Commission was inadmissible against them at their committal and trial by virtue of s 6DD of the Royal Commission Act 1902 (Cth).

Before the High Court decided the *Giannarelli* case it was unclear whether the legislation fusing the profession in 1891 removed barristers' immunity.[205] It stated that:[206]

---

203. See n 202 (above) at 210ff.
204. *Feldman v A Practitioner* (1978) 18 SASR 238.
205. See P Heerey, 'Looking Over the Advocate's Shoulder: An Australian View of *Rondel v Worsley*' (1968) 42 *ALJ* 3, 8.
206. Now s 10(2) of the Legal Profession Practice Act 1958 (Vic).

... every barrister shall be liable for negligence as a barrister to the client on whose behalf he [or she] has been employed to the same extent as a solicitor was [on the date of adoption of the Act] liable to his client for negligence as a solicitor.

There seemed little doubt that at the time it was enacted the intention of the parliament was to abolish immunity for all Victorian lawyers. This view was supported by three of the judges (Deane, Toohey and Gaudron JJ), but the majority (Mason CJ, Brennan, Wilson and Dawson JJ), some using very contorted reasoning, found that immunity had not been removed. The main reason given was that nineteenth-century cases did not establish that a solicitor was liable to a client in negligence for work undertaken as an advocate in court. The decision was based on the lack of authority for finding negligence and the fact that solicitors did not have a right of audience before a superior court in England or Victoria. Therefore, the legislation did not make barristers liable for work undertaken as an advocate.[207] Toohey J, with Gaudron J agreeing, looked at *Cordery* and analysed the nineteenth-century cases dealing with solicitors. He came to the conclusion that there was no distinction made between the conduct of solicitors in or associated with court and other work. Solicitors had been held liable in a number of cases and the legislation extended this right to being sued to barristers.[208]

10.59 In relation to the common law right, the court decided by 4:1 (Toohey and Gaudron JJ not deciding), that the immunity extended to all lawyers for work intimately associated with litigation. Mason CJ, Wilson and Dawson JJ used as their reasons relitigation of the case and the immunity of other participants to express their views. Another reason adopted by Mason CJ, Wilson and Brennan JJ, was the advocate's duty to the court.[209] Three judges, Mason CJ, Wilson and Dawson JJ, directly or indirectly approved of the test in *Rees v Sinclair*[210] while Brennan J indirectly approved the test by approving the view taken in *Saif Ali*.[211]

It would appear that even with very different reasoning the High Court has entrenched the immunity doctrine in Australia and the court is unlikely to reverse its decision. The notion that every wrong should attract a remedy is still very strong in our community and even within the judiciary. A number of cases have already been decided as to the scope of the doctrine. In a case similar to *Saif Ali*, the Court of Appeal in New South Wales found a barrister negligent for advising that the matter could only be brought in Queensland where there was a three-year statute of limitation, when it could be brought in New South Wales where there was a six-year statute of limitation.[212]

---

207. See Mason CJ in *Giannarelli v Wraith* (1988) 81 ALR 417 at 423–4.
208. *Giannarelli* (above) at 457–9.
209. *Giannarelli* (above) at 421–3, 433–6, 439, 449–51.
210. *Giannarelli* (above) at 424, 437, 451.
211. *Giannarelli* (above) at 439.
212. *MacRae v Stevens* (unreported, CA(NSW), Full Court, No 40118/93, 18 October 1996, BC9604869).

Scope of the immunity

Applying the intimately connected test

We have already pointed out in the *Feldman* case that a solicitor–barrister **10.60**
can be found negligent when performing solicitor work for failure to obtain
material such as relevant witnesses. That case did not apply the intimately
connected test. It therefore has limited application in light of the adoption
of that test by the High Court. Another New Zealand case which did apply
the test is *Biggar v McLeod*.[213] In that case the plaintiff alleged that her
lawyer acting for her in matrimonial proceedings had misinformed her of
the terms of settlement. The solicitor–barrister talked to the client after oral
evidence had been taken and then settled the matter. It was held that the
immunity covered advice given by a lawyer concerning a settlement
proposed during the course of a trial.[214]

This settlement took place during the trial, but the vast majority of **10.61**
settlements are prior to trial. The English Court of Appeal recently had to
deal with a settlement of a family dispute prior to trial. It looked at the
proximity of the settlement to the hearing and since it occurred the day
before the hearing it was held to be 'intimately connected' with the conduct
of the case.[215] Many of these settlements are either reached at a pre-trial
conference and are often then ratified by the court or are without prejudice
agreements reached during the course of the action. It would appear that
advice and negotiations in this area are 'intimately connected' to litigation
because they affect the conduct of the case. If the settlement is before a
court officer the arguments for the doctrine would come into play.
Furthermore, encouraging pre-trial settlements is supported by the courts
and the community and there is a good public policy argument that these
settlements would be impeded if they became subject to collateral attack.[216]
The fact that the immunity doctrine has been removed in the United
Kingdom now means that settlement offers are subject to negligence claims.
But as seen in the most recent House of Lords decision, proving the
negligence of the advocate in this area will be difficult[217] (see below).

This approach may fail in light of the New South Wales Court of Appeal **10.62**
decision in *Donellan v Watson*.[218] In that case a solicitor made a simple error
in the mention of a matter in court. He had provided the incorrect terms of
a settlement to the District Court. As a result of the solicitor's actions the
convictions were quashed but the appeals were not withdrawn. The matter
was not contested and the orders were made by consent. The solicitor was
doing what most lawyers would consider a mechanical task. He was sued
and the Court of Appeal rejected the application of the immunity doctrine.
The reasons given by Mahoney J (Waddell J agreeing) were that the
rationale for the doctrine given in *Saif Ali* and *Giannarelli*, as mentioned
above, were not present. Since this was an uncontested hearing there was
no question of collateral attack on the court's findings. Furthermore, there

---

213. *Biggar v McLeod* [1978] 2 NZLR 9 (CA).
214. *Biggar's* case at 10–12.
215. *Kelley v Corston* [1997] 4 All ER 466.
216. Mills (above), pp 33–4.
217. *May v Pettman Smith (a firm)* [2005] 1 WLR 581.
218. (1990) Aust Torts Reports ¶81–066.

was no problem of freedom to speak freely, nor was the counsel under attack for the manner in which he presented the case. The third judge, Handley J, applied the law of agency. He found that the agent solicitor had negligently acted in excess of his authority and the question of immunity did not arise in these circumstances.

10.63 Mills has pointed out that the *Donellan* case shows not only how the immunity doctrine can be restricted and modified:[219]

> ... but it also highlights the complexity of the law concerning professionals' liability. For not only is there the dichotomy of the law of contract and tort, but also the law of agency and fiduciary duties, not to mention the potential liability under the Trade Practices Act.

The issue of whether the immunity doctrine applies to liability under the Trade Practices Act is a very present issue. Two judges of the High Court had opposite views on the issue. Gaudron J said that once s 52 of that Act applies, the law of negligence is not applicable and there is no need to consider the immunity doctrine.[220] By contrast, Callinan said that the immunity doctrine did not apply only to a claim of negligence but also to statutory liability.[221]

10.64 Another area of controversy has been that of the drafting of pleadings. The English Court of Appeal in the *Somasundaram* case[222] found that advice as to the pleadings was intimately connected to litigation, but refused to extend the immunity to solicitors in the drafting of the pleadings. The court held that their immunity was only present when solicitors acted as advocates. The New South Wales Court of Appeal agreed that the immunity does extend to a barrister's advice on the pleadings. In the *Keefe* case[223] the barrister failed to advise the appellant prior to and during the trial to seek interest. The statement of claim was drafted without this provision. The inclusion of interest is something that is a mechanical item and was not essential to the conduct of the litigation. Gleeson CJ (with whom Meagher J agreed) approved the application of the immunity doctrine. He found that work done out of court was 'inextricably interwoven so that the immunity must extend' to this work. He said this included such matters as interviewing the plaintiff and any other potential witnesses, giving advice and making decisions about what witnesses to call and not to call, working up any necessary legal arguments, giving consideration to the adequacy of the pleadings and, if appropriate, causing any necessary steps to be undertaken to have the pleadings amended. Matters of that kind would ordinarily be under active consideration, as required, not only prior to the commencement of the hearing, but also

---

219. Mills (above), p 33. The author could also have included liability under the Corporations Act 1989 (Cth). See T Middleton, 'Liability of Solicitors Under the Corporations Act 1989 (Cth)' (October 1992) *Queensland Law Society J* 429. For example, under s 1006(2)g a solicitor is liable for a deceptive or misleading statement in a prospectus.
220. *Boland v Yates* (2000) 74 ALJR 209 at 281.
221. *Boland v Yates* (2000) 74 ALJR 209 at 281. For a discussion of this issue see G Hancock and A Baron, 'Practitioner Immunity following *Boland v Yates*' (June 2000) *Law Institute J(Vic)* 52, 56–57.
222. *Somansundaram v M Julius Melchior & Co* [1989] 1 All ER 129.
223. *Keefe v Marks* (1989) 16 NSWLR 713.

throughout the hearing and right up until the time of the conclusion of the proceedings.[224]

In light of the decision in *Donellan* I believe the views of the dissenting judge are more accurate. Priestly JA argued that the interest claim was not 'sufficiently significant' to have a bearing on the conduct of the hearing:

10.65

> In many cases the only preparation necessary in regard to the interest component of a claim, which is not part of the cause of action, will be the need to bear in mind that the claim should be made and readiness to put some simple arithmetical submissions to the court. These matters are essentially incidental and not integral to the establishment of the cause of action in a negligence case and hence the conduct of that case in court.

Thus, his Honour concluded that failing to include the interest component in the claim should not fall under the protection of the category of intimately connected with the conduct of the litigation.[225]

The Western Australian decision in *Laird v Mossenson*[226] allowed a claim in negligence by a client on the grounds that her solicitor had improperly presented her case. As a result of the solicitor's court action she lost any chance of having a successful application under the Inheritance (Family and Dependants Provision) Act 1972. The court rejected the immunity doctrine on the basis that the solicitor was not acting as counsel. Wallace J (Pidgeon J agreeing) relied on Toohey J's minority judgment in *Giannarelli* that found a number of cases holding solicitors liable for negligence in the conduct of litigation. Toohey J did point out that there 'was room for debate as to whether any of the cases cited are truly cases of in-court negligence'. But, as Marks J (in the lower court) pointed out, in those cases 'no distinction was made between conduct in or associated with court and other work'.[227] It is debatable whether this decision is correct in light of the High Court stating in the *D'Orta-Ekenaike* case that solicitors are to be treated like barristers in applying the intimately related test.[228]

10.66

The judges in the *Laird* case appeared to have a similar problem to that faced by Bray CJ in the *Feldman* case: see **10.57**. The difficulty is determining what a solicitor's duties are in a fused profession, when a solicitor is acting as a solicitor–barrister. As I just stated, the judges of the High Court have stated there is no distinction between a solicitor advocate and a barrister advocate. Handley JA in the *Donellan* case does find that the immunity between them is not co-extensive. He said:[229]

10.67

> ... [a] solicitor enters into a binding contract with the client which may either expressly or by necessary implication limit the solicitor's authority as the agent of the client, in the conduct of the litigation ... For example, a solicitor ... is bound to take reasonable care to properly instruct competent counsel ... [A] solicitor who briefs himself [or herself] may be liable in negligence of briefing an incompetent advocate although not liable in negligence as advocate.

---

224. *Keefe* (above) at 718.
225. *Keefe* (above) at 725.
226. (1990) Aust Torts Reports ¶81–058 (SC Full Ct).
227. *Giannarelli v Wraith* (1988) 81 ALR 417 at 458.
228. [2005] HCA 12 at para 90.
229. (1990) Aust Torts Reports ¶81–066 at 68,377.

What will happen in reference to the scope of the immunity doctrine, in light of the *D'Orta-Ekenaike* case, will have to still be decided on a case-by-case basis.

Liability for advice and to be disciplined

10.68   In *Tahche v Abboud*[230] the court found no immunity when an accused sought to sue prosecuting counsel and solicitors for failing to disclose information relevant to the accused's trial. The court said that 'discovery cannot be said to be "intimately connected" to the presentation in court of the case of the party giving discovery'.

It appears that the giving of advice by a barrister will not be protected by the immunity doctrine. This is what happened when a barrister was found negligent for his advice in *NRMA Ltd v Morgan*[231] and also in *Hodgins v Cantrell.*[232] In England the courts have made a distinction between tactical planning, which comes under the doctrine, and strategic planning, which does not attract the immunity.[233] These distinctions are no longer relevant in England due to the House of Lords decision in *Hall*: see **10.76**. They are still of use for courts in Australia while we deal with the complications that result from applying the flexible 'intimately related' test.

The inability to sue because of the immunity doctrine is not a barrier to disciplinary action. A barrister negligently drew up terms of a settlement agreement that was read and adopted by the court and had not been agreed to by the client. The barrister was immune but the New South Wales Legal Services Tribunal unanimously found that the barrister's failure amounted to negligence that constituted 'unsatisfactory professional conduct'. One of the two barristers' members felt that there could be no penalty because the immunity doctrine extended to disciplinary proceedings, but the other two members, including one barrister, held that the doctrine did not extend to the proceedings and invoked the penalty.[234]

High Court revisits the doctrine

10.69   In *Boland v Yates,*[235] decided before the House of Lords *Hall* case, the High Court had a chance to re-examine the doctrine. In *Boland* only Gaudron and Kirby JJ felt that the doctrine adopted in *Giannarelli* should be reopened. Gaudron J in a short opinion stated she would have reopened the immunity matter if the question had arisen. She said: 'In my view, proximity — more precisely, the nature of the relationship mandated by that notion — may exclude the existence of a duty of care on the part of legal practitioners with respect to work in court. Whatever the position, it

---

230. [2002] USC 42.
231. [1999] NSWSC 407. The barrister was held liable for $7m but the decision was reversed on appeal in *Heydon v NRMA Ltd* [2000] NSWCA 374. The fact that the barrister won on appeal does not negate the fact that he still had been exposed to a negligence action for his advice.
232. (1997) MVR 481 SC(NSW).
233. *Atwell v Perry & Co* [1998] 4 All ER 65; *Hall & Co v Simons* [1999] 1 FLR 679. These cases are referred to in B Hocking, 'Barristers' immunity: an update' (October 1999) *Proctor (Queensland Law Society J)* 29.
234. 'Unsatisfactory Professional Conduct in respect of a barrister' (1998) 3 *Legal Profession Disciplinary Reports* 1.
235. *Boland v Yates* (2000) 74 ALJR 209.

is one that derives from the law of tort, not notions of "immunity from suit".[236]

Kirby J, unlike the other judges in *Boland* felt that the immunity issue needed to be addressed as the primary issue in the case. He said if immunity was found there would be no need to look at the complex issues involved in determining the standard of care. Kirby J approved the approach of Priestly J in the *Keefe* case and that of the Full Federal Court in the present case. He argued that a barrister's negligent advice as to whether a cause of action exists does not fall within the ambit of the doctrine. His reasons are that immunity derogates from the 'normal accountability for wrong-doing to another which is an ordinary feature of the rule of law and fundamental civil rights'. He says other professions are held accountable who make 'decisions at least as difficult and often as urgent as those typically made by legal practitioners, including advocates'. Secondly, he argues that the 'historical, social and professional circumstances' on which the doctrine is founded have radically changed leading to the need to reconsider its foundations or at least the scope of the doctrine. Thirdly, many of the circumstances under which the doctrine was developed in England are now 'inapplicable to contemporary Australia'. The structure of the present profession in Australia is vastly different with a far larger bar and many solicitor advocates from large firms. Furthermore, professional indemnity insurance is now a standard requirement. He then dealt with issues such as duty to the court, the floodgate argument and that solicitor advocates are included. He pointed out that in *Boland* the solicitors should not have protection of the doctrine because at no time did they act as advocates. Instead they should be judged by the proper standard of care in relation to their actions. Finally, he extensively examines *Giannarelli*, which was a criminal case. He points out that in criminal cases more 'stringent safeguards are adopted ... to prevent a miscarriage of justice. The highly developed rules and practices established to consider a suggestion of wrongful conviction may make it more appropriate to recognise further restrictions on the availability of proceedings against a practitioner in respect of the conduct of criminal rather than civil proceedings.' Kirby J then rejected the adoption of the 'intimately connected' test. He found the test as 'impermissibly vague'. He said the doctrine should be confined to the 'in-court conduct during proceedings before a court or like tribunal'. He concluded that the practitioner's actions did not fall within the doctrine. He then examined the standard of care and found that they were not negligent.[237]

Since the *Boland* case the immunity doctrine was upheld by Burchett AJ in the Supreme Court of New South Wales in *Abriel v Rothman*,[238] rejected by the Supreme Court in Victoria, in relation to discovery, in *Tahche v Abboud*,[239] and by the High Court in the *D'orta-Ekenaike* case. In the latter case Kirby J rejected his view in *Boland* and held that the doctrine should be totally removed.

---

236. *Boland* (above) at 230–1.
237. *Boland* (above) at 234–9.
238. [2002] NSWSC 1056.
239. [2002] VSC 42.

The position in the United States, Canada, Europe and other countries

10.70   The immunity doctrine has never found favour in the United States. It has been accepted that mere errors in judgment do not bring liability, but this has never been extended to a broad view of no liability for errors in litigation. The arguments given for immunity have been rejected by commentators either because they have no basis or are irrelevant in American law.[240] United States courts have recognised a common law immunity for prosecutors. The prosecutors are seen as in the same category as judges and there is a 'concern that harassment by unfounded litigation would cause a deflection of the prosecutor's energies from his public duties, and the possibility that he would shade his decisions instead of exercising the independence of judgment required by his public trust'.[241] The United States Supreme Court said the immunity for prosecutors was absolute for conduct 'intimately associated with the judicial phase of the criminal process' and qualified in other areas.[242] The courts in several states have upheld the immunity granted by statute to public defenders.[243] Furthermore, as a prerequisite to suing defence counsel some courts have required that defendants prove they were not guilty.[244]

10.71   The Canadian position established in 1863 in *Leslie v Ball*[245] was that lawyers could be sued for the manner in which they conducted a case in court. The matter was not litigated for more than 100 years. In *Demarco v Ungaro*, Krever J in the Ontario High Court of Justice applied *Leslie v Ball* and held that there was no immunity doctrine. Krever J had the benefit of the House of Lords decision in *Rondel* and concluded that the development of law in Ontario under a fused profession had taken a different path to that in England. He said there was no empirical evidence that dire consequences would result from not having an immunity doctrine.[246] As Wilson J pointed out in the *Giannarelli* case, this decision has received general acceptance from many commentators.[247] The House of Lords in the *Hall* case also uses this decision and the Canadian experience as important support for removing the immunity doctrine.

The position for countries in the European Union is there is no immunity. Lord Steyn in the *Hall* case does point out that 'the control of a civilian judge over the proceedings is greater than is customarily exercised by a judge in England', but recent reforms to civil procedure has reduced the differences. In the criminal law area the role of an English judge continues to be far more passive. But even accepting the differences, Lord Steyn states

---

240. *Wolfram* (above), pp 216–7.
241. *Imbler v Pachtman* 424 US 409 at 422–4.
242. *Imbler* (above), p 430.
243. *Morgano v Smith* 879 P 2d 735 (Nev 1994); *Browne v Robb* 583 A 2d 949 (Del 1990); *Bradshaw v Joseph* 666 A 2d 1175 (Vt 1995); and *Coyazo v State of New Mexico* 897 P 2d 234 (NM 1995). These cases are cited by Lord Hope of Craighead in the *Hall* case.
244. For example, see *Carmel v Lunney* 511 N E 2d 1126 (NY 1987). See also G Hazard Jr, S Koniak and R Crampton, *The Law and Ethics of Lawyering*, 2nd ed, Foundation Press, Westbury, NY, 1994, pp 218–19.
245. (1863) 22 UCQB 512 at 517.
246. (1979) 95 DLR (3d) 385.
247. Wilson J lists a number of articles at 437–8.

that the 'absence of an immunity has apparently caused no practical difficulties' and this 'is of some significance'.

Other countries that have no immunity doctrine include Singapore,[248] India[249] and Malaysia.[250]

Arguments for and against the immunity doctrine

The following comments are a brief outline of the arguments. The issues will also be looked at in the next part in outlining the *Hall* and *D'Orta-Ekenaike* cases. The Law Reform Commission of Victoria has succinctly outlined the arguments for and against the immunity doctrine.[251] The first argument is that an advocate's duty to the court would be impaired because of the fear of being sued. This might cause lawyers to choose their clients over their duty to the court 'in face of a close call'. The argument against this is that errors in situations of 'close calls' would not be negligence, nor would it be negligence to err in favour of their duty to the court. Another fear is that:

> ... every disappointed and angry client would be a threat to counsel. One has to wonder how readily clients would take it upon themselves to sue a lawyer, particularly in face of advice ... that great deference will be given by the courts to an advocate's judgment of how a trial should have been run.

The Commission pointed out that in Canada, which has had no immunity doctrine for more than 100 years, actions against lawyers for in-court negligence 'had not attained serious proportion'. Furthermore, the argument that extra work would need to be done is unconvincing because it applies equally to other professions and trades which do not have immunity. Doctors, for example, are not immune from the public interest in efficient health that is nearly equal to that of efficient administration of justice. There is less reason for advocates' immunity because judges have the authority to control the asking of unnecessary questions and the calling of unnecessary witnesses.[252]

The second reason for immunity is that it prevents collateral attacks on final judgments that would undermine public confidence in the courts. There is a strong public interest in finalising litigation but there is also one in favour of giving the right to compensation to those negligently harmed by others. An action in negligence would allow relitigation, but it is no different from replaying at trial the professional conduct of a surgeon being sued for negligence: 'The fact is that negligence action against an advocate only looks like "re-litigation" because the courtroom is an advocate's operating theatre.'[253] Furthermore, it is not self-evident that public confidence would be undermined by collateral attacks on judgments. An

10.72

10.73

---

248. *Chong Yeo & Partners v Guan Ming Hardware & Engineering Pty Ltd* [1997] 2 SLR 729 at 744.
249. *Kaur v Deol Bus Service Ltd* 1989 P&H 183 at 185.
250. *Miranda v Khoo Yew Boon* [1968] 1 MLJ 161.
251. *Access to the Law: Accountability of the Legal Profession*, Discussion Paper, 24 July 1991, pp 17–23. This was one of several controversial reports issued by the Victorian Law Reform Commission. Perhaps this was one of the reasons the Commission was abolished by a conservative government. In May 2000 the new Labor Government announced it was going to re-establish the Commission: Australian Associated Press, 4 May 2000.
252. *Access to the Law* (above), pp 18–20.
253. *Access to the Law* (above), p 21.

action against the lawyer may be perceived as meaning that the case was not properly conducted and not that the judge or jury in the earlier case was wrong.[254]

10.74 The Commission pointed out that failure to provide any remedy may lead to 'far more harm to public respect for the law' than having a matter relitigated.[255] Another consideration is mentioned by Wilson J in *Giannarelli*. His Honour said the immunity may lead to:[256]

> ... the likely perception in the community ... that 'barristers with the connivance of the judges, [have] built for themselves an ivory tower and have lived in it ever since at the expense of their clients'.

Finally, the Commission says that the idea of relitigation is not foreign to the courts. In criminal cases a conviction can be set aside outside the permissible period for an appeal, where a miscarriage of justice has occurred because the accused's counsel was incompetent.[257] The Commission failed to point out that the approach in criminal cases is not allowed in civil cases, leaving an incongruity in relation to remedies. Negligence of a lawyer in civil cases that attracts the immunity and causes the loss of the suit leaves the client without any remedy. The Chief Justice of the Federal Court, Black CJ, has suggested that in civil appeals, where courts already provide remedies for lawyers' 'procedural blunders', they should be able to take into consideration other trial blunders made by lawyers.[258] More recently, right after the *D'Orta-Ekenaike* decision, the former President of the New South Wales Bar Association and Law Council of Australia, Brett Walker SC, agreed with Black CJ's views when he said parliament should adopt legislation that appeals in civil cases be allowed on the basis of inadequate representation. He also stated that parliament could legislate to remove the immunity in cases where 'flagrant incompetence of counsel or perhaps other reprehensible factors' caused a 'miscarriage of justice'.[259] The Commission concluded that the immunity should be removed.[260] It quoted with approval Deane J's dissenting judgment in *Giannarelli*:[261]

> I do not consider that the considerations of public policy ... outweigh or even balance the injustice and consequent public detriment involved in depriving a person, who is caught up in litigation and engages the professional services of a legal practitioner, of all redress under the common law for 'in-court' negligence, however gross and callous in its nature or devastating in its consequences.

10.75 A leading Australian tort expert, Professor Yeo, made two suggestions before the House of Lords' decision. The first was that the immunity doctrine could be replaced by a barrister [I would suggest the appropriate term should be 'advocate'] determined standard of care. He argued that the courts could determine the proper standard either by themselves or with the

254. *Access to the Law* (above), p 21.
255. *Access to the Law* (above), pp 21–2.
256. Wilson J at 435–6 citing *Rondel* at 468.
257. *Re Knowles* [1984] VR 751 (Full Court).
258. M Black, 'In Court Immunity' (Spring 1992) 82 *Victoria Bar News* 32–3.
259. M Pelly, 'Litigants should be able to appeal: SC', *Sydney Morning Herald*, 16 March 2005, p 3.
260. *Accountability of the Legal Profession* (above), pp 22–3.
261. *Giannarelli & Shulkes v Wraith* (1988) 81 ALR 417 at 445.

help of members of the bar. His second alternative approach would be to limit the scope of the doctrine by taking into consideration fully the immunity test in *Rees v Sinclair*. He correctly pointed out that Australian courts have failed to give sufficient weight to the second part of that test that the doctrine should be restricted by not giving it 'any wider application than is absolutely necessary in the interests of the administration of justice'. The courts by failing to limit the doctrine by referring to public policy reasons have made it too wide. If consideration of the public policy were applied by the courts limiting its scope, more remedies would become available. Yeo also suggested that the courts modify the 'intimately connected' test by including with it the need for the work to be performed in circumstances which required an immediate response from counsel. This would predominately apply when the 'barrister is representing the client's case at a hearing'.[262]

Removal of the doctrine in England

In *Hall & Co v Simons*[263] the House of Lords upheld the decision of the Court of Appeal[264] that the claims against solicitor firms in three separate cases, heard together on appeal, were wrongly struck out. Two of the cases involve allegations of negligent advice in family proceedings and the third negligent advice on the settlement concerning the claim for a share of the matrimonial home after a divorce. The allegations had not been investigated until the issue of immunity was resolved. Although the case concerned only civil law matters, the main issue of contention was the removal of the immunity in criminal law. The decision was unanimous to abolish the civil law immunity and by 4:3 to remove the immunity in relation to criminal law.   **10.76**

Lord Steyn and Lord Hoffmann wrote the main judgments. Lord Millett and Lord Browne-Wilkinson agreed with their views. Lord Steyn rejected the first argument for the immunity, the 'cab-rank' principle — that barristers have to take on unwanted briefs. He said that it is easy for barristers to avoid taking on unwanted work. He then rejected the argument that barristers are to be treated the same as other actors in the court proceedings that enjoy the immunity and found that this is based on freedom of speech in court, which has no relevance to an immunity for the advocates. Lord Hoffmann pointed out that the reason for immunity for witnesses is to help them come forward to tell the truth. This reason has no relevance to the way advocates perform in court.   **10.77**

Lord Steyn then examined the argument for immunity based on the notion that there would be an abuse of public policy to allow the relitigation of a competent court's decision. He said there can be no problem with this issue in cases where there was not a verdict by a jury or a decision by the court. The major issue is in criminal cases. He found that the problem here has been cured. *Hunter v Chief Constable of the West Midlands Police*[265] held that a defendant, who wishes to challenge a guilty

---

262. S Yeo, 'Dismantling Barristerial Immunity' (1998) 14 *QUTLJ* 12, 14–20.
263. *Hall & Co v Simons* [2000] 3 All ER 673.
264. *Hall v Simons (a firm)* [1999] 3 WLR 873.
265. [1982] AC 529.

verdict, cannot do so by first suing his or her advocate for negligence. The verdict must be challenged by appeal. If the appeal is successful and defendant wants to sue the advocate the defendant still needs to prove that he or she has a meritorious cause of action. Lord Steyn said it is far easier for a court, since the 1999 changes to the Civil Procedure Rules, to throw out frivolous actions. Furthermore, courts set the standard of care and 'can be trusted to differentiate between errors of judgment and true negligence'.

10.78 Lord Hoffman pointed out that there would ordinarily be an abuse of process to ask a civil court to find that a conviction in another court was wrong. 'The resulting conflict of judgments is likely to bring the administration of justice into disrepute ... Once the conviction has been set aside, there can be no public policy objection to an action for negligence against the legal advisers.' A finding by a civil court of negligence by the advocate in this situation does not result in a 'conflict of judgments'.

Lord Steyn found the barrister's duty to the court to be the 'critical factor'. He stated that other professionals also have conflicting duties. He gave as an example a doctor with an AIDS patient who asks the doctor not to reveal the condition to his wife. Lord Steyn then looked at other countries without an immunity doctrine and accepted there are differences in the legal system from that in England. He then pointed out the Canadian experience, where there is a similar system, and that without an immunity doctrine 'there is no evidence that the work of Canadian courts was hampered in any way by counsel's fear of civil liability'. Lord Steyn concluded by pointing out the most important benefit to be gained by ending the immunity is that it will end 'an anomalous exception to the basic premise that there should be a remedy for a wrong'.

10.79 Lord Hoffmann in his opinion pointed out the difficulties the Court of Appeal had with this case because that court had to stay within the 'intimately connected' test. He said that the distinction under this test 'is very difficult to apply with any degree of consistency. That is perhaps another reason why the immunity should be altogether abolished.'

The minority view was expressed by three Lords. Lord Hope of Craighead said that the immunity needed to be maintained for advocates when engaged in criminal law activity in court. This he called 'the core immunity'. His argument was based on the need to protect the efficient administration of the criminal justice system, which would be at risk if the immunity were removed. This would occur because criminal advocates would not be able to exercise independent judgment if they feared being liable in negligence. They would pursue every conceivable point and make every possible argument so that 'no stone was left uncovered'. They would be at the mercy of clients that insist on pursuing everything without any regard to the administration of justice.

Lord Hope also rejected as being a 'satisfactory substitute' for the core immunity the principle in the *Hunter* case. He argued if the appeal is successful, even though it has nothing to do with the advocate's alleged incompetency, a disgruntled client's allegations 'can no longer be dismissed or struck out as an abuse of process'. He also pointed out that if the *Hunter* principle is applied too widely to deny a remedy, the case could become 'vulnerable to attack on the ground that it is inconsistent with the client's fundamental right of access to a court for the determination of his civil rights'. Thus, the *Hunter* principle could be overruled as contrary to the European Convention on Human Rights.

Lord Hutton disagreed with Lord Hoffmann's views that advocates are different from other participants who are granted immunity in court. He said that advocates are like judges who are given 'immunity because the law considers that it is in the public interest that they should not be harassed by vexatious litigation'. He argued that defence advocates, like judges, are performing an important public duty. By defending the accused they perform a task that is 'essential for the proper administration of justice'. They should therefore be protected from harassment by disgruntled clients. Lord Hutton would maintain the 'intimately connected' test in the area of criminal law, 'notwithstanding the difficulty of drawing a clear line in respect of pre-trial work'. **10.80**

Lord Hobhouse of Woodborough used the *Rondel v Worsley*[266] decision to show why the *Hunter* principle only works in a limited fashion. The claim in *Rondel* was not that the advocate caused the conviction. Nor was it an attack, direct or collateral, upon the verdict of the jury. The claim was only that the advocate had failed to pursue with sufficient force Rondel's allegation that the injuries inflicted came from his use of his teeth and hands. Thus, the *Hunter* principle would not have helped to stop the action in *Rondel*. He then argued that if advocates were treated differently from other participants in a criminal trial they would be unique. This would be illogical because their role is also to discharge a public duty the same as the other participants.

Lord Hobhouse concluded that the civil and criminal justice systems have essential differences, which result in the need for the immunity for the criminal one. 'The advocate's role, the purpose of the criminal process, the legitimate interest of the client, the inappropriateness of the tort remedy, the fact that it would handicap the achievement of justice, the fact that it would create anomalies and conflict with the statutory policy for the payment of compensation for miscarriages of justice, all demonstrate the justification for the immunity in the public interest and, indeed, the interests of defendants as a class.' **10.81**

The fact that the Lords have abolished the doctrine does not mean a plaintiff will be successful. In a recent case, *May v Pettman Smith (a firm)*,[267] the House of Lords reversed the Court of Appeal decision finding the barrister negligent. The case dealt with a last minute offer of settlement and the barrister's advice to reject the offer. The Court of Appeal had found a breach of duty that caused financial loss to the plaintiff. Lord Carswell emphasised the need for advocates not to adopt 'defensive' advocacy. He found that the barrister's assessment of the prospects of success of adducing new evidence was not negligent. Therefore her advice to proceed with the action and to reject the highest offer by the hospital was not negligent.[268] If this matter had taken place in Australia, the issues of breach and causation **10.82**

---

266. [1969] 1 AC 191.
267. [2005] 1 WLR 581.
268. Ibid, para 60.

would not have been heard, as the immunity doctrine would have protected the barrister.[269]

Retention of the doctrine in Australia

10.83 We will again outline the facts of *D'Orta-Ekenaike v Victoria Legal Aid*[270] which were given at **9.54**. The accused at all times believed he was innocent of the rape charge but, because of the pressure of his solicitor and counsel, he pleaded guilty at the committal hearing. He had been told that 'he did not have a defence', that if he pleaded guilty he would get a 'suspended sentence' and if he did not 'he would receive a custodial penalty'. There was also no requirement that he enter a plea at the committal hearing. On the advice of new counsel he withdrew the guilty plea at trial. He testified that he was 'virtually forced' to enter the guilty plea. The committal plea was led as evidence and he was found guilty. On appeal the Court of Appeal quashed the verdict because the lower court had failed to properly instruct the jury on the use that might be made of the defendant's original guilty plea. On retrial the evidence of his guilty plea was not admitted and he was acquitted. The defendant later sued Victorian Legal Aid and the barrister who had represented him at the committal hearing. He alleged that they had negligently exercised 'undue pressure and influence' upon him. His claim was summarily terminated on the basis he had no cause of action because of the immunity doctrine and the High Court granted special leave.

10.84 The High Court by a 6:1 vote upheld the doctrine under common law and held it was not abrogated by s 10(2) of the Legal Profession Practice Act 1891. The main judgment of Gleeson CJ, Gummow, Hayne and Heydon JJ, again upheld an interpretation of s 10(2) like the majority in *Giannarelli*, that the section did not remove the immunity. The main judgment only briefly touched on the meaning of the section. They stated 'that a disputed question of construction was finally resolved in *Giannarelli*. This Court should not depart from that decision without powerful reasons to do so. A mere preference for one construction over the other would not suffice'.[271] Kirby J, the only dissent, adopted and added to the minority view in *Giannarelli* that the section removed the immunity. He stated that Toohey J was the only judge in that case who 'clearly identifies the legal points that were before the Court'. Kirby J argued that the reasoning of the majority resulted in no clear ratio as there were three separate theories as to the meaning of s 10(2). He therefore stated that the interpretation of that section is open to a 'fresh determination'. Kirby J referred to Toohey J's judgment and added additional case law to come to his conclusion that solicitors did not have an immunity at the time of the adoption of the statute. Therefore s 10(2) removed the immunity from barristers.[272]

10.85 In relation to the common law immunity doctrine the main judgment rejected most of the reasons given in *Giannarelli* for maintaining the

---

269. For a discussion of the *May* case and other relevant cases in the United Kingdom and Australia, see A Abadee, 'The further divergence between UK and Australian law on barristers' negligence', *Bar News (NSW)*, winter 2005, p 36.
270. [2005] HCA 12.
271. Ibid, para 24.
272. Ibid, paras 250–257, 260–269.

doctrine. They rejected the contract, duty to the court and the 'cab-rank' principle arguments as being irrelevant to upholding the doctrine. They also rejected the argument that advocates have to make quick decisions because 'so too do many others have to make equally difficult decisions'. Finally, they rejected the 'chilling' effect of civil suit argument that would result in longer trials. They find that this threat should not be underestimated, nor does it 'distract from the importance of the immunity', but it does not 'provide support in principle for its existence'.[273]

They find the reasons for sustaining the doctrine are found on 'considerations of public policy', and that the removal of the immunity would result in 'injury to the public interest'. The main reason they find is the need to have finality. 'Once a controversy has been quelled, it is not to be relitigated. Yet relitigation of the controversy would be an inevitable and essential step in demonstrating that an advocate's negligence in the conduct of litigation had caused damage to the client ... [T]he central justification for the advocate's immunity is the principle that controversies once resolved, are not to be reopened except in a few narrowly defined circumstances. This is a fundamental and pervading tenet of the judicial system, reflecting the role played by the judicial process in the government of society.'[274]

In rejecting the removal of the immunity by the *Hall* case, they pointed out that the High Court had decided more than 40 years ago that it would no longer 'follow decisions of the House of Lord, at the expense of our own opinions and cases decided here'.[275] Furthermore, the arguments for the decision in *Hall* were based on social and other changes in England that affected their administration of justice. They said: '[T]here can be no automatic transposition of the arguments found persuasive there to the Australian judicial system.' They argued that the main reason for the *Hall* decision was the 'imminent coming into operation of the Human Rights Act 1998 (UK) and the consequent application of Art 6 of the European Convention for the Protection of Human Rights and Fundamental Freedoms'. Thus, the *Hall* decision had been 'significantly affected by European considerations', which should not have any influence in Australia.[276]

The judges realised that there would be many who would criticise their decision. They stated: 'There may be those who will seek to characterise the result ... as a case of lawyers looking after their own, whether because of personal inclination and sympathy, or for other base motives. But the legal principle which underpins the Court's conclusion is fundamental. Of course, there is always a risk that the determination of legal controversy is imperfect. And it may be imperfect because of what a party's advocate does or does not do. The law aims at providing the best and safest system of determination that is compatible with human fallibility. But underpinning the system is the need for certainty and finality of decision. The immunity of advocates is a necessary consequence of that need.' The judges also held that the immunity applied equally to criminal and civil cases.[277]

273. Ibid, paras 25–29.
274. Ibid, paras 34–36, 43–45.
275. Ibid, para 59 referring to *Parker v R* (1963) 110 CLR 610 at 632.
276. Ibid, paras 56 and 60.
277. Ibid, paras 76–80.

10.86   Justice Kirby in his dissent said: 'The cards are now stacked' against maintaining the immunity doctrine. He then listed numerous places where it no longer exists or never existed.[278] The main focus of his judgment was to show that the statutory interpretation of s 10(b) by the majority in this case and in the *Giannarelli* case was wrong.[279] He also found that the common law did not support the maintenance of the doctrine. He stated:

> [A]n immunity from liability at law is a derogation from the rule of law and fundamental rights. The special solicitude of the law for its own practitioners has been noted by judges. It has been contrasted with the high measure of accountability demanded of other professions. Such an immunity diminishes justifiable loss distribution in a generally inelastic market. Effectively, it reduces equality before the courts.[280]

He pointed out that the Australian rule originated in England and has now been removed. Furthermore, similar legal systems within and outside the common law world 'operate perfectly well without the immunity'. He stated that most of the judges in the *Hall* case did not even refer to the European Convention for the Protection of Human Rights and Fundamental Freedoms. The Convention was also not the basis for the House of Lords' decision because at that time it had not become part of the English domestic law.[281] He agreed with the *Hall* case that the foundations for the doctrine need to be looked at in the contemporary setting. He argued that none of the traditional arguments for retaining the immunity, including the arguments of public policy, are sufficient within the modern context. Justice Kirby rejected the main reasons of public policy of the majority. In reference to the argument that barristers need to have the same immunity afforded to judges, jurors and prosecutors, he said: 'None of these persons owes any duty of care to a litigant.'[282] Advocates do have such a duty. In reference to the finality argument he said 'that virtually all legal systems of the world, including many that are at least as worthy of respect as our own, flourish without the supposed indispensable immunity'. He gives a number of other reasons to meet the public policy arguments of the other two judgments of the majority by Callinan and McHugh JJ.[283]

10.87   The decision in the *D'Orta-Ekenaike* case has caused a public outcry. The editorials of the main newspapers condemned the decision with headings such as 'Justice must come first',[284] 'It's time to raise the bar'[285] and 'Gentlemen's club protects its own'.[286] All three of these editorials pointed out that the only remedy was parliamentary reform. As the one in the *Sydney Morning Herald* said, politicians 'must resolve to banish this unjust anachronism from all state and federal jurisdictions'.[287] Ackland pointed out that the need for finality left an important victim — D'Orta-Ekenaike.

278. Ibid, para 211.
279. Ibid, paras 247–309.
280. Ibid, para 314.
281. Ibid, paras 313 and 315.
282. Ibid, para 323.
283. Ibid, paras 333–339.
284. *Sydney Morning Herald*, 14 March 2005, p 12.
285. *Australian Financial Review*, 18 March 2005, p 82.
286. *Australian*, 12–13 March 2005, p 18.
287. *Australian*, 14 March 2005, p 12.

He cannot sue his lawyers. He ended his column by stating: 'One fervently hopes that D'Orta-Ekenaike is now happy that his controversy has been quelled.'[288]

Community expectation that every wrong should attract a remedy strongly opposes the continuation of the immunity doctrine. There appears to be a sense of injustice that law is the only occupation that is exempt from this rule. Mills has said that as tort law has been developing, lawyers, like members of other professions, have been made more accountable for their actions. He thought the reform would come through the courts:[289]

> No doubt, these expectations will be translated into increasing standards of care being required and modern business conditions producing new sources of potential liability. Ultimately, it may also mean the dissolution of the advocate's immunity.

Mills' view of judicial removal of the doctrine has proven wrong for Australia. It has made Australian law in this area diverge dramatically from that in the United Kingdom.[290] The *D'Orta-Ekenaike* decision has made, at least for the foreseeable future, the immunity doctrine safe from removal by judicial interpretation. What about the possibility of it being abolished by legislation? None of the legislative reforms in Victoria or elsewhere have removed the immunity; on the contrary, the new Legal Profession Act 2004 (Vic) Pt 7.2.11 re-enacted the almost identical provision found in the Legal Practice Act 1996 (Vic) s 442. It states that nothing in the Act 'abrogates any immunity from liability for negligence enjoyed by Australian lawyers'. Furthermore, in 1997 the New South Wales Attorney-General in a reference to the Legal Advisory Council asked whether the immunity of advocates should be removed. The Council recommended that the doctrine be maintained and quoted with approval Branson J's comments in *Yates v Boland*. These were that the relevant work in that case by the solicitors would be viewed as 'work done out of court which leads to a decision affecting the conduct of the case in court' and fell within the doctrine.[291] The main judgment in *D'Orta-Ekenaike* pointed out that a number of statutes have recently been adopted by state legislatures under what was called 'tort law reform'. The court said: 'In none of that legislation has there been any reference to the immunities from suit of advocates, witnesses or judges.'[292] Justice Kirby, agreeing with the judges in the *Hall* case also stated that the court should remove the doctrine and not have to leave it to parliament.[293] Justice Kirby may have no other choice to have his views accepted. Perhaps there may be a different approach by the legislative bodies in light of the *Hall* and *D'Orta-Ekenaike* cases. The Standing Committee of Attorneys-General has placed the issue on their agenda and

---

288. R Ackland, 'Majority ruling gives minnows little chance', *Sydney Morning Herald*, 11 March 2005, p 11.
289. Mills (above), p 38. For an article arguing against an immunity doctrine, see M Newman, 'The Case Against Advocates' Immunity: A Comparative Study' (1995) 9 *Georgetown J of Legal Ethics* 267.
290. See article by Abadee (above), fn 269.
291. 'Advocates immunity from civil action to continue' (1998) 36 *Law Society J (NSW)* 80.
292. [2005] HCA 12 at para 53.
293. Ibid, paras 341–344.

most of the state attorneys favour abolishing the immunity.[294] At their March 2005 meeting they decided to have an options paper to consider at their July meeting.[295] One of the reports prepared for the Committee found that abolition of the immunity would be unlikely to increase insurance premiums.[296]

PROFESSIONAL INDEMNITY INSURANCE

10.88   Compulsory liability insurance schemes have spread rapidly in the last 25 years. All the provinces in Canada and the United Kingdom adopted schemes and were soon followed by all jurisdictions in Australia except Western Australia, which only adopted a scheme in 1987. Many barristers belong to the voluntary liability insurance scheme of the Australian Bar Association.[297] A compulsory scheme was adopted by the Victorian Bar in 1985[298] and by the New South Wales Bar in 1994.[299] In the fused states — Western Australia and South Australia — barristers must participate in a scheme. In the United States most states have voluntary insurance plans, although a few have made it compulsory, for example Wisconsin and Oregon.[300]

The need for professional indemnity insurance has been expanding, especially in light of the increasing value of the awards being made by courts and juries.[301] As the number of claims and the amount of the awards increased in the 1980s and 1990s the master policy schemes increased in the amount of coverage and in the yearly premium.

10.89   In New South Wales and the Australian Capital Territory the number of claims reported under the LawCover scheme rose by 124 per cent from 557 in 1987–88 to 1247 in 1992–93. The estimated ultimate cost of these claims rose by over 244 per cent from $13.4m to $46.1m in the same period. For 1993–94 the LawCover premium was $5530 for sole practitioners and all partners in firms. For 1994–95 the premiums rose dramatically to meet additional estimated claims of close to $84m. There was a revision of the way in which the burden of the cost of the LawCover scheme's protection was spread across the members of the legal profession involved in the scheme in 1994–95. Sole practitioners and partners were required to contribute for the 1994–95 insurance year a basic $8015, and loadings for employees, for past claims and for representing more than one party to transactions.

---

294. C Merritt and K Towers, 'States to break barrier', *Australian Financial Review*, 18 March 2005, p 58.
295. C Merritt and Sean Parnell, 'A-Gs fight immunity for lawyers', *Australian*, 21 March 2005, p 4.
296. M Priest, 'Immunity not a big issue', *Australian Financial Review*, 5 August 2005, p 51.
297. D Weisbrot, *Australian Lawyers*, Longman Cheshire, Melbourne, 1990, p 213.
298. Disney et al (above) (1986), p 749.
299. Legal Profession Reform Act 1993 (NSW) s 38R.
300. See T Morgan and R Rotunda, *Professional Responsibility*, 5th ed, Foundation Press, Westbury, NY, 1991, pp 114–15 and Wolfram (above), pp 240–1.
301. For an article discussing the problem for all professionals, see M Forde, 'Professional Indemnity — Expanding Horizons' (April 1991) *Queensland Law Society J* 157.

Before 1994–95, all sole practitioners and partners paid the same contribution and there was no loading of the contributions payable by individual members of the profession because they appeared to pose a greater risk. The contributions payable for the 1994–95 insurance year purchased up to $1,100,000 per claim. This coverage can still be increased by paying additional premiums. The premiums for sole practitioners (typically) rose from $8815 for 1995–96 to $11,097 for 1997–98, while those of partners (typically) rose from $9215 for 1995–96 to $11,831 for 1997–98. Estimated claims rose from $47.2m for 1995–96 to $58.9m for 1997–98.[302]

As a result of the number of claims falling substantially in the late 1990s **10.90** and early 2000s, LawCover moved to full risk rating, and premiums have sometimes been reduced. In the low risk group a principal pays the minimum rate of $8500, while those in the high risk group can pay up to the maximum rate of $16,500. These minimum and maximum figures were fixed from 1 July 1998 to 1 July 2001.[303] For the insurance year 2002–03 the following factors determined the amount of premium to be paid by a new firm: '1) The size of the firm measured by estimated annual gross fee income; 2) The risk profile of the firm (considering such factors as the claims experience of the firm, the risk management training of principals, and any practice management certification); 3) The level of excess selected by the firm; and 4) Whether the firm succeeds a prior practice.'[304]

The increase in the number of negligence claims in the 1980s and 1990s and the awards given, leading to massive increases in the cost of insurance premiums, led to a discussion on limiting professional liability.[305] One rationale for limiting liability is that the community has to pay for unnecessary preventive measures. It is costing millions to do extra work to eliminate risk because of the fear of a negligence suit.[306] This is quite evident from the over-servicing in the medical area.[307] The extension of the scope of tort liability for lawyers has also led to a more cautious approach. As we have discussed (see **10.1**) all states have placed restrictions on plaintiffs in seeking a tort remedy and the new forms of practice, incorporation and MDFs, have also raised many problems for clients. New South Wales has also adopted the Professional Standards Act 1994 which allows a cap on liability for approved mandatory liability schemes: see **10.28**. A similar Act, the Professional Standards Act 1997, has been

---

302. This information comes from Tim Webber of LawCover in June 1997.
303. LawCover (March 1998) 2 *Bulletin* and LawCover *1999 Annual Report*, pp 6–8.
304. B MacDermott, F – 'Risk Management', F150-19 (above).
305. For the arguments for limiting liability and allowing incorporation, see M Lawrence, 'The Fortified Law Firm: Limited Liability Business and the Propriety of Lawyer Incorporation' (1995) 9 *Georgetown J of Legal Ethics* 207.
306. See M Sweet, 'Medicine of Fear', *Sydney Morning Herald*, 8 April 1995, Section 5, Spectrum, p 4A. In contrast, see the Department of Human Services and Health (Cth) Report, *Review of Professional Indemnity Arrangements for Health Care Professionals*, February 1994, which states: 'According to the usual measures of medical malpractice crisis there has been no crisis in Australia.'
307. See, generally, the New South Wales Attorney-General's proposals to limit professional liability in discussion paper, *Professional Liability, Regulation, Insurance and Risk Management*, 1990.

enacted in Western Australia. The New South Wales Act was warmly received by the Law Society and the accountancy professional bodies, but as would be expected, not by the Australian Consumers' Association.[308]

In the early 2000s there was strong reaction by large corporate clients, especially the banking and property sectors, to the capped liability. In 2004 and 2005 the national law firms, representing approximately 2500 solicitors, reacted to this pressure from their clients and abandoned the system. As a result the New South Wales Law Society applied to the Professional Standards Council to allow firms to vary their limitations on liability between clients, types of work and particular projects. There still was the requirement that some kind of capping had to be adopted.[309] The banks and large corporations have stated that if opting out is not permitted they might move their legal work offshore.[310]

308. S Kirk, 'Bid to limit client claims for damages', *Sydney Morning Herald*, 29 January 1994, p 3.
309. C Merritt, 'Angry lawyers decide cap doesn't fit', *Australian Financial Review*, 4 February 2005, pp 1 and 58.
310. K Towers, 'Capping foe warns of move offshore', *Australian Financial Review*, 20 May 2005, p 58.

11

CONFIDENTIALITY

INTRODUCTION

The following problem concerns confidentiality issues that will arise during this chapter:

11.1

> The Australian Taxation Office (ATO) and the Commonwealth Police with information from the Australian Customs Service carried out raids on the offices of David Garfunkel, a barrister, and those of the New South Wales Bar Association. The tax officers had proper documentation for their raid on the Bar Association under s 263 and s 264 of the Income Tax Assessment Act 1936. The police had a warrant under s 10 of the Crimes Act 1914. There were two teams of four each that went to the premises. Jill Booth, who was in charge of the raids, had been discussing the problem the previous week with Alice Parkinson, who is employed by the Bar Association, but not with David.
>
> The ATO was looking for the details of money made from the sale of the drug ecstasy. No criminal charges had been laid before the raid. The customs officials believe that Jim Sly, also known as Sukarni (his name received from his guru, Ragi) who is in the import–export of artefacts business, had been bringing the drug in using freight containers. Although he had not been caught with the drug, there is some evidence that he was involved with it. In the last two years he has opened four new shops around Australia, bought a million dollar house on the harbour, a BMW sports car, and was arrested for kissing a police officer while he was obviously in a state of ecstasy. Jim has as his lawyer David Garfunkel, also known as Suli. David was admitted to the bar 10 years ago and practised as a barrister for a few years before going to study with Ragi in India. Since his return to Australia four years ago, he has served as legal adviser to the members of the Ragian movement and has a current practising certificate but no chambers. He has established several corporations to deal with his business interests and a number of Ragians who are his clients have invested in these businesses. One of his companies went into bankruptcy last year and several of his clients who had invested in it complained to the Bar Association that David had negligently advised them. The Association has also in its files his problems with the ATO. The file states he has far too many assets in light of the income he has declared on his tax return, and allegations from some former clients that they have bought ecstasy from him. All this information has been gathered by Alice Parkinson

who is employed by the Bar Association to assist the Association's complaints committee. She was admitted as a solicitor last year but does not have a current practising certificate. In light of this information the Bar Association's complaints committee has had a member interview David, with his barrister present, concerning the above matters. David was cooperative on most aspects, but refused to give information concerning the ecstasy.

Jill Booth's officers surprised Alice when they arrived at her doorstep and she surrendered the file on David Garfunkel that also contained information on Jim Sly. At David's office, from which his companies also carried out their business, the police officers were confronted by a young first year barrister who is doing her practical qualification experience by being supervised by David. She has been in practice for only two months. She had been doing some filing, a little research and a few mentions in court, but had no other legal experience. No one else was in the office since the raid took place at 5.30 pm on Friday. The officers took only documents that they were authorised to take under the warrant but David feels some of them were privileged.

As a result of the raids both Jim and David have been charged in the Federal Court with conspiracy to import and sell a prohibited drug. During the trial both defendants objected to use of documents taken during the raids, saying they were privileged. Their objections were denied and they requested a stay in proceedings to appeal to the Full Federal Court that upheld their appeal. The Department of Public Prosecutions has now been granted special leave to appeal to the High Court.

11.2   As the problem shows, the area of lawyers maintaining clients' confidences raises many conflicting issues. The duty of confidentiality stems from contractual requirements and is a broader rule than the narrower legal professional privilege which prevents lawyers from testifying against their present or former clients. The confidentiality requirement can be overruled by courts within their inherent powers and by the ATO, police and other administrative agencies that have been granted specific statutory powers. It places an obligation on lawyers not to reveal clients' information in other contexts. The obligation has been recognised by the professional associations. For example, the Law Society of New South Wales says that solicitors should 'act confidentially and in the protection of all client information'.[1]

11.3   The law does recognise other 'privileges' to withhold certain types of information. For example, public interest immunity privilege (not really a privilege because it does not benefit private interests or relationships),[2] privilege against self-incrimination, marital privilege, without prejudice privilege,[3]

---

1.   *Statement of Ethics*, 1994, revised 11 December 2003. See also for more detailed rules Law Council of Australia, Model Rules and Professional Conduct and Practice Rules (NSW) rr 2.1 and 2.2, and Professional Conduct Rules (WA) r 6.3; (SA) r 9.2 and (NT) r 9.2.
2.   S McNicol, *Law of Privilege*, Law Book Co, Sydney, 1992, p 3.
3.   These privileges are dealt with extensively in McNicol (above), Ch 8; J Hunter, C Cameron and T Henning, *Litigation 1 — Civil Procedure*, 7th ed, LexisNexis Butterworths, Sydney, 2005, Chs 7.26–7.45 and 8; and A Ligertwood, *Australian Evidence*, 4th ed, LexisNexis Butterworths, Sydney, 2004, pp 325–407. The common law on the 'without prejudice' privilege (also called 'privilege in aid of settlement') has been modified by the Evidence Acts 1995 s 131 — Exclusion of evidence of settlement negotiations. The provision does not allow 'any judicial discretion to overcome the privilege in circumstances within the listed exceptions. For example, the common law admitted of a possible exception where delay is in issue, as in proceedings involving alleged want of prosecution or laches ... There is no comparable exception in s 131': S Odgers, *Uniform Evidence Law*, 3rd ed, Federation Press, Sydney, 1998, p 431.

but we will deal predominantly with legal professional privilege.[4] The term 'legal professional privilege' is a misnomer, as the right to the privilege belongs to the client. This has been recognised in the Uniform Evidence Acts (virtually identical in the Australian Capital Territory, New South Wales, Tasmania, Norfolk Island and the Commonwealth Federal Courts[5], hereafter the Evidence Act) where it is called 'client legal privilege'. The Evidence Act modifies the common law in a number of instances but privilege is only protected when 'adducing' evidence. This approach has been criticised because the vast majority of privilege issues arise in reference to pre-trial procedures.[6] A Review of the Uniform Evidence Acts by the Australian Law Reform Commission (ALRC), in conjunction with the New South Wales Law Reform Commission (NSWLRC), began in July 2004. The project is a joint venture. An issues paper, IP 28, was published in November 2004. A discussion paper (for the ALRC it is DP 69 and for the NSWLRC it is DP 47) was published in July 2005 (with the addition of the Victorian Law Reform Commission) and the final report is to be presented to the Commonwealth Attorney-General by 5 December 2005.[7] There is one chapter of the review that deals with privilege; we will refer to the discussiuon paper as DP 69.[8]

The privilege covers a wide range of communications obtained by lawyers in dealing with their clients' legal problems and includes original and derivative materials. Thus, the lawyers' notes and other materials (lawyer work product) in relation to pursuing litigation for the client are protected because to deny this protection would tend to reveal material that is protected in its own right as being privileged. For example, the Third Circuit Court in the United States has found that the use of trial consultants in witness preparation is protected under work product.[9] Another example was when a lawyer sent letters containing his work on the case to an auditor on behalf of his client, a California court held that there was no waiver of the privilege.[10] 'This privilege finds its justification in the adversary notion that the lawyer's brief is sacrosanct ... [and also] provides an incentive to lawyers and parties to collect information and argument for presentation at trial.'[11] Thus, there are two privileges. One is the communication privilege and the other a narrower litigation privilege.[12]

The work product doctrine was extended by the Evidence Act s 120. This section protects confidential documents and communications made by an unrepresented litigant in the preparation and presentation of his or her

4.   There is only one book in Australia that deals solely with this topic. See R J Desiatnik, *Legal Professional Privilege in Australia*, 2nd ed, LexisNexis Butterworths, Sydney, 2005.
5.   Victoria has stated it intends to adopt the Uniform Evidence Act: see State Government of Victoria, *New Directions for the Victorian Justice System 2004–2014: Attorney-General's Justice Statement*, 2004, p 26.
6.   Anderson J, Hunter J and Williams N, *The New Evidence Law: Annotations and Commentary on the Uniform Evidence Acts*, LexisNexis Butterworths, 2002, p 416.
7.   ALRC, Issues Paper 28, *Review of the Evidence Act 1995*, November 2004, Chapter 1.
8.   ALRC, Discussion Paper 69, *Review of the Uniform Evidence Acts*, July 2005, Chapter 13.
9.   *In re Cendant Corporation Securities Litigation*, No 02-4386.
10. *Laguna Beach County Water District v Superior Court of Orange County*, 15 December 2004, No G034238.
11. Ligertwood (above), para 5.21 at p 275.
12. Ibid, paras 5.21 and 5.22 at pp 275–6.

case.[13] Of course, courts are used to and rely upon qualified legal practitioners to claim the privilege:[14]

> A court may be more reluctant to rely upon the integrity of a litigant in person who makes a claim for privilege, because of the litigant's personal involvement in the proceedings and because of the absence of disciplinary jurisdiction over the litigant. And unless the litigant is reasonably experienced with legal proceedings, the court may also not be able to assume that the litigant will be able to be relied upon to apply the provisions of s 120 with the same facility as a lawyer.

11.4 Finally, the communication has to be confidential. The Evidence Act s 117(1) defines 'confidential communication' as where: (a) the person who made it; or (b) the person to whom it was made, was under express orders or implied obligation not to disclose its contents, 'whether or not the obligation arises under law'. It should be noted that the Full Court in Western Australia has said that confidentiality is not essential when a document is brought into existence for the sole purpose of litigation and comes under litigation privilege. The document was an executed affidavit of a deceased person, which had been prepared solely for litigation.[15] *Cross on Evidence* says that this view is contrary to the preponderance of authority which 'requires that the document be confidential in the sense that it is brought into existence with the expectation that it will not be circulated beyond the camp of the party in whose cause it was prepared, at least for a time'.[16]

THE DUTIES OF LAWYERS UNDER CONFIDENTIALITY

Ethical duties

11.5 As I have stated, lawyers have been advised by their professional bodies to keep the affairs of clients confidential. In 1997 the Law Council's Model Rule r 2.1 stated: 'A practitioner must not, during, or after termination of, a retainer, disclose to any person ... any information which is confidential ...'. The revised Model Rules in 2002 state in r 3.1: 'A practitioner must never disclose to any person ... any information, which is confidential to a client and acquired by the practitioner ... during the client's engagement ...'. In the United States the old ABA Model Code includes under confidential communications the term 'secrets'. Secrets are defined as:[17]

---

13. Unrepresented persons at common law had no right to the privilege. See Mason J in *National Employers' Mutual General Insurance Association v Waind* (1979) 141 CLR 648 at 654. The 'work product privilege' is an American concept (see *Hickman v Taylor* (1947) 329 US 495) that has been approved in Australia: see *Southern Equities Corp Ltd v West Australian Government Holdings Ltd* (1993) 10 WAR 1 (FC). The High Court has not given its approval but Brennan CJ did approve it in *Australian Federal Police v Propend* (1997) 141 ALR 545 at 548.
14. K Smark, 'Privilege Under the *Evidence Acts*' (1995) 18 *UNSW LJ* 95, 99. The author does point out that the court can control the lay person through its contempt power.
15. *Southern Equities Corporation Ltd v West Australian Government Holdings Ltd* (1993) 10 WAR 1 (FC).
16. J D Heydon, *Cross on Evidence*, 7th ed, Butterworths, Sydney, 2004, para 25225, p 803, fn 363.
17. DR 4-101(A).

... information gained in the professional relationship that the client has requested be held inviolate or the disclosure of which would be embarrassing or would be likely to be detrimental to the client.

Secret information also includes information known to the public.[18] This is a broad coverage but is limited to information 'gained in the professional relationship'. Thus, like the revised Australian Model Rule, information obtained before or after the relationship is not protected. The ABA Model Rules (now adopted in 43 states) in r 1.6 state that a lawyer 'shall not reveal information relating to representation of a client'. The Comment [3] to r 1.6 states that it applies 'to all information relating to the representation, whatever its source'. Furthermore, unlike the Code, information is confidential if obtained before, during or after the representation.[19] Finally, information is confidential whether or not it will embarrass or work to the detriment of the client. The Canadian Bar Association's Code of Professional Conduct as of May 2005 differs from the ABA Model Rules. Chapter 4 states: 'The lawyer has a duty to hold in strict confidence all information concerning the business and affairs of the client acquired in the course of the professional relationship.' Under Guiding Principles 1 it states: '... [M]atters disclosed to or discussed with the lawyer will be held secret and confidential.' Under Principle 2 it points out that this ethical rule is wider than the evidentiary rule of lawyer and client privilege because it 'applies without regard to the nature or source of the information or to the fact that others may share the knowledge'.

The idea of lawyers keeping confidences has its historical roots in the fact that 'gentlemen' (barristers) did not reveal confidences. In the modern context it supports the idea that in fulfilling their role lawyers should be trustworthy. The development of trust in the lawyer–client relationship stems from clients feeling confident that what they tell their lawyers will not be passed on to anyone else. There is a further ethical obligation for lawyers in the revised Law Council's Model Rules general introduction: 'Relations with clients'. It states practitioners should 'always deal with their clients fairly, free of the influence of any interest which may conflict with a client's best interests'. Implicit in this idea is for them not to 'take an unfair advantage over their clients'.[20] Thus, lawyers should not use privileged or unprivileged information to the disadvantage of their clients or for their own selfish ends.[21] The use of such information is also a breach of agency principles violating the lawyer's fiduciary duty to the client.[22] The 1997 Australian Model Rule 2.2 stated:

11.6

> A practitioner's obligation to maintain the confidentiality of a client's affairs is not limited to information which might be protected by legal professional privilege, and is a duty inherent in the fiduciary relationship between the practitioner and the client.

---

18. EC 4-4 states that client secrets are protected 'without regard to the nature or source of information or the fact that others share the knowledge'.
19. See ABA, Formal Opinion, 90-358, 'Protection of Information Imparted by Prospective Client'.
20. This language is found in the 1997 Law Council's Model Rules r 8.
21. DR 4-101(B)(2), (3); MR 1.6 and MR 1.8(b).
22. See *Law Society of New South Wales v Harvey* [1976] 2 NSWLR 154.

The concept of the practitioner's fiduciary obligation is now present in the revised Model Rules under 'Relations with Clients'. It states: 'They should be acutely aware of the fiduciary nature of their relationship with their clients.'

11.7   The problem of the lawyer's fiduciary duty will be discussed in more detail in Chapter 12.

The maintaining of secret information may also be necessary even when lawyers do not consider the information to be confidential. The line between the communication of confidential and non-confidential information is difficult to discern. We know that even outside the lawyer–client relationship there are often good moral reasons for not passing on information. To do so might embarrass the communicators, interfere with their interests, thwart their plans, invade their privacy, or cause harm to third parties. Sometimes this information is not given confidentially, but there is implicit the fact that the personal information may be damaging and that it should not be revealed. This information will not be disclosed because of respect for the needs of the communicators, the bad consequences for them or others and a sense of duty to maintain implicit confidences.[23]

Exceptions to maintaining confidentiality

11.8   There are exceptions to the rule that lawyers should keep confidential all personal information received from clients. The first is when lawyers are required by law, rule of court or court order to disclose them.[24] Even in those circumstances lawyers must take all reasonable steps to test the validity of the law. A perplexing question is whether lawyers should take such steps of testing the law if they know that maintaining the confidences is not in the public interest.[25]

A second exception is when lawyers have to defend themselves against a charge or complaint of criminal or professional misconduct, usually instigated by a client. Such action by clients is similar to a waiver of their right to confidentiality, but the lawyer can only reveal matters bearing on the subject matter.[26] An undecided issue is what happens when clients criticise or attack their lawyers for the way in which they conducted their affairs. Can lawyers defend themselves by revealing confidential information? The situation in Australia is not clear.

The South Australian Law Society has said that lawyers are bound to maintain secrecy.[27] They must refrain from using this information to answer such criticism if no proceedings have commenced against them. The professional rules in Queensland and Western Australia come to the same conclusion.[28] In New South Wales the new Legal Profession Act 2004

---

23.   B Landesman, 'Confidentiality and the Lawyer–Client Relationship' in D Luban, *The Good Lawyer* (1964), pp 194–6.
24.   Law Council's Model Rules r 3.1.2 and 3.1.3.
25.   See K Koomen, 'Breach of Confidence and the Public Interest Defence: Is it in the Public Interest?' (1994) 10 *Queensland University of Technology LJ* 57.
26.   *Lillicrap v Nalder & Son* [1993] 1 WLR 94. See also ABA Model Code DR 4-101(C)(4) and ABA Model Rules r 1.6(b)(2).
27.   J Disney, J Basten, P Redmond and S Ross, *Lawyers*, 1977, pp 582–3.
28.   See *Solicitors Handbook* (Qld), para 4.02.1 and Professional Conduct Rules (WA) r 6.3(b). These rules allow confidential information to be revealed only in defending a criminal or professional misconduct charge.

states: 'If a client of an Australian legal practitioner makes a complaint about the practitioner, the complainant is taken to have waived client legal privilege, or the benefit of any duty of confidentiality, to enable the practitioner to disclose to the appropriate authorities any information necessary for investigating and dealing with the complaint.'[29] The English Law Society's *Guide to the Professional Conduct of Solicitors* allows solicitors to reveal confidential information to the extent that it is 'reasonably necessary to establish a defence', not only for disciplinary investigations, but also to any civil claim or criminal charge.[30] In the United States such behaviour by a client appears to constitute a waiver and the lawyer can respond even if no proceedings have been taken.[31] Finally, in Canada the Code of Professional Conduct says disclosure is justified when lawyers or their associates or employees need to defend an allegation of malpractice or misconduct brought by the client, 'but only to the extent necessary for such purposes'.[32]

The third exception is when clients waive their rights by expressly or impliedly allowing disclosure.[33] If the client waives the privilege inadvertently or accidentally there is still no waiver. If clients do not expressly limit lawyers' authority they have extensive implied authority to make disclosures that are in the best interests of their clients.[34]

The fourth exception is where the confidential information becomes public knowledge and therefore it is not necessary to maintain the protection.[35]

There is a fifth category of general duties that may override the confidentiality rule. What if a lawyer feels a moral responsibility to reveal confidential material of a client (who has acted improperly or illegally) in order to protect another person against physical or financial harm? What if the client is going to commit a fraud or crime or has committed it with the lawyer's help unbeknownst to the lawyer? What if the client is a large corporation that is using its lawyers to hide information that shows its products are defective and harmful to the public?[36] How far should the discretion of the lawyer extend in deciding what can be revealed and when it can be revealed? It can be argued that lawyers can disclose such confidences for higher purposes such as in the interest of justice, but it would be difficult for lawyers to maintain such a defence to disclosure.[37]

11.9

---

29. Legal Profession Act 2004 (NSW) s 604(1).
30. p 333.
31. ABA Model Rule 1.6(b)(2) and Comment [17]; Model Code DR 4-101(c)(4). See also Note, 'ABA Code of Professional Responsibility: An Attorney's Right to Self-Defense' (1975) 40 *Mod L Rev* 327.
32. Chapter 4, Guiding Principles, 10.
33. Evidence Act s 122 and Law Council's Model Rule 3.1.1. There is an interesting example of a client's waiver in *Benecke v National Australia Bank* (1993) 35 NSWLR 110.
34. This has been recognised under ABA Model Rule 1.6(a) which permits disclosures that are impliedly authorised in order to carry out the representation.
35. Model Rule 3.1.4. and Barristers' Rules (NSW) r 103(a) and (Qld) r 109(a).
36. See R Nader and W Smith, *No Contest: Corporate Lawyers and Perversion of Justice in America*, Random House, New York, 1996, Ch 2, pp 60–99. The authors outline a number of cases where this has occurred in the United States. They also make a strong argument against the use of confidential settlements, calling for their removal.
37. G Dal Pont, *Lawyers' Professional Responsibility in Australia and New Zealand*, 2nd ed, LBC Information Services, Sydney, 2001, p 273. Dal Pont refers for more detail to G Dal Pont and D Chamlers, *Equity and Trusts in Australia and New Zealand*, 2nd ed, LBC Information Services, Sydney, 2000, pp 167–75.

There is a general broad exception in the Law Council's Model Rules r 3.1.3 allowing disclosure 'for the sole purpose of avoiding the probable commission or concealment of a serious criminal offence'. A similar broad exception exists under the ABA Model Code.[38] The exceptions to the ABA Model Rules are far narrower than the broad exception in Australia and under the ABA Model Code. ABA Model Rule 3.3(b) requires a lawyer to take remedial action with respect to client perjury. ABA Model Rule 1.6(b)(1) permits (no requirement) a lawyer to reveal confidential information if it is necessary to prevent a 'criminal act likely to result in imminent death or substantial bodily harm'. In New Zealand there is a special exemption to protect clients and not third parties. It states that the practitioner may disclose when he or she believes that 'there is a serious and imminent risk to the health or safety of the client'.[39] The exceptions in Australia and the United States will be discussed in more detail in **11.92–11.95**.

Legal duties

11.10 Lawyers, by entering into a contract of retainer, have a contractual duty to maintain the confidentiality of their clients' affairs. Lawyers have a similar duty to other agents, if their principal so intends, to treat information from and about their clients as confidential. There is an important exception to this obligation. As Lord Diplock stated:[40]

> Such a duty of confidence is subject to, and overridden by, the duty of any party to that contract to comply with the law of the land. If it is the duty of such a party to a contract ... to disclose in defined circumstances confidential information, then he must do so, and any express contract to the contrary would be illegal and void.

As will be seen in Chapter 12, the duty of a lawyer to maintain confidences continues after the lawyer–client relationship has ended.[41] It would even appear that this duty continues after the client dies, but as is shown later in the chapter, this can cause considerable distress to others.

The scope of the contractual and agency duty and the exceptions are similar to those under the ethical duty. Breach of the contractual duty to maintain confidences is a breach of the fiduciary duty and could render a lawyer liable for damages in contract or tort. A lawyer has to protect clients' confidences adequately. Conferences with clients should be arranged to avoid the presence of third parties. Procedures need to be adopted to prevent third parties from obtaining confidential information. Lawyers must maintain the security of clients' files and make sure all their employees understand the need to maintain strict confidentiality in relation to clients' affairs.[42] Securing clients' confidences is even more difficult with modern methods of communication such as mobile phones, fax machines and email and thus lawyers must be careful in using these forms of communication. Failure to maintain proper standards can lead not only to negligence or breach of contract actions, but can also constitute behaviour falling below

38.   DR 4-101(C)(3).
39.   Rules of Professional Conduct for Barristers and Solicitors (NZ) r 108(ix).
40.   *Parry-Jones v Law Society* [1969] 1 Ch 1 at 9 (C of A). This view has been adopted by the High Court in *O'Reilly v Commissioner of State Bank of Victoria* (1982) 57 ALJR 130.
41.   See, for example, *In the Marriage of Griffis* (1991) 14 Fam LR 782.
42.   C Wolfram, *Modern Legal Ethics*, West Publishers, St Paul, 1986, p 303.

professional standards and lead to disciplinary action. It is good practice to place a disclaimer on all emails and faxes that the communication is confidential and privileged. This now appears to be common practice in Australia.

The contractual obligations did not apply to barristers until recently **11.11** because they did not have contractual capacity. Barristers had relationships with solicitors and not with clients. An equitable remedy was the only avenue open for a client to use against a barrister. An action for breach of confidence is such a remedy. The action arises independently of any contractual obligation. In order for such an action to succeed:[43]

> ... the information must have the necessary quality of confidence, the defendant must be under an obligation to the plaintiff not to disclose or use it, and an unauthorised disclosure or use must have occurred or be in contemplation. A successful plaintiff may be granted an injunction, other equitable relief, or damages.

Although breach of confidence actions have occurred frequently in the area of trade secrets there is no reason they could not be used against barristers. With recent changes to the laws regulating barristers throughout Australia this remedy may not be necessary in a number of circumstances. Now that barristers are entitled to enter into contractual relationships and at times to deal directly with clients, they will be subjected to the same avenues of redress as other lawyers for breaching clients' confidences.

LEGAL PROFESSION PRIVILEGE

Historical background

There is a dispute as to the history of the privilege. One view, attributed to **11.12** Wigmore, is that the privilege stems from ideas in Roman law. Under Roman law the accused's advocate, relatives and slaves were all prohibited from testifying as witnesses. The original reason for the prohibition was to maintain the stability of the family. It was later deemed that such evidence was unreliable because such witnesses would be motivated to lie.[44] Wigmore wrote that these views were recognised in English law during the reign of Elizabeth I (late sixteenth century) and then applied throughout the common law ever since.[45] During the seventeenth and eighteenth centuries the privilege was that of the legal adviser. He was a man of honour and such a man would not betray the confidences of his clients. A shift then occurred away from the gentleman's honour notion, that barristers should not be made to be embarrassed by being asked to reveal sordid things about their clients, to the modern version that the privilege serves the interests of clients to obtain effective legal advice.[46]

---

43. J Disney, J Basten, P Redmond and S Ross, *Lawyers*, Law Book Co, Sydney, 2nd ed, 1986, p 659.
44. M Radin, 'The Privilege of Confidential Communication between Lawyer and Client' (1928) 16 *California LR* 487. See also D Boniface, 'Professionalism, privilege and public policy: legal professional privilege' (1989) 27 *Law Society J* 66.
45. Wolfram (above), pp 242–3, citing J Wigmore, *Evidence*, 3rd ed, Little Brown & Co, Boston, 1940, para 2290.
46. *Greenough v Gaskell* (1833) 1 Myl & K 98, High Court of Chancery, England. For a discussion of its history in Australia see Desiatnik (above), Ch 2.

11.13   More recently, the High Court of Australia has seen privilege to be of paramount importance because it is an essential part of the 'perfect administration of justice'.[47] The court has also said that the privilege facilitates the 'rule of law'[48] and is a 'practical guarantee of fundamental, constitutional or human rights'[49] and thus protects 'the weak, the frightened, the unpopular and the disadvantaged'.[50]

Hazard has a different view of the development of the privilege in English law. He argues that although it was recognised as early as the sixteenth century, it was only applied sporadically and not fully accepted until after 1800.[51] Furthermore, the scope of the privilege was constantly changing and there was no predictable direction.[52] Today the privilege is well established in many countries outside the common law.[53]

The rationale and critique of the rule

11.14   The modern justification for retaining the privilege rests on a three-step syllogism. First, in order for an effective adversary system, it is useful for people to have the assistance of competent legal advisers. Second, in order for lawyers to be effective, to give accurate and appropriate legal advice, they must have open communication with their clients to obtain all the necessary information.[54] Third, it is argued that people will be more willing to make use of lawyers' services and more willing to make disclosures, if they are assured that their communications will remain secret. Therefore, in order to have orderly and efficient adversarial justice, we must maintain lawyer–client confidentiality.[55] This rationale was originally stated in a leading nineteenth-century case in England,[56] and the High Court has enunciated a similar rationale in recent decisions.[57] Lawyers have also argued that additional rationales for the privilege are that it improves the 'dignity' of the lawyer–client relationship by promoting obedience to the law. By having the doctrine lawyers can discover, by obtaining information, spurious claims and planned wrongdoings and be able to persuade clients to not go through with their plans.[58] The privilege therefore 'is specifically

---

47.   *Carter v Managing Partner, Northmore Hale Davy & Leake* (1995) 129 ALR 593, 601 per Deane J.
48.   *Carter* (above) at 596 per Brennan J.
49.   *Australian Federal Police v Propend Finance Pty Ltd* (1997) 141 ALR 545 at 584 per McHugh J.
50.   *Carter* (above) at 604 per Deane J.
51.   G Hazard, 'An Historical Perspective on the Attorney–Client Privilege' (1978) 66 *California LR* 1061, 1070.
52.   Hazard (above), p 1087, fn 120.
53.   For example, Belgium, Denmark, Germany, France, Greece, Italy, Luxembourg and Holland are mentioned in *AM & S Europe v Commission of the European Communities* [1983] 3 WLR 17 at 26–8.
54.   This rationale has strong support for enabling lawyers to be effective negotiators; but this aspect is covered by the without prejudice privilege: see *Lukies v Ripley (No 2)* (1994) 35 NSWLR 283. See also S McNicol (above), 1992, Ch 8; and Desiatnik (above), Ch 4.
55.   Wolfram (above), p 243.
56.   *Greenough v Gaskell* (1833) 1 Myl & K 98 at 102.
57.   See the majority judgment in *Grant v Downs* (1976) 51 ALJR 198 at 202 and Dawson J (one of the majority) in *Baker v Campbell* (1983) 153 CLR 52; 57 ALJR 749 at 780–1.
58.   S Watson, 'Keeping Secrets that Harm Others: Medical Standards Illuminate Lawyer's Dilemma' (1992) 71 *Nebraska LR* 1123, 1129.

aimed at reducing the amount of litigation … by promoting the peaceful settlement of disputes out of court'.[59] It can just as easily be argued that the privilege shields as many groundless suits and planned wrongful activities as those that it stops.[60]

The granting of the privilege also removes from the adversarial process **11.15** information that can aid in the search for truth. Frankel J has urged that the premise for placing the right to privilege above the search for truth needs to be examined.[61] He does see problems in reversing the present situation:

> If the lawyer is to be more truth-seeker than combatant, troublesome questions of economics and professional organization may demand early confrontation. How and why should the client pay for loyalties divided between himself and the truth? Will we not stultify the energies and resources of the advocate by demanding that he judge the honesty of his cause along the way? Can we preserve the heroic lawyer shielding his client against all the world — and not least against the state — while demanding that he or she honour a paramount commitment to the elusive and ambiguous truth? It is strongly arguable, in short, that a simplistic preference for the truth may not comport with more fundamental ideals — including notably the ideal that generally values individual freedom and dignity above order and efficiency in government …

Frankel J's worries show that clients may have expectations and reliance and will feel a sense of unfairness or betrayal if their confidences are revealed. We have discussed earlier (see **11.5–11.7**) the moral basis for maintaining confidences in our society and these concerns are increased by the nature of confidences given to lawyers. The placing of strict limits on the privilege may also induce uncertainty as to what to disclose, and induce clients to lie or seek out lawyers who have a reputation for maintaining confidences.[62]

Historically the English courts have said that privilege is more important **11.16** than truth. Knight Bruce VC in 1846 said:[63]

> Truth, like all other good things, may be loved unwisely — may be pursued too keenly — may cost too much. And surely the meanness and mischief of prying into a man's confidential consultations with his legal adviser, the general evil of infusing reserve and dissimulation, uneasiness and suspicion and fear, into those communications which must take place, and which, unless in a condition of perfect security, must take place uselessly or worse, are too great a price to pay for truth.

This statement was approved by Deane J of the High Court in 1995 in the *Carter* case.[64]

All these arguments for the privilege do not justify an unqualified privilege. **11.17** The claim to the privilege can also lead to a 'moral blindness to the real issues of potential conflict and abuse that a broad and unqualified claim of confidentiality can mask'.[65] This was the approach of Gibbs CJ of the High

---

59.   McNicol (above), p 2.
60.   Wolfram (above), p 244.
61.   M Frankel, 'The Search for Truth: An Umpireal View' (1975) *U Pa LR* 1031, 1055.
62.   Watson (above), pp 1129–30.
63.   *Pearse v Pearse* (1846) 1 De G & Sm 12 at 28–9; 63 ER 950 at 957.
64.   *Carter v Managing Partner, Northmore Hale Davy & Leake* (1995) 183 CLR 121; 129 ALR 593 at 600.
65.   S Bok, *Secrets*, Pantheon Books, New York, 1982, p 123.

Court in the *Baker* case. He said the privilege is 'in conflict with another principle of equal importance, namely, that all evidence which reveals the truth should be available for presentation to the court'.[66] This view was repeated very recently by Lord Carswell in the *Three Rivers District Council* case where he said:

> Determining the bounds of privilege involves finding the proper balance between opposing imperatives, making the maximum relevant material available to the court of trial and avoiding unfairness to individuals by revealing confidential communications between their lawyers and themselves ... There is considerable public interest in each of these. The importance of keeping to a minimum the withholding of relevant material from the Court ... is self-evident.[67]

As will be seen, there are a number of exceptions to the privilege rule. They usually do not allow a case-by-case balancing of the interests of society for disclosure against the need for maintaining the privilege.[68] Although there was evidence from several cases that the Australian High Court was more willing to use the balancing approach, in the *Carter* case it rejected this approach by a 3:2 majority,[69] and Lord Scott of Foscote in the *Three Rivers District Council* case in 2005 also rejects the balancing exercise.[70]

Arguments for and against privilege

11.18   The right to privilege was first attacked as being anti-utilitarian by Jeremy Bentham almost 180 years ago. He argued that removal of the privilege would be beneficial to society; the making available of all relevant material in a trial would enable the court to achieve a just decision. The consequences would be that 'a guilty person will not in general be able to derive quite so much assistance from his law adviser, in the way of concerting a false defence': the privilege only protected the guilty and those who are innocent do not need to be protected.[71]

Dean Wigmore defends privilege against these arguments. He claims that Bentham did not consider the innocent who are accused because of suspicious circumstances, but only those plainly innocent or guilty. In relation to those who are guilty it is not clear that lawyers will give them as much assistance. Wigmore argued that Bentham assumed that lawyers will invariably proceed to assist unjust causes, when in fact many would decline to act or persuade their client that the cause is hopeless and plead guilty. In relation to the unprotected innocent person in suspicious circumstances, such a person would be harmed by being exposed to the same risks as if the right against self-incrimination were absent. The accused would refrain from stating incriminating matters to their lawyers. Furthermore, if lawyers

---

66. *Baker v Campbell* (1983) 153 CLR 52 at 69.
67. *Three Rivers District Council v Governor and Co of the Bank of England (No 6)* [2005] 1 AC 610 at 667–8.
68. Ibid.
69. Important High Court cases taking this approach include *Re Bell; Ex parte Lees* (1980) 146 CLR 141, *Baker v Campbell* (1983) 153 CLR 52 and *Grant v Downs* (1976) 135 CLR 674. The High Court in a later case rejected the balancing approach, see *Carter v Managing Partner, Northmore Hale Davy & Leake* (1995) 129 ALR 593.
70. [2005] 1 AC 610 at 646.
71. J Bentham, *Rationale of Judicial Evidence* (1827) Vol VII, p 474 (Banring ed), extracted in M Pirsig and K Kirwin, *Professional Responsibility: Cases and Materials*, 4th ed, West Publishing, St Paul, 1984, pp 113–14.

were forced to testify to damaging admissions, the result would be to discourage these accused from seeking out lawyers.[72]

Wolfram states that the defenders of privilege do not argue against Bentham's utilitarian framework. Instead they argue that the harm of concealing the truth is more than balanced by the essential good of helping an innocent victim in suspicious circumstances.[73] This is a libertarian philosophical approach that the privilege 'is of great importance to the protection and preservation of the rights, dignity and freedom of the ordinary citizen under the law';[74] and 'individual rights and interests should be protected against undue interference from the law'.[75] Simon still believes that the various rationales are 'perverse' because they protect and encourage clients to act irresponsibly by withholding information, sometimes at the expense of innocent third parties.[76] Furthermore, having the right is no guarantee that an accused will speak freely with his or her lawyers. The accused will be more hesitant to speak to lawyers who usually cannot be discharged or who might have conflicting loyalties in the eyes of the accused, for example legal aid lawyers.[77] **11.19**

Wigmore also argued that in civil cases there is no hard and fast line between the guilty and the innocent; and in civil cases the guilt is not all on one side. The loss of truth is also less in civil cases because the opponent can be compelled to take the stand and be subjected to interrogation. Wigmore does concede that there is still a loss in getting to the truth in civil cases. Therefore the privilege in this area should be 'strictly confined within the narrowest possible limits consistent with the logic of its principle'.[78]

There are strong arguments that more disclosure, especially in civil proceedings, would make little if any difference to the willingness of clients to share confidences with their lawyers. Rhode has summarised other reasons for such disclosure:[79] **11.20**

- clients often have no realistic alternative to confiding in counsel;
- lawyers acquire much adverse information through means other than direct client communication;
- clients already are unaware of the scope of confidentiality protections; and
- the bar in many countries and in this nation [the United States] historically has managed to provide adequate representation without sweeping confidentiality protections.

There is no objective evidence to support the arguments for maintaining the privilege and empirical research is needed,[80] especially in Australia.

72. J Wigmore, *A Treatise on the Anglo-American System of Evidence in Trials at Common Law*, revised ed, Little Brown & Co, Boston, 1961, para 2291.
73. Wolfram (above), p 247.
74. Deane J in *Attorney-General (NT) v Maurice* (1986) 161 CLR 475; 65 ALR 230.
75. McNicol (above), p 1.
76. W Simon, 'Ethical Discretion in Lawyering' (1988) 101 *Harvard LR* 1083, 1142.
77. H Subin, 'The Lawyer as Superego: Disclosure of Client Confidences to Prevent Harm' (1985) 70 *Iowa LR* 351, 382–3.
78. Wigmore (above), (1961), para 2291.
79. D Rhode, *Professional Responsibility: Ethics by the Pervasive Method*, Little Brown, Boston, 1994, p 478.
80. F Zacharias, 'Rethinking Confidentiality' (1989) 74 *Iowa LR* 351. The author discusses data that is opposed to the rationale for retaining the privilege: pp 379–408.

A 1962 American study of lawyers and non-lawyers concerning the effectiveness of privilege in opening up communications concluded that a greater number of lawyers than non-lawyers believed that the privilege encourages disclosures. Furthermore, it found that most non-lawyers were either unaware that the privilege existed or erroneously assumed that the privilege was also found within other professional relationships.[81] A later study of lawyers and clients in the late 1980s found the following: lawyers rarely inform clients about confidentiality; clients had a great misunderstanding of the scope of confidentiality; only 30 per cent of former clients surveyed said they would have withheld information they had given if they were not given a guarantee of confidentiality.[82]

11.21 It is difficult to determine the extent of the effect on clients' disclosures of maintaining the privilege. If empirical studies show that the number of clients needing a broad privilege doctrine is small, the interests of society should then prevail, allowing, or even mandating, disclosures.[83] Lawyers will vigorously oppose such a change. Lawyers' privilege doctrine has improved their competitive position in relation to other professionals. This was patently obvious after the ATO raided the offices of Citibank in 1988. Several law firms doing tax work ran advertisements pointing out that their clients' communications were protected by the privilege. The major accountancy firms could not make such a claim and therefore the services they were offering would necessarily have to be considered less valuable by clients.[84] Wolfram accurately sums up the situation:[85]

> One can confidently predict that if professors or members of another occupational group could convene a court or legislature of their kind to consider whether communications in their secret conclaves should be absolutely privileged, they too would solemnly decide to enact the privilege for compelling reasons. But courts are peopled only by lawyers, and no other occupational group has been benefited by an unqualified privilege recognised in all tribunals.

Privilege for other occupations

11.22 The clergy has been granted the privilege in relation to confessions under statute in six jurisdictions.[86] The provision, s 127 of the Evidence Act, is the only section of the Act relating to privilege that does not have the

81. Note, 'Functional Overlap between the Lawyers and Other Professionals: Its Implication for the Privilege Communication Doctrine' (1962) 71 *Yale LJ* 1226, 1232.
82. F Zacharias (above), pp 382–3. See also L Levin, 'Testing the Radical Experiment: A Study of Lawyer Response to Clients who Intend to Harm Others' (1994) 47 *Rutgers LR* 81. Levin found (pp 103–4) that 79.1 per cent of clients claimed to know of lawyer–client confidentiality and 42 per cent mistakenly believed it was absolute.
83. Watson (above), p 1131.
84. S Ross, *Ethics for Tax Practitioners*, Australian Tax Research Foundation Research Study No 18, Sydney, 1993, p 50. The accountants brought strong pressure on the Australian Taxation Office and they were granted limited rights to confidentiality in the ATO Guidelines.
85. Wolfram (above), p 247.
86. Evidence Act (NSW, ACT and Cth (1995) and Tas (2001)) s 127; Evidence Act 1958 (Vic) s 28(1); Evidence Act 1939 (NT) s 12(1). See also American Law Institute Model Code of Evidence r 219. In *R v Lynch* [1954] Tas SR 47 it was held that the confession must be for a spiritual purpose. The above statutory provisions also state that a confession is not protected if it discloses a criminal purpose.

'adducing evidence' requirement. In other jurisdictions it would appear most judges would exercise their discretion and not compel a clergyman to disclose confidential communications.[87] The Anglican Church in Australia, in light of revelations to the Police Royal Commission concerning criminals being sheltered by the confessional, re-enacted in October 1997 the right of clergy to reveal confessions in 'extreme cases'. This right had been removed in 1993.[88] Physicians have the privilege by statute in three jurisdictions in civil cases.[89] Ritter JR of the Industrial Relations Court of Australia rejected an argument that the legal advice given by industrial officers of a union was entitled to privilege because of industrial officers' right to represent union members under s 170EA of the Industrial Relations Act 1988 (Cth) in applications before the court.[90] There is statutory protection for a registered patent attorney and his or her client for intellectual property matters under s 200(2) of the Patents Act 1990 (Cth).[91] This section does not cover a foreign patent attorney.[92] Gyles J has also stated that it was 'far from axiomatic' that the privilege extends to foreign lawyers.[93] Richard Ackland pointed out that this decision had important implications in light of 'an increasingly globalised business environment ... Suddenly the rules of the protection game have changed. No wonder there is panic abroad'.[94] It would appear that foreign lawyers admitted to practice in Australia do have the privilege.

There are many other confidential relationships, such as with accountants, **11.23** journalists, bankers, teachers, tax agents, and so on, where there is no specific statutory protection. There is protection in most jurisdictions only if a judge exercises his or her discretion to protect the confidences[95] either under their common law power or if granted by statute.[96] New South Wales amended its Evidence Act to create a 'professional confidential relationship privilege'.[97] Section 126B(1) grants judges the right to direct that evidence not be adduced in court if such disclosure would result in revealing a protected confidence, or a document containing a protected confidence, or information revealing a protected identity. 'Protected confidence' under s 126A(1) is a communication made by a person in confidence to a confidant acting in a professional role, where there was an obligation for

---

87. *Cross on Evidence* (above), para 25320 at p 845.
88. *Sydney Morning Herald*, 15 October 1997, p 6 and 24 October 1997, p 5.
89. Evidence Act 1958 (Vic) s 28(2)–(5); Evidence Act 2001 (Tas) s 127A; Evidence Act 1939 (NT) s 12(2). The American Law Institute Model Code of Evidence r 221 grants privilege in civil cases and in prosecutions for misdemeanours.
90. *Wood v Commonwealth Bank of Australia* (1996) 67 IR 46, 63–5.
91. The privilege provision for a patent attorney is more restricted than that for a lawyer and client. The protection for the former extends to a communication or document brought into existence that directly relates to the purpose of that communication. See *Cross on Evidence* (above), para 25245, fn 446 at p 814.
92. *Eli Lilly & Co v Pfizer Ireland Pharmaceuticals (No 2)* [2004] FCA 850.
93. *Kennedy v Wallace* [2004] FCA 332 at para 57.
94. R Ackland, 'Ruling leaves Kennedy less privileged', *Sydney Morning Herald*, 2 April 2004, p 13.
95. *Cross on Evidence* (above), para 25340.
96. For an example of the statutory right, see Order 15, r 11 of the Industrial Relations Court Rules (Cth). Also see *Wood v Commonwealth Bank of Australia* (1996) 67 IR 46 at 65–7 when a statutory discretion was used to order production of the document.
97. Evidence Act 1995 (NSW) Pt 3.10 Div 1A.

the latter not to disclose the contents. This provision has been interpreted to include journalists.[98] There is an obligation under s 126B(3) on the court to suppress the confidential information if it will likely cause harm to the confider and that harm outweighs the benefit from adducing the evidence. Harm includes both physical, financial, emotional, psychological harm and damage to one's reputation.[99] There are also detailed instructions as to what the court needs to take into account for making its decision.[100] Victoria has also created under its Evidence Act 1958 provisions for 'confidential communications' privilege.[101] The ALRC in Proposal 13-7 of DP 69 favours the adoption in other jurisdictions of the New South Wales provisions and in proposal 13-8 that it be extended to 'pre-trial discovery and the production of documents in response to a subpoena and non-curial contexts such as search warrants and notices to produce documents'.[102]

11.24 Judges will also at times accept a public interest argument to maintain confidences; for example, rape counsellors' notes on victims.[103] Changes to the Evidence Act 1995 (NSW) also include a separate Part (Pt 3.10 Div 1B) for 'Sexual Assault Communications Privilege'.[104] There are similar provisions in the Northern Territory and Tasmania (absolute confidentiality provision).[105] The ALRC in DP 69 has recommended in Proposal 13-7a that Pt 3.10 Div 1B be amended to include a discretionary sexual assault counselling privilege and in Proposal 13-8 that the sexual assault communication privilege be extended to 'pre-trial discovery and the production of documents in response to a subpoena and non-curial contexts such as search warrants and notices to produce documents'. Judges in the past have not often used their general discretion to protect confidences and there have been a number of cases of people being fined or gaoled for contempt; for example, journalists refusing to reveal their sources.[106] A recent example has been the Howard Government's action in Victoria against two *Herald-Sun* journalists for publishing leaked information from a federal bureaucrat. The journalists refused to reveal their source and were held in contempt of court.[107] In a strong editorial criticising the court action, the *Sydney Morning Herald* said: 'In the interests of a free media and an open society, the Federal Government should terminate this witch-hunt immediately.'[108] There are a number of arguments for extending a lawyer-

---

98. See *NRMA v John Fairfax Publications Pty Ltd* [2002] NSWSC 563.
99. Evidence Act 1995 (NSW) s 126A(1).
100. Evidence Act 1995 (NSW) s 126D(4).
101. Pt II Div 2A; the provisions are discussed in detail in *Cross on Evidence* (above), para 25340, pp 852–5.
102. See Appendix 1 of DP 69 for draft provisions of s 126A.
103. For a discussion of this problem see A Cossins and R Pilkinton, 'Balancing the Scales: The Case for the Inadmissibility of Counselling' (1996) 19 *UNSWLJ* 222.
104. See *Cross on Evidence* (above), para 25340 at pp 849–52 for a detailed analysis of the provisions. See also Desiatnik (above), Ch 11 and M Liverani, 'Confidential Communications' (April 1998) *Law Society J (NSW)* 42.
105. Evidence Act 1939 (NT) ss 56–56G and Evidence Act 2001 (Tas) s 127B.
106. An excellent example is the gaoling of a New York Times reporter for failing to reveal her source. See D Nason, 'Reporter jailed for her source', *Australian*, 8 July 2005, p 7. By contrast, protection was given in New South Wales to a journalist in *NRMA v John Fairfax Publications Pty Ltd* [2002] NSWSC 563.
107. C Merritt, 'Flintstones case against journalists', *Australian*, 26 August 2005, p 5.
108. Editorial, 'Court threat to free speech', *Sydney Morning Herald*, 26 August 2005, p 12.

like privilege to other occupations, but movements to broaden it for lawyers or for extending it to other occupations arouse strong opposition.[109] By contrast, the New Zealand Government in 2005 introduced legislation to grant a privilege for giving and receiving tax advice for registered tax practitioners.[110] Perhaps the changes creating a general 'professional confidential relationship privilege' granting discretion to the court will help to overcome some of these problems.

Statement of the rule and general scope

Cross on Evidence succinctly states the rule:[111]

11.25

> In civil and criminal cases, confidential communications passing between a client[112] and a legal adviser need not be given in evidence or otherwise disclosed by the client and, without the client's consent, may not be given in evidence or otherwise disclosed by the legal adviser[113] if made either (1) to enable the client to obtain, or the adviser to give, legal advice, or (2) with reference to litigation that is actually taking place or was in the contemplation of the client.

The definition may be even broader in light of the High Court using the expression 'legal advice or assistance'.[114] There was a distinction between communications from third parties and those coming from the client or his or her agent, but this may have been changed by the Full Federal Court in the *Pratt Holdings* case (see below). In the case of third parties it has been held that the protection only covers confidential communication made with reference to actual or contemplated litigation.[115] If the third party is an agent of either the lawyer or the client, for example a secretary, investigator, or expert, whose advice was sought, and who acts as an intermediary for either one, the communication is privileged.[116] The requirement of actual or contemplated litigation for third parties may no longer be valid. In *Pratt Holdings Pty Ltd* the Full Federal Court felt that the distinction between expert assistance by an agent or alter ego of the client

---

109. See, for example, the editorial 'Tax agents don't need privilege', *Australian Financial Review*, 22 October 1993, p 22.
110. DP 69 at footnote 98. The ALRC paper refers to a New Zealand Government Press Release, 'Statutory Privilege for Legal Advice Extended', 14 September 2004, and to an article 'Follow NZ Lead Say Accountants', *Australian Financial Review*, 17 September 2004.
111. *Cross on Evidence* (above), para 25210 at pp 798–9.
112. There must be a client for the privilege to exist: see *Somerville v Australian Securities Commission* (1995) 131 ALR 517.
113. In a Californian case the court tried to make a lawyer give evidence against his client in a criminal matter that constituted a communication from the lawyer to the client. It was held that the lawyer cannot be forced to make such a disclosure, since it was privileged: see *Re Navaerro* 155 Cal R 522 (1977).
114. *Attorney-General (NT) v Maurice* (1986) 161 CLR 457 at 487 (Mason and Brennan JJ).
115. *Cross on Evidence* (above), para 25210 at p 799. This view is based on *Wheeler v Le Marchant* (1881) 17 Ch D 675. Wood J confirmed this distinction in *Nickmar Pty Ltd v Preservatrice Skandia Insurance Ltd* (1985) 3 NSWLR 44 at 53–4. See also *Southern Equities Corporation Ltd v West Australian Government Holdings* (1993) 10 WAR 1. In *Mitsubishi Electric Australia Pty Ltd v Victorian WorkCover Authority* (2002) 4 VSCA 59 the Court of Appeal upheld an appeal in finding that litigation was comtemplated when reports were obtained from third parties for the purpose of legal advice.
116. *Attorney-General (NT) v Maurice* (1986) 161 CLR 475; 65 ALR 230 at 235 per Woodward J.

was an artificial distinction in the modern world of complex legal arrangements, where companies need expert advice from many different sources. Thus, in *Pratt* the advice came from a third party, the client's accountants, Price Waterhouse, and was not for purposes of litigation, but still held to be privileged. The client here gave the instructions for the documents to be prepared. The court said if the instructions has come from the solicitors the documents would not have been privileged.[117] The court sent the case back to the lower court where Kenny J found that the valuation documents prepared by Price Waterhouse were not privileged as they were not prepared for the dominant purpose of providing legal advice.[118]

The Full Federal Court's decision has been criticised for making a distinction between third party advice sought by the client and that requested by the solicitor. Desiatnik states that: 'These are neither principled nor coherent reasons for so expanding the doctrine of legal professional privilege.'[119] He also points out that Finn J states in *Pratt Holdings* that, while 'legal advice privilege is capable of extending to non-agent, third party authored documentary communications', at times there are great difficulties in meeting the dominant purpose test.[120] The ALRC in DP 69 agrees with the decision in *Pratt Holdings* and in Proposal 13-4 states that s 118(c) of the Evidence Act be amended from reading 'the client or a lawyer' to read 'the client, a lawyer or another person'. The High Court has so far not dealt with the extension of privilege as decided in the *Pratt Holdings* case.

11.26 In the 1990s the definition was also broadened by a clarification of what constitutes a 'common interest' privilege and a 'joint interest' privilege.[121] The common interest privilege occurs when a privileged communication is given to a third party who has a 'common interest' in relation to that communication. It is also found in the Evidence Act 1995 in s 122(5)(b) where the privilege is not lost by communications made to a person who comes under the common interest privilege. Although a third party is involved the communication does not have to be made with reference to actual or contemplated litigation but has to be received by the third party subject to a duty of confidence.[122] The fact that the communication is made does not constitute a waiver and the third party also has the right to

---

117. *Pratt Holdings Pty Ltd v Federal Commissioner of Taxation* [2004] FCAFC 122 at paras 40–3, 103–6. In *GSA Industries (Aust) Pty Ltd v Constable* [2002] 2 Qld R 146, with similar facts to *Pratt*, Holmes J upheld the privilege on the basis that the accountants were the agent of the client. Finn J in *Pratt* at para 41 disagreed with this view by finding that the accountants were a third party. See also J O'Neil, 'Loosening the Shackles on Advice Privilege' (2004) 42 *Law Society J (NSW)* 60.
118. S Scott, 'Third parties mean advice may not be privileged', *Australian Financial Review*, 9 September 2005, p 60.
119. Desiatnik (above), p 25.
120. Ibid at pp 25–6, and *Pratt Holdings Pty Ltd v Commissioner of Taxation* (2004) 207 ALR 217 at 227–8.
121. See S McNicol, 'Professional privilege spreads its wings' (1996) 70 *Law Institute J (Vic)* 32. A joint interest privilege has been present in a number of cases during the last 100 years. See *Cross on Evidence* (above), para 25265, p 724.
122. *State of South Australia v Peat Marwick Mitchell* (1995) 65 SASR 72.

claim a privilege concerning that communication. Lockhart J has clearly defined 'common interest' privilege. He said it is:[123]

> ... a privilege in aid of anticipated litigation in which several persons have a common interest. It often happens in litigation that a plaintiff or defendant has other persons alongside him [or her] — who have the self-same interest as he — and who have consulted lawyers on the self-same points as he — but these others have not been made parties to the action.

The common interest holder does not have to be a client of the same lawyers.[124] What is required is that there exists 'a sufficient identity or commonality of interest'. This means that the interests do not have to be identical but they must be common.[125] As Giles CJ has stated:[126]

> ... two persons interested in a particular question will not have a ... common interest privilege if their individual interests in the question are selfish and potentially adverse to each other.

The Federal Court has also stated that if a conflict of interest develops between the parties the common interest privilege is waived.[127]

A 'joint interest' privilege can be shown when there is a joint retainer or **11.27** when the facts show that two clients jointly sought and received legal advice. It is also found in s 122(5)(a) of the Evidence Acts. Young J in *Farrow Mortgage Services Ltd v Webb* stated that when a joint interest privilege exists, unlike common interest, all must join in for a waiver to take place.[128] The majority of the Court of Appeal in the *Farrow Mortgage Services* case upheld a joint privilege when legal advice had been sought by both a company and its directors even though it had not been jointly commissioned by both. In that case Meagher JA issued a strong dissent on the basis that the company was the client who sought and paid for the advice and thus the directors had no legal interest in the advice.[129] Another way of proving a joint interest was accepted by Simos J in *Pioneer Concrete (NSW) Pty Ltd v Webb*, where his Honour found that the clients had proved they 'believed' on reasonable grounds the lawyers were acting for both parties.[130] In a joint interest situation where a solicitor represents both parties, if an actual conflict of interest develops between the joint parties the waiver between them ceases. This does not happen when one of the clients is deceived by the other client or the solicitors 'into believing that information sought was required for the purposes of the joint retainer'.[131] The common law is modified by s 124(2) of the Evidence Act.

---

123. *Somerville v Australian Securities Commission* (1995) 131 ALR 517, 528. In this case it was found that the Commission did not have the self-same interest as the client who was the party to the litigation.

124. *Network Ten Ltd v Capital Television Holdings Ltd* (1995) 36 NSWLR 275.

125. McNicol (above), 1996, pp 32–3. See *Theiss Contractors Pty Ltd v Terokill Pty Ltd* [1993] 2 Qd R 341 (common interest of an insurer and insured); *Southern Cross Airlines Holdings Ltd (in liq) v Arthur Andersen & Co* (1998) 84 FCR 472 (liquidator and creditors).

126. Giles CJ, *Ampolex v Perpetual Trustee Co* (1995) 37 NSWLR 405 at 410.

127. *Patrick v Capital Finance Corp* (2004) 211 ALR 272.

128. (1995) 13 ACLC 1329 at 1333; see also the judgment of Giles CJ in *Ampolex v Perpetual Trustee Co* (1995) 37 NSWLR 405 at 412.

129. (1996) 14 ACLC 1240.

130. (1995) 13 ACLC 329; see also *Global Funds Management (NSW) Ltd v Rooney* (1994) 36 NSWLR 122.

131. *Cross on Evidence* (above), para 25265 at p 824, which refers to *TSB Bank plc v Robert Irving & Burns* [2000] 2 All ER 826 at 831–4 (CA).

When two or more clients have jointly retained a lawyer in the same civil matter the Act does not prevent one of them from adducing evidence of: (a) a communication made by any one of them to the lawyer; or (b) the contents of a confidential document prepared by or at the direction or request of any one of them.

Lockhart J stated in the *Sterling* case that the privilege would also cover other situations such as communications between the client's various legal advisers, for example lawyers and their partners or their city agent. Thus, the numerous notes, memoranda, minutes or other documents made by these lawyers or their agents or by clients or their agents, can also be privileged.[132] File or diary notes have to be related to the giving of legal advice,[133] and documents that were not regarded as privileged material are not protected just because they are included as part of a 'bundle' in a brief given to a barrister. The privilege can be 'original' or 'derivative' material. The latter receives protection because to deny such protection would lead to revealing of the original privileged material.[134] The knowledge, information or belief of clients that come from privileged communication made to them by their lawyers or agents is also privileged.[135] The fact that the documents, notes, and so on are not used does not destroy the privilege.[136] Under common law if the privileged communication is leaked or overheard or intercepted by a third party,[137] or a copy is obtained by the opposing party,[138] the privilege is lost.

Fairness doctrine and waiver

11.28   As we will see, the harshness of this doctrine is being tempered by more recent cases. It is also lost if clients impliedly or expressly waive their rights. Even an express partial disclosure of some of the contents of the legal advice can result in denying privilege to the whole communication.[139] In *Goldberg v Ng*[140] a solicitor waived the privilege, even though an officer of the Law Society had given an undertaking that the documents would remain privileged. The High Court held by a 3:2 decision that the client had lost his privilege by bringing the complaint against the solicitor to the Law Society, and in the interests of fairness the solicitor, by submitting his documents, should also be considered to have waived his privilege. The fairness doctrine was applied in another case[141] where an expert witness read the privileged document to refresh his memory. He did this for the

132. *Trade Practices Commission v Sterling* (1978) 36 FLR 244 at 247.
133. *Anford Pty Ltd v GCI Properties Pty Ltd* (SC(Qld), Muir J, No 56355 of 1999, 7 December 1999, unreported). This case was handed down just before the sole purpose test was removed by the High Court. The judge found most of file and diary notes did not meet the test and granted the privilege only for 2 of the 17 documents. The documents were files and diary notes of the former solicitors for the plaintiff recording telephone discussions with a director of the plaintiff concerning negotiations for a lease with the defendants.
134. *Cross on Evidence*, para 25055 at pp 768–70.
135. *Trade Practices Commission v Sterling* (1978) 36 FLR 244 at 247.
136. *Sterling* (above).
137. *Rumping v DPP* [1964] AC 814.
138. *Calcraft v Guest* [1898] 1 QB 759.
139. *Ex parte Cohen* (unreported, SC(WA), Scott J, no CIV 2075 of 1998, 17 November 1998, BC9806429).
140. *Goldberg v Ng* (1995) 132 ALR 57.
141. *Mgica (1992) Ltd v Kenny & Good Pty Ltd (No 2)* (1996) 135 ALR 743.

purpose of giving evidence for the benefit of the privilege holder and the court held that the privilege was lost. Finally, the fairness doctrine was applied by Hill J in finding that a voluntary waiver had taken place in relation to witnesses' statements that had been filed and served on another party in the proceedings.[142]

The fairness doctrine has been removed for adducing evidence in court under the Evidence Act. Thus, the High Court's decision in *Ng* appears to be modified by the Act. Section 122(2) states that the privilege is not available 'if a client or party has knowingly and voluntarily disclosed to another person the substance of the evidence' subject to certain exceptions. Furthermore, under s 122(4) the privilege is lost 'if the substance of the evidence has been disclosed with the express or implied consent of the client or party', but again is subject to exceptions. This subsection deals with disclosures by third parties who are not a client or party as defined under s 117. Furthermore, the Full Federal Court in *Adelaide Steamship Pty Ltd v Spalvins*[143] held that notions of fairness from the common law were not applicable to s 122.

Kirby J interpreted s 122(2) in *Ampolex Ltd v Perpetual Trustee Co (Canberra) Ltd.*[144] He said that the 'mere reference to the existence of legal advice would not amount to a waiver of the contents' of a document under the section. But waiver did take place because Ampolex said that the substance of the legal advice supported its assertion that it was applying a correct ratio formula. Kirby J said the privilege was waived as to the 'precise content of the legal advice on that point'. Thus, parties must be careful in quoting the use of legal advice to support their views, which can be found to be inconsistent with evoking the privilege. This is obvious from the *Telstra Corp Ltd v BT Australasia Pty Ltd*[145] case, which appears to oppose the *Adelaide Steamship* case by using the fairness doctrine. In the *Telstra* case waiver was found as imputed consent under the common law fairness doctrine. The majority of the Full Federal Court stated that the client had opened up the issue of his state of mind because of stating that he had relied on representations made by another in undertaking his actions. The Full Federal Court also held that the determination of waiver had to be done on common law principles. In *Perpetual Trustees (WA) Ltd v Equuscorp Pty Ltd*[146] the Full Court found waiver because the client asserted it had relied on legal advice in formulating the privileged document. The court referred to *Ampolex* in stating that the state of mind of Equus was central to its claims and the security document had to be examined.[147] Waiver is thus

---

142. *Complete Technology Pty Ltd v Toshiba (Aust) Pty Ltd* (1994) 124 ALR 493.
143. (1998) 81 FCR 360.
144. (1996) 137 ALR 28. In contrast to Kirby J's views, Rolfe J in the Supreme Court (NSW) came to the opposite conclusion: (1996) 40 NSWLR 12.
145. (1998) 156 ALR 634.
146. [1999] FCA 925.
147. For a case where waiver was not found although there was a reliance, see *Temwell Pty Ltd v DKGR Holdings Pty Ltd; mCom Solutions Inc v Temwell Pty Ltd* [2003] FCA 1296. Ryan J at para 43 said that he did not understand the High Court majority opinion in *Mann v Carnell* (1999) 201 CLR 1. He said 'to have held that the putting in issue of reliance or some other state of mind does not in every case amount to a waiver of privilege attaching to legal advice relevant to the formation of reliance or other state of mind'. Ryan J still felt bound to apply the general principle but found it inapplicable in the case because of the 'impossibility of identifying any relevant legal advice' in the disputed file.

present when a party acts in a way that is inconsistent with the otherwise confidential communication.

McLelland CJ has made an extensive analysis of the relationship between the provisions in s 122(2) and (4). He shows by examining the language that subs (2) deals with disclosures by the client or party (including employees and agents) as defined in s 117, and not by subs (4), while subs (4) deals with disclosures by any other person or entity.[148] This view has also been recently adopted in *British American Tobacco Australia Services Ltd v Eubanks (for the USA)*.[149] He also held that the provisions extend derivatively, although not directly, to processes ancillary to the trial, such as interrogatories, discovery and production of documents under a notice to produce or a subpoena.[150] This view was rejected by the High Court in *Mann v Carnell* where it was held that the Evidence Act does not modify the common law and is inapplicable to pre-trial proceedings.[151] In that case the appellant sought pre-trial discovery and inspection of copies of documents that were a legal report and legal advice. The copies had been given in confidence by the Chief Minister of the Australian Capital Territory to a member of the Legislative Assembly. Although it was accepted that they were privileged, the appellant argued that by her actions the Chief Minister had waived the privilege. The court found that waiver had not taken place because she was only performing functions of her office. Thus, her actions were not 'inconsistent with the maintenance of the confidentiality which the privilege is intended to protect'.[152] Although the High Court did not rely on the fairness doctrine it did say that the fairness doctrine was relevant to s 122(2).[153] The courts have also found that circulation of legal advice among managers, members of the board of directors and employees, will not constitute a waiver by being considered a disclosure to strangers.[154]

11.29 Sometimes part of a privileged document can be waived while the rest remains privileged. In *Ashfield Municipal Council v RTA*[155] a privileged advice by a barrister was referred to in two letters to the RTA. In one of the letters the Council quoted the conclusion to support its point from the barrister's advice concerning certain statutes. The conclusion dealt with only a portion of the opinion dealing with the statutes and waiver of that portion was found, while the remainder was held to be privileged.[156]

Desiatnik, in an excellent analysis of the implied waiver cases,[157] finds that 'fairness as a test per se for implied waiver has given way to the primary test of inconsistency. This is not just a change in emphasis — it is a

148. *Telstra Corp v Australis Media Holdings Pty Ltd and News Corp Ltd v Australis Media Holdings Pty Ltd* (1997) 41 NSWLR 346 at 350–1.
149. [2004] NSWCA 158.
150. Ibid.
151. (1999) 201 CLR 1.
152. Ibid, p 13.
153. Ibid, pp 14–15.
154. *CC Bottlers v Lion Nathan Ltd* [1993] 2 NZLR 445; *Brambles Holdings Ltd v TPC (No 3)* (1981) 58 FLR 452 at 458–9; *Waterford v Commonwealth* (1987) 163 CLR 54 at 85 per Deane J.
155. [2004] NSWSC 917.
156. See also *Great Atlantic Insurance Co v Home Insurance Co* [1981] 2 All ER 485. Desiatnik (above), discusses this case and others in a section on partial disclosure at pp 163–7,
157. Desiatnik (above), pp 157–63.

seachange'.[158] He is also very critical of the Full Federal Court's decision in the *Telstra* case where waiver took place when determining the issues for the litigation. He argues that the High Court should adopt a more restrictive test based on the inconsistency doctrine.[159] The ALRC in DP 69 states that there are a number of inconsistent decisions in relation to s 122 but does recognise that 'inconsistency' is the appropriate test. The ALRC in Proposal 13-5 recommends that s 122(2) be amended 'to allow that evidence may be adduced where a client or party has knowingly and voluntarily disclosed to another person the substance of the evidence or has otherwise acted in a manner inconsistent with the maintenance of the privilege'.[160]

It should be noted that the New South Wales Supreme Court and District Court have adopted rules of court to extend the privilege provisions under Pt 3.10 of the Evidence Act to ancillary and pre-trial civil proceedings.[161] Section 5 of the Civil Procedure Act 2005 continues the application of the Evidence Act to pre-trial proceedings. A rule under this Act extends the privilege provisions to ancillary processes for all civil proceedings.[162] The Federal Court, after the High Court decision in the *Mann* case, changed its court rules to allow the privilege provisions to apply to certain aspects of pre-trial disclosure.[163] 'However the scope of the amendment is unclear.'[164]

Under the rules of the superior court, in most civil cases there is an exchange of the statements of witnesses. It is in all likelihood that these statements maintain their privilege status under s 122(2)(c) of the Evidence Act which protects the privilege against disclosure 'under the compulsion of law'.[165] The common law cases probably lead to the same view.[166]

The ALRC in DP 69 recommends the extension of the client legal privilege provisions to pre-trial civil proceedings and other matters. In Proposal 13-1 it states that this privilege 'should apply to pre-trial discovery and production of documents in response to subpoena and non-curial contexts such as search warrants and notices to produce documents, as well as court proceedings'.[167]

Types of communications

The definition covers oral, written or other communications. There has to be an intention for a communication. Thus, documents and information prepared for an expert to be used in his report 'were not communicated or intended to be communicated to anyone' and were not privileged.[168] It

11.30

---

158. Ibid, p 163.
159. Ibid, p 171.
160. The problem of inconsistency is discussed at paras 13.124–13.139.
161. Supreme Court Rules Pts 23-4, 36 and 75 and District Court Rules Pts 22, 22A and 29.
162. Rule 5.7 of the Uniform Civil Procedure Rules 2005.
163. See O 33, r 11, Federal Court Rules.
164. Hunter et al (above), para 8.1.
165. Ibid, para 8.57.
166. Ibid. Hunter et al (above) refer to a number of cases. See *Nilsen Industrial Electronics Pty Ltd v National Semiconductor Corporation* (1994) 48 FCR 337; *Complete Technology Pty Ltd v Toshiba (Aust) Pty Ltd* (1994) 124 ALR 493; and *State Bank of South Australia v Smotthdale (No 2) Ltd* (1995) 54 SASR 224.
167. For the discussion of this recommendation see paras 13.29–13.49.
168. *Interchase Corporation Ltd (in liq) v Grosvenor Hill (Queensland) Pty Ltd (No 1)* (1999) 1 Qld R 141 at 162.

would appear to cover documents and other forms of recording communication, but not physical objects.[169] A videotape can be privileged if it is an actual communication but if it was just a recording that was an observation it would not be protected.[170] The fact that the documents are stamped 'commercial-in-confidence' does not automatically make them privileged. Thus, stamped documents being discovered that concerned various tenders for government contracts, minutes of committee meetings and other correspondence were found not to contain any proprietary or secret information. If there was genuine 'secret information about a trade rival's operations' that information would be protected if communicated to a lawyer.[171] It does not cover information. Therefore, although the communication may be privileged, the information that it contains may be proved by other means.[172] The High Court in *Grant v Downs*[173] had added another requirement, which greatly narrowed the privilege. It is that the communication must have been made, or brought into existence, for the sole purpose of legal advice or assistance being given or sought, or for use in existing or contemplated litigation. The sole purpose test was finally removed by the court in 1999 and replaced by the dominant purpose test.[174] Either test places restrictions on the privilege. By contrast, the High Court expanded the privilege in *Baker v Campbell*[175] by extending it to non-judicial or quasi-judicial contexts or, in other words, to 'non-testimonial, non-curial context[s]'.

Public interest exception

11.31   There are a number of other limitations or exceptions to the privilege which will be discussed later, for example future crime. The scope of the privilege can also be modified by statute or the public interest. The latter states that the privilege is an aid in the administration of justice and thus at times will need to be balanced against other public interests that *affect* the administration of justice. In *Re Bell; Ex parte Lee*[176] a mother disappeared with her child after the Family Court had awarded custody to the father. A warrant was issued by the court but the mother was not found. The mother subsequently instructed a solicitor, Lees, in relation to a different matter, the matrimonial home. Lees was told how to contact her but he was expressly asked to keep the information confidential. Lees was ordered by the court to reveal her address, but claimed the privilege. The court rejected his claim, and he sought a writ of prohibition.

---

169. See Dawson J in *Baker v Campbell* (1983) 153 CLR 52 at 122–3. In *J-Corp Pty Ltd v Australian Builders Labourers Federation Union* (WA Branch) (1992) 110 ALR 510, the Federal Court held that videotapes could not come under the privilege because they were not taken in confidential circumstances. A similar holding was given in *Konia v Casino Canberra Ltd* BC300004722; [2000] ACTSC 67. In *Sony Music Entertainment (Australia) Ltd v University of Tasmania* (2003) 198 ALR 367 it was stated that electronic backup tapes, CD-ROMs and computer hard drives can all be subject to privilege.
170. *Daniel v Western Australia* (1999) 94 FCR 537 at 544.
171. *ACCC v Baxter Healthcare Pty Ltd* [2003] FCA 994 at para 24.
172. Disney et al (above), 2nd ed, p 660.
173. (1976) 135 CLR 674.
174. *Esso Australia Resources Ltd v FCT* (1999) 168 ALR 132.
175. (1983) 153 CLR 52.
176. (1980) 146 CLR 141.

The High Court held that he had to reveal the address. Gibbs J found an exemption to the privilege existed at common law. His Honour said that the privilege does not apply where the communication is part of a criminal or unlawful proceeding or made in utterance of an illegal object. Gibbs J said the order for custody made the child a ward of the court. Therefore, the welfare of the child was a paramount public interest that prevailed over the privilege.[177] Stephen J said that if the privilege was granted it would subvert its purpose which is to further and not impede the administration of justice. He argued that one must weigh competing public interests and the interest of the welfare of the child in these circumstances prevails.[178]

Wilson J (Aickin J agreed) pointed out that the address of a client is usually merely a collateral fact that does not arise out of any professional confidence. It does become a confidence if the client has communicated it confidentially. He argued that the privilege is grounded in public policy and by extending it in the present circumstances it does nothing to facilitate 'the perfect administration of justice'. Instead, in this case the privilege aids the continuing contempt of court by the wife, as it 'bears on its face the taint of illegality'.[179] Neither Gibbs J nor Wilson J noted that the communication which was made to the solicitor by the wife was in relation to a different matter and did not concern the custody issue. An earlier New South Wales Supreme Court decision in *Clarkson v Clarkson*[180] supports the High Court but goes further, stating that in custody and access matters the interests of the child are always paramount and come before those of the lawyer's client. This would imply that the privilege would almost invariably be denied when it conflicts with the interests of the child.

In the *Carter* case,[181] a majority (Brennan, Deane and McHugh JJ) of the High Court would see the best interests of the child not prevailing over the privilege, but as one of the exceptions to the privilege rule. In that case they held that privilege was part of the perfect administration of justice and involved a balancing process. Deane J expressed the majority's view when he said that 'legal professional privilege is itself the outcome of a balancing process and is conclusive when it attaches'. Thus, once it is identified the privilege is absolute and unqualified. Just after the High Court reached its decision the House of Lords in *R v Derby Magistrates' Court; Ex parte B* came to a similar conclusion stating the following:[182]

11.32

> Legal professional privilege is thus much more than an ordinary rule of evidence … It is a fundamental condition on which the administration of justice as a whole rests.

---

177. *Esso Australia Resources Ltd* (above) at 144.
178. *Esso Australia Resources Ltd* (above) at 151.
179. *Esso Australia Resources Ltd* (above) at 161.
180. [1972] 19 Fam LR 112 at 114.
181. *Carter v Managing Partner, Northmore Hale Davy & Leake* (1995) 129 ALR 593. Deane J's quote is at 601, but see also per Brennan J at 596, per Deane J at 600–4 and per McHugh J at 624. For an application of the *Carter* principle see *Somerville v Australian Securities Commission* (1995) 131 ALR 517.
182. [1995] 4 All ER 526 at 540–1.

Statutory removal

11.33   The second important modification is that made by statute. It is rare to find a statute that explicitly removes the privilege while there are many statutes specifically retaining the privilege.[183] The courts have also been reluctant to find that the privilege has been overridden unless it is expressly stated in the statute.[184] The judgment of Deane J in the *Baker* case[185] clearly enunciates this approach:

> It is a settled rule of construction that general provisions of a statute should only be read as abrogating common law principles or rights to the extent made necessary by express words or necessary intendment ... Both logic and authority support the present-day acceptance of ... confidentiality as a fundamental and general principle of common law. It is to be presumed that if the Parliament intended to authorise the impairment or destruction of that confidentiality by administrative action it would frame the relevant statutory mandate in express and unambiguous terms.

11.34   The High Court has reiterated more recently its approach first taken in the *Baker* decision. Kirby J stated in *Commissioner of Australian Federal Police v Propend Finance Pty Ltd* that to remove the privilege the statute has to 'be made plain because of the high public interest which the privilege defends'.[186] The High Court has in one case taken a different approach. In a 3:2 decision in the *Yuill* case,[187] the court showed at that time that it was willing to find parliamentary statutory intent that overrides the privilege in situations where there is a strong public interest to deny privilege. The *Yuill* case dealt with the New South Wales Company Code, but was later deemed applicable to the Commonwealth statute in *Australian Securities Commission v Dalleagles Pty Ltd*.[188] The *Yuill* case was a rare exception to the strict interpretation of statutes that stop the abrogation of the privilege.[189]

The case upset the legal profession, which felt it was wrongly decided. There was a campaign by the Law Council to have it overturned by

---

183. A statute removing the privilege is Legal Services Commission Act 1977 (SA) s 22. In the United States see Internal Revenue Code s 6050(1) which compels lawyers to reveal any cash transaction of a client that is $10,000 or more. An example of a statute preserving the privilege is the Freedom of Information Act 1982 (Cth) s 42.
184. *Baker v Campbell* (1983) 153 CLR 52, the majority judgments. In Canada see *Re Director of Investigation and Research and Canada Safeway Ltd* (1972) 26 DLR 745; in New Zealand see *Commissioner of Inland Revenue v West-Walker* [1954] NZLR 191 at 210.
185. *Baker v Campbell* (1983) 153 CLR 52 at 116.
186. (1997) 188 CLR 501 at 582.
187. *Corporate Affairs Commission (NSW) v Yuill* (1991) 172 CLR 319; 100 ALR 609 dealt with the interpretation of ss 295 and 296(2) of the old Companies Code (NSW). The case also affects the successor to these provisions, s 68 of the Australian Securities Commission Act 1989 (Cth). See T Middleton, 'Search of a Solicitor's Premises Under the Australian Securities Commission Act 1989 (Cth) and the Crimes Act (Cth)' (December 1992), *Queensland Law Society J* 499 and D Boniface, 'Legal Professional Privilege and Disclosure Powers of Investigative Agencies: Some Interesting and Troubling Issues Regarding Competing Public Policies' (1992) 16 *Crim LJ* 320.
188. (1992) 108 ALR 305.
189. Upholding the privilege by the Full Federal Court see *FCT v Citibank Ltd* (1989) 109 ALR 119 (Income Tax Assessment Act (Cth) s 263) and *Re Compass Airlines Pty Ltd* (1992) 109 ALR 119 (Corporations Law (Cth) s 597). See also Ryan J in *Re Steel; Ex parte Official Trustee in Bankruptcy v Clayton Utz* (1994) 126 ALR 58 (Bankruptcy Act (Cth) s 77AA). For a recent case where privilege was overridden by a Law Society's power to investigate complaints see *Rogerson v Law Society (NT)* (1993) 88 NTR 1.

legislation.[190] It was feared that if *Yuill* was followed by the courts in relation to interpretation of other investigative agencies' legislation, privilege would be further eroded.[191] The High Court in *Daniels Corporation International Pty Ltd v ACCC*[192] put an end to the debate of the significance of the case by distinguishing *Yuill*. The court said that the case had been interpreted in relation to the state of the law of privilege when the New South Wales Company Code had been enacted in 1981. This was before the decision in *Baker v Campbell*[193] and the view at that time was that privilege was only available in judicial and quasi-judicial proceedings.[194] The court in *Daniels* held that *Yuill* was only relevant to the 1981 Act which no longer exists and that 'it may be that *Yuill* would now be decided differently'.[195]

The *Daniels* case dealt with an interpretation of s 155 of the Trade Practices Act (Cth) which permits the ACCC to issue notices to produce documents and to have the right to inspect documents. The statute had a provision which stated that persons had to comply with notices 'to the extent that the person is capable of complying', but the High Court still decided that the statute did not negate the privilege. The court also applied *Baker v Campbell*[196] to uphold the privilege against the seizure of documents under s 155.[197] The *Daniels* case emphasises that there is a strong presumption in the maintaining of privilege unless legislation for its removal states clearly that it is removed or by necessary implication.[198] The High Court did not state that for the privilege to be removed by statute it had to be by express words. Therefore, the question of whether a statute removes the privilege is still open to interpretation,[199] unless parliament expressly states that the privilege is denied. 'Parliament's usual procedure is far more obscure and problematic, namely to make no mention of legal professional privilege but to word a provision so that it may be taken to negate the doctrine — by implication.'[200]

Sole and dominant purpose tests

Australia was unique in adopting the sole purpose test. The leading case that first enunciated the principle is *Grant v Downs*.[201] The plaintiff was

11.35

---

190. The Law Council of Australia has asked the government to legislate to overcome the decision. See its letter to the government in *Australian Law News*, August 1992, p 10. See also K White, 'Legal Professional privilege: the bridling of a common law right', *Law Society J (NSW)*, November 1991, p 69.
191. Boniface (above), p 348.
192. (2002) 192 ALR 561.
193. (1983) 153 CLR 52.
194. *O'Reilly v Commissioners of the State Bank of Victoria* (1982) 153 CLR 1.
195. This is from the main judgment of Gleeson CJ, Gaudron, Gummow and Hayne JJ (2002) 192 ALR 561 at para 35.
196. (1983) 153 CLR 52.
197. Paras 29–31.
198. Para 11.
199. Ligertwood (above), para 5.72 at p 308. Before the High Court made its decision in *Daniels* some academics thought the Full Federal Court had made the right interpretation that s 155(1) of the Trade Practices Act 1974 abrogates the privilege. See A Bruce, 'The *Trade Practices Act 1974* (Cth) and the Demise of Legal Professional Privilege' (2002) *Fed L Rev* 13.
200. Desiatnik (above), p 123.
201. *Grant v Downs* (1976) 135 CLR 674.

the widow of a patient who had died in the hospital grounds of a government psychiatric centre. In her action for damages against the government, she sought discovery of certain reports relating to the death made by the Department of Public Health. The defendant claimed the privilege. The report was drawn up for various purposes including receiving legal advice. Some of the other purposes included:

❑ to assist in determining whether there had been any breaches of discipline by the staff; and

❑ to find out if there were any faults in the security and general running of the institution, in order to prevent future possible death or injury to patients.

The majority (Stephen, Mason and Murphy JJ) confined the privilege to: 'those documents which are brought into existence for the sole purpose of submission to legal advisers for advice or for use in legal proceedings.'[202] The High Court supported its views by pointing out that 'the privilege does little, if anything, to promote full and frank disclosure of truthfulness'. The privilege also 'makes it more difficult for opposing parties or individuals to test the veracity of the party claiming privilege by removing' from inspection documents which may be inconsistent with the case. In the case of a statutory authority or a company these difficulties are accentuated because of the enormous number of documents brought into existence which may serve various different purposes, one of which may be legal advice. The non-legal purposes that aid management are unconnected to the privilege and cannot therefore be privileged.[203] Barwick CJ came to the same result but did so by adopting the dominant purpose test. He said:[204]

> I prefer the word 'dominant' to describe the relevant purpose. Neither 'primary' nor 'substantial', in my opinion, satisfies the true basis of the privilege.

11.36 Barwick CJ's test was adopted in England by the House of Lords[205] and in New Zealand for reasonably contemplated or in progress litigation.[206]

Murphy J, commenting on the *Grant* case[207] a few years later, said that it was the most important civil liberties case he had decided up to that time while sitting on the court. *Grant v Downs* contraposed freedom of information versus privacy and resulted in opening up the files of government and big corporations. The decision also led to criticism that the rule would lead to uncertainty of status of documents because of determining the 'purpose'. Furthermore, those making routine reports following accidents, or loss assessors to insurance companies informing underwriters of whether or not a claim is fair by the insured, would be unwilling to express an opinion fearing it could be used against their principals.[208] One author felt that the 'decision could result in more work for the lawyers, more secrecy in organisations and more expense for the

---

202. *Grant* (above) at 688.
203. *Grant* (above) at 682–7.
204. *Grant* (above) at 678.
205. *Waugh v British Railways Board* [1980] AC 521. See also *Guinness Peat Properties Ltd v Fitzroy Robinson Partnership* [1987] 2 All ER 716.
206. See *Carlton Cranes Ltd v Consolidated Hotels Ltd* [1988] 2 NZLR 555 at 557 and referring to *Guardian Royal Assurance v Stuart* [1985] 1 NZLR 596.
207. Private communication to the author made at a conference in 1979.
208. *Cross on Evidence*, 2nd Australian ed, Butterworths, Sydney, 1980, p 275.

community'.[209] There was also fear that it could lead to widespread destruction of documents and that the shredder would work overtime.

Rejection of sole purpose test

It took the High Court 23 years, but in *Esso Australia Resources Ltd v Federal Commissioner of Taxation*[210] the majority (Gleeson CJ, Gaudron, Bummow and Callinan JJ) decided that all along the common law was the dominant purpose test as stated by Barwick CJ in the *Grant* case.[211] The minority (McHugh and Kirby JJ) felt that the court was overruling the decision in *Grant* and wanted to maintain the sole purpose test.[212] We will look at this decision in more detail below.

11.37

Under the dominant purpose test, the purpose needs to exist at the time the documents are created or communication takes place, and even if the documents could be used or are later used for other purposes, they still remain privileged.[213] The burden of proof is on the party seeking to claim the privilege to show, as a question of fact, that the document or communication was used for the dominant purpose of legal advice.[214] Purpose also requires an investigation of the state of mind of clients when they are communicating with their lawyers, and lawyers' minds when communicating with third parties.[215] What if the document is brought into existence by several government or corporation employees? It would appear that the court in these situations has to find or make up some kind of governmental or corporate purpose.[216] Tompkins J, in the New Zealand case *Carlton Cranes Ltd v Consolidated Hotels Ltd*,[217] said in relation to finding a purpose:

> This is to be judged not only by the purpose of the person creating the document … but also regard is to be had to the intention of the person or authority under whose direction, whether particular or general, it has been produced or brought into existence.

If the document takes a long time to prepare, when will the state of mind be examined? For example, the report of a loss assessor takes some time to prepare before it is produced in a final form. What started as a normal investigation of a fire may have assumed important legal significance as it progresses. It appears that the relevant time for determining the purpose is when the actual document is produced and delivered to the lawyer.[218]

11.38

The idea of 'purpose' was important for the High Court in *Commissioner, Australian Federal Police v Propend Finance Pty Ltd*. In upholding the right to

209. M Rosser, *Going to Court*, Legal Books, 2nd ed, Sydney, 1980, p 49.
210. (1999) 169 ALR 123.
211. at pp 137–8, paras 54–61.
212. at pp 139 and 150, paras 64 and 99.
213. Mohr J in *Electricity Trust of SA v Mitsubishi Australia Ltd* (1991) 57 SASR 48.
214. *Waterford v Commonwealth* (1987) 163 CLR 54 at 66 per Mason and Wilson JJ, at 78 per Brennan J.
215. Third party communications also come under the test: see *Hongkong Bank of Australia Ltd v Murphy* [1993] 2 VR 419.
216. *Cross on Evidence* (above), para 25240. See also *Hartogen Energy Ltd v The Australian Gas Light Co* (1992) 8 ACSR 277 and *Aydin v Australian Iron and Steel Pty Ltd* [1984] 3 NSWLR 684.
217. [1988] 2 NZLR 555 at 557.
218. *Cross on Evidence* (above), para 25240 citing *Electricity Trust of SA v Mitsubishi Australia Ltd* (1991) 57 SASR 48.

privilege for copies of original documents McHugh J said that 'legal professional privilege turns on purpose, and no argument is needed to show that the purpose of a client or lawyer in making a copy document may be very different from the purpose of the person who created the original'.[219]

11.39   What about routine documents that have been submitted or not submitted to legal advisers in the past? In *National Employers Mutual General Insurance Association Ltd v Waind*[220] it was determined that there was no litigation in 90 per cent of the claims investigated to determine liability. Furthermore, 99 per cent of the cases of the investigators' and doctors' reports were not submitted to the solicitors for the company. The High Court held that these documents were not privileged because the primary reason they were brought into existence was for the insurance company to make a decision in its ordinary course of business. The only time the documents were submitted to the solicitors was if a decision was made to discontinue payments.[221] If a company had a routine of submitting its documents to its legal advisers it would be able to establish readily the sole purpose test.[222]

11.40   Before the *Esso* decision the High Court had to find reasons to get around the sole purpose test. For example, what if a document which is brought into existence solely for a privileged purpose contains information that is outside that purpose? *Waterford v Commonwealth of Australia*[223] presented such documents and both Mason and Wilson JJ granted the privilege even though the documents contained 'extraneous materials'. The better view would have been, if it were possible, to sever or blank out the offending sections of the document.[224] If that was not possible 'it would be necessary to determine whether the contents as a whole were outside the protection of legal professional privilege' because they did not satisfy the sole purpose test.[225] Smith J in *Hongkong Bank of Australia Ltd v Murphy*[226] interpreted the majority view in *Waterford* as a 'shift in emphasis in formulation of the sole purpose test'; that the High Court was moving towards the dominant purpose test. His view was later proven correct.

11.41   Even before the High Court's decision in *Esso* there were strong arguments that the dominant purpose test would be a better approach because of its adoption in the Evidence Act 1995. The Evidence Act 1995 states:

> **s 118.** Evidence is not to be adduced if, on objection by a client, the court finds the adducing of the evidence would result in disclosure of:
>
> (a) a confidential communication between the client and a lawyer; or
>
> (b) a confidential communication made between two or more lawyers acting for the client; or

---

219. (1997) 188 CLR 501 at 552–3.
220. *Waind* (1979) 141 CLR 648.
221. *Waind* (above).
222. See *Guinness Peat Properties Ltd v Fitzroy Robinson Partnership* [1987] 2 All ER 716.
223. (1987) 163 CLR 54; the non-legal part consisted of some policy advice.
224. *Great Atlantic Insurance Co v Home Insurance Co* [1981] 1 WLR 529; *Grofam Pty Ltd v Australia and New Zealand Banking Group Ltd* (1993) 116 ALR 535. By contrast Smith J in *Hongkong Bank of Australia Ltd v Murphy* [1993] 2 VR 419 said privilege could not attach to part of a document.
225. Deane J in *Waterford v Commonwealth of Australia* (1987) 163 CLR 54 at 85. Dawson J supports this view at 103.
226. [1993] 2 VR 419.

(c) the contents of a confidential document (whether delivered or not) prepared by the client or a lawyer;

for the dominant purpose of the lawyer, or one or more lawyers, providing legal advice to the client.

s 119. Evidence is not to be adduced if, on objection by a client, the court finds that adducing evidence would result in disclosure of:

(a) a confidential communication between the client and another person, or between a lawyer acting for the client and another person, that was made; or

(b) the contents of a confidential document (whether delivered or not) that was prepared for the dominant purpose of the client being provided with professional legal services ...

Under ss 118–119 the privilege conferred cannot be maintained unless clients or their representatives object to the use of the privileged material. The sections appeared to limit the dominant purpose test to 'adducing' evidence, that is, presenting it in court. It therefore appeared that another test, the sole purpose test, then the common law, would apply in other contexts. The courts adopted an inconsistent view. It was unclear whether the common law continued to apply outside of litigation. Therefore, for example, was privilege in discovery procedures still governed by the common law sole purpose test, or by the dominant purpose test under the Act?[227]   **11.42**

The problems have now been resolved by the *Esso* decision. The case dealt with the issue of whether the dominant purpose test in the Evidence Act applied to discovery and inspection of written confidential communications between lawyer and client. The majority upheld the decision of the Full Federal Court[228] that the Evidence Act did not apply to discovery and inspection of written confidential communication before the commencement of the trial.[229]

The majority in a detailed analysis of the views of those adopting the sole purpose test found that they had gone too far and mistakenly interpreted the common law. For example, the court said that in *Grant* one of the fears of allowing the privilege was that it was 'unduly protective of written communications within corporations and bureaucracies. The sole purpose test goes to the other extreme ... [Thus for example] a document primarily directed to lawyers is incidentally directed to someone else as well means that privilege does not attach, the result seems to alter the balance too far the other way'.[230] The court pointed out that Barwick CJ's dominant purpose test in the *Grant* case was sufficient to defeat the claims for privilege. It rejected the need to formulate a new test as causing only confusion. The court concludes that the dominant purpose test 'strikes a just balance ... and it brings the common law of Australia into conformity with other common law jurisdictions'.[231]   **11.43**

---

227. Branson J in *Trade Practices Commission v Port Adelaide Wool Co Pty Ltd* (1995) 132 ALR 645 at 648.
228. *Esso v FCT* (1998) 159 ALR 664.
229. *Esso* (above) at pp 128–9, para 17.
230. *Esso* (above) at p 139 para 59.
231. *Esso* (above) at p 139 para 61. For a discussion of the case see A Palmer, 'Legal professional privilege — the demise of the sole purpose test' (April 2000) *Law Institute J (Vic)* 50.

In the most recent case, *Seven Network Ltd v News Ltd*,[232] Graham J in the Federal Court found that the dominant purpose of a summary of legal advice by Seven was to advance Seven's commercial interests, and not for obtaining legal advice. The summary concerned Seven's bidding process for AFL broadcast rights and had been provided to the Australian Competition and Consumer Commission as part of an investigation. Graham J also found that the ACCC was not under any obligation to maintain the confidentiality of the legal summary. This meant that if the dominant purpose test had been met, the summary would still not have been privileged because a waiver had taken place.[233]

Investigations and other non-judicial inquiries — general principles

11.44   The High Court in *O'Reilly v Commissioner of State Bank of Victoria*[234] in a 3:2 judgment said that s 264 of the Income Tax Assessment Act 1936 could require a solicitor to produce documents relating to a client to the Australian Taxation Office (ATO). The High Court held that the privilege applies only to judicial or quasi-judicial proceedings and therefore was not relevant to the ATO's power under s 264. Mason J in the majority pointed out the need for confidential communications between solicitor and client, but he said that since privilege is an obstacle to truth it should be strictly enforced within the narrowest possible limits connected with the logic of its principles. He found that the common law did not extend the privilege to administrative inquiries.

The decision went contrary to those in other common law jurisdictions where the privilege had been extended to administrative and legislative inquiries.[235] It is obvious that if a client is made to disclose privileged communications before these bodies there is no longer any protection if the client is later brought to court. The decision in *O'Reilly* caused widespread concern and criticism from the legal and business community.[236] It was not surprising that the High Court reopened the issue the next year in *Baker v Campbell* and by a 4:3 decision overruled *O'Reilly*. In the *Baker* case Gibbs CJ in his dissent gave as his reason for reviewing the *O'Reilly* case, and not resting on that authority, the fact that the decision was only made by five judges. The *Baker* case, by contrast, had been argued before the Full Court.[237]

11.45   In *Baker* the defendant had attempted to seize documents of the plaintiff held by his solicitor. The documents had been brought into existence for the sole purpose of legal advice in devising a tax scheme to minimise liability for sales tax. A warrant was issued under s 10(b) of the Crimes Act

---

232. [2005] FCA 864.
233. For another recent case where the dominant purpose was not met see Full Federal Court decision in *Kennedy v Wallace* [2004] FCAFC 337.
234. (1983) 153 CLR 1; (1982) 44 ALR 27.
235. *Commissioner of Inland Revenue v West-Walker* [1954] NZLR 191; *Re Director of Investigation and Research and Shell Canada Ltd* (1975) 55 DLR (3rd) 713; *AM & S Europe v Commission of the European Community* [1983] 3 WLR 17; and *United States v Calandra* 414 US 338, 94 S Ct 613 (1974).
236. See, for example, S Charles, 'Legal Professional Privilege: Continued Erosion' (1983) *Law Institute J (Vic)* 832.
237. *Baker v Campbell* (1983) 153 CLR 52; 49 ALR 385 at 388.

1914. This section empowers a justice of the peace to grant a warrant to seize 'anything as to which there are reasonable grounds for believing that it will afford evidence as to the commission' of offences against the Commonwealth. The issue before the court was whether the privilege attached to the documents or whether they could be subjected to a search warrant which applied to areas outside legal proceedings.

Gibbs CJ pointed out that until recent times it was not necessary to determine whether the privilege applied outside legal proceedings. Before the twentieth century there were few administrative hearings and administrative powers. When these did come into existence the question of non-judicial privilege did not arise:

> ... possibly because the nature of the things for which the warrant authorised a search to be made (such as things with which a crime was committed, or which were the fruits of a crime or evidence of the commission of a crime) made it unlikely that they would be found in a solicitor's office.

Gibbs CJ reviewed cases from many jurisdictions and came to the **11.46** conclusion that the common law did not extend the privilege outside judicial or quasi-judicial proceedings. He examined s 10 of the Crimes Act and found that it did not expressly protect the privilege against warrants which is 'supported by the fact that the section provides no machinery for determination of the disputed question as to whether the privilege exists'. Gibbs CJ in dictum recommended that parliament give consideration to extending the privilege to s 10 and s 264 of the Income Tax Assessment Act and provide a procedure for an independent authority to determine claims about whether documents should be privileged.[238]

Mason J in his dissent recognised that privilege was important in non-procedural areas. This occurs because where relevant materials are used in preliminary investigation to litigation, disclosure would impair the exercise of privilege in pending or future litigation. His Honour did find countervailing considerations where a statute requires answers, and the provision of information or production of documents, which contain a strong public interest in obtaining the materials. The parliament in adopting such statutes did not want administrative hearings disturbed while waiting for a decision on the privilege. Mason J said adherence to the *O'Reilly* rule 'will produce greater certainty than the adoption of a case-by-case approach in which the court seeks to balance opposing public interest considerations' to see if statutes abrogate the privilege.[239]

Murphy J, in the majority, pointed out that the privilege is now a **11.47** fundamental human right. The privilege is needed to protect the public against official and unofficial eavesdropping and other invasions of privacy. Individuals 'should be able to seek and obtain legal advice and legal assistance for innocent purposes'. Denying the exercise of the privilege 'against a search warrant would only have a minimal effect in securing convictions, but a major damaging effect on, lawyer–client relationship'. In dictum his Honour said that as far as the privilege has been held to exist not only for situations of pending or anticipated litigation there is a strong argument that legal advice should not be elevated above medical or

---

238. *Baker v Campbell* (above) at 387–9, 396.
239. *Baker v Campbell* (above) at 401, 404.

financial advice. Murphy J was also worried that if there was no privilege available outside court proceedings there would be a tendency for law enforcement authorities to press for more extra-judicial methods of investigation and decision-making. Furthermore, he said that search and seizure in pre-trial investigation had a close connection with judicial proceedings and therefore the privilege should apply to all areas.[240]

11.48 All of the majority in *Baker* agreed that the privilege was a substantive principle and not just a rule of evidence. Dawson J (Wilson J agreeing) expressed this view when he said the privilege was firmly established as a principle of common law 'not merely as a rule of evidence, but as a matter of public policy with a natural application wherever compulsory disclosure of evidence is involved, whether in judicial proceedings or not'. Destroying the privilege in administrative inquiries, Dawson J held, would result in the destruction of freedom of communication as much as if there were compulsory disclosure of those confidences in court.[241]

Investigations and other non-judicial inquiries — specific problems

Search warrants and privilege

11.49 The *Baker* case did not remove the concern for lawyers when the police or other bodies vested with compulsory powers of investigation sought access to clients' files. Two years before *Baker* was decided the Full Federal Court looked at the matter. In *Crowley v Murphy*[242] Lockhart J discussed the problem of what should happen if the police arrived with a search warrant to obtain evidence from a client. He said that the materials requested in a search warrant to overcome the privilege needed to be well-defined. The officers had the right to open and read the file of the client in the warrant, but they did not have a right to conduct a fishing expedition 'in the hope of finding something that might be of probative value'. Lockhart J did state that there was a problem of limiting the scope of the search. He was concerned as to how a police officer could know that he or she has seen all the documents that bear on the alleged offence and fall within the warrant, without looking at them all. The latter results in a 'negative search'. If the solicitor's filing system is haphazard and disorganised, the officers may need to search in all the files because they cannot rely on the system. Thus they are entitled to conduct a negative search. In other situations they have no rights to look at files not related to the warrant and the officers do not have the authority to turn a solicitor's office upside down.[243]

11.50 After the *Baker* case, Ian Temby, then President of the Law Council of Australia, wrote that although a search warrant pursuant to s 10 of the Crimes Act was subject to the privilege, there still existed some problems. How could lawyers assert that right in the face of police officers that demand to search their office immediately to find valuable evidence of a crime that has been committed? Temby said the first step is to persuade the officers to delay in order to enable clients to be advised. The client in the

---

240. *Baker v Campbell* (above) at 408, 411–12.
241. *Baker v Campbell* (above) at 442, 445.
242. (1981) 34 ALR 496 (Full Fed Ct).
243. *Baker v Campbell* (above) at 520, 525–7.

warrant can then consider whether to take proceedings to challenge the validity of the warrant or its efficacy as against particular documents for which the privilege is claimed. Second, lawyers should not simply hand over documents to which the privilege actually or arguably attaches. Refusal to do so may lead to a lack of cooperation with the police and may result in the office being turned upside down, but this is highly unlikely to happen today. Third, do not hinder, obstruct or use force or respond to force used by the police officer. Such action by the lawyer will usually result in charges being laid.[244]

To stop a negative search lawyers can point out that they have an organised and efficient filing system. The officers can be shown the index of files and only be allowed access to files of clients named that are relevant to the details of the warrant. This access should only be granted in the presence of the lawyer who should record all documents seized or copied. The lawyer must make sure the documents seized fall within the terms of the warrant. If an invalid search takes place or the warrant is invalid the solicitor then goes to court to obtain an injunction.[245] This is an obviously unsatisfactory solution if the solicitor does not act immediately. Temby points out that even if documents that are seized are later declared to be privileged, the damage will have been done as the officers will have read their contents.[246] Furthermore, one author argued that the *Baker* case protected the seizure of privileged documents under a search warrant, but it was unclear that the decision protects these documents from being inspected.[247] One solution to stop a possible unlawful seizure is to make use of a duty judge, who in an emergency can issue a temporary injunction to protect privileged documents. **11.51**

Temby, in 1997, in his capacity as an Acting Justice, declared invalid the search warrants use by the Police Royal Commission (NSW). He said that: **11.52**

> … the searching officers could seize every photograph, including one showing the occupant when a toddler and others of his late grandmother … The concluding words … can be in my view read in no other way than that the warrants authorise seizure of anything whether documentary or not.

The warrant authorised the police to:[248]

> … search the premises for prohibited drugs, drug paraphernalia, documents, correspondence, facsimiles, photographs, audio or video cassettes, video production equipment, banking and financial records, monies, bullion and other precious metals, jewellery, gems and other precious stones, antiques, credit cards, safety deposit box keys, post office box keys, forms of identification, diaries, notebooks, personal organisers, telephone indexes, computers, computer disks or records or any other documentation or things found in or about these premises and to deliver these things so seized, to the Royal Commission.

---

244. I Temby, 'Protecting the Lawyer's Office from Intrusion' (June 1984) *Australian Law News* 15–16. A solicitor who sought to prevent police removing what he considered privileged documents was arrested and charged with hindering the police: see *Allitt v Sullivan* [1988] VR 621.

245. J Hanlon, 'Confrontation with a Search Warrant — A Check List for the Practitioner' (1982) 56 *Law Institute J* 469. See also N Petroulias, 'Tax Raids: Lessons on Challenging Search Warrants' (April 1992) 66 *Law Institute J (Vic)*.

246. Temby, see n 244 (above), p 16.

247. A Sing, 'Search Warrants and Legal Professional Privilege' (1986) 10 *Criminal LJ* 32.

248. *Sydney Morning Herald*, 24 April 1997, p 6.

11.53   The then Premier, Bob Carr, immediately ordered retrospective legislation to validate the warrants due to fears that 'illegal warrants could jeopardise prosecutions of corrupt police and paedophiles'.[249]

The courts have recognised these problems in several cases. In *Arno v Forsyth*[250] a warrant was issued to enter the chambers of a Queen's Counsel and to seize documents that supposedly related to tax avoidance schemes. The Full Federal Court held that the warrant was void for uncertainty. The judges did not resolve the problem of whether the privilege should be raised at the warrant stage. Lockhart J said that the question of the privilege may need to be considered by justices when determining to issue it in searching a lawyer's office and the warrant be endorsed with a stipulation that it is subject to the privilege.[251] In contrast, Fox J stated that the privilege is 'to be dealt with when it is sought to execute the warrant'.[252] Should it be at the time it was issued or at the time it was executed or both? If we adopt Lockhart J's approach we do not have a solution because the affected party has no opportunity to argue that the material is privileged, or may want to waive the right, and what if the seizure does not take place in the lawyers' offices?[253]

11.54   A related issue is the seizing of documents, from a firm of lawyers, by the Complaints Committee of the Law Society of South Australia under a s 10 warrant. The Federal Court held that the privilege did not invalidate the warrant.[254] In *Finch v Grieve*[255] the court held that the Bar Council had the right to claim public interest immunity in relation to disclosing documents in a disciplinary matter. The court said that a balancing exercise was involved and the public interest was served by disclosing relevant portions of the documents because a legitimate forensic purpose was served.[256]

11.55   In a Victorian Supreme Court case, *Allitt v Sullivan*,[257] although the court was dealing with specific provisions of s 465 of the Victorian Crimes Act 1958, the judges were more concerned with determining the claims for privilege at the execution stage. Under the statute the executing officer has the right to 'carry away' relevant documents to a justice to be 'dealt with according to law'. Murphy J stated that if the solicitor objected to certain documents being seized he or she should secure the documents in a box or envelope, and accompany the officer to the justice to obtain a definitive ruling on the privilege. He also followed Lockhart J's general view that a warrant is bad if it fails to state matters relating to the privilege.[258]

In dissent Hampel J strongly argued that justices need to consider the privilege issue on issuing the warrant. At that stage the justice needs to

249. *SMH* (above), p 1.
250. (1986) 65 ALR 125.
251. *Arno* (above) at 136–7.
252. *Arno* (above) at 128.
253. *Cross on Evidence* (above), para 25250.
254. *Lander v Mitson* (1988) 83 ALR 466.
255. (1991) 22 NSWLR 579.
256. For another case dealing with the public interest argument by a law society see *Law Institute v Irving* [1990] VR 429. There are cases involving legal professional bodies where the profession's right to investigate and conduct a complaint overrode the privilege: see *Goldberg v Ng* (1995) 132 ALR 57 and *Rogerson v Law Society* (NT) (1993) 88 NTR 1.
257. *Allitt* [1988] VR 621.
258. *Allitt* (above) at 630–1.

determine what are the 'safeguards by way of appropriate procedures to ensure that the search and seizure is not unlawful. A justice does not act merely as a rubber stamp for requests for search warrants'.[259] McNicol argues that the minority view is to be preferred because it protects a fundamental right at 'every stage where it could foreseeably arise'. She does note that the preponderance of authority supports the majority view.[260]

The resolution of the problem of exercising privilege is focused on the execution stage.[261] This is supported by the taxation raid in *Citibank*,[262] and in *Allen, Allen and Hemsley v Deputy Commissioner of Taxation*[263] where authorisations for the seizure of documents issued by the Commissioner of Taxation were held to be valid. In both cases the courts held that there was no requirement that the authorisation (the equivalent of 'issuing' a warrant) needed to specify the premises to be entered or the documents or class of documents to be inspected. Furthermore, the guidelines agreed upon by the Law Council of Australia and the ATO[264] and between the Law Council and the Commissioner of the Australian Federal Police outline the procedures to be followed at the execution and further stages and not when the authorisation is made.   **11.56**

Guidelines for searches

The guidelines adopted by the Law Council of Australia and the Australian Federal Police have solved many of the problems discussed above. They were adopted in 1986[265] and revised in 1997[266] in light of changes to the Crimes Act 1914 (Cth). The 1997 changes also extended the guidelines to the offices of professional associations. The Federal Police guidelines state that where practicable a search warrant shall only be sought from a magistrate or a legally qualified justice, and after consultations with the Office of the Director of Public Prosecutions. The search team should be kept to the lowest number of persons reasonably necessary in all the circumstances. If no lawyer is present, if practicable the premises should be sealed off, and the execution delayed to enable a lawyer to be present. A reasonable time should be allowed to enable lawyers to consult with their clients and/or obtain legal advice. Therefore, it is desirable for the execution of warrants to take place during normal working hours. If a warrant is executed at other times allowances should be made for delays. The lawyers should, if consistent with their clients' instructions, cooperate with the police in locating all documents which may be within the warrant. If the lawyer does not cooperate, the police officer will advise the lawyer that the search will proceed.   **11.57**

---

259. *Allitt* (above) at 660.
260. McNicol (above), 1992, pp 59–60.
261. For a discussion of the execution of search warrants, see *Cross on Evidence* (above), para 25250 at p 816.
262. *Commissioner of Taxation v Citibank* (1989) 89 ATC 4268.
263. (1989) 89 ATC 4294.
264. Other Guidelines (OG) 53. These Guidelines can be found on the Law Council's website, www.lawcouncil.asn.au. There are also specific guidelines for access to accounting advisers' papers: see Other Guidelines (OG) 69.
265. The 1986 guidelines are set out in (September 1991) *Australian Law News* 23.
266. The 1997 guidelines are set out in (1997) 32 *Australian Lawyer* 29 and are also found at the Law Council's website, www.lawcouncil.asn.au.

Since the search team is unfamiliar with the filing system, the search may entail looking at all files and documents in the office. The officer will also advise the lawyer that documents will not be seized if they are not within the warrant or privilege. All documents for which privilege is claimed should be placed by lawyers or their staff in a container under the supervision of the police, which shall then be sealed. A list of these documents should be prepared showing general information as to the nature of the documents. The list and the container shall be delivered into the possession of a third party who will hold them pending resolution of the claims. The lawyer or the professional association has to inform the executing officer, within three working days or a reasonable period agreed upon by the parties, that instructions have been received to institute proceedings to establish the privilege list and documents will be delivered to the Registrar of the court in which the proceedings have commenced. If the executing officer has not been informed that proceedings will be commenced within the stated time period, he or she shall request consent of the third party for the release of the documents.[267] Similar guidelines or procedures to deal with these problems have been established by state law bodies and state police forces.[268]

11.58 The tax guidelines have solved the main problems resulting from the Citibank raid. The raid involved 37 ATO officers who were divided into six teams who sought documents in relation to a tax avoidance scheme. The raid took place under a letter of authorisation from the Commissioner and a 'wallet authorisation' from the Deputy Commissioner of Taxation. Each team had an adviser with experience to determine whether a claim for the privilege was valid.[269] The Full Federal Court upheld the validity of the authorisations, but found that the privilege restricted the powers of the Commissioner to seize documents under s 263. The court also held that the officer in charge of the raid did not give adequate opportunity to Citibank to protect its clients' documents and to assert their rights to the privilege.[270]

11.59 In a case handed down immediately after *Citibank* the Full Federal Court in *Allen, Allen and Hemsley v Deputy Commissioner of Taxation*[271] again found the authorisations valid under s 263, but held that entries in a trust account ledger were not privileged and thus access by the ATO was not denied.[272] Furthermore, unlike *Citibank*, there was no precipitous raid since the matter had been discussed by the parties over a period of many months. Therefore, the solicitors had ample opportunity to make a claim of privilege to entries in the trust accounts.[273] As a result of the bad publicity over the Citibank raid the ATO entered into an agreement with the Law Council for

---

267. (1997) 32 *Australian Lawyer* 30–2.
268. *Cross on Evidence* (above), 6th ed, para 25250.
269. *Federal Commissioner of Taxation v Citibank Ltd* (1989) 89 ATC 4268 at 4271–3.
270. *Citibank Ltd* (above) at 4274–80, 4293.
271. (1989) 89 ATC 4294.
272. Lawyers' trust account records were also found not to be privileged in *Packer v Deputy Federal Commissioner of Taxation* (1984) 84 ATC 4666 (SC(Qld)). It should be noted that a solicitor's detailed bill of costs is privileged because it lists work done for the client which could tend to disclose the nature of the advice involved in the relationship.
273. *Allen, Allen and Hemsley v Deputy Commissioner of Taxation* (1989) 89 ATC 4294 at 4297–8.

guidelines to deal with the matter. The guidelines were adopted even before these two decisions were handed down as to the access by ATO officers to documents in lawyers' offices. The guidelines are similar to those made with the Commonwealth Police and stop access to documents, for which the privilege is claimed, until the claim can be determined in a legal proceeding.[274] The guidelines have been applied on a number of occasions. In June 2005, the ATO seized a number of documents from four large firms concerning offshore tax evasion. The firms had a few days' notice before the Federal Police officers arrived and claimed privilege for many of the documents that were seized.[275]

California has established under Penal Code para 1524(c)–(f) a system of unpaid special masters, comprising a list of neutral experienced lawyers (at least five years at the bar) who mediate between the police, lawyers, physicians, psychotherapists and the clergy. Materials can be submitted to the special masters to determine whether a search of the listed occupations' office is necessary and to determine if the documents are privileged. If the special master determines a search should be carried out he or she is empowered to seize any items listed in the search warrant. The special masters go with the police and accurately conduct the search. They seal and keep all the alleged privileged documents until a hearing is held, which usually occurs within three days.[276] A Minnesota case goes further in restricting the police.[277] The court held that a warrant to search a law office could not be issued unless the police were able to show sufficient evidence that the lawyer was involved in the client's criminal activity or that there was a threat that the matter searched for would be destroyed because of prior warning. The court based its decision on the detrimental impact of a search warrant upon the attorney–client privilege, the work product doctrine and the constitutional right to counsel. The court was troubled by the fact that in executing the warrant the police would be able to read files of innocent clients and read non-seizable material of the suspect client. **11.60**

RESTRICTIONS ON THE PRIVILEGE

Lawyer–client relationship

In order for the privilege to come into existence there needs to be a lawyer–client relationship or at least the contemplation of such a relationship. Thus, if the communication is made to a lawyer in the capacity of a friend, or advice is sought in a social setting, there may not be such a relationship, nor are some of these kinds of communications intended to be confidential. Communications made by parties acting for themselves seem not to attract the privilege[278] (this has been changed for adducing evidence under the **11.61**

---

274. See OG 53.
275. M Priest, 'Solicitors draw line in the sand', *Australian Financial Review*, 17 June 2005, p 53.
276. N McCarthy, 'Special masters search, protect the privilege', *California Bar J*, July 2003, pp 1 and 20. McCarthy states at that time there were 375 approved special masters. See also Wolfram (above), p 823.
277. *O'Connor v Johnson* 287 NW 2d 400 (Minn 1979).
278. *National Employers Mutual General Insurance Association v Waind* (1979) 141 CLR 648 at 654. For an opposing view see Murphy J in *Baker v Campbell* (1983) 153 CLR 52; 49 ALR 385 at 412. He states: 'This protection [the privilege] should apply not only to client–lawyer communications, but also to preparation by a litigant in person …'.

Evidence Act s 120), but if the communication is made to clients who then pass it on to their lawyers it is privileged.[279] If the advice or documents sought were in order to decide whether to obtain legal advice they will not be privileged.[280]

11.62 In the *Waterford* case Dawson J stated: 'In order to attract that privilege, the communications must be confidential and the legal adviser must be acting in his [or her] professional capacity.'[281] If the lawyer is approached to commit an illegal act or to do work that does not require legal expertise, there will be either no professional relationship or the lawyer is not acting in his or her professional capacity.[282] Statements taken by witnesses for the purpose of litigation are not covered by the privilege, but are usually still protected by the courts.[283] Documents that are evidence of a transaction such as conveyances,[284] contracts, receipts, offers, and so on,[285] or any public documents, are not protected, while a copy of a privileged document will be protected.[286] The High Court in *Commissioner, Australian Federal Police v Propend Finance Pty Ltd*[287] held by a 5:2 majority that a copy of an unprivileged document given to a lawyer for the sole purpose of legal advice is privileged. Finally, the privilege belongs to the client, and cannot be waived by their lawyers or any agents (lawyer or client) without consent of the client.[288]

11.63 An area in which the existence of the lawyer–client relationship may become difficult to define is in relation to 'in-house' corporate lawyers and government lawyers. In these situations the communications made between lawyers and other members of the organisation are often in different capacities and for mixed purposes. The *Waterford* case[289] highlights these problems. In that case Waterford, a journalist, sought access to documents regarding the estimated number of persons who would receive unemployment benefits from the Department of the Treasury under s 15 of the Freedom of Information Act 1982 (Cth). Access to them, and also his application for review, were denied by the Administrative Appeals Tribunal and subsequent appeal to the Federal Court, as most of the documents were held to be privileged. A majority of the High Court, Mason, Wilson and Brennan JJ (in a 3:2 decision) held that the privilege applies to communications and documents between governmental agencies and their salaried legal officers, where the communications are made for the sole purpose of

---

279. *Cross on Evidence* (above), para 25245.
280. *Wheeler v Le Marchant* (1881) 17 Ch D 675.
281. (1987) 163 CLR 55 at 95. The requirement of confidentiality may not always be needed to claim the privilege. There may be circumstances where it is not present and the privilege is granted: see S Zindel, 'Waiver and legal professional privilege: *Derby v Weldon*' (1991) NZLJ 132, 133. The *Derby* case has been reported nine times.
282. *Minter v Priest* [1930] AC 558; *Leary v Federal Commissioner of Taxation* (1980) 47 FLR 414; *Medina v R* (1990) 2 WAR 21.
283. *Dingle v Commonwealth Development Bank of Australia* (1989) 91 ALR 239.
284. Note, however, that communications made in the course of a conveyancing transaction can be privileged: see *Balabil v Air India* [1988] 2 All ER 246.
285. *Sharp v Deputy Commissioner of Taxation* (1988) 18 FCR 475.
286. *Cross on Evidence* (above), paras 25015, 25227 and 25275.
287. (1997) 141 ALR 545.
288. *Attorney-General (NT) v Maurice* (1986) 161 CLR 475; 165 ALR 230 at 235.
289. *Waterford v Commonwealth* (1987) 163 CLR 54.

providing legal advice. They had a broad definition of legal advice stating it could be made in relation to both administrative and policy decision-making. The High Court also required that the lawyers employed by the Commonwealth, or as in-house lawyers, must be able to provide advice of an independent character.

Mason and Wilson JJ referred to the European Court of Justice case, *AM & S Europe Ltd v Commission of European Community*,[290] which ruled that there is a need for the lawyer to be 'independent'. Mason and Wilson JJ stated that this case was not a ruling in a common law context and all other authorities are against it. They quote Denning JJ in *Alfred Crompton Amusement Machines Ltd*,[291] who said that government lawyers: **11.64**

> ... are regarded by the law as in every respect ... as those who practise on their own account. The only difference is that they act for one client only and not for several clients ... They are subject to the same duties to their client and to the court. They must respect the same confidences.

Denning recognised that at some times government lawyers did work in a non-lawyer capacity, which was not privileged. He also said:[292]

> Being a servant or agent too, he may be under more pressure from his client. So he must be careful to resist it. He must be as independent in the doing of right as any other legal adviser.

The same approach to Denning has been followed in cases in the United States,[293] Ireland[294] and Canada.[295]

Mason and Wilson JJ in the *Waterford* case stated that s 42(1) of the Freedom of Information Act 1982 mentions the privilege. Thus, this expressly acknowledges that legal advice tendered in connection with administrative decision-making will attract the privilege. They still upheld the privilege even though the tribunal failed to inspect documents. The tribunal was satisfied enough by the government's statements concerning the documents that it did not ask to see them.[296] There is no requirement for a tribunal or judge to look at the documents to determine if they are privileged. This may cause problems in trials by judges without juries. A judge can take sworn evidence as to whether the documents are privileged, but if the judge has some doubt as to whether they are privileged he or she has no choice but to look at them.[297] If this occurs, judges in some circumstances may have difficulties in eliminating 'the poison' from their mind.[298] More recently the High Court has stated that: 'A court has power to examine documents in cases where there is a disputed claim [for **11.65**

290. [1983] QB 878.
291. *Alfred Compton Amusement Machines Ltd* [1972] 2 QB 102 at 129.
292. *Alfred Compton Amusement Machines Ltd* (above).
293. *National Labor Relations Board v Sears, Roebuck & Co* 421 US 132 (1975). For a detailed analysis of government lawyers' role in the United States, see R Cramton, 'The Lawyer as Whistleblower: Confidentiality and the Government Lawyer' (1991) 5 *Georgetown J Legal Ethics* 291.
294. *Geraghty v Minister for Local Government* [1975] IR 300 at 312.
295. *Re Director of Investigation & Research and Shell Canada Ltd* [1975] 55 DLR (3d) 713 at 721.
296. *Waterford* (above), at 64 and 68.
297. *Trade Practices Commission v Sterling* (1978) 36 FLR 244.
298. Young J made this comment in *Ng v Goldberg* (SC(NSW), No 5342 of 1989, 17 August 1993, unreported).

privilege] and it should not be hesitant to exercise such power. In appropriate cases, there is also power to allow cross-examination of a deponent of an affidavit claiming privilege.'[299]

Brennan J, unlike Mason and Wilson JJ, gave great weight to the *AM & S Europe* decision that an independent lawyer is 'one who is not bound to his client by a relationship of employment'.[300] He rejected Denning J's views as sounding 'pious and unreal'. Brennan J found that 'the employment relationship creates a conflict between the independence necessary for a legal adviser and the loyalties, duties and interest of an employee'. He said that although other courts had followed Denning J it was in relationship to government salaried legal advisers. Thus, these decisions needed to be limited because Crown lawyers by statute were independent by being granted security of tenure. Brennan J makes a distinction in that a communication brought into existence for the purpose of seeking or giving advice as to the government's policy in *administering* the Act, as distinct from the policy of the Act itself, would not be privileged. The former is executive policy and a matter of fact, while the latter is statutory policy and a matter of law.[301] Dawson J pointed out that when the government adviser is dealing with legal process, privilege applies, but in the 'purely executive function of decision-making' then it does not apply.[302]

Deane and Dawson JJ, in their dissenting opinions, supported Brennan J in rejecting Denning J's view of what constitutes independence. Deane J says besides academic or practical qualifications independence depends on whether the lawyers are on the 'roll of current practitioners, or worked under the supervision of such a person'.[303] Dawson J required that the 'legal adviser must be qualified to practise law and, it seems, subject to the duty to observe professional standards and professional discipline'.[304]

Need for independence

11.66 The Administrative Appeals Tribunal has summarised the effect of *Waterford*. The tribunal said that for the privilege to attach the lawyer must be acting in his or her professional capacity pursuant to a lawyer–client relationship. The legal advice must be given where the lawyer has the necessary degree of independence:[305]

> Thus, for instance, an advice prepared subject to direction as to its contents and conclusions by a person who was not a lawyer would not be privileged.

Section 117 of the Evidence Act permits in-house lawyers to fall within its definition and does not call for a practising certificate. In an examination of *Waterford* the Federal Court found that even when the Commonwealth Department of Public Prosecutions (DPP) acted ultra vires, in giving advice to the ATO and the Australian Federal Police, the clients had sought that advice in a lawyer–client context and thus it was privileged. Furthermore,

---

299. *Esso Australia Resources Ltd v Federal Commissioner of Taxation* (1999) 201 CLR 49 at 70.
300. *AM & S Europe v Commission of the European Communities* [1983] QB 878 at 951.
301. *Waterford* (above) at 71, 73, 77.
302. Ibid, at 100.
303. Ibid, at 81–2.
304. Ibid, at 96.
305. *Re Proudfoot and Human Rights and Equal Opportunity Commission* (1992) 28 ALD 734 (AAT).

the privilege was present also because the DPP was both independent and competent and there were no unacceptable risks that the privilege would be subverted.[306]

In *Australian Hospital Care v Duggan (No 2)*[307] (discussed below) an in-house lawyer did not have a current practising certificate. Gillard J upheld the finding of privilege on the basis of the independence of the lawyer who gave the advice. The need for independence, and not a practising certificate, was also the essential criterion in a recent Administrative Appeals Tribunal case.[308] Privilege was also upheld in a recent case by the Full Federal Court for advice given by an overseas lawyer who did not have an Australian practising certificate.[309] In a Queensland case it was decided that an adviser, who was an accountant with a law degree, must also be admitted to practice.[310] Also in a very recent case in the Australian Capital Territory, *Vance v McCormack*,[311] Crispin J found that advice given by legal and military officers employed by the Department of Defence, without a current practising certificate and having no statutory right to practise, was not privileged. On appeal, in *Commonwealth v Vance*, the Court of Appeal reversed. The court said that Crispin J had failed to apply ss 117 and 118 of the Evidence Act, which allows client privilege with in-house lawyers who do not have a practising certificate. The court also found that the lawyers did have independence.[312] In a very surprising decision it was held by O'Keefe J that legal advice given by the Director of Public Prosecutions *may* not attract the privilege. The judge said this is because the Director performs mainly administrative tasks and does not perform the functions of a solicitor or barrister.[313]

The ALRC in DP 69 reviews most of these cases and finds that the main criterion should be 'the substance of the relationship ... rather than a strict requirement that the lawyer hold a practising certificate'.[314] The ALRC thus feels that if independence is present there is no need for a current practising certificate because the required standards of practice are met when a lawyer is admitted to practice. In Proposal 13-3 the ALRC recommends that the definition of lawyer in the Act be amended 'to allow that a lawyer is a person who is admitted to practice as a legal practitioner, barrister or solicitor in an Australian jurisdiction or in any other jurisdiction'.

There are also serious problems of conflict of interest, confidentiality and **11.67** privilege with the establishment of new government legal structures. We discussed one of these developments in Chapter 4 (**4.31–4.35**), the restructuring of the Commonwealth Attorney-General's Department as suggested in the Report of the Attorney-General's Legal Practice. The

306. *Grofam Pty Ltd v Australia and New Zealand Banking Group Ltd* (1993) 117 ALR 669 (FC).
307. [1999] VSC 131.
308. *McKinnon and Secretary of Department of Foreign Affairs and Trade* [2004] AATA 1365.
309. *Kennedy v Wallace* (2004) 213 ALR 108.
310. *Glengallan Investments Pty Ltd v Anderson* [2002] 1 Qld R 233; *GSA Industries (Aust) v Constable* [2002] 2 Qld R 146.
311. [2004] ACTSC 78.
312. [2005] ACTCA 35. This view is also found in *Sydney Airports Corporation Ltd v Singapore Airlines & Qantas Airways* [2005] NSWCA 47.
313. *Nye v State of New South Wales* [2002] NSWSC 1270.
314. At para 13.67.

restructuring took place in 1998. The department still retained its main functions — the giving of policy advice, coordinating the provision and purchase of legal services, dealing with constitutional and international law problems and involvement in legislative drafting. The legal practice section has become a statutory authority, the Australian Government Solicitor (AGS), which is a body corporate,[315] and is within the portfolio of the Attorney-General, but no longer part of his department.[316] The AGS is totally competitive with the private sector and charges normal legal fees. The AGS continues to provide legal services to government depart-ments.[317] There was no indication in the report whether AGS lawyers needed to have practising certificates. As of 2005 most lawyers in the AGS do not have practising certificates because government lawyers under the Judiciary Act 1903 (Cth) can practise without one. There was also no discussion in the report of the problems the AGS would have maintaining confidential government information, while seeking other legal business. Part of the confidentiality problem has been alleviated by the fact that the AGS is no longer subject to the Freedom of Information Act.[318] The AGS maintains its own ethical rules to maintain high standards of ethics but these rules are internal and not available to clients or the public.[319] It should be noted that the New South Wales Law Society in 2003 adopted 'Guidance on Ethical Issues for Government Solicitors'. There are special provisions under 4.1–4.4 on the duty of confidentiality and under 3.2 a provision for the need to maintain the independence of the advice.

Privilege for corporations

11.68   The problems of privilege within the corporate area are not dealt with by the High Court in *Waterford*. The Victorian Supreme Court, in dealing with the problem of corporate lawyers, reiterated the need for in-house lawyers to be independent. In *Australian Hospital Care Pty Ltd v Duggan (No 2)*[320] Gillard J had to deal with a challenge to a claim for privilege concerning four internal memoranda that had been prepared by a solicitor who was general counsel and secretary of the plaintiff's parent company. The judge assumed that he was acting for the plaintiff. Gillard J said that for privilege to be claimed a general counsel must act at that time in the capacity as a lawyer. He assumed that when so acting the lawyer 'must act independently of any pressure from his employer and if it is established he was not acting independently at the particular time then the privilege would not apply or if there was any doubt the court should in those circumstances look at the documents'. Gillard J found that the privilege existed even though the practitioner did not have a current practising certificate. He said when a client issues a sworn affidavit claiming privilege

---

315. See Judiciary Act 1903 s 55M, in Part VIIIB (ss 51I–55ZI). There is a class called 'AGS lawyers' and another class under s 55E who are admitted to practice and called 'Attorney-General's lawyers'.

316. See the Secretary's overview of the Department in its Annual Report for 2001–02.

317. *Report of the Review of the Attorney-General's Legal Practice*, March 1997, Chs 9 and 10.

318. Email communication from Laureen Honcope, Senior Government Solicitor, AGS, 28 July 2000.

319. Private communication from an AGS lawyer.

320. [1999] VSC 131.

there is a 'prima facie position that the legal adviser was acting independently at the relevant time … thus the burden falls on the party disputing the privilege to establish facts, which prima facie rebut the presumption'. If the party presents such facts the burden then falls on the party claiming the privilege to establish the claim. Gillard also pointed out that just because in-house counsel may perform non-legal work, this will not deny their employer the right to claim privilege, as long as at the time the legal work was performed counsel was acting independently.[321]

Kyrou in analysing the *Australian Hospital Care* case warned that there are problems facing general counsel who perform multiple roles in claiming privilege for their client. He said that in seeking to challenge claims for privilege a party should make the following inquiries: 'general counsel's place in the organisational hierarchy of the company; whether counsel's remuneration is linked in some way to the performance of his or her business unit or the company as a whole; and whether counsel owns shares in the company.' [322]

The issue of corporate privilege was dealt with in detail by the United States Supreme Court in *Upjohn v United States*.[323] The Supreme Court rejected for lack of certainty the 'control group test'. The test to find privilege was that the person communicating or receiving advice from the lawyer had to be a member of the 'control group' that had managerial responsibility for taking action in response to the lawyer's recommendation concerning the matter.[324] The Supreme Court in *Upjohn* had to deal with a widespread confidential inquiry of employees conducted by the company's lawyers concerning knowledge of illegal overseas payments. The Supreme Court's decision did not bring certainty to the area. It adopted a broad subjective test extending privilege to communications to a corporate lawyer by all employees of a corporation.[325] Since the Supreme Court did not adopt any general standard for corporate privilege, the area has been left open for future adjudication. The decision also affects only federal litigation and some of the state courts have rejected *Upjohn* in favour of the more restrictive 'control group' test.[326] Finally, there are five other doubts cast on the broad scope of the decision:

11.69

- ❏ Documents must be kept confidential and many corporate documents have a wide circulation thereby losing this status.
- ❏ *Upjohn* involved consultation concerning possible illegal payments made by its overseas employees to foreign officials. These were completed acts and consultations about ongoing or future payments which would probably come under the crime/fraud exception to the privilege rule.

---

321. Ibid, paras 67–71, 81.
322. E Kyrou, 'Dual Roles: Implications for legal professional privilege' (April 2000) *Law Institute J (Vic)* 53 at 55.
323. 449 US 383 (1981).
324. The test was first articulated in *City of Philadelphia v Westinghouse Electric Corporation* 210 F Supp 483 (ED Pa 1962).
325. Berger CJ would have extended the privilege even further, covering former employees of a corporation: see (1981) 449 US 383 at 403. His view was followed in subsequent federal cases.
326. For example, see *Consolidation Coal Company v Bucyrus-Eire Company* (1982) 432 NE 2d 250 (Ill). Note also that if a case is governed by state law federal judges have to apply state law under Federal Rules of Evidence, s 501.

- ❑ *Upjohn* did not deal with communications conducted by corporate lawyers with non-employees or with employees about matters outside the scope of employment.[327]
- ❑ After the *Upjohn* decision, the American Uniform Rules of Evidence were amended in 1986 to incorporate its rejection of the control test. Rule 502(a)(2) defines 'representative of the client' as including:[328]

    any ... person who, for the purpose of effectuating legal representation for the client, makes or receives a confidential communication while acting in the scope of employment for the client.

- ❑ The Restatement (Third) of the Law Governing Lawyers adopts a subject matter approach. It states for an organisational client the privilege 'extends to a communication that: ... (3) concerns a legal matter of interest to the organization; and (4) is disclosed only to: (a) [lawyers and their agents]; and (b) other agents of the organization who reasonably need to know of the communication in order to act for the organization'.

The broad scope of the privilege in *Upjohn* has allowed corporate lawyers to hide important information. It leads to cover-ups of corporate wrong-doings and blocks regulatory investigation and control. Examples of such cover-ups in the United States are the *Dalkon Shield*, *Enron*, *Ford Pinto* and the tobacco cases. In a number of these cases the reports of research by company scientists were directed to the company lawyers and then fell within a deep 'black hole' — the privilege.[329]

Sarbanes-Oxley Act

11.70   Since 2002 corporate lawyers around the world have been keeping an eye on developments in the United States after the adoption of the Sarbanes-Oxley Act. The Act was a response to the recent corporate scandals and covers not only American corporations but also foreign companies listed in the United States — including Australian companies. Under s 307 the Securities and Exchange Commission (SEC) has adopted regulations known as Part 205 Rules. Rule 205.3b(1) requires lawyers practising before the Commission to 'report evidence of a material violation of securities law or any breach of fiduciary duty' to the company's chief legal officer. If no action is taken lawyers have to report the information to an audit committee of the corporation and up the corporate ladder as high as the board of directors. An alternative to this process is to report the wrongdoing to a 'Qualified Legal Compliance Committee' of the corporation.

The SEC has also adopted new 'minimum standards' for lawyers practising before the SEC. These include the controversial Rule 205.3(d)(2) which permits lawyers in certain circumstances, for example to prevent a fraud or to rectify a fraud, to disclose confidential information relating to their representation to the SEC without the consent of the issuer of the

---

327. Wolfram (above), p 286.
328. For a discussion of the principles see Comment, 'The Attorney–Client Privilege and the Corporate Client: Where do we go after *Upjohn*?' (1983) 81 *Mich L Rev* 665. For criticism of the corporate lawyer–client privilege see E Thornburg, 'Sanctifying Secrecy: The Mythology of the Corporate Attorney–Client Privilege' (1993) 69 *Notre Dame LR* 157.
329. For a discussion of the pros and cons of the corporate privilege and for a detailed discussion of the tobacco cases, see D Rhode and D Luban, *Legal Ethics*, 4th ed, Foundation Press, New York, 2004, pp 255–73.

information. Although the new rules govern only these lawyers, the result has greater ramifications. The rules have created national standards for all lawyers representing public companies. There are problems of interpretation. What constitutes 'a material violation' or 'breach of fiduciary duty'? How does the lawyer determine whether the chief executive officer or general counsel has adequately responded to the evidence? These are judgment decisions and place great pressure on lawyers as to whether they should or should not act.[330]

There has been extensive criticism of the provisions, largely on the grounds that they violate legal professional privilege. The Californian State Bar issued an Ethics Alert stating the provisions on revealing confidences of Part 205 Rules conflict with s 6068(e) of the California Business and Professions Code on protection of legal professional privilege and the SEC rules may not pre-empt this state law. The bar stated that 'it may be safer for California attorneys' not to make a disclosure to the SEC because they could be 'subject to State Bar discipline and/or breach of fiduciary duty claims'.[331]

Corporate lawyers also have anecdotal evidence as to what happens to lawyers when they bypass management and go to the Board; they are soon looking for another job. Karpman has pointed out that many corporate lawyers have persuaded corporate agents to refrain from doing illegal acts and have helped these agents rectify corporate misconduct already committed. She said that the Act appears to assume that lawyers have not been doing this and instead has transformed them into informants.[332]

In C C Bottlers Ltd v Lyon Nathan Ltd,[333] a New Zealand case, it was held there was no waiver of 'without prejudice' privilege in respect of documents sent to accountants for comment. The court in dictum used, as an example for the scope of privilege within a company, the circulation among corporate officers of a privileged document. It said such an action would still result in the document maintaining its privilege. It would appear unlikely in the Australian/New Zealand context that if a document was circulated to many more employees that it would be able to maintain that status.

11.71

Privilege after death

There are also problems concerning the fact that the privilege does not die with the client and must be maintained except with the consent (waiver) of the client's successors in title, for example his or her executor.[334] A case arose in Scotland in 1976 when a media debate took place after a solicitor disclosed that for seven years he had kept secret that a client had confessed

11.72

---

330. Y Ross, 'US corporate lawyers asked to become whistleblowers', *Australian Financial Review*, 25 October 2002, p 57.
331. *California Bar J*, April 2004, pp 1 and 8.
332. D Karpman, 'New law turns lawyers into informants', *California Bar J*, September 2002, p 23.
333. [1993] 2 NZLR 445.
334. *Dunesky v Elder* (1992) 107 ALR 573; *R v Molloy* [1997] 2 CrApp R 283. See also T Neoh and A Eu, 'The Duration of a Claim of Legal Professional Privilege' (1982) 12 *Hong Kong LJ* 66; M Frankel, 'The Attorney–Client Privilege After the Death of the Client' (1992) 6 *Georgetown J of Legal Ethics* 45, 78–9; Ho, 'Legal Professional Privilege After the Death of a Client' (1999) 115 *LQR* 27 and McNicol (above), 1992, p 81.

to him that he had committed a murder, for which another person was serving life imprisonment. When the client died, the solicitor, with the consent of the client's executor, revealed the confession. Due to widespread public criticism the English and Scottish law societies asserted that he had behaved correctly; that a solicitor had to maintain the privilege, and reveal it only with the client's consent or, after he died, with the consent of the executors.[335]

What happens if the executor refuses to waive the privilege? Section 123 of the Evidence Act 1995 may overcome this problem because it provides that the privilege cannot be used to 'prevent a defendant from adducing evidence' unless the evidence is a confidential communication made by a co-accused. There is nothing in s 123 that deals with the posthumous rule but it would logically follow that the privilege could not be maintained by lawyers for deceased clients, including a co-accused, who had committed a crime where the information could help someone wrongly accused or wrongly incarcerated. In jurisdictions without the Uniform Evidence Act it would appear that the privilege would be able to be maintained. The present situation is unfair to defendants in these jurisdictions where a wrongly accused will remain in gaol because the posthumous rule will prevail.

The common law rule that the privilege does not die was upheld by the United States Supreme Court in *Swidler and Berlin and James Hamilton v United States*.[336] I have stated elsewhere that:[337]

> ... the Supreme Court by placing the privilege in a sacrosanct position has jeopardised the lives of those wrongly found guilty of a capital crime committed by another. What should a lawyer do working in common law countries that have capital punishment when they receive information from a client that they have committed a murder that someone else has been found guilty of and who faces the death penalty? If that client has deceased, in the interests of justice the lawyer should be free to violate the posthumous privilege rule and reveal the deceased client's communication. California has modified the rule by statute. The California Evidence Code [ss 954 and 957] allows lawyers to assert the posthumous privilege only so long as the holder of the privilege, the executor of the estate, exists. Therefore the privilege appears to terminate when the estate is wound up.

11.73 The approach taken by Lord Taylor of Gosforth CJ in the *Derby Magistrates' Court*[338] case appears to be a better solution. He said (speaking for the Lords) in dictum: 'I would not expect a law, based explicitly on consierations of the public interest, to protect the right of a client when he has no interest in asserting the right and the enforcement of the right would be seriously prejudicial to another in defending a criminal charge or in some other way.'[339] This test would result in waiver of the privilege by the court. It may cause damage to the reputation of deceased clients and their heirs but this result would appear to be greatly outweighed by protecting the innocent.

335. Disney et al (above), 2nd ed, p 677. See also J Beltrami, *A Deadly Innocence*, Mainstream, Edinburgh, 1989, p 19.
336. 118 SCt 2081 (1998).
337. For a discussion of the *Swidler* case see Y Ross, 'Confidentiality after death', *Law Institute J (Vic)*, August 1999, p 41.
338. *R v Derby Magistrates' Court; Ex parte B* [1995] 4 All ER 526 at 546 (HL).
339. Ross (above), p 546.

Obviously, public indignation is justified if the posthumous privilege rule is maintained and an innocent person is executed.

Third party rule

If a third party finds out about privileged material can the client still assert **11.74** the privilege especially to prevent submission of the privileged material in court proceedings? What happens if privileged documents are stolen or wrongfully obtained or obtained because of negligence? Under common law, according to *Calcraft v Guest*,[340] the documents are no longer privileged. If a solicitor is the negligent party the client has an action in negligence or breach of contract, but the loss may be very serious.[341] The rule arose before the development of eavesdropping devices, photocopying machines, faxes, and cellular communications and interception of communication was difficult and rare. One of the biggest concerns today is the confidential problems that arise from the use of email.[342]

Today, even when clients take reasonable precautions, privileged material is difficult to protect from disclosure. These developments led to the modification of the rule under modern rules of evidence in the United States by extension of the privilege to cover third parties that gain knowledge of privileged communications.[343] Under the common law rule clients were also not protected against faithless lawyers who disclosed the material in bad faith. The rule did not apply when a lawyer attempted to violate the privilege in court.[344] In the United States the privilege is protected if the breach occurs as a result of a lawyer's voluntary conduct in or out of court.[345]

There has been a trend to modify or reject the *Calcraft* rule by the use of **11.75** equitable principles but no Australian court has specifically overruled the decision.[346] In the *Baker* case Gibbs CJ said in dictum that although documents obtained by accident, trickery or even theft may be given in evidence, the person asserting the privilege can get an injunction in

340. [1898] 1 QB 759 (C of A); the court used as authority an earlier case, *Lloyd v Mostyn* (1842) 10 M&W 478.
341. A good example is Lord Denning's judgment in *Frank Truman Export Ltd v Metropolitan Police Commission* [1977] 3 ALL ER 431. In that case a solicitor negligently turned over privileged documents and it was held that he had waived the client's privilege.
342. See Comment, 'Cellular Communications and Confidentiality: Can Waiver Occur on the Way to the Office?' (1992) 25 *Creighton LR* 1185. The article points out the dangers of losing the privilege by using a mobile telephone and having the communication intercepted because these devices are not a secure (protect confidentiality) form of communication. The problem is not as serious today as digital phones are supposed to be secure. More serious may be the use of email. See S Masciocchi, 'Email confidentiality: legal and practical considerations' (1998) 24 *Legal Practice Management* 42. For an opposing view that email is not such a big problem see D Hricik, 'Lawyers Worry Too Much about Transmitting Client Confidences by Internet Email' (1998) 11 *Georgetown J of Legal Ethics* 459.
343. Uniform Rules of Evidence 26; Federal Rules of Evidence r 503(a)(4); California Evidence Code s 954.
344. J Heydon, 'Legal Professional Privilege and Third Parties' (1974) 37 *Modern LJ* 601, 607.
345. Wolfram (above), p 256.
346. For a summary of the history of the rule and recent changes to its scope see N Andrews, 'The Influence of Equity Upon the Doctrine of Legal Professional Privilege' (1989) 105 *Law Quarterly R* 608.

separate proceedings to stop them from being placed in evidence. This must be done before the revealed material has been put into evidence. Gibbs CJ also said that the material may be excluded by the court if it was obtained in a fashion that amounted to contempt of court. Mason J in *Baker* said that the cases in this area are open to criticism and rules may need to be qualified, especially when documents are 'obtained by illegal means or by deception'.[347]

In a more recent case, *Attorney-General for Northern Territory v Maurice*,[348] also in dictum, the High Court held that in most situations waiver required a *mens rea* — an intentional decision to give up the rights — and those attacking the privilege have the burden to show that the intention existed. *Cross on Evidence* states: 'Where a privileged document is stolen or otherwise comes into the possession of another party without the knowledge of the party possessing the privilege there can be no question of waiver.'[349] The Evidence Act s 122(2), (3) and (5) also supports this view by providing that privilege is not waived unless it is done knowingly and voluntarily. Thus, for example, under s 122(2)(b) if the action is taken under duress or by deception there is no waiver.[350]

11.76 Unlike the Australian courts, in *R v Uljee* the New Zealand Court of Appeal specifically rejected the *Calcraft* principle by finding inadmissible the evidence of a police officer who had 'accidentally' overheard discussion between the accused and his solicitor. The court said that if the accused knew outsiders were within earshot there would be no privilege. In this case he intended confidentiality and that was enough to maintain his right to the privilege. Richardson J was worried by the inhibiting effect on the 'free and confidential communication between solicitor and client which lies at the foundation of the use and service of the solicitor to the client'. He held that the 'exclusion of overheard communications is ... a logical extension of the privilege as it applies to solicitors and clients'.[351]

11.77 The idea that clients do not waive the privilege by acting negligently has been supported in a number of recent cases. In *Guinness Peat Properties Ltd v Fitzroy Robinson Partnership*[352] developers (the plaintiffs) engaged defendants to act as architects for the construction of an office building. They notified them of an alleged design fault, intending to hold the defendants liable for the cost to remedy it. In the course of discovery procedures in this action the architects' solicitors inadvertently failed to claim privilege for the letter to the insurers and left it in the file that was disclosed and a copy was taken. When the defendants' solicitors realised this had occurred they applied for an order restraining the developers from making use of it at the trial. The court used its equity jurisdiction to deny waiver of the privilege on the basis that the plaintiffs' solicitors must have realised when they saw the document the mistake made by the defendants' solicitors. Furthermore,

---

347. *Baker v Campbell* (1983) 153 CLR 52 at 67, 80.
348. (1987) 61 ALJR 92 at 94, 98–9.
349. *Cross on Evidence* (above), para 25020 at p 759.
350. See also *Hartogen Energy v Australian Gas Light Co* (1992) 109 ALR 177.
351. [1982] 1 NZLR 561 at 567, 574. In a case where no privilege was found the accused did not intend confidentiality. This confession of guilt to his solicitor was listened to by the police: see *R v Braham and Mason* [1976] VR 547.
352. [1987] 2 All ER 716.

in realising the mistake the defendants had acted promptly to claim privilege. In *Spedley Securities Ltd (in liq) v Bank of New Zealand*[353] it was held that privilege is waived when no objection is made when a privileged document is placed into evidence or if it was used in cross-examination.

In *Hooker Corp Ltd v Darling Harbour Authority*[354] notes on legal advice given to the defendant were inadvertently included in a list of documents given to the plaintiffs. The plaintiffs sought to use the notes in court and the defendants claimed the privilege. Rogers J in upholding the right to the privilege by granting injunctive relief approved *Guinness Peat*[355] and applied a leading United States case, *Transamerica Computer Co Inc v IBM*.[356] In that case IBM had been compelled to produce within a three-month period 17 million pages of documents and inadvertently had included 1138 privileged documents. The Circuit Court of Appeals upheld the privilege. Rogers J said in the present case the task of discovery was just as burdensome and this resulted in the mistake. He held that the privilege had not been waived.[357] Rogers J is accurate in recognising that modern discovery cases frequently involve a large volume of documents with many lawyers and others scrutinising the material. In these circumstances it is likely that some mistakes will be made in disclosing privileged documents and mistakes will also be made in not knowing that disclosure was accidental or intentional. It will therefore be difficult for courts to apply the exception to *Calcraft*. In Australia it seems to be that *Calcraft* will be ignored if the court is able in its equitable jurisdiction to preserve the privilege.[358]   **11.78**

In a more recent decision, *Meltend Pty Ltd v Restoration Clinics of Australia Pty Ltd*, the Federal Court said that an expressed waiver may result if there is knowledge by the solicitor of the right to claim privilege although there was a mistake made concerning either the correct principle or the relevant facts.[359] The court also said that if the documents are disclosed as part of discovery and inspection, and the party receiving them could not be criticised, the court may restrict the use of the documents. Fairness would require that the party who received the documents is not disadvantaged by how the documents could be used in the proceedings.[360] According to *Cross on Evidence* the 'more complete the knowledge gained of the inadvertently disclosed documents by the opposing party the less likely it is that their confidentiality, so far as it continues, will be protected'.[361] This view seems consistent with the need to find out about the inadvertence early enough to allow the courts to exercise equitable remedies.   **11.79**

Cases in other jurisdictions

Several other cases in New Zealand and England support the view that notions of fairness and equity will be applied in deciding whether the   **11.80**

---

353. (1991) 26 NSWLR 711.
354. (1987) 9 NSWLR 538.
355. *Guinness Peat Properties Ltd v Fitzroy Robinson Partnership* [1987] 2 All ER 716.
356. 573 F 2d 646 (9th Cir 1978).
357. (1987) 9 NSWLR 538 at 542–3.
358. *Hongkong Bank of Australia Ltd v Murphy* [1993] 2 VR 419.
359. *Meltend Pty Ltd* (1997) 145 ALR 391 at 402–3.
360. *Meltend Pty Ltd* (above), p 404.
361. *Cross on Evidence* (above), para 25020 at p 761.

privilege has been lost by inadvertence or fraud. In the case of fraud the courts are more inclined to help the person claiming the privilege, but in any situation where inspection has been made it is harder to protect the privilege unless the solicitors opposing the privilege had realised they had obtained privileged documents.[362] These issues were discussed in detail in the English decision, *Derby v Weldon*.[363] In the *Derby (No 8)* case[364] the Court of Appeal accepted *Guinness Peat* as authority that no party should be granted waiver of the privilege when knowingly taking advantage of an obvious mistake. The Court of Appeal went even further in *International Business Machines Corp v Phoenix International (Computers) Ltd*.[365] In that case an injunction was granted protecting the privilege even though the solicitor who received the disclosed material did not realise on inspection that it was privileged. The court held that if a reasonable solicitor would have realised the mistake and that the material was privileged, the court would grant the exception to the waiver rule.

11.81 A more recent example in New South Wales adopted the same approach as the English Court of Appeal. It concerned a privileged document that was accidentally included with a letter sent by the DPP to solicitors. It was evident that the document was privileged, and Hunt CJ adopted the view that even if this fact was not realised by the actual recipient of the document, the test to be applied would be an objective standard of the reasonable solicitor receiving such a document.[366]

Andrews feels that the balancing approach is not a proper solution to the problem. He suggests the following principles:

(a) The general principle should be that waiver requires an uncoerced and intentional decision. Accordingly it should not be possible to lose the privilege inadvertently …;

(b) Waiver should be analysed as a unilateral act. Only the privileged party's conduct should be relevant to the process of waiver. Accordingly, it should be unnecessary to examine the conduct and state of mind of the other side;

(c) The privilege is property belonging to the client so that he [or she] alone, and not his lawyer, should be capable of extinguishing it.

The author includes as his major qualifications implied waivers, including open documents and waiver to only part of a document and not the whole.[367]

---

362. The ABA has adopted this view in Formal Opinion 92-368, 'Inadvertent Disclosure of Confidential Materials'.
363. The case involved three-and-a-half years of interlocutory proceedings and 10 reported judgments. It was similar to the *IBM* case in that over one million documents were involved and many privileged documents were inadvertently disclosed. The case is discussed in some detail in Zindel's article, see n 281 (above). Two important reported judgments are *Derby v Weldon (No 7)* [1990] 1 WLR 1156 and *Derby v Weldon (No 10)* [1991] 1 WLR 660. See D Hunt (1992) 136 *The Solicitors' J* 430.
364. [1991] 1 WLR 73 at 100.
365. [1995] 1 All ER 413.
366. *DPP v Kane* (1997) 140 FLR 468 at 485. This case is discussed by V Shirvington, 'A slip of the fax lands solicitor in ethical quandary' (May 1999) *Law Society J (NSW)* 30.
367. Andrews (above), pp 628–35.

American perspective

The general rule in the United States has been that where there is a **11.82** voluntary waiver of any portion of a privileged communication this will result in waiver of the rest of the material. The attitude about carefully guarding the privilege was summed up by one judge saying that one 'must treat the confidentiality of attorney–client communications like jewels — if not crown jewels'.[368] We have seen in the *Transamerica Computer Co Inc* case that American courts are willing to apply a reasonable and fair standard on waiver. Some American courts have rejected the traditional waiver rule,[369] while others adhere to it strictly.[370] In a Californian case where 7000 pages were discovered, but unintentionally included 273 privileged documents, the court upheld the privilege. There were highly visible markings on the privileged documents differentiating them from the other documents.[371] The American Law Institute's proposed *Restatement of the Law Governing Lawyers*[372] adopts a cautious middle-of-the-road approach. Paragraph 129, Comment (i) states:[373]

> The question is whether the client, lawyer, or other agent was inattentive to the need to maintain confidentiality of the communication and turns on whether reasonable precautionary measures were taken to protect against disclosure or, if an inadvertent disclosure has already occurred, to recover the communication. What is reasonable depends on all the relevant circumstances ...

In contrast, ABA Formal Opinion 92-368 states that lawyers receiving **11.83** materials that on their face appear to be privileged or 'otherwise confidential' *should* not examine them when it is obvious that the disclosure was unintentional. The lawyer should then notify the sending lawyer and abide by that lawyer's instructions. There is a slightly different ruling on privileged information received from an unauthorised source such as a whistleblower. In that situation ABA Formal Opinion 94-832 allows the receiving lawyer either to contact the adversary's lawyer or refrain from using the material until a court rules on its proper disposition. In 2002 ABA Model Rule 4.4(b) was modified. It requires a lawyer who inadvertently receives privileged material to promptly notify the sender. In Comments [2] and [3] there appears to be no obligation under the Rules to return the document, nor to refrain from reading or using the document. The obligations to do so are to be determined by a court as part of the process as to whether or not waiver has taken place.

Third party rule in criminal cases

One area where some of the cases oppose the claiming of the privilege is **11.84** when documents are inadvertently revealed to a prosecutor in a criminal context. In *Butler v Board of Trade*[374] an English court held that although

---

368. *Re Sealed Case* 877 F2d 976, 980 (DC Cir 1989).
369. *Mendenhall v Barber-Greene Co* 531 F Supp 951 (ND Ill 1982).
370. *International Digital Systems Corp v Digital Equipment Corp* 120 FRD 445, 450 (D Mass 1988).
371. *State Compensation Insurance Fund v WPS Inc* (1999) 70 Cal App 4th 644.
372. This is from the 1989 Tentative Draft No 1.
373. This approach is also found in *Lois Sportswear USA Inc v Levi Strauss & Co* 104 FRD 103 (SD NY 1985).
374. [1971] 1 Ch 680.

there had been a breach of confidence by a solicitor who had inadvertently handed over his client's documents, the duty of the state to prosecute offenders prevailed over the private right of an individual in equity to claim the privilege. The *Butler* case was followed in *R v Tompkins*.[375] In that case the prosecution found a note on the floor written by the accused to his lawyer admitting perjury. The court allowed the prosecution to use the privileged note to cross-examine the accused on its content. By contrast, Hunt J, in a New South Wales criminal case in which a defendant's solicitor obtained important prosecution letters by mistake of a clerk, restrained the solicitor from using the documents. The solicitor also was made to give them back.[376]

Exceptions to the privilege

Fair trial in criminal cases

11.85 The maintenance of the privilege in criminal cases has led to conflicting results. In *Adams v Anthony Bryant & Co*[377] charges were brought under the Trade Practices Act 1974. The defendants wanted statements of witnesses and in the alternative their names if they were to be called or relied upon. They argued that without the statements they lacked the usual advantages of the accused in criminal matters in committal proceedings at which the prosecution evidence is disclosed before trial. The court has general powers to order production of statements but the prosecution claimed the privilege. Wilcox J said that the primary duty of the court is to ensure a fair trial. If it cannot be provided without waiver of the privilege then the court should take note that it arose. In this case he was not persuaded that a trial, without the prior supply of proofs of evidence, would be likely to prove unfair. Wilcox J did order the prosecutor to furnish in advance of the trial a list of the witnesses the prosecutor intended to call so as to leave the defendant time to make investigations as to their credibility. In dictum Wilcox J said it would be highly desirable if, upon reflection, the prosecution decided voluntarily to supply proofs of the evidence expected to be adduced from the witnesses to be called because that would not prejudice the prosecution's case. By so acting the prosecution would save considerable time at the hearing and lessen objections by the defendant which could arise from unfounded fears of what was to come. Furthermore, the defendant would be more willing to admit facts, which he or she realises, cannot realistically be contested.

11.86 In *R v Barton*[378] a partner in a firm testified for the prosecutor against the accused, a former employee (legal executive). The defence asked the partner to produce documents, which had come into existence in his office in a legal matter and he had claimed privilege. The trial judge ruled for the defendant and enumerated a new principle based on natural justice:[379]

---

375. (1977) 67 Cr App R 181 at 184; for criticism of this case see T Allan, 'Legal Privilege and the Principle of Fairness in the Criminal Trial' [1987] *Criminal LR* 449.
376. *Director of Public Prosecutions v Kane* (No 11386 of 1997).
377. (1987) 15 FCR 513 at 517–19.
378. *R v Barton* [1972] 2 All ER 1192.
379. *R v Barton* (above) at 1194.

If there are documents in the possession or control of a solicitor which ... help to further the defence of an accused man ... no privilege attaches. [Our system would not allow privilege when information] would perhaps enable a man to establish his innocence or resist an allegation made by the Crown.

In *R v Ataou*[380] the English Court of Appeal clarified the *Barton* principle. The court held that in criminal proceedings when privilege is claimed the court could waive that privilege. The accused has to show on the balance of probabilities that the claim of privilege could not be sustained either because:

❑ there was no ground on which the client could any longer reasonably be regarded as having a recognisable interest in asserting the privilege; or

❑ the legitimate interest of the accused in seeking to breach the privilege outweighed that of the client in seeking to maintain it.

The court found that both these conditions were present.

The *Barton* and *Ataou* cases were later overruled by the House of Lords in *R v Derby Magistrates' Court; Ex parte B* because it was found that the 'client must be sure that what he tells his lawyer in confidence will never be revealed without his consent'. It was held that the privilege 'is a fundamental condition on which the administration of justice as a whole rests'.[381]

In Australia the High Court in the *Carter* case[382] also rejected the accused's **11.87** submission that no privilege exists in criminal proceedings based on the general statement in *R v Barton*. The majority (Brennan, Deane and McHugh JJ) said that there are no exceptions to the privilege at common law in favour of an accused person. The court considered the privilege to be part of the perfect administration of justice and it prevailed over the needs of the accused, even to a fair trial. The minority (Toohey and Gaudron JJ) felt strongly that an accused's right to a fair trial had to be balanced against the privilege and then a determination would be made whether the privilege was to be overridden.

Although the decision in *Carter* was not by the Full High Court, the majority view was accepted more recently by the Full Court in *Commissioner, Australian Federal Police v Propend Finance Pty Ltd*.[383] Thus, it appears that the *Carter* doctrine, with its rejection of the balancing principle, will not readily be overturned by the High Court. The Evidence Act, enacted shortly after the *Carter* case, limits some of its effect. Section 123 provides that in a criminal proceeding the privilege cannot be used to:

... prevent a defendant from adducing evidence unless it is evidence of:

(a) a confidential communication made between an associated defendant and a lawyer acting for that person in connection with the prosecution of that person; or

(b) the contents of a confidential document prepared by an associated defendant or by a lawyer acting for that person in connection with the prosecution of that person.

---

380. [1988] 2 All ER 321 (C of A).
381. [1995] 4 All ER 526 at 540–1.
382. (1995) 129 ALR 593.
383. (1997) 183 CLR 121; 141 ALR 545; see in particular Kirby J, a new member of the court, applying the majority view from *Carter* (above) at 141 ALR 608.

It would appear that the section will have limited application because it only applies when adducing evidence. Thus: '[D]efendants will be unable by compulsory process to obtain a privileged document in order to be able to adduce evidence of it, and will rarely know the content of otherwise privileged oral communications in order to be in a position to ask questions of witnesses about them. The only privileged material to which defendants will ordinarily have access is that involving associated defendants, which remain privileged under s 123.'[384] The section may still cause problems for prosecutors in light of its interpretation by the New South Wales Court of Criminal Appeal in *R v Pearson*.[385] Gleeson CJ stated that the privilege would not prevent the access to subpoenaed documents 'in circumstances where a legitimate forensic purpose of the accused at a criminal trial is served by giving access to such documents for the purpose of potential use at the trial'.[386] The New South Wales Department of Public Prosecutions in its submission to the ALRC in DP 69 states that privilege arises for prosecutors 'most commonly in the context of pre-trial subpoenas'. Thus, if the ALRC's recommendation that client–lawyer privilege be extended to pre-trial is adopted, the DPP could lose its common law claim to privilege over confidential documents containing advice prepared by Crown Prosecutors, the private bar and the DPP's solicitors. The ALRC agreed with the DPP. It states in Proposal 13-6 that if Proposal 13-1 is adopted s 123 be amended to preserve the client legal privilege provided to DPPs and other non-DPP prosecutors under ss 118 and 119.[387]

11.88   Section 123 recognises one of the main problems in applying the *Barton* principle: when the privilege is set aside for the accused it might be unfair to the co-accused or others charged with related offences. In *R v Dunbar and Logan*,[388] a Canadian case, the Ontario Court of Appeal dealt with a situation where Bray (B) and two others were enjoined for murder. After the other two had testified, B testified, incriminating his co-accused. Counsel for one of the accused had acted for a period for both those accused and for B. During that time some documents were prepared which indicated that B's former lawyer had attempted to persuade B to change his story and to incriminate the two accused. Counsel for the co-accused wished to cross-examine B on these documents and a third document which appeared to be a note prepared by B's former lawyer and found by one of the accused in B's cell. The trial judge held that all three documents were privileged during cross-examination of B. B on several occasions testified that his first lawyer had attempted to 'make a deal' with the Crown which required B to perjure himself.

B further testified that when the present lawyer of one of the co-accused was representing both of them he had directed the accused as to what B should write in certain documents. Counsel for one of the co-accused sought to reopen his case and call the two lawyers against whom the imputation had been made. The trial judge refused this request. The appeal was

---

384. Anderson J et al, para 5-123, p 429.
385. (NSW Court of Criminal Appeal, 5 March 1996, unreported).
386. Ibid.
387. DP 69, paras 13.146–13.158.
388. (1983) 138 DLR 221; balancing was also considered to be possible in *R v Craig* [1975] 1 NZLR 597.

allowed and a new trial granted. The interests of B as well as his co-accused had to be balanced in deciding whether privilege must yield in the interest of the co-accused. B being acquitted, the interest was now balanced in favour of the co-accused and against privilege. Applying the balancing test two factors were looked at in allowing the right to maintain the privilege:

❑ if disclosing the statement might have an adverse influence on the judge when sentencing him; and

❑ whether the disclosure might expose him to a risk of prosecution for perjury.

The trial judge did not balance the issue because no authority for the proposition was cited to him.

The court stated that if the trial judge had balanced the factors he would likely have resolved this issue in favour of the appellant and thus the latter was not given an opportunity to impugn the credit of an important Crown witness. Therefore the conviction was rendered unsafe or unsatisfactory. The court in dictum criticised the firm of solicitors for giving information to counsel about former clients even though a clerk and not a solicitor did it. In such cases the firm had a conflict of interest and the court doubted it should act for either client.

The House of Lords in the *Derby Magistrates' Court* case supports the views in *Dunbar* and *Logan*. Lord Taylor of Gosforth CJ, speaking for the Lords, states by way of dictum:[389]   **11.89**

> I would not expect a law, based explicitly on considerations of the public interest, to protect the right of a client when he has no interest in asserting the right and the enforcement of the right would be seriously prejudicial to another in defending a criminal charge or in some other way.

The issue of the privilege being protected when the client no longer has any interest in asserting it was not an issue in the *Carter* case. Desiatnik therefore believes that it is open to the High Court to adopt the principle that there is no privilege when it is no longer of any use to its holder. This would allow the courts to gain access to communications that will help them to arrive at the truth.[390]

Communication relating to unlawful acts

American cases

Acts committed prior to the time of communication with a lawyer are considered to be privileged. In the vast majority of instances these communications of past unlawful acts are privileged unless the communication is made outside the professional relationship. There have been occasions, such as the case in Scotland (discussed at **11.71**) of an innocent party remaining in gaol because of the privilege, that have led to public criticism of this rule. The most notorious case of such public criticism took place in the United States concerning the actions of the lawyers in the *Lake Pleasant* case.[391]   **11.90**

The accused in that case had kidnapped four young campers. He killed them and by the time his two lawyers were appointed two bodies had been

---

389. *R v Derby Magistrates' Court; Ex parte B* [1995] 4 All ER 526 at 546.
390. Desiatnik (above), p 49.
391. The facts come from the case against one of the lawyers: *People v Belge* 83 Misc 2d 186, 372 NYS 2d 798 (1975).

found. He told the lawyers where the other two bodies were buried and the lawyers went to the gravesite and took photographs. The lawyers did not actively 'conceal' the bodies, but used the information to bargain for a plea of insanity. When at the trial for murder it was revealed that the lawyers knew of the location of the bodies months before they were found, it caused a wave of public indignation and a debate about lawyers' ethics. Under public pressure one of the lawyers, Belge, was indicted under the New York public health laws for failure to give a dead person a decent burial and for failure to report the death of a person without medical attendance. The court and an appellate court dismissed the charges on the basis that Belge had acted properly in protecting a privileged communication. The New York State Bar later issued an ethical opinion finding no impropriety in the lawyers' conduct.[392] Finally, a county court in granting the lawyers' request for higher compensation, because of the unusual expenditure of time and the damage to their practices resulting from the public outcry, stated that they had 'acted in the highest tradition of the profession'.[393]

The courts in this case did not have to deal with a charge of 'obstruction of justice'. Would such a charge prevail over the privilege? If you were the lawyer in such a situation could you anonymously disclose the whereabouts of the bodies? Could this lead to disciplinary problems? Do you think that lawyers have a positive duty of candour in these situations?

11.91 In a later, but similar case to *Lake Pleasant*, *Morrell v State*,[394] the lawyer turned over evidence to the prosecution prejudicial to his client, which was held not to be privileged because it came from a third party. In the United States cases have made a number of exceptions to the privilege in criminal cases. The cases state that lawyers cannot become 'a repository for the suppression of criminal evidence'.[395] In *Re Ryder*[396] the lawyer was suspended from practice for 18 months for taking possession of money and a shotgun that he suspected to have been involved in a robbery. He actively concealed the money and the weapon in a safe deposit box in his name. In another case it was held that if defence counsel removes evidence from the scene of the crime to examine or test it, the original location and condition of that evidence loses the protection of the privilege.[397]

---

392. New York State Bar Formal Opinion 479 (1978).
393. *Re Armani* 83 Misc 2d 252, 371 NYS 2d 563 (1975). A leading legal ethics scholar argues that the lawyers acted properly because their obligations to the client and the system of justice prevented them from divulging the information. See M Freedman, 'Where the Bodies are Buried: The Adversary System and the Obligation of Confidentiality' (1975) 10 *Criminal Law Bulletin* 979. Rhode gives a more complete account surrounding the case, including the fact the outcry against the two lawyers was so great that they became targets for 'hate mail, death threats, and public vilification. Armani had to lay off his three associate lawyers and staff; Belge left the country': D Rhode, *Professional Responsibility: Ethics by the Pervasive Method*, Aspen Law and Business, New York, 2nd ed, 1998, pp 241–2.
394. 575 P2d 1200 (Alaska 1978).
395. *State ex rel Somers v Olwell* 64 Wash 2d 681 (Wash 1964). The lawyer had to turn over a knife believed to belong to his client to the prosecution, but did not have to reveal its source.
396. 263 F Supp 360 (ED Vir 1967).
397. *People v Meredith* 631 P 2d 46 (Ca 1981).

In *People v Meredith*[398] the evidence, a wallet stolen from the victim, was thrown into a trash bin and burnt. The lawyer had the wallet retrieved by an investigator. The court said that the removal of the evidence interfered with the investigation and thus destroyed the privilege. If it had been left, the lawyer's observations derived from communication with his client would be privileged. The evidence here was that the wallet was a container for the fruit of the crime — the money. The lawyer was required to turn it over to the police but when the prosecutor offered it into evidence he could not allude to its source so as to maintain the privilege. In *State v Olwell*[399] the court said that the lawyer who has relevant evidence, here it was a knife, had the right to retain the evidence for a reasonable time for testing purposes.

A situation where the lawyers never faced any charges was the Ford *Pinto* case.[400] This case involved a car that was produced with a faulty petrol tank that exploded on impact at low speeds. A number of people involved in these accidents died and many had serious burns. The Ford Motor Company had done an actuarial study that came to the conclusion that it was far cheaper to take a chance on the cost of paying costs per victim and per vehicle burnt (estimated $49.5m) than replacing all the tanks ($137m). After losing several cases, with large damages being assessed, receiving tremendous negative publicity and a dramatic drop in sales, Ford recalled all the Pintos with the faulty design tanks. This was too late for at least 27 people who were killed and also the many more who were injured. **11.92**

If you were a lawyer working for Ford and knew about the actuarial study, what would you have done? Would it make any difference if you had the information while working as Ford's lawyer with a large law firm? What kind of factors did Ford fail to take into consideration in deciding not to recall the cars?

It should be noted that a leading American torts expert, Professor Schwartz, has argued that there are a number of significant factual misconceptions concerning the Ford *Pinto* case and these mistakes had made the case take on a 'mythical quality'. In his analysis of the safety of the Pinto, Schwartz says that its 'overall fatality rate was roughly in the middle of the subcompact range; its record was better than the subcompact average with respect to fatalities-with-fire; yet for the quite small category of fatalities-with-rear-end-fire, its design features apparently gave it a worse-than-average record'. He argues thus that Ford was liable for the harm done by the fires, but it was difficult to justify the award of substantial punitive damages.[401] **11.93**

---

398. (1981) 29 Cal3d 682.
399. 64 Wash 2d 828, 394 P 2d 681 (1964).
400. This information comes from R Nader and W Smith (above), pp 70–5 and D Luban, *Lawyers and Justice: An Ethical Study,* Princeton University Press, Princeton, 1988, pp 206–13. Luban discusses the moral issues involved in the *Pinto* saga in great detail. Nader and Smith (pp 72–3) point out that both General Motors and Chrysler also had fuel tank troubles. General Motors had drawn up a similar cost-benefit memo to the one for the Pinto, but lawyers were able to keep the damaging information confidential. Chrysler also kept its files secret.
401. G Schwartz, 'The Myth of the Ford Pinto Case' (1991) 43 *Rutgers LR* 1013, 1066-67.

Cardozo J of the United States Supreme Court said:[402]

> The privilege takes flight if the relationship is abused. A client who consults an attorney for advice that will serve him in the commission of a fraud, will have no help from the law.

Crime or fraud exception

11.94 There is no privilege if a lawyer assists a client to commit a crime or fraud. In these circumstances the lawyer can also be prosecuted. The crime or fraud exception applies to ongoing activity as well as future activity. A fraud can be a continuing event and some crimes involve a continuing conspiracy.

In *R v Cox and Railton*[403] the defendants were found guilty of conspiracy to defraud another party. Their solicitor was approached to obtain advice to help them carry out the fraud. The court held that the solicitor could testify to giving that advice and the communication was not privileged. The court said the communication with the solicitor was a step preparatory to the commission of the criminal offence. It said that if a crime is involved there is the possibility that either the clients conspired with the solicitor or deceived him. The latter situation lacks professional confidence and in the former there is no professional employment.

11.95 The *Cox* case has been applied in civil contexts to include 'all kinds of fraud and dishonesty such as fraudulent breach of trust, fraudulent conspiracy, trickery and sham contrivances'.[404] It has also been used to deny privilege to documents created to pervert the course of justice even where the illegality is that of a third party rather than the client or the practitioner.[405] In *Re Kearney; Ex parte Attorney-General for the Northern Territory*[406] the High Court extended the *Cox* doctrine to include furtherance of an 'illegal purpose'.

The case concerned an inquiry by the Aboriginal Land Commission. The Northern Land Council sought Northern Territory Government documents for which privilege was claimed. The law was being evaded by the adoption of regulations not contemplated under the Act for the purpose of defeating a traditional land claim. The communications in question were made in preparation for, in furtherance of, or as part of the evasion of the law. Gibbs CJ said that the exemption to privilege is present when communication by the client is for the purpose of being guided or helped in the commission of a crime or fraud. The exception is not limited only to cases of crime or fraud but extends to communications made to further an illegal purpose. The abuse here was of a statutory power to prevent others from exercising their rights under the law. The majority of the court supported this proposition.

Gibbs CJ took an expanded view of the public interest overcoming the privilege when the fair processes of the law would be frustrated if the

402. *Clark v United States* 53 S Ct 465 at 469 (1936).
403. (1884) 14 QBD 153 at 165.
404. *Crescent Farm (Sidcup) Sports Ltd v Sterling Offices Ltd* [1971] 3 All ER 1192 at 1200; *Finers v Miro* [1991] 1 WLR 35. In Australia see *Conlon v Lensworth Interstate (Vic) Pty Ltd* [1970] VR 293; *Sut v Nominal Defendant* [1968] 2 NSWR 78. For a recent example in the criminal context see *Capar v Commissioner of Police* [1994] 34 NSWLR 715.
405. *Capar v Commissioner of Police* [1994] 34 NSWLR 715.
406. (1985) 59 ALJR 749 at 752ff; the views in this case have been generally enacted in the Evidence Act s 125.

privilege was upheld. His Honour pointed out that some prima facie evidence is required to displace the claim of privilege — not just allegations of crime, fraud or that the powers have been exercised for illegal purposes. He found that there was prima facie evidence in the present case of communications being made to legal advisers as part of a plan to defeat land claims. Illegal purpose was more recently found to have occurred by actions seeking to obtain evidence to be used in litigation.[407]

The common law is broader than the Evidence Act because the common law denies the privilege when an illegal or improper purpose is present. Under the Evidence Act the burden of proof is on the party alleging that the privilege has been lost. Section 125(1)(a) of the Act states that the privilege is lost if it is furtherance of a crime or fraud or is an act attracting civil penalty. Section 125(1)(b) states that the privilege is lost when made in furtherance of a deliberate abuse of power, by the client or lawyer. The loss can occur when the client's communication both threatens a crime and by itself constitutes a crime.[408] In *Ath Transport v Jas International (Australia) Pty Ltd*,[409] the defendant argued that the s 125 fraud exception applied to privileged documents. He argued that fraud existed because of a 'clandestine plan by the plaintiff and its associated interests to bring about the commercial downfall of the defendant and then to take steps to introduce itself into the commercial position the defendant had previously occupied or, perhaps more accurately, to introduce its associated interests into that position'. The defendant alleged a plot that involved placing the company into liquidation. The plaintiff said that there were 'genuine grievances about alleged irregularities in the conduct of the affairs of the defendant, and within the defendant a loss of mutual confidence among the shareholders of the defendant, of whom there are three, one of them being the plaintiff'. Barrett J accepted the plaintiff's argument that the fraud exception 'is a statutory emanation of the principle that there is no privilege in iniquity'. An iniquity is present when there is 'a crime, civil wrong or serious misdeed of public importance, and the confidence is relied upon to prevent disclosure to a third party with a real and direct interest in redressing such crime, wrong or misdeed'. In finding fraud there must be an 'element of dishonesty'. He concluded that the conduct of the plaintiff was not 'infected by dishonesty as distinct from being legitimate business tactic, even if a hard one'. The case gives wide scope in allowing people in business to play 'hardball'. It means that when legitimate business manoeuvres or 'sharp practices'[410] are present, courts will refrain from interfering and maintain the privilege. Business leaders need to keep secret their tactics when they seek to achieve their goals. Barnett J has a broad view of what constitutes a fraud — it can be just dishonesty or deception.[411]

In *Kennedy v Wallace* Gyles J recently said that legal advice that is given in order to frustrate the enforcement of Australian statutes would not be

---

407. *Dubai Aluminium Ltd v AlAlawi* [1999] 1 All ER 703.
408. *C v C (Privilege: Criminal Communications)* [2002] Fam 42 at paras 14–15, 22.
409. [2002] NSWSC 956.
410. See *Southern Equities Corporation Ltd (in liq) v Arthur Anderson and Co* (1997) 70 SASR 166 at 174.
411. This is also the view of Odgers. See S Odgers, *Uniform Evidence Law*, 6th ed, LBC, Sydney, 2004, 1.3.11620.

protected by the privilege. He said such advice 'would be contrary to the better administration of justice, the public interest in which privilege is designed to secure …'.[412] This view falls within the concept of improper purpose and views expressed above by Gibbs CJ in *Re Kearney; Ex parte Attorney-General for the Northern Territory*.

11.96 Wolfram has argued that courts in the United States should expand the fraud/crime exception to include any intentional wrongdoing 'involving a client acting with bad faith'. The exceptions for wrongdoing concern the denial of the right to claim the privilege. But is there a positive duty to stop a client who is going to commit a fraud or crime? How far should the discretion of the lawyer extend in deciding what can be revealed and when it can be revealed?

In Australia until recently there was no explicit rule covering these problems.[413] There was one case supporting the view that if serious bodily harm or death is imminent then the lawyer should reveal the client's confidences. In New South Wales, a barrister sought a ruling in a custody suit when the mother, his client, threatened to shoot her children if she lost custody. The barrister and the instructing solicitor believed that the mother's state of mind was of such a nature that she was likely to carry out the threat. The Bar Council ruled that the barrister had a duty to inform the judge and his opponent and advise the police of the threat and their fears in relation to it.[414] The Law Council of Australia Model Rules r 3.1.3 allows a practitioner to disclose confidential information:

> … in circumstances in which the law would probably compel its disclosure …
> and for the sole purpose of avoiding the probable commission or concealment
> of a felony.

11.97 There is a general broad exception in the ABA Model Code for information relating to a client's intention to commit a crime.[415] The exceptions to the ABA Model Rules are far narrower than the broad exception of the Code. There is no provision for disclosure of client fraud to third parties, but in ABA Model Rule 4.1 the lawyer cannot knowingly assist the client in carrying out this fraud. There is an exception to Model Rule 4.1 by reference to r 1.6. It requires lawyers to remain silent about a client's material omissions even when disclosure 'is necessary to avoid assisting a criminal or fraudulent act by the client'. This exception appears to leave the lawyers open to charges of fraud in civil and criminal law, but removes any disciplinary proceedings by the profession.

11.98 The ABA Model Rules on dealing with clients' frauds are at times conflicting and often unclear. It has resulted in various jurisdictions and agencies adopting different rules. The resolution of the problem has been highlighted by lawyers knowingly assisting a prominent savings and loan institution to defraud investors of nearly $200 million. The lawyers either omitted or misrepresented material facts in submissions to federal agencies. The case is the *Lincoln Savings and Loan* case,[416] which has aroused a great

412. (2004) 208 ALR 424 at 447.
413. The problem has been discussed: see G Lewis, 'Client Threats' (1983) 57 *Law Institute J* (Vic) 846.
414. New South Wales Bar Association, *Annual Report* (1981), p 12.
415. DR 4-101(C)(3).
416. *Lincoln Savings and Loan Association v Wall* 743 F Supp 901 (DDC 1990).

deal of criticism of the Model Rules and the need for more disclosure of clients' frauds.[417] The debate has surrounded the situation where lawyers discover that their services are being, or have been used to commit a crime or fraud.[418] At present the inconsistent rules in different jurisdictions and agencies can result in a lawyer who discovers that the client has misused his or her services 'from being required to disclose the fraud in one forum and prohibited from revealing it in another'.[419] Even California with its strict rule on confidentiality has an exception to the rule for future crime or fraud.[420] In 2004 California also modified its strict confidentiality rule by amending its Professional Conduct Rules. Rule 3-100(B) states confidential information may now be revealed if the lawyer 'reasonably believes the disclosure is necessary to prevent a criminal act that ... is likely to result in the death of, or substantial bodily harm to, an individual'.

The other rules include ABA Model Rule 3.3(b), which requires (mandatorily) a lawyer to take remedial action with respect to client perjury; and r 1.6(b)(1), which permits (no requirement) a lawyer to reveal confidential information if it is necessary to prevent a 'criminal act likely to result in imminent death or substantial bodily harm'. There is considerable diversity among the states as to the requirements under r 1.6(b)(1). Some states have rules with mandatory requirements based on earlier discussion drafts of the Model Rules or based on the old Model Code or have a mandatory requirement using r 1.6(b)(1) or have a broader mandatory requirement or adopt the permissive approach under the Model Rule.[421] We should ask ourselves whether most lawyers would disclose confidences to prevent death or substantial bodily harm to others in light of the fact that even in those states with mandatory requirements, disclosure is very low because lawyers do not want to be known as 'whistleblowers'.[422]   **11.99**

The distinction between future fraud prevention and past fraud rectification has been under attack. It seems illogical to prevent lawyers having the discretion to rectify the consequences of the deliberate misuse of their services. It makes no sense to have an applicable timeframe for when the wrong takes place.[423] Hazard has stated that it is difficult to maintain the distinction between past and future acts in maintaining the privilege both in theory and practice. He argues that the planning of future illegal acts should be kept secret because this can help the lawyer dissuade a client from doing them; or there may be moral grounds for helping a client to breach the law.   **11.100**

---

417. Drexler (above), p 393.
418. D Rhode and D Luban, *Legal Ethics*, Foundation Press, Westbury, NY, 1992, p 239.
419. Drexler (above), p 413.
420. California Evidence Code, s 956. Under s 956.5 of the Code there is a further exception when it is necessary to disclose confidential information to 'prevent the client from committing a criminal act that the lawyer believes is likely to result in death or substantial bodily harm'.
421. For a discussion of the different state approaches see S Gillers and R Simon, *Regulation of Lawyers: Statutes and Standards*, Aspen Law & Business, New York, 1999, pp 74–8. There are (as of 1994) 11 states requiring disclosure and 39 that permit disclosure. See Attorney's Liability Assurance Society, *State by State Analysis of Ethics Rules on Client Confidences*, 1997, published in T Morgan and R Rotunda, *Selected Standards on Professional Responsibility*, Foundation Press, Westbury, 1998, Appendix A, pp 133–42.
422. Gillers and Simon, see n 421 (above), pp 406 and 413. For a discussion of the effectiveness of the rule see Levin (above).
423. Drexler (above), p 412.

He argues that in contrast it could be said that even communications about a past crime may not be privileged. An accused has:[424]

> ... no right ... to attack or discredit proofs against him unless he is willing to join in the search for 'the whole truth', which would include revealing any admissions he might have made to anyone.

11.101   This would include disclosures made to his or her lawyer. Hazard also finds that in modern business practice the lawyer has a continuous relationship with the client which makes the distinction between past and future conduct difficult to maintain. Many business transactions overlap and what is in the past continues into the present and has manifestations in the future. Hazard's arguments are open to attack, but they do point out the arbitrary nature of the past/future distinction.[425]

Non-legal activities

11.102   In *Leary v Federal Commissioner of Taxation*[426] a taxpayer gave $10,000 to charity as part of a tax scheme. He then bought back the money for a small sum and claimed a deduction for the $10,000. The scheme was established by accountants and lawyers. Brennan J found that the lawyers were performing the role of entrepreneurs and advisers at the same time. Since both roles were present the former prevails and this falls outside the field of professional activity: 'Entrepreneurial activity does not attract the same privilege nor the same protection as professional activity.'

11.103   In *Minter v Priest*[427] two prospective clients approached a solicitor, Priest, to obtain a loan to purchase a house. If Priest lent them the money they said they would employ him for the purchase. He refused the request and in his discussions with them slandered the vendor. Priest then offered to buy the house for them and resell it at a profit which he would share with them. The vendor sued Priest for defamation and the evidence of the slander stemmed from this conversation. Priest claimed the privilege.

Lord Buckmaster said merely to lend money is outside the ordinary scope of a solicitor's business, but in some cases it is an added factor of a contemplated relationship of solicitor and client and this was sufficient for the discussions to be privileged. The conversation must be in reference to the solicitor–client relationship. In the present situation the discussions were not of this nature being no more than a malicious scheme to deprive the vendor of any chance of effecting a contract with a view to Priest making and sharing the profit. Lord Warrington said that as soon as Priest refused the loan there was no solicitor–client relationship and therefore there was no privilege. Lord Atkin held there was no discussion in relation to legal advice, but rather one to carry out a speculation in real property. The latter is not covered by the privilege. The ideas in these two cases are reflected in the Evidence Act 1995 s 118 which requires the provision of 'legal advice', or in s 119 the provision of 'professional legal services' in order for the communication or document to be protected.

11.104   The above cases highlight the difficulty of determining in modern times what constitutes legal work. The definition is in flux and many activities

---

424. G Hazard Jr, *Ethics in the Practice of Law*, Yale University Press, New Haven, 1978, pp 28–9.
425. Hazard (above), pp 27–31.
426. (1980) 47 FLR 414 at 434.
427. [1930] AC 558 at 584 (HL).

that in the past may have been considered outside the scope of legal work are now done by lawyers. An obvious area is lawyers' business activities, but others include work in immigration, tax, alternative dispute resolution and administration.

Facts discovered in the course of the relationship

In a famous old case, *Brown v Foster*,[428] the lawyer saw an entry in a book **11.105** and did not receive the information from the client. The court said the privilege does not attach to 'matters which the counsel sees with his eyes'. The exception is not only the eyes, but what is patent to the senses, except those that are communicated (orally) or written; also any facts which lawyers have obtained that have not been given in confidence, for example the names and addresses of clients. In *Cook v Leonard*[429] the defendant's solicitor was called as a witness. He revealed to the court that he had prepared a document but claimed privilege as to who had instructed him to prepare it. The court made him answer the question. Young CJ in *Southern Cross Commodities Pty Ltd v Crinis*[430] held that a solicitor cannot keep the name of a client secret even if the client expressly asked him to do so. His Honour said that it was not necessary in the present case to keep a name as part of privilege and that since the privilege is founded in public policy the client cannot by contract extend its scope. What if the client's life is under threat or his or her name must not be revealed because of national defence? Young CJ said the name would be protected from being revealed if it was necessary for the public interest or where the client's identity would be incriminating information. In *Commissioner of Taxation (Cth) v Coombes*[431] the Full Federal Court held that the client's name can be kept privileged when revealing it would lead to the disclosure of confidential communications. In a very recent case, *ACCC v Baxter Healthcare Pty Ltd*, Whitlam J in the Federal Court said there is no automatic guarantee of anonymity just because the ACCC was requested not to reveal the names. A nurse and physician had been interviewed by the Commission. They argued that their names should be concealed because their 'professional relationship' with Baxter gave them a public interest immunity. The judge said: 'It is true that the Commission is an investigatory body with extensive powers of compulsion under s 155(1) of the [Trade Practices] Act. No doubt, too, it wishes to encourage information about prohibited practices from so-called "whistle-blowers". But the fact that someone may have a "professional relationship" with a corporation being pursued by the Commission does not suggest that suppression of his or her identity is necessarily required in the public interest.'[432]

In *Ex parte Campbell; Re Cathcart*[433] a solicitor did not want to reveal the **11.106** residence of the client. The court held that it was not privileged information because it is a 'mere collateral fact which the solicitor knows without

428. (1857) 1 H & N 73 at 740.
429. [1954] VLR 591 at 592.
430. [1984] VR 697 at 700, 702.
431. (1999) 164 ALR 131 (Fed C of A).
432. [2003] FCA 994 at para 25. See also the analysis of this case by C Jay, 'Secret papers not always secret', *Australian Financial Review*, 9 July 2004, p 69.
433. (1870) 5 Ch D 703 at 705 (C of A).

anything like professional confidence'. The court did say that if the client communicated his or her address only to the solicitor in confidence and wanted to keep it secret from the rest of the world, then the privilege would apply because the confidentiality of the residence was contingent on the solicitor taking on his affairs. This rule is not in conflict with the High Court decision in *Re Bell; Ex parte Lees*,[434] where the address was revealed because the interests of the child were paramount or other cases where there is an exception to the privilege rule.

CONCLUSION

11.107 In the future the privilege will continue to evoke the tension between having all the necessary evidence revealed in seeking the truth and the maintenance of the sacred confidences of the client. The courts recently have been more willing to be flexible and deny the privilege, in order to negate a glaring injustice. This has been achieved by finding numerous exceptions and by applying the doctrine of waiver.[435] Desiatnik concludes his book, *Legal Professional Privilege in Australia*, by stating that the law of privilege today can be stated as follows:

> Legal professional privilege can be successfully claimed only when a court decides that, provided all the elements of the doctrine have been strictly satisfied, such a result is not prevented by fairness, good conscience, and the proper administration of justice.[436]

---

434. (1980) 146 CLR 141.
435. Desiatnik (above), p 232.
436. Ibid, p 232.

12

CONFLICT OF
INTEREST: LOYALTY

The following real life problem reveals various conflict of interest issues:[1]   **12.1**

In a civil antitrust action, *Berkey Photo Inc v Eastman Kodak Corp*,[2] during
routine discovery of notes and letters of an economist by the plaintiff,
Mahlon Perkins Jr, a senior partner in the leading Wall Street firm of
Donovan Leisure, Newton & Irvine (known as Donovan Leisure), lied
stating that a certain letter and related documents had been accidentally
destroyed because he thought they were duplicates of material that he still
retained. The letter, from a leading economics professor, says that he could
not explain how the early acquisition of rival companies by Kodak could not
be relevant to its present domination of the market. This view could be used
in opposition to Kodak's argument that it historically obtained its dominant
market position because of its innovative product development and not by its
acquisition of rival companies, but this was not of great importance to
Berkey's case.

Two weeks later, Perkins submitted a sworn affidavit to the court confirming
what he had stated. It was later discovered during the hearing that the
documents had not been destroyed but were reposing in a suitcase in Perkins'
office. The false statements under oath led to Perkins pleading guilty to a
reduced misdemeanour contempt of court charge (instead of perjury, which is
a felony) and his resignation from the firm. He later received a severe censure
on disciplinary charges from the New York Court of Appeals.[3] The disclosure
contributed to a jury verdict against Kodak for $113m, then reduced to $87m

---

1. For a detailed discussion of the story see J Stewart, 'Kodak and Donovan Leisure — The
   Untold Story' (January 1983) *American Lawyer* 24.
2. 74 FRD 613 (SD NY) 457 F Supp 404 (NY 1977).
3. D Rhode, *Professional Responsibility: Ethics by the Pervasive Method*, Aspen Law and
   Business, New York, 2nd ed, 1998, p 85. Rhode quotes from the court's judgment:
   'Having served a term of imprisonment, suffered resignation from partnership in a major
   law firm, tarnishing of his previously impeccable reputation with consequent
   humiliation and disgrace, we believe that the conduct is not likely to recur …'.

and later reversed on appeal and finally settled for almost $7m. As a result, Kodak also fired Donovan Leisure as its antitrust counsel.

We are concerned with the role of Joseph Fortenberry, a senior associate who at the age of 33 was possibly on the path to being made a partner in one year.[4] He was one of the 20 lawyers working full-time on the *Kodak* case, the firm's biggest case, and worked very closely for six months with his senior partner, Perkins. When Perkins lied, Fortenberry was sitting at his side. He had worked with the 'missing' documents in the suitcase and had carried the case containing those documents for Perkins.

The New York State Bar Code of Professional Responsibility requires a lawyer to reveal information that comes to his or her attention which clearly establishes that a person other than a client has perpetrated a fraud upon a tribunal. The Code also requires a lawyer who knows that another lawyer has engaged in dishonesty, deceit or misrepresentation to report that lawyer to the proper prosecutorial authorities. Fortenberry was obliged to speak up, but, instead, decided to say nothing to anyone — neither to the judge nor to anyone in the firm. Perkins alleged that Fortenberry did help him; he told the prosecutors that Fortenberry had whispered in his ear to remind him of the existence of the documents when he first alleged he had destroyed them. Fortenberry denied this allegation. He was later investigated by the New York Bar Association, but was not charged with any disciplinary violation.

If you were in Fortenberry's situation what would you do? Contrast Fortenberry's behaviour with that of the New York lawyer in *Wieder v Skala* discussed in Chapter 7: see **7.87**.

INTRODUCTION

12.2 Conflict of interest problems overlap with a number of other areas, including confidentiality and duties of representation. They are not unique to the lawyer–client relationship, being found in all social relationships, but lawyers have far more of these problems due to the nature of their work. Conflict of interest problems have become one of the most frequent ethical problems facing lawyers today.

For example, I looked at the issues over the last few years of the *Law Institute Journal* in Victoria and found that a majority of requests for an Ethical Committee ruling concerned conflict of interest. Connock states[5] the situation in Australia thus:

---

4. This description of Fortenberry's situation comes from S Brill, 'When a Lawyer Lies', *Esquire Magazine*, 19 December 1978, pp 23–4 and from Stewart (above). Stewart (p 62) differs from Brill, saying that Fortenberry had been rejected for a partnership before the incident and this was concealed by Donovan Leisure to increase his chances of finding other employment. According to Rhode (above), p 85, there is no dispute from commentators on the case that Fortenberry failed to receive any employment offers from other firms.

5. M Connock, 'Restraining Lawyers from Acting in the Face of Conflict: Discussion and Advice in Australia' (1995) 12 *Australian Bar R* 244, 278. Connock's article is the most comprehensive one written on the subject in Australia and contains a valuable summary of propositions and guidelines on pp 259–63 and some practical advice for applicants and respondents involved in restraining order litigation on pp 271–7. See also A Mitchell, 'Whose Side Are You On Anyway? Former Client Conflict of Interest' (1998) 26 *Australian Business LR* 418 and C Edmonds, 'Trusting Lawyers with Confidences — Conflicting Realities (A Review of the Test and Principles Applying to Lawyers' Conflict of Interests)' (1998) 15 *Australian Bar Review* 222.

The growth of national and multi-national legal firms and the increased mobility of partnerships and individuals within the profession has highlighted and accentuated conflict of interest problems in commercial, and other, litig-ation. Indeed, it is perhaps trite to say that handling conflicts of interest has become an increasingly important day to day concern of the modern lawyer.[6]

The courts have also recognised the problems, but at times have not been sympathetic. There is a view by some judges that loyalty to clients is important to the image of the profession. For example, Byrne J of the Victorian Supreme Court stated:[7]

> It is a notorious fact that a good deal of commercial litigation in this state is conducted by a handful of very large firms. How is a client to obtain the services of one of them if the conflict rule is applied too strictly? To my mind, this is the price which clients of such firms and firms themselves must pay. The firms have found it commercially convenient to become large. This is but one disadvantage of this trend. It is certainly no reason for the courts to weaken the traditionally high standard of a practitioner's loyalty to the client which have characterised the practice of law in this State.

In light of the complexity of modern practice, the Law Institute in Victoria and the New South Wales Law Society in late 2005 are in the process of drafting new conflict guidelines to act as a national model.[8]

Another development causing increased conflict of interest is the growth of specialisation, with lawyers becoming very narrow in their field of technical expertise, especially in areas such as intellectual property.[9] Evidence of the problem is shown by the increasing use of motions to disqualify opposing counsel and the increasing number of important judicial pronouncements on the issue in recent cases. Many law firms have computer programs to assist them in keeping track of their clients and cases in order to determine if a conflict problem has arisen. Even the most sophisticated software is only as good as the input it receives. For example, a misspelling of a name can result in a serious conflict problem. A fairly recent case has shown that some firms still have not installed proper software. In *World Medical Manufacturing Corp v Phillips Ormonde & Fitzpatrick Lawyers (a firm)*[10] Gillard J said: 'It is clear that the recording mechanisms used by both defendants in the past left a lot to be desired. Even the old card system employed in solicitors' offices in days long gone, in both offices of the defendants would have picked up the potential for conflict and an efficient

12.3

---

6.   Busby and Bashman make a similar observation in the American context. They say the realities of large firm practice include: 'many lawyers; many clients; many matters; corporate clients with complex interrelationships; law firm branch offices in different jurisdictions; lateral hiring of lawyers and law firm mergers; complex, multiparty lawsuits that change over time and that last a long time; class action lawsuits; the constant search for new business by all lawyers in the firm, especially partners; and the demands of large institutional clients': L Busby and H Bashman, 'Conflicts of Interest in Large Law Firms' (1996) 23(1) *Litigation* 25.

7.   *Village Roadshow Ltd v Blake Dawson Waldron* [2003] VSC 505, para 49.

8.   M Priest, 'Draft guidelines — a national model', *Australian Financial Review*, 12 August 2005, p 60.

9.   In the United States 'high tech' companies have repeatedly been involved in conflict of interest disqualification motions: see R Flamm and P Vapnek, 'Conflicts of Interest and Disqualification in Intellectual Property Litigation' (1996) 32 *California Western LR* 257.

10. [2000] VSC 196 at [275].

computer system should have made it a very simple task. The fact is that the control mechanisms within the defendants' offices were lamentably inadequate.'

Firms have also established conflicts committees to deal with the numerous problems that now occur. For example, these committees would be responsible for determining whether or not to hire a practising lawyer on the basis of how much the new employee's past experience will cause conflict problems for their clients. If there are important conflicts involved the lawyer may not be hired. These situations can lead to limitations on the mobility of lawyers in the pursuit of their careers. Conflict problems are also a major concern when firms seek to enter into a merger. The committees also have to decide situations where the firm is asked by two of its clients to represent them when opposing each other. This can lead to conflicts between partners concerning their own client and create damaging office politics.

No matter how many techniques are used, tracking software, circulation of memorandums concerning new business, and regular meetings, large firms still have to deal with thousands of current and past clients. No matter how thorough the searches and checks, large firms just have to hope that they avoid a conflict situation.

Conflicts with clients

12.4   The modern lawyer–client relationship is fraught with conflict. A lawyer used to be able to expect confidence and understanding in his or her relationship with a client and vice versa. Today, lawyers must anticipate claims, litigation and possible disciplinary proceedings from their clients. The relationship has become much more adversarial.[11] The lawyer–client relationship has always had a possible conflict of interest based on the contract for services, that is, the lawyer's fee. When negotiating their fees lawyers must always remember they have a fiduciary obligation to the client. Within the relationship lawyers are expected to avoid conflicts with clients under their fiduciary duty. Conflict problems with clients are at the core of the fiduciary relationship. Within that relationship clients depend on a lawyer's expert knowledge, fairness, integrity and judgment. Lawyers have also obtained confidential information which places them in a power position in negotiations with the client. Finally, it is difficult for clients to change lawyers; they are more likely to remain economically or psychologically dependent on their lawyers.[12]

There are other conflict problems which stem from the lawyer–client relationship, which is supposed to be at arms' length. 'As fiduciaries, solicitors are bound to act in the interests of their clients, and not pursue their own interest.'[13] The most common example is when the lawyer will receive a material gain for being involved with the client; even when the gain is made with the client's consent (in the case of a gift or a loan) this

---

11.   Mahoney JA, *Sedgwick v Law Society of New South Wales*, Legal Profession Disciplinary Reports, No 3, 1994, p 26 at p 32.
12.   S Gillers, *Regulation of Lawyers*, 5th ed, Aspen Law & Business, New York, 1998, p 67. See also Mitchell (above), pp 419–22.
13.   Mitchell (above), p 423.

may not obviate the problem.[14] Furthermore, lawyers cannot be involved in a business or transaction that is in secret competition with the client. This can result in a civil action for breach of the duty.[15] Another important situation is when lawyers cannot give the client full representation by enforcing the rights of the client because of the lawyer's representation of a former or present client.[16] What should be done if different members of a firm are on opposite sides of the same matter? These situations highlight the fiduciary principle, including the maintenance of confidences; that is, the loyalty owed to clients or prospective clients. The professional conduct rules emphasise the need for lawyers to give 'undivided fidelity' to a client's interest.[17] As Street CJ stated: 'There cannot be any doubt that the duty of a solicitor to his client is paramount, and that he must not prefer his or the interest of another to that of his client.'[18] The need for loyalty to a client will at times be detrimental to the lawyer's business, requiring the rejection of another client.

However, clients may still want to employ a particular lawyer despite a known conflict of interest. The rejected clients may have revealed important confidences, and spent time and money in informing the lawyer about their legal problem. Furthermore, there is strong support to maintain the principle that clients should have the freedom of choosing their own lawyers. How do lawyers determine that there is a conflict? If there is one, how can lawyers determine if their representation is proper in a given situation? In other words, what level of awareness of the conflict and its potential harm is needed to allow an effective waiver by the affected clients? If the clients agree to waive it, will the professional responsibility rules or the courts permit this waiver?

Professional codes

The various professional codes and rules require lawyers to be fully open and candid with their clients. The lawyer can thus make full disclosure to all those who are in actual or potential conflict and continue to act if they all agree to that course of action. For example, under r 3.1.1 of the Law Council's Model Rules, a client can authorise disclosure of confidential information. The ABA Model Rule 1.7(b) says that by providing the clients with full information and receiving their consent, it will not be enough if the lawyer reasonably believes the representation of these clients will be adversely affected.[19] The lawyer can withdraw or decline to act for all the clients involved or can decide to act for only one of them. This course of action also presents a number of problems.

12.5

---

14. For example, see Professional Conduct Rules (WA) r 7.2; Professional Conduct Rules (SA) r 9.3; Professional Conduct Rules (ACT) r 8; Professional Conduct Rules (NT) r 8.19A2; Law Council of Australia Model Rules r 9; and Professional Conduct and Practice Rules (NSW) r 10.
15. Gillers (above), pp 68–9.
16. Law Council's Model Rules r 4 and Professional Conduct and Practice Rules (NSW) r 3.
17. Professional Conduct Rules (WA) r 7.1.
18. *Law Society of NSW v Harvey* [1976] 2 NSWLR 154 at 170.
19. There is a similar requirement under Professional Conduct Rules (WA) r 7.3 and (SA) r 8.3. The ABA Model Rules have six sections solely dealing with conflict problems, rr 1.7 to 1.12 and r 1.13 (deals partly with the problem in the corporate context).

The ABA Ethics Committee has also issued *Formal Opinion* 93-372, which allows clients to waive future conflicts of interest. This kind of waiver needs to meet all the requirements of ABA Model Rule 1.7 on full disclosure plus the lawyers obtaining the waiver have to explain clearly all the possible future conflicts that can be perceived. This would include identifying either the potential opposing party or at least the class of potentially conflicting clients. Failure to do so would result in the waiver being inoperative.[20]

Possibility of a conflict

12.6 Ideally, lawyers should refrain from acting if there is even a possibility of a conflict. Many situations seem conflict-free, but a conflict may suddenly develop during the course of employment. It can be argued that the possibility of a conflict is always present during the course of employment. Perhaps the only way to solve these problems is to apply a balancing process in every situation of potential conflict; weighing up the potential harm to the client against the factors which favour allowing the employment of the lawyer. The possible areas of harm would include restrictions on full representation, the degree to which the lawyer and client interests differ, and how the lawyer will be influenced by these differences. The factors favouring representation would include familiarity with the client's problem, the desire for the parties involved to have the lawyer act as a mediator, and the lawyer's expertise in the area. Lawyers will have to balance out both sides and if the potential harm to the client is considerable and the benefits minimal the lawyer should cease being employed or avoid being employed. If, on the other hand, the potential harm is minimal and the benefits considerable, employment should be undertaken.[21]

Today it is accepted that conflict problems are one of the major concerns of the profession. In New South Wales, under the auspices of the Attorney-General, the OLSC established in 2003 a Conflict of Interest Working Party. It has a broad representation from leaders of the legal profession bodies, the Law Reform Commission, the law schools, representatives from large firms and solo practice, and several other bodies.[22] The OLSC has brought the various conflicting views together in a discussion paper in 2005. There is also an initiative by the Law Council to seek uniform conflict rules and to press for greater use of arbitration and mediation to solve conflict disputes.[23]

I have divided this chapter into two parts: concurrent representation — opposing a current client; and successive representation and vicarious disqualification — opposing a former client.

20. Rhode (above), p 340.
21. S Weddington, 'A Fresh Approach to Preserving Independent Judgment — Canon 6 of the Proposed Code of Professional Responsibility' (1969) 11 *Arizona LR* 31, 34.
22. See *Without Prejudice*, OLSC, Issue 30, December 2004, p 3 and Issue 31, February 2004, p 3.
23. M Priest, 'States share interest in resolving conflicts', *Australian Financial Review*, 1 July 2005, p 55. The author also received a copy of the OLSC's discussion paper, *Conflicts of Interests: Discussion Paper of the Conflicts of Interests Working Party*, May 2005, to submit comments.

CONCURRENT REPRESENTATION — OPPOSING A CURRENT CLIENT

The general rule

The general rule is that lawyers need to give full and effective representation to their clients and this may not be possible if the interests of the two clients actually or potentially clash. In *Blackwell v Barroile Pty Ltd*[24] Davies and Lee JJ stated:

> [Full and effective representation to clients] is an ethical rule of long standing which goes to the core of the solicitor–client relationship, the maintenance and protection of which is a matter of public interest reflected in the doctrine of professional privilege. It is central to the preservation of public confidence in the administration of justice.

As the Bible says in Matthew 6:24: 'No man can serve two masters.'

This notion is supported by r 7.4 of the Professional Conduct Rules (WA), which provides:

> A practitioner shall not give legal advice to a person where he [or she] knows that the interests of that person are in conflict or likely to be in conflict with the interests of his client other than advice to secure the services of another practitioner.

The ABA Model Rule 1.7(a) states that a lawyer:

> ... shall not represent a client if the representation involves a concurrent conflict of interest. A concurrent conflict of interest exists if: ...
>
> (2) there is a significant risk that the representation of one or more clients will be materially limited by the lawyer's responsibilities to another client, a former client or a third person, or by the personal interest of the lawyer.

The rules here take a risk avoidance approach; that certain risks of conflicts developing are too great for lawyers to represent the party or parties.

12.7

Rule 8.3–8.4 of the Law Council of Australia's Model Rules takes a different approach. Under r 8.3–8.4 the practitioner must be satisfied, before acting for multiple parties, that each of the parties is aware that the practitioner intends to work for the other parties and all the parties consent to such representation. The parties must have knowledge that by giving that consent the practitioner may be prevented from disclosing to each party all information relevant to the transaction or proceedings, may be prevented from giving advice to one party which is contrary to the interests of another, and will also have to cease acting for all the parties if the practitioner is obliged to act in a manner contrary to the interest of one or more of the parties.

12.8

In some Australian jurisdictions even if the risk of a conflict is great the rule is waived for non-litigious matters. A practitioner may act for more than one party if all parties to the transaction are kept fully informed and no situation arises where the lawyer has to withhold information or advice from one of the parties because of a duty owed to one of the other parties.[25] Failure to keep one of the parties informed about relevant activities of the

12.9

---

24. (1994) 123 ALR 81 at 93.
25. See, for example, Professional Conduct Rules (SA) r 8.3–8.4; and Victorian Lawyers Professional Conduct and Practice Rules 2003 r 8.

other party can lead to a finding of negligence.[26] In reality lawyers represent multiple parties all the time, especially in non-litigious matters such as conveyancing and business mediation, and the problem is deciding the likelihood and seriousness of the harm to interests of each party that may be caused by the concurrent representation. The important question is how the lawyers are impaired by the conflict. For example, if the lawyer is involved in a business transaction with the client the impairment and unfairness to the client is considered to be too great.[27] In the case of a liquidation of a company sometimes a lawyer has been allowed to represent the liquidator and a party interested in the liquidation. In a recent Western Australian case the Supreme Court refused this request. McKechie J stated that in this case 'there is a clear perception that, fulfilling their role to provide impartial and sound advice to the liquidator, it would be difficult, if not impossible, for the solicitors to put to one side, their role in representing [an interested party] ...'.[28]

Lawyers also have to be careful in representing multiple interests because if a serious conflict of interest develops the lawyer may be disqualified from representing not only one party, but possibly all the parties involved. In any event, as soon as a serious conflict develops lawyers must cease to act for at least one of the parties and advise him or her to seek alternative representation. Lawyers who fail to cease acting may be in breach of their ethical and contractual obligations and may be found negligent.[29] Disciplinary action may also result.[30]

Litigation conflicts

12.10   In litigious matters the possibility of a conflict is far greater than in non-litigious matters. If a lawyer is representing two or more defendants this can lead to a conflict over the presentation of their defence, whether or not to waive a jury trial, or whether the defendants should testify. They may have different stories to tell, different alibis and their testimony may affect the decision as to who is the principal culprit and who is the accessory. If a conflict develops in a criminal case it can lead to a miscarriage of justice because the accused did not have effective legal representation.[31] The

---

26.   A good example was a Full Federal Court decision finding the Sydney law firm of Westgarth Middletons negligent when acting for both parties in a business negotiation for failing to keep one of them informed about relevant obligations and activities of the other party: *Blackwell v Barroile Pty Ltd* (1994) 123 ALR 81.

27.   Law Council Model Rules r 9.1.

28.   *Re LPO Transact Pty Ltd (in liq)*; *Williamson v Nilant* [2002] WASC 225.

29.   *Blackwell v Barroile Pty Ltd* (1994) 123 ALR 81. See also R Zitrin, 'Gambling with Multiple Interests' (April 1989) *California Lawyer* 73.

30.   For an example of a finding of 'unsatisfactory professional conduct' due to a conflict of interest see *In the matter of Patrick William Bird*, Disciplinary Reports, Administrative Decisions Tribunal, No 1, 1999, p 26.

31.   The United States Sixth Amendment requires a right to fair trial by having adequate legal representation; multiple representation can cause a conflict of interest situation that violates this right. See *Cuyler v Sullivan* 44 US 335 (1980). Comment [23] to Model Rule 1.7(a)(2) recognises that: 'The potential for conflict of interest in representing multiple defendants in a criminal case is so grave that ordinarily a lawyer should decline to represent more than one co-defendant.' It is unclear who decides whether to continue such a representation. In *Holloway v Arkansas* 435 US 475 at 485 (1978) the Supreme Court said it was the defendants' lawyer who was in the best position to determine when a conflict exists. In *Wheat v United States* 486 US 153 at 163 (1988) the court held it was in the trial judge's discretion whether to override a criminal defendant's choice of having joint representation.

benefits of multiple representation in criminal cases are that it can reduce costs, lead to the lawyer having more complete information concerning the defendants' strategies, and weaken the prosecution's case by providing a united front and denying the prosecutor valuable information.[32] Furthermore, in political criminal trials a united front is essential if the defendants are to have any chance against the power of the state.

The lawyer in such a case can also face disciplinary charges for not adequately preparing the defence due to a conflict of interest.[33] The clearest conflict in litigious matters is representing opposing parties. The English/ Australian position appears to recognise clearly:[34]

    12.11

> ... an absolute ban on the same firm acting simultaneously for two clients with opposing interests although even that rule may be subject to rare exceptions. The reason for it ... is that the firm will be paid by each side to win; there will be a conflict between the interests of its clients and therefore a conflict of duties resting on the firm.

Will this ban be imposed on a firm that represents opposite interests in a litigation, but from offices in different cities? Such a situation occurred in the United States in *Westinghouse Electric Corp v Kerr-McGee Corp*.[35] In an antitrust action by Westinghouse against a group of uranium producers, the firm's Chicago office was retained by Westinghouse. Meanwhile the Washington branch had been asked by the uranium producers trade association to compile a legislative report as part of a lobbying effort and had received confidential information. The court refused to accept the arguments of the Chicago office that the building of a 'Chinese Wall' (see below) between its Chicago lawyers and those in Washington, keeping the lawyers from communicating on the case, was sufficient to avoid a conflict of interest. The court emphasised that there was a greater danger of disclosure of confidences in this concurrent representation than if the representation of one of the parties had taken place in the past. Thus, American courts generally will not allow screening in concurrent litigation conflicts cases because the possibility of divided loyalties is too great. As we have seen, the possible combination of conflicting interests in every matter is so large that it is necessary to look at each situation to decide whether or not representation should continue.

In *Australian Liquor Marketers Pty Ltd v Tasman Liquor Traders Pty Ltd*[36] [TLT], a case concerning two different matters, the defendant sought an injunction to restrain a large firm, Deacons, from acting for the plaintiff in Melbourne. The defendant argued a fiduciary breach because Deacons's Brisbane office was acting for the defendants in another matter. It was conceded by TLT's counsel that the Melbourne and Brisbane proceedings were unrelated and that there was no problem in the passing of confidential information between the two offices. Justice Habersberger distinguished other cases where an appearance of disloyalty had resulted in an injunction because they dealt with solicitors acting adversely to a client in the same

    12.12

---

32. Rhode (above), p 346.
33. See Ethics Committee ruling 8506.93, November 1985, Law Institute of Victoria, (1988) 62 *Law Institute J* 865.
34. *Re a Firm of Solicitors* [1992] 2 WLR 809 at 820.
35. 580 F 2d 1311 (7th Cir 1978).
36. [2002] VSC 324.

matter. He said that there was no specific information from the Brisbane action that could be used in Melbourne. He did find that there was the problem of the 'getting to know you' factor; that the Brisbane office would obtain information concerning the client's strengths, weaknesses, tactics, emotions etc. He allowed Deacon to continue to act because it had when taking the case immediately adopted adequate safeguards (Chinese Wall) and on the basis that the two solicitors from the Melbourne office involved in the case give the court certain undertakings. The undertakings required them to refrain from any requests or discussions with the Brisbane office concerning TLT. Furthermore, if they did become aware of any information concerning the Brisbane action, they were obliged to immediately inform TLT's Melbourne solicitors.

This case is to be contrasted to the recent English case, *Marks & Spencer v Freshfields Bruckhaus Deringer*.[37] The defendant, Freshfields, represented a company, Revival Acquisitions, considering to purchase the plaintiff. Freshfields was acting for Marks & Spencer in another contract matter with designer George Davies. The plaintiff alleged that the retainer in this matter had not been terminated. The Court of Appeal applied *Prince Jefri's* principle of double employment to disqualify Freshfields from acting for Revival. It said that the contract with Davies would be a factor in Revival's possible offer for the plaintiffs. Freshfields had promptly erected a number of barriers, including moving the bid legal team to a different location, to protect the confidentiality of Marks & Spencer, but these were rejected because of the large amount of confidential information already received from the plaintiff. The court also said that even if the retainer had ended Freshfields would not be able to act against its former client because of its extensive knowledge of Marks & Spencer's affairs. We will discuss these cases, and others, under the topic Chinese Walls, later in the chapter.

The *Freshfields* case has 'now prompted the major law firms in the United Kingdom to write to their clients seeking approval for the firm to act for their client's rivals, whilst in Australia clients are now demanding loyalty agreements'.[38]

Professional rules

12.13   As we just saw, the appearance of disloyalty can lead to an injunction when acting in the same matter. The courts also use the term 'appearance of impropriety' for other situations. This means that clients only have to prove that it is possible some adverse effects will take place. This is a low standard adopted to eradicate any possibility of an appearance of impropriety and to maintain high professional standards.[39] This notion is found in the ABA Model Code EC 5-6 ('care should be taken by the lawyer to avoid even the appearance of impropriety'). The idea is that lawyers should not be seen to be in a situation that appears to be one of conflict of interest even if there is no actual mischief, because clients have reasonable grounds in these situations to fear disloyalty from the lawyers because they may misuse

---

37.   [2004] EWCA Civ 741.
38.   OLSC, *Conflicts of Interests: Discussion Paper of the Conflicts of Interests Working Party*, para 2.54, May 2005.
39.   *IBM v Levin* 579 F 2d 271; 280 (3d Cir 1978); for a discussion of this case and other relevant principles see D Donoghue, 'Conflicts of Interest: Concurrent Representation' (1998) 11 *Georgetown J of Legal Ethics* 319.

confidential information.[40] The more recent ABA Model Rules, however, do not mention the 'appearance of impropriety' and have adopted a flexible approach frequently allowing representation. Model Rule 1.7(a) states: '... a lawyer shall not represent a client if ... (1) the representation of one client will be directly adverse to another client ...'. Comment [6] to r 1.7(a) states that a lawyer:

> ... may not act as an advocate in one matter against a person the lawyer represents in some other matter, even when the matters are wholly unrelated ... On the other hand, simultaneous representation in unrelated matters of clients whose interests are only economically adverse, such as representation of competing economic enterprises in unrelated litigation, does not ordinarily constitute a conflict of interest and thus may not require consent of respective clients.

Comment [24] to r 1.7(a) also states:

> Ordinarily a lawyer may take inconsistent legal positions in different tribunals at different times on behalf of different clients. The mere fact that advocating a legal position on behalf of one client might create precedent adverse to the interests of a client represented by the lawyer in an unrelated matter does not create a conflict of interest. A conflict of interest exists, however, if there is a significant risk that a lawyer's action on behalf of one client will materially limit the lawyer's effectiveness in representing another client in a different case; for example, when a decision favoring one client will create a precedent likely to seriously weaken the position taken on behalf of the other client ...

Appearance of a conflict

There are many firms in both Australia and the United States that will not take antagonistic positions to their steady clients; for example, firms that are known as 'defendant firms' in the insurance industry, or trade union firms in the industrial relations area, will not switch to the other side. This attitude to a positional conflict may be a barrier to these firms taking on pro bono or legal aid work that is against the interests of their important clients. In the United States refusing such cases would be against the spirit of Model Rule 6.4 which states that lawyers may be involved in law reform activities 'notwithstanding that the reform may affect the interests of a client of the lawyer'.[41] In contrast to Australian law firms, barristers are usually willing to take antagonistic positions on a legal question to former or present clients in different cases.[42]

12.14

There is no specific rule in Australia that 'appearance of impropriety' by itself will be enough to disqualify a lawyer from acting, but at times law societies have ruled that a lawyer should cease to act.[43] Australian courts

12.15

---

40. A Kaufman, *Problems in Professional Responsibility*, 3rd ed, Little Brown & Co, Boston, 1989, p 39.
41. Comment [1] to this rule states: 'Lawyers involved in organizations seeking law reform generally do not have a client–lawyer relationship with the organization ...'. These are similar views to those expressed in Model Rule 6.4 in the Model Code, EC 8-1 and EC 7-17.
42. For an interesting discussion of positional conflicts see G Hazard Jr, *Ethics in the Practice of Law*, Yale University Press, New Haven, 1978, p 90.
43. See, for example, the Ethics Committee ruling of the Law Institute of Victoria in R 1161, December 1986, (1988) 62 *Law Institute J* 865. It dealt with a situation where the firm represented the husband in a claim for damages in one car accident, and the wife in a claim for damages against the husband regarding another car accident. The Committee stopped the firm from acting on behalf of the wife due to a perception of a conflict of interest.

'are less concerned with the appearance of justice, and, thus, a possible conflict will not generally be actionable'.[44] The appearance of impropriety has still played a role in stopping legal representation. For example, when Ian Temby QC was replaced as counsel for the police in the Royal Commission into the police force in New South Wales in 1994, it was the appearance of impropriety that was a major factor in this decision. The Royal Commission had been set up as a result of inquiries conducted by the New South Wales Independent Commission Against Corruption, when Temby was its director. The main fears were those of potential whistle-blowers from whom Temby had obtained confidential information when he was director.[45]

Another more recent example of the 'appearance of impropriety' occurred in Victoria when a part-time member of a statutory tribunal sought to appear in an appeal to a court from a decision of that tribunal. The barrister was not on the tribunal for the case. The Ethics Committee decided that it was improper for the barrister to appear under Rule 92(q) of the Rules of Conduct. Rule 92(q) provides that: 'A barrister must refuse to accept or retain a brief or instructions to appear before a court: ... (q) where to do so would compromise the barrister's independence, involve the barrister in a conflict of interest, or otherwise be detrimental to the administration of justice.'[46]

Who is the client?

Professional rules

12.16 Sometimes lawyers are paid by other parties for services to their client. For example, parents may pay the legal fees of their child and want the matter handled according to their instructions or a political organisation may pay the legal costs of one of its members who has violated the law and wants the lawyer to espouse his or her cause. Who is the lawyer's client? Is it the person paying or the person represented? In those situations the lawyer must follow the instructions of the client and can only accept payment if the client is informed and consents to the arrangements.[47]

As we have seen in Chapter 11, corporate and government lawyers are required to maintain the same standards of ethical duties as lawyers in private practice.[48] These would include the fiduciary duties of loyalty. The problem for these lawyers is determining which members of the organisation represent the views of the organisation and are therefore their client. There are no clear guidelines in Australia for these lawyers to deal with these conflict situations. For example, 'client' is defined under the Barristers'

---

44. R Teele, 'The Necessary Reformulation of the Classic Fiduciary Duty to Avoid a Conflict of Interest or Duties' (1994) 22 *Australian Business LR* 99, 110.

45. Editorial, 'Temby was bound to go', *Sydney Morning Herald*, 28 July 1994, p 10. When there is a genuine conflict 'the appearance provided to the public is that the interests of the solicitors as partners are in conflict with, and may be preferred to, the interests of one or both clients': *Blackwell v Barroile Pty Ltd* (1994) 123 ALR 81.

46. Ethics Committee, Victorian Bar Association, Bulletin 4 (2002), 'Appearance as counsel by part-time tribunal members on appeals from the Tribunal'.

47. See Comment [13] to ABA Model Rule 1.7 and Model Rule 1.8(f).

48. See also Law Council of Australia Model Rules and the Professional Conduct and Practice Rules (NSW) r 4 and Professional Conduct Rules (ACT) r 5.

Rules, r 15 (NSW), r 14 (Qld), r 15 and r 9(f) (Vic) to include 'those officers, servants or agents of a client which is not a natural person who are responsible for or involved in giving instructions on behalf of the client'. The Law Council Model Rules r 5 states:

> A practitioner, who is employed by a corporation … must not, despite any contrary direction from the practitioner's employer, act as a practitioner in the performance of any legal service in breach of any of the provisions of the [relevant legislation applicable to practitioners] or these rules.

What are lawyers' duties to shareholders, officers, directors, employees and creditors? The issue is further blurred in that there is no distinction made in any of the rules or rulings between public corporations and closely held corporations. The latter present a different situation because the stock is concentrated in a few hands and there is usually little distinction between the corporate entity's interests and those of the shareholders.[49]   **12.17**

American rules

In the United States, Model Rule 1.13 gives us some guidance. The rule was extensively changed in August 2003 in response to the Sarbanes-Oxley Act (2002) (see Chapter 11) and recommendations of an ABA task force. The changes go beyond the requirements of the Act as the House of Delegates of the ABA adopted the extensive recommendations of the ABA's Task Force on Corporate Responsibility. Rule 1.13(a) states: 'A lawyer employed or retained by an organization represents the organization acting through its duly authorized constituents.' The rule recognises that while an organisation is a legal entity it cannot act except through various human beings conducting its operations. Comments [1] and [9] to the rule state that it applies to unincorporated associations and governmental organisations. Comment [9] recognises that rules applying to governmental organisations are different because public business is involved. This means that lawyers have additional duties; for example, perhaps in relationship to disclosures which are defined by statutes and regulations. The latter may authorise more extensive questioning of the conduct of governmental officials than would be permitted for a lawyer working for a private organisation. The client may be a governmental department, but it is generally considered to be the government as a whole.[50]   **12.18**

The ABA Model Rule 1.13 has more detailed provisions and does give some guidance: **12.19**

> (b) If a lawyer for an organization knows that an officer, employee or other person associated with the organization is engaged in an action, intends to act or refuses to act in a matter related to the representation that is a violation of a legal obligation to the organization, or a violation of law which reasonably might be imputed to the organization, and that is likely to result in substantial injury to the organization, then the lawyer shall proceed as is reasonably necessary in the best interest of the organization. Unless the lawyer reasonably believes that it is not necessary in the best

---

49. W Kilbride, 'Identifying the Client in the Corporate Setting and the Attorney–Client Privilege' (1993) 6 *Georgetown J of Legal Ethics* 1129, 1135.

50. For an excellent article on identifying a government lawyer's client see R Cramton, 'The Lawyer as Whistleblower: Confidentiality and the Government Lawyer' (1991) 5 *Georgetown J Legal Ethics* 291. It is also necessary to look at the Preamble and Scope, para [18], to help clarify the role of government lawyers.

interest of the organization to do so, the lawyer shall refer the matter to higher authority in the organization, including, if warranted by the circumstances, to the highest authority that can act on behalf of the organization as determined by applicable law.

(c) Except as provided in paragraph (d), If,

(1) despite the lawyer's efforts in accordance with paragraph (b), the highest authority that can act on behalf of the organization insists upon or fails to address in a timely and appropriate manner an action or a refusal to act, that is clearly a violation of law, and

(2) the lawyer reasonably believes that the violation is reasonably certain to result in substantial injury to the organization,

then the lawyer may reveal information relating to the representation whether or not Rule 1.6 Permits such disclosure, but only if and to the extent the lawyer reasonably believes necessary to prevent substantial injury to the organization.

(d) Paragraph (c) shall not apply with respect to information relating to a lawyer' representation of an organization to investigate an alleged violation of law, or to defend the organization or an officer, employee or other constituent associated with the organization against a claim arising out of an alleged violation of law.

(e) A lawyer who reasonably believes that he or she has been discharged because of the lawyer's actions taken pursuant to paragraph (b) or (c), or who withdraws under circumstances that require or permit the lawyer to take action under either of those paragraphs, shall proceed as the lawyer reasonably believes necessary to assure that the organization's highest authority is informed of the lawyer's discharge or withdrawal.

(f) In dealing with an organization's directors, officers, employees, members, shareholders or other constituents, a lawyer shall explain the identity of the client when the lawyer knows or reasonably should know that the organization's interests are adverse to those of the constituents with whom the lawyer is dealing.

(g) A lawyer representing an organization may also represent any of its directors, officers, employees, members, shareholders or other constituents, subject to the provisions of Rule 1.7 [directly adverse interest]. If the organization's consent to the dual representation is required by Rule 1.7, the consent shall be given by an appropriate official of the organization other than the individual who is to be represented, or by the shareholders.

12.20 Comment [10] clarifies the lawyer's role when the organisation's interest may be or become adverse to those of one or more of its constituents. The lawyer must inform the latter of that conflict and advise that person that he or she cannot represent them, and they should seek independent representation. Colorado has clarified this situation in its rule 1.13(c) which permits a lawyer to represent both the entity and its constituents 'only in those instances in which the representation will not affect the lawyer's allegiance to the entity itself'. The Model Rule's requirement under r 1.13 that the organisation may possibly suffer 'substantial injury' has been criticised; in Minnesota that requirement has been deleted.[51] Model Rule 1.13 does not solve the problem lawyers face in deciding what is in the

---

51. S Gillers and R Simon, *Regulation of Lawyers: Statutes and Standards*, Aspen Law & Business, 1998, p 145.

best interests of the organisation and when an organisation is facing possible substantial injury. There is still the problem of who, within the organisational structure, decides the objectives of the body and can act as 'the client' in dealing with the lawyer's suggestions.[52] In other words: whose directions should the lawyer take and on what subject? There are further questions such as whose confidences need to be protected and to whom certain 'confidences' can be revealed. Finally, the old rule permitted only internal whistleblowing by the lawyer, but the new rule now allows it externally in limited circumstances.

Problems for in-house lawyers

By contrast to the American rule there is no whistleblowing rule in Australia for in-house lawyers. There may be an implied right for internal whistleblowing and a right to withdraw under the Law Council Model Rule section 'Relations with clients', which states: '... Practitioners should not, in the service of their clients, engage in, or assist, conduct that is calculated to defeat the ends of justice or is otherwise in breach of the law.' This rule calls for a lawyer to complain, but of course this step could lead to a loss of employment. The other choice is not to act and thus tender one's resignation. Lawyers who do whistleblow can be violating their professional duty to maintain confidences but there is no duty of confidentiality for illegal actions. There appears to be a need for legislation protecting whistleblowing corporate lawyers who seek to maintain their independence and who are willing to report illegal activities.

12.21

The questions posed above probably cause the most problems for in-house lawyers.[53] When in-house lawyers 'lose' their client they become unemployed. The pressure on them to disregard ethical standards and illegal activities is far greater than for the lawyer in private practice. As Jeffrare's has stated in discussing Australian corporate lawyers: 'A lawyer can become unpopular by having to protect the organisation against some of its more zealous employees. The system of evaluation [of the lawyer's performance] needs to ensure that this does not reflect adversely on those lawyers.'[54]

12.22

Thus, corporate lawyers are forever in the situation of balancing what is best for the corporation by giving effective independent legal advice and looking after their future in the organisation by meeting the desires of those in power who may oppose this advice. In most corporations these lawyers

---

52. In *Waggoner v Snow, Bechen, Knoll, Klaris and Krauss*, 991 F2d 1504 (9th Cir 1993) it was held that corporate counsel was not responsible to the CEO but to the corporation because counsel did not assume any personal duties to the CEO.
53. See G Giesel, 'The Ethics of Employment Dilemma of In-House Counsel' (1992) 5 *Georgetown J of Legal Ethics* 535; H Lowell Brown, 'Ethical Professionalism and At-Will Employment: Remedies for Corporate Counsel when Corporate Objectives and Counsel's Ethical Duties Collide' (1996) 10 *Georgetown J of Legal Ethics* 1; S Weaver, 'Client Confidences in Disputes Between In-House Attorneys and Their Employer-Clients: Much Ado About Nothing — or Something?' (1997) 30 *University of California Davis LR* 483; T Schneyer, 'Professionalism and Public Policy: The Case of House Counsel' (1988) 2 *Georgetown J of Legal Ethics* 449; and B Martin, 'When Corporate Counsel Get Caught in the Middle' (December 1989) *California Lawyer* 75.
54. P Jeffares, 'The Practical Perspective, from a Corporate Lawyer' (March 1988) *The Australian Corporate Lawyer* 21 at 23.

are regarded as an important part of the management team.[55] The general counsel will often report directly to managing directors because of the significance of legal matters in determining corporate policy. The in-house lawyer has considerable knowledge of how the organisation works. By working so closely with top management they also become trusted co-workers and therefore are able to influence the corporation's decisions. This can be a positive influence, sensitising management to its social responsibilities and to ethical issues. But this close involvement with their client can cause in-house lawyers to be placed under severe pressure to support unethical or illegal activities. They have far more knowledge of these actions than the corporation's private lawyers do. If corporate lawyers approve or are involved in unethical and/or illegal activities they will not only face criminal liability but can also receive professional disciplinary sanctions. Furthermore, by having their lawyers involved in the business aspects of the corporation, there is a greater likelihood that the client will not be able to claim legal privilege.

12.23 The world of the in-house lawyer is very different to that of the lawyer working in private practice. Jackall has described the corporate world setting:[56]

> The moral ethos of managerial circles emerges directly out of the social context ... It is an ethos most notable for its lack of fixedness. In the welter of practical affairs ... morality does not emerge from some set of internally held convictions or principles, but rather from ongoing albeit changing relation-ships with some person, some coterie, some social network, some clique that matters to a person. Since these relationships are always multiple, contingent, and in a flux, managerial moralities are always situational, always relative.

Jackall then describes the problems faced by Brady, an accountant, who discovers financial irregularities, including large bribery payments made overseas and a pension fund scam. Assume that Brady is a lawyer. What should he do? Brady does basically what is advised in r 1.13 of the ABA Model Rules and gets no results in changing the practices:

> Brady refused to recognize, in the view of the managers ... that truth is socially defined, not absolute, and that therefore compromise, about anything and everything, is not moral defeat, as Brady seems to feel, but simply an inevitable fact of organizational life.

Brady of course is fired. Jackall summarises the views of the managers he interviewed as to what Brady did wrong:

---

55. For an article on how young corporate lawyers are incorporated into a company see S Williams, 'In-house lawyers: a career choice second to none' (December 1990) *The Australian Corporate Lawyer* 15. The corporate lawyer is expected to be an active participant in the business affairs of the company. See D Aiton, 'Companies turn to in-house for legal advice' (October 1981) *Australian Law News* 14 and J Stockdale, 'Corporate Lawyers on the Move: What does the future bring?' (March 1998) *The Australian Corporate Lawyer* 10.

56. R Jackall, *Moral Mazes: The World of Corporate Managers*, Oxford University Press, New York, 1988, pp 19–21 and 106–12, extracted in Rhode (above), pp 286–91.

His basic failing was, first, that he violated the fundamental rules of bureaucratic life ... (1) You never go around your boss. (2) You tell your boss what he [or she] wants to hear, even when your boss claims that he wants dissenting views. (3) If your boss wants something dropped, you drop it. (4) You are sensitive to your boss's wishes so that you anticipate what he wants; you don't force him ... to act as boss. (5) Your job is not to report something that your boss does not want reported, but rather to cover it up. You do what your job requires, and you keep your mouth shut.

Jackall lists three other matters:

12.24

1. Everyone, including top executives, knew about the pension fund scam and did nothing. They were just 'playing the game'. The problem was not Brady's but was the responsibility of others.

2. The violations that disturbed Brady, 'irregular payments, doctored invoices, shuffling numbers in Accounts', were seen by the managers 'as small potatoes indeed, commonplaces of corporate life in doing business overseas'.

3. The managers felt that 'Brady's biggest error was insisting on acting according to a moral code, his professional ethos, that had simply no relevance to his organizational situation'.

Under ABA Model Rule 1.16(a)(1) it is mandatory for a lawyer to withdraw if the 'representation will result in violation of the rules of professional conduct or other law'. Furthermore, they may withdraw if they find out that the client is using them or has used them to commit a crime or fraud. As set out above, r 5 of the Law Council's Model Rules and the section 'Relations with Clients' appear to imply a similar mandatory withdrawal.

Wrongful discharge

When in-house lawyers abide by these rules they will threaten severely their own employment. Lawyers in such situations have been discharged or assigned to a lesser position within the organisation. If the lawyer goes above his or her immediate supervisor to higher management, and has that supervisor's decision reversed, the lawyer is in a perilous situation unless the supervisor is removed. If the supervisor remains he or she can later take action to have the lawyer demoted or discharged. In *Norling v Northern States Power Company*[57] the lawyer discovered that his supervisor planned to spy on employees in their homes. He believed such action could lead to corporate liability. Norling expressed these views to the supervisor and when he did not heed the advice, Norling took the matter to the general manager. The spying plan was rejected, but the supervisor allegedly manufactured a situation in order to discharge the lawyer. The Minnesota Supreme Court said that the lawyer–client contractual relationship was not a barrier to Norling making a claim for wrongful discharge.

12.25

There has been divided opinion over whether a lawyer has a right to sue for wrongful discharge. The argument against compensation is that the

---

57. 478 NW 2d 498 (Minn 1991).

lawyer has entered into a contract at will because of being in a lawyer–client relationship and can be dismissed at any time.[58] In *GTE Products Corporation v Stewart*[59] a Massachusetts court held that a lawyer had a right to sue when he alleged he was 'squeezed out' because his suggestions concerning the need to protect consumer safety and also to avoid corporate liability were not well received by the company. The court upheld Stewart's right to sue but rejected his claim. The court said that the:[60]

> ... public interest is better served if in-house counsel's resolve to comply with ethical and statutorily mandated duties is strengthened by providing judicial recourse when an employer's demands are in direct and unequivocal conflict with those duties.

12.26   In *Kachmer v SunGard Data Systems, Inc*[61] the Third Circuit Court of Appeal allowed an in-house lawyer to sue for retaliatory discharge. The case is important because the court allowed the case to proceed even though there were substantial risks to confidential information of the client. It is interesting to note that the American Corporate Counsel Association, the body which represents in-house lawyers, has filed a brief in one of the cases supporting the corporation's right of dismissal because the lawyer's disloyalty destroyed the confidence of corporate executives in their in-house lawyers and deprived them of 'the opportunity to police corporate activities and advise their corporate clients to comply with our laws'.[62] Nader and Smith believe that the association might have been worried that if in-house lawyers are compensated for wrongful dismissal corporations will give more work to outside counsel, who are independent contractors and thus cannot claim retaliatory discharge.[63]

12.27   In-house lawyers will find it difficult to reject unethical or illegal requests, knowing that to do so can lead to dismissal. Therefore, they will have a difficult time in maintaining their independence. Giesel and Brown suggest

58.   In *Herbster v North American Co for Life and Health Insurance* 501 NE2d 343 (Ill 1986) the court denied the lawyer any damages for retaliatory discharge after Herbster had refused the request by management to destroy documents that were subject of a discovery motion. A similar result was found in *Balla v Gambro* 584 NE 2d 104 (Ill 1991) where the lawyer was fired for threatening to turn his company in for importing kidney machines that he said were dangerous. See also *Willy v The Coastal Corp*, 939 SW 2d 193 (Tex Ct App 1996) where the court did not allow the lawyer to prove his claim because he could only do so by using his client's confidences. By contrast in *Mourad v Automobile Club Insurance Association* 465 NW 2d 395 (Mich 1991) the Court of Appeal upheld a finding of a constructive discharge, granting the lawyer damages. For a discussion of similar cases in California see (June 1994) *California Lawyer* 45.
59.   653 NE 2d 161 (Mass 1995).
60.   653 NE 2d 161 at 166. This statement was modified by the court at 166–7. The court said a remedy would be allowed only in 'narrow and carefully delineated circumstances' where the retaliatory discharge came about because of '(1) explicit and unequivocal statutory or ethical norms, (2) which embody policies of importance to the public at large in the circumstances of the particular case, and (3) the claim can be proved without any violation of the attorney's obligation to respect client confidences and secrets'.
61.   109 F 3rd 173 (3d Cir 1997).
62.   R Nader and W Smith, *No Contest: Corporate Lawyers and the Perversion of Justice in America* (1996), p 350. The authors discuss (pp 347–50) in detail *Balla v Gambro* 584 NE 2d 104 (Ill 1991) in which the brief was filed.
63.   Nader and Smith (above).

that lawyers who maintain high ethical standards should be rewarded. If they are dismissed for such actions they should be compensated. Giesel says this in turn will improve professional responsibility compliance:[64]

> ... furthering professional independence, creating potential business benefit to the organisation, creating systemic benefit to business as a whole and ensuring a measure of fairness to the individual attorney who has taken a personally more arduous course in the interest of the law or the rules of professional conduct.

Brown would 'strictly circumscribe' wrongful dismissal actions:[65]

> First, the claim must be predicated on a clear violation of legal or ethical requirements, not on disputes over personal moral values or ambiguities in the law. Second, the substance of the dispute must involve policies affecting the public at large, not simply the various parties directly involved in the dispute. Third, the litigation must be able to be conducted in a way that preserves client confidences as both an evidentiary and an ethical matter ... [W]here appropriate confidentiality cannot be protected, the claim should be dismissed, and, if improper disclosure has been made, counsel should be referred to the bar for discipline. Finally, corporate counsel should be required to submit the dispute for resolution by the bar as a prerequisite to litigation. Such an 'administrative remedy' would go a long way in assuring that only the exceptional case, firmly grounded in ethics and law, would become the subject of litigation.

I have stated elsewhere that:[66]

12.28

> Even if senior management is pursuing illegal policies that may be financially profitable in the short term, there are strong arguments that they may be very financially damaging in the long run and thus not in the best interests of the corporation. A corporation that gets a bad name for hiding defective products, for following unsound environmental policies, for giving bribes etc, will eventually have large financial losses because of these policies. Furthermore, senior management is not the only stakeholder that the lawyer has to keep in mind. The views and interest of other stakeholders such as shareholders, directors, creditors and fellow employees will also need to be considered by the corporate lawyer in determining what is in the best interests of the company.

> There is a need to provide support for those corporate lawyers who do the right thing — uphold their professional rules. It should be part of any lawyer's employment contract that refusal to adhere to any requirement for him or her to pursue a corporate policy that leads to violation of the professional rules will not be grounds for dismissal. There are strong public policy arguments for upholding such contracts.

Besides getting a bad name, companies now face large fines and even, at times, possible criminal penalties for violating government regulations. The increased regulation has meant that many more companies now have ethics officers. In the United States, according to a 1992 survey, approximately one-third of these officers are senior in-house counsel. Furthermore, there is now an active and rapidly growing corporate Ethics Officers Association

---

64. Giesel (above).
65. Brown (above), pp 30–1.
66. Stan Ross, 'Corporate lawyer whistleblowing' (September 1998) *Law Institute J (Vic)* 27, 28.

that was established in 1992.[67] Similar developments are starting to occur in Australia.

Conveyancing, family and insurance matters

Conveyancing problems — rules

12.29 Conveyancing, family and insurance matters are the three main areas causing conflict problems where lawyers act for more than one party. In most jurisdictions in Australia it is not uncommon for a solicitor to represent both the vendor and purchaser, or lessor and lessee, in a conveyance. Solicitors also are very likely to act for both mortgagor and mortgagee.[68] Of course, in South Australia and Western Australia most of the conveyancing work is done by non-lawyers. It is not illegal for solicitors or land agents to act for both parties, but in South Australia changes to the Land and Business (Sale and Conveyancing) Act 1994 provide new regulations that state they cannot act for both except in limited circumstances.[69] The courts do frown on this practice for both land agents and solicitors.[70] Under the Law Council's Model Rule 8.5 practitioners cannot act for both parties in a sale of land transaction, in lease or mortgage transactions for a builder, developer or sub-divider and at the same time for anyone that person or entity contracts with in relation to that business unless they are fully informed in writing concerning the potential disadvantages and both parties sign a designated consent form. Victoria has a similar provision.[71]

12.30 The Australian Capital Territory also has restrictions on acting for both parties in sale of land transactions, except when both parties are existing clients or are related.[72] Queensland has an interesting prohibition against dual representation when either party offers (1) to pay both parties' fees or (2) offers any other kind of financial inducement to have dual representation.[73]

New South Wales r 9 includes conveyancing as part of the general rule on acting for more than one party. Under r 45, in relation to loan or security documents, the practitioner cannot act for the lender when giving advice to anyone concerning these documents. The solicitor needs to be independent in giving the advice to the borrower or guarantor.

12.31 The advantages of having one solicitor act for both parties are mainly those of convenience, speed and the ability of both parties to have the solicitor of their choice. With increased competition from licensed conveyancers,

---

67. R Zitrin and C Langford, *The Moral Compass of the American Lawyer: Truth, Justice, Power, and Greed*, Ballantine Books, New York, 1999, p 111. This book has an excellent chapter on corporate whistleblowing especially in the tobacco industry: Chapter 5.
68. J Disney, J Basten, P Redmond and S Ross, *Lawyers*, 2nd ed, Law Book Co, Sydney 1986, p 761.
69. The Act was amended in 1995 and the provisions are found in the Land and Business (Sale and Conveyancy) Regulations, regs 17–19.
70. *Re a Practitioner* (1975) 12 SASR 166 at 168; *Jennings v Zilahi-Kiss* (1972) 2 SASR 493 at 511–12; *Fox v Everingham* (1983) 50 ALR 337 at 345; *Tubby Trout Pty Ltd v Sailbay Pty Ltd* (FC, February 1994, unreported).
71. Victorian Lawyers RPA *Professional Conduct and Practice Rules 2003* r 8.5.
72. Professional Conduct Rules (ACT) rr 8.4 and 8.5.
73. *Solicitors Handbook* (Qld), para 8.05.

clients can also usually negotiate a lower fee. The disadvantages are numerous: possible conflicts in negotiating the terms of the contract, the finance aspects and carrying out the instructions of each client during the course of the transaction. The right to dual representation may have some validity in country areas. Acting for both parties is perhaps more justifiable in sparsely populated areas (jurisdictions such as Tasmania), on the basis that there are few solicitors practising in such areas and clients do not have much of a choice. Country solicitors act for both parties in a large number of conveyancing matters and depend on these matters for a major part of their fees. If they were no longer permitted to continue this type of dual representation they could be forced out of practice.[74]

The Law Society in England and Wales has adopted a general prohibition against acting for both parties in conveyancing transactions. The exceptions to the rule are if the parties are related, or are established clients, or if there are no other solicitors in the vicinity whom the client can consult.[75] The English rules are in the process of being replaced by a new Code of Conduct to be adopted at the end of 2005, but this rule will essentially be the same.[76] In the United States there is no general prohibition on acting for both parties in a conveyancing transaction in either the Model Code or Model Rules. Some states have adopted rules against such representation but they are in a small minority.[77]

Property problems — cases

Although some jurisdictions in Australia allow dual representation in conveyancing transactions, as has been stated previously, there has been considerable criticism of the practice. Wootten J summarised this view when he said:[78]   **12.32**

> It seems to me that the practice of a solicitor acting for both parties cannot be too strongly deprecated. It is only because of the possibility that something may be wrong in a transaction, or may go wrong during its implementation, that the employment of highly trained professional people at professional scales of remuneration can be justified ... [The client] is entitled to assume that that person will be in a position to approach the matter concerned with nothing but the protection of his client's interests against [those] of the other party. He should not have to depend on a person who has conflicting allegiances and who may be tempted either consciously or unconsciously to favour the other client, or simply to seek a resolution of the matter in a way

74. Submission of the Law Society of NSW to the Law Reform Commission of NSW, 1979, extracted in Disney et al (above), p 767.
75. Rule 6, Solicitors' Practice Rules (1999). See also *The Guide to the Professional Conduct of Solicitors*.
76. See www.lawsociety.org.uk.
77. See, for example, the New Jersey Advisory Committee on Profession Ethics Opinion 243 (1972) 95 *New Jersey LJ* 1145. The rule states that in a real estate transaction 'in all circumstances it is unethical for the same attorney to represent buyer and seller in negotiating the terms of a contract of sale'. The New Jersey Supreme Court has not accepted this rule in disciplining lawyers for ignoring it. The court stated that it would consider the facts of each case before deciding whether dual representation was permissible: *In re Dolan* 384 A 2d 1076 (NJ 1978). By contrast the Oregon Supreme Court has been willing on numerous occasions to discipline lawyers for improper simultaneous representation of multiple interests: Kaufman (above), p 88.
78. *Thompson v Mikkelsen* (SC(NSW), Wootten J, No 584/74, 3 October 1974, unreported).

which is least embarrassing to himself ... No doubt every solicitor thinks when he accepts ... a [dual representation] role that nothing unfortunate can possibly happen in that particular transaction. That of course was the attitude of the solicitor in this case, and in nearly all of the other cases where unfortunate consequences flow from the acceptance of the dual role. It seems to me that this is a matter in which the Law Society of New South Wales should take a very strong line, stronger than it has, so far as I can ascertain, taken up to the present time ...

12.33 Wootten J's warning and those of other judges[79] were recognised in the Residential Property Conveyancing Code of Conduct (NSW) s 2.1.4, but the Code was repealed in October 2000. Solicitors are warned that dual representation can lead to damage actions. These warnings have been shown to be valid. There have been numerous cases of solicitors found to be negligent in dual representation for not taking reasonable care in a conveyancing transaction when a conflict arose. The negligence usually arises for failure to completely keep one of the parties informed as to problems encountered by the other party.[80] Solicitors who act for developers and their purchasers, and also arrange the finances, are now also confronted with serious conflict problems that can easily lead to successful negligence actions.[81] Preferring the interests of one party over another can also lead to a finding of professional misconduct.[82]

12.34 In contrast to these cases, in a Privy Council case, *Clark Boyce v Mouat*,[83] a law firm successfully appealed a New Zealand Court of Appeal decision finding it to be negligent in a dual representation mortgage matter. In this case a mother and son used the same solicitor to have a mortgage placed on the mother's property for a loan for the son. The loan was taken out with the mother as the mortgagor and the son as the guarantor. The son was primarily responsible for the payment of interest. Three times the solicitors pointed out to the mother that she should obtain independent legal advice. She also signed a written acknowledgment that she had been advised of the legal implications of the transaction and the need for independent legal advice and that she did not wish to seek it. The son failed to meet his obligations and was later adjudicated a bankrupt. The mother sued the solicitors for breach of contract and of duty of care.

12.35 The judgment of the Privy Council was delivered by Lord Jaucey of Tullichettle. He stated that there was no general rule of law that a solicitor should never act for both parties in a transaction where there is a possible conflict of interest. A solicitor can act if both parties have given informed consent, meaning that the parties know there is a conflict that may disable the solicitor from disclosing to each party the full information the solicitor

79. See, for example, in the English context, Megarry J, *Spector v Ageda* [1971] 3 WLR 498 at 512.
80. See *Stewart v Layton* (1993) 111 ALR 687; *Farrington v Rowe McBride & Partners* [1985] 1 NZLR 83; *Wan v McDonald* (1992) 105 ALR 473.
81. See J Anderson, 'Duties of Care in Conveyancing, Dangers of acting for several parties exemplified: O'Briens case' (1993) 31 *Law Society J (NSW)* 54. O'Brien's case was discussed in **10.19**.
82. See, for example, *In the matter of Douglas Alan Perry*, Legal Profession Disciplinary Reports (NSW), No 3, 1996, pp 25–6. In this case the vendor's interests were preferred to the detriment of the purchaser.
83. [1993] 3 NZLR 641 (PC).

possesses as to the transaction or may stop the solicitor from giving information to one party if it conflicts with the interests of the other. In other words, the clients can waive their rights if they fully understand what is involved. His Lordship did say there were certain situations where full disclosure would not be enough because the conflict was too detrimental to one of the parties, for example 'where one client sought advice on a matter which would involve disclosure of facts detrimental to the interests of the other client'. In the present case their Lordships found that the solicitor had done all that was reasonably required of him before accepting the plaintiff's instructions. The solicitor also had no duty to give unsought advice on the wisdom of the proposed transaction since this was not part of his instructions.[84] This means that a solicitor can be employed under a limited retainer to complete documentation in respect of a transaction where the client or clients have already made the decision to proceed.[85]

The Privy Council's view seems to be opposed to the position in Australian courts that solicitors acting for two parties have a duty to disclose all material facts within their knowledge which are relevant to either client's consideration of the transaction.[86] However, a statement by the Law Society of New South Wales in 1995 and that Council's and the Law Council of Australia's adoption of r 9 and r 8, respectively, seems to approve the *Clarke Boyce* principle of informed consent.[87] Rule 45 in New South Wales (see above) by contrast appears to modify the general provisions and that of the earlier views adopted by the Law Society's Council. Windeyer J has recently applied the *Clarke Boyce* principle in rejecting a client's allegation of breach of fiduciary duty where a solicitor had acted for two parties entering into a loan agreement.[88] An English court has also stated in reference to a dual conveyancing matter that:[89]

12.36

> A solicitor must put at his client's disposal not only his skill but also his knowledge, so far as is relevant; and if he is unwilling to reveal his knowledge to his client, he should not act for him. What he cannot do is to act for the client and at the same time withhold from him any relevant knowledge that he has …

The ABA recently issued an ethical opinion[90] concerning a conflict problem in drafting a will. A lawyer was asked to change a will to disinherit a beneficiary whom the lawyer was representing in an unrelated matter. The ABA opinion found that no conflict took place unless it could be shown that the representation of the testator was materially limited because of the lawyer's representation of the beneficiary in the other matter.

---

84. [1993] 3 NZLR 641 at 646–8.
85. For a discussion of this case see 'The extent of a practitioner's duties — the successful Privy Council appeal in *Clark Boyce v Mouat*' (1993) 405 *Law Talk (NZ Law Society)* 8–11.
86. *Clark v Barter* (1989) NSW ConvR ¶55–483.
87. See (1995) 33 *Law Society J (NSW)* 15 for the views of the Law Society on the *Clarke Boyce* case.
88. *Lowy v Alexander* [2000] NSWSC 661.
89. *Spector v Ageda* [1973] 1 Ch 30 at 48.
90. ABA, Formal Ethical Opinion 05-434, December 2004.

Family problems

12.37　These cases show the type of problem lawyers frequently confront when handling the affairs of different members of a family.[91] For example, a situation arose in New South Wales where a solicitor acted for the father in the purchase of land in the name of his minor daughter for tax reasons. Later, when the daughter was no longer a minor, the father sought to give a security to a bank over the property and the daughter refused to sign the document after being advised by the same solicitor that she was not bound to sign the document. The father instructed another firm to act for him to have the daughter declared a trustee of the company for the father. The solicitor asked the Law Society whether it was possible for him to act for the daughter. The ruling of the Council was that he could not act for either of them in the contemplated proceedings and that the communications to and from both of them were equally privileged.[92] The matter has been further complicated with the adoption of the Married Persons (Equality of Status) Act 1996 (NSW), which makes it necessary for practitioners when instructed to act for both husband and wife, for example in the purchase of a property or a loan transaction, to obtain instructions from both spouses. If instructions are obtained only from one spouse, it may not be binding on the other spouse.

In a New Zealand Court of Appeal case, *Black v Taylor*,[93] a practitioner had acted for various members of the Taylor family for a number of decades. He was prevented from acting for the nephew who had sued the estate of his late uncle or for anyone else in the matter. The court declared his ineligibility on the basis that it would cause the community to lose confidence in the judicial system.

12.38　The conflict problems for lawyers who have represented various members of a family for a long time are not adequately dealt with under the present rules in both Australia and the United States. The multiple representation of a family will frequently lead to disputes concerning estate planning and domestic relations. Lawyers are strongly advised that it is undesirable to act for both parties in any proceedings under the Family Law Act.[94] This advice is also present in the Professional Conduct Rules (WA), Sch 4, 'Some Family Law Guidelines'. It states that: 'It is highly undesirable for a practitioner to act for both parties to a marriage in proceedings under the Family Law Act.' The guidelines further state that if both parties request joint representation it 'should always be recommended that one of them seek separate legal advice and representation, even in circumstances in which the Family Law Rules envisage that one practitioner may act for both parties'. There is a provision under s 44(1A) of the Family Law Act 1975 allowing joint representation for decrees of dissolution or nullity of marriage, but it is highly undesirable to act in such cases if there are children under the age of 18 or there are any matters in dispute between

---

91.　We have dealt with other conflict situations concerning the family in Chapters 8, 9 and 11.
92.　This ruling is produced in Disney et al (above), p 751.
93.　[1993] 3 NZLR 403.
94.　For example, see Family Law Advisory Code of Practice (1992) Law Society of New South Wales paras 3.5–3.7.

the husband and wife.[95] Section 79(9) of the Act also has mandatory mediation requirements.

Under our present rules, as we have seen from the above Law Society of New South Wales ruling and court decisions,[96] there is a justified fear that lawyers will be disqualified from representing any of the clients in such situations. This is unfortunate because lawyers who have been representing a family for some time will know best how to deal with the family's legal problems. One suggested solution has been that the family as a unit should be considered to be the client. This would overcome the present conflict rules on multiple representation and allow the lawyer to mediate and work out the disputes with members of the unit.[97]

In the United States the traditional approach is found in the American **12.39** Academy of Matrimonial Lawyers Standards. It states: 'An attorney should not represent both husband and wife even if they do not wish to obtain independent representation.' The Comment on this Standard states that: '[I]t is impossible for the attorney to provide impartial advice to both parties, and even a seemingly amicable separation or divorce may result in bitter litigation over financial matters or custody.'[98]

There are a number of American cases that have supported the notion that when joint representation takes place and the clients are aware of each other's relationship to the firm, there is waiver of the confidences involved. Thus, the firm should not be disqualified for deciding to represent one of the two parties in a related transaction when a conflict develops.[99] Furthermore, the ABA has adopted the Divorce and Family Mediation: Standards of Practice 1986. The preamble states that the Standards set down rules for the 'process in which a lawyer helps family members resolve their disputes in an informative and consensual manner'. It also says that mediation may be an alternative conflict resolution but is 'not a substitute for the benefit of independent legal advice'. Joint representation may also be appropriate in Australia because of the large number of ethnic minorities here. The cultural attitude of some of these groups emphasises the need to subordinate the needs of the individual to that of the family.[100] Thus, in family law a practitioner may have to be sensitive to the cultural needs. For example, an Aboriginal couple may want to use only an Aboriginal lawyer who understands their cultural values.

---

95. Schedule 4 of the Professional Conduct Rules (WA) gives further guidance in relation to s 44(1A). There is also a warning to not act for both parties in drawing up a maintenance agreement and that the party needs to seek separate legal advice. If that party refuses, the practitioner can only give advice to the client he or she chose to prepare the agreement.

96. See, for example, *Simmons v Simmons* (1991) FLC ¶92–919 where it was held a consensus between the parties did not preclude a conflict of interest. See J Eades, 'Acting for Both Parties in Family Law: A practice fraught with difficulty' (1992) 30 *Law Society J* 68.

97. See P Batt, 'The Family Unit As Client: A Means to Address the Ethical Dilemmas Confronting Elder Law Attorneys' (1992) 6 *Georgetown J of Legal Ethics* 319.

98. (1991) Standard 2.20.

99. See in the family law area *Levine v Levine* 436 NE2d 476 (NY 1982) and *Halvorsen v Halvorsen* 479 P2d 161 (Wash Ct App 1970). In other areas see Allegaert *v Perot* 565 F 2d 246 (2nd Cir 1977) and *American Special Risk Insurance Co v Delta America Insurance Co* 634 F Supp 112 (SD NY 1986).

100. A Ray, 'Cultural Issues in Family Law' (1990) 15 *Legal Services Bulletin* 168.

Insurance problems

12.40   Another important area of non-litigious conflict is the representation of the insured by the insurer's lawyer. The vast majority of insurance policies contain a provision that gives control over conduct of the matter to the insurance company. The insured in reality has no choice but to accept this provision. The insurers choose the lawyers to negotiate and appear for the insured. They pay these lawyers and the lawyers' performance will dictate whether the insurers will use them again. The insured has again no choice but to accept these lawyers. The contracts usually contain a clause that forfeits coverage if the insured rejects the company's lawyer. These lawyers are therefore fully aware that if they want to act for the insurers on a continuing basis they have to satisfy them, rather than their client (the insured). The conflict has become even more serious because rising legal fees have forced some insurance companies to use their own in-house lawyers to represent the insured.

Although the interests of the insured and the insurer frequently coincide, the lawyer will have no difficulty in representing the insured. When these interests differ the lawyer may have obtained confidential information that is usually to the detriment of the insured. For example, some information will result in loss of coverage under the insurance policy or an offer of settlement may be within the terms of the policy, but be considered too high by the insurer. In the latter situation the insured may want to settle while the insurer wants to fight the matter. Sometimes insurers want to settle and admit negligence because of 'knock for knock' agreements with other insurers (each taking turns for liability in a particular matter) or just to settle in order to save the cost of litigation. The insured may not want to be named for being at fault and courts have held that insurers can be liable for making such settlements without the insured's agreement.[101]

12.41   The Council of the Law Society of New South Wales issued a ruling which is now only for guidance. It states:[102]

> A solicitor who files a defence on behalf of an insured defendant thereby establishes the relationship of solicitor and client with him and notwithstanding that the solicitor's instructions came from the insurer, the solicitor is under an absolute obligation not to disclose to anyone confidential information obtained from his client, the insured, unless there has been a waiver by the client of his privilege.

The Council stated that it considered the English position as outlined in Lund, *Professional Conduct of Solicitors*, but disagreed with its conclusion.[103] Lund states that there is a solicitor–client relationship between both the solicitor and insured and the solicitor and the insurer. The solicitor has a duty to inform both clients of any facts that come to his or her knowledge as a result of the relationship which are material to the insurance.[104] The

---

101. See *Rogers v Robson* 407 NE 2d 47 (Ill 1980) (medical malpractice settlement) and *Groom v Crocker* [1939] 1 KB 194 ('knock for knock' agreement admitting negligence in collision accident).

102. F Riley, *New South Wales Solicitors Manual*, LexisNexis Butterworths, Sydney, 2004, looseleaf, para 12016.

103. Riley (above).

104. Lund, *A Guide to the Professional Conduct and Etiquette of Solicitors*, Law Society of England and Wales, London, 1960, p 103.

Law Society in England has adopted a similar view, stating that the solicitor:[105]

> ... should advise both clients that he is acting on the basis that he will fully disclose to both clients matters of common interest coming to his knowledge. If this is not accepted as the basis for his instructions, then he should decline to act for the insured.

The English view was adopted by Kearney J in a Northern Territory case, *Kennedy v Cynstock Pty Ltd*.[106] His Honour pointed out that although the insurer conducted the litigation under the insurance policy, the insured was the one subject to the court's orders. Therefore, unless the insured waived his or her right to confidentiality, the lawyer had a lawyer–client relationship with both the insured and the insurer.[107]

12.42

A Queensland decision, *Northumberland Insurance Co Ltd v Castner*,[108] seems to oppose the position taken by courts in the United States and the Law Society (NSW) and would be of concern to the insured. The insured had been involved in a driving accident and on the morning of the hearing revealed to the clerk of the insurer's solicitors that he had been drinking prior to the accident. The insured had lied concerning this matter in answering a question on the accident report. There was the usual proviso in the insurance policy that 'the truth of all statements made in writing by the insured for the purposes of the policy shall be a condition precedent to any liability of the insurer to make any payment under the policy'. The information was given to the solicitor and the insurer then claimed to be indemnified by the insured under the policy for the expenses it had incurred. The insured claimed that the information given to the clerk was privileged and could not be placed in evidence. The court said that the insured had failed to meet the terms of the policy by providing all necessary information and assistance. Furthermore, he had been uncooperative because he had to be subpoenaed to give evidence. As a result the court held that no solicitor–client relationship existed with the insured and thus his admission to the clerk was not privileged.[109] The court appears implicitly to find a waiver of the right of confidentiality by the insured in light of his behaviour. It may also have been applying the doctrine of 'utmost good faith' — perfect good faith by both the insured and the insurer in carrying out the terms of the policy.[110]

In the United States the ABA issued an opinion that: 'The essential point of ethics involved is that the lawyer so employed [in an insurance matter] shall represent the insured as his client with undivided fidelity ...'.[111] A much later opinion states that if a conflict develops between the insured and the insurer, and cannot be resolved, the lawyer must withdraw.[112] ABA

12.43

---

105. *A Guide to Professional Conduct of Solicitors*, Law Society of England and Wales, London, 1974, p 11.
106. (1993) 3 NTLR 108.
107. For a discussion of this case, see N Rein, 'Acting for the insured on instructions of the insurer' (1995) 33 *Law Society J (NSW)* 31.
108. [1975] 3 *Queensland Lawyer* 246 (D Ct).
109. [1975] 3 *Queensland Lawyer* 246 at 247.
110. See A Tarr, 'Dishonest Insurance Claims' (1988) 1 *Insurance LJ* 42.
111. ABA Formal Opinion 282 (1950).
112. ABA Formal Opinion 403 (1996).

Model Rules r 1.8(f) and r 5.4(c) caution that a third party who pays the lawyer must not be permitted to influence the lawyer's independent representation of the client. This view is also supported by s 133 of the *Restatement of the law Governing Lawyers*, but the comment to this section points out that conflicts may not be able to be settled by the ethical codes, but by looking at the terms of the insurance contract. The vast majority of court decisions have held that when a conflict arises, the lawyer must treat the insured as the client. For example, when a lawyer gained confidential information from the insured to help deny the insured coverage under the policy, an Arizona court held that such conduct constituted a waiver of the policy provisions. The action was deemed to be against public policy and the insurance company was estopped from disclaiming liability.[113] Some American courts have held when there is a conflict between the insured and the insurer the insured is entitled to be provided with independent counsel.[114] Under legislation in California the independent counsel has to maintain the client's confidences, but when those confidences are not in issue counsel has a duty to cooperate with the insurer within the terms of the contract.[115]

12.44   Although the courts support the concept of the insured as the client they have not interfered with the insurers' right to select the lawyer to deal with the matter.[116] The right for the insurers to conduct, control and defend proceedings has been upheld in both England and Australia.[117] The ABA has also adopted Guiding Principles that have been accepted by the majority of casualty and liability insurance companies in the United States.[118] These principles appear to conflict with the court cases in that they contain Paragraph IV which states that if the lawyer discovers a problem concerning coverage he or she needs to inform both the company and the insured, and should invite the insured to retain counsel at his or her own expense. Paragraph VI says that if the insured reveals information denying coverage which the insured believed to be confidential, the lawyer should not tell the company, but neither should he or she discuss with the insured the legal significance of the disclosure or the nature of the coverage in question. This paragraph conflicts with ABA Model Rule 1.4(b), which requires lawyers to explain matters to their clients to help them make informed decisions. The Guiding Principles cause more confusion with Paragraph IX, which provides that if the lawyer decides to withdraw:[119]

113. *Parsons v Continental National American Group* 550 P 2d 94 (Ariz 1976).
114. See *San Diego Credit Union v Cumis* 162 Cal App 3d 358, 208 Cal Rptr 494 (1984) and *Wolpaw v General Accident Insurance Co* 639 A 2d 338 (NJ 1994). For a general discussion of the principles see R O'Malley, 'Ethics Principles for the Insurer, the Insured and Defense Counsel: The Eternal Triangle Reformed' (1991) 66 *Tulane LR* 511.
115. California Civil Code, s 2860.
116. See J Morris, 'Conflicts of Interest in Defending Under Liability Insurance Policies: A Proposed Solution' (1981) *Utah LR* 457. Riopelle states that an insured has the right to loyalty from the insurer's lawyer: see Riopelle, 'When May an Insurer Fire Counsel Hired to Represent an Insured?' (1993) 7 *Georgetown J Legal Ethics* 247, 249.
117. *Groom v Crocker* [1939] 1 KB 194; *Club Motor Insurance Agency Pty Ltd v Swann* [1954] VLR 745; *Yellow Express Couriers Ltd v GIO* (1959) 76 WN (NSW) 622.
118. They were adopted in 1972 and are reprinted in (1972) 20 *Federal Insurance Counsel Q* 95. Although they were repealed in 1980, they are still influential: Rhode (above), p 850.
119. See, for example, *Employers Casualty Co v Tilley* 496 SW 2d 552 (Texas 1973).

The insured should be fully advised of such decision and the reasons therefore … This provision appears to be in conflict with Paragraph VI. Courts have held that when the Guiding Principles conflict with those of the state's Code of Professional Responsibility, the latter will prevail.

The ABA has adopted Ethics Formal Opinion 1476-81 which, like the principles, calls for disclosure upon discovery of any conflict, including coverage under the policy, to both insured and insurer. The role expected in these situations by insurance company lawyers is:[120]

12.45

> … unrealistic because it ignores the extent to which insurance contracts qualify the rights of representation (particularly concerning settlement), and the extent to which insurance defense lawyers inevitably feel loyalty toward the source of past and future business.

Lawyer and client

Professional rules

The Law Council's Model Rules r 9 states:

12.46

> 8.1 A practitioner must not, in any dealings with a client:
>
> > 8.1.1 allow the interests of the practitioner or an associate of the practitioner to conflict with the client's interest;
> >
> > 8.1.2 exercise any undue influence intended to dispose the client to benefit the practitioner in excess of the practitioner's fair remuneration for the legal services provided to the client;
>
> 8.2 A practitioner must not accept instructions to act or continue to act for a person in any matter when the practitioner is, or becomes, aware that the person's interest in the matter is, or would be, in conflict with the practitioner's own interest or the interest of an associate.

Rule 10.2 states that a practitioner cannot draw a will where he or she or an associate will or may receive a substantial benefit outside any reasonable entitlement as an executor. In such circumstances the client must be referred to another solicitor who is not an associate of that solicitor. There are exceptions for members of the solicitor's immediate family or people working for or with the solicitor. Rule 11 stops solicitors borrowing from clients unless the solicitor does not act, nor provide advice concerning this transaction and the client obtains independent legal advice.

There are identical rules in Victoria (rr 9–11) and in New South Wales (rr 10–12), but r 12 in New South Wales has additional provisions dealing with prohibitions from maintaining a private finance company. There are also similar rules in other jurisdictions.[121] ABA Model Code DR 5-101(A) and ABA Model Rule 1.7(b) preclude lawyers from representing clients if the lawyers' personal interest might interfere with the representation. The rules take into account similar considerations when assessing a conflict between two clients. The Code allowed the representation if the client consented, while the Model Rule requires, besides consent, that the lawyer believes the representation will not be adversely affected and it is not in the same litigation or proceeding. Under Model Rule 1.8(a) lawyers cannot enter into business transactions, property transactions or dealings with other financial interests that are adverse to the client unless the particular

12.47

---

120. Rhode (above), p 797.
121. See, for example, Professional Conduct Rules (WA) rr 7.2 and 8.1; Professional Conduct Rules (SA) rr 9–10; Professional Conduct Rule (NT) rr 8–10.9A2.

transaction is fair and reasonable to the client and its terms are fully disclosed in writing to the client. The client must also be given a reasonable opportunity to seek independent legal advice and the client has to consent in writing to the transaction. Rule 1.8(c) prohibits lawyers or their relatives from receiving a substantial gift from the client (unless the client is related to the donee) by way of an instrument drawn up by the lawyer for that client.[122]

Case law

12.48
There are no specific rules prohibiting sexual relations between lawyers and clients in Australia, but as discussed in **7.31–7.32**, such rules exist in some jurisdictions in the United States. It appears that the general rules on conflict of interest in Australia cover most situations. It is also debatable whether specific rules prohibiting sexual relations should be adopted in Australia in light of the difficulty of applying them to all situations. For example, in situations where clients may be powerful, independent, wealthy or influential people who are not in the least intimidated or influenced by their lawyer, why should a sexual relationship be prohibited? It can be argued that in this situation lawyers may need to be protected against themselves because of a loss of objectivity.

The case law in Australia and elsewhere has supported the ethical rules. For example, professional misconduct has been found when solicitors borrow from a client or have business dealings with a client, and fail to make adequate disclosure of their personal interests and ensure that the client obtains independent legal advice.[123] The fact that the client has suffered no loss is irrelevant.[124] In *Law Society of New South Wales v Harvey*[125] the Court of Appeal held that solicitors must not prefer their own interests to their clients' and if a conflict arises must make full disclosure. *Harvey* emphasised that even with full disclosure the lawyer should not continue to act. In a more recent Full Supreme Court (ACT) decision the court said that:[126]

> ... a solicitor who deals with the client while remaining the client's solicitor undertakes a heavy burden and it will be a rare case where the solicitor should not at least advise the client to take independent legal advice.

In that case the practitioners were suspended from practice for only two years because the court felt they had not 'acted disgracefully or dishonourably. Their errors arose from inexperience and general lack of understanding of a solicitor's duties to his client'.[127] In a recent Victorian case, *Woods v Legal Ombudsman*,[128] a practitioner gave migration advice to Chinese clients with little or no English. The advice included the formation of a company in which the practitioner had an interest. Although the client was presented with a letter that said he had an obligation to seek

---

122. In *Monco v Janus* 222 Ill App 3d 280, 583 NE 2d 575 (1991) a lawyer received 50 per cent ownership in his client's company for inadequate consideration. The client had not received independent legal advice and was granted relief by the appellate court.
123. *Law Society of NSW v Moulton* [1981] 2 NSWLR 736.
124. *Moulton* (above); this solicitor was still struck off the rolls.
125. [1976] 2 NSWLR 154.
126. *Re Fabricius and McLaren; Legal Practitioners Ordinance 1970* (1989) 91 ACTR 1 at 7–8.
127. *Re Fabricius* (above).
128. [2004] VSCA 247, paras 13 and 75–78.

independent legal advice, it was found that the client did not understand the meaning of the letter, nor did the client receive an explanation of the meaning of the documents or the need to obtain independent legal advice. The Court of Appeal upheld the finding of misconduct and upheld the finding of costs against the practitioner.

A High Court decision shows the need for lawyers who help arrange finance   **12.49**
for their clients to explain the situation carefully and advise them to obtain independent legal advice. In *Maguire v Makaronis* the solicitor did explain to the clients all the details of the mortgage, including that the funds were coming from the Commonwealth. He failed to tell the clients that he and his partner were the mortgagees of the loan. This failure was held by Ashley J in the lower court to be a breach of fiduciary duty because there was a 'real and sensible' possibility of a conflict present in this situation. His Honour emphasised the need for fully informed consent which in the present case included being advised to seek independent legal advice. He said that the fact that the solicitor had complied with the requirements of the Solicitors' (Professional Conduct and Practice) Rules 1984 (Vic) r 10 did not satisfy his equitable fiduciary obligations. Ashley J concluded that because of the breach of fiduciary duties it 'is to be assumed that the securities were given by reason of the breach'. The securities were unconditionally set aside.[129]

  The Court of Appeal dismissed the solicitor's appeal and the High Court in a *per curiam* decision reversed it, stating that the mortgage be set aside but that the clients pay the moneys owed, that is, the unpaid principal together with the interest to be calculated by the Court of Appeal.[130] The High Court upheld Ashley J's findings including his rejection of compliance with r 10 as satisfying the fiduciary obligations. The court said that the solicitor had failed to show that the respondents had informed consent: 'What is required for a fully informed consent is a question of fact in all the circumstances of each case and there is no precise formula ...'. The court found that in this case the circumstances included the obtaining of 'independent and skilled advice from a third party'.[131] Thus, the solicitor had failed to take the necessary steps to negate the charge of breach of fiduciary duty. It should be noted that the court did not reject or accept the 'real and sensible possibility' test.

Courts have also been very suspicious of situations where clients make gifts   **12.50**
to their lawyers. In a famous English case, *Wright v Carter*,[132] Stirling LJ stated:[133]

> ... that transactions between solicitor and client are watched and scrutinised by the Court with utmost jealousy ... [T]he Court ... starts with the presumption that undue influence exists on the part of the donee, and throws upon him the burden of satisfying the Court that the gift was uninfluenced by the position of the solicitor. Secondly, this presumption is not a presumption

---

129. Digested in [1995] ANZ Conv R 457.
130. *Maguire v Makaronis* (1997) 144 ALR 729 per Brennan CJ, Gaudron, McHugh and Gummow. Kirby J wrote a separate judgment including numerous references to the views of the Court of Appeal.
131. *Maguire* (above) at 739.
132. [1903] 1 Ch 27 (C of A).
133. [1903] 1 Ch 27 at 57.

which is entirely irrebuttable, though it is one which is extremely difficult to be rebutted … [I]n order to uphold a gift … the donor must have competent independent advice in conferring the gift … [T]he Court has still to be satisfied that the influence arising from the relationship can no longer be supposed to exist. The [independent] solicitor does not discharge his duty by satisfying himself simply that the donor understands and wishes to carry out the particular transaction. He must also satisfy himself that the gift is one that it is right and proper for the donor to make under all the circumstances; and if he is not so satisfied, his duty is to advise his client not to go on with the transaction, and to refuse to act further for him if he persists.

Lawyer as witness

12.51   The Barristers' Rules r 87 (NSW) (r 92 (Vic) and r 91 (Qld)) is one of the mandatory exceptions to the 'cab-rank' rule. It states that:

> a barrister must refuse a brief … if:
>
> …
>
> (c) the barrister has reasonable grounds to believe that the barrister may, as a real possibility, be a witness in the case;
>
> (d) the brief is to appear on an appeal and the barrister was a witness in the case at first instance.

There are similar rules for other legal practitioners.[134]

A lawyer who is likely to be a material witness but is not to be instructed in a case, may still provide a conflict of interest for his or her firm, if the firm represents a client in that matter. The Queensland Supreme Court in the *Chapman* case indicated in dictum that it may be unwise for such a firm to continue to represent a client in that case. The court felt it was 'desirable to avoid any suggestion of real or apparent conflict between the duty to the court and the obligation to the client'.[135] Another Queensland judge, Thomas J, pointed out that a lawyer becoming a witness will compromise his or her objectivity and independence.[136]

12.52   The *Chapman* case has been approved and followed in two recent Supreme Court cases in Western Australia. In *Clay v Karlson*[137] Templeman J relied on the reasoning not only of Campbell CJ in *Chapman*, but also on Marks J from an older Victorian case, *Commissioner for Corporate Affairs v Harvey*.[138] In a recent decision, *Miles v Hughes*,[139] Parker J says: 'At the heart of the matter is the desirability of avoiding any suggestion of real or apparent conflict between the duty owed by a practitioner to the court and the obligation of the practitioner to the client or to the self-interest of the practitioner.'

---

134. See, for example, Law Council's Model Rules r 13.4 and the identical rule, r 13 (ACT) and r 19 (NSW), where the practitioner cannot act if he or she will be a material witness. The Queensland Law Society Rules r 1 states that the solicitor shall not accept instructions in a case in which he or she 'has reason to believe that he is likely to be a witness'. See also *Solicitors Handbook* (Qld) paras 5.01.8 and 5.04; Professional Conduct Rules (SA) r 16(2)(e); Professional Conduct Rules (NT) r 13 and Professional Conduct Rules (WA) r 13.11.

135. *Chapman v Rogers* [1984] 1 Qld R 542 at 544.

136. *Jeffrey v Associated National Insurance Co Ltd* [1984] 1 Qd R 238 at 245.

137. (1996) 17 WAR 493.

138. [1980] VR 669.

139. (unreported, SC(WA), Parker J, No CIV 1438 of 1998, 11 November 1998, BC9807243).

The *Miles* case dealt with a motion to disqualify a firm from acting for the defendant — a partner in the firm. The issues involved the legality of a will and the appointment of the defendant as executor. The court reviewed the adequacy of the firm's actions in the adoption of a new will and the testamentary capacity of the plaintiff's father at the time of accepting instructions to prepare his will. There was also the issue of whether the defendant in the administration of the estate acted in his personal capacity or as a partner of the firm. Parker J found that 'there is a clear prospect that evidence will need to be led for the firm from one or more of its practitioners and it is likely that this would include evidence from the defendant ... More significantly, ... members of the firm ... have a direct pecuniary interest in the outcome of this litigation'. He felt that the latter reason provided a 'determinative reason' for disqualifying the firm. 'It gives rise to the potential liability with respect to its profit costs and the potential for practitioners of the firm to be called as witnesses also make it undesirable that the firm should continue to act.'

12.53 By contrast to this line of cases, Drummond J has stated that the general disapproval of so acting did not mean that 'there is jurisdiction to restrain a solicitor for a party continuing to act for that party on the basis that it is apparent that he is going to be required as a witness for one side or the other on contentious issues, even though, by so acting, the solicitor may fall short of meeting a proper standard of professional conduct'.[140] Byrne J followed Drummond J's view in *Executive Homes Pty Ltd v First Haven Pty Ltd*, a more recent case than *Miles*. Byrne J allowed a solicitor to continue to act even though he was to be a witness. The judge emphasised that this was not a case where the solicitor had acquired confidential information from the opposing party nor was it a case where he was going to act as the advocate.[141]

Although there have been few cases, the case law appears to have supported the general prohibition on lawyers who are likely to be witnesses from acting. There will be exceptions to this rule and in each case the court will have to look closely at the facts. Two possible exceptions will be: (1) when a lawyer is not acting as an advocate but only as an instructing solicitor and (2) when the lawyer does not have confidential material related to the issues in the case. In general, lawyers who try to act in a dual capacity of advocate and witness usually compromise their objectivity and independence. Furthermore, if the action takes place before a jury there will be considerable confusion for jurors. What weight should jurors give to the lawyer's evidence? Will their views be affected by their admiration or distaste for the lawyer stemming from his or her advocacy role? Finally, what confusion will remain in light of the fact that the lawyer goes back from the witness role of giving an opinion to one where opinions are forbidden?[142]

12.54 In the United States both the ABA Model Code DR 5-101(B) and DR 5-102, and the Model Rules 3.7, prevent lawyers who are likely to be

---

140. See *Yamaji v Westpac Banking Corporation (No 1)* (1993) 115 ALR 235 at 236.
141. *Executive Homes Pty Ltd v First Haven Pty Ltd* BC9904117; [1999] VSC 261 at [10] and [11]. See also *Grimweade v Meagher* [1995] 1 VR 466.
142. See Note, 'Disqualification of Law Firms Under the Attorney-Witness Rule' (1980) 54 *Tulane LR* 521

witnesses from acting for a client. Model Code DR 5-102(A) is far stricter in imposing vicarious disqualification on the firm in all cases in which their lawyers are likely to be a witness. Model Rule 3.7(b) would disqualify the firm only if a prohibited conflict of interest is involved, for example adverse testimony by the lawyer to the client's case. There are exceptions to the rule if their testimony relates to an uncontested issue or if the disqualification of the lawyer would result in a substantial hardship for the client. The courts generally have narrowly interpreted the exceptions and have applied the disqualification rule strictly.[143] An exception to this strict approach would be if the court felt that the disqualification motion was being used as a delaying tactic.[144] There are various provisions allowing lawyers to continue to represent clients (even when it becomes apparent to them that they are likely 'to be a witness on a material question of fact') if it is not 'possible to withdraw without jeopardising the client's interest'.[145]

The Comment [1] to Model Rule 3.7 gives the reason for the disqualification: 'Combining the roles of advocate and witness can prejudice the tribunal and opposing party and can also involve a conflict of interest between the lawyer and client.' Comment [2] states:[146]

> ... A witness is required to testify on the basis of personal knowledge, while an advocate is expected to explain and comment on evidence given by others. It may not be clear whether a statement by an advocate-witness should be taken as proof or as an analysis of the proof.

SUCCESSIVE REPRESENTATION AND IMPUTED DISQUALIFICATION — OPPOSING A FORMER CLIENT

Introduction

12.55   Where representing a current client who has interests which are opposed to a former client, the focus in this area has primarily been on the problem of past receipt of confidential information, breach of the fiduciary duty (loyalty) and the appearance of impropriety.

The rules and cases have been concerned that the lawyer may be inhibited in exercising his or her judgment in the present representation because of loyalty to the former client and that the appearance of justice will be subverted. The former client may also fear that the lawyer will divulge or make use of the past confidences to help the present client. As has already been discussed in relation to concurrent clients, there is also the problem for lawyers of taking a position that can lead to a legal result that is contrary to that achieved for a former client. Finally, there is the modern problem of imputed disqualification because of the movement of lawyers between firms and between government and private practice.

---

143. Kaufman (above), p 84. He cites as an example *MacArthur v Bank of New York* 524 F Supp 1205 (SD NY 1981). The *Solicitors Handbook* (Qld) para 5.04 agrees with these exceptions.
144. Kaufman (above).
145. *Guide to Professional Conduct and Etiquette* (ACT) para 12.11(2); *Solicitors Handbook* (Qld) para 5.04.4; and Professional Conduct Rules (WA) r 13.11(2).
146. For an analysis of the ABA rules and cases in the area see B Moss, 'Ethical Prohibitions Against a Lawyer Serving as Both Advocate and Witness' (1993) 23 *Memphis State University LR* 555.

First, we will examine the different professional rules and rulings adopted to deal with successive representation in Australia and the United States and how the courts have applied the rules. Second, we will look at the rules and cases dealing with the vexed problem of imputed disqualification.

Successive representation

Professional rules

The Law Council's Model Rules r 4 states that: **12.56**

> 4.1 A practitioner must not accept an engagement to act for another person in any matter against, or in opposition to, the interest of a person ('the former client')
>
> > 4.1.1 for whom the practitioner or the practitioner's current or former firm or the former firm of a partner, director or employee of the practitioner or of the practitioner's firm has acted previously and has thereby acquired information confidential to the former client and material to the matter; and
> >
> > 4.1.2 from whom the practitioner or the practitioner's firm has thereby acquired information confidential to that person and material to the action or proceedings; and
>
> if the former client might reasonably conclude that there is a real possibility the information will be used to the person's detriment.

There are similar rules or rulings in other jurisdictions.[147] The Australian rules and cases concentrate on the confidentiality aspects and are far narrower and less flexible than the American rules and cases. American courts have delineated between concurrent conflicts and successive conflicts. In the former it is generally sufficient for a court to find the existence of adverse interests, while for successive conflicts adverse effects are required. This means that even if there are potential conflicts the courts will generally find them not to be sufficient to warrant disqualification. According to Donoghue: 'These different standards exist because of a belief that where two clients with adverse interests are represented by a firm at the same time the risk of impropriety is greater than where each client is represented by separate counsel.'[148]

The ABA Model Rule 1.9(a) provides that a lawyer shall not: **12.57**

> ... represent another person in the same or substantially related matter in which that person's interests are materially adverse to the interests of the former client unless the former client gives informed consent, confirmed in writing.

The rule adopts a 'substantial relationship test' but it applies only when the new client's interests are 'materially adverse' to those of the former client. Although Model Rule 1.9 applies to both private and government lawyers, the latter are also bound by r 1.11. We will discuss r 1.11 below: see **12.74–12.75**. This rule differs from r 1.9 in that former government lawyers are restricted from representing new clients even when the

---

147. For example, see Professional Conduct and Practice Rules (NSW) r 3; Professional Conduct Rules (WA) r 7.4; (NT) r 39.4; Professional Conduct and Practice Rules (Vic) r 4; Conflict of Interest Guidelines, Council of Law Institute of Victoria, (1991) 65 *Law Institute J* 351; Barristers' Rules (NSW) rr 103, 107–10.

148. D Donoghue, 'Conflicts of Interest: Concurrent Representation' (above), p 319. See also J Wong, 'Conflicts of Interest in Successive Representation' (1998) 11 *Georgetown J of Legal Ethics* 275.

new clients' interests are in harmony with the former government client. There is obviously a feeling that the inside information that lawyers carry from their government association gives their new clients too much of an advantage.

12.58 There are also restrictions under r 1.9(c) on the use of confidential information obtained from the former client. The Comment [2] to r 1.9 does not preclude lawyers who have handled a type of problem for a former client from representing another client in 'a factually distinct problem of that type even though the subsequent representation involves a position adverse to the prior client'.

The American courts have been concerned with whether or not the previous person or entity was a client. Even in situations where it might appear that the services provided were limited, a lawyer–client relationship will have been established if the client reasonably believed the relationship existed. Thus, information passing to the lawyer in such a situation will have been believed by the client to have been communicated in confidence.[149] A second problem has been in defining what is a 'matter' in which the lawyer represented the former client. This may be easily worked out where both parties are private clients, but if one of the clients is a government department it is difficult to determine what is a 'matter'. An example is a lawyer who drafts legislation and then is later employed in private practice to challenge it.[150] A third issue is determining whether the matters are 'substantially related'. The courts are concerned with whether the lawyer involved is likely to possess confidential information relevant to the present case because of that lawyer's past relationship with the protesting party. In the *Analytica* case Posner J was concerned with a strict test of the 'possibility of real mischief'.[151] This standard 'would seem to apply whether or not the matters are substantially related' and hence could be read as *broader* than the 'substantial relationship' test.

Case law and various tests

12.59 The courts in the United States have taken different approaches to the problem and there is no clear answer. The main task is for the court to assess the risk to the confidences without revealing the confidences that the test seeks to protect. How inferences will be drawn will depend on the practice experience of the judge and his or her attitude towards client loyalty. If the court finds that the matters are substantially related there will be a presumption, that is ordinarily irrebuttable, that the lawyer possesses

149. *Westinghouse Electric Corporation v Kerr-McGee Corp* 580 F 2d 1311 (7th Cir 1978). See *Brennan's Inc v Brennan's Restaurants* Inc 590 F 2d 168 (5th Cir 1979) where the court did not find a lawyer–client relationship existed for co-counsel of a lawyer who had such a former relationship. This lawyer would not be disqualified unless he received confidential information from his disqualified co-counsel.
150. G Hazard Jr, S Koniak and R Cramton, *The Law and Ethics of Lawyering*, 2nd ed, Foundation Press, Westbury, New York, 1994, p 740.
151. In *Analytica v NPD Research* 708 F 2d 1263 (7th Cir 1983) the court said the two matters are substantially related: 'if the lawyer could have obtained confidential information in the first representation that would be relevant to the second'. This case seems to apply the test related to confidences obtained and it does not concern whether the matters involved were substantially related.

confidential information and that the information will be used to the client's detriment, even if only inadvertently.[152]

Perhaps the American courts have difficulties in establishing clear standards and have narrowed the issue to one of protecting confidences because of 'the courts' growing impatience with disqualification motions used for tactical purposes'. There is a 'deeper problem' according to Hazard, Koniak and Cramton. They say that:[153]

> ... the courts are not of one mind on whether to demand relatively strict loyalty to a former client, at the cost of requiring one or both parties to get new lawyers if they have a falling out, or to avoid that cost through a more relaxed standard of loyalty.

It may also be because the courts are more interested in protecting the interests of large firms that have frequent conflict problems over the interests of clients.

12.60 Australian courts have taken a number of different approaches when solicitors act against former clients. The courts have at times followed the principle established in the English case, *Rakusen v Ellis, Munday & Clarke*.[154] Rakusen had consulted Munday, while the only other partner, Clarke, was away, about an action for wrongful dismissal from a company. The partners never discussed the matter. Rakusen changed solicitors and the company employed Clarke. Rakusen sought a restraining order stopping the firm from acting. The court rejected the request. The principle adopted by the English High Court was that solicitors employed to act for a client in a particular matter could later act against him or her in the same matter, unless the court was 'satisfied that real mischief and real prejudice will in all human probability result if the solicitor is allowed to act'.[155] The rule in *Rakusen* has at times been reaffirmed in England,[156] but was overruled by the House of Lords in December 1998 in *Prince Jefri Bolkiah v KPMG (a firm)*.[157] Although this case concerns accountants it is clear from the Lords' reasoning that they did not draw any distinction between accountants and solicitors.

12.61 The facts are that the defendants had acted for the plaintiff in a complex litigation over a period of 18 months for which the firm had used 168 personnel. This matter settled, but the defendants had during their representation acquired confidential information about the plaintiff's assets and financial affairs. The Brunei Government then commenced an investigation into the affairs of an investment agency of which the plaintiff had been the chairman. The government sought to retain the defendants to assist in this investigation. By this time the firm had ceased to act for the

---

152. Hazard, Koniak and Cramton (above), pp 694–5.
153. Hazard et al (above), p 704.
154. [1912] 1 Ch 831.
155. [1912] 1 Ch 831 at 835.
156. *Re a Solicitor* (1981) 131 *Solicitors J* 1063. In this case the court noted that there was no indication that the lawyer had acquired relevant confidential information and the evidence showed that the former client could not recollect having given any confidential information to that lawyer.
157. *Prince Jefri Bolkiah's* case [1999] 1 All ER 517. This case is the subject of a 'Case Note'. See A Mitchell, 'Chinese Walls in Brunei: *Prince Jefri Bolkiah v KPMG (a firm)* (1999) 22 UNSWLJ 1.

plaintiff and thus accepted the instructions. In order to avoid any possible conflict of interest the defendants had erected a 'Chinese Wall' (see below) around the department carrying out this investigation.

The House of Lords overruled the Court of Appeal and granted an injunction prohibiting the firm from acting for the government. The Lords found that there was a risk of disclosure and the firm had not 'discharged the heavy burden of showing that there is no risk' that confidential information 'may unwittingly or inadvertently come to the notice' of those working on the new project. Thus, the Chinese Wall was found to be ineffective. Lord Hope pointed out one of the main views that the duty to preserve confidentiality 'extends well beyond that of refraining from deliberate disclosure'. He said that it included an obligation to ensure that former clients were not at risk that confidential information 'obtained from that relationship may be used against him in any circumstances'.[158] This general language was clarified in the main judgment by Lord Millett.

12.62 Like Lord Hope, Lord Millett based the need for intervention 'on the protection of confidential information' but rejected the need for intervention in order to avoid the perception of possible impropriety.[159] His Lordship said that there was no need for court intervention 'unless two conditions were satisfied: (i) that the solicitor was in possession of information which was confidential to the former client and (ii) that such information was or might be relevant to the matter on which he was instructed by the second client'. This makes the possession of confidential information the test of what is comprehended within the expression 'the same or a connected matter'.[160]

Lord Millet then clarified the difference between concurrent and successive client conflicts. In discussing former clients he said:

> The court's jurisdiction cannot be based on any conflict of interest, real or perceived, for there is none. The fiduciary relationship, which subsists between solicitor and client, comes to an end with the termination of the retainer. Thereafter the solicitor has no obligation to defend and advance the interests of the former client. The only duty to the former client ... [is] a continuing duty to preserve the confidentiality of information imparted [by the client during the relationship].

Lord Millet then spoke about the two conditions. He said:

> Although the burden of proof is on the plaintiff it is not a heavy one. The former [first condition] may readily be inferred, the latter will often be obvious. I do not think that it is necessary to introduce any presumptions rebuttable or otherwise, in relation to these two matters. But given the basis on which the jurisdiction is exercised, there is no cause to impute or attribute the knowledge of one partner to his fellow partners. Whether a particular individual is in possession of confidential information is a question of fact which must be proved or inferred from the circumstances of the case.

As to the issue of how far the duty to the client extends, he held that although there cannot be complete protection, the client 'is entitled to prevent his [or her] former solicitor from exposing him to any avoidable risk; and this includes the risk of the use of the information to his prejudice

---

158. *Prince Jefri Bolkiah* (above) at 519.
159. *Prince Jefri Bolkiah* (above) at 526.
160. *Prince Jefri Bolkiah* (above) at 527.

arising from the acceptance of instructions to act for another client with an adverse interest in a matter to which the information is or may be relevant'. The test that he adopted was 'that the court should not intervene unless it is satisfied that there is no real risk or disclosure. It goes without saying that the risk must be a real one, and not merely fanciful or theoretical. But it need not be substantial'.[161]

The rule adopted in *Prince Jefri* appears to have been modified by the English Court of Appeal in *Freshfields*, discussed above, because preserving confidentiality at times may not be enough. This is also the view of some but not all judges in Australia (see below).

Rakusen has also been rejected in New Zealand[162] and, as we have seen, the rule in the United States is a 'possibility of real mischief'. The new English rule adopted by the House of Lords has shifted the focus and burden of proof to the defendant. It is thus easier under this approach to disallow representation.

12.63

The *Rakusen* rule has been quoted in a number of Australian cases including recent cases allowing and disallowing representation. In *Australian Commercial Research and Development Ltd v Hampson*[163] a QC was disqualified from acting for a defendant bank where a year before he had advised the plaintiff in writing as to whether there was a cause of action.[164] In *South Black Water Coal Ltd v McCullough Robertson (a firm)*[165] Muir J said that doubt had been cast on the *Rakusen* approach by a number of recent cases and rejected the rule. He found that a solicitor, Mr McCosker, had been involved in giving advice to the plaintiff while an employee of their solicitors and was now a partner in the firm giving advice to the defendant. Muir J said that McCosker did have confidential information concerning the dispute and this inform-ation resulted in a conflict of interest that could be imputed to the entire firm. He did not disqualify the firm because the plaintiff had known that McCosker was acting for the defendant for 14 months and had not objected. Thus, the plaintiff had acquiesced to the representation. Muir found that the motion for disqualification was 'motivated by anything other than a desire to make the litigation as difficult and as uncomfortable as possible'.

There are also several cases using the *Rakusen* rule concerning offers of establishing 'Chinese Walls': in *D & J Constructions Pty Ltd v Head*[166] Bryson J rejected the Chinese Wall concept and followed the test in *Rakusen*; in *Mallesons v KPMG Peat Marwick*[167] Ipp J followed Bryson J in refusing to allow the erection of a wall and rejected the *Rakusen* test. He stated that 'a real and sensible possibility' of misuse of confidential information of a former client was sufficient to create a conflict and he thus issued an injunction.[168] In *Newman as Trustee for the Estates of Littlejohn v*

12.64

---

161. *Prince Jefri Bolkiah* (above) at 527–8.
162. See *Equiticorp Holdings Ltd v Hawkins* [1993] 2 NZLR 737.
163. [1991] 1 Qd R 508.
164. See also *Newman as Trustee for the Estates of Littlejohn v Phillips Fox (a firm)* BC9905941; [1999] WASC 171.
165. (unreported, SC(Qld), Muir J, No 353 of 1997, 8 May 1997, BC9701879).
166. (1987) 9 NSWLR 118.
167. (1990) 4 WAR 357.
168. (1990) 4 WAR 357 at 362–3.

Phillips Fox (a firm) Steytler J rejected the offer of erection of a wall by applying the principles from *Prince Jefri Bolkiah*.[169] Meanwhile, in *Freuhauf Finance Corp Pty Ltd v Feez Ruthning (a firm)*,[170] Lee J permitted a wall to be established because there was no 'risk of prejudice or mischief' and 'no prospect of detriment to the plaintiff'; and in *World Medical Manufacturing Corp v Phillips Ormonde & Fitzpatrick Lawyers (a firm)* Gillard J felt that the risk of disclosure was so slight that there was not even a need for an offer of a wall.[171] We will discuss these cases and 'Chinese Walls' in more detail in the next section (**12.71ff**) on vicarious disqualification.

12.65 Several cases that do not discuss any screening mechanism — *Mytton's Ltd v Phillips (a firm)*;[172] *Unioil International Pty Ltd v Deloitte Touche Tohmatsu*;[173] and *Boyce v Goodyear Australia Pty Ltd*[174] — give us some insights into the problems of successive representation.

In *Mytton's Ltd v Phillips Fox (a firm)* the plaintiff had a product recall concerning a faulty valve. It notified its insurer of a possible claim for the cost of the recall. The insurance underwriters appointed a partner in the defendant firm to advise the insurer on the matter. Another firm represented the plaintiff, but for the defendant to give its advice to the underwriters it received a number of documents from the plaintiff's firm concerning the valve. The defendant advised the insurer that product liability would be denied.

The defendant never had verbal communication with the plaintiff nor did it represent the plaintiff. Five years later the plaintiff sued the state of Victoria, seeking damages for the recall because the government had certified the fitness of the value. The government retained a different partner in the defendant firm. Coldrey J said that the protection afforded to avoid a conflict of interest could be broader than the solicitor–client relationship. The protection could extend to a third party giving information to a solicitor if that information could be used to the third party's detriment. Although it was unclear how the defendant made use of the information in the present litigation, Coldrey J concluded that 'the trial process is a dynamic one and the capacity for misuse of the confidential information is ongoing with the twists and turns of the litigation'.

12.66 In *Unioil* Ipp J found that the law firm Corrs Chambers Westgarth (Corrs) had breached its fiduciary duty when its Perth office failed to investigate all relevant information concerning a company, UFI Group, which its client, Unioil, wanted to invest in. The investment proved to be a disaster and the client sued. Corrs' Sydney office had discovered that UFI faced a number of claims for warranty breaches for pools it manufactured. An email was sent to all Corrs offices by a Sydney partner stating that he had been instructed to act for a client, BSC, in relation to a possible agreement with UFI and that he should be notified of any potential conflicts.

---

169. *Newman's* case, see n 164 (above).
170. [1991] 1 Qd R 558 at 571.
171. BC200002633; [2000] VSC 196.
172. (unreported, SC (Vic), Coldrey J, No 6908 of 1997, 23 September 1997, BC9704847).
173. (1997) 17 WAR 98.
174. (unreported, CA(NSW), Full Ct, No CA 40313 of 1995, 16 September 1997, BC9504603).

A partner in Perth then telephoned stating that he was acting for a possible investor in UFI. The Sydney partner did not reveal all the information he knew about UFI but he revealed enough for the Perth office to know that UFI was in trouble. The discussions as to possible conflicts between these two partners resulted in the Sydney office not acting for BSC.

Ipp J found that even though there was not a partnership between the two Corrs' offices there was enough of a common interest to connect them. He found therefore that there existed a 'real and sensible possibility' of a conflict concerning the degree of investigation of BSC involvement with UFI handled by the Sydney office, and the need to give proper investment advice to Unioil by the Perth office.

The second aspect dealt with imputation. For the purposes of dealing with this issue Ipp J assumed that Corrs' different offices were treated as one partnership. Ipp J held that there was a presumption that lawyers who work together will share confidences. This presumption could be rebutted by showing clear and convincing evidence that reasonable measures had been taken to prevent any disclosure. In this case the presumption was rebutted because only some of the confidences had been given and only to one partner in Perth. Therefore, the knowledge of the Sydney partner was not to be imputed to all of Corrs' partners. Ipp made an important point that in the modern world of mega law firms information that an individual partner has on his or her personal client that is helpful to other clients of the firm does not have to be given to all clients. In this case the Sydney partner therefore did not owe any fiduciary duty to the firm's client in Perth who was not his personal client. Ipp J realised the nature of these fiduciary duties would have to be 'determined by the exigencies of particular circumstances, and no fixed or absolute rule applies'.[175]

In *Boyce* the New South Wales Court of Appeal upheld the issuing of an injunction by Windeyer J[176] in a civil case restraining Hunt & Hunt from acting for the National Employers Mutual Ltd (NEM), an insurer, on a cross-claim. NEM denied any liability under an insurance policy held by Goodyear Australia Ltd in relation to a case concerning exposure to asbestos dust allegedly resulting in mesothelioma. Hunt & Hunt had acted for Goodyear in other proceedings before the Dust Disease Tribunal related to claims by other employees. These employees had worked at the same factory as the present employee who sought compensation. Giles AJA in the Court of Appeal stated that Hunt & Hunt had privileged material that was confidential as between Goodyear and NEM but which had not previously been made available to Goodyear. He said that there was a real prospect of this material being used on appeal 'in the interests of NEM and against the interests of Goodyear. That remains, in the words of Windeyer J, an impossible situation'. Giles AJA applied the 'real and sensible possibility' test and stated:

12.67

> At the heart of impermissible disclosure of information is prejudice to the client, and prejudice to the client may come about by impermissible use of the information otherwise than by disclosure. It is present when the

---

175. 17 WAR 98, 109–10.
176. *Goodyear Australia Pty Ltd v Boyce* (unreported, SC(NSW), Windeyer J, No 2213 of 1995, 12 May 1995, BC9504603).

information is denied to the client but made available to the client's adversary for which the solicitor is acting, and it may be present if the solicitor acts against the client even if there not be overt disclosure.

12.68 The other principle followed in Australia stems from an early Queensland Supreme Court case, *Mills v Dan Dawn Block Gold Mining Co Ltd*.[177] In that case the court held that solicitors had a duty to make sure they did not place themselves 'in such a relation as might lead to there being even an unwitting breach of duty'. This principle was upheld in two recent cases. In *Wan v McDonald*[178] the Federal Court said that it was only in rare and very special cases that solicitors could act against former clients and this principle was relevant whether or not confidentiality was an issue. It also said that *Rakusen* was no longer accepted as suitable to modern conditions.[179] In *Carindale Country Club Estate Pty Ltd v Astill* the Federal Court reinforced this view. Drummond J, granting an injunction against the firm of solicitors, said the test should be that:[180]

> ... a solicitor is liable to be restrained from acting for a new client against a former client if a reasonable observer, aware of the relevant facts, would think that there was a real, as opposed to a theoretical possibility that confidential information given to the solicitor by the former client might be used by the solicitor to advance the interests of a new client to the detriment of the old client.

12.69 The *Prince Jefri Bolkiah* strict approach appears to be in line with the views of Drummond J in the *Carindale* case and this case is referred to by Lord Millett. Thus, the House of Lords appears to implicitly approve the line of cases following *Mills*. The Australian cases thus vary from the strict prohibition approach stemming from *Mills*[181] to the need to consider the facts of each case,[182] to a new test from *Mallesons v KPMG Peat Marwick* of a 'real and sensible possibility of misuse' of confidential information,[183] to the 'real mischief and real prejudice' test from *Rakusen*.[184] Courts have also been worried about the appearance of impropriety. Bryson J, in *D & J Constructions Pty Ltd v Head*, stated: 'The appearance that a lawyer can change sides during the currency of a case is very subversive of the appearance of justice being done.'[185] The appearance of impropriety was important in a recent Victorian Supreme Court case, *Village Roadshow Ltd v Blake Dawson Waldron*.[186] Blake Dawson Waldron (BDW) had drafted a trust deed for Permanent Trustee that was then used by the plaintiff in seeking to execute a preference share buy-back scheme. BDW later

177. (1882) 1 QLJ 63.
178. (1992) 33 FCR 491.
179. (1992) 33 FCR 491 at 514.
180. (1993) 115 ALR 112 at 118.
181. See also *Commonwealth Bank of Australia v Smith* (1991) 102 ALR 453. Aitken says that this strict test 'has much to commend it': see L Aitken, '"Chinese Walls" and Conflicts of Interest' (1992) 18 *Monash Univ LR* 91, 117.
182. *Murray v Macquarie Bank* (1991) 33 FCR 46.
183. (1994) 4 WAR 357 at 362–3 per Ipp J.
184. This is also the conclusion of Teele (above), p 107. The *Rakusen* test at this time was still very much alive in Australia and was applied in *Macquarie Bank Ltd v Myer* and *Toycorp Ltd (Receivers and Managers Appointed) v Myer* [1994] 1 VR 350 and no conflict of interest was found.
185. (1987) 9 NSWLR 118 at 123.
186. [2003] VSC 505.

represented Boswell who was attacking the preference share buy-back. Byrne J in disqualifying BDW said: 'I was presented with the unsavoury spectacle of a solicitor acting now for a client whose objective was to strike down an arrangement which another client or former client had an interest in upholding.' He also comments on what the 'supposed well-informed reasonable bystander' would think. He said that 'the person is likely to find it distasteful that a solicitor, having accepted a client's coin for its labours, can on its client's behalf, go over to the other side and accept a fee for striving to disadvantage the client in the same or a similar matter'.[187]

Present situation in Australia

The Australian courts have been moving away from the probability test of *Rakusen* and are taking a middle path between that decision and the approach in *Mills*.[188] The test increasingly used is the 'real and sensible possibility of misuse' of confidential information.[189] In other words, the shift is towards the more stringent approach of the House of Lords. Its principles have now been applied and adopted in South Australia,[190] Victoria[191] and Western Australia.[192]

12.70

For example, in the Western Australian case, *Newman as Trustee for the Estates of Littlejohn v Phillips Fox (a firm)*, Steytler J (applying the Lords' test), said:[193]

> ... [there is] little practical difference between that test and the test adopted in such cases as *Mallesons* and *Farrow Mortgage Services*. Indeed it seems to me that the test applied in *Carindale Country Club Estate*, referred to by Lord Millett ... is no different from ... that expressed in *Mallesons* ... If there is any difference in degree between 'a real and sensible possibility' of misuse of confidential information and no 'reazl' risk of disclosures ... then it must ... be slight. Moreover any additional stringency which might be comprehended by the test espoused by the House of Lords when coupled with a shifting of the evidential burden is ... justified by the need to safeguard the proper administration of justice ... That cannot be done unless every client can be satisfied that confidential disclosures to his or her solicitor will be kept secret, especially in circumstances in which the solicitor appears to have changed camps.

This test was also used in a later Victorian case, *Spincode Pty Ltd v Look Software Pty Ltd*.[194] The case involved a firm who had represented the

---

187. Ibid, paras 27 and 46.
188. This is the approach taken by Gummow J in *National Mutual Holdings Pty Ltd v Sentry Corp* (1989) 87 ALR 539 and approved by the Full Federal Court in *Blackwell v Barroile Pty Ltd* (1994) 123 ALR 81 at 93 per Davies and Lee JJ. See also L Aitken, (above).
189. See *Farrow Mortgage Services Pty Ltd v Mendell Properties Pty Ltd* [1995] 1 VR 1. In applying this test Hayne J found that the solicitors when acting for the plaintiff had received information which dealt with matters of the very kind that were involved in present proceedings. This test has also been applied in numerous cases. Aitkin (above), p 117, finds problems with the flexible approach because: 'There is probably little hope, in practice, of obtaining a timeous ruling from relevant ethical committees, and the flexible approach does impose a strain on the conscience of the solicitor.' For some interesting conflict of interest situations not found in any reports, see V Shirvington, 'Conflict of interest not always so clear cut' (1996) 34 *Law Society J (NSW)* 26–7.
190. *Pradhan v Eastside Day Surgery Pty Ltd* BC9903476; [1999] SASC 256.
191. *World Medical Manufacturing Corp v Phillips Ormonde & Fitzpartrick (a firm)*, see n 171 (above).
192. *Newman as Trustee for the Estates of Littlejohn v Phillips Fox (a firm)*, see n 164 (above).
193. *Newman's* case (above), paras 63–4. The firm was disqualified from acting.
194. [2001] VSC 287 and [2001] VSCA 248.

defendants and helped set up that corporation. The firm now sought to represent the major shareholders in the defendant company. The 'real and sensible possibility' test was used to disqualify the firm in the Supreme Court where Warren J approved of the *Prince Jefri* case, but she pointed out it was a narrow test. In the Court of Appeal Brooking J upheld the disqualification and in dictum said that the test in Australia was wider than that in *Prince Jefri*. He said Australian courts also considered as very important the issue of loyalty to clients, which is in the public interest. Brooking's view is that even if there is not a likelihood of misuse of confidential information, the duty to a former client may require a court to prevent the practitioner from acting. This is also the view discussed above in *Village Roadshow*.

This expansive view of a conflict has not been adopted by some other Australian courts. In a very recent case, *APT v Optus Networks Pty Ltd*,[195] the firm of Clayton Utz had been involved in an earlier matter, that was very similar to the present one, for Gilsan International Ltd against Optus. In the Gilsan matter, Clayton had been asked by E-New Media, related to the plaintiffs, to give assistance in answering questions asked by Gilsan. Clayton claimed the information it had provided was not confidential but it still put in place arrangements to protect any possible breach of confidentiality. The practitioners involved in the E-New Media matter gave an undertaking that they would not release any confidential information and the team acting for Optus issued an affidavit that they had not discussed and would not discuss any matter with the E-New Media team about the Gilsan matter or the present matter. Bergin J applied *Prince Jefri*: that two conditions needed to be met — the solicitor was in possession of confidential information from the former client and the information was or might be relevant to the present matter. Her Honour said that the court would only intervene for the protection of confidential information and not to avoid any perception of possible impropriety.[196] Although the solicitors on the Optus team worked on the same floor as those from the Gilsan matter, her Honour found no conflict. She said that Clayton had satisfied her that there was no risk of disclosure to the Optus team. She emphasised that there were 'confidentiality undertakings in place and a willingness to give undertakings to the Court. Undertakings to the Court would be expected to heighten the consciousness for sensitivity and diligence in ensuring that the information remains confidential'. The judge felt that there was no need for undertakings to the court because there was no real risk of misuse of confidential information and refused to restrain Clayton from acting. She also distinguished the *Spinicode Pty Ltd* case (discussed above), and found Brooking J's views on the requirement of a duty of loyalty as being *obiter*, and were views followed only in Victoria.[197]

---

195. [2005] NSWSC 550.
196. To support this view her Honour referred to her views in *Belan v Casey* [2002] NSWSC 58 and the case of *British American Tobacco Australia Services Ltd v Blanch* [2004] NSWSC 70.
197. See paras 99–102. Her Honour says that Brooking JA's view has been adopted in a later Victorian case, *Sent v Fairfax Publications Pty Ltd* [2002] VSC 429.

The recent decisions show a willingness to apply the 'real and sensible risk' test, but sometimes look at the fiduciary duty and confidentiality aspects while at other times they are concerned primarily with the confidentiality aspect.

IMPUTED DISQUALIFICATION

Introduction

ABA Model Code DR 5-105(D) states as a general rule that if any lawyer in a firm is disqualified from representing a client because of a conflict of interest, all the lawyers in the firm are disqualified. The Code has a simple approach based on the notion that lawyers within a firm talk to each other and share confidences. Furthermore, these lawyers share in the financial rewards that would flow from preventing disqualification and keeping the clients. This means that the lawyers' interests would be more important than loyalty to the clients. The Code is also concerned with the 'appearance of impropriety' which would be present if a 'contaminated' firm were allowed to continue to represent a client. As will be shown, because of modern practice the ABA Model Rules have taken a much more complicated approach to the problem. Modern lawyers are very likely to move between firms or between government and private practice and vice versa. It has been argued that to adopt the Model Code approach leads to unfair prejudice against lawyers changing firms. There are still concerns for the welfare of clients, and the poaching of clients because of the increased inability of lawyers to move.[198]

12.71

As we have seen, one line of cases stemming from the *Rakusen* case has established in the Australian/English context that lawyers can continue to act in these situations unless a 'real mischief or real prejudice' will 'probably' occur. *Rakusen* always seems to be an extreme case, since there were only two partners involved, and the likelihood of communication concerning clients was very high. Thus, it has been appropriate that Australian courts have moved away from the *Rakusen* test and now appear to be following the more stringent test of the House of Lords. Furthermore, the *Unioil* case shows a willingness to take into consideration the complications of this problem in the context of modern 'mega' law firms.

Rules and cases in the United States

Rules in the United States dealing with vicarious disqualification are far more detailed and applied more extensively than elsewhere. The general rule on imputed disqualification is found in ABA Model Rule 1.10. This rule was amended in 1989 with specific aspects placed in r 1.9(b). In 2003 this rule and its Comments were amended. Rule 1.10(a) states that a prohibition against representing a client by one member of a firm because of any conflict of interest rules will be deemed to be a prohibition against

12.72

---

198. The Council of the Law Society of NSW adopted on 25 September 1998 a 'Best practice protocol for conduct of firms and solicitors (employees and partners) leaving firms': see (1998) 36 *Law Society J* (NSW) 30.

other members of the firm.[199] This rule only governs lawyers concurrently associated with a firm, and if a lawyer moves to another firm the situation is governed by rr 1.9(b) and 1.10(b). Rule 1.10(b) allows representation by the firm of clients whose interests are materially opposed to the interests of clients of a lawyer formerly associated with that firm, unless:

- ❏ the matter is the same or substantially related to that in which the formerly associated lawyer represented the client; and

- ❏ any lawyer remaining in the firm has information protected by Rules 1.6 [confidentiality] and 1.9(c) [former client's confidences] that is material to the matter.

12.73 ABA Model Rule 1.9(b) states that a lawyer cannot represent a person in the same or a substantially related matter in which a firm, with which the lawyer was formally associated, had previously represented a client whose interests are materially adverse to that person and the lawyer had acquired confidential information, unless the client gives informed consent in writing. Rule 1.9(c) prohibits the use of information from a former client to disadvantage that client except when the rules permit or require the use of that information or when the information becomes generally known. Comments [4]–[9] recognise the problems of modern legal practice when lawyers leave a firm and undertake representation that appears to conflict with their former association and attempt to balance the competing considerations:

> [4] ... First, the client previously represented by the former firm must be reasonably assured that the principle of loyalty ... is not compromised. Second, the rule should not be so broadly cast as to preclude other persons from having reasonable choice of legal counsel. Third, the rule should not unreasonably hamper lawyers from forming new associations and taking on new clients after having left a previous association. In this connection, it should be recognized that today many lawyers practice in firms, that many lawyers to some degree limit their practice to one field or another, and that many move from one association to another several times in their careers. If the concept of imputation were applied with unqualified rigor, the result would be radical curtailment of the opportunity of lawyers to move from one practice to another and of the opportunity of clients to change counsel.

> [5] Paragraph (b) operates to disqualify the lawyer only when the lawyer involved has actual knowledge of information protected by Rules 1.6 [confidentiality] and 1.9(c). Thus, if a lawyer while with one firm acquired no knowledge or information relating to a particular client of the firm, and that lawyer later joined another firm, neither the lawyer individually nor the second firm is disqualified from representing another client in the same or related matter even though the interests of the two clients conflict

> ...

---

199. Firm has been defined to include situations where there are office sharing arrangements by individual lawyers. In *Matter of Sexson* 613 NE2d 841 (Ind 1993) the court said: '[I]t is crucial to look at the level of association, the appearance of the association to the public, any specific agreements, accept to confidential information, and the purpose of the rule. But in the end, as stated in [the Comment to Rule 1.10] ... if attorneys "present themselves to the public in a way suggesting that they are a firm or conduct themselves as a firm, they should be regarded as a firm for purposes of the Rules".'

[6] Application of paragraph (b) depends on a situation's particular facts, aided by inferences, deductions or working presumptions that reasonably may be made about the way in which lawyers work together. A lawyer may have general access to files of all clients of a law firm and may regularly participate in discussions of their affairs; it should be inferred that such a lawyer in fact is privy to all information about all the firm's clients. In contrast, another lawyer may have access to the files of only a limited number of clients and participate in discussions of the affairs of no other clients; in the absence of information to the contrary, it should be inferred that such a lawyer in fact is privy to information about the clients actually served but not those of other clients. In such an inquiry, the burden of proof should rest on the firm whose disqualification is sought.

ABA Model Rule 1.11 concerns government lawyers and is the counterpart to r 1.9(b). It prevents lawyers from exploiting their public office by using confidential government information for the benefit of their private clients unless the law expressly permits the lawyers to act. Model Rule 1.11(a) and (b) disqualifies these lawyers and their firms from acting against the government if the lawyers were associated with the matter involved unless: **12.74**

- ❑ the disqualified lawyer is timely screened from any participation in the matter and is apportioned no part of the fee therefrom; and
- ❑ written notice is promptly given to the government agency to enable it to ascertain compliance with the provisions of the rule.

Rule 1.11(c) has similar provisions for disqualifying lawyers having confidential information about the matter, despite the lawyers not being personally involved.

Rule 1.11(d) deals with situations where a lawyer moves to government service from private practice.[200]

Chinese Walls

The screening process in this rule is an explicit recognition of the use of 'Chinese Walls'. Comment [4] to r 1.11 points out that it was enacted to enable governments to attract legal talent. If the government had maintained a strict disqualification rule, there would be a barrier to lawyers leaving the public service to enter private practice. This would obviously be a severe deterrent against initially entering public service. Although the screening process is not mentioned in rr 1.9(b) or 1.10 there is a possible argument that it is allowed in certain contexts because of the explanation in the Comments to those rules. For example, Illinois,[201] Pennsylvania, Massachusetts, Oregon[202] and Michigan have gone further, modifying the Model Rules to explicitly allow effective use of screening for lawyers   **12.75**

---

200. For a discussion of this provision, see R Rotunda, 'Ethical Problems in Federal Agency Hiring of Private Attorneys' (1987) 1 *Georgetown J Legal Ethics* 85.
201. Even under this permissive screening rule it has been held that it was insufficient to institute screening procedures five weeks after the new lawyer (causing the conflict) had joined the office: see *S K Handtool Corp v Dresser Industries* 619 NE 2d 1282 (Ill 1993).
202. The Oregon rule DR 5-105(I) (Massachusetts is very similar) requires the disqualified lawyer to give the former firm an affidavit attesting he or she 'will not participate in any manner in the matter or the representation and will not discuss the matter or representation with any other firm member'. The lawyer can also be requested to provide an affidavit when the dispute is finished 'describing the lawyer's actual compliance with these undertakings'. The third requirement is that a lawyer in the new firm must also provide the first affidavit and, if asked, the second one.

moving between private practices,[203] while New Jersey[204] and Arizona[205] have rejected screening, strengthening the protection for clients. As of 2005 the vast majority of states accepted the Model Rules, but many had not modified the rules to explicitly allow 'Chinese Walls'. Some states still follow the Model Code. Therefore, 'Chinese Walls' are still not accepted in a majority of the states.

12.76 The 'Chinese Wall' principle was adopted in some jurisdictions in the United States for two purposes:

❑ The first was to allow a firm to continue to represent a client although another member of the firm had confidential information about the opposing side. Related to this was the need for a flexible rule to enable firms to keep established clients although a conflict existed with another or former client in relation to a matter.

❑ The second was to allow lawyers to move between firms. Lawyers were becoming increasingly specialised and if they could not work against former clients in their areas of expertise they would be prejudiced in their careers. Also if lawyers leaving a firm were imputed to have obtained the knowledge of the confidences of all clients of that firm, it would have been difficult for them to set up their own firm or go to another firm. If they went to another firm their knowledge would be imputed to members of that firm and lawyers moving around could be considered like a 'typhoid Mary', infecting every place they went with the 'conflict of interest' virus. This would lead to 'typhoid Mary' law firms, according to the court in *Analytica Inc v NPD Research Inc.*[206] The court said: 'This would have a drastic impact on the careers of attorneys in entire firms, would impede clients' rights to be represented by attorneys of their choice and would discourage attorneys with expertise in a particular field of law from handling cases in their respective specialities.' Coull warned judges to 'exercise caution not to paint with a broad brush under the misguided belief that coming down on the side of disqualification raises the standard of legal ethics and the public's respect. The opposite effects are just as likely — encouragement of vexatious tactics and increased cynicism by the public.'[207]

12.77 The case law in some jurisdictions has been supportive of lawyers' mobility by adopting the view that the presumption of imputed shared confidences could be rebutted. One court pointed out that if screening can be effective for government lawyers moving to private practice it can also be used for

---

203. Gillers and Simon (above), pp 122–3. See also M Moser, 'Chinese Walls: A Means of Avoiding Law Firm Disqualification When A Personally Disqualified Lawyer Joins the Firm' (1990) 3 *Georgetown J of Legal Ethics* 399, 411. It should be noted that the *Restatement of the Law Governing Lawyers* (tent. draft, no 4), para 204, allows screening for all migrating lawyer situations.

204. See F Hamermesh, 'In Defense of a Double Standard in the Rules of Ethics: A Critical Revaluation of the Chinese Wall and Vicarious Disqualification' (1986) 26 *J of Law Reform* 245, 269–70 (fn 26). Although New Jersey does not have a screening rule, its courts will sometimes use equity principles to allow representation to continue even when there is an imputed conflict situation: see *Dewey v RJ Reynolds Tobacco Co* 109 NJ 201, 536 A2d 243 (1988) and *Barnes v RJ Reynolds Tobacco Co* 587 A2d 667 (NJ 1991).

205. See *Towne Development of Chandler Inc v Superior Court* 173 Ariz 364, 842 P 2d (1992).

206. 708 F2d 1263, 1277 (7th Cir 1983).

207. D Coull, 'Typhoid Marys: The Ethical Dilemma of Lawyers Who Switch Firms' (1998) 28 *Victoria University Wellington LR* 41, 55.

private lawyers moving between firms.[208] In *Silver Chrysler Plymouth Inc v Chrysler Motors Corp*,[209] a young lawyer had established his own firm after working for a large firm. He represented a client against a client of his former firm. In dismissing the application to disqualify him the Second Circuit Court of Appeal pointed out that his former employer was a large firm and had a rapid turnover of lawyers. The court said it was absurd to think that young associates were privy to confidences of all files relating to clients of their firm. It held that the presumption of imputed knowledge was rebuttable and that the associate had little or no possibility of having been privy to client confidences. In *Freeman v Chicago Musical Instrument* the Seventh Circuit Court said factors to be considered included the size of the firm, the lawyer's specialisation and his or her position in the firm.[210] The court has continued to support the use of screening as an effective tool, stating that disqualification is a 'drastic measure'.[211]

The case law has also coined a new term for Chinese Walls, a 'cone of silence'.[212] In a very permissive case, the Sixth Circuit Court allowed the screening of a disqualified lawyer formerly involved as the chief attorney for the opposing side. His new firm was not disqualified because the lawyer was hired to do non-litigation work. The court emphasised that the firm seeking to avoid disqualification had the burden of establishing 'objective and verifiable evidence' of effective screening. The factors to be looked at were 'size and structural divisions' of the firm, what rules were used to keep the infected lawyer from gaining access to files in the matter and whether this lawyer would share in any fees coming from the case.[213] One writer has listed seven factors to consider in appraising a 'Chinese Wall'. They include: **12.78**

- ❑ the substantiality of the relationship between the former and current matters;
- ❑ the time elapsing between the matters;
- ❑ the size of the firm;
- ❑ the number of tainted attorneys;
- ❑ the nature of the disqualified attorney's involvement in the former matter;
- ❑ the speed with which the wall is erected; and
- ❑ the strength of the wall.[214]

More recently Dunnigan has stated that to make a screen viable there would be a burden on the firm erecting the screen to show the following possible actions: (1) intra-firm education; (2) prohibited access to files; (3) no sharing in fees from the representation to the tainted lawyer; (4) physical separation of the tainted attorney from the members of the firm **12.79**

---

208. *INA Underwriters Insurance Co v Rubin* 635 F Supp (ED Pa 1983). This case quotes this proposition from Note, 'The Chinese Wall Defense To Law-Firm Disqualification' (1980) 128 *U Pa LR* 677, 701.
209. 496 F 2d 800 (2nd Cir 1974).
210. 689 F 2d 715 at 722 (7th Cir 1982).
211. See *Cromley v Board of Education* 17 F 3d 1059 (7th Cir 1994) certiorari denied, 513 US 816 (1994).
212. See *Nemours Foundation v Gilbane, Aetna, Federal Insurance Co* 632 F Supp 418 (D Del 1986) and *INA Underwriters Insurance Co v Rubin* 635 F Supp (ED Pa 1983).
213. *Manning v Waring, Cox, James, Sklar and Allen* 849 F 2d 222 (6th Cir 1988). See also *Geisler v Wyeth Laboratories* 716 F Supp 520 (D Kan 1989).
214. Note, 'The Chinese Wall Defense To Law-Firm Disqualification' (1980) *U Pa LR* 677.

working on the case in question; (5) affidavits by tainted members of the firm; (6) no informal meetings regarding the representation in question; (7) named party responsible for supervising and maintaining the screen.[215]

Support for erecting 'cones of silence' comes not only from some of the courts. Modification of the American Law Institute *Restatement (Third) of the Law Governing Lawyers* is currently being considered so as to permit the use of screening mechanisms. Various drafts of changes to the *Restatement* contemplate using screening devices in order to remove the imputation of shared confidences. The ABA has adopted Formal Opinion 90-358. The opinion rejects the adoption of a broad concept of screening. It does allow screening but states it may be used only when the confidential information of the former client is not extensive or sensitive. A proposal by the ABA's Ethics 2000 Commission, that when a lawyer moves to a new firm, screening with or without the consent of the client be permitted to cure imputed disqualification, was rejected by the ABA's house of Delegates.[216]

12.80 It should be noted that, even in cases where the screening mechanism was approved, courts have often found that it was not properly implemented,[217] and there are still courts which take a strong position against screening. For example, in the *Atasi Corporation* case[218] the Ninth Circuit disqualified a law firm from acting because one of its lawyers had previously been counsel to the other firm in the case. This lawyer had had direct but minimum contact with the matter in dispute with his former firm, but was not participating in the matter for his new firm. The court held that there was a presumption he had gained and shared confidences from the earlier matter. There was no evidence that his new firm had made any effort to screen him from lawyers working on the matter.

According to Dunnigan the lack of any firm endorsement of screening by the ABA has led to a split on the approach to screening. Currently five Federal Circuit Courts, the Second, Third, Sixth, Seventh and Eleventh, have allowed some screening, while the First, Fourth, Fifth, Eighth and Tenth Circuit Courts of Appeal have rejected the concept.[219] The Ninth Circuit has indicated it may be willing to allow it. He also points out that the courts have no knowledge of the effectiveness of the screens, as there has been no study concerning the effectiveness of the screens.[220]

---

215. C Dunnigan, 'The Art Formerly Known as the Chinese Wall: Screening in Law Firms: Why, When, Where, and How' (1998) 11 *Georgetown J of Legal Ethics* 291, 300–1.
216. For a discussion of the screening problems related to the Commission, see C Wolfram, 'Ethics 2000 and Conflicts of Interest: The More Things Change ...' (2001) 70 *Tenn LR* 27 and S Shapiro, 'If it ain't broke ... : An Empirical Perspective on Ethics 2000, Screening and the Conflict of Interest Rules' (2003) *U Illinois LR* 1299.
217. See M Brodeur, 'Building Chinese Walls: Current Implementation and a Proposal for Reforming Law Firm Disqualification' (1988) 2 *The Review of Litigation* 167, 181.
218. See *Atasi Corp v Seagate Technology* 847 F 2d 826 at 831–2 (9th Cir 1988). For a discussion of Californian cases on vicarious disqualification see I Ruvolo, 'An Antidote for Typhoid Mary' (June 1990) *California Lawyer* 65. Some other cases opposing screening are: *Chen v GAF Corp* 631 F 2d 1052; *Parker v Volkswagenwerk* 245 Kan 580, 781 P2d 1099 (1989); and *Casco Northern Bank v JBI Associates Ltd* 667 A 2d 856 (Me 1995).
219. C Dunnigan (above) at 295, 303. He also stated that the DC Circuit Court of Appeals had not dealt with the issue.
220. *United States v Lynn Boyd Stites* 56 F 3d 1020, 1025 (1995).

Firms have also been disqualified when employing non-lawyers. In *Re Complex Asbestos Litigation*[221] a paralegal who worked for defence firms in similar asbestos cases joined a plaintiff firm which was disqualified in an asbestos case. In *Allen v Academic Games Leagues of America, Inc*[222] a newly qualified lawyer had his new employer disqualified because he had worked for the other side while he was a law student. There are also courts that have taken a permissive approach and allowed screening.[223]

12.81

There is opposition to screening and the more flexible approach to conflict problems because the new rules are in the interest of large firms and detrimental to clients. It is pointed out that as firms get larger potential conflicts of interest multiply. Since these firms are more interested in maintaining their clients because of the financial interests involved, they have made demands to have more flexible ethical rules. In these circumstances lack of full loyalty to clients is secondary and the ethical standards are therefore lowered.[224]

There is academic support for allowing a flexible approach because disqualification is expensive, vexing and inefficient for those involved. Green has even proposed that disqualification motions should be granted only if a former client has actually suffered harm.[225]

Rules and cases in Australia and elsewhere

Chinese Walls in Australia

In Australia only the Law Institute of Victoria has issued a ruling on the matter of Chinese Walls. It is only a guideline and states that a conflict of interest may still exist 'notwithstanding that the firm had arrangements in place to exclude the person in possession of the confidential information from having any involvement with the file'.[226] The New Zealand Law Society issued r 1.07 stating that a practitioner shall cease to act in the event of a conflict or likely conflict among clients 'even though a notional barrier known as a "Chinese Wall" may be or may have been constructed. Such a device does not overcome a conflict situation'.[227]

12.82

There is legislation in Australia under the Corporations Law allowing the use of a Chinese Wall. The provisions are used in the area of representation or recommendations about securities.[228] There are also provisions for erecting a Chinese Wall as a defence to insider trading offences.[229] Tomasic has pointed out that the 'use of the Chinese Wall in the securities industry

---

221. 283 Cal Rptr 273 (Cal App 1991). See also *Smart Indus. Corp v Superior Court* 876 P 2d 1176 (Ariz 1994).
222. 831 F Supp 785 (CD Cal 1993). For a more recent case with the same result, see *Actel Corp v QuickLogic Corp* 1996 WL 297045 (ND Cal 1996). For an article stating the law on the subject is unsettled, see I Schein, 'Legal Secretaries and the Conflict of Interest Rule' (1992) 14 *Advocates Quarterly* 81.
223. For example, see *Phoenix Founders Inc v Marshall* 887 S W 2d 831 (Tex 1994).
224. M Riger, 'Disqualifying Counsel in Corporate Representation — Eroding Standards in Changing Times' (1980) 34 *University of Miami LR* 995, 1041.
225. B Green, 'Conflicts of Interest in Litigation: The Judicial Role' (1996) 65 *Fordham LR* 71, 129.
226. Conflict of Interest Guidelines r 2, *Law Institute J*, May 1991, p 351.
227. *Rules of Professional Conduct for Barristers and Solicitors*, July 1994.
228. Corporations Law ss 849(2) and 850(2).
229. Corporations Law s 1002M (corporation) and s 1002N (partnership).

has been extended further in Australia and Britain than in the United States'.[230] In contrast, courts in the United States have been more willing to extend Chinese Walls to overcome conflicts for large law firms than courts in Australia or the United Kingdom.

12.83   Out of the cases dealing with Chinese Walls in Australia several have rejected the concept. Bryson J in *D & J Constructions Pty Ltd v Head*[231] (dictum) said:

> I would think that the court would not usually undertake attempts to build walls around information in the office of a partnership, by accepting undertakings or imposing injunctions as to who should be concerned in the conduct of litigation or as to whether communications should be made among partners or their employees. The new client would have to join in such an arrangement and give up his right to the information held by such parties and staff as held it. Enforcement by the court would be extremely difficult and it is not realistic to place reliance on such arrangements in relation to people with opportunities for daily contact over long periods, as wordless communication can take place inadvertently and without explicit expression, by attitudes, facial expression or even by avoiding people one is accustomed to see, even by people who sincerely intend to conform to control ... [T]here is a thriving, diverse and talented legal profession and the court need not fear that a litigant who is deprived of the services of one firm will not be able to retain adequate representation.

12.84   Ipp J in *Mallesons v KPMG Peat Marwick*[232] quoted with approval Bryson J's views. In *Mallesons* the firm had been retained by the Commissioner for Corporate Affairs (WA) in relation to the prosecution of criminal charges of a partner of the accounting firm KPMG Peat Marwick. Mallesons had been previously consulted for advice concerning audits that were done by the accountants and the confidential information given (including by the partner facing criminal charges) was related to the transactions under question in the criminal matter. The lawyers representing the Commissioner were different to those who had acted for the accountants, no communication had taken place between these lawyers concerning the matter, and undertakings were made by the Commissioner not to use any confidential information, if any was obtained. Furthermore, a 'Chinese Wall' was to be kept in place to stop communication between the lawyers working for the Commissioner from those who had acted for the accountants. Ipp J nevertheless found that a conflict existed and disqualified the firm from acting. Ipp J said that 'even with the best will in the world that the [confidential] information would colour, at least subconsciously, the approach of the solicitors and influence them in the performance of the tasks'.

12.85   In *Newman as Trustee for the Estates of Littljohn v Phillips Fox (a firm)* the firm of Hely Edgar withdrew its representation in an arbitration when the firm was dissolved. Two lawyers, two article clerks and the administrative staff

---

230. R Tomasic, 'Chinese Walls, Legal Principle and Commercial Reality in Multi-Service Professional Firms' (1991) 14 *University of New South Wales LJ* 46, 48–9.
231. (1987) 9 NSWLR 118 at 122–3.
232. (1990) 4 WAR 357. In *Freuhauf Finance Corp Pty Ltd v Feez Ruthning (a firm)* [1991] 1 Qd R 558 the court found, due to undertakings by the new client to limit the representation and a Chinese Wall constructed within the firm, there was no 'real risk of prejudice or mischief'.

then joined Phillips Fox who was acting in the same matter against the client. One of these lawyers was to become a partner when the matter was settled. Phillips Fox said that the lawyers would give written undertakings to maintain the confidences they had obtained in the representation. Furthermore, the lawyer working on the arbitration case would undertake to have no consultation with either of them in respect to this matter. Steytler J rejected the proposed 'wall' and applied the test for an effective wall as stated by Lord Millett in the House of Lords: see **12.62**. He said that the proposed wall was to be established ad hoc and there was no proposal for an educational program, nor one for monitoring and record keeping, nor an offer of imposition of disciplinary sanctions if the 'wall' was breached. Steytler J said it could be assumed that the lawyer who was to become a partner would have 'frequent interaction, both professional and social, between him and others at Phillips Fox'. He said a similar interaction would take place between the articled clerks and other young lawyers in the firm. He was concerned by the lack of adequate safeguards as regards the administrative staff from Hely Edgar that had joined Phillips Fox. Finally, he said that even if an effective wall could be established it was too late. The Hely Edgar personnel had already been employed for several months and there was no way to satisfy the former client that there already could have been some inadvertent disclosure.[233]

In *Freuhauf Finance Corp Pty Ltd v Feez Ruthning (a firm)*[234] Lee J of the Queensland Supreme Court refused to issue an injunction requested by a former client disqualifying the firm from acting. In this case Freuhauf sought the injunction to stop the firm from representing Westpac in an action against them. The law firm had advised Freuhauf some time earlier concerning a different matter. Freuhauf based its argument on the fact that the firm had confidential information as to how Freuhauf ran its operation. Lee J found for the law firm for two reasons:

12.86

- the new client had given undertakings to limit the representation of the firm; and
- the firm had established internal systems that had placed walls around information concerning two of the items involved in the litigation, so that it would not be passed on to those working for the new client from those that had worked for the old client.

Lee J found that there had been no communication of confidential information within the firm and thus there was no 'real risk of prejudice or mischief' and no 'prospect of detriment to the plaintiff'.

In *World Medical Manufacturing Corp v Phillips Ormonde & Fitzpatrick (a firm)* Gillard J applied the principles from *Prince Jefri Bolkiah* but rejected the disqualification application. The firm had been retained by the plaintiff to pursue an application for a patent in Australia. In the present proceedings the firm was in opposition to its former clients but it involved Federal Court litigation having nothing to do with patent application. Gillard J found that the confidential information was not relevant to the present case. Different lawyers in the firm were involved in the patent application from those involved in the litigation. Gillard J approved the

12.87

---

233. *Newman's* case, see n 164 (above).
234. [1991] 1 Qd R 558.

action of the firm in not even pursuing the establishment of a wall. He said there was no need for a wall as the confidential information guarded by the lawyers involved in the patent application was of 'such little moment in relation to the issues in the Federal Court proceedings'. Thus, the litigation lawyers would have had little interest in receiving it. Furthermore, the firm had ceased to represent the plaintiff, knew little about their client and had not had face-to-face meetings or telephone conversations (all correspondence was by letters or facsimiles). Gillard J concluded that even assuming some of the communications would be privileged there was no evidence that there was any risk of the former lawyer disclosing any privileged information.[235]

12.88   In the *Freuhauf Finance* and *World Medical Manufacturing Corp* cases the confidential information was of a general character and not relevant to the present matter. It could therefore not be used to the detriment of the former client. By contrast, in the *Mallesons* and *Newman* cases the information related to the very transactions involved with the new or former clients. The cases also differed in that *Freuhauf Finance* and *World Medical Manufacturing Corp* concerned civil cases where the firm had acted for the other party in an unrelated matter, while in *Mallesons* serious criminal charges were involved and the firm had acted for the previous client in the same matter.[236] Although *Newman* was also a civil case, like *Mallesons*, the issue involved was representation concerning the same matter of a former client.

12.89   Two very recent cases, *Australian Liquor Marketers Pty Ltd v Tasman Liquor Traders Pty Ltd*[237] and *APT Ltd v Optus Networks Pty Ltd*,[238] discussed earlier in the chapter, were cases where firms were not disqualified. In the former case the practitioners with confidential information were in Brisbane while those running the case were in Melbourne. It also concerned a different matter in relation to its client in Brisbane and arrangements had been promptly put in place. These facts plus the requirement of undertakings to the court were enough to avoid disqualification. In the latter case, *APT*, although the matter was very similar, the court accepted arrangements had been adopted to avoid any real risk of the leaking of confidential information, and undertakings by the firm were considered enough.

12.90   Australian courts have adopted a stricter standard in family law cases because of the sensitive nature of the confidential information. It would be less likely in these cases that courts would consider allowing a Chinese Wall. In the leading case of *In the Marriage of Thevenaz*[239] Frederico J stated:

> It may well be that the risks were … more theoretical than practical. However, it is asserted and not contradicted that material in the files does relate to confidences exchanged in the course of the former firm previously acting on behalf of both parties and would embarrass the husband. It is of the utmost importance that justice should not only be done but should appear to be done.

---

235. *World Medical*, see n 171 (above), paras 144–47, 242–52 and 271.
236. See M Keith, 'Berlin Wall Down, Chinese Walls Next?' (December 1992) *Law Society Bulletin (SA)* 12–16; and I Tunstall, 'Acting for the Corporate Regulator: A Potential Conflict of Interests' (September 1991) *Law Society J (NSW)* 57.
237. [2002] VSC 324.
238. [2005] MSWSC 550.
239. (1986) 86 FLR 10.

In the circumstances of the present case, there is a risk which may well be merely theoretical but still exists, that justice might not appear to be done.

This case has been cited with approval in the more recent case of *In the Marriage of Magro*.[240] A firm was disqualified from representing the husband in property proceedings that were bitterly contested, because the former lawyer of the wife had joined the firm. Even though the new lawyer did not deal with the matter, and he and the solicitor dealing with the matter made an undertaking to not discuss the matter, the court disqualified the firm. In contrast, the *Thevenaz* case was criticised for concentrating on the appearance of justice by Mackenzie J in *Australian Commercial Research and Development Ltd v Hampson*, but later on in his judgment Mackenzie J does comment on the 'special nature' of family law matters.[241] It also appears that criminal law, like family law, is to be treated differently. In both these areas the courts have recognised the importance that justice be seen to be done.[242]

Chinese Walls in other countries

Australian courts are not the only courts uneasy about the reliability and effectiveness of Chinese Walls. The Supreme Court of Canada, Canada's highest court, dealt with the issue in *Martin v MacDonald Estate*.[243] The court unanimously disqualified a firm from acting in the matter, but was divided in its approach. In this case one of the young associates of the firm had formerly been actively involved with a matter that was now being opposed by her firm. Although she had had no involvement in the case since joining the firm, and swore an affidavit that she had not discussed the matter with any member of the firm, and made an undertaking not to discuss it in the future, the firm was disqualified from acting. The majority decision written by Sopinka J rejected the then English standard of a 'probability of mischief' as being insufficiently high to satisfy the public requirement of the 'appearance of justice'. He adopted a more stringent test because of the difficulties in determining whether confidential information had been used. His test was whether 'the public represented by the reasonably informed person would be satisfied that no use of confidential information would occur'. This test was approved by the House of Lords in the *Prince Jefri Bolkiah* case. Sopinka J asked two questions:

❑ Did the lawyer receive the confidential information attributable to a solicitor and client relationship relevant to the matter at hand?

❑ Is there a risk that it will be used to the prejudice of the client?[244]

He said that once a relationship is established there is an inference that relevant confidential information was imparted to the lawyer, unless the

12.91

---

240. (1993) 93 FLR 365. An earlier case, *Gagliano v Gagliano* (1989) FLC ¶92–014 used the expression 'the appearance of a possible injustice'.
241. [1991] 1 Qd R 508 at 516, 518. Connock states: 'There is no authority for the proposition that "stricter rules apply in family law cases"'. He cites for this proposition the Law Institute of Victoria, *Members Handbook*, 1994, p 391. Connock also believes that, like the commercial law cases, no injunction would be issued in family law cases if there was 'only theoretical risks of breach of confidence or prejudice' despite what was stated in *Thevenaz*: Connock (above), p 261 and fn 114.
242. C Edmonds (above), p 232.
243. [1990] 3 Supreme Court Reports 1235.
244. *Martin* (above) at 1259–60.

lawyer satisfies the court that no information was imparted that could be relevant. This would be a difficult burden to discharge because the lawyer has to discharge it without revealing the specifics of the privileged communication. He also said that there was a strong inference that lawyers working together share confidences. This inference could be rebutted by the use of screening devices like Chinese Walls and cones of silence, but only if such devices have been approved by the professional governing bodies and are considered to be sufficiently effective by a court.[245] The minority judgment of Cory J established more stringent restrictions. He said that where a lawyer has actually received confidential information before joining a firm that is acting for those opposed to the interests of the former client, there is an irrebuttable presumption that these lawyers working together will share each other's confidences, as opposed to the majority's rebuttable inference.[246]

12.92   In another Canadian case, *Canada Southern Petroleum v Amoco Canada Petroleum Co Ltd*,[247] the court allowed a wall to be erected around a lawyer who had confidential information from his former client on the same matter where the lawyer's new firm was on the opposing side. The wall was effective because the lawyer (the subject of the wall) was in an office located in a different city than the lawyers acting in this same matter. A more recent case, *ASA v Queen's University of Kingston*,[248] follows the principles of *Prince Jefri*, allowing representation if the confidentiality of the former client can be maintained. The Canadian Bar Association's Code of Professional Conduct, Chapter 6.1, has detailed rules concerning 'Conflicts Arising as a Result of Transfer' between firms.[249] The Canadian Bar has also adopted specific Guidelines for Chinese Walls. They are:

1. The screened lawyer should have no involvement in the current representation.

2. (a) The screened lawyer should not discuss the current matter or any information relating to the representation of the former client (the two may be identical) with anyone else in the new firm.

   (b) No member of the new firm should discuss the current matter or the prior representation with the screened lawyer.

3. The current client matter should be discussed only within the limited group who are working on the matter.

4. (a) The files of the current client, including computer files, should be physically segregated from the regular filing system, specifically identified, and accessible only to those lawyers and support personnel in the firm who are working on the matter (or require access for other specifically identified and approved reasons).

   (b) No member of the firm should show the disqualified lawyer any documents relating to the case.

5. The measures taken by the firm to screen the lawyer should be stated in a written policy explained to all lawyers and support personnel within the firm, supported by an admonition that violation of the policy will result in sanctions, up to and including dismissal.

---

245. *Martin* (above) at 1260–3.
246. *Martin* (above) at 1271.
247. (1997) 144 DLR (4th) 30.
248. (2002) FCA 905.
249. See www.lawsociety.mb.ca/code.htm.

6. Affidavits should be provided by the appropriate firm members, setting out that they have adhered to and will continue to adhere to all elements of the screen.

7. (a) Former client should be informed that the screened lawyer is now with the firm representing the current client.

(b) The former client must be advised of the measures adopted by the firm to assure there will be no misuse of the confidential information.

8. It may prove helpful if the screened lawyer does not participate in the fees generated by the current client matter.

9. The lawyer's office should be located away from the offices of those working on the matter.

10. The screened lawyer should use associates and support personnel different from those working on the current client matter.

11. Every effort should be made to obtain the former client's consent to the new firm's representation. If that consent is given, it must be on the basis of a fully informed appreciation of the situation and only after receiving independent legal advice.[250]

The English Court of Appeal in *Re a firm of solicitors*, by a 2:1 majority, has adopted three different approaches to the use of Chinese Walls. Parker LJ said that he doubted whether an 'impregnable wall can ever be created'. He said that some confidential information might permeate a 'wall'. He also regarded it as:

> ... astonishing that the plaintiffs should be faced with solicitors on the other side to whom, over a considerable period, they have afforded much confidential information concerning matters being investigated in the main action.

Parker LJ did state that 'only in very special cases that any attempt should be made' to establish a Chinese Wall. Sir David Croom-Johnson was not as rigid as Parker LJ and rejected Chinese Walls if there was a real, not just possible, risk of leakage. The dissenting judge, Staughton LJ, was willing to accept the 'information barrier' that had been erected and thus remove the injunction.[251]

The facts in *Prince Jefri Bolkiah* were discussed above. In order to avoid any possible conflict of interest the defendants had in this case erected a 'Chinese Wall' around the department carrying out the investigation for the Brunei Government. Lord Millett did accept the notion that Chinese Walls or similar other arrangements could be used. He said they could be used to eliminate the risk but there was an assumption that information would be disclosed within a firm and thus there was a need to take special measures. He referred to the English Law Commission's 'Consultation Paper on Fiduciary Duties and Regulatory Rules' 1992, which stated the type of arrangements that needed to be established to constitute a Chinese Wall. They are:[252]

---

250. These guidelines are from OSLC, *Conflicts of Interests Discussion Paper*, May 2005, Annexure D, which refers to www.practicpro.ca.

251. *Re a Firm of Solicitors* [1992] 1 All ER 353 at 363, 367, 370. This case was applied in a Chancery Division decision, but the judge there refused to issue an injunction on the basis of the possible perception of impropriety. Lightman J rejected the American test and applied the real risk test: *Re A Firm of Solicitors* [1996] 3 WLR 16.

252. *Prince Jefri Bolkiah* (above) at pp 527–8.

(i)   The physical separation of the various departments in order to insulate them from each other — this often extends to such matters of detail as dining arrangements;

(ii)   an educational programme, normally recurring, to emphasise the importance of not improperly or inadvertently divulging confidential information;

(iii) strict and carefully defined procedures for dealing with a situation where it is felt that the walls should be crossed and the maintaining of proper records where this occurs;

(iv)   monitoring by compliance officers of the effectiveness of the wall;

(v)   disciplinary sanctions where there has been a breach of the wall.

I would add a sixth requirement — the rapid bringing into existence of these complicated arrangements.

In the latest English case, *Marks & Spencers v Freshfields Bruckhaus Deringer*,[253] discussed above, Freshfields offered to adopt various arrangements, which included relocating staff to separate premises, obtaining affidavits from those that had been involved with the previous client, that they had not received any confidential information, and obtaining undertakings from them that they would not be involved with the new matter. All of these were rejected by the Court of Appeals. It stated that there existed:

> ... [a] huge amount of confidential information within Freshfields in relation to Marks & Spencer's affairs through acting for it over the years, some of which may be material to the bid, if only to be discarded. I cannot see, even with a firm the size of Freshfields, that effective information barriers can be put in place given the very large number of people involved, even on the two matters ... I am satisfied that the Chinese walls cannot be or be seen to be — perception is very important here — sufficient.

12.93   In New Zealand Tompkins J has stated: 'In my view, once a potential conflict of interest situation has arisen or an allegation of breach of fiduciary duty is made, the protection thought to be given by a "Chinese Wall" will almost always prove illusory.'[254] In a more recent New Zealand High Court case, *Equiticorp Holdings v Hawkins*,[255] Henry J also rejected 'what is called a Chinese Wall'. He did state that representation could be continued by the firm's 'implementing some other safeguards' to isolate the lawyer who had been involved in the case for the defendant's law firm before seeking to join as a partner in the plaintiff's law firm. This is a curious observation because the 'implementation of safeguards' in reality is a Chinese Wall! Henry J also rejects the *Rakusen* case and adopts the 'reasonable possibility of disclosure' test.[256]

12.94   The cases in Australia, Canada, New Zealand and England show that the courts are more uneasy in deciding to allow the erection of screening devices than the courts in the United States. There is scepticism towards Chinese Walls and a hardening of attitudes towards potential conflict of interest. Although the walls are accepted by the House of Lords, the necessary arrangements are stringent and difficult to carry out. The courts

---

253. [2004] EWCA Civ 741.
254. *McNaughten v Tauranga City Council (No 2)* (1987) 12 NZ TPA 429 at 431.
255. [1993] 2 NZLR 737 at 741.
256. *Equiticorp Holdings* (above) at 739.

also often appear less willing to believe in the honour and integrity of members of the legal profession. There is less willingness to believe that undertakings to keep confidences from other members of a firm will be adhered to, although in two recent Australian cases, *APT* and *Australian Liquor Marketers*, discussed above, undertakings were considered sufficient to avoid disqualification.

This lack of trust in most Australian cases is in stark comparison to the attitude of courts in the United States where screening is allowed because of the courtesy that is extended to lawyers as professionals.[257] Even when the courts espouse the integrity and honesty of the profession they find that unless action is taken quickly there is an assumption that some disclosure, even though by inadvertence, will have taken place. Although Australian courts still stick to a concept of fiduciary duty to former clients, there may be a trend to allow more flexibility in balancing the interests of the lawyer, the new client and the former client. This flexibility is especially important with the development of national and international mega firms. The presumption of imputed knowledge seems appropriate within small firms. It appears out of place for mega firms, especially for lawyers in offices located in different cities.[258]

Rules and cases for government lawyers

Screening in the United States has allowed lawyers to move more easily between government and private practice. Model Rule 1.11(a) states that a substantial involvement in a matter for a government body would lead to the disqualification of the lawyer when acting for a new firm.[259] When an effective screen has been put into place courts have upheld the right of the firm to continue to represent a client, although one of its lawyers worked for the government agency involved in the matter.[260] There are tremendous variations in the rules in this area among the states and further complications because of federal and state criminal statutes that deal with the misuse of government confidential information.[261] Furthermore, there will be a lack of tolerance, especially in criminal law, if the representation will lead to a lack of due process. Thus, a court disqualified the entire prosecutorial office because the main prosecutor in the case had represented the accused when he was a public defender on similar related matters.[262] The use of a screen for former government lawyers appears to Hazard to be the:[263]

12.95

---

257. L Winslow, 'Federal Courts and Attorney Disqualification Motions: A Realistic Approach to Conflicts of Interest' (1987) 62 *Washington LR* 863, 871.
258. Mitchell (above), p 430.
259. This was the situation before the Model Rule. See *General Motors Corp v City of New York* 501 F 2d 639 (2nd Cir 1974). For a case since Model Rule 1.11(a) disqualifying the lawyers, see *Securities Investor Protection Corp v Vigman* 587 F Supp 1358 (Dist Ct Cal 1984).
260. See *Armstrong v McAlpin* 625 F 2d 433 (2nd Cir 1980); *Telectronics Pty Ltd v Medtronic Inc* 836 F 2d 1332 (Fed Cir 1988); *Chambers v Superior Court* 121 CA 3rd 893 (1981).
261. For a discussion of the rules, statutes and cases see G Dawson, 'Working Guidelines for Successive Conflicts of Interest Involving Government and Private Employment' (1998) 11 *Georgetown J of Legal Ethics* 329.
262. *State v Tippecanoe County Court* 432 NE 2d 1377 (Ind 1982).
263. G Hazard Jr, *Ethics in the Practice of Law*, Yale University Press, New Haven, Conn, 1978, p 113.

... epitome of naive legalism. No one who is anxious about the fidelity of former government lawyers will regard such a rule as adequate; and everyone who thinks the problem is primarily one of an individual's trustworthiness will regard the rule as obnoxious.

12.96   Australian courts do not make a distinction between the movement of lawyers between private firms and those moving from organisations, such as government departments. Chapter 13 of the *Guidelines on Official Conduct of Commonwealth Public Servants 1987* deals with possible conflict of interests in accepting employment after leaving the public service. The *Guidelines* are not binding and allow flexibility in obtaining new employment. Under paras 13.8–13.11 public servants with knowledge of confidential procedures should apply for consent to be employed 'if there is a possibility that the employment could give rise to an actual or apparent conflict of interest'. Under paras 13.16–13.20 the policy is strongly in favour of granting consent to take up new employment. Where there is a strong conflict of interest the Commonwealth can impose restrictions for up to two years on contacts to be made by the former employee with the public service. The fact that many prominent senior legal public servants have taken up employment with private law firms without any restrictions is an indication that the *Guidelines* will rarely be enforced. Former civil servants still need to be aware of the restrictions under s 70(2) of the Crimes Act 1914. It prohibits the disclosure of confidential information obtained while working for the public service. The penalty for breaching the provision is two years' imprisonment.

CONCLUSION

12.97   In light of the increase in conflict of interest situations Zitrin says there is a need for law firms to have in place a system of checks to identify all potential conflicts. There has to be a review of possible conflicts when new lawyers, law clerks, legal secretaries and even administrative staff enter the firm. A firm needs to have written materials for waivers discussing all ramifications of a conflict, the effect of the waiver on confidential communications, the lawyer's role in the event the conflict ripens and a warning that the waiver can only be used where the client is not disadvantaged. Firms need to adopt a system that keeps control over the integrity of files in order to preserve absolute client confidentiality. This includes protection for clients when they change firms or the firm withdraws or declines to represent them. There have to be procedures to discuss with clients the type of fee involved for their matter and the effect of a third party paying their fee. Guidelines need to be issued on restricting personal relationships between lawyers and clients. Firms should create administrative procedures manuals covering all of the above matters. Lawyers have to be aware of protecting confidential information when speaking on mobiles, using email and fax machines. For lawyers working for government or corporations, guidelines have to be issued to establish clearly the ground rules defining who is the client.[264] A database containing detailed information as to the affiliated interests of each corporate client

---

264.   R Zitran, 'Attorney, Heal Thyself' (July 1991) *California Lawyer* 38.

also needs to be created. In the United States lawyers can obtain this information from several companies. For example, the Attorneys' Liability Assurance Society (Bermuda) Ltd (ALAS), on a per search fee basis, will conduct a search of the publicly available corporate information in its database.[265]

Zitrin envisages that conflict of interest problems may take years to ripen and that preventive care is necessary.[266] There seems to be very little activity among firms in Australia to heed this advice. Anecdotal evidence indicates that only the large firms have established routines to avoid conflicts and that not many of the small or medium-size firms have a committee to deal with conflict of interest problems when they occur. The approach has been one of dealing with issues on an ad hoc basis. Obviously, as more lawyers are disqualified from acting, law firms will heed such advice.

---

265. See Busby and Bashman (above), p 71. To the author's knowledge no such organisation exists in Australia.
266. Zitrin (above), p 38.

PART FOUR

The Adversary System

13

OUTLINE OF THE ADVERSARY SYSTEM

INTRODUCTION

In the last part of this book we will primarily examine the ethical standards for lawyers within the context of the adversary system. The final chapter, Chapter 16, discusses the future of the profession. We have discussed in Chapter 2 that one of the main reasons for the 'amoral' lawyer is the adversary system. This part of the book deals with what ethical restrictions are placed on lawyers within this system. A discussion of the nature of the adversary system and its comparison with the inquisitorial system will set the basis for looking at lawyers' obligations within this adversary system. Chapter 14 will deal with the concept of fairness and candour, while Chapter 15 looks at the application of fairness and candour in the context of the criminal trial.

13.1

ADVERSARY AND INQUISITORIAL SYSTEMS

There are two main systems under which lawyers represent clients in the Western world: the adversary (common law) and inquisitorial (civil law). The adversary system is sometimes called the adversarial system, but this is a misnomer — both systems are adversarial, and at times the adversary system is inquisitorial. For example, the adversary system has discovery of documents which is a purely inquisitorial tool, while in Germany, which has an inquisitorial system, discovery is not used.[1] In adversary systems of law the parties and their lawyers play the main role in gathering evidence and questioning witnesses in court, and the court (the judge) plays a less active role. The inquisitorial system, in contrast, has the court playing the

13.2

---

1. B Walker SC, 'Adversaries on paper: ALRC raises legal hackles' (1997) 32 *Australian Lawyer* 8.

main role in gathering evidence and questioning witnesses.[2] The Australian Law Reform Commission aptly summarises the differences: 'Civil code proceedings represent, in procedural theory, "judicial prosecution" of the parties' dispute, as opposed to "party prosecution" of the dispute under the common law system.'[3]

Inquisitorial system

13.3   German civil law litigation cases commence with lawyers alleging the basis for the action and proposing means of proving the material allegations. Lawyers will include or identify in the complaint pertinent documents and the names of potential witnesses. The defendant's lawyer will follow the same pattern. Generally, what is made available to the presiding judge is information and documents provided by clients, whose lawyers will not have conducted any significant investigation. The presiding judge assesses the material, seeks additional documentation, and undertakes several hearings with the lawyers and sometimes with their clients and witnesses. Judges will at this stage seek to promote a settlement, but if the parties cannot agree the judge establishes a schedule for taking proof and chooses the witnesses, documents and experts needed for the action. The judges are also responsible for 'examining witnesses and summarizing their testimony for the record, although lawyers may occasionally ask supplemental questions or suggest changes in wording ... If a new question unexpectedly surfaces, the judge can delay the proceedings to allow investigation. Civil cases are resolved without juries and generally by a panel of judges; appellate review involves a de novo consideration of the record, supplemented if necessary by additional evidence'.[4]

Lawyers play a circumscribed role in this kind of litigation. They can make suggestions as to additional areas that need investigation and comment on the court's findings through oral and written submissions. They cannot influence witnesses and should not try to contact them. They have some obligation to determine if their clients' statements are true before verifying them and have a duty not to contradict any opposition representations if they hold a belief that they are true. Finally, their fees are established by statute and based on the category of the case and the financial amount in dispute. Thus, there is no charging by the hour.[5] In a more recent account of the German civil system, Koetz claims that the lawyers can contact witnesses in order to clarify the testimony they may give at the trial, but

---

2.   See *Review of the Adversarial System of Litigation: Rethinking the Federal Civil Litigation*, Australian Law Reform Commission, Issues Paper 20, April 1997, paras 2.6–7.

3.   Australian Law Reform Commission, DP 62, *Review of the federal civil justice system*, August 1999, para 2.25.

4.   D Rhode, *Professional Responsibility: Ethics by the Pervasive Method*, 2nd ed, Aspen Law & Business, New York, 1999, p 183.

5.   Rhode (above), pp 183–4, does point out that even with these constraints: 'German lawyers generally believe that their primary loyalty is to the client rather than to the state. German and American attorneys often report similar economic pressures and distortions of the decision-making process.' But the billing practices in Germany control any extreme abuses that are not controlled in the United States. For a brief summary of the French criminal procedures see A Bullier, 'Evidence in French Criminal Procedure: A Short Note' (September 1999) *Brief (Law Society of WA)* 12.

such contact is unusual.[6] Although there are these differences in the German civil law system from the adversarial system there are, according to the Australian Law Reform Commission, also similarities. 'Parties present the facts to the court and their lawyers have comparable roles ... The court may only consider those facts brought before it; it may not investigate on its own.'[7]

It has been said that the judge in the inquisitorial system is more concerned with the interests of justice and discovering the 'truth', the substance of the matter and not the procedural aspects. Judges in the adversary system are said to be passive. Lawyers dominate in this system as to what and how much evidence is presented, which therefore determines the length of the hearing. Judges are mainly concerned that the procedures are followed and do not seek the truth.[8] Marks J of the Supreme Court of Victoria supports this view. He said:[9]

> Many of the procedures under the [inquisitorial system] are a great deal more sensible than ours, and behind them is the philosophy that the aim of the law is the discovery of the truth.

Criticism of the inquisitorial system

The inquisitorial system has been criticised because judges in criminal cases fail to take a dispassionate look at a case before forming relatively firm conclusions. This is because the dossier, a complete file on the accused including witnesses' statements, is presented to the judge before the hearing. The dossier, which is usually prepared by the police and the committing magistrate, is so complete that there is little room for change.[10] Furthermore, there is no cab-rank rule and an advocate can make his or her own judgment about the accused. The dossier can thus influence the advocate in deciding whether or not to represent the accused.[11] The judge has to be persuaded that the person is not guilty. This is why some comments have been made that under the inquisitorial system an accused is guilty unless he or she proves otherwise. Contrary to this view, as a result of the thorough dossier many more criminal cases are dropped before trial than in the adversary system.[12]

13.4

---

6. H Koetz, 'Civil Justice Systems in Europe and the United States' (2003) 13 *Duke J of Comparative and International Law* 61, 67–8.
7. ALRC, DP 62 (above), para 2.26.
8. See A Rosett, 'Trial and Discretion in Dutch Criminal Justice' (1972) 19 *UCLA LR* 53; see also A Goldstein, 'Reflections on Two Models: Inquisitorial Themes in American Criminal Procedure' (1974) 26 *Stanford LR* 1017. For an excellent fictional scenario comparing the two systems see M Moskovitz, 'The O.J. Inquisition: A United States Encounter With Continental Criminal Justice' (1995) 28 *Vanderbilt J of Transnational Law* 1121.
9. Quoted in J Slee, 'The change we need in the law', *Sydney Morning Herald*, 6 November 1992, p 10.
10. C Wolfram, *Modern Legal Ethics*, West Publishers, St Paul, 1986, p 566. Germany and Italy no longer use a committing magistrate. See Jean-Marc Baissus, 'Common v Continental: A Reaction to Mr Evan Whitton's 1998 Murdoch Law School Address' (1998) 5 *Murdoch University Journal of Law* 15, 34.
11. J Leubsdorf, *Man in his Original Dignity: Legal Ethics in France*, Aldershot, Hants, England, 2001, p 26.
12. Rosett (above).

The differences in the conduct of a criminal case in the two systems was recently highlighted in the well-publicised Indonesian drug possession case of Schappelle Corby. The Indonesian system was defended against intense criticism in the Australian media by Asian law experts, Tim Lindsey and Simon Butt. They pointed out that the active role of the judges in the case was a normal aspect in most inquisitorial systems, as well as the absence of a jury. They also stated that the media's comments that Corby was held to be guilty until she proved otherwise was not true. There was a presumption of innocence under article 18 of the Indonesian Human Rights Law and article 66 of the Indonesian Code of Criminal Procedure states that 'the obligation of proof is not to be imposed upon the accused or defendant'.[13]

Justice Ronald Sackville, reflecting on the strong negative reaction by the Australian public to Corby's sentence to 20 years gaol, said: 'Rightly or wrongly, [most Australians] have insufficient confidence in the Indonesian justice system to accept the verdict as legitimate.'[14] Richard Ackland, a leading legal journalist, stated: 'Even though law reform in Indonesia is in progress ... perversions from the Soeharto ... eras are unravelling only slowly. The close relationship that existed between the courts and the prosecution is something that many Indonesian lawyers have fought to end, but complete independence still has a way to go. The zealousness of the prosecution is an element of Indonesian criminal law that to us also seems intolerable. The function of dispassionately laying out the facts is something that has not yet fully permeated the thinking of the Indonesian prosecution service.'[15] It would appear that Ackland's criticism of the role of the prosecutor in Indonesia as compared to Australia is projecting an idealistic view of the role and actions of prosecutors in Australia.

Adversary system — lack of truth?

13.5 Some writers have argued that truth becomes lost in the adversary system because it is more concerned with preserving procedural fairness. The lawyer in the adversary system shows respect for the law of procedure by showing disrespect for the substantive law.[16] Frankel has stated that the 'adversary system rates truth too low among the values that institutions of justice are meant to serve'. He argues that the legal profession in the United States is held in low regard because of the attitude that finding truth has a low priority. Frankel feels that there is too much emphasis placed on the advancement of the client's interest:[17]

> The struggle to win, with its powerful pressures to subordinate the love of truth, is often only incidentally, or coincidentally, if at all, a service to the public interest.

13. T Lindsey and S Butt, 'Justice system not getting a fair trial hearing in high-profile drugs cases', *Sydney Morning Herald*, 3 May 2005, p 13.
14. R Ackland, 'Indonesian legal system doesn't inspire trust', *Sydney Morning Herald*, 3 June 2005, p 13.
15. Ibid. See also by contrast, T Lindsey, 'Facts and Fiction in the Corby Case', *Sydney Morning Herald*, 27 May 2005, p 15.
16. D Luban, *Lawyers and Justice: An Ethical Study*, Princeton University Press, Princeton, 1988, p 50.
17. M Frankel, 'The Search for Truth: An Umpireal View' (1975) 123 *University of Pennsylvania LR* 1031.

Frankel concludes that in the area of human rights — confrontations against the state — truth may have to give way. But he feels that clients' rights can be protected and that 'we can hope to preserve the benefits of a free, sceptical, contentious bar while paying a lesser price in trickery and obfuscation'.[18]

Freedman believes that the adversary system must maintain 'respect for human dignity, even at the expense of the search for truth'. Freedman also states that he does not mean:[19]

13.6

> ... to deprecate the search for truth or to suggest that the adversary system is not concerned with it. On the contrary, truth is a basic value, and the adversary system is one of the most efficient and fair methods designed for determining it.

He has also pointed out truth has been a very elusive concept throughout history — from Plato to Shakespeare to the present day. He concludes therefore 'that those who devised the adversary system took account of the illusive nature of truth — particularly the elusive kind of truth that is sought in resolving a dispute between two or more contesting parties'.[20] Freedman also devotes all of Chapter 2 of his latest book, *Understanding Lawyers' Ethics*, to explaining and justifying the adversary system.[21]

Freedman's sentiments are also voiced in Australia. For example, David Bennett QC has stated: 'The adversary system with its emphasis on cross-examination is probably the finest engine devised by man for determining the truth.' Bennett based his argument on the fact that the oral advocacy skills of Australian advocates help judges to change their views and thus arrive at the truth. Bennett could have supported his argument by pointing out that the Australian emphasis on 'fearless' advocacy, as compared to 'zealous' advocacy in the United States, is more likely to provide less tampering with evidence. This thus provides us with a better chance of arriving at the truth than the American system. Our advocacy rules adopted in the Law Council's Model Rules rr 12–20, which are almost the same as the Barristers' Rules throughout Australia, place a greater emphasis on maintaining a more even balance between the advocate's duty to the client, and to the court and the

13.7

---

18. See Frankel (above).
19. M Freedman, *Lawyers' Ethics in an Adversary System* (1975), p 2.
20. M Freedman, 'The Trouble with Postmodern Zeal' (1996) 38 *William and Mary LR* 63, 64–5. Bjorgum finds that there are two conceptions of truth functioning in the legal system: (1) truth as coherence — under this concept 'truth or falsity of any statement depends upon others in the system. Observations are formulated as statements and absorbed into the system with reference to statements already accepted as true'. This continues until the system becomes 'so unworkable and observations' become 'so untenable that new beliefs' are embraced; (2) truth as correspondence — under this concept there is a 'belief that statements are true by virtue of their correspondence to states of affairs in the world. Most members of the non-legal community (and lawyers in their personal lives) live according to this definition of truth'. The author concludes that lawyers have to make use of both concepts and perform a difficult balancing act between the 'conflicting roles of genesis and necessity' as to what they can disclose: E Bjorgum, 'Pursuing Truth in the Adversary System: An Ideal Criterion' (1996) 9 *Georgetown J of Legal Ethics* 1211, 1214–15, 1219–20. For how truth is manipulated in a hypothetical case in order to help Jesus to be born under a roof, see S Goldberg, 'A Little Known History of Truth' (1996) 9 *Georgetown J of Legal Ethics* 1199.
21. M Freedman, *Understanding Lawyers' Ethics*, Matthew Bender, New York, 1990, pp 13–42.

administration of justice, than the ABA Model Code or Model Rules. The American Model Rules according to Higgins 'license lawyers to engage in ethically questionable conduct by allowing them, for example, to disregard the moral rights of people other than their client'.[22]

Canadian concept of integrity

13.8   One provision we do not have in our rules, and which I feel we need to adopt, is found in the Canadian Bar Association (CBA) Code of Professional Conduct as of June 2005, Chapter 1 'Integrity': 'The lawyer must discharge with integrity all duties owed to clients, the court, other members of the profession and the public.' The CBA Code defines integrity as being 'soundness of moral principle, especially in relation to truth and fair dealing; uprightness, honesty, sincerity, candour'.[23] *Commentary* 1 states: 'Integrity is the fundamental quality of any person who seeks to practise as a member of the legal profession ... If personal integrity is lacking the lawyer's usefulness to the client and reputation within the profession will be destroyed regardless of how competent the lawyer may be.' *Commentary* 2 states: 'The principle of integrity is a key element of each rule of the Code.' There is also a quote from Sir Thomas Lund (British expert on legal ethics) where he states, among a number of things, that: '*Integrity is the fundamental quality, whose absence vitiates all others.*'[24]

According to Woolley the Integrity provision has helped Canadian lawyers to temper the ideal of zealous advocacy and retain 'a commitment to maintaining a lawyer's *personal* integrity'. She summarises the Canadian position in terms of the ideal lawyer:[25]

> ... the lawyer acts to further the interests of her client but does so taking into account that she is not simply a servant of her client; that she has a responsibility to further the administration of justice; that she cannot act, or assist her client in acting, in a way she considers dishonourable; that she has a responsibility to the community; and that, most importantly, she must ensure that she retains her personal integrity.

It should be noted that the International Bar Association's Code of Conduct in its 'Introductory' states: 'The rules of professional conduct enforced in various countries ... uniformly place the main emphasis upon the essential need for integrity and, thereafter, upon the duties owed by a lawyer to his client, to the Court, to other members of the legal profession and to the public at large.'[26]

---

22.   S Higgins, 'Ethical Rules of Lawyering: An Analysis of Role-based Reasoning from Zealous Advocacy to Purposivism', (1999) 12 *Georgetown J of Legal Ethics* 639.
23.   See fn 1 to Chapter 1.
24.   See fn 2 to Chapter 1. For the complete CBA Code of Professional Conduct see www.lawsociety.mb.ca/code_rules/chapter1.htm.
25.   A Woolley, 'Integrity in Zealousness: Comparing the Standard Conceptions of the Canadian and American Lawyer' (1996) 9 *The Canadian J of Law & Jurisprudence* 61, 63, 92. Woolley compares the CBA Code to the ABA Model Rules. In contrast to Woolley's 'ideal' type of Canadian lawyer others have found similar problems in Canada as exist in the United States: see G MacKenzie, 'Breaking the Dichotomy Habit: The Adversary System and the Ethics of Professionalism' (1996) 9 *The Canadian J of Law & Jurisprudence* 33.
26.   See Canadian Bar Association Code of Professional Conduct, Chapter 1, fn 1.

Adversary system — criticism

The adversary system has come under great scrutiny in Australia and   **13.9**
elsewhere. There have been a number of conferences[27] to discuss its faults
and improvement and several judges and academics have made various
suggestions for reform.[28] A comprehensive review was undertaken by the
Australian Law Reform Commission (ALRC) which published discussion
paper, DP 62, *Review of the federal civil justice system*, in August 1999 and
final report, No 89, *Managing Justice: A review of the federal civil justice
system*, in February 2000. In its earlier Issues Paper 20 — *Review of the
adversarial system of litigation: Rethinking the federal civil litigation system*,
para 1.7, the ALRC describes the traditional features of our system and
explains why, according to its critics, they have been deemed
'counterproductive or inefficient' — the system is about winning which
places emphasis on confrontation; the lawyers' role is strictly partisan which
is not tempered enough by their duties to the court; although the judge is
responsible for making sure the hearing is conducted fairly, the judge is not
responsible as to how evidence is collected, what arguments and points are
submitted and how long this will take; the judge is not responsible for
discovering the truth, but only adjudicating questions of fact and law.

In para 1.8 the ALRC quotes from Lord Woolf's report on the civil justice   **13.10**
system in England and Wales. He found the following defects:[29]

> ... it is too expensive — costs often exceed the value of the claim; it is too
> slow in bringing cases to conclusion; it is unequal — there is a lack of
> equality between the powerful, wealthy litigant and the under-resourced
> litigant; it is uncertain — the difficulty in forecasting what litigation will cost
> and how long it will last; it is incomprehensible to many litigants.

The ALRC also points out that the adversary system has possibly had a detrimental effect on the ethical behaviour of lawyers. In para 11.15 it states:[30]

> Formally, duties to the administration of justice are paramount and take
> precedence over duties to the client. However, in practice, it is generally
> recognised that interests of the client are given greater weight by lawyers.
> Duties to the administration of justice may also be interpreted narrowly so
> that they do not restrict a lawyer's ability to present the best possible case for
> their client ...

The Commission in DP 62 comes to the conclusion that although there
are many defects in our system there are also defects in other systems. For
example, there are high costs and delays that permeate the German and

---

27. See reports from speeches at conferences in (1995) 30 *Australian Lawyer* 16 and
    A Marfording, 'Taming the adversary system' (1996) 31 *Australian Lawyer* 10.
    Marfording discusses the reforms suggested by the Queensland Litigation Reform
    Commission. The Australian Law Reform Commission co-sponsored a conference
    examining comparative legal systems in July 1997 and a conference to discuss its final
    report in May 2000.
28. See the excellent articles by Justice Ipp: D Ipp, 'Reforms to the Adversarial Process in
    Civil Litigation — Part I and Part II' (1995) 69 *Australian LJ* 705 and 69 *Australian LJ*
    790 and 'Lawyers' duties to the court' (1998) 114 *Law Quarterly Review* 63.
29. The Commission refers to Lord Woolf, *Access to Justice: Final Report to the Lord
    Chancellor on the Civil Justice System in England and Wales*, HMSO London, 1996, p 2.
30. See also Ipp (above), pp 725–30.

French legal systems.[31] There are numerous articles showing that the adversary system does not measure up to its own self-image and that it contains numerous internal contradictions,[32] but as Lowenfield commented at a common law and civil code systems symposium: '[O]ne result of listening to and reading about each other's problem was the realization that none of the observers and commentators was satisfied with the system he or she knew best.'[33]

13.11 Luban sets forth six justifications for the adversary system:

- ❏ It is the best system for discovering the truth.
- ❏ It is the best way of defending the rights of clients.
- ❏ It has developed checks and balances that prevent excesses.
- ❏ The nature of the lawyer–client relationship is intrinsically good.
- ❏ By giving everyone a voice, it honours human dignity.
- ❏ It is so woven into our social fabric that it would be too disruptive to adopt another system.

Luban examines each justification and decides that only the last has validity. He comes to the conclusion that the system has merit in that it is 'not demonstrably worse than other systems'. He says therefore that since it is the system we are used to, we should retain it, because to adopt another would cause too much dislocation with little benefit. Luban also finds that there is no sound evidence that either the inquisitorial or the adversary system is better at finding the truth.[34]

13.12 Luban, defending his book against criticism, concedes that the adversary system has merit for the 'criminal defense paradigm'. He states:[35]

> In the criminal defense paradigm, adversary advocacy is a crucial device for protecting, and indeed overprotecting, the rights of individuals against a powerful and potentially dangerous bureaucratic institution.

Luban probably did not mean to include in the 'criminal defense paradigm' wealthy white collar defendants. He also extends his coverage to any situation where individuals are confronted by powerful bureaucratic organisations, including private powerful corporations, 'since these too pose a chronic threat'.

Luban came to his conclusions by making a comparison between the adversary system and the inquisitorial German legal system. He found that the German system did not have procedural safeguards to protect the litigants' civil rights. The system depended a great deal more than the American system on trusting the integrity and impartiality of a civil service judiciary. He also found that the judges in Germany have a 'slightly condescending, paternalistic attitude ... toward litigants of lower social

---

31. DP 62, *Review of the federal justice system*, August 1999, para 2.29.
32. See, for example, MacKenzie (above); Ipp (above); W Simon, 'The Ideology of Advocacy' (1978) *Wisconsin LR* 1; C Menkel-Meadow, 'The Trouble with the Adversary System in a Postmodern, Multicultural World' (1996) 38 *William and Mary LR* 5.
33. A Lowenfield, 'Introduction: The elements of procedure: Are they separately portable?' (1997) 45 *American J of Comparative Law* 649, 651.
34. Luban (above), pp 67–93, 102–3.
35. D Luban, 'Partnership, Betrayal and Autonomy in the Lawyer–Client Relationship: A Reply to Stephen Ellmann' (1990) 90 *Columbia LR* 1004, 1019.

class'. He therefore felt that Americans would not trust such a judiciary using informal procedures to protect their basic human rights.[36]

Luban's comparison can be criticised because his study of the German system was almost 20 years ago and there may have been important changes since then. Furthermore, other inquisitorial systems may be far less paternalistic and more protective of the litigants' rights than the German one of the 1980s. For example, the judiciaries in both Italy and France are probably more liberal. This has occurred because a large number of the young radical law students of the late 1960s are now in positions of judicial power.[37] A comparison made of the American system with these two countries and modern-day Germany might lead to a finding of less paternalistic attitudes and more respect for the human dignity of the litigants. If this was the case perhaps the dislocation of adopting a different system would have merits.

Ideal model of adversary system

13.13 It appears that the ALRC's view that there is limited usefulness in listing the possible advantages and disadvantages of the two systems has great merit. The Commission also points out there are many texts taking either side of the argument.[38]

The ideal model of the adversary system would have the following features:

❑ an impartial judge sitting alone or with a jury;

❑ the litigants decide what evidence to marshal and present;

❑ the advocates for each side [with similar skills and experience] by using investigation, pre-trial discovery, cross-examination of opposing witnesses, present to the judge or jury in the best possible light their view of the case;

❑ the judge or jury then are in the best possible position to make an accurate and fair judgment and this leads to ascertainment of the truth.[39]

13.14 Even if this ideal model was followed in all adversary jurisdictions and in all their courts, which it is not, there is no reason to believe it would lead to the truth. Hazard has stated that we have 'no proof that the adversary system yields truth more often than any other system of trial …'.[40] Rhode supports this view:[41]

> Lawyers are concerned with the production of belief, not of knowledge. Why assume that the fairest results will necessarily emerge from two advocates arguing as unfairly as possible on opposite sides?

The party who can best persuade that it has truth, rather than the party that in fact has truth, is rewarded by the adversary system. Is such a system

---

36. Luban (above) (1988), pp 93–103.
37. The author was told of the influence of law students in the early 1970s into the judiciary when he was a visiting fellow in 1984 at an Institute of Criminology and Sociology in Vaucrasson just outside of Paris.
38. Report No 89, *Managing Justice: A review of the federal civil justice system*, February 2000, paras 1.121–1.125. Also see DP 62 (above), paras 2.30–2.41.
39. M Freedman, *Lawyers' Ethics in an Adversary System* (1975), p 2. For the ideal form of the adversary system see R Aronson, 'Professional Responsibility: Education and Enforcement' (1976) 51 *Washington LR* 273, 293ff.
40. G Hazard Jr and D Rhode, *The Legal Profession: Responsibility and Regulation*, 2nd ed (1988), pp 170–1.
41. Quoted in P Rizzo, 'Morals for Home, Morals for Office: The Double Ethical Life of a Civil Litigator' (1993) 35 *Catholic Lawyer* 79, 89.

necessarily the fairest, such that unfair tactics can be justified in order to preserve it?[42]

Ipp J still feels that truth, within the bounds of fairness, should be the goal of a civil trial. To achieve this goal he suggests in particular more judicial intervention to limit the length of a trial, that is, limiting the number of witnesses, the time to address the court or 'simply fixing an appropriate period for the trial'.[43] Perhaps an important justification for the adversary system is that it allows aggressive behaviour to be played out in a safe environment. This assumes that the system allows aggressive behaviour that would otherwise be acted out in a destructive and socially harmful manner to be replaced and deflected. There is an argument and some evidence that the adversary system creates more conflict and that it is socially more desirable to settle matters by the use of alternative dispute resolution.[44]

Comparison of the systems — conclusions

13.15 The ALRC concluded that the debate concerning the two systems was a 'non debate'. It said the 'debate assumes that transplants from different political and cultural systems will function in similar ways when rooted in our legal system, that such change can be engineered, and that it will improve the system rather than introducing a new host of problems in comparing the systems'.[45] The ALRC pointed out that none of the countries in either system 'operates strictly within the prototype models'.[46]

The argument over the merits or faults of the inquisitorial and adversary systems is losing its importance as each system increasingly adopts aspects of the other, although some important aspects may not change in the near future.[47] The most hybrid system is the new Italian criminal court system. While it still has lawyers trained to be passive, it has given them the power to present evidence and taken that power away from the judges. The Italian prosecutor, by contrast to the Anglo-American prosecutor, still has limited authority. The system is having problems because of the inadequate legal training given to Italian lawyers in adversarial techniques.[48] The Italian

---

42. P Rizzo (above), p 89.
43. Ipp, 'Reforms to the Adversarial Process in Civil Litigation — Part I and Part II' (above), p 821.
44. Wolfram (above), p 568. Menkel-Meadow states: 'A culture of adversarialism, based on our legal system, has infected a wide variety of social institutions ... [It has] dominated journalism, both print and electronic media, political campaigns, educational discourse, race relations, gender relations, and labor and management relations, to name only a few examples.': see Menkel-Meadow, n 32 (above), p 11.
45. Report No 89 (above), paras 1.111–1.112.
46. Report No 89 (above), para 1.116.
47. For example, the use of contempt law in common law, which virtually does not exist in civil law. See M Chesterman, 'Contempt: In the Common Law, But not the Civil Law' (1997) 46 *International and Comparative LQ* 521.
48. For a discussion of the new Italian system and its various problems see L Fassler, 'The Italian Penal Procedure Code: An Adversarial System of Criminal Procedure in Continental Europe' (1991) 29 *Columbia J of Transnational L* 245; M Zander, 'From inquisitorial to adversarial — the Italian experiment' *New Law J*, 17 May 1991, pp 678–9; W Pizzi and L Marafioti, 'The New Italian Code of Criminal Procedure: The Difficulties of Building an Adversarial Trial System on a Civil Law Foundation' 1992) 17 *Yale LJ* 1.

experiment, and other changes in Europe, such as increased procedural protections and greater reliance on lawyers, show a movement towards the adversary system. Judges in the adversary system, on the other hand, according to Alan Rose QC, former President of the ALRC, have become:[49]

> ... much more involved in the progress of court cases ... and are acting 'managerially' to drive the pace of litigation, to help the parties to define the issues, to eliminate some of these issues before a trial and to encourage them to think about other ways of resolving the dispute.

According to Ipp J, reforms substantially modifying the adversarial ethic in the United States, England and Australia have already been implemented or are being proposed. These reforms emphasise cooperation, candidness and respect for truth. He also states that there is a strong movement by judges in these countries 'to extend the judicial power of intervention and implement greater judicial control over litigation'.[50] This control over litigation and a more activist role for judges is found in the adoption of case management and managerial judging.[51] Former High Court Chief Justice Anthony Mason has issued a warning about these developments: 'The judge must remain a judge, despite the temptation in the world of case management to call him a manager. It is vital to build up and maintain public confidence in the court system. Accordingly, there is a risk that, if we put too much emphasis on speedy disposition of cases, we shall prejudice the just disposition of cases. This is just what we cannot afford to do.'[52]

13.16

Damaska states that the purpose of the 'inquest' is to solve a problem by the implementation of state policy, while the purpose of a 'contest' is to have the state legitimate the resolution of a dispute between two or more parties. Both 'inquest' and 'contest' are present in Western legal systems. The adversary system is in fact rarely adversarial (a contested trial). It can be viewed as a system of inquiry by both sides to reach a negotiated settlement. The ideal types of both systems would be quite exceptional because in the modern state most systems for resolving disputes are hybrids.[53]

13.17

49. A Rose, 'Multiskilling the bench', *Sydney Morning Herald*, 5 May 1997, p 17. Rose's view should be contrasted with the comment by the New South Wales Law Reform Commission that judges were reluctant to make use of these extensive powers: *Evidence*, Report 56, Sydney, 1988, para 6.30. The ALRC in Issues Paper 21, para 11.3, states: 'While recognising that judges may intervene significantly in the trial process, for example by calling a witness, judges generally view the exercise of such powers as appropriate only in exceptional circumstances.' Furthermore, the High Court is strongly opposed to judges calling witnesses in criminal cases, except in exceptional circumstances: *R v Apostilides* (1984) 154 CLR 563.

50. Ipp (above), pp 722–5. See also D Ipp, 'Judicial impartiality and judicial neutrality: Is there a difference?' (2000) 19 *Australian Bar Review* 212.

51. See H Astor and C Chinkin, *Dispute Resolution in Australia*, 2nd ed, LexisNexis Butterworths, Chatswood, New South Wales, 2002, pp 237–42.

52. A Mason, 'The courts as community institutions' (1998) 9 *Public Law Review* 83, 85.

53. M Damaska, *The Faces of Justice and State Authority*, Yale University Press, New Haven, 1986, pp 3–6, 10–12, 69, 224–5.

Twining examines this hybrid world of dispute settlement in the English context and finds that many English tribunals are adversarial although they were set up to make inquiries into matters such as welfare, tax and immigration: 'There is in a sense "dispute" and hearings have some "adversarial" characteristics.'[54] Twining's views are supported in the Australian context by Aronson and Franklin who state that in the administrative decision-making context: 'Lawyers instinctively turn to the adversary model as providing the greatest measure of procedural protection.' Thus, they state a fair hearing needs 'notice and disclosure, orality, confrontation and cross-examination and a reasoned decision ... based on the evidence presented'.[55]

13.18 The ALRC states: 'A duty to act fairly is also consistent with non-adversarial procedures. A judge who conducts the investigation, assists the parties to clarify the issues and pleadings and questions witnesses is not proceeding unfairly. However, the adoption of some inquisitorial features into the Australian legal system may interfere with accepted notions of procedural fairness. For proceedings to be fair in an adversary system, a judge must be independent of the state, impartial and seen to be impartial, with clear limitations to a judge's participation, investigation and management of a matter.'[56]

Within the court systems of the common law countries, the demands of modern litigation and pressure on public funds has led to an erosion of the basic characteristics of the adversary model. There is a more interventionist and regulatory role being performed by the judiciary. We are moving towards a 'quasi-adversary system of civil procedure'.[57] As Damaska has pointed out, the modern goal of conflict resolution is for the state to have a coordinated system backed up by its authority and providing different avenues of redress.[58] It still should be noted that, as the ALRC says, it is not that the systems are becoming the same: 'it is more an indication of the adoption by one system of the principles and procedure used in another. Some important differences remain. These may be so entrenched that there is never complete convergence.'[59] A good example of these differences is that in the Australian context the High Court has stated in dicta in *Bass v Permanent Trustee Co Ltd*[60] that the adoption of an inquisitorial approach is inconsistent with procedural fairness, because it would contradict the

54. W Twining, 'Theories of Litigation, Procedure and Dispute Settlement' (1993) 56 Mod LR 380, 391. Lawyers sometimes view fairness in the tribunal setting through a 'prism of adversarialism' and this has an 'inhibiting and often inappropriate influence ... in the wider context of the administrative process': M C Harris, 'Fairness and the Adversarial Paradigm: An Australian Perspective' (1996) *Public Law* 508, 526–7. See also T Thawley, 'Adversarial and inquisitorial procedures in the Administrative Appeal Tribunal' (1997) 4(2) *Australian J of Administrative Law* 67.
55. M Aronson and N Franklin, *Review of Administrative Action*, Butterworths, Sydney, 1987, p 146.
56. Report No 89 (above), para 1.143.
57. In the English context see C Glasser, 'Civil Procedure and the Lawyers — The Adversary System and the Decline of the Orality Principle' (1993) 56 Mod LR 307, 317.
58. Damaska (above), pp 78–9.
59. Report No 89 (above), para 1.126 and fn 199.
60. (1999) 161 ALR 399, 425.

requirements of the 'Constitution governing the exercise of the judicial power of the Commonwealth'.

ALTERNATIVE DISPUTE RESOLUTION

The removal of many matters from the adversary system for conflict resolution has been very evident in the modern state. In the United States the use of alternative dispute resolution (ADR) has skyrocketed in the last few years with the vast majority of courts establishing procedures for its use. There were also pilot programs looking at mandatory use of ADR and it is already mandatory in domestic relations cases in 33 jurisdictions.[61] In the federal sphere there was a Federal Court Pilot Project in selected districts which may require parties in money disputes of $100,000 or less to submit to arbitration[62] and the Administrative Dispute Resolution Act which requires the adoption by all federal agencies of an ADR policy when all parties consent.[63] The various pilot programs resulted in the widespread adoption of mandatory ADR throughout the federal and state court systems. In 2005 the President of the American Arbitration Association (AAA), William Slate, stated: 'Ten years ago we were doing 50,000 matters a year, last year we did 240,000 cases. That is more than all the civil cases filed in all federal courts in America last year.'[64]

13.19

In Australia the adversary system has already been deemed to be inappropriate in a number of tribunals which bar the use of lawyers, such as the Consumer Tribunal. In the area of family law many of its characteristics are considered detrimental by the Family Court because it sees its role 'as much as a therapeutic agency as a judicial institution'.[65] Furthermore, the different avenues of redress that are being created include the increased referral by courts of parties to arbitration or mediation.

13.20

The fact that lawyers have been barred from some tribunals should be heeded as a warning. Ardaugh says lawyers are imbued with an adversary culture and thus may bring this legal 'baggage' with them. She states:[66]

> In lawyers' education and management of disputes there is little or no recognition of parties' underlying needs and how these might be satisfied outside legal norms. Asking lawyers to practise facilitative mediation is anomalous without a radical change in legal education, philosophy, training

---

61. F Woods, *Report, ABA Section of Dispute Resolution*, 30 June 1995.
62. Section 901 of the Judicial Improvements and Access to Justice Act, 28 USC ss 651–658.
63. Public Law No 101-552, 104 Stat 2736.
64. M Priest, 'US courts in quiet revolution', *Australian Financial Review*, 17 June 2005, p 54.
65. J Crawford, *Australian Courts of Law*, Oxford University Press, Melbourne, 2nd ed, 1988, p 197. The Family Law Act 1995 (Cth) was amended by the Courts (Mediation and Arbitration) Act 1991. As a result a new Order 25A of the Family Law Rules was adopted. It provides a detailed scheme for the conduct of mediation in family law matters. See T Altobelli, 'Mediation in family: Statutory provisions and the solicitor's role' *Law Society J* (NSW) Vol 32, August 1994, p 36. The use of mediators in family law in England and problems in their education and training is discussed in L Neilson, 'Mediators' and Lawyers' Perceptions of Education and Training in Family Mediation' (1994) 12 *Mediation Quarterly* 165.
66. A Ardagh, 'Lawyers and Mediation: Beyond the Adversarial System?' (1998) 9 *Australian Dispute Resolution J* 72, 74.

and development of skills. Lawyers' concerns are with facts and certainty, from this follows a legal solution to the dispute. Mediation's focus is with feelings and ambiguity; and from the drawing out of feelings and perceptions comes resolutions to the conflict. If lawyers are to be mediators and/or participate as lawyers in mediation sessions, a lessening of emphasis on legal methods and solutions is necessary.

This view of lawyers today hopefully may be incorrect. Many more lawyers are being trained in mediation skills at university and in courses conducted by the legal profession and by professional mediation bodies. The problem is that the lawyers still dominating ADR have had many years of training and practice in adversarial skills.

13.21 The courts are more willing than they used to be to recommend ADR to clear up their backlog of cases, to save public funds and reduce legal costs. This view was supported by a study of Federal Court judges' attitudes to ADR which showed they prefer matters to be settled before trial and advise parties to consider using ADR. The judges did not feel they had a role to play in the preliminary search for solutions and the Registrars of the Federal Court usually conduct the pre-trial settlement conferences. Judges also generally believed that participation in seeking pre-trial solutions should not be mandatory.[67] The views of the judges in this survey have in some aspects been rejected. Judges now have a much greater role in case management and overseeing ADR.[68] Furthermore, there has been an adoption of compulsory mediation in some Australian courts. The widespread acceptance of ADR by the courts has led to a huge increase in the number of referrals since the late 1990s.[69] Astor and Chinkin stated in 2002: 'It is difficult to think of a court or tribunal that does not have available to it one or more forms of dispute resolution in addition to trial.'[70]

A survey in New South Wales by the Justice Research Centre supported the need for alternatives to the adversary system. The centre questioned 255 people involved in personal injury cases. The survey compared the perception of fairness and satisfaction of the approximately 60 per cent who went through the formal court hearing or formal arbitration with the perception of the rest, who used pre-trial procedures or mediation to solve the dispute. The detailed comparison showed a far higher satisfaction and fairness rating with the pre-trial/mediation system than the more formal court/arbitration system.[71] Two other interesting findings were that 40 per cent of all those surveyed thought that their lawyers had not provided good value for money, and 44 per cent felt they could not completely trust their lawyer to act in their best interest.[72]

---

67. A De Garis, 'The role of federal court judges in the settlement of disputes' (1994) 13 *University of Tasmania LR* 217, 223–5. Regarding the arguments for judges having powers of mandatory mediation referral see T Altobelli, 'ADR Legislation some recent developments' (1996) 3 *Commercial Dispute Resolution J* 1, 10. For arguments against mandatory participation see R Ingleby, 'Court sponsored litigation: the case against mandatory participation' (1993) 56 *Modern LR* 441.
68. Astor and Chinkin (above), pp 237–57.
69. M Priest (above), p 54.
70. Astor and Chinkin (above), p 235.
71. M Delaney and T Wright, *Plaintiffs' Satisfaction with Dispute Resolution*, Justice Research Centre, Sydney, 1997, pp 21–69.
72. Delaney (above), p 73.

Professional rules

The professional bodies also emphasise the need for compromise and the need to avoid litigation. For example, the Professional Conduct Rules (WA) r 5.7 states: 'A practitioner shall when in his [or her] client's best interests endeavour to reach a solution by settlement out of court rather than commence or continue legal proceedings.' Lawyers have a duty to inform clients about alternative possibilities for solving their disputes, which would include various forms of ADR.[73] The Law Society of New South Wales in several of its guides and codes of good practice 'has encouraged solicitors to advise clients of the advantages of alternative dispute resolution'.[74] The Law Council's Model Rules for advocates, and the Barristers' Rules in New South Wales and Queensland state the advocate 'must inform the client or the instructing solicitor about the alternatives to fully contested adjudication of the case which are reasonably available to the client' unless there are reasonable grounds for the barrister to believe that the client already understands those alternatives.[75]

13.22

The then New South Wales Attorney-General, Jeff Shaw, said that settlement rates in excess of 70 per cent had taken place under the Law Society's mediation program. He added: 'It is in the interests of the profession to resolve as many disputes without litigation and formal hearings, except for more complex cases.' Shaw was launching a mediation kit. The kit includes guidelines for practitioners involved in mediation, precedent documents including the 'Agreement to Mediate', an ADR clause, and the Charter on Mediation Practice.[76]

13.23

We have already discussed the lawyer's role as a mediator in family law disputes in Chapters 7, 8 and 12. There are many other professionals who play a role in solving disputes in the family law system. Staying away from adversarial proceedings has become the norm in family matters. It has become known in the family law context as primary dispute resolution (PDR). PDR includes mediation, arbitration and counselling. It is available under numerous provisions of the Family Law Act 1975 (Cth).[77] The Law Council of Australia initiated a plan, which has been endorsed by the Standing Committee of Attorneys-General, under which courts have been able to apply substantially uniform national rules on referring disputes to mediation. The plan includes court-annexed mediation model legislation and model rules of court.[78] The Law Council has also adopted Ethical Standards for Mediations which was revised in February 2000.

Evaluation of ADR

It is very difficult to evaluate whether ADR processes are better than traditional court processes. According to the ALRC in Issue Paper 20:[79]

13.24

---

73. For example, see *Solicitors Handbook* (Qld), para 7.00.
74. See the introduction to the *Guidelines for Legal Representation in a Meditation* and fn 2.
75. Barristers' Rules (NSW) r 17A, (Qld) r 18 and Model Rules r 12.3.
76. 'Practical ADR resources for a changing culture' (August 1999) *Law Society J* (NSW) 72. The mediation kit is available at www.lawsocnsw.asn.au/resources/ mediation_kit.
77. See ss 14F–G, 16, 16A–16B, 19A–19D, 62B–62F. For a detailed discussion of these provisions and of PDR see Astor and Chinkin (above), pp 330–41.
78. The plan is published in 'Mediation plan endorsed' (1995) 30 *Australian Lawyer* 15–16.
79. Issues Paper 20 (above), para 9.34.

... the increased use of ADR may lead to a decrease in litigious or adversarial behaviour, foster a better relationship between parties to a dispute or result in a higher level of compliance with outcomes. These benefits are very difficult to measure.

There are a number of Australian reports which have tried to evaluate ADR programs. The ALRC in Issue Paper 20 states:[80]

While there is no conclusive evidence about the cost and benefits of court related ADR, many studies suggest that there are significant benefits for some types of disputes. For example, evaluation by the Federal Court of its mediation program suggests that court related mediation is beneficial and worthy of expansion.

The ALR in its discussion paper and final report came to the conclusion that ADR was no panacea for curing the problems of the adversary system, that it was not suitable for all cases and there were difficulties in evaluating the effectiveness of ADR programs.[81] The Commission refers to the fact that ADR has had in the United States 'too little impact on overcrowded dockets and litigation expenses'.[82] The ALRC quotes Sir Gerard Brennan, former Chief Justice of the High Court, that litigants may find that 'solutions reached by diversionary procedures may deliver cheaper but also a less satisfying form of justice'.[83]

Chief Justice Brennan's views are at the heart of the debate as to whether or not the use of ADR is detrimental to the rights of litigants. People who are from disadvantaged groups and cannot afford litigation, such as women in family law, may be forced into ADR. Governments may support inappropriate ADR programs in order to save money, but to the detriment of the rights of litigants.[84] Those who oppose ADR also argue that litigants who choose or are referred to ADR are giving up their rights to adequate discovery, appeal and other protections of the court system.[85] Furthermore, ADR prevents people from fully airing their grievances by diffusing rather than resolving a conflict. It 'privatises' disputes, removing them from the public area and thereby eliminates any precedent value or any public scrutiny.[86]

As a result ADR helps maintain the present structure and its unequal distribution of power, discriminating against women and other weak

---

80.   Issues Paper 20 (above), para 9.35. For the evaluation by the Federal Court see M Black, 'The courts, tribunals and ADR' (1996) 7 *Australian Dispute Resolution J* 138, 143.

81.   ALRC Report No 89 (above), para 6.59 and ALRC DP 62 (above), paras 9.35–9.36 and fn 62.

82.   ALRC Report No 89 (above), para 6.59.

83.   ALRC Report No 89 (above), para 6.60.

84.   ALRC DP 62 (above), para 9.36 quoting from the Access to Justice Advisory Committee (AJAC) report, para 11.5.

85.   See R Reuben, 'The Dark Side of ADR' (February 1994) *California Lawyer* 53. He argues that ADR may help to unclog the courts, but it endangers constitutional protections and provides justice only for those who can afford to pay for it. D Luban, 'Settlements and the Erosion of the Public Realm' (1995) 83 *Georgia LJ* 2619, 2622–40 argues that litigation involving 'public questions' needs to be contested in open court where fairness rules prevail. See also J Resnik, 'Many Doors? Closing Doors? Alternative Dispute Resolution and Adjudication' (1995) 10 *Ohio State J of Dispute Resolution* 211.

86.   ALRC DP 62, para 9.36 quoting from the AJAC report, para 11.5.

groups.[87] Judges have thus been warned that encouraging parties to utilise ADR may not be in the best interests of the clients. Judges should be made aware that they may be sending the parties to solve their problems under a lower standard of ethics.[88] There is a countervailing argument that ADR is a remedy for the disadvantaged in the sense that, sometimes, it is available only to the wealthy who can afford to 'rent a judge': these people are thus able to jump the queue and have their dispute heard before those in the traditional court.[89] Furthermore, the disadvantaged may not be able to afford an expensive court action and ADR offers them a remedy.

In Australia the Federal Court has offered a voluntary Assisted Dispute Resolution program for most civil matters in New South Wales since 1987, which spread to the rest of the country by 1991.[90] The Federal Court eventually was granted the right to refer proceedings or a part of a proceeding for mediation, without the consent of the parties, but not for arbitration.[91] The Federal Court programs have been facilitated by courts in New South Wales since 1994.[92]

13.25

The New South Wales Supreme Court has made arbitration available for personal injury matters, for partnership and family disputes, and commercial matters.[93] In late 2000 amendments were adopted in New South Wales that permitted the Supreme Court, except in criminal cases, to refer proceedings or a part of a proceeding for mediation, without the consent of the parties.[94] Section 26 of the Civil Procedure Act 2005 (NSW) extended compulsory mediation to other courts in New South Wales. There are programs available in other courts throughout Australia, and the Law Council of Australia has on its website (www.lawcouncil.asn.au) a 'Summary of ADR Procedures in Australian Courts, Tribunals and Commissions', last updated in January 2001. Some examples of these programs are: the Family Law

---

87. D Rhode and D Luban, *Legal Ethics*, 2nd ed, Foundation Press, Mineola, 1995, pp 783–4. They state: 'Mediation between parties with unequal power may reinforce their inequality and encourage negotiation of rights that should be non-negotiable. For example, divorcing wives have often traded necessary child support to avert custody battles and battered wives may agree to avoid "nagging" in exchange for their husbands' promises to refrain from physical assaults.' This quote has been removed from later editions of this book. In the latest edition, D Rhode and D Luban, *Legal Ethics*, 4th ed, Foundation Press, New York, 2004, the authors state at p 496: 'Given the difficulties for mediators in simultaneously addressing power disparities and maintaining impartiality, many experts believe that certain cases involving such disparities are inappropriate for mediation.' There is a comprehensive discussion of mediation at pp 488–97.
88. J Parke, 'Lawyers as Negotiators: Time For a Code of Ethics' (1993) 4 *Australian Dispute Resolution J* 216, 218–19.
89. Rhode and Luban (above) (2nd ed), p 783.
90. See H Astor and C Chinkin (above), pp 11–22, for the history of ADR and also pp 23–51 for its theoretical basis. See also Federal Court of Australia Act 1976 (Cth) ss 53A–53C and Federal Court Rules, Order 72.
91. Federal Court of Australia Act 1976 (Cth) s 53A(1A).
92. Courts Legislation (Mediation and Evaluation) Act 1994 (NSW).
93. Supreme Court Act 1970 (NSW) Pt 7B and s 76B; Commercial Arbitration Act 1984 (NSW); Arbitration (Civil Actions) Act 1983 (NSW); Supreme Court Rules, Pts 72A–72B and Practice Notes No 88 and 89.
94. Supreme Court Act 1970 (NSW) with new ss 110K–110L. For criticism of the changes, see B Walker and A Bell, 'Bar News' (Spring 2000) *Journal of NSW Bar Association* 7–8.

Court,[95] which has mandatory mediation requirements,[96] the Supreme Court of South Australia,[97] the Supreme Court of Victoria,[98] the Supreme Court of the Northern Territory,[99] the Supreme Court of Queensland[100] and the Supreme Court of Tasmania, which has mandatory mediation,[101] and any other court in Tasmania.[102]

Lawyers and ADR

13.26   ADR has traditionally been the basis for solving disputes in the industrial relations area. There are also developing ADR systems outside court jurisdiction.[103] There are many organisations that are conducting courses and training for mediation and other ADR processes but there is no single body, within any state or federally, to set standards of competence.[104] There is thus a need for a national certification process with proper and uniform standards for accreditation. A pilot program for national certification of family mediators that was carried out in Canada and later[105] implemented could serve as a basis for our own programs.[106]

---

95.   Family Law Act 1975 (Cth) ss 14–19B and s 43(d). There are other areas where mediation may be more appropriate within the family law context. For example, there are strong arguments for giving less power to judges in dealing with access or custody to children in spouse abuse cases and instead concentrating on promoting change through collective action. See L Neilson, 'Spousal Abuse, Children and the Courts: The Case for Social Rather than Legal Change' (1997) 12 *Canadian J of Law and Society* 101.

96.   Family Law Act 1995 (Cth) s 79(9).

97.   The Supreme Court has adopted rules that virtually compel its judges to be involved in mediation. See *Current Topics* (1994) 68 *ALJ* 555. See also Supreme Court Practice Direction No 12 and Civil Procedure Rule 76.

98.   Supreme Court Rules, Orders 48:12 and 50; Supreme Court Act 1986 (Vic), s 24A and s 27.

99.   Supreme Court Rules, Order 48.

100.   Supreme Court Act 1991 (Qld) ss 94–116.

101.   See 'Summary of ADR Procedures in Australian Courts, Tribunals and Commissions 2001' at www.lawcouncil.asn.au, which states that mandatory rules are to be adopted.

102.   The Alternative Dispute Resolution Act, January 2001, s 5 allows referral for mediation or neutral evaluation session by any court. Under s 6 the parties to the mediation have the right to withdraw at any time.

103.   For a number of interesting articles on ADR see (1993) 56 *The Mod LR*.

104.   Australian Law Reform Commission, Issues Paper 20 (above), para 9.21.

105.   Priest (above), p 54.

106.   P English and L Neilson with W Hacking, *National Certification Implementation Pilot Project Report*, 1999, Department of Justice, Canada, Kitchener, Ontario: Family Mediation Canada. See also L Neilson and P English with J Bradley, 'The Role of Interest-Based Facilitation in Designing Accreditation Standards: The Canadian Experience', July 2000, to be published.

The various legal professional bodies and private mediation organisations in Australia have set up systems to certify lawyers and others to act as mediators and arbitrators[107] and many practitioners are urging clients to make use of ADR. In the United States in some jurisdictions it is considered poor professional conduct if an attorney does not first try to recommend ADR to a client. We have already referred to the Law Society's Model Rules and the Barristers' Rules in Queensland and New South Wales which require the communication to clients of the availability of ADR. In civil litigation the Law Society of New South Wales *Guidelines for Legal Representatives in a Mediation* states that the Law Society in various directives has 'encouraged solicitors to advise clients of the advantages of ADR'.

The New South Wales Law Society has also issued *Revised Guidelines for Solicitors Who Act as Mediators*. The guidelines are not binding but do provide an important framework for mediators.

ADR organisations have formulated their own standards that are more comprehensive than those of legal professional bodies, but their power to sanction is limited. The ALRC approved of 'harmonisation of relevant standards and rules of ethical conduct for legal and non-legal ADR practitioners'.[108] The ALRC recommended that the Law Council of Australia should include in its national ADR model practice rules that practitioners acting for clients in ADR processes and lawyer-neutrals be required to participate in 'good faith'.[109]

Access to the system

Parker has pointed out in *Just Lawyers* that in the past lawyers have dominated access to the legal system.[110] As Kafka wrote in *The Trial*, his famous parable of the futility of one man trying to gain entry into the system: 'Before the law stands a doorkeeper.' Parker argues that lawyers have blocked legal justice by their domination of access. Without a lawyer it is difficult to gain this access. Although, as Parker states, lawyers are 'doorkeepers to many rooms';[111] often the use of a lawyer results in access being restricted to one 'room' — the court system. She feels that lawyers are

13.27

---

107. Private bodies such as Lawyers Engaged in Alternative Dispute Resolution, the Institute of Arbitrators and Mediators Australia, Australian Dispute Resolution Association and the Australian Commercial Dispute Centre have established registration or accreditation schemes. Various law societies and bar associations have also established ADR schemes. ALRC DP 62, *Review of the federal civil justice system*, August 1999, para 4.35 and fn 73. Also see the qualifications required in *Revised Guidelines for Solicitors Who Act as Mediators* (NSW) r 3.1. These guidelines now have been followed by the Commercial Dispute Resolution Committee. See also Professional Conduct Rules (WA) r 7A. There are other bodies involved with ADR, such as the Australian Institute of Family Law Arbitrators and Mediators, Centre of Dispute Resolution and Mediation Association of Victoria, Mediation Association of the Northern Territory, National Dispute Centre, South Australian Dispute Resolution Association and Western Australian Dispute Resolution Association: see www.lawcouncil.asn.au.
108. ALRC Report No 89, *Managing Justice*, February 2000, paras 3.118–3.120.
109. ALRC Report No 89 (above), Recommendation 20, at pp 26 and 240.
110. C Parker, *Lawyers' Just, Lawyers: Regulation and Access to Justice*, Oxford University Press, New York, 1999.
111. Parker (above), Chapters 1 and 3.

important for access to the many new rooms being made available, but other actors have a part to play. She says that:[112]

> Improvements in access to justice could be made if we free access to justice policy-making from legalistic over-reliance on processes of law. This does not mean severing issues of justice from law, but seeking out the potential for interdependence between legal and non-legal means of justice. Set within a broader context of participation in social movement politics, democratic representation, and civic education for the respect of rights. The aim is a culture which maximises both the doing of justice spontaneously and informally under the shadow of the law, and the accessibility of legal and semi-legal remedies when injustice is done.

13.28   Parker's views as summarised in this quote are found in Chapter 4. They involve a system of checking injustice by moving up and down a pyramid of access to justice options. Parker's pyramid has formal legal justice at the apex, informal justice in the middle and justice according to indigenous ordering on the bottom. The formal justice at the top would act as a check on 'problems of oppression and domination' lower down, while indigenous ordering can go up the pyramid to access increased options for meaningful resolution of their own disputes. Parker says:[113]

> As informal justice was made more accountable to public justice the base of the pyramid would get larger because people prefer to settle matters lower down when they found that matters could be settled in a way that protected their rights at that level. Such institutions of dispute resolution would maximise the effect of law in encouraging voluntary aversion to injustice, and provide means and techniques to restore justice quickly at the most informal level. Formal justice would remain (or rather become) available whenever necessary ... In an integrated pyramid of access to justice options, communal relations of justice are enhanced by formal justice and vice versa.

This system works when access to other levels is available to the vast majority in our society.

13.29   Menkel-Meadow also warns that the fact that lawyers are getting more involved in ADR makes it even more important that these doors to justice do not become 'corrupted by the persistence of adversarial values. Lawyers and third party neutrals will clearly have to learn new roles to play in mediation'.[114] These new roles are complicated in our multicultural society in which the adversary system seems even more inadequate.[115] There is already criticism that opportunistic lawyers have created an 'ADR industry' and usurped the mediation field.[116] De Maria has said that 'the colonisation of mediation by lawyers ... will mean that mediation skills will become professional artefacts ... locked up within the lawyering role, not to be shared, but to be given down, at a fee'.[117] De Maria's comments were

---

112. Parker (above), p 81.
113. Parker (above), p 76.
114. See Menkel-Meadow, n 32 (above), p 37.
115. Australia has similar problems to those in the United States, with the adversary system not being able to deal with multiculturalism dispute settlement. On the United States see Menkel-Meadow (above), pp 28–38.
116. Ardagh (above), p 75.
117. W De Maria, 'Social Work and Mediation: Hemlock is the Flavour of the Month?' (1992) 45 *Australian Social Work* 17, 18.

written in 1992 and since then lawyers have dominated the field of ADR turning it into a very profitable business.

As more litigants make use of ADR there seems to be the necessity for ethical rules for the many lawyers acting as mediators and arbitrators. Such rules have already been adopted in some jurisdictions[118]and by the Law Council of Australia.[119]

It is debatable whether traditional ethical rules for lawyer mediators are the answer. Given the fact that lawyers are already making ADR legalistic, do we need more rules to apply and decipher? A leading Canadian expert on mediation, Linda Neilson, writes:[120]

13.30

> ... creating and memorizing rules is not what professional ethics is about. Rules are not of much help; mediators need to understand, not so much rules, as why certain mediator behaviours are necessary in the context of mediation. In the absence of a framework which promotes self-reflection and analysis of ethics in social, interpersonal contexts, the only way to guide practitioner conduct is to create new rules. Commonly those new rules are wrong as new social contexts arise. If, however, one defines and analyses ethics in terms of interests and values, codes can be of some assistance — can guide practitioners towards ethical professional conduct — when new circumstances, not specifically considered in the codes, arise. What is needed is to take a course of action, not from specific rules, but from their analysis of the interests and values operating in the context of the mediation setting.

Neilson said that if ethical issues are to be examined they have to be applied to:

13.31

1. *Client interests* (needs) — for example, self-empowerment, enhanced understanding of conflict and enhancement of communication skills to resolve conflict, confidentiality and so on;

2. *Mediator interests* (needs) — for example, promoting client self-determination — resisting pressure to impose solutions, working with clients so as to be able to effectively and equitably participate, full disclosure from clients, facilitating agreements that produce no harm, generating public confidence in mediation process and so on;

3. *Interests of the Mediation Discipline* — qualified, competent and ethical practitioners, promotion and development of the discipline, generating client demand — public confidence in equity and fairness of mediation, client satisfaction and so on; and

4. *Social Interests in Mediation* — development of fair, equitable, affordable conflict resolution processes the public can trust, reduction of the social costs of conflict management/resolution, promotion of peace and harmony and so on.[121]

Neilson is thus calling for a flexible use of the ethical rules and for lawyers and participants in the process to see the underlying values of the rules.

13.32

---

118. *Revised Guidelines for Solicitors Who Act as Mediators* (NSW) and Professional Conduct Rules (WA) r 7A. Rule 9 of the Rules of Practice (Tas) prohibits a practitioner from being a mediator without the permission of the Tasmanian Law Society. By contrast r 74 ((d) and (g)) of the Barristers' Rules (NSW and Qld) permits barristers to represent a client in mediation and to act as an arbitrator or mediator.
119. Law Council 'Ethical standards for mediators', updated February 2000 at www.lawcouncil.asn.au.
120. Private email communication to the author, August 2000.
121. Private email communication (above).

Vial, a Victorian lawyer working exclusively as a mediator, says that the important question to be addressed is: 'Whose mediation is it and why is it being conducted? ... Working as a mediator is about understanding and working with the dynamics of how people are relating with each other during the whole mediation process.'[122] The use of lawyers' ethical rules in this context must be flexible and not only for the benefit of the profession.

As legal costs have escalated, clients are also more willing to accept negotiated settlements. In the past when there has not been a third party (judge, arbitrator, mediator) lawyers negotiated within a context of different ethical standards. It was thought different rules operated outside the adversary system because there were different expectations as to ethical behaviour.[123]

Today, negotiation is an important area of ADR and the development of ethical rules to control lawyers' behaviour is essential.[124] In the next chapter we will look at the rules that have developed within the context of duties of fairness and candour. As will be shown, these rules have placed certain restrictions on how far lawyers can go in representing their clients.

---

122. R Vial, 'Mediation: Who For?' (1997) 101 *Victorian Bar News* 30.
123. See M Schwartz, 'The Professionalism and Accountability of Lawyers' (1978) 66 *U of California LR* 669, 677.
124. Parke (above). See also M Gaines, 'A proposed conflict of interest rule for attorney-mediators' (1998) 73 *Washington LR* 699.

14

DUTIES OF FAIRNESS AND CANDOUR

INTRODUCTION

In the first part of this chapter we will look at the professional rules on duties of fairness and candour in the context of negotiation. In the second part we will discuss the duties of fairness, the means and methods lawyers pursue in their clients' interests, and in the third part the duties of candour and the use of honesty in promoting the merits of their clients' cases. In Chapter 15 we will discuss the special problems of candour and fairness in certain aspects of the criminal trial.[1] The questions that we must ask are — What are the limits placed on lawyers in representing their clients? May a lawyer, for example, use trickery or deception or make unsupported allegations or try to intimidate the opposing party? May a lawyer file frivolous actions, seek unnecessary adjournments, abuse discovery or court procedures? May a lawyer knowingly make false or misleading statements or conceal or fail to disclose information required to be disclosed by law? May a lawyer assist his or her client in conduct that the lawyer knows to be illegal or fraudulent?

Lawyers sometimes by their behaviour will breach both their duties of fairness and candour, for example acting unfairly while at the same time knowingly misleading the court. Breaches of these duties can lead to disciplinary action, contempt of court, orders to pay costs, awards of damages and disapproval from their colleagues and judges, leading to future mistrust.

14.1

---

1. The outline in these two chapters generally follows that in our book and the chapters were a research source for some of my material: see J Disney, J Basten, P Redmond and S Ross, *Lawyers*, 2nd ed, Law Book Co, Sydney, 1986, Chapters 24 and 25.

DUTIES OF FAIRNESS AND CANDOUR IN NEGOTIATION[2]

Negotiation problem

14.2 Gurnsey has set up a problem where a borrower wishes to obtain at least $5 million from a bank (lender) at no greater price than the prime interest rate plus 4 per cent:[3]

> The borrower is in great need of the funds as all other lenders have turned him down. The lender wants to expand its business loans and is actively seeking new customers. Its preliminary investigation of the borrower's books leads the lender to believe he is a good credit risk. The lender is willing to lend him $8 million at the prime rate plus 2 per cent.
>
> May the borrower's lawyer, who knows all the facts state:
>
> (1) My client has been investigating the possibility of borrowing money. Bank X has agreed to lend him $10 million at the prime rate plus 2 per cent. Can you match that? ... [Is this statement a lie?]
>
> Knowing that the past years have been progressively decreasing sales, however, may the lawyer ... say:
>
> (2) My client's company is on the move and poised for an expansion which will double sales. [Is this a lie, or is it merely acceptable puffery? ...]
>
> (3) My client *does not want* to accept less than $10 million at prime plus 2 per cent ... [Is this a truthful statement?]
>
> (4) My client *will not agree* to borrow any of your money unless you agree to charge no more than prime plus two and agree to lend $10 million ... [Is this an excessive demand?]

Does it make a difference that most people are aware that the normal rule is that people will ask for as much as they can get? Is there any distinction as to truthfulness even if there is this expectation? The use of a term such as 'will not' is very different to 'does not want to'.[4] What is the truth in these statements by the borrower's lawyer? Is the borrower's lawyer acting fairly by making these statements?

Lawyers acting unfairly

14.3 We seem to have accepted that in negotiations lawyers will act unfairly and lack candour, and many clients expect this. The joke often told is: a client is informed by email or fax from his or her lawyer stating, 'we have achieved a fair settlement for all'. The client responds with 'I could have reached a fair settlement by myself!'. Statements such as: 'My client won't accept a dollar less than' a specific sum are made all the time, when the lawyer knows that the client will accept less. Lawyers will still use what is called 'puffery' and make believe they have no authority to accept a different settlement. Rhode says that: 'Those who argue that exaggeration or equivocation is harmless generally assume that the opposing party will recognize puffing for what it is. But if that were always true, the practice would also be ineffective. Puffing continues because sometimes it works and some opponents are deceived.'[5]

For a discussion of the types, approaches and meaning of negotiation see H Astor and C Chinkin, *Dispute Resolution in Australia*, 2nd ed, LexisNexis Butterworths, Sydney, 2002, Chapter 4.

3. T Guernsey, 'Truthfulness in Negotiation' (1982) 17 *U of Richmond LR* 99, 103.

4. Guernsey (above).

5. D Rhode, *Professional Responsibility: Ethics by the Pervasive Method*, 2nd ed, 1998, p 347.

Lawyers will even state at a pre-trial conference to the judge and the opposition that they have no settlement authority, although they have been given settlement instructions. As Rubin states:[6]

> ... estimable members of the Bar support the thesis that a lawyer may not misrepresent a fact in controversy but may misrepresent matters that pertain to his [or her] authority or negotiating strategy because this is expected by the adversary.

A leading American expert, Professor Charles Craver, who taught courses and workshops on legal negotiation and settlement, would begin by stating: 'I've never been involved in legal negotiations where both sides didn't lie.'[7]

Sometimes if a lawyer is so misleading in the negotiations, he or she will be found to be in breach of the doctrine of fairness. In a New Jersey case the lawyer for the owner failed to inform the lessee that the shopping centre where the shop was located was going into foreclosure. When this occurred the lessee was evicted by the new owner and suffered significant losses from refurbishing the premises. The court, in holding the lawyer liable, said that besides a lawyer's duties to his or her client there was also a duty to 'act fairly and in good faith'. The lawyer should have at least informed his client to disclose the information and, if the client refused, to withdraw from the representation.[8]

Professional rules

The duties of fairness and candour have been expressed generally by a number of professional bodies in Australia. The Law Council's Model Rules r 18.1 states: 'A practitioner must not knowingly make a false statement to the opponent in relation to the case (including its compromise).' There are identical rules for solicitors and barristers in New South Wales.[9] The Professional Conduct Rules (WA) r 3.1 states: 'A practitioner shall not attempt to further his [or her] client's case by unfair or dishonest means.'[10] The Council of the Law Society of New South Wales has taken a very strong 'general duty' approach in Caveat No 99, issued March 1997. It states:[11]

> The Law Society is of the view that a solicitor who lies to another party, whether on behalf of, or on the instructions of, a client acts dishonourably and is guilty of professional misconduct. A solicitor has a clear duty to act honestly and fairly in all dealings not only with the solicitor's own client but also with courts and third parties.

14.4

The Law Council's Model Rules r 28 (also r 34 of the Professional Conduct and Practice Rules (NSW)) states:

14.5

---

6. A Rubin, 'A Causerie on Lawyers' Ethics in Negotiation' (1975) 35 *Louisiana LR* 577, 585.
7. L Lempert, 'In Settlement Talks, Does Telling the Truth have its Limits' (1988) 2 *Inside Litigation* 1, extracted in D Rhode and D Luban, *Legal Ethics*, 4th ed, 2004, Foundation Press, New York, NY, p 470.
8. *Davin v Daham* (2000) 746 A 2d 1034 (NJ Super AD).
9. Barristers' Rules (NSW) r 51 [(Qld) r 52 and Professional Conduct and Practice Rules (NSW) r 23-A.51].
10. A similar rule exists for barristers: see Barristers' Rules (NSW) rr 3 and 51 [(Qld) r 3 and Law Council's Model Rules r 52]   also discuss the matter in the introduction to 'Relations with other practitioners' and the introduction to 'Relations with third parties'.
11. See F Riley, *New South Wales Solicitors Manual*, Law Society of New South Wales, Sydney, 1988, looseleaf, paras 3390, 4595. In the new edition, Law Society of NSW and Butterworths, Sydney, 2000, there is no reference to the caveat.

> A practitioner must not, in any communication with another person on behalf of a client:
>
> 28.1 represent to that person that anything is true which the practitioner knows, or reasonably believes, is untrue; or
>
> 28.2 make any statement that is calculated to mislead or intimidate the other person, and which grossly exceeds the legitimate assertion of the rights or entitlement of the practitioner's client ...

Academic views

14.6   These are noble expressions, but at least two textbooks[12] in Australia by lawyers ignore the concept of fairness and candour in the art of negotiation. McCarthy lists the following tactics among others:

- ❑ make extreme demands to lower the opponents' expectations and thus widen the bargaining area;
- ❑ place the opposition under a long period of physical and mental strain to impair their competence and thus make it easier to obtain concessions;
- ❑ become impatient, brusque, show frustration and issue deadlines;
- ❑ make knowingly false statements (lying).[13]

14.7   In another text Hawkins et al state that the negotiator should use false demands. These include the following: (1) bluffing or presenting false material that you have more than you do; (2) feinting by moving in a different direction to the real goal; (3) using paradoxical attention, having the other lawyer take action on a particular item by falsely making him or her believe that you do not want them to consider that action. This text also gives as strategy:

- ❑ discredit the opposing lawyers or their client by associating them with some unsavoury connection;
- ❑ provide biased statistical information;
- ❑ threaten the opposition by stating you will behave in a manner that will be detrimental to them, unless they make a concession.[14]

14.8   It would appear that the use of 'irrational', 'aggressive' and 'posturing' tactics is 'already well entrenched in negotiation practice in Australia'.[15] Negotiations, unlike courtroom practice, allow unethical lawyers to engage in unfair and untruthful tactics. They can act in such a way knowing that they will rarely be discovered and, even if they are, there are few if any effective available sanctions. The main sanction is that lawyers who 'encounter each other repeatedly will penalize aggressive bargainers; cooperation works better over the long run'.[16] When the negotiations are

---

12. The views from these books and two important American books are outlined in J Parke, 'Lawyers as Negotiators: Time for A Code of Ethics?' (1993) 4 *Australian Dispute Resolution J* 216, 221–2.

13. P McCarthy, *Developing Negotiating Skills and Behaviour*, CCH Australia, North Ryde, 1989, Chapter 6.

14. Hawkins et al, *The Legal Negotiator: A Handbook for Managing Legal Negotiations More Effectively*, Longman Professional, Melbourne, 1991, pp 136–44.

15. Parke (above), p 223.

16. D Rhode (above), p 338. For 'principled' negotiation that rejects adversarialism see C Menkel-Meadow, 'Toward Another View of Legal Negotiation: The Structure of Problem-Solving' (1984) 31 *UCLA LR* 754 and R Harris, 'Contrasting "principled negotiation" with the adversarial model' (1990) 20 *Victoria University of Wellington LR* 91.

under a provision in a contract to negotiate in 'good faith', courts can apply this provision if it has been breached.[17]

Need for code of ethics

There is obviously a need for a code of ethics in negotiation, which would include effective sanctions.[18] Fisher has proposed a code of negotiation practices:[19]

> Do not look upon those on the other side as enemies but rather as partners with whom cooperation is essential and greatly in the interest of your client … It is not enough to seek a fair result. Among results that fall within the range of fairness, you should press with diligence and skill toward that result that best satisfies your client's interest consistent with being fair and socially acceptable … Another of your roles is to help your clients take long-term considerations properly into account, come to understand their enlightened self-interest, and to pursue it … Two lawyers, negotiating with each other, sometimes best function as co-mediators, trying to bring their clients together. Finally, as a lawyer and negotiator, you behave toward those with whom you negotiate in ways that incorporate the highest moral standards of civilization. Your conduct should be such that you regard it as a praiseworthy model for others to emulate and such that, if it became known, it would reflect credit on you and the bar. You should feel no obligation to be less candid for a client than you would be for yourself, and should not behave in ways that would justifiably damage your reputation for integrity.

14.9

If ethical rules are adopted, any information or admissions that are disclosed during negotiation would be subject to a 'without prejudice' requirement, that is, the information or admissions cannot be later used in court against either party if the negotiations fail. The 'without prejudice' requirement developed under the common law for civil cases makes the contents of the discussions confidential. The main reason for the policy is the desire to support effective negotiated agreements and thus avoid litigation. It should be noted that the 'without prejudice' privilege does have exceptions and is not a blanket prohibition of evidence of what was discussed.[20] The common law in this area has been restated in the Evidence Act 1995 (Cth) s 131.[21]

14.10

American professional rules

ABA Model Rules r 4.1 calls for fairness and candour. It requires lawyers not to 'knowingly make a false statement of material fact or law' when representing a client in their dealings with third parties. Comment [1] to r 4.1 says the requirement does not include any:

14.11

---

17. *Aiton v Transfield* (1999) NSWSC 996 and *WA v Taylor (Njamal People)* (1996) 134 FLR 211.
18. Parke (above), pp 223, 225–8.
19. R Fisher, 'A Code of Negotiation Practices for Lawyers' (1985) 1 *Negotiation J* 105. Fisher includes seven goals in negotiating which include: clients get the best available outcome and their interests are well-satisfied, the settlement is reasonably fair to all and thus future negotiations will be easier.
20. See Hunter, Cameron and Henning, *Litigation 1 — Civil Procedure*, 7th ed, LexisNexis Butterworths, Sydney, 2005, paras 8.92–8.100 for more details on the 'without prejudice' privilege.
21. The wording of s 131 was found to be clear in a recent case, *Silver Fox Pty Ltd v Lenard Pty Ltd* (2004) 214 ALR 261.

... affirmative duty to inform an opposing party of relevant facts. A misrepresentation can occur if the lawyer incorporates or affirms a statement of another person that the lawyer knows is false. Misrepresentations can also occur by partially true but misleading statements or omissions that are the equivalent of affirmative false statements ...

Comment [2] says that 'statements of material fact' depend on the circumstances. Under general conventions accepted in negotiation certain statements are not taken as material facts. Examples given are estimates of price or value placed on the subject of a transaction or the intention of one's client as to what is acceptable. The Model Rules thus support Rubin's view that there are different rules as to fairness and candour in the context of negotiation.[22] This approach that permits puffing as a generally 'accepted convention' has been criticised because it 'offers no criteria for identifying which conventions count, and tolerates practices that should be subject to critical re-examination'.[23] The ABA Model Rules for negotiation are so general that White argues that it would be 'better to have no rule than to have one so widely violated as to be a continuing hypocrisy that may (compromise) the application of the remaining rules'.[24] Rhode disagrees, stating: 'Even where non-compliance is common, legal and ethical requirements serve important societal functions. They clarify standards, remove excuses, and provide some support for lawyers who wish to resist client or collegial pressure to cut ethical corners.'[25]

DUTIES OF FAIRNESS

Hopeless cases, unreasonable expense or delay

Professional rules

14.12 Western Australia, Victoria and New South Wales appear to be the only Australian jurisdictions with rulings on this subject. Rule 13.4(b) of the Professional Conduct Rules (WA) states: 'Counsel shall at all times: ... (b) use his best endeavours to avoid unnecessary expense and waste of the court's time ...'. There is a similar American rule. ABA Model Rules r 3.2 states: 'A lawyer shall make reasonable efforts to expedite litigation consistent with the interests of the client.' In Victoria the Professional Conduct and Practice Rules 2003 r 1.2 states: 'A practitioner must ... use the practitioner's best endeavours to complete legal work as soon as reasonably possible.'

14.13 There were new rules adopted in January 2000 for New South Wales barristers and later by the Law Society. Under the section 'Efficient

---

22. ABA Formal Opinion 93-370 gives as a reason for non-disclosure to a judge of the limits of settlement authority the fact that it is a material fact. Thus, the judge should not ask this information.

23. Rhode (above), p 369. Rhode refers to E Norton, 'Bargaining and the Ethics of Process' (1989) 64 *NYU LR* 493, 538.

24. J White, 'Machiavelli and the Bar: Ethical Limitations on Lying in Negotiations' (1980) *American Bar Foundation Research J* 926, 937–8.

25. Rhode (above), pp 359–60. Rhode refers to an ABA study of 2500 litigators which found that the ethical rules did act as some guidance on negotiation behaviour. Over 40 per cent believed that amending the rules was an effective way of improving standards.

administration of justice', Barristers' Rules r 41 requires barristers to seek to ensure that they do work 'in sufficient time to enable compliance with' requirements of the court. They must give a warning as soon as they have reasonable grounds to believe that they 'may not complete any such work on time'. Under r 42 the barrister must seek to: '(a) confine the case to identified issues which are genuinely in dispute; (b) have the case ready to be heard as soon as practicable; (c) present the identified issues in dispute clearly and succinctly; (d) limit evidence, including cross-examination, to that which is reasonably necessary to advance and protect the client's interest ...; and (e) occupy as short a time in court as is reasonably necessary to advance and protect the client's interests ...'.[26] The identical rules for advocate solicitors are under r 23-A15 of the Professional Conduct and Practice Rules (NSW).

These rules have caused advocates to be more aware that their work affects the court's business. The Bar Association said: 'The timeliness of a barrister's work should not, therefore, be left solely to regulation by engagements between counsel and instructing solicitors and clients.'[27]

Rule 42 already had support from existing Barristers' Rules r 19. Rule 19 protects barristers from pressure by clients or solicitors. It allows barristers to exercise independent forensic judgment by confining the case to the real issues, presenting it quickly and simply and by informing the court of any persuasive authority against the client's case. Rule 19 combined with r 42 makes clear that 'barristers cannot justify dilatory or delinquent conduct with respect to the procedural rules or directions of a court by invoking the instructions or desires of the client'. These rules make it more evident that the duty to the court is paramount.[28] Under the Barristers' Rules (NSW) r 100(d) [(Qld) r 106(d)] there is also a right for a barrister to return a brief accepted under a conditional costs agreement if 'the barrister has the firm view that the client has no reasonable prospects of success or of achieving a result better than the offer'. **14.14**

Case law

The New South Wales Barristers' Rules concerning delay were seen by some commentators as the 'Callinan amendment' — named after the judge on the High Court.[29] The rules were designed to prevent delaying tactics such as those of Justice Callinan (when acting as senior counsel), his co-counsel and the instructing solicitor in the famous case of *White Industries (Qld) Pty Ltd v Flower & Hart*.[30] The *White* case has been widely discussed.[31] **14.15**

---

26. There is also r 42A which requires barristers to inform the opponent as soon as possible of an application to adjourn any hearing.

27. *Bar Brief* (Newsletter of the NSW Bar Association) Special Edition, February 2000, p 5.

28. *Bar Brief* (above).

29. R Ackland, 'Lawyers in limbo as bar raised', *Sydney Morning Herald*, 10 March 2000, p 17.

30. (1998) 156 ALR 169. See also Goldberg J's judgment upheld on appeal (1999) 87 FCR 134. The 1993 Federal Court hearing is (1993) 45 FCR 134 and the original judgments by Ryan J were unreported in 1989 and 1990.

31. See L Hoffman, 'Solicitors Acting "Unreasonably"' (November 1998) *Protor (Queensland Law Society J)* 28; T Di Lallo, 'Personal Liability for Costs' (1999) 73 *Law Institute J (Vic)* 48; and M Yorkston, 'Practitioners' duties: Steady or increasing, clear or conflicting? Costs' (1999) 73 *Law Institute J (Vic)* 57, 59–60.

In the *White Industries* case Goldberg J found that the action filed was not to vindicate any right, but only to stall the collection of money due under the contract. Goldberg J found that the action was filed expressly to delay proceedings and that the instructing of counsel was part of these delaying tactics. Goldberg J said that the solicitor's actions in fighting everything might be considered legitimate litigation strategy but 'it is quite a different matter continuously to attempt to delay the progress of an action and avoid it being set down for trial'.

Goldberg J held that the solicitors, by initiating hopeless proceedings, had knowingly obstructed the course of justice. He ordered them to pay the opposing party's costs.[32] He fined the firm, Flower & Hart, \$3.6 million. Goldberg J also found that Justice Callinan, who was the senior counsel, and the junior counsels had given advice that, even if there was sufficient evidence of facts alleged, the client had an arguable, but a weak case. The judge found that counsel had advised the solicitors to institute proceedings immediately and not to wait until there was sufficient evidence because the defendant (White) was about to institute their own proceedings. Justice Callinan was a witness in the case and there were calls for his resignation or removal from the bench.[33] The Full Federal Court relied on *White Industries* when it said that 'unreasonable conduct must be more than acting on behalf of a client who has little or no prospect of success. There must be something akin to abuse of process; that is, using the proceeding for an ulterior purpose or without any, or any proper, consideration of the prospects of success'.[34] The *White Industries* case has become an important authority for abuse of process and has also been cited in other cases.[35] There are inherent and statutory powers for courts to order costs against lawyers. In *Myers v Elman*[36] the House of Lords used this inherent power because the lawyer's actions constituted 'negligence of a serious character' leading to 'useless costs to the other parties'. In criminal cases the courts will only make such an order if the lawyer's actions are 'serious misconduct'.[37]

Statutory rules

14.16   The court's statutory power is applied 'where costs are incurred improperly or without reasonable cause, or are wasted by undue delay or by any other misconduct or default'.[38] The court may also:[39]

---

32.   For his conclusions see 156 ALR 169 at 248.
33.   See the profile of Justice Callinan in the *Sydney Morning Herald*, 12 June 1999, p 11; see also the *Sydney Morning Herald*, 30 April 1998, p 5; the *Melbourne Age*, 26 June 1999, p 12; and C Merritt, 'The High Court judge who could hang his profession', *Australian Financial Review*, 25 July 1998, p 22. It is debatable that counsel behaviour in the *White Industries* case was unethical because the Queensland Bar Rules on the use of the court process are narrow in scope. There is not any rule that directly deals with the delay problem.
34.   *Levick v Deputy Commission of Taxation* [2000] FCA 674 at para 44.
35.   *Johnson Tiles Pty Ltd v Esso Australia Ltd* (1999) ATPR ¶141–679; *Abriel v Australian Guarantee Corp* BC9900134; [1999] FCA 50; *Cook v Pasminco (No 2)* (2000) 107 FCR 44.
36.   [1940] AC 282 at 290. See also *Sinclair Jones v Kay* [1988] 2 All ER 611 and *Gupta v Comer* [1991] 1 All ER 289.
37.   *Holden and Co v CPS* [1990] 1 All ER 368 (C of A).
38.   See, for example, Supreme Court Rules (NSW) Pt 52, r 66.
39.   Supreme Court Act 1970 (NSW) s 76C(1).

… in respect of a solicitor whose serious neglect, serious incompetence or serious misconduct delays, or contributes to delaying those proceedings … direct the solicitor to indemnify any party other than his or her client against the whole or any part of the costs payable by the party indemnified.

The Supreme Court Rules 1970 (NSW) were amended in March 2000 to tighten up procedures dealing with delay in the civil law cases. Chief Justice Spigelman said that their overriding purpose is 'to facilitate the just, quick and cheap resolution of the real issues in civil proceedings'. Spigelman said that the rules identify:[40]

❑ An obligation on the court to give effect to this purpose and on a party to civil proceedings to assist the court to further the purpose.

❑ Legal practitioners need to refrain from engaging in conduct that breaches their obligation to the court and any failure by them would be taken into consideration by the judge when awarding costs.

The Court Rules were followed and simplified in the Civil Procedure Act 2005 (NSW) and, under that Act, the Uniform Civil Procedure Rules 2005. The purpose of the Act is found under s 56 which states:

(1) The overriding purpose of this Act and of rules of court, in their application to civil proceedings, is to facilitate the just, quick and cheap resolution of the real issues in the proceedings.

(2) The court must seek to give effect to the overriding purpose when it exercises any power given to it by this Act or by rules of court and when it interprets any provision of this Act or of any such rule.

(3) A party to civil proceedings is under a duty to assist the court to further the overriding purpose and, to that effect, to participate in the processes of the court and to comply with directions and orders of the court.

(4) A solicitor or barrister must not, by his or her conduct, cause his or her client to be put in breach of the duty identified in subsection (3).

(5) The court may take into account any failure to comply with subsection (3) or (4) in exercising a discretion with respect to costs.

Under s 57 of the Act the objectives of case management are:

(1) For the purpose of furthering the overriding purpose referred to in section 56(1), proceedings in any court are to be managed having regard to the following objects:

(a) the just determination of the proceedings,

(b) the efficient disposal of the business of the court,

(c) the efficient use of available judicial and administrative resources,

(d) the timely disposal of the proceedings, and all other proceedings in the court, at a cost affordable by the respective parties …

14.17 The New South Wales courts now have the power to limit the number of witnesses and their time for testifying, and the time spent on submissions and on the case. A practitioner can be directed to notify a party estimating the trial length, the practitioner's costs and disbursements and estimated party to party costs payable when unsuccessful. The court can also specify maximum costs recoverable by one party from another. The court can instruct parties to refrain from making or maintaining issues unless it is reasonable to do so and order payment of costs, on an indemnity basis, by parties who breach this obligation.

40. J Spigelman, 'Just, Quick and Cheap: A New Standard for Civil Procedure' (February 2000) *Bar Brief* (Newsletter of the NSW Bar Association) Special Edition 6.

The court can also issue an order that a party pay the costs when they cause unreasonable delays or protract the proceedings. This provision overcomes abuse of process and the use of the courts as a weapon by rich litigants against poor ones. Finally, the court can make a cost order against a person who fails to comply with a direction of the court. This provision will make legal practitioners meet deadlines and stop unnecessary delay.[41]

A practitioner can also be held responsible under Supreme Court Rules Pt 52A, r 43 when proceedings are interrupted because the practitioner failed:

a) to attend in person or by a proper representative;
b) to file any document which ought to have been filed;
c) to deliver any document which ought to have been delivered for the use of the court;
d) to be prepared with proper evidence or account;
e) to comply with any provision of the rules or any judgment or order or direction; or

otherwise to proceed.[42]

14.18	The court also issued Practice Note 108 which points out that the courts rely on practitioners to act themselves and to advise their clients 'to observe listing procedures, rules and court directions'. Practitioners also have to 'ensure readiness for trial, to provide reasonable estimates of length of hearings, to present written submissions on time and to give the earliest practicable notice of an adjournment application'. A late amendment of pleadings may also attract a costs order. Failure to observe these practices will lead to a referral of the practitioner for possible disciplinary sanctions.

Hopeless cases

14.19	It has been stated in an old English case, *Re Cooke*,[43] that it is 'dishonourable' for solicitors to take instructions from a client if they know that the client's case is 'absolutely and certainly hopeless'. The English Court of Appeal in this case also said that if the proceedings could be legally taken, but were taken 'in order to gratify' the client's 'own anger or malice, then if the solicitor knew all this he [or she] would be unfair and wrong' to take the proceedings.[44] In another English case Lord Goddard CJ found that the solicitor knew he was filing a fictitious cause of action under instructions from his client. The taking of these proceedings was a contempt.[45] A New South Wales case found a breach of duty to the court when an obvious hopeless appeal was lodged as a delaying tactic. The appeal denied the respondent his just payment and was used as a tool to negotiate a lower settlement.[46]

41.	Spigelman (above), pp 6–7 and Supreme Court Rules 1970, Pt 15A — Limiting Issues.
42.	Supreme Court Rules 1970, Pt 52A, r 43 (solicitors) and r 43A (barristers).
43.	(1889) 5 TLR 407 at 408 (C of A).
44.	*Re Cooke* (above). It should be noted that the new Civil Procedure Rules, adopted in 1999, make it easier for English courts to throw out 'frivolous and vexatious' actions. Rule 24.2 allows a court to give summary judgment if it considers that 'the claimant has no real prospect of succeeding on the claim'.
45.	*R v Weisz* [1951] 2 KB 611.
46.	*Saragas v Martinis* [1976] 1 NSWLR 172. This case and the *Weisz* case are discussed briefly in an excellent article by Justice Ipp. See D Ipp, 'Lawyers' Duties to the Court' (1998) 114 *The Law Quarterly R* 63, 80.

In *Clyne v NSW Bar Association*, the Australian High Court said there is no misconduct in acting for a client 'who has a perfectly good cause of action but is inspired by ill-will towards the defendant'.[47] More recent English cases show that it would be unusual for an English court to find an abuse of process has taken place. In *Mainwaring v Goldtech Investments Ltd* the solicitor was held not to be liable for bringing a hopeless case for being 'too trusting' or accepting their client's account of a dispute. The client's account was later proved unfounded, thereby putting the opposition to the expense and trouble of disproving the case.[48] In *Ridehalgh v Horsefield*, in relation to 'wasted costs', Sir Thomas Bingham MR stated:[49]

14.20

> A legal representative is not to be held to have acted improperly, unreasonably or negligently simply because he [or she] acts for a party who pursues a claim or defence which is plainly doomed to fail ... [It is his duty to] advise clients of the perceived weakness of their case and risk of failure. But clients are free to reject advice and insist that cases be litigated. It is rarely if ever safe for a court to assume that a hopeless case is being litigated on the advice of the lawyers involved.

By contrast the New South Wales Court of Appeal in *Ian Cameron Miller v Commissioner of Police NSW*[50] recently found that the legal representatives ought to have been aware that the appeal was futile. The court requested the lawyers to give an undertaking 'that they will not look to the appellant for his costs of the appeal and that they will indemnify him in respect of the order that he pay the respondent's costs of appeal'.[51] The court exercised its inherent power to request the undertaking. In its orders the court said if the undertaking was not given it would then consider issuing a show cause notice under Supreme Court Rules Pt 52A, r 43(e), discussed above.

Legal Profession Act provisions

The court in the *Miller* case did not apply the provisions of the Legal Profession Act 1987 Div 5C, which are identical to ss 344–349 under the new Legal Profession Act 2004 (NSW). Section 345 states:

14.21

(1) A law practice must not provide legal services on a claim or defence of a claim for damages unless a legal practitioner associate responsible ... reasonably believes on the basis of provable facts and a reasonably arguable view of the law that the claim or defence (as appropriate) has reasonable prospects of success.

(2) A fact is provable only if the associate reasonably believes that the material then available to him or her provides a proper basis for alleging the fact ...

(3) A claim has reasonable prospects of success if there are reasonable prospects of damages being recovered on the claim. A defence has reasonable prospects of success if there are reasonable prospects of the defence defeating the claim or leading to a reduction in the damages recovered on the claim ...

Under s 347, bringing an action without reasonable prospects of success is capable of being unsatisfactory professional conduct or professional

---

47.   (1960) 104 CLR 186 at 196.
48.   *Mainwaring v Goldtech Investments Ltd, The Times*, 19 February 1991.
49.   *Ridehalgh v Horsefield* [1994] 3 WLR 462 at 479.
50.   [2004] NSWCA 356.
51.   Ibid, para 32.

misconduct. Furthermore, under s 348 the court *may* make an order for the practitioner to repay his or her client 'the whole or part of the costs that the party has been ordered to pay to any other party' and/or 'an order … to indemnify any party other than [the client] … against the whole or any part of the costs payable by the party indemnified'.

Reasonable prospects of success

14.22　The important phrase in the Act, 'reasonable prospects of success', was discussed in an article by Justice Beaumont. He argues, by interpreting the second reading speeches of the Act and other precedents, that 'reasonable prospects of success' exist if a case is not hopeless or entirely without merit.[52] The courts have also interpreted the phrase. In *Momibo Pty Ltd v Adam*[53] Neilson DCJ set up a detailed five-element test to determine whether reasonable prospects were present. The first was that the practitioner subjectively held the reasonable belief based on logical argument from an objective sense. Second, there must be a reasonable belief based on an objective foundation from the available material. Third, that material can be a proper basis for alleging the relevant facts. Fourth, that there need to be present reasonable arguments of law that can also be innovative. Finally, there needs to be a reasonable chance that damages can be recovered. Neilson applied this test and held that recovery of some or any damages was enough to constitute reasonable prospects of success.

This test and Beaumont J's article were then applied by Barrett J in dismissing a request for a cost order in *Degiorgio v Dunn (No 2)*.[54] He found that 'without reasonable prospects of success' meant the claim was 'so lacking in merit or substance as to not be fairly arguable'.[55] The approach by Barrett J was then approved by the Court of Appeal in *Lemoto v Able Technical Pty Ltd*.[56]

Migration lawyers

14.23　Migration law in recent years has been the major concern in relation to frivolous actions. There have been many statements by the government and others criticising the misuse of the courts by lawyers in these matters. One Adelaide lawyer, Mark Clisby, had according to allegations by another migration lawyer about 600 matters before the courts and was not properly serving his clients.[57] The then Immigration Minister, Phillip Ruddock, tried to stop this lawyer from inundating the courts with migrant appeals, but was unsuccessful.[58] In 2005, Ruddock, now Attorney-General, introduced the Migration Litigation Reform Bill 2005 to stop serial litigation. The Bill adds

---

52.　N Beaumont, 'What are reasonable prospects of success?' 78 *ALJ* 812, 814. Other relevant articles are A Moses, 'Costs: personal liability of legal practitioners', *Bar News*, Winter 2005, pp 42–5 and D Cassidy, 'Reasonable prospects revisited', *Bar News*, Winter 2005, pp 46–8.

53.　(2004) 1 DCLR (NSW) 316.

54.　[2005] NSWSC 3.

55.　Ibid, para 28.

56.　[2005] NSWCA 153. These cases are discussed and analysed in detail by Moses, see n 52 (above).

57.　R DiGirolamo and N O'Brien, 'A case of déjà vu?', *Australian*, 4–5 October 2003, p 21.

58.　R DiGirolamo, 'Ruddock tried to halt serial litigator', *Australian*, 23–24 August 2003, p 21.

a new Pt 8B to the Migration Act 1958. Part 8B is headed 'Costs orders where proceedings have no reasonable prospect of success'. Section 486E states:

(1) A person must not encourage another person (the *litigant*) to commence or continue migration litigation in a court if:
(a) the migration litigation has no reasonable prospect of success; and
(b) either:
(i) the person does not give proper consideration to the prospects of success of the migration litigation; or
(ii) a purpose in commencing or continuing the migration litigation is unrelated to the objectives which the court process is designed to achieve.

(2) For the purposes of this section, migration litigation need not be:
(a) hopeless; or
(b) bound to fail;
for it to have no reasonable prospect of success.

The definition is a narrow interpretation of 'no reasonable prospect of success'. Under s 486F, if there is a violation of s 486E, the court can order that the lawyer is not to be paid and that he or she has to repay any litigation costs already paid by the litigant.

The legislation may be unconstitutional because it may be deemed to be an intrusion into the 'judicial power' of the Commonwealth in contravention of Chapter III. Furthermore, it may result in lawyers refraining from giving advice and as a result leading to more unrepresented applicants. This in turn would result in 'applications which would take much longer to hear and would generate more appeals'.[59]

Use of legal aid funds

The use of legal aid funds to bring a frivolous or futile action has also led to penalties for lawyers. In an English 'wasted costs' case Aldous J in *Filmlab Systems International Ltd v Pennington*[60] rejected the application against counsel made before trial. The counsel had advised legally aided defendants to apply for discovery. The application for discovery was dismissed as being wholly misconceived. Aldous J said that the application should be made after the trial when it was possible to assess the counsel's conduct in the context of the whole proceedings. The plaintiffs had argued that if they succeeded it was unlikely they would recover costs from the legally aided defendants. Thus, the only way that they had to be recompensed was by a 'wasting costs' order against counsel. Aldous J said the same standard applied for all cases. 'No lawyer who acts in the public interest by accepting legally aided clients, should stand any greater risk of being ordered to pay costs than if he acted for a paying client.'

14.24

In *Davy-Chiesman v Davy-Chiesman*[61] the English Court of Appeal ordered a solicitor to pay both parties' costs because he had pursued a hopeless case. The court said lawyers will be made to pay costs if they continue an action when there is no chance or substantially no chance of success. In this case

---

59. Cassidy, p 48, see n 52 (above). Cassidy refers extensively to the explanatory memorandum issued with the Bill, that highlights these issues.
60. [1995] 1 WLR 673; [1994] 4 All ER 673.
61. [1984] 2 WLR 291 at 305–6 (Ct of Appeal).

the solicitor had sought costs from the Law Society's legal aid fund. The Law Society was successful in its argument on appeal that the solicitor should pay the costs of both parties. The South Australian Professional Conduct Rules r 34.3 supports this decision. Rule 34.3 states:

> Subject to any requirements of any legal aid agency:
>
> (a) a practitioner who forms the view that a client in receipt of legal aid no longer has a reasonable prospect of success, the practitioner shall inform the legal aid agency accordingly and take such steps as may reasonably be necessary to ensure that the furnishing of aid is either terminated or reduced to reflect the opinion so formed; ...

14.25 Rule 34.3 does not indicate what sanctions can be applied. The *Davy-Chiesman* case shows that sanctions can include denial of legal aid funds to the lawyer or greatly reducing the amount of these funds.[62] All legal aid commissions in Australia in civil matters apply a 'merit' test, that the case is not frivolous, before granting legal aid. It has been stated that there is a duty of lawyers to the Legal Aid Commission to conduct a legal aid case in the same manner as they would a private client's case. Lawyers must pursue the legal aid matter in a reasonable way and thus not squander public funds for non-meritorious cases.[63]

Advocacy problems

14.26 Lord Denning has indicated that costs can also be awarded against a lawyer who 'knowingly takes a bad point and thereby deceives the court' eventually causing delay and unnecessary expense, for example the cost of an appeal. Lord Denning added that if lawyers argue a point that they believe to be fair and is later held to be bad by the court, there is no misconduct.[64] Lord Denning did not indicate how a court would be able to determine that counsel was 'knowingly' taking a bad point. Would it be an objective or subjective test? Furthermore, can lawyers make a legal argument they feel sure is incorrect, but which they think may be accepted by the court? What if they think it only has a small chance of being accepted?

14.27 There is an English authority that, even in a serious criminal case such as murder, counsel is under no duty:[65]

> ... to attack a summing-up which is quite impeccable and which has put the case fairly and properly to the jury. There is no obligation on counsel in such a case to endeavour to find some minute points which could have no bearing on the case ... [W]hen it is perfectly clear that there is no ground for appeal, there is no duty on counsel other than to tell the court that he represents the appellant, and that if the court has discovered anything in the case on which they wish to hear him, he is prepared to do his best to assist the court.

This attitude was more recently rejected in the United Kingdom by the Seabrook Report which said that there probably was no such thing as a hopeless criminal case.[66] As Mack and Anleu have stated:[67]

---

62. See Statement on *R v McFadden* (1975) 119 *Solicitors J* 868.
63. J Evans, 'Legal Aid — A Lawyer's Professional Responsibilities' (1982) 8 *Australian Law News* 17.
64. *Abraham v Jutsun* [1963] 2 All ER 402 at 404 (C of A).
65. *R v Reynolds* (1948) 32 Criminal App R 39 at 40.
66. Seabrook, *The Efficient Disposal of Business in the Crown Court*, General Council of the Bar, London, 1992, para 508.
67. K Mack and S Anleu, *Pleading Guilty: Issues and Practices*, Australian Institute of Judicial Administration, Carlton, 1995, p 109.

It is important to remember that likely conviction and actual guilt are not necessarily the same. Even accurate advice that an accused is likely to be convicted is not the same as proof of guilt. It is possible for a prosecution to be strong in circumstances where the accused still has an arguable claim.

There has been a call for a general ethical rule for hopeless cases in Australia. Parker has proposed the following rule:[68]

> It is unethical for a lawyer to take a step in litigation where the client's prospects of success are not sufficiently good to justify the expense and inconvenience caused to third parties and to the administration of justice as a whole.

American perspective

Under American due process constitutional requirements, lawyers in criminal cases would have to pursue the matter more thoroughly and failure to do so could result in an unfair trial. Model Rules r 3.1 states:

14.28

> ... A lawyer for the defendant in a criminal proceeding, or the respondent in a proceeding that could result in incarceration, may ... defend the proceeding as to require that every element of the case be established.

The Supreme Court has stated in the *Anders* case that the constitutional requirements of substantial equality and fair process can only be attained where counsel is an active advocate for his or her client. Lawyers must support a client's appeal to the best of their ability.[69] Counsel can still meet this requirement even when he or she refuses to raise every nonfrivolous issue requested by the defendant.[70] They can only request permission to withdraw if they find and prove to the court that the appeal is 'wholly frivolous'. The court will make the decision and if it finds any of the legal points arguable on their merits, and therefore not frivolous, provide counsel to the accused to argue the appeal. When a court appointed counsel sought to withdraw after concluding there were no grounds for appeal the Supreme Court said that his motion had to include an *Anders* 'brief referring to anything in the record that might arguably support the appeal'.[71] In a later case the Supreme Court said that the defence counsel must not only 'cite the principal cases and statutes and the facts in the record that support the conclusion that the appeal is meritless', but must also add 'a brief statement of why these citations lead the attorney to believe the appeal lacks merit'.[72] This requirement means that defence counsel has to make sound arguments against his or her own client. The Supreme Court in the most recent case, *Smith v Robbins*,[73] held that an *Anders* brief is not a constitutional requirement. The court said alternative procedures can be used. For example, an appellate court can conduct an independent review of the record.

There have been suggestions that the Supreme Court should change its position and lawyers should not be allowed to withdraw from frivolous

14.29

68. S Parker, Senate Standing Committee on Legal and Constitutional Affairs, *Cost of Legal Services and Litigation*, February 1992, para 4.37.
69. *Anders v California* 386 US 738 (1967) at 744.
70. *Jones v Barnes* 463 US 745 (1983).
71. *Anders v California* (above) at 743–5 (1967).
72. *McCoy v Court of Appeals* 486 US 429 at 440–3. The Supreme Court upheld the Wisconsin requirement of the need to assert the basis for the lawyer's conclusion.
73. 528 US 259 (2000).

appeals. A draft of the Advisory Committee on ABA Standards, *The Prosecution Function and the Defense Function*, says lawyers are of greater aid to the court by not withdrawing from weak or groundless appeals:[74]

> He [or she] can, in good conscience, communicate to the court the issues and whatever can be said in support of them without, at the same time, advising the court that he is aware of the weakness of the position.

It has been rare for lawyers in Australia to be penalised for pursuing cases which have little chance of success. Lawyers often use the courts for the benefit of their clients. For example, wealthy corporations, as well as those suing them, have made use of litigation for nuisance value. Many actions are also pursued or defended by using tactics that cause delay and expense. In actions where insurers are involved (usually as defenders) it is widely known that they use their advantageous financial position to extract favourable settlements. It is also not too disadvantageous for large organisations to use the court system to defeat opponents because their legal fees are deductible, while often those of individuals are not deductible.[75] There was an unsuccessful campaign by the Australian Plaintiff Lawyers' Association (now the Australian Lawyers' Alliance) to have the government abolish the tax deduction that large organisations can claim for legal expenses. The Australian Law Reform Commission has stated that businesses claimed in 1995 deductions of $700 million for litigation costs.[76]

14.30 The United States Supreme Court has lamented the social cost of discovery procedures. It said that these procedures allow a plaintiff with a:[77]

> ... largely groundless claim to simply take up the time of a number of people, with the right to do so representing an *in terrorem* increment of the settlement value, rather than a reasonably founded hope that the process will reveal relevant evidence ...

Wealthy clients can afford to make extensive abusive use of procedures causing poorer litigants to drop or compromise an action, even if the latter have a good case.[78] It has been stated that in Australia:[79]

> Generally speaking, the courts have been remarkably lax and ineffective in seeking to prevent the abuses of the legal system, and the injustices, which so frequently arise from conduct of this kind.

Abusing discovery procedures

14.31 The scenario where the poorer litigant is flooded with thousands of documents could no longer occur under changes to the Supreme Court Rules

---

74. (1970) pp 298, 300–2.
75. See *Cost Shifting — who pays for litigation*, Report 75, pp 38–9, Australian Law Reform Commission, 1995 and *Review of the adversarial system of litigation: Rethinking of the federal civil litigation system*, Issues Paper 20, paras 12.17 and 12.18, Australian Law Reform Commission, April 1997.
76. C Merritt, 'Bid to ban expenses as a tax deduction', *Australian Financial Review*, 31 March 2000, p 31.
77. *Blue Chips Stamps v Manor Drug Stores* 421 US 723 (1975) at 741.
78. For an interesting example of the poor against the rich, see the Uranium Moratorium Organisation's case against the Uranium Producers in S Ross, *Politics of Law Reform*, Penguin Books, Ringwood, Victoria, 1982, pp 196–7. There are numerous examples of these practices in Nader and Smith, *No Contest: Corporate Lawyers and the Perversion of Justice in America*, Random House, New York, 1996.
79. Disney et al (above), p 845.

in New South Wales. Under this change the party supplying huge amounts of material to the one seeking discovery must help in sorting it out. The former needs to provide a person to assist in locating and identifying particular documents and classes of documents.[80] Furthermore, under the new Supreme Court Rules adopted in March 2000, as discussed above, many of the abuses will lead to severe penalties for the parties as well as the lawyers.

The Australian Law Reform Commission commented that there is an abuse of discovery procedures where it has been used as a 'delaying tactic, a fishing expedition or as a process to add to the other side's litigation costs'. The Commission noted that discovery worked well in cases where there are few documents. The concerns were in large cases with 'significant documents and costs and the few cases where discovery may be used tactically'.[81] The ALRC suggested that compliance with discovery orders and sanctions for failure to comply could not be dealt with by a 'blanket rule as judges need to exercise their discretion in this area'. The Commission also suggested the use of timetables to meet discovery directions, agreed to by the parties, and the need for more strict enforcement. The Commission quotes from a submission that monetary sanctions were ineffective in large complex cases. The most effective sanction would be to use preclusionary sanctions where the court denied reliance on documents improperly discovered.[82]

14.32

The Federal Court sought to meet some of the problems by the adoption of a new disclosure test which requires parties to reveal documents that are 'directly relevant' to allegations made in the pleadings. The 'directly relevant' test is found in the Federal Court's amended Order 15 and Practice Note 14 adopted December 1999.

14.33

The ALRC outlines and approves the changes by the Federal Court in its final report in February 2000. It also approves the use of directions hearings by the court to argue and determine the scope of discovery and to help the court to enunciate clearly its discovery orders.[83] The ALRC also recommends the adoption of a practice note and/or guidelines for electronic discovery and discovery of electronic documents dealing with general procedures and problems encountered by parties, including:[84]

- ❏ requirements for parties to disclose search terms and mechanisms;
- ❏ arrangements for authenticating documents;
- ❏ fixing documents in time; and,
- ❏ the restoration and retrieval of electronic data by parties …

Unfair use of the court system

Another tactic taken by large corporations is to threaten those seeking remedies against them. This can be done by either a preliminary strike — seeking an injunction or instituting legal action, against disgruntled consumers or shareholders — or by cross-claiming. The former is

14.34

---

80. Supreme Court Rules (NSW) s 23.3(10)(b). For details on discovery see Hunter, Cameron and Henning, Chapter 7 (see n 20 (above)).
81. ALRC DP 62, *Review of the federal civil justice system*, August 1999, para 10.93.
82. ALRC DP 62 (above), para 10.100. These comments are also found in the final report. See ALRC Report No 89, *Managing Justice: A review of the federal civil justice system*, para 7.182.
83. ALRC Report No 89 (above), paras 7.174–7.184.
84. ALRC Report No 89 (above), Recommendation 89.

widespread in the United States: Pring and Canan have called it SLAPP — Strategic Lawsuit Against Public Participation. These suits often lack merit and are used to intimidate and silence critics. The corporations sue usually for defamation or tortious interference with business. It is a method of punishing citizens who are exercising their legal rights. It is estimated that around 80 per cent of SLAPP suits are dismissed before trial, but they are effective as defendants are so intimidated by the possibility of enormous legal costs that they often agree to cease their protests.[85] There is a movement in the United States to adopt anti-SLAPP legislation. Sometimes this legislation can be too effective. For example, California has one of the strongest statutes, but some Californian lawyers 'complain that Goliaths as well as Davids claim to be victims of SLAPPs, so that what was supposed to be a shield has turned into a sword'.[86]

14.35   In Australia such activities do not seem to be widespread, but at times other forms of intimidation will work. The most notorious is the use of the defamation laws. Another is to contact those who are seeking a remedy against you and threaten them. In a legal action by Drambo Pty Ltd against Westpac concerning losses incurred by Westpac clients who had borrowed offshore, Westpac's solicitors, Feez Ruthning, sent letters to four businessmen funding the legal action, warning them that they may incur large costs including some of the bank's legal costs. It was reported that Westpac had used a similar approach in two other offshore loss cases.[87] One of those receiving the letters stated: 'It stinks. The bank has been using gutter tactics to date and is continuing to use them.' He added how unfair the litigation was because the bank had no compunction about using its 'bottomless bucket', funded by shareholders and investors, to contest the action.[88]

Lawyers' tactics

14.36   The tactics that lawyers use to delay the discovery process in the United States include:[89]

- ❑ construing inquiries and requests as narrowly as possible;
- ❑ refusing to respond to written requests not free of ambiguity, imprecision, overbreadth, irrelevance, or other technical deficiencies;
- ❑ claiming privilege or work product as often as possible;
- ❑ burying significant documents in mountains of innocuous or irrelevant materials;
- ❑ refusing to respond until compelled to do so.

Brazil has found in a survey of lawyers' discovery practices in the United States that the abuses in smaller cases ($25,000 or less) were substantially less than in larger cases. He states that the lawyers interviewed said: 'The real need is to devise a system of restraints and rewards that will combat the

---

85.   See, generally, G Ping and P Canan, *SLAPPs: Getting Sued for Speaking Out*, Temple University Press, Philadelphia, 1996. For some SLAPP cases see R Zitrin and C Langford, *The Moral Compass of the American Lawyer*, Ballantine Books, New York, 1999, pp 68–72.

86.   Zitrin and Langford (above), p 72.

87.   R Lamperd, 'Backers shy off Westpac action', *Courier-Mail*, 11 November 1996, p 9 and A Lampe, 'Westpac in threat row', *Sydney Morning Herald*, 9 November 1996, p 35.

88.   *Sydney Morning Herald* (above).

89.   W Brazil, 'The Adversary Character of Civil Discovery: A Critique and Proposal for Change' (1978) 31 *Vanderbilt LJ* 1295, 1323–5.

pervasive problem of evasion and curb misuse of the system's tools.'[90] In the United States, the Supreme Court agrees with this approach and has called for sanctions for unreasonably extending court proceedings, especially by use of discovery procedures.[91] Discovery abuses have also been carried out by government counsel. The Fifth Circuit Court of Appeal in *Chilcutt v United States*[92] upheld a District Court's decision preventing the government from reimbursing a lawyer for the sanction imposed upon him personally for discovery abuse. ABA Model Rules r 3.2 states: 'A lawyer must make reasonable efforts to expedite litigation consistent with the interests of the client.' The Comment to Model Rules r 3.2 emphasises the profession's view of the problem. It states: 'Dilatory practices bring the administration of justice into disrepute.' The problem is that the American profession's ethical boards have been very lax about applying any sanctions, let alone harsh sanctions, for discovery abuse. As Nader and Smith state:[93]

> If you get caught it might cost you money, it might even cost you a case, but it will not endanger your right to practice law. That message needs to be amended.

MacKenzie, a Canadian author, says that judges are also at fault because **14.37** they do little about discovery abuses. This is because they treat the discovery process as incidental and preliminary to the important process — the trial. Lawyers at the trial will avoid 'overly aggressive and unfair conduct that is likely to alienate judges and juries. There is less incentive for them to avoid overzealousness on discovery'.[94] The Canadian professional conduct rules, like those in Australia, do not specifically deal with discovery abuse. And, as in Australia, 'disciplinary proceedings have been brought in only a few egregious cases'. MacKenzie feels that the abuses are a logical result because discovery is 'an intentional erosion of the pure adversarial process'. The discovery process:[95]

> … has been engrafted onto what otherwise remains a thoroughly adversarial process. Full, efficient and meaningful pre-trial disclosure requires co-operation that many lawyers consider to be incompatible with the furtherance of their clients' objectives.

Kirby J has sought to stop some of these practices in Australia. In *Garrad v* **14.38** *Email Furniture Pty Ltd*,[96] which dealt with a dispute over costs and a certificate of taxation, he commented that professional discourtesy existed in the case. The lawyers had secured a certificate for want of objection, knowing that particulars had been sought, and objections were intended. He said the lawyers won a momentary battle:

---

90. W Brazil, 'Civil Discovery: How Bad Are the Problems?' (1981) 67 *American Bar Association J* 450–6.
91. *Roadway Express Inc v Piper* 447 US 752 (1980) at 757 n 4.
92. 4 F3d 1313 (5th Cir 1993). See also *United States v Shaffer Equipment Co* 158 FRD 80 (SD W Va 1994) where two Justice Department lawyers were sanctioned. The court also had earlier on dismissed the government's claim. On appeal the dismissal was reversed but still found the lawyers were at fault: *United States v Shaffer Equipment Co* 11 F 3d 450 (4th Cir 1993).
93. Nader and Smith (above), p 132.
94. G MacKenzie, 'Breaking the Dichotomy Habit: The Adversary System and the Ethics of Professionalism' (1996) 9 *The Canadian J of Law & Jurisprudence* 33, 36.
95. See MacKenzie (above), pp 36–7.
96. (1993) 32 NSWLR 662.

But in the end those engaged in such tactics, without complete candour to the court run the risk of ... causing delay and inconvenience. They become known for their rigid adherence to the rules. Those who act in this way also generally attract retaliation ... A limit must be placed upon undue procrastination by lawyers or their clients. The Rules of court exist to protect the interests of parties beyond the professional relationships of their lawyers. But sensible relationships between lawyers usually rebound to the advantage of clients.

Kirby J said that professional discourtesy was on the rise and could possibly lead to conflict and higher costs for clients.[97] There are obviously problems with abusing court and discovery procedures in Australia but they do not as yet appear to be as serious as those in the United States.[98]

American approach to discovery problems

14.39   In the United States there have been a number of moves to remedy these problems. ABA Model Rules r 3.1 states:

> A lawyer shall not bring or defend a proceeding, or assert or controvert an issue therein, unless there is a basis in law and fact for doing so that is not frivolous, which includes a good faith argument for an extension, modification or reversal of existing law ...

Comment [2] to r 3.1 says an action is frivolous if the 'lawyer is unable either to make a good faith argument on the merits of the action taken or to support the action taken by a good faith argument for an extension, modification or reversal of existing law'. We have pointed out that Model Rules r 3.2 calls for lawyers to expedite matters. The Comment to this rule states:

> ... The question is whether a competent lawyer acting in good faith would regard the course of action as having some substantial purpose other than delay. Realizing financial or other benefit from otherwise improper delay in litigation is not a legitimate interest of a client.

The implication of the Comment is that delay is usually allowed if it is in the interests of the client. In addition, Model Rules r 3.3 deals with candour towards the tribunal and will be discussed later.

American statutes

14.40   In civil litigation in the United States there are also three relevant rules — rr 26, 38 and 11 of the Federal Rules of Civil Procedure.[99] Rule 26 deals with discovery misstatements. Rule 26(a)(1) states that 'a party must, without awaiting a discovery request, provide to other parties' information which includes the names of people with 'discoverable information that the disclosing party may use to support its claims or defenses, unless solely for impeachment, identifying the subjects of the information'. If the party has control it shall also provide a 'copy' or 'description by category' of 'all documents, data compilations, and tangible things ... that the disclosing party may use to support its claims or defenses, unless solely for impeachment'. If the party later finds other information that helps to clarify or complete the material already supplied, the party has to disclose this information.[100]

---

97. *Law Society J* (NSW) Vol 31, December 1993, p 14.
98. See, generally, Hunter, Cameron and Henning, Chapter 7 (see n 20 (above)). This is a vast subject area and is better dealt with in a course on litigation.
99. There are also sanctions for frivolous legal arguments on appeal under r 38 of the Federal Rules of Appellate Procedure.
100. Rule 26 is entitled 'The General Provisions Governing Discovery: Duty of Disclosure' [as amended, effective 1 December 2000]. See r 26(e) concerning the duties related to supplementation of disclosures and responses.

Rule 38 states: 'If a court of appeals determines that an appeal is frivolous, it may ... award damages and single or double costs to the appellee.' In *Beam v Bauer*[101] the Third Circuit Court of Appeals upheld a decision of the United States District Court that found the action was barred by the *res judicata* doctrine and dismissed the suit for being frivolous. The District Court judge imposed r 11 sanctions on the lawyer, who was also the lawyer for the appeal. The Third Circuit pointed out that r 38 sanctions were discretionary, but that it has 'consistently held represented clients, and specifically their counsel, to a higher standard'. The court held counsel responsible for the damages, which were determined to be the amount expended by the appellees.[102]

The present r 11 was revised in 1983 and 1993. It requires lawyers to sign pleadings, motions or other papers. By signing, lawyers certify that to the best of their:

> ... knowledge, information and belief, formed after an inquiry reasonable under the circumstances, — (1) it is not being presented for any improper purpose, such as to harass or to cause unnecessary delay or needless increase in the cost of litigation; (2) the claims, defences, and other legal contentions therein are warranted by existing law or by a nonfrivolous argument for the extension, modification, or reversal of existing law or the establishment of new law; (3) the allegations and other factual contentions have evidentiary support or, if specifically so identified, are likely to have evidentiary support after a reasonable opportunity for further investigation or discovery; and (4) the denials of factual contentions are warranted on the evidence or, if specifically so identified, are reasonably based on a lack of information or belief.

If the rule is violated a court can, upon a motion or upon its own initiative, impose an appropriate sanction. The sanction may include an order to pay 'the party or parties the amount of the reasonable expenses incurred' because of the lawyer's actions, including a reasonable lawyer's fee. This is an important sanction in the United States. Unlike in Australia where the loser pays some of the winner's costs,[103] each party is responsible for its own costs.[104]   **14.41**

Every state in the United States has adopted some equivalent to r 11. Many of the state rules are modelled on the pre-1983 version of the rule

---

101. US Court of Appeals, 3rd Circuit, Nos 03-1874, 03-2194, 9 September 2004.
102. The court applied one of its earlier decisions, *Hilmon Co (VI) Inc v Hyat International* 899 F2d 250 (3rd Cir 1999), in coming to its conclusion.
103. The loser pays only the winner's reasonable or 'party and party' costs. Parker found that some lawyers use two-thirds as a rule of thumb, but one study in Victoria in 1986 showed that 83.6 per cent of total costs were recovered when the costs indemnity rule was applied. See S Parker, *Costs of Legal Services and Litigation, Discussion Paper No 5*, 'Legal Ethics' Senate Standing Committee on Legal and Constitutional Affairs, February 1992, paras 4.17 and 4.18.
104. The ALRC, in *Costs shifting — who pays for litigation*, (1995) Report No 75, recommended maintaining the present system with certain important exceptions. These included the 'material effect' exception. The rule would not apply 'to people whose ability to present their case properly or to negotiate a fair settlement is materially and adversely affected by the risk of having to pay the other party's costs'. The second important exception to the costs allocation rules is to prevent the rules from inhibiting public interest litigation that is of significant benefit to the community. For a discussion of fees terminology and application see Disney et al (above), Chapter 13. See also G E Dal Pont, *Lawyers' Professional Responsibility in Australia and New Zealand*, Law Book Co, Sydney, 1996, pp 279–83.

that required a showing of 'bad faith', a subjective standard, before imposing sanctions. The post-1983 r 11 has instead the 'reasonable inquiry' standard. Besides the sanctions listed under r 11 and the state versions, lawyers also face the possibility of disciplinary action and may even be subject to malpractice claims by their clients.

Application of Rule 11

14.42 There have been some large awards under r 11. In *Uniol Inc v EF Hutton & Co Inc*[105] the Ninth Circuit Court awarded nearly $300,000, plus counsel fees and expenses of $166,000. Counsel had undertaken 'representation of plaintiffs with conflicting interests and failed to conduct a reasonable inquiry into the factual bias of the complaint'. In *Brandt v Schall Associates Inc* $443,000 was granted on request from the defendant's lawyers who had spent more than 3000 hours opposing a civil racketeering suit. The suit was eventually withdrawn voluntarily.[106] The largest r 11 sanction imposed so far has been more than $1 million in *Avirgan v Hull*.[107]

A controversial case involved one of the largest law firms in the Pacific Northwest, Boyle & Gates, and its client, the large drug company Fisons. It was sanctioned for $325,000 under that state's discovery rules.[108] Boyle & Gates had truthfully, from a literal point of view, answered the interrogatories but the answers were misleading and evasive. The case highlights the deceptive attitude of some large firms and support they receive from other members of the profession. The sanction did not scare the firm as they were found two years later in another case to have 'obfuscated, stonewalled, and "gave answers that were just plain wrong"'.[109] Although they may have sullied their reputation the sanction imposed was minute in comparison to fees it had received. Furthermore, Zitrin and Langford point out that 'the two lawyers primarily responsible for the Fisons discovery remained with the firm in good standing. The younger one was even promoted to partner'.[110]

14.43 The Supreme Court in *Chambers v NASCO Inc*[111] upheld a sanction of $996,645 against a party imposed by a Federal District Court. The lower court assessed that amount as the total of the opposing party's litigation expenses, less a contempt fee. The judge had found that the party sought to deprive the court of jurisdiction, filed false and frivolous pleadings and tried to discourage the opposing party through delay. Although only the second ground was sanctionable under r 11, the Supreme Court by a 5:4 vote held that a federal court may use its:[112]

> ... inherent power to police itself, serving the dual purpose of 'vindicating judicial authority ... and making the prevailing party [wholly responsible] for the expenses caused by his opponent's obstinacy'.

105. 809 F 2d 548 (9th Cir 1986).
106. 960 F 2d 640 (7th Cir 1992).
107. 932 F 2d 1572 (11th Cir 1991).
108. *Washington State Physicians Insurance Exchange & Association v Fisons Corp* 122 Wash 2d 299, 858 P2d 1054 (1993).
109. R Zitrin and C Langford (above), 1999, pp 64–5.
110. Zitrin (above), p 65.
111. *Chambers v NASCO Inc* 111 S Ct 2123 (1991).
112. *Chambers* (above) at 2133. The District Court also disbarred one of the lawyers.

This case shows that inherent powers can still be used and may be needed in light of the post-1993 changes to r 11.

The cases under r 11 have varied greatly. For example, the Second Circuit Court has granted sanctions for a single improper count in a complaint, even though all other counts were well founded,[113] while the Ninth Circuit Court stated it reserved sanctions only for 'rare and exceptional cases' thereby preserving 'the strongest presumption of open access to all levels of the judicial system'.[114]

14.44

The United States Supreme Court in *Cooter & Gell v Hartmarzx Corp*[115] gave some guidance on how r 11 should be applied. A class action had been voluntarily dismissed in 1984. The defendant's lawyers filed a r 11 application, which was not heard by the court until 1987 when it imposed sanctions on the lawyer and his client. O'Connor J, writing the majority opinion (8:1), said that federal courts could consider r 11 sanctions after an action is no longer pending and a 'voluntary dismissal' does not affect this right (now overruled by 1993 amendments: see below). She said that what constituted a 'reasonable standard' would be determined by the trial courts, which are acquainted with the local bar's litigation practices and thus best suited to determine when sanctions were warranted.[116]

The Supreme Court in *Business Guides Inc v Chromatic Communications Enterprises*[117] upheld the lower court's r 11 sanction against a client who had signed an offending application for a restraining order. In *Pavelic & Le Flore v Marvel Entertainment Group*[118] the court refused to extend liability to an entire firm or other lawyers working on the case. The only lawyer held responsible was the lawyer signing the offending document (now overruled by the 1993 amendments).

14.45

There were only a handful of cases under the pre-1983 rule, while there have been several thousand under the post-1983 rule. There are those that oppose it as denying poorer litigants access to lawyers. A study conducted on Third Circuit Court r 11 cases found that civil rights plaintiffs and their attorneys were sanctioned at a rate of 47.1 per cent as compared to 8.4 per cent for plaintiffs in non-civil rights cases. As a result it has had a chilling effect on the civil rights bar's willingness to file cases.[119] The reason for these results is that 'civil rights lawyers and litigants have more incentive and inclination than most others to file and pursue cases they know are long shots'.[120] One judge has stated that r 11 has:[121]

---

113. *Cross & Cross Properties v Everett Allied Co* 886 F 2d 497 (2nd Cir 1989).
114. *Operating Engineers Pension Trust v A-C Co* 859 F 2d 1336 (9th Cir 1988).
115. 496 US 384 (1990).
116. Comments on this case are found in *The National Law J*, 25 June 1990, pp 1 and 27.
117. 498 US 533 (1991).
118. 493 US 120 (1990).
119. *The National Law J*, 30 July 1990, p 32. Similar conclusions were reached by the *Federal Judicial Center's Study of Rule 11*, 2 FJC Directions, November 1991.
120. C Yablon, 'The Good, The Bad, and The Frivolous Case: An Essay on Probability and Rule 11' (1996) 44 UCLA LR 65.
121. *New York Times*, 2 October 1986, pp 30–1 quoted in T Morgan and R Rotunda, *Problems and Materials on Professional Responsibility*, 5th ed, Foundation Press, Westbury, NY, 1991, p 212.

... become another way of harassing the opponent and delaying the case. It has increased the tensions in litigation, and increased the amount of extra motions and extra appeals.

Changes to Rule 11

14.46   In response to the 'chilling effect' on advocacy, amendments to r 11 were adopted in 1993. Under r 11(c) these motions now have to be served separately from other motions. This can only be done after the accused lawyer has had the opportunity to withdraw or correct, 'within 21 days after the service of the motion (or such other period the court may prescribe), the challenged paper, claim, defence, contention, allegation, or denial'. The Committee's notes explaining the amendment state:[122]

> ... a party will not be subject to sanctions on the basis of another party's motion unless, after receiving the motion, it refuses to withdraw that position or to acknowledge candidly that it does not currently have evidence to support a specified allegation.

14.47   Other changes in 1993 protecting lawyers include: (1) a provision in r 11(b)(3) which protects lawyers who, when making a factual allegation, state that the allegation is 'likely to have evidentiary support after a reasonable opportunity for further investigation or discovery'; (2) under r 11(b)(4) a lawyer is protected when denying a factual contention when stating the denial is 'reasonably based on a lack of information and belief'. The reasonable test is evaluated by an objective standard. Sanctions under these provisions must be 'limited to what is sufficient to deter repetition of such conduct or comparable conduct'. If a party is voluntarily dismissed or settles a claim before the court issues a show cause order, the court cannot award a monetary penalty.

14.48   It appears that the changes have had the effect of reducing the number of r 11 cases.[123]

It should be noted that Ipp J has said that:[124]

> Rule 11 could well be a model in Australia for legislative regulation of the conduct of lawyers. It is strongly arguable that the time has come for lawyers' obligations to the court (and the system) to be defined in specific terms so as to ensure the speedy and efficient administration of justice.

Should Australia adopt a rule 11?

14.49   The Law Council of Australia is opposed to the total adoption of r 11. In its submission to the Australian Law Reform Commission the Council expressed its 'concern at the suggestion that advocates should believe the allegations and factual contentions their clients are making'. It stated that 'this confuses the role of an advocate with that of an investigator'. The Council also found it inappropriate to regulate practitioners' conduct through costs orders.[125] By contrast the ALRC has recommended that 'the thrust of Rule 11 ... should be incorporated into Australian federal court and tribunal rules and professional practice rules, although the requirement should be couched in terms of "to the best of the practitioner's knowledge

---

122. 146 FRD 591 explaining the amendment to r 11(c).
123. A Westlaw search shows the numbers have fallen since 1993.
124. Ipp (above), p 730.
125. ALRC Report No 89, *Managing Justice: A review of the federal civil justice system*, February 2000, para 3.95.

or information" rather than "to the best of his or her knowledge, information or belief".[126]

Courtesy codes

Besides the ABA Model Rules and r 11 a number of 'courtesy codes' have been circulated; for example, the Proposed Code of Litigation Conduct 1988. This Code establishes certain rules of courtesy among lawyers for civil cases. The Code disapproves of the following practices:[127]

14.50

> ... taking advantage of an opponent's known absence from the office to serve papers; writing letters that ascribe to one's adversary a position she has not taken; making *ad hominem* arguments in legal papers; and falsely holding out the possibility of settlement as a means of delaying discovery or trial.

Hazard and Koniak have criticised such codes as being ineffective because they do not have support among the legal community:[128]

> Without a community capable of imposing informal sanctions, such as ostracism, there is little hope for improvement. Moreover, however lofty their purpose, 'courtesy codes' may increase ambiguity about what is actually prohibited.

Even if these codes are ineffective, they can help raise lawyers' consciousness and eventually lead to some amelioration of 'hardball' litigation techniques. They can also 'serve a valuable purpose, by creating a community standard that encourages a "kinder, gentler" way of thinking and, perhaps, some amount of peer pressure to conform to what have been defined as reasonable behavioural norms'.[129]

Unsupported or irrelevant allegations

Professional rules

The rules in this area pertain to lawyers acting fairly in litigious matters. In Australia fairness in litigation is found in the Barristers' Rules and Bar Rules adopted by other bar associations, by the Model Rules and by law societies.[130] The Barristers' Rules in New South Wales dealing with fairness were drastically changed in June 1997 and March 2000. The Law Council of Australia later amended the Model Rules to include these rules as

14.51

126. ALRC Report No 89 (above), para 3.96 and Recommendation 16.
127. G Hazard Jr and S Koniak, *The Law and Ethics of Lawyering* (1990), Foundation Press, Westbury, New York, pp 449–50. See also the Los Angeles County Bar Association's Litigation Guidelines 1989 which include refraining from: acting other than in a 'civil and courteous' fashion; using interrogatories etc as a 'means to harass or to generate expense; engaging in conduct during a deposition that would not be allowed before a judicial officer; coaching deponents while a question is pending; and refrain from reading interrogatories or document demands in an artificially restrictive manner to avoid disclosure': Rhode (above), p 209.
128. Hazard and Koniak (above), p 450.
129. R Zitrin and C Langford, *Legal Ethics in the Practice of Law*, Michie Company, Charlottesville, Virginia, 1995, p 320. The book reprints two of these codes at pp 321–6.
130. The Barristers' Rules in New South Wales up to January 2000 were the same as those in Queensland, and the old rr 35–44 had also been adopted by the Law Society of NSW and in the Law Council's Model Rules. The changes made in January 2000 by the NSW Bar are now being reviewed by the Law Council of Australia and other professional associations; see also Professional Conduct Rules (SA) r 16.3; and Professional Conduct Rules (WA) rr 13.6–13.8, 14.3.

rr 16.1–16.5 and the Queensland Bar adopted them as rr 37–41. The New South Wales Rules rr 35–39 state:

> 35. A barrister must, when exercising the forensic judgments called for throughout the case, take care to ensure that decisions by the barrister or on the barrister's advice to invoke the coercive powers of a court or to make allegations or suggestions under privilege against any person:
>
> (a) are reasonably justified by the material already available to the barrister;
>
> (b) are appropriate for the robust advancement of the client's case on its merits;
>
> (c) are not made principally in order to harass or embarrass the person; and
>
> (d) are not made principally in order to gain some collateral advantage for the client or the barrister or the instructing solicitor out of court.
>
> 36. A barrister must not allege any matter of fact in:
>
> (a) any court document settled by the barrister;
>
> (b) any submission during any hearing;
>
> (c) the course of an opening address; or
>
> (d) the course of a closing address or submission on the evidence;
>
> unless the barrister believes on reasonable grounds that the factual material already available provides a proper basis to do so.
>
> 37. A barrister must not allege any matter of fact amounting to criminality, fraud or other serious misconduct against any person unless the barrister believes on reasonable grounds that:
>
> (a) available material by which the allegation could be supported provides a proper basis for it; and
>
> (b) the client wishes the allegation to be made, after having been advised of the seriousness of the allegation and of the possible consequences for the client and the case if it is not made out.
>
> 38. A barrister must not make a suggestion in cross-examination on credit unless the barrister believes on reasonable grounds that acceptance of the suggestion would diminish the witness's credibility.
>
> 39. A barrister may regard the opinion of the instructing solicitor that material which is available to the solicitor is credible, being material which appears to the barrister from its nature to support an allegation to which rr 36 and 37 apply, as a reasonable ground for holding the belief required by those rules (except in the case of a closing address or submission on the evidence).

14.52   The explanatory note to the new rr 36–39 states that the changes have 'broadened counsel's obligation to apply professional judgment to the adequacy of the available material to justify allegations made under privilege ... The obligation now covers all matters of fact — it is no longer confined to matters amounting to allegations of disgraceful conduct'.[131]

It should be noted there has been added to r 15 a new definition for the word 'allege'. Allege now 'includes conduct constituted by settling or opening on pleadings, affidavits or witness statements, and reading or tendering affidavits or witness statements filed or prepared for the client (whether or not they were drawn or settled by the barrister)'. The notes say that the new rules are intended to cause counsel to exercise their

---

131. *Bar Brief* (Newsletter of the NSW Bar Association) Special Edition, February 2000, p 5.

professional and ethical judgment in order to reduce 'contested litigation, which has been begun or fought without justification'.[132] It should be noted that under r 39, barristers can still hide behind the opinion of instructing solicitors as to the credibility of material made available to the barrister. I believe there should be a greater onus on barristers to make more extensive investigations to validate the credibility of the material presented.

Rule 40 (r 44 in Queensland) is identical to old rule 42. It states: **14.53**

> A barrister who has instructions which justify submissions for the client in mitigation of the client's criminality and which involve allegations of serious misconduct against any other person not able to answer the allegations in the case must seek to avoid disclosing the other person's identity directly or indirectly unless the barrister believes on reasonable grounds that such disclosure is necessary for the robust defence of the client.

There are also two other important rules that are relevant to this section. They are:

> 43. A barrister must not suggest or condone another person suggesting in any way to any prospective witness (including a party or the client) the content of any particular evidence which the witness should give at any stage in the proceedings. [r 45 in Queensland]
>
> 44. A barrister will not have breached Rule 43 by expressing general admonition to tell the truth, or by questioning and testing in conference the version of evidence to be given by a prospective witness, including drawing the witness's attention to inconsistencies or other difficulties with the evidence, but must not coach or encourage the witness to give evidence different from the evidence which the witness believes to be true. [Rule 46 in Queensland]

American professional rules

The ABA Model Rules r 3.4 requires lawyers to be fair to the opposing **14.54** party and counsel.

> A lawyer shall not:
>
> (a) unlawfully obstruct another party's access to evidence or unlawfully alter, destroy or conceal a document or other material having potential evidentiary value. A lawyer shall not counsel or assist another person to do any such act;
>
> (b) falsify evidence, counsel or assist a witness to testify falsely, or offer an inducement to a witness that is prohibited by law;
>
> (c) knowingly disobey an obligation under rules of a tribunal except for an open refusal based on an assertion that no valid obligation exists;
>
> (d) in pretrial procedure, make a frivolous discovery request or fail to make reasonably diligent effort to comply with a legally proper discovery request by an opposing party;
>
> (e) in trial, allude to any matter that the lawyer does not reasonably believe is relevant or that will not be supported by admissible evidence, assert personal knowledge of facts in issue except when testifying as a witness, or state a personal opinion as to the justness of a cause, the credibility of a witness, the culpability of a civil litigant or the guilt or innocence of an accused;[133] or

---

132. *Bar Brief* (above), p 5.
133. See its application in *Pappas v Middle Earth Condominium Association* 963 F 2d 534 (2nd Cir 1992) where defence counsel aroused the jury's bias against out of state parties.

(f) request a person other than a client to refrain from voluntarily giving relevant information to another party unless:

(1) the person is a relative or an employee or other agent of a client; and

(2) the lawyer reasonably believes that the person's interests will not be adversely affected by refraining from giving such information.[134]

According to Comment [1] to r 3.4 the adversary system secures fair competition 'by prohibitions against destruction or concealment of evidence, improperly influencing witnesses, obstructive tactics in discovery procedure, and the like'. Comment [2] points out that in many jurisdictions it is an offence to destroy evidence so as to impair any proceedings and that falsifying evidence is also usually a criminal offence. There have been a number of cases finding that lawyers have acted unethically by using prohibited forensic tactics, such as making impermissible arguments.[135]

Destruction of evidence

14.55   The destruction of relevant evidence became a national issue in Australia in *McCabe v British American Tobacco Australia Services Ltd* (hereafter BAT).[136] McCabe was dying from lung cancer and died before the appeal was heard. Eames J struck out BAT's defence and gave judgment for Mrs McCabe. He based his decision on the fact that the defendant's lawyers had deliberately destroyed thousands of relevant documents and subverted the discovery process. The documents had been destroyed before proceedings had commenced but was done because, as Eames J said, it was 'not only merely likely, but a near certainty' that further proceedings would take place.[137] Eames J said the action by the lawyers meant that a fair trial could no longer possibly take place as the trial process had been contaminated. He only allowed the trial to go to jury to decide the quantum of damages and McCabe was awarded $700,000. Eames J had found that between November 1990 and March 1998 there were 'holding orders' prohibiting BAT from destroying documents concerning its internal affairs because of litigation concerning smoking-related disease. The final holding order was removed when litigation ended in Australia in March 1998 and at that point thousands of documents were then destroyed as a matter of urgency.[138]

The Court of Appeal in *British American Tobacco v Cowell*[139] reversed the decision on all major issues. It was not disputed before this court that thousands of documents had been destroyed and that further litigation was anticipated. The court said there was no authority directly on the point dealing with the destruction of evidence before the commencement of proceedings. It thus formulated a new test for allowing a court to interfere when this occurred. It said that what the plaintiff had to prove in order for the 'court's intervention (otherwise than by the drawing of adverse inferences, and particularly if the sanction sought is the striking out of the

---

134. This provision allows lawyers for large organisations to advise their employees and agents to 'refrain from voluntarily giving relevant information'. See *Niesig v Team 1* 76 Ny2d 363, 558 NE2d 1030 (1990).

135. See C Wolfram, *Modern Legal Ethics* (1986), para 12.1.2.

136. [2002] VSC 73.

137. Ibid, para 289.

138. Ibid, paras 58–59 and 289.

139. [2002] VSCA 197.

pleading) is whether that conduct of the other party amounted to an attempt to pervert the course of justice or, if open, contempt of court ...'.[140] The court did not find an attempt to pervert the course of justice and upheld the appeal. The Court of Appeal focused on the lawfulness of BAT's conduct and not on the effect the destruction of documents had on the ability of the court to reach a just and fair decision.[141] The focus should have been on the doctrine of fairness and not on whether criminal sanction was appropriate.

The High Court decided not to grant special leave and so the Court of Appeal decision is still authority. As a result of the decision McCabe's estate was burdened with huge legal costs. BAT won the appeal but the information concerning destruction of valuable evidence as a worldwide policy has been used against the tobacco industry in the large lawsuits in the United States.[142] The Court of Appeal decision has been widely criticised.[143] In an excellent analysis of how the court asked the wrong question, Cameron and Liberman conclude their article by stating:

> The criterion of fairness is equally relevant to the destruction of evidence both before and after the commencement of proceedings. That is because the role of a court is to do justice between the parties to the case it is adjudicating, and that role may be prejudiced equally by the destruction of evidence before commencement as after. This is not to say that the deliberate destruction of evidence ... is not a serious matter worthy of punishment. Indeed, it is. It represents a fundamental attack on the role and rationale of courts. However, its punishment ought to occur through the criminal offences of attempting to pervert the course of justice and contempt of court, rather than in the civil proceeding (or proceedings) it has prejudiced. In *BAT v Cowell*, the Court of Appeal erroneously focused on the lawfulness or unlawfulness of the destruction of documents (an issue which had not been argued at trial) and lost sight of the primary issue, namely the extent to which the destruction of evidence had affected the plaintiff's capacity to obtain a fair trial of her allegations.

As a result of the *BAT* decision, New South Wales adopted cl 142A of the Legal Profession Regulation 2002 on destruction of documents. It states:

> (1) A legal practitioner must not give advice to a client to the effect that a document should be destroyed, or should be moved from the place at which it is kept or from the person who has possession or control of it, if the legal practitioner is aware that:
>
>   (a) it is likely that legal proceedings will be commenced in relation to which the document may be required, and
>
>   (b) following the advice will result in the document being unavailable or unusable for the purposes of those proceedings.

---

140. Ibid, para 41.

141. C Cameron and J Liberman, 'Destruction of Documents before Proceedings Commence: What is a Court to Do?' (2003) MULR 12.

142. R Ackland, 'Missing documents haunt tobacco giants', *Sydney Morning Herald*, 7 September 2004; C Pirani and R Yallop, 'Big tobacco "sanitised" its paperwork', *Australian*, 12–13 February 2005.

143. See Cameron and Liberman (above); R Ackland, 'Missing documents haunt tobacco giants' (above); M McLachlan, 'Smoking gun still relevant for litigation', *Australian Financial Review*, 10 October 2003, p 53.

(2) A legal practitioner must not destroy a document or move it from the place at which it is kept or from the person who has possession or control of it, or aid or abet a person in the destruction of a document or in moving it from the place at which it is kept or from the person who has possession or control of it, if the legal practitioner is aware that:

(a) it is likely that legal proceedings will be commenced in relation to which the document may be required, and

(b) the destruction or moving of the document will result in the document being unavailable or unusable for the purposes of those proceedings.

(3) Subclauses (1) and (2) apply even if there has been no indication that a specific person intends to commence proceedings in relation to which the document concerned may be required.

(4) A contravention of this clause is declared to be professional misconduct.

The regulation was still effective under the Legal Profession Act 1987 (NSW) as of 1 July 2005 and will continue under the Legal Profession Act 2004 (NSW). Although lawyers can be held responsible for their actions, the courts still may decide to apply the *BAT* decision.

Lawyers' privileges and responsibilities

14.56 Lawyers have a responsibility to the court to make reasonable inquiries concerning their clients' allegations of fraud, dishonesty or misconduct of others. These allegations may be placed into pleadings and can lead to serious damage to the reputation of others. Lawyers are protected absolutely against any defamation actions for what they say in court, to ensure freedom of speech.[144] The protection granted to lawyers places them under an obligation to obtain all relevant information on serious allegations in order to make a fair assessment as to whether to make the allegations in court. Failure to do so would be an abuse of their privilege of immunity.[145] If after investigating the lawyer concludes that the allegations are unsubstantiated, but the client insists that they be made, the lawyer has a duty to refuse to follow the instructions or to withdraw.[146]

14.57 In a famous case of abuse of this privilege, *Clyne v NSW Bar Association*,[147] Clyne was struck off the rolls for allegations he made concerning the solicitor for the opposing party. Clyne represented the husband in a matrimonial dispute and persuaded him to bring an action against the wife's solicitor for criminal maintenance. The purpose of the action was to intimidate the solicitor into ceasing to act for the wife. In opening the proceedings Clyne alleged, according to the High Court, that the solicitor had engaged in 'fraud, perjury and blackmail'. The High Court said Clyne:

> ... knew that he had no evidence to substantiate such allegations. At the end of the opening he invited the [solicitor] ... to defend himself before any evidence had been given against him and intimated that, if he were to cease to act for his client, the criminal proceedings would have achieved their object and could be discontinued.

---

144. *Cabassi v Vila* (1940) 64 CLR 130 at 141 following *Munster v Lamb* (1883) 11 QBD 588.

145. See Lord Macmillan, *Law and Other Things*, Cambridge University Press, Cambridge, 1937, p 191 cited by Jordan CJ in *Oldfield v Keogh* (1941) 41 SR (NSW) 206 at 211.

146. D Ipp, 'Lawyers' Duties to the Court' (above), p 85. Justice Ipp cites *Thatcher v Douglas* [1996] *Times Law Reports* 6, to support this statement.

147. (1960) 104 CLR 186 at 188.

Some of Clyne's allegations for which there was no evidence were:

❑ The solicitor was 'in financial difficulties' as a result of his partner's defalcations. The court pointed out that this statement was highly damaging to a solicitor.

❑ The solicitor had signed a false affidavit on behalf of the wife.

❑ The solicitor had deliberately protracted the litigation to serve his own ends, that is, making costs for himself.

❑ The solicitor was conducting proceedings that he knew to be hopeless.

The High Court upheld the right to absolute privilege against defamation for advocates' statements in court, but held that:[148]   **14.58**

> ... from the point of view of a profession which seeks to maintain standards of decency and fairness, it is essential that the privilege ... is not abused ... It is obviously unfair and improper in the highest degree for counsel, hoping that, where proof is impossible, prejudice may suffice, to make such statements unless he definitely knows that he has, and definitely intends to adduce, evidence to support them. It cannot, of course, be enough that he thinks that he may be able to establish his statements out of the mouth of a witness for the other side.

Clyne alleged that he was the only advocate in a common law jurisdiction in the last 300 years to be struck off the rolls for his advocacy in court.[149] Usually, unsupported or irrelevant allegations do not lead to disciplinary action against the lawyer making them. In *Taylor v Edwards*[150] counsel in a jury trial opened and closed a civil case with allegations that he had not and could not prove. Counsel had been warned by the judge after his opening address that counsel might not prove the allegation and still counsel repeated similar remarks in his closing address. The Court of Appeal upheld the judge's action of aborting the trial, discharging the jury, and ordering that the case not be relisted for one year and that the plaintiff pay the costs of the trial. It would appear that such an order penalises the client unfairly, leaving the lawyer with no sanction.

English perspective

In *Strange v Hybinett*[151] a police officer who attended the scene of an   **14.59** accident drew plans to show that the plaintiff's motorcycle was lying some 400 yards from the point of collision. He later modified the distance to 200 yards, severely affecting the plaintiff's case, after revisiting the scene with an inspector. The Court of Appeal said that a submission to the jury that the police officer had been 'leant on' by his superiors to change his evidence would not have been considered improper. But counsel went further in his submission, asserting corruption on the part of the defendant's solicitor and others. He said that they had leant on various witnesses and 'orchestrated' their evidence, which according to the Court of Appeal unfairly affected the jury's minds. It therefore ordered a new trial.

---

148. For similar views in an American case see *Kiefel v Las Vegas Hacienda, Inc* 39 FRD 592 (ND Ill 1966).
149. Clyne made this allegation to the author and, by my investigations, seems to be correct: see also P Clyne, *Outlaw Among Lawyers*, Cassell, North Ryde, 1981, pp 3–7.
150. [1967] 1 NSWLR 689 at 690. For similar views on opening address see *Frazier v Cupp* 394 US 371 at 376 and on closing remarks *Ayoub v Spencer* 550 F 2d 164 (3rd Cir 1977).
151. [1988] VR 418.

Lawyers have a difficult time with courts concerning unsupported or irrelevant allegations in protecting the rights of 'political offenders'. Political cases have been focused on mainly in Europe and the United States.[152] In political cases in Australia[153] and England lawyers have to show that police practices have been unfair. These lawyers usually allege that police fabricate confessions and evidence, and have difficulty in proving these allegations,[154] although it has been successfully done at times in Australia.[155] Judges have in the past not been supportive of such allegations against police and have usually reprimanded the lawyers, but this may change in light of the revelations of police corruption, including fabrication of evidence, found by the New South Wales Police Royal Commission conducted from 1995–97.

14.60   A good example of the typical behaviour of judges was Stevenson J's comments on defence counsel in a famous IRA case in England. He said:

> One would have hoped that judgment and experience would have spared the police and their witness the insulting suggestions made in this case. It has been a mud-slinging defence.

The judge expressed his opinion to the taxing officer that legal aid costs paid to defence counsel should exclude the time spent in making allegations against the police. The taxing officer heeded this advice and reduced counsel fees by one-third. The Bar Council defended the actions of the barrister and the Professional Conduct Committee found that the barrister had properly conducted the defence of his client. The Court of Appeal also acquitted counsel of any deliberate wasting of the court's time for personal advantage or other motives.[156]

Insults, intimidation and obfuscation

Professional rules

14.61   As stated above, r 35 of the Barristers' Rules [Model Rules r 16.1] states that:

> A barrister [practitioner in Model Rules] must, when exercising the forensic judgements ... take care to ensure that decisions by the barrister or on the barrister's advice to involve the coercive powers of a court or to make allegations or suggestions under privilege against any person: ...
>
> (c) are not made principally in order to harass or embarrass the person ...

---

152. For an excellent book on the issue in the United States see N Dorsen and L Friedman, *Disorder in the Court*, Pantheon Books, New York, 1973; see also G Hazard Jr, 'Securing Courtroom Decorum' (1970) 80 *Yale LJ* 433.
153. They occur rarely in Australia but one such case was the Alister, Dunn and Anderson trial according to Justice Murphy. See *R v Alister* (1984) 154 CLR 404; *R v Anderson* (1991) 53 A Crim R 2/21 (CCA, NSW). See T Anderson, *Take Two*, Transworld Publishing, Sydney, 1992. See also I Turner, *Sydney's Burning*, Heinemann Books, Melbourne, 1967 for a political trial of members of the International Workers of the World in 1915.
154. R Douglas, 'Restrained Dissent: Restrained Repression: Political Offenders and the Victorian Courts' (1989) 22 *ANZ Journal of Criminology* 237, 249.
155. See, generally, Anderson (above).
156. 'Statement on *R v McFadden*' (1975) 119 *Solicitors J* 868. See also *R v McFadden* (1976) 62 Cr App R 187.

There are similar provisions in other jurisdictions.[157] ABA Model Rules r 3.5 states: 'A lawyer shall not: (d) engage in conduct intended to disrupt a tribunal.' Comment [4] to the rule states:

> ... Refraining from abusive or obstreperous conduct is a corollary of the advocate's right to speak on behalf of litigants ... An advocate can present the cause, protect the record for subsequent review and preserve professional integrity by patient firmness no less effectively than by belligerence or theatrics.

Although the ABA Model Rule calls for lawyers to behave with decorum and to avoid abusive practices, lawyers in the United States have rarely been disciplined or punished for such behaviour.[158] In Australia courts have been willing to criticise such behaviour, but there are not many cases that have used sanctions.[159] The *Clyne* case (see **14.57**) is an example of the imposition of a harsh sanction and there are other cases that have, for example, ordered a new trial[160] or cited the lawyer for contempt.[161]

Advocate's court behaviour

In a more recent case, *NSW Bar Association v di Suvero*,[162] the barrister was suspended from practice for three months for 'unsatisfactory professional conduct'. The disciplinary action arose out of the actions of the barrister during a 10-week trial where his client, the leader of a transformational group, was charged with sexual abuse. The trial was highly contentious from its start when, on the application of the Crown, the judge closed the court for most of the Crown's case. The barrister accused the court of creating a 'Star Chamber' by closing the court to the public, which is exactly how the Star Chamber operated. In a later proceeding, an appellate court said the court closure had been a serious error. The barrister also on five occasions used the word 'improper' concerning the actions of the prosecutor. The prosecutor took offence at these descriptions and claimed that this was an attack on his integrity and holding the potential tendency to inflame the jury against him.[163] In handing down its suspension the tribunal said that it accepted the Bar Council's submission that 'the conduct of the barrister was serious and that he did not display any understanding that his misconduct was wrong or that it was unsatisfactory'. The tribunal did point out that it thought it was 'unlikely that he would offend again'.[164]   **14.62**

There are also statutory provisions giving the court power to stop abusive questioning of witnesses in all jurisdictions in Australia,[165] but a study,   **14.63**

---

157. For example, Professional Conduct Rules (WA) rr 13.8 and 14.11.
158. Wolfram (above), para 12.1.3.
159. Disney et al (above), pp 860–4. An example where barristers were criticised but not punished is found in J Basten, 'Barristers; More Self-Protection' (1981) 6 *Legal Service Bulletin* 152; *Albrighton v Royal Prince Alfred Hospital* [1980] 2 NSWLR 542.
160. *Uren v Australian Consolidated Press* [1965] NSWLR 371 at 375 where the barrister introduced false issues, to prejudice and obscure the facts from the jury.
161. See *Ex parte Bellanto; Re Prior* [1963] NSWR 1556 at 1557 (C of A).
162. [2000] NSWADT 5 May 2000 and penalty decision handed down 28 July 2000.
163. See Y Ross, 'Fearless crusader pays the price for his principles', *Australian Financial Review*, 11 August 2000, p 35. The article criticises the decision of the tribunal.
164. [2000] NSWADT, 28 July 2000.
165. See, for example, Evidence Act 1906 (WA) ss 25–26; Evidence Act 1929 (SA) ss 22–25; Evidence Act 1958 (Vic) ss 37, 39–40; Evidence Act 1995 (NSW) and (Cth) s 41.

entitled *Heroines of Fortitude*, found that the courts failed to exercise their power. The study recorded sexual assault hearings (sentencing and trial) of adult women in the District Court of New South Wales between May 1994 and April 1995, and revealed many dubious ethical practices. There was excess adversarialism in cross-examination of complainants by both prosecutors and defence lawyers. These practices caused great distress and unfairness to the complainants. Furthermore, the report stated: 'Crown Prosecutors and Judges often failed to interject when cross-examination was irrelevant, intimidating and harassing.'[166] Some of the recommendations of the report included: (1) the need to 'develop and encourage alternative mechanisms by which complainants may give their evidence such as through the production of written statements, closed circuit television and computer technology'; (2) the need to utilise provisions of the Evidence Act 1995 and the Bar Association Rules to 'limit questions that are insulting, degrading, humiliating or irrelevant'.[167]

Intimidation

14.64   In an English case a solicitor was struck off the rolls for intimidation of witnesses. He had placed in the well, normally reserved for solicitors and close to the witness box, a person known 'to be active in the twilight world' and known to witnesses for the prosecution. The purpose was to intimidate these witnesses.[168]

In a more recent disciplinary hearing in 2000 in Queensland, *In the Matter of Greg Gregory*, a solicitor had deliberately sought in a conversation to influence a Crown witness to change her proposed testimony to be more favourable towards his client. The solicitor was found guilty of contempt. The Solicitors Complaints Tribunal found him guilty of professional misconduct and suspended him from practice for two years and to pay $4500. The tribunal considered striking him off but accepted his sincere regrets. It said it was 'satisfied that the offence was committed on the spur of the moment' and that the practitioner, who had limited criminal law experience, did not fully appreciate the seriousness of what he did and 'that his judgment was clouded and pressured'.[169]

14.65   In a separate matter arising out of the retrial of *Strange v Hybinett*, discussed above, the plaintiff's lawyer, Taylor, was charged with contempt for attempting to intimidate Strange who was a main witness in the case. Serious allegations had been made in court concerning Taylor just before the luncheon adjournment. The incident related to the contempt occurred during this adjournment. While walking past Strange in the street he said 'You're gone, son' and kept on walking. Strange alleged that the words 'were spoken quietly accompanied by a physical movement towards him and a thrusting forward of the head'. The court cited *Westcott v Lord*[170] as clear authority that 'threatening or intimidating a witness is capable of

---

166. *Heroines of Fortitude: The experiences of women in court as victims of sexual assault*, Report of Department of Women (NSW), Sydney, November 1996, p 181.
167. *Heroines of Fortitude* (above), pp 147, 181.
168. *Re a Solicitor* (1978) 122 *Solicitors' J* 96 (HC).
169. 'Bi-Annual Report of Disciplinary Action' (June 1998) Supplement to *Proctor* (*Queensland Law Society J*) 13. The Attorney-General lodged an appeal in this matter.
170. [1911] VLR 452.

amounting to contempt'. Gobbo J looked at the surrounding circumstances of the conduct. He concluded that he was unable to be satisfied beyond a reasonable doubt that Taylor's actions were 'in reckless disregard of the likely effect of the threat on Strange. Thus there was not the necessary intention to interfere with the course of justice'. Gobbo J did comment that Taylor's 'conduct was belligerent, arrogant, vulgar and generally fell short of what one would expect from a member of a learned profession'.[171]

Although the rules prohibit abusive practices, there are numerous articles and books on trial advocacy on various strategies to be adopted to insult, intimidate or obscure in order to discredit disadvantageous evidence.[172] Wigmore said approvingly:[173]

14.66

> An intimidating manner in putting questions may so coerce or disconcert the witness that his [or her] answers do not represent his actual knowledge on the subject. So also, questions which in form or subject cause embarrassment, shame or anger in the witness may unfairly lead him to such demeanour or utterances that the impression produced by his statements does not do justice to its real testimonial value.

Even in the United States, where there is more leeway than in Australia or England on cross-examination,[174] the courts have criticised harassment of witnesses. They state that these actions distort the fact-finding process, are offensive to witnesses and cause potential witnesses to be discouraged from testifying.[175] As in Australia, there are evidence rules that require judges to protect witnesses from undue harassment and embarrassment.[176]

Direct communications with other parties or their witnesses

The doctrine of fairness requires lawyers to be careful in their communications with other parties or their witnesses. In fact there is a general prohibition on communication, with certain exceptions.[177] The purpose of the restrictions as stated by the professional bodies is the fear that such communications by a lawyer will tend to intimidate, coerce or harass. Communications to opposing parties that are misleading and calculated to intimidate can constitute professional misconduct. For example, the High Court in *Kennedy v Incorporated Law Institute of New South Wales*[178] held that a lawyer who attempts to influence a defence witness has committed professional misconduct. In that case a solicitor was struck off the rolls for going to the home of an adverse witness, and trying to persuade her to change her testimony.

14.67

---

171. *R v Taylor* (unreported, SC(Vic), Gobbo J, No 3051 of 1989, 14 December 1989, BC8902930).
172. See R Keeton, *Trial Tactics and Methods*, 2nd ed, Little Brown & Co, Boston, 1973, which analyses the unfair tactics urged by others in light of the ABA Model Code of Professional Responsibility.
173. See J Frank, *Courts on Trial*, Princeton University Press, Princeton, 1949, pp 82–3.
174. For the Australian position, see Aronson and Hunter (above), Chapter 21.
175. Wolfram (above), para 12.4.5.
176. For example, see Federal Rules of Evidence r 611(a)(3).
177. See Professional Conduct and Practice Rules (NSW) r 31; Solicitors' Handbook (Qld) r 4.01.3; Barristers' Rules (NSW)) rr 54 and 55, (Qld) rr 55 and 56; Law Council of Australia's Model Rules rr 25.1–25.2.
178. (1939) 13 ALJ 563.

Professional rules

14.68   The professional rules have three main consequences:

- ❑ they may lead to reducing the risk of excessive coercion by opposing lawyers;
- ❑ they enable lawyers to have greater control over their clients;
- ❑ they prevent clients from saving on legal fees because of the need always to communicate through their lawyers.

14.69   The first of these consequences is 'clearly desirable, but the second and third are of dubious merit'.[179]

Rule 49 of the Barristers' Rules (NSW) [r 50 (Qld) and Model Rules r 17.7] allows communication with any witness willing to discuss the matter involved and prohibits barristers from preventing or discouraging witnesses from being interviewed by opposing counsel. Rule 50 (NSW) [r 51 (Qld) and Model Rules r 17.8] says a barrister will not have breached r 49 simply by 'telling ... a witness that the witness need not agree to confer or to be interviewed'. Solicitors are entitled to the same rights.[180]

There is a lack of guidance in these rules in relation to a corporation instructing its in-house advisers. It may be difficult for lawyers to decide which persons among the opponent corporation's employees are to be considered clients and therefore come under the rules.[181] There is no doubt that seeking to talk with chief executives would be unethical but there is scope to have contact with other employees of the opponent corporation. But, Jones says, even if contact with other employees is technically within the rules, this 'communication should be limited to requests for information for facts which are not privileged or in dispute and should avoid sharp practice on the part of a solicitor initiating communication, in both substance and form'.[182]

DUTIES OF CANDOUR

Introduction

14.70   In the beginning of this chapter, in the context of negotiation, the various general statements of professional bodies that lawyers need to act honestly and truthfully in their dealings with other parties have been discussed. The courts depend on lawyers' honesty and vigilance for the system to operate efficiently. For example, legal practitioners are under a duty to ensure that their clients, especially corporate clients, understand the need for full disclosure under discovery procedures. The clients should be made aware that they must search and disclose any material documents and not destroy them. The practitioner's 'burden extends ... to taking steps to ensure that in any corporate organisation [this] knowledge is passed on to any who may be

---

179. Disney et al (above), p 866.
180. Professional Conduct and Practice Rules (NSW) rr 18, 23–A54; Law Council's Model Rules r 12 or r 17.55.
181. 'Ethical Restraints on Interviewing Witnesses' (1990) 64 *Law Institute J (Vic)* 910.
182. A Jones, 'Speak No Evil, Hear No Evil?: Rule 4.01.3 and the Corporate Client' (March 1998) *Proctor (Queensland Law Society J)* 11, 13.

affected by it'.[183] Obviously, the lawyers in the *McCabe* case knew about these duties, but discovery only takes place after an action is initiated.

Can lawyers be trusted?

Ipp J feels that judges cannot depend on lawyers today as they did in the past. He says lawyers give greater weight to the interest of their clients than to the paramount formal duties to the administration of justice. Furthermore, he argues that the power of collegiate disapproval has dissipated: as litigation has increased, the profession has grown larger and there is wide geographical dispersal of lawyers.[184] The Australian Law Reform Commission (ALRC) in Issues Paper 20, para 11.15 states:[185]   **14.71**

> Duties to the administration of justice may also be interpreted narrowly so that they do not restrict a lawyer's ability to present the best possible case for their client. For example distinctions are made between fabricating evidence and not disclosing evidence. The consequences of this lack of candour in litigation may include:
>
> ❑ the deliberate suppression of relevant but unfavourable evidence
> ❑ the selective presentation of part of the evidence
> ❑ the promotion of biased expert evidence
> ❑ the unwarranted failure to admit the truth of the facts asserted by the opposition
> ❑ the use of cross-examination to suggest the falsehood of a matter known to be true
> ❑ the use of tactical attacks on the credibility of witnesses to suggest that the witness cannot be believed on oath, even though their evidence is known to be true.

This section will discuss the duties of candour that limit what lawyers can do for their clients, mainly in the context of litigation because most discussion has been in this area. We will look at the following areas: **14.72**

❑ failure to proffer material;
❑ proffering material known to be false or misleading;
❑ tricks in presenting and discrediting material.

Lawyers are only held to duties of candour to disclose things that they know or should know in relation to the subject matter in question. These duties are in addition to various obligations for disclosure under procedural rules, for example discovery, answering interrogatories and inspection of documents. Our problem is what should be done if reasonable lawyers in the particular context 'would have known, whether by deduction from facts disclosed or by pursuing investigations' and the lawyer alleges he or she did not know.[186] As Frankel has pointed out, American lawyers are experts at losing certain senses at critical moments. The 'sharp eye of the cynical lawyer becomes at strategic moments a demurely averted and filmy gaze'.[187]

---

183. *Rockwell Machine Tool Co Ltd v E P Barrus (Concessionaires) Ltd* [1968] 2 All ER 98 (HC).
184. D Ipp, 'Reforms to the Adversarial Process in Civil Litigation — Part I' (1995) 69 *ALJ* 705, 726–7.
185. Ipp (above). The ALRC refers to T Thawley, 'Adversarial and inquisitorial procedures in the Administrative Appeal Tribunal' (1997) 4(2) *Australian J of Administrative Law* 67.
186. Ipp (above).
187. M Frankel, 'The Search for Truth: An Umpireal View' (1975) *Univ of Penn LR* 1031, 1039.

14.73   In the English context, the famous 'Rumpole of the Bailey', an eccentric criminal barrister who is depicted in various books and on television, uses all kinds of devices to avoid hearing material that may be detrimental to his client. These include telling the witness or client to 'shut up', making believe he is 'temporarily deaf' or just getting out of the interviewing room before the incriminating information is revealed.[188] Similar practices have been found among Australian barristers.[189]

Failure to proffer material — generally

Professional rules

14.74   Barristers' Rules New South Wales state:[190]

21. A barrister must not knowingly make a misleading statement to a court on any matter.

22. A barrister must take all necessary steps to correct any misleading statement made by the barrister to a court as soon as possible after the barrister becomes aware that the statement was misleading.

23. A barrister must take all necessary steps to correct any express concession made to the court in civil proceedings by the opponent in relation to any material fact, case-law or legislation:

    (a) only if the barrister knows or believes on reasonable grounds that it was contrary to what should be regarded as the true facts or the correct state of the law;

    (b) only if the barrister believes the concession was an error; and

    (c) not (in the case of a concession of fact) if the client's instructions to the barrister support the concession. [substituted for old rule, January 2000]

24. A barrister seeking any interlocutory relief in an ex parte application must disclose to the court all matters which:

    (a) are within the barrister's knowledge;

    (b) are not protected by legal professional privilege; and

    (c) the barrister has reasonable grounds to believe would support an argument against granting the relief or limiting its terms adversely to the client.

24A A barrister who has knowledge of matters which are within Rule 24(c):

    (a) must seek instructions for the waiver of legal professional privilege if the matters are protected by that privilege, so as to permit the barrister to disclose those matters under Rule 24; and

    (b) if the client does not waive the privilege as sought by the barrister:

        (i) must inform the client of the client's responsibility to authorise such disclosure and the possible consequences of not doing so; and

        (ii) must inform the court that the barrister cannot assure the court that all matters which should be disclosed have been disclosed to the court.

25. A barrister must, at the appropriate time in the hearing of the case and if the court has not yet been informed of that matter, inform the court of:

    (a) any binding authority;

---

188. See, generally, J Mortimer, *Rumpole of the Bailey*, Penguin Books, Ringwood, 1979.

189. E Proust, 'Observing the Legal Profession' in P Cashman (ed), *Research and the Delivery of Legal Services*, Law Foundation of NSW, Sydney, 1981, p 296; E Beecker, 'A Quotient of Conscience', *The Age*, May 13, 1978, p 17.

190. The Queensland Bar Rules, rr 23–33, and the Model Rules, rr 44, 14.1–14.12, are similar.

(b) any authority decided on by the Full Court of the Federal Court of Australia, a Court of Appeal of a Supreme Court or a Full Court of a Supreme Court;

(c) any authority on the same or materially similar legislation as that in question in the case, including any authority decided at first instance in the Federal Court or a Supreme Court, which has not been disapproved; or

(d) any applicable legislation;

which the barrister has reasonable grounds to believe to be directly in point, against the client's case.

26. A barrister need not inform the court of matters within Rule 25 at a time when the opponent tells the court that the opponent's whole case will be withdrawn or the opponent will consent to final judgment in favour of the client, unless the appropriate time for the barrister to have informed the court of such matters in the ordinary course has already arrived or passed.

27. A barrister who becomes aware of a matter within Rule 25 after judgement or decision has been reserved and while it remains pending, whether the authority or legislation came into existence before or after argument, must inform the court of that matter by:

(a) a letter to the court, copied to the opponent, and limited to the relevant reference unless the opponent has consented beforehand to further material in the letter; or

(b) requesting the court to relist the case for further argument on a convenient date, after first notifying the opponent of the intended request and consulting the opponent as to the convenient date for further argument.

28. A barrister need not inform the court of any matter otherwise within Rule 25 which would have rendered admissible any evidence tendered by the prosecution which the court has ruled inadmissible without calling on the defence.

29. A barrister will not have made a misleading statement to a court simply by failing to disclose facts known to the barrister concerning the client's character or past, when the barrister makes other statements concerning those matters to the court, and those statements are not themselves misleading.

30. A barrister who knows or suspects that the prosecution is unaware of the client's previous conviction must not ask a prosecution witness whether there are previous convictions, in the hope of a negative answer.

31. A barrister must inform the court in civil proceedings of any misapprehension by the court as to the effect of an order which the court is making, as soon as the barrister becomes aware of the misapprehension.

The Professional Conduct Rules (WA) state: **14.75**

13.1 Subject to these Rules, counsel shall conduct each case in such manner as he [or she] considers will be most advantageous to his client.

13.2 A practitioner shall not knowingly deceive or mislead the court ...

13.4 Counsel shall at all times: ... (e) subject to these Rules, inform the court of any development which affects the information already before the court.

13.5 Counsel shall ensure that the court is informed of any relevant decision on a point of law or any legislative provision of which he is aware and which he considers to be relevant, whether it be for or against his contention.

There is little guidance given in applying the professional rules. In 1995 the New South Wales Bar Association issued a clarification to r 21 concerning the service of medical reports. Rule 21 states: 'A barrister must not knowingly make a misleading statement to the court on any matter.' The Association stated:

> The tender of a medical report in common law proceedings where counsel making the tender is aware that in a subsequent report the doctor has changed his opinion constitutes making a misleading statement to the court.

Counsel should 'either tender the second report or, alternatively, withdraw the tender of the first report'.[191] The Australian Law Reform Commission has noted the problem of interpreting the ethical rules for litigation and has recommended that commentaries and examples be included with the text of the Law Council's Model Rules.[192]

American professional rules

14.76   In the United States ABA Model Rules r 3.3 has similar requirements to avoid misleading the court. It states:

> (a) A lawyer shall not knowingly:
>
> (1) make a false statement of fact or law to a tribunal or fail to correct a false statement of material fact or law previously made to the tribunal by the lawyer;
>
> (2) fail to disclose to the tribunal legal authority in the controlling jurisdiction known to the lawyer to be directly adverse to the position of the client and not disclosed by the opposing counsel; or
>
> (3) offer evidence that the lawyer knows to be false. If a lawyer, the lawyer's client, or a witness called by lawyer, has offered material evidence and the lawyer comes to know of its falsity, the lawyer shall take reasonable remedial measures …

This rule is most likely to be applicable to pre-trial discovery and has thus been applied in conjunction with r 26 of the Federal Rules of Civil Procedure: see **14.40**.[193] The adoption and application of r 3.3 has led to a vigorous debate, especially in relation to perjury in a criminal trial. We will discuss this debate in the next chapter.

Examples of failure to proffer materials

14.77   The general rule appears to be that a passive withholding of material is permissible, but the active concealment or misleading of the court is prohibited. The rule is based on the notion that in an adversary system each side has to discover and present its own evidence to best present its case. But does it make sense to distinguish between active or passive conduct in civil litigation if both result in giving the court a false impression and possibly leading to an unfair result? This general rule on passive conduct is

---

191. *Bar News* (NSW) 1995 edition, p 2.
192. Report No 89 (above), paras 3.141–3.147 and Recommendation 23.
193. ABA Opinion 92-376, which applies r 3.3. concludes that 'the only remedial measure in the client fraud situations most likely encountered in pre-trial proceedings' may be revelation. For a thorough application of r 3.3 to a case where Justice Department lawyers failed to divulge the perjury in a deposition of one of its witnesses see *United States v Shaffer Equipment Company*, 11 F3d 450 (4th Cir 1993).

modified by the specific professional rules stated above. Lord Diplock has stated the general rule:[194]

> A barrister must not wilfully mislead the court as to the law nor may he actively mislead the court as to facts, although, consistently with the rule that the prosecution must prove its case, he may passively stand by and watch the court being misled by reason of its failure to ascertain facts that are within the barrister's knowledge.

Comment [3] to ABA Model Rules r 3.3 also appears to modify this statement. It states: **14.78**

> ... There are circumstances where failure to make a disclosure is the equivalent of an affirmative misrepresentation. The obligation prescribed in R 1.2(d) not to counsel a client to commit or assist the client in committing a fraud applies to litigation.

This provision is also relevant to lawyers dealing with criminal defendants involved in perjury under r 3.3(b) and Comments [8]–[11] to that rule. We will discuss these provisions in the next chapter. A good example of the application of r 1.2(d) is *People v Lewis*.[195] In that case the court held that defence counsel had acted properly in informing the court that his client was feigning inability to communicate. The client was trying to have the court find him too incompetent.

The case law has illustrated the general rules. A New South Wales barrister was found to have committed professional misconduct by knowingly misleading a magistrate by stating that the defendant had no prior convictions. The barrister argued that at the time he made the allegations he had not fully recollected the facts as to the defendant's history. The tribunal said that if the barrister's recollection was limited he should not have taken the course of providing information about the defendant's previous convictions without seeking an adjournment to ascertain the facts.[196] **14.79**

In the English case of *Tombling v Universal Bulb Co Ltd*[197] the barrister received an affirmative reply when he asked a witness whether he lived at a certain residential address. The witness then replied in the affirmative when asked whether he had been a prison governor. The witness had left the prison service after being convicted of an offence. He was presently in prison, but brought to court by a warder and both of them were in plain clothes. The fact that he was in prison was unknown to the defendants' lawyers, but known to the plaintiff's lawyers.

Somervell LJ disapproved of the method of questioning but found that what happened was not a 'trick'. He added that even if there had been a trick that in itself would not be enough for a new trial. A new trial 'must depend on the nature of the evidence and not on the circumstances that prevented its being available'. He denied a new trial but did say that if there was a failure by the lawyers to carry out their duties to the court there were ways **14.80**

---

194. *Saif Ali v Sydney Mitchell & Co* [1980] AC 198 at 220.
195. 393 NE 2d 1380 (Ill 1979).
196. *In the matter of Everard Andrew Englebrecht*, Legal Services Tribunal, Disciplinary Reports No 5, 1995, p 1.
197. [1951] 2 TLR 289 at 291–7 (C of A).

to deal with that matter. Denning LJ emphasised that counsel's duty to their clients:

> ... is to make every honest endeavour to succeed. He must not, of course, knowingly mislead the court, either on the facts or on the law, but, short of that, he may put such matters in evidence or omit others as in his discretion he thinks will be most to the advantage of his client.

Lord Denning found nothing improper in the conduct of the case, but said it would have been improper if the question on his address had been done to knowingly mislead the court. Singleton LJ, in dissent, interpreted the facts differently and was critical of the conduct of the plaintiff's solicitors.

14.81   The *Tombling* case needs to be compared to another English case, *Meek v Fleming*.[198] In this case the Court of Appeal found that there was deliberate misleading by the lawyer and ordered a new trial. The plaintiff had sought damages against a police officer for assault and false imprisonment. At that time the officer had been a chief inspector, but had been demoted to sergeant; this was not known to the plaintiff. At the trial the defendant came in plain clothes, while all the other police witnesses were in uniform. If he had been in uniform it would have been obvious that he had been demoted. His counsel addressed him throughout the trial as 'Mr' and not according to his status. Furthermore, he was never asked his rank. In cross-examination he was asked if he was a chief inspector and lied. The judge also referred to him as inspector or chief inspector.

Holboyd Pearce LJ said that the misleading of the court as to his status was an important matter to his credibility as a witness. Unlike the *Tombling* case the failure to reveal was a 'premeditated line of conduct' and the judge and jury in this case were misled on an important matter:

> Where a party deliberately misleads the court in a material matter, and that deception has probably tipped the scale in his favour ... it would be wrong to allow him to retain the judgment thus unfairly procured.

14.82   Willmer LJ distinguished this case from the *Tombling* case. In the latter case failure to disclose the prison record was only of incidental significance. In this case the evidence of character not disclosed was of one of the parties to the suit, which was of vital significance, so as to present 'the whole case on a false basis'. Furthermore, unlike the *Tombling* case, here the deception was knowingly and deliberately implemented.

The law may be moving towards requiring advocates to make more disclosures if the information that is withheld would change the basis of how the court understands the case. If the situation is such that the court will be seriously misled, the advocate needs to disclose this information. In a recent English case, *Vernon v Bosley (No 2)*,[199] counsel failed to reveal that his client had given inconsistent evidence in other proceedings to that tendered in the present proceeding. In finding that the counsel had a duty to disclose this information, Stuart-Smith LJ said that 'where the case has been conducted on the basis of certain material facts which are an essential part of the party's case' there is a duty on that party's counsel to correct the misunderstanding by the court.[200]

198. [1961] 2 QB 366 at 375.
199. [1997] 3 WLR 683.
200. This case is discussed by Justice Ipp. See D Ipp, 'Lawyers' Duties to the Court' (above), p 68.

Failure to proffer material

Regulatory bodies

An area of deception that has been of great importance in Australia and the **14.83** United States is that of practices before regulatory agencies. Lawyers appear-ing before these bodies have to be wary of the fact that these bodies usually have powers to discipline them. The disciplinary powers include the right to suspend or revoke their rights of appearance before the regulatory body. Some of these problems are apparent in the tax area. The ethical rules for lawyers may be in conflict with adopting a non-adversarial approach in the tax area. As was discussed in Chapter 12, lawyers must give 'undivided fidelity' to the client's interest, subject only to their duty to the court. The duty to the court places on lawyers affirmative duties that can oppose their client's interests, but these duties appear only to arise in the context of litigation. This situation arises out of the historical foundations of professional legal ethics in criminal cases, especially criminal defence work. Although these rules have been extended to other areas of law they cannot possibly cover all the functions now performed by lawyers. The fact that the criminal defence model is still retained by the profession as a main source of lawyer obligations would seem to result in 'maximum immunity from responsibility'.[201]

Another problem is that if practitioners do not give their clients full **14.84** information they may be subject to negligence,[202] although it would be almost impossible to win a suit against a practitioner who did not offer advice on a position that fell into the grey area between legality and illegality. It can also be argued that cooperation at the early stages of dealing with the ATO, return preparation and filing, may reveal information that will prejudice your client if the client is later audited and may also be a breach of the rules of confidentiality. The problem for Australian lawyers, unlike American tax lawyers, is that they frequently arrive on the scene after the early stages. Finally, it can be argued that lawyers in Australia should adopt the same position as stated in the United States in Opinion 85-352 (see below), which is that ethically they have to take an adversary position towards the government.

Accountants' Taxation Standards

It is of interest to note that the accountants' statement of Taxation **14.85** Standards in Australia, APS 6 issued in 1982 and not amended as of August 2005, tries to balance the accountant's obligations to the client and to the government. Paragraph 11 states:

> In the absence of specific instructions from his client, a member is not responsible for the accuracy of the particulars or information forming part of the return. However, where a member relies on the particulars and information supplied by the client for the preparation of returns or submissions to the revenue authorities, he must make reasonable inquiries as to their accuracy and completeness.

---

201. G Hazard, *Ethics in the Practice of Law*, Yale University Press, New Haven, 1978, p 150.
202. D Hill, 'Ethics of Tax Practice' in G Cooper and R Vann (eds), *Decision Making in the Australian Tax System*, Australian Research Tax Foundation, Sydney, 1986, p 164.

14.86   In a similar vein, para 10 requires members, when associated with a return, a financial statement submitted with a return, or a submission to a revenue authority, to:

> ... take reasonable steps to ensure that it is not misleading and that it does not omit or obscure material information. Subject to these requirements he must present the information in a way which best supports the client's interests.

It would appear that accountants are more willing to judge the ethical behaviour of their clients than lawyers. Collie and Marinis have argued that the difference between lawyers and accountants in the perception of their role for their clients is due to the fact that accountants do not see themselves as advocates.[203] Lawyers in their professional codes and rules frequently emphasise the need to provide undivided loyalty to their client. If a conflict of interest or a problem of confidentiality arises which can lead to less than total service for the client, the lawyer must fully inform the client. The lawyer can act if the client waives the right to total service. In contrast, accountants' professional roles sometimes lead them to act as go-betweens for the government and their clients. Historically, accountants adopted this mediation position because their initial job is frequently to certify financial statements and in this capacity they must act independently of, and even sometimes against, their client.

If accountants ignore this role and act solely for their clients, they can become liable to creditors and the public, who are third parties whose interests may be adversely affected. It is only since the early 1970s that accountants expanded their tax role to one of adviser and advocate, causing the schizophrenic effect found in the statement of Taxation Standards. In effect, the government is seen as a creditor and the accountant as acting in a certification role. Accountants, unlike lawyers, will therefore at times be required to divulge confidential information that is adverse to their client's position. This problem may cease to exist as the mega accountancy firms develop large legal departments staffed with qualified lawyers.

14.87   Some legal firms tried to take advantage of their tax clients' right to legal professional privilege after the Federal Court held that professional legal privilege modified s 263 of the Income Tax Assessment Act 1936 (access to documents by ATO) in relation to the ATO raid on Citibank.[204] They advertised that, unlike clients of accountants, lawyers' clients were protected by professional legal privilege. The accountancy profession was outraged and protested to the Commissioner over the unequal treatment. As a result, the Commissioner issued guidelines in 1989 which were modified in 1992, that give some protection to independent accountants' clients' papers.[205] Furthermore, the large accounting firms now have legal departments, with tax lawyers admitted to practice. The clients of these lawyers do have the right to legal professional privilege. The differences

---

203. M Collie and T Marinis, 'Ethical Considerations of Discovery of Errors in Tax Returns' (1968– 69) 22 *Tax Lawyer* 455, 464–5.
204. *FCT v Citibank Ltd* (1989) 85 ALR 588. Due to the criticism over the nature of the raid the Commissioner issued guidelines for his officers in exercising their access power, restricting their activities in light of professional legal privilege: Other Guidelines (OG) 53.
205. See OG 69.

between lawyers and accountants may be changing. As we discussed in Chapter 13, lawyers are becoming more involved in the processes of mediation and these developments have become reflected in lawyers' professional codes.

American rules

In the United States the ABA and the American Institute of Certified Public Accountants (AICPA) have both issued ethical standards in relation to return preparation and advice. The ABA Formal Opinion 314 permits tax lawyers to advise their clients to take a position that has a 'reasonable basis' when they believe the law is uncertain.[206] A 'reasonable basis' opinion from a lawyer to a client usually results in a particular transaction being non-taxable. When a transaction falls outside the concept of income there is no need to disclose it in a tax return. Such a transaction may be held taxable if tested in court, but it is highly unlikely that it will be discovered because of the limited number of audits. The AICPA's Statement on Responsibilities, Tax Practice No 10, states that a certified public accountant may 'resolve doubt in favour of his client as long as there is reasonable support for his position'.

14.88

In 1985 the ABA modified Opinion 314 by adopting Formal Opinion 85-352. The latter reiterates the position taken by Opinion 314 with the additional requirement that the lawyer has to have a 'good faith belief' that the position has 'some realistic possibility of success if the matter is litigated'.[207] The relevant part of Opinion 85-352 states that:[208]

14.89

> [A] lawyer may advise reporting a position on a return even where the lawyer believes the position probably will not prevail, there is no 'substantial authority' in support of the position, and there will be no disclosure of the position on the return. However, the position to be asserted must be one which the lawyer in good faith believes is warranted in existing law or can be supported by a good faith argument for an extension, modification or reversal of existing law. *This requires that there is some realistic possibility of success if the matter is litigated.* In addition, in his role as adviser, the lawyer should refer to potential penalties and other legal consequences should the client take the position advised. [emphasis added]

The ABA Ethics Committee, by adopting Opinion 85-352, rejected its tax section's proposed higher standard which required that a position be 'meritorious'.[209] This proposal required lawyers to 'honestly' believe that the position is 'meritorious'. The 'meritorious' requirement would have meant that both 'a practical and realistic possibility of success, if litigated' standard would need to be met.[210] Perhaps even more important is the fact that the ABA failed to adopt the tax section's statement that the filing of a 'tax return is not a submission in an adversarial proceeding' and 'prior to commencement of such an adversarial relationship different considerations

---

206. ABA on Ethics and Professional Responsibility, Formal Opinion 85-352 (1985).
207. Formal Opinion 85-352 (1985).
208. ABA Standing Committee on Ethics and Professional Responsibility, Formal Opinion 85-352 in 39 *Tax Lawyer* 631, 672 (1985).
209. ABA Section of Taxation Proposed Revision to Formal Opinion 314 (1984) in B Wolfman and J P Holden, *Ethical Problems in Federal Tax Practice*, 2nd ed, Michie Co, Charlottesville, Va, 1985, pp 71–4. A third edition of this book was issued in 1995.
210. Holden (above), p 73.

apply'.[211] Instead it reaffirmed the adversarial view stated in Opinion 314. The ABA focused on the lawyer's obligation under its ethical codes and failed to look at the client's duty under law. The ABA Committee emphasised that both roles of a lawyer were involved even at the tax return stage — adviser and advocate. It said that frequently:[212]

> ... a lawyer must realistically anticipate that the filing of the tax return may be the first step in a process that may result in an adversary relationship between the client and the IRS [Internal Revenue Service] ...

14.90 In 1988 the AICPA followed the ABA by repealing the 'reasonable support test' and adopting a requirement of a 'good faith belief that the position has a realistic possibility of being sustained administratively or judicially on its merits if challenged'.[213] This requirement is modified by the fact that the Institute has said a certified public accountant may take a position that does not meet the standard if the position is not frivolous and is adequately disclosed on the return or claim for refund. The latter requirement at least gives the revenue service the opportunity to scrutinise the position taken but this will still be rare under the self-assessment system.

Many American tax lawyers and tax accountants have been or are involved in helping clients establish tax shelters. The big four accountancy firms have the largest stake. There is a continuous battle by the promoters of shelters with the IRS and legal academics about the validity of the schemes. Bankman says that, unlike the accountants, lawyers have somewhat more freedom, but those who are very involved have conflicts with their clients. Even if these lawyers want to be ethical about a particular scheme they have to protect their client and not take a public stand on the issue. Bankman points out that when the government wants to make a high level appointment in this area, it is difficult to find a tax expert who has not been compromised by working on dubious schemes.[214]

Is a tax audit adversarial?

14.91 According to most practitioners an audit is the first stage in a potential adversarial proceeding. Often it is also the last step and there will be no need for litigation. The role of the tax practitioner is made more complicated in these situations by the fact that the tax officers treat the audited taxpayer as a 'client'. Unlike the rules for lawyers, which regard contact with an opposing party as being unethical,[215] tax officers do not have similar restrictions. If we accept the audit as being non-adversarial such access to the taxpayer would appear to be for the benefit of both the government and the taxpayer. The problem is that taxpayers often lack the knowledge and experience, nor understand the legal ramifications of their situation in comparison to a tax officer. A tax practitioner may not need to

---

211. Holden (above), p 71.
212. Formal Opinion 85-352 (above), p 632.
213. Revised Statement on Responsibilities in Tax Practice (No 1).
214. J Bankman, 'An Academic's View of the Tax Shelter Battle' in J Selmrod and H Aaron (eds), *The Crisis in Tax Administration*, 2003, extracts in D Rhode and D Luban, *Legal Ethics*, 2004, pp 534–6.
215. See Law Council's Model Rules r 23.1; Professional Conduct and Practice Rules (NSW) r 31.1; Solicitors' Handbook (Qld) r 4.01.3 and Professional Conduct Rules (SA) r 10(3).

be present at all stages of the audit, but should have at least the initial access to the taxpayer to discuss the legal aspects of the situation.

An audit can be either adversarial or non-adversarial. If during the audit, for example, a possible fraud is revealed, the audit would immediately become adversarial. In such a situation practitioners would have to represent their client with undivided loyalty and to the best of their ability. There is also a view that as soon as the taxpayer's position is challenged by the tax officer an adversarial relationship exists between the client and the ATO.

Corneel realises the need for a balanced approach to the revenue service in the case of an audit. He says:[216]

14.92

> Both we and the client should cooperate with the Service, where this can be done without harm to the client's situation. We must remember, however, that it is not the Service but the courts that have the last word in determining what information — including information relating to third parties — the Service has a right to obtain from the client. In a particular case there is nothing wrong with politely informing an agent that a summons will be required or that the propriety of a summons that has been issued will be tested in court.

He emphasises the need to be truthful with the revenue service at all times and 'use our best efforts to ensure that the client is also truthful'.[217]

Lawyers' responsibilities during an audit/litigation

The question for a legal practitioner during an audit and litigation is — what are their duties of loyalty and confidentiality to the client and how do they differ from the tax return preparation and advice stage? The accounting profession provisions state that an accountant 'may act as an advocate for his client when representing or assisting him before certain tribunals'.[218] This calls for an adversarial position and undivided loyalty in the various stages of litigation. But does this include such representation at the audit stage? There appear to be no professional standards for taking an adversarial position during an audit, but many accountants do take such a position, especially if their client appears to be threatened with litigation. Furthermore, there is an increasing number of accountants with law degrees doing tax work who have been trained to be adversarial.

14.93

The provisions on loyalty for the Australian accountancy professions are almost identical and are found in the separate professional standards. The Institute of Chartered Accountants Standards state:[219]

> It is recognised that from time to time, unavoidable conflicts of interest or of duty will occur ... there may be an actual or perceived conflict between the respective interests of two or more clients of a *firm*; or there may be an actual or perceived conflict between the duty owed by the *firm* or a person in the *firm* to a client, and the personal interest of the *firm* or a person in the *firm*.

There are other provisions concerning keeping clients informed and the use of safeguards (Chinese Walls) within a firm to manage a conflict

216. F Corneel, 'Guidelines to Tax Practice Second' (1990) 43 *Tax Lawyer* 297, 308.
217. Corneel (above).
218. APS 6, para 6.
219. Institute of Chartered Accountants, Professional Statement, F.1, para 20, issued May 2002 and revised December 2004.

between two or more clients.[220] There are also provisions which prohibit representation, for example in a takeover situation, except with permission of both parties. Furthermore, a firm shall not represent both parties when there is potential for actual litigation.[221]

14.94 There is no guidance in Australia as to what position to take when a conflict develops between obligations to the client and those to the Tax Office. These often result in a problem over confidential information. Accountants face the problem discussed above of having defined public obligations as well as those to their clients. This is reflected in the general principles adopted by the profession which emphasise the need for objectivity and independence.

These provisions emphasise that an accountant's duty in the area of conflict of interests (loyalty) is in relation to the public and not the client. It includes this requirement in 'all professional work'. Perhaps this is why a survey found that accountants are more cooperative and less adversarial than lawyers in their dealings with the ATO.[222]

Other Taxation Standards provisions

14.95 One further problem facing Australian accountants is that they do the vast majority of return preparation. Thus, if litigation does occur they are far more likely than lawyers to be called as a witness in their client's case. This has been recognised by the accountancy profession in APS 6 para 7, which states:

> A member acting as a witness before any court or tribunal must ensure that his client is aware that the member has an obligation to assist in establishing the truth and to safeguard his professional independence. He must inform the client that he cannot, in his capacity as a witness, act as an advocate for the client.

It has been stated that accountants do not have as stringent requirements in the area of confidentiality as lawyers. The accounting profession's statement of Taxation Standards para 14 states:

> Confidential information acquired by a member in the course of his work for a client must not be used for any purposes other than the proper performance of his professional duties for that client.

Paragraph 15 states:[223]

> Unless he has a legal or professional duty to disclose, a member must not convey any information relating to a client's affairs to a third party without his client's permission.

Accountants and privilege

14.96 Accountants, unlike lawyers, have not been granted by common law the right to professional legal privilege. Therefore, in relation to para 15 on the exception to confidentiality, when required by the law the need to disclose is far more extensive for accountants than for lawyers. It was for this reason that the accountancy profession feared loss of clients if they were not

---

220. Ibid, paras 21–3.
221. Ibid, paras 23 and 24.
222. See R Tomasic and B Pentony, 'Tax Compliance and the Rule of Law: From Legalism to Administrative Procedure?' (1991) 8 *Australian Tax Forum* 85.
223. APS 6.

granted some rights of confidentiality in relation to ATO investigations. The Commissioner has granted accountants some rights to confidentiality in relation to access to documents made in the course of any access request administered by the Commissioner. This includes access to documents made in the course of all income tax audits. The guidelines are only a guide for the ATO to determine what is the appropriate circumstance for requesting accounting advisers to furnish information or produce papers.[224] Also, as previously stated, the large accountancy firms now have legal departments and/or employ many qualified tax lawyers who can maintain professional legal privilege.

American scandals — Savings and Loan Bank

The problem of dealing with regulatory agencies has come to the forefront in the United States because of the actions of several large law firms. The firm that received the most publicity was the Wall Street, New York law firm of Kaye, Scholer, Fierman, Hays & Handler (known as Kaye Scholer). They were the lawyers for Charles Keating Jr's infamous Lincoln Savings and Loan Bank and between 1984–89 received fees of about $13 million. The action of the law firm delayed regulators from discovering the slipshod business practices that resulted in the government performing a $2.6 billion bail out.[225] Some of the charges brought by the regulatory body, Office of Thrift Supervision (OTS), against the firm were that it engaged in a pattern of omitting or misrepresenting material facts in the various submissions it made to a regulatory agency (the now defunct Federal Home Loan Bank Board). It was alleged that these submissions were false or misleading. The OTS sought from the law firm restitution of losses of at least $275 million. **14.97**

Professor Hazard issued a favourable legal opinion for the firm based on a summary of OTS' documents on the affair.[226] Hazard said that the firm had not violated the professional responsibility rules. He based his decision on the fact that the matter had become adversarial. This had occurred because by the time these submissions were made Lincoln had already been told that it violated the Board regulations and had to act immediately to remedy the problem. Therefore, under the Comment to Model Rules r 1.3, the firm had acted with 'commitment and dedication to the interests of the client and with zeal in advocacy upon the client's behalf'. Furthermore, it had met the 'good faith' requirement under Model Rules r 3.1 for testing the existing law, as long as it was not making frivolous statements to the opposition. The opposing argument would be that a lawyer who cannot do anything for a client except to assist in fraudulent behaviour is in violation of r 1.2(d). A lawyer in such a situation should withdraw. Even if we assume that Hazard's argument is correct and the situation was adversarial, Comment [2] to r 3.3 states that the obligation under r 1.2(d) of not assisting a client in committing a fraud applies in the litigation context. Furthermore, more relevant than r 3.1 is r 8.4. Rule 8.4 states: 'It is professional misconduct for a lawyer to: … (c) engage in conduct involving dishonesty, fraud, deceit or misrepresentation.' **14.98**

---

224. See *Other Guidelines* (OG) 69.
225. S Goldberg, 'Welcome to the New Uncertainty' (1992) 78 *ABA J* 51.
226. J Podgers, 'Changing the Rules' (1992) 78 *ABA J* 53, 54.

14.99 The question of characterisation in Kaye Scholer is similar to one asked of tax lawyers. When does a matter become adversarial when dealing with a government agency? Is the adversarial position the correct approach to take in all regulatory situations? There are other questions here as to when lawyers need to take positive action to make their corporate client conform with regulatory law. Does there have to be in the lawyers' opinion 'substantial injury' to the corporation or can the lawyers decide what is in 'the best interests' of the corporate client? Weinstein, general counsel for OTS, who was involved in most of the cases against the law firms said he could not understand:[227]

> ... how we can claim that a lawyer is free to deceive a third party when the client could not? If that were the rule, if a lawyer were permitted to do that, what would be left of the liability risked by client's deception? Any client could overcome that liability simply by hiring a lawyer to do the dirty work for him.

14.100 Wolfram stated that to help clarify the situation regulatory agencies need to promulgate rules explicitly stating what is required from lawyers.[228] There are similar problems for lawyers in Australia when dealing with regulatory bodies.

It should be noted that Kaye Scholer eventually paid $41 million to the OTS and accepted restrictions placed on two of its partners preventing them from representing federally insured depository institutions. This settlement was forced on the firm after the OTS placed a freeze order on Kaye Scholer's assets. This order caused the firm's New York banks to threaten to 'pull the firm's line of credit if the case wasn't settled. Since the firm couldn't meet its payroll without credit, it had to accept the settlement'.[229] Other firms also settled in relation to the Lincoln Savings and other savings and loans institutions. They are: Jones Day Reavis & Pogue (Cleveland — the second largest firm in the United States), $51 million; Paul Weiss Rifkind Wharton & Garrison (New York), $45 million; Troutman Sanders (Atlanta), $20 million; Kirkpatrick & Lockhart (Pittsburgh), $9 million; and Sidley & Austin (Chicago), $7.5 million.[230] Nader and Smith recently interviewed a leading partner in Kaye Scholer as to whether the firm's reputation had been damaged and whether they had lost clients. The partner said:

> We know we haven't lost clients. We have gotten a lot of new business. The firm is very healthy and very prosperous. Our clients are bigger and more prosperous than they have ever been.

14.101 Nader and Smith conclude: 'So it appears that in the corporate and corporate law communities in which Kaye Scholer operates, the firm's conduct was viewed as standard, acceptable, even commendable legal work.'[231] It can only be concluded that unethical conduct can be very profitable. It should also be noted that no lawyer was disciplined by the professional associations for their actions. Simon states that: 'Kaye Scholer

---

227. H Weinstein, 'Attorney Liability in the Savings and Loan Crisis' (1993) *U of Illinois LR* 53, 61.
228. Podgers (above), p 55.
229. D Rhode (above), p 632.
230. *No Contest: Corporate Lawyers and the Perversion of Justice in America* (1996), pp 47–8. The authors cite various sources for this information in fn 109 of Chapter 1.
231. *No Contest* (above), pp 46–7.

indicates limitations on the profession's willingness and ability to set and enforce plausible standards of practice. Its instincts throughout the affair appear to have been self-protective rather than self-regulatory.'[232] Simon shows that a number of leading members of the profession and various professional institutions 'failed to seriously confront the issues raised by the OTS complaint, instead producing a panoply of evasions'.[233] One good ethical change that appeared to result from the case was that New York became the first state bar to allow an entire law firm to be disciplined for the unethical conduct of one or more of its lawyers.[234]

American scandals — Enron

Leading members of the accountancy and legal profession did not learn their lessons from the Savings and Loan Bank scandals and as result the stage was set for the Enron, WorldCom and other financial scandals at the beginning of the twenty-first century. The Sarbanes-Oxley Act, adopted in 2002, was a response to these fraudulent activities. We have already discussed how the Act makes corporate lawyers more accountable for fraudulent activities of their corporate clients: see **11.70**.   **14.102**

The scandals that erupted with the collapse of Enron in 2001 were based on manipulation of financial statements to make the corporations appear profitable or more profitable. The companies hoped to trade themselves out of their financial problems. The intention was to keep the companies out of bankruptcy and to maintain or increase the share price. 'Enron's manipulation consisted of extremely intricate transactions designed to move losses off Enron's books and onto the books of "special purposes entities" (SPEs) that were nominally independent from Enron but actually created by Enron for no purpose other than parking losses.'[235]

The big accounting firms were largely held responsible for the 'cooking' of the books, even though Enron had 250 in-house lawyers, and numerous other lawyers. It was estimated that Enron had spread the work out to over 100 law firms. The lawyers saw only certain transactions and supposedly did not know substantial parts of what was taking place. If one set of lawyers would not solve the problems given to them, or refused because they found the request to be fraudulent, Enron would give the work to another more amendable firm. Gordon points out that two large outside law firms, Vinson & Elkins and Andrews & Kurth, did work closely with Enron's accountants in setting up the SPEs. He still states that many times the lawyers did not understand the financial transactions and thus the lawyers 'seem to have played a relatively minor part in the theater of deception and self-dealing that has led to the collapse of Enron Corporation'.[236]

---

232. W Simon, 'The Kaye Scholer Affair: The Lawyer's Duty of Candor and the Bar's Temptations of Evasion and Apology' (1998) *Law and Social Inquiry* 243, 244.
233. Simon (above), Part II, pp 259–67. See also Zitrin and Langford, *The Moral Compass of the American Lawyer* (above), pp 172–8.
234. Simon (above), p 178.
235. Rhode and Luban (above), p 290.
236. R Gordon, 'A New Role for Lawyers? The Corporate Counselor After Enron' (2003) 35 *Conn LR* 1185 extracted and referred to in Rhode and Luban (above), pp 290–1 and 508–14.

Koniak disagrees with Gordon's assessment. She points out that some of the nation's best legal talent represented the leading banks in establishing fraudulent transactions with Enron and setting up the SAEs. She says: 'Are we also to believe that all the lawyers who worked on these deals were incapable of grasping just what it was they were doing? I rest my case.'[237] The court-appointed examiner's report into Enron's collapse states that the lawyers did not blow the whistle because they did not always understand the financial transactions, in part because they chose to close their eyes and in part because they relied on the accountants. The examiner still said that substantial grounds did exist to bring malpractice actions against some of the lawyers. He based this conclusion on the fact that 'these lawyers took no remedial measures in the course of papering deals that they often recognized to be improper'.[238]

Why did these lawyers act for their corporate clients against the public good? Gordon believes that the lawyers identified too closely with their business clients and took on their values. He says the lawyers' argument is: 'We help our clients work around the constraints on their autonomy and wealth-maximizing activities.' But according to Gordon, when the lawyers and accountants got around the regulators 'they were not helping heroic outlaws add value to the economy and society by defying timid convention, but enabling, if not abetting, frauds and thieves'.[239]

Gordon says that the notion that the corporate advocates need to take an adversary position is wrong because it is based on the false premise that the role of corporate advocates is the same as that of a criminal defence lawyer. A lawyer's activities outside the litigation process are different. Acting in an adversarial manner in outside activities 'is more likely to help parties overstep the line to violate the law, and to do so in such ways as are likely to evade detection and sanction, and thus frustrate the purposes of law and regulation ...'. He recommends that corporate lawyers need to recognise that besides representing their clients they need to be public agents of the legal system. They need to accept that they cannot act to 'frustrate, sabotage, or nullify the public purposes of the laws'.[240] What has been the result of the scandals and adoption of the Sarbanes-Oxley Act? It will take years to see if the Act results in less fraudulent activity. The Act has already been a new profit-making measure for the legal profession by requiring their advice on the implications of the Act. One Canadian journalist, Terence Cororan, takes a strong view of what has happened. He says lawyers have not fallen on hard times because of the scandals they helped to create. 'We may not know where the lawyers were when all the documents were drafted and alleged frauds committed, but we have no difficulty knowing where they are today ... They are everywhere, hosting seminars, issuing press releases, running full-page newspapers ads, and promoting the hell out of their new careers aboard the compliance bandwagon created by Sarbanes-Oxley.'[241]

---

237. S Koniak, 'When the Hurlburly's Done: The Bar's Struggle with the SEC' (2003) 103 *Columbia LR* 1236.
238. Rhode and Luban (above), p 291. See also D Rhode and P Paton, 'Lawyers, Ethics, and Enron' (2002) 8 *Stanford JL Bus & Fin* 9.
239. Gordon (above).
240. Ibid.
241. T Corcoran, 'Stop the Lawyers', *National Post* (Canada), 28 September 2002, p 11.

It is debatable whether legislation can result in corporate lawyers negating the fraudulent activities of their clients. Cororan points out that the Canadian Council of Chief Executives rejected the need for a similar Act in Canada. They said: 'We believe that by building on Canada's traditional strengths and values, our country can craft a more effective strategy … Market forces have made commitment to values such as fairness, honesty and integrity into an important source of competitive advance for companies and countries alike.' Cororan concludes by saying that 'the market has already killed off Enron and WorldCom, delivering a stronger message to boards and CEOs than all the crap that's packed into Sarbanes-Oxley'.[242] Perhaps in Australia we also do not need to follow America's example of corporate regulation.

Proffering false material

False material can be presented by clients, witnesses or by lawyers. We have already discussed the tendering of false material in the area of negotiations and we will now discuss this problem in the context of civil litigation. We will discuss in the next chapter situations where criminal defendants commit perjury or confess to being guilty.   **14.103**

There are numerous questions to be examined. Are lawyers under an obligation to advise their clients at the beginning of the lawyer–client relationship of the consequences of the lawyer discovering that false information has been tendered or that there is an intention to proffer false material? What are lawyers' duties to prevent clients from proffering such material? What if clients or witnesses have already proffered such material — are the lawyers under a duty to insist on disclosure of the falsity? What if at the time they proffered the material the clients and/or witness did not know it was false? What if they refuse to remedy their actions — can lawyers cease to act and what must they do if they choose this course of action? If they do not cease to act, what are the lawyers' obligations?[243] Some of these questions have definite guidelines, but for others the answer is unclear and will depend on the circumstances.

Professional rules

We have already discussed some of the professional rules on not misleading the court that are also relevant to the proffering of false materials. There are also specific rules. Barristers' Rules (NSW) r 32 states:[244]   **14.104**

> A barrister whose client informs the barrister, during a hearing or after judgement or decision is reserved and while it remains pending, that the client has lied to the court or has procured another person to lie to the court or has falsified or procured another person to falsify in any way a document which has been tendered:
>
> (a) must refuse to take any further part in the case unless the client authorises the barrister to inform the court of the lie or falsification;
>
> (b) must promptly inform the court of the lie or falsification upon the client authorising the barrister to do so; but
>
> (c) must not otherwise inform the court of the lie or falsification.

---

242. Ibid.
243. Disney et al (above), pp 883–4.
244. The Barristers' Rules (Qld) r 34 and Model Rules r 15.1 are identical.

14.105 The Western Australian Professional Conduct Rules r 13.3 is similar to these rules but is limited to situations before judgment is delivered in civil cases.[245] It would appear that the rule also applies to the proffering of false material by witnesses, even though they are not mentioned. Justice Ipp states: 'If counsel discovers that a witness intends or is likely to give false testimony, he is duty bound not to produce that individual as a credible witness.'[246] None of these rules deal with situations where the client threatens to commit perjury. Justice Ipp has stated that if this occurs during the trial in a civil case counsel should continue to act if he or she can do so 'without advancing a case that to his knowledge is dishonest ... But counsel must never assert as true that which he knows to be false; nor connive at or attempt to substantiate a fraud. If the case cannot be otherwise conducted, counsel must withdraw, no matter the stage of the proceedings'.[247]

Disney et al have stated:[248]

> One might conclude that if withdrawal from the case is required when the client refuses to allow disclosure of past perjury, it must also be required when the client indicates that he or she intends to commit perjury and cannot be persuaded to the contrary. Another possibility is that the lawyer has the power, and is obliged, to refuse to call the client as a witness. The first of these two approaches appears to be generally acceptable in Australia. However, where the perjury is to be committed by a witness other than the client, it is arguable that the lawyer may either withdraw from the case or continue without calling the witness (unless, of course, the client decides to dismiss the lawyer).

American professional rules

14.106 These rules lead to an obvious prejudice against the client's case if the lawyer withdraws without giving reasons. The judge and the opposing counsel will immediately know a client perjury issue is involved. This may be a reason why the California courts require counsel to give the judge reasons. The lawyer can protect confidentiality and privacy by requesting an in camera hearing.[249] In a criminal case it would also appear to deny the basic civil liberties of an accused. The Americans have a very different approach in both criminal and civil cases. We will discuss the former in the next chapter. ABA Model Rules r 3.3 states:

> (a) A lawyer shall not knowingly:
>
> ...
>
>> (3) offer evidence that the lawyer knows to be false. If a lawyer, the lawyer's client, or a witness called by the lawyer, has offered material evidence and the lawyer comes to know of its falsity, the lawyer shall take reasonable remedial measures, including, if necessary, disclosure to the tribunal. A lawyer may refuse to offer evidence, other than the

245. There is a similar rule in England: see r 137 Code of Conduct for the Bar of England and Wales.
246. D Ipp, 'Lawyers' Duties to the Court' (above), p 92. Justice Ipp refers to *Brand v College of Surgeons* (1990) 83 Sask R 218; reversed on other grounds (1990) 80 Sask R 18.
247. Ipp (above), pp 87–8.
248. Disney et al (above), p 885.
249. *Manfredi & Levine v Superior Court* 78 Cal Rptr2d 494 (Cal App 2 Dist 1998). In this case counsel had requested to withdraw and not give any facts in a civil case by stating only that a conflict of interest had occurred.

testimony of a defendant in a criminal matter, that the lawyer reasonably believes is false.

(b) A lawyer who represents a client in an adjudicative proceeding and who knows that a person intends to engage, is engaging or has engaged in criminal or fraudulent conduct related to the proceeding shall take reasonable remedial measures, including, if necessary, disclosure to the tribunal.

Comments [5]–[6] state that if he or she knows a witness is providing false evidence the rule 'requires that the lawyer refuse to offer [this] evidence … regardless of the client's wishes'. When material false evidence is offered by the client, the lawyer should seek to persuade the client not to offer it. If persuasion fails, the lawyer must refuse to offer the false evidence. Comment [10] deals with the situation where evidence has been given and the lawyer later finds out it is false or a witness or the client offers testimony the lawyer knows is false. The lawyer must first seek to have the client withdraw or correct the false statements. If the client refuses and withdrawal from representation by the lawyer will not remedy the situation, the lawyer has to make disclosure to the tribunal, even though he or she is violating confidentiality. Comment [11] states: 'The disclosure of a client's false testimony can result in grave consequences for the client including not only a sense of betrayal but also loss of the case and perhaps a prosecution for perjury. But the alternative is that the lawyer cooperate in deceiving the court, thereby subverting the truth-finding process which the adversary system is designed to implement.' Clients, knowing that this is a lawyer's duty, will also be less likely to coerce the lawyer into being silent (which would make the lawyer a party to a fraud on the court). The Comment does not point out that such a duty of disclosure will also cause clients to keep untruths from being discovered by their lawyers. **14.107**

In an important case interpreting this duty of candour and disclosure, *Doe v Federal Grievance Committee*, the lawyer suspected an adverse witness of perjury. The lawyer's client had told him that the witness had been told to lie at a deposition. After the deposition the client reported that the witness had told him he had lied at the deposition. The lawyer did not reveal this information to the court. He said he did not believe the first statement by his client, but after the second comment he did suspect the witness had committed perjury. The lower court found that he had violated his duty to reveal a fraud on the tribunal. The Court of Appeals reversed and held that 'information clearly establishing' a fraud on a tribunal requires actual knowledge and not just suspicion or belief. The test is what the lawyer 'reasonably knows to be a fact'.[250] **14.108**

Pleadings

Courts depend on lawyers to make sure that in settling pleadings and in drawing up sworn affidavits that the allegations and facts are not false. Part of this requirement is stated in the Barristers' Rules (NSW) as changed in January 2000:[251] **14.109**

---

250. 847 F2d 57, 63 (2nd Cir 1988).
251. The old rule is still present in the Barristers' Rules (Qld) r 37 and Model Rules r 16.1.

R 36 A barrister must not allege any matter of fact in:

(a) any court document settled by the barrister;

(b) any submission during any hearing;

(c) the course of an opening address; or

(d) the course of a closing address or submission on the evidence;

unless the barrister believes on reasonable grounds that the factual material already available provides a proper basis to do so;

14.110 The case law supports this rule.[252] In *Myers v Elman*[253] the House of Lords upheld a trial judge's order for costs against the solicitors. The court found that one of the solicitors had made allegations which he must have known or suspected to be false. Furthermore, the solicitor had allowed his clients to make affidavits that were incorrect and false. Viscount Maugham LC said that solicitors are not entitled to assist clients in any way in dishonourable conduct in court. The solicitor is under a duty not to assist in the swearing of affidavits which are untrue. If clients wish to omit relevant documents from their affidavits, solicitors have to cease to act for those clients. If solicitors only find out that the affidavits are incomplete or untrue after they have been tendered in court, they must seek the client's permission to inform the opposing party's solicitor. Failure by clients to permit the solicitor to disclose the information means that the solicitor must cease to act. Lord Atkin in *Myers*[254] said that solicitors had a duty to make sure clients' affidavits of documents are accurate before lodging them. This includes an affirmative duty to take reasonable steps to ascertain the truth, if they have reasonable grounds to believe there are missing relevant documents and to make sure that clients have included all relevant documents in their affidavit.[255] A failure to do so could lead to the solicitor being charged with aiding and abetting a criminal activity.[256]

14.111 In a more recent case a legal practitioner was struck off the rolls by the Full Supreme Court of South Australia for improper administration of an oath. The practitioner allowed a client, as was his usual practice, to swear answers to interrogatories on a dictionary. The client, who was later charged for perjury for his answers, was therefore able to conduct a good defence to the charge.[257]

There were also serious charges made in 1995 at the New South Wales Police Royal Commission that the courts in criminal cases could not rely on evidence provided by lawyers. The example cited by Woods J, Commissioner in charge, was an unreliable report of an expert concerning an alleged drug dealer. A former Crown prosecutor, Mr Frank Holles QC, told the Commission that the pressures in getting business done by the courts was so great, it was not difficult for lawyers to manipulate evidence, such as character references and experts' reports. Woods J commented at

---

252. See *Re Thom* (1918) 18 SR (NSW) 70.
253. *Myers v Elman* [1940] AC 282 at 292.
254. *Myers v Elman* (above) at 294.
255. *Woods v Martins Bank Ltd* [1959] 1 QB 55, 60.
256. These views are followed by *Y v M* [1994] 3 NZLR 581. Temm J found a misleading affidavit in a custody dispute because of 'the unquestioning acceptance by the partner in the firm as to what the mother had to say'.
257. *In the matter of Mirza* (unreported, SC(SA), Full Ct, No 2225 of 1996, 8 May 1996, BC9602072).

the time that he was 'somewhat shattered' to find his trust in lawyers to investigate ethically the evidence they presented had been misplaced. Woods J in his final report in 1997 did not make any recommendations in this area.

It was suggested that the practice was much wider than the one example that was given. An editorial said:[258]

> Lawyers cannot stop their clients telling lies, but how scrupulous are lawyers about ensuring that material they see put before a court is not fraudulent? Lawyers should do their very best to represent their clients, but do they always ensure that they do not step over the line between strong representation and abuse of the processes of the court? ... Lawyer corruption should be investigated, but not by a lawyer from NSW. A retired judge from elsewhere, perhaps New Zealand would be best.

The government did not heed the editorial and no Royal Commission or other investigation has been initiated.

Tricks in presenting or discrediting material[259]

Cinema example

In the 1959 film *The Young Philadelphians*, Paul Newman conducted a cross-examination of a crucial prosecution witness in a murder trial. The witness, the butler, claimed to have the ability to differentiate different alcoholic spirits by their smell. Newman has the witness sniff three different glasses filled with spirits. He correctly states that the first contains scotch and the second rye. But by deeply inhaling these two he loses his sense of smell. Newman then has the witness sniff some strong gin that the witness assumed was water and he says so and arrogantly adds 'with a slight hint of chlorine'. The witness did not know that Newman had substituted gin for the water in his jug, which he drank throughout the trial. Newman thus discredited a truthful witness and won the case. Should Newman be allowed to conduct this type of investigation? Should the court condone his activity? According to Bergman, the judge's ruling allowing the experiment is questionable, because there were different conditions than those that existed at the night of the murder, under which the butler is asked to identify the spirits. On that night he only had to identify two glasses, one with expensive scotch, normally the drink of the victim, and other cheap rye, normally the drink of the accused.[260]

14.112

Role of advocate in cross-examination

There appears to be a good argument that the defence counsel in a criminal case may cross-examine a witness he or she knows is telling the truth in order to discredit that witness before the jury. It seems to be fair tactics,

14.113

---

258. Editorial, 'Lawyers too', *Sydney Morning Herald*, 23 August 1995, p 20.
259. For a number of 'dirty tricks' used by lawyers in the American context see R Underwood, 'Adversary Ethics: More Dirty Tricks' (1982) *American J of Trial Advocacy* 265.
260. P Bergman, 'Pranks for the Memory' (1996) 30 *U of San Francisco LR* 1235, 1238–9. Bergman discusses tricks or pranks in 17 different movies, showing which are permissible and which could not occur or should not occur. What he calls 'a shining example' of a permissible use of an experiment comes from the film *Trial* (1955). The defence lawyer uses a spotlight to show how difficult it is to identify someone who has screamed in the dark when a spotlight shines on them. Bergman also refers for greater detail on the films to Bergman and Asimow, *Reel Justice* (1996).

within the adversarial context where a person faces incarceration, for counsel to test the prosecution's evidence and have the prosecution prove its case. The defence counsel should be allowed to search for weaknesses in the witness's character or testimony, even though it has no relationship to accuracy. Wolfram states that such action is supportable in the criminal context. He does find it 'extremely doubtful that it should be extended to civil cases and, it is entirely clear, should form no part of a prosecutor's arsenal'.[261]

14.114 The ABA Prosecution Standards para 3-5.7 prohibits a prosecutor from discrediting or undermining a witness who the prosecutor knows is testifying truthfully. There are general rules in Australia for prosecutors to seek the truth and they imply that they will not discredit truthful witnesses.[262] We have already stated that under the Barristers' Rules (NSW and Qld) r 38, when dealing with cross-examination barristers cannot suggest criminality, fraud or other serious misconduct unless 'the material already available to the barrister provides a proper basis for the suggestions'. They can ask questions which go only to credit when they have reasonable grounds for believing 'that affirmative answers to the suggestion would diminish the witness's credibility'.

Some commentators have stated that sometimes counsel should refrain from discrediting a truthful and fair witness. For example, if your question will reveal something from a witness's distant past that is true and will possibly destroy his or her credibility, you should refrain from using it. To use this information would be 'to deal a cowardly blow' at the witness.[263] Of course, it might hurt your case if the witness has maintained an unblemished record since his or her misdeed. The judge or jury may feel you have committed an indiscretion by bringing up the matter.

Courtroom tricks

14.115 Lawyers are known to use various tricks to confuse witnesses and jurors, and thereby discredit the opposition's case. In a previous era when smoking was allowed, Clarence Darrow, a famous American criminal defence lawyer, was known to light up a long cigar when the prosecution was giving its closing arguments to the jury. The ash on the cigar would get longer and longer, and the jurors would cease listening to the presentation, focusing their attention on the cigar. Darrow had a number of these cigars in which he had placed some wire, which held onto the ash.

Successful trial lawyers use various tricks to win and maintain their reputation. The attitude is that clients do not pay for justice but only for victory. Lawyers will use various methods of manipulation to win over witnesses or jurors. These tactics can include playing on emotional weaknesses, playing on class and racial prejudices and even the use of sex appeal. For example, a lawyer who is wealthy and dresses immaculately outside the courtroom, may dress shabbily (in comparison) in court, in order to win sympathy from juries while defending insurance companies in

261. Wolfram (above), para 12.4.5.
262. Barristers' Rules (NSW and Qld) Rules 62 and 63.
263. Lord Macmillan (above), p 192, quoted in Disney et al (above), p 898.

large tort suits.[264] This might work in America but in the Australian context most large tort actions are without juries. Perhaps such attire might help a criminal defence lawyer, as long as he or she is not a barrister.

The following three cases are examples of lawyers being disciplined for using tricks. In *United States v Thoreen*[265] during a criminal proceeding, counsel substituted another person, Mason, who resembled his client, and placed his client in an area normally reserved for the press. He did this without the court's knowledge or consent. As a result of his action two government witnesses misidentified the accused. After the government had presented its case, he called Mason as a witness and disclosed the substitution. The court then called a recess and allowed the government to reopen its case.

The lawyer was charged with criminal contempt. He argued that his conduct was a good faith tactic in aid of cross-examination and fell within the notion of zealous advocacy. He also argued that defence counsel in a criminal case had no obligation to help the court to ascertain the truth and had the right to confuse witnesses with misleading questions. The Ninth Circuit Court said there was a right for counsel to confuse truthful witnesses and conduct zealous advocacy, but the action here became actual obstruction in impeding the court's search for truth. The court quoted ABA Standards for Criminal Justice, 4.9 which requires defence counsel to be scrupulously candid and truthful in representation before a court. The court upheld the lawyer's conviction stating that he intentionally caused a misidentification, resulting in the misleading of the court, opposing counsel and witnesses. The action also caused delay as the government was forced to reopen its case to identify the defendant.

In a similar New Zealand case, counsel tried to mislead the court and witnesses by coming to the hearing with his client and a 'ringer'. The two women sat apart, came in separately, but were similar in appearance. Counsel entered the courtroom with the ringer and made a point of talking to her. The ringer was wrongfully identified as the defendant, but despite this action the defendant was convicted. The Law Society Council said that such activity constituted unprofessional conduct. The Council said that:[266]

14.116

> ... there is a difference between testing the identifying witness's evidence without deliberately misleading the witness, and creating a situation where the witness is bound to be unfairly misled in a manner known to counsel to be false.

In *Re Metzger*[267] a lawyer tried to discredit the testimony of a witness whom he believed was wrong. During an adjournment, while cross-examining a handwriting expert, the lawyer substituted for the evidence being examined his own copy of it. He then used this in cross-examination to discredit the witness. The court suspended him from practice for 10 days because what he did was a 'falsehood and a misrepresentation'. The dissenting judge felt that as a defence lawyer in a criminal case he had not

---

264. Morgan and Rotunda, *Professional Responsibility*, 5th ed (1991), pp 220–2. The authors give other examples of questionable litigation tactics used in tort actions.
265. 653 F 2d 1332 (9th Cir Court 1981).
266. (1981) 7 *Commonwealth Law Bulletin* 285.
267. 31 *Hawaii Reports* 929, 931 (1939).

acted unethically because he had not treated the witness unfairly. The judge said he had the 'right to impeach by every proper means' the expert witness's opinion. Metzger had testified that he was an expert on handwriting and believed the expert witness was wrong in his identification of the writing as being that of the defendant. His purpose was therefore not to mislead the jury but a 'laudable one of exposing what he believed to be an erroneous opinion'.

15

FAIRNESS AND CANDOUR: CRIMINAL TRIALS

INTRODUCTION

In this chapter we continue our discussion of duties of fairness and candour within the criminal context. We have already touched on the subject in the last chapter and at other times throughout the book. Some of the professional ethical rules already discussed are also relevant to this chapter.

15.1

Advice to witnesses

One area we will examine briefly is the advice to witnesses, including clients who will be witnesses, known as 'coaching'. There are formal ethical rules in Australia prohibiting the manipulation of witnesses' evidence.[1] Legal practitioners have a right during the consultations with witnesses to help prepare them for the trial. Such preparation is not unethical when the witnesses are provided with necessary information about the issues in the case, which will help them produce relevant information. Although stated in the civil context, Ipp J's comments are also relevant in the criminal context:[2]

15.2

> Without an understanding of the underlying facts, witnesses may be flustered at trial by statements of other persons or by documents of which they are unaware. Accordingly, it is regular practice for competent lawyers to protect witnesses from unknowingly contradicting themselves or even, by mistake,

1. See Barristers' Rules (NSW) rr 43–44 and 46–50 and (Qld) rr 45–51; Model Rules r 17.1–17.8; Professional Conduct Rules (WA) r 13.9; 'Ethical Restraints on Interviewing Witnesses' (1990) 64 *Law Institute J (Vic)* 910–11.
2. D Ipp, 'Reforms to the Adversarial Process in Civil Litigation — Part II' (1995) 69 *ALJ* 790, 799.

contradicting others … A careful lawyer will accordingly clarify these matters with witnesses before they testify. In addition, memory will be refreshed, relevance will be explored and advice will be given as to how best to present the evidence …

There is nothing improper in preparing witnesses this way. It is indeed desirable for the lawyers to prepare witnesses, especially those who are to give lengthy and complex evidence, for trial. This enables lawyers to present witnesses who are thoroughly familiar with the subject matter of their testimony and who are prepared to say what they know in a clear, coherent manner. Individual witnesses are likely to testify more intelligently and relevantly if they understand the factual and legal significance of their observations and know what to expect. Efficient witness preparation also prevents trials from getting bogged down in apparent contradictions that, if considered carefully, are illusory or irrelevant.

15.3   Ipp J points out that this witness preparation plus guidance on the witness's demeanour — dress, speech and being trained to avoid nervousness — has a detrimental effect on the value of oral evidence.[3] Others may not agree with this approach. Defence counsel, Sophia Beckett, has stated: 'I hate to do it, but if I have a conservative magistrate/judge I still politely suggest to my clients that they might "tone down" the jewellery, or consider dressing more conservatively for their hearing/trial.' Furthermore, she feels that helping clients to avoid nervousness is not coaching, 'but simply an attempt to have the client get their message across to the trier of fact in the most simple and coherent manner possible'.[4] Ipp J has also more recently stated that: 'Witnesses may not be placed under pressure to provide other than a truthful account of their evidence nor may witnesses be rehearsed, practised or coached in relation to their evidence or the way in which it should be given.'[5] This quote is almost identical to r 6.5 of the Law Society in England and Wales Code for Advocacy.[6] The Law Society of Victoria has adopted similar guidelines for solicitors in interviewing witnesses.[7] There is of course a fine line between 'preparation' and 'coaching' a witness. The coaching of witnesses, and helping them make up a story, not only breaches ethical obligations, but can also lead to criminal charges for subornation of perjury and/or obstructing justice.

15.4   The New South Wales Court of Appeal recently allowed an appeal because of coaching of three witnesses. Sheller JA stated:

It has long been regarded as proper practice for legal practitioners to take proofs of evidence from lay witnesses separately and to encourage such witnesses not to discuss their evidence with others and particularly not with other potential witnesses. For various reasons, witnesses do not always abide by those instructions and their credibility suffers accordingly. In the present case, it is hard to see that the intention of the teleconference with witnesses discussing amongst themselves the evidence that they would give was for any

3.   Ipp (above), pp 799–800 finds more benefits in written statements, especially when these statements have been exchanged at pre-trial.
4.   S Beckett, 'Preparing your client for giving evidence', Legal Aid Commission of NSW, Duty Solicitors Conference, July 2003.
5.   D Ipp, 'Lawyers' Duties to the Court' (1998) 114 *The Law Quarterly Review* 63, 91–2. Ipp refers to *Re Spedley Securities Ltd (in liq)*; *Reed v Harkness* (1990) 2 ACSR 117.
6.   Adopted and amended January 2003 under the Solicitors' Practice Rules 1990, updated February 2005.
7.   'Ethical Restraints on Interviewing Witnesses' (1990) 64 *Law Institute J (Vic)*.

reason other than to ensure, so far as possible, that in giving evidence the defendant's witnesses would all speak with one voice about the events that occurred. Thus, the evidence of one about a particular matter which was in fact true might be overborne by what that witness heard several others say which, as it happened, was not true. This seriously undermines the process by which evidence is taken. What was done was improper.[8]

The court referred the actions of the two solicitors to the Legal Services Commissioner for investigation.[9]

In another recent case, Justice Wilcox found that an expert witness had been coached in preparing his testimony by solicitors from Clayton Utz. Wilcox J said he would not 'place much weight' on the expert's testimony. The three lawyers from Clayton Utz are being investigated by the New South Wales Law Society for their actions in the matter.[10]

15.5

Coaching witnesses in the United States

Coaching appears to be far less prevalent in Australia than in the United States, probably because of the divided profession and the professional rules that maintain the integrity of evidence. The extremes in the United States have been portrayed in films such as *Anatomy of a Murder* (1959) and *The Verdict* (1982),[11] and have been described by various American authors.[12] In the United States lawyers routinely 'prepare' witnesses and clients:[13]

15.6

It would be considered poor advocacy to call someone 'cold' unless there were no choice. Witness preparation is ethical.

Frankel sees the practice in the United States as going beyond helping organising what the witness knows, and moving in the direction of helping witnesses to know new things:[14]

At its starkest, the effect is called subornation of perjury, which is a crime ... Somewhat less stark, short of criminality but still to be condemned, is the device of telling the client 'the law' before eliciting the facts — that is, telling the client what facts would constitute a successful claim or defence, and only then asking the client what the facts happen perchance to be.

The latter approach is the one used in the famous novel *Anatomy of a Murder*. The lawyer in the novel educates a murder defendant about various defences including impaired mental capacity. The defendant then

15.7

8. *Day v Perisher Blue Pty Ltd* [2005] NSWCA 110, para 30.
9. Ibid, para 37.
10. *Universal Music Australia Pty Ltd v Sharman License Holdings* [2005] FCA 1242. See K Towers, 'Role of the expert witness called into question', *Australian Financial Review*, 9 September 2005, p 58; G Montgomery, 'Clayton Utz in hot water over witness', *Australian*, 9 September 2005, p 27; G Montgomery, 'Lawyers "coached" expert witness', *Australian*, 16 September 2005, p 3; and 'Clayton Utz trio facing inquiry', *Australian*, 16 September 2005, p 25.
11. For a summary and an analysis of these two films see P Bergman and M Asimow, *Reel Justice*, 1996, pp 232–8, 301–5.
12. See, for example, M Freedman, *Lawyers' Ethics in an Adversary System*, Bobbs-Merrill, Indianapolis, 1975, pp 63ff, and D Rhode, *Professional Responsibility: Ethics by the Pervasive Method*, 2nd ed, Aspen Law and Business, New York 1998, pp 195–200.
13. S Gillers, *Regulation of Lawyers: Problems of Law and Ethics*, 5th ed, Aspen Law and Business, New York, 1998, p 429. Gillers, to support this statement, refers to: District of Columbia Opinion 79 (1980) and R Wydick, 'The Ethics of Witness Coaching' (1995) 17 *Cardozo L Rev* 1.
14. M Frankel, *In Partisan Justice*, Hill and Wang, New York, 1980, pp 14–16.

conveniently recounts his facts to the lawyer to fit that defence.[15] Monroe Freedman supports this approach on the basis that it is not lawyers' role to prejudge the client as a perjurer. A lawyer 'cannot presume that the client will make unlawful use of his [or her] advice ... [T]here is a natural predisposition in most people to recollect facts, entirely honestly, in a way most favorable to their own interest ... Before he begins to remember essential facts, the client is entitled to know what his own interests are ... To decide otherwise would ... penalize the less well-educated defendant'.[16]

We will look first at the rules of acting for a client who has committed perjury or intends to commit perjury. We will then discuss the rules when acting for a client whom the lawyer knows to be guilty, and also the rules governing the behaviour of prosecutors.

PERJURY IN CRIMINAL TRIALS

Professional rules

15.8   Up until the nineteenth century there was no problem concerning perjury by a party to an action. All parties to an action, including criminal defendants, were disqualified from testifying 'on the ground that the temptation to falsify would put [their] soul in jeopardy'.[17] The present Australian professional rules on perjury are the same in criminal or civil cases in most jurisdictions. The general rule is if a client has committed perjury or intends to commit it, counsel must refuse to take any further part in the case, unless the client corrects the perjury, or refrains from committing it. We have outlined this rule, Barristers' Rules r 32 (NSW) [r 34 (Qld) and the Model Rules r 15.1], in **14.104**.[18] If counsel has come to the conclusion that the client will commit perjury during the trial he or she must advise the client of the ramifications of his or her actions. This occurred in *Sankar v State of Trinidad and Tobago*[19] where counsel advised the client to be silent and not to testify and then in closing argument only put the prosecution to proof. The Privy Council found a miscarriage of justice had taken place and set aside the conviction because counsel had failed to explain various options that were available to the client. The Privy Council said the advocate could have obtained an adjournment and could have sought to withdraw from the trial if, after explaining the alternatives, the client still wanted to testify against counsel's advice.

15.9   Sawer has stated that the practice in Australia in the case of perjury is in all cases, whether civil or criminal, for counsel to request permission to withdraw. It is not clear exactly what counsel should tell the court when seeking permission to withdraw. It appears that lawyers will usually say that

---

15. See Robert Traver, *Anatomy of a Murder*, St Martin's Press, New York, 1958.
16. M Freedman, 'Professional Responsibility of the Criminal Defense Lawyer: The Three Hardest Questions' (1966) 64 *Michigan L Rev* 1460, 1479, 1481.
17. G Hazard Jr and S Koniak, *The Law and Ethics of Lawyering*, Foundation Press, Westbury, New York, 1990, p 369.
18. See also the identical rule in Professional Conduct and Practice Rules (NSW) rr A.32 and 21 and (ACT) rr 20.1 and 15; see also Australian Bar Rules Code of Conduct (1993) r 5.6.
19. [1995] 1 WLR 194.

they 'are embarrassed'. Such a statement serves notice to judges, prosecutors and perhaps the counsel subsequently briefed, that the client has committed perjury or intends to commit perjury.[20] The withdrawal by counsel also serves as a warning to the accused not to inform his or her next counsel. 'Leave will normally be given if counsel informs the court that he would be "forensically embarrassed" by continuing.'[21] It appears that if the court refuses the request to withdraw because of, for example, too much disruption to the court process, counsel must not do anything further in the case. This will also inform others that a perjury has been committed or will be committed.

As we have stated in Chapter 14, Western Australia differs from other jurisdictions on the perjury issue. Rule 13.3 of its Professional Conduct Rules limits the right not to take any further part in the case to civil cases.[22] In criminal cases there are no specific rules as to what a lawyer should do. Rule 14.6 prohibits defence lawyers from absenting themselves unless 'there are exceptional circumstances which he could not reasonably have foreseen'. It can be argued that in cases of perjury in a criminal case defence counsel can request permission to withdraw because of 'exceptional circumstances'. In jurisdictions with divided professions, the number of times which barristers have to deal with perjury issues is reduced because solicitors conduct initial interviews with clients and witnesses in advance of the trial. This may be changing with the right of direct access to barristers. **15.10**

American professional rules

The rules in the United States are different in this area from those in Australia and have caused a lively debate. We have outlined ABA Model Rules r 3.3 and some of its Comments in **14.106–14.107**. Rule 3.3 states: **15.11**

(a) A lawyer shall not knowingly:

   (1) make a false statement of fact or law to a tribunal; or fail to correct a false statement of material fact or law previously made to the tribunal by the lawyer;

   …

   (3) offer evidence that the lawyer knows to be false. If a lawyer, the lawyer's client, or a witness called by the lawyer has offered material evidence and the lawyer comes to know of its falsity, the lawyer shall take reasonable remedial measures, including, if necessary, disclosure to the tribunal. A lawyer may refuse to offer evidence, other than the testimony of a defendant in a criminal matter, that the lawyer reasonably believes is false …

Comment [7] states that these duties apply to all lawyers, including criminal defence lawyers. However, some jurisdictions require criminal defence counsel 'to present the accused as a witness or to give a narrative statement if the accused so desires, even if counsel knows that the testimony or statement will be false'. These state requirements prevail over the Model Rules.

---

20. G Sawer, 'The Guilty Accused' (1971) *The Summons* 30, 33.
21. Ipp, 'Lawyers' Duties to the Court' (above), p 88. Ipp J cites *R v Lyons* (1978) 68 Cr Ap R 104 to support this statement.
22. The rule in England is similar to the Western Australian rule: Code of Conduct for the Bar of England and Wales r 137.

15.12 What we said (see **14.107**) on candour in civil matters is also relevant here. Comment [10] deals with the situation where evidence has been given and the lawyer later finds out it is false or a witness or the client offers testimony the lawyer knows is false. The lawyer must first seek to have the client withdraw or correct the false statements. If the client refuses and withdrawal from representation by the lawyer will not remedy the situation, the lawyer has to make disclosure to the tribunal, even though he or she is violating confidentiality. Comment [11] states: 'The disclosure of a client's false testimony can result in grave consequences for the client including not only a sense of betrayal but also loss of the case and perhaps a prosecution for perjury. But the alternative is that the lawyer cooperate in deceiving the court, thereby subverting the truth-finding process which the adversary system is designed to implement'. Clients, knowing that this is a lawyer's duty, will also be less likely to coerce the lawyer into being silent (which would make the lawyer a party to a fraud on the court). The Comment does not point out that such a duty of disclosure will also cause clients to keep untruths from being discovered by their lawyers.

15.13 After the publication of an earlier version of the Comment to r 3.3, the United States Supreme Court decided *Nix v Whiteside*.[23] The court unanimously held, on the perjury issue, that a criminal defendant has no right to the assistance of counsel in giving false testimony. The court said that lawyers who refuse to give such assistance, and who threaten to disclose the client's future perjury, have not denied the client effective legal assistance under the Sixth Amendment to the Constitution.

The court was upholding the notion expressed by Bronaugh that 'while every person has a legal right to go to court, no one has the *moral* right to conceal or lie about wrongdoing, or hire others for that purpose'.[24] This is consistent with r 3.3 and the Comment. Furthermore, the ABA adopted Formal Opinion 87-353 which requires lawyers to divulge client perjury. The Opinion advises lawyers to disclose testimony that they know is false. There is no definition or guidance as to what constitutes 'know'.

15.14 Freedman points out that the *Whiteside* case also did not clarify how certain lawyers must be before taking action on their judgment that the client will commit perjury.[25] A later Second Circuit court decision in a civil case, *John Doe, Esquire v The Federal Grievance Committee*,[26] said that the potential perjury has to become 'clearly established'. This was interpreted as meaning that the lawyer has 'actual knowledge', that is, must 'clearly know, rather than suspect'.[27] The *Whiteside* case also did not state what lawyers must do when confronted with client perjury in criminal cases. The case only tells lawyers what they may do in order to conform with ethical standards and still

---

23. 106 S Ct 988 at 994–7 (1986).
24. R Bronaugh, 'Thoughts on Money, Winning, and Happiness in the Practice of Law' (1996) 9 *The Canadian J of Law & Jurisprudence* 101, 108.
25. M Freedman, 'Client Confidences and Client Perjury: Some Unanswered Questions' (1988) 136 *Univ of Penn LR* 1939.
26. 847 F 2d 57 (2nd Cir 1988).
27. For a discussion of the knowledge issue see H Sabin, 'The Criminal Lawyer's "Different Mission": Reflections on the "Right" to Present a False Case' (1987) 1 *Georgetown J Legal Ethics* 125, 136–43.

not violate the client's constitutional rights. It leaves open the issue of what action by lawyers will violate criminal defendants' constitutional rights.[28]

In *US v Litchfield*,[29] the Tenth Circuit Court of Appeals held that effective **15.15** assistance of counsel is not denied when counsel speaks to the judge about a possible perjury by his or her client. The judge in this case told the lawyer it was the jury's role to decide what was true and untrue.[30] The Eighth Circuit Court in *United States v Long*[31] disagreed with this approach. In *Long* the lawyer revealed his belief that the client would commit perjury when he testified. The court stated that 'a clear expression of intent to commit perjury is required before the attorney can reveal client's confidences'.[32] The Supreme Court, after *Whiteside*, in *Rock v Arkansas*,[33] upheld the constitutional right of criminal defendants to testify, but confirmed *Whiteside* by stating that this right did not include the right to testify falsely.

The ABA House of Delegates in 2002 tried to clear up the problem by **15.16** adding Comment [8] to r 3.3. It states: 'The prohibition against offering false evidence only applies if the lawyer knows that the evidence is false. A lawyer's reasonable belief that the evidence is false does not preclude its presentation to the trier of fact. A lawyer's knowledge that the evidence is false, however, can be inferred from the circumstances. See Rule 1.0(f) ["Knowingly," "known," or "knows" denotes actual knowledge of the fact in question. A person's knowledge may be inferred from circumstances.] Thus, although a lawyer should resolve doubts about the veracity of testimony or other evidence in favor of the client, the lawyer cannot ignore an obvious falsehood.' The new Comment [8] stills leaves the lawyer a certain amount of flexibility on deciding what to do.

The ABA, in Formal Opinion 87-353, while approving *Whiteside*, states **15.17** that its effect may not overcome some states' own applicable constitutional provisions. These provisions may still prohibit disclosure of the client's perjury by defence counsel.[34] The Opinion concludes that *Whiteside* combined with Model Rules r 3.3(a)(2) means that a 'lawyer can no longer rely on the narrative approach to insulate the lawyer from a charge of assisting the client's perjury'. The Californian Supreme Court does not appear to agree with this conclusion, especially when the trial judge permits the accused to take the narrative format.[35] Other jurisdictions have also adopted the narrative approach as a 'commonly accepted method of dealing

---

28. G Hazard, S Koniak and R Cramton, *The Law and Ethics of Lawyering*, 2nd ed, Foundation Press, Westbury, NY, 1994, p 372.
29. 959 F 2d 1514 (10th Cir 1992).
30. A lawyer was surprised by his client's perjured testimony and immediately requested, without giving any reason, permission to withdraw. The appeal court held that even though the request to withdraw was denied it deprived the client of a fair trial because it announced to the jury and judge that his client had just lied. *Lowery v Cardwell* 575 F2d 727 (9th Cir 1978). See also *State v Jones* 923 O2d 560 (Mont 1996) where inadequate representation was found because a lawyer moved to withdraw on the unsubstantiated belief that his client intended to commit perjury.
31. 857 F2d 436 (8th Cir 1988).
32. *United States v Long* (above) at 445.
33. 107 S Ct 2704 (1987).
34. Formal Opinion 87-353, ABA, p 5.
35. *People v Guzman* 755 P 2d 917 (1988).

with client perjury'.[36] Furthermore, a leading textbook has stated that 'the narrative approach may have more acceptance in actual practice than in formal recognition'.[37] The narrative approach can be criticised because defence lawyers, by not questioning their client, will appear to be turning their back on the evidence. Furthermore, in giving closing arguments they will not refer to the narrative, nor argue the probative value of this false testimony. It will be obvious to the jury that the defendant's testimony is flawed.[38]

15.18 The perjury issue in criminal cases has caused a lively debate in the United States. Freedman[39] set up a hypothetical situation where a lawyer has an innocent client who happened to be near the scene of a serious crime. There are two witnesses for the prosecution who have identified him. The first has done so mistakenly, but with a certain degree of persuasiveness. This witness may or may not be believed by the jury. The second witness, corroborating the first witness, is an elderly woman who has truthfully identified the client as having been one street from the scene of the crime five minutes before it occurred. On cross-examination her testimony and credibility are thrown into doubt because she is shown to become easily confused and to have poor eyesight. The client still feels that the only way to overcome her corroboration is to commit perjury by testifying he was not there. If he testifies truthfully, the jury would be more likely to accept the inaccurate testimony of the first witness. What should the lawyer do?

15.19 Freedman said that lawyers face a 'trilemma' — 'the lawyer is required to know everything, to keep it in confidence, and to reveal it to the court'. They need to determine 'all relevant facts known to the accused' in order to know the truth and thus to 'properly perform their duties'. Second, lawyers need to maintain in strict confidence all disclosures made to them during the relationship. Finally, as officers of the court, lawyers' conduct before the court 'should be characterised by candour'. For a criminal defence lawyer the conflicting obligations are more acute. This is because of the 'presumption of innocence, the burden on the state to prove its case beyond a reasonable doubt, and the right to put the prosecution to its proof'. Hazard and Koniak state that lawyers have a fourth responsibility 'to refrain from assisting criminal activity'.[40] This last responsibility is also found in various ethical codes in Australia.[41]

15.20 Freedman applies these views to his hypothetical example. He approves of the cross-examination of the elderly lady, making her appear to be mistaken

---

36. *Shockley v State* 565 A2d 1373, 1380 (Del 1989). See also *Commonwealth v Jermyn* 620 A2d 1128 (Pa 1993) that advising a client to take the narrative approach does not lead to ineffective assistance.
37. Hazard, Koniak and Cramton (above), pp 380–1.
38. Freedman (above) (1975), pp 27ff.
39. These views were first expressed in M Freedman, 'Professional Responsibility of the Criminal Defense Lawyer: The Three Hardest Questions' (1966) 64 *Michigan LR* 1469. The discussion here comes from an expanded version of the argument in Freedman (above), pp 27ff. The latter version is found also in M Freedman, *Understanding Lawyers' Ethics*, Matthew Bender, New York, 1990, p 167.
40. Hazard and Koniak (above), p 369.
41. Professional Conduct Rules (SA) r 9.9 and the introduction to Relations with Clients of Law Council's Model Rules and Professional Conduct and Practice Rules (NSW).

or lying, even though she is telling the truth.[42] He says that the lawyer should advise the client that his or her proposed testimony is perjurous, but if the client decides to testify the lawyer should proceed with the case in a normal fashion. Freedman says that the lawyer in such circumstances should withdraw but only if the client's confidences can be maintained. If the confidences cannot be maintained the lawyer is setting up a further perjurous situation. By withdrawing, the lawyer will cause the client to realise that he or she should withhold incriminating information, on perjury or being guilty, from the next lawyer. The result will be that the perjured evidence will still be presented. He says that by disclosing the client's actions the lawyer would violate two basic foundations of the lawyer–client relationship: confidentiality and adversarial zeal. Furthermore, the trial will be conducted on an unfair basis because the judge and the prosecution will now know what the client has done, and this may not be known to the new lawyer.

Freedman's hypothetical example poses various vexing questions. When can one justify harming another person who is doing his or her civic duty for the interest of someone who may have tricked you into believing he or she is innocent? Is such conduct by lawyers in the best interests of society where it is difficult to find citizens who are willing to testify? Selinger asks further questions: When there is moral justification for the accused to lie, does this justification extend to the lawyer? Second, if there is moral justification for some defendants to lie, does this require lawyers to assist all defendants to lie? The failure to do otherwise would require lawyers to decide the issue of guilt or innocence. Finally, Selinger asks — if lawyers are morally justified in assisting some defendants to lie, does this therefore permit lawyers to exercise discretion on whether or not to assist a perjury? Does this mean that the ethical rules need to be amended to require lawyers to assist perjury? Selinger comes to the conclusion that to avoid being imprisoned unfairly, innocent defendants have a moral justification in perjuring themselves. He also concludes that there cannot be a rule which would allow lawyers to assist in 'good' lying as opposed to 'bad' lying. The application of such a rule would be inconsistent, and it would be too difficult for lawyers to determine when they were applying it correctly.[43]

15.21

Bress argues that Freedman's views are wrong. He says that the accused would have been advised by that lawyer 'of the strong possibility that the prosecutor will expose his perjured defence, thus seriously jeopardising his chance for acquittal by calling his credibility into question before the jury'. If the accused wanted to continue his or her perjury with the second lawyer he or she would not disclose it. This would result in the new lawyer not knowing the truth. As a result the 'onus for the perjury would not rest upon a member of the Bar, but rather upon the defendant alone'.[44] Subin would change the role of the defence counsel, making it:

15.22

---

42. Freedman (above) (1990), pp 167–8.
43. C Selinger, 'The Perry Mason Perspective and Others: A Critique of Reductionist Thinking about the Ethics of Untruthful Practices by Lawyers for "Innocent" Defendants' (1978) 6 *Hofstra LR* 631. The issues are explored in greater depth in S Bok, *Lying*, Pantheon Books, New York, 1979, pp 154–73.
44. D Bress, 'Professional Ethics in Criminal Trials: A View of Defense Counsel's Responsibility' (1966) 64 *Michigan LR* 1493, 1495.

> ... improper for an attorney who knows beyond a reasonable doubt the truth of a fact established in the state's case to attempt to refute that fact through the introduction of evidence, impeachment of evidence, or argument.

Subin does add that if clients still insist on having their day in court the lawyer would have the responsibility 'to assure that all of the elements of the crime were proven beyond a reasonable doubt, on the basis of competent evidence' and then argue to the jury that the prosecution's evidence does not 'sustain the burden of proof'.[45] Subin's views do not appear to be acceptable in the American context.[46]

15.23 Freedman's views were widely criticised. There was an attempt by a group of judges, including the then Chief Justice of the Supreme Court, Berger J, to have him struck off the roll and fired from his position as a law professor. Berger J argued that the actions of lawyers who aided their clients in the presenting of known false testimony were morally indefensible. He also said that the adoption of such practices by a lawyer would destroy the trust and confidence placed in that lawyer by the judges and his or her fellow lawyers.[47] In contrast, Mann has stated that notwithstanding the ethical rules a large number of practising lawyers believe they have a duty to present perjured testimony if their client insists. Mann quotes a lawyer as saying:[48]

> It's my mission and obligation to defend the client, not to sit in moral, ethical or legal judgment of him ... [W]hatever he does of his own impetus ... is a decision he has to make independent of what I do. I must inform him of the consequences and significance of his action, but not punish him ... or in other ways initiate law enforcement actions against him. My role in the adversary system is to protect him.

15.24 It is interesting to note that Mann's general view was enunciated by a New South Wales court in 1926. In *R v Tighne and Maher*[49] the court said that a lawyer:

> ... may be called upon to advise and to act for all manner of clients, good, bad or indifferent, honest and dishonest, and he [or she] is not called to sit in judgement beforehand upon his client's conduct. [emphasis added]

Freedman more recently maintained his views by arguing that perjury is different to other crimes that abuse the court process:[50]

> [B]ribery is clandestine, usually not suspected when committed and difficult to detect. Perjury, by contrast, takes place in the goldfish bowl of the courtroom, before a skeptical judge and jury, and is subject to immediate impeachment. Also, when perjury is detected by the court, the defendant faces the likelihood of an increased sentence ...

> Further, ... the lawyer's knowledge of the client's perjury is usually the direct outcome of lawyer–client communications about the crime that has been

---

45.   Subin (above), pp 149–50.

46.   See J Mitchell, 'Reasonable Doubts Are Where You Find Them: A Response to Professor Subin's Position on the Criminal Lawyer's "Different Mission"' (1987) 1 *Georgetown J of Legal Ethics* 339. See also H Subin, 'Is This Lie Necessary? Further Reflections on the Right to Present a False Defence' (1988) 1 *Georgetown J Legal Ethics* 689.

47.   W Burger, 'Standards of Conduct for Prosecution and Defense Personnel' (1966) 5 *American Criminal LQ* 11, 12.

48.   K Mann, *Defending White Collar Criminals: A Portrait of Attorneys at Work*, Yale University Press, New Haven, 1985, p 121.

49.   (1926) 26 SR(NSW) 108.

50.   Freedman (above) (1988), p 1951.

charged. Thus, knowledge of the 'future crime' of perjury is inextricably interwoven with the crime that is the subject of the representation. A client's announcement of an intent to kill a witness, on the other hand, is a fact that stands separate and apart from communications about the crime that is the subject of the representation, such as what Whiteside did or did not see in the victim's hand just before he stabbed him.

THE GUILTY ACCUSED

Introduction

Some of the problems facing lawyers representing clients involved with perjury are present when the client is known to be guilty. Ascertaining the client's guilt presents similar problems to determining whether a client has committed or intends to commit perjury. There is also the problem of what steps are required by lawyers to investigate whether their client is guilty. Do lawyers have a role in aiding the administration of justice by helping to find this out? In advising clients, what can lawyers tell them to say when dealing with the police? Can they be advised to stay silent to avoid confessing their guilt? If they are guilty, can silence be advised to negotiate a more lenient charge?[51] Finally, a guilty accused who wants to testify as being innocent is committing perjury. Some commentators have stated that lawyers will rarely be able to conclude from the available facts that their client is guilty. Even if it is rare, there will be times when lawyers will be very confident in concluding that their client is guilty. Can lawyers, knowing their client to be guilty, still conduct a defence leading to their acquittal? Should such lawyers refuse to provide a proper defence? Under what circumstances can lawyers cease to act for a guilty client? These problems are not present in the civil law system. In this system there is no need to enter a plea and if defendants confess their guilt lawyers are prohibited from arguing that their clients are innocent.

15.25

Professional rules

The Barristers' Rules (NSW) r 33 and (Qld) r 35 [Model Rules r 15.2] states:[52]

15.26

> A barrister briefed to appear in criminal proceedings whose client confesses guilt to the barrister but maintains a plea of not guilty:
>
> (a) may return the brief, if there is enough time for another legal practitioner to take over the case properly before the hearing, and the client does not insist on the barrister continuing to appear for the client;
>
> (b) in cases where the barrister keeps the brief for the client:
>
> (i) must not falsely suggest that some other person committed the offence charged;
>
> (ii) must not set up an affirmative case inconsistent with the confession; but
>
> (iii) may argue that the evidence as a whole does not prove that the client is guilty of the offence charged;

---

51. For a discussion on advising concerning the right to silence see D Dixon, *Law in Policing Legal Regulation and Police Practices*, Clarendon Press, Oxford, 1997, pp 246–56.
52. The English Bar has similar rules: see W Boulton, *A Guide to Conduct and Etiquette at the Bar*, 6th ed, Butterworths, London, 1975, pp 70–2.

(iv) may argue that for some reason of law the client is not guilty of the offence charged; and

(v) may argue that for any other reason not prohibited by (i) and (ii) the client should not be convicted of the offence charged.

15.27 According to Sawer the type of withdrawal required by these rules can lead to 'musical chairs'. This is because a confession of guilt to the next lawyer will require a further change of lawyers and so on, until one unlucky lawyer finds out too late to withdraw. Of course, the client may finally decide not to defend the case or to withhold the information of his or her guilt. The restrictions placed on the barristers under the rules who retain the brief means they are conducting a 'frozen defence'. In such a situation it will be obvious to both the judge and prosecutor, but probably not to the jury, that the defendant is a guilty accused.[53] It should be noted that if defendants confess to their lawyers that they are guilty and then change their minds and decide to plead not guilty, counsel would have the right to withdraw if there is sufficient time to be replaced. This appears to be what occurred in the Port Arthur massacre, where the defendant Martin Bryant's first lawyer withdrew and refused to make any public comment on the reason for the withdrawal.[54]

Tuckiar case

15.28 The most famous case in Australia dealing with the rights of a guilty accused is *Tuckiar v The King*.[55] During the trial of an 'uncivilised' Aborigine, the accused admitted to his lawyer, through an interpreter, that he had committed the murder. In open court counsel said he wanted to discuss with the judge 'the worst predicament that he had encountered in all his legal career'. The jury retired and counsel discussed the matter with the judge in chambers. The case then resumed and the accused was found guilty. Before pronouncing sentence counsel told the court that the accused had confessed to the crime. The judge sentenced the accused to death. He also stated:[56]

> It did not occur to me at the time, but I think I should have stated publicly that immediately that confession had been made to you, you consulted ... me about the matter and asked my opinion as to the proper course for you, as counsel to take, and I then told you that if your client had been a white man and had made a confession of guilt to you I thought your proper course would have been to withdraw from the case; but as your client was an aboriginal, and there might be some remnant of doubt as to whether his confession to you was any more reliable than any other confession he made, the better course would be for you to continue to appear for him, because if you had retired from the case it would have left it open to ignorant, malicious and irresponsible persons to say that this aboriginal had been abandoned and left without any proper defence.

---

53. Sawer (above), p 31. It should be noted that an accused at common law can choose to enter a plea of *noli contendre*, which means the charges are not contended but guilt is not admitted.
54. A Barby, 'Why Bryant changed plea', *Sydney Morning Herald*, 9 November 1996, p 9.
55. *Tuckiar v The King* (1934) 52 CLR 335.
56. *Tuckiar* (above) at 343–4.

The High Court quashed the verdict on various grounds of irregularity and **15.29**
misdirection by the judge and ordered Tuckiar to be released.[57] The court
did not understand why counsel found himself in so great a predicament.
He had a duty to press the arguments for acquittal or conviction only of
manslaughter. It did not matter whether in fact he was guilty or not. The
accused was:

> ... entitled to acquittal from any charge which the evidence fails to establish
> that he committed, and it is not incumbent on his counsel by abandoning his
> defence to deprive him of the benefits of such rational arguments as fairly
> arise on the proofs submitted.

The court said that the open statement to the court after the jury verdict
of the accused's guilt was 'wholly indefensible'.[58]

The facts surrounding the *Tuckiar* case are written up by Rowley. They
reveal a strong concern by the police, the defence lawyer and the trial judge
to uphold white supremacy.[59] Rowley says Tuckiar was released from prison
and sent home because of the High Court's decision that it was impossible
for him to receive a fair trial in Darwin, but he never reached his home:
'There have been stories of foul play ever since. That he was murdered is
highly probable.'[60]

American professional rules

In the United States the applicable provisions are ABA Model Rules rr 3.1, **15.30**
3.3 (discussed above) and 6.2. Rule 3.1 states that:

> A lawyer shall not ... defend a proceeding ... unless there is a basis in law
> and fact for doing so that is not frivolous ... A lawyer for the defendant in a
> criminal proceeding ... may nevertheless so defend the proceeding as to
> require that every element of the case be established.

Rule 6.2 outlines the lawyer's duty to act, which is discussed in Chapter 8.

Comment [10] to Rule 3.3 states that if withdrawal will not remedy the
situation or is impossible, the 'advocate must make such disclosure to the
tribunal as is reasonably necessary to remedy the situation, even if doing so
requires the lawyer to reveal information that otherwise would be protected
by Rule 1.6 [confidentiality]. It is for the tribunal then to determine what
should be done — making a statement about the matter to the trier of fact,
ordering a mistrial or perhaps nothing'.

Standard 4-7.7 also states:

(a) If the defendant has admitted to defense counsel facts which establish guilt
and counsel's independent investigation established that the admissions
are true but the defendant insists on the right to trial, counsel must
strongly discourage the defendant against taking the witness stand to
testify perjurously.

(b) If, in advance of trial, the defendant insists that he or she will take the
stand to testify perjurously, the lawyer may withdraw from the case, if that
is feasible, seeking leave of the court if necessary, but the court should not
be advised of the lawyer's reason for seeking to do so.

---

57. *Tuckiar* (above) at 342–4.
58. *Tuckiar* (above) at 336.
59. C Rowley, *The Destruction of Aboriginal Society*, Penguin Books, Ringwood, 1972, pp 290–7.
60. C Rowley (above), p 297.

American cases

15.31 There is a problem in the United States that a 'frozen defence' may lead to a denial of an accused's Sixth Amendment constitutional right to effective assistance of counsel as required by the Supreme Court in *Strickland v Washington*.[61] In *Johns v Smyth*[62] a lawyer was so convinced of his client's guilt of first degree murder that he was unable to give his client the 'undivided allegiance and faithful devoted service' required by the Supreme Court. In this case the accused did not testify. No proposed instructions were submitted to the trial judge on behalf of the defendant, although it was possible for a defence of involuntary manslaughter. The defence lawyer made an agreement with the prosecutor that the case would be submitted to the jury without argument of counsel. The defence lawyer did this because he felt that to make an argument defending the client would be factually untrue. He said:

> I think an argument to the jury would have made me appear ridiculous in the light of evidence that was offered. I ... would have been a hypocrite and falsifier if I had gone before the jury and argued in the light of what Johns told me that the statement was accurate.

15.32 The court ordered a new trial because counsel also admitted that 'his conscience prevented him from effectively representing his client according to customary standards'.

The *Johns* case is the exception in finding ineffective counsel. In a Texas case, *McFarland v State*,[63] an accused faced the death penalty, and was represented by a lawyer who fell asleep at various times during witnesses' testimony. The Texas Court of Appeals found that falling asleep could have been a 'strategic' method to gain the jury's sympathy. A federal trial judge in reviewing the decision made the following amazing comment: 'The Constitution says that everyone is entitled to an attorney of their choice. But the Constitution does not say that the lawyer has to be awake.'[64] By contrast there are cases in some jurisdictions that find ineffective represent-ation if there is sleeping during any 'substantial portion of a trial'.[65]

15.33 The United States Supreme Court recently gave some hope in finding inadequate representation in *Wiggins v Smith*[66] and *Rompilla v Beard*.[67] In *Wiggins* the court overturned a death conviction because the accused's lawyers failed to do a proper investigation of mitigating circumstances. It was obvious to any reasonable lawyer that the accused had experienced abuse that could have influenced the jury's deliberations. In *Rompilla*, decided in 2005, the court overturned a death sentence. It found ineffective representation because the defence lawyer had failed to read the files concerning the defendant's prior convictions and failed to investigate his client's possible abuse and mental retardation. Even with these decisions

---

61.   467 US 1267 (1984). Sawer (above), p 31, also supports this view.
62.   176 F Supp 949 (ED Va 1959).
63.   928 SW2d 482 (Tex Crim App 1996).
64.   Ibid, p 506, fn 20.
65.   *Javore v United States* 724 F2d 831 (9th Cir 1984). For other cases on the approach to or jurisprudence of sleeping or napping, see D Rhode and D Luban, *Legal Ethics*, 4th ed, Foundation Press, New York, 2004, p 321.
66.   123 S Ct 2527 (2003).
67.   125 S Ct 2456 (2005).

the vast majority of ineffective assistance claims have been[68] and will be unsuccessful.

Rhode and Luban have summed up the situation:

> Courts have declined to find inadequate representation where attorneys were drunk, on drugs, or parking their car during key parts of the prosecution's case. And defendants have been executed despite their lawyers' lack of any prior trial experience, ignorance of all relevant death penalty precedents, or failure to offer any witnesses, closing argument or mitigating evidence.[69]

The ineffectual defence lawyers in the *Johns*, *Wiggins*, *Rompilla* and other cases give us an indication that a 'frozen defence' may constitute ineffective representation. The attitude of the lawyers in these cases can be compared to that of one lawyer quoted by Mann in relation to handling multiple criminal defendants:[70]

15.34

> My own belief is that the more information you control as defense lawyer, the more effective you are, meaning that the only weapon you have as a defense lawyer in my view is control of information. You do not have much else. The prosecution has all the cards — they have ... all the investigative agencies, they have awesome powers. The only thing you have is sometimes you can stonewall an investigation. Now some people claim that that is obstructing justice. I don't, if you do it ethically and you do it out front, it's not.

Rationale for the rule

The problem with lawyers determining clients' guilt is that a lawyer will not really 'know' that the client is factually guilty unless the client admits all the facts making up the offence. This is so even in those cases where the client may be lying, mentally ill or mistaken. For example, a client who 'confesses' may not understand that certain legal defences exist such as provocation or self-defence. The admitting of guilt may result in the lawyer failing to explore fully these possible defences. Furthermore, the prosecution has to prove to a jury that the client is guilty beyond a reasonable doubt. Thus, a client is not legally guilty without the full scrutiny of a trial.[71] There is an important difference between a client who may be 'factually' guilty and one who is 'legally' guilty.[72] Pool makes this distinction and says that defence counsel 'defends the basic rights of all members of society by assuring that a client who is presumed innocent is accorded every protection which is rightfully his [or hers] under the laws of our society'.[73] It would appear that in the Anglo-Australian context lawyers have to be

15.35

---

68. One survey found that over 99 per cent of ineffective counsel claims failed. See V Flango and P McKenna, 'Federal Habeas Corpus Review of State Court Convictions' (1995) 31 *Calif West LR* 237, 259–60.

69. D Rhode and D Luban (above), p 320.

70. Mann discusses the importance of keeping multiple accused together to avoid giving the prosecution vital information. He includes the need for defence lawyers to counsel friends and associates of the accused. Of course, in the process defence counsel may compromise the interests of an individual client, in order to protect the others: see Mann (above), pp 169–73.

71. M Schwartz, *Lawyers and the Legal Profession: Cases and Materials*, 2nd ed, Michie Company, Charlottesville, Virginia, 1985, p 49.

72. J Pool, 'Defending the "Guilty" Client' (1979) 64 *Mass LR* 11, 15. See also F Gedicks, 'Justice or Mercy? — A Personal Note on Defending the Guilty' (1988) 13 *The Journal of the Legal Profession* 139.

73. Pool (above), p 19.

virtually certain of the client's guilt before returning a brief or conducting a frozen defence. The standard usually stated is that the lawyer has to have proof of guilt by credible evidence that meets the beyond reasonable doubt standard.[74] Some American commentators go even further, stating that lawyers need not only be certain of guilt, but 'that a conviction will be obtained, and doubt whether such certainty can ever be justified'.[75]

Rejection of the rationale

15.36 Bargaric and Dimopoulos criticise this rationale for being inconsistent. A client who confesses that he or she is guilty but still wants to plead not guilty can do so, but the lawyer cannot allow the client to give dishonest evidence. They say, therefore, 'we have the interesting situation where the client can, effectively, lie regarding the ultimate issue, but not tell "small lies" during the course of the proceedings where the ultimate aim is to determine guilt or innocence'.[76]

Bargaric and Dimopoulos say the argument that the lawyer will not really 'know' is not persuasive because a competent lawyer will not be stopped from exploring the facts and will go beyond the client's confession and find out information that could be used to make a defence. The second reason is that the prosecution has the burden of proving beyond a reasonable doubt and thus the lawyer should not take on the role of the judge or jury and decide the guilt of the client. They say this argument 'begs the question. It distinguishes legal from substantive guilt (prioritising the former over the latter), and hence *assumes* — rather than establishes — that judges and juries should be put to the task of deciding legal guilt or innocence in cases where the lawyer is aware of the client's guilt'.[77]

Defending the guilty

15.37 Criminal defence lawyers have different attitudes concerning the guilt of their clients. I once heard one New York lawyer say he had no trouble with defending a guilty accused because 'all of my clients are guilty'! Some lawyers have said: 'I never know whether a client is guilty'![78] Another response is that 'truth cannot be known. Facts are indeterminate, contingent, and in criminal cases, often evanescent'.[79] Famous Melbourne criminal lawyer Frank Galbally would agree with that view. He says:

> I wasn't present when the crime was committed and I have no better reason to believe a man [or woman] charged with a crime who says he is guilty than one who says he is not.

15.38 He consciously avoids asking his clients if they have committed the crime. He carefully and deliberately stops short of allowing his clients to confess their guilt.[80] This is also the attitude adopted by Rumpole, a fictional

74. See H Subin, 'The Criminal Lawyer's "Different Mission": Reflections on the "Right" to Present a False Defense' (1987) 1 *Georgetown J of Legal Ethics* 125, 143.

75. Sawer (above), p 31.

76. M Bargaric and P Dimopoulous, 'Legal Ethics is (Just) Normal Ethics: Towards a Coherent System of Legal Ethics' (2003) 3 *QUTLJJ* 21.

77. Ibid.

78. Freedman (above) (1975), p 51.

79. B Babcock, 'Defending the Guilty' (1983) 32 *Cleveland State L Rev* 175.

80. E Becker, 'A Question of Conscience', *The Age*, 13 May 1978, p 17.

criminal defence barrister created by John Mortimer.[81] For criminal defence lawyers justice is not part of the equation. As Mills stated:[82]

> Criminal law to the defense lawyer does not mean equity or fairness or proper punishment or vengeance. It means getting everything he [or she] can for his client ... Justice is a luxury enjoyed by the district attorney. He alone is sworn 'to see that justice is done'. The defense lawyer ... finds himself most often working for the guilty and for a judicial system based upon the sound but paradoxical principle that the guilty must be freed to protect the innocent.

All of these lawyers seem to have screened themselves from the lay person's question: How can you represent people who are so evil, especially either knowing they are guilty or being pretty sure that they are guilty? How can you, by the use of your skills or tricks, get them off?

There are a number of reasons lawyers can present for defending the guilty. **15.39** The first is that, by providing criminal defendants with competent counsel, whether they have committed a heinous offence or are innocent, their human dignity is upheld. Freedman expresses this view by stating that the 'right to counsel is one of the most significant manifestations of our regard for the dignity of the individual'.[83] The dignity aspect includes the need to maintain defendants' human spirit by providing them with someone to trust and confide in who will remain loyal throughout this terrible ordeal.

The second reason is that lawyers have an obligation to protect their clients and not to sit in judgment on them. The determination of guilt or innocence of a client is not the lawyer's function. In the famous exchange between Boswell and Dr Johnson, Boswell asked: 'But what do you think of supporting a cause which you know to be bad?' Dr Johnson replied:

> Sir, you do not know it to be good or bad till the Judge determines it ... It is his business to judge; and you are not to be confident in your own opinion that a cause is bad, but to say all you can for your client, and then hear the judge's opinion.

Dr Johnson also said:[84]

> [A] lawyer has no business with the justice or injustice of the cause which he undertakes ... [It] is to be decided by the judge ... A lawyer is not to tell what he knows to be a lie; he is not to produce what he knows to be a false deed; but he is not to usurp the province of the jury and of the judge and determine what shall be the effect of evidence — what shall be the result of legal argument.

A third reason is to make sure that those operating the system do so **15.40** properly. Criminal defence lawyers in this context not only make prosecutors prove their case but also ensure that they do so legally and ethically.

A fourth reason is that the adversary system requires lawyers to present for their clients a fearless defence. Lawyers can argue that they are just doing what is required under the adversary system. Schwartz states:[85]

81. J Mortimer, *Rumpole of the Bailey*, Penguin Books, Ringwood, 1979.
82. J Mills, 'I Have Nothing to Do with Justice', *Life*, 12 March 1971, pp 56–7 quoted in D Rhode (above), p 603. Mills is quoting and referring to the views of Martin Erdmann who in 25 years had defended more than 100,000 criminals 'who have robbed, raped, burglarized and murdered tens of thousands of people'. Erdmann finds the idea that he had a 'very personal and direct hand in all that mayhem ... as boring and irrelevant ... "If you say I have no moral reaction to what I do, you are right"'.
83. Freedman (above) (1975), pp 2 and 4.
84. Quoted in J Barry, 'The Ethics of Advocacy' (1941) 15 *ALJ* 166, 168.
85. Schwartz (above), p 50.

The lawyer is a functionary in that system and may properly conclude that the ethics of the role outweigh any immoral consequences stemming from a particular instance of advocacy. Can a lawyer shield himself [or herself] from the moral consequences of his actions by saying as did Eichmann ..., 'I was a functionary in the system and I was only obeying orders'?

As we saw in **2.71–2.72**, according to Sartre such an attitude leads lawyers frequently to act in 'bad faith'.

A fifth reason is that lawyers have an obligation as key-holders to the legal system to provide their services to all who are in need. Shaffer says that by serving the guilty, lawyers are fulfilling their Christian role of service to those in need. Shaffer's view is based on lawyers having fidelity to, and caring for, their clients. It is the notion of the role Jesus played when he ministered to the sinners.[86] Thus, criminal defending is an act of Christian charity for helping, and not judging, one's neighbour.[87] Similar ideas about helping others are found in all major religions.

15.41   Shaffer's view of service involves a certain degree of empathy which can lead to lawyers becoming too involved in their client's case. This is against the general professional role of being objective, as we discussed in Chapter 2. Ogletree says: 'Without the benefit of critical distance, a [public] defender may be tempted to overstep ethical boundaries in her zeal to help her client.' Another model used to justify and conduct criminal defences is the 'hero of the oppressed'. This role can also cause lawyers to feel they do not have to play by society's rules. Such a lawyer may thus be inclined to present a perjurous witness in order to win the case.[88] Ogletree believes that lawyers defending the accused can justify their work and receive personal satisfaction by combining the best elements of the 'empathy' and 'heroic' models. He says: 'Empathy enables the "heroic" defender to broaden her understanding of what "winning the case" really means.' This allows lawyers to attain the client's objectives as defined by the client. In contrast, the heroic approach enables empathetic lawyers to focus on the goal of winning and helps them to avoid being 'tempted to devote too much time or attention to other problems or needs of the client'.[89]

15.42   A sixth reason given by some defence lawyers for their work is that they may keep people from going to gaol who are guilty but who do not deserve to be in gaol. This is especially true when the prison system is so brutal that it will destroy a person who may have a chance for redemption and rehabilitation by remaining outside the gaol system. Mitchell has stated that: 'Those guilty of serious crime merit the wrath of our society. But almost no one deserves the hellholes we call jails and prisons. There is almost no case I would not defend if that meant keeping a human being, as condemnable as he or she may be, from suffering the total, brutal inhumanity of our jails and prisons.'[90]

---

86.   T Shaffer, *On Being a Christian and a Lawyer* (1981), pp 55–6. Shaffer quotes from Mark 2:15–2:17. Gedicks (above), pp 140, 147–8.
87.   Gedicks (above), p 148. The author sees the choice of defending the guilty as 'holding the promise of reforming and redeeming the lives of both lawyer and client'.
88.   C Ogletree Jr, 'Beyond Justifications: Seeking Motivations to Sustain Public Defenders' (1993) 106 *Harvard LR* 1239, 1278.
89.   Ogletree (above), p 1281.
90.   J Mitchell, 'The Ethics of the Criminal Defense Attorney — New Answers to Old Questions', (1980) 32 *Stanford L Rev* 293, 334.

Duties of the prosecution

We have already discussed in Chapter 9 the prosecutor's role in plea bargaining and charge bargaining. In this section we will look first at the professional rules. We will then look at the prosecutor's obligation to call witnesses and disclose potential evidence. Finally, the role of the prosecutor's office in Australia and the United States will be discussed.

15.43

Professional rules

The Barristers' Rules (NSW) rr 62–71 and (Qld) rr 63–74 state:

15.44

62. A prosecutor must fairly assist the court to arrive at the truth, must seek impartially to have the whole of the relevant evidence placed intelligibly before the court, and must seek to assist the court with adequate submissions of law to enable the law properly to be applied to the facts.

63. A prosecutor must not press the prosecution's case for a conviction beyond a full and firm presentation of that case.

64. A prosecutor must not, by language or other conduct, seek to inflame or bias the court against the accused.

65. A prosecutor must not argue any proposition of fact or law which the prosecutor does not believe on reasonable grounds to be capable of contributing to a finding of guilt and also to carry weight.

66. A prosecutor must disclose to the opponent as soon as practicable all material (including the names of and means of finding prospective witnesses in connexion with such material) available to the prosecutor or of which the prosecutor becomes aware which could constitute evidence relevant to the guilt or innocence of the accused, unless:

   (a) such disclosure, or full disclosure, would seriously threaten the integrity of the administration of justice in those proceedings or the safety of any person; and

   (b) the prosecutor believes on reasonable grounds that such a threat could not be avoided by confining such disclosure, or full disclosure, to the opponent being a legal practitioner, on appropriate conditions which may include an undertaking by the opponent not to disclose certain material to the opponent's client or any other person.

66A. A prosecutor who has decided not to disclose material to the opponent under Rule 66 must consider whether:

   (a) the defence of the accused could suffer by reason of such non-disclosure;

   (b) the charge against the accused to which such material is relevant should be withdrawn; and

   (c) the accused should be faced only with a lesser charge to which such material would not be so relevant.

66B. A prosecutor must call as part of the prosecution's case all witnesses:

   (a) whose testimony is admissible and necessary for the presentation of the whole picture;

   (b) whose testimony provides reasonable grounds for the prosecutor to believe that it could provide admissible evidence relevant to any matter in issue;

   (c) whose testimony or statements were used in the course of any committal proceedings;

   (d) from whom statements have been obtained in the preparation or conduct of the prosecution's case;

   unless:

(e) the opponent consents to the prosecutor not calling a particular witness;

(f) the only matter with respect to which the particular witness can give admissible evidence has been dealt with by an admission on behalf of the accused; or

(g) the prosecutor believes on reasonable grounds that the administration of justice in the case would be harmed by calling a particular witness or particular witnesses to establish a particular point already adequately established by another witness or other witnesses;

provided that:

(h) the prosecutor is not obliged to call evidence from a particular witness, who would otherwise fall within (a)–(d), if the prosecutor believes on reasonable grounds that the testimony of that witness is plainly untruthful or is plainly unreliable by reason of the witness being in the camp of the accused; and

(i) the prosecutor must inform the opponent as soon as practicable of the identity of any witness whom the prosecutor intends not to call on any ground within (f), (g) and (h), together with the grounds on which the prosecutor has reached that decision.

[(j) omitted in the Barristers' Rules: see below]

67. A prosecutor who has reasonable grounds to believe that certain material available to the prosecution may have been unlawfully obtained must promptly:

(a) inform the opponent if the prosecutor intends to use the material; and

(b) make available to the opponent a copy of the material if it is in documentary form.

68. A prosecutor must not confer with or interview any of the accused except in the presence of the accused's representative.

69. A prosecutor must not inform the court or the opponent that the prosecution has evidence supporting an aspect of its case unless the prosecutor believes on reasonable grounds that such evidence will be available from material already available to the prosecutor.

70. A prosecutor who has informed the court of matters within Rule 69, and who has later learnt that such evidence will not be available, must immediately inform the opponent of that fact and must inform the court of it when next the case is before the court.

71. A prosecutor must not seek to persuade the court to impose a vindictive sentence or a sentence of a particular magnitude, but:

(a) must correct any error made by the opponent in address on sentence;

(b) must inform the court of any relevant authority or legislation bearing on the appropriate sentence;

(c) must assist the court to avoid appealable error on the issue of sentence;

(d) may submit that a custodial or non-custodial sentence is appropriate; and

(e) may inform the court of an appropriate range of severity of penalty, including a period of imprisonment, by reference to relevant appellate authority.

15.45 Model Rules r 20.1–20.12 and Professional Conduct and Practice Rules (NSW) r 23, A.62–71 are identical to the Barristers' Rules except for an important additional provision, r 20.7.4(iii) and r A66B(j), which states that 'the prosecutor *must* call any witness whom the prosecutor intends not to call on the ground in (i) [the same as (h) in r 66B above] if the opponent requests the prosecutor to do so for the purpose of permitting the opponent to cross-examine that witness' [author's italics].

Under the Legal Profession Act 2004 (NSW) the Solicitors' and Barristers' Rules are now recognised by statute as being binding and having a normative effect.[91] The ethical rules have also been adopted by the Director of Public Prosecutions (DPP) in New South Wales. But r A66B(j) of the Solicitors' Rules (above) has been explicitly rejected by the DPP in New South Wales in its Guidelines. The DPP refers to A66B(j) but states only that it '*should* assist the accused to call such a witness by making him or her available for cross-examination without adducing relevant evidence in chief'[92] [author's italics]. I believe that this results in solicitor advocates in New South Wales, who ignore the provision and obey the Guideline of their office, being in breach of the Act and their professional rules. The DPP has accepted all of the other provisions. These developments may now make the judiciary more willing to apply the rules to the conduct of advocates, including prosecutors, instead of just relying on case law.

The Professional Conduct Rules (WA) state: **15.46**

15.1   Prosecuting Counsel *shall* not seek to obtain a conviction by any improper means. It is his duty to present before the jury the case for the prosecution fairly, impartially and in a competent manner. [author's italics]

15.2(1) If Prosecuting Counsel knows of the existence of a person who may be able to give evidence relevant to the case, but who is not proposed to be called before the jury by the prosecution, he *shall* cause the defence to be informed of the identity and location (if known) of that person prior to the trial ...

15.3   Prosecuting Counsel *shall* assist the court at all times before the verdict is returned by drawing attention to any apparent errors or omissions of fact or law or procedural irregularities which, in his opinion, ought to be corrected [author's italics] ...

American professional rules

ABA Model Rules r 3.8, reflecting the constitutional needs of a fair trial in the United States, states: **15.47**

The prosecutor in a criminal case shall:

(a) refrain from prosecuting a charge that the prosecutor knows is not supported by probable cause;

(b) make reasonable efforts to assure that the accused has been advised of the right to, and the procedure for obtaining, counsel and has been given reasonable opportunity to obtain counsel;

(c) not seek to obtain from an unrepresented accused a waiver of important pretrial rights, such as the right to a preliminary hearing;

(d) make timely disclosure to the defense of all evidence or information known to the prosecutor that tends to negate the guilt of the accused or mitigates the offense, and, in connection with sentencing, disclose to the defense and to the tribunal all unprivileged mitigating information known to the prosecutor, except when the prosecutor is relieved of this responsibility by a protective order of the tribunal; ...

---

91.   Section 711.
92.   *Prosecution Policy and Guidelines*, Office of the DPP (NSW), October 2003, Guideline 26. See www.odpp.nsw.gov.au for the Guidelines.

Comment [1] to the rule states the prosecutor has the responsibility of a minister of justice. This role carries the obligations of ensuring that defendants receive procedural justice and that guilt is decided upon the basis of sufficient evidence. How far a prosecutor can go to uphold this rule varies in different jurisdictions. This is recognition that the prosecutor's office in some jurisdictions will have a far more political role than in others. There is a great variation in the nature of prosecution agencies in the United States. Comment [1] says many jurisdictions have adopted the ABA Standards of Criminal Justice Relating to the Prosecution Function.

15.48   In 1990, r 3.8 was amended with the inclusion of subs (e). It calls for the prosecutor not to subpoena lawyers in criminal proceedings except in exceptional circumstances. Comment [4] to the rule states that it was added to allow prosecutors to intrude into the lawyer–client relationship only when there is a genuine need. This requirement is relevant to our discussion in Chapter 11 in relation to confidentiality.

In 1994 rule 3.8 was amended with the inclusion of subs (f) which states:

> ... except for statements that are necessary to inform the public of the nature and extent of the prosecutor's action and that serve a legitimate law enforcement purpose, refrain from making extrajudicial comments that have a substantial likelihood of heightening public condemnation of the accused
> ...

Comment [5] states that (f) supplements rule 3.6, which prohibits out of court statements that have a substantial likelihood of prejudicing a hearing. It was felt that a special rule was needed to prevent prosecutors from inflaming the public against an accused.

15.49   The ABA Standards Relating to the Administration of Criminal Justice in 3-1.2 state:

> (b) The prosecutor is an administrator of justice, an advocate and an officer of the court; the prosecutor must exercise sound discretion in the performance of his or her functions.
>
> (c) The duty of the prosecutor is to seek justice, not merely to convict.

Standard 3-1.2(e) says prosecutors are subject to the same standards of professional conduct as defined in codes and cannons of the legal profession as other lawyers. Prosecutors can be found to have committed unprofessional conduct by violating these provisions. There are specific rules under Pt III concerning the investigation and the instituting of criminal charges, Pt IV rules concerning plea discussions, Pt V rules relating to the conduct of the trial and in Pt VI in relation to sentencing. Finally, the prosecutor has under Standard 3-1.2(d) a general obligation to improve the administration of criminal justice and when they discover defects in the system they should seek remedial action. It is noteworthy that a similar general obligation has been placed on the Commonwealth DPP in Australia.[93]

Duty to call witnesses and disclose relevant evidence

15.50   Lawyers are generally not under a duty to call witnesses or disclose information that may assist the opposition. As we have seen earlier, the

---

93. *Information Booklet*, Commonwealth DPP, 1989, p 6.

professional rules state that prosecutors *must* (NSW, Qld and WA) make available to the accused all relevant material, including the names of material witnesses, concerning the accused's culpability unless the disclosure threatens the public interest. Although he was writing in 1982, Lane has aptly summarised the position of the Australian courts when he said that they have:

> ... avoided imposing any enforceable obligation which would require disclosure of information by prosecutors; consequently they have also failed to specify what information prosecutors should disclose.

The courts have granted wide discretionary powers to prosecutors in conducting criminal cases, including whether or not to call any witnesses.[94]

Cases on duty to call witnesses

The High Court was originally critical of the prosecution's actions of not calling a credible material witness. In *Ziems v Prothonotary*[95] both Fullagar and Taylor JJ used the failure to call a police sergeant by the prosecutor as grounds for reducing the penalty of a barrister from disbarment to suspension. The barrister had been convicted for involuntary manslaughter for drunken driving. The barrister had used as a defence that the accident was caused by his confusion after a fight, witnessed by the sergeant, rather than being drunk. Fullagar emphasised that the prosecution is bound to call all material witnesses, even if they give inconsistent accounts and harm the Crown's case. Fullagar said the only possible reason for not calling the sergeant was to place the defence:[96]

15.51

> ... under the tactical disadvantage which resulted from the inability to cross-examine him. Such tactics are permissible in civil cases, but in criminal cases, in view of what is at stake, they may sometimes accord ill with the traditional notion of the functions of a prosecutor for the Crown.

Since that decision the Australian courts have retreated from making prosecutors disclose witnesses or evidence to the defence. In *Re Van Beelen*[97] some time after an accused had been found guilty of murder, his lawyer found that during the committal the prosecution had suppressed important evidence. The lawyer found that the prosecution had in its possession the confession of another person, together with statements of four witnesses who had seen this person in the vicinity of the murder. Van Beelen's counsel appealed on the basis that this 'fresh evidence' alone showed there was a miscarriage of justice; that the evidence led to a reasonable doubt as to his guilt. The appeal was rejected for two reasons. First, the confessional evidence would not have been admissible at the trial. Second, the prosecutor was not under any obligation to disclose the information because the confessional statement was not credible. The court gave the prosecution and/or the police the power to determine what is

15.52

---

94.   W Lane, 'Fair trial and the adversary system; withholding of exculpatory evidence by prosecutors' in J Basten et al (eds), *The Criminal Injustice System*, Australian Legal Workers Group, Sydney, 1982, pp 174–5.
95.   *Ziems v Prothonotary* (1957) 97 CLR 279.
96.   *Ziems v Prothonotary* (above) at 293.
97.   [1974] SASR 163.

credible evidence. If they decided evidence was not credible there was no obligation to call the witnesses nor to disclose the evidence.[98]

15.53   In *Richardson v R*[99] the High Court retreated from *Ziems* by deciding that prosecutors have the discretion not to call an eyewitness when they have sufficient reason for not calling him or her. In this case the prosecutor did not call a Miss Gardiner, who gave evidence in favour of the accused. His reason for not calling her was that she was not a credible and truthful witness. The court said the failure to call a particular witness by the Crown:[100]

> ... can only constitute a ground for setting aside a conviction and granting a new trial if it constitutes misconduct which, when viewed against the conduct of the trial as a whole, gives rise to a miscarriage of justice.

15.54   The High Court continued this view in *Lawless v R*.[101] Lawless had appealed against a murder conviction on the basis that fingerprint evidence had been planted by the police and that the prosecution had suppressed material evidence. The main Crown witness had said that Lawless was alone when the shooting occurred, while another person, Mrs Telford, had told the police that she had seen two men. Mrs Telford's evidence was suppressed. Other suppressed evidence included the psychiatric history of the main Crown witness, the statements of two other witnesses and police notes of an earlier interview with their main witness which supported Lawless's alibi.[102]

The High Court held by a 4:1 majority that the suppressed material did not constitute 'fresh evidence' resulting in a miscarriage of justice. The court upheld the discretion of the prosecutor not to disclose material favourable to the accused. In fact, two of the judges, Barwick and Mason JJ, said that the suppressed material was not 'fresh evidence' because the defence could have discovered it by exercising 'reasonable diligence'. Mason J said that it was like the rule in the *Richardson* case where there was no duty to call particular witnesses. There was no rule of law making the Crown 'provide the defence with statements of people whom it does not propose to call as witnesses'.[103]

The High Court's views should be compared to the American view. American courts have stated that prosecutors must provide items 'the existence of which is known, or by the exercise of due diligence may become known'.[104]

98.   The court selectively quoted Lord Denning from *Dallison v Caffery* [1965] 1 QB 348, 369 and failed to quote his statement that: 'If the prosecuting counsel ... knows, not of a credible witness, but a witness whom he does not accept as credible, he should tell the defence about him so that they can call him if they wish.' The court's approach in *Re Van Beelen* should be contrasted with the more recent Privy Council case of *Berry v R* [1992] 2 AC 364 in which the Board said that the prosecutor had an obligation not only to disclose the identity of material credible witnesses, but also to provide the statements of these witnesses if it would help the defence in questioning the witnesses at the trial.
99.   *Richardson v R* (1974) 131 CLR 116.
100. *Richardson v R* (above) at 121.
101. (1978) 53 ALJR 733.
102. The defence only found out about some of this information because of the revelations of police misconduct in the *Beach Report*, 1978, p 39. Lawless was also an important witness against the police before the Beach Commission.
103. (1979) 53 ALJR 733 at 736, 740–1.
104. *United States v Gladney* 563 F 2d 491 at 493 (1st Cir 1977). See also *United States v Bailleaux* 685 F 2d 1105 (9th Cir 1982).

Murphy J wrote a strong dissent, adopting the American view of the need for a fair trial. He said:[105]

> Those prosecuting on behalf of the community are not entitled to act as if they were representing private interests in civil litigation. The prosecution's suppression of credible evidence tending to contradict evidence of guilt militates against the basic element of fairness in a criminal trial ... [T]he guilty verdict was brought about by conduct which departed from the standard required of those prosecuting on behalf of the community.

Since the *Lawless* case the High Court has made an effort to clarify its position, but has still maintained the fresh evidence rule and the complete discretion granted to the prosecution. In *Whitehorn v R*[106] Deane J said that all material witnesses should be called that were necessary for the presentation of the whole picture by the Crown unless valid reasons exist, such as in the interests of justice, for not calling them. Material witnesses generally included all eyewitnesses of 'any events that go to prove the elements of the crime charged and will include witnesses, notwithstanding that they give accounts inconsistent with the Crown case'. Deane J pointed out that prosecutors do not have to call such witnesses if they judge them to be 'unreliable, untrustworthy or otherwise incapable of belief'.[107]   **15.55**

In *R v Shaw*,[108] a Victorian case, a murder conviction was quashed because the Crown prosecutor failed to call a reliable eyewitness to the fatal stabbing. The prosecution came to the conclusion that the witness was unreliable but failed to interview the witness or take into consideration information offered by the defence counsel showing the substance of the witness's evidence. The defence had to call this witness, allowing the prosecution to have an unfair advantage by allowing cross-examination by the prosecution and denying it to the defence.[109] Nathan J stated:[110]   **15.56**

> ... eye witnesses do not belong to a camp, but are within the class of persons from whom juries expect and are entitled to hear. The characterisation of witnesses being in camps is unfortunate. It necessarily implies that the prosecution might choose to call only those witnesses favourable to his or her camp. This is an absolute derogation of a prosecutor's responsibilities.

In a Victorian case, *R v Lewis Hamilton*,[111] the Full Court of Appeal found that a miscarriage of justice had occurred. Charles JA said that this occurred because the prosecution failed to reveal the complainant's victim impact statement until after the verdict. The statement contained information that 'was sufficiently solid reasonably to lead to the view that cross-examination based upon it might elicit answers materially affecting the credibility of the complainant'.   **15.57**

---

105. *Lawless v R* (1978) 53 ALJR 733 at 742. It seems likely that the High Court today would view *Lawless* differently.
106. *Whitehorn v R* (1983) 57 ALJR 809; 152 CLR 657.
107. *Whitehorn v R* (above) at 811.
108. *R v Shaw* (1991) 57 A Crim R 425 (Vic CCA).
109. In allowing the appeal in *Grey v R* (2001) 184 ALR 593, the High Court pointed out the importance of allowing defence counsel to cross-examine a material and relevant witness.
110. *Shaw* (above) at p 450.
111. [1998] 1 VR 630.

In another Victorian case, *R v Garofalo*,[112] evidence of prior convictions for dishonesty of the principal Crown witness only came to light after the trial. Ormiston JA of the Court of Appeal stated that 'there is, in general terms, a common law duty to make disclosure of previous convictions of prosecution witnesses, though the precise manner in which this duty should be worked out and applied may depend upon the court in which the prosecution has been brought, the means of obtaining that information and possibly other circumstances relevant to the individual case'.[113] The court found a miscarriage of justice and said the verdict was unsafe and unsatisfactory.

15.58 In *R v Wilson*[114] the Queensland Court of Appeal quashed a conviction for attempted murder because of the failure of both the prosecution and the self-represented accused to call an essential witness. This witness, a Dr Fama, was needed to testify about the accused's mental condition when he stabbed the victim. The Court of Appeal said that the trial judge had failed to inquire 'why the prosecutor was not calling the medical evidence and to encourage him to do so. While the prosecutor could not be required by the trial judge to call Dr Fama ... his Honour could have reminded the prosecutor what was said in *Whithorn v R* by Deane J' (see above).[115]

15.59 In a more recent important New South Wales Court of Appeal decision, *R v Kneebone*,[116] a new trial was ordered because the prosecutor used tactics that enabled him to avoid calling a material eyewitness. The only witness to an alleged sexual assault on the accused's de facto daughter was possibly the accused's de facto wife, the mother of the complainant. The complainant had alleged her mother saw the assault and said 'That's enough' or something similar. Neither the Crown nor the defence called the mother. The mother's affidavit denied seeing the assault. According to the accused's solicitor, the Crown approached him at the end of the first day of the trial to inquire whether the defence intended to call the mother. Defence counsel pointed out that the mother's statement 'formed part of the brief upon which the appellant had been committed to trial'. She had been listed as a potential witness and should be called by the Crown. The next day the Crown said to the defence that she probably would not be called, as she was an unreliable witness. The defence did not demand reasons for the decision and stated that he had refrained from interviewing the mother because he believed that the Crown would call her.

James J (who wrote the main judgment) applied the *Apostilides* case, both the New South Wales Bar Rules and the Guidelines of the Director of Public Prosecutions (see below), and cited cases from the United Kingdom,[117] New Zealand[118] and the United States[119] as being consistent

112. [1999] 2 VR 625.
113. Ibid, at 634.
114. [1998] 2 Qd R 599.
115. (1983) 152 CLR 657, 664.
116. (1999) 47 NSWLR 450.
117. *R v Russell-Jones* [1995] All ER 239.
118. *R v Wilson* [1997] 2 NZLR 500.
119. *Commonwealth of Pennsylvania v Horn* 150 Atlantic Reporter 872 (1959).

with the Australian view, while noting a differing position in Canada.[120] He rejected the notion that a witness, whose evidence is inconsistent or contradicts other evidence, is necessarily untrue. He says a prosecutor needs to be able to point to 'identifiable facts which can justify a decision not to call a material witness on the ground of unreliability'. In order to form a proper opinion it is necessary for a prosecutor to interview witnesses. James J found that the prosecutor's view on the mother's unreliability, that the mother was in the enemy's camp, was wrongly based on the grounds that the mother's account did not accord with his 'case theory'.

'An approach, whereby the witness is not called at all or is left to the defence to call because the witness' evidence is seen as not fitting the prosecution's view of the case is likely to lead to a miscarriage of justice.' James J relied on Fullagar J in *Ziems v Prothonotary* in holding that failure to call a material witness 'without having a principled basis for not so doing [calling the witness] accorded ill with the traditional notion of the functions of a prosecutor for the Crown'.[121] James J, in ordering a new trial, pointed out the lack of a principled basis for not calling the mother for reasons of presumed unreliability:

> There was, for example, no evidence that the witness was unwilling to speak to the police; there was no attempt to conduct a conference with the witness; and the witness' statements to the police concerning the physical assault may have been explicable on a basis other than being in the accused's 'camp'.

15.60 It should be remembered that a prosecutor still has the right not to call an unreliable and untruthful witness. The New South Wales Court of Appeals in *R v Gibson*[122] found that when the prosecutor did not call such a witness, a miscarriage of justice did not occur. The court said that the jury would have soon realised that the witness was not being put forward by the prosecutor as a witness of truth, which would have become even more evident when she would have had to cross-examine the witness.

High Court standards for calling witnesses

15.61 In *R v Apostilides*[123] the High Court had to deal with the failure of the prosecution to call known witnesses, the two main witnesses to circumstances surrounding the alleged rape. The two witnesses were a couple who had been present at the house and saw the initial stages of the sexual advances made by the accused. The prosecutor gave no reason for his actions, but did make available to the defence copies of the statements made by the witnesses. The defence decided it had to call these witnesses (thus allowing the prosecutor to cross-examine them).

The High Court upheld the setting aside of the conviction by the Full Victorian Supreme Court. The Victorian court had based its decision on the ground that the prosecutor's actions were not justified. It said that the trial judge should have called the witnesses, thereby allowing them to be cross-

---

120. *R v Cook* 114 CCC3d 481. James J says the different position in Canada may be explained because of the development of 'pre-trial disclosure and the availability there of an opportunity for an accused to cross-examine its own witness'.
121. (1957) 97 CLR 279, 294.
122. [2002] NSWCA 401.
123. (1984) 154 CLR 563.

examined by the defence. The High Court rejected this approach and said that the failure of the prosecutor to call a witness:[124]

> ... whose evidence is essential to the unfolding of the case for the Crown the central question is not whether his decision constitutes misconduct but whether in all circumstances the verdict is unsafe or unsatisfactory.

The court in a *per curiam* joint judgment of Gibbs CJ, Mason, Murphy, Wilson and Dawson JJ laid down some 'general propositions':[125]

(1) The Crown prosecutor alone bears the responsibility of deciding whether a person will be called as a witness for the Crown.

(2) The trial judge may but is not obliged to question the prosecutor in order to discover the reasons which led the prosecutor to decline to call a particular person. He is not called upon to adjudicate the sufficiency of those reasons.

(3) Whilst at the close of the Crown case the trial judge may properly invite the prosecutor to reconsider such a decision and to have regard to the implications as then appear to the judge at that stage of the proceedings, he cannot direct the prosecutor to call a particular witness.

(4) When charging a jury, the trial judge may make such comment as he thinks to be appropriate with respect to the effect which the failure of the prosecutor to call the particular person as a witness would appear to have had on the course of the trial. No doubt that comment, if any, will be affected by such information as to the prosecutor's reasons for his decision as the prosecutor thinks it proper to divulge.

(5) Save in the most exceptional circumstances, the trial judge should not himself call a person to give evidence.[126]

(6) A decision of the prosecutor not to call a particular person as a witness will only constitute a ground for setting aside a conviction if, when viewed against the conduct of the trial taken as a whole, it is seen to give rise to a miscarriage of justice.

The High Court more recently in *Dyers v The Queen*[127] upheld and applied the principles established in *Apostilides*.

Summary of possibilities for the judge

15.62 There appear to be a number of possibilities open for a judge if the prosecutor refuses to call a witness. According to *Cross on Evidence* the judge may 'include a direction as to the possibility of an inference that the witness would not have assisted the Crown case, and may include a direction as to the unfairness of the position in which the accused has been placed'.[128] Other possible courses of action could be:

---

124. For a case applying this test of a safe and satisfactory verdict in favour of the prosecution even though he had suppressed evidence, see *R v Warner* (unreported, CA(NSW), Full Ct, No 60432 of 1993, 10 June 1994, BC9402639).
125. See also *Wakeley v R* (1990) 64 ALJR 321 and *Maxwell v R* (1996) 184 CLR 501.
126. In *R v Griffis* (1996) 67 SASR 170 the trial judge called the witness and allowed both sides the right to cross-examination. This action occurred after the defence closed its case because the defence had asked the judge why this witness was 'essential to the case'. The conviction was quashed on appeal and a new trial ordered on the basis of *Apostilides*.
127. [2002] HCA 45.
128. J Heydon, *Cross on Evidence*, 7th ed, Butterworths, Sydney, 2004, para 17130. Each possible approach is supported by various cases cited in the book. There is also a discussion of a number of the cases presented above. See paras 17070–17125.

(a) The judge may call the witness, subject to the constraints indicated above [see *Apostilides* case].

(b) The judge may adjourn the trial to enable the attendance of the witness to be procured if requested.

(c) The judge may discharge the jury and remand the accused for retrial.

(d) The judge may dismiss the case as an abuse of process: a power to be exercised sparingly, and only if there is no alternative course such as the judge calling the witness.[129]

Other principles for prosecutors

There are also additional principles concerning the prosecutor. The prosecutor has to give reasonable notice if there is an intention to use a witness at trial who did not give evidence at the committal proceedings. If the Crown has a statement from a person that contains relevant material or of a credible witness who can testify concerning material facts and decides not to call such a person, these witnesses need to be made available to the defence. In summary proceedings the prosecutor must notify the defence of additional witnesses that the prosecutor knows about but intends not to call. Where a witness for the prosecution gives evidence that is materially inconsistent with any statement, written or oral, made by the witness to the prosecutor, the prosecutor should inform and provide copies to the defence. If a witness for the prosecution is of known bad character there is an obligation to inform the defence, but there is no duty on the prosecution to tell the jury this information.[130]

15.63

It is also obvious from the cases that the Australian courts until recently did not apply the ethical rules or the Guidelines of the Director of Public Prosecutions. The *Kneebone* case appears to be a major change as James J did make use of the Guidelines. In the past the Guidelines have had little relevance to the courts. A good example was the unfair use of evidence by the prosecution to achieve a conviction in the *Hilton Bombing* case. The tactics of the prosecution in that case led to a successful appeal because the verdicts of the jury were unsafe and unsatisfactory.[131]

15.64

Prosecution guidelines

Guidelines issued by the Director of Public Prosecutions (NSW) are respectively pursuant to s 13 of the Director of Public Prosecutions Act 1986 (NSW).[132] They thus operate under legislation and in New South Wales under the Professional Advocacy Rules rr 62–72.[133] Guideline 3 states that counsel prosecuting for the Crown in assisting the court to arrive

15.65

---

129. Ibid, para 17130.
130. *Cross on Evidence* (above), para 17130. There is another obligation in England for the Crown to inform the defence of any 'convictions and disciplinary findings against any police officers or other persons involved in the case, together with transcripts of any Court of Appeal decisions in which convictions had been quashed, or trials stopped or discontinued, by reason of misconduct or lack of veracity on the part of identified police officers or other persons': *R v Guney* [1998] 2 Cr App R 242 (CA).
131. *R v Anderson* (1991) 53 A Crim R 421 (CCA, NSW).
132. *Prosecution Policy Guidelines*, Office of the DPP (NSW), October 2003 . There are DPP guidelines in other jurisdictions.
133. *Prosecution Guidelines*, Office of the DPP (NSW), March 1998, p 11. Appendix A sets out the Barristers' Rules (NSW) and Law Society of NSW Solicitors' Rules rr 62–72.

at the truth must act impartially and fairly towards the accused. 'This will involve the prosecutor in informing the defence and the court of directions, warnings or authorities which may be appropriate in the circumstances of the case, even where unfavourable to the prosecution. It will also involve identifying portions of evidence which may be objectionable and declining to open on such evidence.' Guideline 18 states:

> Prosecutors are under a continuing obligation to make full disclosure to the accused in a timely manner of all material known to the prosecutor which can be seen on a sensible appraisal by the prosecution:
>
> ❏ to be relevant or possibly relevant to an issue in the case;
> ❏ to raise or possibly raise a new issue whose existence is not apparent from the evidence the prosecution proposes to use; and/or
> ❏ to hold out a real as opposed to fanciful prospect of providing a lead to evidence which goes to either of the previous two situations ...
>
> The duty of disclosure extends to any record of a statement by a witness that is inconsistent with the witness's previously intended evidence or adds to it significantly, including any statement made in conference (recorded in writing or otherwise) and any victim impact statement ...[134]

Guideline 26 states that it is appropriate to inform the defence of prior convictions and/or indemnities of Crown witnesses. It states that all apparently credible and material witnesses should generally be called by the Crown. If a decision is made not to call a witness then the Crown should notify the accused within a reasonable time before the commencement of the trial and give reasons for the decision. The Crown should also, where possible, assist the accused to call such witness by making him or her available.

Fresh evidence rule

15.66   The Australian courts can also be criticised for failing to realise that what they call fresh evidence is not really 'fresh'. The suppressed evidence does not come from a neutral source after the trial, but from the prosecution that possessed it during the trial. The author has heard the term used by a Crown prosecutor for non-suppressed evidence that has been uncovered as 'real fresh' evidence. Lane finds that the adoption of the fresh evidence rule is inappropriate. He states that courts have ignored the special position of prosecutors in criminal trials to 'ensure that fundamental principles of fairness are observed'. The fresh evidence rule results in prosecutors having no incentive 'to disclose exculpatory evidence or to ensure that doubtful cases are resolved in favour of disclosure'.[135] These views are still relevant, but as we saw above in the more recent cases of *R v Shaw; R v Glenn Carson Lewis-Hamilton; R v Wilson* and *R v Kneebone*, Australian courts are more willing to quash convictions and uphold appeals when prosecutors' actions have led to the prosecutor having an unfair advantage.

---

134. There is protection for witnesses under this guideline. The DPP will not disclose addresses or telephone numbers of witnesses. There is also special protection for victims. See New South Wales Charter of Victim Rights, Appendix D, *Policy and Guidelines* (above).
135. Lanem (above), p 181.

It should be noted that in each of these cases the courts found a miscarriage   **15.67**
of justice had occurred. In *Bradshaw v R*[136] the Crown had failed to disclose
material relevant to the defence that went to the credibility of the main
Crown witness and to other witnesses. The court found that even if there
was an innocent failure to disclose, such failure by the prosecutor may
constitute a miscarriage of justice. In this case the court rejected the appeal
for a new trial on the basis that the additional material would not have
changed the views on corruption already established in cross-examination.

It also should be noted as more jurisdictions adopt caseflow management
techniques, suppression of evidence will become less frequent. As both the
prosecution and defence will have to outline their cases, prosecutors will
become more willing to reveal all the witnesses. Such obligations of
disclosure are present in the Victorian Crimes (Criminal Trials) Act 1999
and the English Criminal Procedure and Investigations Act 1996.

American approach

In the United States the Supreme Court in *United States v Agurs*[137] held   **15.68**
that such suppressed evidence is not considered to be fresh. The court thus
did not place a burden on the accused to show that if it had been available
it would have resulted in acquittal. The court has also said in the *Brady* case
that exculpatory evidence not made available to the accused can result in
denial of the constitutional right to a fair trial and a new trial will be
ordered.[138] Furthermore, there is a duty on prosecutors to disclose any
exculpatory evidence, even if it has not been requested by the defence.[139]
Besides evidence that is directly exculpatory, the Supreme Court has said
that prosecutors also have to disclose evidence that is useful for the defence
to impeach prosecution witnesses.[140]

The *Brady* doctrine is also supported by ABA Standards Relating to the
Administration of Justice. The Prosecution Function Standard 3-4.1 states
that: 'A prosecutor should not knowingly make false statements or representations as to fact or law in the course of plea discussions with defense
counsel or the accused.' Furthermore, withholding of information and
knowingly making false statements by a prosecutor in court or to a special
prosecutor can lead to charges of perjury and obstruction of justice.[141]

The Supreme Court has stepped back a little on controlling prosecutors. In   **15.69**
US v Bagley[142] the court held that a prosecutor's failure to disclose evidence
that could have been used to impeach government witnesses does not

---

136. (unreported, CCA(WA), Full Ct, No CCA 142 of 1996, 13 May 1997, BC9701944).
137. (1976) 427 US 97.
138. *Brady v Maryland* (1963) 373 US 83.
139. *US v Agurs* (1976) 427 US 97. Note that under the Federal Rules of Criminal Procedure
     r 16(c) both prosecutors and defence counsel must promptly notify the other side or the
     court if they discover 'additional evidence or material previously requested or ordered'.
140. *Banks v Dretke* 124 S Ct 1256.
141. Such charges were brought against the prosecutor, Bill Johnston, who helped send
     several Branch Davidians to prison in the famous Waco incident: *New York Times*, 1 and
     2 September 2000, National section. He made a plea bargain and admitted to a felony of
     withholding information about the use of tear gas in the Waco siege: *Associated Press*,
     6 February 2001 and the *Dallas Morning News*, 7 February 2001.
142. 473 US 667.

automatically lead to an unfair trial. Five justices did say in *Bagley* that the due process clause requires prosecutors to disclose such evidence. It said that disclosure also needs to be made for evidence that favours defendants with respect to guilt on the merits or is relevant to punishment for the offence. The court emphasised that a case needs to be reversed only if the prosecutor's non-disclosure 'undermines confidence in the outcome of the trial' and thus 'deprives the defendant of a fair trial'. This requirement is met if there is a 'reasonable probability' of a different result if the suppressed evidence had been disclosed. In a more recent Supreme Court case, *United States v Ruiz*,[143] the court said that the *Brady* doctrine is fundamentally a trial right. Prosecutors are not required to reveal material impeachment evidence before plea bargaining because this would undermine the government's ability to secure 'those guilty pleas that are factually justified, desired by defendants, and help to secure the efficient administration of justice'. Rhode and Luban point out that the Supreme Court 'decision leaves open whether prosecutors ever have an ethical, if not constitutional obligation, to make such disclosures'.[144]

15.70   Luban says that 'an unscrupulous prosecutor needs to get caught before *Brady* does any good and it is a matter of conjecture how often the prosecutor gets away with undisclosed *Brady* material'.[145] Defence lawyers have argued that 'public pressure' and an 'adversarial mindset' encourage prosecutors to withhold *Brady* materials and that 'neither judges nor disciplinary committees have provided adequate enforcement'.[146] A study of the effect of the *Brady* doctrine during its first 25 years supports these perceptions by finding 'only nine cases in which discipline was even considered for suppressing *Brady* material'.[147] The reason for a lack of enforcement is that the concerned parties, defendants, defence lawyers and judges, all have few incentives in pursuing a district attorney on their own initiative.[148] If they do, there can be retaliatory measures taken by an upset district attorney.

The *Brady* doctrine has not fulfilled its promise of making the system fairer. Rhode and Luban say that judges are 'reluctant either to condone *Brady* violations or to overturn guilty pleas'. The compromise has been to allow defendants to 'withdraw their plea if they can prove that undisclosed exculpatory material would have materially affected' their guilty plea. 'However, the absence of a record indicating what considerations most influenced a decision has made it easy for courts to find that the undisclosed information was not material. Moreover, this compromise offers least to those who need it most … [P]rosecutors offer greatest inducements in their weakest cases, which are the ones where innocence is most likely. Yet, because defendants in those cases receive the most generous offers, they will

---

143. 122 S Ct 2450 (2002).
144. Rhode and Luban (above), p 383.
145. Ibid, p 384.
146. Rhode (above), p 645.
147. Rhode (above). Rhode at p 653, fnn 126 and 127, cites C Carmody, 'The *Brody* Rule: Is It Working?' (17 May 1993) *National Law J* 30, which refers to a 1987 study by R Rosen, 'Disciplinary Sanctions Against Prosecutors for Brady Violations: A Paper Tiger' (1987) 65 *North Carolina L Rev* 693, 720.
148. F Zacharias, 'The Professional Discipline of Prosecutors' (2001) *North Carolina LR* 721.

also have the most difficulty showing that the *Brady* material would have altered their plea decision.'[149]

Approach in England and Canada

In both England and Canada the courts have required a higher standard of disclosure by the prosecution than that demanded in Australia. This has been evident in recent cases in England quashing convictions against members of the IRA, some of whom had been in prison for 17 years.[150] In the famous *Birmingham Six* case the court said:[151]   **15.71**

> A disadvantage of the adversarial system may be that the parties are not evenly matched in resources ... But the inequality of resources is ameliorated by the obligation on the part of the prosecution to make available all material which may prove helpful to the defence.

The English cases were under the common law and disclosure is now covered by the Criminal Procedure and Investigations Act 1996, while in Canada the common law cases now come under the Charter of Rights.

The role of the prosecutor

The first independent prosecuting office in Australia, the Office of Crown Advocate, was created in 1973 in Tasmania.[152] The creation of Departments of Public Prosecutions in Australia is a more recent development starting in Victoria with the enactment of the Director of Public Prosecutions Act 1982 and then in March 1984 with the establishment of a Commonwealth Office.[153] The Office, and others like it, have been given the power to decide whether or not to proceed with criminal prosecutions. The DPP offices are independent from the agencies responsible for investigating and commencing proceedings.[154] This independence is viewed as enhancing public confidence in the criminal justice system and providing 'a high degree of consistency and expertise' for serious and complicated criminal cases.[155] The common law has also granted the prosecutorial service certain rights that protect its independence. McKechie QC, DPP for Western Australia, states:[156]   **15.72**

> In a series of cases it has been held that prosecuting counsel's undoubted duty of fairness nonetheless does not give rise to a cause of action; that an action for malicious prosecution cannot be sustained against prosecuting counsel while a conviction remains on record; that a DPP is not ordinarily responsible for any malice there may be on the part of prosecuting counsel; and there is no duty of care owed to private individuals aggrieved by careless decisions of prosecution service lawyers.

---

149. Rhode and Luban (above), pp 384–5.
150. *R v Ward* [1993] 2 All ER 577 and *McIlkenny v R* (1991) 93 Cr App R 287. See also the film *In the Name of the Father*.
151. *McIlkenny v R* (1991) 93 Cr App R 287 at 312. See also P O'Connor, 'Prosecutions' Disclosure: Principle and Justice' (1992) *Crim LR* 464.
152. Crown Advocate Act 1973 (Tas).
153. Director of Public Prosecutions Act 1983 (Cth).
154. See J Tombs, 'Independent Prosecution Systems' in G Zdenkowski et al (eds), *The Criminal Injustice System Vol II*, Australian Legal Workers Group, Sydney, 1987.
155. Editorial, 'Independence of the DPP', *Sydney Morning Herald*, 23 October 1995, p 14.
156. McKechie (above), pp 274–5. He cites as authority *Whitehorn* (1983) 152 CLR 657; *Love v Robbins* (1989) 2 WAR 510; *Riches v DPP* [1973] 1 WLR 1019; and *Elguzouli-Daf v Metropolitan Commission of Police* [1995] QB 335 respectively.

This does mean that a prosecuting lawyer, whether a member of the DPP's office or an advocate briefed by the DPP, cannot be held responsible in a civil suit for malfeasance. Such action was allowed in *Tahche v Abboud*,[157] where material evidence was suppressed during discovery.

Concept of independence

15.73   The independence of the DPP has usually been secure in most jurisdictions in Australia. In Victoria the repeal of the 1982 Act and enactment of the Public Prosecutions Act 1994 (Vic), and pressure on the Director by the Attorney-General, leading to his resignation, caused concern within the legal profession and the community.[158] The pressure to secure the Director's independence was successful and the Public Prosecutions Act was amended. In 1995 and 1996 the DPPs in New South Wales and Queensland had confrontations with their governments because of their criticism of government legislation. The argument posed by government is that legislation is the carrying out of policy decisions which are in their realm and any criticism by the independent DPP is political activism. The New South Wales DPP, Nicholas Cowdery QC, is of the view that their role is apolitical and it is in the best traditions of their independent office that they comment on legislation that is not in the public interest.[159] He warned the Carr Government to stop its attacks on his independence. He said the DPP needed to be free:[160]

> ... of any improper or untoward influence by government ... If there is even a reasonable perception that I am subject to the dictates of politicians, the independence and effectiveness of my office are at risk.

15.74   The attacks against the DPP in New South Wales stopped for several years, but were renewed in 2003 when the Leader of the Opposition proposed that the Office be made accountable by the establishment of a parliamentary committee to monitor and review how the DPP exercises its functions.[161] Mr Cowdery in defending his Office pointed out that the politicians did not understand the need for the complete independence of the Office.[162] The New South Wales Law Society issued a media release supporting Cowdery and stating the DPP must remain independent of government.[163] As of August 2005, no parliamentary committee has been set up. Mr Cowdery has continued to be outspoken on subjects such as making hard drugs available

---

157. [2002] VSC 42.
158. There are numerous articles on the confrontation. See C Corns, 'Politics of prosecutions' (1994) 68 *Law Institute J (Vic)* 276. For related events see Editorial, *Sydney Morning Herald*, 13 April 1995, p 20; *Australian*, 13 April 1995, p 6 and 15–16 April, p 6. See also J McKechie QC, 'Directors of Public Prosecutions: Independent and Accountable' (1996) 26 *Western Australian LR* 269.
159. See the *Weekend Australian*, 3–4 August 1996, p 10 on attacks on Queensland DPP; *Sydney Morning Herald*, 10 October 1995, p 6, 20 October 1995, p 6, on attacks on NSW DPP; editorial supporting the NSW DPP, 23 October 1995, p 14 and 7 November 1995, p 1.
160. *Sydney Morning Herald*, 7 November 1995, p 1 and article by N Cowdery, 10 November 1995, p 13.
161. A Tink, 'Turn down the volume and clear the air', *Australian Financial Review*, 11 July 2003, p 53.
162. N Cowdery, 'Independence under threat', *Australian Financial Review*, 8 August 2003, p 53.
163. Media Release, NSW Law Society, 25 February 2004.

to addicts. In one incident, the then Premier, Mr Carr, demanded that the DPP appeal an inadequate prison sentence in a controversial case. Mr Cowdery refused to listen and independently decided not to appeal. The Premier had to back down and protect Mr Cowdery from attack from the then Opposition shadow Attorney-General, Mr Hartcher. He had called Mr Cowdery's behaviour like that of a 'high priest of a religious cult accountable to no-one'. Mr Hartcher had sought to legislate for better monitoring of the DPP.[164] In late 2003 Mr Cowdery criticised the government for its indifference as to whether people were receiving a fair trial and that the government was more interested in police numbers and full gaols.[165]

South Australia is the latest state to have a confrontation. In 2005 the DPP, Paul Rofe QC, had to resign after public outrage and political criticism of his handling of two high-profile cases. His replacement, a leading Western Australian barrister, Stephen Pallares QC, was hired by the government 'to lock up the bad guys', but he also immediately spoke out. He said in a talk to the South Australian Press Club that the independence of the Office was essential and that justice did not always produce a popular result. He attacked those who had criticised the DPP in the past, saying they were 'political populists with a lot to say, who see an advantage to be gained, but contribute little'. He soon also had a confrontation with the government just before a state election, when he demanded greater funding for his Office and criticised the government for trying to influence the judiciary. The Treasurer, Mr Foley, accused Pallaras of picking a fight with the government and whingeing. He said: 'The truth is that he doesn't seem to like public or private criticism, but he doesn't mind dishing it out.' Pallaras responded by calling Foley's attack a 'personal vilification at its most objectionable and the office of the DPP will not descend to such behaviour'.[166] A few weeks later Pallaras was required to give evidence at a public parliamentary hearing into the corruption trial of Randall Ashbourne, which was a potentially politically damaging issue for the government. Pallaras testified that the Premier's office had threatened one of his prosecutors, which he said was an attempt to 'improperly influence my prosecutor'.[167] The confrontations have continued as this book goes to print.[168] **15.75**

Even with these confrontations, the establishment of the DPPs has given lawyers an expanded role in the conduct of criminal prosecutions. We will deal with the prosecution policy of the Commonwealth DPP, but there are similarities with the state prosecution policies.[169]

---

164. See the *Sun-Herald*, 27 August 2000, p 15 and *Sydney Morning Herald*, 29 August 2000, p 3.
165. G Noonan, 'Fair trials have been neglected, says DPP', *Sydney Morning Herald*, 11–12 December 2003, p 4.
166. 'DPP rocks boat', *Sunday Times* (Perth), 5 June 2005.
167. M Bockmann, 'Premier's office "threatened" DPP', *Weekend Australian*, 16–17 July 2005, p 7.
168. See R Eccleston, 'The Premier versus his prosecutor', *Weekend Australian*, 6–7 August 2005, p 19.
169. For example, the provisions concerning the decision to prosecute in New South Wales are almost identical to those of the Commonwealth. See *Prosecution Policy of the Commonwealth*, 2nd ed, Commonwealth DPP, as of August 2005, www.cdpp.gov.au, paras 2.1–2.13 and *Prosecution Policy and Guidelines*, Office of the DPP (NSW), October 2003, guideline 4.

policy and guidelines

approved as 'worthy objectives' a comment made in a Report
, Commission on Criminal Procedure (UK).[170] The Report
the system needed to be judged by standards of fairness,
,nd accountability, and efficiency:[171]

system fair; first in the sense it brings to trial only those against whom
ther is an adequate and properly prepared case and who it is in the public
interest should be prosecuted ..., and secondly, in that it does not display
arbitrary and inexplicable differences in the way that individual cases or
classes of case are treated locally or nationally? Is it open and accountable in
the sense that those who make the decisions to prosecute or not can be called
publicly to explain and justify their policies and actions as far as that is
consistent with protecting the interest of suspects and accused? Is it efficient
in the sense that it achieves the objects that are set for it with the minimum
use of resources and the minimum delay?

The DPP adopted this view in establishing the criteria governing the
decision to prosecute. The basic rule is that there needs to be a prima facie
case and after that is established the 'prosecution should not proceed if
there is no reasonable prospect of a conviction being secured'. The criteria
listed include a large number of ways to evaluate the evidence to see if there
is a reasonable prospect. If this is satisfied the prosecutor moves to the next
step. He or she then has to decide whether 'in light of the provable facts
and the whole of the surrounding circumstances, the public interest requires
a prosecution to be pursued'. The more serious the offence the more likely
the prosecution will be pursued.[172]

15.77 There are numerous factors used to determine the public interest and their
applicability and weight will be determined by the particular circumstances
of each case. The main factors listed are: the mitigating or aggravating
circumstances; the youth, age, intelligence, physical health, mental health
or special infirmity of the alleged offender, a witness or victim; the
seriousness or triviality of the alleged offence; degree of culpability of the
alleged offender; the obsolescence or obscurity of the law; the effect on
public order and morale; the staleness of the action; availability and efficacy
of any alternatives; the prevalence of the alleged offence and the need for
deterrence; whether the consequences of any resulting conviction would be
unduly harsh and oppressive; the attitude of the victim and of the alleged
offence to a prosecution; the willingness of the alleged offender to cooperate
with the investigation; the likely length and expense of a trial and the
necessity to maintain public confidence in such basic institutions as the
parliament and the courts.[173]

One important ethical guideline is that the decision to prosecute must not
be influenced by personal feelings, possible political advantage or
disadvantage for the government or any other political party, or the possible
effect on the career of the prosecutors. It also must not be based on grounds

170. *Prosecution Policy of the Commonwealth* (above), para 1.4.
171. *Prosecution Policy of the Commonwealth* (above), quoting from Cmnd 8092, Report
(1981) pp 127–8.
172. *Prosecution Policy of the Commonwealth* (above), paras 2.1–2.9.
173. *Prosecution Policy of the Commonwealth* (above), para 2.10.

of 'race, religion, sex, national origin or political associations, activities or beliefs of the alleged offender or any other person involved'.[174]

In making the decision as to whether or not a prosecution is to be started or continued, and on what charge or charges, the DPP will carefully take into consideration the views of the police or the responsible department. The ultimate decision on what action will be taken is made by the DPP. This also includes the decision on whether to discontinue a prosecution.[175]   **15.78**

The Commonwealth DPP's prosecution policy does not give any guidance as to the prosecutor's role in relation to sentencing. The New South Wales Guideline 28[176] says that the 'prosecution has an active role to play in the sentencing process'. It then refers to the Barristers' Rules r 71 and Solicitors' Rules (NSW) r A71. This rule is like the professional ethical rules in other jurisdictions and calls for a neutral role and a halt to the adversarial process. The prosecutor's role is to aid the court to determine a fair and appropriate sentence and he or she 'must not advocate for a vindictive sentence'. At times prosecutors have taken a more active role in seeking to have a harsher sentence imposed[177] but the professional ethical rules appear to support the better approach.[178] In relation to appeals against sentences the DPP has adopted a policy that the prosecution's right 'should be exercised sparingly' and only if there is 'some confidence that the appeal will be successful'.[179] The New South Wales guideline concerning appeals, Guideline 29, says that 'prosecution/Crown appeals are and ought to be rare, as an exception to the general conduct of the administration of criminal justice'. [180]

In New Zealand the Prosecution Guidelines were changed making the prosecutor more actively involved in the sentencing process because of the 'Crown's right to appeal against a sentence considered to be manifestly inadequate or wrong in principle'. The prosecution at sentencing 'should be prepared to assist the court, to the degree the Judge indicates is appropriate, with submissions on' matters such as 'the accused's criminal history, if any' and 'the relevant sentencing principles and guideline judgement'. The guideline does emphasise that the prosecution 'should not press for a particular term or level of sentence'.[181]   **15.79**

By having a virtual monopoly over the prosecution process[182] the DPP can influence the ethical standards of its client investigative agencies. If an

---

174. *Prosecution Policy of the Commonwealth* (above), para 2.13.
175. *Prosecution Policy of the Commonwealth* (above), paras 3.8 and 4.3. For a discussion of the DPP (Cth) discretion to prosecute, see I Temby, 'Prosecution Discretions and the Director of Public Prosecutions Act 1983' (1985) 59 *ALJ* 197.
176. *Prosecution Policy and Guidelines* (NSW) (above).
177. See G Campbell, 'The Role of Crown Prosecutor on Sentence' (1985) 9 *Criminal LJ* 202.
178. Campbell (above). There is a discussion of both sides of the issue in this article.
179. *Prosecution Policy of the Commonwealth* (above), para 5.32.
180. *Prosecution Policy and Guidelines* (NSW) (above).
181. *Prosecution Guidelines*, 9 March 1992, r 8. New Zealand does not have a DPP: see *Criminal Prosecution: A discussion paper*, Preliminary Paper No 28, Law Reform Commission, Wellington, New Zealand, March 1997, paras 337–41.
182. Private prosecutions occur, but they are rare. For a discussion of this right to prosecute privately see *Who can sue? A review of the law of standing*, Discussion Paper 61, Australian Law Reform Commission, October 1995, pp 41–3.

agency objects to high ethical standards being imposed by the DPP, it has no remedy. The agency cannot take its cases elsewhere. Grabosky says:[183]

> A tactful withholding of cooperation from a wayward client is one way in which a prosecutor may exercise such power. It might also be appropriate to disclose client illegality to the responsible minister or to the court in appropriate circumstances. A tactful threat of public disclosure may be a potent instrument of organisational social control.

If the DPP adopts a policy of introducing evidence that has been tainted by government misconduct, the prosecutor's own integrity becomes tarnished.

Disciplining prosecutors

15.80   As previously stated, in New South Wales a breach of the professional advocacy rules can constitute professional misconduct or unsatisfactory professional conduct. In the United States the ABA Standards Relating to the Administration of Criminal Justice, The Prosecution Function, Standard 3-1.2 states that prosecutors are to be guided by the professional rules of their jurisdiction. Prosecutors are subject to those rules and if they violate the professional rules they will be found to have committed professional misconduct. Prosecutors in Australia, like those in the United States, still fall under other professional rules and can be found to have committed professional misconduct, but the chances of that happening would be slight. Those prosecutors who have been disciplined have usually been involved in criminal activities or other personal misdeeds.[184] A good example was the case of a senior DPP prosecutor who offered and then delivered prosecution documents in the DPP's $1 billion fraud case against Alan Bond, asking for approximately $4 million from Bond's son John.[185] When criminal charges are dropped against a DPP lawyer the actions will come under close scrutiny and the DPP will be faced with criticism for not pursuing the matter.[186] Those working for the DPP are also subject to public service rules. Mark Weinberg QC, former Director of the Commonwealth DPP, and now a Federal Court judge, said when he was Director, if they violated their ethical duties under the Office's policy, they would be penalised.[187] There has also been an increased emphasis in DPP

---

183. P Grabosky, 'Prosecutors, Informants, and the Integrity of the Criminal Justice System' (1992) 4 *Current Issues in Criminal Justice: J of Institute of Criminology* 47, 56–7.
184. See *In the matter of Duncan Mark McKenzie Fine*, Legal Profession Disciplinary Tribunal Reports, No 3, 1994, p 11. A DPP solicitor was found guilty of professional misconduct for abusing his position by writing three letters on DPP letterhead to the Police Department seeking waiver of traffic and parking infringements for himself and a friend. He was treated leniently, ordered to pay costs and refused a practising certificate for one year, because of his prompt, full and frank admission to his deeds.
185. P McGeough, 'Bond case prosecutor faces disclosure charge', *Sydney Morning Herald*, 19 August 1995, p 13. The prosecutor was eventually found guilty and sentenced to gaol.
186. See F Walker, 'Storm over DPP solicitor's case', 23 July 2000, p 31. The charges were against a former DPP solicitor for making false statements for an insurance claim. The magistrate criticised the Crown for dropping the charges. The Crown solicitor stated it had acted on advice of senior counsel that there was insufficient evidence to proceed. The DPP Mr Cowdery stated that his office had nothing to do with 'the conduct of the prosecution or any decisions made in relation to it'.
187. Private communication.

offices on 'continuous ethical policy training'.[188] Prosecutors are required by the professional ethical rules to play fair, but as we have seen there has been a history in Australia of prosecutors suppressing witnesses and evidence. It has been rare in Australia for prosecutors to be criticised for their conduct of a trial, but if the prosecution is grossly unfair this can be grounds for a miscarriage of justice and quashing of any conviction.[189] In contrast, courts have not found the suppression of information by a prosecutor to be unfair when the defence counsel initiated the reason for the prosecutor's action.[190]

Prosecutorial misconduct has drawn very little attention in Australia. This may be because there is far less prosecutorial misconduct in this country than elsewhere, such as the United States. When charges were brought against a high-profile Australian prosecutor the authorities were eventually unable to pursue the matter because of extensive delays in getting a hearing and over technicalities concerning the jurisdiction over the matter.[191] In the United States there have been a number of reported cases of misconduct by prosecutors: some stem from 'overzealousness' in order to win, but most of these cases involve issues such as conflict of interest, failure to enforce the law and embezzlement.[192] Rhode says that 'neither defendants nor their lawyers have incentives to bring a complaint that might invite retaliation, and courts rarely make referrals to bar regulatory agencies. Empirical surveys indicate that disciplinary actions for improper argument are extremely rare'.[193] Like Australia, prosecutorial misconduct

15.81

---

188. Western Australia has had such a program for three years: McKechie (above), p 280. The New South Wales DPP has an ethics officer to train staff and at times runs workshops for its staff by using outside experts. The author ran such workshops in July 1998.

189. See *R v Anderson* (1991) 53 A Crim R 421 (CCA(NSW)): the most notorious example of unfair behaviour was the highly prejudicial cross-examination by the prosecutor in the supposed Ananda Marga conspiracy to murder the National Front leader, Robert Cameron, and their involvement in the Hilton bombing. The High Court in an earlier case dealing with the bombing found that, although some aspects of the cross-examinations by the prosecution were improper, they had not caused a miscarriage of justice. Murphy J in his dissent outlines the cross-examination in finding a miscarriage of justice: *R v Alister* (1984) 154 CLR 404.

190. *R v Jamieson* (1992) 60 A Crim R 68 (CCA(NSW)).

191. Charges were lodged by the Legal Services Commissioner (NSW) against senior Crown prosecutor Mark Tedeschi QC concerning his conduct in the Ananda Marga conspiracy trial. These charges were dismissed by Rolfe J. He held that the Commissioner had no power to investigate, since the matter had already been dismissed by the Bar Council: *Tedeschi v Legal Services Commissioner* (1997) 43 NSWLR 20. This problem has now been remedied by amendments in 2000 to the Legal Profession Act 1987. Two other cases filed in 1993 against Tedeschi in the Disciplinary Tribunal were also unsuccessful. One was dismissed by the ADT on 25 November 1999 because it found that it lacked jurisdiction ([1999] NSWADT 92), now on appeal to the Supreme Court. The other was withdrawn and dismissed by the Bar Association on 23 August 1999. I was told by an official at the tribunal that the hearings took such a long time to be heard because of the court case and the fact that at one hearing date the prosecutor had an important murder trial — the Ivan Milat case.

192. See Annotation, 'Disciplinary Action Against Attorney for Misconduct Related to Performance of Official Duties as Prosecuting Attorney' (1981) 10 *ALR* 605, 610–11. See also C Wolfram, *Modern Legal Ethics,* West Publishers, St Paul, 1986, para 13.10.2.

193. Rhode (above), p 643.

rarely leads to courts reversing criminal conviction or to professional discipline.[194]

Gershman has said that the United States Supreme Court has failed to control prosecutorial behaviour. He states that the court has refused 'to articulate or even require ethical standards' and has even been encouraging to 'prosecutorial overreaching'.[195] There have been times when the Supreme Court has condemned prosecutorial behaviour,[196] but these are rare. The courts have also adopted the view that they cannot impose sanctions for improper behaviour of prosecutors because their action would violate the principles of sovereign immunity.[197] When the Illinois Disciplinary Commission censured a prosecutor, on appeal it was reversed. The State Supreme Court said that the prosecutor had acted improperly but decided not to discipline him because he was motivated by 'a sincere, if misguided, desire to bring corrupt attorneys to justice'.[198] In cases of prosecutorial misbehaviour the United States courts 'generously apply doctrines of fundamental fairness, harmless error and "invited response" to uphold convictions'.[199] Although there are cases where defence counsel has gone too far. For example, the Ninth Circuit Court of Appeals threw out a number of bribery convictions because the Californian prosecutor had painted the defence counsel as a liar who had set out to mislead the jury from the beginning of the case.[200] Allen has stated that in the United States the problem of controlling and 'minimizing prosecutorial excesses is one of ... [the] great unsolved problems in criminal law administration'.[201]

15.82   What is the prosecutorial role in light of the ethical requirements? Grabosky states that in Australia prosecutors 'have a duty to prevent, detect, and disclose illegal or unethical conduct by agents of government' because the 'prosecutor is the keystone of the criminal justice system'.[202] If our system malfunctions, and we have miscarriages of justice, this will be blamed on the prosecution's office to a significant extent.[203]

These views support one important function of prosecutorial work, the duty to achieve justice — to assist the court to arrive fairly at the truth. It is a quasi-judicial role and also includes guarding the criminal defendant's rights. What if the accused has incompetent counsel? For example, if the lawyer has not adequately presented all the material facts that would help his or her client to be acquitted? In such a situation the prosecutor would

---

194. For an outrageous case where no disciplinary action was taken against a prosecutor for suppressing exculpatory information, see *Read v Virginia State Bar* 357 SE 2d 544 (Va 1987).
195. B Gershman, *Prosecutorial Misconduct*, C Boardman Co, New York, 1987, p 218.
196. See the famous judgment of Justice Sutherland in *Berger v United States* 295 US 78 at 88 (1935).
197. See *US v Horn* 29 F3d 754 (1st Cir 1994). By contrast, where the principles of separation of powers was ignored, see *Chilcutt v US* 4 F3d 1313 (5th Cir 1993).
198. *In re Friedman* 392 NE2d 1333, 1336 (Ill 1979).
199. S Fisher, 'In Search of the Virtuous Prosecutor: A Conceptional Framework' (1988) 15 *American J of Criminal Law* 197, 198–9.
200. *United States v Rodrigues* 98 Daly Journal DAR 11153, 29 October 1998.
201. F Allen, 'A Serendipitous Trek Through the Advance-Sheet Jungle: Criminal Justice in the Courts of Review' (1985) 70 *Iowa LR* 311, 335.
202. Grabosky (above), p 58.
203. Grabosky (above).

have to make sure that these facts were presented. In such a situation the prosecutor would have to see his or her primary role as achieving a just result.[204]

The other role is to protect the state and the public by having convicted those who disturb the public order. This role is adversarial and requires 'fearless' or 'zealous' advocacy. Prosecutors face the dilemma of balancing these two roles. They have to decide what interests to pursue without the help of a particular 'client'. They have various constituencies, that is, the police, victims,[205] the media, but their true client is the public — their duty is representing the public interest. In the Northern Territory, the DPP in its Mission Statement has included 'fairness to victims *and* the accused'[206] [author's italics]. The accused is not mentioned, for example, in the Mission Statement of the New South Wales DPP.

Conviction mentality?

Prosecutors representing the public essentially have to make their decisions without the help of a client, which is similar to representing incompetent clients. Prosecutors have to place themselves in the shoes of those clients (the public) and decide what is best for them. Thus, prosecutors have an important role in creating public policy within criminal proceedings.[207]

15.83

Prosecutors in Australia's DPP offices do not have a 'conviction psychology' to the same extent that it is prevalent in America.[208] Many American district attorneys, especially in the large cities, need a high-profile conviction rate. This profile includes the need to win the big public cases that arouse strong passions. Failure to win these cases can lead to loss of office in the next election.[209] This need to win can result in the courts finding prosecutorial misconduct when prosecutors break their professional rules and are overzealous.[210] Although the ability to win is the dominant feature of prosecutorial practice, there are counter-pressures from professional codes and standards, academic, judicial and professional sources to be fair. Some prosecutors do follow the notion of fairness because it can help their careers when leaving the office. Fairness and reasonableness by these prosecutors can impress judges and private lawyers, providing them with career opportunities.[211] A good example of fairness is the program begun by the San Diego County District Attorney, which has a policy of offering free

---

204. Fisher (above), pp 224–5.
205. A special Charter of Victims Rights has been adopted in New South Wales for victims. *Prosecution Policy and Guidelines* (above), Appendix D and Guideline 19.
206. DPP, Northern Territory, *Annual Report*, 2003–2004, p 10.
207. DPP, Northern Territory (above), pp 219–24.
208. A Blumberg, *Criminal Justice*, 2nd ed, Quadrangle Books, Chicago, 1967, p 117.
209. Even when in office these failures can result in a public investigation on the effectiveness of the office. A good example was the grand jury investigation of the Los Angeles District Attorney Gil Garcetti who was voted in because his predecessor also did not win some important cases: see 'Garcetti on Trial' (July 1994) *California Lawyer* 25.
210. The Los Angeles County District Attorney's office has recently been criticised by the courts for misconduct in two homicide cases. This led to a reversal of first-degree murder convictions. See *People v Contreras* 98 CDOS 7229 and *People v Hill* 17 Cal 4th 800.
211. Fisher (above), pp 205–14.

DNA testing to prison inmates. The office has even taken the initiative in searching for cases where DNA tests had not been performed.[212]

15.84   The DPPs, like American district attorneys, have as their 'clients' government agencies, such as the police. Although, unlike their American counterparts, they will not need the approval of these clients for their actions to the same extent, they still need their cooperation. Therefore, like American prosecutors, there will be pressure to act firmly with criminal defendants rather than upholding the ethical requirements of fairness.[213] As one American writer said: 'A prosecutor must give the people what they want — someone who is tough on crime. Seeking the death penalty helps prove the prosecutor running for election is not soft on crime like his opponents.'[214] American prosecutors have been described as gladiators battling on behalf of a 'team'. The team extends beyond the victim and includes a subculture composed of their peers, the police, probation and court officers, the media and even sympathetic judges. These prosecutors will receive warm congratulations from this subculture after winning. When they lose they take it more personally because the losses 'are experienced as losses to society'.[215]

15.85   The DPP lawyers also have elements of pressure from a similar subculture. They have the advantage of more easily withstanding these pressures because they are not as involved as American lawyers in the investigative process. This allows them to maintain a distance from their 'clients' and to be able more readily to uphold ethical standards. Although there has been a call for prosecutors to be more involved in the investigative process, in order to control the ethical behaviour of their clients,[216] investigative agencies in several Australian jurisdictions oppose this idea.[217] For example, in 1986 when Tasmania changed the name of the Office of Crown Advocate and its Act to a DPP it removed the obligation to provide advice and representation to the police. The reason for this change was to establish the independence of the function of the DPP and that of the investigator, the police.

The Commonwealth DPP[218] and state DPPs[219] already have the power to be more involved in the investigation by issuing directions and guidelines to the investigative agencies. For example, in New South Wales the DPP issued guidelines in January 1995, under s 14 of its Act, to the Commissioner of Police.[220] These guidelines ask for more detailed information concerning proposed witnesses in light of some past problems in the use of police informers. The DPP also amended its own guidelines to

212. Private communication.
213. Blumberg (above), p 87.
214. A Halphen, 'Prosecutorial Misconduct: Goliath's Slingshot', *Victorian Bar News*, No 125 (Winter 2003) 40, 41.
215. Fisher (above), pp 208–9.
216. Grabosky (above), pp 56–63.
217. Grabosky (above), p 63. Grabosky quotes a Report of the Royal Commissioner the Honourable Justice J A Lee, *Royal Commission of Inquiry into the Arrest, Charge and Withdrawal of Charges Against Harold James Blackburn and Matters Associated Therewith*, 1990, pp 364–6.
218. Director of Public Prosecutions Act 1983.
219. See, for example, Director of Public Prosecutions Act 1986 (NSW) s 14.
220. *Prosecution Policy and Guidelines* (above), Guidelines 13 and 14, as of October 2003.

better protect the confidentiality of police informers.[221] This involves consultations with the police before disclosing any sensitive information or material to the defence and adopting better procedures to make the documents and other material secure. In August 1997 a further guideline was issued, requiring DPP officers to consult with the police whenever they are considering whether or not to discontinue a local court prosecution or to offer no evidence in an appeal to the District Court. Thus, the DPP has the choice of becoming further involved in investigations to help create a fairer justice system by raising ethical standards or to close its eyes to unethical behaviour by its clients. There is also a danger that, by becoming more involved, prosecutors will become more identified with the investigative agencies and thereby lose some of their independence, resulting in lower ethical standards.

---

221. Ibid, Guideline 16.

16

CONCLUSION

DISSATISFACTION WITH WORK

16.1   I wrote in the first three editions of this book that I had found more and more articles on lawyers being dissatisfied with their work and their profession, feeling that they were working too hard and sacrificing their health for money, and I believe that this is still the case. A 1999 article stated: 'Six-day working weeks, 2 am finishes and high burnout. That's the reality for many of Sydney's top young lawyers.' The article said that lawyers have 'never worked harder or longer'.[1] A survey in Western Australia that year of why people leave the profession found frustration with the billing system and lack of professional support, both of which added to high levels of stress. It said that the lawyers had 'little sense of what was happening in the firm'; 'lack of challenging work'; and 'failure to have proper supervision and feedback'. 'You only knew you had done a good job when you didn't get yelled at or chastised.' It also found that recruiting was in the 'image of the existing partners to the extent that diversity was discouraged'. The attitude was 'to recruit in the image of the existing partners, "The Culture was very sexist, often [holding] bad attitudes towards minority groups, very Waspish"'.[2]

As I pointed out in Chapter 2 (see **2.59**), the large firms have in recent years adopted various programs in order to keep valuable staff. These include flexible work hours and part-time work, and in some firms even day care facilities. There are also life-style perks such as lunchtime yoga and in-house massage. Even with these changes there still is concern over the key issue of the long working hours.[3] The senior partners at times still do not appear to be too concerned about this problem. For example, the managing partner of Allens Arthur Robinson in 2005 stated in an interview that staff

---

1.   J Freeman, *Sydney Morning Herald*, 1E, 5 June 1999. This article is referred to in M Conners, 'Quality of Life ... Quality of Law' (September 1999) *Law Society J (NSW)* 45.
2.   C Thompson, 'Greener Pastures: Why people leave the legal profession' (July 1999) *Brief (Law Society of Western Australia)* 6–7.
3.   A Clelland, 'Family-friendly practice: team effort required', Corporate Legal Services, Special Report, *Australian Financial Review*, 14 November 2002, p 7.

members did not have a right to any free time and the firm expected them to treat clients 'as if they were God'.[4] The then president of the Australian Young Lawyers, Nathan Laird, said in 2005: 'Long hours are the norm in the bigger firms. A lot of young lawyers regularly work until 10 pm or midnight and working weekends is standard.'[5] It is therefore not surprising that a 2004 survey by legal recruiter Seek found that 55 per cent of the profession are 'unhappy or very unhappy' with their present work.[6]

LEAVING THE PROFESSION

Lawyers also continue to leave the profession out of sheer boredom, dissatisfaction, burn-out and the stress of dealing with distressed clients day after day. They are leaving for a wide range of occupations: teaching meditation and inner well-being (even to corporate Australia), driving trucks or taxis, working as machinists or fishermen, or high-profile jobs such as film-making or entertainment.[7] Some are just having a seachange, moving out of the large cities, while others are leaving Australia seeking interesting overseas experiences. The number of lawyers leaving the profession is increasing rapidly, unlike past generations of lawyers who had financial and work satisfaction and thus stayed in the profession.[8] The modern generation of lawyers have far fewer incentives to stay in their jobs; and a Victorian Law Foundation survey in 1995 revealed very high levels of dissatisfaction with their choice of a profession.[9] A survey in 2004 by the Australian Young Lawyers found that almost half of those who responded did not see themselves as legal practitioners in five years' time.[10]

In North America there are currently indications that many lawyers are leaving the profession because of dissatisfaction.[11] A Canadian lawyer withdrawing from a large city firm said:[12]

> If I practised law any longer, I felt my entire soul would be swallowed up; that the practice being what it is, I'd never be able to do the things in life that had personal meaning for me or even remain capable of appreciating those things.

16.2

---

4. L Schmidt, 'Perils of young guns dying to be lawyers', *Australian Financial Review*, 13 May 2005, p 1.
5. Ibid.
6. S Scott, 'Those jokes aside, lawyers are an unhappy bunch', *Australian Financial Review*, 13 May 2005, p 62.
7. J Fife-Yeomans, 'Lawyers invoke the escape clause', *Australian*, 12 October 1994, p 7.
8. See, for example, the study by the Law Institute of Victoria of 1000 law graduates from 1935–88 in J Ewing, L Dennerstein, C Bartlett and J Hopper, *The Career Pattern of Law Graduates*, Law Institute of Victoria, Melbourne, 1990.
9. See, for example, *Job Satisfaction Survey — Interim Report*, Victoria Law Foundation, June 1995.
10. Ibid.
11. F Iacobucci, 'Striking A Balance: Trying to Find the Happy and Good Life Within and Beyond the Legal Profession' (1992) 36 *Gazette (Law Society of Upper Canada)* 205. See also *Transitions in the Ontario Legal Profession: A Survey of Lawyers called to the Bar between 1975 and 1990*, Law Society of Upper Canada, May 1991, p 101. On 5–6 April 1991, the ABA held a national conference on the emerging crisis in the quality of lawyers' health and lives — its impact on law firms and client services: see *The Breaking Point*. See also a 1992 ABA report, *Beyond the Breaking Point: A Report and Plan for Action*, 28 December 1992.
12. M Otvos, 'Why I'm Leaving Law', *Canadian Lawyer*, February 1992, p 12.

16.3   This practitioner, Mary Otvos, had similar complaints as those found in Australia. She was disturbed by the need to increase output in order to accumulate billable hours. More disturbing for her was the stress she experienced from being under constant scrutiny. Finally, she was greatly dissatisfied with the legal issues in her work which she found 'meaningless and, more often than not, motivated by greed or spite'.[13] Otvos' most damning indictment of her work was her view of legal goals:[14]

> What ... is lacking is a defined end — a goal. No one is ever told where it ends. What is the ultimate goal? To have a certain amount of money? To have a certain amount of partnership points? To have a certain size office? To work less or to work more?

NEW FORMS OF PRACTICE

16.4   For many legal practitioners modern legal practice has changed for the worse. The number of lawyers in the profession has dramatically increased. This is one of the factors leading to a highly competitive atmosphere. Lawyers feel that they must work harder in order to keep up their business's profitability. This in turn has led to unusual practices, some quite questionable, in order to retain existing clients and to attract new ones.

Lawyers also have to market their product to meet new desires in the marketplace. Legal services are now available via the internet at reduced rates, increasing the market nature of legal services and further eroding the service ideals. 'Small firms ... will face competition from online interactive legal services which will have the advantage in terms of cost ... and convenience.'[15] In Victoria in 1996 a 'frequent lawyer' scheme called LAWYERloyalties was established. It is now available in other states. It arranges substantial discounts on legal services for clients who are frequent users of legal services. It is a brokerage service that matches the specialty that clients require for their problems with skills available from the firms on their database.[16] By July 2005 it had referred over 177,000 clients. It offers to pay for the client's legal fees if the client is dissatisfied with the services as long as the request is made within 30 days and it does not involve a criminal matter.[17]

There is also a need for capital to support the increasing costs of legal actions. Rene Rivkin, the infamous and now deceased businessman, established in 1998 with his partners, Justice Corporation Pty Ltd. Since then a number of other operators have entered the field. Today the largest are IMF (Australia), which is listed on the stock exchange, and Litigation Lending Services. They offer to finance civil litigation in return for a percentage of any damages awarded. When Justice Corporation was established it received a hostile welcome from the profession,[18] but the concept of outside funding was endorsed by the Australian Law Reform

---

13.   Otvos (above), p 13.
14.   Otvos (above), p 15.
15.   ALRC, Report No 89, *Managing Justice: A review of the federal civil justice system*, February 2000, para 3.22.
16.   *Australian Financial Review*, 25 November 1996, p 6.
17.   See www.primelawbrokers.com.au.
18.   Editorial, 'A new way to access justice', *Australian*, 18 May 1998, p 12.

Commission. The ALRC said that such funding provided access to the courts being denied by inadequate legal aid.[19] There has been in recent years a dramatic increase in the funding of actions by these companies. There seemed to be ethical problems with such funding as percentage contingent fees are considered champerty,[20] but the Full Federal Court has found the funding to be valid. The court said: 'The Courts must be seen as willing to move with the times.' The court also said that high costs of litigation had denied access to the courts and if others were willing to provide funds for litigation these actions should be 'no cause for instant alarm'.[21] The welcoming of this funding has recently come under criticism because the companies, unlike lawyers, are not regulated. The Attorney-General of New South Wales, Bob Defus, said these companies 'initiate, manage and influence the running of court cases' and that is a concern because 'consumers are poorly protected'. As a result Mr Defus brought the problem before the Standing Committee of Attorneys-General to seek national regulation of the industry.[22]

LAWYERS AND LARGE ORGANISATIONS

16.5

Many more lawyers in Australia are working for large organisations, law firms, government or corporations.[23] The number of sole practitioners has remained at a similar percentage for a number of years, while the percentage of those working for the larger firms has rapidly increased. The national figures show that in 1972 it was estimated that 28 per cent of solicitors were sole practitioners and by 1985 the proportion of sole practitioners had fallen to 23 per cent.[24] The Law Council of Australia national figures, March 1997, showed that 25.7 per cent were sole practitioners, while the latest figures, November 2000, were almost identical at 25.8 per cent.[25] There will be new figures in 2006. In the meantime, large firms have grown considerably. In 1972 firms with 10 or more partners made up 6 per cent of solicitors; this grew to 12 per cent by 1985.[26] The Law Council of Australia figures in 1997 showed that there were 49 firms with 11–20 partners having a total of 709 partners and 908 employee lawyers, while in late 2000 there were 44 firms with 654 partners and 999 employee lawyers. There were also in 1997 45 firms with 20 or more partners having a total of 1575 partners and employing 2922 lawyers, while by late 2000 there were 50 firms with 2023 partners and 4352 employee lawyers. If these figures are added

19. ALRC Report No 89, *Managing Justice*, February 2000, para 5.3.
20. M Saville, 'Punting on the barristers', *Sydney Morning Herald*, 24 April 2000, p 35.
21. *Gore v Justice Corp Pty Ltd* [2002] 189 ALR 712 at 733.
22. M Pelly, 'State seeks greater control of firms funding litigation', *Sydney Morning Herald*, 26 July 2005, p 6.
23. See S Ross, 'Economic Integration of the Australian Legal Profession' (1997) 4 *International Journal of the Legal Profession* 267, 282–5.
24. J Disney, J Basten, P Redmond and S Ross, *Lawyers*, 2nd ed, 1986, p 58.
25. These figures are taken from the Australian Legal Directory and compiled by Bruce Timbs of the Law Council of Australia. The latest statistics are headed 'Law Firm Statistics', 2001 issue, but they are from source data of November 2000. Furthermore, Mr Timbs did not include the figures from Queensland from that date because they were clearly incorrect. He instead used the figures from the previous year.
26. Disney et al (above), p 60.

together, 27 per cent of practising solicitors in 1997 were in firms with 11 or more partners, while by 2000 it was 30.5 per cent. The largest firms, 20 or more partners, had in 1997 4497 out of 22,686 solicitors in private practice, which was 19.8 per cent and by late 2000 they had 6375 solicitors out of 26,288 which was 24.3 per cent. The biggest increase therefore has been in firms with 20 or more partners.

The trend to increase numbers in the top firms is not a continuous one. For example, in 2004 Australia's largest firms shrank by 5.9 per cent of their total number. It was stated that: 'The top-end of the legal profession faces an uncertain future as the big law firms battle unprecedented levels of staff turnover and a loss of crucial market share to mid-tier players.'[27] This development may have only been a small dip in the growth of these firms, as in the previous year there had been substantial growth.[28]

POOR IMAGE OF THE PROFESSION

16.6   Lawyers at the top have become organisers and paper pushers, while those at the bottom feel a loss of community and autonomy. As one lawyer said, 'when we have a firm party, we have to have name tags'.[29] Furthermore, the public image of the profession has continued to decline. A Morgan poll in December 2004 showed that only 33 per cent of those polled thought lawyers had very high or high standards for ethics and honesty, as compared to 43 per cent in its 1976 poll, and there is continuous publicity about the greed of lawyers. Mr Cowdery, Director of the New South Wales DPP, in the St James Ethics Centre Lecture, in August 1997, described many lawyers as 'useless and expensive parasites' and said that their professional associations were 'essentially parochial and mean spirited' and 'selfish, elitist ... and unreasonably self-protective'.

He also said:[30]

> In the new age of economic rationalism, firms pursue profit and measure the performance — the worth — of their lawyers by the profit they generate. The public worth of a barrister is measured by the fees commanded. Rewards depend on profit, not on the quality of service — insurance companies cover lapses in that area.

The *Sydney Morning Herald*'s editorial comment was: 'This is a sorry picture, but true. It is just as well that the best lawyers want to change it.'[31] The image was not helped by the ATO's figures for failure by lawyers to lodge their tax returns for 2003–04. They were 7658 for solicitors (20 per cent of total), 133 for barristers (2.95 per cent) and 31 judges.[32] A

---

27.   C Merritt and K Towers, 'Partners turn their back on big law firms', *Australian Financial Review*, 17 December 2004, pp 1 and 46.
28.   Ibid, p 1.
29.   R Cranston, 'The Changing Legal Profession' (1990) 17 *Cornell Law Forum* 11.
30.   This quote is taken from the unpublished version of the paper, which was to be published in late 1997. See also for a summary of the main points of the paper, *Sydney Morning Herald*, 27 August 1997, p 2.
31.   Editorial, 'The greed of lawyers', *Sydney Morning Herald*, 30 August 1997, p 44. The leaders of the professional bodies had reacted strongly to his comments and attacked Mr Cowdery for his views: *Sydney Morning Herald*, 28 August 1997, p 4. The editorial took the view that the attack by the professional bodies proved that Mr Cowdery was right.
32.   C Merritt, 'Law societies ask ATO to name names', *Australian*, 12 August 2005, p 25.

profession with such a poor image does not support a feeling of doing worthwhile work.

FUTURE OF THE PROFESSION

Any book written mainly for law students on their profession should seek to look into the future and make some predictions of what trends in modern legal practice will be like in the twenty-first century. I am not clairvoyant, but certain trends are already developing.

16.7

There will probably be an increase in the percentage of lawyers working as salaried employees for large organisations, either as in-house lawyers or employees of large firms. These lawyers will very likely view their work, like many other employees, as just paid labour[33] and be more willing to organise in a trade union. They will thus have less loyalty, and many will not be interested in becoming a partner, nor in staying for a long time. The number of women lawyers, which by 2003 constituted 38.6 per cent of the profession in New South Wales, will substantially increase.[34] The legal profession will in the future have many more experts in alternative dispute settlement[35] and less in litigation. The conveyancing business will be run mainly by licenced conveyancers.

A survey by Urbis consultants, commissioned by the Law Society of New South Wales in 2004, found that by 2015 women will outnumber men in the profession. Furthermore, it found that lawyers in 2015 will be doing more corporate work and less conveyancing and the number of large firms with 20 or more partners in New South Wales will increase from 24 to 33. The survey said that there had been a recent sharp increase in the number of lawyers advising in the areas of trade practices, intellectual property and industrial relations.[36]

Large firms

As we have seen in the 1990s and early 2000s, many more lawyers were working in large law firms. This trend started after World War II and was accentuated by the mineral boom of the 1960s. There was a very large in-flow of capital which led to an enormous increase in multinational and Australian corporate activity, which led to a need for highly complex specialised services to be provided by group work, monitored and tailored for the individual corporate client. As a result, Australian law firms came under the influence of multinational companies and branches of international firms such as Baker & McKenzie, from Chicago, the largest law firm in the world[37] (which arrived in Australia in 1964) — and adopted

16.8

---

33. Cranston (above), p 15.
34. M Pelly, 'Laying down the law: women to take lion's share of legal profession jobs by 2015', *Sydney Morning Herald*, 16 December 2004, p 2.
35. See, for example, this development in M Priest and S Scott, 'Case closed: disputes head out of court', *Australian Financial Review*, 22 July 2005, pp 1 and 46, and M Priest and S Scott, 'Mediation, arbitration on the rise', *Australian Financial Review*, 22 July 2005, p 46.
36. Ibid.
37. M Galanter and T Palay, *Tournament of Lawyers: The Transformation of the Big Law Firm*, University of Chicago Press, Chicago, 1991, p 47.

the features of the American large firm.[38] There also developed in the 1990s smaller specialised mid-size firms known as 'boutique firms'.[39]

16.9 Baker & McKenzie, as of June 2005, had 3246 lawyers in 69 offices in 38 countries.[40] In July 1999 the second largest firm in the world, Clifford Chance of London, with more than 2000 lawyers, merged with Rogers and Wells of New York and with the German firm of Puender, Volhard, Weber & Axster, to create a firm of over 2700 lawyers, claiming that it was then the largest firm.[41] The latest available figures in November 2004 place it in second place. It had 28 offices in 19 countries with 2688 lawyers.[42] The third largest firm in 2004 was Freshfields Bruckhaus Dennger of London with 2225 lawyers,[43] while the fourth largest was a tie between Jones Day Revis & Pogue of Cleveland[44] and Skedden Arps Slate Meagher and Flom of New York with 1822 lawyers.[45]

The United States as of 1995 had 875,000 practising lawyers; there were over 1.2 million in 2005.[46] The state of New York, the largest bar in the United States, had by January 2005 over 214,000 lawyers, while California, the second largest had by March 2005 over 200,000 of which over 148,000 were practising.[47] The 1000-lawyer firm has also arrived in Australia. As of November 2004 Minter Ellison was the 13th largest firm in the world and had 1236 lawyers with 279 partners working in eight countries.[48] The second largest firm in Australia was Freehills with 997 lawyers and 210 partners working mainly in Australia[49] and the third largest was Mallesons Stephen Jaques with 901 lawyers and 207 partners working in four countries.[50]

---

38. See G Mendelshon and M Lippman, 'The Emergence of the Corporate Law Firm in Australia' (1979) 3 *University of New South Wales Law J* 78 and D Weisbrot, *Australian Lawyer*, Longman, Melbourne, 1990, pp 256–7.
39. These firms, such as film, entertainment and media law, technology and communications and tax firms, developed rapidly in the late 1980s and 1990s: see *The Australian*, 19 May 1995, p 17.
40. See www.bakernet.com. According to the website there were 3200, but a more accurate number is given at www.ilrg.com, which is 3246. A November 2004 survey, 'The Global 110 Law Firms', said Baker & McKenzie had 3053 lawyers. See www.thelawyer.com/global100.html.
41. These figures are from M Todd, 'Mallesons may join law merger', *Sydney Morning Herald*, 13 July 1999.
42. See www.cliffordchance.com for the number of offices. The website does not list the number of lawyers. According to the November 2004 survey, 'The Global 110 Law Firms', Clifford Chance had 2684 lawyers. See www.thelawyer.com/global100.html.
43. Ibid, in the 'Global 110' survey.
44. This is according to www.ilrg.com.
45. This figure is from the 'Global 110' survey (above).
46. T Morgan and R Rotunda, *Professional Responsibility: Problems and Materials*, 6th ed, 1995, p 2 and private communication from Professor Klee of UCLA.
47. As of 1 March 2005 total membership was 200,269 — active members 148,885. See (April 2005) *California Bar Journal* 3. It should be noted that a number of the active members do not reside in California. The New York Bar, which has the greatest number of non-resident members, had 207,413 registered lawyers at the end of 2003 and another 7000 registered in 2004. See (February 2005) *California Bar Journal* 1.
48. According to its website, www.minterellison.com, it had over 1100 lawyers, but 'The Global 110' had the number at 1236.
49. According to its website, www.freehills.com, it had around 1000 lawyers, but 'The Global 110' had the number at 997.
50. Its website, www.mallesonscom, did not have any figures on the number of lawyers, but 'The Global 110' had the number at 901.

Other future changes

The present increase in specialisation, bureaucratic work and competition will continue.[51] The information technology revolution will accelerate, making lawyers even more dependent on machines and leading to less personal contact and more isolation.[52] To maintain legal expertise lawyers will increasingly need to develop the 'capacity to use data and information technology tools'.[53] As a result of these trends, many law students will seek non-legal work on graduating from law school and many others will leave the profession early on in their careers. The trend to seek non-law careers is confirmed by a 1994 study by the Centre for Legal Education in New South Wales of almost 5000 first and final year law students throughout Australia. The study showed that only 55 per cent of first-year students planned to be admitted within two years of completing their degree, as compared to 70 per cent of final year students.[54] Other possible trends are that the profession will decline in status as the right to self-regulation is replaced by public regulation. Lawyers will probably become more accountable to their clients and be held more responsible for their actions both by courts and disciplinary authorities.

16.10

In this profession of the future how will lawyers be able to find a happy, meaningful and good life and still remain in the profession? A prominent Canadian judge wrote just before he died:[55]

16.11

> Good lawyers should not be leaving the law. The profession of law must reclaim its traditions of meaningful engagement with issues of justice while developing a new tradition of providing for a lawyer's involvement in equally meaningful work of raising a family and fulfilling broader civic obligations in the community.

Hoffmaster gives further insight into a 'meaningful' practice. He says:[56]

> Eating at home is a convergent good. Looking at the moon out of your window is a convergent good. Making a living from the law is a convergent good. But using the law to promote the public interest is a shared good. It transcends the individual pursuit of self-interest in two ways: it aims at something beyond self-interest, and it requires a collective effort. The pursuit of a shared good is what makes the practice of law intrinsically worthwhile, not just instrumentally rewarding.

Hoffmaster quotes from the famous Nigerian novelist Chinua Achebe's *Things Fall Apart* to illustrate 'shared goods'. An elder is giving thanks for a feast:[57]

---

51. See K Wilson, 'Law Practice in 1991 and beyond — a forecast' (1991) 65 *Law Institute J* (Vic) 18; F Riley, 'Future of the legal profession in New South Wales: An invitation to enquiry and reflection' (1992) 30 *Law Society J* (NSW) 50; a report of the Law Society's Development and Practice Management Committee, *The Future of the Private Profession* (1995), extracted in the (1995) 33 *Law Society J* (NSW) 28; and K Elgar, 'The way ahead' (1997) 32 *Australian Lawyer* 16.
52. See A Clark, 'Information Technology in Legal Services' (1992) 19 *J of Law and Society* 13.
53. R Volpato, 'Legal Professionalism and Informatics' (1991) 2 *J of Law and Information Science* 206, 225.
54. C Roper, *Career Intentions of Australian Law Students*, AGPS, Canberra, 1995.
55. Iacobucci (above), pp 217–18.
56. B Hoffmaster, 'Hanging Out a Shingle: The Public and Private Services of Professionals' (1996) 9 *The Canadian J of Law & Society* 127, 137.
57. C Achebe, *Things Fall Apart*, Heinemann Books, London, 1958, p 118.

It is good in these days when the younger generation consider themselves wiser than their sires to see a man doing things in the grand, old way. A man who calls his kinsmen to a feast does not do so to save them from starving. They all have food in their own homes. When we gather together in the moonlit village ground it is not because of the moon. Every man can see it in his own compound. We come together because it is good for kinsmen to do so.

16.12 Nader and Smith call for a greater effort to help those without access to legal services:[58]

A corporate lawyer who is personally committed to and has experience in representing individuals can develop empathy for real people. That empathy would serve the ideals of professionalism — aiding society as well as clients — too often lacking today in lawyering for impersonal corporations. Such pro bono involvement, by pricking their consciences, may make it harder for lawyers to stomp on the little guy and still get a good night's sleep.

Nader and Smith do point out that increased pro bono will not be enough without further changes:[59]

Achieving a critical mass of enduring lawyer energy to expand public interest law, and to organise it in conjunction with millions of citizens, demands a desire for fundamental self-renewal ... Once the process of professional regeneration is under way the challenge becomes one of restructuring abusive power systems — public and private — and not simply becoming another legal charity, sponsoring palliatives and congratulatory dinner ceremonies.

16.13 All these views are noble sentiments, but are they the solution for the present and future malaise of lawyers and law students? I believe that more is needed than just fulfilling the views of traditional family values, community involvement, restructuring abusive power systems and seeking justice in legal practice. The present cry goes deeper into the meaning of life, which includes the examination of age-old questions of why are we here and what is our soul or human purpose? Kirby J of the High Court recognised the situation when he said 'there is a deeper malaise which I believe underlines the problem' of modern legal practice. He found it difficult to speak about because we live in a secular society. He was worried his words 'should be misinterpreted as inappropriate, hypocritical or self-righteous'. He still felt he 'must' mention it. He said:[60]

I refer to the void which is left in many lives by the absence of any spiritual construct and by the increasingly general rejection of any spiritual dimension whatever to life. By a life in law that has no reflection on the amazing fact of existence and its brevity.

16.14 I believe that one avenue to the salvation of lawyers' souls is the willingness of more and more lawyers to practise tithing. All major religions in the world emphasise the need to give to others freely our services or some of our wealth without the expectation of any financial or spiritual reward. There are lawyers who donate their time to various legal programs in order to obtain new clients or advance their careers within professional associations, but there are also a number of lawyers who willingly do services without

---

58. R Nader and W Smith, *No Contest: Corporate Lawyers and the Perversion of Justice in America*, Random House, New York, 1996, pp 339–40.
59. Nader and Smith (above), p 370.
60. M Kirby, *An Honourable Profession?*, The Inaugural Lawyers Lecture, St James Ethics Centre, Sydney, 23 June 1996, pp 15–16.

seeking reward or recognition. The latter are fulfilling a deep soul connection that enriches their lives and enables them to be at peace with themselves in both their work and private lives.

There may also be new ways of practising law that create a wholesome atmosphere with less strain and more fulfilment. There has developed in North America an organisation called the International Alliance of Holistic Lawyers (IAHL). The members are dedicated to practise law in a humanistic manner and to seek creative methods to solve clients' problems by avoiding conflict. An annual international conference has also been organised by the IAHL.[61] Holistic law is defined as being 'the practice of law as a healing profession. It seeks to maintain the dignity of the people involved and seeks to maintain justice without bitterness. Integrity and honesty are important aspects of a holistic law practice'.[62]

16.15 An ethical framework needs to be developed in legal practice. A South Australian lawyer, John Harley, said that the proliferation of laws (I would also add the proliferation of detailed ethical codes) represents the failure of morality in the community.[63] The more we mistrust each other, the more we seek detailed words to control our behaviour. Harley says that legislation and sanctions cannot solve the failure of moral standards. The problems have to be solved within our own business organisations by teaching people the following principle:[64]

> Your word is your bond. The truth is what we live by. If you expect something else, don't use our services! If you practise differently, don't represent yourself as one of our partners, associates or staff.

16.16 The choosing of truth is a difficult task when done from the intellect. We all know what rings true and that truth is from the heart. It is spelt not as truth but as 'Truth'. Choosing to practise in this fashion will not be just left in the office, but will become an integral part of these lawyers' everyday life.

Many of the students reading this book will never practise law, while many others will have law as one of several different occupations during their life. There is as much relevance for the ideas and materials in this book for these students as for those who remain in the profession. These practices continue into one's life, no matter what occupation, and are a basis for living a far more satisfactory personal life. The more each law student decides that concepts such as seeking the 'Truth' or being of service are important in their work, the more they will find that their actions reflect these choices. They will also find more joy in their work and more peace and harmony in their lives. In order to develop legal skills there is a need to practise them continuously. And to develop ethical skills there is a need also to practise them continuously. Nicholas Cowdery QC, the DPP of New South Wales said: 'The Dalai Lama's motto is: "Be happy and useful". It's a fine ambition and I urge it upon everyone.'[65]

---

61. For more information see its website at www.iahl.org or write to: IAHL, PO Box 753, Middlebury, Vermont 05753, USA; email HJC1@aol.com or fax 802-388-4079.
62. See www.holisticnetworker.com.
63. J Harley, 'Managing Personal and Organisational Ethical Practices: Ethics, Professionalism and Success' (1993) 15 *Law Society Bulletin (SA)* 16.
64. J Harley (above).
65. 'Hot Seat — or Siberia?' (1995) *Bar News* 8.

INDEX

References are to paragraph numbers

References are to paragraph numbers

References are to paragraph numbers